MACMILLAN STUDENT'S DICTIONARY

General Editor
Martin H. Manser

Compilers
Jane Deam
Gillian A. Rathbone
Maurice Waite

Macmillan

Special thanks are due to Ruth Swan
and Michael Croza-Ross who formed part of the editorial
team and to Andrew Butcher for checking the
phonetic transcriptions.

First published 1984
Reprinted 1984, 1985 (twice), 1986

Published by *Macmillan Publishers Ltd*
London and Basingstoke
*Associated companies and representatives in Accra,
Auckland, Delhi, Dublin, Gaborone, Hamburg, Harare,
Hong Kong, Kuala Lumpur, Lagos, Manzini, Melbourne,
Mexico City, Nairobi, New York, Singapore, Tokyo.*

Illustrations by Malcolm Stokes, Linden Artists

ISBN 0 333 34836 2

Printed in Hong Kong

Contents

Introduction

This dictionary is written for students with a basic knowledge of the English language but who have not yet reached an advanced level of ability. It has been prepared with two particular groups of users in mind: students for whom English is a Second Language, that is those who are taught school subjects such as geography, mathematics, physics, and literature in English; and students studying for examinations at intermediate level. The choice of entries and meanings given reflects the needs of both such groups: for example, greater attention has been paid to 'study language' — words and phrases common to many subjects — than is usual in dictionaries of a similar size.

Students sometimes use a learner's dictionary that is too advanced for their real needs. It is hoped that this medium-sized dictionary will indeed be a useful reference book and will be found to develop the knowledge and abilities of the intermediate learner of English.

Martin H. Manser

Why a dictionary is helpful

This dictionary gives help in three areas of language skills: how to speak English, how to write it, and how to read it.

Speaking English

To be able to speak English well, you must pronounce the words accurately. English spelling is unreliable as the same written letter may represent different sounds. For example, the letter *a* stands for different sounds in the words *cat, came, mare,* and *ago.* For this reason we use a phonetic spelling in this dictionary. This is a way of writing the pronunciation where one symbol always represents one sound. To check how to pronounce the word, look it up in the dictionary, and you will find its phonetic spelling. A list of the symbols used is given on page v.

Writing English

If you want to write good English, you must be able to spell words correctly. A dictionary will help you to check the right spelling of a word. To find out how a word is spelt, look up the ways you think it might be spelt and you will find the one that is right. In writing it is often not enough to know how to spell a word; you also want to know how to use it. The grammatical information, notes on the kinds of situation in which a word is suitable, and examples given, will guide you in this.

Reading English

When you meet a word whose meaning you do not understand, think and try to work out what the word means from the rest of the sentence. Then, if you still can't understand it, look it up in the dictionary. Remember that many of the dictionary entries have more than one definition, so it is important to look at all the meanings of the word to find the one that fits your particular sentence.

The dictionary will be found helpful in these three ways. But to get the best use from your dictionary, you should read the next few pages to discover how it works.

How to use this dictionary

1 Headwords

The information in the dictionary is arranged in entries and the first word in the entry is called the *headword*. This word is printed in thick type. The headwords are all listed in alphabetical order from A to Z.

> **collect** (kə'lekt) 1 *vti* gather together: *I collected everyone's books; Water collected in the bucket. vt* 2 obtain and put with others for interest: *I collect stamps.* 3 fetch; call for: *I'll collect you tomorrow.* 4 regain control of (oneself). **collection** 1 *ncu* (an example of) collecting. *nc* 2 a body of collected things or material. 3 a collected sum of money. **collective** *adj* 1 formed by or forming a collection. 2 to do with a group of people acting together: *collective bargaining.* ●*nc* something, such as a farm, that is run collectively. **collectively** *adv* **collector** *nc*
> **college** ('kɒlɪdʒ) *nc* 1 (a part of) a university. 2 a place of education of a particular kind: *an art college.*
> **collide** (kə'laɪd) *vi* strike violently together: *The car collided with the bus.*

If you want to look up the word *college,* you look among the words beginning with *C.* But there are many such words, so you look at the next letter: *co.* Words beginning *co-* come after words beginning *cl-* and before those beginning *cu-.* But there are still many such words, so you look at the third and fourth letters, and so on, until you find the word *college.*

Not every word that you want to look up will be a headword. Some will be derived words—see section 7 below.

The words printed at the top of each page help you to find a word quickly. At the top of a left-hand page the first new headword on that page is printed; at the top of a right-hand page, the last headword on that page. Some headwords have small raised numbers by their sides.

> **case¹** (keɪs) *nc* 1 an example of something. 2 a situation; state of affairs: *If that is the case, I'll go.* 3 an example of or a person with a disease: *a bad case of smallpox.* 4 an example of a crime to be solved: *Sherlock Holmes' most famous case.* 5 *law* a court action: *a murder case.* 6 a set of reasons for a court action: *He hasn't a good case.* 7 *grammar* a class of nouns in some languages: *the genitive case.* **in any case** whatever may happen; anyway: *Is it raining?—I'll go in any case.* **in case** so as to be safe (if): *He took his umbrella in case (it rained).* **in case of** *formal* in the event of; should... happen: *In case of fire, shout 'Fire!'*
> **case²** *nc* 1 a container or covering. 2 short for **briefcase** or **suitcase.**

This means that they are spelt the same, but have different histories, and are best thought of as different words.

Other information about the headword is given where needed:

> **calf**[1] (ka:f) *nc, pl* **calves** 1 (of cattle) a young cow or bull. 2 a young seal, elephant, etc.

irregular plurals

> **calm** (ka:m) *adj* **-er, -est** 1 peaceful; not worried. 2 (of the sea) flat; without

comparative and superlative forms of an adjective

> **caster** (also **castor**) ('ka:stə*) *nc* 1 a small wheel fixed to furniture for moving it

other English spellings

> **colour** *US* **color** ('kʌlə*) *nc* 1 a quality of the light produced or reflected by something,

American spellings

Notes

1 Irregular forms of verbs are included as headwords, for example there are entries for *brought* and *written*. A full list of irregular verbs is on page xvi.

2 There are a number of differences in spelling between American and British English, and many of these are noted at the entries. The main differences are:

American	British
ONE OR TWO CONSONANTS	
canceling	cancelling
focusing	focussing or focusing
traveler	traveller
OR ⟶ OUR	
color	colour
favor	favour
ER ⟶ RE	
center	centre
theater	theatre
S ⟶ C	
defense	defence
-IZE ⟶ -ISE	
realize	realise

(The *-ize* spelling is also becoming more common in British English)

2 Pronunciations

Each of the headwords has its pronunciation shown in the phonetic spelling of the International Phonetic Association. The form of speech shown is the kind of British English spoken by educated native speakers in England. The symbols used for the phonetic transcriptions are from *Everyman's English Pronouncing Dictionary* by Daniel Jones, revised by A.C. Gimson (14th edition, Dent 1977). Here is a list of symbols used in this dictionary (a comparison is made with the symbols in the Macmillan *New Basic Dictionary* where slightly different symbols are used for some sounds):

List of phonetic symbols

Consonants		Vowels		
p	*p*ad	iː	s*ee*	
b	*b*ig	ɪ	*i*t	NBD i
t	*t*oo	e	g*e*t	
d	*d*og	æ	c*a*t	
k	*k*eep	ɑː	f*a*ther	
g	*g*o	ɒ	h*o*t	NBD ɔ
tʃ	*ch*in	ɔː	s*aw*	
dʒ	*j*am	ʊ	p*u*t	NBD u
f	*f*ish	uː	t*oo*	
v	*v*ase	ʌ	*u*p	
θ	*th*in	ɜː	b*ir*d	NBD əː
ð	*th*en	ə	driv*er*, Chin*a*	
s	*s*it	eɪ	d*ay*	NBD ei
z	*z*ero	əʊ	g*o*	NBD əu
ʃ	*sh*ip	aɪ	fl*y*	NBD ai
ʒ	mea*s*ure	aʊ	h*ow*	NBD au
h	*h*ot	ɔɪ	b*oy*	NBD ɔi
m	*m*an	ɪə	h*ere*	NBD iə
n	*n*o	eə	th*ere*	NBD ɛə
ŋ	lo*ng*	ʊə	p*oor*	NBD uə
l	*l*eg			
r	*r*ed			
j	*y*es			
w	*w*in			

Stress

Where a word has more than one syllable, one syllable is given more emphasis or *stress* than the other. The mark ' is placed before the syllable that has the main stress, for example *camera* ('kæmərə). In other (especially longer) words, other syllables may also be given more emphasis than the rest, but with a stress that is not as strong as that marked '. The mark , is used to show this, for example *chronological* (ˌkrɒnəˈlɒdʒɪkəl).

Notes

1 ə is included before an *l* or *n* sound in some words. An alternative pronunciation is to omit it, the *l* or *n* becoming a syllable, for example in *bottle, button.*

2 * is used to show an *r* sound at the end of a word. This is heard in British speech when there is a suffix or a word beginning with a vowel immediately following, for example in *law-abiding* ('lɔː*əˌbaɪdɪŋ). Otherwise it is not pronounced.

3 Two pronunciations are given where both are acceptable.

> **controversy** ('kɒntrəˌvɜːsɪ, kənˈtrɒvɜːsɪ) *nc,*
> *pl* **-sies** an argument, usually on public

4 When words with raised numbers by their sides are pronounced the same, the pronunciation is shown only by the first word.

> **case¹** (keɪs) *nc* **1** an example of something. **2** a situation; state of affairs: *If that is the case, I'll go.* **3** an example of or a person with a disease: *a bad case of smallpox.* **4** an example of a crime to be solved: *Sherlock Holmes' most famous case.* **5** *law* a court action: *a murder case.* **6** a set of reasons for a court action: *He hasn't a good case.* **7** *grammar* a class of nouns in some languages: *the genitive case.* **in any case** whatever may happen; anyway: *Is it raining?—I'll go in any case.* **in case** so as to be safe (if): *He took his umbrella in case (it rained).* **in case of** *formal* in the event of; should... happen: *In case of fire, shout 'Fire!'*
> **case²** *nc* **1** a container or covering. **2** short for **briefcase** or **suitcase.**

5 The same word may consist of two parts of speech. Different parts of speech may have different pronunciations. This is clearly shown.

> **contrast** ('kɒntrɑːst) *nc* something seen to be not like something else when put next to it. ●(kənˈtrɑːst) *vti* **1** compare so that differences are clear. **2** show differences.

3 Parts of speech

Each of the headwords is given a part-of-speech marker, that is a word to show it is a noun, verb, adjective, etc. The following markers are used:

adj	adjective	*big*	
adv	adverb	*fast*	
conj	conjunction	*and*	
determiner		*my*	(See note 1)
interj	interjection	*ha!*	
n	noun	*February*	
nc	countable noun	*book*	(See note 2)
ncu	countable and uncountable noun	*charm*	(See note 4)
n pl	plural noun	*cattle*	(See note 5)
nu	uncountable noun	*milk*	(See note 3)
prep	preposition	*into*	
pron	pronoun	*it*	
v	verb	*shall*	
vi	intransitive verb	*come*	(See note 6)
vt	transitive verb	*kick*	(See note 7)
vti	transitive and intransitive verb	*check*	(See note 8)

Notes

1 The marker *determiner* is used for words such as *my, that, this*. A determiner limits the meaning of a noun and comes before any adjective describing that noun.

2 *nc* A countable noun is one that can be used with *a* or *an*, can be counted as separate units, and may be used in the plural with *many*. An example is *book: a book, four books, many books*.

3 *nu* An uncountable noun is one that takes a singular verb and is usually not used with *a* or *an, one* or other numbers, and does not have a plural. It can be used in the singular with words like *more, much, some*. An example is *milk: more milk, much milk, some milk*.

4 *ncu* Some nouns are both countable and uncountable, such as *charm*.

> **charm** (tʃɑːm) **1** *ncu* an attractive or pleasing quality: *a country cottage with great charm*.

You can say: *The house has a certain charm* and *a country house with great charm*.

5 *n pl* Some nouns are only used in the plural, such as *cattle*.

> **cattle** (ˈkætəl) *n pl* bulls and cows kept by farmers for meat and milk.

6 *vi* An intransitive verb is one that does not take a direct object, such as *come* in: *John came when I called him.*

7 *vt* A transitive verb is one that takes a direct object, such as *kick* in *John kicked the ball.*

8 *vti* Some verbs are both transitive and intransitive, such as *check.*

> **check** (tʃek) *vti* **1** make sure that (something) is correct, safe, etc.: *Have you checked your petrol?*

You can say: *'Have you checked your work?'* and *'Do you have enough sugar?'—'I'll just check.'*

The part-of-speech markers are placed at the beginning of a definition. Where the marker refers to more than one numbered definition, it comes before all the relevant ones.

> **chance** (tʃɑːns) **1** *nu* the accidental nature of events: *It was only chance that brought me here.* *nc* **2** the degree to which something is probable; likelihood: *There's not much chance of it raining.* **3** an opportunity: *Go while you have the chance.* **4** a lucky event.

The word *chance* is an uncountable noun in definition **1**, and a countable noun in definitions **2**, **3**, and **4**.

Where the entry for a word has more than one part of speech, the symbol ● is used to separate the parts of the entry.

> **copy** ('kɒpɪ) *nc*, *pl* **-pies 1** something made to be or look like something else: *Please make a copy of this letter.* **2** (of a book, etc.) one example: *They published thousands of copies of the newspaper.* ● *vt* make a copy of; reproduce.

4 Definitions

The definitions are explanations of the meaning of a word. They have been written in simplified language, and you should be able to understand them fully. If you sometimes find a word you do not understand in the definition, look up that word itself in the dictionary; you should find it listed. Numbers are used to separate different meanings of a word.

> **chain** (tʃeɪn) *nc* **1** a line of rings, esp. of metal, one passing through the next. **2** a series: *a chain of events.*

Because a lot of information has been put into the small space of the dictionary, some special styles of writing have been used.

1 A definition may contain the phrase (of...). This gives information about the words that the headword goes with:

> **clash** (klæʃ) **1** *vti* strike together. *vi* **2** not go or fit together. **3** fight or play against each other. **4** (of colours) look ugly together. **5** (of events) happen at the same time.

These show that definition **4** describes *colours* clashing and **5** *events* clashing.

2 A definition may contain words in round brackets ( ). These are used for two purposes:
—to show words that need not be chosen for the definition:

> **chair** (tʃeə*) *nc* **1** a seat with a back for one person. **2** the position of a professor at a university: *the chair of English.* **3** (the position of) the person in charge of a meeting: *Mr Jones took the chair.*

This means that definition **3** can be either 'the position of the person in charge of a meeting' or 'the person in charge of a meeting'.
—to show the direct object of a verb:

> **circulate** ('sɜːkjʊ,leɪt) *vti* **1** (cause to) travel round and round in a space or endless system; move freely. **2** pass (news, a book, etc.) round a circle of people.

This shows that *news* or *a book* are common objects of *circulate* in this sense.

5 Style

Some of the words and definitions are marked to show that they are thought suitable only in particular situations or are used only by certain people. The main ones are:

formal   used in formal writing, official meetings; not used in everyday conversation or in letters to friends

infml   (short for *informal*) used between friends in everyday conversation; not used in, for example, business letters

slang   used between close friends or members of a group that feel they belong together, such as young people; not accepted in general standard English

Brit	only used in British English and variants of English related to it
US	only used in the English spoken in the United States of America and variants of English related to it

Other style markers, such as *not standard, derogatory;* specialist subject markers, such as *economics, history;* and markers showing older words: *old-fashioned* (used especially by older people), *archaic* (no longer in use) are also used. The marker *Trademark* is included where a word is believed to be a proprietary name, but the presence or the absence of such a marker should not be taken as affecting the legal status of such a word.

Labels are placed at the beginning of the definition referred to:

> **come over 1** (of a person or message) have an (intended) effect. **2** *infml* feel: *I came over all hot.* **3** visit one or someone.

6 Examples and grammatical information

It is important to know how to use a particular word. For this reason, the dictionary includes many examples and notes on grammatical information to help you use the word correctly.

> **come out 1** go to a social occasion: *Can you come out for dinner?* **2** become known: *If you don't tell us now, it will come out later.* **3** appear; be produced: *My book comes out tomorrow.*
>
> **consist** (kən'sıst) *vi* **1** (followed by **of**) be made of: *The team consists of six people; Water consists of hydrogen and oxygen.* **2** (followed by **in**) have as the only or most important thing.

7 Compound and derived words

In a particular entry compound words and derived words connected with the headword may be given. These kinds of words are printed in thick type towards the end of an entry.

Compound words are made up of two or more words joined together, such as *cassette recorder.*

> **cassette** (kə'set) *nc* **1** a holder for recording-tape that fits into a tape-recorder. **2** a film holder that fits into a camera. **cassette recorder** a tape-recorder that records on and plays cassettes.

Derived words are words formed from other words, by adding an ending (suffix) to the main part of the word, such as *caller* from *call.*

> **call** (kɔːl) *vti* 1 say loudly; shout. 2 telephone or radio (someone). *vt* 3 tell (someone or something) to come: *I'll call the waiter.* 4 consider as: *I call that cheap.* 5 say that someone or something is: *Don't you call me stupid!* 6 name: *I'm called Maurice.* 7 wake: *Please call me at seven o'clock.* *vi* 8 also **call by** or **in** pay a short visit. ● *nc* 1 a shout. 2 a short visit. 3 a telephone or radio conversation. 4 need: *There's no call to worry.* **caller** *nc* 1 a person who visits. 2 a person who telephones.

Sometimes derived words are included but not defined, for example *comfortably.*

> **comfort** ('kʌmfət) 1 *nu* a feeling of being at ease, in body or mind. 2 *nc* a person or thing that brings comfort. ● *vt* bring comfort to. **comfortable** *adj* 1 bringing comfort. 2 enjoying comfort. 3 with plenty of money. **comfortably** *adv*

The meaning of such words can be worked out easily by taking the meaning of the main part of the word and joining it to the meaning of the ending. The pronunciation of such words is given where it may be difficult to work out. For a list of such endings see page xiii.
Idioms and phrasal verbs are also treated as compounds.

> **cash** (kæʃ) *nu* coins and banknotes. ● *vt* obtain cash for (a cheque, etc.). **cash in on** *infml* take advantage of.

8 Cross-references

Some of the words have cross-references to other places in the dictionary. This means that you should turn to the word after the 'See' to find the meaning you want—here, *track,* definition 5.

> **caterpillar** ('kætə,pɪlə*) *nc* the young form of a butterfly or moth, with many legs and no wings. **caterpillar track** See **track** (def. 5).

Beginnings and endings of words

Many English words are made up by using parts of words, such as *-er* in *speaker*, where the ending *-er* means a person who does something. Here is a list of the more common word parts.

Beginnings of words

a-	1 without; not: *asymmetrical* 2 in; on; at: *ashore*
aero-	aircraft: *aeronautics*
ambi-	both; two: *ambidextrous*
ante-	before: *antenatal*
anthropo-	human: *anthropology*
anti-	against: *anti-aircraft*
arch-	chief: *archenemy*
astro-	stars: *astronomy*
audio-	hearing or sound: *audiovisual*
auto-	self: *autobiography*
be-	(used to make verbs): *becalm*
bi-	two; twice: *bicycle*
biblio-	book: *bibliography*
bio-	life: *biography, biology*
by-	less important: *by-election*
centi-	one hundredth: *centimetre*
chron-	time: *chronological*
co-, col-, com-, con-, cor-	together; with: *collect, combine*
contra-	against; opposite: *contradict*
counter-	1 opposite: *counteract* 2 corresponding; matching: *counterpart*
de-	1 take away something: *dethrone* 2 go back: *decode*
di-	two: *diphthong, dioxide*
dia-	through; across: *diameter*
dis-	1 not: *disagree, dissimilar* 2 opposite: *disconnect*
electro-	electricity: *electrolysis*
em-, en-	1 (used to make verbs): *enthrone, enrich, enable* 2 in; into: *enlist*
equi-	equal: *equidistant*
ex-	1 former: *ex-president* 2 out of: *expel*
extra-	outside: *extraterrestrial*
fore-	1 front: *foreword* 2 before: *foretell*
geo-	earth: *geology*
haemo-	blood: *haemorrhage*
hect-, hecto-	one hundred: *hectare*
hemi-	half: *hemisphere*
hepta-	seven: *heptagon*
hexa-	six: *hexagon*
homo-	same: *homogeneous*

hydro-	water: *hydroelectricity*
hyper-	much more than normal: *hypermarket*
hypo-	under: *hypodermic*
ig-, il-, im-, in-, ir-	not: *ignoble, illogical, impossible*
il-, im-, in-, ir-	in; into: *income, irrigate*
infra-	below: *infra-red*
inter-	1 between: *intermediary* 2 from one to another *interchange*
intra-	inside: *intravenous*
kilo-	one thousand: *kilometre*
mal-	bad: *malfunction*
mega-	1 million: *megawatt* 2 big: *megaphone*
micro-	small: *microscope*
mid-	middle: *mid-day*
milli-	one thousandth: *millimetre*
mini-	small: *minibus*
mis-	bad; badly: *mislead*
mono-	one: *monotony*
multi-	many: *multicoloured*
neo-	new: *neoclassical*
neuro-	mind or nerves: *neurosis*
non-	not: *non-stop*
ob-	against: *obstruct*
octa-, octo-	eight: *octagon, octopus*
omni-	all: *omnipotent*
ortho-	correct: *orthodox*
out-	1 greater than: *outlast* 2 outside: *outbuilding*
over-	1 above: *overhang* 2 too much: *overdo*
penta-	five: *pentagon*
peri-	around: *perimeter*
photo-	1 light: *photosynthesis* 2 photography: *photocopy*
physio-	nature: *physiology*
poly-	many: *polygon*
post-	after: *postscript, post-war*
pre-	before: *prelude*
pro-	1 in favour of: *pro-African* 2 substitute: *pronoun*
proto-	first; original: *prototype*
pseudo-	not real; pretended: *pseudonym*
psycho-	mind; behaviour: *psychology*

quad-	four: *quadrangle*	**techno-**	practical skill and science: *technology*
quin-	five: *quintet*		
re-	again: *reappear*	**tele-**	distant: *telephone, television*
retro-	back: *retrograde*	**theo-**	God: *theology*
self-	oneself: *self-confident*	**thermo-**	heat: *thermometer*
semi-	half: *semi-circle*	**trans-**	across: *transcontinental*
sept-	seven: *septet*	**tri-**	three: *triangle*
sex-	six: *sextet*	**ultra-**	beyond: *ultraviolet*
socio-	social; society: *sociology*	**un-**	1 not: *unhappy* 2 opposite: *undo, untie*
sub-	1 under: *subsoil* 2 less than: *sub-normal*	**under-**	1 below: *undergrowth* 2 too little: *underdeveloped*
super-	1 over: *superimpose* 2 greater: *supersonic*	**uni-**	one: *unity*
sym-, syn-	together with: *sympathy, synthesis*	**vice-**	assistant: *vice-president*

Since the way a word is said may change from one word to another, a phonetic spelling is not shown here. To find out how to pronounce the word, look it up in the main part of the dictionary.

Endings of words

-able (əbəl), **-ible** (ıbəl) 1 able to be... : *enjoyable* 2 that may cause: *objectionable* 3 that belongs to: *fashionable*

-age (ıdʒ) an action, condition, or charge: *breakage, postage*

-al (əl) 1 an action: *removal* 2 relating to: *postal, central, dental*

-an (ən), **-ian** (ıən) 1 (a person) coming from a country: *Canadian* 2 a person who is an expert at something: *mathematician*

-ance, -ence (əns), **-ancy, -ency** (ənsı) a quality, state, or action: *assistance, ascendancy*

-ant, -ent (ənt) (a person or thing) that does something: *pleasant, student, dependent*

-ar (ə) like; belonging to: *solar, molecular*

-ary (ərı) 1 connected with: *monetary* 2 a person doing something· *missionary* 3 a place for: *aviary*

-ate 1 (ət) having a quality: *fortunate* 2 (eıt) a chemical compound: *carbonate* 3 (eıt) cause to have or become: *hyphenate*

-atic (ətık) (used to make adjectives): *problematic*

-ation (eıʃən) an action, state, or condition: *pronunciation, moderation*

-cide (saıd) killing: *insecticide*

-cy (sı) a state or quality: *secrecy*

-dom (dəm) 1 a state or condition: *freedom* 2 an area ruled: *kingdom* 3 a group of persons: *officialdom*

-ed (ıd, d, t) 1 (used to make the past tense and past participles of verbs): *extended, gained* 2 showing or having a quality or state: *surprised, long-sighted*

-ee (iː) 1 a person to whom something is done or given: *addressee* 2 a person in a particular state or condition: *refugee*

-eer (ıə*) a person who does something or is concerned with something: *mountaineer*

-en (ən) 1 (cause to) become: *harden* 2 made of: *wooden*

-ence, -ency See **-ance**

-ent See **-ant**

-er (ə*) 1 (also **-r**) (used to make the comparative of adjectives): *faster, nicer, tidier* 2 (also **-or**) a person or thing that does something: *cooker, sailor, transmitter* 3 a person working in a job: *writer, painter* 4 a person who lives in a place: *Londoner* 5 a person or thing that has or is something: *teenager*

-ery (əri), **-ry** (ri) 1 a place where an activity or business is done: *bakery* 2 a group of things: *cutlery* 3 a condition: *bravery* 4 the practice of: *cookery*

-es See **-s**

-ese (iːz) a place of origin or language: *Chinese, journalese*

-ess (ɪs) (used to make the feminine of nouns): *lioness, countess*

-est (ɪst) (used to make the superlative of adjectives): *fastest, tidiest*

-ette (et) 1 small: *cigarette* 2 (used to make feminine nouns): *usherette*

-fold (fəʊld) having a number of parts or multiplied by a number: *fivefold*

-ful (fʊl) 1 having a quality: *painful* 2 the amount that a... can hold: *spoonful*

-fy (faɪ), **-ify** (ɪfaɪ) make or become: *simplify, liquefy*

-gon (gən) an angle: *polygon*

-hood (hʊd) a state or condition; time of being something: *manhood, childhood*

-i (ɪ) (a person) belonging to a religion or people: *Iraqi, Bangladeshi*

-ian See **-an**

-ible See **-able**

-ic (ɪk), **-ical** (ɪkəl) related to: *poetic, fanatical*

-ice (ɪs) (used to make abstract nouns): *cowardice*

-ics (ɪks) a science, subject, or group of activities: *physics, politics, acrobatics*

-ide (aɪd) a chemical compound: *cyanide*

-ie See **-y**

-ify See **-fy**

-ine (aɪn) made of; like; connected with: *crystalline*

-ing (ɪŋ) 1 (used to make the present participle of verbs): *eating* 2 an action, process, or result; thing: *meeting, wedding, welding*

-ion (ʃən) an action, process, or state: *creation, tension*

-ious (əs) having a quality: *suspicious*

-ise, -ize (aɪz) make: *equalise*

-ish (ɪʃ) 1 (belonging to) a country or language: *Swedish* 2 about: *seventyish* 3 like, having the bad qualities of: *childish, foolish* 4 to some extent: *brownish, tallish*

-ism (ɪzəm) 1 a system of beliefs, etc.: *socialism* 2 a quality, practice or action: *heroism, criticism*

-ist (ɪst) 1 (a person) following a system of beliefs, etc.: *communist* 2 a person who does something: *motorist*

-ite (aɪt) (used in the name of a chemical substance): *bauxite*

-itis (aɪtɪs) a disease: *tonsillitis*

-ity (ɪtɪ), **-ty** (tɪ) a quality, state, or condition: *stupidity, flexibility*

-ive (ɪv) that will cause something; having a quality: *productive, digestive*

-ize See **-ise**

-less (lɪs) not having: *harmless*

-let (lɪt) something small: *droplet*

-like (laɪk) like: *hair-like*

-ling (lɪŋ) someone or something small: *duckling*

-logy (lədʒɪ) a science or subject: *biology, geology*

-ly (lɪ) 1 (used to make adverbs): *nicely* 2 having qualities of: *brotherly* 3 happening at regular times: *yearly*

-man (mən) a person who lives in a place or does something: *Frenchman, fireman*

-ment (mənt) a state, condition, quality, result or process: *enjoyment, management, arrangement*

-most (məʊst) the furthest: *eastmost*

-ness (nɪs) a state, quality, or condition; example of this: *kindness, brittleness*

-oid (ɔɪd) like: *humanoid*

-or See **-er**

-ory (əri) 1 a place for: *observatory* 2 having a quality: *contributory*

-ous (əs) having a quality: *poisonous*

-phile (faɪl) (a person) liking something very much: *francophile*

-phobia (fəʊbɪə) fear: *claustrophobia*

-proof (pruːf) resisting something: *waterproof*

-r See **-er**

-ry See **-ery**

-s, -es (s, z, ɪz) 1 (used to make plurals): *books, pencils, horses* 2 (used to make the third person singular of present tense of verbs): *eats, rides*

-'s (s, z, ɪz) of... : *John's, house's, children's, houses'*

-ship (ʃɪp) 1 a state: *friendship* 2 a skill: *craftsmanship*

-some (səm) causing: *troublesome*

-th (θ) 1 (used to make adjectives from numbers): *fifth* 2 a state: *width*

-tion (ʃən) an action, process, or state or result; thing: *completion, imagination*

-ty See **-ity**

-ward (wʊd), **-wards** (wʊdz) in a direction: *homewards*

-ways (weɪz) showing direction: *sideways*

-wise (waɪz) 1 in such a way: *crosswise* 2 as far as... is concerned: *weatherwise*

-woman (wʊmən) a woman who lives in a place or does something: *saleswoman*

-y (ɪ) 1 having a quality: *dusty, sandy, sunny* 2 (also **-ie**) (used as affectionate name) small: *bunny, daddy, auntie* 3 the act of doing something; condition or state: *inquiry, envy*

Many of the words made with the endings in this list are not given separate definitions or pronunciations in the main part of the dictionary. But, by looking at this list, you will be able to work out what the whole word means and how it is pronounced.

Grammatical words

The English language contains grammatical and other words that have a function rather than a clear meaning in a sentence. This dictionary deals with such words better than other similar-sized dictionaries. But for a complete description of the words listed below, you should look in a good grammar book.

a, an	as	could	her
about	at		here
across	away	do	hers
after		down	herself
again	back	during	him
against	backwards		himself
ago	be	either	his
ahead	because	enough	how
all	before	ever	
along	behind	every	I
already	below		if
always	beneath	far	in
and	beside	few	inside
another	between	for	it
any	beyond	forth	its
anybody	both	forwards	itself
anyone	but	from	
anything	by		just
apart		have	
around	can	he	less

like	off	somebody	us
lot	on	someone	
	once	something	very
many	one	sometimes	
may	oneself	still	we
me	only		what
might	onto	than	when
mine	or	that	where
more	other	the	which
most	our	their	while
much	ours	theirs	who
must	ourselves	them	whom
my	out	themselves	whose
myself	outside	then	why
	over	there	will
near		these	with
neither	past	they	within
never		this	without
next	quite	those	would
no		through	
nobody	round	till	yes
none		to	yet
no-one	same	together	you
nor	shall	too	your
not	she		yours
nothing	should		yourself
now	since	under	yourselves
	so	until	
of	some	up	
		upon	

Irregular verbs

Infinitive	Past Tense	Past Participle	Infinitive	Past Tense	Past Participle
abide	abode, abided	abode, abided	bespeak	bespoke	bespoken
arise	arose	arisen	bet	bet, betted	bet, betted
awake	awoke	awaked, awoken	bid	bade, bid	bidden, bid
			bide	bode, bided	bided
be	was; were	been	bind	bound	bound
bear	bore	borne	bite	bit	bitten, bit
beat	beat	beaten	bleed	bled	bled
become	became	become	bless	blessed, blest	blessed, blest
befall	befell	befallen	blow	blew	blown
beget	begot	begotten	break	broke	broken
begin	began	begun	breed	bred	bred
behold	beheld	beheld	bring	brought	brought
bend	bent	bent	broadcast	broadcast, broadcasted	broadcast, broadcasted
beseech	besought	besought			
beset	beset	beset	build	built	built

xvi

Infinitive	Past Tense	Past Participle	Infinitive	Past Tense	Past Participle
burn	burnt, burned	burnt, burned	know	knew	known
burst	burst	burst	lay	laid	laid
buy	bought	bought	lead	led	led
cast	cast	cast	lean	leant, leaned	leant, leaned
catch	caught	caught	leap	leapt, leaped	leapt, leaped
choose	chose	chosen	learn	learnt, learned	learnt, learned
cleave	clove, cleft	cloven, cleft	leave	left	left
cling	clung	clung	lend	lent	lent
come	came	come	let	let	let
cost	cost	cost	lie	lay	lain
creep	crept	crept	light	lighted, lit	lighted, lit
cut	cut	cut	lose	lost	lost
deal	dealt	dealt	make	made	made
dig	dug	dug	mean	meant	meant
do	did	done	meet	met	met
draw	drew	drawn	mislay	mislaid	mislaid
dream	dreamt, dreamed	dreamt, dreamed	mislead	misled	misled
			mistake	mistook	mistaken
drink	drank	drunk	misunderstand	misunderstood	misunderstood
drive	drove	driven	mow	mowed	mown
dwell	dwelt	dwelt	partake	partook	partaken
eat	ate	eaten	pay	paid	paid
fall	fell	fallen	put	put	put
feed	fed	fed	read	read (red)	read (red)
feel	felt	felt	rend	rent	rent
fight	fought	fought	ride	rode	ridden
find	found	found	ring	rang	rung
flee	fled	fled	rise	rose	risen
fling	flung	flung	run	ran	run
fly	flew	flown	saw	sawed	sawn
forbid	forbade, forbad	forbidden	say	said	said
			see	saw	seen
forecast	forecast, forecasted	forecast, forecasted	seek	sought	sought
forget	forgot	forgotten	sell	sold	sold
forgive	forgave	forgiven	send	sent	sent
forsake	forsook	forsaken	set	set	set
freeze	froze	frozen	sew	sewed	sewn, sewed
get	got	got; gotten (US)	shake	shook	shaken
			shear	sheared	shorn, sheared
			shed	shed	shed
gild	gilded, gilt	gilded	shine	shone, shined	shone, shined
gird	girded, girt	girded, girt	shoe	shod	shod
give	gave	given	shoot	shot	shot
go	went	gone	show	showed	shown, showed
grind	ground	ground			
grow	grew	grown	shrink	shrank, shrunk	shrunk
hang	hung, hanged	hung, hanged	shut	shut	shut
have	had	had	sing	sang	sung
hear	heard	heard	sink	sank	sunk
heave	heaved, hove	heaved, hove	sit	sat	sat
hew	hewed	hewed, hewn	slay	slew	slain
hide	hid	hidden	sleep	slept	slept
hit	hit	hit	slide	slid	slid
hold	held	held	sling	slung	slung
hurt	hurt	hurt	slink	slunk	slunk
inlay	inlaid	inlaid	slit	slit	slit
keep	kept	kept	smell	smelt, smelled	smelt, smelled
kneel	knelt	knelt	smite	smote	smitten
knit	knitted, knit	knitted, knit	sow	sowed	sown, sowed

IRREGULAR VERBS

Infinitive	Past Tense	Past Participle	Infinitive	Past Tense	Past Participle
speak	spoke	spoken	take	took	taken
speed	sped, speeded	sped, speeded	teach	taught	taught
spell	spelt, spelled	spelt, spelled	tear	tore	torn
spend	spent	spent	tell	told	told
spill	spilt, spilled	spilt, spilled	think	thought	thought
spin	spun, span	spun	thrive	throve, thrived	thriven,
spit	spat	spat			thrived
split	split	split	throw	threw	thrown
spoil	spoilt, spoiled	spoilt, spoiled	thrust	thrust	thrust
spread	spread	spread	tread	trod	trodden, trod
spring	sprang	sprung	unbend	unbent	unbent
stand	stood	stood	undergo	underwent	undergone
stave	staved, stove	staved, stove	understand	understood	understood
steal	stole	stolen	undertake	undertook	undertaken
stick	stuck	stuck	underwrite	underwrote	underwritten
sting	stung	stung	undo	undid	undone
stink	stank, stunk	stunk	upset	upset	upset
strew	strewed	strewn,	wake	woke, waked	waked, woken
		strewed	wear	wore	worn
stride	strode	stridden	weave	wove	woven
strike	struck	struck	wed	wedded, wed	wedded, wed
string	strung	strung	weep	wept	wept
strive	strove	striven	win	won	won
swear	swore	sworn	wind (waɪnd)	wound	wound
sweep	swept	swept	withdraw	withdrew	withdrawn
swell	swelled	swollen,	withhold	withheld	withheld
		swelled	withstand	withstood	withstood
swim	swam	swum	wring	wrung	wrung
swing	swung	swung	write	wrote	written

Abbreviations used in this dictionary

abbrev.	abbreviation		*ncu*	countable and
adj	adjective			uncountable noun
adv	adverb		*nu*	uncountable noun
Brit	British English		*pl*	plural
conj	conjunction		*prep*	preposition
def.	definition		*pron*	pronoun
defs.	definitions		*US*	American English
esp.	especially		*v*	verb
etc.	et cetera		*vi*	intransitive verb
infml	informal		*vt*	transitive verb
interj	interjection		*vti*	transitive and
n	noun			intransitive verb
nc	countable noun			

A

a (eɪ unstressed ə) (also, before a vowel or sometimes h, an) determiner 1 (used to indicate a person or thing not already mentioned): *A strange man spoke to me.* 2 in or for each: *three meals a day; twice a year.* 3 a person or thing like: *He is quite a Romeo.* 4 one kind of: *Here is a flower you will like.* 5 some sort of: *She really has a love of life.*

aback (ə'bæk) adv take aback surprise; shock.

abacus ('æbəkəs) nc, pl -cuses, -ci (saɪ) a frame holding wires with sliding markers on them, used for adding, multiplying, etc.

abandon (ə'bændən) vt 1 leave, esp. alone or without help. 2 give up; stop: *We abandoned the game because of the storm.* ● nu freedom from care or control: *They joined in the dance with complete abandon.* abandonment nu

abase (ə'beɪs) vt humble or lower (someone, something, or oneself): *an abased form of poetry; He refused to abase himself.*

abashed (ə'bæʃt) adj ashamed; made to feel silly.

abate (ə'beɪt) vti make or become less or weaker: *The storm is abating.* abatement nu

abattoir ('æbətwɑː*) n See slaughterhouse.

abbess ('æbes) nc a nun in charge of an abbey.

abbey ('æbɪ) nc 1 a building where monks or nuns live, governed by an abbot or abbess. 2 a church that was once part of an abbey.

abbot ('æbət) nc a monk in charge of an abbey.

abbreviate (ə'briːvɪˌeɪt) vt shorten (esp. a word). abbreviation (ə,briːvɪ'eɪʃən) 1 nc a part, or only the first letter, of a word standing for the whole word: *etc.* (for 'et cetera'); *UNO* (for 'United Nations Organisation'). 2 nu the act of abbreviating.

abdicate ('æbdɪkeɪt) vti (esp. of a king or queen) give up (one's position, duty, or rights). abdication (,æbdɪ'keɪʃən) ncu (an example of) abdicating.

abdomen ('æbdəmən) nc 1 *anatomy* the lower half of the main part of the body, containing the stomach, etc. 2 *zoology* the rear part of an insect, spider, etc. abdominal (æb'dɒmɪnəl) adj

abduct (əb'dʌkt) vt take (a person) away by force.

aberration (,æbə'reɪʃən) nc 1 a movement away from what is usual or normal; a mistake in behaviour. 2 an example of forgetting something. 3 a fault in a mirror or lens.

abet (ə'bet) vt help (someone) in (a crime, etc.): *He's charged with aiding and abetting a robbery.*

abeyance (ə'beɪəns) n in abeyance not in use or in force for a period of time: *The school's rules were in abeyance during the holiday.*

abhor (əb'hɔː*) vt hate; consider disgusting. abhorrence (əb'hɒrəns) nu abhorrent (əb'hɒrənt) adj causing hatred and disgust.

abide (ə'baɪd) archaic vi live. cannot abide dislike or hate. abide by keep to (a rule, promise, etc.).

ability (ə'bɪlɪtɪ) 1 nu cleverness; the state of being able. 2 nc, pl -ties a cleverness in doing one or more particular things.

abject ('æbdʒekt) adj 1 miserable, hopeless: *an abject liar.* 2 cowardly: *an abject apology.*

ablaze (ə'bleɪz) adj on fire; burning.

able ('eɪbəl) adj clever; good: *He's an able speaker.* be able (to do something) (used esp. in place of missing parts of the verb 'can') can: *Will you be able to go?* ablebodied (,eɪbəl'bɒdɪd) adj having a fit, healthy body, esp. not disabled.

ablution (ə'bluːʃən) nc (usually pl) the act of washing, esp. at a religious occasion: *perform one's ablutions.*

abnormal (æb'nɔːməl) adj not normal; strange. abnormality (,æbnɔː'mælɪtɪ) ncu, pl -ties (an example of) being abnormal.

aboard (ə'bɔːd) adv, adj, prep on, onto, in, or into (a ship, plane, train, etc.).

abode¹ (ə'bəʊd) nc a place to live in; home.

abode² past tense and past participle of abide.

abolish (ə'bɒlɪʃ) vt put an end to (a law, practice, etc.). abolition (,æbə'lɪʃən) nu

abominable (ə'bɒmɪnəbəl) adj 1 causing hate or disgust. 2 *infml* very bad or unpleasant: *work of abominable quality.*

abominate (ə'bɒmɪneɪt) vt hate. abomination (ə,bɒmɪ'neɪʃən) 1 nu hate or disgust: *an abomination of violence.* 2 nc an abominable person, thing, or action.

aborigine (,æbə'rɪdʒɪnɪ) nc a member of the original people living in a part of the world. aboriginal adj Aboriginal nc (also Aborigine) an Australian aborigine.

abort (ə'bɔːt) vt 1 cause (a child) to be born too early so that it dies. 2 end (a space flight or other undertaking) earlier than planned. abortive (ə'bɔːtɪv) adj (of an attempt, etc.) unsuccessful.

abortion (ə'bɔːʃən) ncu the causing of a child to be born too early so that it dies.

abound (ə'baʊnd) *vi* exist in large quantities. **abound in** or **with** contain or possess much or many: *The book abounds with photographs.*

about (ə'baʊt) *prep* 1 to do with; in connection with: *What's this book about?* 2 on or occupied with: *Go about your business.* ● *adv* roughly; near enough: *about twenty people.* ● *prep, adv* 1 in or near: *He's somewhere about (the place).* 2 around: *My enemies are all about me.* 3 from place to place (in): *Just drive about for a bit.* 4 here and there: *There were a lot of plants about the house.* **be about (to do something)** be on the point of or intending (to do something) very soon. **how** or **what about...?** *infml* I suggest (having, doing, etc.): *How about lunch?*

above (ə'bʌv) *prep, adv* in, at, or into a higher position (than): *Trees grow above the ground.* ● *prep* 1 more or greater than: *numbers above 100.* 2 beyond; not open to: *above suspicion.* 3 having too good a character for (doing something bad): *above stealing.* ● *adj, adv* (mentioned) at an earlier place in a book, letter, etc.: *the above-named people.* **above all** more (important) than anything else: *Above all, don't forget your camera.* **the above** what has gone before in a book, letter, etc.

abrasion (ə'breɪʒən) 1 *nu* wearing away by rubbing. 2 *nc* a place where abrasion happens. **abrasive** (ə'breɪsɪv) *adj* 1 causing abrasion. 2 making other people annoyed: *abrasive remarks.*

abreast (ə'brest) *adj* 1 side by side and facing the same way; level: *The soldiers marched four abreast.* 2 (followed by **of**) aware (of); up to date (with): *A businessman should keep abreast of new products.*

abridge (ə'brɪdʒ) *vt* shorten (a book, story, etc.). **abridgement** 1 *ncu* (an example of) abridging. 2 *nc* something abridged.

abroad (ə'brɔːd) *adv* 1 in or to a foreign country. 2 (of news, etc.) current; about: *There is an uneasy feeling abroad.*

abrupt (ə'brʌpt) *adj* 1 sudden: *an abrupt stop.* 2 not gentle or polite in speech or manner. 3 steep: *abrupt cliffs.* **abruptly** *adv*

abscess ('æbses) *nc* a sore in which pus collects.

abscond (əb'skɒnd) *vi* go away secretly, esp. with something stolen.

absent ('æbsənt) *adj* not present; away; not in existence. ● (æb'sent) *vt* make (oneself) absent; keep (oneself) away. **absence** ('æbsəns) *nu* 1 the fact of being absent. 2 lack; non-existence. 3 *nc* a period of absence. **absentee** (ˌæbsən'tiː) *nc* a person who is absent, esp. from work. **absent-minded** (ˌæbsənt'maɪndɪd) *adj* forgetful or

not giving one's full attention.

absolute ('æbsəluːt) *adj* 1 complete; total: *an absolute victory.* 2 (of a measurement, etc.) having no conditions or restrictions: *absolute ownership; an absolute majority.* 3 pure: *absolute alcohol.* **absolutely** ('æbsəluːtlɪ, ˌæbsə'luːtlɪ) *adv* 1 completely. 2 (used to agree with a comment or in reply to a question)

absolution (ˌæbsə'luːʃən) *ncu* (an example of) absolving.

absolve (əb'zɒlv) *vt* 1 (often followed by **from**) free (someone from guilt or duty). 2 say that (someone) is not guilty.

absorb (əb'zɔːb, əb'sɔːb) *vt* 1 soak up (liquid). 2 occupy the attention of (someone): *He was absorbed in his book.* 3 not reflect (heat, light, etc.). 4 include: *We've got all the people we need, but we can probably absorb a few more.* **absorbent** *adj* able to absorb (defs. 1, 3). **absorbing** *adj* interesting; occupying the attention of (someone). **absorption** (əb'zɔːpʃən, əb'sɔːpʃən) *nu*

abstain (əb'steɪn) *vi* 1 not vote. 2 (usually followed by **from**) not use, do, etc.: *abstain from drinking alcohol.* **abstinence** ('æbstɪnəns) *nu* the act of not doing or using something, esp. the drinking of alcohol.

abstract ('æbstrækt) *adj* 1 not to do with actual objects: *abstract art.* 2 not to do with actual practice: *Our plans are still rather abstract.* ● *nc* 1 a very short version of a book, article, etc. 2 an abstract painting, sculpture, etc. ● (əb'strækt) *vt* consider (a quality, etc.) in an abstract way. **abstraction** (æb'strækʃən) 1 *nu* the condition of not paying attention to anything. 2 *ncu* (an example of) abstracting. 3 *nc* something abstracted.

abstruse (æb'struːs) *adj* (of a remark, book, etc.) difficult to understand.

absurd (əb'sɜːd) *adj* unreasonable; silly. **absurdity** (əb'sɜːdɪtɪ) 1 *nu* the quality of being absurd. 2 *nc, pl* **-ties** something absurd. **absurdly** *adv*

abundant (ə'bʌndənt) *adj* 1 plentiful. 2 (followed by **in**) having plenty of: *a field abundant in flowers.* **abundance** *nu* (usually preceded by **in** or followed by **of**) plenty; a plentiful quantity: *There was food in abundance at the feast; an abundance of books in almost every room.* **abundantly** *adv*

abuse (ə'bjuːz) *vt* 1 use badly or not properly. 2 insult; speak unkindly about or to (someone). ● (ə'bjuːs) *nu* 1 improper use. 2 insults. **abusive** (ə'bjuːsɪv) *adj*

abysmal (ə'bɪzməl) *adj* 1 (of bad things) very great: *abysmal stupidity.* 2 *infml* very bad; of very poor quality.

abyss (ə'bɪs) *nc* a very deep narrow hole or valley.

acacia (ə'keɪʃə) *nc* a tree or bush with yellow or white flowers.

academic (ˌækə'demɪk) *adj* **1** to do with schools, universities, etc., or with learning or teaching. **2** not practical or to do with actual experience: *My interest in cars is only academic as I can't afford one.* ●*nc* a member of a university, college, etc., esp. a teacher.

academy (ə'kædəmɪ) *nc, pl* **-mies 1** a college of higher learning, usually for a particular subject: *a music academy.* **2** a society for encouraging science or the arts: *the Royal Academy of Arts.*

accede (ək'siːd) *vi* (usually followed by **to**) **1** enter or obtain (a position, esp. as king or queen): *When the King dies, his son will accede to the throne.* **2** agree (to a demand, etc.).

accelerate (ək'seləreɪt) *vti* (cause to) move or happen faster; speed up. **acceleration** (əkˌselə'reɪʃən) *nu* **accelerator** *nc* something that accelerates something else, esp. the part of a vehicle pressed by the driver with his right foot.

accent ('æksənt) *nc* **1** a way that people from a particular place speak: *You can recognise an American by his accent.* **2** extra force given to part of a word in speech. **3** a mark written above or below a letter in a word to show how it is said. **4** a part of something, to which the maker, author, or organiser gives more attention or importance. ●(æk'sent) *vt* say or write with an accent.

accentuate (æk'sentjʊeɪt) *vt* give extra force, weight, or importance to.

accept (ək'sept) *vt* **1** (agree to) receive (a gift, etc.). **2** say yes to (an invitation). **3** consider or deal with in a kind or friendly way: *Foreigners here are soon accepted by most people.* **4** believe (an explanation, story, etc.). **acceptable** *adj* **1** satisfactory; all right: *He produces acceptable work.* **2** (esp. of a gift) welcome. **acceptance** *ncu* an act of accepting or an act or the state of being accepted: *His plans found acceptance everywhere; The idea slowly gained acceptance.*

access ('ækses) *nu* entrance or approach: *Access to the house is from the road.*

accessible (ək'sesəbəl) *adj* (often followed by **to**) able to be entered or reached: *The information is accessible to anyone who wants it.*

accession (ək'seʃən) *nu* the act of acceding (**accede** def. 1).

accessory (ək'sesərɪ) *nc, pl* **-ries 1** an extra part of a car, camera, or of any other machine or device. **2** a small piece of women's dress, such as a scarf or a handbag. **3** a person who has a part in the planning of a crime without actually committing it.

accident ('æksɪdənt) *nc* **1** an unfortunate event, esp. causing damage or injury. **2** an unintended or chance event: *The fact that these numbers are the same is an accident; We met by accident.* **accidental** (ˌæksɪ'dentəl) *adj* **1** unintended; chance: *accidental damage.* **2** extra or unnecessary. **accidentally** *adv*

acclaim (ə'kleɪm) *vt* **1** express one's approval of, esp. by shouting, clapping, etc. **2** welcome (someone) on becoming: *He was acclaimed king.* **3** recognise publicly the quality of (someone or something): *She was acclaimed the best star in the film.* ●*nu* **1** (esp. shouted) welcome or approval. **2** popularity: *The book won wide acclaim.* **acclamation** (ˌæklə'meɪʃən) *ncu* (a) welcome or approval, esp. shouted.

acclimatise (ə'klaɪmətaɪz) *vti* (cause to) become used to new conditions or surroundings.

accolade ('ækəˌleɪd) *nc* a show or expression of praise or strong approval.

accommodate (ə'kɒmədeɪt) *vt* **1** provide (someone) with something, esp. somewhere to stay or live. **2** contain: *a room to accommodate several hundred books.* **3** (usually followed by **to**) alter so as to suit or fit in with: *We can accommodate ourselves to a new timetable.* **accommodation** (əˌkɒmə'deɪʃən) *nu* **1** the act of accommodating. **2** somewhere to live.

accompany (ə'kʌmpənɪ) *vt* **1** travel, be put, or exist with: *He accompanied me on the train.* **2** (followed by **with**) add to: *She accompanied her welcome with a kiss.* **3** music play a less important part than: *I accompanied the song on the piano.* **accompaniment** *nc* something that accompanies (**accompany** def. 3), such as a musical part. **accompanist** *nc* a person who plays a musical accompaniment.

accomplice (ə'kʌmplɪs) *nc* a person who takes part in a crime with another person.

accomplish (ə'kʌmplɪʃ) *vt* manage to do. **accomplished** *adj* good; clever: *an accomplished singer.* **accomplishment** *nc* **1** the act of accomplishing something. **2** something that has been accomplished. **3** a well-learned ability.

accord (ə'kɔːd) *n* harmony. **of one's own accord** gladly or without being asked to.

according (ə'kɔːdɪŋ) *adj* **according to 1** in a manner suitable for: *Each person is paid according to his needs.* **2** in the words of; as said by; as written by or in: *According to one report, three people had been hurt in the crash.* **3** also **in accordance with** in a manner ordered or recommended by (the law, etc.). **accordingly** *adv* suitably: *This is a* *serious crime and you will be punished accordingly.*

accordion (ə'kɔːdɪən) *nc* a musical instrument in which air is blown across reeds, the notes being controlled by one's fingers and the wind being produced by pumping with one's arms: see picture at **musical instruments.**

accost (ə'kɒst) *vt* approach and speak to (someone, usually a stranger), esp. in the street.

account (ə'kaʊnt) *nc* **1** an arrangement by which a person or business keeps money at a bank or receives money from it. **2** a report or description. **3** a statement of the money paid and received by a business. **on account of** because of. **take (something) into account** or **take account of** consider; allow for. **accountable** *adj* **1** responsible to someone for something. **2** able to be explained. **account for 1** provide an **account** (def. 3) of (money). **2** explain; give a reason for. **3** kill; destroy; get rid of.

accountant (ə'kaʊntənt) *nc* a person who organises and checks the accounts of a business and advises on the use of money. **accountancy** *nu* the work of an accountant.

accredited (ə'krɛdɪtɪd) *adj* (esp. of a representative of a country) formally recognised.

accrue (ə'kruː) *vi* (esp. of an amount of money) increase by being added to.

accumulate (ə'kjuːmjʊleɪt) *vti* (cause to) increase or collect. **accumulation** (ə,kjuːmjʊ'leɪʃən) **1** *nu* the act of accumulating. **2** *nc* something that has accumulated. **accumulator** *nc* also (**rechargeable**) **battery** a device for storing electricity.

accurate ('ækjʊrət) *adj* exactly right or true: *an accurate report; an accurate measurement.* **accuracy** *nu* **accurately** *adv*

accursed (ə'kɜːsɪd, ə'kɜːst) *adj* hateful; annoying.

accuse (ə'kjuːz) *vt* say that (someone) did something wrong, esp. a crime: *He was accused of murder.* **the accused** the person or persons accused of a particular crime. **accusation** (,ækjuː'zeɪʃən) *nc* **accuser** *nc*

accustom (ə'kʌstəm) *vt* make used (to something): *You must accustom your eyes to the light.* **accustomed** *adj* **1** usual. **2** used (to something).

ace (eɪs) *nc* **1** the playing-card in each suit that counts as the 'one': *the ace of hearts.* **2** a person who is very good or clever at something: *a flying ace.*

acetate ('æsɪteɪt) *chemistry ncu* a (particular) salt of acetic acid, used esp. in man-made cloths.

acetic (ə'siːtɪk) *adj* to do with vinegar: *acetic acid.*

acetylene (ə'sɛtɪliːn) *nu* a poisonous gas that can be burned, esp. to produce a very hot flame for cutting and joining metal.

ache (eɪk) *nc* a dull, lasting pain. ●*vi* feel an ache: *My feet ache from all that walking.*

achieve (ə'tʃiːv) *vt* succeed in obtaining or doing: *With a lot of work, you could achieve a good result.* **achievement 1** *nu* the act of achieving. **2** *nc* something achieved.

acid ('æsɪd) *ncu* a (type of) substance, that, dissolved in water, can attack metals and form salts. ●*adj* **1** to do with acid, esp. sour-tasting. **2** (of something said) bitter; biting: *an acid remark.* **acidity** (ə'sɪdɪtɪ) *nu*

acknowledge (ək'nɒlɪdʒ) *vt* **1** say or show that one knows of the truth, existence, presence, etc., of: *I acknowledge your success.* **2** let the sender know that one has received (a letter, etc.). **acknowledgement 1** *nu* the act of acknowledging. **2** *nc* a statement or message of acknowledgement.

acme ('ækmɪ) *ncu* the highest point or point of greatest excellence.

acne ('æknɪ) *nu* a skin disease common in young people, causing spots, esp. on the face.

acorn ('eɪkɔːn) *nc* the fruit of the oak tree: see picture.

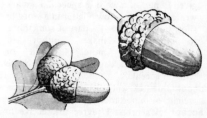

acorn

acoustics (ə'kuːstɪks) *nu* **1** *(with singular verb)* the study of sound. **2** *(with plural verb)* the properties of a room, etc., that affect sound heard in it: *This hall has poor acoustics.* **acoustic** *adj* to do with sound or acoustics.

acquaint (ə'kweɪnt) *vt* (usually followed by **with**) make (someone) familiar: *I've acquainted myself with the rules; I think we ought to get better acquainted.* **acquaintance 1** *nc* a person whom one knows slightly. **2** *nu* familiarity; knowledge: *He has little acquaintance with other languages.* **make (someone's) acquaintance** meet or get to know (someone).

acquiesce (,ækwɪ'es) *vi* (often followed by **in**) silently agree (to), perhaps unwillingly: *Seeing that he had no other choice, he acquiesced in the plan.*

acquire (ə'kwaɪə*) *vt* get; become the owner or possessor of. **acquisition** (,ækwɪ'zɪʃən)

1 *nu* the act of acquiring. 2 *nc* something acquired, esp. of great value.

acquit (ə'kwɪt) *vt* declare (someone) to be not guilty: *He was acquitted of murder.* **acquit oneself** behave (well, bravely, etc.). **acquittal** *nc*

acre ('eɪkə*) *nc* a measure of area = 4046.86 sq m **acreage** ('eɪkərɪdʒ) *nc* an area expressed in acres.

acrid ('ækrɪd) *adj* 1 having a sharp unpleasant smell. 2 (of a person, argument, etc.) bitter.

Acrilan ('ækrɪlæn) *Trademark nu* a manmade material used for clothes, carpets, etc.

acrimonious (,ækrɪ'məʊnɪəs) *adj* (of a person, argument, etc.) bitter.

acrobat ('ækrəbæt) *nc* a person who entertains with various jumping and balancing acts, such as walking a tightrope: see picture. **acrobatic** (,ækrə'bætɪk) *adj* **acrobatics** (,ækrə'bætɪks) *nu (with singular verb)* the art of an acrobat.

acrobat

acronym (,ækrənɪm) *nc* a name made from the first letters of words, such as 'UNESCO' from 'United Nations Educational, Scientific, and Cultural Organisation'.

across (ə'krɒs) *prep, adv* from one side to the other (of): *He walked across the road; The lake is four kilometres across.*

act (ækt) 1 *vti* play (a part in a film or play). *vi* 2 behave; carry out actions: *to act for someone in court.* 3 do a particular action: *The government should act to prevent war; Who'll act as leader?* ●*nc* 1 something done: *an act of kindness.* 2 a part of a stage play. 3 a short piece of entertainment. 4 a law passed by a parliament. **act of God** a sudden natural event, such as lightning or a flood.

acting ('æktɪŋ) *nu* the activity of playing parts in films and plays. ●*adj* doing something in someone else's place: *the acting governor of the district.*

action ('ækʃən) *nu* 1 the state of doing something or being active. 2 energy; activity: *I want to see some action here!* 3 fighting in a war: *He was killed in action. nc* 4 something done; an act. 5 a movement or manner of moving. 6 a case brought by one party against another in a court of law. **out of action** (of a machine, etc.) not working.

activate ('æktɪveɪt) *vt* make active.

active ('æktɪv) *adj* 1 doing something; in action. 2 using body movements: *active sports.* 3 having or using energy: *He's very young and active.* 4 to do with a verb of which the action described is actually carried out by its subject to something else: *In 'I wrote the book', 'wrote' is an active verb.* **actively** *adv*

activity (æk'tɪvɪtɪ) 1 *nu* the state of being active. 2 *nc, pl* **-ties** a particular action or occupation: *Reading is usually an indoor activity.*

actor ('æktə*) *nc* a man who acts in a film or play.

actress ('æktrɪs) *nc* a woman who acts in a film or play.

actual ('æktʃʊəl) *adj* real; really in existence; true. **actually** *adv* in actual fact; really.

actuate ('æktʃʊeɪt) *vt* cause (someone or a machine) to work, move, or act.

acumen (ə'kjuːmen, 'ækjʊmen) *nu* good judgement or understanding: *business acumen.*

acupuncture ('ækjʊ,pʌŋktʃə*) *nu* the treatment of medical complaints by sticking needles into the skin at various special points.

acute (ə'kjuːt) *adj* 1 showing good judgement or insight. 2 strong, sharp, or serious: *acute pain.* 3 (of a disease) serious but not long-lasting. 4 (of an angle) of less than ninety degrees.

ad (æd) *infml n* short for **advertisement**.

adamant ('ædəmənt) *adj* refusing to give up a course of action.

Adam's apple ('ædəmz) *anatomy nc* the lump at the front of the neck, esp. in men, made by the larynx.

adapt (ə'dæpt) *vti* change, esp. so as to fit in with (something or someone else): *Dogs adapt easily to new homes.* **adaptable** *adj* **adaptation** (,ædæp'teɪʃən) 1 *nu* the act of adapting. 2 *nc* something resulting from adaptation.

add (æd) *vt* 1 also **add up** join (numbers) to produce a total: *If you add two and three, you get five.* 2 join (something) to something else: *Add some water to the milk.* 3 (followed by **to**) make greater in size or quantity: *This wood will add to the fire.* 4 go on (to say); say further: *'And make sure that you're not late,' she added.* **add up** 1 See **add** (def. 1). 2 produce a correct total. 3 *infml* seem probable or logical. **add up to** produce a total of; amount to.

addendum (ə'dendəm) *nc, pl* **-enda** (endə) something added, esp. something missed out of a book and printed at the end instead.

adder (ˈædə*) nc also **viper** a poisonous snake.

addict (ˈædɪkt) nc **1** a person who is dependent on something, esp. a drug. **2** infml a person who is very keen on something: a television addict. **addicted to** (əˈdɪktɪd) dependent on; unable to do without. **addiction** (əˈdɪkʃən) nu the state of being addicted to something.

addition (əˈdɪʃən) **1** nu the act of adding. **2** nc something added. **in addition (to)** besides; as well (as). **additional** adj added; extra.

additive (ˈædɪtɪv) nc a substance added to something to change or improve it.

addled (ˈædəld) adj **1** (of an egg) rotten. **2** confused.

address (əˈdres) nc **1** a description of where a home, office, etc., is, as used for sending letters. **2** the place described in an address. **3** a speech. ●vt **1** write an address on (an envelope, etc.). **2** also **address oneself** to speak or write to (someone). **3** direct (remarks) to someone: Please address your questions to me. **addressee** (ˌædreˈsiː) nc the person, business, etc., to whom a letter, etc., is addressed.

adduce (əˈdjuːs) vt supply (a fact, etc.) as proof or an example.

adenoids (ˈædəˌnɔɪds) n pl a part of the body, at the back of the nose and throat, that can grow and make it difficult to breathe through the nose.

adept (ˈædept) adj clever; skilled.

adequate (ˈædɪkwət) adj enough or sufficient (for something). **adequately** adv

adhere (ədˈhɪə*) vi **1** (usually followed by **to**) stick; be fixed. **2** (followed by **to**) follow (a rule, etc.). **3** (followed by **to**) support (an opinion, political party, etc.). **adherence** nu **adherent** nc someone who adheres (**adhere** def. 2). ●adj adhering.

adhesive (ədˈhiːsɪv) nu a substance used for sticking things together. ●adj adhering; sticky.

ad hoc (ˌæd ˈhɒk) Latin adj, adv for a particular purpose: an ad hoc arrangement.

adieu (əˈdjuː) French interj, nc, pl **-s**, **-x** (z) goodbye.

ad infinitum (ˌæd ɪnfɪˈnaɪtəm) Latin adv forever; endlessly.

adjacent (əˈdʒeɪsənt) adj nearby, esp. touching: Their house is adjacent to ours.

adjective (ˈædʒɪktɪv) nc a word describing a noun or pronoun, such as 'big' or 'red'. **adjectival** (ˌædʒɪkˈtaɪvəl) adj

adjoin (əˈdʒɔɪn) vt be next to; touch.

adjourn (əˈdʒɜːn) vti stop or put off until sometime in the future: This court is adjourned until tomorrow. **adjournment** ncu

adjudicate (əˈdʒuːdɪkeɪt) vti decide or judge (a court case) or in a competition, etc. **adjudicator** nc

adjunct (ˈædʒʌŋkt) nc something or someone added or extra.

adjust (əˈdʒʌst) **1** vt alter (something) slightly, esp. to correct a position, setting, etc. **2** vti change to suit a new situation or new surroundings. **adjustable** adj **adjustment** ncu

ad lib (ˌæd ˈlɪb) Latin adv **1** as much or long as one likes. **2** without preparation: He did his whole act ad lib. ●adj done **ad lib** (def. 2). **ad-lib** vi speak, entertain, etc., ad lib. ●nc something done **ad lib** (def. 2).

administer (ədˈmɪnɪstə*) vt **1** manage; carry out (government, business, etc.). **2** give out; distribute. **administration** (ədˌmɪnɪˈstreɪʃən) **1** nu the act of administering. **2** nc a group of people who administer, esp. a government. **administrative** (ədˈmɪnɪstrətɪv) adj to do with administration. **administrator** nc

admirable (ˈædmərəbəl) adj deserving admiration; splendid. **admirably** adv

admiral (ˈædmərəl) nc an important officer in a navy, usually in charge of a large number of ships.

admire (ədˈmaɪə*) vt consider to be good or praiseworthy: His work is much admired. **admiration** (ˌædməˈreɪʃən) nu **admirer** nc **admiring** adj showing or feeling admiration: an admiring visitor.

admission (ədˈmɪʃən) nu **1** permission to enter. **2** the act of entering or being allowed to enter. **3** the price charged for **admission** (def. 1). **4** the act of confessing something one has done or not done.

admit (ədˈmɪt) vt **1** allow to enter: They admitted him to the private rooms. **2** confess: I admit to having lied. **3** recognise the truth of: He admitted that the mountain was difficult to climb. **admittance** nu the act of allowing or being allowed to enter. **admittedly** adv **1** without saying something is untrue; by general agreement: He was admittedly a good worker. **2** (esp. when beginning a sentence) I admit or agree (that): Admittedly, it was cold.

admixture (ædˈmɪkstʃə*) nc something added to a mixture; mixture.

admonish (ədˈmɒnɪʃ) formal vt **1** scold. **2** urge; warn: I admonish you to be careful.

ado (əˈduː) nu activity; business: without further ado.

adolescence (ˌædəˈlesəns) nu the period of human life during which a child becomes an adult. **adolescent** adj to do with adolescence. ●nc an adolescent person.

adopt (ə'dɒpt) *vt* **1** take (something or a child) over as if it were one's own. **2** choose (a course of action, etc.). **adoption** (ə'dɒpʃən) *ncu*

adore (ə'dɔː*) *vt* **1** love deeply. **2** *infml* like very much. **adorable** *adj* very pleasing or attractive. **adoration** (ˌædə'reɪʃən) *nu* deep love.

adorn (ə'dɔːn) *vt* make beautiful: *She was adorned with jewellery.* **adornment** *nc* something that adorns.

adrenalin (ə'drenəlɪn) *nu* a substance produced in the body that allows the blood to flow faster, etc., when one needs to be more active.

adrift (ə'drɪft) *adj* **1** floating in water and being moved only by currents and the wind. **2** *infml* not as intended: *I'm afraid our plan has gone adrift.*

adroit (ə'drɔɪt) *adj* clever; skilful.

adulation (ˌædjʊ'leɪʃən) *nu* praise that is more than is deserved or needed.

adult ('ædʌlt, ə'dʌlt) *adj* grown up; fully developed. ●*nc* an adult person, animal or plant.

adulterate (ə'dʌltəreɪt) *vt* mix something of lower value or quality into (food, etc.).

adultery (ə'dʌltərɪ) *nu* voluntary sexual union between a married man or woman and someone to whom they are not married.

advance (əd'vɑːns) **1** *vti* move forwards. *vt* **2** cause to happen earlier. **3** put forward or suggest (an idea, etc.). **4** lend (money). **5** improve; further: *This discovery has advanced our understanding of animal behaviour.* ●*ncu* **1** (a) forward movement. **2** (an) improvement; progress. *nc* **3** an amount of money lent. **4** a part of an amount of money paid before it is due. ●*adj* early; before the event: *advance warning.* **in advance (of)** before: *You'll be told in advance if you're going to be chosen; They arrived in advance of the others.* **advanced** *adj* far on in progress, knowledge, etc.: *advanced lessons in French.* **advancement** *nu* **1** being moved to a more important position or job: *He's due for advancement to manager.* **2** the act of improving or furthering: *the advancement of science.*

advantage (əd'vɑːntɪdʒ) **1** *nc* a better or more favourable position: *Your money gives you an advantage over most people.* **2** *nu* something extra that is gained: *There's no advantage in arriving early.* **take advantage of** make use of, sometimes unkindly or unfairly. **advantageous** (ˌædvən'teɪdʒəs) *adj* giving advantage: *a special advantageous price.*

advent ('ædvent) *literary or formal nc* a coming.

adventitious (ˌædven'tɪʃəs) *adj* **1** accidental; arriving unexpectedly. **2** (of roots) growing in an unusual position.

adventure (əd'ventʃə*) **1** *nc* a dangerous, exciting, or risky action or journey. **2** *nu* the state of adventure; risk; excitement. **adventurer** *nc* a person who undertakes adventures. **adventurous** *adj* like an adventure.

adverb ('ædvɜːb) *nc* a word that adds to the meaning of a verb, adjective, sentence, or other adverb, such as 'luckily' or 'well' in 'Luckily, he did it well'. **adverbial** (æd'vɜːbɪəl) *adj*

adversary ('ædvəsərɪ) *nc, pl* **-ries** an enemy or person with whom one is in competition.

adverse ('ædvɜːs) *adj* against or hurting one: *adverse criticism.* **adversely** *adv* **adversity** (əd'vɜːsɪtɪ) **1** *nu* adverse conditions: *brave in adversity.* **2** *nc, pl* **-ties** an adverse event.

advertise ('ædvətaɪz) *vt* make (a fact, product, etc.) known. **advertisement** (əd'vɜːtɪsmənt) (*infml abbrev.* **ad**, *Brit* **advert**) *nc* a sign, notice in a newspaper, short television film, etc., advertising something. **advertiser** *nc*

advice (əd'vaɪs) *nu* **1** a recommendation as to what action to take: *Let me give you some advice.* **2** information.

advise (əd'vaɪz) *vt* **1** give advice to; recommend: *I advise great care; We were advised to wait.* **2** inform; tell formally. **advisable** *adj* recommended; wise: *It would be advisable to wait.* **adviser** *nc* someone who gives advice, esp. one whose job is to do this. **advisory** (əd'vaɪzərɪ) *adj* giving advice.

advocate ('ædvəkeɪt) *vt* recommend (an action, etc.). ●('ædvəkət) *nc* **1** a person who advocates something: *an advocate of peace.* **2** a lawyer who tries to prove or disprove a case in court.

aegis ('iːdʒɪs) *nu* protection: *I'm doing this work under the aegis of the University.*

aerate ('eəreɪt) *vt* **1** add air or gas to (water, etc.), esp. to make a fizzy drink. **2** make (something) fresh, clean, or pure by making it open to air: *He dug the soil well so as to aerate it.*

aerial ('eərɪəl) *adj* to do with (the) air. ●*nc* also **antenna** a wire or metal pole, etc., used to send or receive radio and television signals.

aerobatics (ˌeərə'bætɪks) *nu (with singular verb)* dangerous flying in a plane, that is done for show.

aerodrome ('eərədrəʊm) *nc* a place where mainly small planes take off and land.

aerodynamics (ˌeərəʊdaɪ'næmɪks) *nu (with singular verb)* the study of objects moving through gases.

aerofoil ('eərəʊfɔɪl) *US* **airfoil** *nc* an object,

such as a plane wing, with surfaces shaped to produce lift when it is moved through the air.

aerogramme ('eərə,græm) *nc* also **aerogram, air letter** a letter sent by air on a single folded sheet of thin paper without an envelope.

aeronautics (,eərə'nɔːtɪks) *nu (with singular verb)* the study or practice of flight through the air.

aeroplane ('eərəpleɪn) *US* **airplane** (often shortened to **plane**) *nc* a heavier-than-air flying vehicle that has fixed wings and needs power to rise: see picture.

aeroplane

aerosol ('eərəsɒl) *nc* a container for a liquid, such as paint, that is held under pressure and can be let out in a spray.

aerospace ('eərəʊspeɪs) *nu* **1** the air round the earth together with the space beyond it. **2** the building of vehicles that fly in both air and space: *the aerospace industry.*

aesthetic (iːs'θetɪk) *adj* to do with a proper understanding of pure beauty, esp. in art, architecture, etc. **aesthetically** *adv* **aesthetics** *nu (with singular verb)* the study of the laws of beauty and good taste.

afar (ə'fɑː*) *archaic adv* a long way away.

affable ('æfəbəl) *adj* friendly or kind. **affability** (,æfə'bɪlɪtɪ) *nu* **affably** *adv*

affair (ə'feə*) *nc* **1** a matter; business: *The whole affair is a mystery.* **2** a sexual relationship between two people not married to each other.

affect[1] (ə'fekt) *vt* have an effect on; make a difference to: *This weather could affect the harvest.*

affect[2] *vt* pretend to feel or have (a quality or condition); put on a show of doing or being (something one is not): *Hearing him walk towards her, she decided to affect deafness if he spoke.* **affectation** (,æfek'teɪʃən) *nc* a pretence put on for show: *His foreign appearance is only an affectation.* **affected** *adj* **1** done as an affectation. **2** (of a person) having affectations.

affection (ə'fekʃən) *nu* a kindly or loving feeling: *affection for one's children.* **affectionate** (ə'fekʃənət) *adj* showing or feeling affection. **affectionately** *adv*

affidavit (,æfɪ'deɪvɪt) *nc* a sworn written statement for use in a court of law.

affiliate (ə'fɪlɪeɪt) *vt* connect (a person, society, etc.) to a (larger) organisation: *a local club affiliated to the national body.* ●

(ə'fɪlɪət) *nc* an affiliated person, society, etc. **affiliation** (ə,fɪlɪ'eɪʃən) *nu*

affinity (ə'fɪnɪtɪ) *nc, pl* **-ties 1** a liking: *an affinity for sport.* **2** a likeness; similarity: *an affinity between brothers.*

affirm (ə'fɜːm) *vt* declare or confirm to be true. **affirmation** (,æfə'meɪʃən) *ncu* **affirmative** (ə'fɜːmətɪv) *adj* affirming: *'Yes' is an affirmative answer.*

affix (ə'fɪks) *formal vt* fix; fasten: *A stamp should be affixed to the envelope.* ● ('æfɪks) *grammar nc* a part added at the beginning or end of a word to change its meaning such as 're-' in 'rewrite'.

afflict (ə'flɪkt) *vt* cause suffering or worry to: *Old age afflicts us all.* **affliction 1** *nu* the state of being afflicted. **2** *nc* something that afflicts.

affluent ('æflʊənt) *adj* wealthy; rich. **affluence** *nu*

afford (ə'fɔːd) *vt* **1** be able to spare: *I can't afford the time.* **2** have the means, time, or money for: *I can't afford a new coat; Can you afford to take a day off work?* **3** *formal* provide (with): *We may not be afforded such an opportunity again.*

affront (ə'frʌnt) *vt* insult. ● *nc* an insult.

afield (ə'fiːld) *adv* to or at a distance; away, esp. from home: *He hasn't gone far afield.*

afire (ə'faɪə*) *adj* on fire.

aflame (ə'fleɪm) *adj* in flames.

afloat (ə'fləʊt) *adj* floating.

afoot (ə'fʊt) *adv* about; happening: *There's evil afoot.*

aforementioned (ə'fɔː,menʃənd) *formal adj* already mentioned.

aforesaid (ə'fɔːsed) *formal adj* already mentioned.

afraid (ə'freɪd) *adj* **1** (often followed by **of**) feeling fear: *afraid of death; He's afraid that she won't be there.* **2** (followed by an infinitive) unwilling because of fear: *afraid to fight.* **I'm afraid** regretfully; unfortunately: *I'm afraid I've got bad news.*

afresh (ə'freʃ) *adv* again.

aft (ɑːft) *nautical, aviation, adj, adv* at or towards the back of a boat or plane.

after ('ɑːftə*) *prep, adv* **1** during the time following; later than. **2** in a place following; behind. ● *prep* **1** about: *He asked after you.* **2** hoping to find or receive: *I'm after that job.* **3** in the manner or style of: *a painting after the Italian masters.* **4** by the name of: *The city was called New York after York in England.* **5** *US* See **past** *prep* (def. **2**). ● *conj* following the time when: *You played after I did.* **after all 1** in spite of expectations: *So you went, after all!* **2** what is more important: *After all, it wouldn't have worked.*

after-effect ('ɑːftərɪ,fekt) *nc* an effect that

happens a long time after its cause.

aftermath ('ɑːftəmæθ, 'ɑːftəmɑθ) *ncu* results: *the aftermath of war.*

afternoon (ˌɑːftə'nuːn) *nc* the part of a day between midday and evening.

afterthought ('ɑːftəθɔːt) *nc* something thought of or added later.

afterwards ('ɑːftəwədz) *adv* after a particular event: *I'm in a meeting now, but I can see you afterwards.*

again (ə'gen, ə'geɪn) *adv* 1 (yet) another time; once more. 2 besides; in addition: *half as much again.* 3 on the other hand: *That could be right, but then again I can't prove it.* **now and again** occasionally; every so often. **time and (time) again** many times; repeatedly.

against (ə'genst, ə'geɪnst) *prep* 1 in opposition to: *the fight against crime; I'm against killing animals for food.* 2 (into a position) onto: *He hit his head against the wall; He's leaning against our car.* 3 as protection from: *I had to wear gloves against the cold.*

agape (ə'geɪp) *adj, adv* (with the mouth) open wide because of surprise, fear, etc.

agate ('ægɪt) *ncu* (a piece of) a hard stone used in jewellery.

age (eɪdʒ) *nc* 1 the length of the life or existence of someone or something: *What's the age of this horse?* 2 a period of life: *old age.* 3 a period of history: *the modern age.* 4 *infml (often pl)* a long time: *I did it ages ago.* 5 *nu* the quality of being old: *One gets slower with age.* ● *vti* make, become, or begin to seem old or older: *He has aged much under the heavy work of his new job.* **come** or **be of age** reach or have reached the age at which one becomes responsible for one's actions. **aged** *adj* 1 ('eɪdʒɪd) (of a person) old. 2 (eɪdʒd) having the age of: *a man aged forty.* **ageing** (also **aging**) ('eɪdʒɪŋ) *adj* old: *my ageing parents.* ● *nu* the process of growing old. **age-group** ('eɪdʒgruːp) *nc* people who are of a similar age. **age-old** ('eɪdʒəʊld) *adj* (of a thing) very old.

agency ('eɪdʒənsɪ) 1 *nc, pl* **-cies** the business or office of an agent: *a travel agency.* 2 *formal nu* action; help; influence: *I was separated from my family through the agency of war.*

agenda (ə'dʒendə) *nc* a list of matters to be dealt with, esp. by a committee.

agent ('eɪdʒənt) *nc* 1 a person who acts, esp. on business, for another: *an insurance agent; a travel agent.* 2 a substance that has an effect on something else: *a cleaning agent.*

agglomeration (əˌglɒmə'reɪʃən) *nc* a large collected quantity of something, esp. buildings forming a town, or rocks from a vol-

cano melted together in a disordered way.

agglutination (əˌgluːtɪ'neɪʃən) *nu* 1 *grammar* the building of words from parts that keep their meaning. 2 a group of things joined together with glue.

aggravate ('ægrəveɪt) *vt* 1 make worse. 2 *infml* annoy. **aggravation** *nu*

aggregate ('ægrɪgeɪt) *vt* join (esp. numbers) together. ● ('ægrɪgɪt) 1 *nc* something produced by aggregating; a total. 2 *nu* sand and stones used with cement to make concrete.

aggression (ə'greʃən) 1 *nc* an attack, esp. by one country on another. 2 *nu* the feeling of wanting to attack someone or something. **aggressive** (ə'gresɪv) *adj* showing or feeling aggression. **aggressor** (ə'gresə*) *nc* an attacker.

aggrieved (ə'griːvd) *adj* unfairly dealt with.

aghast (ə'gɑːst) *adj* horrified or very surprised.

agile ('ædʒaɪl) *adj* able to move quickly. **agility** (ə'dʒɪlɪtɪ) *nu*

aging ('eɪdʒɪŋ) *adj, n* See **ageing** under **age**.

agitate ('ædʒɪteɪt) *vt* 1 worry; excite. 2 shake (a liquid mixture, etc.). 3 *vi* (often followed by **for** or **against**) try to persuade people to have opinions for or against something. **agitation** (ˌædʒɪ'teɪʃən) *nu* **agitator** *nc*

aglow (ə'gləʊ) *adj* giving off light without burning.

agnostic (æg'nɒstɪk) *nc* a person who believes that it is impossible to know anything about a god. ● *adj* to do with this belief or with agnostics.

ago (ə'gəʊ) *adv* before now: *He was here ten minutes ago.*

agog (ə'gɒg) *adj* eager; curious.

agony ('ægənɪ) *nc, pl* **-nies** great pain or worry. **agonise** ('ægənaɪz) *vti* (cause to) suffer agony.

agrarian (ə'greərɪən) *adj* to do with land, esp. farmland.

agree (ə'griː) *vi* 1 (often followed by **with**) have the same opinion: *I agree with you that I should go.* 2 (often followed by **to**) approve; allow: *I won't agree to his going.* 3 (followed by **with**) (esp. of food) suit: *Milk doesn't agree with me.* 4 (often followed by **with**) match; be similar: *These figures don't agree with each other.* *vt* 5 (sometimes followed by **on**) decide together: *We've agreed on where to meet.* 6 *grammar* (often followed by **with** or **in**) match in number, person, etc.: *In many languages adjectives must agree with nouns.* **agreeable** *adj* 1 pleasing; acceptable. 2 willing to agree. **agreeably** *adv* **agreement** 1 *nu* the act or state of agreeing. 2 *nc* an arrangement reached by agreement.

agriculture ('ægrɪkʌltʃə*) *nu* (the science or

practice of) the use of land for growing food and raising animals. **agricultural** (ˌægrɪˈkʌltʃərəl) *adj*

aground (əˈɡraʊnd) *adj, adv* (of a boat) on(to) the bottom of the sea, a lake, etc., in shallow water: *run aground.*

ah (ɑː) *interj* (used to express surprise, admiration, pain, etc.)

aha (ɑːˈhɑː) *interj* (used to express surprise, pleasure at a victory, etc.)

ahead (əˈhed) *adj, adv* in front; further forward. **ahead of** in front of; further forward than.

ahoy (əˈhɔɪ) *nautical interj* (used to attract attention): *Ship ahoy!*

aid (eɪd) 1 *nu* help, esp. money. 2 *nc* something that gives aid: *a walking aid.* ● *vt* give aid to; help. **first aid** help given immediately to an injured person. **in aid of** in support of; for the purpose of.

aide-de-camp (ˈeɪddəkɒŋ) *nc, pl* **aides-de-camp** (ˈeɪdzdəkɒŋ) an officer in an army, etc., serving as assistant to one above him: *abbrev.* ADC.

ail (eɪl) 1 *vi* be ill or in a bad state. 2 *vt* trouble; be wrong with: *What ails you?* **ailment** *nc* an illness, esp. a slight one.

aim (eɪm) 1 *vt* (often with **at** after direct object) point; direct: *Never aim a gun at anybody.* *vi* 2 (followed by an infinitive) intend; hope: *We aim to leave soon.* 3 (followed by **at** or **for**) try to get or bring about: *I'm aiming for a low price.* ● *nc* 1 the action of aiming. 2 something aimed at or for. **aimless** *adj* with no purpose or direction.

ain't (eɪnt) *not standard v* am not, are not, is not, have not, or has not.

air (eə*) 1 *nu* the mixture of gases that surrounds the earth. *nc* 2 a tune. 3 an appearance; manner: *He has the air of a happy man.* ● *vt* 1 let fresh, cool air reach (a room, etc.); let fresh, warm air reach (clothes, etc.). 2 express or make known (opinions, etc.). **airborne** (ˈeəbɔːn) *adj* (travelling or carried) in the air: *an airborne attack.* **air-conditioned** (ˌeəkənˈdɪʃənd, ˈeəkəndɪʃənd) *adj* (of a room, building, car, etc.) containing air that is cooled for comfort. **aircraft** (ˈeəkrɑːft) *nc, pl* **aircraft** a flying vehicle, such as a plane or helicopter. **aircraft carrier** a warship with a mainly flat top on which planes can take off and

aircraft carrier

land: see picture. **airfield** (ˈeəfiːld) *nc* a place where planes are kept and take off and land. **airfoil** (ˈeəfɔɪl) *US n* See **aerofoil**. **air force** a country's aeroplanes and men who fly them, used for defence and war. **air letter** See **aerogramme**. **airline** (ˈeəlaɪn) *nc* a business that transports people or goods by air. **airmail** (ˈeəmeɪl) *nu* mail carried in planes. **airman** (ˈeəmən) *nc, pl* **-men** (mən) a man who flies or helps to fly aircraft, esp. a pilot. **airplane** (ˈeəpleɪn) *US n* See **aeroplane**. **airport** (ˈeəpɔːt) *nc* a place where large aircraft for passengers or goods are kept and take off and land. **air raid** *nc* an attack by aircraft, esp. dropping bombs. **airship** (ˈeəʃɪp) *nc* a flying machine that gets its lift from a very large bag filled with a gas that is lighter than air: see picture. **airstrip** (ˈeəstrɪp) *nc* a piece of ground where planes take off and land. **airtight** (ˈeətaɪt) *adj* not allowing air in or out: *an airtight door.*

airship

airy (ˈeərɪ) *adj* **-ier, -iest** 1 (esp. of a room, etc.) containing much (fresh) air. 2 hopeful; not realistic: *airy plans.*

aisle (aɪl) *nc* a path between rows of seats in a church, plane, or theatre.

ajar (əˈdʒɑː*) *adj* (of a window or door) slightly open.

akin (əˈkɪn) *adj* (often followed by **to**) similar; related.

alacrity (əˈlækrɪtɪ) *nu* speed; haste.

alarm (əˈlɑːm) 1 *nu* frightened expectation of danger: *The noise of shouting filled him with alarm.* 2 *nc* a device that gives a warning of danger: *a fire alarm; a burglar alarm.* ● *vt* cause alarm in (someone). **alarm clock** a clock that rings a bell or gives some other signal at a set time: see picture. **alarming** *adj* giving cause for alarm.

alarm clock

alas (əˈlæs) *interj* also **alack** (used to express disappointment, sorrow, etc.)

albatross (ˈælbətrɒs) *nc* a large sea-bird.

albeit (ɔːlˈbiːɪt) *conj* even though.

albino (æl'biːnəʊ) *nc, pl* **-nos** a person or animal born with white skin and hair and pink eyes.

album ('ælbəm) *nc* **1** a book for keeping photographs, stamps, etc., in. **2** a set of gramophone records. **3** a gramophone record of several pieces of music. **4** a protective cover for a gramophone record.

alchemist ('ælkɪmɪst) *nc* a person who tries to make gold out of other metals.

alcohol ('ælkəhɒl) *nu* a clear liquid that is in drinks such as beer, wine, and spirits and is burnt to run engines, etc. **alcoholic** (,ælkə'hɒlɪk) *adj* to do with alcohol: *alcoholic drink.* ●*nc* a person who depends on taking alcoholic drink. **alcoholism** ('ælkəhɒlɪzəm) *nu* the state of being an alcoholic.

alcove ('ælkəʊv) *nc* a space set into the wall of a room.

alderman ('ɔːldəmən) *nc, pl* **-men** (mən) (in England and Wales until 1974) a senior member of a local council, serving under a mayor.

ale (eɪl) *n* See **beer**.

alert (ə'lɜːt) *adj* fully awake; ready for action. ●*nc* **1** a warning, esp. of an attack. **2** the period for which such a warning lasts. ●*vt* warn; make alert: *Has he been alerted to the danger?*

alfalfa (æl'fælfə) *nu* a plant, esp. grown as food for animals.

algae ('ælgiː, 'ældʒiː) *n pl* plants that grow in water, esp. seaweeds.

algebra ('ældʒɪbrə) *nu* a branch of mathematics using letters to represent numbers. **algebraic** (,ældʒɪ'breɪɪk) *adj*

alias ('eɪlɪəs) *adv* also known as: *Eric Warburton alias John Smith.* ●*nc, pl* **-ses** a name other than one's original name.

alibi ('ælɪbaɪ) *nc, pl* **-bis** a defence by an accused person that he was somewhere else at the time the crime took place.

alien ('eɪlɪən) *adj* foreign. ●*nc* a foreigner.

alienate ('eɪlɪəneɪt) *vt* turn away; cause to become unfriendly. **alienation** (,eɪlɪə'neɪʃən) *nu* the state of being or feeling alienated, esp. from the rest of society.

alight[1] (ə'laɪt) *formal vi* **1** (often followed by from) step out (of) or off: *Do not alight from a moving bus.* **2** land; settle after coming down from the air: *The bird alighted on a branch.*

alight[2] *adj* **1** burning. **2** lit up.

align (ə'laɪn) *vt* place in a line. **alignment** *nc* a line made by aligning.

alike (ə'laɪk) *adj, adv* like each other; similar(ly).

alimentary (,ælɪ'mentərɪ) *adj* to do with feeding: *Food travels down one's alimentary canal.*

alimony ('ælɪmənɪ) *nu* money ordered by a court to be paid by a man to his former wife.

alive (ə'laɪv) *adj* **1** living. **2** active; full of life. **alive to** paying attention to; making use of: *alive to new ideas.* **alive with** containing large numbers of: *The lake is alive with fish.*

alkali ('ælkəlaɪ) *nc, pl* **-lis, -lies** a chemical substance that cancels out the effect of an acid. **alkaline** ('ælkəlaɪn) *adj*

all (ɔːl) *determiner, pron* the whole number or quantity of: *all the time; That's all we have left; Are they all here?* ●*determiner* **1** the greatest possible: *with all speed.* **2** any; every: *beyond all doubt.* ●*adv* completely: *Everything suddenly went all quiet.* **after all** See under **after**. **all at once 1** together; at the same time. **2** suddenly. **all of** no less than; as much as: *She's all of ninety.* **all over 1** on the whole surface (of): *There's paint all over the carpet.* **2** completely finished: *His life's work was all over now.* **3** acting normally; just like (someone): *That's him all over!* **4** very or too friendly or helpful towards: *Learning of his great wealth, she was suddenly all over him, attending to his every need.* **all right** (also *not standard* **alright**) **1** good or well enough. **2** safe(ly): *Did you get home all right?* **3** definitely: *It's him all right.* **4** (used to agree to a request): *Will you do this for me, please? — All right.* **all the same** See under **same**. **in all** altogether: *I have five in all.* **not at all 1** in no way or not even the slightest amount: *I don't like him at all.* **2** (used to accept thanks.) **all-important** (,ɔːlɪm'pɔːtənt) *adj* most important. **all-round** ('ɔːlraʊnd) *adj* good in all respects: *an all-round footballer.*

Allah ('ælə) *n* the Arabic word for God.

allay (ə'leɪ) *vt* lessen or get rid of (pain, fear, etc.).

allege (ə'ledʒ) *vt* state without proof: *He is alleging that I am a thief; the alleged crime.* **allegation** (,ælɪ'geɪʃən) *nc* something alleged.

allegiance (ə'liːdʒəns) *nu* loyalty, esp. to one's country.

allegory ('ælɪgərɪ) *nc, pl* **-ries** a story, picture, etc., of which the elements represent things with deeper meaning. **allegorical** (,ælɪ'gɒrɪkəl) *adj*

allergy ('ælədʒɪ) *medicine nc, pl* **-gies** a condition in which something, such as dust, has an unusual effect on the body. **allergic** (ə'lɜːdʒɪk) *adj* (usually followed by **to**) to do with, esp. having, an allergy: *I'm allergic to feathers.*

alleviate (ə'liːvɪeɪt) *vt* lessen (pain, suffering, etc.).

alley ('ælɪ) *nc, pl* **-s** a path or narrow road between buildings.

alliance (ə'laɪəns) **1** *nu* the state of agreement or connection. *nc* **2** an agreement, esp. between political parties or countries, to act in the common interest. **3** the parties, countries, etc., that make such an agreement. **4** a marriage.

alligator ('ælɪgeɪtə*) *nc* a large American animal with powerful jaws and tail that lives on land and in water: see picture at **reptiles**.

alliteration (ə,lɪtə'reɪʃən) *nu* the use of a particular sound in several words close together, as in *'Sister Susie sews socks for sailors'*.

allocate ('æləkeɪt) *vt* give to use, etc., as one's share: *You've been allocated this room to work in*. **allocation** (,ælə'keɪʃən) **1** *nu* the act of allocating. **2** *nc* something allocated.

allot (ə'lɒt) *vt* share out; give a share of. **allotment 1** *nu* the act of allotting. *nc* **2** something allotted. **3** *Brit* a small piece of public land rented by someone to grow flowers or vegetables on.

allotrope ('ælətrəʊp) *nc* any of two or more forms, all either solid, liquid, or gas, of a chemical element: *Diamond and graphite are allotropes of carbon*.

allow (ə'laʊ) *vt* **1** permit. **2** admit or accept (a point of argument, etc.): *The judge allowed the claim*. **3** prepare or expect to need: *I should allow three metres of cloth for that jacket*. **4** give; agree to give; let (someone) have (money). **allowance** *nc* something allowed, esp. an amount of money given regularly. **allow for** (prepare, add, or take away in order to) take into consideration. **make allowances for** take account of (something, esp. an excuse for bad behaviour, etc.): *He's late, but we must make allowances for the distance he has to come*.

alloy ('ælɔɪ) *nc* a mixture of metals, such as brass. ● *vt* mix (metals).

allude (ə'luːd) *vi* (followed by **to**) mention indirectly: *Are you alluding to something I have written?* **allusion** (ə'luːʒən) *ncu*

allure (ə'ljʊə*) *vt* attract: *alluring colours*. ● *nu* attraction.

alluvial (ə'luːvjəl) *adj* to do with earth left behind by rivers: *the alluvial plain:* see picture.

alluvial

ally ('ælaɪ) *nc, pl* **-lies** a country, person, etc., agreeing with one or more others that they should act in their common interest. ● ('ælaɪ, ə'laɪ) *vt* make an ally of: *We should ally ourselves to our neighbours*. **allied** *adj* **1** joined by agreement or treaty. **2** related; connected.

almanac ('ɔːlmənæk) *nc* a yearly book of information.

almighty (ɔːl'maɪtɪ) *adj* **1** more powerful than any other. **2** *infml* very great: *an almighty crash*.

almond ('ɑːmənd) *nc* a nut of the almond tree.

almost ('ɔːlməʊst) *adv* nearly.

alms (ɑːmz) *n pl* money or goods given to poor people.

aloe ('æləʊ) *nc* a plant with thick leaves, of which the juice is used as a medicine.

aloft (ə'lɒft) *adj, adv* in or to a higher place.

alone (ə'ləʊn) *adj, adv* without other people or other things. ● *adv* only: *I alone can help you*. **leave** or **let alone** not disturb or annoy. **let alone** still less: *I haven't got a bicycle, let alone a car*.

along (ə'lɒŋ) *prep, adv* for (any part of) the length (of): *We walked along the road*. ● *adv* **1** with; in one's company: *Would you like to come along?* **2** *infml* over, across, up, down: *Why not come along and see us sometime?* **all along** for or through the whole length of: *There are trees all along the road*. **along with** together with; and: *I bought the vegetables, along with a nice piece of meat*. **be along** come: *I'll be along in a minute*.

alongside (əlɒŋ'saɪd) *prep, adv* along the side (of): *The other ship is alongside us*.

aloof (ə'luːf) *adj, adv* **1** apart; independent; without fear or favour: *The judge must stand aloof from the case*. **2** *often derogatory* without sympathy: *He is too aloof to make friends with anyone*.

aloud (ə'laʊd) *adv* **1** in a normal speaking voice. **2** in a voice able to be heard at a distance.

alpha ('ælfə) *nc* the first letter of the Greek alphabet.

alphabet ('ælfəbet) *nc* a set of letters used for writing a language. **alphabetical** (,ælfə'betɪkəl) *adj* in the order in which the alphabet is generally used: *an alphabetical list of names*.

alps (ælps) *n pl* **1** any range of high mountains: *New Zealand's alps are in its South Island*. **2 the Alps** the mountain range in western Europe. **alpine** ('ælpaɪn) *adj* to do with the Alps or with any mountains: *alpine flowers*.

already (ɔːl'redɪ) *adv* **1** before a particular time: *I have already seen it*. **2** earlier than expected: *It's already quite late.*

alright (ɔːlˈraɪt) *not standard adj, adv* See **all right** under **all**.

also (ˈɔːlsəʊ) *adv* as well; besides.

altar (ˈɔːltə*) *nc* a block or table used for religious sacrifices or, in Christian churches, for Communion.

alter (ˈɔːltə*) *vti* change. **alteration** (ˌɔːltəˈreɪʃən) *ncu*

altercation (ˌɔːltəˈkeɪʃən) *nc* an angry conversation; argument.

alternate (ˈɔːltəneɪt) *vti* (often followed by **with** or **between**) (of two or more things), (cause to) do something or happen by turns: *Day alternates with night; She alternates between moods of anger and joy; He and I alternate as driver.* ●(ɔːlˈtɜːnət) *adj* 1 alternating: *alternate mountains and valleys.* 2 every second: *He works on alternate weeks.* **alternately** *adv* **alternating current** electricity that changes direction regularly: *abbrev.* AC

alternative (ɔːlˈtɜːnətɪv) *adj* possible as a choice instead of something else. ● *nc* one of two possible choices. **alternatively** *adv*

although (ɔːlˈðəʊ) *conj* in spite of the fact that; though.

altitude (ˈæltɪtjuːd) *nc* the height at which something is situated, esp. above sea level.

alto (ˈæltəʊ) *nu* 1 also **contralto** the lowest female singing voice. 2 also **counter-tenor** the highest male singing voice. 3 *nc, pl* **-s** a male or female singer with an alto voice.

altogether (ˌɔːltəˈgeðə*) *adv* in total; with everything considered; completely.

altruism (ˈæltruːɪzəm) *nu* kindness, generosity, or helpfulness to other people. **altruistic** (ˌæltruːˈɪstɪk) *adj*

aluminium (ˌæljʊˈmɪnjəm) *US* **aluminum** (əˈluːmɪnəm) *nu* a chemical element; light, silvery-coloured metal that is used for aircraft, etc., and does not need protecting from air or water.

always (ˈɔːlweɪz) *adv* 1 each time: *It always rains when I go out.* 2 whatever happens: *You can always feed it to the dog!* 3 at all or most times; again and again: *There's always someone causing trouble.*

am (æm unstressed əm) *v* (used with **I**) a form of **be**.

amalgamate (əˈmælgəmeɪt) *vti* (cause to) combine or join. **amalgamation** (əˌmælgəˈmeɪʃən) *ncu*

amass (əˈmæs) *vti* (cause to) gather or collect: *his amassed wealth.*

amateur (ˈæmətə*, ˈæmətjʊə*) *nc* a person who does something, esp. sport, for pleasure not money. ● *adj* 1 to do with amateurs. 2 poor; badly done: *an amateur piece of work.*

amaze (əˈmeɪz) *vt* surprise greatly; astonish.

amazement *nu* **amazing** *adj* **amazingly** *adv*

ambassador (æmˈbæsədə*) *nc* a person representing his country abroad.

amber (ˈæmbə*) *nu* 1 a hard, dark yellow substance formed from a liquid in trees that grew thousands of years ago. 2 the colour of amber. 3 the yellow colour of traffic lights used as warnings.

ambidextrous (ˌæmbɪˈdekstrəs) *adj* able to use both hands equally well.

ambiguous (æmˈbɪgjuːəs) *adj* having more than one possible meaning. **ambiguity** (ˌæmbɪˈgjuːɪtɪ) 1 *nu* the state of being ambiguous. 2 *nc, pl* **-ties** something ambiguous.

ambition (æmˈbɪʃən) *ncu* (a) desire to do or succeed in something: *an ambition to climb Mount Everest.* **ambitious** *adj*

ambivalence (æmˈbɪvələns) *nu* having opposite opinions or feelings at the same time.

amble (ˈæmbəl) *vi* walk slowly.

ambrosia (æmˈbrəʊzɪə) *nu* anything with a particularly pleasant taste or smell.

ambulance (ˈæmbjʊləns) *nc* a road vehicle for carrying sick or injured people: see picture.

ambulance

ambush (ˈæmbʊʃ) *nc* an attack by hidden waiting soldiers, etc. ● *vt* attack in an ambush.

ameliorate (əˈmiːljəreɪt) *vti* make or become better; improve.

amen (ˌɑːˈmen, ˌeɪˈmen) *interj, adv* (used at the end of a Christian prayer) so be it; in truth.

amenable (əˈmiːnəbəl) *adj* 1 open to suggestions; likely to be persuaded. 2 (usually followed by **to**) responsible.

amend (əˈmend) *vt* change, esp. to correct or improve. **make amends for** do something to put right or make up for (a wrong). **amendment** *ncu* (an example of) amending.

amenity (əˈmiːnɪtɪ, əˈmiːnətɪ) *nc, pl* **-ties** a pleasant or useful place or service, esp. public, such as shops, a library, or a park.

amethyst (ˈæmɪθɪst) *ncu* (a piece of) a purple or violet precious stone.

amiable (ˈeɪmɪəbəl) *adj* (esp. of a person) pleasant; friendly.

amicable (ˈæmɪkəbəl) *adj* (esp. of an action) friendly: *The argument was settled in an amicable way.*

amid (əˈmɪd) *prep* also **amidst** (əˈmɪdst) in the middle of.

animals

badger

bear

bison

beaver

boar

camel

cat

chimpanzee

deer

dog

donkey

antelope

fox

elephant

gazelle

giraffe

animals

goat
gorilla
hedgehog
hippopotamus
horse
hyena
kangaroo
leopard
lion
lynx
mongoose
monkey
ox
panda
seal
wolf
reindeer
tiger
zebra

amiss (ə'mıs) *adj, adv* incorrect(ly); wrong(ly): *Something has gone amiss.* **take (something) amiss** feel hurt or insulted by (something).

ammeter ('æmıtə*) *nc* an instrument for measuring electrical current in amperes.

ammonia (ə'məʊnıə) *chemistry nu* a colourless, strong-smelling gas containing nitrogen and used esp. for making fertilisers: symbol NH_3 **ammonium** (ə'məʊnıəm) *nu* the radical of ammonia salts: symbol NH_4 or NH_4^+ : *ammonium hydroxide.*

ammunition (,æmjʊ'nıʃən) *nu* **1** bullets, shells, etc., fired by guns. **2** information, etc., used to support an argument.

amnesia (æm'niːzıə) *nu* loss of memory.

amnesty ('æmnəstı) *nc, pl* **-ties** an act of cancelling punishments or promising not to punish people who confess to a crime.

amoeba *US* **ameba** (ə'miːbə) *nc, pl* **amoebas, amoebae** (biː) a tiny animal that lives in water and has only one cell.

amok (ə'mɒk) *adv* See **amuck.**

among (ə'mʌŋ) *prep* also **amongst** (ə'mʌŋst) **1** surrounded by; within: *among a crowd of people.* **2** between: *Divide it amongst yourselves; There's agreement among us.* **3** (followed by a comparative or superlative adjective and a plural of the noun) one of: *London is among the biggest cities in the world.*

amorous ('æmərəs) *adj* to do with love.

amorphous (ə'mɔːfəs) *adj* having no particular shape.

amount (ə'maʊnt) *nc* a quantity, esp. a total. ● *vi* (followed by **to**) add up or be equal (to) in quantity, meaning, etc.: *His unenthusiastic answer amounted to a refusal.*

ampere ('æmpeə*) (often shortened to **amp**) *nc* a measure of electrical current = the current flowing when one watt is being produced at one volt: *abbrev.* **A**

amphibian (æm'fıbıən) *nc, adj* **1** (an animal) able to live on land and in water. **2** (a vehicle) able to travel on land and water. **amphibious** *adj* **1** able to live on land or in water. **2** to do with an army attack on land from water: *an amphibious landing.*

amphitheatre *US* **amphitheater** ('æmfı,θıətə*) *nc* a room or open space with rows

amphitheatre

of seats banked up round a central space used for plays, etc.: see picture.

ample ('æmpəl) *adj* **-r, -st** large; more than enough. **amply** *adv*

amplify ('æmplıfaı) *vt* make (esp. sound signals) stronger, louder, etc. **amplification** (,æmplıfı'keıʃən) *nu* **amplifier** *nc* a device used to amplify an electrical signal, esp. sound from a record, etc.

amplitude ('æmplıtjuːd) *ncu* a size or width, esp. of a sound or other wave.

amputate ('æmpjʊteıt) *vt* cut off (part of a living body, esp. (part of) an arm or leg).

amuck (ə'mʌk) *adv* (also **amok**) **run amuck** run about with a desire to kill or do other violence.

amulet ('æmjʊlət) *nc* something worn as a protection against evil.

amuse (ə'mjuːz) *vt* **1** cause to laugh or smile. **2** interest pleasantly; entertain. **amusement** (ə'mjuːzmənt) **1** *nc* something that amuses, such as a game. **2** *nu* the state of being amused.

an (æn unstressed ən) *determiner* See **a.**

an' (ən) *infml conj* short for **and.**

anachronism (ə'nækrənızəm) *nc* a person, thing, or event that is not in the right period of time.

anaemia *US* **anemia** (ə'niːmıə) *medicine nu* a shortage of red blood cells, or of haemoglobin in them, that produces a pale appearance to the body.

anaesthetic *US* **anesthetic** (,ænəs'θetık) *nc, adj* (a substance) used to stop one feeling pain in all or part of the body. **anaesthetist** (ə'niːsθətıst) *US* **anesthesiologist** (,ænəsθiːzɪ'ɒlədʒıst) *nc* a person who uses anaesthetics on patients in hospital, etc. **anaesthetise** *US* **anesthetize** (ə'niːs,θətaız) *vt* stop (someone) feeling pain by the use of anaesthetics.

anagram ('ænəgræm) *nc* a word whose letters can be put in a different order to make another word, such as: *evil* and *live.*

analogy (ə'nælədʒı) *ncu* (a) similarity or comparison, esp. in part: *There's an analogy between the movements of the sun and the hands of a clock.* **analogous** (ə'næləgəs) *adj*

analyse *US* **analyze** ('ænəlaız) *vt* examine (something) in detail, esp. by splitting it up into its parts. **analysis** (ə'næləsıs) *ncu, pl* **-lyses** (ləsiːz) (an example of) analysing something. **analyst** ('ænəlıst) *nc* a person who carries out analyses. **analytical** (,ænə'lıtıkəl) *adj*

anarchy ('ænəkı) *nu* the absence of government (and order) in a society. **anarchist** *nc* a supporter of anarchy.

anathema (ə'næθəmə) *nc* a hated person or thing: *He is anathema to me.*

anatomy (ə'nætəmɪ) **1** *nu* the study of human or of other animal bodies or of the structure of plants. **2** *infml nc* a human body. **anatomical** (,ænə'tɒmɪkəl) *adj*

ancestor ('ænsestə*) *nc* a person from whom one is descended, esp. further back than a grandparent. **ancestral** (æn'sestrəl) *adj* handed down from or to do with ancestors: *an ancestral home*. **ancestry** ('ænsestrɪ) *ncu, pl* -**ries** (a line of) ancestors.

anchor ('æŋkə*) *nc* **1** a heavy metal device on a chain that is dropped to the bottom of the sea from a ship to stop the ship moving: see picture. **2** anything that holds something in place. **drop anchor** (of a ship) anchor. ● *vti* use an anchor to (cause to) stay in place. **anchorage** *nc* a place where a ship anchors.

anchor

anchovy ('æntʃəvɪ) *nc, pl* -**vies** a small sea fish with a strong salty taste.

ancient ('eɪnʃənt) *adj* **1** very old. **2** of long ago, esp. to do with Rome and Greece before the year 476. ● *nc* a person belonging to an ancient civilised society such as Rome or Greece.

ancillary (æn'sɪlərɪ) *adj, nc, pl* -**ries** (someone or something) dependent or secondary: *Hospital cleaners are ancillary workers.*

and (ænd *unstressed* ənd, ən) (*infml abbrevs.* **an'**, **'n'**) *conj* **1** together with; as well as; in addition to: *men and women; both tall and wide*. **2** (used before a repeated word to indicate a great quantity, time, force, etc.): *louder and louder; It took hours and hours to find*. **3** (used after **nice** or **good** to indicate approval): *The ground's nice and dry*. **4** *infml* (used instead of **to** in an infinitive after **try**): *Do try and come!* **5** good... but also bad... : *There are films and films*. **6** (in place of an *if*-clause) because then; so that; in order that: *Try just a little harder and you will succeed.* **and so on** See under **so**.

anecdote ('ænɪkdəʊt) *nc* an amusing story.

anemone (ə'nemənɪ) *nc* a plant that grows in temperate woods: see picture at **flowers**.

aneroid ('ænərɔɪd) *adj* **aneroid barometer** a device that measures the pressure of the air with a metal box from which some of the air has been removed.

anew (ə'njuː) *formal adv* **1** again. **2** differently.

angel ('eɪndʒəl) *nc* an attendant or messenger of God, usually represented as a human being with wings. **angelic** (æn'dʒelɪk) *adj* **1** to do with angels. **2** *infml* beautiful. **3** *infml* well-behaved.

anger ('æŋgə*) *nu* great annoyance or displeasure. ● *vt* make angry.

angle¹ ('æŋgəl) *nc* **1** the space between two lines or surfaces that meet. **2** the amount by which two directions differ, measured esp. in degrees. ● *vt* move (something) so that it forms an angle with something else.

angle² *vi* (follwed by **for**) **1** try to obtain compliments, an invitation, etc., in an indirect way. **2** try to catch fish with a hook on a line. **angler** *nc* someone who angles.

Anglican ('æŋglɪkən) *adj* to do with the Church of England or any connected Church. ● *nc* a member of an Anglican Church.

anglicise ('æŋglɪsaɪz) *vt* make (someone or something) English.

angry ('æŋgrɪ) *adj* -**ier**, -**iest** **1** showing or feeling anger. **2** appearing to be angry: *dark, angry clouds*. **3** sore: *an angry wound*. **angrily** *adv*

anguish ('æŋgwɪʃ) *nu* great pain or worry.

angular ('æŋgjʊlə*) *adj* **1** to do with angles. **2** having points or corners; not round or smooth.

anhydrous (æn'haɪdrəs) *chemistry adj* containing no water.

animal ('ænɪməl) *nc* **1** any living creature, including man, with well-developed senses and the ability to move as it likes: see picture. **2** any animal other than man. **3** a wild, cruel, or fierce person. ● *adj* **1** to do with animals. **2** to do with man's bodily urges.

animate ('ænɪmeɪt) *vt* **1** make alive. **2** make lively: *an animated speaker*. ● ('ænɪmət) *adj* having life. **animated cartoon** See **cartoon** (def. 2).

animism ('ænɪmɪzəm) *nu* the belief that all natural things have souls.

animosity (,ænɪ'mɒsɪtɪ) *ncu, pl* -**ties** a great dislike or hatred.

ankle ('æŋkəl) *nc* the joint between the foot and the leg.

annex (æ'neks) *vt* **1** add; join. **2** take over (neighbouring land): *Germany annexed Austria in 1938*. **annexation** (,ænek'seɪʃən) *ncu*

annexe (also *esp. US* **annex**) ('æneks) *nc* **1** something added. **2** a usually smaller building used to provide extra space or services for a main building: *There are extra bedrooms in the hotel's annexe.*

annihilate (ə'naɪɪleɪt) *vt* destroy completely. **annihilation** (ə,naɪɪ'leɪʃən) *nu*

anniversary (,ænɪ'vɜːsərɪ) *nc, pl* -**ries** a day that is the return each year of the date on which something happened in an earlier year: *our fiftieth wedding anniversary.*

annotate ('ænəʊteɪt) *vt* write notes explaining points in (a written work).

announce (ə'naʊns) *vt* 1 make known. 2 announce the arrival of (a guest) or the start of (a radio or television programme). **announcement** *nc* **announcer** *nc*

annoy (ə'nɔɪ) *vt* (esp. in passive) displease; make mildly angry. **annoyance** *nu* 1 the state of being annoyed. 2 the act of annoying. 3 *nc* someone or something annoying.

annual ('ænjʊəl) *adj* done, paid, lasting, happening, etc., once a year. ●*nc* 1 a book brought out under the same title once every year. 2 a plant that lives no longer than a year. **annually** *adv*

annuity (ə'njuːɪtɪ) *nc, pl* **-ties** a fixed amount of money received annually, esp. in return for a lump payment made at the start.

annul (ə'nʌl) *vt* put an end to (a marriage etc.); cancel.

anode ('ænəʊd) *physics nc* the part by which electrons enter a battery or leave an electrical device, a positive electrode.

anoint (ə'nɔɪnt) *vt* 1 pour or rub (oil) onto (someone's head): *He anointed him with oil.* 2 anoint as a sign of (one's) having the duty and title of: *He was anointed King.*

anomaly (ə'nɒməlɪ) *nc, pl* **-lies** something not regular or normal. **anomalous** *adj*

anon (ə'nɒn) *chiefly archaic or literary adv* soon.

anonymous (ə'nɒnɪməs)· *adj* 1 (of a person) having no known name: *the anonymous writer of this letter.* 2 *abbrev.* **anon.** (of music, a book, painting, etc.) written by someone whose name is not known: *The letter was anonymous.* **anonymity** (ˌænə'nɪmɪtɪ) *nu*

anorak ('ænəræk) *nc* a waterproof jacket with a covering for the head.

another (ə'nʌðə*) *determiner, pl* **other,** *pron, pl* **others** 1 (one of) a different (kind or type): *If you don't like this type of apple, try another.* 2 (of the same type) one more; a further: *Have another cake.*

answer ('ɑːnsə*) *nc* 1 a reply to a question, letter, etc. 2 a solution to a problem. ●*vt* 1 give an answer to. 2 respond to a call to (the door, telephone, etc.). 3 *vi* (often followed by **to**) respond (to): *My dog answers to 'Rover'; The plane isn't answering to the controls.* 4 *vti* (when *vi,* often followed by **to**) fit (a description): *He answers (to) this description exactly.* **answerable** *adj* (usually followed by **for** or **to**) responsible (for something or to someone). **answer for** be responsible for (bad behaviour, etc.).

ant (ænt) *nc* a small insect that lives in large groups: see picture at **insects. ant-eater**

('ænt,iːtə*) *nc* a Central or South American animal with a long mouth for getting at ants to eat. **ant-hill** ('ænthɪl) *nc* a pile of earth, leaves, etc., over an ants' nest.

antagonism (æn'tægənɪzəm) *nu* opposition or unfriendliness, esp. between two people or two groups of people. **antagonise** *vt* make unfriendly; annoy. **antagonist** *nc* an opponent. **antagonistic** (æn,tægə'nɪstɪk) *adj*

antarctic (æn'tɑːktɪk) *adj* to do with the land and sea around the South Pole. **the Antarctic** or **Antarctica** the land and sea around the South Pole.

antecedent (ˌæntɪ'siːdənt) *nc* 1 *grammar* the noun, etc., to which a pronoun, esp. a relative pronoun, refers, such as *'day'* in *'the day on which you arrived'.* 2 an event that happens earlier than another. ●*adj* happening or existing before in time or order.

antedate (ˌæntɪ'deɪt) *vt* 1 put an earlier date on a (letter, cheque, etc.). 2 be older than; come before.

antediluvian (ˌæntɪdɪ'luːvɪən) *derogatory or humorous adj* very old, esp. old-fashioned.

antelope ('æntɪləʊp) *nc, pl* **antelope, antelopes** any of various chiefly African deer-like animals, such as the gazelle or impala: see picture at **animals.**

antenatal (ˌæntɪ'neɪtəl) *adj* happening or existing before birth: *antenatal classes for mothers.*

antenna (æn'tenə) *nc* 1 *pl* **-nae** (niː) one of two stalks on the head of an insect, crustacean, etc., used chiefly for feeling or tasting: see picture. 2 *pl* **-nas** See **aerial.**

antenna

anterior (æn'tɪərɪə*) *adj* 1 (further) forward. 2 earlier.

anthem ('ænθəm) *nc* a short piece of church music for a choir. **national anthem** the special song or hymn used by a particular nation to express loyalty to it.

anther ('ænθə*) *nc* the male part of a flower containing pollen.

anthology (æn'θɒlədʒɪ) *nc, pl* **-gies** a printed collection of poems, pictures, etc.

anthracite ('ænθrəsaɪt) *nu* a hard form of coal containing a lot of carbon.

anthrax ('ænθræks) *nu* a disease of cattle and sheep that can be passed from one animal to another and also to people.

anthropoid ('ænθrəpɔɪd) *adj, nc* (a creature) looking like man or one of the apes.

anthropology (ˌænθrə'pɒlədʒɪ) *nu* the study of man. **anthropological** (ˌænθrəpə-'lɒdʒɪkəl) *adj* **anthropologist** *nc*

anti-aircraft (ˌæntɪ'eəkrɑːft) *adj* (of guns, etc.) used as defence against attacks by planes, etc.

antibiotic (ˌæntɪbaɪ'ɒtɪk) *nc* a drug, such as penicillin, made by bacteria and used to cure a disease by killing the bacteria that cause it.

antibody ('æntɪˌbɒdɪ) *nc, pl* **-dies** a substance in the blood that joins an antigen and makes it harmless.

anticipate (æn'tɪsɪpeɪt) *vt* **1** expect: *I anticipate that he will arrive today.* **2** act in expectation of: *He anticipated his prize by spending the money before he won it.* **anticipation** (ænˌtɪsɪ'peɪʃən) *nu*

anticlimax (ˌæntɪ'klaɪmæks) *nc* a disappointing ending.

anticlockwise (ˌæntɪ'klɒkwaɪz) *US* **counterclockwise** *adv, adj* in the opposite direction to the movement of the hands of a clock.

antics ('æntɪks) *n pl* curious or foolish actions.

anticyclone (ˌæntɪ'saɪkləʊn) *nc* a body of high-pressure air over the earth.

antidote ('æntɪdəʊt) *nc* a drug that stops the effect of another one, esp. of a poison.

antifreeze ('æntɪfriːz) *nu* a liquid added to another, esp. the cooling water in an engine, to lower the temperature at which it freezes.

antigen ('æntɪdʒən) *nc* a substance that gets into the blood from outside the body and can cause a disease but is usually prevented from doing so by an antibody.

antimony ('æntɪmənɪ) *nu* a chemical element; light grey metal used esp. mixed with other metals: symbol Sb

antipathy (æn'tɪpəθɪ) *nu* a feeling of strong dislike.

antique (æn'tiːk) *nc, adj* (to do with) an old-fashioned but valued object such as a plate or a piece of furniture. **antiquarian** (ˌæntɪ'kweərɪən) *nc* a person who studies, collects, or buys and sells antiques or antiquities. ● *adj* to do with antiques. **antiquated** ('æntɪˌkweɪtɪd) *adj* old; out of date.

antiquities (æn'tɪkwɪtɪz) *n pl* very old objects, esp. from Greek and Roman times.

antiquity (æn'tɪkwɪtɪ) *nu* **1** the quality of being very old. **2** very early times, esp. before the European Middle Ages.

antiseptic (ˌæntɪ'septɪk) *nc, adj* (a sub-

stance) able to kill tiny organisms that cause disease.

antithesis (æn'tɪθəsɪs) *nc, pl* **-theses** (θəsiːz) **1** a complete opposite. **2** the comparison of two opposite things.

antitoxin (ˌæntɪ'tɒksɪn) *nc* a substance produced in the blood that stops a poison having any effect.

antler ('æntlə*) *nc* one of the two horns, esp. branched, of a deer.

antonym ('æntənɪm) *nc* a word with the opposite meaning of another: *'Hot' is the antonym of 'cold'.*

anus ('eɪnəs) *nc* the hole at the end of the body, by which undigested food leaves as solid waste.

anvil ('ænvɪl) *nc* a metal block on which hot metal is hammered into shape: see picture.

anvil

anxiety (æŋ'zaɪətɪ) *ncu, pl* **-ties 1** the state of being very worried or nervous. **2** great eagerness. **anxious** ('æŋkʃəs) *adj* feeling anxiety. **anxiously** *adv*

any ('enɪ) *determiner, pron* no matter which or how much or many: *Come on any day you like; Any you get will be yours.* ● *determiner, pron, adv* (usually used with a negative or in a question) even the smallest amount (of): *I haven't any (food); Do you feel any better?* ● *determiner* a great (number or amount): *There's any number of things to do.* **anybody** ('enɪˌbɒdɪ) *pron* also **anyone 1** any person. **2** an important or famous person: *Was that man we saw anyone?* **3** (esp. after **just**) any unimportant person: *He's not just anyone.* **4** somebody, someone: *Is there anyone there I can speak to?* **anyhow** ('enɪhaʊ) *adv* **1** also **anyway** in any case. **2** in any way or manner. **3** carelessly: *He did it anyhow, and just look at it!* **anyone** ('enɪwʌn) *pron* See **anybody. anything** ('enɪθɪŋ) *pron* any object, idea, event, etc.; something: *Did anything go wrong?* ● *n* a thing of any kind; something: *Is there anything you want?* ● *adv* in any way: *Your photograph isn't anything like you.* **anytime** ('enɪtaɪm) *adv* at any time. **anyway** ('enɪweɪ) *adv* See **anyhow** (def. 1). **anywhere** ('enɪweə*) *adv, pron* (in or to) any place; somewhere; no matter where.

apace (ə'peɪs) *adv* quickly.

apart (ə'pɑːt) *adj, adv* **1** in or to pieces: *My pen has come apart.* **2** at or to a distance;

distant: *a place far apart from here.* **3** which is separate; separate(ly): *They are in a room apart.* **4** separated: *The pages of the book have come apart.* **apart from** except for; besides; other than.

apartheid (ə'pɑːthaɪt, ə'pɑːtheɪt) *nu* (in South Africa) the separation of white, black, and coloured people.

apartment (ə'pɑːtmənt) *nc* **1** *chiefly US* See **flat¹. 2** *(pl)* a set of rooms, esp. rented.

apathy ('æpəθɪ) *nu* a lack of interest. **apathetic** (æpə'θetɪk) *adj*

ape (eɪp) *nc* a tailless monkey, such as a gorilla. ●*vt* imitate; act like.

aperitif (ə'perɪtiːf) *nc* an alcoholic drink taken just before a meal.

aperture ('æpətʃə*) *nc* a hole or opening, esp. one that can be altered to allow more or less light into a camera, etc.

apex ('eɪpeks) *nc, pl* **apexes, apices** ('eɪpɪsiːz) **1** the highest point of something. **2** a pointed end of something, such as a cone.

apiece (ə'piːs) *adv* each: *We had three apiece.*

aplomb (ə'plɒm) *nu* confident calmness.

apocryphal (ə'pɒkrɪfəl) *adj* (of a story, etc.) probably not true.

apologise (ə'pɒlədʒaɪz) *vi* say or write that one is sorry (to someone or for something). **apologetic** (ə,pɒlə'dʒetɪk) *adj* apologising. **apology** *nc, pl* **-gies** an act of apologising.

apoplexy ('æpəpleksɪ) *nc, pl* **-xies** a loss of consciousness caused by a burst or blocked blood vessel to the brain.

apostle (ə'pɒsəl) *nc* an early supporter, esp. one of the twelve followers of Jesus Christ. **apostolic** (,æpə'stɒlɪk) *adj*

apostrophe (ə'pɒstrəfɪ) *nc* the sign (') used in writing mainly to indicate missing letters or numbers, as in *doesn't* or *the '39-'45 war* or to indicate possession, as in *John's coat.*

appal *US* **appall** (ə'pɔːl) *vt* shock; horrify: *He was appalled at the waste.* **appalling** *adj* **1** shocking. **2** *infml* very great: *an appalling waste of time.*

apparatus (,æpə'reɪtəs) **1** *nu* devices, instruments, etc. *nc* *(pl* rarely used) **2** a device or instrument. **3** a means of organisation, esp. political: *the party apparatus.*

apparel (ə'pærəl) *chiefly archaic nu* clothing.

apparent (ə'pærənt) *adj* clear to see or understand. **apparently** *adv*

apparition (,æpə'rɪʃən) *nc* (an appearance of) a ghost or spirit.

appeal (ə'piːl) *vi* (often followed by **to**) **1** (often also followed by **for**) ask or beg, esp. for help: *I appeal to you for understanding.* **2** ask a higher person or court to change another's decision: *If I'm found guilty, I shall appeal.* **3** please: *The idea doesn't ap-*

peal *to me.* ●*nc* **1** the act of appealing (**appeal** defs. 1, 2). **2** *nu* the quality of being appealing. **appealing** *adj* pleasing; attractive.

appear (ə'pɪə*) *vi* **1** be in view or come into view. **2** seem; look: *That appears to be so.* **3** (of printed work) be brought out; be produced: *Most newspapers appear every day.* **4** present oneself (in a play, etc., or in court). **appearance** *nc* the act or state of appearing.

appease (ə'piːz) *vt* **1** calm or quieten (a possible enemy, etc.) esp. by giving in to demands. **2** satisfy (hunger, etc.).

appellation (,æpə'leɪʃən) *formal nc* a name or title.

append (ə'pend) *vt* add (something extra). **appendage** *nc* something appended, eg. a leg.

appendicitis (ə,pendɪ'saɪtɪs) *nu* inflammation of the **appendix** (def. 1).

appendix (ə'pendɪks) *nc, pl* **-dixes, -dices** (dɪsiːz) **1** a small narrow bag near the end of the path that food takes through the body. **2** a part of a book or article printed separately at the end, esp. a list or other information.

appetite ('æpɪtaɪt) *nc* **1** the feeling of wanting to eat or drink. **2** a feeling of wanting to satisfy any needs of the body. **appetiser** ('æpɪtaɪzə*) *nc* a small amount of food eaten to give one an appetite. **appetising** ('æpɪtaɪzɪŋ) *adj* giving one an appetite; tasty.

applaud (ə'plɔːd) *vt* express one's approval of, esp. by clapping one's hands. **applause** (ə'plɔːz) *nu* the noise of clapping one's hands to applaud.

apple ('æpəl) *nc* the hard round green or red fruit of the apple tree: see picture at **fruits.**

appliance (ə'plaɪəns) *nc* a machine or device, esp. electrical, such as a food mixer.

applicable (ə'plɪkəbəl, 'æplɪkəbəl) *adj* (often followed by **to**) able to be applied; suitable or intended (for).

applicant ('æplɪkənt) *nc* a person who applies for something, such as a job.

application (,æplɪ'keɪʃən) *nc* **1** the act of applying. **2** a use; value: *the applications of science.* **3** *nu* hard work; effort.

apply (ə'plaɪ) (often followed by **to**) *vi* **1** be intended or suitable (for); have to do (with): *These rules apply to everyone.* **2** (often followed by **to** and **for**) ask formally (for): *You apply to the government for a licence.* *vt* **3** put onto: *Apply oil to all moving parts.* **4** use in connection with: *You can't apply your arguments to this case.* **5** work (one's self) hard: *He really applied himself to that task.* **applied** *adj* put to practical use: *applied science.*

appoint (ə'pɔɪnt) *vt* **1** give to (someone the job or position of): *I was appointed a director*. **2** fix; agree: *at the appointed time*. **appointment** *nc* **1** a planned meeting with someone. **2** the act of appointing someone.

apportion (ə'pɔːʃən) *vt* share out.

apposite ('æpəzɪt) *adj* suitable; fitting.

apposition (,æpə'zɪʃən) *grammar nu* the following of a noun or pronoun by another to add to its meaning: *In 'Smith, the teacher', the word 'teacher' is in apposition to 'Smith'; In 'Smith is a teacher' the words 'Smith' and 'teacher' are in apposition*.

appraise (ə'preɪz) *vt* judge the value, quality, or importance of. **appraisal** (ə'preɪzəl) *nc* such a judgement.

appreciable (ə'priːʃəbəl) *adj* enough to be noticed or make a difference; considerable. **appreciably** *adv*

appreciate (ə'priːʃɪeɪt) *vt* **1** understand; realise. **2** be grateful for. **3** value highly: *I appreciate a good meal*. **4** *vi* rise in value. **appreciation** (ə,priːʃɪ'eɪʃən) *nu* **1** thanks; gratefulness. **2** rise in value. **3** *ncu* (a) judgement of the value of something. **appreciative** (ə'priːʃətɪv) *adj* **1** grateful. **2** able to make an **appreciation** (def. 3).

apprehend (,æprɪ'hend) *vt* **1** (of the police, etc.) arrest. **2** grasp; understand. **apprehension** *nu* **1** fear of what may happen. **2** understanding. **3** *ncu* (an instance of) arresting. **apprehensive** *adj* fearful of what may happen.

apprentice (ə'prentɪs) *nc* a person who learns a trade while working for someone else. ● *vt* place (someone) as an apprentice. **apprenticeship** *nu* **1** the state of being an apprentice. **2** *nc* the period for which someone is an apprentice.

approach (ə'prəʊtʃ) **1** *vti* come nearer (to). *vt* **2** be like, esp. nearly as good as. **3** make a suggestion or request to: *Have you approached him about your idea?* **4** start on (a task, etc.). ● *nc* **1** the act or a means of approaching. **2** a way or method of dealing with a problem.

approbation (,æprə'beɪʃən) *nu* **1** formal approval. **2** praise.

appropriate (ə'prəʊprɪət) *adj* suitable; fitting. ● (ə'prəʊprɪeɪt) *vt* **1** take, esp. unjustly. **2** set (money) aside for a particular purpose. **appropriately** (ə'prəʊprɪətlɪ) *adv* **appropriation** (ə,prəʊprɪ'eɪʃən) *nu*

approval (ə'pruːvəl) *nu* the act of approving. **on approval** (of goods for sale) taken away and to be bought or returned.

approve (ə'pruːv) **1** *vti* (often followed by **of**) consider to be good. **2** *vt* allow (a plan, etc.) to be put into practice. **approvingly** *adv*

approximate (ə'prɒksɪmət) *adj* not exact; very near. ● (ə'prɒksɪmeɪt) *vti* (cause to)

be near or similar (to). **approximately** (ə'prɒksɪmətlɪ) *adv* **approximation** (ə,prɒksɪ'meɪʃən) *nc* a result worked out approximately or by a guess.

apricot ('eɪprɪkɒt) *nc* the soft yellow fruit, containing a stone, of the apricot tree.

April ('eɪprəl) *n* the fourth month of the year, after March and before May.

apron

apron ('eɪprən) *nc* **1** a garment worn on the front of the body, tied round the waist, to protect clothes underneath: see picture. **2** a piece of ground with a hard surface on which planes stand, load, etc., at an airport. **3** the part of a theatre stage in front of the curtain.

apropos (,æprə'pəʊ, 'æprəpəʊ) *adv* (often followed by **of**) in respect (of); with regard (to): *I was talking apropos of the meeting yesterday*.

apt (æpt) *adj* **1** (followed by an infinitive) likely or tending (to do something). **2** suitable; fitting: *an apt description*. **3** clever; good at learning. **aptitude** ('æptɪtjuːd) *ncu* **aptly** *adv*

aqualung ('ækwəlʌŋ) *nc* a device for breathing underwater, using metal bottles of compressed air and a pipe to the mouth: see picture.

aqualung

aquarium (ə'kweərɪəm) *nc, pl* **-riums, -ria** (rɪə) a tank, esp. made of glass, in which fish or plants are kept in water.

aquatic (ə'kwætɪk) *adj* living or done in water: *aquatic animals*.

aqueduct ('ækwɪdʌkt) *nc* a channel built to carry water, esp. on a bridge: see picture.

aqueduct

aqueous ('ækwɪəs) *adj* made of or like water: *an aqueous solution.*

Arabic numeral ('ærəbɪk) *nc* any of the written signs for the numbers zero, one, two, three, etc.: *0, 1, 2, 3, etc.*

arable ('ærəbəl) *adj* (of land) suitable for growing crops, such as corn and vegetables.

arbitrary ('ɑːbɪtrərɪ) *adj* (of a decision, choice, etc.) based merely on opinion or preference. **arbitrarily** *adv*

arbitration (ˌɑːbɪ'treɪʃən) *nu* the settlement of a quarrel or disagreement by someone outside it. **arbitrate** ('ɑːbɪtreɪt) *vti* settle by arbitration. **arbitrator** ('ɑːbɪtreɪtə*) *nc*

arbour *US* **arbor** ('ɑːbə*) *nc* a place surrounded and covered by plants or trees.

arc (ɑːk) *nc* a curve, esp. part of a circle. ● *vi* make an arc. **arc light** a lamp in which light is produced by electricity flowing through air.

arcade (ɑː'keɪd) *nc* 1 a covered passage with shops along the side. 2 a row of arches and pillars.

arch[1] (ɑːtʃ) *nc* something built as or made into a curve over an opening: see picture. ● *vti* make (into) an arch: *A cat can arch its back.*

arch

arch[2] *adj* 1 main, chief: *his arch enemy.* 2 experienced; well-practised: *an arch criminal.* **archly** *adv*

archaeology (ˌɑːkɪ'ɒlədʒɪ) *nu* the study of man's existence long ago from remains dug out of the ground. **archaeological** (ˌɑːkɪə-'lɒdʒɪkəl) *adj* **archaeologist** *nc* a person who does archaeology.

archaic (ɑː'keɪɪk) *adj* belonging to an earlier age.

archangel ('ɑːkeɪndʒəl) *nc* a chief angel.

archbishop (ˌɑːtʃ'bɪʃəp) *nc* a chief bishop.

archer ('ɑːtʃə*) *nc* a person who shoots with a bow and arrows. **archery** *nu* the practice of shooting with bows and arrows.

archipelago (ˌɑːkɪ'peləgəʊ) *nc, pl* **-s, -es** a group of islands.

architect ('ɑːkɪtekt) *nc* a person who plans buildings and who is responsible for their construction. **architectural** (ˌɑːkɪ'tektʃərəl) *adj* to do with architecture. **architecture** ('ɑːkɪˌtektʃə*) 1 *nu* the art or science of planning buildings. 2 *nc* a style of building: *Modern architecture is quite plain.*

archives ('ɑːkaɪvz) *n pl* letters, photographs, maps, etc., kept as the history of a business, family, town, etc.

archway ('ɑːtʃweɪ) *nc* a passage or entrance under an arch.

arctic ('ɑːktɪk) *adj* to do with the region around the North Pole. **the Arctic** the land and sea around the North Pole.

ardent ('ɑːdənt) *adj* very keen or eager: *an ardent lover.* **ardour** *US* **ardor** ('ɑːdə*) *nu* great keenness or eagerness.

arduous ('ɑːdjʊəs) *adj* (of a task, conditions, etc.) hard; difficult.

are (ɑː* unstressed ə*) *v* (used with **we, you,** or **they**) a form of **be.**

area ('eərɪə) *nc* 1 an amount of a surface, such as land, measured by multiplying the length by the width: *The area of this floor is ten square metres; an area of grass.* 2 a particular area of the world: *A great lack of food in this area.* 3 a subject of study, discussion, etc.

arena (ə'riːnə) *nc* a space or stage surrounded by seats, used for sports competitions, etc.: see picture.

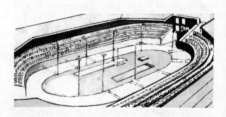

arena

aren't (ɑːnt) *v* are not.

argon ('ɑːgɒn) *nu* a chemical element; gas that reacts very little and is used esp. in light bulbs: symbol Ar

argue ('ɑːgjuː) *vi* 1 quarrel: *He's arguing about the price.* 2 (usually followed by **for** or **against**) defend or oppose (a plan, etc.): *to argue against hanging murderers.* *vt* 3 try to show or prove: *I argued that it would be* *unfair.* **4** discuss: *They argued the point.* **5** persuade: *She tried to argue him into doing it.* **argument** (ˈɑːgjʊmənt) *nc* **1** a quarrel. **2** a discussion in which an idea is defended and opposed. **3** a set of reasons used in arguing: *My argument is very simple.* **argumentative** (ˌɑːgjʊˈmentətɪv) *adj* fond of arguing.

aria (ˈɑːrɪə) *nc* a long song in an opera, cantata, etc., for one voice with instruments.

arid (ˈærɪd) *adj* (of land) hot and dry.

arise (əˈraɪz) *vi* **1** come into being. **2** (followed by **from** or **out of**) result (from): *Three main points arose out of our talk.* **3** *formal or archaic* stand up, get out of bed, etc.

arisen (əˈrɪzn) past participle of **arise.**

aristocrat (ˈærɪstəkræt) *nc* a noble. **aristocracy** (ˌærɪˈstɒkrəsɪ) *nc, pl* **-cies** a class of nobles. **aristocratic** (ˌærɪstəˈkrætɪk) *adj*

arithmetic (əˈrɪθmətɪk) *nu* adding, subtracting, multiplying, and dividing numbers. **arithmetical** (ˌærɪθˈmetɪkəl) *adj*

ark (ɑːk) *nc* a large ship, esp. the ship built by Noah in the Bible, for himself, his family, and two of every animal during the flood.

arm[1] (ɑːm) *nc* **1** either of the parts of the body from the shoulder to the hand. **2** a part of a garment covering an arm; sleeve. **3** a part of a chair that supports an arm. **4** something like an arm: *an arm of the sea; a record-player arm.* **with open arms** in a friendly way; welcomingly. **armchair** (ˌɑːmˈtʃeə*) *nc* a chair with arms. **armhole** (ˈɑːmhəʊl) *nc* a hole in a garment for an arm, often leading to a sleeve. **armpit** (ˈɑːmpɪt) *nc* the hollow under a shoulder.

arm[2] *vt* **1** provide with weapons. **2** provide with protection: *He was armed with answers to all our questions.* **3** make (a bomb, etc.) able to explode. **4** *vi* provide oneself with weapons. **armed forces** the army, navy, and air force, etc., of a nation, or those of several nations.

armada (ɑːˈmɑːdə) *nc* a large group of ships, esp. warships.

armadillo (ˌɑːməˈdɪləʊ) *nc, pl* **-los** a mainly South American animal that is covered in bony armour and digs holes in the ground for itself.

armament (ˈɑːməmənt) **1** *nc* (often *pl)* guns, shells, missiles, etc. used for war. **2** *nu* the process of arming for war.

armature (ˈɑːmətʃʊə*) *nc* the moving coil of an electric motor, with wire wound onto it.

armistice (ˈɑːmɪstɪs) *nc* an agreement between armies to stop fighting each other in order to discuss peace terms.

armour *US* **armor** (ˈɑːmə*) *nu* **1** metal covering for the body, worn esp. by soldiers in the Middle Ages. **2** protective metal plates on ships, cars, etc. **3** armoured vehicles. **armoured** *adj* covered with armour (def. 2): *armoured cars.* **armourer** *nc* a person who makes or repairs weapons. **armoury** *nc, pl* **-ries** a store for weapons.

arms (ɑːmz) *n pl* **1** weapons. **2** a family or city sign. **lay down one's arms** stop fighting. **take up arms** prepare to fight. **up in arms** angry or protesting (about something).

army (ˈɑːmɪ) *nc, pl* **-mies** **1** (a large group of) a nation's soldiers. **2** a large organised number of people or animals: *an army of ants.*

aroma (əˈrəʊmə) *nc* a smell, esp. pleasant. **aromatic** (ˌærəˈmætɪk) *adj*

arose (əˈrəʊz) past tense of **arise.**

around (əˈraʊnd) *adv, prep* **1** on every side (of); outside: *a rope around his neck.* **2** at a number of places (in or on): *There are several policemen around.* **3** from place to place (in): *I've travelled around Europe.* **4** near: *It's somewhere around here.* ● *prep* **5** past in a curve: *Walk around the outside of the house.* **6** (in) about (a number, date, etc.): *It happened around 1900.*

arouse (əˈraʊz) *vt* **1** wake from sleep. **2** give rise to (anger, suspicions, etc.).

arrange (əˈreɪndʒ) *vt* **1** put into an order. **2** agree about; settle. **3** alter (music) for playing by other instruments. *vti* **4** make plans (for); cause to happen: *I've arranged a party; Can you arrange for everyone to be there?* **5** agree with someone on a plan: *We've arranged with them where to stay.* **arrangement** **1** *nu* the act of arranging. *nc* **2** a way of arranging. **3** an arranged piece of music. **4** an agreement. **5** a plan.

array (əˈreɪ) *nc* a fine or splendid show or arrangement of things. ● *vt* **1** arrange in an array. **2** dress (in fine clothes).

arrears (əˈrɪəz) *n pl* something owed, such as rent. **in arrears** late in making a payment.

arrest (əˈrest) *vt* **1** (of the police, etc.) seize (a person or a ship). **2** stop or slow the growth or spread of (a disease, etc.). **3** catch and hold (one's attention). ● *nc* **1** the act of arresting. **2** *nu* the state of having been arrested: *under arrest.*

arrive (əˈraɪv) *vi* **1** (often followed by **at** or **in**) come to (a place, esp. the end of a journey). **2** (followed by **at**) reach (agreement, a decision, etc.). **3** *infml* (of a baby) be born. **4** (of a time) come; be reached. **arrival** (əˈraɪvəl) *nc* **1** the act of arriving. **2** a person or thing that appears or arrives. **3** *infml* a new baby.

arrogant (ˈærəgənt) *adj* thinking too highly of oneself. **arrogance** *nu*

arrow (ˈærəʊ) *nc* **1** a pointed stick shot from

a bow as a weapon: see picture. **2** a sign or mark like an arrow, used to indicate a direction.

arrow

arsenal (ˈɑːsənəl) *nc* a store for weapons.

arsenic (ˈɑːsnɪk) *nu* **1** a chemical element. **2** a poisonous compound of arsenic.

arson (ˈɑːsən) *nu* setting fire to buildings.

art¹ (ɑːt) **1** *nu* (the making of) things such as music and paintings. **2** *nc* a method or skill: *There's an art to writing business letters.* **the arts** non-scientific subjects of study, such as music, languages, and history.

art² *archaic v* (used with **thou**) a form of **be**.

artefact (also **artifact**) (ˈɑːtɪfækt) *nc* an object made by man.

arterial (ɑːˈtɪərɪəl) *adj* to do with arteries.

artery (ˈɑːtərɪ) *nc, pl* **-ries** a blood vessel carrying blood from the heart.

artesian (ɑːˈtiːzɪən) *adj* **artesian well** a deep hole in the ground up which water flows naturally.

artful (ˈɑːtfʊl) *adj* deceiving.

arthritis (ɑːˈθraɪtɪs) *nu* a disease; inflammation of joints.

artichoke (ˈɑːtɪtʃəʊk) *nc* a plant of which the large flower head is cooked and partly eaten: see picture at **vegetables**.

article (ˈɑːtɪkəl) *nc* **1** an object; piece: *an article of clothing.* **2** a separate piece of writing in a newspaper, magazine, etc. **3** a section of a written agreement, contract, etc. **definite article** the word 'the' or a word that means the same thing in another language. **indefinite article** the word 'a' or 'an' or a word that means the same thing in another language.

articulate (ɑːˈtɪkjʊlət) *adj* able to speak or write clearly. ● (ɑːˈtɪkjʊleɪt) *vt* speak (words, etc.) clearly. **articulated lorry** (ɑːˈtɪkjʊleɪtɪd) *US* **trailer truck** *Brit* a lorry jointed between the tractor and the trailer.

articulation (ɑːˌtɪkjʊˈleɪʃən) *nu* the act or a manner of speaking.

artifact (ˈɑːtɪfækt) *n* See **artefact**.

artifice (ˈɑːtɪfɪs) **1** *nc* a clever way of doing something. **2** *nu* cleverness, esp. at deceiving.

artificial (ˌɑːtɪˈfɪʃəl) *adj* **1** not natural; man-made: *artificial stone.* **2** pretended; insincere: *artificial politeness.* **artificially** *adv*

artillery (ɑːˈtɪlərɪ) *nu* large guns used for fighting on land.

artisan (ˌɑːtɪˈzæn) *nc* a skilled worker.

artist (ˈɑːtɪst) *nc* **1** a person who practises art, esp. painting, drawing, or sculpture. **2** a person who does something with the quality or skill of an artist. **artistic** (ɑːˈtɪstɪk) *adj* to do with art. **artistry** *nu* the quality of work or ability of an artist.

artiste (ɑːˈtiːst) *nc* an entertainer, esp. a singer or dancer.

artless (ˈɑːtlɪs) *adj* natural; not intending to deceive.

as (æz unstressed əz) *conj* **1** since; because: *As you don't know, I'll tell you.* **2** while; when: *I saw you as I came in.* **3** (of) which fact: *It's important, as you know.* **4** in the way that: *Did you behave as was proper?* **5** that which: *Do as I do.* ● *prep* **1** being: *As your father, I forbid it.* **2** like: *He was as a brother to me.* ● *pron* that; who: *the same book as I have.* **as... as** (used to indicate an equality of amount): *I am as old as you; You have done it as badly as before.* **as far as** See under **far. as for, to,** or **regards** in respect of; with regard to. **as if** or **though** as it would be if: *He looked as though he were in a hurry.* **as regards** See **as for. as though** See **as if. as to** See **as for. as well (as)** See under **well¹. as yet** until now or then; so far. **so as to** in order to.

asbestos (æzˈbestɒs) *nu* a substance got from the ground that is made into cloth and stiff sheets used as protection from heat.

ascend (əˈsend) *vti* go up (stairs, a hill, etc.). **ascendancy** *nu* having control over someone or something. **ascent** (əˈsent) *ncu* (an example of) ascending.

ascertain (ˌæsəˈteɪn) *vt* discover (the truth or facts about something) for certain.

ascetic (əˈsetɪk) *nc, adj* (a person) refusing pleasures and comfort.

ascribe (əˈskraɪb) *vt* (followed by **to**) consider to belong to or come from: *music ascribed to Beethoven.*

aseptic (æˈseptɪk) *adj* (to do with being) free from micro-organisms that cause disease.

asexual (eɪˈseksʃʊəl) *biology adj* without sex: *asexual reproduction.*

ash¹ (æʃ) *nc* **1** (often *pl*) a usually grey or black powder left after something has been burnt. **2** (*pl*) the remains of a human body after burning. **3** *nu* fine material thrown out of a volcano.

ash² *nc* a European and Asian tree with winged seeds; see picture at **trees**; (also *nu*) the wood of this tree.

ashamed (əˈʃeɪmd) *adj* (often followed by **of**) feeling sorrow or shame (because of): *He's ashamed of having lied.*

ashore (əˈʃɔː*) *adv, adj* on(to) land (from water).

aside (ə'saɪd) *adv* **1** at or to one side: *Move aside to let us through.* **2** away; apart: *They went aside to talk privately.* ● *nc* a remark intended for only some of the people present, esp. for a theatre audience.

ask (ɑːsk) *vt* **1** put (a question) about (something) to (someone): *I asked him the time.* **2** (usually followed by **for**) request; try to get: *I'll ask her to move; Are you asking for money?* **3** invite: *I've been asked to dinner.* **ask after** ask about the health of (someone). **ask for it** or **trouble** behave in a way likely to cause trouble.

askance (ə'skæns) *adv, adj* **1** (looking) sideways. **2** (considering) with suspicion.

askew (ə'skjuː) *adv, adj* not straight, square, or upright.

asleep (ə'sliːp) *adj* sleeping.

asp (æsp) *nc* a small poisonous European and North African snake.

asparagus (ə'spærəgəs) *nc* a plant of which the young shoots are cooked and eaten: see picture at **vegetables;** (usually *nu*) these shoots.

aspect ('æspekt) *nc* **1** a look, appearance, or view. **2** a side (of a house, etc.). **3** an element (of a problem, etc.).

aspen ('æspən) *nc* a tree with leaves that tremble in the wind.

aspersion (ə'spɜːʃən) *nc* a remark attacking someone's reputation: *Are you casting aspersions on my honesty?*

asphalt ('æsfælt) *nu, vt* (cover a road, etc. with) a thick, black liquid made from oil.

asphyxiate (əs'fɪksɪeɪt) *vti* (cause to) breathe too little oxygen (and die): *She may have been asphyxiated by an electric shock.*

aspic ('æspɪk) *nu* an unsweetened jelly made from meat and used to cover meat, vegetables, etc.

aspire (ə'spaɪə*) *vi* (usually followed by **to** or **for**) have an ambition: *to aspire to greatness.* **aspiration** (,æspɪ'reɪʃən) *nc* an ambition.

aspirin ('æsprɪn) *ncu* (a tablet of) a drug widely used to relieve pain and fever.

ass (æs) *nc* **1** See **donkey.** **2** a foolish person.

assail (ə'seɪl) *vt* **1** attack (an enemy, task, etc.). **2** trouble: *He was assailed by money worries.* **assailant** (ə'seɪlənt) *nc* an attacker.

assassin (ə'sæsɪn) *nc* a murderer, esp. of a politician, ruler, etc. **assassinate** *vt* murder (a politician, ruler, etc.). **assassination** (ə,sæsɪ'neɪʃən) *ncu* (an example of) assassinating.

assault (ə'sɔːlt) *vt* attack violently. ● *nc* a violent attack.

assay (ə'seɪ) *vt* **1** test (metal, esp. gold or silver) for quality or purity. **2** attempt. ● ('æseɪ) *nc* a test of metal.

assemble (ə'sembəl) *vti* come or bring or

put together: *A crowd assembled; an easily assembled model.* **assemblage** *nc* a number of assembled people or things. **assembly 1** *nu* the act of assembling. *nc, pl* **-lies 2** a group of people who meet formally: *the General Assembly of the United Nations.* **3** a group of machine parts fitted together. **assembly line** a row of machines or workers working one after the other on the same product: see picture.

assembly line

assent (ə'sent) *nu* agreement. ● *vi* give one's assent.

assert (ə'sɜːt) *vt* demand recognition of (a right, oneself, a fact, etc.): *He asserted that the story was true.* **assertion** *ncu* (an example of) asserting. **assertive** *adj* given to asserting oneself.

assess (ə'ses) *vt* **1** find out the (value) of (something). **2** work out the (tax) to be paid by (someone). **3** judge the (importance or size) of. **assessment** *nc* **1** an amount assessed. **2** a judgement. **3** *nu* the act of assessing. **assessor** *nc*

asset ('æset) *nc* a possession or someone or something useful.

assiduous (ə'sɪdjʊəs) *adj* (of a worker or a piece of work) careful; thorough.

assign (ə'saɪn) *vt* **1** decide on or appoint (a person, place, time, etc.): *This office has been assigned to you.* **2** give or hand over (work, property, etc.). **assignment 1** *nc* something assigned, esp. a task. **2** *nu* the act of assigning.

assimilate (ə'sɪmɪleɪt) *vti* (often followed by **to** or **with**) (cause to) become (a)like or fit in (with): *to assimilate to one's new surroundings.* **assimilation** (ə,sɪmɪ'leɪʃən) *nu*

assist (ə'sɪst) *vt* help. **assistance** *nu* help. **assistant** *nc* **1** a helper. **2** See **shop assistant.**

associate (ə'səʊsɪeɪt) *vt* **1** connect in the mind: *I associate the sea with my childhood.* **2** join as a friend, business partner, etc: *I refuse to associate myself with that affair.* *vi* **3** join to form a group. **4** mix (with other people): *He associates with bankers.* ● (ə'səʊsɪət) *nc, adj* (a person) associated with and esp. less important than another: *an associate member of the society.* **association** (ə,səʊsɪ'eɪʃən) **1** *nc* an organisation of people; club; society. **2** *nu* the act of associating or state of being associated. **association football** also **soccer** football between teams of eleven players using a round ball that may not be handled except by the goalkeepers.

assorted (ə'sɔːtɪd) *adj* of different kinds mixed together: *a very assorted group of people.* **assortment** *nc* an assorted group.

assuage (ə'sweɪdʒ) *vt* relieve (thirst, pain, guilt, etc.).

assume (ə'sjuːm) *vt* 1 accept as true: *I assume that you're right.* 2 take or put (a job, clothes, etc.) on oneself: *The king assumed control of the army.* **assumption** (ə'sʌmpʃən) *ncu* (an example of) assuming.

assure (ə'ʃʊə*) *vt* cause to be or feel certain; promise: *I can assure you I'm right; The comfort of passengers is assured.* **assurance** 1 *nc* a promise. *nu* 2 *chiefly Brit* insurance. 3 confidence. **assured** *adj* confident. **assuredly** (ə'ʃʊərɪdlɪ) *adv* certainly; to be sure.

aster ('æstə*) *nc* a plant with large colourful flowers.

asterisk ('æstərɪsk) *nc* the sign (*) used in writing to indicate both a note and the word or passage which it is about.

astern (ə'stɜːn) *nautical, aviation adv, adj* 1 at, behind, or towards the back of a boat or plane. 2 backwards.

asteroid ('æstərɔɪd) *nc* any of the very small planets or pieces of rock that are mainly between Mars and Jupiter.

asthma ('æsmə) *nu* difficulty in breathing that is often a reaction to dust, etc.

astigmatism (æ'stɪgmətɪzəm) *nu* an imperfection in the shape of a lens, esp. in the eye.

astir (ə'stɜː*) *adj* 1 out of bed. 2 moving.

astonish (ə'stɒnɪʃ) *vt* surprise greatly. **astonishing** *adj* **astonishment** *nu*

astound (ə'staʊnd) *vt* surprise and shock or cause to wonder.

astray (ə'streɪ) *adv, adj* 1 away from the right direction: *My letter must have gone astray.* 2 to bad or evil actions: *The devil leads people astray.*

astride (ə'straɪd) *adv, prep* (with one's legs) on either side (of): *sitting astride a horse.*

astringent (ə'strɪndʒənt) *adj, nc* (a medicine) causing parts of the body, such as muscles or blood vessels, to close or tighten up.

astrology (ə'strɒlədʒɪ) *nu* the study of what effect the positions of the stars and planets have on people's fate and behaviour. **astrologer** *nc* a person who practises astrology.

astronaut ('æstrənɔːt) *nc* a space traveller. **astronautics** *nu (with singular verb)* the science of space travel.

astronomy (ə'strɒnəmɪ) *nu* the study of the stars and planets. **astronomer** *nc* a person who studies astronomy. **astronomical**

(ˌæstrə'nɒmɪkəl) *adj* 1 to do with astronomy. 2 huge: *an astronomical failure.*

astute (ə'stjuːt) *adj* with a quick or sharp mind.

asunder (ə'sʌndə*) *archaic adv* apart; in(to) pieces.

asylum (ə'saɪləm) 1 *nu* also **political asylum** protection in one country from arrest under the laws of another. 2 *becoming archaic nc* a home for people needing care and protection, esp. (also **lunatic asylum**) with sick minds.

asymmetrical (ˌeɪsɪ'metrɪkəl) *adj* not symmetrical.

at (æt unstressed ət) *prep* 1 (used to indicate position): *at the North Pole; sitting at a table.* 2 (used to indicate a time, esp. a time of day): *at six o'clock.* 3 towards: *He shot at the enemy.* 4 (used to indicate a condition): *at rest; at war.* 5 doing: *What are you at?* 6 for a price of... (each): *The books are for sale at two pounds.* 7 (with adjective) in the action of: *He's good at figures.*

ate (eɪt unstressed et) past tense of **eat**.

atheist ('eɪθɪɪst) *nc* a person who does not believe in God. ● *adj* to do with atheism. **atheism** *nu* belief that there is no God.

athlete ('æθliːt) *nc* a person who takes part in running races and other physical competitions. **athletic** (æθ'letɪk) *adj* to do with athletes. **athletics** *nu (with singular verb)* athletic competitions.

athwart (ə'θwɔːt) *chiefly nautical prep, adv* across; from one side to the other (of).

atlas ('ætləs) *nc* a book of maps.

Atman ('ɑːtmən) *n* (in the Hindu religion) the one Self in everyone and everything.

atmosphere ('ætməs,fɪə*) *nc* 1 the gas surrounding a star or planet, esp. the air round the earth. 2 a feeling or mood: *There's a friendly atmosphere where I work.* 3 a measure of pressure = 101,325 N/m² **atmospheric** (ˌætməs'ferɪk) *adj*

atoll ('ætɒl) *nc* a ring of coral islands.

atom ('ætəm) *nc* the smallest part of a chemical element. **atomic** (ə'tɒmɪk) *adj* **atomic** or **atom bomb** a powerful exploding device in which the nucleus of an atom is split in two.

atone (ə'təʊn) *vi* (usually followed by **for**) make up (for wrongdoing). **atonement** *nu* **Day of Atonement** a Jewish religious holiday, spent in prayer and fasting.

atop (ə'tɒp) *prep, adv* on top (of).

atrium ('ɑːtrɪəm) *nc, pl* **-ria** (rɪə) also **auricle** the upper space in either half of the heart.

atrocious (ə'trəʊʃəs) *adj* 1 *infml* very bad or poor. 2 very cruel.

atrocity (ə'trɒsɪtɪ) 1 *nc, pl* **-ties** a very cruel action. 2 *nu* great cruelty.

atrophy ('ætrəfɪ) *nu* wasting away of part of

the body through disease, lack of use, etc. ●*vti* (cause to) suffer atrophy.

attach (əˈtætʃ) *vt* 1 join, fasten, or add: *Attach the lid before using the machine.* 2 join in love or friendship: *He's very attached to her.* 3 *vti* (usually followed by **to**) connect or be connected (with): *There are several conditions attached to the sale.* **attachment** 1 *nu* the act of attaching or state of being attached. 2 *nc* something that is attached.

attaché (əˈtæʃeɪ) *French nc* a person working in an embassy: *a trade attaché.* **attaché case** a small, hard, flat case for carrying papers in.

attack (əˈtæk) *vt* 1 act with force against; start fighting. 2 set to work on (a problem, task, etc.). 3 criticise as bad. 4 (of chemicals) affect or be harmful to. ●*ncu* 1 (an example of) attacking. 2 a sudden illness: *a heart attack.* **attacker** *nc*

attain (əˈteɪn) *vt* 1 reach; arrive at. 2 manage to do (a task, ambition, etc.). **attainable** *adj* **attainment** *ncu*

attempt (əˈtempt) *vt, nc* (a) try. **attempt on (someone's) life** an attempt to kill (someone).

attend (əˈtend) *vt* 1 be present at (school, a meeting, etc.). 2 be present with: *The rain was attended by high winds.* *vi* 3 (followed by **to**) deal (with); take care (of): *He attended to a customer in the shop.* 4 (often followed by **to**) listen with one's whole mind: *Attend while I show you what to do.* **attendance** 1 *nu* the act of attending (**attend** defs. 1, 2, 3). 2 *nc* the number of people present. **attendant** *nc* 1 a person providing a service: *a beach attendant.* 2 a person who is present or notice with another: *The King arrived with his attendants.* ●*adj* also present: *all the attendant difficulties.*

attention (əˈtenʃən) *nu* 1 the act or state of attending (**attend** def. 4): *His attention wandered from what he was doing; Something has come to my attention.* 2 the position of a soldier standing still and upright: *to come to attention.* 3 *nc* (usually *pl*) kind or loving behaviour: *She welcomed his attentions.* ●*interj* (an order to soldiers to come to attention.) **pay attention (to)** 1 **attend** (def. 4) (to). 2 take care (over). **attentive** (əˈtentɪv) *adj* paying attention. **attentively** *adv*

attenuate (əˈtenjʊeɪt) *vti* make or become weak or thin.

attest (əˈtest) *vti* (when *vi*, usually followed by **to**) show or declare to exist or be correct or true: *This painting is an attested original.*

attic (ˈætɪk) *nc* the space inside a roof.

attire (əˈtaɪə*) *vt, nu* dress, esp. (in) fine or unusual clothes.

attitude (ˈætɪtjuːd) *nc* 1 a state of mind, way of thinking, or an opinion: *a strange attitude towards other people.* 2 a position of a body or an aircraft.

attorney (əˈtɜːnɪ) *chiefly US nc, pl* **-s** a lawyer.

attract (əˈtrækt) *vt* 1 draw towards oneself: *Magnets attract iron; Don't attract attention!* 2 be pleasing to: *He's attracted by dogs.* **attraction** 1 *nu* the act of attracting. 2 *nc* a person or thing that attracts. **attractive** *adj* attracting, esp. beautiful. **attractively** *adv*

attribute (æˈtrɪbjuːt) *vt* consider (something) to belong (to) or come (from): *a play attributed to Shakespeare.* ● (ˈætrɪbjuːt) *nc* a quality.

attune (əˈtjuːn) *vti* (cause to) become used (to): *New members quickly attune to the way of life.*

aubergine (ˈəʊbəʒiːn) *nc* a dark purple fruit eaten as a vegetable: see picture at **vegetables.**

auburn (ˈɔːbən) *adj* reddish-brown. ●*ncu* an auburn colour.

auction (ˈɔːkʃən) *nc* a sale at which things are sold to the person who offers the most money for each one. ●*vt* offer for sale at an auction. **auctioneer** (ˌɔːkʃəˈnɪə*) *nc* a person who runs an auction.

audacious (ɔːˈdeɪʃəs) *adj* bold; daring. **audacity** (ɔːˈdæsɪtɪ) *nu*

audible (ˈɔːdəbəl) *adj* able to be heard.

audience (ˈɔːdɪəns) *nc* 1 a group of people watching or listening to a speech, film, etc. 2 a formal meeting with a king, president, religious leader, etc.

audit (ˈɔːdɪt) *nc* an examination of business accounts. ●*vt* carry out an audit of (business accounts). **auditor** *nc*

audition (ɔːˈdɪʃən) *nc* a test for a dancer, musician, actor, etc., applying for a job. ●*vti* test or be tested at an audition.

auditorium (ˌɔːdɪˈtɔːrɪəm) *nc, pl* **-riums, -ria** (rɪə) a hall used for concerts, etc., or the part of one in which the audience sits.

auditory (ˈɔːdɪtərɪ) *adj* to do with hearing.

aught (ɔːt) *archaic or literary pron* anything.

augment (ɔːgˈment) *vti* make or become greater.

augur (ˈɔːgə*) *formal* 1 *vt* indicate that (something) will happen. 2 *vi* indicate (how something will go): *This fine weather augurs well for our holiday.*

August (ˈɔːgəst) *n* the eighth month of the year, after July and before September.

august (ɔːˈgʌst) *adj* respected and influential: *The Royal Society is an august body.*

aunt (ɑːnt) *nc* 1 a sister of one's father or mother. 2 the wife of an uncle. 3 (used by and to children in naming a female friend of their parents.) **auntie** (also **aunty**) ('ɑːntɪ) *infml, children nc, pl* **-ties** an aunt.

au pair (əʊ'peə*) *nc* also **au pair girl** a foreign girl who works for a family in order to learn the local language. ● *vi* work as an au pair.

aura ('ɔːrə) *nc* a mood or feeling produced by a person or place.

auricle ('ɔːrɪkəl) *nc* **1** the part of an ear outside the head. **2** See **atrium**.

auspices ('ɔːspɪsɪz) *n pl* guidance or approval: *A concert was given under the auspices of the music club.*

auspicious (ɔː'spɪʃəs) *adj* favourable; indicating a good future: *A wedding is an auspicious occasion.*

austere (ɔː'stɪə*) *adj* **1** serious or strict. **2** (of clothes, etc.) very plain or simple. **austerity** (ɔː'sterɪtɪ) *nu*

authentic (ɔː'θentɪk) *adj* real; true. **authenticate** (ɔː'θentɪkeɪt) *vt* prove to be true. **authenticity** ('ɔːθen'tɪsɪtɪ) *nu*

author ('ɔːθə*) *nc* **1** a person who writes books. **2** a person who causes things to happen: *the author of these evils.*

authorise ('ɔːθəraɪz) *vt* give permission for (something).

authority (ɔː'θɒrɪtɪ) *nu* **1** the right to give orders and be obeyed. **2** a manner that expresses this right. **3** *nc pl* **-ties** a person or group whose opinions are accepted. **4** a council that governs a district or organises a service: *a local authority; the water authority.* **authoritative** (ɔː'θɒrɪtətɪv) *adj* **1** (having opinions) that ought to be accepted. **2** expressing authority.

auto ('ɔːtəʊ) *nc, pl* **-os** *US infml* short for **automobile.**

autobiography ('ɔːtəʊbaɪ'ɒgrəfɪ) *nc, pl* **-phies** a written account of one's own life. **autobiographical** ('ɔːtə'baɪə'græfɪkəl) *adj*

autocrat ('ɔːtəkræt) *nc* **1** an all-powerful ruler. **2** a person who expects to control the affairs of those around him. **autocratic** ('ɔːtə'krætɪk) *adj* like an autocrat.

autograph ('ɔːtəgrɑːf) *nc* a person's own name which he or she has written by hand. ● *vt* write one's name on (a book, etc.), esp. one written by oneself.

automate ('ɔːtəmeɪt) *vt* make (production) completely mechanical. **automatic** ('ɔːtə'mætɪk) *adj* **1** that works by itself. **2** done without thinking: *It's automatic to hold your breath under water.* ● *nc* a small gun that reloads itself. **automatically** ('ɔːtə'mætɪkəlɪ) *adv*

automation ('ɔːtə'meɪʃən) *nu* completely mechanical production.

automobile ('ɔːtəməbiːl) (often shortened to **auto**) *chiefly US nc* a car.

automotive ('ɔːtə'məʊtɪv) *adj* that drives itself.

autonomous (ɔː'tɒnəməs) *adj* (esp. of a country) governing itself. **autonomy** (ɔː'tɒnəmɪ) *nu*

autopsy ('ɔːtɒpsɪ) *nc, pl* **-sies** the medical examination of a body after death.

autumn ('ɔːtəm) *nc* the season between summer and winter, when corn and fruit are harvested and the leaves fall off some trees. **autumnal** (ɔː'tʌmnəl) *adj*

auxiliary (ɔːg'zɪljərɪ) *adj* helping someone or something more important. ● *nc, pl* **-ries** a trained person who helps in the health services, etc.

avail (ə'veɪl) **avail oneself of** *vt* take advantage of or use (opportunities, etc.). **to no avail** with no success.

available (ə'veɪləbəl) *adj* **1** that can be obtained. **2** free to do work. **availability** (ə'veɪlə'bɪlɪtɪ) *nu*

avalanche ('ævəlɑːnʃ) *nc* **1** a sudden movement of snow down a mountain. **2** *infml* a huge quantity coming all at once: *an avalanche of letters.*

avant-garde ('ævɒn'gɑːd) *adj* (of music, an idea, etc.) new and accepted by only a small number of people. ● *nu* people who are ready to accept new ideas.

avarice ('ævərɪs) *nu* greed for money. **avaricious** ('ævə'rɪʃəs) *adj*

avenge (ə'vendʒ) *vt* give punishment for (a crime or a defeat). **avenge oneself** gain a victory over someone who has harmed or defeated one.

avenue ('ævɪnjuː) *nc* **1** a straight road, often with trees on each side. **2** a means of doing something: *avenues of enquiry.*

aver (ə'vɜː*) *vt* say firmly.

average ('ævərɪdʒ) *adj* normal; most common. ● *nc* the amount found by adding different quantities and dividing this total by the number of quantities: *The average of 1, 6, and 8 is 5.* ● *vt* **1** work out the average of. **2** *vi* give an average of: *Steel production in the Republic of Korea averages 20 million tons a year.*

averse (ə'vɜːs) *formal adj* opposed: *I am not averse to helping you.* **aversion** (ə'vɜːʃən) **1** *ncu* a strong dislike. **2** *nc* a person or thing one dislikes strongly.

avert (ə'vɜːt) *vt* turn away: *He averted his eyes from the terrible sight.*

aviary ('eɪvjərɪ) *nc, pl* **-ries** a place for keeping birds.

aviation ('eɪvɪ'eɪʃən) *nu* flying in planes. **aviator** ('eɪvɪeɪtə*) *old-fashioned nc* a person who flies a plane.

avid ('ævɪd) *adj* greedy; eager.

avocado ('ævə'kɑːdəʊ) *nc, pl* **-dos** a green pear grown in tropical America: see picture at **fruits.**

avoid (ə'vɔɪd) *vt* stay away from (something

unpleasant). **avoidable** *adj* **avoidance** (ə'vɔidəns) *nu*

avoirdupois ('ævwɑːdjuː'pwɑː) *nu* the system of weights in which sixteen ounces equal one pound.

avow (ə'vaʊ) *vt* declare or confess (feelings, etc.).

avuncular (ə'vʌŋkjʊlə*) *adj* in the manner of a (kind) uncle.

await (ə'weit) *vt* wait for.

awake (ə'weik) *adj* conscious before or after sleep. ● *vti* wake up from sleep.

awaken (ə'weikən) 1 *vti* wake up from sleep. 2 *vt* bring (feelings) to life. **awakening** *nc*

award (ə'wɔːd) 1 *nc* a prize given for something well done. 2 *nu* the giving of such a prize. ● *vt* give (such a prize).

aware (ə'weə*) *adj* 1 conscious. 2 having knowledge. **awareness** (ə'weənis) *nu*

awash (ə'wɒʃ) *adj* 1 (of a boat) with seawater flowing over it. 2 *humorous* very full: *The place was awash with wedding presents.*

away (ə'wei) *adv* 1 from a place. 2 at a distance. 3 to a place other than home, work, etc.: *They have gone away.* 4 aside; out of the way: *Stop work and put your books away.* 5 disappearing or coming to an end: *The noise died away.* 6 on and on; without stopping: *He's working away at his car.* ● *adj* (of a game) for which a team has to travel to the other team's ground. **away from** 1 in a direction not towards. 2 at a distance of... from. 3 not at (home, work, etc.). **right** or **straight away** immediately.

awe (ɔː) *nu* great wonder or respect. ● *vt* overcome (a person) with deep respect.

awe-inspiring ('ɔːinspaiəriŋ) *adj* which causes awe or admiration. **awesome** ('ɔːsəm) *adj* which causes awe.

awful ('ɔːfʊl) *adj* terrible; very bad. **awfully** *adv* 1 ('ɔːfʊli) very badly. 2 ('ɔːfli) *infml* very: *That's awfully kind of you.*

awhile (ə'wail) *adv* for a short time.

awkward ('ɔːkwəd) *adj* 1 (of movement, language, etc.) not easy, smooth, or pleasing. 2 difficult to use or deal with. **awkwardly** *adv*

awl (ɔːl) *nc* a tool for making small holes, esp. in leather.

awning ('ɔːniŋ) *nc* a canvas shade for a door or window.

awoke (ə'wəʊk) past tense of **awake.**

awoken (ə'wəʊkən) past participle of **awake.**

awry (ə'rai) *adj, adv* 1 off course; wrong. 2 crooked; not straight.

axe (æks) *US* **ax** *nc* a tool with a blade set at the end of a handle, used for cutting wood, etc.: see picture at **tools. have an axe to grind** have personal, often selfish, reasons for doing something. ● *vt infml* end (someone's job); stop (payments).

axial ('æksiəl) *adj* to do with an axis.

axiom ('æksiəm) *nc* a statement, principle, or rule that is generally accepted to be true. **axiomatic** ('æksiə'mætik) *adj*

axis ('æksis) *nc, pl* **axes** ('æksiːz) an imagined line around which a turning object spins.

axle ('æksəl) *nc* the pin or rod in the centre of a wheel, around which it turns.

ay (also **aye**) (ei) *archaic adv* ever.

ayatollah ('aiə'tɒlə) *nc* a Muslim religious leader.

aye (also **ay**) (ai) *adv, interj, nc* yes.

azalea (ə'zeiliə) *nc* a kind of plant with pink flowers.

azure ('æʒʊə*) *adj* sky-blue. ● *ncu* an azure colour.

B

baa (bɑː) *nc* the sound made by a sheep. ● *vi* make this sound.

babble ('bæbəl) *vi* 1 talk all the time, often without making sense. 2 make a continuous sound like the noise of a stream flowing over stones.

babe (beɪb) *literary nc* a baby.

baboon (bəˈbuːn) *nc* a large kind of monkey.

baby ('beɪbɪ) *nc, pl* -**bies** 1 a young human. 2 *infml* a favourite project. 3 *infml* the youngest member of a group. ● *adj* of smaller size than usual. **babysit** ('beɪbɪˌsɪt) *vi* stay in the house with small children while their parents are out. **babysitter** *nc*

bachelor ('bætʃələ*) *nc* a man who has never been married. **Bachelor of Arts** or **Science** a man or woman who has passed the examinations for a first degree in arts or science.

back (bæk) *nc* 1 the side of an animal's body that is opposite the front or (of four-footed animals) highest from the ground. 2 the part of an object that is opposite or furthest away from the front or that is out of sight. ● *adj* 1 that is behind: *the back door of the house.* 2 late; that should have been paid sooner: *back rent.* 3 past: *a back issue of a magazine.* ● *adv* 1 away from the front or the scene of action. 2 (to) where the person or thing was before: *They were back for lunch; Put that back, you naughty boy.* 3 in return: *Don't hit back if you're attacked.* 4 ago; in the past. ● *vti* 1 move backwards. *vt* 2 support; encourage. 3 put money into (a project); bet on (horses, etc.). **be back** return: *I'll be back soon.* **get off (someone's) back** stop annoying (someone). **get one's own back** See under **own**. **put one's back into** put all one's effort into. **put (someone's) back up** annoy (someone). **backache** ('bækeɪk) *nu* a continuing pain in one's back. **backbone** ('bækbəʊn) *nc* 1 the long line of bones inside the back of humans and some animals. 2 the enthusiastic people who keep an organisation going. 3 *nu* determination. **backbreaking** ('bækˌbreɪkɪŋ) *adj* (of work) very tiring. **backfire** ('bækfaɪə*) *nc* the noise of petrol, etc., exploding too soon in an engine. ● *vi* (ˌbækˈfaɪə*) make a backfire. 2 *infml* go wrong. **background** ('bækgraʊnd) *nc* 1 the part of a scene that is behind the action. 2 the conditions, events, etc., that exist when something happens. 3 the social class from which a person comes.

backhand ('bækhænd) *nc* a stroke in tennis in which the racket is held with the back of the hand facing the ball. **back out of** not do (something one had promised to do). **backstage** (ˌbækˈsteɪdʒ) *theatre adv* behind the scenery. **back up** 1 support (someone, a plan, etc.). 2 move, esp. drive, backwards. **backward** ('bækwəd) *adj* late in developing. ● *adv* also **backwards** 1 in the direction in which the back is facing. 2 from the end to the beginning. **know backwards** know thoroughly. **backyard** (ˌbækˈjɑːd) *nc* the enclosed space at the back of a house.

backgammon (bækˈgæmən, 'bækˌgæmən) *nu* a game in which two people move pieces on a board according to the throw of a dice.

bacon ('beɪkən) *nu* smoked or salted pig meat.

bacteria (bækˈtɪərɪə) *n pl* tiny animals that cause illnesses or changes in the nature of substances. **bacteriology** (bækˌtɪərɪˈɒlədʒɪ) *nu* the study of bacteria.

bad (bæd) *adj* **worse, worst** 1 of poor quality. 2 morally wrong; evil. 3 harmful. 4 unsuitable for a particular purpose. 5 serious: *a bad cold.* 6 (of food) rotten; sour. **not (so) bad** fairly good. **badly** ('bædlɪ) *adv* 1 in a bad way. 2 very much: *I badly need to go.* **bad-tempered** ('bædˈtempəd) *adj* angry by nature.

bade (beɪd) past tense of **bid**.

badge (bædʒ) *nc* a device, usually worn, which shows membership of an organisation or ability in some skill.

badger ('bædʒə*) *nc* an animal that lives in a hole in the earth and comes out at night: see picture at **animals**. ● *vt* keep on asking (someone) for something.

badminton ('bædmɪntən) *nu* a game rather like tennis in which a cork with feathers is used instead of a ball.

baffle ('bæfəl) *vt* confuse (a person).

bag (bæg) *nc* 1 a soft container for carrying things, that can be opened at the top. 2 the amount a bag will hold. 3 *(pl) infml* plenty: *We've got bags of time.* 4 *(pl) infml* trousers. ● *vt* 1 kill (wild animals). 2 *infml* take (something not one's own). **let the cat out of the bag** tell a secret.

baggage ('bægɪdʒ) *nu* cases and bags used to carry belongings on a journey.

baggy ('bægɪ) *adj* -**ier, -iest** (of clothes) hanging loosely on the body.

bagpipes ('bægpaɪps) *n pl* a musical instrument played in Scotland: see picture at **musical instruments.**

bail¹ (beɪl) *nu* the money demanded by a

court of law to release a person from arrest until his trial. **bail out** pay bail to a court to release (someone) from arrest until his trial.

bail² (also **bale**) *v* **bail out 1** empty (seawater) out of (a boat). **2** parachute out of an unsafe plane.

bail³ *cricket nc* one of two short pieces of wood laid across the top of the stumps.

bailiff ('beɪlɪf) *nc* **1** a law officer who carries out the decisions of a court. **2** a manager who acts for a property-owner.

bait (beɪt) *nc* something attractive intended to trap a person or animal. ● *vt* tempt, tease, or provoke (a helpless person or animal).

bake (beɪk) **1** *vt* cook (food) or heat (pots) in an oven. **2** *vi infml* be very hot. **baker** *nc* a person who makes and sells bread. **bakery** ('beɪkərɪ) *nc, pl* **-ries** a place where bread is made. **baking powder** a powder that makes cakes, etc., rise during baking.

balance ('bæləns) *nu* **1** an upright position kept by the even spread of weight. **2** the state of containing the right amount of each of the elements of a thing. *nc* **3** (in accounts) an amount of money still owed. **balance sheet** the accounts of a business showing money paid out and received. **4** an instrument for measuring weight. **hang in the balance** be uncertain. ● *vti* **1** (cause to) be in **balance** (def. 1). *vt* **2** consider the force of (various arguments). **3** (in accounts) cause (amounts of money paid and received) to be equal; *(also vi)* (of amounts of money paid and received) be equal.

balcony ('bælkənɪ) *nc, pl* **-nies 1** a place outside a window, above ground-level, where people may stand or sit. **2** a bank of seats above ground-level in a theatre or cinema.

bald (bɔːld) *adj* **-er, -est** with little or no hair on one's head.

bale¹ (beɪl) *nc* a large, tightly-packed quantity of hay, wool, etc.

bale² *v* See **bail²**.

balk (also **baulk**) (bɔːk) **1** *vi* (usually followed by **at**) refuse (to do something): *They were angry but balked at fighting.* **2** *vt* prevent (someone) from doing or getting (something). ● *nc* something that prevents one from doing something.

ball¹ (bɔːl) *nc* a round object, esp. made to be thrown or hit in a game. **ballpoint pen** ('bɔːlpɔɪnt) a pen in which the ink is carried to the paper by a little ball. **ball bearing** a device in which a moving part of a machine turns on steel balls.

ball² *nc* a large, formal dance. **ballroom** ('bɔːlruːm) *nc* a large room used for balls.

ballad ('bæləd) *nc* a song that tells a story.

ballast ('bæləst) *nu* heavy material put in the bottom of a ship to keep it upright.

ballerina (ˌbælə'riːnə) *nc* a female ballet dancer.

ballet ('bæleɪ) **1** *nu* an artistic form of dancing that often tells a story. **2** *nc* a dance of this kind.

ballistic (bə'lɪstɪk) *adj* to do with rockets, bullets, etc. **ballistics** *nu* the study of rockets, bullets, etc.

balloon (bə'luːn) *nc* **1** a very light rubber bag filled with air for children to play with. **2** a large bag that floats in the air when filled with a gas that is lighter than air. **balloonist** (bə'luːnɪst) a person who flies in a balloon which carries a basket or car for people.

ballot ('bælət) *nc* an election in which each voter indicates his choice on a piece of paper. ● *vti* (ask (someone) to) vote in this way. **ballot-box** *nc* a box into which voters put their pieces of paper at an election.

balm (bɑːm) *nc* **1** an oil or cream used to heal the skin or make it more comfortable. **2** something comforting. **balmy** ('bɑːmɪ) *adj* **-ier, -iest** (of air, an evening, etc.) mild and soft.

balsa ('bɔːlsə) *nu* a wood that is very light in weight.

balustrade (ˌbælə'streɪd) *nc* a bar supported by small pillars that forms a wall: see picture.

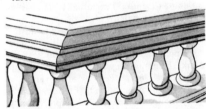

balustrade

bamboo (bæm'buː) *nu* a plant with hard, hollow stems that grows esp. in East Asia: see picture.

bamboo

ban (bæn) *vt* forbid (something). **2** refuse membership, etc., to (a person). ● *nc* the act of banning or state of being banned.

banal (bə'nɑːl) *adj* boring; uninteresting; too ordinary.

banana (bə'nɑːnə) *nc* a curved yellow fruit which grows esp. in the West Indies: see picture at **fruits.**

band¹ (bænd) *nc* **1** a group of people. **2** a group of musicians who play popular music. **band together** form a group.

band² *nc* **1** a strip of material, esp. for putting round things to hold them together. **2** a strip of something in a different colour from the rest.

bandage ('bændɪdʒ) *nc* a strip of cloth used to cover the dressing on a wound. ● *vt* put a bandage round (a wound or a part of the body).

bandit ('bændɪt) *nc* a robber, esp. in lonely country.

bandy¹ ('bændɪ) *adj* **-ier, -iest** (of legs) bent so as to be apart at the knees.

bandy² *vt* exchange (words), esp. angrily.

bane (beɪn) *nc* the chief nuisance; an evil.

bang (bæŋ) *nc* **1** a short, loud noise made by an explosion, etc. **2** a hit: *If it won't go in, give it a bang.* ● *vti* make such a noise (by hitting). ● *adv* **1** with a bang: *The gun went bang.* **2** exactly: *bang in the middle.*

bangle ('bæŋgəl) *nc* a round ornament for the arm or leg.

banish ('bænɪʃ) *vt* **1** drive (a person) out of a country or society. **2** get rid of (ideas). **banishment** *nu* the act of banishing or state of being banished.

banister ('bænɪstə*) *nc (*usually *pl)* a railing fixed beside stairs.

banjo ('bændʒəʊ) *nc, pl* **-os, -oes** a musical instrument played by plucking the strings: see picture at **musical instruments.**

bank¹ (bæŋk) *nc* **1** a wall of earth, often sloping. **2** the land at the edge of a river.

bank² *nc* an organisation that looks after money for its customers. ● *vt* **1** put (money) into a bank. **2** *vi* have an account (with a bank). **bank on** depend on; be sure of. **Bank Holiday** (in the UK) a public holiday. **banker** *nc* a person holding a high position in a bank. **banknote** ('bæŋknəʊt) a piece of paper money produced by a bank.

bankrupt ('bæŋkrʌpt) *adj* with no money left to pay one's debts. ● *nc* a bankrupt person. ● *vt* make bankrupt. **bankruptcy** ('bæŋkrʌptsɪ) *ncu, pl* **-cies**

banner ('bænə*) *nc* a piece of cloth expressing an organisation's aims that is carried in a procession.

banns (bænz) *n pl* the notice of a future marriage, read out in church.

banquet ('bæŋkwɪt) *nc* a big formal meal attended by many people. ● *vi* feast.

banter ('bæntə*) *nu* teasing, joking conversation. ● *vi* exchange banter.

baptism ('bæptɪzəm) *nc* the acceptance, shown by the use of water, of a person into Christianity. **baptise** (bæp'taɪz) *vt* give baptism to. **Baptist** ('bæptɪst) a member of the Church which believes that one should go completely under water at baptism.

Bar (bɑː*) *n* **the Bar** (in England) barristers.

bar (bɑː*) *nc* **1** a piece of a hard substance, longer than it is wide. **2** a stripe or ring of colour, etc. **3** something that prevents or forbids. **4** a regular division of a piece of music. **5** the place where drinks are served in a pub, etc. ● *vt* **1** forbid (an action); keep (a person) out. **2** block (a road). **3** mark with bars (**bar** def. **2**). **bar chart** a kind of drawing in which quantities are represented by bars (**bar** def. **2**): see picture.

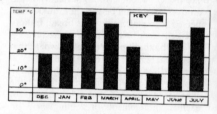

bar chart

barmaid ('bɑːmeɪd) *nc* a woman who serves drinks in a bar. **barman** ('bɑːmən) *nc, pl* **-men** a man who serves drinks in a bar.

barb (bɑːb) *nc* a sharp point facing backwards on an arrow, fishing hook, etc. **barbed wire** wire with regular sharp points along it used for fences.

barbarian (bɑː'beərɪən) *adj* uncivilised ● *nc* an uncivilised person. **barbaric** (bɑː'bærɪk) *adj* **barbarous** ('bɑːbərəs) *adj* **barbarism** ('bɑːbərɪzəm) also **barbarity** (bɑː'bærɪtɪ) *ncu* a barbaric state or act.

barbecue ('bɑːbɪkjuː) *nc* **1** a picnic at which meat is cooked over a fire. **2** a frame on which meat is cooked over a fire. ● *vt* cook (meat) on a **barbecue** (def. **2**).

barber ('bɑːbə*) *nc* a person who cuts men's hair and shaves their beards.

barbiturate (bɑː'bɪtjʊrət) *nc* a drug that causes sleep.

bard (bɑːd) *literary nc* a poet; poet and singer.

bare (beə*) *adj* **-r, -st** **1** not covered, esp. naked. **2** unprotected. **3** empty: *The cupboard was bare.* **4** simple: *the bare facts.* ● *vt* uncover. **bareback** ('beəbæk) *adv, adj* on a horse without a saddle. **barefoot** ('beəfʊt) *adv, adj* without shoes or socks. **bareheaded** ('beə'hedɪd) *adj, adv* without a hat or other head covering. **barely** *adv* **1** only just: *It is barely six o'clock.* **2** simply· poorly: *a barely furnished room.*

bargain ('bɑːgɪn) *nc* **1** something bought cheaply. **2** an agreement, esp. to buy or sell something ● *vi* discuss the price of a sale or the terms of an agreement. **get more than one bargained for** find that one has accepted more than one expected or wanted.

barge (bɑːdʒ) *nc* a wide-bottomed boat chiefly for carrying goods, used on inland waters. ● *v infml* **barge in** interrupt rudely. **barge into** knock against.

baritone ('bærɪtəʊn) **1** *nu* the middle male singing voice. **2** *nc* a man with this voice.

barium ('beərɪəm) *nu* a chemical element that is a soft silver-white metal: symbol Ba.

bark¹ (bɑːk) *nu* the short cry of a dog. ● *vi* (of a dog) give a bark.

bark² *nu* the covering of the trunk and branches of a tree.

barley ('bɑːlɪ) *nu* a plant producing seeds which are used to make beer, whisky, and bread.

barn (bɑːn) *nc* a large farm building for corn, hay, animals, etc.

barnacle ('bɑːnəkəl) *nc* a small sea-animal with a shell that sticks to boats, rocks, etc., under the water.

barometer (bə'rɒmɪtə*) *nc* an instrument for measuring air pressure.

baron ('bærən) *nc* **1** (in the UK) a male noble of the lowest rank. **2** a powerful person: *a press baron.*

barracks ('bærəks) *nu* (*with singular verb*) a group of buildings where soldiers live.

barrage ('bærɑːʒ) *nc* **1** a long period of firing from many guns. **2** a dam across a river. **3** a series of questions put to a person at the same time.

barrister ('bærɪstə*) *nc* (in England) a lawyer who argues cases in the higher courts.

barrow¹ ('bærəʊ) *nc* **1** short for **wheelbarrow**. **2** a stand on wheels used for selling fruit and vegetables.

barrow² *nc* a very old grave covered by a heap of earth.

barter ('bɑːtə*) *nu* the exchange of goods for other goods (instead of money). ● *vti* exchange (goods) in this way.

base¹ (beɪs) *nc* **1** the bottom of a thing; foundation. **2** the chief substance in a mixture. **3** a place where an army, group of explorers, etc., keeps its stores, and from which it operates. ● *vt* develop (figures, an argument, etc.) from something: *I base my criticism on the figures before us.* **baseboard** ('beɪsbɔːd) *US n* See **skirting-board**.

base² *adj* **-r, -st** **1** (of behaviour, etc.) mean; low. **2** (of metals, etc.) of low value.

baseball ('beɪsbɔːl) *nu* a game, played by two teams of nine players, in which a member of one team hits a ball thrown by a member of the other.

basement ('beɪsmənt) *nc* the rooms of a building that are below ground-level.

bash (bæʃ) *infml nc* **1** a violent hit. **2** a try: *Let's have a bash!* ● *vt* hit violently.

bashful ('bæʃful) *adj* modest; not welcoming attention.

basic ('beɪsɪk) *adj* **1** acting as a base or basis: *basic education.* **2** plain; simple: *basic facts.* **basically** ('beɪsɪklɪ) *adv* at bottom; essentially.

basil ('bæzɪl) *nu* a plant with a sweet smell used in cooking.

barrel

barrel ('bærəl) *nc* **1** a round container usually with curved sides: see picture. **2** the tube of a gun. **barrel organ** a mechanical musical instrument played in the streets.

barren ('bærən) *adj* **1** (of animals) unable to produce young; (of plants) unable to produce fruit; (of land) unable to produce crops. **2** (of a discussion, etc.) that fails to produce results.

barricade (,bærɪ'keɪd) *nc* a barrier built across a street, esp. during fighting.

barrier ('bærɪə*) *nc* **1** a bar or fence used to keep people within or out of a place. **2** something that keeps people apart: *barriers of race.*

basin

basin ('beɪsən) *nc* **1** a round open container, esp. for food: see picture. **2** the amount a basin will hold. **3** a low area of land into which rivers run. **4** **wash-basin** See under **wash**.

basis ('beɪsɪs) *nc, pl* **bases** ('beɪsiːz) something on which an argument, etc., is based. **on the basis of** using... as a guide.

bask (bɑːsk) *vi* lie somewhere pleasantly warm, esp. in the sun.

basket ('bɑːskɪt) *nc* **1** an open container, usually made from cane or reeds, with a handle, for carrying things: see picture. **2** the amount a basket will hold.

basket

basketball ('bɑːskɪtbɔːl) *nu* a game played by two teams of five players, in which the aim is to throw the ball through a metal ring high above the ground.

bass¹ (beɪs) **1** *nu* the lowest male singing voice. **2** *nc* a man with this voice. ● *adj* (of a voice, instrument, etc.) in the lowest range.

bass² (bæs) *nc, pl* **bass** any of several fishes of the perch family.

bassoon (bə'suːn) *nc* a large woodwind instrument with keys and a double reed and which makes a deep sound: see picture at **musical instruments.**

bastard ('bɑːstəd) *nc, adj* (a child) born to parents who are not married. **2** *derogatory* (something) very annoying or difficult. ● *nc derogatory* someone one dislikes strongly.

baste (beɪst) *vt* pour juice or oil over (food being cooked).

bastion ('bæstɪən) *nc* a strongly built, safe place.

bat¹ (bæt) *nc* a flying animal; mammal that lives in dark places and is active at night.

bat² *nc* a long piece of wood with a handle for hitting the ball in cricket, baseball, etc. ● *vt* hit (a ball) with a bat.

bat³ *v* **not bat an eyelid** *infml* appear not to be surprised or worried.

batch (bætʃ) *nc* a convenient quantity of things, esp. one coming at intervals. ● *vt* put into convenient quantities.

bated ('beɪtɪd) *adj* **with bated breath** with breath held back (through anxiety, etc.).

bath (bɑːθ) *nc, pl* **baths** (bɑːðz) **1** a container that one fills with water to sit and wash oneself in. **2** the act of washing oneself in a bath: *I'm going to have a bath.* **3 the baths** See **swimming-bath** under **swim.** ● *vti* wash in a bath. **bathrobe** ('bɑːθrəub) *US nc* a dressing-gown. **bathroom** ('bɑːθruːm) *nc* **1** a room with a bath in. **2** *US* a toilet. **bathtub** ('bɑːθtʌb) *nc* a **bath** (def. 1). **bathe** (beɪð) **1** *vi* swim. *vt* **2** clean (a wound) with water. **3** put (a tired part of the body) into water. ● *nc* a swim. **bathing costume** *nc* a garment to swim in.

batman ('bætmən) *nc, pl* **-men** an army officer's personal servant.

baton ('bætɒn) *nc* a short stick, esp. carried by army officers or policemen or used to direct musicians.

batsman ('bætsmən) *cricket nc, pl* **-men** a player who tries to hit the ball with his bat.

battalion (bə'tæljən) *nc* a part of an army, containing several companies and being part of a brigade.

batten ('bætən) *nc* a long, thin piece of wood for fixing tiles to, etc. **batten down** fix (something) down with battens.

batter¹ ('bætə*) *vti* hit or knock hard and for a long time.

batter² *nu* a mixture of eggs, milk, and flour used to make pancakes, etc., or to coat food to be fried. ● *vt* coat (food) with batter.

battery ('bætərɪ) *nc, pl* **-ries 1** a device which stores electricity. **2** a group of heavy guns. **3** a row of cages in which hens are kept. **battery charger** See **charger** (def. 1).

battle ('bætəl) *nc* a big fight, esp. between armed forces. ● *vi* (often followed by **against** or **with**) fight (against difficulties, etc.). **battlefield** also **battleground** *nc* the place where a land battle is fought. **battlement** ('bætəlmənt) *nc* a wall with holes through which to shoot. **battleship** *nc* a large warship with heavy guns.

baulk (bɔːk) *v, n* See **balk.**

bauxite ('bɔːksaɪt) *nu* a substance dug out of the ground from which aluminium is obtained.

bawl (bɔːl) *vi* shout or cry loudly.

bay¹ (beɪ) *nc* an inward curve of the coast.

bay² *nc* a part of a room that curves outwards from the line of the walls. **bay window** a window in a bay.

bay³ *nc* a laurel tree of which the dried leaves are used to add taste in cooking: see picture at **trees.**

bay⁴ *vi* (of a dog) give a deep bark or howl. **keep at bay** hold off (an enemy, disease, etc.).

bay⁵ *adj* of a colour between red and brown. ● *ncu* a bay colour or horse.

bayonet ('beɪənet) *nc* a knife fixed to the end of a rifle. ● *vt* stick a bayonet into.

bazaar (bə'zɑː*) *nc* a market where all kinds of goods are sold.

be (biː unstressed bɪ) *vi* **1** exist; live. **2** (used to describe): *I am ill; She is a doctor.* **3** take place: *The concert is tonight.* **4** occupy space: *I'm upstairs.* **5** (used in continuous verbs): *He was reading; What are you doing?* **6** (used in passive verbs): *The window had been broken.* **7** go: *Have you been to India?* **8** have as a task: *We're to report for duty.* **bride-to-be** a future wife.

beach (biːtʃ) *nc* land, esp. sand, at the edge of the sea. ● *vt* run or pull (a boat) onto a beach. **beachhead** (ˈbiːtʃhed) *nc* land near the sea occupied by soldiers who have arrived in boats to attack.

beacon (ˈbiːkən) *nc* a bright light which can be seen from far away and acts as a guide or signal.

bead (biːd) *nc* a small piece of glass, coloured stone, etc., a number of which can be put on a string and worn round the neck as an ornament. **2** a drop, esp. of sweat. **beady** (ˈbiːdɪ) *adj* **-ier, -iest** (esp. of the eyes) round and hard in appearance.

beagle (ˈbiːgəl) *nc* a kind of dog.

beak (biːk) *nc* the horny mouth of a bird.

beaker (ˈbiːkə*) *nc* **1** a tall cup without a handle. **2** a tall glass container with a lip, used in scientific experiments.

beam (biːm) *nc* **1** a piece of wood that goes across a room and helps to support the ceiling or the roof. **2** a light that shines straight from the sun or a lamp. **3** a broad smile. ● *vi* **1** shine brightly. **2** smile broadly. **3** *vt* direct (a broadcast) towards a particular place.

bean (biːn) *nc* **1** any of several plants of which the seeds are eaten as vegetables. **2** one of these seeds. **full of beans** very energetic; not at all tired. **spill the beans** tell a secret.

bear¹ (beə*) *vt* **1** *formal* carry. **2** put up with (grief, etc.). **3** (of a tree, etc.) produce (fruit, etc.). *vi* **4** turn slightly: *Bear left onto the main road.* **5** be patient: *Bear with me for a few more minutes.* **bear in mind** See under **mind. bearable** *adj* able to be borne (**bear¹** def. 2). **bear up** face a blow with courage.

bear² *nc* a large powerful animal with thick fur: see picture at **animals. bearskin** (ˈbeəskɪn) *nc* **1** the skin and fur of a bear. **2** a tall, black fur cap worn by some British soldiers.

beard (bɪəd) *nc* the hair that grows on the lower part of a man's face. ● *vt* face (a difficult person). **bearded** *adj* (of a man) with a beard.

bearer (ˈbeərə*) *nc* **1** a person who carries (in former times, in India and Africa) a porter or personal servant. **2** the person who brings a cheque to a bank for payment. **3** a person who brings: *the bearer of good news.*

bearing (ˈbeərɪŋ) *nu* **1** the way a person behaves and moves: *a man of military bearing.* **2** a direction described by its relationship to north: *East is the same as a bearing of 90 degrees.* **3** a connection: *That has no bearing on the case.* **4** *nc* a support for a moving part in a machine. **get** or **lose one's bearings** find out or forget where one is or the direction one wants to go in. **ball bearing** See under **ball¹**.

beast (biːst) *nc* **1** an animal, esp. one with four feet. **2** a cruel or dirty person. **beastly** (ˈbiːstlɪ) *adj* **-ier, -iest 1** like a beast. **2** nasty.

beat (biːt) *nc* **1** a sound that is repeated regularly, as of a drum or the heart. **2** a rhythm in music. **3** a conductor's movements indicating this to the musicians. **4** a way regularly walked by someone such as a policeman. ● *vt* **1** hit repeatedly. **2** stir (food) fast and thoroughly. **3** defeat. **4** *vi* (esp. of the heart) make regular movements that can be heard. **beat about the bush** avoid an important matter by not talking about it plainly. **beat off** win the fight against (an attack, etc.). **beat up** knock (someone) about violently. **beating** (ˈbiːtɪŋ) *nc* **1** repeated hits. **2** a defeat.

beaten (ˈbiːtən) past participle of **beat.** ● *adj* **1** (shaped by being) hit repeatedly: *beaten metal.* **2** (of food) mixed thoroughly: *beaten egg.* **3** defeated. **off the beaten track** away from big towns and main roads.

beater (ˈbiːtə*) *nc* a person who makes birds fly up so that they can be shot.

beauty (ˈbjuːtɪ) **1** *nu* the quality of being attractive to look at or pleasing to the mind. *nc, pl* **-ties 2** a woman who is attractive to look at. **3** something that is big, well made, etc.: *This potato is a beauty!* **beautiful** *adj* **beautifully** *adv* **beautify** (ˈbjuːtɪfaɪ) *vt* make (more) beautiful.

beaver (ˈbiːvə*) *nc* **1** a furry animal that builds its home in a river: see picture at **animals. 2** *infml* a hard worker. **3** *nu* beaver fur. ● *vi infml* (often followed by **away**) work hard.

becalm (bɪˈkɑːm) *vt* (*usually passive*) stop (a ship) from moving, from lack of wind.

became (bɪˈkeɪm) past tense of **become.**

because (bɪˈkɒz) *conj* for the reason that: *It is hot because the sun is shining.* **because of** owing to; by reason of: *We stayed at home because of the bad weather.*

beckon (ˈbekən) **1** *vi* make a sign (to someone that he should come nearer). **2** *vt* make a sign to (someone) that he should come nearer.

become (bɪˈkʌm) **1** *v* come to be; change into (being): *After the storm it became very cold; She became a doctor.* **2** *vt* suit (someone) well: *Long hair becomes you.* **become of** happen to: *Whatever became of her?* **becoming** (bɪˈkʌmɪŋ) *adj* that suits a person well.

bed (bed) *nc* **1** a piece of furniture for sleeping on. **2** a part of a garden where a particular plant is grown: *a flower bed.* 3 the bottom of a sea, river, etc. **bedclothes** ('bedkləʊðz) *n pl* also **bedding** *nu* blankets, sheets, etc., used on a bed. **bedroom** ('bedrʊm) *nc* a room that contains a bed or beds. **bedside** ('bedsaɪd) *nu* the place beside the bed of a sick person. ●*adj* that is placed beside a bed. **bedsitter** ('bed'sɪtə*) *nc* a room used as bedroom and sitting-room in one. **bedspread** ('bedspred) *nc* a cloth spread over the rest of the bedclothes. **bedstead** ('bedsted) *nc* the frame of a bed. **bedtime** ('bedtaɪm) *ncu* the time at which someone, esp. a child, ought to go to bed.

bedecked (bɪ'dekt) *adj* ornamented (with jewels, etc.).

bedlam ('bedləm) *nu* a state of noise and confusion.

Bedouin ('bedəʊɪn) *nc, pl* **Bedouin** an Arab who moves from place to place in the desert.

bedraggled (bɪ'drægəld) *adj* dirty with water or mud.

bedrock ('bedrɒk) *nu* 1 solid rock that lies some way under the soil. 2 the basic facts.

bee (biː) *nc* 1 a winged insect that produces honey: see picture at **insects.** 2 a meeting or competition, esp. for spelling words.

beehive

beehive ('biːhaɪv) (often shortened to **hive**) *nc* a box built for bees to live and make honey in: see picture. **make a beeline for** ('biːlaɪn) go straight to.

beech (biːtʃ) 1 *nc* a tree with smooth grey bark that produces nuts. 2 *nu* the wood of this tree.

beef (biːf) 1 the meat of a bull, cow, or ox. 2 physical strength. 3 *infml nc* a complaint. ●*vi infml* complain. **beefsteak** ('biːf'steɪk) *nc* a thick piece of beef with little fat.

been (biːn unstressed bɪn) past participle of **be.**

beep (biːp) *nc, vi* (make) a simple, steady sound made esp. as a warning by an electrical device such as a horn.

beer (bɪə*) also **ale** 1 *ncu* an alcoholic drink made from malt and hops. 2 *nc* a glass of beer.

beet (biːt) *ncu* any of various plants with thick roots that can be eaten as vegetables or made into sugar. **beet sugar** sugar made from the roots of white beet. **beet-**

root ('biːtruːt) *nu* the root of the red beet: see picture at **vegetables.**

beetle ('biːtəl) *nc* any of a great many types of insect with hard wing-cases: see picture at **insects.**

befall (bɪ'fɔːl) *formal* 1 *vi* happen. 2 *vt* happen to (someone).

befallen (bɪ'fɔːlən) past participle of **befall.**

befell (bɪ'fel) past tense of **befall.**

befit (bɪ'fɪt) *formal vt* suit; be fitting for.

before (bɪ'fɔː*) *prep* 1 in front of. 2 earlier than: *before three o'clock.* ●*adv* already; earlier: *I've never seen that before.* ●*conj* sooner than: *Before she could move, the thief had taken the ring.* **beforehand** (bɪ'fɔːhænd) *adv* before some event; already.

befriend (bɪ'frend) *vt* act as a friend towards (someone).

beg (beg) 1 *vi* ask people in the street for money. 2 *vti* ask (for): *She begged £5 from us; I beg your pardon.*

began (bɪ'gæn) past tense of **begin.**

beget (bɪ'get) *vt* 1 (be the) father (of). 2 *literary* cause: *Fear begets jealousy.*

beggar ('begə*) *nc* a poor person who asks people for money. ●*vt* make poor.

begin (bɪ'gɪn) *vti* start. **beginner** (bɪ'gɪnə*) *nc* a person who is new to an activity. **beginning** *nc* a start; first part. **to begin with** as a start; first.

begone (bɪ'gɒn) *literary interj* go away!

begot (bɪ'gɒt) past tense of **beget.**

begotten (bɪ'gɒtən) past participle of **beget.**

begrudge (bɪ'grʌdʒ) *vt* give (something to someone) when one would rather not do so: *I don't begrudge you money that you earn.*

beguile (bɪ'gaɪl) *vt* 1 (esp. of women) cheat. 2 charm. 3 pass (the time) with amusements.

begun (bɪ'gʌn) past participle of **begin.**

behalf (bɪ'hɑːf) *n* **on behalf of** for, on the part of, or representing (someone).

behave (bɪ'heɪv) *vi* act, esp. with good manners. **behave well** or **badly** have good or bad manners.

behaviour *US* **behavior** (bɪ'heɪvjə*) *nu* 1 a way of behaving; one's manners. 2 the way that a machine, chemical, or animal acts under given conditions.

behead (bɪ'hed) *vt* cut off the head of.

beheld (bɪ'held) past tense and past participle of **behold.**

behest (bɪ'hest) *old-fashioned nc* an order or request: *I have come at the behest of the King.*

behind (bɪ'haɪnd) *prep, adv* 1 at or to the back of. 2 not as far on as (one ought or would like to be): *We're getting behind the others — we must work faster.* ●*prep* in support of: *We're right behind you in your* plan. ●*adv* remaining after someone or something else has left: *I left my hat behind at work.* ●*nc infml* the soft part of the body on which one sits. **behindhand** (bɪˈhaɪndhænd) *adv* late.

behold (bɪˈhəʊld) *old-fashioned vti* look (at); see.

beholden (bɪˈhəʊldən) *old-fashioned adj* grateful or in debt (to someone) for a kindness, etc.

beige (beɪʒ) *adj* very light brown. ●*ncu* a beige colour.

being (ˈbiːɪŋ) present participle of **be.** ●*nu* 1 life; existence. *nc* 2 a person. 3 something thought to exist or have life, such as a god or a creature from a star.

belabour (bɪˈleɪbə*) *vt* talk about something for too long: *to belabour a point.*

belated (bɪˈleɪtɪd) *formal adj* late: *Their belated good wishes arrived two days after his birthday.*

belay (bɪˈleɪ) *nautical, mountaineering vt* fix (a rope) by turning it round a strong pin or with some other device.

belch (beltʃ) 1 *vi* make a noise of allowing gas from the stomach out through the mouth. 2 *vti* pour out.

beleaguered (bɪˈliːgəd) *adj* under attack.

belfry (ˈbelfrɪ) *nc, pl* **-fries** the part of a church tower where the bells are.

belie (bɪˈlaɪ) *vt* 1 give a false idea of. 2 show (something) to be untrue or a lie: *The report of his death was belied by his appearance the next day.*

belief (bɪˈliːf) *nu* 1 faith; trust. 2 acceptance of something as true. 3 *nc* an opinion. 4 *ncu* (acceptance of) a religion.

believe (bɪˈliːv) *vt* 1 have faith in; trust. 2 accept as true. 3 have as an opinion. **believable** (bɪˈliːvəbəl) *adj* that can be believed. **believe in** 1 have faith in; trust. 2 accept the existence of. 3 agree with (an idea). **believer** (bɪˈliːvə*) *nc* a person who has faith (in a religion, political system, etc.).

belittle (bɪˈlɪtəl) *vt* speak of (someone's work, etc.) as less important than it is.

bell (bel) *nc* a hollow metal object containing a movable hanging part that makes a ringing sound when the bell is shaken: see picture.

bell

belligerent (bɪˈlɪdʒərənt) *adj* 1 taking part in a war. 2 warlike; aggressive. ●*nc* a power that takes part in a war.

bellow (ˈbeləʊ) *vti* roar; shout very loudly. ●*nc* a roar; very loud shout.

bellows (ˈbeləʊz) *n pl* also **pair of bellows** a device for feeding air to a fire to make it burn faster, or to an organ, etc., to make it sound.

belly (ˈbelɪ) *nc, pl* **-lies** 1 the lower front part of the body above the legs. 2 the stomach.

belong (bɪˈlɒŋ) *vi* 1 be normally kept or put: *The plates belong in the cupboard.* 2 fit in; match the surroundings. **belongings** (bɪˈlɒŋɪŋz) *n pl* possessions. **belong to** 1 be owned by (someone). 2 be a member of (an organisation).

beloved (bɪˈlʌvɪd) *old-fashioned adj, nc* a person who is dearly loved.

below (bɪˈləʊ) *prep* 1 under; lower than. 2 less than (a figure). 3 less important than: *He's below me at work.* ●*adv* 1 underneath; at or to a lower place. 2 (on a ship) lower than the decks; down inside: *They went below.* 3 further on (in a book).

belt (belt) *nc* 1 a band that goes round the waist, usually to hold a garment up or in. 2 a stretch of country: *the green belt round London.* 3 a band connecting wheels in a machine. **hit below the belt** attack a person unfairly. ●*vt* 1 fasten with a belt. 2 hit with a belt. 3 *infml vi* move fast: *We belted along the road.*

bemoan (bɪˈməʊn) *vt* be sad about.

bench (bentʃ) *nc* 1 a long seat with room for several people. 2 a work table. 3 *nu* the people who judge others accused of crimes.

bend (bend) 1 *vti* curve. 2 *vi* fold one's body so as to reach down, etc. ●*nc* a curve, esp. in a road. **the bends** sickness caused by a sudden change in air pressure. **be bent on** be determined to (do something).

beneath (bɪˈniːθ) *formal or literary prep. adv* under(neath). ●*prep* too ordinary, common, etc., for: *Now he's manager, he thinks dirty work is beneath him.*

benediction (ˌbenɪˈdɪkʃən) *nc* a (Roman Catholic service of) blessing.

benefactor (ˈbenɪfæktə*) *nc* someone who gives money to a person or organisation.

beneficent (bɪˈnefɪsənt) *adj* (of a person) generous.

beneficial (ˌbenɪˈfɪʃəl) *adj* bringing good; having a good effect.

beneficiary (ˌbenɪˈfɪʃərɪ) *nc, pl* **-ries** a person who receives money from someone.

benefit (ˈbenɪfɪt) *nc* 1 an advantage: *Education is a great benefit in life.* 2 money paid to people by a government, insurance company, etc.: *unemployment benefit.* **for the benefit of** for the good of (someone). **give (someone) the benefit of the doubt** not accuse (someone) when the truth of a matter is not clear. ●*vt* 1 do good or give an advantage to (someone). **2** *vi* profit; receive an advantage. **benevolent** (bɪˈnevələnt) *adj* **1** kindly, friendly. **2** (of an organisation) giving help to people; not intended to make a profit. **benevolence** (ləns) *nu* **1** kindness. **2** generosity.

benign (bɪˈnaɪn) *adj* **1** favourable. **2** (of a disease) mild.

bent[1] (bent) past tense and past participle of **bend**.

bent[2] *nc* an inclination; ability; nature.

benumbed (bɪˈnʌmd) *literary adj* with no feeling (in the body or the mind).

benzene (ˈbenziːn) *nu* a liquid obtained from coal tar, used to make plastics, etc.

benzine (ˈbenziːn) *nu* a liquid obtained from mineral oil, used in cleaning, etc.

bequeath (bɪˈkwiːð) *formal vt* give (something) away after one's death or departure. **bequest** (bɪˈkwest) *nc* **1** something bequeathed. **2** the act of bequeathing.

berate (bɪˈreɪt) *vt* scold.

bereave (bɪˈriːv) *vt* (usually passive) (of death) take a loved person away from (someone): *He was bereaved of his wife.* **bereavement** *nc*

bereft (bɪˈreft) *literary adj* **bereft of** having lost: *They were bereft of all hope.*

beret (ˈbereɪ) *nc* a soft round cap.

beriberi (ˌberɪˈberɪ) *nu* a disease common in the East and hot parts of the world, caused by lack of foods containing vitamin B₁.

berry (ˈberɪ) *nc, pl* **-ries** any of many kinds of small fruit without stone that grow on bushes and small trees.

berserk (bəˈsɜːk, bəˈzɜːk) *adv* **go berserk** (of persons and animals) run wild; lose control; go mad.

berth (bɜːθ) *nc* **1** a bed fixed to a wall in a ship, train, or plane. **2** a place in a port where a ship can be tied up. ● *vt* tie up (a ship) in a port; *(also vi)* (of a ship) tie up in a port. **give a wide berth** keep well away from (something or someone unpleasant).

beseech (bɪˈsiːtʃ) *old-fashioned vt* ask or beg (someone to do something).

beset (bɪˈset) *vt* surround; trouble: *a task beset with difficulties.*

beside (bɪˈsaɪd) *prep, adv* at the side of or next to (something). ● *prep* compared to: *Beside last year's loss, this year's is small.* **beside the point** not connected with the matter being discussed. **be beside oneself** not in control of oneself; overcome (with anger, etc.).

besides (bɪˈsaɪdz) *prep, adv* in addition (to); as well (as).

besiege (bɪˈsiːdʒ) *vt* **1** attack (a town). **2** crowd round (a popular person). **3** flood (someone) with questions, telephone calls, etc.

besought (bɪˈsɔːt) past tense and past participle of **beseech**.

bespeak (bɪˈspiːk) *vt* **1** order (something) in advance. **2** indicate (a person's nature).

bespoke (bɪˈspəʊk) past tense of **bespeak**. ● *adj* **bespoke tailoring** clothes made to personal order.

bespoken (bɪˈspəʊkən) past participle of **bespeak**.

best (best) *adj* having the highest qualities; most attractive, useful, etc. ● *adv* **1** the most: *He's the one I like best.* **2** most efficiently, easily, etc.; with the greatest effect: *She sings best before a small audience.* **the best** the most attractive, useful, etc., person(s) or thing(s). See also **good** and **well**[1]. **all the best** all good wishes. **make the best of a bad job** do as well as possible in a difficult situation. **best man** a friend who attends the bridegroom at a wedding. **bestseller** (ˈbestselə*) *nc* a book of which very large numbers are sold.

bestial (ˈbestɪəl) *adj* **1** natural to a beast. **2** (of behaviour) inhuman; cruel.

bestir (bɪˈstɜː*) *vt* cause or start to move.

bestow (bɪˈstəʊ) *formal vt* give (a present or prize): *He had many things bestowed on him.*

bet (bet) also **wager** *nc* a promise of money to be paid or not according to the unpredictable result of an event. ● *vt* promise (money) in this way: *I bet £5 that the black horse will win.*

beta (ˈbiːtə) *nc* the second letter of the Greek alphabet.

betide (bɪˈtaɪd) *old-fashioned vti* (of unpleasant things) happen to (someone): *Woe betide the man who goes to sea in a storm.*

betray (bɪˈtreɪ) *vt* **1** put (a person who trusts one) into the power of an enemy. **2** show or make clear (what one would wish to hide): *Her pale face betrayed her worry.* **betrayal** (bɪˈtreɪəl) *ncu*

betrothed (bɪˈtrəʊðd) *old-fashioned adj* promised in marriage (to someone). **betrothal** (bɪˈtrəʊðəl) *nc*

better (ˈbetə*) *adj* **1** having higher qualities; more attractive, useful, etc. **2** improved: *You'll be (the) better for a holiday.* ● *adv* more efficiently, easily, etc.: *A car goes better on a well-made road.* **the better** the one that is more attractive, useful, etc. See also **good** and **well**[1]. ● *vt* improve (on): *I shall better their offer.* **better oneself** improve one's position. **better off 1** in a more pleasant situation. **2** having more money. **get the better of** defeat; overcome. **had better** ought to or must (do something): *We had better go or she won't be pleased.*

between (bɪˈtwiːn) *prep* connecting or separating: *There are many flights between Lon-*

don and New York. **between you and me** as a secret.

betwixt (bɪˈtwɪkst) *old-fashioned prep, adv* between.

bevel (ˈbevəl) *vt* slope (the edge of a glass, card etc.). ● *nc* a sloping edge.

beverage (ˈbevərɪdʒ) *old-fashioned nc* a drink, esp. one without alcohol.

bevy (ˈbevɪ) *nc, pl* **-vies** a group (of girls or birds).

bewail (bɪˈweɪl) *vt* express grief for.

beware (bɪˈweə*) *vti* (when *vi*, followed by **of**) guard (against): *Beware of the dog.*

bewilder (bɪˈwɪldə*) *vt* confuse (a person). **bewildering** *adj*

bewitch (bɪˈwɪtʃ) *vt* **1** put a spell on. **2** charm; enchant. **bewitched** *adj*

beyond (bɪˈjɒnd) *prep, adv* further (than), past, or on the other side (of). **the beyond** what happens after death. **beyond a joke** (of a trick or piece of fun) no longer funny. **beyond one's means** too expensive(ly), (spending) more than one can afford.

bias (ˈbaɪəs) *ncu* an unfair preference; prejudice. ● *vt* influence (someone) too much in favour of something: *He's biased, so take no notice of his opinion.*

bib (bɪb) *nc* **1** a cloth tied round a child's neck to protect its clothes from dropped food. **2** the part of an apron that is above the waist.

Bible (ˈbaɪbəl) *nc* the holy book of Christians. **bible** a book of important or reliable information on a particular subject. **biblical** (ˈbɪblɪkəl) *adj*

bibliography (ˌbɪblɪˈɒgrəfɪ) **1** *nc, pl* **-phies** a list of the books used in writing a book or article. **2** *nu* the study of books and their history. **bibliographer** *nc* the writer of a bibliography. **bibliographical** (ˌbɪblɪəˈgræfɪkəl) *adj*

bicarbonate (baɪˈkɑːbənɪt) *chemistry nc* an acid salt, esp. sodium Rydrogen carbonate, which is used as baking powder.

bicentenary (ˌbaɪsenˈtiːnərɪ) *US* **bicentennial** (ˌbaɪsenˈtenɪəl) *nc, pl* **-ries** the two-hundredth anniversary of an event.

biceps (ˈbaɪseps) *nc, pl* **biceps** the large muscle in the upper arm.

bicker (ˈbɪkə*) *vi* argue or quarrel over small matters.

bicycle

bicycle (ˈbaɪsɪkəl) (*infml abbrev.* **bike**) *nc* a two-wheeled vehicle on which one must balance to ride: see picture. ● *vi* ride a bicycle.

bid (bɪd) *nc* **1** an attempt (to seize power, etc.). **2** an offer to buy (in competition with other people). ● *vt* **1** *formal* say or wish (something to someone): *I bid him goodbye.* **2** *old-fashioned* order (someone to do something). **3** offer (a price).

bidden (ˈbɪdən) past participle of **bid** (defs. **1**, **2**).

bide (baɪd) *vi archaic* stay. **bide one's time** wait for the right moment.

biennial (baɪˈenɪəl) *adj* **1** that happens every two years. **2** that lasts for two years. ● *nc* a plant that flowers in its second year and then dies.

bier (bɪə*) *nc* a vehicle on which a dead body is taken to be buried.

bifocals (ˌbaɪˈfəʊkəlz) *n pl* glasses with lenses of which the upper half gives a different focus from the lower half.

big (bɪg) *adj* **-ger, -gest 1** large. **2** on a grand scale: *He has big ideas.* **3** generous in spirit: *It was big of him to take no notice of insults.* **4** important: *He's a big man in his firm.* ● *adv* on a grand scale: *We must think big.* **bigwig** (ˈbɪgwɪg) *infml nc* an important person.

bigamy (ˈbɪgəmɪ) *nu* getting married to someone when one is already married to someone else.

bigot (ˈbɪgət) *nc* a person with narrow fixed opinions, esp. about religion. **bigoted** *adj* (of a person) with narrow fixed opinions. **bigotry** (ˈbɪgətrɪ) *nu*

bike (baɪk) *infml n* short for **bicycle.**

bikini (bɪˈkiːnɪ) *nc* a woman's two-piece bathing costume.

bilateral (baɪˈlætərəl) *adj* with two sides (taking part): *bilateral talks.*

bile (baɪl) *nu* **1** a substance that is produced by the human liver. **2** bad temper.

bilge (bɪldʒ) **1** *nc* the space inside the very bottom of a ship. *nu* **2** seawater that has come into a ship's bilge in small quantities. **3** *infml* rubbish; nonsense.

bilharzia (bɪlˈhɑːzɪə) *nu* a disease caused by flat worms in the blood.

bilingual (baɪˈlɪŋgwəl) *adj* **1** speaking two languages perfectly. **2** of or in two languages: *a bilingual dictionary.*

bilious (ˈbɪlɪəs) *adj* **1** to do with bile: *a bilious attack.* **2** bad-tempered. **3** (of colours) violent, such as to make one feel sick.

bill¹ (bɪl) *nc* **1** *US* **check** an account presented as a demand for payment in a restaurant, by a shop-keeper, etc. **2** a notice advertising a public meeting, play, etc. **3** *US* a banknote. **4** the text of a law that a government asks a parliament to approve. ● *vt* send a **bill¹** (def. 1) to. **fill the bill** be exactly what is needed.

bill² *nc* the horny mouth of a bird.

billboard ('bɪlbɔːd) *US n* See **hoarding** (def. 2).

billet ('bɪlɪt) *nc* a place for a soldier to live, esp. in a private house. ● *vt* provide a billet for (a soldier).

billiards ('bɪljədz) *nu* (*with singular verb*) a game in which balls are hit across the top of a table with a long stick.

billion ('bɪljən) *determiner, n* **1** *Brit* the number 1,000,000,000,000; a million million. **2** *US* the number 1,000,000,000; a thousand million.

billow ('bɪləʊ) *literary nc* (usually *pl*) a wave in the sea. ● *vti* roll, fill, or be filled like a sail in the wind. **billowy** *adj*

billy-goat ('bɪlɪgəʊt) *nc* a male goat.

bin (bɪn) *nc* **1** a large, usually round container for food, rubbish, etc. **2** See **dustbin** under **dust**.

binary ('baɪnəri) *adj* which has two parts.

bind (baɪnd) *vt* **1** tie (things) together with (string, etc.). **2** put a bandage round: *bind (up) a wound.* **3** put tape, etc., round (an edge) of a garment, etc., **4** fix (someone or something to something else): *bind the man with ropes.* **5** put (the pages of a book) together. **6** make (substances) stick together. **7** make (someone) promise to do something. ● *nu infml* an unpleasant duty; nuisance: *It's a bind having to stay at home.* **binder** *nc* **1** a person who binds things, esp. books. **2** a substance used to hold a mixture together. **3** a case for keeping loose papers, etc., together. **binding** *nc* the material that covers the outside of a book. ● *adj* (of a promise, etc.) that must be kept or observed.

bingo ('bɪŋgəʊ) *nu* a game of chance in which the first person to have all his numbers called out wins a prize. ● *interj* (used to express pleasure at a success.)

binoculars (bɪ'nɒkjʊləz) *n pl* a device with lenses in two tubes through which one can see distant things larger: see picture.

binoculars

biochemistry (ˌbaɪəʊ'kɒmɪstrɪ) *nu* the study of the chemistry of living things.

biography (baɪ'ɒgrəfɪ) *nc, pl* **-phies** a written

account of someone's life by another person. **biographer** *nc* a person who writes a biography. **biographical** (baɪə'græfɪkəl) *adj*

biology (baɪ'ɒlədʒɪ) *nu* the study of living things. **biological** (baɪə'lɒdʒɪkəl) *adj* **biologist** *nc* a person who studies biology.

bionics (baɪ'ɒnɪks) *nu* the study of the ways of living things applied to computers, etc.

biplane ('baɪpleɪn) *nc* a plane with two pairs of wings.

birch (bɜːtʃ) *nc* **1** any of a variety of trees with a thin, smooth outer covering that grow in northern countries; (also *nu*) the wood of these trees. **2** a stick of birch twigs formerly used in Britain to beat criminals. ● *vt* beat with the birch.

bird (bɜːd) *nc* **1** any of a great variety of animals with two legs and two wings, most of which can fly: see picture. **2** *infml* a girl. **bird's eye view** a view of the whole of a place or situation. **birdwatching** ('bɜːdˌwɒtʃɪŋ) *nu* the observation of the habits of birds in their natural surroundings.

biro ('baɪərəʊ) *Trademark nc* a ballpoint pen.

birth (bɜːθ) *nc* **1** the coming to life of an animal. **2** the beginning of an idea, a political movement, etc. **birth control** the prevention of giving birth to children. **birthday** ('bɜːθdeɪ) *nc* the date on which a person was born in an earlier year. **birthplace** ('bɜːθpleɪs) *nc* the house or town where a person was born or a movement started.

biscuit ('bɪskɪt) *nc* a small hard cake, esp. a sweet one.

bisect (baɪ'sekt) *vt* cut into two (equal) parts: *The new road bisects the town.* **bisection** (baɪ'sekʃən) *nu* **bisector** (baɪ'sektə*) *nc* a line that bisects.

bishop ('bɪʃəp) *nc* **1** an important Christian priest. **2** a chess piece.

bismuth ('bɪzməθ) *nu* a chemical element; reddish-white metal, of which compounds are used as medicines.

bison ('baɪsən) *nc* a kind of wild cattle in North America: see picture at **animals.**

bit¹ (bɪt) *nc* a strip of metal put inside a horse's mouth that can be pulled to control the horse.

bit² *nc* a small piece or amount: *Have a bit of cake.* **a bit** (even) a little: *I don't like it a bit.* **bit by bit** little by little, a little at a time.

bit³ past tense and past participle of **bite.**

bitch (bɪtʃ) *nc* **1** a female dog or wolf. **2** *derogatory* an unpleasant or spiteful woman.

bite (baɪt) **1** *vt* break (something, esp. food) with one's teeth. **2** *vti* (of an animal) dig its teeth into (a human): *Does your dog bite?* **3** *vi* have an unpleasant effect: *The new taxes will soon begin to bite.* ● *nc* **1** the act of bit-

birds

blackbird

crow

cuckoo

dove

falcon

hawk

eagle

pelican

magpie

parrot

pigeon

robin

rook

sparrow

thrush

vulture

woodpecker

swallow

bluetit

ing. 2 the result of being bitten by an insect, etc. 3 a mouthful. 4 *nu* sharpness (of weather or words). **biting** (ˈbaɪtɪŋ) *adj* 1 (of a remark) sharp. 2 (of a wind) very cold.

bitten (ˈbɪtən) past participle of **bite**.

bitter (ˈbɪtə*) *adj* -er, -est 1 with a sharp and unsweet taste. 2 (of weather) very cold. 3 (caused by) feeling angry and hurt. 4 (of an experience) painful. **bitterly** *adv* **bitterness** *nu*

bitty (ˈbɪtɪ) *adj* -ier, -iest (of a story, film, etc.) made of parts that seem to be unconnected.

bitumen (ˈbɪtjʊmɪn) *nu* a natural, thick black liquid used on roads, etc. **bituminous** (bɪˈtjuːmɪnəs) *adj*

bivouac (ˈbɪvʊæk) *vi, nc* (a) camp in the open air.

bizarre (bɪˈzɑː) *adj* odd; strange.

blab (blæb) *vti* let out (secrets), talk unwisely (about).

black (blæk) *adj* -er, -est 1 of the very darkest colour; the opposite of white. 2 (of a person) with a dark skin. 3 sad: *It was a black day for lovers of freedom.* 4 angry: *a black look.* 5 (of coffee or tea) without milk. 6 declared out of bounds (by a trade union). ● *nc* 1 a person with black skin. 2 *ncu* a black colour. 3 *nu* black clothes. ● *vt* 1 cover (one's face) with black make-up; clean (shoes, etc.) with black polish. 2 (of a trade union) refuse to handle or give service to. **in the black** having money in the bank. **blackberry** (ˈblækbərɪ) *nc, pl* -ries a black or very dark red soft fruit that grows wild in hedges. **blackbird** (ˈblækbɜːd) *nc* a singing bird common in Europe: see picture at **birds**. **blackboard** (ˈblækbɔːd) *nc* a large black board on which teachers write with chalk. **blacken** (ˈblækən) *vt* 1 apply black colouring to. 2 make accusations about (someone's character). **black eye** dark marks around an eye after it has received a blow. **blackish** (ˈblækɪʃ) *adj* rather black. **blackmail** (ˈblækmeɪl) *nu* a threat to tell of a person's crimes, etc., unless he pays money. **black market** an unlawful trade, esp. at very high prices and in goods in short supply. **blackness** (ˈblæknɪs) *nu* **black out** *infml vi* lose consciousness suddenly. **black-out** *nc* 1 a forbidding of the publishing of news about a subject. 2 a sudden loss of consciousness. 3 a failure of electric power in a district. 4 *nu* the hiding of lights during a war. **blacksmith** (ˈblæksmɪθ) *nc* a person who makes things from iron by heating and hammering.

bladder (ˈblædə*) *nc* 1 (in animals) the bag in which urine collects before being passed out of the body. 2 a bag of rubber, etc., that can be filled with air.

blade (bleɪd) *nc* 1 the metal cutting part of a knife, sword, etc. 2 a straight flat leaf (of grass, etc.).

blame (bleɪm) *nu* 1 accusation of guilt; criticism. 2 responsibility for something that has gone wrong. ● *vt* accuse (someone) of guilt; criticise. **blameless** (ˈbleɪmlɪs) *adj*

blanch (blɑːntʃ) 1 *vi* turn pale suddenly (with shock, etc.). 2 *vt* make pale; take the colour from.

blancmange (bləˈmɒndʒ) *nc* a sweet, firm but soft food made with milk and cornflour.

bland (blænd) *adj* -er, -est (of food, someone's manner, etc.) smooth; mild.

blank (blæŋk) *adj* -er, -est 1 with nothing written on it: *blank paper.* 2 empty of ideas: *My mind went blank.* 3 without expression: *a blank face.* 4 (of a gun cartridge) without a bullet. 5 (of verse) without rhymes. ● *nc* 1 a space for words to be written in (on a printed form, etc.). 2 a blank cartridge. 3 *nu* emptiness. **blank cheque** 1 a signed cheque without the amount of money written in. 2 freedom to act, esp. to spend money, as one chooses. **draw a blank** find nothing after a search.

blanket (ˈblæŋkɪt) *nc* 1 a thick, warm cloth for a bed. 2 a thick covering of snow, fog, etc. ● *vt* (of snow etc.) cover thickly. ● *adj* (of directions, etc.) which cover anything that might happen or many things: *a blanket rule.* **wet blanket** *infml* a person who dampens the enthusiasm of others.

blare (bleə*) *vi* (of a radio, car horn, etc.) make a very loud noise. ● *nu* a very loud noise.

blaspheme (blæsˈfiːm) *vti* speak or write without respect for (sacred things). **blasphemous** (ˈblæsfəməs) *adj* **blasphemy** (ˈblæsfəmɪ) *ncu, pl* -mies

blast (blɑːst) *nc* 1 a loud sound (from a horn, etc.). 2 a strong wind. 3 the rush of air after a big explosion. ● *vt* blow up with explosive. ● *interj* (used to express annoyance.) **blast furnace** a container in which iron ore is melted by a blast of hot air. **blast off** the launching of a space rocket.

blatant (ˈbleɪtənt) *adj* undisguised; unashamed: *blatant lies.*

blaze (bleɪz) *nc* 1 a big fire. 2 a great show (of publicity, etc.). 3 a violent fit (of anger, etc.). ● *vi* burn fiercely. **blazing** *adj* 1 burning fiercely. 2 very angry.

blazer (ˈbleɪzə*) *nc* a sports jacket, often with the crest of a school, club, etc., that is worn by members.

bleach (bliːtʃ) *vt* make whiter; lighten the colour of. ● *nc* a liquid used for whitening cloth, etc.

bleak (bliːk) *adj* **-er, -est 1** cold. **2** (of a place) bare; unwelcoming. **3** not hopeful: *a bleak future.*

bleary ('bliəri) *adj* (of the eyes) clouded; unable to see properly.

bleat (bliːt) *vi, nc* **1** (make) the noise made by a sheep. **2** (make) a weak complaint.

bled (bled) past tense and past participle of **bleed.**

bleed (bliːd) **1** *vi* (of a person or wound) lose blood. **2** *vt* draw blood from (a person). **3** take away the strength or money of (a person or country).

bleep (bliːp) *nc* the high, steady sound made by personal radios and other electronic calling devices. ● *vi* give a bleep.

blemish ('blemɪʃ) *nc* a fault or mark on the skin, etc.

blend (blend) **1** *vt* mix (teas, tobaccos, etc.) to give a pleasant result. **2** *vi* (of musical instruments, colours, etc.) mix to give a pleasant effect. ● *nc* a mixture.

bless (bles) *vt* **1** speak or express God's goodwill towards. **2** make (something) holy. **3** express goodwill towards. **blessed** (blest) past tense and past participle of **bless.** ● ('blesɪd) *adj* **1** approved by God. **2** happy. **3** *infml* (used to express annoyance): *Where is the blessed key?* **blessing** ('blesɪŋ) *nc* **1** the speaking of God's goodwill towards someone or something. **2** something to be thankful for. **3** *nu* the making holy (of something). **blessing in disguise** an event that appears bad but brings good.

blest (blest) past tense and past participle of **bless.**

blew (bluː) past tense of **blow.**

blight (blaɪt) *nu* **1** a disease of plants. **2** something that spoils something else. ● *vt* destroy or spoil (hopes, etc.).

blind (blaɪnd) *adj* **-er, -est 1** without the power of sight. **2** (often followed by **to**) unable to see, unaware of: *blind to the beauty of music.* ● *nc* **1** a piece of cloth that can be unrolled downwards to cover a window: see picture. **2** something intended to deceive someone. ● *vt* **1** make (someone) blind. **2** confuse (someone) with one's knowledge, etc.: *Don't blind me with science.* **the blind** blind people. **blind alley**

a street which can be entered from only one end. **blindfold** ('blaɪndfəʊld) *nc, adj, adv* (with) a cloth tied around the head so that one cannot see. ● *vt* put a blindfold on (someone). **blindly** *adv* **blindness** *nu*

blind spot 1 a spot on the back of the eye with which one cannot see. **2** a space, esp. on a road, that one cannot see. **3** an inability to understand one particular subject.

blink (blɪŋk) **1** *vti* shut (one's eyes) for a moment and open them again. **2** *vi* shine irregularly; twinkle. **3** *vti* shut one's eyes to; take no notice of (facts).

blinkers ('blɪŋkəz) *n pl* **1** pieces of leather partly covering a horse's eyes to prevent it seeing to the side. **2** something that prevents a person from seeing what is happening around him.

bliss (blɪs) *nu* great happiness. **blissful** ('blɪsfʊl) *adj* **blissfully** ('blɪsfʊlɪ) *adv* in complete happiness: *He was blissfully unaware of the danger.*

blister ('blɪstə*) *nc* a small lump on the skin that forms when a part of the body has been rubbed. ● *vt* (cause to) form blisters.

blithe (blaɪð) *adj* **-r, -st** happy; untroubled.

blitz (blɪts) *nc* **1** a period of many bombing attacks from planes. **2** a great effort to complete a task: *Let's have a blitz on the garden!*

blizzard ('blɪzəd) *nc* snow falling in a strong wind.

bloated ('bləʊtɪd) *adj* swollen.

bloater ('bləʊtə*) *nc* a herring salted and dried in smoke.

blob (blɒb) *nc* a spot, usually of colour.

bloc (blɒk) *nc* a group of countries or politicians who agree and act together.

block (blɒk) *nc* **1** a piece of a solid substance with square corners. **2** a large building containing many flats or offices. **3** *US* the buildings between one street and the next. **4** See **road-block** under **road. 5** *nu* (in the past) the piece of wood on which a person laid his neck when his head was to be cut off. ● *vt* prevent (the movement of something) along (a road, pipe, etc.). **blockade** (blɒ'keɪd) *vt* prevent traffic travelling to and from (a town, etc.) ● *nc* the prevention of traffic to and from a town, etc. **blockage** ('blɒkɪdʒ) *nc* **1** something that stops the flow of liquid along a pipe, etc. **2** the blocking of a pipe, etc. **blockhead** ('blɒkhed) *nc* a stupid person. **blockhouse** ('blɒkhaʊs) *nc* a strong building intended for soldiers to shoot from.

bloke (bləʊk) *infml, Brit nc* a man.

blond (blɒnd) *adj, nc* (a man) with fair hair.

blonde (blɒnd) *adj, nc* (a woman) with fair hair.

blood (blʌd) *nu* **1** the red body liquid in animals. **2** a family relationship: *blood re-*

blind

lations. ● *vt* mark with blood. **in cold blood** without pity; without feeling. **blood donor** a person who gives some of his blood to be used in a hospital. **blood group** one of the types of human blood. **bloodhound** ('blʌdhaʊnd) *nc* a kind of dog that can follow the track of a person by smell. **bloodless** ('blʌdlɪs) *adj* 1 without blood. 2 without energy or spirit. 3 without fighting: *a bloodless coup.* **blood pressure** the force with which the blood presses against the sides of the blood-vessels. **bloodshed** ('blʌdʃed) *nu* killing, esp. as a result of fighting. **bloodshot** ('blʌdʃɒt) *adj* (of eyes) reddened with blood. **bloodstream** ('blʌdstriːm) *nc* the blood as it goes round the body. **bloodthirsty** ('blʌdθɜːstɪ) *adj* liking fighting and killing. **bloodvessel** ('blʌd,vesəl) *nc* one of the tubes that carry blood round the body.

bloody ('blʌdɪ) *adj* 1 covered with blood. 2 (of fighting) that causes serious wounding. 3 *derogatory* (used to express annoyance.) **bloody-minded** (,blʌdɪ'maɪndɪd) *adj* unhelpful on purpose.

bloom (bluːm) 1 *nc* a flower. *nu* 2 freshness (of youth, etc.). 3 the fine powder on a ripe fruit. ● *vi* produce blooms.

blossom ('blɒsəm) *nc* a flower or the flowers of a fruit tree. ● *vi* 1 produce blossom. 2 develop well.

blot (blɒt) *nc* 1 a spot, esp. of ink. 2 a stain (on someone's reputation). ● *vt* 1 make a blot on (paper). 2 use paper to suck up (ink, etc.). **blot out** 1 cover or hide completely. 2 destroy completely. **blotter** ('blɒtə*) *nc* sheets of blotting-paper in a pad. **blotting-paper** a thick kind of paper used to suck up ink.

blotch (blɒtʃ) *nc* an irregular spot of colour, etc.

blouse (blaʊz) *nc* a woman's light garment for the upper part of the body.

blow (bləʊ) *nc* 1 a hit. 2 a piece of bad luck; shock. ● *vi* 1 (of wind, etc.) move along. 2 send air out through the mouth. *vt* 3 drive air on or into. 4 play by blowing air into (a musical instrument). **blower** *nc* 1 a device that blows air. 2 *infml, old-fashioned* the telephone. **blowlamp** ('bləʊlæmp) *nc* a device producing a very hot flame used to remove old paint, etc. **blow out** 1 stop (a flame) with a puff of air. 2 (of a blast) remove (windows, etc.) by force. 3 (of a flame) be blown out. **blow-out** *slang* a very large meal. **blow up** 1 *vti* explode. *vt* 2 make (a photograph, etc.) bigger. 3 make (an issue) important.

blown (bləʊn) past participle of **blow.**

blubber ('blʌbə*) *nu* the fat under the skin of whales and other sea-animals from which oil is obtained. ● *vi infml, derogatory* weep; cry loudly.

bludgeon ('blʌdʒən) *nc* a short stick for hitting people. ● *vt* 1 hit (someone) with a bludgeon. 2 try to force (someone into doing something).

blue (bluː) *adj* -**r**, -**st** 1 of the colour of a clear sky, for example. 2 *infml* rude; indecent. ● *ncu* a blue colour. **bluebell** ('bluːbel) *nc* a plant with flowers like small blue bells. **blueberry** ('bluːbərɪ) *nc, pl* -**ries** a small soft black or dark blue fruit that grows wild in America. **blue blood** relationship to a family of noble birth. **bluebottle** ('bluː,bɒtəl) *nc* a dark blue fly that buzzes and lays its eggs on meat. **blueprint** ('bluːprɪnt) *nc* 1 a photographic print in white on blue paper. 2 a plan in full detail. **the blues** 1 a mood of depression. 2 sad tunes which began as popular songs of black Americans. **out of the blue** unexpectedly; without warning. **bluish** ('bluːɪʃ) *adj* rather blue.

bluff¹ (blʌf) *nc* a steep cliff beside the sea. ● *adj* 1 rough but kind. 2 blunt; plain-speaking.

bluff² *vi* pretend; make empty threats. ● *nc* a pretence; empty threat.

blunder ('blʌndə*) *nc* a careless mistake. ● *vi* 1 make a blunder. 2 move carelessly.

blunt (blʌnt) *adj* -**er**, -**est** 1 (of a knife, etc.) not sharp. 2 (of words) plain; undisguised. 3 (of a person) lacking smoothness of manner. ● *vt* make (a knife, etc.) blunt. **bluntly** *adv* plainly; without disguise: *Tell me bluntly what I did wrong.*

blur (blɜː*) *vti* make or become unclear or indistinct: *a blurred photograph.* ● *nu* something that cannot be seen clearly.

blurb (blɜːb) *nc* a description of a book on its cover.

blurt (blɜːt) *vt* (usually followed by **out**) speak carelessly of (a secret).

blush (blʌʃ) *vi* (of a person) have a rush of blood to the cheeks (from strong feeling). ● *nc* a sudden reddening of the cheeks.

bluster ('blʌstə*) *nu* 1 over-confident talking with the intention of deceiving someone. 2 (of the wind) blowing with great force. ● *vi* 1 talk over-confidently with the intention of deceiving someone. 2 (of the wind) blow with great force.

boa ('bəʊə) *nc* a large South American snake that kills animals by winding itself tightly around them.

boar (bɔː*) 1 *nc* a large wild pig: see picture at **animals.** 2 *nu* the meat of the boar.

board (bɔːd) *nc* 1 a piece of wood cut into oblong shape. 2 a flat piece of strong material: *an ironing-board.* **3** the group of directors who govern a business company. **4** *nu* meals (provided in a hotel, etc.). ● *vt* **1** go onto (a ship or plane). **2** (followed by **up**) cover (parts of a building) with boards. **boarder** ('bɔːdə*) *nc* a child who lives at his school during school terms. **boarding-house** ('bɔːdɪŋhaʊs) *nc* a private house in which people pay to live and eat. **boarding school** *nc* a school where some or all of the children live during school terms. **above board** done honestly and openly. **go by the board** be cancelled; come to nothing. **on board** on or onto a ship; in or into a plane.

boast (bəʊst) *vi* praise oneself or things with which one is connected. ● *nc* praise of oneself. **boastful** ('bəʊstfʊl) *adj*

boat (bəʊt) *nc* a small ship. ● *vi* travel in a boat. **boathouse** ('bəʊthaʊs) *nc* a building at the edge of a river, etc., where boats are kept. **boatman** ('bəʊtmən) *nc, pl* **-men 1** a man who carries paying passengers in a boat. **2** a man who is in charge of boats that can be hired. **boatswain** ('bəʊsən) *nc* a seaman who is in charge of other seamen on a ship. **(all) in the same boat** (all) in the same (unwelcome) situation.

bob¹ (bɒb) *vi* (usually followed by **up and down** or **about**) float on moving water.

bob² *nc* a style of short haircut.

bobbin ('bɒbɪn) *nc* a stick round which cotton, string, etc., is wound.

bobby ('bɒbɪ) *infml nc, pl* **-bies** a British policeman.

bobsleigh ('bɒbsleɪ) *nc* a racing sledge for sliding down steep slopes in the snow.

bode¹ (bəʊd) *formal or literary vti* be a sign (of): *The sunny weather bodes well for the harvest.*

bode² past tense of **bide.**

bodice ('bɒdɪs) *nc* the part of a woman's dress between the neck and the waist.

bodily ('bɒdɪlɪ) *adj* to do with the body. ● *adv* all together; completely.

body ('bɒdɪ) *nc, pl* **-dies 1** the physical frame of a living animal. **2** the main part of this, without the head, legs, and arms. **3** a dead body; corpse. **4** *infml* a person. **5** a group (of people): *a large body of soldiers.* **6** the main part of anything. *nu* **7** the physical nature of humans. **8** the strength (of wine, etc.). **bodyguard** ('bɒdɪgaːd) a strong man who protects royal persons, etc.

bog (bɒg) *nc* a large stretch of spongy ground. **be bogged down** be unable to make progress. **boggy** ('bɒgɪ) *adj* **-ier, -iest.**

bogey ('bəʊgɪ) *nc* **1** a cause of fear. **2** an evil spirit.

bogie ('bəʊgɪ) *nc* **1** a trolley. **2** the frame to which the wheels at each end of a railway carriage are attached.

bogus ('bəʊgəs) *adj* false.

bohemian (bəʊˈhiːmɪən) *adj, nc* (a person) with a way of life that takes no notice of the conventions of society.

boil¹ (bɔɪl) *vt* heat **1** (a liquid) until it starts to turn to gas. **2** cook (food) in boiling water. **3** wash (garments, etc.) in boiling water. **4** *vi* (of a liquid) start to turn to gas. **boiler** *nc* **1** a device for heating water. **2** a container in which things can be boiled. **boiling-point** ('bɔɪlɪŋpɔɪnt) *nc* the temperature at which a liquid boils. **on the boil** at boiling-point. **boil down to** (of a problem) be reduced to (something simple).

boil² *nc* a red, painful swelling on the skin, caused by an infection.

boisterous ('bɔɪstərəs) *adj* (of a person or the wind) strong; wild; noisy.

bold (bəʊld) *adj* **-er, -est 1** courageous; daring. **2** (of writing, etc.) that can be clearly seen. **boldly** *adv* **boldness** *nu*

boll (bɒl) *nc* the seed-box of the cotton plant.

bolster ('bəʊlstə*) *nc* a long round pillow. ● *vt* support or help (someone's courage, etc.).

bolt (bəʊlt) *nc* a small metal bar on a door that can be slid across to fasten it. ● *vt* **1** fasten (a door) with a bolt. **2** *infml* eat (a meal) fast. **3** *vi* (of a horse) gallop away out of control through fright. **4** (of a person) rush away, esp. because of guilt. **bolt upright** (sitting) with one's back very straight.

bomb (bɒm) *nc* **1** a device containing explosive, intended to kill people or destroy buildings. **2** *infml* a lot of money: *This suit cost a bomb.* ● *vt* drop bombs on (a town, etc.). **bomber** *nc* **1** a person who plants a bomb in a car, shop, etc. **2** a plane that drops bombs. **bombshell** ('bɒmʃel) *nc* a complete surprise or shock.

bombard (bɒmˈbaːd) *vt* aim shells from heavy guns at (a town, etc.). **bombardment** *nc* an attack against a town, etc., with gunfire or bombs; (sometimes *nu*) the practice of bombarding: *Aerial bombardment caused many deaths.*

bombast ('bɒmbæst) *nu* pompous, empty talk.

bond (bɒnd) *nc* **1** a tie that connects people: *bonds of affection.* **2** (*pl*) a prisoner's chains. **3** a promise. **4** a promise by a government, etc., to repay money that has been borrowed.

bondage ('bɒndɪdʒ) *nu* slavery.

bone (bəʊn) **1** *nc* one of the hard parts inside an animal's body that form a frame or skeleton. *nu* **2** the material of which these parts are made. **3** bones as material for manufacture: *bone china.* ● *vt* **1** remove the bones from (meat, etc.). **2** put bones into (corsets, etc.). **have a bone to pick** have something to argue about. **make no bones 1** not hesitate. **2** not object or complain. **bone up on** learn the facts about. **bony** *adj* **-ier, -iest 1** (of a person or animal) so thin that the shape of the bones can be seen through the skin. **2** (of meat) full of bones.

bonfire ('bɒnfaɪə*) *nc* a fire lit in the open air to burn rubbish, etc.

bonnet ('bɒnɪt) *nc* **1** a woman's hat that ties under the chin, now worn only by babies. **2** *US* **hood** the front part of a car, usually covering the engine. **have a bee in one's bonnet** have an obsession (about something).

bonny ('bɒnɪ) *adj* **-ier, -iest** (esp. of babies) healthy or pretty.

bonus ('bəʊnəs) *nc* something extra received or paid, esp. in an employee's wages.

boo (buː) *nc, pl* **boos,** *interj* a cry of scorn or disapproval from an audience. ●*vti* shout boo at (actors, etc.).

boobyprize ('buːbɪpraɪz) *nc* a prize sometimes given to the player with the lowest number of points in a game or competition.

boobytrap ('buːbɪtræp) *nc* **1** a trick that will surprise someone and make him look foolish. **2** a bomb set to explode when something ordinary is touched.

book (bʊk) *nc* a number of pages bound together inside a cover. ●*vt* **1** order (a theatre seat, place on a holiday, etc.). **2** record the name of (someone guilty of a slight offence). **bookcase** ('bʊkkeɪs) *nc* shelves in a frame, for keeping books so that they can be easily seen. **bookie** ('bʊkɪ) *infml n* short for **bookmaker. booking-office** ('bʊkɪŋ-ɒfɪs) *nc* a room where tickets, etc., are sold. **book-keeper** ('bʊkkiːpə*) *nc* a person who keeps the account books of an organisation in order. **book-keeping** ('bʊkkiːpɪŋ) *nu* the work of a book-keeper. **booklet** ('bʊklɪt) *nc* a book of a few pages. **bookmaker** ('bʊkmeɪkə*) (*infml abbrev.* **bookie**) *nc* a person who takes bets from others on horse-races, etc. **bookmark** ('bʊkmaːk) *nc* a piece of paper, leather, etc., left in a book at the page where one has stopped reading. **bookseller** ('bʊkselə*) *nc* a person who sells books. **bookshelf** ('bʊkʃelf) *nc, pl* **-shelves** a shelf on which books are kept. **bookshop** ('bʊkʃɒp) *nc* a shop selling books.

boom¹ (buːm) *vi, nu* (make) a deep sound like the firing of heavy guns.

boom² *nc* **1** a pole that keeps the bottom of a sail in place. **2** a barrier across the entrance to a harbour.

boom³ *nc* a time when trade goes very well. ●*vi* (of trade) go very well.

boomerang ('buːməræŋ) *nc* a curved piece of wood which returns to the thrower if it hits nothing. ●*vi* (of an action) affect the person who has done it when he had expected it to affect other people only.

boon (buːn) *nc* a great help; big advantage.

boost (buːst) *vt* **1** encourage (confidence, etc.). **2** increase (sales, etc.). ●*nc* **1** an encouragement. **2** an increase. **booster** *nc* a device that gives extra power to something.

boot (buːt) *nc* **1** a shoe that reaches anywhere above the ankle, sometimes to below the knee: see picture. **2** *US* **trunk** a place in a car for luggage, etc., esp. at the back. ●*vt infml* kick.

boot

booth (buːð) *nc* **1** a small, often temporary building used for selling goods in a market, etc. **2** a compartment used by voters at an election: *a polling booth.*

bootlegger ('buːtlegə*) *chiefly US, old-fashioned nc* a person who carries or sells alcoholic drinks illegally.

booty ('buːtɪ) *nu* goods taken by invading armies, thieves, etc.

booze (buːz) *infml nu* alcoholic drinks. ●*vi* take alcoholic drink.

border ('bɔːdə*) *nc* **1** an edge: *the Mexican border;* (sometimes *pl): the borders of the town.* **2** a strip along the edge of something: *Their garden has a rose border; a coat with a fur border.* ●*vti* **1** (when *vi,* followed by **on**) be next to: *My garden borders on the road.* **2** *vt* provide (a garment, etc.) with a border. **border on** be very nearly: *Such an action borders on stupidity.* **borderline** ('bɔːdəlaɪn) *nc* a line that divides two conditions or categories: *a borderline case.*

bore¹ (bɔː*) *vt* be without interest to (someone). ●*nc* a boring person, task, etc. **boredom** ('bɔːdəm) *nu* the state of being bored. **boring** *adj* that lacks interest.

bore² *vt* drive or drill (a hole) into something. ●*nc* **1** a hole driven into something, esp. the ground. **2** the size of the inside of a gun barrel.

bore³ past tense of **bear¹.**

born (bɔːn) *adj* **1** with the original name of: *Elizabeth Jones, born Smith.* **2** having a natural ability for something: *He is a born musician.* **be born** come out of one's mother; start life.

borne (bɔːn) past participle of **bear¹.**

borough ('bʌrə) *nc* a town or part of a large city that is important enough to control some of its own affairs.

borrow ('bɒrəʊ) *vt* ask for and receive (something belonging to someone else) to use for a time and then give back.

borstal ('bɔːstəl) *nc* (in Britain) a special training school for young offenders.

bosom ('bʊzəm) *nc* 1 the human breast. 2 one's innermost being. 3 *nu* a safe, comforting centre: *in the bosom of his family*.

boss[1] (bɒs) *infml nc* a person who is in command, esp. an employer. ● *vt* (often followed by **about**) give orders to, treat (someone) like an employee. **bossy** *adj* **-ier, -iest** enjoying giving (unnecessary) orders.

boss[2] *nc* a circle sticking out from a ceiling, etc.: see picture.

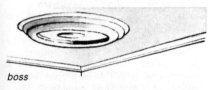

boss

botany ('bɒtənɪ) *nu* 1 the study of plants. 2 a kind of fine wool. **botanical** (bə'tænɪkəl) *adj* **botanist** *nc* a person who studies botany.

both (bəʊθ) *determiner, pron* one and the other of two; each of the two: *Both (roads) go near the sea.* ● *conj* (used in front of the first of two nouns or pronouns joined by **and**): *Both he and his brother were politicians.* ● *adv* **both... and...** not only... but also...: *She is both a singer and an actress.*

bother ('bɒðə*) *nu, vt* trouble; worry: *Don't bother him when he's busy.* ● *vi* take trouble: *She didn't bother to come.* ● *interj* what a nuisance!

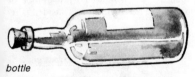

bottle

bottle ('bɒtəl) 1 *nc* a container with a narrow neck, usually of glass and with a lid or cork: see picture. 2 the amount a bottle will hold. ● *vt* 1 put in a bottle. 2 (followed by **up**) hold back or restrain (anger, etc.).

bottom ('bɒtəm) *nc* 1 the lowest part. 2 *infml* the soft part of the body on which one sits. 3 *nu* the ground under the sea. **bottom out** (of a downward movement) reach its lowest point. **bottomless** *adj* 1 without a bottom (that can be seen). 2 (of stores, money, etc.) having no limit.

botulism ('bɒtjʊlɪzəm) *nu* a kind of food poisoning.

boudoir ('buːdwaː*) *old-fashioned nc* a small room where the lady of a house received close friends.

bough (baʊ) *nc* a thick branch of a tree.

bought (bɔːt) past tense and past participle of **buy**.

boulder ('bəʊldə*) *nc* a large rock.

boulevard ('buːləvaːd) *nc* a road in a town with trees on each side.

bounce (baʊns) *vti* 1 (cause to) hit something and then jump back. *vi* 2 move suddenly. 3 *infml* (of a cheque) be returned as worthless by a bank. ● *nu* 1 the ability of a ball, etc., to jump back. 2 liveliness; joy.

bound[1] (baʊnd) past tense and past participle of **bind**. ● *adj* 1 (of a book) with the outside covered (with cloth, etc.). 2 (of a person) with a duty (to do something): *Don't feel bound to come.* 3 certain: *He's bound to find out.* **be bound up with** be closely connected with; be impossible to separate from.

bound[2] *nc, vi* (a) jump, leap.

boundary ('baʊndərɪ) *nc, pl* **-ries** 1 the outside edge, esp. of a region: *The boundaries of the country are marked on the map.* 2 the limit (of human abilities). 3 the edge of a cricket ground; hitting the ball outside the boundary: *He scored three boundaries during the match.*

boundless ('baʊndlɪs) *adj* without limit; very plentiful.

bounds (baʊndz) *n pl* the limits: *It was expressed within the bounds of politeness.* **out of bounds** where one is forbidden to go.

bounteous ('baʊntɪəs) also **bountiful** ('baʊntɪfʊl) *adj* 1 generous. 2 plentiful; in good supply. **bounty** ('baʊntɪ) 1 *nu* generosity. 2 *nc, pl* **-ties** a government payment for activities it wants to encourage.

bouquet (bʊ'keɪ) 1 *nc* a bunch of flowers carefully and attractively arranged. 2 *nu* a smell (of wine, etc.).

bourgeois ('bʊəʒwaː) *nc, pl* **-geois,** *adj* (a) middle-class (person). **bourgeoisie** (ˌbʊəʒwaː'ziː) *nu* the middle class.

bout (baʊt) *nc* a period of an activity, esp. illness or a fight.

bow[1] (baʊ) *vti* 1 bend (one's head or upper body) forward with respect or to acknowledge applause. 2 *vi* accept defeat; yield. ● *nc* the act of bowing.

bow[2] ('bəʊ) *nc* 1 a curved piece of wood with

bow

a string stretched between the ends, for shooting arrows with: see picture. **2** *music* a piece of wood with horsehair stretched between the ends, for playing stringed instruments. **3** a knot pulled out into loops. ● *vt music* play (an instrument) with a bow.

bow³ (baʊ) *nc* (often *pl*) the pointed front of a ship or boat.

bowel (ˈbaʊəl) *nc* (usually *pl*) the lowest part of the tube through which food passes through the body; intestines.

bowl¹ (bəʊl) *nc* **1** a round open container; basin: see picture. **2** the amount a bowl will hold.

bowl

bowl² *vt* **1** *cricket* throw (a ball) to a batsman. **2** (often followed by **out**) *cricket* get (a batsman) out by hitting the wicket with a bowled ball. **3** *vi* go quickly and smoothly (along a road) in a wheeled vehicle.

bowler¹ (ˈbəʊlə*) *nc* **1** *cricket* the person who throws balls to a batsman. **2** a person who plays bowls.

bowler² also **bowler hat** *nc* a man's hat with a hard, curved top: see picture.

bowler hat

bowls (bəʊlz) *n pl* a game in which heavy balls are rolled along the ground.

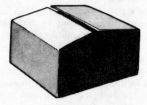

box

box¹ (bɒks) *nc* **1** a container, usually with a lid: see picture. **2** a group of seats that are walled off in a theatre, etc. **3** a very small room, often specially built, used by commentators at sports events, etc. ● *vt* put (something) in a box. **box in** shut in; limit the freedom of. **box-office 1** the room in a

theatre, etc., where tickets are sold. **2** the money taken in the box-office.

box² *vti* fight (someone) by hitting with the hands wearing thick gloves. **box someone's ears** hit someone on the ears with one's hand. **boxing** *nu* the sport of boxing.

boxer (ˈbɒksə*) *nc* a person who boxes.

Boxing Day (ˈbɒksɪŋ) (in Britain) the day after Christmas Day, and a public holiday.

boy (bɔɪ) *nc* **1** a male child. **2** (formerly, in some countries) a male servant. **boyfriend** a girl's special male friend. **boyhood** *nu* the state or period of being a boy. **boyish** *adj* like a boy; with feelings, an appearance, etc., like a boy's.

boycott (ˈbɔɪkɒt) *nu* a refusal to handle or deal with (goods produced by) a company, country, etc., with which one is in dispute. ● *vt* refuse to handle or deal with.

bra (brɑː) *infml n* short for **brassiere**.

brace (breɪs) *nc* **1** a support; something that holds tight (the walls of a building, etc.). **2** *(pl)* US **suspenders** two elastic straps by which men's trousers may be kept up, one passing over each shoulder. **3** *pl* **brace** a pair of wild birds that have been shot for eating. ● *vt* strengthen; make firm.

bracelet (ˈbreɪslɪt) *nc* a piece of jewellery that is put round the arm or leg.

bracing (ˈbreɪsɪŋ) *adj* (of exercise, fresh air, etc.) strengthening; refreshing.

bracken (ˈbrækən) *nu* a plant; a fern that grows in open, sandy ground.

bracket (ˈbrækɪt) *nc* **1** a support on a wall for a shelf, etc.: see picture. **2** a small holder for a plant, etc., that is fixed to a wall. **3** the sign (⎰) drawn beside words or numbers to show that they are connected. **4** a range of more or less similar things. **5** *(pl)* the signs ( ), written one before and one after words that are separate from the main flow of a sentence. ● *vt* (followed by **together** or **with**) put in the same class; consider as related.

bracket

brackish (ˈbrækɪʃ) *adj* (of water) with a slightly salty taste.

brag (bræg) *vi* boast.

Brahma (ˈbrɑːmə) *n* the highest Hindu god.

Brahmanism (ˈbrɑːmənɪzəm) *nu* the worship of Brahma.

braid (breɪd) *nu* a kind of ornamental ribbon used on garments, esp. round the edges, and on uniforms to indicate rank. ● *vt* **1** tie (long hair) with a ribbon. **2** put braid on (a garment).

Braille (breɪl) *nu* a writing system for blind people, using raised dots in paper.

brain (breɪn) **1** *nc* the part of the body inside the head that controls the nervous system in animals and is also the means of thought in man. **2** *nu* the ability to think. ● *vt infml* hit (someone) hard on the head. **brains** *infml n pl* great cleverness: *None of my children has brains.*

braise (breɪz) *vt* cook (meat) slowly in a covered pot.

brake (breɪk) *nc* **1** a device for stopping a vehicle. **2** something that slows down (an activity, etc.): *Lack of money put a brake on their enthusiasm.* ● *vti* use a brake to (cause to) slow down.

bramble ('bræmbəl) *nc* a thorny plant that bears blackberries.

bran (bræn) *nu* the outside coverings of grains, separated from the flour after grinding.

branch (braːntʃ) *nc* **1** one of the main arms that grow out of the trunk of a tree and bear leaves. **2** a department of a business that is under the control of the head office. **3** a division (of knowledge, etc.). ● *vi* divide: *The main railway line branches at Rugby.*

brand (brænd) *nc* **1** a particular (type of) product: *Which brand of washing powder do you prefer?* **2** *poetic* a piece of burning wood. ● *vt* **1** burn the owner's name or symbol into the flesh of (cattle, etc.). **2** give a bad reputation to (someone): *He was branded as a coward.* **brand new** completely new; not yet used.

brandish ('brændɪʃ) *vt* wave (a sword, etc.).

brandy ('brændɪ) *nc* a strong alcoholic drink made by distilling wine.

brash (bræʃ) *adj* over-confident; too loud.

brass (braːs) *nu* **1** a metal made of copper mixed with zinc. **2** *infml* money. **3** (the players of) musical instruments made of brass. **4** *nc* an engraved brass plate on a tomb.

brassiere ('bræsɪə*) (*infml abbrev.* **bra**) *nc* a garment that supports a woman's breasts.

brat (bræt) *nc* **1** a tiresome, naughty child. **2** *derogatory or humorous* a child.

bravado (brə'vaːdəʊ) *nu* a show of false courage.

brave (breɪv) *adj* **-r, -st 1** courageous. **2** *old-fashioned* splendid; fine: *Brave New World.* ● *nc* a North American Indian fighter. ● *vt* dare to go out into or face (a storm, etc.). **bravely** (breɪvlɪ) *adv* **bravery** (breɪvərɪ) *nu* courage.

bravo (bræ'vəʊ) *interj* (used esp. at concerts, etc.) well done!

brawl (brɔːl) *nc* a noisy quarrel or fight. ● *vi* quarrel or fight noisily.

brawn (brɔːn) *nu* **1** physical strength. **2** meat from a pig's head in jelly. **brawny** *adj* **-ier, -iest** (of a man) big and strong.

bray (breɪ) *vi, nc* (make) the cry of a donkey.

brazen ('breɪzən) *adj* **1** made of brass. **2** (of a person) shameless.

brazier ('breɪzɪə*) *nc* a metal basket for an open-air fire.

breach (briːtʃ) *nc* **1** a breaking (of an agreement, etc.). **2** a hole or break (in defences, etc.). ● *vt* **1** break or act against the terms of (an agreement). **2** force a way through (a wall, etc.).

bread (bred) *nu* **1** a soft, solid food baked from flour, water, and usually yeast. **2** the food necessary for life: *She managed to earn her daily bread.* **3** *slang* money. **bread and butter** slices of bread with butter spread on one side. **breadcrumb** ('bredkrʌm) *nc* a very small piece of bread. **breadwinner** ('bred,wɪnə*) *nc* the person who earns money for the whole family.

breadth (bredθ) *nu* **1** width; the distance from one side of something to the other. **2** width or range (of opinion, etc.).

break (breɪk) *vt* **1** knock or cut (something) into pieces. **2** fail to follow (a promise, etc.). **3** destroy (self-confidence or a business). **4** interrupt (a silence, etc.). **5** go beyond (a record): *She broke the world record.* *vi* **6** come to pieces. **7** (of a machine) be damaged so that it will not work. **8** (of a day, storm, etc.) begin. **9** (of news) become known. **10** (of a boy's voice) change to a lower range. ● *nc* **1** a stopping of contact. **2** an interruption; gap. **3** a holiday; rest. **4** *infml* an opportunity; chance. **break down 1** divide into smaller units. **2** (of a machine, service, etc.) fail to work (properly). **3** (of talks) end without completing business. **4** burst into tears. **breakdown** ('breɪkdaʊn) *nc* **1** a failure of a car, the nervous system, etc., to work (properly). **2** the ending of talks without completing their business. **3** a separation of a number, etc., into its parts. **break in 1** force an entrance into a building. **2** interrupt a conversation. **3** cause (a horse) to be no longer wild. **break off 1** separate (a piece of something). **2** put an end to (a relationship, talks, etc.). **break out 1** (of a war, disease, etc.) start. **2** (of a prisoner) escape. **breakthrough** ('breɪkθruː) *nc* a sudden important discovery. **break up 1** break into pieces. **2** destroy. **3** (of a marriage, etc.) come to an end.

breaker ('breɪkə*) *nc* **1** a big sea wave, the top of which rolls over. **2** a person whose business is to break up old ships or cars.

breakfast ('brekfəst) *nc* the first meal of the day, eaten in the morning. ● *vi* eat breakfast.

breakwater ('breɪk,wɔːtə*) *nc* a wall in the sea around a port, etc., that breaks the force of the waves.

breast (brest) *nc* 1 the upper front part of the human body; the chest; the part of an animal's body between the neck and the (front) legs. 2 one of the parts of the body of an animal that produce milk for its young. 3 *literary* the heart; feelings. ● *vt* have one's breast on a level with; face: *He breasted the waves*. **breastbone** ('brestbəʊn) *nc* (in humans or animals) the bone down the middle of the breast, to which some of the ribs are attached.

breath (breθ) *nu* 1 the air that a human or animal draws in and lets out. 2 life. 3 *nc* a drawing in of air: *take a deep breath*. **breathless** *adj* also **out of breath** breathing very fast, for example after exercise. **breathlessly** *adv* **under one's breath** in a whisper.

breathe (briːð) *vi* 1 draw in and let out air. 2 *literary* have life. 3 *vt* draw in (air, etc.).

bred (bred) past tense and past participle of **breed**.

breech (briːtʃ) *nc* the part of a gun where the cartridge or shell is placed.

breeches ('brɪtʃɪz) *n pl* 1 a kind of trousers that come to just below the knees, where they fit tightly round the legs. 2 *infml* trousers.

breed (briːd) 1 *vti* produce (young). 2 *vt* arrange the breeding of (animals). 3 cause: *Poverty breeds poor health*. ● *nc* 1 a group of people or animals who have the same qualities produced by breeding. 2 a type of person or animal. **breeder** *nc* 1 a person who arranges the breeding of animals. 2 a nuclear reactor that can produce more radioactive material than it uses. **breeding** *nu* 1 the production of young. 2 the arranged reproduction of animals. 3 the good manners resulting from many generations of careful training.

breeze¹ (briːz) *nc* a light wind. **breeze in** come in casually and cheerfully. **breezy** *adj* **-ier, -iest** 1 (of a place) windy. 2 (of a person) cheerful; lively.

breeze² *n* **breeze block** a building brick made from ash and cement.

brethren ('breðrɪn) *religious or archaic n pl* brothers.

brevity ('brevɪtɪ) *nu* shortness, esp. of time or speech.

brew (bruː) *vt* 1 make (beer). 2 make (a drink such as tea) using leaves, etc., by soaking and boiling in water. 3 *vi* (of beer, tea, etc.)

be being made by brewing. ● *nc* a drink made by brewing. **be brewing** be coming; be heating up: *A revolution was brewing*.

brewery ('bruːərɪ) *nc, pl* **-ries** a place where beer is made.

briar (braɪə*) *nc* any of various kinds of prickly bush; (also *nu*) the wood of the root of this bush.

bribe (braɪb) *vt* offer money, etc., to (someone) to persuade him to do something he should not do. ● *nc* a gift made in this way. **bribery** ('braɪbərɪ) *nu* the practice of bribing.

bric-a-brac ('brɪkəbræk) *nu* furniture and ornaments kept for their interest.

brick (brɪk) *nc* a hard block of baked clay, used in building. **brick up** fill (an opening) with bricks. **bricklayer** ('brɪk,leɪə*) *nc* a person who lays bricks to make buildings. **brickwork** ('brɪkwɜːk) *nu* construction in brick.

bridal ('braɪdəl) *adj* to do with a bride or a wedding.

bride (braɪd) *nc* a woman about to be married or newly married. **bridegroom** ('braɪdgruːm) (sometimes shortened to **groom**) *nc* a man about to be married or newly married. **bridesmaid** ('braɪdzmeɪd) *nc* a girl who helps a bride during the wedding.

bridge¹ (brɪdʒ) *nc* 1 a stretch of road or railway built crossing a river, another road, etc. 2 the place high up in a ship from which it is directed. 3 a wooden support for the strings of a violin, etc. 4 a means of connecting things: *Sport is a bridge between nations*. ● *vt* be (like) or make a bridge over.

bridge² *nu* a game of cards for two pairs of players, the cards of one player being played by his partner.

bridle ('braɪdəl) *nc* the part of a horse's harness that goes over its head. ● *vt* 1 put a bridle on. 2 control. 3 *vi* (often followed by **at**) show one's anger or dislike: *He bridled at being given such a humble job*.

brief (briːf) *adj* short. ● *nc* 1 a report on the facts of a person's position prepared for his lawyer. 2 a detailed plan of action. ● *vt* give detailed instructions to (someone). **briefly** *adv*

briefcase ('briːfkeɪs) *nc* a case in which papers can be carried.

briefs (briːfs) *n pl* panties or underpants without legs.

brigade (brɪ'geɪd) *nc* 1 a part of an army that is part of a division. 2 a group of people organised for a particular task: *a fire brigade*. **brigadier** (,brɪɡə'dɪə*) *nc* an army officer in charge of a brigade.

bright (braɪt) *adj* **-er, -est** 1 (of a light) shining strongly. 2 happy; cheerful. 3 (of a person) clever. **brighten** *vti* (often followed by **up**) make or become bright or brighter. **brightly** *adv* **brightness** *nu*

brilliant ('brɪljənt) *adj* **1** (of a light) very bright. **2** (of a person or idea) very clever. **3** splendid; showy: *brilliant flowers*. **4** *infml* very good: *It was a brilliant concert.* ●*nc* a diamond or other precious stone cut in a particular way with many faces. **brilliance** also **brilliancy** *nu* **brilliantly** *adv*

brim (brɪm) *nc* **1** the top edge of a container for liquids. **2** the flat part of a hat sticking out around the bottom: see picture. ●*vi* (often followed by **over**) be full to the top (with liquid, excitement, etc.).

brim

brimstone ('brɪmstəʊn) *old-fashioned nu* sulphur.

brine (braɪn) *nu* **1** very salty water. **2** the sea.

bring (brɪŋ) *vt* **1** cause to come with one: *I've brought my cousin to the meeting.* **2** cause: *The war brought great suffering.* **3** cause to reach a certain state: *bring into being.* **bring about** cause; make (something) happen. **bring back 1** return with (what was taken away). **2** restore (a former practice). **3** cause one to remember (past events). **bring in 1** cause (a person) to enter with one, carry in (a thing). **2** introduce (a law, etc.). **3** produce (money): *Farming brings me in enough to live on.* **bring off 1** succeed in doing (something). **2** take (people) away from a sinking ship, etc. **bring out 1** produce (a book, etc.). **2** put (a new product) on sale. **3** make clear(er); emphasise. **4** cause (flowers) to open. **bring round** bring (an unconscious person) back to consciousness. **bring up 1** train or teach (a child). **2** cause (food) to come back up from the stomach. **3** mention (a subject).

brink (brɪŋk) *nu* the edge of water, a cliff, etc. **on the brink of** close to (a discovery, a war, doing something, etc.).

brisk (brɪsk) *adj* **-er, -est 1** quick in movement. **2** lively. **briskly** *adv*

bristle ('brɪsəl) *nc* **1** a stiff hair such as grows on pigs. **2** a similar object made for use in brushes. ●*vi* **1** show anger or indignation. **2** be full of (something awkward): *The situation bristles with difficulties.*

brittle ('brɪtəl) *adj* (of a hard substance) easily broken.

broach (brəʊtʃ) *vt* **1** start discussion of (a subject). **2** make a hole in (a container of wine, etc.) to draw off the liquid.

broad (brɔːd) *adj* **-er, -est 1** wide. **2** (of opinions, etc.) of wide range; liberal. **3** having the width described: *six metres broad.* **4** (of a description) general; without detail. **5** (of an accent in speech) strong; noticeable. ●*nc US infml* a girl or woman. **broadly** *adv* **broad-minded** (,brɔːd 'maɪndɪd) *adj* accepting others' opinions; not easily shocked. **broad-shouldered** (,brɔːd 'ʃəʊldəd) *adj* having wide shoulders.

broadcast ('brɔːdkɑːst) *nc* a message, programme, etc., sent by radio or television. ●*vt* **1** send (something) by radio or television. **2** make (something) known.

broaden ('brɔːdən) *vt* make or become broad or broader.

broadside ('brɔːdsaɪd) *nc* **1** the firing of all the guns on one side of a ship. **2** a strong written or spoken attack.

brocade (brə'keɪd) *ncu* (a) cloth with a raised pattern on it.

broccoli ('brɒkəlɪ) *ncu* a kind of cauliflower with small heads of flowers, which are eaten cooked.

brochure ('brəʊʃə*) *nc* a small book, for example produced by a business to describe its products or services.

broil (brɔɪl) **1** *vti* cook or be cooked by grilling. ●*vi* **2** be very hot.

broke (brəʊk) past tense of **break.** ●*adj infml* without any money.

broken ('brəʊkən) past participle of **break.** **broken-hearted** (,brəʊkən'hɑːtɪd) *adj* overcome with grief.

broker ('brəʊkə*) *nc* a person paid by others to buy and sell shares, insurance, etc., for them.

bromide ('brəʊmaɪd) *nc* a chemical containing bromine, esp. potassium bromide, which calms the nerves.

bromine ('brəʊmiːn) *nu* a non-metallic chemical element; red liquid with a sharp smell: symbol Br

bronchial ('brɒŋkɪəl) *adj* to do with the bronchi.

bronchitis (brɒn'kaɪtɪs) *nu* an illness; inflammation of the bronchi in the lung.

bronchus ('brɒŋkəs) *nc, pl* **-chi** (kaɪ) either of the two tubes into which the windpipe divides before reaching the lungs.

bronze (brɒnz) **1** *nu* a metal made of copper mixed with tin. **2** *nc* a bronze object, esp. a work of art. **3** *ncu* a bronze colour. ●*adj* of the colour of bronze; between yellow and brown. ●*vt* (of the sun) turn (a person's skin) brown.

brooch (brəʊtʃ) *nc* a piece of jewellery on a pin by which it is fastened to a garment.

brood (bru:d) *vi* **1** (of a hen) sit on its eggs to make them hatch. **2** (often followed by **over**) think for long periods about something sad. ●*nc* **1** the young produced together by a bird. **2** *humorous* the children in a family.

brook[1] (brʊk) *nc* a stream; small river.

brook[2] *formal vt* (usually followed by **no** and a noun) allow; permit: *I will brook no interference.*

broom (bru:m) **1** *nc* a brush with a long handle for sweeping floors. **2** *nu* a bush with bright yellow flowers. **broomstick** (ˈbru:mstɪk) *nc* the handle of a broom.

broth (brɒθ) *nu* a thin kind of soup made with water in which meat has been boiled.

brother (ˈbrʌðə*) *nc, religious or archaic pl* **brethren 1** a male child of the same parents as another child. **2** a male member of a Christian religious order. **3** a male member of the same religion, trade union, etc., as another. **brotherhood** (ˈbrʌðəhʊd) **1** *nu* the state of being (like) brothers: *the brotherhood of man.* **2** *nc* a community or group of men. **brother-in-law** (ˈbrʌðərɪnˌlɔ:) *nc, pl* **brothers-in-law 1** the brother of one's husband or wife. **2** the husband of one's sister. **brotherly** (ˈbrʌðəlɪ) *adj* like (the behaviour of) a brother.

brought (brɔ:t) past tense and past participle of **bring**.

brow (braʊ) *nc* **1** the forehead; part of the face above the eyes. **2** the top of a hill, esp. above a steep slope.

browbeat (ˈbraʊbi:t) *vt* frighten (someone) with looks or words, esp. into doing something.

brown (braʊn) *adj* **-er, -est** of the colour of, for example, dark earth or dead leaves. ●*ncu* a brown colour. ●*vt* **1** cook (meat, etc.) until it is brown. **2** *vi* (of meat, etc.) turn brown in being cooked. **brownish** (ˈbraʊnɪʃ) *adj* rather brown.

Brownie (ˈbraʊnɪ) *nc* a junior Guide, aged from seven to eleven, who wears a brown uniform.

browse (braʊz) *vi.* **1** examine a book, goods in a shop, etc., in an unhurried way. **2** (of a sheep, etc.) eat grass, leaves, etc., off the ground. ●*nc* a period of browsing.

bruise (bru:z) *vt* **1** hurt (a person, animals, or fruit) so that a mark is left under the unbroken skin. **2** wound (someone's feelings). ●*nc* a mark caused by bruising.

brunette (bru:ˈnet) *adj, nc* (a woman) with dark brown hair.

brunt (brʌnt) *nu* the main force of an attack, etc.: *Our best soldiers bore the brunt of the attack.*

brush (brʌʃ) *nc* **1** a large number of stiff hairs, etc., fixed into a board which often

has a handle, for smoothing or sweeping. **2** the tail of a fox. *nu* **3** a stretch of shrubs and small trees. **4** the act of brushing. ●*vt* **1** smooth (hair), clean (teeth), sweep (a floor), etc., with a brush. **2** remove (dust, etc.) with a brush. **3** touch lightly in passing. **brush aside** refuse to consider (a person, argument, etc.). **brushed** *adj* with the surface roughened by a brush: *brushed nylon.* **brush up (on)** refresh one's knowledge (of).

brusque (bru:sk) *adj* short or blunt in one's abrupt manner.

brutal (ˈbru:təl) *adj* very cruel; without feeling. **brutality** (bru:ˈtælɪtɪ) *ncu, pl* **-ties** (an act of) cruelty. **brutally** *adv*

brute (bru:t) *nc* **1** a strong wild animal. **2** a very cruel person. **3** *infml, sometimes humorous* something very difficult: *That examination paper was a brute.* ●*adj* purely physical: *brute force.* **brutish** (ˈbru:tɪʃ) *adj*

bubble (ˈbʌbəl) *nc* **1** a thin ball of liquid filled with air. **2** a small amount of air in a liquid. ●*vi* **1** (of a liquid) give off bubbles. **2** be lively (with joy, etc.). **bubble-gum** (ˈbʌbəlgʌm) *nu* a sweet that is chewed but not swallowed and can be blown out into bubbles. **bubbly** (ˈbʌblɪ) *adj* **-ier, -iest** full of bubbles. ●*nu infml* champagne wine.

buccaneer (ˌbʌkəˈnɪə*) *nc* **1** *historical* a person who attacked and stole from ships at sea. **2** a person who carries on business by unfair competition with other traders. ●*vi* behave like a buccaneer.

buck[1] (bʌk) *nc* a male deer, goat, rabbit, or hare. ●*vi* (of a horse, etc.) jump in an attempt to throw its rider. **buck up** *infml* **1** get moving; hurry. **2** make (someone) cheerful.

buck[2] *infml, US nc* a dollar.

bucket (ˈbʌkɪt) *nc* **1** an open container with a handle: see picture. **2** the amount a bucket will hold. ●*vi* **1** travel very fast. **2** *vt* ride (a horse) very hard. **3** *infml vi* rain heavily: *It's bucketing down.* **kick the bucket** *slang* die.

bucket

buckle (ˈbʌkəl) *nc* a fastener for a belt or strap. ●*vt* **1** fasten the buckle of: *buckle your shoe.* **2** *vti* bend or be bent in folds by heat, a blow, etc. **buckle down (to)** apply oneself seriously to (a task).

buckler (ˈbʌklə*) *nc* a small round shield, once used by soldiers for their protection.

buckskin (ˈbʌkskɪn) *nu* a soft leather made from the skin of a deer, goat, or sheep.

bud (bʌd) *nc* a young flower that has not yet opened. ● *vi* (of a plant) grow buds. **taste buds** the parts of the tongue with which one tastes things. **budding** *adj* developing: *He's a budding politician.*

Buddha ('budə) the Indian who started Buddhism. **Buddhism** ('budɪzəm) *nu* an important religion of India, Japan, etc., with no god. **Buddhist** ('budɪst) *adj* to do with Buddhism. ● *nc* a follower of Buddhism.

budge (bʌdʒ) *vti (usually negative)* **1** move: *The handle is so tight it won't budge.* **2** (cause to) change an opinion: *I can't budge him on this question.*

budgerigar ('bʌdʒərɪˌgɑː*) *nc* a small singing bird originally from Australia, widely kept as a pet.

budget ('bʌdʒɪt) *nc* **1** a plan for spending and saving money, for example made by a government. **2** the money set aside for something. ● *vi* make a **budget** (def. 1): *I'm budgeting for an early holiday this year.*

buff (bʌf) *adj* brownish-yellowish. ● *ncu* **1** a buff colour. **2** *nu* a soft, thick leather. **3** *nc infml* an enthusiast: *a film buff.*

buffalo ('bʌfələʊ) *nc, pl* **buffalos, buffaloes, buffalo** an African or an Asian member of the cattle family.

buffer ('bʌfə*) *nc* **1** a device that reduces the force of a collision, esp. as on a railway carriage. **2** someone or something that lessens shock or gives protection: *a buffer state.*

buffet¹ ('bufeɪ) *nc* **1** a table, etc., where food is served out. **2** a meal at which one can help oneself to food.

buffet² ('bʌfɪt) *vt* **1** (esp. of the wind) strike repeatedly; knock about. **2** strike or hit (someone) with the hand. ● *nc* a blow with the hand.

buffoon (bə'fuːn) *nc* **1** a clown; amusing person. **2** a fool.

bug (bʌg) *nc* **1** one of many kinds of insect, esp. the bed-bug. **2** a problem or fault, esp. in a computer program. **3** *infml* a germ that causes a short, slight illness. ● *vt infml* **1** put a device in (a room) with which to listen to or record conversation. **2** annoy.

bugbear ('bʌgbeə*) *nc* a cause of great (unnecessary) fear or worry.

buggy ('bʌgɪ) *nc, pl* **-gies** a two-wheeled horse-drawn carriage or other light vehicle.

bugle ('bjuːgəl) *music nc* a wind instrument made of brass, used esp. in armies to give signals. **bugler** a person, esp. a soldier, who plays the bugle.

build (bɪld) *vt* **1** make or form (a house, etc.). **2** set up or establish (a business etc.). ● *nu* the height, weight, and size of a person. **build on** add (extra rooms, etc.) to a build-ing. **build up 1** (cause to) increase: to build up a business. **2** make (someone) strong and healthy. **build-up** ('bɪldʌp) *nc* **1** an increase. **2** a preparation for the appearance or arrival of someone or something special.

builder *nc* a person who puts up buildings.

building ('bɪldɪŋ) **1** *nc* a place with walls and a roof, such as a house or church. **2** *nu* the practice of putting up buildings. **building society** an organisation that lends money to people so they can buy their own homes.

built (bɪlt) past tense and past participle of **build**. **built-in** *adj* that is part of something else: *The kitchen has built-in cupboards.* **built-up** *adj* **1** (of a district) full of buildings. **2** (of a shoe) with extra material fixed underneath to raise it.

bulb (bʌlb) *nc* **1** the round underground part of plants such as the onion. **2** a plant that grows from a bulb, esp. a garden flower. **3** an object shaped like a bulb, such as an electric light bulb.

bulge (bʌldʒ) *vi* curve outwards; swell. ● *nc* **1** a place where something bulges. **2** a temporary increase in numbers.

bulk (bʌlk) *nu* **1** the size of a thing. **2** a large quantity: *We buy apples in bulk to save money.* **3** the greater part; the greater number: *the bulk of the population.* ● *vi* **1** (often followed by **large**) be large or important; have an important place (in someone's thinking). **2** *vt* (often followed by **out**) increase the size of; add to. **bulky** *adj* **-ier, -iest** (awkwardly) big.

bulkhead ('bʌlkhed) *nc* a wall in a ship, plane, etc.

bull (bʊl) *nc* **1** an uncastrated male of the cattle family. **2** a male elephant, whale, etc. **take the bull by the horns** deal boldly with a difficulty. **bulldog** ('bʊldɒg) *nc* a strongly-built kind of dog. **bulldozer** ('bʊlˌdəʊzə*) *nc* a tracked vehicle with a large blade at the front for levelling ground, etc. **bull's eye 1** the circle at the centre of a target. **2** a hard boiled sweet with black and white stripes.

bullet ('bʊlɪt) *nc* a ball or pointed piece of metal fired from a small gun.

bulletin ('bʊlɪtɪn) *nc* a report of news or on the condition of someone famous who is ill.

bullion ('bʊljən) *nu* gold or silver in heavy bars.

bullock ('bʊlək) *nc* a castrated bull.

bully ('bʊlɪ) *vt* (often followed by **into**) use force on or threaten (someone), to make him do something: *I was bullied into giving up.* ● *nc, pl* **-lies** a person who bullies others.

bulrush ('bʊlrʌʃ) *nc* a tall, thick grass that grows in or near fresh water.

bulwark ('bʊlwək) *nc* **1** a wall that acts as a defence. **2** a protection: *a bulwark against poverty in old age.*

bum¹ (bʌm) *slang, Brit nc* the soft part of the body on which one sits.

bum² *infml, chiefly US nc* **1** a person without a proper home who wanders around begging. **2** an unpleasant person.

bumblebee ('bʌmbəlbiː) *nc* a large kind of bee.

bump (bʌmp) **1** *vt* hit: *I bumped my head on the window.* **2** *vi* move in bounces. **bump into** meet (someone) by chance. ● *nc* **1** a jolt. **2** the noise of something hitting something else. **3** a lump in a surface, such as a body or road. **bumpy** *adj* **-ier, -est.**

bumper¹ ('bʌmpə*) *nc* a bar across the front or back of a car or lorry to protect it.

bumper² *adj* unusually good or large: *a bumper harvest.*

bumpkin ('bʌmpkɪn) *nc* a simple country person.

bun (bʌn) *nc* **1** a bread roll, usually sweet. **2** hair rolled up on the back of the head.

bunch (bʌntʃ) *nc* several things held or joined together, such as flowers or fruit.

bundle ('bʌndəl) *nc* several things held or fastened together, such as clothes.

bung (bʌŋ) *nc* a stopper for a bottle, drum, etc.

bungalow ('bʌŋɡələʊ) *nc* a house with all its rooms at ground level.

bungle ('bʌŋɡəl) *vti* do (something) badly: *The army bungled its attack on the town.*

bunion ('bʌnjən) *nc* a lump that hurts where the big toe joins the foot.

bunk (bʌŋk) *nc* also **bunk bed** a bed fixed to a wall, often one of two, one above the other.

bunker ('bʌŋkə*) *nc* **1** a space for storing coal. **2** a hole filled with sand on a golf course. **3** an underground shelter in a war.

bunny ('bʌnɪ) *infml, children nc, pl* **-nies** a rabbit.

bunsen burner ('bʌnsən) *nc* a gas burner used for heating in scientific experiments: see picture.

bunsen burner

buoy (bɔɪ) *nc* a fixed marker floating in water to show boats where to go.

buoyant ('bɔɪənt) *adj* **1** able to float. **2** cheerful; happy. **buoyancy** ('bɔɪənsɪ) *nu*

bur (bɜː) *nc* a seed-case that sticks to clothes and hair.

burden ('bɜːdən) *nc* **1** a load to be carried. **2** a nuisance; something annoying. ● *vt* give (someone) a difficult or annoying job to do. **burdensome** ('bɜːdənsəm) *adj* difficult.

bureau ('bjʊərəʊ) *nc, pl* **bureaux** ('bjʊərəʊz) **1** a writing desk with a cover. **2** an office: *an information bureau.*

bureaucracy (bjʊə'rɒkrəsɪ) *ncu, pl* **-cies** the governing of a country by officials. **bureaucrat** ('bjʊərə,kræt) *nc* a (government) official. **bureaucratic** (,bjʊərə'krætɪk) *adj*

burette (bjʊə'ret) *nc* a glass tube with a tap for measuring liquids.

burglar ('bɜːɡlə*) *nc* a person who steals from a building. **burglar-proof** *adj* (of a building) unable to be stolen from. **burglary** ('bɜːɡlərɪ) *ncu, pl* **-ries** (an example of) stealing from a building. **burgle** ('bɜːɡəl) *vti* steal from (a building).

burial ('berɪəl) *ncu* (an example of) burying a dead person.

burlesque (bɜː'lesk) *ncu* (a book or play) that makes fun of someone or something.

burly ('bɜːlɪ) *adj* **-ier, -iest** (of a person) big and strong.

burn (bɜːn) *vti* **1** (cause to) be destroyed by fire: *She burned my letter to her; Paper burns easily.* **2** (cause to) be damaged by fire or heat: *The cakes are burnt.* **burn down** (of a building), (cause to) be destroyed by fire. ● *nc* a part damaged by fire or heat: *a burn on my arm.* **burner** *nc* (the part of) a cooker, lamp, or heater that makes a flame. **burning** *adj* **1** on fire. **2** important; urgent: *a burning question.*

burnish ('bɜːnɪʃ) *vt* polish by rubbing.

burnt (bɜːnt) past tense and past participle of **burn.**

burp (bɜːp) *infml vi* let air noisily come out of the stomach through the mouth. ● *nc* an example of doing this.

burrow ('bʌrəʊ) *vi* dig into the ground or through something. ● *nc* the underground home of an animal, esp. a rabbit.

bursar ('bɜːsə*) *nc* a person in charge of the money of a school, university, etc.

burst (bɜːst) **1** *vti* (cause to) break open, letting something out: *A burst tyre; The river will burst its banks if we have more rain.* *vi* **2** move suddenly: *He burst into the room.* **3** start suddenly: *She burst into tears.* **burst out 1** go or come out suddenly. **2** start suddenly: *We all burst out laughing.* ● *nc* **1** an example of something bursting: *a burst in the water pipe.* **2** a period: *a burst of firing.*

bury ('berɪ) *vt* **1** put (something, esp. a dead person) underground. **2** put (something) deep into something else.

bus (bʌs) *nc, pl* **buses, busses** a large road vehicle that carries people. **bus-stop** *nc* a place where buses stop for passengers.

bush (buʃ) *nc* a thick, woody plant smaller than a tree. **the bush** wild uncultivated area, esp. in Africa or Australia. **bushy** (ˈbuʃɪ) *adj* **-ier, -iest** (of plants or hair) growing thickly.

bushel (ˈbuʃəl) *nc* a measure of volume in the UK 0.036 cubic metres (in the USA 0.035 cubic metres).

busily (ˈbɪzɪlɪ) *adv* in a busy way.

business (ˈbɪznɪs) *nu* **1** buying and selling goods and work. **2** affair; concern: *Where I go is my business. nc* **3** a job. **4** a shop or factory. **mind your own business** See **mind. business-like** *adj* efficient; serious. **businessman** *nc, pl* **-men** a man whose job is in **business** (def. 1), esp. in industry. **on business** to do with one's job.

bust¹ (bʌst) *nc* **1** a woman's breasts. **2** a model of someone's head and shoulders.

bust² *infml vti* **1** (cause to) break. **2** (cause to) fail in business.

bustle (ˈbʌsəl) *vti* move busily; hurry: *She bustled around getting ready; I was bustled out of the room.*

busy (ˈbɪzɪ) *adj* **-ier, -iest 1** doing something; occupied. **2** with many things happening: *I've got a busy day.*

but (bʌt *unstressed* bət) *conj* **1** in spite of that: *It will be cold but bright.* **2** also **but then** except that; however: *I wanted to come but forgot.* ● *prep* except: *all but one.* **but for** if it were not for: *I would have come but for the rain.*

butane (ˈbjuːteɪn) *nu* a natural gas burned for heat and light.

butcher (ˈbutʃə*) *nc* a person who kills animals for their meat or sells it. **butchery** (ˈbutʃərɪ) *nu* **1** cruel and unnecessary killing. **2** meat for sale.

butler (ˈbʌtlə*) *nc* the chief male servant in a private house.

butt¹ (bʌt) *nc* **1** the part of a rifle held against the shoulder. **2** a cigar or cigarette end.

butt² *nc* a person or thing that is made fun of: *the butt of a joke.*

butt³ *vti* hit with the head or horns. **butt in** interrupt a conversation.

butter (ˈbʌtə*) *nu* a yellow food made from cream. ● *vt* spread butter on. **butter up** talk nicely to.

butterfly (ˈbʌtəflaɪ) *nc, pl* **-flies** an insect with brightly-coloured wings: see picture at **insects.**

buttock (ˈbʌtək) *anatomy nc* (usually *pl*) either of the two fleshy parts one sits on.

button (ˈbʌtən) *nc* **1** a flat, round object sewn onto clothes for fastening them. **2** a switch pressed to start or stop a machine. ● *vti* (cause to) fasten with a button: *He buttoned up his coat.* **buttonhole** (ˈbʌtən,həʊl) *nc* a narrow hole on clothes for fastening a button through.

buttress (ˈbʌtrəs) *nc* a piece added to a wall to support it.

buxom (ˈbʌksəm) *adj* (of a woman) fat and healthy.

buy (baɪ) *vt* **1** obtain for money or something else of value. **2** be used to obtain in exchange: *Money buys most things.* **buyer** (ˈbaɪə*) *nc*

buzz (bʌz) *nc* a noise like the sound (z). ● *vi* make this noise. **buzz off** *slang* go away. **buzzer** (ˈbʌzə*) *nc* an electric signalling machine that buzzes.

buzzard (ˈbʌzəd) *nc* a large brown bird that catches small animals for food.

by (baɪ) *prep* **1** (used to show who or what performs the action of a passive verb): *I was hit by a ball.* **2** near; beside: *sitting by the fire.* **3** past: *I walked by him.* **4** using; by means of: *He succeeded by hard work; Come in by the front door.* **5** (used with the -ing form of a verb): *We finished early by working harder.* **6** (used to show who made something): *a play by Shakespeare.* **7** during: *by day.* **8** not later than; before: *Be home by ten o'clock; By this time next week, we'll be on holiday; He should be here by now.* **9** (used with units of measurement): *We are paid by the hour; Cloth is sold by the metre; a piece of wood three centimetres by two centimetres.* **10** to the amount or degree of: *He missed the train by ten minutes.* **11** according to; judging by: *By the expression on his face, he looked angry.* **12** with (a type of transport): *I often travel by plane.* **13** with (a part of the body): *He grabbed me by the arm.* ● *adv* past: *I walked by.* **by and by** *infml* soon. **by and large** generally.

bye-bye (ˈbaɪˈbaɪ) *infml interj* goodbye.

bye-law (baɪ) also **by-law** *nc* a local law.

by-election *nc* an extra election for a new member of parliament.

bygone (ˈbaɪɡɒn) *adj* past: *a bygone age.* **let bygones be bygones** forget the past.

by-pass *nc* a road built to avoid a town.

by-product *nc* something made during the making of something else: *by-products of oil.*

bystander (ˈbaɪstændə*) *nc* a person who watches something without taking part.

byway (ˈbaɪweɪ) *nc* a small country road.

C

cab (kæb) *nc* 1 a taxi. 2 the part of a train, lorry, etc., where the driver sits.

cabaret ('kæbəreɪ) *ncu* singing and dancing, etc., in a restaurant or nightclub.

cabbage ('kæbɪdʒ) *nc* a green leafy vegetable: see picture at **vegetables**; (sometimes *nu*) the leaves of this vegetable eaten as food.

cabin ('kæbɪn) *nc* 1 a small house; hut: *a log cabin.* 2 a room in a boat; passenger's bedroom in a ship. 3 the space for passengers in a plane, spacecraft, etc.

cabinet ('kæbɪnət) *nc* a piece of furniture with drawers and cupboards. **Cabinet** the chief members of a government.

cable ('keɪbəl) *nc* 1 a strong metal rope used in ships, cranes, etc. 2 a wire or bundle of wires used for carrying electricity. 3 a telegram. ● *vti* send (a message) by cable to (someone). **cable-car** *nc* a cabin that travels from a cable up a mountain.

cacao (kə'kɑːəʊ) *nc* a tree with brown seeds from which cocoa is made.

cackle ('kækəl) *vi* 1 (of a hen that has just laid an egg) cluck. 2 laugh loudly, like a hen cackling.

cactus ('kæktəs) *nc, pl* **-tuses, -ti** (taɪ) a plant with spikes and thick leaves that lives in very dry country.

cadence ('keɪdəns) *nc* 1 rhythm; beat. 2 rise and fall in the voice.

cadet (kə'det) *nc* a young person training to work in the army or police.

café ('kæfeɪ) *nc* a restaurant that sells generally cheap, ordinary meals. **cafeteria** (,kæfə'tɪərɪə) *nc* a restaurant where people themselves take the food to their tables.

caffeine ('kæfiːn) *nu* the mild stimulant in coffee.

cage (keɪdʒ) *nc* a room or box with walls of metal bars for keeping animals in.

cagey ('keɪdʒɪ) *infml adj* **-ier, -iest** not wanting to say much about something.

cairn (keən) *nc* a rough pile of stones built as a memorial or marker on top of a mountain.

cajole (kə'dʒəʊl) *vt* persuade (someone), esp. by flattery.

cake (keɪk) *nc* 1 a food, baked with flour, fat, eggs, and usually sugar and other things such as fruit: *a rich chocolate cake.* 2 a solid piece of food: *a fish cake.* 3 anything in a hard lump: *a cake of soap.* **caked** (keɪkt)

adj covered with something dried: *His face was caked with blood.*

calabash ('kælə,bæʃ) *nc* a tree with large gourds that are used as containers.

calamity (kə'læmɪtɪ) *nc, pl* **-ties** a terrible event; disaster.

calcium ('kælsɪəm) *nu* a metal found in chalk and in foods such as milk, necessary for growth: symbol Ca

calculate ('kælkjʊ,leɪt) 1 *vti* work out with numbers: *Can you calculate the cost of these?* 2 *vt* guess; estimate. 3 plan; intend: *a speech calculated to confuse people.* **calculation** (,kælkjʊ'leɪʃən) *ncu* (an example of) working out a number problem. **calculator** *nc* a machine that works out number problems: see picture. **calculating** *adj* selfishly planning.

calculator

calculus ('kælkjʊləs) 1 *nu* a way of working out problems to do with variable numbers. 2 *medicine nc* a hard, loose ball formed in the body.

calendar ('kælɪndə*) *nc* 1 a system of names and numbers for the days of the year. 2 a list of the days of the year.

calf¹ (kɑːf) *nc, pl* **calves** 1 (of cattle) a young cow or bull. 2 a young seal, elephant, etc.

calf² *nc, pl* **calves** the back of the lower leg.

calibrate ('kælɪ,breɪt) *vt* mark (a measuring instrument) so that readings can be taken.

calibre *US* **caliber** ('kælɪbə*) 1 *nc* the distance across something round, esp. the inside of a gun barrel. 2 *nu* quality: *his calibre as a painter.*

calico ('kælɪkəʊ) *nu* cheap, strong, cotton cloth.

caliph ('keɪlɪf) *nc* (formerly) a Muslim ruler: *the Caliph of Baghdad.*

call (kɔːl) *vti* 1 say loudly; shout. 2 telephone or radio (someone). *vt* 3 tell (someone or something) to come: *I'll call the waiter.* 4 consider as: *I call that cheap.* 5 say that someone or something is: *Don't you call me stupid!* 6 name: *I'm called Maurice.* 7 wake: *Please call me at seven o'clock.* *vi* 8 also **call by** or **in** pay a short visit. ● *nc* 1 a shout. 2 a short visit. 3 a telephone or radio conversation. 4 need: *There's no call to worry.* **caller** *nc* 1 a person who visits. 2 a person who telephones. **call for** 1 go and collect. 2 make necessary: *This calls for a party.* **call-**

ing *nc* **1** a strong wish to follow a particular life. **2** a profession or way of life. **call off** stop; not carry out: *If many people are ill, I'll call the party off.* **call on 1** pay (someone) a short visit. **2** tell; ask: *I call on you to help me.* **call out** shout. **call up 1** telephone or radio (someone). **2** tell (someone) to join the army, etc. **call-up** *ncu* (an example of) this.

calligraphy (kə'lɪgrəfɪ) *nu* beautiful writing.

calliper *US* **caliper** ('kælɪpə*) **1** *nc* a pair of metal bars for supporting a weak leg. **2** *(pl)* a tool with two arms for measuring the size of objects.

callous ('kæləs) *adj* unkind; not caring.

calm (kɑːm) *adj* **-er, -est 1** peaceful; not worried. **2** (of the sea) flat; without waves. ●*vti* also **calm down** (cause to) become calm. **calmly** *adv* **calmness** *nu*

calorie ('kælərɪ) *nc* **1** a measure of heat = 4.187 joules. **2** the amount of any food that produces 1000 calories as energy.

calorific (,kælə'rɪfɪk) *adj* to do with heat.

calorimeter (,kælə'rɪmɪtə*) *nc* an instrument for measuring heat.

calve (kɑːv) *vti* give birth to (a calf).

calves (kɑːvz) plural of **calf**.

Calvinism ('kælvɪnɪzəm) *nu* the Christian beliefs started by John Calvin.

calypso (kə'lɪpsəʊ) *nc, pl* **-sos** a popular West Indian song.

cam (kæm) *nc* a wheel that has a bump that moves something else every time it goes round: see picture.

 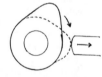

cam

camber ('kæmbə*) *nu* the curve on a road surface.

came (keɪm) past tense of **come**.

camel ('kæməl) *nc* a large animal with either one or two humps on its back: see picture at **animals.**

cameo ('kæmɪəʊ) *nc, pl* **cameos** a piece of jewellery with someone's head pictured on it.

camera ('kæmərə) *nc* a device for taking

camera

photographs on film: see picture; or for producing a television picture.

camouflage ('kæmə,flɑːʒ) *nu* **1** a disguise, esp. for guns, factories, etc. **2** the ability of some animals to look like their surroundings. ●*vt* disguise (something) in order to hide it.

camp (kæmp) *nc* a temporary home of tents or huts, esp. for soldiers: *a training camp.* ●*vi* **1** set up a camp. **2** live in a tent, esp. on holiday. **camper** *nc* **camping** *nu*

campaign (,kæm'peɪn) *nc* **1** a number of connected army actions: *the North African Campaign.* **2** a number of connected activities: *an advertising campaign.* ●*vi* take part in a campaign. **campaigner** *nc*

camphor ('kæmfə*) *nu* a substance obtained from the camphor tree and used to make celluloid and relieve colds.

campus ('kæmpəs) *nc* the grounds and buildings of a university.

can¹ (kæn) *nc* a metal container, esp. for liquids: *a can of oil.* ●*vt* put (food) into a can to keep it good.

can² (kæn unstressed kən) *v* (used before a verb) **1** be able to: *I can run fast.* **2** be permitted to: *Can I go home, please?* **3** (used to show possibility): *Can this be real?*

canal (kə'næl) *nc* a waterway dug across land to allow transport by boat or for irrigation.

canary (kə'neərɪ) *nc* a small yellow bird with an attractive song.

cancel ('kænsəl) *vt* **1** stop (something) happening: *The game was cancelled because of the weather.* **2** say that (an order) is no longer valid. **3** mark (a postage stamp or ticket) to show that it has been used. **cancel out** make up for (each other): *What we owe each other exactly cancels out.* **cancellation** (,kænsə'leɪʃən) *ncu*

cancer ('kænsə*) *nu* a growth in the body that can spread from one part to another and cause death.

candid ('kændɪd) *adj* honest; blunt.

candidate ('kændɪdət) *nc* **1** a person who wants to be chosen in an election, etc. **2** a person taking an examination.

candle ('kændəl) *nc* a stick of wax round string, burned to give light. **candlelight** ('kændəl,laɪt) *nu* light from a candle. **candlepower** ('kændəl,paʊə*) *nu* the brightness of a light. **candlestick** ('kændəl,stɪk) *nc* a holder for one or more candles.

candour *US* **candor** ('kændə*) *nu* honesty; openness.

candy ('kændɪ) *chiefly US nc, pl* **-dies** a sweet such as a chocolate or toffee. ●*vt* preserve by boiling in sugar: *candied peel.*

cane (keɪn) **1** *ncu* (a piece of) stick from a bamboo or sugar plant. **2** *nc* a stick for beating someone as a punishment. ● *vt* beat with a cane.

canine ('keɪnaɪn) *adj* 1 to do with dogs. 2 to do with the pointed third tooth from the middle on each side.

canister ('kænɪstə*) *nc* a container, esp. of metal, for food or equipment.

canker ('kæŋkə*) *nc* a bad sore, esp. on the lips or mouth. **cankerous** *adj*

cannabis ('kænəbɪs) *n* See **hemp.**

cannibal ('kænɪbəl) *nc* a person or animal that eats creatures of its own kind.

cannon ('kænən) *nc, pl* **-nons, -non** 1 a large old gun that fired stone or metal balls. 2 an automatic gun that fires shells from a plane.

cannot ('kænɒt) (often shortened in speech to **can't**) *v* can not. See **can².**

canoe (kə'nuː) *nc* a small narrow pointed boat moved through the water with paddles: see picture. **canoeing** (kə'nuːɪŋ) *nu*

canoe

canon¹ ('kænən) *nc* 1 a law or rule. 2 a general principle. **canonise** ('kænənaɪz) *vt* name (someone) as a saint.

canon² *nc* a Christian priest who does work connected with a cathedral.

canopy ('kænəpɪ) *nc, pl* **-pies** a cover over something, esp. a throne or plane cockpit.

canst (kænst) *archaic v* (used with **thou**) a form of **can².**

cant (kænt) *nu* talk spoken in order to deceive people.

can't (kɑːnt) *speech or written speech v* cannot.

cantankerous (kæn'tæŋkərəs) *adj* given to argument and easily angered.

canteen (kæn'tiːn) *nc* 1 a restaurant for the workers in a factory, etc. 2 a water container carried on journeys. 3 a box for a set of knives, forks, and spoons.

canter ('kæntə*) *nu* the second fastest step of a horse, between a trot and a gallop. ● *vi* 1 (of a horse) move with this step. 2 *vt* cause (a horse) to move with this step.

cantilever ('kæntɪˌliːvə*) *nc* an object, such as a bridge or wing, that needs supporting at only one end.

canton ('kæntɒn) *nc* a political district of Switzerland.

canvas ('kænvəs) 1 *nu* a strong cloth used for tents, sails, bags, painting on, etc. 2 *nc* a piece of canvas used for a painting.

canvass ('kænvəs) *vti* attempt to persuade (someone), esp. to vote a certain way.

canyon ('kænjən) *nc* a high-sided river valley, esp. in North America.

cap (kæp) *nc* 1 a hat that fits closely, esp. with a peak at the front: *a cricket cap.* 2 a small, tight cover for something: *a bottle cap.* ● *vt* put a cap on; cover: *snow-capped mountains.*

capable ('keɪpəbəl) *adj* 1 skilful; able. 2 (followed by **of**) able (to do something): *I am quite capable of driving.* **capability** (ˌkeɪpə'bɪlɪtɪ) *ncu, pl* **-ties.**

capacity (kə'pæsɪtɪ) *nc, pl* **-ties** 1 the quantity something can contain: *The capacity of this tank is 200 litres.* 2 (followed by **for**) an ability (to do something): *a great capacity for hard work.*

cape¹ (keɪp) *nc* an outer garment without sleeves.

cape² *nc* a point of land sticking out to sea: *Cape Horn.*

caper ('keɪpə*) *nc* 1 a jump; leap. 2 a playful action; prank. ● *vi* leap about playfully.

capillary (kə'pɪlərɪ) *nc, pl* **-ries** a very narrow tube, esp. a blood vessel.

capital ('kæpɪtəl) *nc* 1 the town from which a country is governed. 2 also **capital letter** a letter such as A, B, or C, as compared with a, b, and c. 3 *nu* money, esp. when being invested. ● *adj* (punishable) with death: *a capital offence; capital punishment.*

capitalise ('kæpɪtəlaɪz) *vi* (followed by **on**) make sure of: *to capitalise on an advantage.*

capitalism ('kæpɪtəlɪzəm) *economics nu* a system in which people can own factories, etc., privately, compete with each other for business, and make profits for themselves. **capitalist** *adj* to do with capitalism. ● *nc* a person who believes in capitalism or works in a capitalist society.

capitulate (kə'pɪtjʊˌleɪt) *vi* give in; surrender. **capitulation** (kəˌpɪtjʊ'leɪʃən) *nu*

capricious (kə'prɪʃəs) *adj* given to do unexpected things; fickle; unpredictable.

capsize (kæp'saɪz) 1 *vi* (of a boat) turn over in the water. 2 *vt* turn (a boat) over.

capsule ('kæpsjuːl) *nc* 1 a small container for medicine. 2 the part of most spacecraft in which the astronauts sit and which comes back to earth. 3 the seed-case of some plants.

captain ('kæptɪn) *nc* 1 a person in charge of a ship or plane. 2 an officer in a navy or an army. 3 a person in charge of a sports team. ● *vt* be captain of.

caption ('kæpʃən) *nc* a piece of writing connected with or describing a picture, as in a newspaper.

captivate ('kæptɪˌveɪt) *vt* cause to pay much attention: *We were captivated by the won-*

derful colours of the tropical sunset.

captive ('kæptɪv) *adj* caught; not free. ●*nc* a person or animal that has been caught; prisoner. **captivity** (,kæp'tɪvɪtɪ) *nu*

captor ('kæptə*) *nc* a person who captures someone or something.

capture ('kæptʃə*) *vt* catch; take prisoner. ●*ncu* 1 (an example) of capturing someone or something. 2 *nc* a captured person or thing.

car (kɑ:) *nc* 1 also **motor car**, *US* **automobile** a road vehicle for carrying between two and five people. 2 a carriage on a railway: *a sleeping-car.* 3 the cabin of an airship or cable-car. **car park** land or a building where cars may be left.

caramel ('kærəməl) 1 *nu* burnt sugar, used in cooking. 2 *nc* a soft sweet made of milk, butter, and sugar.

carat ('kærət) *nc* 1 a measure of the weight of a diamond = 0.2 g 2 a measure of the relative quantity of gold in a mixture with other metals.

caravan ('kærə,væn) *nc* 1 a road vehicle for living in that can be pulled by a car. 2 a group of people travelling through a desert.

carbohydrate (,kɑ:bəʊ'haɪdreɪt) *nc* a substance such as sugar or starch that gives energy when eaten.

carbon ('kɑ:bən) 1 *nu* a chemical element found esp. in carbon dioxide, coal, and oil, and as diamond: symbol C 2 *infml nc* short for **carbon copy** or **carbon paper**. **carbonate** ('kɑ:bənət) *nc* a compound of carbon and oxygen and a metal: *calcium carbonate.* **carbon copy** 1 a copy made with carbon paper. 2 a person or thing exactly the same as another one. **carbon paper** plastic sheet or paper covered with carbon, used for making a copy while writing.

Carboniferous (,kɑ:bə'nɪfərəs) *adj, n* (to do with) the period of the earth's history in which coal was formed in the ground.

carbuncle ('kɑ:bʌŋkəl) *nc* a swollen sore like a boil in the skin.

carburettor *US* **carburetor** (,kɑ:bə'retə*) *nc* the device in an engine that mixes the petrol with air.

carcass (also **carcase**) ('kɑ:kəs) *nc* the dead body of an animal.

card (kɑ:d) *ncu* (a piece of) stiff paper, used for various purposes: *birthday card; computer card; identity card; playing-card.* **on the cards** likely to .happen. **put one's cards on the table** say what one's intentions are.

cardboard ('kɑ:d,bɔ:d) *nu* thick, stiff paper, stiffer than card: *a cardboard box.*

cardiac ('kɑ:dɪæk) *medicine adj* to do with the heart: *cardiac arrest.*

cardigan ('kɑ:dɪgən) *nc* a knitted jacket, esp. made of wool.

cardinal ('kɑ:dɪnəl) *adj* central: *cardinal importance.* ●*nc* 1 one of the chief members of the Roman Catholic Church, after the Pope. 2 also **cardinal number** a number such as 1, 2, or 3, as compared with 1st, 2nd, and 3rd.

care (keə) 1 *vti* be troubled (about); worry (about): *I don't care whether I win.* 2 *vt* (followed by an infinitive) like: *I wouldn't care to guess.* **care about** worry about; have regard for: *Don't you care about your appearance?* **care for** 1 look after: *You must care for your teeth.* 2 like: *I don't care for rude people.* ●*nu* 1 attention; concern. 2 *ncu* (a) worry; thing to worry about: *I've not got a care in the world.* **take care** be careful; beware: *Take care not to fall.* **take care of** 1 look after; preserve: *I take care of my car.* 2 deal with; see to: *The police will take care of the thieves.*

career (kə'rɪə*) *nc* 1 the jobs one has during one's life. 2 a period spent in one job: *His army career was over.* ●*vi* move fast and out of control: *The car careered into several others.*

carefree ('keə,fri:) *adj* (of a person) untroubled; with nothing to worry about.

careful ('keəfəl) *adj* 1 done with care: *a careful piece of work.* 2 taking care; cautious: *a careful driver.* **carefully** ('keəfəlɪ) *adv*

careless ('keəlɪs) *adj* 1 done without care: *a careless mistake.* 2 not taking care: *a careless driver.* **carelessly** *adv* **carelessness** *nu*

caress (kə'res) *vt* stroke lovingly: *He caressed his wife's hair.* ●*nc* an example of caressing.

caretaker ('keə,teɪkə*) *nc* a person whose job is to look after a building.

cargo ('kɑ:gəʊ) *nc, pl* **-es** a load carried by a plane or ship.

caricature ('kærɪkə,tʃʊə*) *nc* a funny drawing, piece of acting, etc., that picks out someone's peculiarities.

caries ('keərɪːz) *medicine nu* rotting of the teeth.

carnage ('kɑ:nɪdʒ) *nu* many bloody deaths, esp. in a battle.

carnal ('kɑ:nəl) *adj* to do with natural desires of the body: *carnal instincts.*

carnation (kɑ:'neɪʃən) *nc* a red, pink, or white flower with a long stem. ●*adj* (reddish-) pink.

carnival ('kɑ:nɪvəl) *nc* a celebration, with parties, processions, etc.; festival.

carnivorous (kɑ:'nɪvərəs) *adj* (to do with) feeding on meat.

carol ('kærəl) *nc* a happy song, esp. a Christmas hymn.

carp[1] (kɑ:p) *nc, pl* **carps**, **carp** a freshwater fish about 35 cm long that lives in rivers, lakes and ponds: see picture at **fish.**

carp² *vi* complain or criticise in an annoying way.

carpenter ('kɑːpɪntə*) *nc* a person who makes things, such as furniture, from wood. **carpentry** ('kɑːpɪntrɪ) *nu* making things from wood or things made from wood; woodwork.

carpet ('kɑːpɪt) *nc* 1 a thick woven floor cover. 2 something like a carpet: *a carpet of snow.* ● *vt* cover (something) with a carpet or something like a carpet.

carriage ('kærɪdʒ) *nc* 1 a road vehicle pulled by horses. 2 *Brit* a railway vehicle for passengers. *nu* 3 carrying; transport. 4 the position of a person's body, esp. when walking.

carrier ('kærɪə*) *nc* 1 a person or thing that carries. 2 *medicine* a person or animal that can catch a disease and pass it on to others without suffering from it. 3 a business that transports people or goods. **carrier bag** a plastic or paper bag with handles, used for carrying shopping, etc.

carrion ('kærɪən) *nu* rotting meat.

carrot ('kærət) *nc* a pointed orange vegetable that grows under the ground: see picture at **vegetables.**

carry ('kærɪ) *vt* 1 move from one place to another: *He carried his books home; The pipes carry oil across the country.* 2 have with one: *I don't carry much money.* 3 have as a result: *Does murder carry the death penalty?* 4 (of a newspaper, etc.) contain: *Most newspapers carry advertisements.* 5 influence in one's favour: *He carried his audience with him.* 6 (of a committee) approve (a proposal); pass. 7 win (an election). 8 *vi* travel: *His voice carries well.* **carried away** very excited. **carry off** 1 take away, esp. by force: *They attacked our town and carried off our women.* 2 win (a prize). 3 manage to do (something) well. **carry on** 1 continue. 2 manage or run (a business). **carry-on** ('kærɪˌɒn) *infml*, *Brit nu* unnecessary activity; fuss. **carry out** do; perform: *The operation was carried out badly.*

cart (kɑːt) *nc* 1 a vehicle pulled by horses, used to carry goods. 2 any other light vehicle without an engine: *a hand-cart.*

cartilage ('kɑːtɪlɪdʒ) *ncu* (a piece of) soft material between bones in a joint.

carton ('kɑːtən) *nc* a cardboard box for goods.

cartoon (kɑː'tuːn) *nc* 1 a funny drawing. 2 a cinema film made from drawings.

cartridge ('kɑːtrɪdʒ) *nc* 1 a case containing explosive and a bullet, for use in a small gun. 2 a holder for film that fits into a camera. 3 a holder for recording tape that fits into a tape-recorder. 4 the part of a record-player that picks up sound from a record.

carve (kɑːv) *vt* 1 make (something) out of (wood) by cutting. 2 cut (meat) for eating. **carver** *nc*

cascade (kæs'keɪd) *nc* a large quantity of water falling or flowing over rocks. ● *vi* fall or flow in large quantities.

case¹ (keɪs) *nc* 1 an example of something. 2 a situation; state of affairs: *If that is the case, I'll go.* 3 an example of or a person with a disease: *a bad case of smallpox.* 4 an example of a crime to be solved: *Sherlock Holmes' most famous case.* 5 *law* a court action: *a murder case.* 6 a set of reasons for a court action: *He hasn't a good case.* 7 *grammar* a class of nouns in some languages: *the possessive case.* **in any case** whatever may happen; anyway: *Is it raining?—I'll go in any case.* **in case** so as to be safe (if): *He took his umbrella in case (it rained).* **in case of** *formal* in the event of; should... happen: *In case of fire, shout 'Fire!'*

case² *nc* 1 a container or covering. 2 short for **briefcase** or **suitcase.**

casement ('keɪsmənt) *nc* a window frame that opens, fixed at one side.

cash (kæʃ) *nu* coins and banknotes. ● *vt* obtain cash for (a cheque, etc.). **cash in on** *infml* take advantage of.

cashier (kæ'ʃɪə*) *nc* a person who collects or gives out cash in a shop, bank, etc.

casing ('keɪsɪŋ) *nc* a cover round something, such as an engine.

casino (kə'siːnəʊ) *nc* a building in which gambling games such as roulette are played.

cask (kɑːsk) *nc* a barrel, esp. used for wine.

casket ('kɑːskɪt) *nc* 1 a small box for money or jewels. 2 *US* See **coffin.**

cassava (kə'sɑːvə) *nu* also **manioc** a root vegetable used to make flour and several foods: see picture at **vegetables.**

casserole ('kæsərəʊl) *nc* 1 a cooking pot with a lid. 2 a dish made in such a pot: *beef casserole.*

cassette (kə'set) *nc* 1 a holder for recording-tape that fits into a tape-recorder. 2 a film holder that fits into a camera. **cassette recorder** a tape-recorder that records on and plays cassettes.

cassock ('kæsək) *nc* a full-length garment like a coat worn by Christian priests.

cast (kɑːst) *vt* 1 throw. 2 cause: *The tree casts a long shadow; She cast a spell on the frog.* 3 express: *He cast doubts on my honesty.* 4 put into a particular form. 5 choose (actors) for (a play or film): *He was cast as Macbeth.* 6 make (metal, wax, etc.) go hard in the shape of (an object): *cast iron; a statue cast in bronze.* ● *nc* 1 a throw. 2 the actors chosen for a play or film. 3 an object cast in metal, wax, etc. **4** a casing, esp. of plaster, for a broken arm, etc.

castanet (ˌkæstəˈnet) *nc* a Spanish musical instrument made of two small shell-shaped pieces of wood that are hit together: see picture at **musical instruments.**

castaway (ˈkɑːstəˌweɪ) *nc* a person who reaches land from a ship that has been wrecked.

caste (kɑːst) *nc* a class of people in Hindu society in India.

caster (also **castor**) (ˈkɑːstə*) *nc* **1** a small wheel fixed to furniture for moving it around. **2** a container with holes in the top for shaking the contents over something: *a sugar caster.* **caster sugar** sugar that is finer than granulated sugar.

castle (ˈkɑːsəl) *nc* a building that protected the people in it from an attacking army: see picture.

castle

castor (ˈkɑːstə*) *n* See **caster. castor oil** oil, made from the castor oil plant, used as a medicine.

castrate (kæsˈtreɪt) *vt* remove the testicles of. **castration** (kæsˈtreɪʃən) *nu*

casual (ˈkæʒjʊəl) *adj* **1** accidental; chance: *a casual encounter.* **2** not regular or not permanent: *casual work.* **3** informal: *casual clothes.* **4** slight; faint: *He's only a casual acquaintance.* **5** not taking care or paying attention. **casually** *adv*

casualty (ˈkæʒjʊəltɪ) *nc, pl* **-ties** a person who is hurt or killed in an accident or war.

cat (kæt) *nc* **1** a furry animal often kept as a pet: see picture at **animals. 2** any animal of the family including the lion, tiger, and lynx.

cataclysm (ˈkætəˌklɪzəm) *nc* a sudden, violent change, esp. a flood or earthquake.

catalogue *US* **catalog** (ˈkætəˌlɒg) *nc* a list of books, paintings, or other objects. ● *vt* make such a list of (something).

catalyst (ˈkætəˌlɪst) *nc* **1** *chemistry* a substance that speeds up a reaction without being used up itself. **2** a person or thing that encourages something to happen.

catapult (ˈkætəˌpʌlt) *nc* a device with a strip of elastic used to fire small stones, etc.: see picture. ● *vti* (cause to) travel very fast.

catapult

cataract (ˈkætəˌrækt) *nc* **1** a steep, narrow stretch of a river; rapids. **2** a condition of the eye, in which the lens becomes difficult to see through.

catarrh (kəˈtɑː*) *nu* inflammation, esp. of the nose and throat.

catastrophe (kəˈtæstrəfɪ) *nc* a disaster; terrible event. **catastrophic** (ˌkætəˈstrɒfɪk) *adj*

catch (kætʃ) *vt* **1** take hold of (esp. something moving): *to catch a ball.* **2** capture, after pursuing: *The police caught the thief.* **3** discover (someone doing something wrong). **4** be in time to join: *to catch a train.* **5** start to suffer from (a disease). **6** hear and understand: *I couldn't catch what he said.* **7** hit: *The ball caught me on the leg.* **8** receive: *I caught a glimpse of him.* **9** cause to become hooked: *I've caught my sleeve on a nail.* ● *nc* **1** an example of taking hold of something. **2** a person or thing that is caught. **3** a quantity of caught fish. **4** a device for fastening something: *a door catch.* **5** a hidden disadvantage or problem: *This looks too easy—there must be a catch.* **catcher** *nc* **catch on 1** become popular. **2** understand. **catch out** show that (someone) has made a mistake. **catch up with** reach (someone one is following) by going faster than him.

catechism (ˈkætəˌkɪzəm) *nc* a number of questions and answers that teach, esp. about the Christian religion.

category (ˈkætɪgərɪ) *nc, pl* **-ries** a class: *What category is this in?* **categorise** (ˈkætɪgəraɪz) *vt* put in a category.

cater (ˈkeɪtə*) *vi* **1** do what is needed (for); allow: *We cater for everyone's wishes.* **2** provide food (for): *to cater for a dance.* **caterer** *nc*

caterpillar (ˈkætəˌpɪlə*) *nc* the young form of a butterfly or moth, with many legs and no wings. **caterpillar track** See **track** (def. **5**).

cathedral (kəˈθiːdrəl) *nc* the chief Christian church building in a diocese.

cathode (ˈkæθəʊd) *physics nc* the part by which electrons leave a battery or enter electrical devices; a negative electrode. **cathode-ray tube** the glass tube that produces the picture in television, radar, etc.

catholic (ˈkæθəlɪk) *adj* relating to many varied people or things; general; wide: *a catholic taste in music*. **Catholic** *adj, n* See **Roman Catholic**.

cattle (ˈkætəl) *n pl* bulls and cows kept by farmers for meat and milk.

caught (kɔːt) past tense and past participle of **catch**.

cauldron (ˈkɔːldrən) *nc* a large pot for cooking in, esp. over a fire.

cauliflower (ˈkɒlɪˌflaʊə*) *nc* a type of cabbage; (sometimes *nu*) the large, white, round flower head of this vegetable eaten as food: see picture at **vegetables**.

cause (kɔːz) *nc* 1 something that makes something else be or happen: *Your absence was the cause of our defeat*. 2 reason: *There's no cause for complaint*. 3 something wanted; interests; a claim: *Our cause is just; in the cause of peace*. ●*vt* make (something) be or happen.

causeway (ˈkɔːzweɪ) *nc* a raised road, etc., across marsh or water.

caustic (ˈkɔːstɪk) *chemistry adj* able to burn or corrode something: *caustic soda*.

caution (ˈkɔːʃən) 1 *nu* care in thinking ahead; prudence: *Caution—men at work!* 2 *nc* a warning; being told to be careful. ●*vt* warn; try to persuade: *He was cautioned against breaking the law again*. **cautious** (ˈkɔːʃəs) *adj* **cautiously** *adv*

cavalcade (ˌkævəlˈkeɪd) *nc* a procession of people on horses or in cars.

cavalier (ˌkævəˈlɪə*) *nc* a soldier who rides a horse. ●*adj* without regard for others.

cavalry (ˈkævəlrɪ) *nc, pl* **-ries** a group of soldiers who ride on horses or travel in vehicles. **cavalryman** *nc, pl* **-men** one of these soldiers.

cave (keɪv) *nc* a natural space under the ground.

cavern (ˈkævən) *nc* a cave, esp. a large one. **cavernous** *adj*

caviar (ˈkævɪɑː*) *nu* the eggs of a sturgeon (a fish), used as food.

cavity (ˈkævɪtɪ) *nc, pl* **-ties** 1 a space inside something; hollow: *a cavity wall*. 2 a rotten part of a tooth.

cayenne (keɪˈen) *nu* also **cayenne pepper** a powder made from dried hot peppers.

cease (siːs) *formal vti* stop. **ceaseless** (ˈsiːslɪs) *adj*

cedar (ˈsiːdə*) *nc* an evergreen tree with cones and flat, spreading branches.

cede (siːd) *vt* 1 give up (esp. land). 2 give in on; admit.

ceiling (ˈsiːlɪŋ) *nc* 1 the inside surface on top of a room. 2 the most that is allowed or possible: *a wage ceiling*.

celebrate (ˈselɪˌbreɪt) *vti* 1 enjoy oneself or hold a special event to mark (an occasion such as a birthday). 2 perform a religious ceremony, esp. Christian Communion. **celebrated** *adj* famous; praised. **celebration** (ˌselɪˈbreɪʃən) *ncu*

celebrity (sɪˈlebrɪtɪ) *nc, pl* **-ties** a popular, famous person.

celery (ˈselərɪ) *nu* a plant whose thick bunch of stalks are eaten: see picture at **vegetables**.

celestial (sɪˈlestɪəl) *adj* 1 to do with the sky or with space: *celestial bodies*. 2 to do with heaven; divine: *celestial thoughts*.

celibate (ˈselɪbət) *adj, nc* (a person who is) unmarried, esp. because of a religious promise not to do so. **celibacy** (ˈselɪbəsɪ) *nu*

cell (sel) *nc* 1 a small space, esp. one of those into which something is divided. 2 the smallest living part of anything living. 3 a room for a prisoner in a prison or police station. 4 a device for making electricity by chemical action; battery. 5 a group of people in a secret organisation.

cellar (ˈselə*) *nc* 1 a room below ground-level in a building. 2 a wine store.

cello (ˈtʃeləʊ) *nc, pl* **-los** a stringed musical instrument played between the knees with a bow: see picture at **musical instruments**.

cellophane (ˈseləˌfeɪn) *nu* a thin, clear material used esp. for wrapping food.

cellular (ˈseljʊlə*) *adj* to do with or made from cells (**cell** def. 2).

celluloid (ˈseljʊˌlɔɪd) *Trademark nu* a clear plastic material used esp. for camera film.

cellulose (ˈseljʊˌləʊz) *nu* a material found in the cell walls of living plants and used for making such things as paper.

Celsius (ˈselsɪəs) *adj* See **centigrade**.

cement (sɪˈment) *nu* 1 a grey powder made of limestone and clay that is mixed with sand and water and used in building. 2 a substance used for sticking something particular: *polystyrene cement*. ●*vt* 1 fix (something) in place with cement. 2 make firm or stronger: *Our journey together cemented our friendship*.

cemetery (ˈsemɪtrɪ) *nc, pl* **-ries** a piece of land where dead people are buried.

censer (ˈsensə*) *nc* a container in which incense is burned.

censor (ˈsensə*) *nc* a person who can forbid something such as the sending of a letter or showing of a film. ●*vt* remove a part of or forbid (a letter, film, etc.) in this way. **censorship** (ˈsensəˌʃɪp) *nu* the act of censoring or the power to censor.

censure (ˈsenʃə*) *vt* say that one disapproves strongly of; condemn. ●*nu* the act of censuring; condemnation.

census (ˈsensəs) *nc* the counting of something, esp. the people in a country.

cent (sent) *nc* See appendix. **per cent** out of every hundred: *five per cent of 200 is ten.* Symbol (with figures): %

centaur (ˈsentɔː*) *nc* a mythological creature supposed to have had the head, arms, and chest of a man and the body and legs of a horse.

centenary (senˈtiːnərɪ) *nc, pl* **-ries** the point in time a hundred years after an event.

center (ˈsentə*) *US n* See **centre.**

centigrade (ˈsentɪˌɡreɪd) *adj* also **Celsius** (used to describe degrees of temperature on a scale on which water freezes at 0 degrees and boils at 100 degrees: *abbrev.* C): *40° C*

centimetre (ˈsentɪˌmiːtə*) *nc* a measure of length = 0.01 m: *abbrev.* cm

centipede (ˈsentɪˌpiːd) *nc* a small, long, thin animal with many legs.

central (ˈsentrəl) *adj* 1 at or to do with a centre. 2 chief; important. **central heating** a heating system in a building in which heat is produced in one place and carried into the rooms.

centralise (ˈsentrəˌlaɪz) *vt* 1 move (something) to a centre. 2 put (something, esp. government) in one place. **centralisation** (ˌsentrəlaɪˈzeɪʃən) *nu*

centre *US* **center** (ˈsentə*) *nc* 1 a middle, esp. the point in the middle of a circle. 2 a place for a particular activity or purpose or where something is sold: *shopping centre; leisure centre.* 3 a group of politicians who are not far to the left or right. ● *vt* move (something) to a centre. **centre on, around,** or **round** have as a centre or central idea: *His talk centred on music.*

centrifugal (ˌsentrɪˈfjuːɡəl) *adj* moving or to do with movement away from a centre: *centrifugal force.*

century (ˈsentʃʊrɪ) *nc, pl* **-ries** 1 a period of one hundred years. 2 a score of one hundred, esp. in cricket.

ceramic (sɪˈræmɪk) 1 *nu* a hard material made by heating clay or another mineral strongly. 2 *nc* an object made of ceramic. ● *adj* to do with ceramics. **ceramics** *nu (with singular verb)* the art or practice of making ceramics.

cereal (ˈsɪərɪəl) *nc* 1 a grass plant that produces edible seeds, such as wheat, rice, or maize. 2 a food made from one of these types of seed.

cerebral (ˈserɪbrəl) *adj* to do with the cerebrum or the whole brain.

cerebrum (ˈserɪbrəm) *nc, pl* **-brums, -bra** the part of the brain controlling thinking.

ceremonial (ˌserɪˈməʊnɪəl) *adj* to do with a ceremony; appointed: *A king has many ceremonial duties.* ● *nu* ceremonial events.

ceremonious (ˌserɪˈməʊnɪəs) *adj* done with ceremony.

ceremony (ˈserɪmənɪ) 1 *nc* a grand or formal event, such as opening a building or remembering dead soldiers. 2 *nu* grandeur or formality: *with due ceremony.* **stand on ceremony** continue to behave formally.

certain (ˈsɜːtən) *adj* sure: *He's certain to come; Are you certain he's here?* ● *determiner* 1 some particular: *I do not understand certain things.* 2 a particular: *a certain Dr Jones.* ● *pron* some (particular ones): *Certain of these are good.*

certainly (ˈsɜːtənlɪ) *adv* 1 in a sure manner: *He faced the danger certainly.* 2 definitely; to be sure.

certainty (ˈsɜːtəntɪ) *nu* 1 the quality of being certain. 2 something that is certain to happen or be true.

certificate (səˈtɪfɪkɪt) *nc* a piece of paper reporting a fact: *a birth certificate.*

certify (ˈsɜːtɪfaɪ) *vt* 1 report (something) to be true or that (something) is true: *I certify that John Smith is ill.* 2 report that (someone) is insane.

cessation (seˈseɪʃən) *formal nu* stop; stopping: *at the cessation of the war.*

cession (ˈseʃən) 1 *nu* the act of ceding. 2 *nc* something ceded.

cesspit (ˈsespɪt) *nc* a tank for storing liquid waste, esp. sewage.

chafe (tʃeɪf) 1 *vti* rub on (something) and (cause to) become sore. 2 *vi* become angry (at). ● *nc* a sore caused by chafing.

chaff (tʃɑːf) *nu* the husks on grains of corn when separated by beating. **separate the wheat from the chaff** separate the important parts from the worthless parts.

chagrin (ˈʃæɡrɪn) *nu* annoyance; displeasure.

chain (tʃeɪn) *nc* 1 a line of rings, esp. of metal, one passing through the next. 2 a series: *a chain of events.* ● *vt* join together with a chain. **chain reaction** the causing of one event by another. **chain smoker** a person who smokes one cigarette immediately after another. **chain store** one of several shops with the same owner or manager.

chair (tʃeə*) *nc* 1 a seat with a back for one person. 2 the position of a professor at a university: *the chair of English.* 3 (the position of) the person in charge of a meeting: *Mr Jones took the chair* ● *vt* be in charge of (a meeting).

chairman (ˈtʃeəmən) *nc, pl* **-men** the person in charge of a meeting.

chaise (ʃeɪz) *nc* a light carriage pulled by horses.

chalet (ˈʃæleɪ) *nc* a Swiss style of house with a broad, shallow, sloping roof.

chalice (ˈtʃælɪs) *nc* a large cup, esp. of silver and used at a Christian Communion.

chalk (tʃɔːk) *nu* a white rock made chiefly of calcium carbonate. **chalky** *adj*

challenge ('tʃælɪndʒ) *vt* 1 (followed by **to**) call on (someone) to take part in: *I challenge you to a fight.* 2 (followed by an infinitive) call on (someone) (to do something that one does not believe is possible). 3 not accept as true, just, etc.: *I challenge your right to question me.* ● *nc* 1 an example of challenging. 2 something such as a job that makes one want to try hard at it. **challenger** *nc*

chamber ('tʃeɪmbə*) *nc* 1 a room used by a parliament, council, or law court. 2 a space inside something such as the space for a shell in a gun. 3 *(pl)* the office of a judge or barrister. **chamberlain** ('tʃeɪmbəlɪn) *nc* a person who organises a royal palace. **chambermaid** ('tʃeɪmbə,meɪd) *nc* a woman who cleans bedrooms, esp. in a hotel.

chameleon (kə'miːlɪən) *nc* a small lizard that can change its colour and pattern to disguise itself.

chamois 1 ('ʃæmwʌ) *nc, pl* **chamois** an animal like a goat. 2 ('ʃæmɪ) also **chamois leather** *ncu* (a piece of) soft leather from the skin of a goat or sheep.

champ (tʃæmp) *vti* chew (food) noisily.

champagne (ʃæm'peɪn) *nu* a sparkling white wine made in NE France.

champion ('tʃæmpɪən) *nc* 1 a person who wins a competition in a game or sport. 2 a person who helps or supports someone or something: *a champion of human rights.* ● *vt* help; support. **championship** ('tʃæmpɪən,ʃɪp) 1 a competition. 2 *nu* the condition of being a champion.

chance (tʃɑːns) 1 *nu* the accidental nature of events: *It was only chance that brought me here.* *nc* 2 the degree to which something is probable; likelihood: *There's not much chance of it raining.* 3 an opportunity: *Go while you have the chance.* 4 a lucky event. **by (any) chance** perhaps; possibly: *Did I by any chance leave my bag here?* **by chance** unexpectedly; by accident. **take a chance** do something that is dangerous or a risk. ● *adj* accidental: *a chance meeting.* ● *vt* 1 dare to do something. 2 *vi* happen unexpectedly. **chance on** or **upon** find by accident: *I chanced on this old map.*

chancellor ('tʃɑːnsələ*) *nc* 1 the leader of some governments. 2 the head of a university.

chandelier (,ʃændə'lɪə*) *nc* a hanging holder for a number of candles or light bulbs.

change (tʃeɪndʒ) *vti* 1 (often followed by **into**) (cause to) become (something else): *They changed their garage into a workshop.* 2 (cause to) become different: *She's changed in the last ten years.* 3 (often followed by **into** or **out of**) put different clothes on: *If we're going out I must change (into something smart); You must change out of those old clothes.* 4 *vt* (often followed by **for**) give (something) and receive (something different): *I want to change pounds for dollars.* ● *nc* 1 an example of changing. 2 something different: *You're early for a change.* 3 a (spare) set of clothes. *nu* 4 small coins. 5 money given back after payment for something with too large a coin or note. **changeable** ('tʃeɪndʒəbəl) *adj* likely to change: *changeable weather.*

channel ('tʃænəl) *nc* 1 a narrow part of the sea: *the English Channel.* 2 a part of an area of water, for use by ships. 3 a broad cut; groove. 4 a path or band for transmitting electrical, esp. radio and television, signals. 5 *(pl)* a way of taking some official action: *You must apply for this grant through the usual channels.* ● *vt* 1 cause to move in a certain direction. 2 make a channel in.

chant (tʃɑːnt) *nc* 1 a simple tune. 2 something spoken by a number of people together. ● *vti* 1 sing (a song) to a chant. 2 speak as a chant.

chaos ('keɪɒs) *nu* a disorganised state; confusion. **chaotic** (keɪ'ɒtɪk) *adj*

chap¹ (tʃæp) *infml, Brit nc* a boy or man.

chap² *vti* (of skin), (cause to) become sore owing to cold or water: *chapped lips.*

chapel ('tʃæpəl) *nc* 1 a small church, esp. in an army camp, hospital, etc. 2 a room like a small church within a larger one.

chaperon (also **chaperone**) ('ʃæpə,rəʊn) *nc* a female companion for an unmarried woman in the company of a man. ● *vt* act as a chaperon for.

chaplain ('tʃæplɪn) *nc* a Christian priest serving people in a school, army, etc.

chapter ('tʃæptə*) *nc* 1 a numbered part of a book. 2 a large number; series: *a chapter of accidents.* 3 the group of people in charge of a cathedral.

char¹ (tʃɑː*) *vti* (cause to) become black from heat, esp. fire.

char² *infml n* short for **charwoman.** ● *vi* work as a charwoman.

character ('kærɪktə*) *nc* 1 nature; the way someone or something is or behaves. 2 *infml* a person, esp. in respect of his nature: *He's a nice character.* 3 *infml* an unusual or interesting person: *Old soldiers can be real characters.* 4 a part in a film or play: *Which character do you play?* 5 a written letter or figure.

characterise ('kærɪktə,raɪz) *vt* 1 be characteristic or typical of. 2 describe the character of.

characteristic (,kærɪktə'rɪstɪk) *adj* in someone's or something's nature; typical: *It's* *characteristic of him not to say hello.* ● *nc* something characteristic: *the characteristics of frogs.*

charade (ʃəˈrɑːd) *nc* **1** *(pl)* a game in which a word is guessed from actions each representing a part of it. **2** an action that is not what it seems to be: *This competition is a charade—the winner has already been chosen.*

charcoal (ˈtʃɑːˌkəʊl) *nu* a dark form of carbon made by heating wood, etc., used for example as a fuel or for drawing.

charge (tʃɑːdʒ) *vt* **1** ask (someone) for (an amount of money) for something: *The doctor charges £20 for one visit.* **2** *law* say that (someone) is guilty (of something); accuse: *He was charged with murder.* **3** fill (with something such as excitement). **4** (often followed by **up**) fill (a battery) with electricity. **5** *vi* (often followed by **up**) (of a battery) fill with electricity. **6** *vti* rush (at) or attack: *The soldiers charged the enemy.* ● *nc* **1** an amount of money asked for for supplying something. **2** an accusation: *He's on a charge of murder.* **3** an amount of explosive. **4** a rush or attack. **5** *ncu* (an amount of) stored electricity. **in charge of** in a position of power over; responsible for: *Our teacher is in charge of games.*

charger (ˈtʃɑːdʒə*) *nc* also **battery charger** a device for charging a battery.

chariot (ˈtʃærɪət) *nc* a vehicle with two wheels pulled by a horse, esp. in ancient times: see picture.

chariot

charitable (ˈtʃærɪtəbəl) *adj* **1** kind. **2** to do with charity, esp. with an organisation that helps people.

charity (ˈtʃærɪtɪ) *nu* **1** kindness. **2** money or help given to people who need it. **3** *nc, pl* **-ties** an organisation that collects money to help people.

charlatan (ˈʃɑːlətən) *nc* a person who pretends to be able to do something he cannot.

charm (tʃɑːm) **1** *ncu* an attractive or pleasing quality: *a country cottage with great charm.* **2** *nc* a small piece of jewellery, supposed to bring luck. ● *vt* **1** influence with one's pleasing quality. **2** put a magic spell on.

charming *adj* very attractive or pleasing.

chart (tʃɑːt) *nc* **1** a drawing giving information in lines, shapes, etc.: *a weather chart.* **2** a map for either ships or planes. ● *vt* **1** show (information) on a chart. **2** follow; record: *This book charts the history of medicine.*

charter (ˈtʃɑːtə*) *nc* **1** the hiring of a plane, ship, or train: *charter flights.* **2** a piece of paper giving demands or one giving the permission of the king or queen for an organisation to be started. ● *vt* **1** hire (a plane, ship, or train). **2** give permission for (someone or something) to work or exist: *a chartered engineer.*

charwoman (ˈtʃɑːˌwʊmən) *nc, pl* **-women** a woman who cleans an office or home.

chase (tʃeɪs) *vt* **1** follow and try to catch: *The police were chasing a thief.* **2** (often followed by **away, off,** etc.) make (someone or something) go away: *Don't chase the birds away.* ● *ncu* (an example of) chasing.

chasm (ˈkæzəm) *nc* a deep hole or crack in the ground.

chassis (ˈʃæsiː) *nc* **1** the frame of a vehicle, with its wheels and engine but no doors, etc. **2** the frame of a radio, television, etc., with no working parts.

chaste (tʃeɪst) *adj* (of a woman) sexually pure. **chastity** (ˈtʃæstɪtɪ) *nu*

chasten (ˈtʃeɪsən) *vt* correct by punishment.

chastise (tʃæˈstaɪz) *vt* punish, esp. by beating. **chastisement** *nu*

chat (tʃæt) *vi* talk informally. ● *ncu* (an) informal talk: *I'll have a chat with her.*

château (ˈʃætəʊ) *French nc, pl* **châteaux** (ˈʃætəʊz) a French castle or country house.

chattel (ˈtʃætəl) *law nc* (often *pl*) an object that belongs to one.

chatter (ˈtʃætə*) *vi* **1** talk on and on about unimportant things. **2** (of birds and animals) make rapid noises. **3** (of the teeth) knock together when one is cold. ● *nu* talking about unimportant things. **chatterbox** (ˈtʃætəˌbɒks) *infml nc* a person who chatters.

chauffeur (ˈʃəʊfə*) *nc* a man who drives a car for someone.

chauvinism (ˈʃəʊvɪˌnɪzəm) *nu* being too much in favour of one's own country, or that one is a man. **chauvinist** *nc*

cheap (tʃiːp) *adj* **-er, -est** **1** not expensive. **2** of poor quality: *cheap and nasty.* **3** unkind; dishonest: *That was a cheap trick.* **cheaply** *adv*

cheat (tʃiːt) *vti* **1** be dishonest with (someone): *He cheats at cards.* **2** (often followed by **out of**) get money from (someone) dishonestly: *I was cheated out of £5.* ● *nc* **1** a person who cheats. **2** a dishonest action, plan, etc.

check (tʃek) *vti* **1** make sure that (something) is correct, safe, etc.: *Have you checked your petrol?* **2** (cause to) pause or stop for a short time: *He checked the car's movement.* *vt* **3** *US* mark with a tick, as in filling up a form. ●*nc* **1** the act of checking (**check** defs. 1, 2). **2** *US* a ticket for something given or handed over. **3** *US* See **cheque**. **4** *US* See **bill¹** (def. 1). **5** a pattern of squares or crossing lines. **6** any position of the king in chess in which it could be taken. **check in 1** arrive and report at a hotel, airport, etc. **2** give in (one's luggage) at an airport, etc. **check out 1** leave a hotel, etc. **2** make sure that (something) is correct, in order, etc.: *to check out the facts of a story.* **check-out** (ˈtʃek,aʊt) *nc* a desk at a shop where one pays. **check up (on)** make a check (on). **check-up** (ˈtʃek,ʌp) *nc* a check or test of something, esp. one's health. **check-mate** (,tʃekˈmeɪt) *nc* a position of the king in chess in which it could be taken and from which it cannot escape.

checkers (ˈtʃekəz) *US n* See **draughts**.

cheek (tʃiːk) **1** *nc* the soft part on each side of the face. **2** *infml nu* behaviour that is too familiar; impudence: *He had the cheek to call me old.* **cheeky** *adj* **-ier, -iest** behaving too familiarly; impudent.

cheer (tʃɪə*) *vti* **1** (often followed by **up**) (cause to) become happier. **2** shout 'hurrah' to express approval or praise (for): *Everyone cheered their team.* ●*nc* a shout of 'hurrah'. **cheerful** *adj* happy; bright. **cheerfully** *adv* **cheers!** *interj* **1** (said before drinking.) **2** *infml, Brit* thank you. **3** *infml, Brit* goodbye.

cheerio (,tʃɪərɪˈəʊ) *infml, Brit interj* goodbye.

cheery (ˈtʃɪərɪ) *adj* **-ier, -iest** happy; cheerful. **cheerily** *adv*

cheese (tʃiːz) *ncu* (a type or whole piece of) a solid food made from milk, usually hard. **cheesecloth** (ˈtʃiːz,klɒθ) *nu* thin, open, cotton material.

cheetah (ˈtʃiːtə) *nc* a large, wild, spotted member of the cat family.

chef (ʃef) *nc* a male cook, esp. the chief cook in a restaurant.

chemical (ˈkemɪkəl) *nc* a substance used in chemistry. ●*adj* to do with chemistry or chemicals. **chemically** *adv*

chemist (ˈkemɪst) *nc* **1** a person who sells medicines. **2** a person who studies or works in chemistry.

chemistry (ˈkemɪstrɪ) *nu* the study of what substances are made of and how they behave when put together.

cheque *US* **check** (tʃek) *nc* a piece of paper telling a bank to pay someone some money.

chequered (ˈtʃekəd) *adj* **1** having a pattern of black and white squares. **2** varied.

cherish (ˈtʃerɪʃ) *vt* **1** value highly; treasure. **2** have; hold onto: *a cherished ambition.*

cherry (ˈtʃerɪ) *nc, pl* **-ries** a small round red or black fruit with a stone.

cherub (ˈtʃerəb) *nc, pl* **cherubs, cherubim** (bɪm) **1** a being in heaven, represented as a child with wings. **2** a pretty or sweet child.

chess (tʃes) *nu* a game played on a board with sixty-four squares by moving one's sixteen pieces and taking one's opponent's.

chest (tʃest) *nc* **1** the upper half of the main part of the body. **2** the lungs: *I've got a bad chest.* **3** a large, strong box for goods or belongings.

chestnut (ˈtʃes,nʌt) *nc* **1** a tree producing nuts that are eaten. **2** one of these nuts. *nu* **3** (esp. of hair) the reddish-brown colour of this nut.

chew (tʃuː) *vt* bite again and again, esp. to soften food for swallowing. ●*nc* an act of chewing. **chewing gum** *nu* a soft substance chewed for pleasure but not swallowed.

chick (tʃɪk) *nc* a young bird, esp. a young chicken.

chicken (ˈtʃɪkɪn) **1** *nc* a bird kept for its meat and eggs. **2** *nu* meat from a chicken. ●*adj slang* afraid to do something. **chicken pox** (pɒks) a disease producing fever and a rash.

chicory (ˈtʃɪkərɪ) *nu* **1** a plant grown for its stalks and its roots. **2** chicory roots, used mixed with or instead of coffee.

chide (tʃaɪd) *archaic vt* scold.

chief (tʃiːf) *adj* most important; main. ●*nc* the most important person of a group; head. **chiefly** *adv*

chieftain (ˈtʃiːftɪn) *nc* a chief, esp. of a group such as a Scottish clan.

child (tʃaɪld) *nc, pl* **children** (ˈtʃɪldrən) **1** a young person up to the age of about fifteen. **2** a son or daughter. **childhood** *nc* **1** the condition of being a child. **2** the period when one is a child. **childless** *adj* not having had any children: *a childless couple.* **childish** *adj* having or to do with the bad qualities of a child, such as being silly or afraid. **childlike** *adj* having or to do with the good qualities of a child, such as trust or innocence.

chill (tʃɪl) **1** *nu* coldness. **2** *nc* a cold. ●*adj* cold. ●*vt* cool or freeze (esp. food).

chilli (ˈtʃɪlɪ) *nc* a small hot pepper used in food.

chilly (ˈtʃɪlɪ) *adj* **-ier, -iest** cold.

chime (tʃaɪm) *vti* **1** (of a bell), (cause to) ring. **2** give (the time) by chiming: *The clock just chimed four.* ●*nc* **1** a bell, esp. one made from a tube. **2** the sound made by a bell.

chimney (ˈtʃɪmnɪ) *nc, pl* **-s** a structure for the smoke from a fire, esp. one of brick on top of a house. **chimneypot** (ˈtʃɪmnɪ,pɒt) *nc* a short pipe on top of a chimney.

chimpanzee (ˌtʃɪmpænˈziː) *(infml abbrev.* **chimp***)* *nc* a small ape; the closest animal to man: see picture at **animals.**

chin (tʃɪn) *nc* the point of the head below the mouth.

china (ˈtʃaɪnə) *nu* 1 a hard material made from baked clay. 2 plates, cups, etc., made from this.

chink[1] (tʃɪŋk) *nc* a tiny hole; crack.

chink[2] *nc* the sound of glasses, coins, etc., touching. ● *vti* (cause to) make this noise.

chintz (tʃɪnts) *nu* shiny, printed cotton cloth.

chip (tʃɪp) *nc* 1 a small piece knocked or cut off something: *wood chips.* 2 the place in china where a piece has been knocked or cut off something. 3 *Brit* a long, thin piece of potato, fried in deep oil. 4 *US* See **crisp.** 5 a tiny piece of silicon containing a large number of electric circuits and used in computers: see picture. ● *vt* 1 knock or cut (a piece) off (something): *This glass is chipped.* 2 *vi* break off in small pieces.

chip

chirp (tʃɜːp) *nc* a fast high sound made by a bird or insect. ● *vi* make this sound.

chisel (ˈtʃɪzəl) *nc* a pointed tool either for cutting wood or for chipping stone, etc.: see picture at **tools.** ● *vt* cut with a chisel.

chivalry (ˈʃɪvəlrɪ) *nu* 1 the honour, courage, and other qualities of a knight in the Middle Ages. 2 (of men) respect for women. **chivalrous** *adj*

chloride (ˈklɔːraɪd) *chemistry nc* a compound of chlorine and a metal, such as sodium: *Sodium chloride is common salt.*

chlorine (ˈklɔːriːn) *nu* a chemical element found mainly in common salt and used esp. for making water pure: symbol Cl

chloroform (ˈklɔːrəˌfɔːm) *nu* a liquid formerly given to people to smell to make them unconscious.

chlorophyll *US* **chlorophyl** (ˈklɔːrəˌfɪl) *nu* the green substance in plants that changes energy from the light of the sun into starch.

chock (tʃɒk) *nc* an object put against a wheel to stop a car, plane, etc., moving. **chock-full** (ˌtʃɒkˈfʊl) *infml adj* completely full.

chocolate (ˈtʃɒklɪt) 1 *nu* a hard, brown, sweet food made from cocoa. 2 *nc* a small piece of chocolate containing a nut, toffee, etc. ● *adj* dark brown.

choice (tʃɔɪs) *nc* 1 the act of choosing. 2 something chosen. 3 an ability to choose: *There's not much choice.* ● *adj* excellent: *choice apples.*

choir (kwaɪə*) *nc* a group of singers that sings in a church, gives concerts, etc.

choke (tʃəʊk) *vti* 1 (cause to) have difficulty in breathing. 2 (cause to) become blocked or held up: *The streets are choked with traffic.* ● *nc* a device that controls the mixture of air and petrol in an engine.

cholera (ˈkɒlərə) *nu* a disease giving esp. bad diarrhoea and carried in water and food.

choleric (ˈkɒlərɪk) *adj* easily angered.

choose (tʃuːz) 1 *vti* decide to have or use (something) rather than one or more other things: *They chose John for the job.* 2 *vt* like; want: *I wouldn't choose to meet him again.* **choosy** *adj* wanting only particular or the best things; fussy.

chop (tʃɒp) *vt* 1 cut by hitting with an axe, etc.: *I chopped a tree down.* 2 cut into small pieces: *chopped vegetables.* ● *nc* 1 the act of chopping. 2 a piece of meat, cut to include a rib: *a lamb chop.* **choppy** *adj* (of the sea) rough. **chopsticks** (ˈtʃɒpˌstɪks) *n pl* a pair of sticks used in one hand for eating with, esp. in China, Korea and Japan.

choral (ˈkɔːrəl) *adj* to do with a choir.

chord (kɔːd) *nc* a number of musical notes produced together.

chore (tʃɔː*) *nc* 1 an unpleasant task. 2 a cleaning, etc., task in the home.

choreographer (ˌkɒrɪˈɒɡrəfə*) *nc* a person who makes up dance movements, esp. for ballet.

chorus (ˈkɔːrəs) *nc* 1 a group of people who sing together; choir. 2 a piece of music sung by a chorus. 3 the part of a song repeated after each verse.

chose (tʃəʊz) past tense of **choose.**

chosen (ˈtʃəʊzən) past participle of **choose.**

Christ (kraɪst) *n* See **Jesus Christ.**

christen (ˈkrɪsən) *vt* 1 give (a Christian name) to (someone) at a baptism. 2 name; call. **christening** *nc*

Christendom (ˈkrɪsəndəm) *nu* all Christians together.

Christian (ˈkrɪstʃən) *adj* to do with (the qualities taught in) Christianity. ● *nc* a follower of Christianity. **Christian name** *nc* a name given at one's baptism; a personal name, as compared with a family name. **Christianity** (ˌkrɪstɪˈænɪtɪ) *nu* the religion started by Jesus Christ. **Christian Science** *nu* the religion of the Church of Christ, Scientist, which includes a belief in healing without medicine.

Christmas (ˈkrɪsməs) *nc* also **Christmas Day** the day on which Christians remember the birth of Jesus Christ; 25 December.

chrome (krəʊm) *nu* (objects covered with) chromium plate.

chromium ('krəʊmɪəm) *nu* a chemical element; a grey metal used to make steel hard and for shiny plating: symbol Cr

chromosome ('krəʊmə,səʊm) *nc* one of the tiny parts of a living cell that contain genes.

chronic ('krɒnɪk) *adj* 1 (esp. of a disease) lasting a long time. 2 *slang* very bad.

chronicle ('krɒnɪkəl) *nc* an account of events. ●*vt* record (an event) in a chronicle.

chronological (,krɒnə'lɒdʒɪkəl) *adj* in the order in which things happen.

chrysalis ('krɪsəlɪs) *nc, pl* **chrysalises, chrysalides** (krɪ'sælɪ,diːz) the form of a moth or butterfly at the stage before becoming adult.

chrysanthemum (krɪ'sænθɪməm) *nc* a plant with brightly coloured flowers: see picture at **flowers.**

chubby ('tʃʌbɪ) *adj* **-ier, -iest** (of a person) fat; plump.

chuck[1] (tʃʌk) *infml vt, nc* (a) throw.

chuck[2] *nc* the part of a machine that holds something, esp. a drill bit, and spins it round.

chuckle ('tʃʌkəl) *vi* laugh a little. ●*nc* a little laugh.

chum (tʃʌm) *infml nc* a good friend.

chunk (tʃʌŋk) *infml nc* a piece.

church (tʃɜːtʃ) *nc* 1 a building used for religious, esp. Christian, services. 2 often **Church** an organisation within Christianity: *the Church of India.* 3 *nu* Christianity.

churchyard ('tʃɜːtʃ,jɑːd) *nc* the land round a church, esp. used for burying the dead.

churlish ('tʃɜːlɪʃ) *adj* (of a person) rude; difficult to deal with.

churn (tʃɜːn) *nc* 1 a large container for milk. 2 a container for making butter in. ●*vt* 1 stir (milk or cream) to make (butter). 2 (often followed by **up**) mix; stir.

chute[1] (ʃuːt) *nc* a slope with sides for sliding or pouring parcels or water down.

chute[2] *infml n* short for **parachute.**

chutney ('tʃʌtnɪ) *ncu* a (type of) food made from fruit, sugar, and vinegar.

cider (also **cyder**) ('saɪdə*) *nu* an alcoholic drink made from apples.

cigar (sɪ'gɑː*) *nc* a roll of dried tobacco leaves for smoking.

cigarette (,sɪgə'ret) *nc* a small quantity of finely cut tobacco rolled in paper, for smoking.

cinch (sɪntʃ) *infml nc* an easy task.

cinder ('sɪndə*) *nc* a piece of a substance left after a fire because it has not burnt.

cinema ('sɪnɪmə) 1 *nc* a building or room in which films are shown. 2 *nu* also **the cinema** the making of films.

cinnamon ('sɪnəmən) *nu* a spice made from the bark of a tree.

cipher (also **cypher**) ('saɪfə*) *nc* 1 any of the figures 0-9. 2 a way of rewriting a message to keep it secret; code.

circa ('sɜːkə) *prep* in about (a year): *circa 1800.*

circle ('sɜːkəl) *nc* 1 an endless line making a round shape: see picture at **shapes.** 2 a round shape. 3 a number of things arranged in a circle: *A circle of people stood round me.* 4 a group of people with a common interest: *a circle of friends.* 5 a group of seats above the main body of a theatre or cinema: *the dress circle.* ●*vti* be or move in a circle (round).

circuit ('sɜːkɪt) *nc* 1 a trip once right round something. 2 an endless racetrack. 3 a complete path for electric current. 4 a number of sports competitions at which the same people play. **circuitous** (,sɜː'kjuːɪtəs) *adj* not following the shortest path.

circular ('sɜːkjʊlə*) *adj* 1 in the shape of a circle. 2 (of an argument) returning to the same point. ●*nc* a letter sent to many different people.

circulate ('sɜːkjʊ,leɪt) *vti* 1 (cause to) travel round and round in a space or endless system; move freely. 2 pass (news, a book, etc.) round a circle of people. **circulation** (,sɜːkjʊ'leɪʃən) *nu* 1 the act of circulating. 2 the movement of blood round the body. 3 *nc* the number of copies sold of a newspaper, magazine, etc.

circumcise ('sɜːkəm,saɪz) *vt* cut the skin at the end of the penis. **circumcision** (,sɜːkəm'sɪʒən) *nc*

circumference (sə'kʌmfərəns) *nc* (the length of) the edge of a circle.

circumnavigate (,sɜːkəm'nævɪ,geɪt) *vt* sail completely round (esp. the world).

circumscribe (,sɜːkəm'skraɪb) *vt* 1 draw a line round. 2 *formal* shut in; restrict.

circumstance ('sɜːkəm,stæns) *nc* 1 the place, time, etc., at which something happens: *The circumstances of his death are suspicious.* 2 an event. **circumstantial** (,sɜːkəm'stænʃəl) *adj* detailed; unimportant.

circus ('sɜːkəs) *nc* 1 a travelling group of people who entertain with physical skills and trained animals. 2 a place in a town where several streets meet: *Piccadilly Circus.*

cirrus ('sɪrəs) *nu* very high, thin cloud made of tiny pieces of ice.

cistern ('sɪstən) *nc* a water tank in a house.

citadel ('sɪtədəl) *nc* a building built for defence inside a city.

cite (saɪt) *vt* mention (a writer, part of a book, etc.) in order to support an argument, etc. **citation** 1 *ncu* an example of citing. 2 *nc* something cited from a book; quotation.

citizen ('sɪtɪzən) *nc* **1** a person who lives in a (particular) town. **2** a person who belongs to a particular country. **citizenship** *nu*

citron ('sɪtrən) *nc* **1** a tree with a fruit like a small lemon. **2** this fruit.

citrus ('sɪtrəs) *nc* any tree of the family including the orange, lemon, and grapefruit. ● *adj* to do with any of these trees.

city ('sɪtɪ) *nc* **1** a large town. **2** *Brit* a town named a city by the king or queen, usually with a cathedral.

civic ('sɪvɪk) *adj* to do with a city, a town, or its citizens.

civil ('sɪvɪl) *adj* **1** to do with ordinary life; not military, legal, or religious: *civil defence; civil marriage.* **2** polite; helpful. **civil service** *nc* the organisations that run a country that are not elected, such as the tax service. **civil servant** *nc* a person who works for a civil service.

civilian (sɪ'vɪljən) *adj* not to do with an army, navy, or air force. ● *nc* a civilian person.

civilise ('sɪvɪˌlaɪz) *vt* improve the society of (a people); stop (a people) being wild, unjust, etc. **civilisation** (ˌsɪvɪlaɪ'zeɪʃən) **1** *nc* a stage of human social development: *ancient Chinese civilisation.* **2** *nu* the act of civilising.

clad (klæd) *literary adj* clothed.

claim (kleɪm) *vt* **1** demand (something) as being one's right: *I won, so I claimed my prize.* **2** say to be true: *He claims that he was here yesterday.* ● *nc* **1** an act of claiming. **2** something claimed.

claimant ('kleɪmənt) *nc* a person who claims something.

clairvoyant (ˌkleə'vɔɪənt) *adj* able to see things that one cannot normally see, such as future events. ● *nc* a clairvoyant person.

clam (klæm) *nc* a kind of sea-animal with a double shell.

clamber ('klæmbə*) *vi* climb with difficulty.

clammy ('klæmɪ) *adj* **-ier, -iest** cold and sticky or wet: *clammy hands.*

clamour *US* **clamor** ('klæmə*) *nu* shouting, as from a large number of people. ● *vi* make a clamour.

clamp (klæmp) *nc* a device for pressing objects together. ● *vt* press (objects) together (with a clamp). **clamp down on** take action against: *The police are clamping down on crime.*

clan (klæn) *nc* all the descendants of one person, esp. in Scotland.

clandestine (klæn'destɪn) *adj* secret, often because not legal: *a clandestine plan.*

clang (klæŋ) *nc* a ringing noise, such as that from a bell. ● *vi* make a clang.

clank (klæŋk) *nc* a rattling noise, such as that of a chain. ● *vi* make this noise.

clap (klæp) *vti* **1** hit (things) together to make a sharp noise: *to clap one's hands.* **2** clap one's hands to show approval: *He was clapped loudly.* **3** *vt* put suddenly or with force: *He was clapped in prison for ten years.* ● *nc* **1** the sound of clapping. **2** the act of clapping.

claret ('klærɪt) *ncu* (a) red wine made in the Bordeaux district of France.

clarify ('klærɪˌfaɪ) **1** *vt* make clear or easy to understand. **2** *vti* make or become pure.

clarinet (ˌklærɪ'net) *nc* a musical instrument blown with the mouth, with keys and a single reed: see picture at **musical instruments.**

clarity ('klærɪtɪ) *nu* the quality of being clear.

clash (klæʃ) **1** *vti* strike together. *vi* **2** not go or fit together. **3** fight or play against each other. **4** (of colours) look ugly together. **5** (of events) happen at the same time. ● *nc* the act or an example of clashing.

clasp (klɑːsp) *vt* hold or take hold of firmly. ● *nc* a device for holding a book, coat, etc., closed.

class (klɑːs) *nc* **1** a group of people who are taught together in a school, college, etc. **2** a lesson in a school, college, etc. **3** a group of similar people or things. **4** a group of people with similar jobs, habits, etc.: *the working class.* **5** *nu* the existence of such groups in society: *the class system.* ● *vt* place in a class (def. 3). **classmate** ('klɑːsˌmeɪt) *nc* another person in one's own class at school. **classroom** ('klɑːsˌrʊm) *nc* a room in a school in which classes are given.

classic ('klæsɪk) *adj* **1** (of art and literature) of the best sort. **2** being a good example of its own type; typical: *classic case of this disease.* **3** famous or popular. ● *nc* a classic person or thing.

classical ('klæsɪkəl) *adj* **1** to do with ancient Greece and Rome or the ancient Greek or Latin languages. **2** to do with music that is studied and listened to seriously.

classify ('klæsɪˌfaɪ) *vt* **1** put in classes. **2** not make (information) public because it might help a country's enemies. **classification** (ˌklæsɪfɪ'keɪʃən) **1** *ncu* (an example of) classifying. **2** *nc* the name of the class into which something is put.

clatter ('klætə*) *nu* a repeated sharp noise, such as that of tins knocking together. ● *vi* make a clatter.

clause (klɔːz) *nc* **1** a part of a sentence containing a subject and a verb. **2** a part of a document, such as an agreement.

claustrophobia (ˌklɒstrə'fəʊbɪə) *nu* fear of being in closed spaces.

clavicle ('klævɪkəl) *anatomy nc* also **collarbone** the bone joining each shoulder blade to the breastbone.

claw (klɔː) *nc* **1** the curved pointed nail on each toe of the feet of birds and some animals, such as cats. **2** the double pointed arm of a shellfish. ●*vt* tear at (something) with claws or one's hands.

clay (kleɪ) *ncu* (a type of) smooth earth that can be made into bricks, pots, etc., by forming and heating.

clean (kliːn) *adj* **-er, -est 1** not dirty; free from material that should not be there. **2** not written on: *clean paper.* **3** not containing bad language: *a clean joke.* **4** simple; smooth: *a plane with clean lines.* **5** with no cause for blame: *a clean record.* ●*vti* **1** make or be made clean. **2** *vt* make something clean by removing: *I cleaned the oil off the floor.* ●*nc* the act of cleaning: *It has had a clean but still looks dirty.* ●*adv* completely; neatly: *The rope was cut clean through.* **clean-cut** ('kliːnkʌt) *adj* neat: *a clean-cut young man.* **clean up 1** clean. **2** get rid of unwanted people or things. **cleanly** *adv*

cleanliness ('klenlɪnəs) *nu* (esp. of a person, room, etc.) the state of being clean.

cleanse (klenz) *vt* make (a soul, etc.) pure.

clear (klɪə*) *adj* **-er, -est 1** able to be seen through: *clear water.* **2** easy to understand. **3** able to understand; sure: *I'm not clear what you want.* **4** without clouds: *clear weather.* **5** firm: *a clear decision.* **6** empty; with nothing in one's way: *a clear road.* **7** free from guilt: *a clear conscience.* **clear-cut** ('klɪəkʌt) *adj* firm; definite: *clear-cut plans.* **clearly** *adv* **keep clear of** avoid. **stand clear** keep away. ●*vti* **1** make or become clear. **2** remove (something) from: *Clear the room! vt* **3** no longer think (someone) guilty: *I was cleared of the charge.* **4** pass without touching: *The bus only just cleared the bridge.* **5** allow to happen or be used: *Has your idea been cleared with the police?* **clear away** remove and put away. **clear off** *infml* go away. **clear out 1** remove (things) from. *infml* **2** go out or away. **3** take all someone's money or something else. **clear up 1** (of the weather) become bright or clear. **2** settle or explain (an affair). **3** remove (things) from; tidy up or away.

clearance ('klɪərəns) **1** *ncu* (an example of) clearing. **2** *nc* a space left when one thing passes another. **3** *nu* permission for something to happen.

clearing ('klɪərɪŋ) *nc* a space in a wood or forest.

cleavage ('kliːvɪdʒ) *nc* the space between a woman's breasts.

cleave (kliːv) *vti* split.

clef (klef) *music nc* a sign to show at what pitch the notes should be played.

cleft (kleft) past tense and past participle of **cleave.** ●*nc* a split; crack.

clemency ('klemənsɪ) *nu* **1** not punishing someone; mercy. **2** (of the weather) being fine.

clench (klentʃ) *vt* **1** close tightly: *clenched teeth.* **2** hold tightly.

clergy ('klɜːdʒɪ) *nc, pl* **-gies 1** the priests and ministers of the Christian Church or any part of it. **2** the leaders of a religion. **clergyman** *nc, pl* **-men** a member of a clergy.

clerical ('klerɪkəl) *adj* **1** to do with clerks. **2** to do with the clergy.

clerk (klɑːk *US* klɜːk) *nc* **1** a person who files letters, keeps the records, etc., in an office. **2** *US* See **salesclerk** under **sale.**

clever ('klevə*) *adj* **-er, -est 1** good at learning or understanding. **2** able to work well with one's hands. **cleverly** *adv* **cleverness** *nu*

cliché ('kliːʃeɪ) *nc* a word or phrase used so much that its original meaning is no longer thought about.

click (klɪk) *nc* a light, sharp noise, as when a light switch is turned on. ●*vti* **1** (cause to) make this noise. **2** *infml vi* become clear.

client ('klaɪənt) *nc* a person or firm to whom one sells goods or a service. **clientele** (ˌkliːɒn'tel) *nc* all one's clients.

cliff (klɪf) *nc* a tall, steep rock face, esp. facing the sea.

climate ('klaɪmɪt) *nc* **1** the weather of a place. **2** a general opinion or condition: *the economic climate.* **climatic** (klaɪ'mætɪk) *adj*

climax ('klaɪmæks) *nc* **1** the most interesting, exciting, etc., point of an event. **2** the most important part in a story, play, piece of music, etc.

climb (klaɪm) *vti* **1** (often followed by **up**) go up (stairs, a hill, etc.). **2** go up (a mountain) as a sport. **3** *vi* rise: *Prices always climb.* ●*nc* an act or place of climbing. **climb down 1** go down (something). **2** give up an opinion, demand, etc.

clime (klaɪm) *literary nc* **1** a place. **2** climate.

clinch (klɪntʃ) *vt* settle (an argument or deal).

cling (klɪŋ) *vi* hold or stick tightly: *Cling on or you'll fall.*

clinic ('klɪnɪk) *nc* a building where sick or hurt people are treated. **clinical** *adj* **1** to do with the treating of sick or hurt people. **2** having a purpose and not meant to please: *a clinical approach.*

clink (klɪŋk) *nc* a high, sharp sound, as of glasses touching. ●*vti* (cause to) make this sound.

clip¹ (klɪp) *vt* **1** cut (a part) off (something), esp. with scissors. **2** make (a hole) in (something, esp. a ticket). **3** *infml* hit.

clip² *nc* a device for holding things together or something closed: *a paper clip.*

clipper ('klɪpə*) *nc* a fast sailing ship.

clippers ('klɪpəz) *nc* a tool for cutting or clipping.

clipping ('klɪpɪŋ) *nc* a piece cut out of something, esp. a newspaper.

cloak (kləʊk) *nc* an outer garment without sleeves. ●*vt* hide; disguise. **cloakroom** ('kləʊkrʊm) *nc* a room for leaving coats in.

clock (klɒk) *nc* 1 a device showing the time of day. 2 a device for measuring distance driven, a taxi fare, etc. **clock in** or **out** arrive at or leave work, esp. stamping a card with the time at which one does so. **clockwise** ('klɒkwaɪz) *adv* round in the same direction as the hands of a clock move. **clockwork** ('klɒkwɜːk) *nu* the device that works a clock or a toy.

clod (klɒd) *nc* 1 a lump of earth. 2 *infml* a stupid or careless person.

clog (klɒg) *vti* block or become blocked. ●*nc* a wooden shoe: see picture.

clog

cloister ('klɔɪstə*) *nc* a covered path round a garden or courtyard, esp. in a monastery. ●*vt* cut off from ordinary life: *a cloistered existence.*

close (kləʊz) *vti* 1 shut; put (a door, cover, etc.) in place or be put in place: *The door won't close.* 2 shut; put a door, cover, etc., on or have a door, cover, etc.: *I closed the box.* 3 bring or come together: *Close the curtains.* 4 (of a shop, etc.), (cause to) stop business: *The shop closes at 5.30.* 5 finish; bring or come to an end: *The meeting was closed.* **close down** (of radio, television, a business, etc.) stop sending, trading, etc. **closed shop** a place of work in which all workers have to be members of a trade union. ● (kləʊs) *adj* **-er**, **-est** 1 near; not far away: *close to my house.* 2 in detail; careful: *Take a close look.* 3 similar: *It's not the same, but it's close.* 4 (of a friend or relationship) good; valued. 5 (of air, the weather, etc.) unpleasantly hot or wet. 6 secretive. **close together** (of two or more things) near to each other. **closely** *adv* **closeness** *nu* ●*adv* near: *Don't get close!* **close-up** ('kləʊsʌp) *nc* a photograph taken near its subject. ●*nc* (kləʊz) 1 the act of closing. 2 an end or finish. 3 (kləʊs) a space between buildings or round a building, esp. a cathedral.

closet ('klɒzɪt) *nc* 1 a small room. 2 a small cupboard.

closure ('kləʊʒə*) *nc* 1 being closed or the act of closing. 2 something, such as a piece of wire, that closes something else.

clot (klɒt) *vti* (cause to) turn into a soft solid: *Blood soon clots in a wound.* ●*nc* 1 a lump of something clotted. 2 *infml, Brit* a stupid or foolish person.

cloth (klɒθ) 1 *ncu* (a type of) material made from wool, cotton, silk, etc. 2 *nc* a piece of cloth used for wiping, covering, etc.

clothe (kləʊð) *vt* 1 dress; put clothes on. 2 cover. **clothes** *nu* articles of dress; shoes, coats, etc. **clothing** *nu* clothes.

cloud (klaʊd) 1 *ncu* a white or grey body of tiny drops of water or ice in the sky. *nc* 2 any other body of things in the air: *a cloud of dust.* 3 something that threatens or brings gloom. ●*vti* 1 (often followed by **over**) make or become cloudy. 2 make or become dark or unclear. **cloudless** *adj* **cloudy** *adj* **-ier**, **-iest** 1 covered with clouds. 2 (of water, etc.) not clear.

clove¹ (kləʊv) *nc* 1 a tree grown esp. in Zanzibar. 2 a dried unopened flower of this tree, used to give food a taste.

clove² past tense of **cleave**. **cloven** (kləʊvən) past participle of **cleave**.

clover ('kləʊvə*) *ncu* a (type of) small plant with leaves in threes.

clown (klaʊn) *nc* a person who entertains with a funny act in a circus or behaves in an amusing way. ●*vi* act as a clown.

club (klʌb) *nc* 1 a stick used as a weapon. 2 See **golf club**. 3 a group of people with a common interest or the building used by such a group: *a cricket club.* 4 a playing-card with a black shape like a clover leaf on it. ●*vt* hit with a club. **club together** give money for a common purpose.

cluck (klʌk) *vi* (of a hen) make a low repeated noise. ●*nc* this noise.

clue (kluː) *nc* a piece of information that helps one guess or discover something.

clump (klʌmp) *nc* 1 a small group, esp. of trees. 2 a lump, esp. of earth. ●*vti* 1 form clumps (from). 2 *vi* walk heavily.

clumsy ('klʌmzɪ) *adj* **-ier**, **-iest** 1 careless or awkward in handling things. 2 awkwardly made: *a clumsy arrangement.* **clumsily** *adv*

clung (klʌŋ) past tense and past participle of **cling**.

cluster ('klʌstə*) *nc* a group of similar things. ●*vti* form a cluster (of).

clutch (klʌtʃ) 1 *vt* hold or take hold of firmly. 2 *vi* (followed by **at**) take hold of firmly. ●*nc* 1 a firm hold. 2 a device for connecting a spinning part of a machine to one that, to start with, is not spinning, as in a car.

clutter ('klʌtə*) *nc* a disorganised group of objects. ●*vt* (often followed by **up**) fill untidily.

coach (kəʊtʃ) *nc* **1** a large motor road vehicle for up to about fifty passengers. **2** a road vehicle pulled by horses. **3** a railway vehicle for passengers. **4** a teacher, esp. of a sport. ●*vt* teach, esp. in a sport. **coachman** *nc*, *pl* **-men** a man who drives a **coach** (def. 2).

coagulate (kəʊˈægjʊˌleɪt) *vti* (of milk, blood, etc.), (cause to) become a soft solid; clot.

coal (kəʊl) *ncu* (a piece of) black rock made of carbon that is burned or used to make coal gas, coke, etc. **coalfield** ('kəʊlfiːld) *nc* a district under which coal is found. **coal gas** gas made from coal and burned for heat or light. **coal mine** a hole or tunnel dug in the ground in order to get coal out.

coalesce (ˌkəʊəˈles) *vi* join together; become one.

coalition (ˌkəʊəˈlɪʃən) *ncu* (an example of) coalescing, esp. of two political parties to form a government.

coarse (kɔːs) *adj* **-r**, **-st 1** made of large, rough, etc., parts: *coarse cloth*. **2** rude: *coarse language*. **coarsely** *adv*

coast (kəʊst) *nc* the edge of land next to the sea. **coastal** *adj* **coastline** ('kəʊstlaɪn) *nc* the shape of a coast. ●*vi* travel without using (much) power.

coat (kəʊt) *nc* **1** an outer garment with arms that covers from the neck to the hips or below. **2** the hair on the body of an animal. **3** a layer of paint, dirt, etc. **coat of arms** a

coat of arms

pattern of pictures representing a family or town: see picture. **coat hanger** an object used for hanging clothes on: see picture. ●*vt* put or be a layer on.

coat hanger

coating ('kəʊtɪŋ) *nc* a layer; coat.
coax (kəʊks) *vt* persuade gently.

cob (kɒb) *n* See **corn cob**.

cobalt ('kəʊbɔːlt) *nu* a chemical element; metal used in steel: symbol Co

cobbler ('kɒblə*) *nc* a person who repairs shoes.

cobblestone ('kɒbəlˌstəʊn) *nc* also **cobble** a rounded stone used to make a road surface.

cobra ('kəʊbrə, 'kɒbrə) *nc* a poisonous snake that can blow up its neck to look like a hood: see picture at **reptiles.**

cobweb ('kɒbweb) *nc* the net spun by a spider to catch insects.

cocaine (kəˈkeɪn, ˌkəʊˈkeɪn) *nu* a drug used as an anaesthetic.

cock (kɒk) *nc* **1** a male bird, esp. the male of the hen kept for its eggs. **2** the part of a gun raised and then loosed to hit the cartridge or charge. **3** a tap for water, etc. ●*vt* **1** turn upwards: *The horse cocked its ears.* **2** set the cock of (a gun) ready for firing.

cock-a-doodle-doo (ˌkɒkəˌduːdəlˈduː) *interj* the noise made by a **cock** (def. 1).

cockatoo (ˌkɒkəˈtuː) *nc* a bird; type of parrot with a crest on its head..

cockle ('kɒkəl) *nc* a shellfish that can be eaten.

cockney ('kɒknɪ) *adj, ncu* (to do with) (the language of) a person born in the East End of London.

cockpit ('kɒkpɪt) *nc* the space in a plane or ship for the pilot.

cockroach ('kɒkrəʊtʃ) *nc* a large brown insect found in some houses: see picture at **insects.**

cocktail ('kɒkteɪl) *nc* **1** a mixed drink containing spirits. **2** a dish made from a particular food: *prawn cocktail*.

cocoa ('kəʊkəʊ) *nu* **1** a powder made from cacao seeds and used to make chocolate. **2** a drink made from this.

coconut ('kəʊkənʌt) *nc* **1** a large, hard, brown fruit with a solid white lining and white liquid inside. **2** also **coconut palm** the tree bearing this fruit.

cocoon (kəˈkuːn) *nc* the case in which an insect develops.

cod (kɒd) *nc*, *pl* **cod** a large fish that is eaten: see picture at **fish.**

coddle ('kɒdəl) *vt* **1** allow (someone) everything he wants. **2** cook (an egg) in water that is not boiling.

code (kəʊd) *nc* a system of letters or other characters used for a message so as to disguise its meaning.

co-ed (ˌkəʊˈed) *infml adj* short for **co-educational.** ●*nc* **1** *Brit* a co-educational school. **2** *US* a girl at a co-educational school.

co-education (ˌkəʊedjuːˈkeɪʃən) *nu* educating boys and girls in the same schools. **co-educational** *adj*

coefficient (ˌkəʊɪˈfɪʃənt) *nc* **1** a number multiplying another quantity: *The coefficient of 2a is 2*. **2** *physics* the measure of a quality of a material.

coerce (kəʊˈɜːs) *vt* force (somebody) to do something.

coffee (ˈkɒfɪ) *nu* **1** a drink made from coffee beans. **2** also **coffee beans** roasted and ground coffee seeds. **3** a light-brown colour. **coffee-pot** *nc* a tall pot with a handle, for making coffee in.

coffer (ˈkɒfə*) *nc* a strong box, esp. for money.

coffin (ˈkɒfɪn) *US* **casket** *nc* a box in which a dead person is buried or burned.

cog (kɒg) *nc* **1** one of the teeth round a wheel that turns another wheel in a machine. **2** also **cog-wheel** a small wheel with teeth round it: see picture.

cog

cognac (ˈkɒnjæk) *nu* a strong French alcoholic drink made from wine.

cohabit (ˌkəʊˈhæbɪt) *vi* (of people who are not married) live together.

cohere (kəʊˈhɪə*) *vi* **1** stick together. **2** (of an argument) make sense. **coherent** (kəʊˈhɪərənt) *adj* cohering. **coherently** *adv* **cohesion** (kəʊˈhiːʒən) *nu* cohering.

coil (kɔɪl) *vti* arrange or be arranged in rings or turns. ● *nc* **1** (a turn of) something coiled. **2** a coil of wire through which electricity is passed.

coin (kɔɪn) *nc* a small, usually round piece of metal used as money. ● *vt* **1** make (a coin). **2** invent (a word). **coinage** (ˈkɔɪnɪdʒ) *nc* **1** a system of coins: *decimal coinage*. **2** an invented word. **3** the inventing of a word.

coincide (ˌkəʊɪnˈsaɪd) *vi* **1** happen at the same time. **2** meet or touch. **coincidence** (kəʊˈɪnsɪdəns) *nc* an example of coinciding; chance event. **coincidental** (ˌkəʊɪnsɪˈdentəl) *adj*

coke (kəʊk) *nu* coal that has been heated to drive off coal gas and is burned for heat.

colander (ˈkɒlɪndə*) *nc* a dish with holes in for straining food.

cold (kəʊld) *adj* **-er, -est** **1** at a low temperature; not warm or hot. **2** unfriendly. **3** without feeling: *a cold decision*. **cold-blooded** *adj* **1** (of an animal) having a blood temperature that changes with the temperature around it. **2** unfeeling; cruel: *cold-blooded*

murder. **coldly** *adv* **cold war** a period in which countries are unfriendly and likely to go to war. ● *nu* **1** the absence of heat. **2** *nc* an illness giving running nose, sore throat, cough, etc.

collaborate (kəˈlæbəˌreɪt) *vi* **1** work together (with someone). **2** help an enemy that has occupied one's country. **collaboration** *nu*

collapse (kəˈlæps) *vi* **1** fall down or in: *The old house collapsed*. **2** (of a person) fall down from tiredness. **3** *vti* (be able to) fold up: *These chairs collapse*. **collapsible** *adj* able to fold up. ● *nc* an example of collapsing.

collar (ˈkɒlə*) *nc* **1** the part of a garment round one's neck. **2** a band, esp. of leather, round an animal's neck. **collarbone** (ˈkɒləˌbəʊn) *n* See **clavicle**.

collate (kəˈleɪt) *vt* collect and arrange (information or pages of a book) in order.

collateral (kəˈlætərəl) *nu* something of value promised to a lender if his money is not paid back.

colleague (ˈkɒliːg) *nc* a person with whom one works.

collect (kəˈlekt) **1** *vti* gather together: *I collected everyone's books; Water collected in the bucket*. *vt* **2** obtain and put with others for interest: *I collect stamps*. **3** fetch; call for: *I'll collect you tomorrow*. **4** regain control of (oneself). **collection 1** *ncu* (an example of) collecting. *nc* **2** a body of collected things or material. **3** a collected sum of money. **collective** *adj* **1** formed by or forming a collection. **2** to do with a group of people acting together: *collective bargaining*. ● *nc* something, such as a farm, that is run collectively. **collectively** *adv* **collector** *nc*

college (ˈkɒlɪdʒ) *nc* **1** (a part of) a university. **2** a place of education of a particular kind: *an art college*.

collide (kəˈlaɪd) *vi* strike violently together.

collie (ˈkɒlɪ) *nc* a dog with a long narrow head and long hair.

colliery (ˈkɒlɪərɪ) *nc, pl* **-ries** a coal mine and the buildings connected with it.

collision (kəˈlɪʒən) *nc* (an example of) colliding.

colloquial (kəˈləʊkwɪəl) *adj* **1** to do with talking, as compared with writing. **2** (of language) familiar; conversational.

cologne (kəˈləʊn) *nu* also **eau de cologne** a liquid put on the body for its nice smell.

colon[1] (ˈkəʊlɒn) *nc* the sign (:) used in writing, esp. in front of an example or quotation.

colon[2] *anatomy nc* the next to last part of the large intestine.

colonel (ˈkɜːnəl) *nc* an important officer in most armies and some air forces.

colonial (kəˈləʊnɪəl) *adj* to do with a colony. ●*nc* a person living in a colony.
colonialism *nu* the practice of owning colonies.
colonise (ˈkɒlənaɪz) *vt* make (a place) into a colony. **colonisation** (ˌkɒlənaɪˈzeɪʃən) *nu* **colonist** (ˈkɒlənɪst) *nc* a person who starts or lives in a colony.
colonnade (ˌkɒləˈneɪd) *architecture nc* a row of columns or pillars.
colony (ˈkɒləni) *nc, pl* **-nies 1** (the people living in) a country owned by another one: *Britain had many colonies.* **2** a group of people living within a larger group: *a colony of artists in Paris.*
colossal (kəˈlɒsəl) *adj* very big; huge.
colossus (kəˈlɒsəs) *nc, pl* **-si** (saɪ), **-ses** a huge person, statue, or other thing.
colour *US* **color** (ˈkʌlə*) *nc* **1** a quality of the light produced or reflected by something, such as red, green, or blue. **2** a paint with a particular colour. **3** the colour of a person's skin: *Colour makes no difference.* ●*vt* **1** give a colour or colours to. **2** influence; affect: *Her opinion was coloured by jealousy.*
colourful *adj* **1** with many or bright colours. **2** interesting. **colourless** *adj* **1** with few or dull colours. **2** uninteresting.
colt (kəʊlt) *nc* a young male horse.
column (ˈkɒləm) *nc* **1** a thick upright supporting a building. **2** a long line of people, vehicles, etc.; series of numbers. **3** a group of printed lines, one below the other, esp. in a newspaper.
coma (ˈkəʊmə) *nc* an unconscious state caused by injury, lack of food, etc.
comb (kəʊm) *nc* a long, narrow object with teeth along one side for arranging one's hair with: see picture. ●*vt* use a comb on (one's hair).

comb

combat (ˈkɒmbæt) **1** *nu* fighting. **2** *nc* a fight. ●*vt* fight against: *to combat disease.*
combatant (ˈkɒmbətənt) *nc* a person who fights.
combine (kəmˈbaɪn) *vti* join together. **combination** (ˌkɒmbɪˈneɪʃən) *ncu* the action or result of combining. **combine harvester** (ˈkɒmbaɪn) a moving machine that cuts and separates corn: see picture.
combustion (kəmˈbʌstʃən) *nu* burning; being changed or destroyed by fire. **combustible** (kəmˈbʌstɪbəl) *adj* able to burn; flammable.

combine harvester

come (kʌm) *vi* **1** move, esp. towards the speaker: *Come here!* **2** arrive or be brought: *Has he come yet?* **3** happen: *Monday comes after Sunday.* **4** reach: *My coat comes down to my knees.* **5** (followed by **from**) live in; be a native of: *Where do you come from?* **6** be or become: *The button is coming loose.*
come about happen. **come across 1** find by chance. **2** (of a person or message) have an (intended) effect: *How did I come across?* **come back 1** return. **2** be remembered: *His name has just come back to me.* **comeback** (ˈkʌmbæk) *nc* a return to power, popularity, etc. **come before** be considered by: *My case comes before the judge next.* **come by 1** get; obtain. **2** visit one or someone for a short time. **come down 1** come to a lower place. **2** (of prices) fall. **3** (of a plane) land. **comedown** (ˈkʌmdaʊn) *nc* a disappointment. **come forward** say one is willing to do something. **come in 1** enter. **2** have a use or something to do: *This is where you come in.* **3** prove to be (esp. useful). **come in for** get. **come into 1** enter. **2** be given (something) by someone when he dies. **come off 1** become loose or separate. **2** succeed. **come on 1** improve; do well. **2** (of electricity, a radio programme, etc.) start. **come out 1** go to a social occasion: *Can you come out for dinner?* **2** become known: *If you don't tell us now, it will come out later.* **3** appear; be produced: *My book comes out tomorrow.* **4** (of flowers) bloom. **5** be clear in a photograph: *You came out well.* **come over 1** (of a person or message) have an (intended) effect. **2** *infml* feel: *I came over all hot.* **3** visit one or someone. **come round 1** become conscious again. **2** visit one or someone. **3** occur again: *My birthday will come round soon.* **come through 1** move to a different room. **2** live, manage, etc., in spite of (a disease, etc.). **come to 1** become conscious again. **2** cost: *This all comes to a lot of money.* **3** be a case of: *If it comes to war, we'll lose.* **come under 1** have as a title or heading: *Poetry comes under literature.* **2** have in charge of one: *Soldiers come under an officer.* **come up 1** come to a higher place. **2** happen: *I can't go—something's come up.* **3** (of the sun) rise. **4** be discussed: *I thought*

that problem would come up. **5** grow out of the ground. **come up against** meet (a difficulty, etc.). **come upon** find by chance. **come up to** be as good as: *You just don't come up to what I expected.* **come up with** *infml* produce: *You've come up with the answer!*

comedy ('kɒmɪdɪ) **1** *nu* the quality of something that makes one laugh; humour. **2** *ncu* (a play or other piece of) entertainment that makes one laugh. **comedian** (kə'miːdɪən) *nc* a person who entertains with comedy.

comely ('kʌmlɪ) *archaic adj* attractive.

comet ('kɒmɪt) *nc* a large bright object with a tail that travels fast through space.

comfort ('kʌmfət) **1** *nu* a feeling of being at ease, in body or mind. **2** *nc* a person or thing that brings comfort. ● *vt* bring comfort to. **comfortable** *adj* **1** bringing comfort. **2** enjoying comfort. **3** with plenty of money. **comfortably** *adv* **comforter** *nc*

comic ('kɒmɪk) *adj* **1** to do with comedy. **2** funny. ● *nc* a comic person; comedian. **comical** *adj* funny.

coming ('kʌmɪŋ) *adj* next; future: *the coming summer.* **up and coming** about to become good; promising: *an up and coming writer.* ● *nc* the act of arriving.

comma ('kɒmə) *nc* the sign (,) used in writing, esp. where one pauses in reading.

command (kə'mɑːnd) *nc* **1** the act of telling someone to do something; order. **2** a knowledge (of a language). **3** *nu* authority; power to give commands: *in command of a ship.* ● *vt* give (someone) a command.

commandant ('kɒməndænt) *nc* an officer in charge of a camp, prison, etc.

commandeer (,kɒmən'dɪə*) *vt* take for use by the army, etc.

commander (kə'mɑːndə*) *nc* **1** a person who commands. **2** an officer in a navy.

commandment (kə'mɑːndmənt) *nc* one of the Ten Commandments in the Bible.

commando (kə'mɑːndəʊ) *nc, pl* **-dos, -does** (a member of) a group of soldiers who attack land from the sea.

commemorate (kə'meməreɪt) *vt* cause people to remember (an event or dead person).

commence (kə'mens) *formal vti* start; begin. **commencement** *nc*

commend (kə'mend) *vt* **1** praise: *Your work is to be commended.* **2** *formal* give to someone to look after. **commendation** (,kɒmen'deɪʃən) *ncu* (an example of) commending. **commendable** *adj* that ought to be praised.

commensurate (kə'mensjʊrət) *adj* in a suitable or the proper amount: *Your pay will be commensurate with your position in the company.*

comment ('kɒment) *ncu* **1** a note; remark. **2** (a) criticism. ● *vi* make a remark: *Would you like to comment on the news?* **commentary** ('kɒməntrɪ) *nc, pl* **-ries** a set of remarks about something, such as literature or a sports event. **commentator** ('kɒmən,teɪtə*) *nc* a person who gives a commentary.

commerce ('kɒmɜːs) *nu* the activity of trading with other people; buying and selling. **commercial** (kə'mɜːʃəl) *adj* to do with commerce. ● *nc* an advertisement on radio or television.

commiserate (kə'mɪzəreɪt) *vi* (often followed by **with**) express sympathy (with).

commission (kə'mɪʃən) **1** *ncu* (an example of) committing something. **2** *nc* a task. **3** *nu* the condition of being an officer in an army, etc. **4** *nc* a group of people appointed to discover or discuss something. **5** *nu* money paid to someone who brings one business. **commissionaire** (kə,mɪʃə'neə*) *Brit nc* a man who meets people as they arrive outside a theatre, hotel, etc. **commissioner** *nc* **1** a member of a commission. **2** a person in a position of power: *a commissioner of police.*

commit (kə'mɪt) *vt* **1** do (something, esp. a crime). **2** give for keeping, etc.: *Commit this to memory.* **commit oneself** promise or decide to do something. **commitment** *nc* **1** (an example of) committing. **2** a promise to attend or pay something.

committee (kə'mɪtɪ) *nc* a group of people who discuss and decide things together.

commodity (kə'mɒdɪtɪ) *nc, pl* **-ties** something that is traded.

common ('kɒmən) *adj* **-er, -est** **1** existing in large quantities or happening frequently. **2** belonging to more than one person: *This is in our common interest.* **3** ordinary: *a common soldier.* **4** *derogatory* ordinary and not nice. **commonly** *adv* **commonplace** ('kɒmənpleɪs) *adj, nu* (something) very ordinary. **common sense** good judgement or sense. ● *nc* a piece of public land. **in common** together or shared: *My brother and I have a lot in common.*

commoner ('kɒmənə*) *nc* a person who is not a noble.

Commons ('kɒmənz) *n* **the (House of) Commons** the elected lower house in the British parliament.

commonwealth ('kɒmənwelθ) *nc* a republic. **the Commonwealth (of Nations)** Britain and countries now or in the past ruled by Britain.

commotion (kə'məʊʃən) *nc* a noisy disturbance.

communal ('kɒmjʊnəl) *adj* belonging to everyone in a particular group.

commune ('kɒmjuːn) *nc* a group of people other than a family who share a home and their belongings.

communicate (kə'mjuːnɪkeɪt) *vti* give (and receive) (information): *I'd like to communicate this news to the president; Can we communicate with the ship by radio?* **communication** (kə,mjuːnɪ'keɪʃən) **1** *ncu* (an example of) communicating. **2** *nc* something communicated; message. **communicative** (kə'mjuːnɪkətɪv) *adj* **1** to do with communication. **2** willing to talk.

communion (kə'mjuːnɪən) *nu* the sharing of thoughts. **(Holy) Communion** the Christian service of giving bread and wine to worshippers.

communiqué (kə'mjuːnɪkeɪ) *nc* an official message from a government, etc., to the public.

communism ('kɒmjʊnɪzəm) *nu* a system in which all factories, etc., are owned by the nation as a whole. **communist** *nc* a person who believes in communism.

community (kə'mjuːnɪtɪ) *nc, pl* **-ties 1** the people living in a place. **2** a group of people of one race, religion, etc.: *the Indian community in Britain.*

commute (kə'mjuːt) **1** *vi* travel to and from work every day, esp. in and out of a big city. **2** *law vt* change (a sentence) into a less serious one. **commuter** *nc* a person who commutes to and from work.

compact (kəm'pækt) *adj* small for its value or usefulness. ● *vt* press together. ●('kɒmpækt) *nc* a small flat tin of face powder.

companion (kəm'pænjən) *nc* a person who keeps one company: *a travelling companion.* **companionship** *nu* being a companion.

company ('kʌmpənɪ) **1** *nu* the fact of being with someone. *nc* **2** a business that trades as itself. **3** a group of people, actors, or soldiers.

comparable ('kɒmprəbəl) *adj* **1** able to be compared. **2** alike.

comparative (kəm'pærɪtɪv) *adj* **1** to do with comparison. **2** by comparison with something else. ● *nc, adj* (to do with) the form of an adjective or adverb meaning 'more... ': *'Slower' is the comparative of 'slow'.* **comparatively** *adv*

compare (kəm'peə*) *vt* **1** (often followed by **with**) consider the difference between (something) and (something else): *I've compared this year's profit with last year's.* **2** (followed by **to**) consider as alike: *Shall I compare thee to a summer's day?* **3** *vi* (often followed by **with**) be alike: *This year's results just don't compare with last year's results.*

comparison (kəm'pærɪsən) **1** *ncu* (an example of) comparing. **2** *nu* likeness: *This one has no comparison with the old one.*

compartment (kəm'pɑːtmənt) *nc* **1** a separate part of a container. **2** a separate part of a railway carriage for six to twelve people.

compass

compass ('kʌmpəs) *nc* **1** an instrument that shows direction by pointing to the north: see picture. **2** also **pair of compasses** an instrument used for drawing a circle or measuring a distance: see picture.

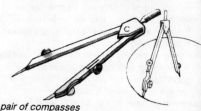

pair of compasses

compassion (kəm'pæʃən) *nu* pity for someone. **compassionate** *adj*

compatible (kəm'pætɪbəl) *adj* (often followed by **with**) able to go or fit together (with).

compatriot (kəm'pætrɪət) *nc* a person from the same country as someone else.

compel (kəm'pel) *vt* force (someone) (to do something): *He was compelled to leave.*

compensate ('kɒmpenseɪt) *vt* (often followed by **for**) give (someone) something, esp. money, to make up (for loss, damage, etc.). **compensation** (,kɒmpen'seɪʃən) *nu*

compère ('kɒmpeə*) *nc* a person who introduces the separate acts in a show. ● *vti* act as compère (for).

compete (kəm'piːt) *vi* try to do better (than other people): *I'm competing with twenty others for this job.*

competent ('kɒmpɪtənt) *adj* **1** able (to do something well). **2** (of a piece of work) well done. **competence** *nu*

competition (,kɒmpɪ'tɪʃən) *nu* **1** rivalry; competing against someone or something. **2** someone or something against which one is competing. **3** *nc* an event in which people compete. **competitive** (kəm'petɪtɪv) *adj* **1** to do with competition. **2** likely to have success in competing: *very competitive prices.* **competitor** (kəm'petɪtə*) *nc*

compile (kəm'paɪl) *vt* gather or collect together: *I've compiled a list of our customers.* **compilation** (ˌkɒmpɪ'leɪʃən) *ncu* **1** (an example of) compiling. **2** something compiled.

complacent (kəm'pleɪsənt) *adj* too pleased with oneself.

complain (kəm'pleɪn) *vi* **1** (often followed by **about**) say one is not satisfied (with): *I want to complain about these shoes—they're worn out already.* **2** (followed by **of**) say one is suffering (from): *to complain of a cold.* **complaint 1** *ncu* (an example of) complaining. **2** *nc* something complained about or of, esp. an illness.

complement ('kɒmplɪmənt) *nc* **1** someone or something that makes something complete. **2** a complete amount. **3** the people needed to run a ship. **4** *mathematics* the difference between a right angle and a smaller angle. **5** *grammar* a noun phrase that follows verbs like 'be' or 'become': *In 'he is my brother', 'my brother' is the complement.* **complementary** (ˌkɒmplɪ'mentrɪ) *adj* forming a complement.

complete (kəm'pliːt) *adj* **1** having everything necessary. **2** thorough: *a complete waste of time.* **3** finished. ● *vt* **1** finish: *to complete one's work; a completed painting.* **2** fill in (a form). **completely** *adv* **completeness** *nu* **completion** (kəm'pliːʃən) *nu*

complex ('kɒmpleks) *adj* **1** made up of parts. **2** (of a problem, etc.) complicated. ● *nc* **1** a group of suppressed ideas that affect one's behaviour: *an inferiority complex.* **2** a group of connected buildings: *a sports complex.*

complexion (kəm'plekʃən) *nc* **1** the appearance of the skin of someone's face: *He has a dark complexion.* **2** a way in which something must be considered.

complexity (kəm'pleksɪtɪ) **1** *nu* the quality of being complex. **2** *nc, pl* **-ties** a thing that makes something else complex.

complicate ('kɒmplɪkeɪt) *vt* make complex. **complicated** *adj* hard to understand, sort out, etc.: *a complicated job.* **complication** (ˌkɒmplɪ'keɪʃən) **1** *nu* the act of complicating. **2** *nc* something that complicates something such as an illness.

complicity (kəm'plɪsɪtɪ) *nu* the fact of being part of something, esp. a crime.

compliment ('kɒmplɪmənt) *nc* **1** an expression of praise: *He made some nice compliments about my dress.* **2** (*pl*) a formal greeting: *with the compliments of the manager.* **complimentary** (ˌkɒmplɪ'mentrɪ) *adj* forming a compliment.

comply (kəm'plaɪ) *formal vi* (usually followed by **with**) obey; follow (a request, etc.).

component (kəm'pəʊnənt) *adj* forming part of something. ● *nc* a component part: *car components.*

compose (kəm'pəʊz) *vt* **1** put together. **2** write (music, poetry, etc.). **3** calm or settle (someone, esp. oneself). **4** *vi* write music. **composed** *adj* (of a person) calm. **composer** *nc* a person who writes music.

composite ('kɒmpəzɪt) *adj, nc* (something) made of parts.

composition (ˌkɒmpə'zɪʃən) **1** *nu* the act of composing. **2** *nc* something composed, esp. a piece of music.

compost ('kɒmpɒst) *nu* animal or vegetable waste used for feeding plants.

composure (kəm'pəʊʒə*) *nu* the quality of being composed.

compound[1] ('kɒmpaʊnd) *adj* made up of parts. **compound interest** interest on the original amount borrowed and on all the unpaid interest. ● *nc* any compound thing, esp. one of chemical elements. ●(kəm'paʊnd) *vt* mix or join (things) to make (a compound).

compound[2] *nc* a piece of land closed in so as to keep something inside.

comprehend (ˌkɒmprɪ'hend) **1** *vti* understand. **2** *formal vt* include. **comprehension** (ˌkɒmprɪ'henʃən) *nu* the act of understanding or ability to understand.

comprehensive (ˌkɒmprɪ'hensɪv) *adj* including or to do with all or many types. **comprehensive school** also **comprehensive** a large school for children of all abilities from about eleven to eighteen.

compress (kəm'pres) *vt* make smaller by pressing together. ●('kɒmpres) *nc* a folded-up wet cloth pressed against a part of the body, to stop swelling or bleeding. **compression** *nu* **compressor** *nc* a machine that compresses a gas.

comprise (kəm'praɪz) *vt* **1** include. **2** form: *The examination is comprised of three papers.*

compromise ('kɒmprəmaɪz) *nc* an agreement reached by both sides giving up some points. ● *vi* **1** reach a compromise. **2** *vt* risk damaging the reputation of, through an unwise action.

compulsion (kəm'pʌlʃən) **1** *nu* being compelled. **2** *nc* a very strong urge.

compulsory (kəm'pʌlsərɪ) *adj* that must be done, followed etc.: *compulsory rules.*

compunction (kəm'pʌŋkʃən) *nu* regrets; hesitation: *I have no compunction about refusing to go.*

computation (ˌkɒmpjʊ'teɪʃən) *ncu* (an example of) working something out with numbers.

compute (kəm'pjuːt) *vt* work out with numbers.

computer (kəm'pju:tə*) *nc* an electric device for working out problems with numbers and for storing, arranging, and supplying information: see picture. **computer language** See under **language. computing** *nc* the use of computers.

computer

comrade ('kɒmrɪd) *nc* a companion. **comradeship** *nu*

con (kɒn) *infml nc* also **con trick** an example of tricking someone, esp. out of money. ●*vt* trick (esp. out of money or into doing something).

concave (,kɒn'keɪv) *adj* having a side that curves in.

conceal (kən'si:l) *formal vt* hide. **concealment** *nu*

concede (kən'si:d) *vt* **1** allow; agree that (something) is true: *I concede most of the points in your argument.* **2** allow someone to win: *to concede the match.*

conceit (kən'si:t) *nu* thinking that one is better than one is. **conceited** *adj* thinking this.

conceive (kən'si:v) **1** *vt* become pregnant with (a child). **2** *vti* (often followed by) *of*) imagine: *I can't conceive of such a stupid idea.* **conceivable** *adj* **conceivably** *adv*

concentrate ('kɒnsəntreɪt) **1** *vti* come or bring together. **2** *vt* make stronger or purer: *concentrated fruit juice. vi* **3** (often followed by **on**) think very hard (about): *I'm trying to concentrate on my work.* **4** (followed by **on**) occupy oneself chiefly (with): *To start with, I'm concentrating on important things.* **concentration** (,kɒnsən'treɪʃən) *nu* **1** the act of concentrating. **2** hard thought. **3** *nc* something concentrated. **concentration camp** a prison camp, esp. during a war but for people other than enemy soldiers.

concentric (kən'sentrɪk) *adj* (of circles) having the same centre.

concept ('kɒnsept) *nc* an idea.

conception (kən'sepʃən) **1** *nu* the act of conceiving. **2** *nc* an idea.

concern (kən'sɜ:n) *vt* affect; be to do with: *Does this concern you?* **concern oneself with 1** (of a thing) be to do with. **2** (of a person) take an interest in. ●*nc* **1** some-

thing that affects or is to do with someone or something; responsibility: *That's no concern of yours.* **2** a business. **3** *nu* worry: *a cause for concern.* **concerned** *adj* **1** that is being discussed: *The play concerned finishes next week.* **2** worried. **concerning** *prep* to do with.

concert ('kɒnsət) *nc* a musical entertainment. **concert hall** a hall in which concerts are given. **concert-master** *US* See **leader.** ●(kən'sɜ:t) *vt* arrange or do together with someone else: *a concerted effort.*

concerto (kən'tʃeətəʊ) *nc, pl* **-tos, -ti** (tɪ) a piece of music for a single instrument and an orchestra.

concession (kən'seʃən) **1** *nu* the act of conceding. **2** *nc* something conceded, such as the right to sell goods made by someone else.

conciliate (kən'sɪlɪeɪt) *vi* try to put a stop to an argument or disagreement between people. **conciliation** (kən,sɪlɪ'eɪʃən) *nu* **conciliatory** (kən'sɪljətrɪ) *adj*

concise (kən'saɪs) *adj* short but not missing anything out: *a concise dictionary.*

conclude (kən'klu:d) **1** *vti* finish. **2** *vt* (followed by **that**) decide; work out: *I conclude from what you said that you don't like me.* **conclusion** (kən'klu:ʒən) *nc* **1** the end. **2** an opinion reached after thinking about the facts. **3** *ncu* (a) settlement.

conclusive (kən'klu:sɪv) *adj* deciding; that proves something: *conclusive facts.*

concoct (kən'kɒkt) *vt* make up or invent (a dish, false story, etc.).

concord ('kɒnkɔ:d) *nu* agreement.

concourse ('kɒnkɔ:s) *nc* a large open space in a public building.

concrete ('kɒnkri:t) *nu* a mix of cement, stones, sand, and water used for building. ●*vt* cover with concrete. ●*adj* real; actually existing; definite.

concur (kən'kɜ:*) *formal vi* **1** happen together. **2** (often followed by **with**) agree. **concurrent** (kən'kʌrənt) *adj* **1** happening together. **2** in agreement.

concussion (kən'kʌʃən) *nu* injury to the brain caused by a blow to the head.

condemn (kən'dem) *vt* **1** say that one disapproves of. **2** (of a judge, etc.) sentence (to a punishment). **condemnation** (,kɒndem-'neɪʃən) *nu*

condensation (,kɒnden'seɪʃən) *nu* **1** the act of condensing or something that has been condensed. **2** water that has condensed on a surface such as a window.

condense (kən'dens) **1** *vti* make or become smaller. **2** *vt* cause (a gas) to become liquid. **3** *vi* (of a gas) become liquid.

condenser (kən'densə*) *nc* a device for condensing gases.

condescend (ˌkɒndɪˈsend) *vi* agree (to do something that one considers too ordinary for one). **condescension** (ˌkɒndɪˈsenʃən) *nu* behaving in this way.

condiment (ˈkɒndɪmənt) *nc* something added to food for its taste, esp. salt or pepper.

condition (kənˈdɪʃən) **1** *ncu* a state: *in good condition*. *nc* **2** something on which something else depends: *conditions of service*. **3** *(pl)* a state of affairs: *weather conditions*. ● *vt* act or cause to act so as to change (something). **on condition that** if, as a condition; providing. **conditional** (kənˈdɪʃənəl) *adj* depending (on something). ● *adj, n grammar* (a verb) expressing a condition: *the conditional form*.

condolence (kənˈdəʊləns) *nc* (often *pl*) an expression of sympathy.

condone (kənˈdəʊn) *vt* say that (an action) is not wrong: *I certainly don't condone crime.*

conducive (kənˈdjuːsɪv) *adj* (often followed by **to**) helpful; permitting: *Noise is not conducive to study.*

conduct (kənˈdʌkt) *vt* **1** lead or guide (a meeting, orchestra, sightseeing group, etc.). **2** manage: *He conducts his affairs well.* **3** allow (electricity, heat, etc.) to pass. ● (ˈkɒndʌkt) *nu* behaviour: *a prize for good conduct.* **conduction** *nu* **conductive** *adj* that can (easily) conduct (heat or electricity). **conductor** *nc* **1** a person who conducts an orchestra. **2** a person who takes the money for tickets on a bus, etc.

conduit (ˈkɒndɪt, ˈkɒndjʊɪt) *nc* a pipe carrying either a liquid or electric wires.

cone (kəʊn) *nc* **1** a solid shape having a circle at one end and a point at the other: see picture at **shapes**. **2** something shaped like a cone, such as the fruit of a pine tree.

confectionery (kənˈfekʃənrɪ) **1** *nu* sweets. **2** *nc, pl* **-ries** a shop selling sweets. **confectioner** *nc* a maker of sweets.

confederacy (kənˈfedərəsɪ) *nc, pl* **-cies 1** a union of nations or peoples formed into one political group. **2** a group of people formed to do something, esp. a crime. **confederate** (kənˈfedərət) *nc* a member of a confederacy. ● (kənˈfedəreɪt) *vti* form (into a confederacy). **confederation** (kənˌfedəˈreɪʃən) *nc* a confederacy, esp. of nations or peoples.

confer (kənˈfɜː) **1** *vi* discuss; talk. **2** *vt* (usually followed by **on**) give (an honour, prize, etc.): *to confer a university degree on a student.*

conference (ˈkɒnfərəns) *nc* a meeting at which something is discussed.

confess (kənˈfes) *vti* say that one did (something wrong): *I confess that I did it; He confessed to murder.* **confession** *ncu*

confetti (kənˈfetɪ) *n pl* tiny pieces of coloured paper thrown at a bride and bridegroom.

confidant (ˌkɒnfɪˈdænt) *nc* someone whom one chooses to trust and confide in.

confide (kənˈfaɪd) *vti* tell one's secrets (to someone).

confidence (ˈkɒnfɪdəns) **1** *nu* believing that one can do something well; trust in oneself, in someone, or in something. **2** *nc* a secret told to someone. **in confidence** as a secret. **confident** (ˈkɒnfɪdənt) *adj* believing in oneself, in someone, or in something. **confidential** (ˌkɒnfɪˈdenʃəl) *adj* to be kept secret. **confidently** *adv*

configuration (kənˌfɪgjʊˈreɪʃən) *nc* a shape or outline; how parts of something are arranged.

confine (kənˈfaɪn) *vt* **1** control. **2** keep in too small a place. **3** put in prison. **confinement** (kənˈfaɪnmənt) *ncu* **1** being put in prison; being controlled. **2** giving birth to a child. **confines** (ˈkɒnfaɪnz) *n pl* limits; borders; the most the mind can understand.

confirm (kənˈfɜːm) *vt* **1** make (an opinion, idea, feeling, etc.) more sure. **2** make (someone) a full member of a Christian Church. **confirmation** (ˌkɒnfəˈmeɪʃən) *ncu* **confirmed** (kənˈfɜːmd) *adj* not likely to change: *a confirmed bachelor.*

confiscate (ˈkɒnfɪskeɪt) *vt* take (something) away from someone as a punishment.

conflagration (ˌkɒnfləˈgreɪʃən) *nc* a very large fire.

conflict (ˈkɒnflɪkt) *nc* a quarrel or fight. ● (kənˈflɪkt) *vi* be in opposition.

conform (kənˈfɔːm) *vti* be in agreement with; do what other people say: *conform to the rules.* **conformity** (kənˈfɔːmɪtɪ) *nu*

confound (kənˈfaʊnd) *vt* **1** cause a little shame to. **2** confuse (and surprise).

confront (kənˈfrʌnt) *vt* face (something unpleasant); oppose. **confrontation** (ˌkɒnfrʌnˈteɪʃən) *ncu*

Confucianism (kənˈfjuːʃənɪzəm) *nu* the study of the teaching of Confucius, a great Chinese who died in 479 BC.

confuse (kənˈfjuːz) *vt* **1** mix up; not be able to tell the difference between. **2** make (someone) puzzled. **confusion** (kənˈfjuːʒən) *nu*

congeal (kənˈdʒiːl) *vti* change to a thick or solid state.

congenial (kənˈdʒiːnjəl) *adj* **1** having the same interests, etc., as someone else. **2** pleasant; that suits one: *congenial work.*

congenital (kənˈdʒenɪtəl) *adj* of a disease or defect existing from birth.

congestion (kənˈdʒestʃən) *nu* being too full: *traffic congestion.* **congested** (kənˈdʒestɪd) *adj* too full.

conglomerate (kən'glɒməreɪt) *vti* gather or collect together into a round mass. ●(kən'glɒmərət) *nc* a large company that consists of smaller companies making many different things. **conglomeration** (kən,glɒmə'reɪʃən) *ncu*

congratulate (kən'grætjʊleɪt) *vt* tell (someone) one is glad about his good news, etc. **congratulations** (kən'grætjʊ'leɪʃənz) *n pl* words that congratulate.

congregate ('kɒŋgrɪgeɪt) *vti* meet together. **congregation** ('kɒŋgrɪ'geɪʃən) a meeting of people, esp. for a church service. **Congregationalist** ('kɒŋgrɪ'geɪʃənəlɪst) *nc* a member of a Christian organisation which believes that each church should be responsible for its own affairs.

congress ('kɒŋgres) *nc* one or more special meetings to discuss important business. **Congress** a national body, esp. of the USA, that makes laws. **congressional** (kəŋ'greʃənəl) *adj* **congressman** *nc, pl* **-men, congresswoman** *nc, pl* **-women** a member of Congress.

congruent ('kɒŋgrʊənt) *adj* 1 agreeing with; suiting. 2 *geometry* having the same size and shape: *congruent triangles*.

conical ('kɒnɪkəl) *adj* having the shape of a cone.

coniferous (kəʊ'nɪfərəs) *adj* (of some trees) having fruit called cones.

conjecture (kən'dʒektʃə*) *formal nc* a guess. ●*vti* guess.

conjugal ('kɒndʒʊgəl) *formal adj* of marriage; of husband and wife: *conjugal love*.

conjugate ('kɒndʒʊgeɪt) *grammar vt* give the forms of a verb. **conjugation** ('kɒndʒʊ'geɪʃən) *ncu*

conjunction (kən'dʒʌŋkʃən) 1 *nc grammar* a word that joins other words, sentences, etc., together. 2 *nu* union. **in conjunction with** together with.

conjure ('kʌndʒə*) *vti* do a trick that looks like magic; make (something) appear. **conjurer** ('kʌndʒərə*) *nc* a person who performs such tricks.

connect (kə'nekt) *vti* join: *Please connect these wires together; I'm connected with the football club*. **connection** (kə'nekʃən) *nc* 1 a link: *an electrical connection*. 2 a train, bus, etc., that takes passengers on the next part of a journey. **in connection with** to do with; about.

connive (kə'naɪv) *vi* 1 work together secretly. 2 (followed by **at**) take no notice, when one should, of (what is wrong).

connoisseur ('kɒnə'sɜː*) *nc* a person who is a good judge in some matter of taste: *a connoisseur of painting*.

connotation ('kɒnəʊ'teɪʃən) *nc* an extra, second meaning suggested by a word.

conquer ('kɒŋkə*) *vt* defeat (an enemy, a country, or bad habits). **conqueror** *nc* **conquest** ('kɒŋkwest) *ncu* the act of conquering or something conquered.

conscience ('kɒnʃəns) *ncu* a feeling that tells one right from wrong.

conscientious ('kɒnʃɪ'enʃəs) *adj* careful to do nothing wrong or badly. **conscientiously** *adv* **conscientiousness** *nc*

conscious ('kɒnʃəs) *adj* awake; noticing: *She was not conscious after the accident.* **conscious of** aware of: *He is conscious of his mistakes.* **consciously** *adv* **consciousness** *nu*

conscript (kən'skrɪpt) *vt* force (someone) by law to join an army, navy, or air force. ●('kɒnskrɪpt) *nc* a person who is conscripted.

consecrate ('kɒnsɪkreɪt) *vt* give (something) completely to God. **consecration** ('kɒnsɪ'kreɪʃən) *nu*

consecutive (kən'sekjʊtɪv) *adj* following on: *One, two, three are consecutive numbers.*

consensus (kən'sensəs) *nc, pl* **-ses** agreement by most of the people.

consent (kən'sent) *vi* agree or allow. ●*nu* agreement.

consequence ('kɒnsɪkwəns) *nc* a result.

consequent ('kɒnsɪkwənt) *adj* following as a result of other causes. **consequently** *adv*

conservation ('kɒnsə'veɪʃən) *nu* the caring for and protection of old buildings, the countryside, wild life, etc.

conservative (kən'sɜːvətɪv) *adj* not liking change; having usual interests, tastes, etc.; cautious.

conservatory (kən'sɜːvətrɪ) *nc, pl* **-ries** a building made of glass for delicate plants to grow in.

conserve (kən'sɜːv) *vt* keep or save from harm.

consider (kən'sɪdə*) *vt* 1 think over carefully. 2 show thought for: *consider people's feelings*. 3 give an opinion: *He's considered a great writer; I consider her a fool.*

considerable (kən'sɪdərəbəl) *adj* very great. **considerably** *adv*

considerate (kən'sɪdərət) *adj* caring about people. **consideration** (kən'sɪdə'reɪʃən) 1 *nu* thinking about; caring. 2 *nc* something that must be thought about as a possible reason.

considering (kən'sɪdərɪŋ) *prep* in spite of: *He is very active considering his age.*

consign (kən'saɪn) *vt* send (goods, etc.). **consignment** *nc*

consist (kən'sɪst) *vi* 1 (followed by **of**) be made of: *The team consists of six people; Water consists of hydrogen and oxygen.* 2 (followed by **in**) have as the only or most important thing.

consistency (kən'sɪstənsɪ) *nu* 1 the degree of thickness of a liquid, etc. 2 agreement or harmony. **consistent with** in agreement with. **consistently** *adv*

console¹ (kən'səʊl) *vt* comfort. **consolation** ('kɒnsə'leɪʃən) *nc*

console² ('kɒnsəʊl) *nc* 1 a piece of wood or metal that supports a shelf. 2 a board for the controls of a plane, car, etc.: see picture. 3 the container of a television set that stands on the floor.

console

consolidate (kən'sɒlɪdeɪt) *vti* 1 make or become stronger. 2 (esp. of companies), (cause to) combine into one. **consolidation** (kən'sɒlɪ'deɪʃən) *ncu*

consonant ('kɒnsənənt) *nc* 1 a speech sound produced by partly stopping the flow of air through the mouth. 2 a letter of the alphabet such as *b*, *d*, or *f*.

consort ('kɒnsɔːt) *nc* the wife or husband of a ruler.

conspicuous (kən'spɪkjʊəs) *adj* easily seen.

conspiracy (kən'spɪrəsɪ) *nc*, *pl* **-cies** a secret plan. **conspirator** (kən'spɪrətə) *nc* a person who makes a secret plan.

conspire (kən'spaɪə*) *vti* make secret plans.

constable ('kʌnstəbəl) *nc* a policeman.

constant ('kɒnstənt) *adj* 1 never changing. 2 loyal; faithful. **constantly** *adv*

constellation ('kɒnstə'leɪʃən) *nc* a group of stars.

consternation ('kɒnstə'neɪʃən) *nu* a feeling of fear and worry.

constipation ('kɒnstɪ'peɪʃən) *nu* difficulty in emptying the body of waste.

constituency (kən'stɪtjʊənsɪ) *nc*, *pl* **-cies** the voters in a town, etc., who choose their own Member of Parliament; the town itself.

constituent (kən'stɪtjʊənt) *nc* 1 a part of something. 2 a voter in a constituency. ● *adj* making up a whole: *the constituent parts of a mixture.*

constitute ('kɒnstɪtjuːt) *formal vt* be a part or the whole of.

constitution ('kɒnstɪ'tjuːʃən) *nc* 1 the health of one's body: *a strong constitution.* 2 the laws of a government. **constitutional** ('kɒnstɪ'tjuːʃənəl) *adj* of the laws, etc., of a government. ● *nc formal* a short frequent walk to keep healthy.

constrain (kən'streɪn) *vt* force (a person) to do something; make (oneself) do something by the force of one's own feelings.

constraint (kən'streɪnt) *nu*

constrict (kən'strɪkt) *vt* press into too small a space. **constriction** *nc*

construct (kən'strʌkt) *vt* build. **construction** (kən'strʌkʃən) *nc* 1 a building. 2 the way words are arranged in a sentence. 3 the meaning of what is said or done. **constructive** *adj* useful and helpful.

construe (kən'struː) *vt* 1 explain the meaning of (words or actions). 2 *grammar* study (the parts of a sentence).

consul ('kɒnsəl) *nc* a member of government living abroad to help his own people there. **consulate** ('kɒnsjʊlət) *nc* the consul's offices.

consult (kən'sʌlt) *vt* get help or information from (a person, book, etc.). **consultant** (kən'sʌltənt) *nc* an expert who gives advice. **consultation** ('kɒnsəl'teɪʃən) *ncu*

consume (kən'sjuːm) *formal vt* 1 eat or drink. 2 destroy: *consumed by fire.* **consuming** *adj* having no control over one's feelings: *consuming anger.*

consumer (kən'sjuːmə*) *nc* a person who buys and uses goods.

consummate ('kɒnsəmeɪt) *vt* make perfect or complete (esp. a marriage) by bodily union. **consummation** ('kɒnsə'meɪʃən) *nc*

consumption (kən'sʌmpʃən) 1 *nc* using up; eating. 2 *nu* a disease of the lungs.

contact ('kɒntækt) 1 *nu* touch: *The wires are in contact with each other.* 2 *nc* a person who one knows in a professional way: *business contacts.* **contact lens** a very small thin lens, usually of plastic, that is placed over the eye to improve vision. ● *vt* get in touch with.

contagious (kən'teɪdʒəs) *adj* (of an illness) likely to be spread by contact (or touch).

contain (kən'teɪn) *vt* 1 have or hold: *This jug contains one litre of water; His report contains some new facts.* 2 control (one's feelings): *Contain your laughter.*

container (kən'teɪnə*) *nc* 1 a box, cup, bucket, etc., made to hold things inside. 2 a large metal box for transporting goods.

contaminate (kən'tæmɪneɪt) *vt* spoil; make unfit for use. **contamination** (kən'tæmɪ'neɪʃən) *nu*

contemplate ('kɒntempleɪt) 1 *vt* (look at and) think about. 2 *vi* think what one might do. **contemplation** ('kɒntem'pleɪʃən) *nu* **contemplative** ('kɒntempleɪtɪv) *adj*

contemporary (kən'temprərɪ) *adj* 1 belonging to the same period of time. 2 modern. ● *nc*, *pl* **-ries** a person of the same age.

contempt (kən'tempt) *nu* a lack of respect (for someone or something). **contemptible** (kən'temptəbəl) *adj* **contemptuous** (kən'temptjʊəs) *adj*

contend (kən'tend) *vi* 1 take part in a race, contest, etc. 2 quarrel or fight. 3 *vt* argue about (something). **contender** *nc*

content¹ (kən'tent) *adj* pleased; happy. **contented** *adj* satisfied. **contentedly** *adv* **contentment** *nu*

content² ('kɒntent) *nc* 1 the amount a container can hold. 2 *(pl)* that which is inside a book, room, pocket, etc.

contention (kən'tenʃən) 1 *nu* quarrelling. 2 *nc* an argument.

contest ('kɒntest) *nc* a race, match, fight, competition, etc. ●(kən'test) *vti* 1 compete. 2 argue (about something). **contestant** (kən'testənt) *nc* a person who fights, competes, etc.

context ('kɒntekst) *ncu* the words before and after a sentence, etc., that help show its meaning.

continent ('kɒntɪnənt) *nc* one of the main large pieces of land in the world. **the Continent** the mainland of Europe. **continental** ('kɒntɪ'nentəl) *adj*

contingency (kən'tɪndʒənsɪ) *nc, pl* **-cies** something that may happen. **contingent** *adj* 1 not certain. 2 (followed by **upon**) that may happen if something else happens first. ●*nc* part of a group of people.

continual (kən'tɪnjʊəl) *adj* seeming never to stop and occurring regularly. **continually** *adv*

continue (kən'tɪnjuː) *vti* keep doing or being; go on speaking, doing, etc., after stopping. **continuation** (kən'tɪnjʊ'eɪʃən) *nu*

continuity ('kɒntɪ'njuːətɪ) *nu* a state of going on and on without a break.

continuous (kən'tɪnjʊəs) *adj* going on for a long time without stopping: *continuous rain*. **continuously** *adv*

contortion (kən'tɔːʃən) *nc* twisting out of its normal shape: *bodily contortions*.

contour ('kɒn'tʊə*) *nc* a line showing the shape or height of something, esp. on a map: see picture.

contour

contraband ('kɒntrəbænd) *nu* goods taken secretly in or out of a country against the law.

contraception ('kɒntrə'sepʃən) *nu* the way to control and esp. stop birth. **contraceptive** *nc, adj* (drug) used in contraception.

contract ('kɒntrækt) *nc* a business agreement. ●(kən'trækt) *vt* 1 make (a business agreement). 2 get (an illness). 3 *vi* get smaller or shorter.

contraction (kən'trækʃən) 1 *nu* getting smaller or shorter. 2 *nc* a short form of a word: *'It's' is a contraction of 'it is'*.

contractor (kən'træktə*) *nc* a person or business that agrees to do work or provide goods.

contradict ('kɒntrə'dɪkt) *vt* 1 say that (something) is not true. 2 say that (someone) is wrong. **contradiction** *nc* **contradictory** ('kɒntrə'dɪktrɪ) *adj*

contraption (kən'træpʃən) *nc* a machine that looks strange.

contrary ('kɒntrərɪ) *adj* opposite: *contrary to the facts*. **on the contrary** (used to oppose what has just been said.)

contrast ('kɒntrɑːst) 1 *nu* putting together different objects to show their differences. 2 *nc* a difference between such objects. ●(kən'trɑːst) *vti* 1 compare so that differences are clear. 2 show differences.

contravene ('kɒntrə'viːn) *vt* go against (the law). **contravention** ('kɒntrə'venʃən) *nc*

contribute (kən'trɪbjuːt) *vt* join with others to buy or give (something). **contribution** ('kɒntrɪ'bjuːʃən) *ncu* **contributor** (kən'trɪbjʊtə*) *nc* a person who contributes.

contrite ('kɒntraɪt) *adj* showing sorrow and guilt. **contrition** (kən'trɪʃən) *nu*

contrive (kən'traɪv) *vti* find a way of doing (something).

control (kən'trəʊl) 1 *nu* power or direction: *The driver has control of the train*. 2 *nc* a way of regulating or directing something. 3 *(pl)* switches for making a machine, car, etc., work. ●*vt* have power over. **controller** *nc* a person who controls something, for example how money is to be spent. **under** or **out of control** able or not able to be kept in order.

controversy ('kɒntrə'vɜːsɪ, kən'trɒvɜːsɪ) *pl* **-sies** an argument, usually on public matters. **controversial** ('kɒntrə'vɜːʃəl) *adj*

convalesce ('kɒnvə'les) *vi* get better after an illness. **convalescence** *nu* **convalescent** *nc* a person getting better after an illness.

convection (kən'vekʃən) *nu* carrying heat by the movement of heated water, air, etc.

convene (kən'viːn) *vti* send for (people) to come, or get together for, (a meeting).

convenience (kən'viːnjəns) *nu* being right or suitable; usefulness. **convenient** *adj* **public convenience** a lavatory. **conveniently** *adv*

convent ('kɒnvənt) *nc* a house in which nuns live.

convention (kən'venʃən) *nc* 1 a number of meetings to discuss one thing, esp. politics.

2 usual behaviour or custom. **conventional** *adj* usual.

converge (kən'vɜːdʒ) *vi* meet at a point, or at the same place. **convergent** (kən'vɜːdʒənt) *adj*

conversant (kən'vɜːsənt) *adj* (followed by **with**) knowing the facts, or a person, well.

conversation ('kɒnvə'seɪʃən) 1 *nu* speaking. 2 *nc* a talk: *conversations with friends*. **conversational** *adj*

converse[1] (kən'vɜːs) *formal vi* talk.

converse[2] ('kɒnvɜːs) *adj* opposite. ●*nu* an opposite statement. **conversely** *adv*

conversion (kən'vɜːʃən) 1 *nu* change from one form, way, use, etc., into another. 2 *nc* a change of faith, opinion, etc.

convert (kən'vɜːt) 1 *vti* change (from one form, way, use, etc., into another). 2 *vt* get (a person) to change his opinion, faith, etc. ●('kɒnvɜːt) *nc* a person who changes, esp. to a different religion.

convertible (kən'vɜːtəbəl) *adj* able to be changed. ●*nc* a car with a roof that can be folded or removed.

convex ('kɒn'veks) *adj* having a side that curves out.

convey (kən'veɪ) *vt* 1 carry. 2 give: *Convey my thanks to her*. **conveyor belt** (in a factory) a belt for carrying goods, etc.: see picture. **conveyance** *nc* a cart, car, etc., for carrying goods or people.

conveyor belt

convict (kən'vɪkt) *vt* prove in a law court that (a person) is guilty. ●('kɒnvɪkt) *nc* a convicted person.

conviction (kən'vɪkʃən) 1 *nu* proving of guilt. 2 *nc* a firm belief in an idea, etc.

convince (kən'vɪns) *vt* make (a person) believe something: *I convinced him of the truth; She convinced me she was right*.

convivial (kən'vɪvɪəl) *adj* merry; enjoying fun with other people.

convocation ('kɒnvəʊ'keɪʃən) *nu* calling together of people to a meeting.

convoy ('kɒnvɔɪ) *vt* (of ships) go with (other ships), esp. in times of war. ●*nc* 1 the ships protecting other ships. 2 the ships being protected.

convulse (kən'vʌls) *vt* make (the body) shake violently: *convulsed with laughter*. **convulsion** *nc* **convulsive** *adj*

coo (kuː) *vi* make a soft sound like a dove or a pigeon. ●*nc* such a noise.

cook (kʊk) *vti* make (food) ready to eat by heating it: *She cooked the meal; These vegetables cook well*. ●*nc* a person who cooks. **cookery** ('kʊkərɪ) *nu* cooking with skill and ability. **cookbook** *nc* a book on how and what to cook. **cooker** *nc* an apparatus for cooking; stove.

cookie ('kʊkɪ) *US nc* a biscuit.

cool (kuːl) *adj* 1 between warm and cold. 2 (of a person) calm; not very friendly. ●*vti* (cause to) become cool. **coolly** *adv* **coolness** *nu*

coop (kuːp) *nc* a cage for hens. **coop up** shut into a small space.

co-operate (kəʊ'ɒpəreɪt) *vi* work together for the same aim. **co-operation** (kəʊˌɒpə'reɪʃən) *nu* **co-operative** *adj* willing to help.

co-ordinate (kəʊ'ɔːdɪneɪt) *vt* 1 make (things or people) work together well or be equally important. 2 bring together (things or people) to increase efficiency. **co-ordination** (kəʊˌɔːdɪ'neɪʃən) *nu* **co-ordinator** *nc* a person who co-ordinates.

cop (kɒp) *slang nc* short for **copper** (def. 4).

cope (kəʊp) *vi* (followed by **with**) deal with (a person, work, difficulty, etc.).

co-pilot ('kəʊpaɪlət) *nc* a second man at the controls in a plane.

coping ('kəʊpɪŋ) *nu* the top line of brick or stone in a wall.

copious ('kəʊpjəs) *adj* more than enough.

copper ('kɒpə*) 1 *nu* red metal: symbol Cu *nc* 2 a coin made of copper. 3 an iron pot for boiling clothes. 4 *slang* a policeman.

copra ('kɒprə) *nu* the dried insides of a coconut.

copse (kɒps) *nc* a small wood with small trees and bushes.

copulation ('kɒpjʊ'leɪʃən) *nc* the union by which a male and female produce children.

copy ('kɒpɪ) *nc, pl* **-pies** 1 something made to be or look like something else: *Please make a copy of this letter*. 2 (of a book, etc.) one example: *They published thousands of copies of the newspaper*. ●*vt* make a copy of; reproduce. **copyright** ('kɒpɪraɪt) *law nu* the right given to a writer of books, music, etc., to be the only producer of the work.

coral ('kɒrəl) *nu* hard red, white, or pink matter produced by small sea animals: see picture.

coral

cord (kɔːd) *nc* **1** a piece of thick string. **2** a part of the body like a cord: *spinal cord*.

cordial ('kɔːdjəl) *adj* polite and kind. ●*nc* a sweet fruit drink.

cordon ('kɔːdən) *adj* a line of police to stop people entering a place. **cordon off** block off (a place).

corduroy ('kɔːdərɔɪ) *nu* a thick cotton cloth with raised lines.

core (kɔː*) *nc* **1** the heart or centre of anything. **2** the part of an apple, etc., with the seeds.

cork (kɔːk) **1** *nu* a light, tough substance from the outer covering of an oak tree. **2** *nc* a piece of this used to close the hole in a bottle. **corkscrew** ('kɔːkskruː) *nc* a steel tool for pulling out corks.

cormorant ('kɔːmərənt) *nc* a large, black, greedy sea-bird.

corn[1] (kɔːn) *nu* **1** *Brit* any of various cereal plants, esp. wheat. **2** *US* also *Brit* **maize** a kind of tall cereal plant grown for its ears of yellow seeds. **corn cob** the hard centre of an ear of **corn**[1] (def. 2): see picture. **cornfield** *nc* a field in which corn is growing.

corn cob

corn[2] *nc* a hard piece of skin, esp. on a toe, that causes pain.

cornea ('kɔːnɪə) *nc* the outer part of the eye that lets light through and covers the iris: see picture.

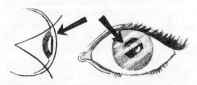

cornea

corner ('kɔːnə*) *nc* **1** a place where two sides or edges meet at an angle, esp. two streets: *a street corner*. **2** a hard place to get out of. ●*vt* stop (someone) from doing something. **cornerstone** ('kɔːnəstəʊn) *nc* a stone, laid at a public event, forming the corner of a building; something on which other things depend.

cornet ('kɔːnɪt) *nc* **1** a small brass musical instrument that is blown: see picture at **musical instruments**. **2** a container shaped like a cone filled with ice cream.

cornflour ('kɔːnflaʊə*) *nu* flour made from maize.

cornflower ('kɔːnflaʊə*) *nc* a plant with blue flowers that grows wild in cornfields.

cornice ('kɔːnɪs) *nc* a strip of decoration, esp. along the top of the wall of a room.

corollary (kə'rɒlərɪ) *nc, pl* **-ries 1** something that needs no proof because it comes from something else that has been proved. **2** the expected result.

corona (kə'rəʊnə) *nc, pl* **-s, -nae** (niː) a circle of white light seen round the sun or moon.

coronary ('kɒrənərɪ) *adj* of the blood-vessels that supply blood to the heart.

coronation ('kɒrə'neɪʃən) *nc* the crowning of a king or queen.

coroner ('kɒrənə*) *nc* a person who finds out the reasons for a violent or unnatural death.

coronet ('kɒrənɪt) *nc* a small crown.

corporal[1] ('kɔːpərəl) *adj* of the body: *corporal punishment*.

corporal[2] *nc* an ordinary soldier.

corporate ('kɔːpərət) *adj* of a group of people, esp. council members elected to govern a town.

corporation ('kɔːpə'reɪʃən) *nc* a group of people acting together, esp. council members or business men.

corps (kɔː*) *n pl* a large organised group of people: *the army corps*.

corpse (kɔːps) *nc* a dead body.

corpuscle ('kɔːpʌsəl) *nc* a red or white cell in the blood.

corral (kɒ'rɑːl) *chiefly US nc* small piece of land with a fence all round, for cattle and horses.

correct (kə'rekt) *adj* **1** right; true: *a correct answer*. **2** proper: *correct behaviour*. ●*vt* **1** make or put right, esp. by showing mistakes. **2** alter: *Correct your course*. **correction** (kə'rekʃən) **1** *nu* making right. **2** *nc* a mistake made right. **corrective** (kə'rektɪv) *adj* making right what was wrong: *corrective training*. ●*nc* something that corrects. **correctly** *adv*

correlate ('kɒrəleɪt) **1** *vi* (followed by **with**) have things in common with. **2** *vt* establish a relationship between. **correlation** ('kɒrə'leɪʃən) *nc*

correspond ('kɒrɪ'spɒnd) *vi* **1** (followed by **with** or **to**) be in agreement with. **2** (followed by **to**) be equal to. **3** (followed by **with**) send and receive letters. **corresponding** ('kɒrɪ'spɒndɪŋ) *adj* same; very like. **correspondingly** *adv*

correspondence ('kɒrɪ'spɒndəns) *ncu* **1** being the same; agreement. **2** writing of letters; set of letters about a particular matter or between certain people: *He kept his correspondence with the bank.* **correspon-**

dent (ˈkɒrɪˈspɒndənt) *nc* **1** a person who writes and receives letters. **2** a person whose job is to get news for a newspaper.

corridor (ˈkɒrɪdɔ:*) *nc* a long narrow passage from which doors open off into rooms.

corroborate (kəˈrɒbəreɪt) *vt* add more proof that (an opinion, etc.) is right.

corrode (kəˈrəʊd) *vti* slowly destroy or be worn away, esp. by chemical action. **corrosion** (kəˈrəʊʒən) *nu*

corrugated (ˈkɒrəgeɪtɪd) *adj* bent into small waves or wrinkles to make stronger: *corrugated iron.*

corrupt (kəˈrʌpt) *adj* (of a person or his behaviour) evil; dishonest. ● *vt* make (someone or something good) go bad: *Pollution corrupts the air we breathe.* **corruption** (kəˈrʌpʃən) *nu*

corset (ˈkɔ:sɪt) *nc* a stiff garment, worn next to the skin round the waist and hips, to improve the shape.

cosmetics (kɒzˈmetɪks) *n pl* creams, powders, etc., used to make the skin and hair beautiful. **cosmetic** (kɒzˈmetɪk) *derogatory adj* changing only the appearance of something.

cosmic (ˈkɒzmɪk) *adj* of stars, planets, and space.

cosmonaut (ˈkɒzmənɔ:t) *nc* a person, esp. a Russian, who travels in a spacecraft.

cosmopolitan (ˌkɒzməˈpɒlɪtən) *adj* **1** of all parts of the world. **2** having wide experience.

cosmos (ˈkɒzmɒs) *nu* the system of all stars and space: see picture.

cosmos

cost (kɒst) *ncu* the amount of money for which something is bought or sold. ● *vt* have as a price: *It costs too much money; This mistake will cost you your job.* **cost of living** money needed to live at a generally accepted level. **at all costs** no matter what happens. **costly** (ˈkɒstlɪ) *adj* **-ier, -iest**

costume (ˈkɒstju:m) **1** *nu* a fashion in dress, esp. of a nation, or of a time: *national costume; period costume.* **2** *nc* clothes for a special purpose: *swimming costume.*

cosy (ˈkəʊzɪ) *adj* **-ier, -iest** warm and comfortable.

cot (kɒt) *nc* a small bed with high sides for a child.

cottage (ˈkɒtɪdʒ) *nc* a small house, esp. in the country.

cotton (ˈkɒtən) *nu* white soft covering of the cotton plant's seeds, used for making cloth; (sometimes *nc*) cloth and thread made from cotton. **cotton wool** *nu* unspun cotton, used esp. for cleaning and protecting wounds.

couch (kaʊtʃ) *nc* **1** a long, comfortable seat for two or more people **2** a bed on which one lies to be examined by a doctor.

cough (kɒf) *vi* make a sharp, violent noise in the throat when pushing air out of the lungs. ● *nc* the sound or act of coughing.

could (kʊd unstressed kəd) past tense of **can²**. **1** used to be able to: *I could do that when I was a child.* **2** (in a question) would: *Could you help me, please?* **3** (to say that something might be possible) were able to: *I would help you if I could.* **4** might: *This could be our chance to escape.*

couldn't (ˈkʊdənt) *v* could not.

council (ˈkaʊnsəl) *nc* a group of people elected to advise, make rules, etc. **councillor** (ˈkaʊnsələ*) *nc*

counsel (ˈkaʊnsəl) *vt* give advice. **counsellor** (ˈkaʊnsələ*) *nc*

count (kaʊnt) **1** *vi* say numbers in order. *vt* **2** add up (numbers, etc.). **3** include. **4** consider. ● *nc* **1** total. **2** a nobleman. **count in** *infml* include. **count on** depend on. **count up** add up. **countdown** (ˈkaʊntdaʊn) *ncu* the (counting of the) amount of time left before a rocket takes off.

countenance (ˈkaʊntənəns) *nc* a face; the look on one's face. ● *vt* accept.

counter¹ (ˈkaʊntə*) *nc* **1** the table in a shop or bank over which goods or money are passed. **2** a small disc used in games.

counter² *adv* **counter to** opposite; against: *counter to my wishes.* ● *vt* **1** oppose; set oneself against. **2** *vi* act after one has been attacked.

counteract (ˌkaʊntəˈrækt) *vt* make of no use by an opposite action.

counterbalance (ˈkaʊntəˌbæləns) *nc* something, esp. a weight, equal to another and balancing it. ●(ˈkaʊntəˌbæləns) *vt* act against and so make less important.

counterclockwise (ˈkaʊntəˈklɒkwaɪz) *US adj, adj* See **anti-clockwise**.

counterfeit (ˈkaʊntəfɪt) *adj* made to copy something else, for a wrong purpose: *counterfeit money.* ● *nc* a copy, usually worthless. ● *vt* copy, for a wrong purpose.

counterfoil (ˈkaʊntəfɔɪl) *nc* a part of a cheque or bill, showing that money has been paid.

counterpart (ˈkaʊntəpɑ:t) *nc* a person or thing exactly like another, or together making a whole.

countersign ('kaʊntəsaɪn) *vt* add one's name on (a paper, etc.) that has already been signed. ●*nc* word or sign needed to get past a guard.

counter-tenor ('kaʊntə'tenə*) *n* See **alto** (def. 2).

countess ('kaʊntɪs) *nc* the wife of a nobleman; noble lady as important as a count.

countless ('kaʊntlɪs) *adj* too many to count.

country ('kʌntrɪ) *nc, pl* **-ries 1** the land of a nation; land where one was born. *nu* **2** land outside towns and cities, esp. used for farming. **3** large area of land: *the North Country.* **4** people of a nation. **countryman** ('kʌntrɪmən) *nc, pl* **-men** a person who is from the same country; person who lives in the **country** (def. 2). **countryside** ('kʌntrɪ saɪd) *nu* the land outside towns.

county ('kaʊntɪ) *nc, pl* **-ties** one of the parts, each under local government, into which a state or country, esp. Britain, is divided.

coup (kuː) *French nc, pl* **-s** (z) a sudden and successful action.

couple ('kʌpəl) *nc* two things or persons, esp. a man and a woman: *They are a happy couple; Wait a couple of minutes.* ●*vt* **1** fasten together. **2** *vi* marry; unite.

couplet ('kʌplɪt) *nc* two lines together in a poem that end in the same sound.

coupling ('kʌplɪŋ) **1** *ncu* (an example of) joining. **2** *nc* a chain that joins two things, esp. railway carriages: see picture.

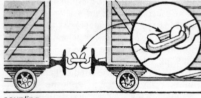

coupling

coupon ('kuːpɒn) *nc* a paper ticket, etc., showing that one has a right to something.

courage ('kʌrɪdʒ) *nu* the ability to be brave. **courageous** (kə'reɪdʒəs) *adj* brave.

courier ('kʊrɪə*) *nc* **1** a person who is paid to help tourists and take them sightseeing. **2** a messenger.

course (kɔːs) **1** *nu* going forward; passing: *the course of events.* *nc* **2** a direction: *the ship's course.* **3** a ground on which a race is run or a game played. **4** a part of a meal: *Soup is the first course.* **5** a series of things coming one after the other: *a course of talks on politics.* **of course** yes; naturally: *Of course we can help you.* **in due course** at the proper time. **in the course of** during.

court (kɔːt) *nc* **1** the judges, etc., who have come together to deal with law cases. **2** short for **courthouse** or **courtroom**. **3** a

courtyard

ground marked out for a game: *tennis court.* *nu* **4** the chief home of a king or queen; all the people attending the king or queen. **5** a name of a building or street: *The address is 5, Westbury Court.* ●*vt* (about a man) try to win the love of (a woman) in order to marry her. **courthouse** *nc* the building in which judges, etc., sit. **courtroom** *nc* the main room in the courthouse. **courtyard** *nc* an open space with walls or buildings on all sides: see picture.

courteous ('kɜːtjəs) *adj* polite. **courteously** ('kɜːtjəslɪ) *adv*

courtesy ('kɜːtəsɪ) *ncu* (an act of) polite behaviour.

courtier ('kɔːtɪə*) *nc* a person who attends at a royal court.

courtly ('kɔːtlɪ) *adj* very polite; respectful.

courtmartial ('kɔːt'mɑːʃəl) *nc, pl* **courtsmartial** a law court held by armed forces for crimes against their law.

courtship ('kɔːtʃɪp) *nc* (about a man) trying to win a woman's love in order to marry her.

cousin ('kʌzən) *nc* the child of one's uncle or aunt

cove (kəʊv) *nc* a place where the coast bends in towards the land and out again; bay.

covenant ('kʌvənənt) *nc* a serious promise; legal agreement.

cover ('kʌvə*) *vt* **1** lay something over (something else): *Cover the bed with a blanket.* **2** lie on top of: *Leaves covered the ground.* **3** travel: *We covered many miles.* **4** deal with; include: *His lecture covered all our questions.* **5** report. **6** watch over; protect: *Cover my escape.* ●*nu* **1** shelter: *Get under cover from the rain.* *nc* **2** thing that covers. **3** the outside of a book. **coverage** ('kʌvərɪdʒ) *nu* reporting of events for television, for a newspaper, etc. **covering** ('kʌvərɪŋ) *nc* something that covers: *a covering of snow.* **coverlet** ('kʌvəlɪt) *nc* the top cover on a bed. **cover up** hide. **take cover** run and hide.

covert ('kʌvət) *adj* secret; sly: *a covert look from the corner of her eye.*

covet ('kʌvɪt) *vt* want (something, esp. belonging to someone else) very much.

cow (kaʊ) *nc* the female of the cattle family;

the female of some other animals. ● *vt* make afraid by threats. **cowboy** ('kaʊbɔɪ) *US nc* man in charge of cattle. **cowhand** ('kaʊhænd) *nc* man who looks after cattle in the fields. **cowhide** ('kaʊhaɪd) *nu* leather made from a cow's skin.

coward ('kaʊəd) *nc* a person who is not brave. **cowardice** ('kaʊədɪs) *nu* **cowardly** *adv* not brave.

cower ('kaʊə*) *vi* bend one's body away from something frightening.

cowl (kaʊl) *nc* a monk's garment with a hood; the hood itself.

cowslip ('kaʊslɪp) *nc* a small yellow flower that grows in fields: see picture at **flowers**.

coxswain ('kɒksən) (*infml abbrev.* **cox**) *nc* a person in charge of a small boat.

coy (kɔɪ) *adj* **-er, -est** modest and shy; pretending to be shy.

coyote ('kɔɪəʊt) *nc* a wolf that lives in the grasslands of N America.

crab (kræb) *nc* a sea creature with a hard shell and ten legs.

crack (kræk) *nc* **1** the line or place at which something has been broken. **2** a sharp blow: *a crack on the head*. **3** a sudden sharp noise: *the crack of a whip*. ● *vti* **1** (cause to) make a sharp noise. **2** (cause to) partly break: *He cracked his skull*. **crack down on** *infml* take action against. **crack up** *infml* get an illness of the mind; become weak and ill, esp. in old age. **cracker** ('krækə*) *nc* **1** a thin, dry biscuit. **2** a kind of firework. **3 Christmas cracker** a paper toy that explodes harmlessly when the ends are pulled.

crackle ('krækəl) *vi* make small cracking noises, one after another.

cradle ('kreɪdəl) *nc* a small bed that rocks, for a baby. ● *vt* hold closely.

craft (krɑːft) **1** *nu* being cunning. **2** *nc* a job or skill, esp. one that needs cleverness with the hands. **3** *nc, pl* **craft** a boat or plane. **craftsman** ('krɑːftsmən) *nc, pl* **-men** one who has a craft (def. 2). **craftsmanship** ('krɑːftsmənʃɪp) *nu* **crafty** ('krɑːftɪ) *adj* **-ier, -iest** cunning.

crag (kræg) *nc* a high, sharp rock. **craggy** ('krægɪ) *adj* **-ier, -iest** rough; not regular.

cram (kræm) *vt* **1** fill too full. **2** push (something) too much into (too small a place): *Don't cram your mouth with food*. **3** *vti* (help someone to) fill the mind with facts just before an examination.

cramp[1] (kræmp) *ncu* (an attack of) sudden pain caused by the muscles getting tight.

cramp[2] *nc* also **cramp-iron** (in building) a metal bar with bent ends used for holding together stone, wood, etc. ● *vt* stop (something) from moving or growing.

cranberry ('krænbərɪ) *nc, pl* **-ries** a red

berry, sharp in taste, that grows on a bush.

crane (kreɪn) *nc* **1** a bird with long legs and neck that stands in water. **2** a machine with a long arm for lifting heavy weights.

cranium ('kreɪnɪəm) *nc, pl* **-nia** the bones of the head that protect the brain.

crank (kræŋk) *nc* **1** a device for changing movement up and down into circular movement; a bent handle for this purpose. **2** *infml* a person with unusual ideas and habits. **crankshaft** ('kræŋkʃɑːft) *nc* a thick metal bar turned by a car or train engine which passes power to the wheels.

cranny ('krænɪ) *nc, pl* **-nies** a narrow opening, esp. in a wall.

crash (kræʃ) *nc* **1** a loud noise caused by something breaking or falling. **2** an accident caused by a car, train, plane, etc. **3** a business failure: *the Wall Street crash*. ● *vi* **1** fall or go violently and noisily into something. **2** cause (a car, etc.) to crash. **crash helmet** a strong hat worn by a driver for protection. **crash landing** the dangerous landing of a plane that is damaged or out of control.

crass (kræs) *adj* stupid; total: *crass stupidity*.

crate (kreɪt) *nc* a large box, made of boards that do not fit closely, for carrying goods.

crater ('kreɪtə*) *nc* an opening in a volcano that sends out fire and ashes: see picture.

crater

cravat (krə'væt) *nc* a piece of cloth worn round the neck.

crave (kreɪv) *v* **crave for** want (something) very much; long for. **craving** ('kreɪvɪŋ) *nc*

crawl (krɔːl) *vi* **1** move slowly on the hands and knees. **2** go or walk slowly: *The traffic crawled along*. **3** *infml* be agreeable to someone just to get something from him. **4** be covered with insects. ● *nu* **1** a slow movement. **2** a way of swimming.

crayfish ('kreɪfɪʃ) *nc, pl* **crayfishes, crayfish** also **crawfish** ('krɔːfɪʃ) an animal with a shell and ten legs that lives in fresh water.

crayon ('kreɪɒn, 'kreɪən) *nc* a stick or pencil of coloured wax or chalk for drawing. ● *vt* draw with a crayon.

craze (kreɪz) *nc* something that interests many people greatly for a short time. ● *vt* make mad or excited. **crazy** ('kreɪzɪ) *adj* **-ier, -iest 1** mad. **2** *infml* fond of; very interested in: *She's crazy about him*. **crazily** ('kreɪzɪlɪ) *adv*

creak (kriːk) *nc* a short, high noise: *the creak*

of a door. ● *vi* make a creak.

cream (kriːm) *nu* 1 the fatty part of milk that rises to the top. 2 the best part of anything. 3 *nc* a soft fat that is used as a cosmetic, a polish, etc.: *face cream; shoe cream.* 4 *nu* a pale yellow or white colour. ● *adj* pale yellow or white. ● *vt* make (something) creamy or add cream to (something). **cream off** take away the best part of (something) esp. for one's own use. **creamy** *adj*

crease (kriːs) *nc* 1 a line made by folding. 2 (in cricket) a white line showing where certain players should be. ● *vt* make a line by folding or crushing.

create (kriːˈeɪt) *vt* 1 bring into being; make: *God created the world.* 2 appoint (someone) to a certain position. **creation** (kriːˈeɪʃən) *nu* the making of something, esp. the world; all things that exist: *the Creation.*

creative (kriːˈeɪtɪv) *adj* full of new ideas; artistic.

creator (kriːˈeɪtə*) *nc* someone who creates. **the Creator** God.

creature (ˈkriːtʃə*) *nc* any human being or animal.

crèche (kreɪʃ, kreʃ) *nc* a place where mothers may leave their babies during the day.

credentials (krɪˈdenʃəlz) *n pl* letters saying that one can be trusted, esp. when applying for a job.

credible (ˈkredəbəl) *adj* that can be believed: *a credible story.* **credibility** (ˈkredəˈbɪlɪtɪ) *nu* ability to be believed or trusted.

credit (ˈkredɪt) *nu* 1 trust, esp. in someone's promise that he will pay what he owes. 2 money owned by a person, business, etc., in a bank account. 3 money lent by a bank. 4 good reputation; recognition for doing something: *The manager takes all the credit for our hard work.* 5 a system in which goods are bought at one time but paid for later: *buy a washing-machine on credit.* ● *vt* 1 believe (someone) has something: *I credited her with more sense.* 2 put money into (a bank account). **credit card** card allowing a person to get money or goods and pay later. **creditor** (ˈkredɪtə*) *nc* a person to whom one owes money. **creditworthy** (ˈkredɪtˈwɜːðɪ) *adj* trusted to pay debts. **creditable** (ˈkredɪtəbəl) *adj* deserving praise.

credulity (krɪˈdjuːlətɪ) *nu* much eagerness to believe. **credulous** (ˈkredjʊləs) *adj* eager to believe.

creed (kriːd) *nc* a set of beliefs on a subject, esp. Christianity.

creek (kriːk) *nc* a stream.

creep (kriːp) *vi* 1 move silently with the body close to the ground, or on tiptoe. 2 (of plants) grow over a wall or along the

ground. 3 feel one's skin to be sticky with fear, etc. ● *nc derogatory* person who tries to make someone important like him or her. **creepy** (ˈkriːpɪ) *adj* **-ier, -iest** giving a feeling of fear.

creosote (ˈkrɪəsəʊt) *nu* an oily liquid obtained from coal, used to prevent decay of wood.

crêpe (kreɪp) *nu* cloth or paper with a wrinkled surface.

crept (krept) past tense and past participle of **creep.**

crescendo (krəˈʃendəʊ) *nc* a gradual increase in the loudness of a piece of music. ● *adj, adv* getting louder.

crescent (ˈkresənt) *nc* 1 the curve of the moon when only partly seen: see picture. 2 anything with this shape, esp. a row of houses. ● *adj* (of the moon) increasing.

crescent

cress (kres) *nu* a plant with leaves that are often included in a salad.

crest (krest) *nc* 1 the feathers on top of a bird's head. 2 the top, esp. of a wave, hill, etc. 3 the design over a coat of arms, or this design by itself. ● *vt* reach the top of. **crest-fallen** (ˈkrestˈfɔːlən) *adj* sad; disappointed.

crevasse (krɪˈvæs) *nc* a deep split in ice on a mountain side.

crevice (ˈkrevɪs) *nc* a small crack in a building, wall, etc.

crew (kruː) *nc* a group of people working together, esp. on a ship or plane.

crib (krɪb) *nc* 1 a large open box with food for animals. 2 a bed for a new baby. ● *vti infml* cheat by copying.

cricket[1] (ˈkrɪkɪt) *nc* a jumping insect that makes a high sound with its wings: see picture at **insects.**

cricket[2] *nu* a ball game played by two teams of eleven men each, on a grass field. **cricketer** *nc*

cried (kraɪd) past tense of **cry.**

crier (ˈkraɪə*) *nc* 1 an officer who gives out notices in a court of law. 2 a person who cries.

crime (kraɪm) *nc* 1 a wrong act that breaks the law. 2 any wrong act: *It's a crime to beat that old horse.* **criminal** (ˈkrɪmɪnəl) *nc* a person guilty of an act that will be punished by law. ● *adj* wrong: *criminal offences.*

crimp (krɪmp) *vt* make (esp. hair) wavy or curly.

crimson ('krɪmzən) *adj* of a deep red colour.

cringe (krɪndʒ) *vi* bend down from fear or shame.

crinkle ('krɪŋkəl) *nc* a small fold in paper, cloth, etc. ●*vti* (cause to) be full of folds.

cripple ('krɪpəl) *nc* a person who has an injury, esp. of the leg or foot. ●*vt* harm or weaken.

crisis ('kraɪsɪs) *nc, pl* **-ses** (siːz) a time when danger or trouble reaches its worst, for example in an illness.

crisp (krɪsp) *adj* 1 hard but easily broken: *crisp toast.* 2 fresh and firm: *a crisp lettuce.* 3 (of the weather) cold and frosty. ●*nc* US **chip** a thin piece of potato cooked in oil. **crispbread** ('krɪspbred) *nu* a thin hard biscuit made from cereal. **crisply** ('krɪsplɪ) *adv*

crisscross ('krɪskrɒs) *adj* with lines crossing each other. ●*vi* 1 make a crisscross pattern. 2 *vt* cover with crossing lines.

criterion (kraɪ'tɪərɪən) *nc, pl* **-ria** (rɪə) the rule or example by which something is measured or valued.

critic ('krɪtɪk) *nc* 1 a person who is paid to make judgements on films, concerts, etc. 2 person who points out faults. **critical** ('krɪtɪkəl) *adj* 1 very important: *a critical time in his life.* 2 (of a person) ready to find fault. 3 to do with the work of a critic.

criticise ('krɪtɪsaɪz) *vti* give an opinion (on something); find fault. **criticism** ('krɪtɪsɪzəm) *ncu*

croak (krəʊk) *nc* a hoarse sound made in the throat, esp. by or like a frog. ●*vti* speak (words) in a croak.

crochet ('krəʊʃeɪ) *nu* a kind of knitting done by passing loops of thread through each other with a small needle. ●*vti* make (something) by doing crochet.

crock (krɒk) *nc* 1 a pot or jar made of baked earth. 2 *infml* a person, horse, car, etc., too broken down to work properly.

crockery ('krɒkərɪ) *n pl* plates, dishes, cups, etc., made of baked earth, and esp. used for eating from.

crocodile ('krɒkədaɪl) *nc* a large water reptile with thick skin and a long tail: see picture at **reptiles**.

crocus ('krəʊkəs) *nc* a small plant that has purple, yellow, or white flowers in spring: see picture at **flowers**.

crony ('krəʊnɪ) *infml nc, pl* **-nies** a close friend.

crook (krʊk) *nc* 1 a stick with a curve at the top, esp. used by a person in charge of sheep. 2 *infml* a person guilty of a crime; person not to be trusted. ●*vti* (cause to) bend: *crook one's finger.* **crooked** ('krʊkɪd)

adj 1 bent. 2 *infml* wrong; against the law.

croon (kruːn) *vti* sing (a song) in a low voice.

crop (krɒp) *nc* 1 the season's produce of fruit, grain, etc.; the plants that form this produce: *Beans are our main crop.* 2 (the handle of) a whip: *riding crop.* 3 short hair. 4 a number of persons or things. ●*vt* cut off; (of animals) bite (grass). **crop up** appear when not expected.

croquet ('krəʊkeɪ) *nu* a game played on grass in which wooden balls are hit with wooden hammers through hoops.

cross (krɒs) *nc* 1 the mark made when one line is drawn over another. 2 two pieces of wood tied across each other, esp. the Cross on which Jesus Christ was put to death. 3 some trouble or suffering one has to bear. 4 (of animals or plants) a mixture of two different kinds. ●*vt* 1 go from one side of to the other: *cross a road.* 2 put (something) over (something else): *cross one's legs.* 3 meet; lie across: *The tracks cross here.* 4 (of animals or plants) mix two different kinds. **cross out** draw a line through a word, etc., to show it is not wanted: *Look for mistakes and cross them out.* ●*adj* angry.

crossbar ('krɒsbɑː*) *nc* a long piece of metal across something, esp. a bicycle frame.

crossbow ('krɒsbəʊ) *nc* a weapon made of a curved piece of wood with a wire stretched between the two ends, and a wooden handle, used for shooting arrows.

crossbreed ('krɒsbriːd) *vt* mix (two different kinds of animals or plants) to produce another kind. ●*nc* animal or plant produced by crossbreeding.

crosscountry ('krɒs'kʌntrɪ) *adj* across fields and not roads: *a crosscountry run.* **crosscountry running** *nu* the sport of running crosscountry.

cross-examine ('krɒsɪg'zæmɪn) *vt* question (a person) to check that that person's or another person's answers were true, esp. in a law court.

crossing ('krɒsɪŋ) *nc* 1 the act of going across: *a ship's crossing.* 2 a place where a road and a railway cross. 3 a place where a street is crossed on foot.

cross-legged ('krɒslegd, 'krɒslegɪd) *adj, adv* (sitting) with one leg crossed over the other.

cross-purposes ('krɒs'pɜːpəsɪz) *n pl* **at cross-purposes** not understanding each other, often because of having different opinions.

cross-reference ('krɒs'refərəns) *nc* a direction to another part of a book for more information.

crossroads ('krɒsrəʊdz) *n pl* 1 the place where two roads cross each other. 2 a time in life when an important decision must be made.

cross-section ('krɒs'sekʃən) *nc* **1** the view of something when seen as if cut straight through. **2** an example; representative group: *a cross-section of the public.*

crosswise ('krɒswaɪz) *adj, adv* lying or placed across.

crossword ('krɒswɜːd) *nc* also **crossword puzzle** a puzzle in which a square has to be filled with words across and down after first solving given clues.

crotchet ('krɒtʃɪt) *US* **quarter note** *nc* (in music) a note with a black head and a long stem, lasting one beat.

crouch (krautʃ) *vi* **1** lower the body with the legs bent, in fear or to hide. **2** (of an animal) lie ready to make a sudden attack.

crow[1] (krəu) *nc* a large black bird: see picture at **birds. crow's nest** *nc* a place at the top of a ship's mast for a watchman. **as the crow flies** in a straight line.

crow[2] *vi* (of a cock) make a sharp cry; (of a baby) make small happy sounds.

crowbar ('krəubɑː*) *nc* a long iron bar used for lifting heavy things: see picture.

crowbar

crowd (kraud) *nc* a large number of people or things gathered together. ●*vti* gather together; fill (a space) with people, etc.: *The hall was crowded.* **crowded** *adj* full.

crown (kraun) *nc* **1** a circle of gold, etc., worn on the head of a king or queen; circle of flowers, etc., worn as a sign of victory. **2** a top (esp. of the head). **the Crown** the powers or property of the king, queen, or government. ●*vt* **1** appoint (someone) king or queen by placing a crown on their head. **2** add the final, best or worst, detail to.

crucial ('kruːʃəl) *adj* very important.

crucible ('kruːsɪbəl) *nc* a pot for melting metals.

crucifix ('kruːsɪfɪks) *nc* a model of Jesus Christ on the Cross. **crucifixion** ('kruːsɪ-'fɪkʃən) *ncu* the punishment of fixing someone (esp. Jesus Christ) to a wooden cross; an example, picture, etc., of this. **crucify** ('kruːsɪfaɪ) *vt* punish (someone) with crucifixion.

crude (kruːd) *adj* **1** in its raw, natural state: *crude oil.* **2** not polite; rough: *crude manners.* **3** not finished properly: *a crude painting.*

cruel ('kruːəl) *adj* **1** (of a person) not caring about, or taking pleasure in, making people suffer. **2** causing pain and suffering: *a cruel winter.* **cruelty** ('kruːəltɪ) *ncu* (an act of) being cruel.

cruise (kruːz) *vti* sail slowly around (a sea or ocean) for pleasure or looking for warships. ●*nc* a holiday on a boat. **cruiser** ('kruːzə*) *nc* a fast warship or motor-powered pleasure boat.

crumb (krʌm) *nc* a very small piece of bread, cake, etc.; very small amount of anything.

crumble ('krʌmbəl) *vti* break or fall into very small pieces; fall slowly into ruin. **crumbly** ('krʌmblɪ) *adj* **-ier, -iest** likely to crumble.

crumple ('krʌmpəl) **1** *vt* crush into folds. **2** become full of folds.

crunch (krʌntʃ) *vti* make a crushing noise with the teeth when eating (something hard) or with the feet when walking (on something hard). ●*nc* crushing noise. **come to the crunch** come to a difficult point where action is needed.

crusade (kruː'seɪd) *nc* **1** one of the wars fought by the Christians against the Muslims in the Middle Ages. **2** any action for a good cause. **crusader** *nc*

crush (krʌʃ) *vt* **1** press so as to break, harm, or put out of shape. **2** press into folds. **3** break (someone's) spirit or resistance: *a crushing defeat.* ●*nu* **1** a crowd pressed together: *a crush at the exit.* **2** a fruit drink.

crust (krʌst) *nc* the hard outer part, esp. of bread or a pie; any hard surface: *the earth's crust.*

crustacean (krʌ'steɪʃən) *nc* a water animal with a hard shell, such as a crab.

crutch (krʌtʃ) *nc* a stick used by a person who cannot walk well through injury or illness; anything which one depends on.

crux (krʌks) *nu* the most difficult or important part.

cry (kraɪ) *vi* **1** (of certain animals) make sounds; call. **2** call out: *He cried for help.* **3** *vti* weep (tears) and make sounds (of pain, joy, fear, grief, etc.). ●*nc, pl* **cries 1** (of an animal) a call. **2** a weep. **3** a shout; calling out.

crypt (krɪpt) *nc* a room under the level of the ground, esp. beneath a church.

cryptic ('krɪptɪk) *adj* secret; with a meaning that is not clear.

crystal ('krɪstəl) **1** *nu* a hard, clear, natural substance. **2** *science nc* a shape some substances take when they change from liquids to solids: *ice crystals.* **crystalline** ('krɪstə-laɪn) *adj* **crystallise** ('krɪstəlaɪz) *vti* (cause to) form crystals.

cub (kʌb) *nc* a young bear, lion, tiger, or fox. **Cub Scout** a young boy belonging to the junior part of the Scouts.

cube (kjuːb) *nc* **1** a block having six equal

square sides: see picture at **shapes. 2** *mathematics* the result when a number is multiplied by itself twice: *the cube of two is eight.* ● *vt* multiply a number by itself twice. **cubic** ('kjuːbɪk) *adj* **1** shaped like a cube. **2** (of a metre, etc.) measuring space in height, depth, and width: *a box of 1.5 cubic metres.* **cuboid** ('kjuːbɔɪd) *adj* shaped like a cube.

cubicle ('kjuːbɪkəl) *nc* a very small room within a larger one.

cubit ('kjuːbɪt) *archaic nc* the length of the arm from the elbow to the wrist, used as a measure.

cuckoo ('kʊkuː) *nc* a bird that has a call like the sound of its name and lays its eggs in the nests of other birds: see picture at **birds.**

cucumber ('kjuːkʌmbə*) *nc* a creeping plant with long green fleshy fruit eaten in salads: see picture at **vegetables.**

cud (kʌd) *nu* the food that a cow, etc., brings back from its stomach and chews.

cuddle ('kʌdəl) *vt* hold in one's arms in a loving way: *cuddle the baby.* **have a cuddle** lie close and warm together.

cudgel ('kʌdʒəl) *nc* a thick stick used as a weapon.

cue¹ (kjuː) *nc* **1** an actor's words or action showing what another actor should say or do. **2** a hint.

cue² *nc* a long stick used for striking balls in a table ball game such as billiards.

cuff¹ (kʌf) *nc* the end of a sleeve, esp. of a shirt or coat. **off the cuff** *infml* without planning.

cuff² *nc* a blow with the hand, often in a friendly way.

cuisine (kwɪˈziːn) *French nu* way of cooking.

cul-de-sac ('kʌldəˈsæk) *nc, pl* **cul-de-sacs, culs-de-sac** a street closed at one end.

culinary ('kʌlɪnərɪ) *adj* having to do with cooking or a kitchen.

cull (kʌl) *vt* **1** choose; pick (a flower, etc.). **2** choose the best animals from (a group), and kill the others.

culminate ('kʌlmɪneɪt) *v* **culminate in** reach the highest point; end in. **culmination** ('kʌlmɪˈneɪʃən) *nc*

culprit ('kʌlprɪt) *nc* a person or thing blamed for a wrong deed.

cult (kʌlt) *nc* **1** (a group of people having) a set of religious beliefs. **2** an interest or enthusiasm, esp. one that is not likely to last for long.

cultivate ('kʌltɪveɪt) *vt* **1** make (land) ready for crops; grow flowers; etc. **2** give time and care to improving (one's mind, a friendship, etc.). **cultivated** *adj* having good manners and good taste. **cultivation** ('kʌltɪˈveɪʃən) *nu* **cultivator** ('kʌltɪveɪtə*) *nc*

a person or machine that prepares land for crops.

culture ('kʌltʃə*) *nu* **1** the ways, art, beliefs, etc., of a people. **2** improvement of the mind and spirit by study and thought; growth of human powers. **3** the growing of something, esp. needing special care, such as silk, bees, or bacteria. **cultural** ('kʌltʃərəl) *adj*

culvert ('kʌlvət) *nc* a large pipe for carrying water, electric wires, or gas under the ground.

cumbersome ('kʌmbəsəm) *adj* awkward to move or carry.

cumulative ('kjuːmjʊlətɪv) *adj* **1** increasing in number or amount. **2** caused by a steady increase.

cumulus ('kjuːmjʊləs) *nc, pl* **-li** (liː) a set of clouds heaped on top of each other.

cuneiform ('kjuːnɪfɔːm) *adj* to do with a kind of writing used by the ancient Assyrians and Babylonians.

cunning ('kʌnɪŋ) *adj* clever, esp. at tricking or deceiving people. ● *nu* cleverness.

cup (kʌp) *nc* **1** a small container that is open at the top, usually with a handle; this container with a drink in it: *a cup of tea.* **2** a vessel, often of gold or silver, given as a prize. **cupful** ('kʌpfʊl) *nc* the amount a cup will hold.

cupboard ('kʌbəd) *nc* a piece of furniture with shelves for keeping things in: *a clothes cupboard.*

cupola ('kjuːpələ) *nc* a small dome.

cur (kɜː*) *derogatory nc* **1** a dog. **2** an unpleasant person.

curate ('kjʊərət) *nc* an assistant priest in a parish.

curator ('kjʊəˈreɪtə*) *nc* a person in charge of a building, esp. a museum or art gallery.

curb (kɜːb) *vt* hold back; keep under control. ● *nc* **1** a chain or strap passing under a horse's jaw to control it. **2** *US* See **kerb.**

curd (kɜːd) *nc* the thick part of sour milk, eaten or used to make cheese.

curdle ('kɜːdəl) *vti* (cause to) turn sour and become solid: *The milk curdled.*

cure (kjʊə*) *nc* **1** healing or being healed; treatment for an illness or disease. **2** something that gets rid of something bad. ● *vt* **1** heal; make healthy. **2** treat (meat, fish, etc.) to keep from going bad.

curfew ('kɜːfjuː) *nc* the time after which people must stay indoors.

curio ('kjʊərɪəʊ) *nc, pl* **-s** a rare object, of value because it is unusual, beautiful, etc.

curious ('kjʊərɪəs) *adj* **1** eager to learn. **2** too interested in other people's affairs. **3** strange. **curiosity** ('kjʊərɪˈɒsɪtɪ) **1** *nu* being curious. **2** *nc* a rare or unusual object. **curiously** *adv*

curl (kɜːl) *nc* a lock of hair made to curve; anything curved like this: *a curl of smoke.* ● *vti* (cause to) turn into curves and waves. **curly** (ˈkɜːlɪ) *adj*

curlew (ˈkɜːljuː) *nc* a water-bird with long legs and a long beak.

currant (ˈkʌrənt) *nc* 1 a small dried grape, esp. used in cakes. 2 a small red, white, or black fruit, or the bush on which it grows.

currency (ˈkʌrənsɪ) *nc, pl* **-cies** 1 the money in use in a country. 2 *nu* the time during which something is in use: *Fashionable ideas of limited currency.*

current (ˈkʌrənt) *adj* 1 in general use. 2 happening in, or belonging to, the present: *the current state of affairs.* ● *nc* a flow of water, air, electricity, etc.

curriculum (kəˈrɪkjʊləm) *nc, pl* **-la** (lə) a course of study; timetable.

curry[1] (ˈkʌrɪ) *nc, pl* **-ries** a dish of meat, eggs, fish, etc., cooked with spices.

curry[2] *v* **curry favour** praise falsely in order to please.

curse (kɜːs) *nc* 1 a set of words calling for evil or punishment to happen to someone or something. 2 a wrong use of God's name to show anger, etc. ● *vt* 1 call for evil to come on (someone). 2 *vi* use bad language. **cursed with** suffering from: *cursed with bad luck.*

curt (kɜːt) *adj* (of a person's manner of speaking) with few words and not very polite.

curtail (kɜːˈteɪl) *vt* cut short: *curtail a speech.*

curtain (ˈkɜːtən) *nc* 1 a cloth at a window to keep out light, etc.; anything that hides or protects. 2 (in the theatre) the cloth between the stage and audience. ● *vt* provide curtains for.

curtsey (ˈkɜːtsɪ) *nc, pl* **-sies** (of a woman) the act of bending one's knees and bowing the head and shoulders in honour of a king, queen, etc. ● *vi* make a curtsey.

curvature (ˈkɜːvətʃə*) *ncu* curving; being curved: *curvature of the spine.*

curve (kɜːv) *nc* a line that is not straight and is without angles. ● *vti* (cause to) bend.

cushion (ˈkʊʃən) *nc* 1 a kind of pillow for sitting on, resting one's back against, etc. 2 something that has a protective effect. ● *vt* protect.

custard (ˈkʌstəd) 1 *nu* a sweet sauce made of milk, sugar, eggs, etc. 2 *nc* a pudding made of milk, sugar, and eggs.

custody (ˈkʌstədɪ) *nu* 1 care: *a child in the custody of her father.* 2 being in prison. **custodian** (kʌˈstəʊdɪən) *nc* keeper.

custom (ˈkʌstəm) 1 *nc* the ways, manners, etc., of a country or people. *nu* 2 the usual way of behaving. 3 the support given to a business, esp. a shop, by its customers.

customary (ˈkʌstəmərɪ) *adj* usual. **customarily** *adv*

customer (ˈkʌstəmə*) *nc* a person who buys, esp. one who buys regularly.

customs (ˈkʌstəmz) *n pl* 1 the tax paid to the government when goods are brought into the country. 2 the place at a port or airport where bags are searched.

cut (kʌt) *vt* 1 harm or injure with a sharp edge: *He cut his finger with the knife.* 2 cut in pieces with scissors, a knife, etc. 3 make shorter or less: *He cut my hair short; The manager cut their wages.* 4 *vi* be able to cut or be cut. **cut across** get somewhere quicker by going straight across rather than around. **cut back (on)** make the size, number, or cost less. **cutback** (ˈkʌtbæk) *nc* a reduction. **cut someone dead** pretend not to have seen a person one knows. **cut down (on)** make less or smaller in number, size, etc. **cut in** enter suddenly; interrupt. **cut off** remove; stop the flow of: *The electricity was cut off.* **cut-off** (ˈkʌtɒf) *nc* a device for stopping the flow of something. **cut out** 1 stop working suddenly: *The engine cut out.* 2 remove or make separate by cutting: *cut an article out of the paper.* 3 stop (eating, doing) something: *cut out smoking.* **cut-out** (ˈkʌtaʊt) *nc* 1 a device for stopping a current of electricity when necessary. 2 a shape cut from something: *paper cut-outs.* **cut up** cut into pieces. ● *nc* 1 act of cutting; blow from something with a sharp edge; wound or mark made by such a blow. 2 something that has been made less: *a wage cut; a hair cut.* 3 *infml* share: *After the bank robbery, everyone will get his cut.* **cutaway** (ˈkʌtəweɪ) *adj* with some parts missing to show the inside.

cute (kjuːt) *adj* **-r, -st** *chiefly US* attractive, pretty; pleasant.

cuticle (ˈkjuːtɪkəl) *nc* the outer layer of the skin, esp. at the lower edge of the nail of a finger or toe.

cutlass (ˈkʌtləs) *history nc* a short sword with a curved blade.

cutlery (ˈkʌtlərɪ) *nu* tools such as knives, forks, and spoons used for eating with.

cutter (ˈkʌtə*) *nc* 1 a person or thing that cuts. 2 a small boat belonging to a ship.

cutthroat (ˈkʌtθrəʊt) *nc* a murderer. ● *adj* fierce, without pity: *cutthroat competition.* 2 *humorous* (of a razor) having a long blade that is not protected.

cutting (ˈkʌtɪŋ) *nc* 1 a passage dug under a hill, etc., for a road, railway, etc. 2 a piece cut from a newspaper. 3 a piece cut from a plant for growing another one. ● *adj* unkind, hurtful (remarks, etc.).

cuttlefish (ˈkʌtəlfɪʃ) *nc, pl* **cuttlefish, cuttlefishes** a sea-animal with ten arms, which sends out black liquid when being chased.

cyanide ('saɪənaɪd) *nu* a very poisonous chemical.

cybernetics ('saɪbə'netɪks) *science nu* the study of the control and passing on of information in animals and machines.

cycle ('saɪkəl) *nc* **1** a set of events arranged and repeated so that each one happens at a regular time. **2** a bicycle. ● *vi* ride a bicycle. **cyclic** ('saɪklɪk) *adj* happening at regular times. **cyclist** ('saɪklɪst) *nc* a person who rides a cycle.

cyclone ('saɪkləʊn) *nc* **1** a violent wind. **2** a large area of low air pressure, around which winds blow. **cyclonic** (saɪ'klɒnɪk) *adj*

cyder ('saɪdə*) *n* See **cider**.

cygnet ('sɪgnɪt) *nc* a young swan.

cylinder ('sɪlɪndə*) *nc* **1** a solid or hollow body shaped like a tube: see picture at **shapes**. **2** a tube-shaped space in an engine with a piston inside it worked by steam, etc. **cylindrical** (sɪ'lɪndrɪkəl) *adj*

cymbal ('sɪmbəl) *nc* one of a pair of round brass plates struck together to make a musical sound: see picture at **musical instruments**.

cynical ('sɪnɪkəl) *adj* not believing that people are good; sneering. **cynicism** ('sɪnɪsɪzəm) *nu*

cypher ('saɪfə*) *n* See **cipher**.

cypress ('saɪprəs) *nc* an evergreen tree that has dark leaves.

cyst (sɪst) *nc* a sac that grows in the body and contains liquid.

czar (zɑː*) *n* See **tsar**.

D

dab¹ (dæb) *vt* touch lightly; put (esp. liquid) (on a surface) briefly and without rubbing. ● *nc* a light touch.

dab² *nc* a small fish with a flat body.

dab³ *infml nc* skilful. **dab hand** an expert in something.

dabble ('dæbəl) *vt* splash (something) about in water: *She dabbled her hands in the stream.* **dabble in** do something from time to time, but not seriously.

dachshund ('dækshʊnd) *nc* a small dog with a long body and short legs.

dad (dæd) *infml nc* daddy.

daddy ('dædɪ) *infml nc*, *pl* **-dies** a father.

daffodil ('dæfədɪl) *nc* a yellow spring flower growing from a bulb: see picture at **flowers.**

daft (dɑːft) *infml, chiefly Brit adj* silly; without much sense.

dagger ('dægə*) *nc* a short knife with two sharp edges used as a weapon.

daily ('deɪlɪ) *adj* happening every day or every day except Sunday and possibly Saturday. ● *adv* every day. ● *nc, pl* **-lies 1** a newspaper that comes out daily. **2** a woman who is paid to come to do housework daily.

dainty ('deɪntɪ) *adj* **-ier, -iest 1** (of a woman or girl) pretty, pleasing in appearance; (of things) pretty, fragile. **2** fussy (over food, cleanliness, etc.). **daintily** ('deɪntɪlɪ) *adv*

dairy ('deərɪ) *nc, pl* **-ries 1** a place where butter, cheese, etc., is made from milk, esp. on the farm; place dealing in milk and milk products. **2** a shop selling milk, butter, eggs, etc.

dais ('deɪɪs) *nc* a platform in a large room.

daisy ('deɪzɪ) *nc, pl* **-sies** a small white field or garden flower with a yellow centre: see picture at **flowers.**

dale (deɪl) *nc* low land between hills or mountains, esp. in N England.

dally ('dælɪ) *vi* **1** (followed by **with**) amuse oneself carelessly with. **2** pass the time by standing around and doing nothing definite.

dam¹ (dæm) *nc* a wall built to hold back water and stop floods, or to raise its level to form a lake for storing water. ● *vt* build a dam to hold back (a river).

dam² *nc* the mother of an animal.

damage ('dæmɪdʒ) **1** *nu* harm, injury, or destruction. **2** *(pl) law* money paid to make up for loss, injury, etc. ● *vt* cause damage to.

damask ('dæməsk) *nu* cloth with patterns on both sides. ● *adj* dark pink.

dame (deɪm) *nc* **1** *archaic* a woman. **2** *Brit* a title of great respect given to a woman. **3** *US slang* a woman.

damn (dæm) *vt* **1** say that (someone or something) is bad. **2** (of God) punish (someone) for ever. **damn!** *slang interj* (cry of anger or unhappiness). **damnation** (dæm'neɪʃən) *nu* being cursed; punishment lasting for ever. **damned** (dæmd) *adj* **1** cursed. **2** *infml* stupid; very bad. ● *adv infml* very.

damp (dæmp) *adj* rather wet. ● *nu* moisture (in the air, a house, etc.). ● *vt* **1** make rather wet. **2** (followed by **down**) put out (a fire) by covering with ashes, etc. **3** make less; get rid of: *The teacher's cruel remarks damped their high spirits.*

dampen ('dæmpən) *vti* (cause to) become damp.

damper ('dæmpə*) *nc* a metal plate in a chimney, etc., that controls the flow of air: see picture. **put a damper on** make less happy.

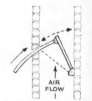

AIR FLOW

damper

damsel ('dæmzəl) *old-fashioned nc* a young woman.

dance (dɑːns) *vi* **1** move in time to music. **2** skip or jump about. **3** *vt* do special steps to music: *dance a waltz.* ● *nc* **1** a set of steps to music; a special form of these steps. **2** an occasion when people come to dance. **dancer** *nc* a person who dances, esp. in public for money.

dandelion ('dændɪlaɪən) *nc* a small yellow field flower.

dandruff ('dændrʌf) *nu* small bits of dead skin which are found in the hair.

dandy ('dændɪ) *old-fashioned nc, pl* **-dies** a man who is too concerned with his clothes and appearance. ● *adj infml, US* of the best.

danger ('deɪndʒə*) *nu* **1** the possibility of harm, injury, or death. **2** something that causes harm, etc.: *Smoking is a danger to health.* **in** or **out of danger** likely to or no longer likely to meet danger. **dangerous** ('deɪndʒərəs) *adj* **dangerously** *adv*

dangle ('dæŋgəl) **1** *vi* hang and move loosely. **2** *vt* hold or carry (something) to hang loosely.

dank (dæŋk) *adj* **-er, -est** cold and damp in an unhealthy way.

dappled ('dæpəld) *adj* marked with spots of colour or shadow.

dare (deə*) **1** *vti* be brave or rude enough to (do something). **2** *vt* test someone's bravery by asking him to do something: *I dare you to climb that tree.* **I daresay** it is very likely. **do something for a dare** do something to prove one is brave. **daredevil** ('deədevəl) *nc* a person who is not afraid of danger. **daring** ('deərɪŋ) *adj* **1** brave. **2** new, unusual: *a daring play.*

daren't (deənt) *v* dare not.

dark (daːk) *adj* **1** with very little or no light. **2** (of colour) almost black. **3** sad: *The war brought dark days for everyone.* **4** secret or bad: *the dark act of murder.* ● *nu* the state of having no light; night. **darkness** *nu* **darken** *vti* **darkly** *adv*

darling ('daːlɪŋ) *nc* a person who is much loved. ● *adj infml* loved very much.

darn (daːn) *vt* mend (esp. clothes) with a needle and cotton. ● *nc* a place that has been repaired in this way.

dart (daːt) *nc* **1** a sudden movement. **2** a small arrow. ● *vti* (cause something to) move quickly. **darts** *nu* a game in which small arrows are thrown at a round board marked with numbers.

dash (dæʃ) *nc* **1** a sudden rush. **2** a small amount added. **3** a short race run quickly. **4** a small line (—) used in writing or printing. **dashboard** ('dæʃbɔːd) *nc* a board in a car with lights, switches, etc.: see picture. ● *vi* **1** make a sudden movement. **2** *vti* throw (something or someone) with violence: *She dashed him to the ground.* **3** *vt* destroy (esp. someone's hopes). **dashing** ('dæʃɪŋ) *adj* lively and gay.

dashboard

dastardly ('dæstədlɪ) *adj* evil.

data ('deɪtə) *n, pl* **1** facts; pieces of information. **2** *(with singular verb)* information stored in a computer. **data processing** (ˌdeɪtə 'prəʊsesɪŋ) *nu* working on data to get information.

date¹ (deɪt) *nc* **1** the time shown by the day, month, year, or all three. **2** *infml* a meeting with someone at an arranged time and place; person of the other sex whom one meets in this way. **out-of-date** old-fashioned. **up-to-date** See **up-to-date**. ● *vt* **1**

put a time on (esp. a letter). **2** connect to a period of time: *pots dated to Roman times.* **3** *vti infml* go out regularly (with someone) on a **date¹** (def. 2). **dated** ('deɪtɪd) *adj* belonging to the past; old-fashioned.

date² *nc* a small, brown, sweet, sticky fruit with a stone.

daub (dɔːb) *vt* **1** cover (a wall) with clay, plaster, etc. **2** make dirty marks on. **3** *vi* paint badly. ● *nc* **1** a covering of clay, etc. **2** a badly done painting.

daughter ('dɔːtə*) *nc* someone's female child. **daughter-in-law** ('dɔːtərɪnlɔː) *nc, pl* **daughters-in-law** the wife of someone's son.

daunt (dɔːnt) *vt* put off from doing something through fear, etc. **dauntless** ('dɔːntlɪs) *adj* brave.

dawdle ('dɔːdəl) *vi* go slowly, wasting time.

dawn (dɔːn) *nc* the start of day as it begins to grow light; the beginning of anything: *the dawn of literature.* ● *vi* begin to get light. **dawn on (someone)** begin to understand.

day (deɪ) *nc* **1** the time between two nights when it is light. **2** the time of twenty-four hours. **3** *(pl)* period: *in the old days.* **4** a person's length of life: *back in grandmother's day.* **call it a day** decide enough work has been done for the day. **day by day** as time goes by: *He grew weaker day by day.* **one day** some time in the past or in the future. **some day** at some time in the future. **the other day** on a recent day. **daybreak** *nc* the time when the sun rises. **daydream** *vi* have dreamy thoughts while awake. ● *nc* events imagined, usually when one should be busy doing something else. **daylight** *nu* the light of the sun. **daytime** *nu* the time when the sun is in the sky.

daze (deɪz) *vt* make (someone) unable to think clearly. ● *nu* **in a daze** in a condition where clear thoughts are impossible.

dazzle ('dæzəl) *vt* **1** make almost blind with bright light. **2** astonish (esp. someone who does not expect something).

dead (ded) *adj* **1** not alive any more. **2** not able to feel or move much because of being cold or hurt. **3** no longer used: *a dead language.* **4** *infml* boring. ● *adv* completely; very: *dead silly; stop dead.* **at dead of; in the dead of** at the quietest time of: *at dead of night.* **the dead** persons who have died. **deaden** ('dedən) *vt* take away feeling, pain, etc. **deadline** *nc* the time by which a piece of work must be finished. **deadlock** ('dedlɒk) *nc* a point at which no agreement seems likely. **deadly** ('dedlɪ) *adj* **-ier, -iest** likely to cause death. ● *adv* **1** as if dead. **2** very: *deadly serious.*

deaf (def) *adj* **1 -er, est** not able to hear. **2** not wanting to hear: *deaf to offers of peace.*

the deaf people who cannot hear. **deafen** ('defən) vt make it difficult to hear because of noise: *a deafening noise.*

deal (diːl) vt give out; hand out. **deal with** handle (a problem, a person, etc.). **deal with someone** do business with someone. ● nc **1** the handing out of cards in a card game. **2** a business agreement. **a deal of** a lot of: *You caused a great deal of trouble.* **dealer** nc **1** a person who buys and sells goods. **2** a person who gives out cards in a card game. **dealings** ('diːlɪŋz) n pl treatment of others, esp. in business.

dealt (delt) past tense and past participle of **deal.**

dean (diːn) nc **1** a priest in charge of other priests. **2** the head of part of a university; person responsible for students' behaviour.

dear (dɪə*) adj -er, -est **1** loved. **2** not cheap. **3** important; precious. **4** a polite way to start a letter: *Dear Madam,...* a lovable person. **dear me!; oh dear!** (cries of surprise, grief, etc.). **dearly** adv very much: *I would dearly like to come.*

dearth (dɜːθ) formal nu a lack.

death (deθ) **1** ncu the end of (someone's) life. **2** nu the state of being dead. **3** nc the end of something. **put to death** kill. **deathless** ('deθlɪs) adj living for ever; never forgotten.

debar (dɪ'baː*) vt (followed by **from**) shut out; prevent from doing or having something.

debase (dɪ'beɪs) vt lower the value or worth of.

debate (dɪ'beɪt) nc a formal talk between two speakers, or two sets of speakers, each taking the opposite side of a question. ● vti consider or argue about (a problem, question, etc.). **debatable** (dɪ'beɪtəbəl) adj

debauchery (dɪ'bɔːtʃərɪ) nu the habit of giving way too much to food, drink, and sexual enjoyment.

debenture (dɪ'bentʃə*) nc a promise made in a written statement by a business, company, etc., to pay a debt.

debilitate (dɪ'bɪlɪteɪt) vt make (esp. a person's health) weak.

debit ('debɪt) nc (the side of an account book showing) money owed or spent from a person's account. ● vt write down money spent from or take (money) out of (an account).

debris ('deɪbriː, 'debriː) nu what is left, usually broken and in pieces: *Clear up the debris after the fight.*

debt (det) nc **1** the money, goods, etc., owing to someone. **2** the state of owing money, or recognition. **be in someone's debt** owe (a person) an act of kindness. **debtor** ('detə*) nc a person who owes.

début ('deɪbuː, 'debjuː) ncu (a person's) first appearance in public as an actor, dancer, musician, etc. **debutante** ('debjʊtɑːnt) nc a daughter of rich parents making her first appearance in society.

decade ('dekeɪd) nc a period of ten years.

decadence ('dekədəns) nu a falling of a former high level, esp. in art, literature, behaviour, etc.

decanter (dɪ'kæntə*) nc a glass bottle for wine, etc., with a small block of glass to close the top.

decapitate (dɪ'kæpɪteɪt) vt cut off the head of.

decay (dɪ'keɪ) vti **1** (cause to) become rotten; go bad. **2** get worse; lose power. ● nu the state of getting worse.

deceased (dɪ'siːst) formal adj dead.

deceit (dɪ'siːt) **1** nu a wrong or false idea, etc., given to a person on purpose. **2** nc a trick. **deceitful** (dɪ'siːtfʊl) adj **deceive** (dɪ'siːv) vt cause (someone) to believe something that is not true.

December (dɪ'sembə*) n the twelfth and last month of the year, after November.

decent ('diːsənt) adj **1** right and proper; modest. **2** Brit kind; good enough.

deception (dɪ'sepʃən) **1** nu causing a person to believe what is false. **2** nc a trick. **deceptive** (dɪ'septɪv) adj

decide (dɪ'saɪd) vt **1** find an answer to (a question, argument, etc.): *Decide the matter now; You decide where to go.* **2** vi make a choice: *I decided to leave home.* **decidedly** (dɪ'saɪdɪdlɪ) adv without doubt.

deciduous (dɪ'sɪdjʊəs) adj (of some trees) having leaves that fall off in winter.

decimal ('desɪməl) adj of the number ten or tenth parts. ● nc a number, such as *.65, 2.31.* **decimalise** ('desɪməlaɪz) vt change to a decimal system.

decimate ('desɪmeɪt) vt **1** kill at least one-tenth of. **2** infml kill almost all of.

decipher (dɪ'saɪfə*) vt work out the meaning that is hidden in (a piece of writing, etc.): *decipher a code.*

decision (dɪ'sɪʒən) nu **1** settling a question; making a judgement. **2** determination. **3** nc a judgement. **decisive** (dɪ'saɪsɪv) adj **1** (of a person) without doubts; definite. **2** deciding a matter: *the decisive battle of the Civil War.*

deck (dek) nc **1** a floor or level of a ship, bus, etc. **2** chiefly US a set of cards for a card game. **deckchair** ('dektʃeə*) nc a folding chair of wood and strong cloth, used outside. ● vt **deck out in** or **with** make attractive.

declaim (dɪ'kleɪm) sometimes derogatory vti talk in a strong voice about (something) and wave one's hands about for effect. **de-**

claim against speak with deep feeling against something.

declare (dɪˈkleə*) *vt* 1 make known: *declare an interest.* 2 confess to having goods on which tax has to be made to the government. 3 say very seriously: *He declared that he would leave.* **declaration** (ˌdekləˈreɪʃən) *ncu*

decline (dɪˈklaɪn) 1 *vti* refuse (an invitation, etc.) 2 *vi* become worse, weaker, less, etc.: *This country's influence is declining.* 3 *vt* grammar give the forms of a word. ● *nc* lessening; lowering; becoming worse.

decode (ˌdiːˈkəʊd) *vt* find the meaning of (a secret message or code).

decompose (ˌdiːkəmˈpəʊz) *vti* 1 (cause to) separate into simpler parts. 2 (cause to) become rotten. **decomposition** (ˌdiːkɒmpə-ˈzɪʃən) *nu*

decorate (ˈdekəreɪt) *vt* 1 make attractive. 2 give (someone) a medal for bravery, etc. 3 *vti* paint, etc., (a room or house). **decoration** (ˌdekəˈreɪʃən) *ncu* **decorative** (ˈdekər-ətɪv) *adj* **decorator** *nc*

decorum (dɪˈkɔːrəm) *nu* correct behaviour.

decrease (diːˈkriːs) *vti* make or become less. ●(ˈdiːkriːs) *ncu* (an example of) getting less.

decree (dɪˈkriː) *nc* an order given by someone in power; judgement made in a law court. ● *vti* demand (something) by law, power of government, etc.

decrepit (dɪˈkrepɪt) *adj* old and weak; in bad condition.

dedicate (ˈdedɪkeɪt) *vt* 1 give up (one's time, etc.) to a special purpose. 2 (of a person who writes a book) write words inside (a book) thanking a friend for his help, etc. **dedication** (ˌdedɪˈkeɪʃən) *ncu*

deduce (dɪˈdjuːs) *vt* reach (an answer, etc.) from the facts or from using one's reason.

deduct (dɪˈdʌkt) *vt* take away (a part of something); take (one number) from a total.

deduction (dɪˈdʌkʃən) 1 *nu* taking away. 2 *nc* that which is taken away. 3 *nu* reaching an opinion, etc. 4 *nc* the opinion reached.

deed (diːd) *nc* 1 an act; something done on purpose: *a brave deed.* 2 *law* a written agreement.

deem (diːm) *formal vt* believe; be of the opinion: *He deemed it necessary to return.*

deep (diːp) *adj* -er, -est 1 going far down from the top, front, or edge: *a deep hole.* 2 needing much thought to understand. 3 (of colour) dark; (of sound) low. 4 intense: *deep thought.* ●*adv* far (into). **deep-freeze** (ˌdiːpˈfriːz) *vt* keep (food) in good condition for a long time by freezing it. ● (ˈdiːpˌfriːz) *nc* a metal box for frozen food. **deep-sea** (ˌdiːpˈsiː) *adj* of the deeper parts of the sea. **deep-seated** (ˌdiːpˈsiːtɪd) *adj*

not easily changed or moved because existing deep in (someone's character, etc.). **deepen** (ˈdiːpən) *vti* **deeply** (ˈdiːplɪ) *adv*

deer (dɪə*) *nc, pl* **deer** a graceful animal, the male having horns like the branches of a tree: see picture at **animals**.

deface (dɪˈfeɪs) *vt* spoil or damage the appearance of (a surface, picture, etc.).

defame (dɪˈfeɪm) *vt* try to harm the reputation of (a person) by saying bad things. **defamation** (ˌdefəˈmeɪʃən) *nu*

default (dɪˈfɔːlt) *vi* fail to do something, esp. to pay a debt or appear in a law court. ● *nu* failure to pay, appear, etc.

defeat (dɪˈfiːt) *vt* 1 win a victory over: *defeat the enemy.* 2 cause (a person, plan, etc.) to fail. ●*ncu* (an example of) being defeated: *Be brave in defeat.*

defect (ˈdiːfekt) *nc* a fault. ● (dɪˈfekt) *vi* run away from one's own country, party, etc., to be loyal to another.

defective (dɪˈfektɪv) *adj* not perfect; wrong or broken.

defence *US* **defense** (dɪˈfens) 1 *nu* the fighting against attack. 2 *nc* something that protects against attack. 3 *law ncu* the facts used to defend a person accused of a crime. **defenceless** *adj*

defend (dɪˈfend) *vt* 1 protect. 2 give reasons for (what one believes, etc.). 3 *sport* guard, to prevent the other team winning. **defendant** (dɪˈfendənt) *law nc* a person who is accused of a crime. **defender** (dɪfendə*) *nc* a person who defends.

defensive (dɪˈfensɪv) *adj* 1 with an aim to protect. 2 (of a person) always defending one's actions, etc. **on the defensive** ready for attack.

defer[1] (dɪˈfɜː*) *vt* put off to a later time.

defer[2] *vi* (followed by **to**) show respect by giving way to another person's opinion, etc. **deference** (ˈdefərəns) *nu*

defiance (dɪˈfaɪəns) *nu* refusal to obey or show respect. **defiant** (dɪˈfaɪənt) *adj*

deficiency (dɪˈfɪʃənsɪ) *nc, pl* **-cies** 1 a lack. 2 *nu* the state of there not being enough. **deficient** (dɪˈfɪʃənt) *adj*

deficit (ˈdefɪsɪt) *nc* the amount by which something, esp. a sum of money, is not enough.

defile (dɪˈfaɪl) *vt* make dirty or evil.

define (dɪˈfaɪn) *vt* give the exact meaning or the points of.

definite (ˈdefɪnɪt, ˈdefənət) *adj* 1 of which there is no doubt; clear. 2 (of a person) firm. **definitely** *adv* **definite article** See under **article**.

definition (ˌdefɪˈnɪʃən, ˌdefəˈnɪʃən) 1 *ncu* the exact meaning of a word; set of words used to show this meaning. 2 *nu* clearness, esp. of a photograph.

definitive (dɪˈfɪnɪtɪv, dɪˈfɪnətɪv) *adj* needing no further change; final.

deflate (dɪˈfleɪt, diːˈfleɪt) **1** *vti* (cause to) let the air or gas out of (a balloon, tyre, etc.). *vt* **2** *economics* lower (prices) or cause (the amount of money to become less), **3** make (someone) feel suddenly sad or let down. **deflation** (diːˈfleɪʃən, dɪˈfleɪʃən) *nu*

deflect (dɪˈflekt) *vti* (cause to) turn aside: *He deflected the blow with his arm.* **deflection** *nc*

deform (dɪˈfɔːm) *vt* make twisted or ugly by putting out of shape. **deformed** *adj* **deformity** (dɪˈfɔːmɪtɪ) *nc, pl* **-ties**

defraud (dɪˈfrɔːd) *vt* cheat (a person) esp. in money matters.

defrost (ˌdiːˈfrɒst) *vt* remove ice from (esp. inside a refrigerator).

deft (deft) *adj* **-er, -est** neat and clever, esp. with the hands. **deftly** *adv*

defunct (dɪˈfʌŋkt) *adj* **1** *formal* (of a person) dead. **2** no longer used.

defy (dɪˈfaɪ) *vt* **1** tell (someone) to be ready to prove or do something difficult. **2** show no respect for (rules, etc.).

degenerate (dɪˈdʒenəreɪt) *vi* become worse in quality. ●(dɪˈdʒenərət) *adj* having sunk from a higher state. ● *nc* something, esp. a person, in a low condition.

degrade (dɪˈɡreɪd) *vt* **1** *science* move to a lower class; decompose. **2** put (a person) to shame. **degradation** (ˌdeɡrəˈdeɪʃən) *nu*

degree (dɪˈɡriː) *nc* **1** a step or stage: *a high degree of ability.* **2** a measure of angles: see picture. **3** a measure of heat. **4** a title given by a university, usually for passing an examination.

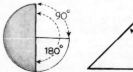

degree

dehydrate (ˌdiːhaɪˈdreɪt) *vti* (cause to) lose water, esp. from food. **dehydration** (ˌdiːhaɪˈdreɪʃən) *nu*

deign (deɪn) *often derogatory or humorous vi* **deign to** do something pleasantly, but show that one feels too good for the task, etc.: *Will you deign to come to my party?*

deity (ˈdiːɪtɪ, ˈdeɪətɪ) *nc, pl* **-ties** a god or goddess.

dejected (dɪˈdʒektɪd) *adj* sad; in low spirits. **dejection** (dɪˈdʒekʃən) *nu*

delay (dɪˈleɪ) *vti* **1** (go slowly to) make (someone or something) late. **2** postpone (something) to a later date. ● *ncu* (an example of) being delayed; pause.

delectable (dɪˈlektəbəl) *adj* (esp. of food) very pleasing.

delegate (ˈdelɪɡət) *nc* a person whose job is to act for others, esp. for the government. ●(ˈdelɪɡeɪt) *vt* appoint (someone) to do something in one's place. **delegation** (ˌdelɪˈɡeɪʃən) **1** *nu* the act of delegating. **2** *nc* a group of delegates: *a trade delegation.*

delete (dɪˈliːt) *vt* draw a line through (a word, sentence, etc.); remove.

deliberate (dɪˈlɪbərət) *adj* **1** done with firm intention. **2** slow and careful. **deliberately** *adv* ●(dɪˈlɪbəreɪt) *vti* think carefully and seriously (on what to do): *He deliberated before making his decision.* **deliberation** (dɪˌlɪbəˈreɪʃən) *ncu*

delicacy (ˈdelɪkəsɪ) *nc, pl* **-cies 1** *ncu* (an example of) pureness of feeling, taste, manners, etc. **2** *nc* a very nice piece of food.

delicate (ˈdelɪkət) *adj* **1** soft; pretty; beautifully made: *delicate pink; delicate silks.* **2** easily injured or broken; (of a person) weak. **3** gentle and tender with the hands, with other people's feelings, etc. **4** needing careful treatment. **delicately** *adv*

delicatessen (ˌdelɪkəˈtesən) *nc* a shop that sells good food, usually cooked.

delicious (dɪˈlɪʃəs) *adj* having a very pleasant taste, smell, etc.

delight (dɪˈlaɪt) *vti* (cause to) be made happy or very pleased: *His success delights me.* ● *ncu* (something that gives) pleasure. **delight in** take great pleasure in. **be delighted** be very pleased. **delightful** *adj* **delightfully** *adv*

delinquency (dɪˈlɪŋkwənsɪ) *ncu* (an example of) breaking of laws; not doing one's duty. **delinquent** (dɪˈlɪŋkwənt) *nc* a person guilty of delinquency, esp. a young person who has broken the law. ● *adj* guilty of delinquency.

delirious (dɪˈlɪrɪəs) *adj* **1** acting and talking in a wild way, esp. in illness. **2** *infml* very excited or happy. **delirium** (dɪˈlɪrɪəm) *nu* an illness of the mind.

deliver (dɪˈlɪvə*) *vt* **1** take or give (something) to a place, person, etc.: *deliver the mail.* **2** (help to) give birth to a baby. **3** set free. **4** speak: *to deliver a speech.* **deliver from** save from. **delivery** (dɪˈlɪvərɪ) *ncu* (an example of) delivering.

dell (del) *nc* a small valley, esp. with trees.

delta (ˈdeltə) *nc* the land between the branches of a river at its mouth: see picture.

delta

delude (dɪˈluːd) vt give (a person) a wrong idea on purpose.

deluge (ˈdeljuːdʒ) nc a flood; huge number or amount. ● vt overwhelm.

delusion (dɪˈluːʒən) 1 nu giving or being given a wrong idea on purpose. 2 nc a wrong idea, esp. in an illness of the mind.

de luxe (dəˈlʊks, dɪˈlʌks) adj of the very best and most expensive kind.

delve (delv) vi **delve into** look into very carefully.

demagogue (ˈdeməgɒg) nc a leader or politician who by his words causes strong feelings among the people.

demand (dɪˈmɑːnd) vti 1 ask (for something), in a way that sounds like an order; claim. 2 vt need: *This letter demands a quick reply.* ● nc 1 a claim. 2 nu a need, esp. for goods that people want to buy: *strong demand for lamb.* **on demand** as soon as asked for. **demanding** adj always needing something, esp. attention.

demarcation (ˌdiːmɑːˈkeɪʃən) nu marking the outer edges or the limits, esp. of the responsibility of someone's job.

demeanour US **demeanor** (dɪˈmiːnə*) nu the way one behaves.

demented (dɪˈmentɪd) adj crazy.

democracy (dɪˈmɒkrəsɪ) nc, pl **-cies** 1 a government chosen by the people in elections; country ruled in this way. 2 nu a system allowing freedom for everyone: *Can a family be a democracy?* **democrat** (ˈdeməkræt) nc a person who believes in the right to choose a government. **democratic** (ˌdeməˈkrætɪk) adj 1 to do with democracy. 2 giving equal rights to everyone.

demography (dɪˈmɒgrəfɪ) nu the study of the numbers of births, deaths, etc., in a country to get information about society.

demolish (dɪˈmɒlɪʃ) vt destroy (esp. old buildings). **demolition** (ˌdeməˈlɪʃən) nu

demon (ˈdiːmən) nc 1 an evil spirit. 2 infml an evil or naughty person; someone full of energy for a particular purpose.

demonstrate (ˈdemənstreɪt) 1 vt show by proving or explaining. 2 vi take part in a public meeting, procession, etc., to show one's feelings about a matter. **demonstration** (ˌdemənˈstreɪʃən) ncu **demonstrator** nc **demonstrative** (dɪˈmɒnstrətɪv) adj showing openly how one feels.

demoralise (dɪˈmɒrəlaɪz) vt make (a person or group) lose respect for their own ability: *Defeat demoralises an army.*

demote (dɪˈməʊt) vt move down to a lower rank, position, etc.

demure (dɪˈmjʊə*) adj quiet and serious; pretending to be shy.

den (den) nc 1 a wild animal's cave. 2 a secret place, esp. for thieves. 3 a room in a

house used esp. by one particular member of a family for work, etc.

denial (dɪˈnaɪəl) nc an act of saying that something is not true or that one does not know about something.

denim (ˈdenɪm) 1 nu strong cotton cloth, esp. used for jeans. 2 (pl) a pair of trousers made of denim; jeans.

denizen (ˈdenɪzən) often literary or humorous nc a person, animal, or plant, living in a place.

denomination (dɪˌnɒmɪˈneɪʃən) nc 1 the name showing the class or kind something belongs to. 2 a group of people with the same religious beliefs. 3 a group of banknotes, weights, etc.

denominator (dɪˈnɒmɪneɪtə*) nc the number below the line in a fraction: *2 is the denominator in ½.*

denote (dɪˈnəʊt) vt be a sign of; show.

denounce (dɪˈnaʊns) vt speak against (a person) in public; accuse.

dense (dens) adj **-er, -est** 1 not easily seen through, esp. mist, steam, etc. 2 with little or no space in between: *a dense crowd.* 3 stupid. **densely** adv

density (ˈdensɪtɪ) 1 nu the state of having very little space in between. 2 ncu, pl **-ties** science the relation of mass or weight to volume (of a substance).

dent (dent) nc a shallow hole in a surface, caused esp. by a blow. ● vti (cause to) have dents.

dental (ˈdentəl) adj of the teeth.

dentist (ˈdentɪst) nc a person whose work is repairing, cleaning, and taking out teeth. **dentistry** (ˈdentɪstrɪ) nu

denude (dɪˈnjuːd) vt make bare.

denunciation (dɪˌnʌnsɪˈeɪʃən) ncu accusing (a person) in public.

deny (dɪˈnaɪ) vt 1 say (something) to be not true or not known to one. 2 refuse to give what is asked for or needed.

deodorant (diːˈəʊdərənt) nc a powder, spray, etc., used to prevent or cover up bad smells, esp. of the body.

depart (dɪˈpɑːt) vi 1 (followed by **from**) leave; go away from, esp. of a train, bus, etc.: *The train departs from platform three.* 2 vt formal or polite die. 3 vi (followed by **from**) turn away from what is the usual or right thing to do: *to depart from the truth.*

department (dɪˈpɑːtmənt) nc a part of a business, university, school, etc.: *the college's science department.* **department store** a large shop with several parts selling different goods in each. **departmental** (ˌdiːpɑːtˈmentəl) adj

departure (dɪˈpɑːtʃə*) ncu 1 (an example of) leaving; going away. 2 a turning away from doing the usual; taking a new direction.

depend (dɪ'pend) vi 1 (followed by **on**) rely on for help; trust. 2 change according to: *The children's interest in this subject depends on the teacher.* **that** or **it all depends on**... that or it is not certain until (something else is known first). **dependable** (dɪ'pendəbəl) adj trustworthy.

dependant (dɪ'pendənt) nc a person, esp. a child, who relies on someone for a home, etc.

dependence (dɪ'pendəns) nu a state of relying on others for their support; trust.

dependency (dɪ'pendənsɪ) nc, pl **-cies** a country that is controlled by another.

dependent (dɪ'pendənt) adj 1 unable to do without something. 2 being not certain until something else is known.

depict (dɪ'pɪkt) vt show in a picture; describe in words.

deplete (dɪ'pliːt) vt almost use up (a store of something).

deplore (dɪ'plɔː*) vt feel deep sorrow for, because one considers (something) to be wrong: *He deplored his son's rudeness.* **deplorable** (dɪ'plɔːrəbəl) adj

deploy (dɪ'plɔɪ) vt spread out (soldiers) to be ready for battle.

deport (dɪ'pɔːt) vt send (esp. a dangerous or bad person) out of a country. **deportation** (ˌdiːpɔː'teɪʃən) ncu

depose (dɪ'pəʊz) vt remove (a person, esp. a king, etc.) from a position of power.

deposit (dɪ'pɒzɪt) nc 1 money put into a bank, etc., for safety; part of an amount of money owed, the rest to be paid later. 2 a layer of solid matter: see picture. ●vt 1 put down. 2 put into a bank, etc. for safety. 3 leave (a layer of matter) behind or at the bottom.

deposit

depositor (dɪ'pɒzɪtə*) nc a person who puts money into a bank.

depot ('depəʊ) nc 1 a place where goods, esp. for soldiers, are kept. 2 a place where buses are kept. 3 *chiefly US* a railway station.

depraved (dɪ'preɪvd) adj choosing to do wrong and evil things, esp. because influenced by bad company. **depravity** (dɪ'prævɪtɪ) ncu

deprecate ('deprɪkeɪt) *formal* vt show one does not approve of.

depreciate (dɪ'priːʃɪeɪt) 1 vti (cause to) become less in value. 2 vt make (a person) feel of little or no value. **depreciation** (dɪ,priːʃɪ'eɪʃən) nu

depress (dɪ'pres) vt 1 press down. 2 make sad or low in spirits. 3 make (esp. trade) less, smaller, etc. **depression** (dɪ'preʃən) ncu

deprive (dɪ'praɪv) vt take away from; prevent from doing or having. **deprivation** (ˌdeprɪ'veɪʃən) ncu

depth (depθ) ncu 1 being deep; distance from the surface to the bottom or from the front to the back. 2 the measure of deep feelings, thoughts, etc. 3 (pl) the deepest part of: *the depths of the sea.*

deputation (ˌdepjʊ'teɪʃən) nc a group of people chosen to speak or act for others.

deputy ('depjʊtɪ) nc, pl **-ties** 1 a person chosen to act for another person. 2 (in certain countries) a member of parliament. **deputise** ('depjʊtaɪz) vi act as a deputy.

derail (dɪ'reɪl) vt cause (a train) to run off the railway lines.

derange (dɪ'reɪndʒ) vt put out of order. **deranged** (dɪ'reɪndʒd) adj mad.

derelict ('derɪlɪkt) adj (esp. of a building or ship) left without an owner; falling to pieces.

deride (dɪ'raɪd) vt laugh unkindly at; make fun of. **derision** (dɪ'rɪʒən) nu

derive (dɪ'raɪv) (followed by **from**). 1 vt get; obtain: *Derive petrol from oil.* 2 vi (of a word) come from. **derivation** (ˌderɪ'veɪʃən) ncu **derivative** (dɪ'rɪvətɪv) adj often derogatory copying something else. ●nc something, esp. a word or substance, coming from something else: *Petrol is one of the derivatives of oil.*

derogatory (dɪ'rɒgətərɪ) adj not respectful.

derrick ('derɪk) nc 1 a tall machine for lifting and moving heavy weights, esp. on a ship. 2 the frame over an oil well: see picture.

derrick

descend (dɪ'send) vti come or go down (something): *descend a hill; descend quickly.* **be descended from** come from (one's ancestors). **descend on** arrive without warning. **descend to** lower or humble oneself. **descendant** (dɪ'sendənt) *nc* a person who has come from an earlier member of the family.

descent (dɪ'sent) *ncu* **1** a coming down; slope. **2** the line of family a person has come from.

describe (dɪ'skraɪb) *vt* **1** show in words what something is like: *Describe his face to me.* **2** *mathematics* draw (a shape).

description (dɪ'skrɪpʃən) *ncu* **1** (an example of) the act of describing. **2** kind: *people of every description.* **descriptive** (dɪ'skrɪptɪv) *adj*

descry (dɪ'skraɪ) *literary vt* see (something, esp. a long way off).

desecrate ('desɪkreɪt) *vt* put (a sacred place) to wicked use.

desegregate (,diː'segrɪgeɪt) *vt* stop the segregation of. **desegregation** (,diːsegrɪ'geɪʃən) *nc*

desert[1] ('dezət) *nc* a large piece of land that is without water and trees, and is covered in sand.

desert[2] (dɪ'zɜːt) *vt* **1** leave (a place) empty. **2** leave (one's duty, esp. one's family) to look after itself. **3** *vti* leave, (esp. the army) without permission. **deserter** (dɪ'zɜːtə*) *nc* a person who leaves, esp. the army, without permission. **desertion** (dɪ'zɜːʃən) *ncu*

deserts (dɪ'zɜːts) *nu* what a person deserves: *A coward gets his just deserts.*

deserve (dɪ'zɜːv) *vt* have a right to (certain treatment) because of good or bad actions, etc. **deservedly** (dɪ'zɜːvɪdlɪ) *adv*

desiccate ('desɪkeɪt) *vt* make (esp. food) dry to keep it and prevent it going bad.

design (dɪ'zaɪn) **1** *nc* a plan or drawing showing how something could be made, built, etc. **2** *nu* the way something is made, built, etc. **3** *nc* a pattern. **4** a plan in the mind. ● *vt* **1** have an idea for; make (something) specially for. **2** draw a plan for. **designer** (dɪ'zaɪnə*) *nc*

designate ('dezɪgneɪt) *vt* **1** appoint (a person) to do a job. **2** mark out clearly. **designation** (,dezɪg'neɪʃən) *ncu*

desirable (dɪ'zaɪərəbəl) *adj* worth having or wanting. **desirability** (dɪ,zaɪərə'bɪlɪtɪ) *nu*

desire (dɪ'zaɪə*) **1** *ncu* a deep wish or want. **2** *nc* that which is wished for or wanted. ● *vt* want very much. **desirous** (dɪ'zaɪərəs) *adj*

desist (dɪ'zɪst, dɪ'sɪst) *formal or humorous vi* stop doing something.

desk (desk) *nc* **1** a piece of furniture like a table, at which to write, study, do business, etc.: see picture. **2** a place in a hotel, etc., where visitors are met: *reception desk.*

desolate ('desələt) *adj* **1** sad and lonely; without friends. **2** (of a place or land) poor and not lived in. **desolation** (,desə'leɪʃən) *nu*

desk

despair (dɪ'speə*) *nu* the feeling of no hope. ● *vi* lose hope.

despatch (dɪ'spætʃ) *n, v* See **dispatch.**

desperate ('despərət) *adj* **1** not caring about danger or the law, because of grief or lack of hope. **2** very serious: *desperate trouble.* **3** wild or dangerous and unlikely to succeed. **desperately** *adv* **desperation** (,despə'reɪʃən) *nu*

despicable ('despɪkəbəl) *adj* shameful and disgusting.

despise (dɪ'spaɪz) *vt* feel contempt for.

despite (dɪ'spaɪt) *prep* in spite of: *Despite his cleverness, he failed the examination.*

despoil (dɪ'spɔɪl) *vt* take goods from (a person or place) by force.

despondency (dɪ'spɒndənsɪ) *nu* sadness; low spirits. **despondent** (dɪ'spɒndənt) *adj*

despot ('despɒt) *derogatory nc* a person who has complete power and uses it badly and cruelly. **despotic** (de'spɒtɪk) *adj* **despotism** ('despətɪzəm) *nu*

dessert (dɪ'zɜːt) *nc* sweet food eaten at the end of a meal.

destination (,destɪ'neɪʃən) *nc* a place to which a person or a thing is going.

destine ('destɪn) *vt* (usually of God or fate) arrange (for something) to happen: *He was destined to become King.*

destiny ('destɪnɪ) **1** *nu* the power that is thought to decide what will happen. **2** *nc, pl* **-nies** a person's fate.

destitute ('destɪtjuːt) *adj* in great need of necessary things, esp. food, clothes, etc.

destroy (dɪ'strɔɪ) *vt* cause the complete ruin of (something); kill; make useless. **destroyer** *nc* a person who destroys; anything that destroys, esp. a fast warship that protects larger ships.

destruction (dɪ'strʌkʃən) *nu* destroying or being destroyed. **destructive** (dɪ'strʌktɪv) *adj* likely to destroy or damage; causing destruction.

desultory ('desəltərɪ) *adj* without plan or purpose; changing often from one subject, piece of work, etc., to another.

detach (dɪ'tætʃ) *vt* separate; unfasten. **detached** (dɪ'tætʃt) *adj* **1** not joined to another: *a detached house.* **2** (of a person) not showing that one likes one person, or thing, more than another; without, or not

101

showing, strong feelings. **detachment** (dɪ-ˈtætʃmənt) *nu* **1** detaching or being detached. **2** being unaffected by the opinions, feelings, etc., of other people, or by things happening around one. **3** *nc* part of an army, etc., separated from the rest for some special purpose.

detail (ˈdiːteɪl) **1** *nc* a small, special, item, point, fact, etc: *details of the battle*. **2** *nu* a small part of a picture, etc.: *The drawing has been spoiled by too much detail*. **in detail** fully. ● *vt* **1** give a very full account of. **2** give a special duty to.

detain (dɪˈteɪn) *vt* prevent from leaving; delay.

detect (dɪˈtekt) *vt* find out; observe. **detector** (dɪˈtektə*) *nc* a device for discovering the presence of something. **detection** (dɪˈtekʃən) *nu* detecting; finding out. **detective** (dɪˈtektɪv) *nc* a person whose job is to find out people guilty of crime or get information.

detention (dɪˈtenʃən) *ncu* (an example of) preventing from leaving or being prevented from leaving: *The naughty child was kept in detention after the rest of the school had gone home*.

deter (dɪˈtɜː*) *vt* discourage (a person) from doing something because of fear, not wanting trouble, etc.: *His gun deterred them from attacking him*.

detergent (dɪˈtɜːdʒənt) *nc* a substance used, often with water, to remove dirt, grease, etc.

deteriorate (dɪˈtɪərɪəreɪt) *vti* make or become worse, less fit for use, etc. **deterioration** (dɪ,tɪərɪəˈreɪʃən) *nu* deteriorating or being deteriorated.

determination (dɪ,tɜːmɪˈneɪʃən) **1** *nu* the state of being fixed and firm in purpose: *He has the determination to succeed in his new job*. *nc* **2** a firm decision. **3** the finding out of a meaning, an amount, etc.

determine (dɪˈtɜːmɪn) *vti* **1** (cause to) decide firmly: *He determined to go abroad as soon as he'd finished his university course*. *vt* **2** find out (something) exactly: *Have we determined how long the journey will take?* **3** fix; decide: *The date for the meeting has now been determined*. **4** be the most important cause of.

deterrent (dɪˈterənt) *nc* something that discourages a person or persons from acting. ● *adj* that discourages action.

detest (dɪˈtest) *vt* hate; dislike strongly.

dethrone (dɪˈθrəʊn) *vt* remove (someone, esp. a king,) from a position of power.

detonate (ˈdetəneɪt) *vti* (cause to) explode. **detonator** (ˈdetəneɪtə*) *nc* a device that explodes, esp. in a bomb, causing the rest of it to explode: see picture.

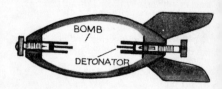

detonator

detour (ˈdiːtʊə*) *nc* a longer way round: *Make a detour to avoid the heavy traffic*.

detract (dɪˈtrækt) *vi* (followed by **from**) make less in value, worth, etc.: *Her unkind nature detracts from her beauty*.

detriment (ˈdetrɪmənt) *nu* harm; loss: *Smoking can be to the detriment of one's good health*. **detrimental** (,detrɪˈmentəl) *adj* harmful.

deuce (djuːs) *nu* **1** (in tennis) the stage reached where each side has won three points and one side must now gain two points, one after the other, to win. **2** the two on dice or cards.

devalue (,diːˈvæljuː) *US* **devaluate** (,diːˈvæljuːeɪt) *vt* make the value of (a country's currency) less. **devaluation** (dɪ,væˈjʊ ˈeɪʃən) *ncu*

devastate (ˈdevəsteɪt) *vt* ruin; damage very badly. **devastation** (,devəˈsteɪʃən) *nc* devastating, or being devastated.

develop (dɪˈveləp) **1** *vt* make larger or more mature; make to progress: *New plans have been developed*. **2** *vi* grow; become: *The story develops into a tale of adventure*. *vt* **3** put (a piece of land) to new use and so make it more valuable. **4** make (a picture on photographic film) able to be seen. **development** (dɪˈveləpmənt) **1** *nu* developing or being developed: *development of a disease*. **2** *nc* a result of something developing: *new developments in medicine*. **developing country** a poor country that has begun to make progress in producing goods, etc.

deviate (ˈdiːvieɪt) *vi* turn away from the truth, usual course of action, etc. **deviation** (,diːvɪˈeɪʃən) **1** *nu* a turning away from. **2** *nc* an example of this or the amount of this.

device (dɪˈvaɪs) *nc* **1** a trick; plan to deceive. **2** something made or made suitable for a particular use or purpose.

devil (ˈdevəl) **1** **The Devil** the spirit of evil and enemy of God. *nc* **2** an evil spirit; cruel or wicked person. **3** (used in an expression of pity) a person: *The poor devil's son has died*. **devilish** (ˈdevlɪʃ) *adj* wicked. ● *adv* very: *devilish bad weather*.

devious (ˈdiːvɪəs) *adj* **1** going a long way round: *a devious route*. **2** hard to understand because complicated; deceitful: *a devious mind*.

devise (dɪˈvaɪz) *vt* think up (an idea, plan, etc.).

devoid (dɪˈvɔɪd) *adj* **devoid of** without: *a lecture devoid of meaning.*

devote (dɪˈvəʊt) *vt* give up (all one's attention, time, etc.) to: *He devoted his life to helping others.* **devoted** *adj* very loving; loyal. **devotee** (ˌdevəˈtiː) *nc* an enthusiastic supporter. **devotion** (dɪˈvəʊʃən) *nu* 1 giving up of all one's time or attention to. 2 strong love.

devour (dɪˈvaʊə*) *vt* 1 eat very hungrily or with greed. 2 destroy by fire. 3 take up all one's interest, attention, etc.: *devour a new book.*

devout (dɪˈvaʊt) *adj* very loyal and sincere, esp. to religious duties. **devoutly** *adv* sincerely; eagerly.

dew (djuː) *nu* very small amounts of water forming on cool surfaces between evening and morning: *The fields were wet with dew.* **dewdrop** (ˈdjuːdrɒp) *nc* a tiny amount of dew. **dewy** *adj* -ier, -iest wet and shining (esp. with dew).

dexterity (dekˈsterətɪ) *nu* ability to do things well with the hands. **dexterous** (ˈdekstərəs) (also **dextrous**) (ˈdekstrəs) *adj* clever with the hands.

diabetes (ˌdaɪəˈbiːtiz) *nu* a disease in which sugar is not properly used when taken into the body. **diabetic** (ˌdaɪəˈbetɪk) *adj* of or to do with diabetes. ● *nc* a person who has diabetes.

diabolical (ˌdaɪəˈbɒlɪkəl) *adj* 1 of, to do with, or like a devil; very cruel. 2 *infml* (of something that makes one angry) very bad: *diabolical rudeness.*

diadem (ˈdaɪədem) *literary nc* a crown; circle of flowers, or leaves, twisted together and worn on the head.

diagnose (ˌdaɪəgˈnəʊz) *vt* find out the nature of (a disease, fault, etc.). **diagnosis** (ˌdaɪəgˈnəʊsɪs) *ncu, pl* -ses (siːz) (a result of) diagnosing.

diagonal (daɪˈægənəl) *nc* a straight line in a figure of four sides that goes across from one corner to the opposite corner. ● *adj* of such a line; sloping. **diagonally** *adv*

diagram (ˈdaɪəgræm) *nc* a drawing or plan, to explain something. **diagrammatic** (ˌdaɪəgrəˈmætɪk) *adj* of or to do with a diagram. **diagrammatically** (ˌdaɪəgrəˈmætɪkəlɪ) *adv*

dial (ˈdaɪəl) *nc* 1 the face of a clock or watch. 2 a flat, round surface with a needle-like device for measuring weight, speed, etc. 3 the flat, round part of a telephone with numbers, letters, etc. 4 the disc on a radio or television set for choosing programmes. ● *vt* make a telephone call to (someone).

dialect (ˈdaɪəlekt) *ncu* the different way of speaking in a part of the country, or by a class of people.

dialectic (ˌdaɪəˈlektɪk) *nu* the skill and practice of deciding whether an idea, opinion, etc., is true by debate.

dialogue *US* **dialog** (ˈdaɪəlɒg) 1 *nc* a conversation between two people. 2 *nu* part of a play or book, that contains conversation; this kind of writing. 3 *nc* a discussion between two leaders, etc.

diameter (daɪˈæmɪtə*) *nc* the line that crosses through the centre of a figure, esp. a circle; length of such a line.

diametrically (ˌdaɪəˈmetrɪklɪ) *adv* completely: *diametrically opposed.*

diamond (ˈdaɪəmənd) *nc* 1 a very hard, bright, precious stone of pure carbon: *a diamond ring.* 2 a figure with four equal straight sides and with angles different from a square. 3 a playing-card with a diamond shape on.

diaphragm (ˈdaɪəfræm) *nc* 1 the wall of muscle that separates the chest from the stomach and bowels. 2 a device in a camera, etc., that changes the size of the opening that lets in light.

diarrhoea (ˌdaɪəˈrɪə) *nu* the frequent emptying of the too liquid contents of the bowels.

diary (ˈdaɪərɪ) *nc, pl* -ries a daily written account of events, thoughts, etc.; book for this purpose.

dice (daɪs) *n pl* (*chiefly US* singular **die**) a small, solid cube, with each side marked with spots, used in games: *Throw a dice.*

dichotomy (daɪˈkɒtəmɪ) *nc, pl* -mies a division into two that is very clearly seen, understood, etc.: *the dichotomy of wealth and poverty.*

dictate (dɪkˈteɪt) 1 *vti* speak or read (words) aloud, usually for someone to write down: *He dictated a letter.* 2 *vt* give orders to, not always with the power and right to do so; govern.

dictation (dɪkˈteɪʃən) 1 *nu* dictating or being dictated to. 2 *nc* a set of words, etc., that are dictated.

dictator (dɪkˈteɪtə*) *derogatory nc* a person with complete power, usually obtained by force. **dictatorial** (ˌdɪktəˈtɔːrɪəl) *derogatory adj* of or like a dictator; forcing others to obey. **dictatorship** (dɪkˈteɪtəʃɪp) *derogatory nc* a country that is governed by a dictator; such a government.

diction (ˈdɪkʃən) *nu* 1 the choice and use of words in speaking or writing. 2 the way the sound of a word is made in speaking or singing.

dictionary (ˈdɪkʃənərɪ) *nc, pl* -ries a book containing a list of words and their meanings, in the order of the alphabet.

did (dɪd) past tense of **do**.

didn't ('dɪdənt) v did not.

didst (dɪdst) *archaic* v (used with **thou**) past tense of **do**.

die¹ (daɪ) vi 1 stop living. 2 come to an end. **be dying for** *infml* want very much: *She's dying for a chance to meet him*.

die² nc 1 *chiefly US* one of two or more dice. 2 a piece of metal with a pattern, shape, etc., cut into it, for use in printing, making coins, etc.

diesel ('diːzəl) nc also **diesel engine** an engine in which power is produced by the burning of oil inside it; vehicle that works with such an engine.

diet ('daɪət) nc 1 the kinds of food one usually eats. 2 a way of eating using special kinds of food for a particular purpose: *The doctor put her on a diet to lose weight.* ● vi eat only certain foods in order to become thinner or for reasons of health.

differ ('dɪfə*) vi 1 be unlike: *Our interests differ*. 2 disagree: *We differ greatly in our political opinions.*

difference ('dɪfrəns) 1 nu being unlike: *the difference between a tree and a bush.* 2 nc the way or measure in which things are unlike: *a difference of two years in our ages.* **different** ('dɪfrənt) adj 1 unlike; not the same. 2 various: *For different reasons he decided not to go to university.* **differently** adv

differential (,dɪfə'renʃəl) adj of or to do with a difference. ● nc the difference in wages between industries.

differentiate (,dɪfə'renʃɪeɪt) vt 1 show or see a difference. 2 make a difference between. **differentiation** (,dɪfərenʃɪ'eɪʃən) nc differentiating.

difficult ('dɪfɪkəlt) adj 1 not easy; hard to do, understand, or explain. 2 (of a person) hard to please; causing trouble: *What a difficult child he is!* **difficulty** ('dɪfɪkəltɪ) nc, pl **-ties** 1 nu being difficult. 2 nc something that gets in the way because it is not easy to do, understand, or explain.

diffident ('dɪfɪdənt) adj having too low an opinion of oneself and one's abilities.

diffraction (dɪ'frækʃən) nc the dividing up of a beam of light into dark and light bands, or into bands of colour.

diffuse (dɪ'fjuːs) adj 1 spread out in every direction: *diffuse light.* 2 using more words than are needed: *a diffuse speech.* ●(dɪ'fjuːz) vti (cause to) spread or send out in every direction. **diffusion** (dɪ'fjuːʒən) nu diffusing or being diffused.

dig (dɪg) 1 vti break up the soil (of a piece of land): *dig the garden.* vt 2 remove soil to make or uncover (something): *The dog dug a hole to bury its bone; They dug up a buried city.* 3 *slang* like. ● nc 1 *infml* a sudden

push. 2 a place where the ground is being dug up to uncover things belonging to times long past; the act of doing this. **digs** *infml, Brit* rented rooms to live in.

digest (dɪ'dʒest, daɪ'dʒest) 1 vt change (food) in the stomach and intestine so that it can be used in the body. 2 vi (of food) be changed so that it can be used in the body. 3 vt take (information, ideas, knowledge, etc.) into the mind: *Has she digested the bad news yet?* ●('daɪdʒest) nc an account of a book, etc., giving the chief points only. **digestion** (dɪ'dʒestʃən, daɪ'dʒestʃən) 1 nu digesting. 2 ncu ability to digest food: *He has a weak digestion.* **digestive** (dɪ'dʒestɪv, daɪ'dʒestɪv) of, or to do with, the digestion of food.

digger ('dɪgə*) nc 1 a person who digs, esp. one who searches for gold. 2 a tool or machine for digging.

digit ('dɪdʒɪt) nc 1 a finger, thumb, or toe. 2 any number from zero up to, and including, nine. **digital** ('dɪdʒɪtəl) adj of, or using, digits: *a digital watch.*

dignified ('dɪgnɪfaɪd) adj having a calm and serious manner.

dignitary ('dɪgnɪtərɪ) nc, pl **-ries** a person of high rank as in the government.

dignity ('dɪgnətɪ) nu 1 high quality of character or worth; nobility. 2 a serious manner.

digression (daɪ'greʃən) 1 nu leaving the main subject in speaking or writing. 2 nc an example of this: *The book is full of digressions.*

dike (daɪk) n See **dyke**.

dilapidated (dɪ'læpɪdeɪtɪd) adj (of buildings, furniture, etc.) in need of repair.

dilate (daɪ'leɪt) vti (cause to) become wider or larger.

dilemma (dɪ'lemə, daɪ'lemə) nc a difficult situation in which neither choice of two courses of action is a good one.

diligence ('dɪlɪdʒəns) nu the giving of all one's attention, energy, etc., to one's work, or to what one has to do. **diligent** ('dɪlɪdʒent) adj giving care, hard work, attention, etc., to what one does. **diligently** adv

dilute (daɪ'luːt) vt make weaker or thinner by mixing with water or another liquid: *to dilute paint.*

dim (dɪm) adj 1 not bright or clear: *dim lights; The old man's memories were very dim.* 2 *infml* not very clever. **dimly** adv

dime (daɪm) *US* nc a coin with the value of ten cents.

dimension (daɪ'menʃən) nc 1 a measurement of any kind, such as height, length, width, volume, etc. 2 (pl) size. **dimensional** (daɪ'menʃənəl) adj having one or more measurements: *A square is two-dimensional, but a cube is three-dimensional.*

diminish (dɪˈmɪnɪʃ) *vti* (cause to) become less or smaller.

diminutive (dɪˈmɪnjʊtɪv) *adj* **1** very tiny; more than usually small. **2** *grammar* letters added to the end of a word showing smallness: *'Duckling' is a diminutive of 'duck'.* • *nc* the word formed by adding letters in this way.

dimple (ˈdɪmpəl) *nc* a tiny hollow place in the cheek or chin: *The baby smiled and showed his dimples.*

dimwit (ˈdɪmwɪt) *infml nc* a foolish person.

din (dɪn) *derogatory nu* a loud noise that goes on for a long time: *the din of the traffic.*

dine (daɪn) **1** *vi* eat dinner. **2** *vt* give dinner to. **diner** (ˈdaɪnə*) *nc* **1** a person who dines. **2** the part of a train where people have meals. **3** *US* a restaurant.

ding-dong (ˈdɪŋˌdɒŋ) *nu* the sound of bells ringing, often in turn. • *adv* with such a sound. • *adj infml* (of an argument, discussion, etc.) in which first one and then the other seems to be winning.

dinghy (ˈdɪŋgɪ) *nc, pl* **-ghies** a small, open boat; rubber boat that is inflated for use in a serious situation, esp. carried by a plane: see picture.

dinghy

dingy (ˈdɪndʒɪ) *adj* **-ier, -iest** dirty and dull in appearance.

dining-room (ˈdaɪnɪŋrʊm) *nc* a room in a house, hotel, etc., where meals are eaten.

dinner (ˈdɪnə*) *nc* the chief meal of the day, eaten in the middle of the day or in the evening.

dinosaur (ˈdaɪnəsɔː*) *nc* **1** a huge reptile that lived in times long past and no longer exists. **2** anything huge, useless, and old-fashioned.

dint (dɪnt) *nc* a hollow place in a hard surface made by a blow.

diocese (ˈdaɪəsɪs) *nc* a district in the care of a bishop.

dioxide (daɪˈɒksaɪd) *chemistry nc* a molecule formed by two atoms of oxygen with one other element.

dip (dɪp) *vt* **1** put into water or other liquid, for a short time only. **2** *vi* go down slightly and come up quickly: *Birds dipped and rose in flight.* **dip into** read bits of (a book). • *nc* **1** dipping. **2** *infml* a short swim; quick bath. **3** a hollow or downward slope: *a dip in the road.*

diphtheria (dɪfˈθɪərɪə) *nu* a serious disease that affects breathing and is easily passed on to others.

diphthong (ˈdɪfθɒŋ) *nc* two letters that together make one sound.

diploma (dɪˈpləʊmə) *nc* a printed statement showing that someone has passed an examination, or is now trained to do something.

diplomacy (dɪˈpləʊməsɪ) *nu* **1** the (skill of) managing of affairs, agreements, etc., between different governments. **2** the ability to deal with people and situations successfully. **diplomat** (ˈdɪpləmæt) *nc* a person who acts for the government of his country in a foreign country. **diplomatic** (ˌdɪpləˈmætɪk) *adj* **1** of diplomacy. **2** dealing with people and situations in a tactful way.

dire (ˈdaɪə*) *adj* very bad or terrible: *They were living in dire poverty.*

direct (dɪˈrekt) *adj* **1** straight; not going round about: *a direct road.* **2** going straight to the point: *a direct insult; His answers were direct.* **3** with nobody and nothing coming between: *I want to speak to him direct.* • *vt* **1** show the way: *Can you direct me to the nearest town, please?* **2** order someone to do something. **3** cause to turn: *Please direct your eyes this way.* **4** send; aim at: *direct a letter; direct a remark.* **5** control; manage: *direct a business.* **direct current** electricity that goes one way only: *abbrev.* DC **direct object** *grammar* showing the chief object of the action of the verb. **direct speech** words repeated, or written, as actually spoken. **directly** (dɪˈrektlɪ) *adv* **1** in a direct manner. **2** at once. **3** soon. **directness** (dɪˈrektnɪs) *nu* being direct.

direction (dɪˈrekʃən) *nc* **1** the course to take or the way to go to reach a point, place, etc. **2** (often *pl*) order; information on what to do, where to go, etc.: *Read the directions on the bottle before taking the medicine; We followed her directions and easily found the house.* **3** *nu* guidance: *He's a good student but needs direction.*

director (dɪˈrektə*) *nc* a person who controls the affairs of a business, industry, etc.

directory (dɪˈrektərɪ) *nc, pl* **-ries** a book with a list of people, businesses, etc., in a district or industry; book with a list of names, addresses, and telephone numbers.

dirge (dɜːdʒ) *nc* a sad song sung over, or at the burial of, a dead person.

dirt (dɜːt) *nu* **1** unclean matter. **2** earth; soil. **3** (information about) bad acts. **dirty** (ˈdɜːtɪ) *adj* **-ier, -iest** **1** unclean; covered with dirt. **2** *infml* (of behaviour) mean, unworthy: *What a dirty trick!* **3** (of the weather) rough, often with rain: *It's a dirty night.*

disability (ˌdɪsəˈbɪlətɪ) *nc, pl* **-ties** **1** *nu* being unable to do something because of a lack, weakness, etc. **2** *nc* a thing that makes someone unable to do something. **disabled** (dɪsˈeɪbəld) *adj* without the power to do something, esp. because of illness or injury.

disadvantage (ˌdɪsədˈvɑːntɪdʒ) **1** *nc* something that makes progress, success, etc., difficult. **2** *nu* harm to one's reputation, etc.; loss.

disagree (ˌdɪsəˈgriː) *vi* not agree; have another opinion. **disagree with** (of food or a climate) not suit: *I like Italy but Italian food disagrees with me.* **disagreeable** (ˌdɪsəˈgriːəbəl) *adj* bad-tempered; unpleasant: *What a disagreeable old man!* **disagreement 1** *nu* disagreeing. **2** *nc* an argument; difference of opinion.

disappear (ˌdɪsəˈpɪə*) *vi* go out of sight, esp. suddenly; be no longer seen. **disappearance** (ˌdɪsəˈpɪərəns) *nc* disappearing.

disappoint (ˌdɪsəˈpɔɪnt) *vt* fail to do something that (someone) expects and so make (someone) sad: *He disappointed his parents by failing the examination.* **disappointed** (ˌdɪsəˈpɔɪntɪd) *adj* sad because what one hoped for or expected has not happened. **disappointment** (ˌdɪsəˈpɔɪntmənt) **1** *nu* being disappointed. **2** *nc* someone or something that causes disappointment.

disapprove (ˌdɪsəˈpruːv) *vi* say or show that one's opinion of someone or something is not good. **disapproval** (ˌdɪsəˈpruːvəl) *nu* disapproving.

disarm (dɪsˈɑːm) *vt* **1** take weapons away from. **2** remove anger or doubt from by being friendly, honest, etc. **3** *vi* (of a nation) give up weapons; reduce the size of an army, etc. **disarming** *adj* friendly and charming. **disarmament** (dɪsˈɑːməmənt) *nu* taking away or giving up weapons.

disarray (ˌdɪsəˈreɪ) *nu* disorder.

disaster (dɪˈzɑːstə*) *nc* a great and serious accident. **disastrous** (dɪˈzɑːstrəs) *adj* of or causing disaster: *a disastrous mistake.*

disband (dɪsˈbænd) *vt* break up (a group of people who have been working, etc., together).

disbelief (ˌdɪsbəˈliːf) *nu* lack of belief; feeling that something is not true.

disc (dɪsk) *nc* a round, thin, flat object such as a record or a coin. **disc jockey** a person who plays records of popular music, esp. on a radio programme.

discard (dɪsˈkɑːd) *vt* throw away as useless or not good enough to keep.

discern (dɪˈsɜːn) *formal vt* **1** see clearly with the mind. **2** manage to see, hear, or feel, esp. in spite of some difficulty. **discernible** (dɪˈsɜːnəbəl) *adj* that is possible to discern.

discharge (dɪsˈtʃɑːdʒ) *vt* **1** carry out; do: *discharge one's duties well.* **2** unload (goods from a ship). **3** allow to go: *After his opera-*

tion he was discharged from the hospital. **4** fire (a gun or other weapon). **5** dismiss (someone) from employment. **6** *vti* give or send out: *Poisonous matter was discharging from his wound.* ●(ˈdɪstʃɑːdʒ) *nc* discharging or being discharged.

disciple (dɪˈsaɪpəl) *nc* a follower and supporter, esp. of a religious leader.

discipline (ˈdɪsəplɪn) *nu* **1** training to bring about self-control and obedience to rules, etc. **2** behaviour produced by such training. *nc* **3** a set of rules for good behaviour or training. **4** a subject of knowledge. ● *vt* **1** use control over. **2** punish. **disciplinary** (dɪsɪˈplɪnərɪ, ˌdɪsəˈplɪnərɪ) *adj* of or to do with discipline.

disclaim (dɪsˈkleɪm) *vt* say that one does not want or has nothing to do with (something): *She disclaimed any responsibility for the accident.*

disclose (dɪsˈkləʊz) *vt* make known.

disco (ˈdɪskəʊ) *n* See **discotheque.**

discolour (dɪsˈkʌlə*) *US* **discolor** *vti* (cause to) become changed or spoiled in colour.

discomfort (dɪsˈkʌmfət) **1** *nu* lack of ease of body or mind. **2** *nc* something that causes discomfort.

disconcert (ˌdɪskənˈsɜːt) *vt* make to feel unsure or unhappy.

disconnect (ˌdɪskəˈnekt) *vt* **1** separate things that were connected or fitted together. **2** cut off (a supply, telephone line, etc.).

disconsolate (dɪsˈkɒnsələt) *adj* sad; without hope.

discontent (ˌdɪskənˈtent) *nu* lack of satisfaction with what one has; wanting more, something better, etc.

discontinue (ˌdɪskənˈtɪnjuː) *vti* (cause to) come to an end; stop.

discord (ˈdɪskɔːd) **1** *nu* disagreement of opinions, feelings, etc.; quarrelling. **2** *nc* a conflict; difference of opinion. **3** *music ncu* (a set of notes that cause) unpleasant sound.

discotheque (ˈdɪskətek) (often shortened to **disco**) *nc* a club where records are played for people to dance to.

discount (ˈdɪskaʊnt) *nc* the amount taken off the real price of goods for some reason, esp. if the rest is paid before a certain date. ● *vt* **1** take off a certain amount from the real price (on condition that the rest will be paid before a certain date). **2** (dɪsˈkaʊnt) ignore as being untrue, of no value, worth, etc.

discourage (dɪsˈkʌrɪdʒ) *vt* **1** take away feelings of courage or confidence. **2** persuade (someone) not to do something.

discourse (ˈdɪskɔːs) *formal nc* a speech. ● *vt* talk or write (on a subject) esp. for a long time.

discourteous (dɪsˈkɜːtjəs) *adj* not polite; bad-mannered.

discover (dɪˈskʌvə*) *vt* 1 find out the existence of (something): *Columbus discovered America.* 2 find out; realise; learn: *I discovered how greedy he is when he came to dinner!; Have the police discovered how she died?* **discoverer** *nc* a person who makes a discovery. **discovery** *nc, pl* **-ries** 1 *nu* discovering, or being discovered. 2 *nc* a thing that is discovered.

discredit (dɪsˈkredɪt) *vt* refuse to believe; show doubt about the value of (something, someone's reputation or worth, etc.). ● *nu* 1 loss of reputation. 2 *nc* a person or thing that causes this loss: *He's a discredit to his family.*

discreet (dɪˈskriːt) *adj* careful and thoughtful in what one says or does, so as not to make someone worried. **discreetly** *adv*

discrepancy (dɪˈskrepənsɪ) *nc, pl* **-cies** 1 *nu* lack of agreement. 2 *nc* a difference: *There are discrepancies between his account of the car crash and the other driver's account of it.*

discretion (dɪˈskreʃən) *nu* 1 the giving of careful thought to what one says or does. 2 one's right to think about and decide what is the proper or best thing to do: *Use your discretion.*

discriminate (dɪˈskrɪmɪneɪt) *vti* make or see a difference between. **discriminate against** decide that one thing should be treated differently or badly. **discriminating** *adj* 1 having the power to see or make small differences. 2 giving a person, thing, etc., special treatment. **discrimination** (dɪˌskrɪmɪˈneɪʃən) *nu* treating one group of people differently from another; discriminating: *racial discrimination.*

discus (ˈdɪskəs) *nc* a heavy disc of wood, metal, or stone, thrown in sports: see picture.

discus

discuss (dɪˈskʌs) *vt* talk over the details of (a matter, problem, etc.). **discussion** (dɪˈskʌʃən) 1 *nu* discussing or being discussed. 2 *nc* a talk about a subject, etc.; argument.

disdain (dɪsˈdeɪn) *vt* feel that (something) is not worth one's notice or attention; refuse: *He disdained to join in the argument.*

disease (dɪˈziːz) 1 *nc* an illness; disorder of the body or mind. 2 *nu* unhealthy state. **diseased** *adj* with or harmed by disease.

disembark (ˌdɪsɪmˈbɑːk) *vi* leave a ship and go on shore.

disenchanted (ˌdɪsɪnˈtʃɑːntɪd) *adj* no longer liking or believing something as one did.

disengage (ˌdɪsɪnˈgeɪdʒ) 1 *vt* separate from; remove (esp. soldiers from battle). 2 *vi* become separated or removed.

disentangle (ˌdɪsɪnˈtæŋgəl) *vti* (cause to) become free of difficulties, knots, disorder, etc.

disfigure (dɪsˈfɪgə*) *vt* spoil or damage the appearance of: *Her face was disfigured in a car accident; Ugly new buildings disfigured the beauty of the city.*

disgrace (dɪsˈgreɪs) *nu* 1 shame; dishonour. 2 a person or thing that brings about loss of honour, respect, etc.: *You're a disgrace to the school!* ● *vt* bring shame, dishonour, etc., on. **disgraceful** *adj* shameful.

disgruntled (dɪsˈgrʌntəld) *adj* in a bad mood, esp. because something has gone wrong; grumpy.

disguise (dɪsˈgaɪz) *vt* 1 change the appearance of (someone or something) in order to deceive. 2 hide: *He disguised his hatred of his job since it would be difficult to find another.* ● *nu* 1 changing of appearance, etc., in order to hide or conceal. 2 *nc* a thing used, action taken, etc., to cause such a change.

disgust (dɪsˈgʌst) *nu* a strong feeling of dislike; anger caused by lack of justice, bad behaviour, etc. ● *vt* cause a feeling of disgust.

dish (dɪʃ) *nc* 1 a broad plate, often oval or square, with a flat bottom, used to hold food: *a vegetable dish; a soup dish.* 2 a particular kind of food, ready to eat. **dish out** *infml* give out (presents, etc.). **the dishes** all the plates, cups, saucers, etc., that are used for a meal: *It's your turn to wash the dishes!* **dishwasher** *nc* a machine for washing dishes.

dishearten (dɪsˈhɑːtən) *vt* cause to lose hope, confidence, or courage.

dishevelled (dɪˈʃevəld) *adj* untidy.

dishonest (dɪsˈɒnɪst) *adj* not honest; intending to cheat, deceive, or steal.

dishonour (dɪsˈɒnə*) *ncu* (someone or something that causes) shame; loss of honour, reputation, or self-respect. ● *vt* 1 treat without respect. 2 bring shame on.

disillusion (ˌdɪsɪˈluːʒən) *vt* make (someone) free from ideas or beliefs that are false. ● *nu* being without false ideas or beliefs; sadness.

disinfect (ˌdɪsɪnˈfekt) *vt* make free from germs: *After her illness we disinfected her bedroom to get rid of infection.* **disinfectant** (ˌdɪsɪnˈfektənt) *nc* a chemical substance used to disinfect.

disintegrate (dɪs'ɪntɪgreɪt) *vti* (cause to) break up or fall into small pieces. **disintegration** (dɪs,ɪntɪ'greɪʃən) *nu* disintegrating.

disinterested (dɪs'ɪntrəstɪd) *adj* 1 having no feelings or opinions of one's own on a matter, and therefore a good judge. 2 *infml* not caring to know or learn about something.

disjointed (dɪs'dʒɔɪntɪd) *adj* not joined up, or put together, in a smooth way: *His speech gets very disjointed when he is nervous.*

disk (dɪsk) *computers nc* a device in which a magnetic head reads and writes information on spinning plates.

dislike (dɪs'laɪk) *vt* think not likable, pleasing, or satisfying. ● *nc* the feeling that someone or something is not pleasant.

dislocate ('dɪsləkeɪt) *vt* 1 put (esp. a bone in the body) out of the proper place: *He dislocated his ankle when he fell off his bicycle.* 2 put out of the usual order: *The trains were dislocated during the rail strike.* **dislocation** (,dɪslə'keɪʃən) *nc* dislocating or being dislocated.

dislodge (dɪs'lɒdʒ) *vt* move (someone or something) from a particular (fixed) place: *The strong wind dislodged several roof tiles.*

disloyal (dɪs'lɔɪəl) *adj* not loyal. **disloyalty** *nc, pl* **-ties** 1 *nu* being disloyal. 2 *nc* disloyal actions, behaviour, etc.

dismal ('dɪzməl) *adj* 1 gloomy; miserable: *What dismal weather we're having!* 2 *infml* very poor in quality: *As a teacher he's dismal.*

dismantle (dɪs'mæntəl) *vt* separate (machinery, etc.) into parts: *The car would not start so he dismantled the engine to see what was wrong.*

dismay (dɪs'meɪ) *nu* a feeling of surprise and fear. ● *vt* cause (someone) to have this feeling.

dismember (dɪs'membə*) *vt* 1 tear or cut off the limbs from (a body). 2 divide (a country, etc.) into parts.

dismiss (dɪs'mɪs) *vt* 1 (of an employer) cause (a person) to leave employment. 2 send away: *At the end of the lesson the teacher dismissed the children.* 3 put out of one's mind as not worth thinking about. **dismissal** (dɪs'mɪsəl) *nc* dismissing or being dismissed.

dismount (dɪs'maʊnt) 1 *vi* get down from a horse, bicycle, etc. *vt* 2 cause to fall down from a horse, etc.: *The wild horse dismounted its rider.* 3 remove from a fixed position.

disobedience (,dɪsə'biːdɪəns) *nu* failure or refusal to do as ordered. **disobedient** (,dɪsə'biːdɪənt) *adj* not obeying.

disobey (,dɪsə'beɪ) *vt* take no notice of (orders, a rule, law, etc.).

disorder (dɪs'ɔːdə*) 1 *nu* lack of order; untidiness. *ncu* 2 lack of order of a political kind; a riot. 3 (an example of) illness of the body or mind. ● *vt* cause (something) to be out of order.

disorganised (dɪs'ɔːgənaɪzd) *adj* without ordered arrangements, plans, thoughts, etc.

disown (dɪs'əʊn) *vt* say one knows nothing about (someone or something); refuse to have anything, or anything more, to do with (someone or something).

disparage (dɪ'spærɪdʒ) *vt* cause (someone or something) to lose value or importance, by making harmful remarks. **disparagement** *nc* disparaging or being disparaging.

disparity (dɪ'spærətɪ) *ncu, pl* **-ties** being unequal or different; an example of this.

dispassionate (dɪ'spæʃənət) *adj* without strong feelings; not affected by one's own feelings, so just in giving judgements, opinions, etc.

dispatch (also **despatch**) (dɪ'spætʃ) *vt* 1 send off by post, on a journey, on special work, etc. 2 get something done quickly: *His business was quickly dispatched; He dispatched his meal in a hurry.* ● *nu* 1 dispatching or being dispatched. 2 *nc* something sent off.

dispel (dɪ'spel) *vt* get rid of: *Her fears were dispelled.*

dispense (dɪ'spens) *vt* 1 give or deal out: *dispense kindness.* 2 prepare and give out medicine according to a doctor's written instructions. **dispense with** do without; make no longer necessary. **dispensary** (dɪ'spensərɪ) *nc, pl* **-ries** a place, usually in a chemist's shop or hospital where medicines are prepared and given out. **dispensation** (,dɪspen'seɪʃən) 1 *nu* giving or dealing out: *dispensation of justice.* *nc* 2 dealing with a person, society, or the world by God or Nature. 3 special permission, esp. by the Christian Church, to do something that is usually not allowed, or not to do something that is usually necessary.

disperse (dɪ'spɜːs) *vti* (cause to) scatter: *The crowds dispersed when the match ended.* **dispersal, dispersion** *nu* dispersing or being dispersed.

displace (dɪs'pleɪs) *vt* 1 take (someone or something) out of the proper or usual place. 2 take the place of. **displacement** (dɪs'pleɪsmənt) *nu* displacing or being displaced.

display (dɪ'spleɪ) *vt* show so as to attract attention. ● *nu* 1 displaying or being displayed. 2 *nc* a show. 3 a collection of things shown in public.

displease (dɪs'pliːz) *vt* annoy; make angry. **displeasure** (dɪs'pleʒə*) *nu* a feeling of annoyance or anger; lack of satisfaction.

disposable (dɪ'spəʊzəbəl) *adj* made in order to be thrown away after use: *disposable paper handkerchiefs.*

dispose (dɪ'spəʊz) *vt* 1 arrange (people or things) in particular positions or in order. 2 *formal* cause (a person) to be willing to do something: *His rudeness does not dispose me to like him.* **dispose of** get rid of; sell; give away. **disposal** *nu* 1 getting rid of by selling, throwing away, or giving away. 2 dealing with; arranging in certain positions or in order. 3 control. **disposition** (,dɪspə'zɪʃən) *nc* 1 a person's character and approach to life: *She has a cheerful disposition.* 2 the arrangement of people or things. 3 a leaning towards a particular thought or action: *a growing disposition to work a four-day week.* 4 the power and right of ordering or dealing with things.

dispossess (,dɪspə'zes) *vt* take land, a house, etc., away from.

disproportionate (,dɪsprə'pɔːʃənət) *adj* not equal to, being either too large, or too small.

disprove (dɪs'pruːv) *vt* show to be false.

dispute (dɪ'spjuːt) 1 *vi* argue; discuss with strong feelings. 2 *vt* declare (an opinion, fact, etc.) to be untrue or doubtful; argue about. ● *nu* 1 argument; discussion with strong feelings, esp. in public. 2 *nc* a quarrel in words; strong disagreement.

disqualify (dɪs'kwɒlɪfaɪ) *vt* make unfit or unable to do something: *His car accident disqualified him from driving.*

disquiet (dɪs'kwaɪət) *vt* fill with worry, distrust, doubt, etc. ● *nu* being troubled or worried.

disregard (,dɪsrɪ'gɑːd) *vt* take no notice of; treat without respect. ● *nu* lack of interest, respect, or attention: *He shows a complete disregard of the rules.*

disrepair (,dɪsrɪ'peə*) *nu* in a bad condition due to lack of repair.

disrepute (,dɪsrɪ'pjuːt) *nu* bad reputation: *Part of the town has fallen into disrepute because of street fighting there.* **disreputable** (dɪs'repjʊtəbəl) *adj* with a bad reputation.

disrespect (,dɪsrɪ'spekt) *nu* lack of politeness or respect.

disrobe (,dɪs'rəʊb) *vti* take off (someone's) formal robes, clothes, etc.

disrupt (dɪs'rʌpt) *vt* break up or delay the progress of, esp. by causing a disturbance: *The meeting was constantly disrupted by people asking difficult questions.*

dissatisfy (,dɪ'sætɪsfaɪ) *vt* fail to satisfy. **dissatisfaction** (dɪ,sætɪs'fækʃən) *nu* being dissatisfied.

dissect (dɪ'sekt, daɪ'sekt) *vt* 1 cut into pieces in order to examine (esp. a body, plant, etc.). 2 look very carefully into all the details of (an idea, argument, etc.). **dissection** 1 *nu* dissecting or being dissected. 2 *nc* something or a piece of something that has been dissected.

dissemble (dɪ'sembəl) 1 *vt* hide (one's real feelings, thoughts, etc.). 2 *vi* pretend to be something or to be doing or thinking something, in order to deceive.

disseminate (dɪ'semɪneɪt) *vt* spread about in various directions: *to disseminate ideas.*

dissent (dɪ'sent) *vi* refuse to agree, esp. to certain beliefs. ● *nu* disagreement; failure to agree with certain beliefs, etc. **dissension** (dɪ'senʃən) *nu* quarrelling due to failure to agree. **dissenter** *nc* a person who dissents.

dissertation (,dɪsə'teɪʃən) *nc* a long speech or written report, esp. for a university degree.

dissident ('dɪsɪdənt) *nc* a person who has a very different opinion from other people in a group on some subject, esp. a political one. ● *adj* disagreeing.

dissimilar (dɪ'sɪmɪlə*) *adj* unlike; of a different kind.

dissipate ('dɪsɪpeɪt) 1 *vti* (cause to) scatter or disappear. 2 *vt* waste (time, money, etc.) by using in a foolish way.

dissociate (dɪ'səʊʃɪeɪt) *vt* separate thought or feeling from; have nothing to do with someone or something: *I dissociate myself from your ideas.*

dissolve (dɪ'zɒlv) 1 *vti* (of a solid), (cause to) become liquid by being put into liquid. 2 *vt* put an end to; break up: *dissolve parliament.* **dissolution** (,dɪsə'luːʃən) *nu* breaking up; ending: *dissolution of a marriage; nc* an example of this.

dissuade (dɪ'sweɪd) *vt* advise (someone) not to do something.

distaff ('dɪstɑːf) *nc* a stick round which wool, etc., is wound for spinning by hand.

distance ('dɪstəns) *nc* 1 a measure of the amount of space between two points, etc.: *It's only a short distance to the station from here.* 2 a large amount of time: *From a distance of fifty years my childhood seemed a happy one.* **in the distance** at a point far away. **distant** ('dɪstənt) *adj* 1 far away: *a distant country; in the distant past.* 2 (of a person's behaviour) not showing an interest in, or wanting to share, the feelings of others: *What a distant manner he has!* 3 not very close or easily seen: *There's only a distant likeness between her and her sister.*

distasteful (dɪs'teɪstfʊl) *adj* unpleasant; not to one's liking.

distemper (dɪ'stempə*) *nu* 1 a coloured substance mixed with water for painting walls, etc. 2 a disease of dogs. ● *vt* to paint with distemper.

distend (dɪ'stend) *biology vti* (cause to) swell out because of something pressing from inside.

distil (dɪ'stɪl) *US* **distill** 1 *vt* make (a liquid) pure by heating, evaporating, then cooling and collecting in a separate container. 2 *vi* (of a liquid) come out of a substance in drops. 3 *vt* obtain (the main points) of a subject, etc. **distillation** (,dɪstɪ'leɪʃən) 1 *nu* distilling or being distilled. 2 *nc* a substance produced by distilling. **distillery** (dɪ'stɪlərɪ) *nc, pl* **-ries** a place where alcoholic liquid is distilled.

distinct (dɪ'stɪŋkt) *adj* 1 clear: *in a distinct voice.* 2 definite: *a distinct smell of curry; There's a distinct change in the weather today.* 3 separate. **distinctly** *adv*

distinction (dɪ'stɪŋkʃən) *nu* 1 difference in quality or kind. 2 being superior or of very high quality: *a writer of distinction. nc* 3 something that shows one thing to be different from another. 4 a special mark of honour, such as a medal or title.

distinctive (dɪ'stɪŋktɪv) *adj* showing a difference or easily seen or noticed among others: *the distinctive uniform of a policeman.*

distinguish (dɪ'stɪŋgwɪʃ) *vt* 1 see, notice, etc., the difference between. 2 bring honour on (oneself) because of actions, behaviour, or qualities: *He distinguished himself at university.* 3 see, hear, etc., with an effort: *Can you distinguish the road clearly in this mist?* 4 show the difference: *How does one distinguish between a lion and a lioness?* **distinguished** (dɪ'stɪŋgwɪʃt) *adj* famous; very high in quality; deserving notice. **distinguishable** (dɪ'stɪŋgwɪʃəbəl) *adj* 1 that can be distinguished between. 2 that can be seen, heard, etc., with an effort: *Our voices were hardly distinguishable in the noise of the traffic.*

distort (dɪ'stɔːt) *vt* 1 change the usual shape of (something) so as to become twisted: *Anger distorted her face.* 2 twist the meaning of: *distort the truth.* **distortion** (dɪ'stɔːʃən) 1 *nu* distorting or being distorted. 2 *nc* something that has been changed out of its usual shape or meaning.

distract (dɪ'strækt) *vt* cause (someone's attention) to move away from something. **distraction** (dɪ'strækʃən) 1 *nu* distracting or being distracted. *nc* 2 something that draws one's attention away from something. 3 something pleasant to see or do when work is done.

distraught (dɪ'strɔːt) *adj* nearly crazy with pain, sorrow, worry, etc.: *distraught with grief.*

distress (dɪ'stres) *nu* great pain, sorrow, trouble, etc. ●*vt* cause distress to. **dis-**

tressing (dɪ'stresɪŋ) *adj* causing distress.

distribute (dɪ'strɪbjuːt) *vt* 1 give out or send out: *The teacher distributed the books to the students.* 2 spread out. **distribution** (,dɪstrɪ'bjuːʃən) *nu* distributing or being distributed; *nc* an example of distributing: *There is an unequal distribution of wealth in most countries.* **distributor** (dɪ'strɪbjuːtə*) *nc* 1 a person or company that distributes. 2 a device in a petrol engine that distributes electricity to the sparking plugs.

district ('dɪstrɪkt) *nc* 1 part of a country: *the Lake District in England.* 2 part of a country, city, etc., marked out for a special purpose: *London is divided into postal districts.*

distrust (dɪs'trʌst) *vt* have no belief or confidence in. ●*nu* lack of trust or belief.

disturb (dɪ'stɜːb) *vt* 1 upset the calm, peace, or rest of: *Don't disturb the baby while she sleeps.* 2 cause worry to (someone). 3 change the usual state of: *disturb the balance of nature.* **disturbance** (dɪ'stɜːbəns) 1 *ncu* (an example of) disturbing or being disturbed. 2 *nc* something that disturbs.

disunity (dɪs'juːnɪtɪ) *nu* lack of agreement; quarrelling.

disuse (dɪs'juːs) *nu* state of not being used any more. **disused** (dɪs'juːzd) *adj* no longer used.

ditch (dɪtʃ) *nc* a narrow channel dug at the side of a road, etc., for carrying off water. ●*vt slang* 1 bring (a plane) down into the sea because of engine trouble, etc. 2 get rid of: *She's ditched her boyfriend.*

ditto ('dɪtəʊ) *nc* the same. **ditto marks** the sign (,,) used to represent a word, for example in a list, to avoid writing it again.

ditty ('dɪtɪ) *nc, pl* **-ties** a short, simple song.

diurnal (daɪ'ɜːnəl) *adj* of or to do with the day; happening every day.

divan (dɪ'væn) *nc* a long, soft seat on which to sit or lie.

dive (daɪv) *vi* 1 jump head first into water, usually from a height. 2 go down quickly; go out of sight: *The large bird dived down onto its prey; His hand dived into his pocket for money.* **diver** ('daɪvə*) *nc* 1 a person who wears a special suit for diving and works under water, esp. in the sea. 2 a person who jumps head first into water.

diverge (daɪ'vɜːdʒ) *vi* gradually move away from the main subject, path, opinion, line, etc. **divergence** (daɪ'vɜːdʒəns) *ncu, pl* **-cies** (an example of) diverging. **divergent** (daɪ'vɜːdʒənt) *adj* diverging: *divergent paths.*

diverse (daɪ'vɜːs) *adj* of various sorts. **diversely** *adv* **diversity** (daɪ'vɜːsɪtɪ) *ncu* a variety: *a diversity of opinions.*

diversify (daɪ'vɜːsɪfaɪ) *vt* increase the variety of: *We diversified our journey, travelling by* *sea and by rail.* **diversification** (daɪ-ˌvɜːsɪfɪˈkeɪʃən) *nc* an attempt to produce diversity.

diversion (daɪˈvɜːʃən) **1** *nu* turning away from the main or usual path; *nc* an example of this: *The road is being repaired so there's a diversion of traffic. nc* **2** something that turns attention away from its usual, or proper, object. **3** something to do, see, etc., to pass the time in a pleasant or restful way.

divert (daɪˈvɜːt) *vt* **1** change the direction of. **2** turn the attention away; amuse.

divest (daɪˈvest) *vt* **1** take off the clothes of. **2** take away from; make free of: *divest of power; He was divested of all responsibility.*

divide (dɪˈvaɪd) **1** *vti* (cause to) split up into smaller parts. *vt* **2** separate from another or into groups. **3** cause a difference of opinion, etc.: *Our thoughts on the matter are divided.* **4** *mathematics* see how many times a smaller number is contained in a greater number: *Twenty divided by ten gives two.*

dividend (ˈdɪvɪdend) *nc* a share of the profit made by a business, divided among its owners.

divider (dɪˈvaɪdə*) *nc* an upright, movable frame or a piece of furniture, used to divide a room into two parts. **dividers** (dɪˈvaɪdəz) *mathematics n pl* a device with two arms joined by a hinge, used for measuring, dividing lines, etc.

divine (dɪˈvaɪn) *adj* **1** of, or to do with, God, or a god; sacred. **2** *infml* lovely; very pleasant: *What a divine hat she's wearing!*

divinity (dɪˈvɪnətɪ) *nc, pl* **-ties** *nu* **1** being divine. **2** the study of the nature of God, and of the beginnings of belief in religion. **3** *nc* a god, etc.

divisible (dɪˈvɪzəbəl) *mathematics adj* able to be divided with nothing left over: *Sixteen is divisible by four.*

division (dɪˈvɪʒən) **1** *nu* dividing or being divided. *nc* **2** that which divides: *Hedges or walls form divisions between fields.* **3** a difference of opinion, view, etc. **4** the part that has been divided off. **5** a certain part of the army, navy, police, etc.

divisor (dɪˈvaɪzə*) *nc* a number which is to be divided into another number.

divorce (dɪˈvɔːs) **1** *nu* the legal separation of a husband and wife; *nc* an example of this. **2** *nc* separation of anything: *A divorce exists between your account and his.* ● *vt* **1** end a marriage between (a man and woman) or to (a husband or wife) by law. **2** separate.

divulge (daɪˈvʌldʒ) *vt* make known (what has been a secret).

dizzy (ˈdɪzɪ) *adj* **-ier, -iest 1** an unpleasant feeling as if everything is turning round and round and one is going to fall. **2** (of a very high place or conditions) making one feel dizzy: *the dizzy heights of the mountains.*

do (duː unstressed də) **1** *v* (used to start a question): *I want to go now. Do you? vt* **2** carry out an action; perform; finish: *Have you done your work yet?* **3** make; produce: *do the dinner; Do six copies of this letter, please.* **4** arrange; deal with: *I'll do the flowers; Could you do the kitchen?—It really needs a good cleaning.* **5** *infml* cheat: *I've been done!* **6** *infml* visit a place, country, etc., to see the sights: *We're doing London this year.* **7** study: *doing history at university.* **8** solve: *do a puzzle.* **9** cook: *How do you do the lamb? vi* **10** act: *You'd do well to get home before the rain starts.* **11** be enough; be all right: *The house is small, but it will do for now.* **do away with** put an end to; get rid of. **do out of** prevent from having. **do with** find useful or necessary: *That child looks as if it could do with a bath!* **do without** be able to continue, or manage, without. **have to do with** be concerned with: *My affairs have nothing to do with you.* **how do you do?** (usual words said when people are introduced.)

docile (ˈdəʊsaɪl) *adj* easily controlled: *a docile child.* **docility** (dəʊˈsɪlətɪ) *nu*

dock¹ (dɒk) *nc* a place by or in a river, etc., where ships are loaded, unloaded, built, or repaired: see picture. ● *vti* (of a ship), (cause to) come into a dock.

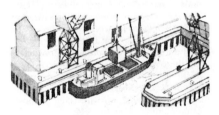

dock

dock² *vt* **1** cut the tail of (an animal). **2** take away a part of (someone's wages, supplies, etc.): *They docked half my pay for being late.*

dock³ *nc* the place in a court of law where a prisoner stands.

doctor (ˈdɒktə*) *nc* **1** a person who gives medical care to people who are ill, injured, etc. **2** a person who has been given the highest degree by a university. ● *vt infml* **1** give medical care to: *Doctor your cold by staying in bed.* **2** repair (a machine, etc.). **3** make false: *These accounts have been doctored.* **4** remove the male or female parts of (an animal). **doctorate** (ˈdɒktərət) *nc* the highest degree given by a university.

doctrinaire (ˌdɒktrɪˈneə*) *adj* wanting to treat beliefs, teachings, etc., as facts, before they have been proved to be true, suitable, practical, etc.

doctrine (ˈdɒktrɪn) **1** *nu* a set of beliefs or teachings. **2** *nc* a religious, political, etc., belief or teaching.

document (ˈdɒkjʊmənt) *nc* a written or printed statement that gives an account or proof of facts. ●(ˈdɒkjʊment) *vt* prove or supply with facts. **documentary** (ˌdɒkjʊˈmentərɪ) *nc, pl* **-ries** *nc* a cinema or television film that is concerned with facts. ● *adj* of or to do with documents.

dodge (dɒdʒ) *vt* **1** move suddenly and quickly in order to get out of the way of: *He ran across the road dodging the traffic.* **2** find a way of not doing (something, one's duty, etc.) by a trick or by deceiving. **3** *vi* move quickly round or behind an object to avoid or escape from someone or something: *He dodged behind a tree hoping he would not be seen.* **dodger** *nc* a person who gets out of doing things and avoids difficulties, etc., by a trick, or by being deceitful.

doe (dəʊ) *nc* a female deer or rabbit.

does (dʌz unstressed dəz) *v* (used with **he**, **she**, or **it**) a form of **do**.

doesn't (ˈdʌzənt) *v* does not.

dog (dɒg) *nc* a common four-legged animal with a tail, often kept as a pet: *There are many varieties of dogs:* see picture at **animals**. ● *vt* follow (someone) very closely: *Bad luck dogged him wherever he went.* **dog collar** *infml* a collar worn by a priest of the Christian Church, that fastens at the back. **dog-eared** (ˈdɒgˌɪəd) *adj* (of a book) having the corners of the pages turned down. **in the doghouse** (ˈdɒgˌhaʊs) *slang* out of favour; in disgrace.

doggedly (dɒgɪdlɪ) *adj* with fixed purpose, or opinion; refusing to yield.

dogma (ˈdɒgmə) **1** *nc* a belief or teaching, esp. by the Church, that is to be believed without questioning it. **2** *nu* a set of such beliefs or teachings. **dogmatic** (dɒgˈmætɪk) *often derogatory adj* putting forward opinions, etc., as if they should be believed without question.

do-it-yourself (ˌduːɪtjɔːˈself) able to be done by an untrained person who is clever at making things, etc. *abbrev.* DIY *adj*

doldrums (ˈdɒldrəmz) *n, pl* **in the doldrums** *infml* feeling miserable; not doing anything.

dole (dəʊl) *vt* (followed by **out**) give out (money, food, etc.) in a careful way without waste, esp. to poor people. ● *nu* something given out, esp. regular payments to people who are unemployed, from money given by workers and the State for this purpose.

doleful (ˈdəʊlfʊl) *adj* sorrowful; sad.

doll (dɒl) *nc* **1** a toy made to look like a person, usually for a child to play with. **2** *often derogatory* a beautiful but silly woman.

dollar (ˈdɒlə*) *nc* See appendix.

dolorous (ˈdɒlərəs) *adj* sorrowful.

dolphin (ˈdɒlfɪn) *nc* a sea-animal like a small whale.

domain (dəʊˈmeɪn) *nc* **1** an area of land controlled by a government, king, etc. **2** a study or activity: *Many discoveries have been made in this century in the domain of science.*

dome (dəʊm) *nc* **1** a rounded roof: see picture. **2** anything rounded like a dome: *The dome of the skies; his dome-shaped head.*

dome

domestic (dəˈmestɪk) *adj* **1** of or to do with the home or family. **2** (of an animal) living with people or kept as a pet. **3** of or belonging to one's own country, not a foreign one: *domestic trade.* **domesticate** (dəˈmestɪkeɪt) *vt* **1** cause to take pleasure in home life, household duties, etc. **2** control (animals), or make used to living with human beings.

domicile (ˈdɒmɪsaɪl) *nc* **1** *formal* one's home. **2** *law* the place in which a person expects or intends to stay.

dominant (ˈdɒmɪnənt) *adj* **1** having power over others; most important. **2** (of a place or position) higher or better than others: *dominant hills.* **dominance** *nu* being dominant.

dominate (ˈdɒmɪneɪt) *vt* **1** have much power over; control. **2** (of a place) look over from a greater height: *The tall tower on the church dominated the village.* **domination** (ˌdɒmɪˈneɪʃən) *nu* dominating or being dominated.

domineer (ˌdɒmɪˈnɪə*) *derogatory vi* try to rule others by force: *That big boy domineers over other children.*

dominion (dəˈmɪnjən) **1** *nu* power to rule. **2** *nc* a land, country, etc., controlled by a government or ruler.

don[1] (dɒn) *literary vt* put on (clothes, etc.).

don[2] *nc* **1** a teacher at a university. **2** the title put before the name of a Spanish nobleman or Spaniard.

donate (dəʊ'neɪt) *vt* give (money, goods, etc.) to a charity or good cause. **donation** (dəʊ'neɪʃən) *nu* giving; *nc* something given.

done (dʌn) past participle of **do**.

donkey ('dɒŋkɪ) *nc* also **ass** an animal with long ears, like a small horse: see picture at **animals.**

donor ('dəʊnə*) *nc* a person who gives money, etc., to a charity, or blood, etc., for a purpose or as a gift.

don't (dəʊnt) *v* do not.

doodle ('duːdəl) *infml vi* make marks on paper that mean nothing because one's thoughts and attention are elsewhere. ●*nc* a meaningless mark on paper.

doom (duːm) *nu* fate, usually an evil one; ruin. **doomsday** ('duːmzdeɪ) *nu* the day when all men will be judged by God.

door (dɔː*) *nc* 1 the thing through which one enters a room, building, etc.; anything that closes an opening: *a cupboard door.* 2 a house: *two doors down the road.* 3 *nu* closeness: *at death's door.* **next door** the next house: *She lives next door to me.* **out of doors** outside; in the open air. **doorbell** *nc* a bell rung by visitors pressing a button, etc., on the front entrance to the house. **doorstep** *nc* a step that leads up to an outer door. **doorway** *nc* an opening filled in by a door.

dope (dəʊp) *nc* 1 *infml* an illegal drug. 2 *slang* information. 3 *infml* a stupid person.

dormant ('dɔːmənt) *adj* that is not in action now but may be so in the future.

dormitory ('dɔːmətrɪ) *nc, pl* **-ries** a large room with several beds in a school, hostel, institution, etc.

dormouse ('dɔːmaʊs) *nc, pl* **mice** (maɪs) a small animal like a mouse that sleeps through the winter.

dorsal ('dɔːsəl) *anatomy adj* of or to do with the back.

dose (dəʊs) *nc* 1 a quantity of medicine to be taken at one time. 2 *infml* something given, or taken, such as punishment. ●*vt* give medicine to.

dost (dʌst) *archaic v* (used with **thou**) a form of **do**.

dot (dɒt) *nc* a tiny, round spot or mark such as that written over an i, or j; anything very tiny: *From the top of the very high tower the cars below looked like dots.* ●*vt* mark with a dot or dots.

dotage ('dəʊtɪdʒ) *nu* a confusion in the mind due to old age.

dote (dəʊt) *vi* (followed by **on** or **upon**) like or love too much, esp. in a foolish way.

doth (dʌθ) *archaic v* (used with **he, she,** or **it**) a form of **do**.

double ('dʌbəl) *adj* 1 twice as big, much, good, etc. 2 meant for two people or things: *a double bed.* 3 having two purposes, qualities, etc. ●*adv* twice. ●*nc* 1 twice the amount. 2 *(pl)* tennis a game between two pairs of partners. 3 a person or thing that looks very like another person or thing. ●*vti* 1 (cause to) become twice as great. 2 *vt* bend one half of something back over on itself. **double back** return the way one has just come. **double bass** *nc* a musical instrument like a very large violin with a very low sound. **double-cross** (ˌdʌbəl'krɒs) *vt* cheat or deceive. **double-dealer** (ˌdʌbəl'diːlə*) *nc* a person who deceives. **double-dealing** *adj* deceitful. ●*nc* deceiving, esp. in business. **double-glazing** (ˌdʌbəl'gleɪzɪŋ) *nu* two layers of glass in a window to keep a room, etc., warm by cutting the loss of heat. **double-jointed** (ˌdʌbəl'dʒɔɪntɪd) *adj* with easy and unusual bending of the fingers and limbs. **double up** *vti* 1 (of a person), (cause to) become bent over because of pain, too much laughter, etc. 2 (of paper, etc.), (cause to) become folded over on itself.

doubly ('dʌblɪ) *adv* to twice the extent: *Look in your pocket to make doubly sure you have your train ticket.*

doubt (daʊt) 1 *nu* being uncertain. 2 *nc* a feeling of not being sure: *I have my doubts as to whether he will come.* ●*vt* 1 feel not certain about. 2 *vi* be uncertain. **in doubt** uncertain: *Please ask questions if in doubt about anything.* **no doubt** 1 certainly. 2 probably: *No doubt you would like an increase in wages?* **doubtful** ('daʊtfʊl) *adj* feeling or causing doubt; not certain. **doubtfully** ('daʊtfʊlɪ) *adv* **doubtless** ('daʊtlɪs) *adv* certainly; probably.

dough (dəʊ) *nu* 1 a mixture of flour and water worked by the hands into a firm paste, used for baking bread, etc. 2 *slang* money. **doughnut** ('dəʊnʌt) *nc* a cake of dough made sweet and cooked in fat.

douse (daʊs) *vt* 1 put into water; throw water over until very wet. 2 put out: *douse the light.*

dove[1] (dʌv) *nc* a grey bird like a pigeon, wild or tame: *A dove is often thought of as a sign of peace:* see picture at **birds.**

dove[2] (dəʊv) *US* past tense of **dive**.

down[1] (daʊn) *adv* 1 moving from a higher position to a lower one: *He fell down the stairs.* 2 in a lower or less important place: *He lives down in the country; He comes from down south.* 3 showing time from earlier to later: *Down the years the old man had become very wise.* 4 to a smaller size or amount: *Turn down the sound on that radio!* ●*prep* 1 along: *He walked down the street.* 2 at or to a lower point in or on: *The chemist's shop is farther down the road.* 3 to a lower position. **be down** be sad or low in spirits. **be down on** not approve of. **down with...!** get rid of (someone or something). **go down with** see under **go**. **down-to-earth** *adj* wise in a practical way; sensible. **downcast** ('daʊnkɑːst) *adj* 1 sorrowful; low in spirits. 2 (of eyes) looking down. **downfall** ('daʊnfɔːl) *nc* 1 a fall from success to failure; ruin. 2 a great fall, esp. of rain. **downhill** ('daʊnhɪl) *adv* towards what is lower, worse, weaker, etc. **downpour** ('daʊnpɔː*) *nc* a great fall, esp. of rain; downfall. **downright** ('daʊnraɪt) *adj* 1 sensible; honest. 2 thorough: *What downright nonsense he talks!* **downstairs** (,daʊn'steəz) *adv, adj* down (the) stairs; to, of, at, or on the floor below. ●*adj* of or to do with downstairs: *a downstairs cloakroom*. **downstream** (,daʊn'striːm) *adv, adj* in the direction in which a river is flowing. **downtown** ('daʊntaʊn) *US adv* to or in the main or lower part of a town. **downward** ('daʊnwəd) *adj* leading, going, or pointing to, what is further down or lower. **downwards** ('daʊnwədz) *adv* towards what is lower.

down² *nu* 1 the first feathers of a baby bird; these feathers used for filling cushions and pillows. 2 fine, soft hair.

dowry ('daʊrɪ) *nc, pl* **-ries** money or goods a woman takes to her husband on her marriage day.

doze (dəʊz) *vi* be not fully asleep. ●*nc* a sleep from which one can easily be awakened.

dozen ('dʌzən) *nc* 1 a set of twelve. 2 (*pl*) lots of: *You've said that dozens of times!* ●*adj* twelve.

drab (dræb) *adj* **-ber, -best** 1 dull; boring: *a drab life*. 2 (of colour) dull: *drab clothes*.

draft (drɑːft) *nc* 1 brief notes of something to be done; outline: *a draft for a letter; a draft for a new building*. 2 a written order for a bank to pay out money; taking out of money by a written order. 3 *US* part of an army, group, etc., chosen for a special duty. 4 *US* See **draught**. ●*vt* 1 write brief notes or draw an outline of something to be carried out. 2 choose a group of men for a special duty. 3 *US* force men by law to go into the army. **draftsman** (drɑːftsmən) *nc, pl* **-men** a person who draws plans for new buildings, machines, etc., or prepares the careful wording for legal statements.

drag (dræg) *vt* 1 pull (something) along with difficulty or force. 2 move or walk slowly in a tired, unwilling, etc., way: *The old woman dragged herself to the shops; dragging his feet on his way to school.* 3 *vi* (of time or anything uninteresting) seem to move slowly. ●*nc* 1 *infml* someone or some-

thing boring, dull, etc. 2 *slang* a puff at a cigarette.

dragon ('drægən) *nc* an imaginary creature, often with wings and claws, that breathes out fire. **dragonfly** ('drægənflaɪ) *nc, pl* **-flies** an insect with two pairs of large wings and a long, narrow body: see picture.

dragonfly

dragoon (drə'guːn) *nc* a horse-soldier. ●*vt* force (someone) into doing something.

drain (dreɪn) *nc* 1 a pipe, etc., through which waste and dirty water is taken away. 2 something that continues to take up a lot of time, money, etc. ●*vti* 1 (of a liquid), (cause to) be taken away by a pipe, etc. 2 (cause to) be made dry by allowing water to flow away. 3 (cause to) be made weaker by taking away: *The effort of calling for help drained his strength*. **drainpipe** ('dreɪnpaɪp) *nc* a pipe that carries away waste, dirty liquid, etc. **drainage** ('dreɪnɪdʒ) *nu* 1 draining or being drained. 2 a set of pipes, etc., for draining. 3 waste matter.

drake (dreɪk) *nc* a male duck.

dram (dræm) *nc* 1 a small measure of weight. 2 a small drink of alcohol.

drama ('drɑːmə) *nc* 1 a play in the theatre or on the radio or television. 2 an exciting event full of strong feelings. **dramatic** (drə'mætɪk) *adj* 1 of or to do with drama. 2 sudden and exciting; having or have a strong effect, like an event or action in a play. **dramatically** *adv* in a dramatic way. **dramatics** *nu* 1 plays acted by people for whom acting is an enjoyable hobby and not a full-time job. 2 behaviour that is better, worse, etc., than normal in order to try and produce a strong effect. **dramatisation** (,dræmətaɪ'zeɪʃən) 1 *nu* the changing of a book, etc., into a play; *nc* an example of this. 2 *nu* the making of an ordinary happening or behaviour into a drama, in order to impress. **dramatise** ('dræmətaɪz) *vt* 1 change (a book, etc.) into a play. 2 try to impress by dramatic behaviour or speech. **dramatist** ('dræmətɪst) *nc* a person who writes plays.

drank (dræŋk) past tense of **drink**.

drape (dreɪp) *vt* 1 cover with a cloth allowing it to lie, or hang in folds. 2 put in a relaxed way: *She draped her legs over the arm of a chair.* ●*nc chiefly US* a curtain.

draper ('dreɪpə*) *Brit nc* a shopkeeper who sells cloth, clothing, etc. **drapery** ('dreɪpərɪ) *nc, pl* **-ries 1** *nu* the trade of such a shop-keeper; draper's goods. **2** *ncu* cloths, curtains, etc. ● *adj* of or to do with a draper: *a drapery store.*

drastic ('dræstɪk) *adj* (of actions and medicines) very strong in order to have a greater effect: *a drastic cure.*

draught *US* **draft** (drɑːft) **1** *nc* a stream of air in a room or anywhere that is shut in: *He opened the door and a draught of cold air came in.* **2** *nu* an amount of liquid that is obtained from a container other than a bottle: *draught beer.* **3** *nc* the amount caught or drunk at one time: *He swallowed a draught of water.* **4** *nc* the depth of water needed for a ship to pass. **draughts** (drɑːfts) *US* **checkers** *Brit nu (with a singular verb)* an indoor game for two people using twenty-four round pieces on a board marked out in thirty-two white, and thirty-two black squares. **draughtsman** ('drɑːftsmən) *nc, pl* **-men 1** a draftsman. **2** one of the round pieces in the game of draughts.

draw (drɔː) *vt* **1** pull, esp. using some effort; move by pulling: *a horse drawing a cart; Draw the curtains.* **2** pull up or out: *draw water from a well; have a tooth drawn.* **3** *vti* make pictures, figures, lines, etc., with a pencil, etc.; give a picture of in words. **4** *vt* attract the attention, interest, etc., of: *The procession drew huge crowds.* **5** *vti* end (a game) without either side having won. **6** *vi* move forward, close, etc.: *They drew near to the town.* ● *nc* **1** a game that ends without either side having won. **2** *nu* taking by chance: *the luck of the draw.* **drawback** ('drɔːbæk) *nc* something that delays or gets in the way of progress; disadvantage. **drawbridge** ('drɔːbrɪdʒ) *nc* a bridge that can be pulled up to stop people crossing or in order to let ships pass. **draw in 1** (of daylight) get shorter: *The nights are drawing in.* **2** encourage to join in: *He was drawn into their conversation.* **3** arrive and stop: *The train drew in at the station.* **draw out 1** (of days) become longer. **2** make longer: *He drew out his visit until we thought he would never go!* **3** leave on a journey: *The ship drew out of port.* **4** take money out of a bank account: *He drew out twenty pounds.* **draw up 1** come to a stop: *The car drew up outside our gate.* **2** put in writing to form (a statement, law, etc.). **3** come, or bring together in regular order.

drawer ('drɔː*) *nc* a long, box-like container that slides in and out of a piece of furniture.

drawing ('drɔːɪŋ) **1** *nu* the art of making pictures, etc., with pencil, chalk, etc., usually without colour. **2** *nc* a picture drawn in this way; plan. **drawing-pin** ('drɔːɪŋpɪn) *US*

thumbtack *Brit nc* a short pin with a round, flat head, used for fastening paper to a notice-board, wall, etc. **drawing-room** ('drɔːɪŋrʊm) *nc* a room for general use in the afternoon, and evening.

drawl (drɔːl) *vti* speak, making the sounds longer than usual. ● *nu* slowness of speech.

drawn (drɔːn) past participle of **draw**.

dread (dred) *vt* be in great fear of. ● *nu* great fear. **dreadful** ('dredfʊl) *adj* **1** causing dread. **2** *infml* very bad: *What dreadful weather!* **dreadfully** *adv*

dream (driːm) *nc* **1** a picture or happening that one seems to see or feel while asleep. **2** hopeful ideas, plans, or pictures of the future that are not likely to come true. **3** an ambition. ● *vti* **1** have a dream (that something happens) while asleep. **2** imagine (something) while awake. **not dream of** not consider: *I wouldn't dream of going.* **dreamer** *nc* **1** a person who dreams. **2** person who has hopes, plans, etc., that are not likely to come true. **dreamy** *adj* **-ier, -iest 1** having hopes, plans, etc., that are not likely to come true. **2** like a dream; not real: *dreamy music.*

dreamt (drempt) past tense and past participle of **dream**.

drear ('drɪə*) *literary adj* sad; gloomy.

dreary ('drɪərɪ) *adj* **-ier, -iest** dull; without happiness or comfort; sad: *dreary weather.* **drearily** ('drɪərɪlɪ) *adv*

dredge (dredʒ) *v* **dredge up** bring up (mud or pieces of plants or rocks), from the bottom of a river or sea. ● *nc* a device for doing this work.

dregs (dregz) *n pl* **1** the waste bits remaining at the bottom of a liquid. **2** the part that is useless and worst: *the dregs of humanity.*

drench (drentʃ) *vt* make thoroughly wet: *We got drenched in the heavy rain.*

dress (dres) **1** *vti* (cause to) have clothes on: *Are you dressed yet?* *vt* **2** put a bandage, etc., on (an injury): *dress wounds.* **3** make attractive: *dress the shop window; They dressed the streets with flags.* **4** prepare for eating or cooking: *to dress a salad with oil and sauces.* **5** *vti* (followed by **up**) put on special clothes: *dress up for a party.* ● *nc* **1** a woman's outer garment covering the body to the knees, or to the feet. **2** *nu* clothing: *They put on evening dress to go to the theatre.* **dressmaker** ('dresmeɪkə*) *nc* a woman who makes clothes for women. **dressmaking** ('dresmeɪkɪŋ) *nu* making clothes for women.

dresser ('dresə*) *nc* **1** a piece of furniture in the kitchen for storing dishes, cutlery, etc. **2** *US* a table with a mirror, used in a bedroom. **3** someone who dresses.

dressing ('dresɪŋ) 1 *nu* putting on clothes. *nc* 2 a bandage, etc., put on an injury. 3 a sauce containing oil, vinegar, etc., added to food to make it tastier. **dressing-gown** ('dresɪŋɡaʊn) *nc* a long garment worn indoors before dressing properly. **dressing-table** *nc* a table with a mirror, used in the bedroom.

drew (dru:) past tense of **draw**.

dribble ('drɪbəl) *vti* 1 (of a liquid), (cause to) flow in drops: *Babies dribble*. 2 *football* (of the ball), (cause to) be kicked forward in short moves.

dried (draɪd) *adj* past tense and past participle of **dry**.

drier ('draɪə*) *n* See **dryer**.

drift (drɪft) *vi* 1 be carried along by a stream of water or air. 2 move through life without a purpose or aim: *He just drifts from one job to another*. ● *nu* 1 being carried along; drifting. 2 *nc* a result of drifting: *a drift of snow collected by the wind*. 3 *nu* most of the meaning: *Do you understand the drift of his speech?*

driftwood ('drɪftwʊd) *nu* pieces of wood carried along by streams of water and onto the beach.

drill¹ (drɪl) *nc* 1 a tool or machine for making holes in hard surfaces, such as wood or metal: see picture at **tools**. 2 army training, such as marching, dealing with weapons, etc. 3 training in the correct way of doing things when quick action is needed: *fire drill*. ● *vt* 1 make (a hole) with a drill; *vi* use a drill to make holes. 2 *vt* train in army matters, or in the correct action to take in a serious or dangerous situation; *vi* be trained in this way.

drill² *nc* a tool or machine for making long cuts in the ground, planting seeds in them, and covering them over with earth.

drill³ *nu* heavy, strong cotton or linen cloth with a rough surface.

drink (drɪŋk) *vt* 1 take in (liquid) through the mouth and swallow: *Drink a cup of tea*. 2 (of a plant, etc.) take in (moisture, liquid, etc.). *vi* 3 take in liquid. 4 take in alcohol, esp. in amounts much larger than is usual. **drink in** listen to with great interest or pleasure: *The children eagerly drank in the exciting stories*. ● *ncu* 1 liquid for drinking. 2 alcohol: *Have we got enough drink for the party?* **drinker** *nc* a person who drinks too much alcohol, or drinks it too often.

drip (drɪp) *vti* (of a liquid), (cause to) fall in drops. ● *nu* 1 dripping. *nc* 2 a small drop of liquid. 3 *infml* a weak, silly person. **drip-dry** (ˌdrɪp'draɪ) *adj* (of a special cloth) best dried by being allowed to drip after being washed. ● *nu* the drying of this special cloth in this way.

dripping ('drɪpɪŋ) *nu* the fat from cooked meat, used for cooking or eating on bread.

drive (draɪv) 1 *vti* (of a vehicle), (cause to) work and move in the same direction. *vt* 2 force (animals and people) to move in the same direction. 3 force (a nail) into something by a hard strike. 4 force (someone) to do something. 5 *vi* go in a car or anything that is not a public vehicle. ● *ncu* 1 (an example of) driving or being driven in a vehicle other than a public one. 2 *nc* a short, private road up to the front of a house. 3 *nu* the power to do things and get things, done: *He hasn't got enough drive for the job*. **be driving at** be meaning: *What's he driving at?* **drive-in** *adj* that can be used, etc., while sitting in one's car: *a drive-in cinema*. ● *nc* a cinema, bank, etc., that can be used in this way. **drive off** 1 chase or frighten away. 2 go off in a vehicle.

driven ('drɪvən) past participle of **drive**.

driver ('draɪvə*) *nc* a person who drives (esp. a car).

drizzle ('drɪzəl) *nu* fine rain. ● *vi* (of rain) fall in very fine drops, often being blown about by the wind.

drone (drəʊn) *nc* 1 a male bee. 2 a person who does no work, passing time in a useless way. 3 *nu* a low, continuous sound like that made by a bee: *the drone of planes*. ● *vi* 1 make a sound like that of a bee. 2 talk or sing with no change in the highness or lowness of the voice, and sounding uninteresting.

droop (dru:p) *vi* hang down, sometimes because of tiredness or sadness. 2 *vt* let (the head) drop forward, or down. ● *nu* a hanging-down position: *the droop of flowers in need of water*.

drop (drɒp) *vti* 1 (of liquid), (allow to) fall in small, rounded amounts. 2 (allow to) fall. 3 (of a person or subject), (cause to) be no longer dealt with: *She dropped most of her friends when she got married; We can't agree, so let's drop the subject*. 4 *vt* allow a passenger to get out of a vehicle: *I'll drop you in town*. ● *nc* 1 a small, rounded amount of liquid: *I felt a drop of rain*. 2 a very small amount. 3 a movement from a higher position to a lower one; fall: *a drop in prices; a drop in temperature; It's a huge drop from the top of those cliffs*. **drop back** move into a position that is further back: *The old man dropped back when they reached the steep hill*. **drop by** or **in** (on) make a short, casual visit to. **drop off** 1 go to sleep. 2 become less in number. **drop out (of)** cease being a part of. **drop-out** ('drɒpaʊt) *nc* a person who ceases to take part in or be a part of something (esp. the usual way of life in a society).

droppings ('drɒpɪŋz) *n pl* the waste matter dropped by animals or birds.

drought (draʊt) *ncu* continuous time of dry weather: *a season of drought*.

drove¹ (drəʊv) past tense of **drive**.

drove² *nc* a large number of animals or people being driven together.

drown (draʊn) **1** *vti* (cause to) die by sinking under water, and being unable to breathe because of this. **2** *vt* (of a sound) be too strong for another sound to be heard: *The noise of the traffic drowned our voices*. **drown with** or **in** be very wet with.

drowsy ('draʊzɪ) *adj* **-ier, -iest** feeling sleepy; causing to feel this way.

drudge (drʌdʒ) *nc* a person whose work is hard and unpleasant. ● *vi* do hard, boring, or unpleasant work as a drudge does. **drudgery** ('drʌdʒərɪ) *nu* hard, unpleasant work.

drug (drʌg) *nc* **1** a substance used as a medicine either on its own or in a mixture. **2** a substance (esp. illegal) that is used like medicine and taken as a habit: *Some drugs can be very harmful if they become a habit*. ● *vt* **1** add drugs, esp. harmful ones to (food, or drink). **2** give drugs esp. harmful ones, to. **drug addict** a person who takes harmful drugs as a habit. **drugstore** ('drʌgstɔː*) *US nc* a chemist's shop that also sells a great variety of other goods, and includes a place to buy and eat food.

drum (drʌm) *nc* **1** a musical instrument made of a round, hollow body with skin stretched over the sides, that is beaten with sticks to produce sound: see picture at **musical instruments**. **2** a container shaped like a cylinder. ● *vt* force (an idea) into someone's mind by repeating it: *I'll drum some sense into him*. **drum up** gather (support) by drawing people's attention. **drummer** ('drʌmə*) *nc* a person who plays a **drum** (def. l).

drunk (drʌŋk) past participle of **drink**. ● *adj* **-er, -est** without self-control because of drinking too much alcohol. ● *nc* a person who is drunk.

drunkard ('drʌŋkəd) *nc* a person who has the habit of drinking too much alcohol.

drunken ('drʌŋkən) *adj* **1** often drunk. **2** caused by, or showing the results of, too much alcohol: *a drunken quarrel*. **drunkenness** *nu*

dry (draɪ) *adj* **drier, driest 1** not wet. **2** *infml* thirsty. **3** not interesting; boring: *a dry book*. **4** (of wine, etc.) not sweet. **5** (of a person's manner) quiet but amused. ● *vti* **1** (cause to) become dry. **2** *vt* keep (food) from going bad by removing moisture: *dried fish*. **dry-clean** (,draɪ'kliːn) *vt* clean (clothes, etc.) with a substance that dis-

solves dirt, etc., without using water. **dry dock** *nc* a place by or in a river, etc., where the water can be let out. **dryer** (also **drier**) ('draɪə*) *nc* a device for drying something: *a hair-dryer*. **dryness** *nu* being dry. **dry rot** *nu* wood that has become diseased through lack of air and has turned to powder. **dry up 1** stop talking because of feeling nervous, or because of not knowing what else to say. **2** make or become dry.

dual ('djuːəl) *adj* of or to do with two; double: *a car with dual controls*.

dub (dʌb) *vt* **1** make (a person) a knight by touching on each shoulder with a sword. **2** give (a person) a name that is not a real name. **3** put words of a different language over (the sound of a film).

dubious ('djuːbɪəs) *adj* feeling or causing doubt.

ducat ('dʌkət) *history nc* a gold coin once used in most countries in Europe.

duchess ('dʌtʃɪs) *nc* the wife or widow of a duke; woman whose position and duties are the same as those of a duke.

duck¹ (dʌk) **1** *nc* a common water-bird with its toes joined by skin; female of this. *nu* **2** the flesh of this bird eaten as food. **3** *infml nc* a failure to make any runs in cricket. **duckling** ('dʌklɪŋ) *nc* a young duck.

duck² **1** *vi* bend the head or body quickly to avoid a blow or being seen. **2** *vt* push (someone) under water quickly, esp. as a joke.

duct (dʌkt) *nc* a small channel, etc., through which liquid is carried, esp. in the body.

ductile ('dʌktaɪl) *adj* easily shaped by pressing or beating: *ductile metals*.

dud (dʌd) *slang adj* useless: *a dud cheque*. ● *nc* a useless person or thing.

due (djuː) *adj* **1** expected at a certain time: *The train is due in ten minutes*. **2** owing: *The rent is due*. **3** proper: *with due respect*. **due to** caused by: *The accident was due to the driver's failure to signal; mistakes due to carelessness*. **dues** (djuːz) *n pl* amounts of money that are to be paid for membership: *club dues*.

duel ('djuːəl) *nc* a fight between two people to settle a quarrel or point of honour with weapons likely to cause death; serious disagreement. ● *vi* fight a duel.

duet (djuː'et) *nc* a piece of music played or sung by two people.

duffel ('dʌfəl) *nu* rough, woollen cloth. **duffel-coat** *nc* a coat made of such cloth.

dug (dʌg) past tense and past participle of **dig**.

dug-out ('dʌgaʊt) *nc* **1** a place dug in the ground used for protection, esp. by soldiers in wartime. **2** a long, light boat made by hollowing out a tree trunk.

duke (djuːk) *nc* a nobleman whose position and duties are below those of a prince.

dull (dʌl) *adj* **-er, -est 1** uninteresting: *a dull book*. **2** grey-looking; not bright: *dull weather*. **3** slow to understand: *a dull mind*. **4** not sharp: *a dull knife; dull pain*. ● *vti* (cause to) become dull. **dullness** *nu* being dull.

duly (ˈdjuːlɪ) *adv* **1** properly; in a right manner: *She was duly sorry for her mistake*. **2** at the right time: *He duly arrived on the day he'd promised*.

dumb (dʌm) *adj* **-er, -est 1** not able to speak. **2** not able to speak for a short time because of surprise, fear, etc. **3** *US infml* stupid.

dumbfound (dʌmˈfaʊnd) *vt* make unable to speak for a short time because of astonishment.

dummy (ˈdʌmɪ) *nc, pl* **-mies** something made to represent and take the place of a person or the real thing (esp. used for making and displaying clothes).

dump (dʌmp) *nc* **1** a place where rubbish, unwanted things, etc., can be left. **2** a place for storing army supplies. **3** *slang* an unpleasant, uninteresting, or dirty place: *This town is a dump!* ● *vt* **1** get rid of (rubbish, etc.) by putting on a dump. **2** put (something) down or let fall with a bump. **3** *commerce* sell goods in large amounts at a lower price abroad than in the home country. **dumping** (ˈdʌmpɪŋ) *commerce nu* the selling of goods in large amounts at a very low price.

dumpling (ˈdʌmplɪŋ) *nc* **1** a round, cooked mixture of flour and water, sometimes filled with meat, apple, etc. **2** *infml* a fat person.

dumpy (ˈdʌmpɪ) *adj* **-ier, -iest** short and fat.

dunce (dʌns) *nc* a person who is slow to learn.

dune (djuːn) *nc* a small hill or ridge of sand, esp. on the seashore: see picture.

dune

dung (dʌŋ) *nu* the waste matter of animals, often spread over soil to make it produce more.

dungarees (ˌdʌŋɡəˈriːz) *n pl (with plural verb)* loose-fitting trousers and bib of strong cotton cloth, worn over clothes to protect them from dirt.

dungeon (ˈdʌndʒən) *history nc* an underground prison.

dupe (djuːp) *vt* deceive. ● *nc* a person who is deceived.

duplicate (ˈdjuːplɪkeɪt) *vt* make an exact copy of. ● (ˈdjuːplɪkət) *nc* something that is an exact copy of another thing. ● *adj* exactly like: *duplicate car keys*. **duplication** (ˌdjuːplɪˈkeɪʃən) **1** *nu* duplicating or being duplicated. **2** *nc* an exact copy. **duplicator** (ˈdjuːplɪkeɪtə*) *nc* a machine that makes copies (of documents, etc.).

durable (ˈdjʊərəbəl) *adj* that is able to last for a long time. **durability** (ˌdjʊərə-ˈbɪlətɪ) *nu* being durable.

duration (djʊəˈreɪʃən) *nu* the length of time that something continues: *of short duration*.

duress (djʊəˈres) *nu* force, esp. violence, or imprisonment used on a person to make him do something.

during (ˈdjʊərɪŋ) *prep* **1** at some point in a length of time: *It rained during the night*. **2** through the whole time of.

dusk (dʌsk) *nu* the time just before night falls.

dust (dʌst) *nu* powdery dirt made up of many tiny pieces of earth, waste matter, etc., lying on surfaces or on the ground. ● *vt* **1** remove dust from. **2** cover lightly with powder. **dustbin** (ˈdʌstbɪn) *Brit nc* a container for rubbish. **dust jacket** See **jacket** (def. 3). **dustman** (ˈdʌstmən) *nc, pl* **-men** *Brit* a man whose job is to collect rubbish from dustbins, etc., and take it away. **dustpan** (ˈdʌstpæn) *nc* a pan used to carry away dust, etc., that has been swept into it. **duster** *nc* a cloth for cleaning dust from furniture, etc. **dusty** *adj* **-ier, -iest** covered with dust.

dutiful (ˈdjuːtɪfʊl) *adj* doing what one must, or is expected to do, willingly and regularly. **dutifully** *adv*

duty (ˈdjuːtɪ) *nc, pl* **-ties 1** *nu* that which one ought to do by law, a promise, a feeling inside oneself, etc. **2** *nc* a particular task or duty: *What are the duties of your new job?* **3** *nu* money to be paid to the government on certain goods made, brought into, or taken out of the country, etc.; *nc* an example of such a payment. **on** or **off duty** at or away from one's regular work.

duvet (ˈdjuːveɪ) *nc* a bed-covering filled with feathers, etc., and used instead of blankets.

dwarf (dwɔːf) *nc* **1** a person who is much smaller than usual; anything that is unusually small. **2** a very small imaginary creature with magic powers. ● *vt* cause to appear small: *He's so tall that he dwarfs everyone else*.

dwell (dwel) *vi* **1** *formal* live (in a place). **2** (followed by **on**) think or talk too much about (something). **dwelling** (ˈdwelɪŋ) *nc formal* a house, flat, etc., in which one lives.

dwelt (dwelt) past tense and past participle of **dwell.**

dwindle ('dwɪndəl) *vi* gradually get less or smaller.

dye (daɪ) *vti* (of cloth, etc.), (cause to) be changed in colour by having been put in liquid. ●*nc* a substance used for dyeing cloth.

dying ('daɪɪŋ) present participle of **die¹**.

dyke

dyke (also **dike**) (daɪk) *nc* a long, thick wall of earth, etc., built to prevent water from a river or sea flooding onto the land: see picture.

dynamic (daɪ'næmɪk) *adj* **1** of or to do with the force that produces motion. **2** (of a person) full of force and energy. **dynamics** *nu (with singular verb)* the part of science that deals with motion and force.

dynamite ('daɪnəmaɪt) *nu* **1** a very powerful explosive. **2** *infml* someone or something dangerous to deal with.

dynamo ('daɪnəməʊ) *nc* a machine that produces electricity.

dynasty ('dɪnəstɪ) *nc, pl* **-ties** a set of kings, related to each other and following one another in time.

dysentery ('dɪsəntərɪ) *nu* a disease with painful emptying of waste matter and blood from the bowels.

E

each (iːtʃ) *adj* (of more than one) every person, thing, etc., treated separately: *A mother loves all of her children but each in a different way.* ●*determiner* each person, thing, etc. ●*adv* to or for every one. **each other** two (or more) members of a group having to do with one another: *We see each other every day.*

eager ('iːgə*) *adj* showing strong desire; very willing to do something. **eagerly** *adv* **eagerness** *nu* being eager.

eagle ('iːgəl) *nc* a large bird that kills and eats other animals: see picture at **birds**.

ear[1] (ɪə*) *nc* the organ of hearing: see picture. **play something by ear 1** play a musical instrument without the help of printed music. **2** behave in a careful way because one is unsure of something: *I don't know if he's still angry with me—I shall have to play it by ear!* **eardrum** ('ɪədrʌm) *nc* the tight skin in the middle part of the ear that is moved by sound. **earmark** ('ɪəmɑːk) *vt* put (something) aside to be used for a special purpose. **earphone** ('ɪəfəʊn) *nc* a device put in or over the ear in order to receive sound from a radio, etc. **earrings** ('ɪərɪŋz) *n pl* rings or ornaments worn on the ears. **earshot** ('ɪəʃɒt) *nu* the distance over which one can hear or that something can be heard: *Stay within earshot in case you need help.*

ear

ear[2] *nc* a head of corn, etc., containing its seeds.

earl (ɜːl) *nc* the title of a British nobleman.

early ('ɜːlɪ) *adj* **-ier, -iest,** *adv* **1** before the usual time. **2** near the beginning of a length of time: *in early summer.*

earn (ɜːn) *vt* **1** get (something) in return for work. **2** deserve. **earnings** ('ɜːnɪŋz) *n pl* money that has been earned.

earnest ('ɜːnɪst) *adj* having serious intentions. **in earnest** in a serious manner. **earnestly** *adv* **earnestness** *nu* being earnest.

earth (ɜːθ) *nu* **1** this planet on which we live.

2 the part of the world that is not sky. **3** soil. **4** *electricity* the connection of an electrical device with the ground; *nc* the wire used for this purpose. **5** the hole in the ground in which a fox or other wild animal lives. ●*vt* connect (an electrical device) with the ground. **earthly** ('ɜːθlɪ) *adj* **1** of or to do with the world in which we live; not to do with heaven. **2** not the slightest: *He hasn't an earthly chance of winning.* **earthquake** ('ɜːθkweɪk) *nc* a sudden shaking of the earth. **earthworm** ('ɜːθwɜːm) *nc* a common worm that lives in the ground. **earthy** ('ɜːθɪ) *adj* **-ier, -iest 1** of or like earth or soil: *an earthy, farmyard smell.* **2** vulgar; to do with the senses not the spirit.

earthenware ('ɜːθənweə*) *nu* dishes, etc., made of baked earth or clay. ●*adj* made of earthenware.

ease (iːz) *nu* freedom from trouble, difficulty, discomfort, pain, etc. ●*vti* **1** (of pain, worry, discomfort, etc.), (cause to) lessen: *I will ease your mind; The pain will soon ease.* **2** (cause to) move gently: *The car eased forward.* **ease off** become less: *The rain is easing off at last; The excitement eased off when the contest was over.*

easel ('iːzəl) *nc* a frame to support a picture or blackboard.

easily ('iːzəlɪ) *adv* **1** without difficulty; with ease. **2** certainly: *She's easily the best in the class.*

east (iːst) *n* **the east** the direction in which the sun rises. **the East** the eastern part of the world, esp. Asia; the Orient. **the Far East** the countries in Asia east of India, such as China and Japan. **the Middle East** the countries in Asia west of India, such as Iran and Israel. ●*adj* **1** in, towards, or facing, the east. **2** (of the wind) coming from the east. ●*adv* towards the east. **easterly** ('iːstəlɪ) *adj* in or from the east. **eastern** ('iːstən) *adj* to the east; to do with the east. **eastward(s)** ('iːstwəd(z)) *adj, adv* towards the east.

Easter ('iːstə*) *nu* the Christian festival celebrating Jesus Christ's rising from the dead.

easy ('iːzɪ) *adj* **-ier, -iest 1** not difficult. **2** comfortable: *an easy chair.* **3** free from trouble, difficulty, etc.: *He has an easy life.* ●*adv* gently; in an easy manner. **easy-going** *adj* (of a person) not worrying about life; taking too little care; lazy.

eat (iːt) **1** *vt* take in (food) through the mouth and swallow it. **2** *vi* have a meal. **3** *vt* slowly destroy: *The sea is eating away the rock.*

eaten ('iːtən) past participle of **eat**.

eaves (iːvz) *n pl* the edge of a roof that hangs over the wall of a building. **eavesdrop** ('iːvzdrɒp) *vi* listen secretly to a private conversation.

ebb (eb) *vi* 1 (of the sea) flow back from the shore. 2 become fainter or less: *Conversation ebbed.* ●*nu* 1 the flowing back of the sea: *the ebb and flow of the sea.* 2 becoming fainter, weaker, or less: *His health is at a low ebb.*

ebony ('ebənı) *nu* hard, heavy, black wood. ●*adj* 1 made of such wood. 2 of the colour of ebony.

eccentric (ık'sentrık) *adj* 1 (of a person's behaviour or habits) not usual; odd; peculiar. 2 (of circles) not having the same centre.

ecclesiastical (ı,kli:zı'æstıkəl) *adj* of the Christian Church or its priests.

echo ('ekəʊ) *nc, pl* **-es** 1 a sound sent back, such as that of one's own voice on top of a hill, in a large room, etc. 2 someone or something very like someone or something else. ●*vi* 1 (of a place) send back an echo. 2 (of a sound) to come back as an echo. 3 *vt* copy (the words, opinions, etc., of another person).

eclipse (ı'klıps) *nc* 1 the darkness, partial or complete, caused when a body such as the moon passes between the sun and the earth, or when the earth's shadow falls on the moon: see picture. 2 loss of fame, power, etc. ●*vt* 1 cut off the light from: *The moon eclipsed the sun.* 2 do much better than; excel.

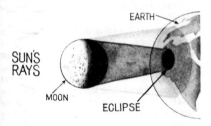

eclipse

ecology (ı'kɒlədʒı) *nu* the study of the relationship of living things to their surroundings. **ecological** (,i:kə'lɒdʒıkəl) *adj* of or to do with ecology. **ecologist** (ı'kɒlədʒıst) *nc* a person who is an expert in ecology.

economic (,i:kə'nɒmık, ,ekə'nɒmık) *adj* 1 of or to do with economics. 2 intended to make a profit or save money. **economical** *adj* not wasteful of money, time, etc.

economics (,i:kə'nɒmıks, ,ekə'nɒmıks) *nu (with singular verb)* the study of the influences that affect the production and distribution of wealth in a country. **economise** (ı'kɒnəmaız) *vi* reduce the money spent on something or the use of something. **economist** (ı'kɒnəmıst) *nc* a person who is an expert in economics.

economy (ı'kɒnəmı) *nc, pl* **-mies** 1 *nu* a way of spending less money or not wasting it; *nc* an example of this. 2 *nu* the control of the wealth, supplies of goods, etc., that a person, country, etc., has; state of a country's wealth, industry, etc.; *nc* an example of this.

ecstasy ('ekstəsı) *nc, pl* **-sies** a state of excited joy. **ecstatic** (ek'stætık) *adj* of or to do with ecstasy.

eddy ('edı) *nc, pl* **-dies** 1 a circular flow of water in a sea, river, etc. 2 smoke, wind, dust, etc., moving in this way.

edge (edʒ) *nc* 1 the thin, sharp side of a tool, or weapon. 2 the outer part or border: *the edge of the forest.* ●*vi* move slowly: *He edged away from the cliff.* **on edge** in a state of being nervous or easily annoyed. **edging** ('edʒıŋ) *nc* a narrow border, esp. one to add decoration.

edible ('edıbəl) *adj* fit for eating.

edict ('i:dıkt) *nc* an order given by a ruler, a king, or by the power of a law.

edifice ('edıfıs) *formal nc* a building, esp. a large, impressive one.

edify ('edıfaı) *vt* improve (the mind or the soul). **edification** (,edıfı'keıʃən) *nu* improvement of the mind or the soul.

edit ('edıt) *vt* 1 prepare (another person's) written work for printing and publishing. 2 put cinema film, tape-recordings, or information into a computer, in a suitable order. **edition** (ı'dıʃən) *nc* 1 the form in which a book is printed. 2 the number of copies of a book, newspaper, etc., printed and published at one time: *A new edition of his book has just been published; Did you get today's edition of the daily paper?* **editor** ('edıtə*) *nc* a person who edits. **editorial** (,edı'tɔ:rıəl) *nc* a special article in a newspaper, magazine, etc., usually written by the editor.

educate ('edjʊkeıt) *vt* teach; train in order to produce a good standard of behaviour. **education** (,edjʊ'keıʃən) *ncu* (an example of) educating or being educated. **educational** (,edjʊ'keıʃənəl) *adj* of or to do with education: *educational books.*

eel (i:l) *nc* a snake-like fish: see picture at **fish.**

e'en (i:n) *poetry adv* even.

e'er (eə*) *poetry adv* ever.

eerie ('ıərı) *adj* **-r, -st** strange; causing feelings of fear and lack of ease.

efface (ı'feıs) *vt* 1 remove by rubbing out. 2 cause to have no more effect; remove.

effect (ı'fekt) *nc* 1 an influence produced on the mind: *a strange effect on him.* 2 a result; result of a happening: *the effect of very hot weather on the garden.* 3 *nu* meaning: *I've told you what she said, or words to that ef-*

fect. ●*vt* **1** cause (something) to happen. **2** succeed in doing (something): *The doctor effected a complete cure.* **in effect** in fact. **into effect** into action: *When does the rule come into effect?* **take effect 1** have a result: *Has the medicine taken effect yet?* **2** begin to act: *Our plans have taken effect.*

effects (ɪ'fekts) *n pl* goods owned by a person; property.

effective (ɪ'fektɪv) *adj* **1** having a result; doing or bringing about what was intended. **2** leaving an impression on the mind: *effective use of colour.* **effectively** *adv* **effectiveness** *nu* being effective.

effectual (ɪ'fektʃʊəl) *adj* having a particular result: *an effectual punishment.*

effeminate (ɪ'femɪnət) *often derogatory adj* **1** (of a man) like a woman.

effervesce (,efə'ves) *vi* **1** *chemistry* give off bubbles of gas. **2** (of a person) be full of excitement and energy.

efficacy ('efɪkəsɪ) *nu* being effective. **efficacious** (,efɪ'keɪʃəs) *adj* able to produce an effect.

efficient (ɪ'fɪʃənt) *adj* **1** (of a person) able to do things well and properly. **2** having the result that is wanted and done with the smallest amount of effort. **efficiency** (ɪ'fɪʃənsɪ) *nu* being efficient. **efficiently** *adv*

effigy ('efɪdʒɪ) *nc, pl* **-gies** a likeness of a person made in wood, metal, etc.

effluent ('eflʊənt) *nc* **1** a stream flowing out from a lake, etc. **2** liquid waste flowing out from factories, etc.

effort ('efət) **1** *nu* trying with force; trying hard: *Put some effort into it!* *nc* **2** an example of using effort. **3** *infml* something done that needed effort: *It was a good effort, but not your best work.* **effortless** ('efətlɪs) *adj* without effort; easy.

effrontery (ɪ'frʌntərɪ) *nu* shameless rudeness and lack of respect.

effusive (ɪ'fjuːsɪv) *adj* (of speech or one's feelings) showing more than enough: *effusive thanks.*

egg (eg) *nc* **1** an oval or rounded object laid by a female animal, fish, bird, etc., containing its young. **2** the female seed that is able to develop into a new life when fertilised by a male seed. **egg-cup** *nc* a small container for holding an egg that has been boiled in its shell. **eggplant** *nc* a plant with a large purple fruit that is eaten as a vegetable. **egg on** urge (someone) to do something.

ego ('egəʊ, 'iːgəʊ) *nc* a person's own special nature, qualities, and knowledge of himself. **egocentric** (,egəʊ'sentrɪk) *derogatory adj* with all one's attention, interest, etc., on oneself.

egoism ('egəʊɪzəm) *derogatory nu* a state in which one is always thinking about oneself. **egoist** ('egəʊɪst) *derogatory nc* a person who is always thinking about himself.

egotism ('egətɪzəm) *derogatory nu* talking too much about oneself. **egotist** ('egətɪst) *derogatory nc* a person who talks too much about himself.

eh (eɪ) *interj* (showing surprise or doubt; asking for agreement or for something to be said again because of not hearing or understanding.)

eiderdown ('aɪdədaʊn) *nc* a thick, outer bedcovering filled with duck's feathers.

eight (eɪt) *determiner, n* the number 8. **eighth** (eɪtθ) *determiner, n, adv* **eighteen** (,eɪ'tiːn) *determiner, n* 18. **eighteenth** (,eɪ'tiːnθ) *determiner, n, adv* **eighty** ('eɪtɪ) *determiner, n* 80. **eightieth** ('eɪtɪɪθ) *determiner, n, adv*

either ('aɪðə*, 'iːðə*) *determiner, pron* **1** one and the other of two: *The two children sat on either side of their father.* **2** each of two: *At either end of the room was a window.* **3** any one of. ●*adv* (used after a phrase containing **not**) what is more; also: *If he is not going, I shall not either; I don't like his brother either.* ●*conj* **either... or** (used to introduce the first of a choice): *We can get there either by bus or by car.*

ejaculate (ɪ'dʒækjʊleɪt) *vt* **1** *formal* say suddenly and quickly. **2** *medicine* send out (liquid, esp. that containing male seed) suddenly and with force.

eject (ɪ'dʒekt) *vt* **1** force (someone) to leave a place. **2** throw out with force.

eke out (iːk'aʊt) *vt* **1** add small amounts to (what one has) for one's needs: *He eked out his low wages by doing extra work in the evenings.* **2** make the best use of (what one has) by being careful, etc.: *The poor family eked out their savings for as long as they could.*

elaborate (ɪ'læbərət) *adj* very carefully planned including the smallest details; made up of many parts: *A very elaborate meal had been prepared for them.* ●(ɪ'læbəreɪt) *vi* give a more detailed account.

elapse (ɪ'læps) *vi* (of time) pass: *Ten days have elapsed since then.*

elastic (ɪ'læstɪk) *adj* **1** that goes back to its normal size or shape after being pulled: *Rubber bands are elastic.* **2** quite easily changed to suit new conditions, etc.: *elastic rules.* ●*nu* elastic substance; *nc* an example of this. **elasticity** (,ɪlæ'stɪsɪtɪ) *nu* being elastic.

elated (ɪ'leɪtɪd) *adj* joyful. **elation** (ɪ'leɪʃən) *nu* very high spirits.

elbow ('elbəʊ) *nc* **1** the place where the two parts of the arm join: see picture. **2** anything with a bend of this shape, such as a corner or a pipe. ● *vt* push (one's way) through (a crowd, etc.).

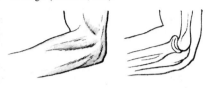

elbow

elder ('eldə*) *adj* older; used in family relationships: *She has an elder brother.* ● *nu* **1** the older of two people: *He is my elder by two years.* *nc* **2** people of greater age: *Children are told to respect their elders.* **3** an officer in some Christian churches who is worthy of respect because of age and wisdom. **elderly** *adj* between middle age and old age; rather old. **eldest** ('eldist) *adj* oldest. ● *nu* the child in a family that is born first: *He's the eldest of three.*

elect (ı'lekt) *vt* **1** choose (someone) for the position of: *He was elected President.* **2** choose; decide. ● *adj* chosen: *President elect.* **election** (ı'lekʃən) *nu* choosing someone for a position by a vote; choosing; *nc* an example of this. **electoral** (ı'lektərəl) *adj* of or to do with an election of a person by vote. **electorate** (ı'lektərət) *nu* all the people having the right to vote for members of government.

electric (ı'lektrık) *adj* **1** of, to do with, or worked by, electricity: *an electric light bulb.* **2** *infml* very exciting. **electrical** (ı'lektrıkəl) *adj* for dealing with electricity. **electrician** (ˌılek'trıʃən) *nc* a person who is trained to deal with electrical equipment, making and repairing it. **electricity** (ˌılek'trısıtı) *nu* **1** the power used to produce heat and light; science and study of this. **2** (the supply of) a continuous flow of electricity.

electrify (ı'lektrıfaı) *vt* **1** put an amount of electricity into (a device, substance, etc.). **2** make very surprised, excited, or shocked: *We were electrified by the news of his death.* **electrification** (ı,lektrıfı'keıʃən) *nu* electrifying.

electrocute (ı'lektrəkjuːt) *vt* kill (a person) by electricity, either by accident, or as a punishment.

electrode (ı'lektrəʊd) *nc* a substance or object, to or from which electricity flows.

electrolysis (ˌılek'trɒləsıs) *science nu* the separation of a liquid into its chemical parts by a flow of electricity.

electron (ı'lektrɒn) *nc* a tiny part of an atom that carries a negative charge of electricity. **electronic** (ˌılek'trɒnık) *adj* of or to do with electronics. **electronics** (ˌılek'trɒnıks) *nu (with singular verb)* **1** the science and

study of the movement of electrons in radio, television, computers, etc. **2** the business of making electronic devices.

electroplate (ı'lektrəʊpleıt) *vt* cover (another metal) with gold, silver, etc., by electrolysis.

elegant ('elıgənt) *adj* graceful; showing good taste; beautiful: *elegant manners.* **elegance** ('elıgəns) *nu* being elegant.

elegy ('elədʒı) *nc, pl* **-gies** a sorrowful poem or song, esp. for the dead.

element ('elımənt) *nc* **1** *chemistry* a substance that cannot be divided into simpler parts by chemical means. **2** a necessary part. **3** *(pl)* the simple beginnings of a subject. **4** a slight sign of: *an element of truth.* **5** a wire in an electrical apparatus that will allow only a certain amount of electricity to pass through. **the elements** the weather. **the four elements** earth, air, fire, and water. **elemental** (ˌelı'mentəl) *adj* like the dangerous forces of nature.

elementary (ˌelı'mentərı) *adj* **1** suitable for a person just starting to learn; simple: *elementary school.* **2** important; basic: *It's an elementary part of his beliefs.*

elephant ('elıfənt) *nc* the largest land animal alive, with a long nose and two curved tusks: see picture at **animals**. **white elephant** a possession that is useless or unwanted.

elevate ('elıveıt) *vt* **1** lift up; raise to a higher position. **2** improve (the mind, etc.): *an elevating conversation.* **elevation** (ˌelı'veıʃən) **1** *nu* elevating or being elevated; *nc* an example of this. *nc* **2** a high place. **3** a plan showing one side of a building: *the front elevation.* **elevator** ('elıveıtə*) *nc* **1** *US* a machine for taking people from one floor of a building to another; lift. **2** a machine for lifting up corn, etc.; place in which corn is stored. **3** any device that raises up something.

eleven (ı'levən) *determiner, n* the number 11. **eleventh** (ı'levənθ) *determiner, n, adv*

elf (elf) *nc, pl* **elves** (elvz) a small, imaginary creature, like a fairy.

elicit (ı'lısıt) *vt* draw out: *to elicit information.*

eligible ('elıdʒəbəl) *adj* fit to be chosen; suitable (esp. for marriage). **eligibility** (ˌelıdʒə'bılıtı) *nu* being fit to be chosen.

eliminate (ı'lımıneıt) *vt* get rid of; remove. **elimination** (ı,lımı'neıʃən) *nu* being got rid of or removed.

élite (eı'liːt) *adj* the people with the most wealth, influence, etc., in a group or in society.

elixir (ı'lıksə*) *nc* **1** *history* an imaginary substance prepared by chemists hoping to change metals into gold or to make life last for ever. **2** something that cures any evil or trouble.

elk (elk) *nc* a kind of large deer found in North America.

ell (el) *history nc* a measure of length = 45 inches (1.14 m).

ellipse (ɪ'lɪps) *nc* a regular oval. **elliptical** (ɪ'lɪptɪkəl) *adj* with the shape of an ellipse.

elm (elm) *nc* a kind of large, tall tree that loses its leaves every autumn: see picture at **trees**; *nu* hard wood of this tree.

elocution (ˌelə'kjuːʃən) *nu* speaking and expressing oneself well, esp. in public; the study of this.

elongate ('iːlɒŋgeɪt) *vti* (cause to) become longer (in space).

elope (ɪ'ləʊp) *vi* run away from home with someone of the opposite sex, esp. in order to marry.

eloquent ('eləkwənt) *adj* expressing oneself clearly and well in speech. **eloquence** ('eləkwəns) *nu* being eloquent.

else (els) *adv* also; besides: *Where else shall we go today?; Who else is coming?* **or else** otherwise: *Hurry, or else you'll be late.* **elsewhere** ('elsweə*) *adv* somewhere that is not where one is.

elucidate (ɪ'luːsɪdeɪt) *vt* make clearer: *elucidate a problem.*

elude (ɪ'luːd) *vt* escape in a skilful way, esp. by means of a trick; avoid; stay away from. **elusive** (ɪ'luːsɪv) *adj* not easy to catch, find, remember, or understand: *an elusive thief; elusive memories.*

'em (əm) *infml pron* them.

emaciated (ɪ'meɪsɪeɪtɪd) *adj* thin and ill in appearance.

emanate ('eməneɪt) *vi* come or flow out.

emancipate (ɪ'mænsɪpeɪt) *vt* make free from control, esp. by others: *emancipate slaves.* **emancipation** (ɪˌmænsɪ'peɪʃən) *nu* emancipating or being emancipated.

emasculate (ɪ'mæskjʊleɪt) *vt* take away the manly strength and energy of; make a coward of.

embalm (ɪm'bɑːm) *vt* keep a dead body from decaying by means of chemicals.

embankment (ɪm'bæŋkmənt) *nc* the sloping bank, or wall of earth, stones, etc., along the side of a river that prevents it overflowing.

embargo (ɪm'bɑːgəʊ) *nc, pl* **-es** an order that forbids the movement of ships or trade; any order that forbids some activity.

embark (ɪm'bɑːk) **1** *vi* go on board a ship. **2** *vt* put on or get on (a ship). **3** *vi* (followed by **on** or **upon**) start; undertake.

embarrass (ɪm'bærəs) *vt* make (a person) feel shy or uncomfortable in the mind (esp. in public). **embarrassment** (ɪm'bærəsmənt) **1** *nu* embarrassing or being embarrassed. **2** *nc* a person or thing that embarrasses.

embassy ('embəsɪ) *nc, pl* **-sies** the building provided for an ambassador living in a foreign country to represent his own country there; the house he lives in.

embed (ɪm'bed) *vt* fix firmly into: *The bullet was embedded in the wall.*

embellish (ɪm'belɪʃ) *vt* add to, with decoration or details; make beautiful: *embellish a story; embellished with jewels.*

ember ('embə*) *nc* one of the pieces of burning coal or wood of a dying fire.

embezzle (ɪm'bezəl) *vt* use (the money belonging to someone else) that has been put in one's care for one's own bad purposes.

embittered (ɪm'bɪtəd) *adj* made bad-tempered and sad because of disappointments in life.

emblem ('embləm) *nc* a device that is a sign of something; symbol: *Our group's emblem is a running bear.*

embody (ɪm'bɒdɪ) *vt* **1** give form to: *His thoughts were embodied in his poem.* **2** contain; be made up of: *Television embodies a variety of programmes.* **embodiment** (ɪm'bɒdɪmənt) *nc* something which embodies or something that is embodied.

emboss (ɪm'bɒs) *vt* make a shape, figure, pattern, etc., stand out from a surface (of something): *notepaper with the address embossed on each sheet.*

embrace (ɪm'breɪs) *vt* **1** hold (someone) closely in one's arms to show affection or love. **2** include: *The study embraced every aspect of the problem.* **3** eagerly agree to (an idea). ●*nc* an act of embracing.

embroider (ɪm'brɔɪdə*) *vt* **1** decorate (a piece of cloth, etc.) with needle and coloured thread. **2** add untrue or imaginary details to (a story). **embroidery** (ɪm'brɔɪdərɪ) *nu* decorative work done with a needle and thread.

embryo ('embrɪəʊ) *nc* **1** *biology* the young of an animal or human in the early part of its development before being born or hatched. **2** anything in the early stages of development: *an embryo of an idea.* **embryonic** (ˌembrɪ'ɒnɪk) *adj* in the first stages of development.

emend (ɪ'mend) *vt* remove mistakes from.

emerald ('emərəld) *nc* a bright green precious stone. ●*adj* colour of this: *emerald green eyes.*

emerge (ɪ'mɜːdʒ) *vi* **1** come out (from water, from being out of sight, etc.). **2** become known: *No new facts emerged from the police inquiry into the murder.* **emergence** (ɪ'mɜːdʒəns) *nu* **emergent** (ɪ'mɜːdʒənt) *adj*

emergency (ɪ'mɜːdʒənsɪ) *nc, pl* **-cies** a sudden, serious or dangerous happening that needs immediate action. ●*adj* of or to do with an emergency.

emery ('emərɪ) *nu* a hard metal used for rubbing surfaces or for crushing them to powder.

emigrate ('emɪɡreɪt) *vi* leave one's own country to settle in another country. **emigrant** ('emɪɡrənt) *nc* a person who emigrates. **emigration** (emɪ'ɡreɪʃən) *nu* emigrating; *nc* an example of this.

eminent ('emɪnənt) *adj* worthy of attention; famous; important. **eminence** ('emɪnəns) 1 *nu* being famous or worthy of attention; *nc* a person like this. 2 *nc* a piece of high ground. **eminently** *infml adv* clearly; plainly: *eminently true*.

emir (e'mɪə*) *nc* the title of an Arab prince. **emirate** (e'mɪərət) *nc* the land ruled by an emir; position of emir.

emissary ('emɪsərɪ) *nc, pl* **-ries** a person sent to take a message or to do some special, often very unpleasant, work.

emission (ɪ'mɪʃən) *nu* the giving out (of heat, light, sound, etc.); *nc* an example of this.

emit (ɪ'mɪt) *vt* give out (heat, light, sound, etc.).

emolument (ɪ'mɒljʊmənt) *formal nc* the money obtained by someone holding authority; wages.

emotion (ɪ'məʊʃən) 1 *nu* strong feeling: *a voice full of emotion*. 2 *nc* any kind of strong feeling: *Anger is an emotion*. **emotional** (ɪ'məʊʃənəl) *adj* 1 of or to do with the emotions. 2 easily excited by strong feelings. **emotive** (ɪ'məʊtɪv) *adj* likely to cause strong feelings: *an emotive film*.

emperor ('empərə*) *nc* the ruler of an empire.

emphasise ('emfəsaɪz) *vt* put extra force on (a word or words) to show a special meaning or importance; put a special meaning or importance on anything. **emphasis** ('emfəsɪs) *ncu, pl* **-ses** emphasising or being emphasised; an example of this. **emphatic** (ɪm'fætɪk) *adj* with emphasis: *emphatic opinions*. **emphatically** *adv*

empire ('empaɪə*) *nc* a number of countries under one government or ruler.

empirical (em'pɪrɪkəl) *adj* relying on what one can see and feel by experiments and observations and not on a theory or idea.

employ (ɪm'plɔɪ) *vt* 1 give work to, for a wage or salary. 2 *formal* use. **employee** (emplɔɪ'iː) *nc* a person who is paid to work. **employer** (ɪm'plɔɪə*) *nc* a person who employs people. **employment** (ɪm'plɔɪmənt) *nu* employing or being employed; one's paid work.

empower (ɪm'paʊə*) *vt* give (someone) power to do something.

empress ('emprɪs) *nc* the wife of an emperor; queen of an empire.

empty ('emptɪ) *adj* **-ier, -iest** 1 with nothing inside: *an empty box*. 2 *infml* hungry. 3 without meaning: *empty promises*. ● *vti* (cause to) become empty. **empty-handed** (emptɪ'hændɪd) *adj* without anything, esp. money, in one's hands. **empty-headed** (emptɪ'hedɪd) *adj* foolish; not sensible. **emptiness** ('emptɪnɪs) *nu* being empty.

emu ('iːmjuː) *nc* a large Australian bird that has long legs and is unable to fly.

emulate ('emjʊleɪt) *vt* try to do as well as or better than (someone else). **emulation** (emjʊ'leɪʃən) *nu* emulating.

emulsion (ɪ'mʌlʃən) *nu* a kind of thick, creamy mixture of liquids in which very small drops of oil or fat float; *nc* a mixture of this kind.

enable (ɪ'neɪbəl) *vt* make able; give (someone) the means to do something: *Having a car enables one to travel.*

enact (ɪ'nækt) *vt* 1 make a law. 2 act (a scene or part) on a theatre stage, or in life.

enamel (ɪ'næməl) *nu* 1 a glass-like material that is melted and used to cover the surface of metal, etc., to decorate or protect it. 2 the hard, shiny covering of the teeth. ● *vt* to cover with enamel.

enamoured *US* **enamored** (ɪ'næməd) *adj* (followed by *of* or *with*) filled with strong liking or love (for).

encamp (ɪn'kæmp) 1 *vt* settle (an army) in a camp. 2 *vi* (of an army) become settled in a camp.

encase (ɪn'keɪs) *vt* put in a case; cover or shut up in a case or covering.

enchant (ɪn'tʃɑːnt) *vt* 1 have or use magic effects on. 2 charm. **enchanting** *infml adj* charming: *What an enchanting hat!* **enchantment** (ɪn'tʃɑːntmənt) 1 *nu* being enchanted. 2 *nc* something that has a magic effect or that charms. 3 *nu* charm.

encircle (ɪn'sɜːkəl) *vt* form a circle round.

enclave ('enkleɪv) *nc* an area of land, or group of people, entirely surrounded by foreign land or people.

enclose (ɪn'kləʊz) *vt* 1 close in on all sides; surround. 2 include with something else: *I've sent a letter to her enclosing a photograph*. **enclosure** (ɪn'kləʊʒə*) 1 *nu* enclosing. *nc* 2 a piece of what was public land with a wall, fence, etc., round it to make it private; any place that is closed in for a special group of people. 3 something that is included with something else.

encompass (ɪn'kʌmpəs) *vt* form a circle round; contain.

encore (ɒŋ'kɔː*) *interj* again; once more. ● *nc* a call from listeners for a piece of music, a song, etc., to be repeated; repeat of a piece of music, a song, etc.

encounter (ɪn'kaʊntə*) *vt* 1 meet with

(danger, trouble, etc.). **2** meet (a friend, etc.) but not on purpose. ●*nc* a meeting; an experience of: *a first encounter with crime.*

encourage (ɪn'kʌrɪdʒ) *vt* give hope to; urge (someone) to do something. **encouragement** (ɪn'kʌrɪdʒmənt) *nu* encouraging; *nc* something that gives hope to or urges one on to do something. **encouraging** *adj* that encourages.

encroach (ɪn'krəʊtʃ) *vi* enter wrongfully (on other people's land, time, or rights).

encumber (ɪn'kʌmbə*) *vt* cause difficulty by adding troubles to or making movement less easy: *encumbered with debts; She was encumbered by shopping bags and parcels.*

encyclopedia *esp. Brit* **encyclopaedia** (en,saɪklə'piːdɪə) *nc* a book, or set of books, containing information in great detail on one, or on very many subjects, arranged in the order from A to Z.

end (end) *nc* **1** the last part of a period of time: *the end of the day.* **2** the finish; last part: *the end of the race.* **3** the farthest point: *the ends of the earth.* **4** a small piece that is left: *a cigarette end.* **5** a death: *He had a peaceful end.* **6** a purpose. ●*vt* **1** bring (something) to an end. **2** *vi* come to an end. **in the end** at last; finally. **end up** finish. **ending** *nc* an end; the way something finishes: *Did the book have a good ending?* **endless** ('endlɪs) *adj* without an end; never stopping: *an endless conveyor belt.* **endlessly** *adv*

endanger (ɪn'deɪndʒə*) *vt* **1** cause danger to, or make danger likely to happen to. **2** threaten the continued existence of.

endear (ɪn'dɪə*) *vt* cause (someone) to love someone else: *Her sweetness endeared her to him.*

endeavour *US* **endeavor** (ɪn'devə*) *vi* try. ●*nc* an attempt.

endemic (en'demɪk) *medicine adj* (of disease) regularly found in certain places or among certain groups of people: *Disease of the lungs is endemic among coal miners.*

endorse (ɪn'dɔːs) *vt* **1** write one's name on (the back of a cheque or written or printed statement). **2** give support to (an opinion, belief, idea, etc.). **endorsement** (ɪn'dɔːsmənt) *nu* endorsing; *nc* an example of this.

endow (ɪn'daʊ) *vt* give money to (a person, college, etc.) in order to provide with a regular amount every year. **be endowed with** have (certain qualities, etc.) from the time one was born. **endowment** (ɪn'daʊmənt) **1** *nu* endowing. *nc* **2** an amount of money that will bring in a regular income. **3** a power one has had from birth to do something well.

endure (ɪn'djʊə*) **1** *vt* suffer (pain, trouble, etc.); put up with: *She endured weeks of pain after her accident; I can't endure that woman!* **2** *vi* last; continue to exist. **endurance** (ɪn'djʊərəns) *nu* being able to bear suffering, pain, etc., with self-control and courage. **enduring** *adj* lasting.

enemy ('enəmɪ) *nc, pl* **-mies 1** a person who feels strong dislike or hatred towards someone or something; person who wishes or tries to do harm. **2** anything that wishes to cause or causes harm: *Time is our enemy.* **3** *nu* the army, etc., of a foreign country that fights against one's own.

energetic (,enə'dʒetɪk) *adj* with force and vigour; very active: *an energetic speech; energetic walk.* **energy** ('enədʒɪ) *nu* **1** force; liveliness: *full of energy.* **2** power (for light, heat, etc.): *Oil is an important source of energy.* **energies** *(pl) infml* one's powers to do things: *Put your energies to good use.*

enfold (ɪn'fəʊld) *vt* put something, esp. one's arms round (something or someone) as in affection or love.

enforce (ɪn'fɔːs) *vt* **1** force (someone) to obey, esp. by force of law. **2** make (something) happen. **enforcement** (ɪn'fɔːsmənt) *nu* enforcing or being enforced.

engage (ɪn'geɪdʒ) **1** *vt* promise (to do something, such as work, give a lecture, etc.), get married, etc.). **2** *vti* (cause to) be locked or joined together. *vt* **3** begin battle with (the enemy); *vi* (of an army, etc.) come into battle with (the enemy). **4** employ. **engage in** take part in; be busy with: *engaged in politics.* **engaged** (ɪn'geɪdʒd) *adj* **1** having agreed to marry. **2** (of a telephone) in use. **3** occupied; working. **engagement** (ɪn'geɪdʒmənt) *nc* **1** a promise to marry. **2** a meeting (with someone); appointment. **3** *nu* the locking or joining together of two parts of a machine, etc.; *(sometimes nc).* **engaging** (ɪn'geɪdʒɪŋ) *adj* charming: *an engaging smile.*

engender (ɪn'dʒendə*) *vt* cause to happen or be.

engine ('endʒɪn) *nc* a machine that produces power or movement, for example, on a train: see picture. **engine-driver** *nc* a man who drives an engine, esp. that of a train.

engine

engineer (,endʒɪ'nɪə*) *nc* **1** a person who is an expert in dealing with engines or who has control of them. **2** a person who designs machines, roads, bridges, etc. ● *vt* **1** build or deal with (roads, bridges, machines, etc.) as an engineer. **2** *infml* think of (a way of doing something), esp. in a cunning way: *engineer a secret plan.* **3** *infml* arrange. **engineering** (ˌendʒɪˈnɪərɪŋ) *nu* the study of the making and use of machines, roads, etc.; the work done by or the job of an engineer.

engrave (ɪnˈɡreɪv) *vt* **1** make (a pattern, picture, etc.). by cutting into the hard surface of (metal, stone, or wood). **2** fix (ideas, feelings, etc.) deeply. **engraving** (ɪnˈɡreɪvɪŋ) *nc* a picture made by cutting into a hard surface.

engross (ɪnˈɡrəʊs) *vt* have one's interest, attention, or time, completely taken up with someone or something: *be engrossed in a book.*

engulf (ɪnˈɡʌlf) *vt* cover or swallow up completely: *The violent seas engulfed the island; engulfed by sorrow.*

enhance (ɪnˈhɑːns) *vt* make better, more beautiful, or more valuable.

enigma (ɪˈnɪɡmə) *nc* a person or thing that is difficult or impossible to understand. **enigmatic** (ˌenɪɡˈmætɪk) *adj* mysterious.

enjoin (ɪnˈdʒɔɪn) *vt* urge; order.

enjoy (ɪnˈdʒɔɪ) *vt* **1** take pleasure in. **2** have the advantage or help of: *He's always enjoyed good health.* **enjoy oneself** pass one's time happily. **enjoyable** (ɪnˈdʒɔɪəbəl) *adj* pleasant: *an enjoyable occasion.* **enjoyment** *nu* pleasure; *nc* something that gives joy or pleasure.

enlarge (ɪnˈlɑːdʒ) *vti* (cause to) become larger. **enlarge on** or **upon** write or speak about (a subject) with more details than before. **enlargement** (ɪnˈlɑːdʒmənt) **1** *nu* enlarging or being enlarged. **2** *nc* a larger copy of (esp. a photograph).

enlighten (ɪnˈlaɪtən) *vt* make something clear to (someone): *Enlighten me about your beliefs.* **enlightenment** *nu* enlightening or being enlightened.

enlist (ɪnˈlɪst) **1** *vti* (cause to) join the army. **2** *vt* get (help or support).

enliven (ɪnˈlaɪvən) *vt* make full of life.

enmity (ˈenmɪtɪ) *nu* hatred.

ennoble (ɪˈnəʊbəl) *vt* make the mind or the spirit better.

enormity (ɪˈnɔːmɪtɪ) *nc, pl* **-ties 1** *nu* very great wickedness. **2** *nc* a serious sin, crime, or mistake. **3** *nu* state of being huge in size.

enormous (ɪˈnɔːməs) *adj* huge; very large. **enormously** *adv* very; very much: *We enjoyed ourselves enormously.*

enough (ɪˈnʌf) *adv, determiner* as much as or many as needed. ● *nu* amount that is enough.

enquire (ɪnˈkwaɪə*) *v* See **inquire. enquiry** *n* See **inquiry.**

enrage (ɪnˈreɪdʒ) *vt* make very angry.

enrapture (ɪnˈræptʃə*) *vt* fill with great pleasure or joy.

enrich (ɪnˈrɪtʃ) *vt* make rich; make better, esp. in quality: *The new baby enriched their lives.* **enrichment** *nu* being enriched.

enrol *US* **enroll** (ɪnˈrəʊl) *vti* (cause to) become a member of a special group. **enrolment** *US* **enrollment 1** *nu* enrolling or being enrolled; *nc* an example of this. **2** *nc* a person who has enrolled.

en route (ɒnˈruːt) *French adv* on the way.

ensemble (ɒnˈsɒmbəl) *nc* **1** a piece of music in which all the musicians join together in playing; a small group of musicians who often play together. **2** a woman's set of clothes in which the colours, etc., go well together.

enshrine (ɪnˈʃraɪn) *vt* put (something precious) in a holy place or place that has special memories or is worthy of great respect.

ensign (ˈensaɪn) *nc* **1** a flag, esp. on a ship. **2** (ˈensən) *US* a naval officer of the lowest rank.

enslave (ɪnˈsleɪv) *vt* make (a person) into an unpaid servant to another; put (a person) completely under the control of (a habit, etc.): *Money enslaves him.*

ensnare (ɪnˈsneə*) *vt* catch in a trap; trick.

ensue (ɪnˈsjuː) *formal vi* happen later or afterwards as a result.

ensure (ɪnˈʃʊə*) *vt* make certain that; make (someone or something) safe against harm, loss, attack, etc.

entail (ɪnˈteɪl) *vt* **1** make (something) necessary; involve. **2** *law* make sure that one's land stays within the family after one's death.

entangle (ɪnˈtæŋɡəl) *vt* cause to become caught up in a trap, net, etc., or in difficulties. **entanglement** (ɪnˈtæŋɡəlmənt) **1** *nu* entangling or being entangled; *nc* an example of this. **2** *nc* a situation that causes being caught up in something.

enter (ˈentə*) **1** *vi* go or come in: *He entered by the back door.* *vt* **2** go or come into (a place, etc.): *The children entered the classroom.* **3** become a member of: *He entered the church as a priest.* **4** write (a person's name, details, etc.) in a book, list, etc.: *He was entered for the competition.* **enter into 1** take part in: *He entered into our conversation.* **2** start to deal with.

enterprise (ˈentəpraɪz) **1** *nc* a task that is often difficult, or that needs courage to do. *nu* **2** the courage and ability needed for such a task. **3** the carrying out of an enterprise. **enterprising** *adj* full of courage; adventurous.

entertain (ˌentəˈteɪn) *vt* **1** welcome as a guest

and give food and drink to. **2** make time pass pleasantly and with amusement for (someone). **3** think about; be prepared to consider: *entertain an idea.* **entertainer** *nc* a person who is paid to make time pass pleasantly, amusingly, etc., for other people. **entertainment 1** *nu* entertaining or being entertained. **2** *nc* a public amusement, such as a play, etc.

enthral (ɪnˈθrɔːl) *US* **enthrall** *vt* **1** have all (someone's) interest and attention: *It's an enthralling book.* **2** have power over, as if by magic: *He was enthralled by her beauty.*

enthrone (ɪnˈθrəʊn) *vt* **1** make (a person) into a king, queen, bishop, etc., with the usual ceremony. **2** give a high place of respect, affection, etc., to: *She was enthroned in her husband's heart.*

enthusiasm (ɪnˈθjuːzɪæzəm) *nu* a strong feeling of interest (for someone or something); eagerness to do something. **enthusiast** (ɪnˈθjuːzɪæst) *nc* a person who has strong feelings of interest or admiration for something. **enthusiastic** (ɪnˌθjuːzɪˈæstɪk) *adj* full of enthusiasm. **enthusiastically** *adv*

entice (ɪnˈtaɪs) *vt* persuade (someone) to do something he does not want to do by promises of good things; tempt: *She enticed him to leave his family.*

entire (ɪnˈtaɪə*) *adj* whole; complete; not broken. **entirely** *adv* completely.

entirety (ɪnˈtaɪərətɪ) *nc, pl* **-ties** *nu* being complete, whole, or unbroken; *nc* an example of this.

entitle (ɪnˈtaɪtəl) *vt* **1** give (a book) a title. **2** give (someone) a right to.

entity (ˈentɪtɪ) *nc, pl* **-ties** something that really exists; its real existence as being different from its qualities, etc. **2** *nu* being; existence.

entomb (ɪnˈtuːm) *vt* **1** bury (a dead body); act as a burial place for. **2** cover up and forget or hide.

entomologist (ˌentəˈmɒlədʒɪst) *nc* a person who studies insects.

entrails (ˈentreɪlz) *n pl* the tubes below the stomach through which food passes; the contents of the abdomen.

entrance[1] (ˈentrəns) **1** *nc* an opening, such as a gate, door, etc., through which someone or something enters. **2** *nu* entering; *nc* an example of this: *She made her entrance.* ● *adj* giving the right to enter: *entrance money.*

entrance[2] (ɪnˈtrɑːns) *vt* fill with complete delight as if dreaming.

entrant (ˈentrənt) *nc* a person entering for an examination, competition, race, etc., or into a profession: *university entrants.*

entrap (ɪnˈtræp) *vt* **1** catch in a trap, net, etc. **2** catch by a trick.

entreat (ɪnˈtriːt) *vt* ask with deep feeling. **entreaty** (ɪnˈtriːtɪ) *ncu, pl* **-ties** (an example of) asking with deep feeling.

entrée (ˈɒntreɪ) **1** *nu* the right or special favour of being allowed entrance; *nc* an example of this. **2** *nc* one of the dishes of food at a meal, served between the fish and meat dishes.

entrench (ɪnˈtrentʃ) *vt* protect by digging a trench or ditch, or by fixing in a safe and firm position.

entrepreneur (ˌɒntrəprəˈnɜː*) *nc* a person who plans and takes on something, esp. trade.

entropy (ˈentrəpɪ) *science nu* **1** the process by which heat, light, etc., gradually spread out, becoming equal everywhere in the universe. **2** a measurement of a lack of order in a system.

entrust (ɪnˈtrʌst) *vt* give into someone's care.

entry (ˈentrɪ) *nc, pl* **-ries 1** *nu* entering in; *nc* an example of this. *nc* **2** a gate, door, etc., through which one enters. **3** the details, names, etc., written or printed in a list or book: *a dictionary entry; a large number of entries for the competition.* **4** a person or thing taking part in a race or contest.

entwine (ɪnˈtwaɪn) *vt* twist or wind (one thing) round another: *Their arms were entwined; Plants climbed and entwined themselves round the tree trunk.*

enumerate (ɪˈnjuːməreɪt) *vt* count; name (items in a list, etc.) one by one.

enunciate (ɪˈnʌnsɪeɪt) **1** *vti* speak (a word) (clearly). **2** *vt* show in clear words what is meant by (an idea, etc.).

envelop (ɪnˈveləp) *vt* wrap or cover up, all round: *The mountains were enveloped in clouds; Mystery envelops the murder.*

envelope (ˈenvələʊp) *nc* a paper container for a letter: *You must address an envelope before posting it.*

enviable (ˈenvɪəbəl) *adj* causing or likely to cause envy.

envious (ˈenvɪəs) *adj* feeling or showing envy.

environment (ɪnˈvaɪərənmənt) *nc* the surroundings in which a person or animal lives. **the environment** mankind's surroundings; the natural balance of animals, plants, etc. **environmental** (ɪnˌvaɪərənˈmentəl) *adj* of or to do with the environment.

envisage (ɪnˈvɪzɪdʒ) *vt* imagine (what one hopes is likely to happen): *I envisage a time when all men will be equal.*

envision (ɪnˈvɪʒən) *vt* envisage.

envoy (ˈenvɔɪ) *nc* a person sent by the government on special work, esp. to another country.

envy (ˈenvɪ) *nu* **1** feeling of ill-will, hate, or

disappointment caused by wanting something that someone else has. 2 the person or thing that causes such feeling. ● *vt* feel envy towards (someone).

enzyme ('enzaɪm), *biology nc* a substance produced by the body that causes chemical changes in other substances but does not itself change.

ephemeral (ɪ'femərəl) *adj* lasting or living for a short time only.

epic ('epɪk) *nc* 1 a very long poem of the deeds of great and noble men. 2 a film or book that deals with this subject, or that is very long. ● *adj* of or to do with an epic: *an epic production.*

epidemic (,epɪ'demɪk) *nc* a situation where a disease spreads quickly among people in a district or country. ● *adj* of or to do with an epidemic.

epidermis (,epɪ'dɜːmɪs) *biology nu* the outer layer of animals and plants.

epigram ('epɪgræm) *nc* a short poem or saying expressing a witty or amusing thought.

epilepsy ('epɪlepsɪ) *nu* a disease of the brain causing a person to fall down, sometimes with violent movements of the body and limbs. **epileptic** (,epɪ'leptɪk) *nc* a person who suffers from this disease. ● *adj* of or to do with epilepsy.

epilogue *US* **epilog** ('epɪlɒg) *nc* 1 a part added at the end of a book. 2 a speech or short poem spoken by an actor to the audience at the end of a play.

episcopal (ɪ'pɪskəpəl) *adj* of or to do with bishops.

episode ('epɪsəʊd) *nc* an event or happening that is one of several of a set: *the nastiest episode of his life.*

epistle (ɪ'pɪsəl) *chiefly formal nc* an important letter.

epitaph ('epɪtɑːf) *nc* a set of words written about a dead person, esp. carved on the stone set up over his grave.

epithet ('epɪθet) *nc* a word that describes a quality of someone or something.

epitome (ɪ'pɪtəmɪ) *nc* the most perfect form or example of something. **epitomise** (ɪ'pɪtəmaɪz) *vt* be an epitome of.

epoch ('iːpɒk) *nc* a certain, esp. great, length of time in which something special takes place; beginning of such a time. **epoch-making** *adj* beginning a new period of time in history or in life because of a special event, etc.

equable ('ekwəbəl) *adj* calm; not easily troubled; not changing much: *an equable temper; equable climate.*

equal ('iːkwəl) *adj* the same in size, weight, value, etc. **equal to** being able to deal with someone or something: *Are you equal to long walks since your illness?* ● *nc* a person

or thing that is equal to another person or thing: *Though younger, she was the equal of her sister in intelligence.* ● *vt* be equal to.

equalise ('iːkwəlaɪz) *vti* make or become equal. **equality** (iː'kwɒlɪtɪ) *nu* the state of being equal. **equally** *adv*

equanimity (,ekwə'nɪmɪtɪ) *nu* calmness of mind; not being easily disturbed: *She bears the death of her son with courage and equanimity.*

equate (ɪ'kweɪt) *vt* believe or treat (two things) as being equal or of the same kind.

equation (ɪ'kweɪʒən) *mathematics nc* an expression in signs and numbers showing that two quantities are equal.

equator (ɪ'kweɪtə*) *nc* an imaginary line round the centre of the earth, drawn on maps halfway between the North and South Poles: see picture. **equatorial** (,ekwə'tɔːrɪəl) *adj* of or near the equator.

equator

equestrian (ɪ'kwestrɪən) *adj* of or to do with horse-riding: *equestrian sports.* ● *nc* a person who is an expert at horse-riding.

equidistant (,iːkwɪ'dɪstənt) *adj* being an equal distance apart.

equilateral (,iːkwɪ'lætərəl) *adj* having all sides equal in length.

equilibrium (,iːkwɪ'lɪbrɪəm) *nu* steadiness or balance; calmness of mind.

equinox ('iːkwɪnɒks) *nc* one of the two times in the year when day and night are of equal length.

equip (ɪ'kwɪp) *vt* supply with what is needed: *Are you equipped for your long journey?* **equipment** (ɪ'kwɪpmənt) 1 *nu* equipping or being equipped. 2 *n pl* supplies needed.

equity ('ekwɪtɪ) *nu* justice; being fair and right. **equities** *n pl.* ordinary stocks and shares in a business. **equitable** ('ekwɪtəbəl) *adj* just; fair: *an equitable decision.*

equivalent (ɪ'kwɪvələnt) *adj* equal in value, amount, or meaning, but expressed differently: *In the metric system 100 centimetres are equivalent to one metre.* ● *nc* something equal: *the local equivalent to this price.* **equivalence** (ɪ'kwɪvələns) *nu* being equivalent; *nc* an example of this.

equivocal (ɪ'kwɪvəkəl) *adj* 1 (of a meaning) doubtful; that can be understood in more than one way. 2 (of a person, his character, etc.) hard to understand; shifty.

era ('ɪərə) *nc* (the beginning of) a time in history when something new or special starts to happen.

eradicate (ɪ'rædɪkeɪt) *vt* to pull up as if by the roots; get rid of; remove.

erase (ɪ'reɪz) *vt* rub out; remove. **eraser** (ɪ'reɪzə*) *nc* a piece of rubber for rubbing out pencil marks, etc.

ere (eə*) *archaic or poetry adv, prep* before.

erect (ɪ'rekt) *vt* 1 build; place something in position: *erect tents.* 2 place in an upright position: *erect a statue.* ● *adj* upright; standing upright. **erection** (ɪ'rekʃən) 1 *nu* erecting or being erected; *nc* an example of this. 2 *nc* a building; anything erected.

ermine ('ɜːmɪn) 1 *nc* a small, meat-eating animal whose fur is brown in summer and white, except for a black tail-tip, in winter. 2 *nu* the fur of this animal; garment made of its winter fur: *ermine robes.*

erode (ɪ'rəʊd) *vt* wear away; slowly destroy as if by eating into. **erosion** (ɪ'rəʊʒən) *nu* eroding or being eroded: *erosion of the coast by the sea.*

erotic (ɪ'rɒtɪk) *adj* of or to do with sexual love.

err (ɜː*) *vi* make a mistake; do wrong.

errand ('erənd) *nc* a short journey (to fetch shopping, take a message, etc.).

erratic (ɪ'rætɪk) *adj* 1 changing often in thought, behaviour, etc. 2 not regular or certain in movement.

erroneous (ɪ'rəʊnɪəs) *adj* mistaken; not correct.

error ('erə*) 1 *nc* mistake; something done wrong. 2 *nu* being mistaken; doing wrong.

erudite ('eruːdaɪt) *adj* having or showing much knowledge.

erupt (ɪ'rʌpt) *vi* 1 (of a volcano) send out smoke, ashes, etc. 2 break out: *erupt into anger.* **eruption** (ɪ'rʌpʃən) *nu* erupting; *nc* the breaking out of a volcano, war, etc.

escalate ('eskəleɪt) *vti* (cause to) increase in size, extent, or amount. **escalation** (ˌeskə'leɪʃən) *ncu* (an example of) escalating: *the escalation of war.*

escalator ('eskəleɪtə*) *nc* a moving set of stairs that carries people from one floor to another in a building: see picture.

escalator

escapade ('eskəpeɪd) *nc* an exciting act with the chance of danger, trouble, etc.

escape (ɪ'skeɪp) 1 *vi* get free from prison or control. *vt* 2 get away from or avoid (an unpleasant person or thing). 3 be forgotten by: *I know his face but his name escapes me.* ● *ncu* 1 (an act of) escaping. 2 *nc* something that offers an escape for a short time from reality: *Listening to music is a form of escape.* **escapist** (ɪ'skeɪpɪst) *nc* a person who tries to avoid the real and often painful facts of life by living in his imagination. ● *adj* that gives an escape for a short time from real life: *escapist literature.*

escarpment (ɪ'skɑːpmənt) *nc* a steep slope between two different levels.

eschew (ɪs'tʃuː) *formal vt* avoid; hold oneself back from.

escort ('eskɔːt) *nc* 1 a person, soldiers, ships, etc., going with others to protect them or as a sign of honour. 2 a man taking out a woman. ● (ɪ'skɔːt) *vt* go with as an escort.

esoteric (ˌiːsə'terɪk, ˌesə'terɪk) *adj* for a special group of people only or for those who have certain knowledge: *esoteric interests.*

especial (ɪ'speʃəl) *formal adj* particular; turning to one as being special or different from others: *my especial friend; He gave her especial attention.* **especially** (ɪ'speʃəlɪ) *adv* particularly; extremely.

espionage ('espɪənɑːʒ) *nu* the work of getting secret information, esp. about another country's armies, etc.

esplanade ('espləneɪd) *nc* a place for walking or riding for pleasure, esp. by the sea.

espouse (ɪ'spaʊz) *vt* 1 support (a cause, idea, etc.). 2 *archaic* (esp. of a man) marry.

esprit ('espriː) *nu* life and spirit; liveliness of mind. **esprit de corps** (ˌespriːdə'kɔː*) *nu* friendly companionship and loyalty of people joined in a group or society.

espy (ɪ'spaɪ) *formal vt* see unexpectedly or with some difficulty; notice.

esquire (ɪ'skwaɪə*) *Brit nc* (the title put after a man's name as a sign of respect): *James Brown, Esq.*

essay ('eseɪ) *nc* 1 a piece of writing, usually short, on one subject. 2 *formal* an attempt. ● (e'seɪ) *vt formal* try to do (something): *essay a difficult task.*

essence ('esəns) *nu* 1 that which belongs naturally to a thing and makes it what it is; most important part. 2 the purest and most important qualities of a substance that remain when the unneeded parts have been taken out; *nc* a pure substance: *vanilla essence.*

essential (ɪ'senʃəl) *adj* 1 necessary: *Honesty is essential for employees in a bank.* 2 that belongs naturally. ● *nc* something that is necessary or the most important part. **essentially** *adv*

establish (ɪˈstæblɪʃ) vt 1 set up (a business, etc.) on a firm basis. 2 prove: *establish a fact.* 3 settle (someone) in a place. **establishment** (ɪˈstæblɪʃmənt) 1 nu establishing or being established; nc an example of this. 2 nc a building or group of persons in a business, etc.

estate (ɪˈsteɪt) nc 1 a piece of land belonging to one person, esp. in the country. 2 a piece of land used for building houses or factories on, owned by one person or by the people governing a district: *a housing estate.* 3 law nu a person's goods and money. **estate agent** a person whose business is to buy and sell houses for other people.

esteem (ɪˈstiːm) formal vt 1 have a high opinion of; consider of great value or worthy of respect. 2 consider. ●nu great respect: *He is held in high esteem.*

estimate (ˈestɪmeɪt) vt make a guess or judgement about (the cost, value, size, etc., of something). ●(ˈestɪmət) nc an opinion on (the cost, size, value, etc., of something); judgement. **estimation** (ˌestɪˈmeɪʃən) nu respect; opinion; judgement.

estrange (ɪˈstreɪndʒ) vt cause to become separated by being unfriendly.

estuary (ˈestjʊərɪ) nc, pl **-ries** the wide mouth of a river into which the sea flows.

et cetera (ɪtˈsetərə) Latin and so on; and other things; abbrev. etc.

etch (etʃ) 1 vti make (a picture) by using a needle and acid on a piece of metal which can be used for making copies. **etching** (ˈetʃɪŋ) 1 nu the skill and practice of a person who etches. 2 nc a picture or copy of it made in this way.

eternal (ɪˈtɜːnəl) adj 1 that will always exist; without beginning or end. 2 infml never seeming to stop: *Stop your eternal chatter!* **eternally** (ɪˈtɜːnəlɪ) adv for ever. **eternity** (ɪˈtɜːnɪtɪ) nu 1 time without end. 2 infml a time that seems endless.

ether (ˈiːθə*) nu a gas used in medicine to make a person unable to feel pain by putting him into a deep sleep.

ethereal (ɪˈθɪərɪəl) adj seeming to be of the spirit or of heaven rather than of this world: *ethereal music.*

ethics (ˈeθɪks) nu the study of the rules of behaviour. **ethical** (ˈeθɪkəl) adj

ethnic (ˈeθnɪk) adj of the different peoples in the world.

etiquette (ˈetɪket) nu the rules for polite behaviour.

etymology (ˌetɪˈmɒlədʒɪ) 1 nu the study of the history of words. 2 nc a description of how a word was formed and developed.

eucalyptus (ˌjuːkəˈlɪptəs) nc an Australian tree with leaves that produce an oil that is used to treat colds.

eugenics (jʊˈdʒenɪks) nu (with singular verb) the study of how to produce healthy children in order to improve the human race.

eulogy (ˈjuːlədʒɪ) nc, pl **-gies** a speech or piece of writing that gives praise.

eunuch (ˈjuːnək) nc a castrated man.

euphemism (ˈjuːfɪmɪzəm) 1 nu the use of a pleasant but less clear word instead of the clear, unpleasant one. 2 nc a word or set of words used in this way.

euthanasia (ˌjuːθəˈneɪzjə) nu bringing about a painless death (of a person in great pain).

evacuate (ɪˈvækjʊeɪt) 1 vti (cause to) leave (a building). vt 2 remove to a safer place, esp. in times of war. 3 empty waste matter from (the body). **evacuation** (ɪˌvækjʊˈeɪʃən) nu

evade (ɪˈveɪd) vt 1 keep away from. 2 avoid (doing something) by cunning.

evaluate (ɪˈvæljʊeɪt) vt decide how much (something) is worth. **evaluation** (ɪˌvæljʊˈeɪʃən) nc

evangelical (iːvænˈdʒelɪkəl) adj of the teachings of the Bible, esp. of Jesus Christ. **evangelist** (ɪˈvændʒəlɪst) nc 1 a writer of one of the four books of the Bible that tell of Christ's life. 2 a person who preaches on Christ's life.

evaporate (ɪˈvæpəreɪt) vi 1 (of a liquid or solid) change into a gas. 2 fade away slowly: *His fear evaporated.* 3 vt cause to change (a liquid or solid) into a gas. **evaporation** (ɪˌvæpəˈreɪʃən) nc

evasion (ɪˈveɪʒən) 1 nu avoiding, esp. by cunning. 2 nc a false reason given to avoid doing something. **evasive** (ɪˈveɪsɪv) adj

eve (iːv) nc the day or evening before (an event); time just before (any event): *the eve of an election.*

even (ˈiːvən) adj 1 level; smooth. 2 equal. 3 (of a number) able to be divided by two. ●adv 1 (used to suggest surprise before something strange or not expected): *He always wears a coat, even on a hot day.* 2 (used to make comparative words stronger): *It is even larger.* **get even (with)** punish (someone) to repay for a wrong done to one. **even if** or **though** in spite of the fact that. **even so** in spite of that.

evening (ˈiːvnɪŋ) nc the hours between late afternoon and going to bed. **evening dress** clothes worn in the evening at a formal event.

evenly (ˈiːvənlɪ) adv 1 equally. 2 smoothly.

event (ɪˈvent) nc 1 anything that happens, esp. something important; happening. 2 the result of something that happens. **in the event of** if; in case of. **at all events** whatever happens. **eventful** adj full of things happening.

eventual (ɪˈventʃʊəl) adj coming as a result at the end. **eventually** adv at last.

ever ('evə*) *adv* **1** at any time: *Do you ever visit him?* **2** always. **3** (used to add force to one's words): *Why ever did you do that?* **ever so** or **such** *infml* very. **ever-present** *adj* here always.

evergreen ('evəgri:n) *adj* (of a tree) keeping its leaves throughout the year.

everlasting (,evə'lɑ:stɪŋ) *adj* lasting for ever.

evermore (,evə'mɔ:*) *adv* for ever.

every ('evrɪ) *determiner* each and all, esp. within a group. **everybody** ('evrɪ,bɒdɪ), **everyone** ('evrɪwʌn) *pron* every person. **everyday** ('evrɪdeɪ) *adj* **1** happening daily. **2** ordinary. **every other** See **other.** **everything** ('evrɪθɪŋ) *pron* all things. **everywhere** ('evrɪweə*) *adv* in all places.

evict (ɪ'vɪkt) *law vt* force (a person) by law to leave (a house or land).

evidence ('evɪdəns) *nu* anything that shows something to be true or false or helps to prove something. **evident** ('evɪdənt) *adj* plain to see or understand. **evidently** *adv*

evil ('i:vəl) *adj* bad; wicked; sinful; harmful. ●*nu* **1** sin. **2** *nc* a wicked or harmful thing.

evince (ɪ'vɪns) *formal vt* show that one has (a special feeling, quality, etc.).

evocative (ɪ'vɒkətɪv) *adj* producing or reminding one of feelings, memories, etc.

evoke (ɪ'vəʊk) *vt* produce or remind of (feelings, memories, etc.).

evolution (,i:və'lu:ʃən) *nu* **1** the gradual way in which something develops or changes. **2** the idea that man, animals and plants developed from simpler forms over millions of years. **evolutionary** (,i:və'lu:ʃənərɪ) *adj*

evolve (ɪ'vɒlv) *vti* develop or be developed by slow change.

ewe (ju:) *nc* a female sheep.

exacerbate (ɪg'zæsəbeɪt) *formal vt* make (a situation, disease, temper, something said) worse.

exact (ɪg'zækt) *adj* correct in every detail. ●*vt* **1** force (someone) to pay money or do (something). **2** demand and get (something) from (someone). **exacting** *adj* needing much work, attention, etc. **exactly** *adv* **1** (used as an answer) just as you say. **2** correctly in every detail. **exactness** *nu*

exaggerate (ɪg'zædʒəreɪt) *vt* say or make (something) seem more than it is. **exaggeration** (ɪg,zædʒə'reɪʃən) *ncu*

exalt (ɪg'zɔ:lt) *vt* **1** give power or a high position to. **2** praise highly. **exaltation** (,egzɔ:l'teɪʃən) *nu* excitement; joyfulness.

exam (ɪg'zæm) *infml n* short for **examination** (def. 1).

examine (ɪg'zæmɪn) *vi* **1** try to learn about (something) by looking at it carefully. **2** put questions to (a person) to find out how much he knows or understands. **examin-ation** (ɪg,zæmɪ'neɪʃən) *nc* **1** (*infml abbrev.* **exam**) a test to find out how much someone knows or how well a person can do something. **2** asking of questions to find out the truth. **3** inspecting (someone) in order to recognise a disease. **examiner** *nc*

example (ɪg'zɑ:mpəl) *nc* **1** a fact, etc., that shows the general rule. **2** something that is like others of the same kind. **3** something to be copied because it is admired: *His life was an example to others.* **for example** to give an **example** (defs. 1, 2): *abbrev.* e.g.

exasperate (ɪg'zæspəreɪt) *vt* make (someone) very annoyed; stir up anger in (someone). **exasperation** (ɪg,zæspə'reɪʃən) *nu*

excavate ('ekskəveɪt) *vt* dig, esp. to find (what has been buried or hidden). **excavation** (,ekskə'veɪʃən) *ncu*

exceed (ɪk'si:d) *vt* **1** go beyond (something that is necessary, expected, or allowed). **2** be more than. **exceedingly** (ɪk'si:dɪŋlɪ) *adv* to an unusual or very great degree.

excel (ɪk'sel) **1** *vi* do better than others. **2** *vt* be better than (other people).

excellence ('eksələns) **1** *nu* being of very good quality. **2** *nc* a very good quality. **excellent** *adj*

Excellency ('eksələnsɪ) *nc, pl* **-cies** the title used when speaking to some officials, esp. ambassadors or governors.

except (ɪk'sept) *prep* but not; not including. **except for** but for. **except that** but for the fact that. ●*vt* not include in; leave out (something) from.

exception (ɪk'sepʃən) *nc* **1** a person or a thing that is not included. **2** something to which the rule does not apply. **take exception to** not agree with. **with the exception of** but for; (but) not including. **exceptional** (ɪk'sepʃənəl) *adj* not usual. **exceptionally** *adv*

excerpt ('eksɜ:pt) *nc* a piece of writing, music, etc., from a book, recording, etc.

excess (,ɪk'ses) **1** *nu* the amount by which something is too much. **2** *nc, pl* **-ses** the very worst kind of behaviour. **in excess of** more than. ●('ekses) *adj* more than is necessary or allowed. **excessive** (ɪk'sesɪv) *adj* **excessively** *adv*

exchange (ɪks'tʃeɪndʒ) *vt* change (something) for another. ●*nc* **1** the changing (of something) for another. **2** the giving and receiving (of things), ideas).

exchequer (ɪks'tʃekə*) *nc* a place where public or private money is kept; the money itself. **Exchequer** *Brit* the government office in charge of public money. **Chancellor of the Exchequer** *Brit* the minister in charge of this government office.

excise[1] ('eksaɪz) *nu* government tax on certain goods made or sold inside a country.

excise² (ɪkˈsaɪz) vt take out (something) from a book, etc.

excite (ɪkˈsaɪt) vt stir up feelings in. **excitable** adj easily excited. **excited** adj with one's feelings stirred up. **excitement** (ɪkˈsaɪtmənt) 1 nu being excited. 2 nc something that causes excitement. **exciting** adj causing excitement.

exclaim (ɪkˈskleɪm) vi cry out suddenly, esp. from surprise. **exclamation** (ˌekskləˈmeɪʃən) 1 nu crying out. 2 nc a sudden short cry. **exclamation mark** the sign (!) used in writing to show a sudden cry, etc. **exclamatory** (ɪkˈsklæmətərɪ) adj

exclude (ɪkˈskluːd) vt 1 keep out (someone or something). 2 prevent; make (something) not possible. **exclusion** (ɪkˈskluːʒən) nu **exclusive** (ɪkˈskluːsɪv) adj keeping out all but the carefully chosen. **exclusively** adv

excommunicate (ˌekskəˈmjuːnɪkeɪt) vt forbid (a person), as a punishment, his rights as a member of the Christian Church.

excrete (ekˈskriːt) vt get rid of (waste) from the body. **excrement** (ˈekskrɪmənt) nu, **excreta** (ekˈskriːtə) n pl waste passed out from the bowels.

excruciating (ɪkˈskruːʃɪeɪtɪŋ) adj causing great pain in the body or mind.

excursion (ɪkˈskɜːʃən) nc a short journey for pleasure.

excuse (ɪkˈskjuːs) nc a reason given or words of regret for one's behaviour. ●(ɪkˈskjuːz) vt 1 give reasons for the behaviour of (someone). 2 forgive. **excuse me** (used to show one is sorry to interrupt, does not agree with someone, etc.) **excusable** (ɪkˈskjuːzəbəl) adj

execute (ˈeksɪkjuːt) vt 1 carry out (a plan, a piece of work, an order, etc.). 2 put (a person) to death, as a punishment. **execution** (ˌeksɪˈkjuːʃən) ncu **executioner** (ˌeksɪˈkjuːʃənə*) nc a person who by order of the law puts people to death.

executive (ɪgˈzekjʊtɪv) adj of or having to do with the carrying out of plans, controlling a business, etc. ●nc a person or a group of people with high positions in a business, company, etc.

executor (ɪgˈzekjʊtə*) nc a person chosen to carry out the wishes of someone after his death.

exemplary (ɪgˈzemplərɪ) adj acting as an example: *exemplary behaviour.*

exemplify (ɪgˈzemplɪfaɪ) vt show or explain by example.

exempt (ɪgˈzempt) vt make free from (a duty, promise, etc.). **exemption** (ɪgˈzempʃən) nc

exercise (ˈeksəsaɪz) 1 nu putting (one's body or mind) to extra use in order to become healthier, stronger, etc. nc 2 something done to cause this: see picture. 3 a task to train the mind. ●vt 1 make healthier or stronger by extra use. 2 vi use.

exercise

exert (ɪgˈzɜːt) vt try hard to do (something) or cause (something) to be done. **exert oneself** try hard. **exertion** (ɪgˈzɜːʃən) 1 nu trying very hard. 2 nc way of doing this.

exhale (eksˈheɪl) vti breathe out. **exhalation** (ˌekshəˈleɪʃən) ncu

exhaust (ɪgˈzɔːst) 1 nu waste vapour or gas given out from an engine. 2 nc a pipe carrying such waste vapour or gas. ●vt 1 use up; finish. 2 make very tired. **exhausted** adj 1 used up. 2 tired. **exhaustion** (ɪgˈzɔːstʃən) nu **exhaustive** (ɪgˈzɔːstɪv) adj complete in every way.

exhibit (ɪgˈzɪbɪt) vt show (something) in a public place for people to see, enjoy, buy, etc. ●nc an object or collection of objects shown to the public. **exhibition** (ˌeksɪˈbɪʃən) nc **exhibitionist** (ˌeksɪˈbɪʃənɪst) nc a person who tries to be noticed, esp. by his strange clothes or behaviour. **exhibitor** (ɪgˈzɪbɪtə*) nc a person who puts paintings, flowers, goods, etc., in an exhibition.

exhilarate (ɪgˈzɪləreɪt) vt make lively and glad. **exhilaration** (ɪgˌzɪləˈreɪʃən) nu

exhort (ɪgˈzɔːt) vt ask (someone) in a serious manner, with deep feeling. **exhortation** (ˌegzɔːˈteɪʃən) nc

exile (ˈegzaɪl) vt send away, esp. to another country, as a punishment. ●ncu 1 being sent away from one's home or country. 2 nc a person punished in this way.

exist (ɪgˈzɪst) vi 1 (continue to) be. 2 live. **existence** (ɪgˈzɪstəns) nu

exit (ˈeksɪt) nc 1 a way out, as from a cinema or theatre. 2 the act of going out, esp. of an actor leaving the stage.

exonerate (ɪgˈzɒnəreɪt) vt make (a person) free from, esp. blame.

exorbitant (ɪgˈzɔːbɪtənt) adj (of a price, demand, etc.) too much or too great.

exorcise (ˈeksɔːsaɪz) vt rid (a person or a place) of evil by prayer.

exotic (ɪgˈzɒtɪk) adj 1 (of plants, fashions, ideas) from another country. 2 strange in an attractive way.

expand (ɪkˈspænd) 1 vti make or become larger. 2 vi (followed by **on**) tell in more detail.

expanse (ɪkˈspæns) *nc* a wide area, esp. of land, sky, or sea.

expansion (ɪkˈspænʃən) *nu* an increase in size: see picture. **expansive** (ɪkˈspænsɪv) *adj* 1 able or likely to get larger. 2 (of a person) ready and willing to show his feelings, thoughts, etc.

expansion

expatriate (eksˈpætrɪət) *nc* a person who has left his own country to live abroad. ● *adj* (of a person) living abroad: exiled. ●(eksˈpætrɪeɪt) *vt* 1 leave one's own country to live abroad. 2 cause (someone) to go into exile. **expatriation** (eks,pætrɪˈeɪʃən) *ncu*

expect (ɪkˈspekt) *vt* 1 believe (something) will happen. 2 wait for (someone) to come. **be expecting** (of a woman) be waiting for the birth of her baby.

expectant (ɪkˈspektənt) *adj* waiting for something to happen. **expectancy** (ɪkˈspektənsɪ) *nu* **expectation** (,ekspekˈteɪʃən) 1 *nu* waiting (for something) to happen. 2 *nc* the thing that is expected.

expedient (ɪkˈspiːdɪənt) *adj* 1 wise or useful at a particular time. 2 not fair, but helpful.

expedite (ˈekspɪdaɪt) *vt* hasten the progress of; finish or send quickly.

expedition (,ekspɪˈdɪʃən) *nc* a journey made in order to explore or discover.

expel (ɪkˈspel) *vt* send (someone) away from a school, country, etc., by force, esp. as a punishment.

expend (ɪkˈspend) *vt* 1 spend (money, time, care, etc.). 2 use up.

expenditure (ɪkˈspendɪtʃə*) *nu* 1 spending. 2 using. 3 *nc* amount of money, etc., spent.

expense (ɪkˈspens) 1 *nu* money spent; cost. 2 *nc* money used (for something). **at the expense of** causing the loss of. **expensive** (ɪkˈspensɪv) *adj* costing a lot of money. **expensively** *adv*

experience (ɪkˈspɪərɪəns) 1 *nu* seeing or living through an event, happening, etc.; knowledge obtained in this way. 2 *nc* an event that has given one knowledge, skill, etc. ● *vt* have (an) experience of. **experienced** (ɪkˈspɪərɪənst) *adj* skilled in or having knowledge of.

experiment (ɪkˈsperɪmənt) *nc* a test to find out what happens, esp. in science. ● *vi* make an experiment. **experimental** (ɪk,sperɪˈmentəl) *adj* **experimentation** (ɪk,sperɪmenˈteɪʃən) *nu* **experimenter** *nc*

expert (ˈekspɜːt) *nc* a person with a lot of knowledge in a particular subject. ● *adj* 1 (of an action) well done, with skill. 2 (of a person) having special knowledge or skill. **expertly** *adv*

expertise (,ekspɜːˈtiːz) *nu* special knowledge about a particular subject.

expire (ɪkˈspaɪə*) *vi* 1 *formal* die. 2 (of a length of time) come to an end. **expiration** (,ekspɪˈreɪʃən) *nu* **expiry** (ɪkˈspaɪərɪ) *nc, pl* **-ries** the end, esp. of a licence or a business agreement.

explain (ɪkˈspleɪn) *vt* 1 make plain or clear. 2 give the meaning of. 3 give reasons for. **explanation** (,ekspləˈneɪʃən) *ncu* **explanatory** (ɪkˈsplænətərɪ) *adj*

explicit (ɪkˈsplɪsɪt) *adj* plainly and clearly said, with nothing left out.

explode (ɪkˈspləʊd) *vi* 1 burst with a loud noise. 2 show anger: *explode with anger.* 3 *vt* make (a balloon) burst with a loud noise.

exploit (ˈeksplɔɪt) *nc* a brave or splendid act. ●(ɪkˈsplɔɪt) *vt* 1 make use of. 2 use (someone) unfairly, esp. for one's own profit. **exploitation** (,eksplɔɪˈteɪʃən) *nu*

explore (ɪkˈsplɔː*) *vt* 1 look carefully into in order to learn. 2 travel round (a country, etc.) to learn more about it. **explorer** *nc* **exploration** (,ekspləˈreɪʃən) 1 *nu* exploring. 2 *nc* an example of this. **exploratory** (ɪkˈsplɒrətərɪ) *adj*

explosion (ɪkˈspləʊʒən) *nc* a sudden bursting with a loud noise: see picture. **explosive** (ɪkˈspləʊsɪv) *adj* likely to **explode** (defs. 1, 2). ● *nc* a substance which can explode. **explosively** *adv*

explosion

exponent (ɪkˈspəʊnənt) *nc* a person or thing that explains the meaning of, or represents something.

export (ɪkˈspɔːt) *vt* send (goods) abroad in order to sell. ●(ˈekspɔːt) 1 *nu* act of exporting. 2 *nc* a thing that is exported. **exporter** (ɪkˈspɔːtə*) *nc*

expose (ɪkˈspəʊz) *vt* 1 uncover. 2 leave unsafe from harm. 3 make known; reveal.

exposition (,ekspəʊˈzɪʃən) 1 *nu* explaining. 2 *nc* an explanation.

expostulate (ɪkˈspɒstjʊleɪt) *vi* make a mild protest; argue.

exposure (ɪkˈspəʊʒə*) **1** *nu* having no protection: *exposure to heat*. **2** *nc* that which has been exposed.

expound (ɪkˈspaʊnd) *vt* explain with the details.

express (ɪkˈspres) *vt* show or represent, esp. in words. ● *adj* **1** clearly and exactly said: *It was his express wish*. **2** fast: *express train*. ● *nc* a train. **expressway** *US nc* a wide road made for fast traffic. **expressly** *adv* clearly and specially. **expression** (ɪkˈspreʃən) **1** *nu* showing one's feelings or meaning by words or actions: *He gave expression to his anger. nc* **2** an example of something expressed. **3** a word or set of words: *Expressions of thanks were given*. **expressive** (ɪkˈspresɪv) *adj*

expulsion (ɪkˈspʌlʃən) *nc* forcing to leave or being forced to leave as a punishment, esp. from school or a country.

exquisite (ˈekskwɪzɪt, ɪkˈskwɪzɪt) *adj* of great beauty. **exquisitely** *adv*

extant (ekˈstænt) *adj* (esp. of a piece of writing or printing) still existing.

extend (ɪkˈstend) *vt* **1** make longer, wider, or larger: *extend one's holiday; extend the garden*. **2** offer: *extend a hand in friendship*. **3** *vi* stretch. **extension** (ɪkˈstenʃən) **1** *nu* extending. **2** *nc* the part, etc., that is added. **extensive** (ɪkˈstensɪv) *adj* stretching very far; that includes much. **extensively** *adv*

extent (ɪkˈstent) *nu* **1** the space or area. **2** degree or amount: *to some extent*.

exterior (ekˈstɪərɪə*) *adj* to do with the outside. ● *nc* the outside.

exterminate (ɪkˈstɜːmɪneɪt) *vt* destroy. **extermination** (ɪkˌstɜːmɪˈneɪʃən) *nu*

external (ekˈstɜːnəl) *adj* of or on the outside. **externally** *adv*

extinct (ɪkˈstɪŋkt) *adj* **1** no longer existing: *Some animals have become extinct*. **2** no longer able to burn or burst out: *an extinct volcano*. **extinction** (ɪkˈstɪŋkʃən) *nu*

extinguish (ɪkˈstɪŋgwɪʃ) *vt* put out (a fire or a light). **extinguisher** (ɪkˈstɪŋgwɪʃə*) *nc* See **fire extinguisher** under **fire**.

extol (ɪkˈstəʊl) *vt* praise highly.

extort (ɪkˈstɔːt) *vt* obtain by force or threat. **extortion** (ɪkˈstɔːʃən) **1** *nu* obtaining by threat. **2** *nc* a way used to do this.

extra (ˈekstrə) *adj* more; more than is needed. ● *nc* an added cost. ● *adv* more than usually.

extract (ɪkˈstrækt) *vt* **1** take out: *extract a tooth*. **2** copy out (a part of a book). **3** obtain (juices, etc.) by pressing, crushing, or boiling. ● (ˈekstrækt) **1** *nc* a part taken from (a book). **2** *nu* the best part obtained by crushing, etc.: *beef extract*. **extraction**

(ɪkˈstrækʃən) *nu* **1** taking or being taken out. **2** the family line of a person, from early times.

extraordinary (ɪkˈstrɔːdnərɪ) *adj* very unusual. **extraordinarily** (ɪkˈstrɔːdnərəlɪ) *adv*

extravagant (ɪkˈstrævəgənt) *adj* (of money, ideas, or behaviour) wasteful; going beyond what is usual. **extravagance** (ɪkˈstrævəgəns) **1** *nu* being wasteful. **2** *nc* a way of being wasteful.

extreme (ɪkˈstriːm) *adj* **1** as far as possible from the middle; at either end of anything. **2** very great: *extreme pain; extreme kindness*. ● *nc* **1** either end of anything. **2** *(pl)* things as different as possible: *extremes of heat and cold*. **extremist** *nc* a person whose opinions, etc., are too strong. **extremity** (ɪkˈstremɪtɪ) *nc, pl* **-ties 1** furthest point. **2** *(pl)* hands and feet.

extrovert (ˈekstrəvɜːt) *nc* a person whose thoughts are turned to life around him rather than to himself.

exuberant (ɪgˈzjuːbərənt) *adj* **1** full of high spirits. **2** (of plants) growing freely and in plenty. **exuberance** (ɪgˈzjuːbərəns) *nu*

exude (ɪgˈzjuːd) **1** *vi* (of a liquid) come out slowly: *Blood exuded from his wound*. **2** *vt* give off (fluid, etc.) slowly.

exult (ɪgˈzʌlt) *vi* feel great joy; show joy because of success or victory over another person. **exultant** (ɪgˈzʌltənt) *adj* **exultation** (ˌegzʌlˈteɪʃən) *nu*

eye

eye (aɪ) *nc* **1** the part of the body with which we see: see picture. **2** a small eye-shaped hole, esp. of a needle. ● *vt* watch or look at (someone or something): *He eyed them carefully*. **have an eye for** have the ability to recognise or judge (esp. beauty, a bargain, or an opportunity). **in the eyes of** in the opinion of. **keep an eye on** take care of; watch carefully. **see eye to eye with** agree with in every way. **eyeball** (ˈaɪbɔːl) *nc* the eye itself behind its lids. **eyebrow** (ˈaɪbraʊ) *nc* the curve of hair above the eye. **eyelash** (ˈaɪlæʃ) *nc* one of a row of hairs on the edge of the eyelid. **eyelid** (ˈaɪlɪd) *nc* the upper and lower covers over the eye. **eyesight** (ˈaɪsaɪt) *nu* the power of seeing. **eye-witness** (ˈaɪˌwɪtnɪs) *nc* a person who sees an event.

F

fable ('feɪbəl) *nc* a short story, sometimes about animals, teaching about good and bad behaviour.

fabric ('fæbrɪk) **1** *ncu* material made from cotton, wool, silk, etc. **2** *nu* something built or put together: *the fabric of society*.

fabricate ('fæbrɪkeɪt) *vt* **1** make (something, esp. a story) in order to deceive. **2** build; put together. **fabrication** (,fæbrɪ'keɪʃən) *ncu*

fabulous ('fæbjʊləs) *adj* **1** *infml* wonderful. **2** almost too difficult to believe. **3** of, in, or from a fable.

façade (fə'saːd) *nc* **1** the part of a building facing the street. **2** a false appearance.

face (feɪs) *nc* **1** the front part of the head. **2** the front part or surface of something: *a clock face*. **3** (of a person) a look: *a smiling face*. **face to face** meeting together. **lose face** lose one's good reputation; lose the respect of. **pull a face** twist the face to show one is not pleased, etc. **face-cloth** *nc* a small cloth for washing the face. **face value** the value of something judged by its appearance. ● *vt* **1** meet without fear: *face danger*. **2** *vti* (cause to) have the face or front towards (a certain direction). **face up to** accept and deal with in a brave way.

facet ('fæsɪt) *nc* **1** one of the sides of a cut diamond, etc. **2** one particular way of looking at something: *one facet of the problem*.

facetious (fə'siːʃəs) *adj* unsuitable and making a joke, esp. at the wrong time.

facial ('feɪʃəl) *adj* of the face.

facile ('fæsaɪl) *often derogatory adj* easily done.

facilitate (fə'sɪlɪteɪt) *vt* (of a thing, not a person) make easy; make (problems, etc.) less.

facility (fə'sɪlɪtɪ) *nc, pl* **-ties 1** *(often pl)* a thing that is useful and makes problems, difficulties, etc., less: *facilities for washing.* **2** *nu* ability to do something without difficulty.

facsimile (fæk'sɪmɪlɪ) *nc* a perfect copy, esp. of a piece of writing, a picture, etc.

fact (fækt) **1** *nc* something that has really happened or is certainly true. **2** *nu* truth: *The story is based on fact*. **in fact** really; (used for emphasis): *He was late—in fact he nearly didn't come at all.*

faction ('fækʃən) *nc* a small group of people, esp. in politics.

factor ('fæktə*) *nc* **1** one of the facts or con-ditions that help to produce a result: *Distance is a factor in speed; Money is an important factor in our discussions.* **2** *mathematics* a number (except one) that divides exactly into a larger number: *Two, four, five, and ten are factors of twenty.*

factorise ('fæktəraɪz) *mathematics vt* change (a number) into the numbers that divide exactly into it.

factory ('fæktərɪ) *nc, pl* **-ries** a building where goods are made.

factual ('fæktʃʊəl) *adj* to do with facts.

faculty ('fækəltɪ) *nc, pl* **-ties 1** a power of the mind or body. **2** a part of a university that teaches on the same subject or group of subjects: *Faculty of Science*.

fad (fæd) *nc* an interest likely to last for a short time only.

fade (feɪd) **1** *vt* cause to lose colour or freshness. **2** *vi* slowly lose colour or freshness. **fade away** slowly lose colour, freshness, or strength; (of sights or sound) get less until no longer seen or heard.

fag (fæg) **1** *slang nc* a cigarette. **2** *Brit nu* an unwanted task: *What a fag!* ● *vi* be very tired after hard work. **fag out** *infml vti* make very tired by hard work.

faggot ('fægət) *nc* **1** a bundle of sticks tied together, used for making a fire. **2** a ball of meat.

Fahrenheit ('færənhaɪt) *adj* (used to describe degrees of temperature on a scale on which water freezes at 32 degrees and boils at 212 degrees: *abbrev*. F): *60 °F*

fail (feɪl) **1** *vt* be not able to succeed in (what one hoped to do); *(sometimes vi)* not succeed. **2** *vt* be not able to do (something): *He failed to come*. **3** *vti* judge or be judged as unsuccessful, esp. in an examination: *The examiners failed the candidate*. **4** *vi* become weak; break down: *Her health failed; The engine failed*. ● *nc* an unsuccessful attempt. **without fail** for certain, whatever happens. **failure** ('feɪljə*) **1** *nu* a failing; lack of success. **2** *nc* a person, something, or an attempt that is not successful.

fain (feɪn) *old-fashioned adv* gladly.

faint (feɪnt) *adj* **-er, -est 1** not clearly seen, heard, tasted, or smelt. **2** (of a person) feeling ill and as if one is about to fall; weak. **3** (of actions) with little force. **4** vague. ● *vi* **1** fall and be no longer awake, because of illness, hunger, fear, etc. **2** become weak ● *nc* being unconscious because of illness, hunger, fear, etc. **faint-hearted** not very brave. **faintly** *adv*

fair[1] (feə*) *adj* **-er, -est 1** just or honest. **2** (of a person's skin or hair) pale; light in colour. **3** quite good. **4** average: *a fair total*. **fair play** the same honest treatment for everyone. **fairly** *adv* **fairness** *nu*

fair² *nc* **1** a gathering of shows and entertainments for the public held outside at certain times. **2** a regular market for cattle, sheep, etc. **3** a large exhibition.

fairy ('feərɪ) *nc, pl* **-ries** a small and magical creature. ● *adj* of or like fairies; magic. **fairy-tale** *nc* **1** a story about fairies. **2** a lie, esp. as told by a child.

faith (feɪθ) **1** *nu* trust or belief (in someone or something). **2** *nc* a religion. **in bad faith** in order to deceive. **in good faith** with a sincere purpose. **faithful** ('feɪθfʊl) *adj* **1** loyal or true to someone or something. **2** exact. **faithfully** *adv* **yours faithfully** (used before one's name at the end of a formal letter.) **faithless** *adj* **1** not loyal to. **2** having no faith.

fake (feɪk) *nc* **1** a copy (of something) made in order to deceive: *fake jewels.* **2** a person who is not what he pretends to be. ● *adj* false or pretended; not real. ● *vt* **1** make a copy (of something), in order to deceive. **2** play at (a state of being ill, angry, etc.).

falcon ('fɔːlkən) *nc* a small meat-eating bird trained to hunt other birds: see picture at **birds**.

fall (fɔːl) *vi* **1** drop down: *The rock fell; She fell and broke her leg.* **2** get less: *prices fell.* **3** happen: *His birthday falls on a Monday this year.* **4** be overcome: *The city fell to the enemy.* **fall back** go back. **fall back on** turn to for help. **fall behind** fail to keep up with others. **fall behind with** do, or make, less than one should of (one's work, regular payments, etc.). **fall for** *infml* be deceived or charmed by. **fall in 1** collapse. **2** (of a soldier) take his place in a line of soldiers. **fall in with 1** meet by chance and join (someone or something). **2** agree with. **fall off** become less in number or size. **fall on** attack. **fall out (with)** quarrel (with). **fall short of** fail to reach the expected (amount, level, etc.). **fall through** not happen when expected to; fail. ● *nc* **1** dropping down: *a fall from his horse; a fall in prices.* **2** *(pl)* place where a river drops over rocks or a cliff. **3** *US* autumn. **4** being overcome: *the fall of the Roman Empire.*

fallacy ('fæləsɪ) *nc, pl* **-cies** a false idea that seems to be true.

fallen ('fɔːlən) past participle of **fall**.

fallible ('fæləbəl) *adj* able to be wrong or to make mistakes.

fall-out ('fɔːlaʊt) *nu* flying radioactive dust after a nuclear explosion.

fallow ('fæləʊ) *adj* (of land) ploughed but in which nothing has been planted.

false (fɔːls) *adj* **1** not true: *a false idea.* **2** not faithful: *a false friend.* **3** deceiving: *a false witness.* **4** not real: *false teeth.* **falsehood** ('fɔːlshʊd) *nc* a lie.

falsify ('fɔːlsɪfaɪ) *vt* **1** make false. **2** give a false account of. **falsification** (,fɔːlsɪfɪ-'keɪʃən) **1** *nu* being false. **2** *nc* a thing done to make false.

falter ('fɔːltə*) **1** *vi* move or walk in an unsteady way through fear, illness, etc. **2** *vti* (of a person) speak unsteadily.

fame (feɪm) *nu* being widely known. **famed** (feɪmd) *adj* well-known; famous.

familiar (fə'mɪljə*, fə'mɪlɪə*) *adj* **1** known; able to be recognised. **2** usual. **familiar to** well-known to (someone). **familiar with 1** not showing enough respect to (someone). **2** friendly with (someone). **be familiar with** know about. **familiarise** (fə'mɪljəraɪz) *vt* make well known, or get to know (something) well. **familiarity** (fə,mɪlɪ'ærɪtɪ) **1** *nu* being familiar. **2** *nc, pl* **-ties** an act showing too little respect.

family ('fæmɪlɪ) *nc, pl* **-lies 1** a unit of parents and children. **2** the children of the same father and mother: *Have you any family?* **3** all the persons coming from the same line of family from early times. **4** a group of animals, plants, etc., that have things in common. ● *adj* of or for a family.

famine ('fæmɪn) *ncu* a (time of) great lack of food in a country.

famish ('fæmɪʃ) *infml vi* feel or be very hungry.

famous ('feɪməs) *adj* very well-known, esp. for something pleasing.

fan 1

fan (fæn) *nc* **1** an object held folded, then spread out for moving air to cool one's face: see picture. **2** a machine for moving air to cool a room, etc.: see picture. **3** *infml* someone who admires a singer, football team, etc. ● *vt* move the air to cool (oneself, a room, etc.).

fan 2

fanatic (fə'nætɪk) *nc* a person with too much, and often unwise, enthusiasm on a certain subject. **fanatical** (fə'nætɪkəl) *adj*

fancy ('fænsɪ) *nc, pl* **-cies 1** *nu* imagination. *nc* **2** something imagined. **3** a desire for. ●*adj* decorated; not plain: *fancy cakes.* ●*vt* **1** imagine. **2** think or feel, but not know with certainty. **3** have a liking or wish for. **fanciful** ('fænsɪfʊl) *adj* using imagination, not reason.

fanfare ('fænfeə*) *nc* the sound of trumpets blown together.

fang (fæŋ) *nc* a long, sharp, pointed tooth, esp. of a dog or snake.

fantastic (fæn'tæstɪk) *adj* **1** very strange. **2** *infml* wonderful; very good.

fantasy ('fæntəsɪ) *nc, pl* **-sies 1** a strange picture in the mind. **2** a strange and wild idea, piece of writing or music.

far (fɑː*) *adj* **farther, farthest; further, furthest** distant. **the Far East** See under **east.** ●*adv* **1** not near; a long way. **2** much: *far better.* **far and away** very much. **far away** to a great distance. **faraway** ('fɑːrəweɪ) *adj* **1** distant. **2** (of a person's eyes) dreamy; full of thoughts. **far back 1** a long way from the front. **2** long ago. **3** the greatest distance from the front. **far-flung** (,fɑː'flʌŋ) *adj* having a wide extent. **far-off** ('fɑːrɒf) *adj* distant. **far out 1** a long way off, esp. at sea, in space, etc. **2** *slang* odd; strange. **far-reaching** (,fɑː'riːtʃɪŋ) *adj* having many effects. **far-sighted** (,fɑː'saɪtɪd) *adj* **1** (of eyes) able to see far things clearly. **2** able to see the future clearly. **so far** up to now. **as** or **so far as 1** up to the place of. **2** as much as: *So far as I know she went abroad.*

farce (fɑːs) **1** *nc* a play or event having absurd situations which make one laugh. **2** *nu* this type of play. **farcical** ('fɑːsɪkəl) *adj*

fare (feə*) *nc* **1** the price of a ticket when travelling. **2** a passenger in a taxi. **3** *nu* food set before one, esp. at an inn, hotel, etc. ●*vi old-fashioned* get on; progress: *How did you fare?*

farewell (,feə'wel) *n, interj* goodbye.

farm (fɑːm) *nc* a piece of land with fields for growing corn, raising cattle, etc. ●*vt* **1** use (land) to grow crops, raise cattle, etc. **2** *vi* lead the life of one who works on the land to produce food. **farm out (to)** send work out for others to do: *The job was farmed out to three people.* **farmer** ('fɑːmə*) *nc* a man who owns or is in charge of a farm. **farmhouse** *nc* **farmland** *nc* **farmyard** *nc* an open space near to farm buildings.

farther ('fɑːðə*) *adj* more distant. ●*adv* to or at a greater distance.

farthest ('fɑːðɪst) *adj* most distant. ●*adv* to or at the greatest distance.

farthing ('fɑːðɪŋ) *nc* a former British coin, worth one quarter of an old penny.

fascinate ('fæsɪneɪt) *vt* **1** attract greatly. **2** take all one's attention. **fascination** (,fæsɪ'neɪʃən) **1** *nu* fascinating or being fascinated. **2** *nc* thing that fascinates.

fascism ('fæʃɪzəm) *nu* a system of government in which the one leader has not been chosen by the people. **fascist** *nc*

fashion ('fæʃən) *nu* **1** a way or manner of doing something. **2** style in clothes, behaviour, etc., that is most popular at a certain time. **3** *nc* an example of this style, behaviour, etc. ●*vt* make or shape. **in** or **out of fashion** be in or not in use, popular, etc., at a certain time. **fashionable** ('fæʃnəbəl) *adj*

fast¹ (fɑːst) *adj* **-er, -est 1** quick. **2** (of a clock or watch) showing a time later than the real time. **3** not easily moved: *The mud has stuck fast to my shoes.* **4** (of colours) not fading. ●*adv* quickly.

fast² *vi* eat no food, esp. for religious reasons. ●*nc* an act or time of fasting.

fasten ('fɑːsən) **1** *vt* fix firmly; tie; join (together); close up, lock: *Fasten the suitcase; Fasten your coat.* **2** *vi* become firmly fixed. **fastener** ('fɑːsnə*) *nc*

fastidious (fə'stɪdɪəs) *adj* difficult to please; finding fault with small things.

fat (fæt) *adj* **-ter, -test** not thin; too heavy. ●*nu* **1** the oily substance found in man and animals. **2** the oily substance used in cooking. **3** *nc* a kind of such a substance: *animal fats.* **fatty** *adj*

fatal ('feɪtəl) *adj* very serious; ending in death or ruin. **fatalism** ('feɪtəlɪzəm) *nu* believing that fate decides all that happens. **fatality** (fə'tælɪtɪ) *nc, pl* **-ties** death caused by an accident; disaster.

fate (feɪt) **1** *nu* the power that is thought to decide all that happens. **2** *nc* a person's future as decided by this power. **fateful** ('feɪtfʊl) *adj* **1** governed by fate. **2** having serious results.

father ('fɑːðə*) *nc (infml abbrevs.* **dad, daddy) 1** a male parent. **2 Father** God. **3** a priest. **father-in-law** ('fɑːðərɪnlɔː) *nc, pl* **fathers-in-law** male parent of one's husband or wife. **fatherhood** ('fɑːðəhʊd) *nu* the state of being a father. **fatherland** *nc* the country of one's birth.

fathom ('fæðəm) *nc* (of water) a measure of six feet or 1.8 m ●*vt* understand; find out.

fatigue (fə'tiːg) **1** *nu* being very tired. **2** *nc* a tiring task, esp. of soldiers.

faucet ('fɔːsɪt) *chiefly US nc* See **tap².**

fault (fɔːlt) *nc* **1** a mark that spoils something. **2** a weakness in a person's character. **3** *nu* responsibility for being wrong. **4** *nc* a break in a layer of rock. **faultless** *adj* **faulty** *adv*

fauna ('fɔːnə) *nu* all the animals living at a certain place and time.

favour *US* **favor** ('feɪvə*) **1** *nu* being friendly, or kindly to; approval. **2** *nc* a small act of kindness. **3** *nu* aid; support: *in favour of helping other people.* ● *vt* **1** treat kindly; show favour to; be helpful. **2** approve; encourage. **3** support (someone or some idea). **do (someone) a favour** be of help to someone. **show favour (towards)** make clear that one likes (someone) rather than someone else. **favourable** (ˈfeɪvərəbəl) *adj* helpful; that produce good results. **favourite** (ˈfeɪvərɪt) *adj, nc* **1** (a person or thing) that is loved or liked more than all others. **2** (a person or horse, etc.), expected to win a race, competition, etc.

fawn (fɔːn) *nc* a young deer. ● *adj* (of colour) pale yellowish-brown.

fear (fɪə*) **1** *ncu* an unpleasant feeling caused by being in danger. **2** *nu* deep respect: *fear of God.* ● *vt* **1** be afraid of. **2** *vi* be afraid; hesitate to do something. **fear for** be afraid about: *fear for their safety.* **for fear of** in case of. **fearful** *adj* **1** afraid. **2** *infml* very great; very bad. **3** terrible. **fearless** *adj* not afraid; brave.

feasible (ˈfiːzəbəl) *adj* **1** able to be done; possible. **2** seeming to be likely or true.

feast (fiːst) *nc* **1** a day to celebrate a joyful religious event. **2** a very large and delicious meal, esp. one for many guests. ● *vi* **1** eat, have, or take part in a feast. **2** *vt* satisfy (the mind, eyes, ears, etc.) as if at a feast: *We feasted our eyes on the beautiful painting.*

feat (fiːt) *nc* a difficult act that is done very well, esp. one needing courage or skill.

feather (ˈfeðə*) *nc* one of the coverings that grow on the skin of a bird: see picture. **feathery** *adj*

feather

feature (ˈfiːtʃə*) *nc* **1** a typical quality of something: *features of his writing.* **2** one of the parts of the face, such as the eyes, nose, etc. **3** a long, important piece of writing in a newspaper. ● *vt* include; bring attention to. **feature film** the main film in a cinema programme.

February (ˈfebruərɪ) *n* the second month of the year, after January and before March.

fed (fed) past tense and past participle of **feed. fed up with** *slang* bored with.

federal (ˈfedərəl) *adj* of a system of government in which states of a country unite in a central government, while each keeps control of some matters. **federalism** (ˈfedərəlɪzəm) *nu*

federate (ˈfedəreɪt) **1** *vi* join together into a federation. **2** *vt* put states into such a system. **federation** (ˌfedəˈreɪʃən) *nc* a federal system.

fee (fiː) *nc* a payment made for a special service, such as from a doctor, lawyer, etc.; money paid to join a club, library, society, etc.

feeble (ˈfiːbəl) *adj* **-r, -st** weak. **feeble-minded** (ˌfiːbəlˈmaɪndɪd) *adj* mentally weak.

feed (fiːd) **1** *vt* give food to, esp. a baby, an animal, or an ill person. **2** *vi* (of animals) eat. ● *nc* **1** a meal for babies or animals. **2** *nu* food for animals.

feedback (ˈfiːdbæk) *infml nu* information, etc., about a product, etc., given, esp. by the user to its maker.

feel (fiːl) *vt* **1** explore by touching. **2** be conscious of: *feel the cold.* **3** be affected by one's feelings, thoughts, etc.: *I feel strongly about it.* **4** have an idea about: *He felt he would win.* ● *nu* **1** the sense of touch. **2** the act of feeling. **3** the quality (of someone or something). **feel like** *infml* want. **feel up to** be able, and ready, to do something. **feeler** *nc* **1** one of two hair-like things on an insect's head, used for feeling. **2** a suggestion. **feeling 1** *nu* ability to feel. *nc* **2** the experience of a mood, quality, or emotion. **3** a sensation (of heat, cold, etc.).

feet (fiːt) plural of **foot.**

feign (feɪn) *formal or literary vt* pretend.

feline (ˈfiːlaɪn) *adj* of or like a cat.

fell[1] (fel) past tense of **fall.**

fell[2] *nc* a stretch of high land without trees but often covered in low shrubs.

fell[3] *vt* make fall; cut down (a tree); knock down (a man).

fellow (ˈfeləu) *nc* **1** *infml* a man. **2** a person's friend. **3** someone who helps to govern a university; member of a learned society, esp. to do with the arts. ● *adj* a person of the same class, group, etc.: *fellow citizens; fellow workers.* **fellowship** (ˈfeləuʃɪp) **1** *nu* friendship. *nc* **2** a group of people with the same interests, etc. **3** the position of a university fellow.

felony (ˈfelənɪ) *nc, pl* **-nies** a very serious crime, esp. murder, burning a building, etc. **felon** (ˈfelən) *nc* a person guilty of such a crime.

felt[1] (felt) past tense and past participle of **feel.**

felt[2] *nu* a kind of thick cloth, made by the pressing flat of wool, hair, etc.: *a felt hat.*

female (ˈfiːmeɪl) *adj, nc* **1** (to do with) a woman, girl, or other animal of the sex that is able to give birth. **2** (to do with) a plant producing fruit.

feminine (ˈfemɪnɪn) *adj* **1** of or like a woman.

2 (in some languages) of a class of nouns usually including female people and animals. **femininity** (ˌfemɪˈnɪnɪtɪ) *nu* **feminism** (ˈfemɪnɪzəm) *nu* a movement to obtain the right of women to be treated as equal to men. **feminist** (ˈfemɪnɪst) *nc* a person who believes in feminism.

femur (ˈfiːmə*) *nc* the bone in the human leg from the hip to the knee.

fen (fen) *nc* an area of low, wet land.

fence¹ (fens) *nc* **1** a wall of upright sticks of wood or metal, used in a field, garden, etc., esp. to keep animals in and people out. **2** *slang* a person who buys and sells stolen goods. **sit on the fence** support neither side in an argument. **fencing** *nu* material such as wood, etc., for making a fence.

fence² *vi* **1** practise fighting with long swords. **2** avoid answering a question. **fencer** (ˈfensə*) *nc* **fencing** *nu* fighting with swords in a skilled way.

fend (fend) *v* **fend for** take care of (oneself). **fend off** defend oneself from (an attack, etc.).

fender (ˈfendə*) *nc* **1** a metal guard put round a fireplace in a room, in case coal falls out. **2** *US* See **mudguard** and **wing** (def. 2).

ferment (fəˈment) **1** *vti* (cause to) go through a chemical change, esp. brought about by yeast, in which sugar becomes alcohol. **2** *vi* become excited. ● (ˈfɜːment) *nc* a substance that causes other substances to go through a chemical change. **(be) in a ferment** (be) very excited. **fermentation** (ˌfɜːmenˈteɪʃən) *nu*

fern (fɜːn) *nc* a plant with long green leaves like feathers, and without flowers.

ferocious (fəˈrəʊʃəs) *adj* very fierce; cruel. **ferocity** (fəˈrɒsɪtɪ) *nu*

ferret (ˈferɪt) *nc* a small animal like a cat, used for killing rats or forcing rabbits from their holes, etc. ● *vi* go hunting with ferrets. **ferret (something) out** find (something) by searching; search out.

ferric (ˈferɪk) *adj* of iron.

ferrous (ˈferəs) *adj* to do with or containing iron.

ferry (ˈferɪ) *nc, pl* **-ries** a boat that takes people or goods from one side of a river, etc., to another. ● *vt* take or go across a river, etc., in a boat.

fertile (ˈfɜːtaɪl) *adj* **1** (of land) producing much; (of a person's mind) full of ideas. **2** able to produce children. **fertility** (fəˈtɪlɪtɪ) *nu*

fertilise (ˈfɜːtɪlaɪz) *vt* make fertile or able to produce. **fertiliser** (ˈfɜːtɪlaɪzə*) *nc* a substance added to earth in order to produce better crops. **fertilisation** (ˌfɜːtɪlaɪˈzeɪʃən) *nu*

fervent (ˈfɜːvənt) *adj* very enthusiastic; eager. **fervently** *adv*

fester (ˈfestə*) *vi* **1** (of a wound, etc.) become full of poison. **2** (of the mind) continue to be bitter and angry.

festival (ˈfestɪvəl) *nc* an occasion of joy, entertainments, etc.

festive (ˈfestɪv) *adj* of a festival or feast day; joyful and gay. **festivity** (feˈstɪvɪtɪ) *nu* being joyful and gay. **festivities** *n pl* happy and joyful events.

festoon (feˈstuːn) *nc* a chain made of coloured paper, ribbons, flowers, across a room, etc., as a decoration. ● *vt* hang or make festoons.

fetch (fetʃ) *vt* **1** go for and bring back: *fetch the doctor; Please fetch my coat.* **2** bring in; sell for (a price).

fête (feɪt) *nc* an entertainment or festival at which money is raised for a special purpose: *church fête; garden fête.* ● *vt* honour; give much attention to.

fetish (ˈfetɪʃ) *nc* **1** something believed to have magic power, by a person who does not believe in any religion. **2** anything to which foolish or unnatural attention is given.

fetter (ˈfetə*) *nc* **1** a chain for a prisoner's feet. **2** *(often pl)* anything that stops a person's progress. ● *vt* **1** put in chains. **2** control or prevent.

fetus (ˈfiːtəs) *n* See **foetus**.

feud (fjuːd) *nc* a quarrel that has continued for a long time, esp. between two persons, families, or groups.

feudal (ˈfjuːdəl) *history adj* of the system of people holding land in return for giving their services to the owner. **feudalism** (ˈfjuːdəlɪzəm) *nu*

fever (ˈfiːvə*) *nu* **1** a high temperature of the body, esp. caused by illness. **2** anxiety or excitement. **3** *nc* an illness causing high temperature of the body. **feverish** *adj* **feverishly** *adv*

few (fjuː) *adj* **-er, -est** *pron (with a plural n)* not many: *He made few mistakes in his work.* **a few** a small number of; some. **few and far between** not happening often.

fiancé (fɪˈɒnseɪ) *nc* a man whom a woman has promised to marry. **fiancée** (fɪˈɒnseɪ) *nc* a woman whom a man has promised to marry.

fiasco (fɪˈæskəʊ) *nc* a complete failure.

fib (fɪb) *infml nc* a lie, esp. not a serious one. ● *vi* tell a fib.

fibre *US* **fiber** (ˈfaɪbə*) **1** *nc* one of the hair-like parts that form a substance: *cotton fibre; nerve fibre: see picture.* *nu* **2** a substance made up of hair-like parts. **3** the way hair-like parts of a substance are arranged: *material of loose fibre.* **fibreglass**

('faɪbəglɑːs) *nu* glass of fibres woven together, made into a material for building or a substance for preventing loss of heat.
fibrous ('faɪbrəs) *adj*

fibre

fickle ('fɪkəl) *adj* likely to change.

fiction ('fɪkʃən) **1** *nc* something that is imagined. **2** *nu* stories. **fictitious** (fɪk'tɪʃəs) *adj* not real; invented.

fiddle ('fɪdəl) *infml nc* **1** a violin. **2** the act of cheating, esp. in business. ● *vi* **1** play the fiddle. **2** make small, useless, movements; do things without a purpose: *He did nothing but fiddle about.* **3** *vt* cheat, esp. in business. **fiddler** *infml nc* **1** a person who plays a fiddle. **2** a person who cheats. **fiddling** *infml adj* useless; unimportant.

fidelity (fɪ'delɪtɪ) *nu* **1** being loyal or faithful. **2** being exact or correct. **high fidelity** See under **high.**

fidget ('fɪdʒɪt) *vi* move about in a restless way. ● *nc* a person who fidgets.

field (fiːld) *nc* **1** a piece of land for cattle or for growing corn, etc., esp. surrounded by stone walls, hedges, etc. **2** any large, open space: *a football field.* **3** a subject of interest, activity, etc.: *His field is politics.* **4** an area of land where minerals are found and removed: *a coalfield.* **fielder** *nc* (in cricket and baseball) a person whose purpose is to stop or catch the ball. **field marshal** the officer with the highest position in the army. **field study** the study of a subject by getting information from visiting and talking to people.

fiend (fiːnd) *nc* **1** a devil; very cruel person. **2** person who gives his whole mind or all his time to something particular: *a fiend for hard work; a drug fiend.* **fiendish** *adj* very cruel.

fierce (fɪəs) *adj* **-r, -st 1** violent; cruel: *fierce temper; a fierce wind.* **2** intense: *fierce heat.* **fiercely** *adv*

fiery ('faɪərɪ) *adj* **-ier, -iest 1** very hot; like fire. **2** (of a person) easily made angry.

fifteen (ˌfɪf'tiːn) *determiner, n* the number 15. **fifteenth** (ˌfɪf'tiːnθ) *determiner, n, adv* **fifth** (fɪfθ) *determiner, n, adv* of the number 5. **fifty** ('fɪftɪ) *determiner, n* 50. **fiftieth** ('fɪftɪɪθ) *determiner, n, adv*

fig (fɪg) *nc* a small, sweet fruit with many small seeds: see picture at **fruits.**

fight (faɪt) **1** *vi* use force, struggle, resist. *vt* **2** use force or struggle against (someone or something). **3** try to overcome: *fight fear; fight disease.* ● *nc* **1** a battle between two or more people or animals. **2** a boxing match. **3** *nu* (of a person) courage; spirit. **fighter** *nc* **1** a person who fights. **2** a fast plane that attacks enemy planes.

figment ('fɪgmənt) *nc* something that is invented or imagined.

figurative ('fɪgjʊrətɪv) *adj* (of words) that represent something rather than give its exact meaning, such as *'I could eat a horse'* meaning *'I am very hungry'.* **figuratively** *adv*

figure ('fɪgə*) *nc* **1** the shape of the human body: *She has a good figure.* **2** *arithmetic* a number, esp. written down: *1, 2; He's not good at figures.* **3** a drawing, painting, or shape cut out in stone, of a person, animal, bird, etc. **4** (esp. in a book) a drawing or plan to explain something. ● *vt* **1** *US infml* think. **2** *vi* appear: *He figures in the new play.* **figure out** solve; understand after working it out. **figure of speech** a set of words that represent something rather than give an exact meaning. **figurehead** *nc* **1** a decorative figure, cut out in wood, placed at the painted front of a ship. **2** a person in an important position but without much influence.

filament ('fɪləmənt) *nc* a hair-like piece; thin metal wire in an electric light.

file¹ (faɪl) *nc* a steel tool with a rough surface for making things smooth or shorter. ● *vt* make smooth or cut with a file: *file nails.*

file² *nc* a container, esp. a box, drawer, or cover, for keeping papers, etc., together and in the right order. ● *vt* **1** place in a file. **2** *vi* march, one behind the other. **rank and file** ordinary soldiers; ordinary people.

filial ('fɪljəl) *adj* to do with a son or daughter.

fill (fɪl) **1** *vi* become full. **2** *vt* make (someone or something) full. **fill in** finish or make complete, by adding what is needed: *He filled in an application form for the job.* **fill out 1** become fatter or larger. **2** *chiefly US* fill in. **fill up** make or become full. **filling** *nc* material used by a dentist to fill up a hole in a tooth. **filling-station** *chiefly US* also **gas station** a place where petrol is bought to fill up a car engine.

fillet ('fɪlɪt) *nc* **1** a ribbon, etc., worn round the hair. **2** a thin piece of meat or fish with the bones removed. ● *vt* take out the bones from meat or fish.

filly ('fɪlɪ) *nc, pl* **-lies** a young, female horse.

film (fɪlm) *nc* **1** a thin layer or covering: *a film of dust.* **2** a roll of thin material used for making photographs. ● *vt* **1** make a cinema or television film. **2** *vi* become covered in a thin layer. **film star** a person who acts in cinema or television films. **film-strip** a long, narrow piece of film with photographs on it. **filmy** *adj* like a thin layer or coating.

filter ('filtə*) *nc* a device for removing solid or impure matter from a liquid when the liquid is passed through it. ● *vt* **1** pass or flow through. **2** *vi* (of news, ideas, a crowd, etc.) pass, flow, or come through.

filth (filθ) *nu* disgusting dirt. **filthy** *adj*

filtrate ('filtreit) *nu* the pure matter obtained after being passed through a device.

fin (fin) *nc* one of the parts, like a small wing, that a fish uses in swimming: see picture.

fin

final ('fainəl) *adj* **1** coming at the end; last. **2** that settles an argument, etc. ● *nc (often pl)* the last of a set of matches, examinations, etc. **finalise** ('fainəlaiz) *vt* finish. **finality** (fai'næliti) *nu* being completely settled or finished with. **finally** *adv*

finale (fi'na:li) *nc* the last part of an opera, play, piece of music, etc.; end.

finance (fai'næns) *nu* the science of controlling public money. **finances** money belonging to a person, a state, or a business. ● *vt* provide money for (a business, plan, etc.). **financial** (fai'nænʃəl) *adj* to do with money matters. **financier** (fai'nænsiə*) *nc* a person with a special knowledge of money matters; person who controls much money.

finch (fintʃ) *nc* a small bird noted for its song.

find (faind) *vt* **1** discover: *They found buried treasure.* **2** get back (something or a person) that was lost, etc. **3** realise or learn. **4** judge: *The court found him guilty.* ● *nc* something found: *Discovering the bar of gold was a good find.* **find out** learn by asking; discover: *Did you find out when the film starts?*

finder *nc* **1** a person who discovers something that was lost. **2** the piece of curved glass in a camera or telescope. **finding** *nc (usually pl)* the result found after investigation, esp. by a court of law.

fine¹ (fain) *adj* **-r, -st** **1** (of weather) bright and clear; with the sun shining. **2** beautiful; good; pleasing: *fine clothes.* **3** of very small pieces; thin: *Salt is a fine white substance; fine cloth.* **fine arts** painting, drawing, and sculpture. **finely** *adv*

fine² *nc* a sum of money to be paid as a punishment for breaking a law or a rule. ● *vt* demand a fine from (someone).

finesse (fi'nes) *nu* a clever way of dealing with people or a difficult situation so that things go well.

finger ('fiŋgə*) *nc* one of the five long, end parts of a hand. ● *vt* touch, feel, or rub with the fingers. **fingernail** *nc* the hard substance at the end of a finger. **fingerprint** *nc* a mark made by the skin of the finger when pressed onto something.

finish ('finiʃ) **1** *vti* bring or come to the end. *Work finishes at five o'clock.* **2** *vt* make perfect. ● *nu* **1** the last part. **2** being perfect or complete, esp. furniture: *The table has a beautiful finish.* **3** the quality of a surface: *The chair has a rough finish.*

finite ('fainait) *adj* having limits; having an end: *Man's knowledge is finite.*

fiord (fjɔːd) *nc* a long, narrow piece of sea, between high cliffs.

fir (fɜː*) *nc* a tree that bears cones and has green, needle-like leaves throughout the year: see picture at **trees**.

fire ('faiə*) **1** *nu* the condition of burning with flames. **2** *nc* a pile of burning coal, wood, etc., in a fireplace to provide heat in a room, etc. ● *vt* **1** excite; *fire the imagination.* **2** shoot (bullets) at someone or something with (a gun). **3** *infml* take away the job of (someone one employs), as a punishment. **on fire 1** burning. **2** excited. **firearm** ('faiərɑːm) *nc* a gun, pistol, etc. **fire brigade** a team of men who are paid to put out unwanted fires. **fire engine** a machine, used by the fire brigade, that throws water onto a large fire. **fire escape** special stairs down the side of a building, to be used if the building is on fire. **fire extinguisher** a device, with a chemical substance inside it,

fire extinguisher

held in the hands to put out a fire: see picture. **firefly** *nc, pl* **-flies** an insect that gives out a small light. **firelight** *nu* the light from a fire, esp. in a fireplace. **fireman** ('faiəmən) *nc, pl* **-men** a member of the fire brigade. **fireplace** *nc* a place in a room where a fire is burning for warmth. **fireproof** *adj* not allowing fire to pass through it. **firework** *nc* a toy containing gunpowder that explodes with a loud noise or burns with pretty lights when lit by a match. **firing squad** a small group of soldiers ordered to fire their guns together at a military funeral, or to shoot someone dead at an execution.

firm¹ (fɜːm) *adj* **-er, -est 1** steady; hard. **2** (of a person's character or mind) not easily changed; showing strength. **firmly** *adv* **firmness** *nu*

firm² *nc* a business company.

firmament (ˈfɜːməmənt) *n* **the firmament** the skies, with their suns, moons, stars, clouds, etc.

first (fɜːst) *adj* **1** coming earlier than or before all others. **2** most important.   ● *adv* before all others. **at first** at the beginning. **first aid** See **aid**. **first-born** (ˈfɜːstbɔːn) *nu* the eldest (child) in a family.   ● *adj* of the first-born. **first-class** (ˌfɜːstˈklɑːs) *adj* of the best quality. **first floor 1** *Brit* the first floor of a building above ground-level. **2** *US* the floor of a building at ground-level. **first-hand** (ˌfɜːstˈhænd) *adj* direct.   ● *adv* directly. **first name** the name given to one, not the family name. **first-rate** (ˌfɜːstˈreɪt) *adj* of the best kind; excellent. **firstly** (ˈfɜːstlɪ) *adv* **First World War** See **World War I** under **world**.

fiscal (ˈfɪskəl) *adj* of money, esp. the money paid to a government.

fish (fɪʃ) *nc, pl* **fish, fishes** a cold-blooded animal that lives in water: see picture.   ● *vi* **1** catch fish. **2** try to get (something) without actually asking: *fish for information*. **fisherman** (ˈfɪʃəmən) *nc, pl* **-men** a man who earns his living by catching fish. **fishery** (ˈfɪʃərɪ) *nc, pl* **-ries** part of the sea where fish are caught. **fishmonger** (ˈfɪʃˌmʌŋɡə*) *nc* a man whose trade is selling fish. **fishy** *adj* **1** smelling like fish. **2** *infml* of doubtful truth.

fission (ˈfɪʃən) *nu* a division, esp. of living matter that splits and produces new matter, and of an atom when an atomic bomb is exploded.

fissure (ˈfɪʃə*) *nc* a deep crack caused by two parts splitting.

fist (fɪst) *nc* the hand with the fingers and thumb closed tightly.

fit¹ (fɪt) *adj* **-ter, -test** healthy. ● *vt* be or make suitable or right for. **fit for 1** good enough for: *food fit for a king*. **2** proper; suitable. **fitness** *nu* **1** being healthy. **2** being suitable or right. **fitting** *adj* proper; suitable. ● *nc* the trying on of a garment to see if it fits. **fittings** *n pl* something fixed in a building: *electric light fittings*.

fit² *nc* **1** a series of sudden uncontrolled movements of the body, esp. caused by illness. **2** a sudden strong feeling that does

fish

carp

eel

cod

haddock

mackerel

halibut

herring

trout

plaice

salmon

pike

not last long: *a fit of anger; a fit of enthusiasm.* **fitful** ('fɪtfʊl) *adj* not regular; not steady.

five (faɪv) *determiner, n* the number 5. **fiver** ('faɪvə*) *infml nc* £5 or $5 note.

fix (fɪks) *vt* **1** make firm; fasten. **2** turn or give (one's attention, eyes, mind, etc.) steadily onto something: *fix one's mind on one's work; She fixed her eyes on his face.* **3** decide on: *Let's fix a date for the party.* **4** arrange: *The meeting has been fixed for tomorrow.* **5** *US infml* repair; put in order. ● *nc* a difficult situation. **fixture** ('fɪkstʃə*) *nc (often pl)* something fixed and permanent in a building; fittings: *The house was sold with all its fixtures.*

fizz (fɪz) *vi* make a sound as when water is poured onto fire. ● *nu* the sound of (something) fizzing. **fizzy** *adj*

fizzle ('fɪzəl) *vi* make a weak, hissing sound. **fizzle out** come to an unsatisfactory end: *Our plans fizzled out.*

flabbergast ('flæbəgɑːst) *infml vt* astonish greatly.

flabby ('flæbɪ) *adj* **-ier, -iest** **1** (of the flesh) not firm; hanging down. **2** (of the character) weak.

flaccid ('flæksɪd) *adj* flabby; hanging limp.

flag[1] (flæg) *nc* a piece of coloured material attached by one edge to a rope or pole, used as a signal or as the sign of a group or nation. **flagpole** ('flægpəʊl) *nc* the strong stick to which a flag is attached.

flag[2] *vi* become tired; weaken. **flag down** stop a vehicle by waving one's arm up and down.

flagon ('flægən) *nc* a glass container with a narrow neck and large broad body, esp. for wine: see picture.

flagon

flagrant ('fleɪgrənt) *adj* (of wrongdoing or a person who does wrong) openly and without shame.

flail (fleɪl) *nc* a wooden tool used for beating the grain out of grain plants. ● *vt* beat (grain) with a flail.

flair (fleə*) *nc* a natural power for doing something well.

flake (fleɪk) *nc* a small, light piece of something: *a snowflake.* ● *vi* come off in small strips.

flamboyant (flæm'bɔɪənt) *adj* **1** with bright colours and much decoration. **2** (of a person) hoping to be noticed by dressing or behaving in a showy manner.

flame (fleɪm) *nc* **1** a piece of burning gas coming up from a fire. **2** *infml* one of a pair in love with each other. ● *vi* **1** burn with flames. **2** become bright in colour: *His face flamed with anger.*

flamingo (flə'mɪŋgəʊ) *nc* a water-bird with a long neck, long legs, and pink feathers.

flammable ('flæməbəl) *adj* easily able to burn.

flan (flæn) *nc* an open pie, containing fruit, etc.

flange (flændʒ) *nc* a round band or outside edge of something, esp. a wheel, to prevent it slipping: see picture.

flange

flank (flæŋk) *nc* **1** the side of a human or animal body. **2** the side of a building, mountain, etc. **3** the right or left side of an army. ● *vt* be placed at the side of.

flannel ('flænəl) **1** *nu* soft, woollen cloth. **2 flannels** trousers made of this cloth. **3** *nc* a square piece of flannel for washing the face, cleaning, etc.

flap (flæp) *nc* a piece of material that is fixed by one side only and hangs down: *a pocket flap; the flap of a table.* ● *vti* move or make move up and down or from side to side.

flare (fleə*) *vi* **1** burn suddenly with a bright flame. **2** (of a skirt or trousers) make wider at the lower end. **flare up 1** burst into flames. **2** suddenly become angry or violent. ● *nc* **1** a bright light used by a ship, boat, etc., in need of help. **2** the widening of a dress, skirt, or trousers at the lower end.

flash (flæʃ) **1** *vi* burst into light, activity, view, etc. *vt* **2** cause (a torch, lamp, or light) to flash. **3** send (a signal). ● *nc* a sudden and short bright light or activity: *a flash of lightning; a flash of inspiration.* **flashback** *nc* (of a cinema film) moving back to an earlier scene. **flashbulb** *photography nc* a bulb that gives light for a moment. **flashlight** *nc* **1** a light used as a signal, a warning, etc. **2** *photography* a device that makes a flash of bright light for taking photographs in otherwise weak light. **3** *esp. US* See **torch** (def. 1). **flashy** *adj* attractive, in a showy way.

flask (flɑːsk) *nc* a bottle with a narrow neck: see picture.

flask

flat¹ (flæt) *US* **apartment** *nc* a set of rooms in part of a house or building, used as a home.

flat² *adj* **-ter, -test 1** even; level; smooth. **2** (of someone or an animal lying down) at full length: *The boy was lying flat on his back.* **3** having too little energy, air, etc.: *a flat tyre; a flat battery.* **4** without interest; lifeless: *a flat party; a flat voice.* **5** *music* below the natural or true note: *He sang flat.* **6** absolute; plain: *flat nonsense.* ●*nc* **1** the flat part of anything: *the flat of my hand.* **2** *music* a flat note. **flat out** *infml* **1** using all one's strength and the things that can help one: *He was working flat out.* **2** very tired. **flatly** *adv* absolutely: *He flatly refused to go.*

flatten (ˈflætən) **1** *vi* become flat. **2** *vt* cause to become flat; destroy.

flatter (ˈflætə*) *vt* **1** praise in a way that is not sincere, in order to please. **2** make (a person) feel pleased, honoured, etc. **3** **flatter oneself** be pleased with oneself. **flattery** (ˈflætərɪ) *nu* praise that is not sincere.

flaunt (flɔːnt) **1** *vt* try to attract notice to (oneself) in a self-satisfied way. **2** *vi* (of flags, etc.) wave proudly.

flavour (ˈfleɪvə*) **1** *nu* the quality of taste or smell. *nc* **2** a taste. **3** a special quality of something: *The book had a flavour of adventure.* ●*vt* give a flavour to. **flavouring** *nu* something used to add a taste to food; (sometimes *nc*)

flaw (flɔː) *nc* a mark that spoils something; crack.

flax (flæks) *nu* a plant produced for making cloth from its stems. **flaxen** (ˈflæksən) *adj* **1** to do with flax. **2** (of hair) pale yellow.

flay (fleɪ) *vt* **1** take the skin off an animal. **2** find fault with someone, in a very angry manner.

flea (fliː) *nc* a tiny jumping insect without wings, that bites humans and animals for blood: see picture at **insects.**

fleck (flek) *nc* **1** a small spot of colour or light. **2** a very small bit: *a fleck of dust.*

fled (fled) past tense and past participle of **flee.**

fledgeling (ˈfledʒlɪŋ) *nc* a young bird. **fledged** (fledʒd) *adj* (of birds) having fully grown feathers. **fully-fledged** having the necessary training, etc.: *a fully-fledged doctor.*

flee (fliː) **1** *vi* run away. **2** *vt* run away from; leave quickly: *flee the country.*

fleece (fliːs) *nc* the woolly covering of a sheep; (sometimes *nu*) the amount of wool cut from a sheep at one time. ●*vt* rob (someone) of money, property, etc., by a trick. **fleecy** *adj* like fleece: *fleecy hair.*

fleet (fliːt) *nc* **1** a large number of warships with one commander. **2** a number of ships, buses, or taxis, etc., with one commander, owner, etc.

fleeting (ˈfliːtɪŋ) *adj* lasting only a very short time.

flesh (fleʃ) *nu* (of the body) the soft substance between the skin and the bones. **one's own flesh and blood** one's own family. **fleshy** (ˈfleʃɪ) *adj* fat.

flew (fluː) past tense of **fly².**

flex (fleks) **1** *nc* a piece of easily bent wire, used for carrying electricity to a lamp, iron, etc. **2** *nu* electric wire. ●*vt* bend (esp. the muscles, limbs, etc.).

flexible (ˈfleksəbəl) *adj* easily bent or changed; (of a person) easy to deal with. **flexibility** (ˌfleksəˈbɪlɪtɪ) *nu*

flick (flɪk) *nc* a light blow, esp. with the ends of the fingers. ●*vt* give a flick.

flicker (ˈflɪkə*) *vi* burn or shine unsteadily, esp. of a fire or light about to go out. ●*nc* (usually singular) a flickering movement of light or flame.

flies (flaɪz) *infml n pl* a piece of cloth over buttons, zip, etc., esp. over the opening at the front of a pair of trousers.

flight¹ (flaɪt) **1** *nu* the flying or moving through the air: *a flight of birds; the flight of an arrow. nc* **2** a journey by plane; distance flown. **3** a set (of stairs), in a straight line or from one landing to the next: *There are two flights of stairs to my room.* **flight path** the planned line along which a plane or spacecraft moves. **flight recorder** a device in a plane that records what happens to the engine, etc., during the flight.

flight² *nu* running away, esp. from danger.

flighty (ˈflaɪtɪ) *adj* **-ier, -iest** (of a person, esp. a woman) unsteady in character, often changing her mind, ideas, etc.

flimsy (ˈflɪmzɪ) *adj* **-ier, -iest 1** (of material or objects) thin and light; easily broken. **2** not solid or real: *a flimsy excuse.*

flinch (flɪntʃ) *vi* make a sudden, small movement back, because of bodily or mental pain: *He flinched at her cruel words; The pain from his injury made him flinch when touched.*

fling (flɪŋ) *vt* **1** throw or push away with force: *She flung the door open.* **2** throw or move in a hurried, angry, violent, etc., way: *She flung her arms around her son.* ● *nc* **1** an attempt at doing something. **2** an energetic dance, esp. in Scotland.

flint (flɪnt) **1** *nu* hard stone in small round lumps, grey inside and covered with white. *nc* **2** a piece of this stone that, if struck, can make fire. **3** a piece of hard metal used in a cigarette lighter to make fire.

flip (flɪp) **1** *vt* move (something) with a quick, short movement of the finger and thumb. **2** *vi* move with a sudden jerk.

flippant (ˈflɪpənt) *adj* talking of serious things without respect.

flipper (ˈflɪpə*) *nc* **1** the part of sea-animals (not fish) used in swimming. **2** a rubber device worn on the feet to increase the speed in swimming: see picture.

flipper

flirt (flɜːt) *vi* **1** pretend that one is in love (with someone of the opposite sex). **2** think about, but not in a serious way: *flirt with an idea.*

flit (flɪt) *vt* move from one place to another in a light, quick way.

float (fləʊt) *vi* **1** rest on the top of water, etc., without sinking. **2** be held up in air, gas, etc.: *Clouds floated by.* **3** *vt* get to go on water without sinking: *The child floated his boat on the lake.* ● *nc* a piece of light material that floats and is used in fishing, supporting a hook or net.

flock (flɒk) *nc* **1** a group of animals of one kind: *a flock of sheep.* **2** a number of birds travelling together. ● *vi* go together, in large numbers: *Crowds flocked to see the football match.*

flog (flɒg) *vt* **1** beat, esp. with a whip or cane. **2** *slang* sell. **flog a dead horse** waste one's time trying to do something that cannot be done.

flood (flʌd) *nc* **1** a bursting in of water over land that is usually dry. **2** an outburst; a sudden rush of something: *a flood of rain; a flood of tears.* ● *vt* **1** cover over (land) with a great amount of water. **2** *vi* come in a large amount or great numbers: *The mail flooded in; The house was flooded with light.* **floodlight** *nc* a lamp with a powerful light that covers a large area. ● *vt* light a place with such a lamp or lamps. **floodtide** *nc* the sea at its highest level.

floor (flɔː*) *nc* **1** the flat surface at the bottom of a room: *thick carpets on the floor;* flat surface at the bottom: *the sea floor.* **2** all the rooms, etc., on one level of a building: *The store has three floors.* **3** the lowest level, esp. of prices, wages, etc. **floorboard** long, narrow, flat, piece of wood as part of a wooden floor.

flop (flɒp) **1** *vi* move, sit, or fall down suddenly and awkwardly. **2** *infml vt* fail completely: *The new play flopped.* ● *nc* a person, book, play, etc., that fails. **floppy** (ˈflɒpɪ) *adj* **-ier, -iest** hanging in a loose way: *Some dogs have floppy ears.*

flora (ˈflɔːrə) *nu* all the flowers, plants, etc., of a particular area or country. **floral** (ˈflɔːrəl) *adj* to do with flowers. **florist** (ˈflɒrɪst) *nc* a person who grows or sells flowers.

floss (flɒs) *nu* the silk threads on the covering of a silkworm: see picture.

floss

flotilla (fləˈtɪlə) *nc* a small fleet or group of small ships, usually of the same kind.

flotsam (ˈflɒtsəm) *nu* **1** the pieces or goods from a wrecked ship found floating at sea. **2** useless things to be thrown away. **3** vagrants. **flotsam and jetsam 1** rubbish found floating on water. **2** tramps; criminals; people with ruined lives.

flounder (ˈflaʊndə*) *vi* **1** make violent but often useless movements, as when trying to get out of deep water, mud, etc. **2** make mistakes, esp. when speaking, because one is uncertain, etc. ● *nc* a small flat fish.

flour (ˈflaʊə*) *nu* fine powder made from grain, used for making bread, cakes, etc. ● *vt* shake flour onto.

flourish (ˈflʌrɪʃ) **1** *vi* grow in a strong and healthy way; become successful. **2** *vt* wave (something) about so that it will be noticed. ● *nc* **1** a waving (by the hand) or movement of something to attract notice: *He took off his hat with a flourish.* **2** an exciting burst of music.

flout (flaʊt) *vt* give no respect to; laugh at and disobey: *He flouted all the rules.*

flow (fləʊ) *vi* **1** move along smoothly: *Rivers flow; Her tears flowed.* **2** (of clothes, hair, etc.) hang down loosely and smoothly: *flowing hair.* **3** come (from), be the effect: *Wealth flows from hard work.* ● *nu* flowing. **flow chart** a chart explaining how a material has been made or the set of actions needed in doing something complicated: see picture.

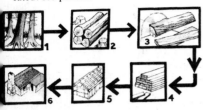

flow chart

flower ('flaʊə*) *nc* **1** the part of a plant that usually has coloured petals and that produces the seeds: see picture. **2** the best part: *in the flower of life.* ● *vi* produce flowers. **flower bed** a piece of garden, etc., kept for growing flowers. **flower-pot** *nc* a pot, of red baked clay or plastic, containing soil in which to grow a plant. **flowery** *adj* **-ier**, **-iest 1** having many flowers. **2** (of speech or language) having too much decoration and praise, sometimes insincere.

flown (fləʊn) past participle of **fly²**.

flu (fluː) *n* See **influenza**.

fluctuate ('flʌktjʊeɪt) *vi* (esp. of levels, or prices) go up and down; rise and fall. **fluctuation** (,flʌktjʊ'eɪʃən) *nc*

flue (fluː) *nc* a pipe that carries smoke out from a fire or leads hot air to or gases from a boiler.

fluent ('fluːənt) *adj* having an easy ability in speaking, esp. a foreign language: *She is fluent in Spanish.*

fluid ('fluːɪd) *adj* **1** able to flow. **2** able to be changed: *fluid plans.* ● *nc* a substance able to flow.

fluke (fluːk) *infml nc* an accidental piece of good luck.

flung (flʌŋ) past tense and past participle of **fling**.

fluorescent (,flʊə'resənt) *adj* (of some substances) taking in radiation and sending out a bright light: *fluorescent lighting.*

fluoride ('flʊəraɪd) *chemistry nu* one of the two parts that make up the chemical substance fluorine (a pale yellow gas).

flurry ('flʌrɪ) *nc, pl* **-ries 1** a sudden rush of wind, snow, etc. **2** hurry and excitement: *She was in a flurry.*

flush¹ (flʌʃ) *adj* **1** level with; even. **2** having plenty of money: *I'm flush this week.*

flush² *nc* **1** a rush of blood to the face making it red. **2** a rush of water, esp. to carry away waste. **3** *nu* freshness; newness: *the first flush of spring.* ● *vi* **1** (of the face) becoming red: *She flushed when she met him.* **2** *vt* make clean by causing a flow of water.

flowers

anemone

chrysanthemum

cowslip

crocus

daffodil

daisy

geranium

iris

lotus

rose

sunflower

tulip

fluster ('flʌstə*) *vt* make or become nervous. ●*nc* condition of being nervous, confused.

flute (fluːt) *nc* a wooden pipe with holes along it, blown into on the side near one end: see picture at **musical instruments**.

flutter ('flʌtə*) 1 *vti* (of birds) flap (the wings) quickly and fly short distances only, or to the ground. *vi* 2 move about in a restless or nervous way. 3 (of wings) flap and make short flights only. ●*nc (usually singular) infml* 1 excitement: *She felt a quick flutter when he spoke.* 2 a gamble: *He had a flutter at the races.*

flux (flʌks) *nu* 1 flowing. 2 in a continuous state of change.

fly¹ (flaɪ) *nc, pl* **flies** 1 a small insect with two wings: see picture at **insects**. 2 a copy of one, put on a fishing line to catch fish.

fly² *vi* 1 move through the air as a bird does or in a plane, etc. 2 move quickly: *We'll be late if we don't fly.* *vt* 3 control (a plane) in the air. 4 raise or make rise: *fly a kite; fly a flag.* 5 run away from, esp. in danger: *fly the country.* **flyer** ('flaɪə*) *nc* a person who flies a plane, esp. the pilot. **flying saucer** an object shaped like a saucer, thought to have been seen in the sky and to have come from another planet. **flyover** ('flaɪ,əʊvə*) *nc* a bridge with a road or railway that passes over another large road. **flywheel** *nc* a heavy wheel that keeps a machine going at a regular speed.

foal (fəʊl) *nc* a young horse.

foam (fəʊm) *nu* a mass of small white bubbles, formed by a liquid. ●*vi* form or give off foam.

fob (fɒb) *vt* **fob (someone) off with** cheat (someone) into accepting (something of no value).

focus ('fəʊkəs) *nc, pl* **-ses, foci** ('fəʊkaɪ) 1 the point at which lines of light, etc., meet. 2 the point where the clearest picture, etc., is seen by the eye, camera, etc. 3 the central point of activity: *the focus of attention.* ●*vi* 1 (of lines of light, etc.) meet at a point. *vt* 2 get (a camera, etc.), into focus. 3 give (one's attention) to something: *Focus on your work.* **focal** ('fəʊkəl) *adj*

fodder ('fɒdə*) *nu* food for cattle.

foe (fəʊ) *poetry nc* an enemy.

foetus ('fiːtəs) (also **fetus**) *nc* the unborn child inside the mother or the young of an animal inside an egg.

fog (fɒg) *nu* a thick mist held in the air at or near the ground and through which it is difficult to see. **foghorn** *nc* a horn used for warning ships in fog. **foggy** *adj* **-ier, -iest** 1 (of air) not clear because of fog. 2 confused: *I haven't the foggiest idea what you mean.*

foil¹ (fɔɪl) 1 *nu* metal beaten into very thin, easily bent, sheets: *Silver foil is put round food to protect it.* 2 *nc* someone or something that contrasts with the qualities of another when compared.

foil² *nc* a sword without a sharp point, used in fighting practice.

foil³ *vt* prevent (someone) from doing something.

fold¹ (fəʊld) 1 *vt* bend (something) over itself: *Fold your clothes before putting them away.* 2 *vi* able to be folded; become folded: *a folding chair.* 3 *vti* cross (one's arms) over one's chest: *She sat with her arms folded.* ●*nc* a line made by folding (paper, cloth, etc.). **folder** ('fəʊldə*) *nc* a stiff cover that is bent in two and used for holding papers, etc.

fold² *nc* a place where sheep are shut in when not in the fields.

foliage ('fəʊlɪɪdʒ) *nu* the leaves of a tree.

folio ('fəʊlɪəʊ) *nc* 1 a sheet of paper folded over to make two or four pages of a book. 2 a book made of such sheets.

folk (fəʊk) *nu (with plural verb)* 1 people. 2 *infml* one's relations. **folk dance** a dance of the ordinary people from early times. **folklore** ('fəʊklɔː*) *nu* knowledge, stories, etc., of the common people from early times.

follicle ('fɒlɪkəl) *nc* 1 a small hole in the skin with the root of a hair. 2 (of a plant) a seed container, opening along one side only.

follow ('fɒləʊ) *vt* 1 go or come after. 2 along (a road, etc.). 3 accept as a guide, leader, etc.: *Follow my advice.* 4 understand: *Do you follow my meaning?* 5 result from; be certainly true: *Because he's a teacher it doesn't follow that he's always right.* 6 *vi* go or come after someone or something. **as follows** as about to be mentioned, told, etc. **following** *adj* these things about to be mentioned. ●*nu* a group of people supporting someone.

folly ('fɒlɪ) *nc, pl* **-lies** 1 *nu* foolishness. 2 *nc* foolish acts, things, etc.

fond (fɒnd) *adj* (of hopes, desires, etc.) believed in, but not likely to happen: *He had fond hopes of success.* **fond of** liking (someone or something) very much. **fondly** *adv* 1 lovingly. 2 in a foolishly hopeful way.

fondle ('fɒndəl) *vt* touch (someone or something) in a loving and tender way.

font (fɒnt) *nc* a container for water that is poured over a person's head when making him a member of the Christian Church, and giving him a first name.

food (fuːd) 1 *nu* that which can be eaten. 2 *nc* food of the same class or group: *frozen foods.* **foodstuff** ('fuːdstʌf) *nc* substance used as food.

fool (fuːl) *nc* a person with little good sense. ● *vi* 1 (often followed by **around** or **about**) act like a fool: *Stop fooling around!* 2 *vt* cheat; deceive: *You can't fool me!* **foolhardy** ('fuːlhaːdɪ) *adj* taking risks when not necessary. **foolish** *adj* with little good sense; silly. **foolishly** *adv* **foolishness** *nu* **foolproof** ('fuːlpruːf) *adj* with no possibility of its going wrong, etc.

foolscap ('fuːlskæp) *nu* a size of paper, 13½ inches × 8 inches (340 mm × 200 mm).

foot (fʊt) *nc, pl* **feet** 1 the lowest part of the leg on which one walks. 2 a measure of length = one third of a yard and equivalent to 0.305 m 3 the lower end (of a bed, a set of stairs, etc.); lowest part (of anything): *at the foot of the hill.* **foot the bill** *infml* pay the bill. **go on foot** walk. **put one's foot down** *infml* be firm (about something); say that something must be stopped. **put one's foot in it** *infml* say or do the wrong thing. **football** 1 *nu* a game in which a ball is kicked between two teams. 2 *nc* the leather ball used in this game. **foothill** ('fʊthɪl) *nc* one of several small hills at the bottom of a mountain. **foothold** ('fʊthəʊld) *nc* 1 a place for the foot when on a difficult surface, esp. in climbing on rocks. 2 a firm beginning from which one can go forward. **footing** 1 *nc* place for standing on. 2 *nu* a person's position with people, relationships, etc.: *He and I are on a friendly footing.* **footman** ('fʊtmən) *nc, pl* **-men** a man servant who serves food, opens the door to visitors, etc. **footnote** *nc* a note at the bottom of a page. **footpath** *nc* a path for people who are walking, esp. one across fields. **footprint** *nc* the mark made by the underneath part of the foot or of a shoe, such as in sand or snow. **footstep** *nc* the sound of (someone) walking. **footwear** ('fʊtweə*) *nu* shoes, boots, socks, etc.

for (fɔː* unstressed fə*) *prep* 1 being intended to be given to, belong to, or used in: *Here is a present for you; We can deliver the goods for you.* 2 in exchange: *I bought it for £5.* 3 in spite of: *For all her friends, she's still not happy.* 4 because of: *I like it for this reason.* 5 considering the nature of; considering that he (she, it, etc.) is: *It's very hot for this time of year; He's very active for his age.* 6 representing: *The letters 'PM' stand for 'Prime Minister'; red for danger.* 7 (used to show purpose): *We went to the restaurant for a meal; You can use this paper for writing on; What is this book for?* 8 instead of: *She did the job for me.* 9 in favour of: *Are you for or against an election?* 10 towards: *setting out for school.* 11 during: *I'm going away for August.* 12 (used to show distance): *After this town, there's not another*

town *for fifty kilometres.* 13 (used to show destination): *The train for Glasgow departs from platform four.* 14 (used to show an aim): *We are all hoping for better times.* 15 as a result of: *I felt better for a good night's rest.* **be for it** *slang* be in trouble, punished, etc. ● *conj formal or literary* because: *The evenings are getting cooler, for it's nearly winter.*

forage ('fɒrɪdʒ) *nu* food for cattle. ● *vi* search for, esp. food.

forbade (also **forbad**) (fə'bæd) past tense of **forbid**.

forbear (fɔː'beə*) *vi* hold oneself back from doing something.

forbid (fə'bɪd) *vt* order someone not to do something. **forbidding** (fə'bɪdɪŋ) *adj* threatening; stern.

forbidden (fə'bɪdən) past participle of **forbid**.

force (fɔːs) 1 *nu* strength; power: *The bomb exploded with great force.* *nc* 2 a body of men trained to work together, etc.: *the police force; a work force; the armed forces.* 3 a person or thing that has much influence: *a force for good in society.* ● *vt* 1 force someone to do something; make something happen. 2 do (something difficult) by trying hard: *She forced a smile in spite of her misery.* **forceful** *adj* (of a person's character) strong. **forcible** ('fɔːsəbəl) *adj* done with force of the body. **forcibly** *adv*

forceps ('fɔːseps) *n pl* a tool used by doctors and dentists for gripping hold of things: see picture.

forceps

ford (fɔːd) *nc* a place in a river where it is not too deep to walk across. ● *vt* cross a river by walking through the water.

fore (fɔː*) *adj* front. **to the fore** towards the front or a more important position.

forearm ('fɔːraːm) *nc* the arm from the elbow to the tips of the fingers.

foreboding (fɔː'bəʊdɪŋ) *nc* a feeling that something unpleasant is about to happen.

forecast ('fɔːkaːst) *vt* say what will happen in the future. ● *nc* act of forecasting: *the weather forecast.*

forecourt ('fɔːkɔːt) *nc* an enclosed space in front of a building.

forefather ('fɔːˌfaːðə*) *nc* a person in one's family line from whom one is descended.

forefinger ('fɔː,fɪŋgə*) *nc* the finger next to the thumb.

forefront ('fɔːfrʌnt) *nu* the extreme front: *in the forefront of battle.*

foregoing (fɔː'gəʊɪŋ) *adj* mentioned earlier.

foregone (fɔː'gɒn) *adj* already known before it happened: *a foregone conclusion.*

foreground ('fɔːgraʊnd) *nu* 1 in the front, esp. of a picture. 2 the most easily seen position.

forehead ('fɒrɪd, 'fɔːhed) *nc* front part of the head above the eyes.

foreign ('fɒrɪn) *adj* of, from or belonging to another country. **foreign to** not natural in; not usual with. **foreigner** ('fɒrɪnə*) *nc* a person not in his own country. **Foreign Secretary** the title of the person in a government who is in charge of foreign affairs.

foreman ('fɔːmən) *nc, pl* **-men** a man in charge of a group of workmen.

foremost ('fɔːməʊst) *adj* first; most important. ● *adv* first in position.

forensic (fə'rensɪk) *adj* to do with the law.

forerunner ('fɔː,rʌnə*) *nc* a person or thing that shows what is to follow.

foresee (fɔː'siː) *vt* see (something that is going to happen) before it does happen.

foreshadow (fɔː'ʃædəʊ) *vt* show or warn what is to come in the future.

foresight ('fɔːsaɪt) *nu* the ability to see and prepare for the future.

forest ('fɒrɪst) 1 *nc* a large piece of land covered with many trees. 2 *nu* land covered in trees. **forested** ('fɒrɪstɪd) *adj* covered in forests. **forester** ('fɒrɪstə*) *nc* a man who is paid to be in charge of a forest; man who works in a forest. **forestry** ('fɒrɪstrɪ) *nu* science of taking care of a forest.

foretell (fɔː'tel) *vt* tell about (an event, etc.) before it happens.

forever (fə'revə*) *adv* for always.

foreword ('fɔːwɜːd) *nc* a section at the beginning of a book to introduce it, esp. by someone who is not the writer of the book.

forfeit ('fɔːfɪt) *nc* something that has to be done, lost, paid for, etc., as a result of something done or as a punishment. ● *vt* suffer something because of an action or as a punishment.

forgave (fə'geɪv) past tense of **forgive.**

forge¹ (fɔːdʒ) *nc* a workshop with a fire where metals are heated, esp. one used for making horses' shoes, etc. ● *vt* 1 shape (metal) by heating it. 2 make a copy of (something written, etc.), in order to deceive: *forge banknotes.* **forgery** ('fɔːdʒərɪ) *nc, pl* **-ries** 1 *nu* the copying of something in order to deceive. 2 *nc* something copied in order to deceive.

forge² *v* **forge ahead** make progress, esp. in spite of difficulties.

forget (fə'get) 1 *vt* be unable or fail to remember: *I've gone out and I've forgotten my keys.* 2 *vi* fail to remember: *He forgot to tell me.* **forgetful** *adj* in the habit of forgetting things.

forgive (fə'gɪv) *vt* 1 stop feeling angry about a wrong (someone) has done. 2 decide not to punish (someone) for a wrong he has done.

forgiven (fə'gɪvən) past participle of **forgive.**

forgiveness (fə'gɪvnɪs) *nu* forgiving or being forgiven.

forgo (fɔː'gəʊ) *vt* do without; give up.

forgot (fə'gɒt) past tense of **forget.**

forgotten (fə'gɒtən) past participle of **forget.**

fork (fɔːk) *nc* 1 a tool with three or more long points used in eating, cooking, serving food, etc. 2 a tool with three or more long points, used in farming or gardening for digging, lifting, etc.: see picture at **tools.** 3 anything that divides into two in a Y-shape, such as a road. ● *vi* 1 divide into two branches. 2 use a fork. **forked** (fɔːkt) *adj* having branches or divisions into a Y-shape. **fork-lift truck** a lorry with a device for lifting and lowering goods.

forlorn (fə'lɔːn) *adj* 1 lonely and sad. 2 deserted.

form (fɔːm) 1 *nu* a shape; appearance. *nc* 2 a person's or animal's figure or shape: *I could see two human forms in the mist.* 3 a general type, kind, or sort of something: *What form of society do you prefer?* 4 a class in a school; *the fourth form.* 5 a printed sheet of paper with spaces in which facts or answers can be written: *an application form.* 6 a long wooden seat without a back. ● *vt* 1 give a shape to (something, habits, thoughts, etc.). 2 organise: *form a theatrical company.* 3 *vi* take shape; start to be.

formal ('fɔːməl) *adj* (of behaviour) according to rules and customs. **formality** (fɔː'mælɪtɪ) *nc, pl* **-ties** 1 *nu* correct attention to rules and customs. 2 *nc* an act that is correct according to rules and customs. **formally** *adv*

formation (fɔː'meɪʃən) 1 *nu* the putting together (of something); being shaped or formed: *the formation of an army.* 2 *nc* something shaped or formed: *unusual rock formations.*

former ('fɔːmə*) *adj* of an earlier time: *in former years; the former president.* ● *pron, adj* the first of two already mentioned: *Of the two, I prefer the former.* **formerly** *adv* in earlier times; before.

formidable ('fɔːmɪdəbəl, fə'mɪdəbəl) *adj* 1 causing fear. 2 likely to be very difficult to deal with: *a formidable task.*

formula ('fɔːmjʊlə) *nc, pl* **-las, -lae** (liː) **1** a fixed form of words for a particular occasion, etc. **2** a rule, facts, etc., written out in signs, numbers, or short form: *'H_2O' is the chemical formula for water.*

formulate ('fɔːmjʊleɪt) *vt* say or show (something) clearly and exactly: *formulate an opinion.* **formulation** (,fɔːmjʊ'leɪʃən) *ncu*

forsake (fə'seɪk) *formal vt* give up; abandon, (esp. one's friends). **forsaken** (fə'seɪkən) past participle of **forsake**.

forsook (fə'sʊk) past tense of **forsake**.

forsooth (fə'suːθ) *archaic adv* truly.

forswear (fɔː'sweə*) *vt* promise to give up (something).

fort (fɔːt) *nc* a strong building used for defence.

forte ('fɔːteɪ) *nc* something a person does very well: *Teaching is his forte.*

forth (fɔːθ) *old-fashioned adv* **1** out: *He set forth on his journey.* **2** onwards: *from this time forth.* **and so forth** and so on. **forthcoming** (,fɔːθ'kʌmɪŋ) *adj* **1** about to come out or appear. **2** (of a person) *infml* answering easily and readily.

forthwith (,fɔːθ'wɪθ) *adv* at once.

fortieth ('fɔːtɪɪθ) *determiner, n, adv* of the number 40.

fortify ('fɔːtɪfaɪ) *vt* **1** strengthen (a place) against attack. **2** strengthen (one's mind, body, spirits, etc.). **fortification** (,fɔːtɪfɪ'keɪʃən) **1** *nu* strengthening against attack. **2** *nc (often pl)* strong buildings, etc., for defence.

fortnight ('fɔːtnaɪt) *Brit nc* a time of two weeks.

fortress ('fɔːtrɪs) *nc* a building or town made strong for defence.

fortunate ('fɔːtʃənət) *adj* lucky; having success, etc., through good luck. **fortunately** *adv*

fortune ('fɔːtʃuːn) **1** *nu* luck; chance. *nc* **2** success; great wealth: *make a fortune.* **3** a person's fate. **fortune teller** a person who can tell what will happen to someone in the future.

forty ('fɔːtɪ) *determiner, n* the number 40.

forum ('fɔːrəm) *nc* **1** in Rome long ago, a market-place or a public place where meetings were held. **2** any place nowadays for a public meeting.

forward ('fɔːwəd) *adj* **1** near or in the front. **2** too eager, esp. in order to attract attention to oneself. ● *vt* send; send on: *I'll forward your mail from your old address to your new one.* **forward(s)** ('fɔːwəd(z)) *adv* **1** onward. **2** onward in time. **3** to the front or to attention: *Bring forward your opinions on the matter.*

fossil ('fɒsəl) *nc* **1** a plant or animal of long ago, found buried and become as hard as rock. **2** an old person who is fixed in his ideas, not accepting new ones.

foster ('fɒstə*) *vt* **1** care for; nurse or bring up (a child who is not one's own). **2** encourage: *foster feelings of goodwill.*

fought (fɔːt) past tense and past participle of **fight**.

foul (faʊl) *adj* **-er, -est 1** causing disgust; very dirty. **2** wicked. **3** (of weather) stormy and wet. **foul play 1** (in sport) against the rules, esp. harming another person. **2** a violent crime, esp. murder. ● *nc* (in sport) an unfair act. **fall foul of** quarrel or get into trouble with.

found¹ (faʊnd) past tense and past participle of **find**.

found² *vt* **1** start the building of: *found a university.* **2** start (something), esp. by giving money: *found a new club.* **3** base on: *proposals founded on new ideas.* **foundation** (faʊn'deɪʃən) **1** *nu* the setting up of a new school, city, etc. *nc* **2** something that is founded. **3** *(usually pl)* the strong and lowest part of a building, esp. under the ground. **4** the most necessary part of anything, on which the rest is built up.

founder¹ ('faʊndə*) *nc* someone who founds or starts (an organisation, state, movement, etc.).

founder² *vi* **1** (of a ship) fill with water and sink. **2** (of a horse) fall or almost fall. *vt* **3** cause (a horse) to stumble.

foundry ('faʊndrɪ) *nc, pl* **-ries** a place where metal or glass is melted and shaped into things.

fountain ('faʊntɪn) *nc* a fast flow of water coming up from a small opening: see picture. **fountain-pen** ('faʊntɪnpen) *nc* a pen able to carry ink inside it.

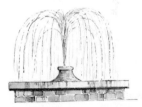

fountain

four (fɔː*) *determiner, n* the number 4. **on all fours** crawling on hands and knees. **fourth** (fɔːθ) *determiner, n, adv* **fourteen** (,fɔː'tiːn) *determiner, n* 14. **fourteenth** (,fɔː'tiːnθ) *determiner, n, adv*

fowl (faʊl) *nc* **1** a bird, kept by man, to be eaten. **2** *old-fashioned* any bird. **3** a bird of a particular kind: *wildfowl; gamefowl.*

fox (fɒks) *nc* a wild animal of the dog family, with red fur and a thick tail: see picture at **animals**.

foyer ('fɔɪeɪ) *nc* a room at the entrance of a theatre, cinema, or hotel, for the use of the public.

fraction ('frækʃən) *nc* **1** a small part of something. **2** part of a whole number: ¼, ½, and ¾ *are fractions.* **fractional** ('frækʃənəl) *adj*

fracture ('fræktʃə*) **1** *nu* being broken or breaking, esp. of a bone. **2** *nc* something that is broken: *She had fractures of both legs.*

fragile ('frædʒaɪl) *adj* easily broken or injured.

fragment ('frægmənt) *nc* a small piece of something that has broken off. **fragmentation** (,frægmen'teɪʃən) *nc* breaking up into small pieces.

fragrance ('freɪgrəns) *nu* a pleasant smell. **fragrant** ('freɪgrənt) *adj*

frail (freɪl) *adj* weak; easily broken or injured. **frailty** ('freɪltɪ) **1** *nu* being frail. **2** *nc* a weakness.

frame (freɪm) *nc* **1** the main form around which something, esp. a building, is built up. **2** the human body: *He has a large frame.* **3** the border of wood, etc., put round a picture, painting, etc. **frame of mind** mood. **framework** ('freɪmwɜːk) *nc* the main part on which the rest is built up: *the framework of society.* ●*vt* put a border round (a picture, painting, etc.).

franc (fræŋk) *nc* See appendix.

franchise ('fræntʃaɪz) *nc* the right to vote at a public election.

frank¹ (fræŋk) *adj* **-er, -est** speaking one's thoughts freely and honestly. **frankly** *adv*

frank² *vt* **1** put (stamps) on letters, etc., by means of a machine, at a post office. **2** put a mark (on a postage stamp) to show it has been accepted.

frankfurter ('fræŋkfɜːtə*) *nc* a sausage of beef or pork with a strong taste that has been preserved with smoke.

frankincense ('fræŋkɪn,sens) *nu* the substance obtained from some trees, used for burning to give off a sweet smell.

frantic ('fræntɪk) *adj* wildly excited with fear, joy, pain, grief, etc. **frantically** *adv*

fraternity (frə'tɜːnɪtɪ) *nc, pl* **-ties 1** *nu* being brothers. **2** *nc* a group of men with the same interest or purpose.

fraud (frɔːd) **1** *nu* dishonesty that can be punished by law. *nc* **2** a dishonest act of this kind. **3** a person or thing that is not what he, she, or it pretends to be. **fraudulent** ('frɔːdjʊlənt) *adj* acting with or got by fraud.

fraught (frɔːt) *adj* **1** (of a person or feeling) nervous, anxious, or like being stretched tightly: *She felt very fraught after the argument.* **2** (of a situation) tense, difficult, or troubled: *The atmosphere was fraught as*

they started to fight.

fray (freɪ) **1** *vt* make (a material, rope etc.) become thin by being used too much; *(also vi)* become like this. **2** make (someone's temper) become worn out; *(also vi)* become like this.

freak (friːk) *nc* person, thing, act, etc., that is very unusual and not normal.

freckle ('frekəl) *nc* (on a person) a small brown spot on the skin. ●*vt* **1** mark with spots. **2** *vi* be covered with spots.

free (friː) *adj* **-r, -st 1** not in someone else's power; not a slave. **2** not in prison. **3** (of a state, its people, etc.) not controlled by another or foreign government. **4** (able) to be obtained without paying. **5** (of a room, telephone, etc.) able to be used; not being used by anyone else. **6** loose; not fixed. **7** relaxed: *Feel free to do what you want.* **8** not having: *free from worry.* **free-and-easy** friendly. **freedom** ('friːdəm) **1** *nu* being free. **2** *nc* a type of freedom. **freehand** ('friːhænd) *adj* (of a drawing) done by hand and without the use of other tools. ●*adv* by hand only. **freehold** ('friːhəʊld) *law nc* land that is completely owned. **freelance** ('friːlɑːns) *nc* a person with no fixed employer, who sells his services where he is able. ●*vi* to work freelance. **free speech** the right to express one's opinions in public. **freeway** ('friːweɪ) *US nc* a very wide road for fast traffic. **free-will** (,friː'wɪl) *nu* a person's power to choose or decide what he will think or do. **freely** *adv* ●*vt* cause (people, animals, etc.) to be set loose from someone else's control: *It took an hour to free the people trapped in the lift; The prisoners were freed.*

freeze (friːz) *vi* **1** be changed into or be covered with ice because of cold. **2** be very cold: *I'm freezing!* **3** be unable to move because of fear, etc.: *She froze with fear.* **4** *vt* put (food, etc.) in a special machine to make it very cold and so prevent it going bad. **5** form ice on or in something. **6** fix (wages and the prices of goods) to stay the same. **freezer** *nc* a machine for freezing food. **freezing-point** *nu* the temperature at which water freezes.

freight (freɪt) *nu* **1** goods carried from one place to another. **2** the money paid for this. ●*vt* send or carry (goods) in this way.

frenzy ('frenzɪ) *nu* wild excitement.

frequency ('friːkwənsɪ) *nc, pl* **-cies 1** the number of times something is repeated. **2** *nu* something that happens often. **frequent** ('friːkwənt) *adj* happening often. **frequently** *adv*

fresco ('freskəʊ) *nc, pl* **-s, -es** a painting done on a wall or ceiling, before the plaster is dry.

fresh (freʃ) *adj* **-er, -est 1** newly grown, made, produced, etc.: *fresh eggs; a fresh pot of tea.* **2** without experience: *fresh from college.* **3** (of water) not containing salt. **4** (of weather) cool and clean: *fresh air.* **5** new; different: *fresh information.* **6** *infml* not showing respect, esp. of a man towards a woman. **freshman** ('freʃmən) *nc, pl* **-men** student in his first year at a university. **freshness** *nu* **freshwater** *adj* not saltwater or seawater. **freshly** *adv*

fret¹ (fret) **1** *vti* make (oneself) suffer thinking about something that has or has not been done. **2** *vt* wear away by rubbing. **fretful** ('fretfʊl) *adj* irritable.

fret² *nc* (on a guitar, banjo, etc.) one of the metal bars across the wood holding the strings, showing where the fingers are to be placed: see picture.

fret

fretsaw ('fretsɔː) *nc* very narrow tool for cutting out patterns in thin wood.

Freudian ('frɔɪdɪən) *adj* of the ways of healing illnesses of the mind advised by Sigmund Freud (1856–1939).

friar ('fraɪə*) *nc* a member of a group of men living together under religious rules.

friction ('frɪkʃən) *nu* **1** the rubbing of one thing on another, esp. with a waste of power. **2** quarrelling.

Friday ('fraɪdɪ) *nc* the sixth day of the week, after Thursday and before Saturday. **Good Friday** the Friday before Easter Day when Christians remember the death of Jesus.

fridge (frɪdʒ) *infml n* short for **refrigerator.**

friend (frend) *nc* **1** a person one knows and likes, who is not a relation. **2** a helper of or one who has sympathy for someone. **friendliness** ('frendlɪnɪs) *nu* **friendly** *adv* **friendship** ('frendʃɪp) **1** *nu* the feeling between friends. **2** *nc* an example of this feeling or the time it lasts.

frieze (friːz) *nc* a narrow, patterned band along the top of a wall, esp. in a room.

frigate ('frɪgɪt) *nc* a small, fast warship.

fright (fraɪt) **1** *nu* a shock of fear. **2** *nc* fear. **frighten** *vt* fill with fear. **frightful** *adj* **1** causing fear. **2** *infml* awful: *What a frightful noise!* **frightfully** *infml adv* very.

frigid ('frɪdʒɪd) *adj* **1** (of the weather) cold. **2** not friendly: *a frigid manner.*

frill (frɪl) *nc* a border of pattern with one edge left loose, such as on a dress: see picture. **frills** adornments of any kind that are not needed. **frilly** *adj*

frill

fringe (frɪndʒ) *nc* **1** a patterned border of loose threads. **2** the outside edge of something: *on the fringes of the forest.* **3** an edge of short hair hanging just above the eyes. ● *vt* put a fringe on; act as a fringe to.

frisk (frɪsk) *vi* jump about in a playful way: *lambs frisking in the fields.* **frisky** *adj* lively.

fritter¹ ('frɪtə*) *v* **fritter away** waste (money, time, etc.) on unimportant things.

fritter² *nc* a mixture of flour, eggs, and milk, that is fried and filled with fruit or meat: *an apple fritter.*

frivolous ('frɪvələs) *adj* **1** not serious; silly: *frivolous behaviour.* **2** (of a person) only interested in pleasures; silly.

fro (frəʊ) *adv* **to and fro** backwards and forwards: *People were hurrying to and fro.*

frock (frɒk) *nc* **1** a woman's dress. **2** a priest's long outer garment.

frog (frɒg) *nc* a small animal without a tail, that lives both on land and in water. **frogman** ('frɒgmən) *nc, pl* **-men** a person able to swim under water, wearing a rubber suit and carrying a device for breathing.

frolic ('frɒlɪk) *vi* play about in a lively and happy way. ● *nc* a time of being joyful and gay; harmless, merry trick.

from (frɒm unstressed frəm) *prep* **1** (showing the starting point): *He came home from work.* **2** (showing the starting point in time): *I'll be in Paris from 14 August.* **3** (showing the lower point): *From fifteen to twenty cars passed me.* **4** (showing a movement away): *He escaped from prison.* **5** (showing a change or difference): *from hot to cold.* **6** showing a reason or cause: *weak from lack of food; From what I know of him, I don't think he's suitable for the job.* **7** (showing distance): *The mountain is a long way from the village.* **8** (showing a material from which something is made): *Wine is made from grapes.* **9** (showing a position from which something is seen or felt): *We can get a good view of the city from the top of the tower.* **10** (showing prevention, stopping, or taking away): *He was prevented from applying for the job.*

front (frʌnt) *nc* **1** *(usually singular with determiner)* the forward or most important part: *the front of the house.* **2** in war, the place where the actual fighting is. **3** a face; outward appearance: *Though afraid, he put on a brave front.* **4** (of the weather) the leading part of a slowly moving mass of cold or warm air. **in front of** before. ● *vt* face towards (something): *Hotels there front the sea for a long way.* ● *adj* leading; being the forward part or the first one: *He got into the front part of the train.* **frontal** (ˈfrʌntəl) *adj* of or on the front.

frontier (ˈfrʌnˌtɪə*) *nc* **1** the part of a country that is next to another. **2** the furthest man can go in knowledge.

frost (frɒst) **1** *nu* the state of the weather when freezing. **2** *nc* a time of freezing weather: *winter frosts.* **3** *nu* white powder of frozen mist that covers the ground, rooftops, etc. ● *vi* become covered with frost: *The windows are frosted over.* **frostbite** (ˈfrɒstbaɪt) *nu* damage to the skin caused by being very cold. **frosty** *adj* **1** cold with frost: *a frosty morning.* **2** not friendly: *a frosty smile.*

froth (frɒθ) *nu* a large number of small bubbles close together. **frothy** *adj*

frown (fraʊn) *vi* move the eyebrows together making lines on the skin above them, as when one is not pleased, or in deep thought. **frown on** not approve of.

froze (frəʊz) past tense of **freeze**.

frozen (ˈfrəʊzən) past participle of **freeze**.

frugal (ˈfruːgəl) *adj* **1** careful not to waste, esp. money or food. **2** small in quantity and costing little: *a frugal meal.*

fruit (fruːt) **1** *nu* the sweet part of a plant that contains the seeds and can be eaten: see picture. *nc* **2** the part of any plant containing the seeds. **3** *(pl)* all that the earth produces that can be eaten. **4** a result of hard work, study, etc. ● *vi* produce fruit. **fruitful** *adj* **1** producing fruit. **2** producing good results. **fruitless** *adj* with no result.

fruition (fruːˈɪʃən) *nu* getting what one hoped for.

frustrate (frʌˈstreɪt) *vt* prevent from doing or being done. **frustration** (frʌˈstreɪʃən) **1** *nu* being frustrated. **2** *nc* a disappointment.

fry[1] (fraɪ) **1** *vt* cook in hot fat: *She is frying some eggs.* **2** *vi* be cooked in hot fat: *The eggs are frying.* **frying-pan** *nc* a shallow pan with a long handle used for cooking food in fat.

fry[2] *nc, pl* **fry** newly born fish.

fudge (fʌdʒ) *nu* soft, brown sweet made of sugar, chocolate, butter, etc.

fuel (fjʊəl) *nu* coal, petrol, oil, etc., used to make a fire burn or to produce power. ● *vt* **1** provide fuel. **2** *vi* get fuel.

fugitive (ˈfjuːdʒɪtɪv) *nc* a person who is running away, esp. from danger or the police. ● *adj* **1** running away. **2** (of books, writings, etc.) of interest for a short time only.

fugue (fjuːg) *nc* a piece of music in which the main tune is repeated by the other parts or singers in turn.

fulcrum (ˈfʌlkrəm) *nc, pl* **-crums -cra** (krə) point on which a lever moves.

fulfil *US* **fulfill** (fʊlˈfɪl) *vt* carry out (a promise, duty, etc.); do (what has been asked, ordered, planned, etc.). **fulfilment** *US* **fulfillment** *nc*

full (fʊl) *adj* **-er, -est** **1** having all that it is possible to contain: *The drawer is full; He ate until he was full.* **2** having many or a lot: *The room was full of people; She's full of energy.* **3** having plenty in one's mind: *He's full of talk about his new car.* **4** reaching the usual or expected size, amount, wholeness, etc.: *The flowers are in full bloom; I waited a full hour for him.* **full stop** the sign (.) to show the end of a sentence. **full-time** *adj, adv* working the normal number of hours each day. **fullness** *chiefly US nc* being full. **fully** *adv*

fumble (ˈfʌmbəl) **1** *vi* feel about with the hands in an awkward way: *He fumbled along in the dark.* **2** *vt* deal with (something) in an awkward or useless way.

fume (fjuːm) *nc* smoke, gas, etc., with a strong smell: *petrol fumes.* ● *vi* **1** give off fumes. **2** show one is controlling anger.

fun (fʌn) *nu* something that is very pleasant to do to pass the time; amusement: *The party was great fun!; We had fun on the beach.* **make fun of** laugh at unkindly, causing others to laugh too.

function (ˈfʌŋkʃən) *nc* **1** a social or public event, formal or for pleasure. **2** a special job or use of a person or thing. ● *vi* do what (one or it) is intended, planned, etc., to do; operate or work: *The lift was not functioning properly.* **functional** (ˈfʌŋkʃənəl) *adj*

fund (fʌnd) *nc* **1** an amount of money to be used for a special purpose. **2** a store of something that is not material: *a fund of knowledge.* **funds** (fʌndz) *nu (with plural verb)* wealth of a person, company, country, etc.

fundamental (ˌfʌndəˈmentəl) *adj* most necessary, as a point from which to build up; basic; most important. ● *nc* the most important or essential part; rule. **fundamentally** *adv*

funeral (ˈfjuːnərəl) *nc* the burial of a dead person.

fungus (ˈfʌŋgəs) *nc, pl* **-gi** (gaɪ) plant that has no leaves or flowers, and grows on other plants or on matter that is going bad.

fruits

apple

avocado

banana

fig

gourd

grape

mango

lemon

melon

orange

peach

pear

pineapple

plum

raspberry

strawberry

funnel ('fʌnəl) *nc* **1** a tube, wide at the top and becoming smaller at the bottom, used for guiding liquids or powders into a small opening: see picture. **2** a metal chimney of a steamship, train, etc. ●*vt* **1** put something through a funnel. **2** *vi* go through a funnel.

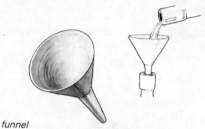

funnel

funny ('fʌnɪ) *adj* **-ier, -iest 1** amusing. **2** strange. **funny bone** the bone at the bend of the arm that tingles if knocked.

fur (fɜː*) **1** *nu* the soft, thick hair that covers some animals. **2** *nc* the skin and hair of an animal, esp. when made into clothes.

furious ('fjʊərɪəs) *adj* very angry; violent: *He was furious when his money was stolen; a furious storm.* **furiously** *adv*

furlong ('fɜːlɒŋ) *nc* a measure of length; 220 yards = 201.168 m

furnace ('fɜːnɪs) *nc* **1** an enclosed, very hot place for heating metals, etc. **2** an enclosed fire for warming a building with hot water in pipes.

furnish ('fɜːnɪʃ) *vt* supply (a room, house, etc.), with furniture; provide. **furnishings** ('fɜːnɪʃɪŋz) *n pl* furniture; things needed for a purpose.

furniture ('fɜːnɪtʃə*) *nu* things needed in a room, house, etc., that can be moved.

furrow ('fʌrəʊ) *nc* a long line made in soil when it is being ploughed.

furry ('fɜːrɪ) *adj* of or like fur; covered in fur.

further ('fɜːðə*) *adv* **1** more forward: *further into the wood.* **2** more: *ask further questions.* **3** moreover: *The ship was hit badly and, further, was beginning to sink.* ●*adj* **1** even more: *further trouble.* **2** another: *a further example.* **3** more distant: *on the further side.* ●*vt* help the progress of: *further our chances of success.* **furthermore** ('fɜːðə-'mɔː*) *adv* and also. **furthest** ('fɜːðɪst) *adj, adv* most distant.

furtive ('fɜːtɪv) *adj* doing things secretly. **furtively** *adv*

fury ('fjʊərɪ) *ncu, pl* **-ries** (a fit of) violent anger.

fuse¹ (fjuːz) **1** *vi* melt because of great heat. **2** *vt* join two things together by heating them. **3** *vi* (of an apparatus using electric current) fail or break, because too much electricity has flowed through. ●*nc* (in an apparatus for using electric current) a piece of metal wire that melts if too much electricity flows through.

fuse² *nc* a length of material or container having in it matter that burns easily, used to make an explosion at a certain time.

fuselage ('fjuːzɪlɑːʒ) *nc* the body of a plane, without the wings, tail, and engine.

fusion ('fjuːʒən) **1** *nu* mixing; joining. **2** *nc* join different things to become one thing.

fuss (fʌs) *nu* unnecessary worry. ●*vi* **1** get into an unnecessary, nervous state. **2** *vt* cause (someone) to be in a nervous state. **fussy** *adj* **1** difficult to satisfy: *She's very fussy about her food.* **2** with too many adornments, details, etc.

futile ('fjuːtaɪl) *adj* useless; not likely to succeed. **futility** (fjuːˈtɪlɪtɪ) *nu*

future ('fjuːtʃə*) *nu* **1** that which will happen after the present; the time to come. **2** what will happen to a person, country, etc. ●*adj* of or in the time to come.

fuzzy ('fʌzɪ) *adj* **-ier, -iest 1** not very clearly seen. **2** (of hair) very curly.

G

gabble ('gæbəl) *vti* speak quickly and unclearly. ● *nu* quick, unclear speaking.

gable ('geibəl) *nc* the wall between two halves of a sloping roof.

gadget ('gædʒɪt) *nc* a small mechanical device or tool.

gag[1] (gæg) *nc* a cloth tied over or put into someone's mouth to stop him speaking. ● *vt* 1 put a gag on (someone). 2 *infml* not allow to speak.

gag[2] *infml nc* a joke.

gaiety ('geɪɪtɪ) *nu* being **gay** (defs. **1, 2**).

gaily ('geɪlɪ) *adv* in a **gay** (defs. **1, 2**) manner.

gain (geɪn) *vt* 1 receive; obtain. 2 win (land, a prize, etc.). 3 arrive at; reach. *vti* 4 increase: *I'm gaining (in) experience.* 5 (often followed by **on**) get further forward (compared to someone or something one is following or that is following one). ● *ncu* 1 (an example of) gaining. 2 *nc* something gained.

gait (geɪt) *nc* a manner of walking; walk.

gala ('gɑːlə) *nc* a special occasion; festival.

galaxy ('gæləksɪ) *nc, pl* **-xies** 1 a star system in space. 2 a gathering of famous, etc., people. **galactic** (gə'læktɪk) *adj*

gale (geɪl) *nc* a strong wind.

gall[1] (gɔːl) *nu* 1 a bitter liquid produced by the liver. 2 *infml* something bitter or unpleasant; bitterness.

gall[2] *nc* a sore on the skin, caused by rubbing. ● *vt* annoy.

gallant ('gælənt) *adj* 1 brave and with honour. 2 (gə'lænt, 'gælənt) (of a man) polite, gentle, and protecting towards women. **gallantly** *adv* **gallantry** *nu* 1 bravery. 2 politeness.

galleon ('gælɪən) *nc* a large sailing ship, esp. of the Spanish navy from the 15th to 17th centuries: see picture.

galleon

gallery ('gælərɪ) *nc, pl* **-ries** 1 a room or corridor open at one side, built over and looking into a larger room. 2 an underground room, esp. in a mine. 3 a room or building in which works of art are shown: *a picture gallery.*

galley ('gælɪ) *nc* 1 a former type of boat with sails and a large number of oars. 2 the kitchen in a boat or plane.

gallon ('gælən) *nc* a measure for liquids (in Britain 4.54 litres, America 3.78 litres).

gallop ('gæləp) *nc* the fastest step of a horse. ● *vi* 1 (of a horse) move with a gallop. 2 *vt* cause (a horse) to move with a gallop.

gallows ('gæləʊz) *n pl (usually with singular verb)* a wooden frame used to kill a person, from which a rope is hung round the person's neck.

galore (gə'lɔː*) *adv* in plenty: *He's got money galore.*

galvanise ('gælvənaɪz) *vt* 1 give a covering of zinc to: *galvanised iron.* 2 make (someone) start doing something: *He was galvanised into action.* **galvanisation** (,gælvənaɪ'zeɪʃən) *nu*

galvanometer (,gælvə'nɒmɪtə*) *nc* an instrument for measuring small electric currents.

gamble ('gæmbəl) 1 *vti* risk (money) on a game of chance. 2 *vt* (followed by **away**) lose (money) by gambling: *He gambled away all his money.* 3 *vi* (often followed by **on**) take a risk in the hope of (something happening): *In planning the trip I'm gambling on being allowed to go.* ● *nc* 1 an example of gambling. 2 a risky act.

gambol ('gæmbəl) *vi* (esp. of lambs) run or jump about playfully.

game (geɪm) *nc* 1 an activity, often organised and with rules, in which there is competition between those taking part, such as football or chess. 2 a single period of such an activity. 3 *infml* any activity, esp. a trick: *What's your game?* 4 *nu* birds and animals killed for food or fun. **give the game away** let out a secret. **gamekeeper** ('geɪm,kiːpə*) a man who looks after game in the country.

gamma ('gæmə) *nc* the third letter of the Greek alphabet.

gammon ('gæmən) *nu* cured meat from the back part and leg of a pig.

gamut ('gæmət) *nc* a range; scale; list: *Red and blue are only two points on the whole gamut of colour.*

gander ('gændə*) *nc* 1 a male goose. 2 *infml* a look: *Have a gander at this!*

gang (gæŋ) *nc* 1 a group of people formed, esp. for crime. 2 a group of people working outside: *a road gang.*

gangplank ('gæŋplæŋk) *nc* a board used for walking onto or off a ship.

gangrene ('gæŋgriːn) *medicine nu* rotting of flesh, caused esp. by a serious injury.

gangster ('gæŋstə*) *nc* a member of a violent gang.

gangway ('gæŋweɪ) *nc* 1 a space between

rows of seats, as in a theatre. **2** a bridge from a ship to land.

gaol (dʒeɪl) *n, v* See **jail. gaoler** *nc*

gap (gæp) *nc* **1** a space; break: *a gap in the wall.* **2** a difference: *an opinion gap.*

gape (geɪp) *vi* **1** stare (at) in surprise or wonder. **2** open one's mouth wide. **3** open or be wide open: *The cave gaped in front of us.* ● *nc* a stare.

garage ('gærɑːʒ, 'gærɪdʒ) *nc* **1** a building in which cars, buses, etc., are kept. **2** a building where petrol is sold and often where cars are sold and repaired. ● *vt* put (a vehicle) in a garage.

garb (gɑːb) *sometimes derogatory nc* clothes; dress. ● *vt (usually passive)* clothe; dress: *He was strangely garbed.*

garbage ('gɑːbɪdʒ) *nu* **1** something worthless or useless. **2** *chiefly US* rubbish; waste.

garble ('gɑːbəl) *vt* mix up (a message, etc.); make difficult to understand.

garden ('gɑːdən) *nc* **1** a piece of land next to a house, used for growing grass, flowers, vegetables, etc. **2** *(pl)* an area of land planted with trees, flowers, etc., and open to the public. ● *vi* look after a garden. **gardener** *nc* **gardening** *nu*

gargle ('gɑːgəl) *vti* wash the mouth and throat by breathing out through (a liquid) held in the mouth. ● *ncu* a liquid used for gargling.

gargoyle ('gɑːgɔɪl) *nc* a pipe with its end shaped like a face, sticking out from a roof to carry rain away from the building: see picture.

gargoyle

garish ('geərɪʃ) *derogatory adj* (of a colour or something coloured) unpleasantly bright.

garland ('gɑːlənd) *nc* a ring of flowers, esp. worn round the head or neck.

garlic ('gɑːlɪk) *nu* a plant root used in food for its strong taste.

garment ('gɑːmənt) *nc* a thing worn to cover the body; piece of clothing.

garnish ('gɑːnɪʃ) *vt* add to (something, esp. food) to make it more attractive: *fish garnished with lemon.* ● *nc* a thing with which something is garnished.

garret ('gærɪt) *nc* a small room in the top of a building.

garrison ('gærɪsən) *nc* the soldiers guarding a town, camp, etc. ● *vt* appoint (soldiers) as a garrison (in a town, camp, etc.).

garter ('gɑːtə*) *nc* a band of elastic cloth worn round the leg to hold up a sock or stocking.

gas (gæs) **1** *ncu, pl* **gases, gasses** a substance, such as air, when it is neither liquid nor solid. *nu* **2** gas burned for heat or light: *natural gas.* **3** *US, infml* short for **gasoline.** ● *vt* **1** use gas on (someone) in order to kill or make unconscious. **2** *infml vi* talk at length. **gas mask** a device worn to remove poisonous gas from the air one breathes. **gasometer** (gæs'ɒmɪtə*) *nc* a very large container for gas. **gas station** *US* See **filling-station. gaseous** ('geɪsɪəs, 'gæsɪəs) *adj* in the form of or to do with a gas.

gash (gæʃ) *nc* a deep cut. ● *vt* make a gash in.

gasket ('gæskɪt) *nc* a thin sheet of paper, rubber, etc., held tightly between two metal surfaces, as in an engine, to keep water, oil, etc., in: see picture.

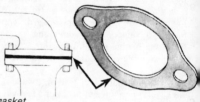

gasket

gasoline ('gæsəliːn) *(infml abbrev.* **gas**) *US n* See **petrol.**

gasp (gɑːsp) **1** *vi* breathe fast or with difficulty, because of lack of air or surprise. **2** *vt* speak while gasping. ● *nc* an example of gasping.

gastric ('gæstrɪk) *adj* to do with the stomach.

gate (geɪt) *nc* **1** a door, either solid or made of bars with spaces in between, used to close a break in a fence, city wall, etc. **2** a way in or out of a large factory, school, etc. **3** a numbered way out of an airport building to a plane. **gatecrash** ('geɪtkræʃ) *vti* get into a party or other social event without having been invited. **gate-post** ('geɪtpəʊst) an upright length of wood, stone, etc., either supporting a gate or to which it is fastened when shut. **gateway** ('geɪtweɪ) an entrance with a gate in it.

gâteau ('gætəʊ) *French nc, pl* **gâteaux** ('gætəʊz) a large rich cake.

gather ('gæðə*) *vti* **1** collect; come or bring together: *to gather flowers; A crowd gathered.* **2** (cause to) increase: *the gathering storm.* **3** *vt* learn; discover: *Did you gather what's happening?* **gathering** *ncu* **1** (an example of) gathering. **2** a meeting of people.

gaudy ('gɔːdɪ) *derogatory adj* **-ier, -iest** very bright, showy, or colourful.

gauge (geidʒ) *nc* **1** an instrument used for measuring: *a rain gauge.* **2** a quantity used for measuring the thickness of wire, fineness of cloth, etc. **3** the distance between the two rails of a railway line. **4** a means of judging something, such as public opinion. ● *vt* **1** measure. **2** judge.

gaunt (gɔːnt) *adj* **1** (of a person) looking very thin. **2** (of a place) bare; unfriendly.

gauntlet[1] ('gɔːntlɪt) *nc* a long heavy glove that widens above the hand. **take up** or **throw down the gauntlet** accept or make a challenge.

gauntlet[2] *n* **run the gauntlet 1** suffer a punishment in which someone is made to run between two lines of men who strike him as he passes. **2** face much criticism.

gauze (gɔːz) *nu* a thin, open cloth.

gave (geiv) past tense of **give**.

gay (gei) *adj* **-er, -est 1** happy; cheerful. **2** bright; showy: *gay colours.* **3** *infml* homosexual.

gaze (geiz) *vi* (often followed by **at**) look long and steadily. ● *nu* a long, steady look.

gazelle (gə'zel) *nc, pl* **gazelles, gazelle** an animal; small type of antelope found in Africa and Asia: see picture at **animals**.

gazette (gə'zet) *nc* a government newspaper containing public notices.

gazetteer (,gæzɪ'tɪə*) *nc* a list of places, with descriptions of them.

gear (gɪə*) *nc* **1** a wheel with teeth round its edge that can turn a similar wheel: see picture. **2** a set of gears built for a purpose: *winding gear.* **3** *ncu* a condition of a set of gears: *low gear; This car has five gears.* **4** *nu* tools, clothes, etc., needed for something:

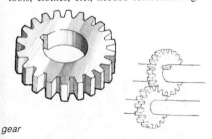

gear

sports gear. **gearbox** ('gɪəbɒks) a box containing the gears in a car or other machine. ● *vt* (followed by **to**) cause to fit in with or be equal to: *My pay is geared to prices.*

geese (giːs) plural of **goose**.

gelatin ('dʒelətɪn) *nu* also **gelatine** ('dʒelətiːn) a substance made from animals' skins and bones and used to make jelly for food, photography, etc.

gelding ('geldɪŋ) *nc* a castrated male horse.

gem (dʒem) *nc* **1** a precious stone, such as a diamond. **2** a particularly good example of something.

gender ('dʒendə*) *grammar* **1** *nc* one of the three types of noun—masculine, feminine, and neuter. **2** *nu* the existence of genders. **3** *nc* the state of being male, female, or neuter.

gene (dʒiːn) *nc* a small part that is inherited; a tiny part of each living cell that controls part of a plant or animal.

genealogy (,dʒiːnɪ'ælədʒɪ) **1** *nc, pl* **-gies** a list of the people of whom one is a descendant. **2** *nu* the practice of making such lists.

general ('dʒenrəl) *adj* **1** to do with everyone in a group or all types of something: *general knowledge; a general strike.* **2** common; frequent: *The rain will be fairly general tonight.* **3** rough; not exact: *I've got the general idea.* ● *nc* an army officer. **in general** generally; most commonly. **general election** an election for all the members of a parliament at once. **generally** *adv* **1** in a general way. **2** most commonly. **general practitioner** a doctor who deals with all types of illness.

generalise ('dʒenərəlaɪz) **1** *vt* (usually followed by **about**) form an idea that may be common to (some but perhaps not all things). **2** *vi* make general statements. **generalisation** (,dʒenərəlaɪ'zeɪʃən) *ncu* (an example of) generalising.

generate ('dʒenəreit) *vt* cause or produce (a result, electricity, etc.).

generation (,dʒenə'reiʃən) *nc* **1** a group of people who are all at the same physical stage in a family or nation. **2** the average time covered by the lives of people in this group, often seen as a single step in a succession of such groups: *three generations ago.* **3** the process of generating.

generator ('dʒenəreitə*) *nc* **1** a person or thing that generates. **2** a machine that generates electricity.

generic (dʒɪ'nerɪk) *adj* to do with a whole group or class; **general** (def. 1).

generous ('dʒenərəs) *adj* **1** glad to give: *He's generous with his money.* **2** large: *a generous amount.* **generosity** (,dʒenə'rɒsɪtɪ) *nu* **generously** *adv*

genetics (dʒɪ'netɪks) *nu* (with singular verb) the study of how plants and animals develop like the ones from which they come. **genetic** *adj* **1** to do with genetics. **2** to do with the origin of something.

genial ('dʒiːnɪəl) *adj* **1** (of a person) cheerful; pleasant. **2** warm; cheering; healthy: *genial surroundings.*

genie ('dʒiːnɪ) *nc* a person supposed to appear by magic to help someone in trouble.

genital ('dʒenɪtəl) *adj* to do with the genitals. **genitals** *n pl* the sexual parts on the outside of the body.

genius ('dʒiːnɪəs) **1** *nc* a very clever person. **2** *nu* the quality of being a genius.

genocide ('dʒenəsaɪd) *nc* the murder of a whole race or nation.

gent (dʒent) *infml n* short for **gentleman.**

gentle ('dʒentəl) *adj* **-r, -st 1** mild; kind. **2** not violent: *Be gentle with those things— they might break.* **3** moderate: *a gentle slope.* **gentleness** *nu* **gently** ('dʒentlɪ) *adv*

gentleman ('dʒentəlmən) *nc, pl* **-men 1** *polite* a man. **2** a polite, educated man.

gents (dʒents) *infml, Brit nc, pl* **gents** *(often with singular verb)* a public toilet for men.

genuine ('dʒenjuːɪn) *adj* **1** real; original. **2** (of a person) sincere. **genuinely** *adv*

genus ('dʒiːnəs) *nc, pl* **genera** (dʒenərə) a group of similar plants or animals.

geography (dʒɪ'ɒɡrəfɪ) *nu* **1** the study of the surface of the earth. **2** *infml* the arrangement of anything, such as the rooms in a house. **geographer** *nc* a person who studies geography. **geographical** (ˌdʒiːə'ɡræf-ɪkəl) *adj*

geology (dʒɪ'ɒlədʒɪ) *nu* the study of what the earth is made of. **geological** (ˌdʒiːə-'lɒdʒɪkəl) *adj* **geologist** *nc* a person who studies geology.

geometry (dʒɪ'ɒmətrɪ) *nu* the study of lines and shapes. **geometrical** (dʒiːə'metrɪkəl) *adj*

geranium (dʒə'reɪnɪəm) *nc* a plant with red, pink, or white flowers: see picture at **flowers.**

geriatrics (ˌdʒerɪ'ætrɪks) *nu (with singular verb)* medicine for old people. **geriatric** *adj* **1** to do with geriatrics. **2** to do with old people.

germ (dʒɜːm) *nc* **1** a tiny creature, esp. one that causes a disease. **2** *(often pl)* a beginning: *the germ of an idea.*

German measles ('dʒɜːmən) *nu* See **rubella.**

germinate ('dʒɜːmɪneɪt) *vti* (cause to) grow or start growing. **germination** (ˌdʒɜːmɪ-'neɪʃən) *nu*

gestation (dʒes'teɪʃən) **1** *nu* the growth of a young animal inside its mother. **2** *nc* the period that this growth takes.

gesticulate (dʒes'tɪkjʊleɪt) *vti* express (a meaning) with movements of the body. **gesticulation** (dʒesˌtɪkjʊ'leɪʃən) *ncu* (an example of) gesticulating.

gesture ('dʒestʃə*) *nc* **1** a movement of the body used to express something. **2** an action that shows one's intentions. ● *vti* use gestures (to indicate): *He gestured me to pass him.*

get (get) *vt* **1** obtain; receive. **2** bring or fetch. **3** take: *I'll get the bus into town.* **4** (followed

by an infinitive after the object) cause: *I got him to come.* **5** *infml* hear or understand: *I didn't get what you said.* **6** *infml* annoy. **7** *vi* (often followed by **to**) reach; arrive at: *We got home safely; Can you get to Nairobi?* **8** suffer from: *I've got a cold.* **9** *vti* (cause to) become: *I got hot; Get your hair cut.* **have got** have; possess: *I have got plenty of time.* **have got to** must: *I've got to go home.* **get across 1** (cause to) cross. **2** (cause to) be understood. **get along 1** (often followed by **with**) be on friendly terms: *I get along well with my cook.* **2** manage; succeed: *We get along without him now.* **3** go away. **get at 1** reach; do something to or with: *I can't get at my car easily when it's in the garage.* **2** mean; intend: *What are you getting at?* **3** annoy; anger. **get away** escape. **getaway** ('getəweɪ) *nc* an escape, esp. just after a crime. **get away with 1** steal. **2** not be punished for. **get back 1** recover (something). **2** return. **get by 1** go past. **2** manage to live, etc.: *I get by without her.* **get down 1** come or go down. **2** bring or take down. **3** write down. **4** eat; swallow. **5** make tired or depressed. **get down to** start (doing). **get in 1** enter. **2** put or bring in. **3** be elected: *He got in at the last election.* **4** manage to do: *I'll try to get all my trips in.* **get into 1** enter. **2** put or bring into. **3** be elected to: *He got into power.* **4** (usually in perfect tense) affect; put into a bad mood: *What's got into you?* **get off 1** leave: *Get off the grass.* **2** come or go down (from). **3** be (or cause to be) punished very little or not at all: *get off lightly.* **get on 1** come or go on. **2** put on. **3** do (well); manage: *How are you getting on?* **4** make progress: *How's the work getting on?* **5** become late or old: *The time's getting on.* **6** (often followed by **with**) be on (friendly) terms with: *We get on well together; She did not get on with him.* **get onto 1** come or go onto. **2** put onto. **3** get a message to: *I'll get onto him about it.* **4** find out: *The police will soon get onto him if he goes on cheating people.* **get out 1** (often followed by **of**) leave. **2** (often followed by **of**) bring or take out. **3** become known: *The news has got out.* **4** (followed by **of**) (cause to) avoid: *I've got out of having to go to school.* **get over 1** (cause to) cross: *Can you get over the wall?* **2** (often followed by **with**) finish: *I'll soon get this over with.* **3** get used to: *I can't get over winning.* **4** overcome: *get over a difficulty.* **5** (cause to) be understood: *I got my message over.* **get round 1** go or come round. **2** put round. **3** avoid having to follow, obey, etc.: *Rules are made to get round.* **4** persuade (someone) to let one do what one wants. **5** travel: *Wait till the news* *gets round.* **get round to** have time to deal with: *I'll get round to you soon.* **get through 1** reach the person one wants to speak to by radio or telephone. **2** (often followed by **to**) make (someone) understand. **3** finish; use up: *I can get through money easily.* **get together 1** collect up. **2** meet to discuss, etc. **get-together** ('getə‚geðə*) *infml nc* a small, informal meeting or party. **get up 1** (cause to) rise from bed. **2** stand up. **3** go or come up. **4** increase: *The train got up speed.* **5** *infml* organise; produce: *I'm getting up a group to go to the theatre.* **get up to** *infml* take part in: *get up to trouble.*

geyser ('giːzə*) *nc* **1** a place where hot water is thrown up out of the ground: see picture. **2** *Brit* a water heater that only heats when water is flowing through it.

geyser

ghastly ('gɑːstlɪ) *adj* **-ier, -iest 1** frightening; terrible. **2** very bad.

gherkin ('gɜːkɪn) *nc* a small cucumber, esp. one put in salt water or vinegar to keep it good.

ghetto ('getəʊ) *nc, pl* **-s, -es** a poor part of a town where a racial group lives.

ghost (gəʊst) *nc* the spirit of a dead person, esp. if seen by someone alive. **ghostly** *adj* **-ier, -iest 1** to do with ghosts. **2** frightening.

giant ('dʒaɪənt) *nc* **1** a very large man, esp. in a story. **2** a very powerful, important, etc., person or thing: *Most petrol is sold by one of the oil giants.* ● *adj* very large.

gibbon ('gɪbən) *nc* an animal; type of ape living in Asia.

giblets ('dʒɪbləts) *n pl* a bird's heart, liver, and other inside parts.

giddy ('gɪdɪ) *adj* **-ier, -iest 1** feeling that one is spinning and may fall over. **2** causing to feel this: *a giddy height.* **giddiness** *nu*

gift (gɪft) *nc* **1** a present. **2** a natural ability.

gigantic (dʒaɪˈgæntɪk) *adj* huge.

giggle ('gɪgəl) *vi* laugh in a silly way. ● *nc* a silly laugh.

gild (gɪld) *vt* cover with gold.

gill¹ (gɪl) *nc* one of the parts of a fish, etc., through which it breathes in water: see picture.

gill² (dʒɪl) *nc* a measure for liquids = 0.148 l or one quarter of a pint.

gilt (gɪlt) past tense of **gild**.

gimlet ('gɪmlɪt) *nc* a small tool for making holes by hand.

gill

gimmick ('gɪmɪk) *infml nc* a device or activity intended to attract attention.

gin (dʒɪn) *nu* a strong, alcoholic, colourless drink made from grain and juniper berries.

ginger ('dʒɪndʒə*) *nu* **1** the hot-tasting root of a plant, used in food, esp. as a powder. **2** this plant. ● *adj* reddish-brown: *ginger hair.* **gingerbread** ('dʒɪndʒəbred) *ncu* (a) cake containing ginger.

gipsy (also **gypsy**) ('dʒɪpsɪ) *nc, pl* **-sies** a member of a wandering people originally from India, now in Europe and North America.

giraffe (dʒɪˈrɑːf) *nc* a very tall African animal with a long neck: see picture at **animals**.

gird (gɜːd) *literary vt* **1** put a belt on (someone or someone's waist). **2** put (clothes) on with a belt: *gird on your clothes.* **3** surround. **gird up one's loins** prepare to do (something).

girder ('gɜːdə*) *nc* a long, strong piece of metal used in buildings and bridges: see picture.

girder

girdle ('gɜːdəl) *nc* **1** a belt, esp. a loose one. **2** a woman's garment, worn under other clothes, from the waist to the upper parts of the legs.

girl (gɜːl) *nc* **1** a female child; young woman. **2** *infml* a woman: *Some old girl told me.* **3** a man's special female friend. **4** a female servant. **5** a young saleswoman. **girlfriend** *nc* a man's special female friend. **girlhood** *nu* the condition or time of being a girl. **girlish** *adj* like a girl.

giro ('dʒaɪrəʊ) *nc, pl* **-s** a system used by banks and post offices for moving money from one person's account to another.

girt (gɜːt) past tense and past participle of **gird**.

girth (gɜːθ) *nc* **1** the distance around something round or nearly round. **2** the strip of leather that is fastened round a horse to keep a saddle on.

gist (dʒɪst) *nc* the main point of a message, etc.

give (gɪv) *vt* 1 pass; hand: *I gave him the bread.* 2 make a present of: *I was given a book for my birthday.* 3 sell: *He gave it me for £5.* 4 pay: *I gave him £5 for it.* 5 offer; show: *Give me your hand.* 6 produce; bring about: *He gave a shout.* 7 provide: *I'm giving a party.* 8 *vi* bend or move when pressed. ●*nu* the amount by which something bends when pressed: *There's not much give in a hard bed.* **give away** 1 make a present of. 2 let out: *to give away a secret.* **giveaway** ('gɪvəweɪ) *nc* the act of giving away a secret, etc. **give back** return (something). **give in** 1 deliver (written work, etc.). 2 admit defeat; surrender. **give off** produce: *A wet fire gives off smoke.* **give out** 1 give (things) to several people: *The teacher gave out our books.* 2 produce: *The man gave out a cry.* 3 stop working; come to an end: *My patience is going to give out soon.* **give over** *infml* stop. **give over to** use or intend to be used for: *Tomorrow is given over to discussion.* **give rise to** cause; bring about. **give up** 1 stop (doing something). 2 admit defeat. 3 lose: *I've given up hope of finding her.* 4 deliver: *The thief gave himself up to the police.* 5 abandon (a belief). **given** past participle of **give. giver** *nc* one who gives.

glacier ('glæsɪə*) *nc* a long mass of ice flowing very slowly down a mountain. **glacial** ('gleɪsɪəl) *adj* to do with ice.

glad (glæd) *adj* **-der, -dest** 1 happy; pleased. 2 ready; willing: *I'd be glad to help you.* 3 causing joy: *glad news.* **gladly** *adv* **gladness** *nu*

glade (gleɪd) *nc* an open space in a wood or forest.

gladiator ('glædɪeɪtə*) *nc* a man who fought with a sword to entertain people in ancient Rome.

glamour *US* **glamor** ('glæmə*) *nu* attractiveness, esp. in a woman or in a job. **glamorous** *adj* having glamour.

glance (glɑːns) *vi* (often followed by **at**) look for short time: *She glanced at her watch.* **glance off** hit (something) and continue in a slightly different direction: *The ball glanced off his arm.* **glance over** or **through** read bits of: *I'll just glance through the newspaper.* ●*nc* 1 a short look. 2 the act of glancing off something. **at a glance** immediately; with one look.

gland (glænd) *anatomy, zoology nc* a part that makes a substance for the body to use or get rid of. **glandular** ('glændjʊlə*) *adj*

glare (gleə*) *vi* 1 (often followed by **at**) look angrily. 2 be very bright or shiny. 3 (often followed by **at**) be clear for (someone) to see or understand: *Doesn't your mistake glare at you?* ●*nu* a bright light or shine.

glass (glɑːs) 1 *nu* a hard, clear substance that lets through light and is used for windows, bottles, etc. *nc* 2 a glass container for drinking from. 3 the amount of drink held by a glass: *a glass of wine.* 4 *(pl)* a pair of lenses in a frame worn in front of the eyes, esp. for improving one's sight. **glassware** ('glɑːsweə*) *nu* objects made of glass, esp. for drinking or eating from. **glassy** *adj* **-ier, -iest** 1 like glass, 2 cold; expressionless: *a glassy stare.*

glaze (gleɪz) *vt* 1 put glass in (windows, etc.). 2 cover (a pot, plate, etc.) with a liquid that turns to glass. 3 give a shiny covering to (food, paper, etc.). ●*nu* 1 the liquid used to glaze a pot, plate, etc. 2 a substance used to make something shiny. **glazier** ('gleɪzɪə*) *nc* a person who glazes.

gleam (gliːm) *vi* shine as a narrow line of weak light that comes and goes. ●*nc* 1 a light that gleams. 2 a short period or small amount: *a gleam of understanding.*

glean ('gliːn) *vt* 1 collect (something, such as information) in small amounts. 2 gather (grain) after corn has been harvested.

glee (gliː) *nu* joy; happiness. **gleeful** *adj*

glen (glen) *nc* a narrow mountain valley.

glib (glɪb) *adj* **-ber, -best** too easy or ready: *a glib answer; a glib speaker.*

glide (glaɪd) *vi* 1 move quietly or smoothly. 2 (of a plane) fly without power. 3 fly a glider. ●*nc* an act of gliding. **glider** *nc* a plane without engines.

glimmer ('glɪmə*) *vi* shine weakly. ●*nc* 1 a weak light. 2 a small amount: *a glimmer of hope.*

glimpse (glɪmps) *nc* a very short look. ●*vt* see for a very short time.

glint (glɪnt) *vi* (of something shiny, esp. metal) shine or flash brightly: *His buttons glinted in the sunlight.* ●*nc* a reflected flash of light.

glisten ('glɪsən) *vi* shine or flash repeatedly: *the glistening stars.*

glitter ('glɪtə*) *vi* shine brightly and repeatedly: *The Queen's jewellery glittered.* ●*nu* showy brightness.

gloat (gləʊt) *vi* (often followed by **over**) be glad (about someone's bad luck, etc.).

globe (gləʊb) *nc* 1 a model of the world: see picture. 2 any round or nearly round object, such as one made of glass round a lamp. **global** *adj* to do with the whole world.

globule ('glɒbjuːl) *nc* a small globe, esp. a drop of liquid. **globular** ('glɒbjʊlə*) *adj*

gloom (gluːm) *nu* 1 darkness. 2 sadness. **gloomy** *adj* **-ier, -iest** 1 (of the sky, etc.) dark. 2 looking sad.

globe

glorify ('glɔːrɪfaɪ) *vt* 1 make glorious. 2 honour; praise. 3 make (something) seem better than it is: *This restaurant is nothing more than a glorified café.*

glorious ('glɔːrɪəs) *adj* 1 having glory. 2 splendid.

glory ('glɔːrɪ) *nu* 1 praise; honour. 2 the quality of being splendid. 3 *nc, pl* **-ries** something glorious. ● *vi* (followed by **in**) pride oneself (on).

gloss[1] (glɒs) *nc* a shine on a smooth surface: *gloss paint.* ● *vt* give a gloss to. **gloss over** give a falsely attractive appearance to. **glossy** *adj* **-ier, -iest.**

gloss[2] *nc* a short explanation or translation of a word or expression. ● *vt* give a gloss for. **glossary** ('glɒsərɪ) *nc, pl* **-ries** a list of glosses, esp. of special words, at the end of a book.

glove (glʌv) *nc* a garment for the hand, usually with separate fingers.

glow (gləʊ) *nu* a steady light, esp. from something hot. ● *vi* 1 give off a glow, esp. by burning without flames. 2 look or feel well, pleased, etc.: *He glowed with pride.* 3 be warm or red in the face. **glow-worm** *nc* a small animal that gives off light.

glower ('glaʊə*) *vi* stare angrily.

glucose ('gluːkəʊz) *chemistry nu* a type of sugar.

glue (gluː) *ncu* a (type of) substance used to stick things together. ● *vt* (often followed by **to**) stick with glue.

glum (glʌm) *adj* **-mer, -mest** looking or feeling unhappy.

glut (glʌt) *nc* too much, for example of something harvested, such as corn.

glutton ('glʌtən) *nc* a greedy person.

glycerol ('glɪsərɒl) *nu* also **glycerine** ('glɪsəriːn) a thick, sweet, clear liquid used in some medicines or for making explosives, etc.

gnash (næʃ) *vti* strike and rub (the teeth) together in anger, etc.

gnat (næt) *nc* a small fly that bites people: see picture at **insects.**

gnaw (nɔː) *vt* wear away (something hard, esp. wood) by biting repeatedly; (sometimes *vi*, followed by **at**): *A mouse has been gnawing at this rope.* 2 make (a hole, etc.) by gnawing.

gnome (nəʊm) *nc* an imagined creature like a little old man, said to guard treasure under the ground: see picture.

gnome

go (gəʊ) *vi* 1 move; travel. 2 leave; depart: *I must go in ten minutes.* 3 lead; point: *The road goes to Rome.* 4 (of a machine, etc.) work: *Is the clock going?* 5 become: *You've gone red!* 6 be; remain: *He had no food, so he went hungry.* 7 make (a noise): *The gun went bang.* 8 act: *Let me show you: go like this.* 9 run; be written: *How does that song go?* 10 run; progress: *It all went well.* 11 fit in; suit: *That chair doesn't go in this room.* 12 fit: *It won't go—it's too big.* 13 be usually put: *Cups go in the cupboard.* 14 be spent: *My money all went on clothes.* 15 be sold: *This house should go for a lot of money.* 16 stop working; break down: *The elastic has gone in my pyjamas.* 17 (often followed by **by**) (of time) pass: *Another hour went by.* ● *nc, pl* **-es** 1 a try: *Have a go at it— you might win!* 2 a turn in a game, etc. **be going to do** be about to do; be on the point of doing. **let oneself go** behave wildly and not mind what other people think. **go about** 1 move from place to place. 2 start working on (a task). 3 be occupied with: *Go about your work!* **go after** follow or chase. **go ahead** 1 start or continue, esp. with permission to do so. 2 travel somewhere before someone else: *I'll go ahead to look for a hotel.* **go along** (often followed by **with**) *infml* agree (with). **go by** 1 pass. 2 judge by: *To go by your face, I'd say you've been running.* **go down with** *infml* start to suffer from (an illness). **go far** help a lot; buy much; extend (to): *This money will go far towards meeting the cost of the new building.* **go for** 1 go to get. 2 apply to: *That goes for you too!* 3 try to get: *I'm going for a prize.* 4 like, prefer, or choose: *I go for the red one.* 5 attack: *When he was rude about my wife, I really went for him.* 6 be to the advantage of: *He's got a lot going for him.* **go in for** 1 enter (a competition). 2 take part in or be keen on: *I go in for wine.* **go off** 1 leave to go (to somewhere or to someone): *He's gone off to work early today.* 2 stop working or coming: *The electricity has gone off again.* 3 (of food) become bad or rotten. 4 stop liking. 5 (of a bomb) explode. 6 happen: *The game went off all* *right*. **go on 1** continue. **2** happen: *What's going on here?* **3** talk a lot. **4** use as a model or example: *This isn't much to go on.* **5** be lit: *The lights went on.* **6** be spent on: *The money will all go on food.* **go out 1** leave a room, house, etc. **2** (of a light or fire) stop shining or burning. **3** stop being fashionable: *Shoes like those went out years ago.* **4** (of a television or radio programme, message, etc.) be sent or broadcast. **5** leave home, etc. to attend an entertainment, party, etc. **6** (of the sea) move out and away from the land: *The sea has gone out.* **go over 1** have an (intended) effect: *His act went over well.* **2** examine; check: *I want to go over our plan again.* **go through 1** examine; check: *Someone has gone through my things.* **2** be approved: *The law has gone through.* **3** use up: *You go through your money quickly.* **4** wear out: *This sock is going to go through soon.* **5** suffer: *She went through great pain.* **go under 1** sink below the surface of water, etc. **2** lose; be beaten; (of a business) fail. **go with 1** travel in the company of. **2** suit; match: *Blue socks don't go with brown shoes.* **go without** not have (something): *I'll go without dinner.*

goad (gəʊd) *vt* (often followed by **into**) cause (someone) to do something, esp. by making him angry: *I was goaded into hitting him.*

goal (gəʊl) *nc* **1** the object or purpose of an action. **2** the end point of a journey. **3** a standing frame through which the ball is to be kicked, etc., in a game such as football. **4** an act of kicking the ball through a goal: *We got five goals.* **goalkeeper** (ˈgəʊl‚kiːpə*) the football player in each team who guards the goal and may handle the ball.

goat (gəʊt) *nc* an animal with horns, kept for its meat, wool, and milk: see picture at **animals.**

gobble (ˈgɒbəl) *vt* eat quickly.

goblet (ˈgɒblɪt) *nc* a metal or glass container for drinking from, without handles and having the drinking bowl connected to the flat bottom by a narrow support.

goblin (ˈgɒblɪn) *nc* an imaginary little creature supposed to do harm.

god (gɒd) *nc* a being or force honoured as the controller of (part of) nature. **God** (gɒd) *n* the being who created and rules everything. **godchild** (ˈgɒdtʃaɪld) *nc, pl* **-dren** a child for whom an adult promises, at its baptism, to see brought up as a Christian. **goddaughter** *nc* a female godchild. **goddess** (ˈgɒdɪs) *nc* a female god. **godfather** *nc* a male godparent. **godly** *adj* **-ier, -iest** (of a person) religious. **godmother** *nc* a female godparent. **godparent** *nc* an adult who promises, at a child's baptism, to see that it is brought up as a Christian. **godson** *nc* a male godchild.

goes (gəʊz) *v* (used with **he, she,** or **it**) a form of **go.** ●*n* plural of **go.**

goggle (ˈgɒgəl) *vi* look with eyes wide open, in surprise, etc. ●*nc* **1** a wide-eyed look. **2** *(pl)* glasses worn to protect the eyes, usually touching the face all round.

go-kart (ˈgəʊkɑːt) *nc* a very small, open racing car.

gold (gəʊld) *nu* a chemical element; a shiny yellow metal used as money and in jewellery, etc.: symbol Au **golden** *adj* **1** made of gold. **2** having the colour of gold. **goldfish** (ˈgəʊldfɪʃ) *nc, pl* **goldfish, goldfishes** a small orange fish. **gold leaf** very thin gold, stuck onto objects as ornament. **goldsmith** (ˈgəʊldsmɪθ) *nc* a person who makes things from gold.

golf (gɒlf) *nu* a game in which a small ball is hit across grass towards and into usually eighteen holes in the ground, one after the other. **golf club** also **club** a metal stick with a flat end used to hit the ball in golf.

golliwog (ˈgɒlɪwɒg) *nc* a soft toy model of a person with a black face.

gondola (ˈgɒndələ) *nc* **1** a boat used in Venice, Italy, to carry about four people and moved with one oar. **2** a container for passengers, under an airship or balloon or one carried on a cable going up a mountain.

gone (gɒn) past participle of **go.**

good (gʊd) *adj* **better, best 1** of high quality; satisfying, suited, enjoyable, valuable, etc. **2** (of food) not rotten. **3** (used after **a**) full; complete; at least: *This job will take a good two hours.* **4** (of a debt) likely to be paid. **5** clever; able: *He's very good at persuading people to do things.* **6** newest or of the best quality: *Don't wear your good shoes in this mud!* **7** large: *A good part of the street is shops.* **good for 1** (of a cheque, etc.) worth (an amount of money). **2** capable of; fit for: *My car's good for another few years.* **have a good time** enjoy oneself. **goodbye** (gʊdˈbaɪ) *interj* (used when leaving someone.) ●*nc* an act of saying 'goodbye'. **good evening** (used when meeting or, sometimes, leaving someone in the evening.) **good-looking** (gʊdˈlʊkɪŋ) attractive. **goodly** (ˈgʊdlɪ) **-ier, -iest 1** pleasing. **2** large: *a goodly fortune.* **good morning** (used when meeting or, sometimes, leaving someone in the morning.) **goodness** *nu* **good night** (used at night when either the speaker or the person spoken to is leaving or going to bed.) **goods** *n pl* things being traded or transported. **goodwill** (gʊdˈwɪl) *nu* **1** kindness. **2** willingness; readiness to do something. **3** the custom of a business that is expected to continue when the business is sold.

goose (guːs) *nc, pl* **geese** a bird that can swim and is larger than a duck.

gooseberry ('gʊzbərɪ) *nc, pl* **-ries** a green, hairy fruit, about 2 cm across, of the gooseberry bush.

gore (gɔː*) *vt* stick a horn or tusk into (a person or animal).

gorge (gɔːdʒ) *nc* a deep, narrow river valley. ● *vti* **1** eat a lot of (food) quickly. **2** *vt* fill (oneself) with food.

gorgeous ('gɔːdʒəs) *adj* **1** very attractive or beautiful. **2** *infml* very pleasant, tasty, etc.

gorilla (gə'rɪlə) *nc* an animal; the largest ape: see picture at **animals**.

gorse (gɔːs) *nu* a bush with yellow flowers and sharp points.

gory ('gɔːrɪ) *adj* **-ier, -iest 1** to do with blood, killings, etc. **2** terrible: *the gory details.*

gosh (gɒʃ) *interj* (used to show surprise.)

gosling ('gɒzlɪŋ) *nc* a young goose.

gospel ('gɒspəl) **1** *nc* the story of the life of Jesus Christ. **2** *nc* a religious message or teaching. **3** *infml nu* complete truth.

gossamer ('gɒsəmə*) *nu* **1** spider's webs. **2** very fine cloth.

gossip ('gɒsɪp) *vi* talk informally, esp. unkindly about other people. ● *ncu* **1** such (a) talk. **2** *nc* a person who gossips.

got (gɒt) past tense and past participle of **get**.

Gothic ('gɒθɪk) *adj, nu* **1** (to do with) the style of buildings put up in Western Europe in the Middle Ages. **2** (to do with) the old-fashioned German printing type.

gotten ('gɒtən) *US* past participle of **get**.

gouge (gaʊdʒ) *vt* **1** cut or pull out: *He gouged a piece out of the tree with his knife.* **2** make by gouging: *He gouged a hole in the tree.* ● *nc* a tool for gouging with.

gourd (gʊəd) *nc* the fruit of certain plants, which is large and hollow, and may be dried and used as a container.

gourmet ('gʊəmeɪ) *French nc* a person with a good judgement of the quality of food or drink.

gout (gaʊt) *nu* a disease causing pain and swelling in joints, esp. in the foot.

govern ('gʌvən) *vt* **1** control the affairs of (a country). **2** influence or control: *What governed such a strange choice?* **governess** *nc* a woman employed to educate children in their own home. **government 1** *nu* the governing of something. **2** *nc* the group of people who govern a country. **governor** *nc* **1** a person in charge of a district, prison, etc. **2** a device that controls the speed of a machine.

gown (gaʊn) *nc* a long garment, such as one worn by a teacher or a woman's evening dress.

grab (græb) *vt* take hold of quickly or with force. ● *nc* **1** an act of grabbing. **2** a device built to pick up things, such as earth.

grace (greɪs) *nu* **1** the beauty of movement, shape, etc. **2** the regard or consideration for others: *She had the grace to go when asked.* **3** *nc* a short prayer said before or after a meal. **graceful** *adj* **gracefully** *adv*

gracious ('greɪʃəs) *adj* **1** showing kindness or courtesy. **2** to do with an easy or comfortable life. **graciously** *adv*

grade (greɪd) *nc* **1** (the people or things in) one of a set of qualities, sizes, abilities, etc.: *These apples are quite big enough for the first grade.* **2** one of a set of marks given for school or university work. ● *vt* put into a grade: *Tea is graded into many different qualities.*

gradient ('greɪdɪənt) *nc* a slope on a road, railway, etc.

gradual ('grædjʊəl) *adj* moving, changing, etc., slowly or a small amount at a time. **gradually** *adv*

graduate ('grædjʊeɪt) **1** *vi* receive a university degree. **2** *vt* put marks on (a container, instrument, etc.) for measuring by. ● ('grædjʊət) *nc* a person who has received a university degree.

graduation (ˌgrædjʊ'eɪʃən) **1** *nu* the act of graduating. **2** *nc* a measuring mark on a container, instrument, etc.

graffiti (grə'fiːtɪ) *n pl* messages, often funny, written on walls, etc., in public places.

graft (grɑːft) *vt* **1** fix (a shoot) from one plant onto another. **2** fix (a part of the body or of someone else's body) onto a part of the body: *He had skin from his leg grafted onto his face.* ● *nc* **1** a grafted shoot. **2** a grafted part of a body. **3** an act of grafting.

grain (greɪn) **1** *ncu* a tall wild grass seed used as food: *grains of corn;* many such seeds: *the grain harvest.* **2** *nu* a particular grass grown for its seeds, such as wheat; corn. **3** *nc* a very small hard piece of something, such as sand. **4** *nu* the direction in which the tiny pieces making up wood, stone, etc., point.

gram (græm) *nc* a measure of weight = 0.001 kg: *abbrev.* **g**

grammar ('græmə*) **1** *nu* the arrangement of the elements of language. **2** *nc* a description of the grammar of a language. **grammar school** *Brit* a school, usually paid for with public money, for children from about eleven to eighteen who are better than others at subjects like languages, mathematics, and science. **grammatical** (grə'mætɪkəl) *adj* **1** to do with grammar. **2** (of language) according to grammar; correct.

gramophone ('græməfəʊn) *old-fashioned n* See **record-player. gramophone record** See **record** (def. 3*).

granary ('grænərɪ) *nc, pl* **-ries** a building for storing harvested grain.

grand (grænd) *adj* **-er, -est 1** large or important: *The grand chief of the district.* **2** splendid: *a grand procession.* **3** final: *The grand total is £40.* **4** *infml* very good: *That's a grand idea.* **grand piano** a piano in which the strings are arranged flat, not upright. **grandstand** ('grændstænd) *nc* a group of seats positioned to give the best view of a game, race, etc.

grandchild ('grændtʃaɪld) *nc, pl* **-ren** a granddaughter or grandson.

granddaughter ('grænd,dɔːtə*) *nc* a daughter of one's child.

grandeur ('grændjʊə*) *nu* the quality of being grand or splendid.

grandfather ('grænd,fɑːðə*) *nc* also *(infml)* **grandad, grandpa** the father of one's father or mother.

grandiose ('grændɪəʊs) *adj* **1** looking grand or splendid. **2** unnecessarily grand.

grandmother ('grænd,mʌðə*) *nc* also *(infml)* **grandma, granny** the mother of one's father or mother.

grandparent ('grænd,peərənt) *nc* a grandfather or grandmother.

grandson ('grændsʌn) *nc* a son of one's child.

granite ('grænɪt) *nu* a very hard light-grey rock much used for building.

grant (grɑːnt) *vt* **1** allow; permit: *My request has been granted.* **2** admit that (something) is true: *I grant you it's cold.* **take (something) for granted 1** suppose (something) to be true. **2** use (something) without knowing its value. ●*nc* an amount of usually public money given for a purpose such as education: *a student grant.*

granule ('grænjuːl) *nc* a **grain** (def. 3). **granulate** ('grænjʊleɪt) *vt* make into grains: *granulated sugar.*

grape (greɪp) *nc* one of a bunch of green or black fruits of the grapevine, eaten or used for making wine: see picture at **fruits.**

grapevine ('greɪpvaɪn) **1** *nc* the plant on which grapes grow. **2** *infml nu* an informal way of hearing news: *I heard about it on the teachers' grapevine.* **sour grapes** a saying that one does not want something because one knows that one cannot get it anyway.

grapefruit ('greɪpfruːt) *nc, pl* **grapefruit, grapefruits** a large, sour, yellow citrus fruit.

graph (grɑːf) *nc* a drawing using lines or dots to represent any number of pairs or sets of figures: see picture.

graphic ('græfɪk) *adj* **1** to do with drawing or writing: *graphic arts.* **2** (of a story, description, etc.) good; clear. **graphically** *adv*

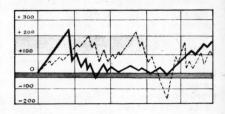

graph

graphite ('græfaɪt) *nu* a type of carbon used as the 'lead' in pencils.

grapple ('græpəl) *vt* **1** grasp (someone), as in a fight. **2** get hold of with a hook. **3** *vi* (followed by **with**) deal (with a problem, etc.). ●*nc* **1** an act of grappling. **2** a kind of hook.

grasp (grɑːsp) *vt* **1** hold or take hold of firmly. **2** understand. **3** *vi* (followed by **at**) try to take hold of. ●*nc* **1** a firm hold. *nu* **2** understanding: *a good grasp of the subject.* **3** ability to do or get: *Victory was within my grasp.*

grass (grɑːs) *ncu* a (type of) plant with long narrow leaves, such as wheat, bamboo or one that is kept cut short in a garden. **grasshopper** ('grɑːs,hɒpə*) *nc* an insect that can jump a long way and make a loud clicking noise: see picture at **insects. grassland** ('grɑːslænd) *ncu* land where mainly grass grows naturally. **grass roots** the basic level of something, esp. politics, as it affects ordinary people. **grassy** *adj* **-ier, -iest.**

grate¹ (greɪt) *nc* a frame of metal bars for holding the burning wood, coal, etc., in a fire.

grate² *vt* **1** cut into small pieces by rubbing against a surface with cutting edges sticking out from it. **2** make a noise by rubbing (rough surfaces) together. **3** *vi* (of rough surfaces) make a noise by rubbing together.

grateful ('greɪtfʊl) *adj* expressing gratitude or feeling thankful. **gratefully** *adv*

gratify ('grætɪfaɪ) *vt* **1** please. **2** act according to (an urge, desire, etc.).

grating ('greɪtɪŋ) *nc* a set of metal bars crossing each other, used, for example, to let water flow through a wall.

gratitude ('grætɪtjuːd) *nu* appreciation of a kindness received.

gratuity (grə'tjuːɪtɪ) *nc* money freely given for a service, on top of any charge; **tip³.**

grave¹ (greɪv) *adj* **-r, -st** serious, esp. dangerous: *in grave difficulty.* **gravely** *adv*

grave² nc a place where a dead person is buried in the ground. **gravestone** (ˈgreɪv-stəʊn) a piece of stone over a grave giving the name of the person buried there. **graveyard** (ˈgreɪvjɑːd) a piece of land where graves are dug, esp. around a church.

gravel (ˈgrævəl) nu small stones dug out of the ground and used to make roads, etc.

graven (ˈgreɪvən) archaic adj carved: a graven image.

gravitate (ˈgrævɪteɪt) vi (followed by **towards** or **to**) 1 be moved by gravity. 2 infml move slowly or be attracted: All the men gravitated to one end of the room.

gravity (ˈgrævɪtɪ) nu also **gravitation** (ˌgrævɪˈteɪʃən) the force that pulls things towards the centre of the earth or another planet or star. 2 graveness; seriousness: the gravity of the situation.

gravy (ˈgreɪvɪ) nu a liquid food made from the juice of cooked meat.

gray (greɪ) US adj see **grey**.

graze¹ (greɪz) vi (of animals) eat (growing grass, etc.) in a field; (sometimes vt) allow (animals) to eat grass, etc.

graze² vti touch or scratch (something, esp. the skin) lightly: I grazed my knee on the ground; The bus was so wide it only just grazed past. ● nc a place where something has been grazed: Is that a graze on your knee?

grease (griːs) nu soft fat or soft, solid oil, used esp. to make machines work smoothly. ● vt put grease on. **greasy** adj **-ier, -iest**.

great¹ (greɪt) adj **-er, -est** 1 large in size or number. 2 lasting a long time; unusually long: a great while; He lived to a great age. 3 important: a great change. 4 very clever, able, etc.: a great writer. 5 keen: a great stamp collector. 6 infml good, enjoyable, etc.: Have a great time! **Great War** See **World War I** under **world**. **greatly** adv **greatness** nu

great² adj (used as a prefix to indicate a child of a grandchild, a parent of a grand-parent, or an aunt or uncle of a father or mother): great-grandchildren; a great-grandfather.

greed (griːd) nu wanting too much of something, esp. food. **greedy** adj **-ier, -iest**.

green (griːn) adj **-er, -est** 1 of the colour of, for example, growing grass. 2 looking ill, esp. seasick. 3 not having had much experience. 4 (of fruit) not yet ripe. 5 (of meat) not smoked or cured: green ham. ● ncu 1 a green colour. nc 2 a piece of land covered with grass in the middle of a village. 3 (pl) green vegetables. **green belt** a ring of land around a town, on which most building is forbidden. **green fingers** infml a great ability to make plants grow: He's got green fingers. **greengage** (ˈgriːngeɪdʒ) nc a fruit; a green variety of plum. **greengrocer** (ˈgriːnˌgrəʊsə*) nc a person who sells fruit and vegetables. **greenhouse** (ˈgriːnhaʊs) nc a building with glass roof and walls, used for growing plants in. **greenish** (ˈgriːnɪʃ) adj of a colour that can almost be called green.

greet (griːt) vt 1 say something, esp. welcoming, on meeting (someone). 2 meet; receive. **greeting** nc 1 an act of greeting. 2 (often pl) a friendly message.

gregarious (grɪˈgeərɪəs) adj 1 fond of being with other people. 2 (of animals) living in groups.

grenade (grəˈneɪd) nc a small bomb thrown by hand or fired from a special gun.

grew (gruː) past tense of **grow**.

grey US **gray** (greɪ) adj **-er, -est** 1 having no colour, but darker than white and lighter than black. 2 having grey hair. 3 unclear; doubtful. ● nc a grey tone. **greyhound** (ˈgreɪhaʊnd) nc a tall, thin dog that can run fast. **greyish** (ˈgreɪɪʃ) adj almost or partly grey. **grey matter** 1 the grey, active parts of the brain. 2 infml, humorous the brain.

grid (grɪd) nc 1 a set of crossing lines, drawn, for example, over a map. 2 a system of pipes or wires by which gas, water, or electricity is fed around a country.

griddle (ˈgrɪdəl) nc 1 a flat metal plate for cooking on. 2 a type of wire net for separating large stones, etc., from small ones.

grief (griːf) nu great sadness, esp. at someone's death. **come to grief** meet with failure, an accident, etc.

grievance (ˈgriːvəns) nc a real or imagined cause for complaining.

grieve (griːv) vti (cause to) feel grief.

grievous (ˈgriːvəs) adj 1 very serious: a grievous crime. 2 causing grief.

grill (grɪl) vt 1 cook (food) by heating from just above or from just below. 2 infml question (someone) forcefully. ● nc 1 a device for grilling food. 2 a set of metal bars on which food is grilled. 3 a dish of grilled food. 4 a restaurant where grills are the main food served.

grille (also **grill**) (grɪl) nc 1 a set of metal bars fastened together in a pattern as a screen, etc. 2 also **radiator grille** a set of metal bars on the front of a car, lorry, etc., to let air flow to the engine.

grim (grɪm) adj **-mer, -mest** 1 cruel, forbidding, or merciless. 2 infml unpleasant or unattractive. 3 determined. **grimly** adv

grimace (ˈgrɪməs) nc an expression of the face indicating dislike, disgust, etc. ● vi make a grimace.

grime (graɪm) *nu* dirt, esp. collected on something over a long time.

grin (grɪn) *vi* smile, showing the teeth. ● *nc* a broad smile.

grind (graɪnd) *vt* 1 (often followed by **down to** or **down into**) make (corn, etc.) into small pieces by rubbing. 2 rub (a knife, etc.) in order to make sharp, smooth, etc. 3 rub hard (together): *He is grinding his teeth in anger; This dirt has been ground into the carpet.* ● *nc* 1 an act of grinding. 2 *infml* a long, hard task. **grinder** *nc* a person or machine that grinds. **grindstone** ('graɪndstəʊn) *nc* a stone for grinding knives, etc., on.

grip (grɪp) *vt* 1 hold tightly. 2 hold (a person's) interest greatly: *a gripping story.* ● *nc* 1 a tight hold. 2 a way of holding something: *use the proper grip.* 3 a soft bag with handles. 4 the part of something by which it is held. 5 *nu* understanding or control of something: *You're losing your grip.*

gripe (graɪp) 1 *vi infml* complain, esp. in an annoying way. 2 *vt* cause (someone) pain just below the stomach. ● *nc* 1 *infml* a complaint. 2 a pain just below the stomach.

grisly ('grɪzlɪ) *adj* **-ier, -iest** frightening or unpleasant: *Some children's stories are really very grisly.*

gristle ('grɪsəl) *nu* tough, smooth, white material found in meat, esp. where bones meet.

grit (grɪt) *nu* 1 small hard pieces of stone, earth, etc. 2 courage; toughness of character. ● *vt* spread grit on (esp. an icy road). **grit one's teeth** hold one's teeth firmly together.

grizzly ('grɪzlɪ) *adj* **-ier, -iest** (esp. of hair) partly grey. ● *nc, pl* **-lies** also **grizzly bear** a large grey-brown North American bear.

groan (grəʊn) *nc* a deep noise made by someone who is disapproving, complaining, in pain, etc. ● *vi* 1 give a groan. 2 (usually followed by **with** or **under**) be weighed down (by) or suffer (under): *The chair groaned with his weight.*

grocer ('grəʊsə*) *nc* a person who sells most types of food. **grocery** *nc, pl* **-ries** a shop used by a grocer. **groceries** *n pl* food sold by a grocer.

grog (grɒg) *nu* a drink of spirits, esp. rum, and water. **groggy** *adj* **-ier, -iest** unsteady; not fully in control of one's movements.

groin (grɔɪn) *anatomy nc* the line at the front of each leg where it joins the rest of the body.

groom (gruːm) *nc* 1 a person employed to look after horses. 2 short for **bridegroom.** ● *vt* 1 make (hair, clothes, etc.) neat and tidy. 2 prepare (someone) for a future job or other activity: *I'm grooming my son to succeed me in the family business.* 3 brush and generally look after (a horse).

groove (gruːv) *nc* a long, narrow cut or hollow, as on a record. ● *vt* make a groove in (something).

grope (grəʊp) *vi* (usually followed by **for** or **after**) 1 feel about (for something), esp. in the dark. 2 try with difficulty to find (the right words, etc.). ● *nc* an act of groping.

gross[1] (grəʊs) *nc, pl* **gross** a measure of quantity = 144.

gross[2] *adj* **-er, -est** 1 (of a person) unpleasantly fat. 2 (of a payment) before tax is taken away: *gross wages.* 3 vulgar: *gross behaviour.* 4 serious: *a gross mistake; gross negligence.*

grotesque (grəʊ'tesk) *adj* very strange or unusual.

grotto ('grɒtəʊ) *nc, pl* **-s, -es** a small attractive cave.

ground[1] (graʊnd) 1 *nu* land: *He's lying on the ground; Tree roots go into the ground.* 2 *nc* a piece of land used for something: *a football ground; a landing ground.* **gain ground** make progress in a chase, battle, etc. **get off the ground** be started successfully. **groundless** *adj* without a cause or reason: *Your fears are groundless.* **ground-nut** ('graʊndnʌt) *nc* 1 part of the root of the ground-nut plant, used for food. 2 See **peanut. grounds** *n pl* 1 land surrounding a building. 2 *formal* reasons: *On what grounds are you refusing to let me in?* 3 ground coffee beans at the bottom of a pot or cup. **groundsheet** ('graʊndʃiːt) *nc* a sheet of material that does not let water through, spread on the ground in a tent, etc.

ground[2] *vt* 1 run (a ship) onto a part of the sea bottom that is near the surface. 2 not allow (a plane, pilot, etc.) to fly.

ground[3] past tense and past participle of **grind.**

group (gruːp) *nc* 1 several people or things together. 2 a small number of musicians who play music together. ● *vti* put into or become a group.

grouse[1] (graʊs) *nc, pl* **grouse** a wild bird that is shot for food.

grouse[2] *vi* complain or grumble.

grove (grəʊv) *nc* a small wood.

grovel ('grɒvəl) *vi* 1 lie or creep on the ground, esp. out of fear. 2 say that one is sorry or admit that one is wrong.

grow (grəʊ) 1 *vti* become bigger; develop: *Apples grow on trees; Their friendship grew with time; He's growing a beard.* 2 *vi* become: *It's growing cold.* 3 *vt* plant and help to **grow** (def. 1): *We grow flowers and sell* *them.* **grower** *nc* a person who grows plants. **grow on** become more liked by: *You may not like this music at once, but it'll grow on you.* **grow up 1** become adult; become like older creatures of the same kind. **2** come into being: *The town grew up a long time ago.*

growl (graʊl) *vi* (of an animal) make a deep noise, usually indicating anger. ● *nc* a deep angry sound, esp. made by an animal.

grown (grəʊn) past participle of **grow. grown-up** (ˈgrəʊnʌp) *nc, adj* (an) adult.

growth (grəʊθ) **1** *nu* the act of growing. **2** *nc* something growing: *a good growth of wool.*

grub (grʌb) *vi* look for something: *He was grubbing around in the box.* ● *nc* **1** the young of some insects. **2** *slang nu* food.

grubby (ˈgrʌbɪ) *adj* **-ier, -iest** dirty.

grudge (grʌdʒ) *nc* a feeling of annoyance at someone who has done something one did not like. ● *vt* **1** not want to give or allow (someone something): *I don't grudge you the money I owe you.* **2** not want to (do something).

gruelling *US* **grueling** (ˈgruːəlɪŋ) *adj* very tiring. ● *nc* a very tiring experience.

gruesome (ˈgruːsəm) *adj* horrible; unpleasant: *a gruesome story of murder.*

gruff (grʌf) *adj* **-er, -est 1** unkind or impolite: *a gruff letter.* **2** (of a voice) deep and rough.

grumble (ˈgrʌmbəl) *vi* complain, esp. for a long time. ● *nc* a complaint.

grumpy (ˈgrʌmpɪ) *adj* **-ier, -iest** unhappy and unfriendly.

grunt (grʌnt) *vi, nc* (esp. of pigs) (make) a deep, short noise.

guarantee (ˌgærənˈtiː) *nc* **1** a promise that an article or service will be as good as is claimed. **2** something that makes something else certain to exist or happen: *A guard is our guarantee of safety.* ● *vt* **1** give a **guarantee** (def. 1) for (an article or service). **2** act as a **guarantee** (def. 2) of (something).

guard (gɑːd) *vt* **1** protect from danger. **2** prevent (a prisoner) from escaping. **3** *vi* (followed by **against**) be ready to prevent: *We have to guard against floods.* ● *nc* **1** a person or group of people (esp. police, soldiers, etc.) who guard someone or something. **2** a device covering a moving part of a machine, etc., that protects the user. **3** *Brit* person in charge of a train. **be off (one's) guard** be unready while not watching. **be on (one's) guard** be watchful or ready to defend. **stand guard** (of a soldier) keep watch, as a sentry.

guarded (ˈgɑːdɪd) past tense and past participle of **guard.** ● *adj* (of a question, etc.) careful; not giving away one's opinion, etc.

guardian (ˈgɑːdɪən) *nc* **1** a person appointed to look after the affairs of someone else, esp. a child whose parents are abroad or dead. **2** a person who guards something.

guerrilla (gəˈrɪlə) *nc* a member of a political armed force, usually fighting against a country's regular army.

guess (ges) *vti* **1** have or express an idea of the quantity or nature of (something) without knowing it. **2** guess correctly: *You've guessed it!* ● *nc* a guessed quantity or nature. **guesswork** *nu* guessing.

guest (gest) *nc* **1** a person invited to have a meal, stay at someone's house, etc., without paying. **2** a person staying in a hotel. **3** a person conducting an orchestra, appearing on a television programme, etc., who does not normally do so. **guestroom** a bedroom in a private house that is kept for visitors to stay in.

guidance (ˈgaɪdəns) *nu* **1** the act of guiding or being guided. **2** advice.

Guide (gaɪd) *nc* a member of the Guides, an international organisation that helps girls to develop skills and responsibility.

guide (gaɪd) *vt* **1** lead; show the way to. **2** steer; direct. **3** advise. ● *nc* **1** a person who guides, esp. visitors round a town, building, etc. **2** a book describing a place or explaining a subject. **3** a device that steers a machine part, etc. **4** something used to help one do something correctly.

guild (gɪld) *nc* an organisation, esp. of people with the same job.

guile (gaɪl) *nu* deceitful behaviour; trickery.

guillotine (ˈgɪlətiːn) *nc* **1** a device for cutting off a person's head with a heavy, falling blade: see picture. **2** a machine for cutting a large number of sheets of paper at once. ● *vt* cut off with a guillotine.

guillotine

guilt (gɪlt) *nu* the fact or state of having done something wrong, esp. broken the law. **guilty** *adj* **-ier, -iest 1** having guilt. **2** showing or feeling guilt.

guinea (ˈgɪnɪ) *Brit nc* an old coin and amount of money = £1.05. **guinea-fowl** (ˈgɪnɪfaʊl) *pl* **guinea-fowl** a dark-grey type of hen. **guinea-pig** (ˈgɪnɪpɪg) **1** an animal about 20 cm long that is related to the rat and much used in experiments. **2** a person or thing used in an experiment.

guise (gaɪz) *nc* an appearance, esp. a pretended one: *The thief got in in the guise of a servant.*

guitar (gɪˈtɑː*) *nc* a stringed musical instrument played by pulling or plucking the strings slightly and letting them go: see picture at **musical instruments.**

gulf (gʌlf) *nc* **1** a large part of the sea that reaches some way into the land: *the Persian Gulf.* **2** something that separates, such as a great difference of opinion.

gull (gʌl) *nc* a mainly white bird that lives on or near the sea.

gullet (ˈgʌlɪt) *n* See **oesophagus.**

gullible (ˈgʌlɪbəl) *adj* easy to deceive or cheat.

gully (ˈgʌlɪ) *nc, pl* **-lies 1** a small valley made by water. **2** a channel built to carry water.

gulp (gʌlp) **1** *vt* swallow quickly. **2** *vi* breathe with difficulty because one is surprised, etc. ●*nc* an act of gulping.

gum¹ (gʌm) *anatomy ncu* the flesh out of which the (upper or lower set of) teeth grow.

gum² **1** *nu* a substance used to stick things together. **2** *nc* a type of sweet: *chewing gum.* ●*vt* cover or stick with gum. **gum up 1** (cause to) become blocked. **2** *infml* (cause something) not to work properly.

gun (gʌn) *nc* a weapon that fires a shell or bullet by means of an explosion. **gunboat** (ˈgʌnbəʊt) *nc* a small navy boat fitted with guns. **gunman** (ˈgʌnmən) *nc, pl* **-men** a man carrying a gun, esp. a criminal. **gunner** *nc* a soldier, sailor, etc., who uses larger guns. **gunpowder** (ˈgʌnˌpaʊdə*) *nu* an explosive mixture of chemicals. **gunsmith** (ˈgʌnsmɪθ) *nc* a person who makes small guns. **gun turret** the (usually revolving) structure for a gun fixed to a plane or ship.

gurgle (ˈgɜːgəl) *vi* make the noise of water flowing over rocks or down a pipe. ●*nc* this noise.

guru (ˈgʊruː) *nc* a Hindu or Sikh religious teacher.

gush (gʌʃ) *vi* flow in large quantities. ●*nc* a sudden large flow.

gust (gʌst) *nc* a sudden, strong rush of wind. ●*vi* (of the wind) blow in gusts. **gusty** *adj* **-ier, -iest.**

gut (gʌt) **1** *nc* the lower part of the passage through which food passes in the body; intestine. **2** *nu* a type of string often made from the gut of an animal and used for sewing parts of the body together after they have been cut; also often used for the strings of a musical instrument, etc. **guts** *n pl* **1** the inside parts of the body. **2** *infml* courage; strength of character. ●*vt* **1** remove the guts of (a fish, etc.). **2** burn or remove the inside of (a building).

gutter (ˈgʌtə*) *nc* a channel under the edge of a roof or at the side of a road to carry rain away.

guy¹ (gaɪ) *nc* a rope, wire, etc., used to hold up a tent, aerial, etc.

guy² *nc* **1** *infml* a man or youth. **2** *Brit* a model of Guy Fawkes, made of old clothes, etc., and burned on 5 November.

gymnasium (dʒɪmˈneɪzɪəm) *nc, pl* **-siums, -sia** (zɪə) a large room used for bodily exercise. **gymnast** (ˈdʒɪmnæst) a person who trains in bodily exercise. **gymnastics** (dʒɪmˈnæstɪks) *nu (with singular verb)* exercises for the body, esp. using things to climb up, jump over, etc.

gynaecology (ˌgaɪnɪˈkɒlədʒɪ) *nu* the study and practice of medicine to do with diseases that women get. **gynaecologist** *nc* a doctor working in gynaecology.

gypsum (ˈdʒɪpsəm) *nu* a substance dug out of the ground and used to make plaster, cement, etc.

gypsy (ˈdʒɪpsɪ) *n* See **gipsy.**

H

something directed somewhere: *A hail of shots came at us.* ● *vi* **1** (of hail) fall. **2** move in large numbers or quantities: *Shots hailed round us.* **hailstone** ('heɪlstəʊn) *nc* a piece of hail.

hail² *vt* **1** greet (someone), esp. in a friendly manner. **2** attract the attention of (a ship) by shouting or (a taxi) by waving. ● *ncu* (an example of) hailing.

hair (heə*) **1** *nc* a fine thread growing out of the skin of an animal. **2** *nu* a number of hairs together, esp. on the head: *I've cut my hair.* **haircut** ('heəkʌt) *nc* **1** an act of cutting someone's hair. **2** a style in which someone's hair is cut. **hairdresser** ('heə,dresə*) *nc* a person who cuts and arranges hair. **hairpin** ('heəpɪn) *chiefly Brit nc* a U-shaped pin used to grip a woman's hair and hold it in place. **hairpin bend** a road that curves so as to turn back on itself, esp. on a steep road. **hairy** *adj* **-ier, -iest.**

hale (heɪl) *adj* **-r, -st** strong and healthy: *hale and hearty.*

half (hɑːf) *nc, pl* **halves 1** one of two equal parts of something. **2** either half of a pitch on which football, etc., is played. **3** either half of the time taken for a game of football, etc. **4** half an hour: *It's half-past two.* **5** half a pint, esp. of beer. ● *determiner* a half of: *half the time.* ● *adj* being a half of: *a half pint.* ● *adv* up to a half: *You've only half cooked it; half-empty.* **half-breed** ('hɑːfbriːd) a person with parents of different races. **half-brother** ('hɑːf,brʌðə*) a male with whom one has one parent in common. **half-hearted** *adj* not keen or eager. **half note** *US n* See **minim. half-sister** ('hɑːf,sɪstə*) a female with whom one has one parent in common. **halfway** (,hɑːf'weɪ) *adj, adv* at or to half the distance.

halibut ('hælɪbət) *nc, pl* **halibuts, halibut** a dark green North Atlantic food fish; the largest flatfish: see picture at **fish.**

hall (hɔːl) *nc* **1** a large building or room used for meetings, concerts, etc. **2** the room, in a house or other building, into which the main door leads and off which other rooms lead. **hall of residence** a university building in which students live. **hallmark** ('hɔːlmɑːk) *Brit* a group of letters, numbers, and pictures stamped onto a gold, silver, or platinum object to show its quality. ● *vt* put a hallmark on.

hallelujah (,hælɪ'luːjə) *interj* (used to praise God or express thanks or relief.)

hallo (hə'ləʊ) *interj* See **hello.**

hallow ('hæləʊ) *vt* make holy.

hallucination (hə,luːsɪ'neɪʃən) *nc* the act of thinking one can see something that is not there.

ha (hɑː) *interj* **1** (used to express surprise, victory, etc.) **2** (used two or more times to represent laughter.)

habit ('hæbɪt) *nc* **1** a custom; practice: *Smoking is a bad habit.* **2** a special garment, esp. of a monk or nun. **be in the habit of doing** be used to doing; do frequently.

habitable ('hæbɪtəbəl) *adj* fit for people to live in.

habitat ('hæbɪtæt) *nc* the natural home of a plant or animal.

habitation (,hæbɪ'teɪʃən) **1** *nc* a place where someone or something lives; home. **2** *nu* living in a home.

habitual (hə'bɪtjʊəl) *adj* regular or usual: *my habitual journey to work.* **habitually** *adv*

hack¹ (hæk) *vt* **1** chop roughly or violently. **2** make (a path, etc.) by hacking. **3** kick (someone), esp. in sport. **4** *vi* (often followed by **at**) chop roughly or violently at (something). ● *nc* an act of hacking. **hacksaw** ('hæksɔː) *nc* a saw for metal, with a thin blade stretched in a frame.

hack² *nc* **1** a horse in poor condition or kept only for riding or driving. **2** a not very good writer.

hackneyed ('hæknɪd) *adj* (of an expression, idea, etc.) used so much that it has become boring.

had (hæd unstressed həd, əd) past tense and past participle of **have.**

haddock ('hædək) *nc, pl* **haddock** a North Atlantic food fish: see picture at **fish.**

hadn't ('hædənt) *v* had not.

hadst (hædst) *archaic v* (used with **thou**) a form of **have.**

haemoglobin *US* **hemoglobin** (,hiːmə'gləʊbɪn) *nu* a substance in red blood cells that carries oxygen round the body.

haemorrhage *US* **hemorrhage** ('hemərɪdʒ) **1** *nu* heavy bleeding from broken blood vessels. **2** *nc* an example of this. ● *vi* bleed heavily.

hag (hæg) *nc* **1** an ugly old woman. **2** a witch.

haggard ('hægəd) *adj* looking thin and unwell, esp. from lack of food or sleep.

haggis ('hægɪs) *nc* a Scottish dish of a sheep's heart, liver, etc., boiled with oatmeal in a bag made from its stomach.

haggle ('hægəl) *vi* argue about the price of something.

hail¹ (heɪl) **1** *nu* little balls of ice falling from clouds. **2** *nc* a large number or quantity of

halo ('heɪləʊ) *nc, pl* **-s, -es** a bright ring around the head of a saint or angel in a painting, etc.

halt (hɔːlt) *nc* a stop or pause. ● *vi* **1** pause; come to a stop. **2** *vt* cause to stop. ● *interj* stop!

halting ('hɔːltɪŋ) *adj* (esp. of speech) hesitating.

halve (hɑːv) *vt* **1** divide into two equal parts. **2** lessen by a half. **halves** plural of **half.**

ham (hæm) *nu* meat from the cured upper part of a leg of pork; (sometimes *nc*) a whole piece of this meat. **hamburger** ('hæm,bɜːgə*) *nc* a fried cake of ground beef, often served in a bread roll.

hamlet ('hæmlət) *nc* a very small village.

hammer ('hæmə*) *nc* **1** a hitting tool with a handle and a metal head: see picture at **tools. 2** a similar part of a device that strikes a bell. **3** one of the parts of a piano that strike the strings. ● *vt* hit with a hammer.

hammock ('hæmək) *nc* a piece of material or net hung by both ends for use as a bed: see picture.

hammock

hamper¹ ('hæmpə*) *nc* **1** a covered basket, used esp. for food. **2** *Brit* a hamper and the food in it.

hamper² *vt* make it difficult for (someone or something) to move or work.

hamster ('hæmstə*) *nc* a small animal related to the rat and often kept as a pet.

hand (hænd) *nc* **1** the end part of each arm, including the thumb, fingers, and palm. **2** a pointer on a clock or watch. **3** an influence or part in something: *You had a hand in this.* **4** a direction or position: *on the left-hand side.* **5** a worker, esp. on a ship or farm: *a deck hand; a farm hand.* **6** a hand-writing: *a clear hand.* **7** *archaic* a promise of marriage: *He asked for her hand in marriage.* **8** *nu* (after **first, second,** etc.) a series of persons through whom something passes: *We heard the news at first hand; The clothes were bought second-hand.* ● *vt* pass (someone something) by hand. ● *adj* for use by or in the **hand** (def. 1): *a hand tool.* **at hand** near; happening soon. **on the one hand... on the other hand** (used before each of two points of comparison or sides of an argument.) **take in hand**

control; organise. **hand down** pass from one generation to the next. **hand in** give (a form, examination paper, etc.) to the correct person or place. **hand on 1** give to the next person. **2** give to those who succeed or come after one. **hand out** give (several things) to different people. **hand-out** ('hændaʊt) **1** food, money, etc., given, esp. to someone poor. **2** a handed-out advertisement, sheet of notes, etc. **hand over** deliver; surrender: *Hand over your money.*

handbag ('hændbæg) *nc* a small bag for personal belongings carried by a woman.

handbook ('hændbʊk) *nc* a book describing a place, how a machine works, etc.

handcuff ('hændkʌf) *nc* one of a pair of rings connected by a chain and locked round a prisoner's wrists. ● *vt* put handcuffs on.

handful ('hændfʊl) *nc* **1** the quantity that a hand can hold. **2** a few: *a handful of soldiers.*

handicap ('hændɪkæp) *nc* **1** something that prevents one from doing something or makes it more difficult. **2** a race or competition in which those taking part are given handicaps so that all have an equal chance of winning. ● *vt* be or give a handicap to **the handicapped** people with handicaps of the mind or body such as blindness.

handicraft ('hændɪkrɑːft) **1** *nc* an activity done with the hands, such as sewing. **2** *n* objects made in such an activity.

handiwork ('hændɪwɜːk) *nu* **1** objects made with the hands. **2** doing; result of someone's efforts: *The new laws are the president's handiwork.*

handkerchief ('hæŋkətʃiːf) *nc* a square of cloth or soft paper carried about and used to blow one's nose on, etc.

handle ('hændəl) *nc* the part of a tool, container, etc., by which it is held or moved. ● *vt* **1** use or feel with the hands. **2** deal with (a customer, situation, etc.); do something about. **handlebar** ('hændəlbɑː* *nc* either of the two handles with which a bicycle is steered.

handmade (,hænd'meɪd) *adj* made by hand not by a machine.

handmaid ('hændmeɪd) also **handmaiden** ('hændmeɪdən) *archaic nc* a female servant

handshake ('hændʃeɪk) *nc* the act of shaking hands.

handsome ('hænsəm) *adj* **-r, -st 1** (esp. of man) good-looking. **2** generous: *a handsome gift.* **handsomely** *adv*

handwriting ('hænd,raɪtɪŋ) **1** *nu* writing done by hand with a pen or pencil. **2** *nc* a style of writing: *They all have good handwritings.*

handy ('hændɪ) *adj* **-ier, -iest 1** close by; easily reached. **2** useful; easy to use. **3** good at doing things with one's hands. **come**

handy be useful. **handyman** ('hændɪmæn) *nc, pl* **-men** a man who does many different jobs with his hands.

hang (hæŋ) *vti* **1** fasten or be fastened, esp. from above: *Hang your coat behind the door; a flag hung from the window.* **2** (past tense and past participle **hanged**) kill or be killed by hanging from a rope round the neck. **3** *vi* be held above something: *Clouds hung in the valley.* **4** *vt* cover or decorate (a wall) with (wallpaper, pictures, etc.). **get the hang of** understand or be able to do: *I can't get the hang of this work.* **hang about** or **around** be present without doing anything useful or important; waste time. **hang back** not want to do something or go somewhere. **hangman** ('hæŋmən) *nc, pl* **-men** a man who hangs criminals. **hang on 1** hold; hold on to: *Hang on or you'll fall off.* **2** *infml* wait: *Can you hang on a minute?* **hangover** ('hæŋ,əʊvə*) *nc* an unpleasant feeling experienced some time after one drinks too much alcohol. **hang up 1** put (something) on a hook, etc. **2** replace a telephone receiver when finishing a call.

hangar ('hæŋə*) *nc* a building in which planes are kept.

hanger-on (,hæŋər'ɒn) *nc, pl* **hangers-on** (,hæŋəz'ɒn) a follower or companion, esp. one who is not welcome, does not help in any way, etc.

hanker ('hæŋkə*) *vi* (usually followed by **after**) want (something) very much: *He's hankering after a bicycle.*

haphazard (hæp'hæzəd) *adj* careless; not regular or in any order. ●*adv* not regularly.

hapless ('hæplɪs) *adj* unlucky.

happen ('hæpən) *vi* **1** (of an event) exist in time; take place. **2** (followed by **to**) (esp. of death) be experienced by: *I shan't know what to do if anything happens to you.* *vt* **3** (used with **it** and followed by a clause) be the case: *It happens that I don't know.* **4** (followed by an infinitive) chance: *We happened to meet.* **happen on** find by chance.

happy ('hæpɪ) *adj* **-ier, -iest 1** joyful: *You look happy; a happy birthday.* **2** lucky: *a happy result.* **happily** *adv* **happiness** *nu* **happy-go-lucky** (,hæpɪgəʊ'lʌkɪ) *adj* not minding what happens.

harangue (hə'ræŋ) *vt* talk to loudly or angrily.

harass ('hærəs) *vt* worry or annoy repeatedly.

harbinger ('hɑːbɪndʒə*) *literary nc* a person or thing indicating an arrival or other event: *a harbinger of bad news.*

harbour *US* **harbor** ('hɑːbə*) *nc* a place where ships can shelter from the open sea. ●*vt* give shelter to.

hard (hɑːd) *adj* **-er, -est 1** firm; not soft. **2** difficult to do, understand, etc. **3** needing much effort: *hard work.* **4** difficult to bear: *a hard life.* **5** unkind, demanding, or cruel: *a hard master.* **6** (of water) containing salts that make more soap necessary for washing. **7** (of drugs and alcoholic drink) strong. ●*adv* with much force or energy: *work hard; hit it hard.* **hard-boiled** ('hɑːd'bɔɪld) *adj* (of an egg) boiled for long enough to make it all hard. **harden** ('hɑːdən) *vti* make or become hard or harder. **hard-headed** (,hɑːd'hedɪd) *adj* tough; not letting one's business decisions be influenced by likes, dislikes, etc. **hardness** *nu* **hard up** not having much money. **hard-working** (,hɑːd'wɜːkɪŋ) *adj* able and willing to work hard.

hardly ('hɑːdlɪ) *adv* **1** only just: *I've hardly had time to sit down.* **2** not; not really: *I can hardly say that!* **hardly ever** very rarely.

hardship ('hɑːdʃɪp) *ncu* (something that causes) suffering, such as lack of food.

hardware ('hɑːdweə*) *nu* **1** metal tools and containers, esp. for gardening or cooking. **2** machines and other devices, esp. making up a computer.

hardwood ('hɑːdwʊd) *nu* the wood of a tree such as oak or elm, as compared with pine or fir.

hardy ('hɑːdɪ) *adj* **-ier, -iest 1** (of a person) tough. **2** (of a plant) able to live outside in winter.

hare (heə*) *nc, pl* **hares, hare** an animal like a rabbit but slightly larger and with longer ears. ●*vi Brit infml* move fast: *He hared off down the road.*

harem ('hɑːriːm) *nc* **1** the part of a Moslem house for wives or other women. **2** the women who live in this.

haricot ('hærɪkəʊ) *nc* also **haricot bean** a white bean used as food and often dried for keeping.

hark (hɑːk) *archaic vi* listen. **hark back** return to a subject or idea.

harlequin ('hɑːlɪkwɪn) *nc* a clown who wears a black mask and clothes made of squares of different coloured materials.

harlot ('hɑːlət) *archaic nc* a prostitute.

harm (hɑːm) *vt, nu* (cause) damage or injury (to). **harmful** ('hɑːmfʊl) *adj* causing harm. **harmless** ('hɑːmlɪs) *adj* not causing harm.

harmony ('hɑːmənɪ) **1** *ncu, pl* **-nies** a group of musical notes played together. **2** *nu* agreement between people. **harmonic** (hɑː'mɒnɪk) *adj* to do with harmony. ●*nc* a part of a musical sound, higher than the note one hears, that determines the quality of the sound. **harmonica** (hɑː'mɒnɪkə) *nc* a small musical instrument in which strips of metal are made to sound by the player blowing and sucking air across them. **harmonious** (hɑː'məʊnɪəs) *adj* **1** in agreement. **2** (of music) having a pleasant harmony. **harmonise 1** *vti* make or become harmonious. **2** *vt* give harmonies to (a tune).

harness ('hɑːnɪs) *nc* **1** the straps tied to a horse by which it pulls a vehicle. **2** the straps used to fasten something to a person: *a parachute harness*. ● *vt* **1** put a harness on (a horse). **2** (followed by **to**) connect (a horse) to a vehicle with a harness. **3** get power from: *to harness the wind*.

harp (hɑːp) *nc* a large musical instrument with strings played directly with the fingers: see picture at **musical instruments. harp on** talk or write about in a long, boring way.

harpoon (hɑː'puːn) *nc* a pointed stick fired or thrown at whales or fish. ● *vt* hit with a harpoon.

harpsichord ('hɑːpsɪkɔːd) *nc* a musical instrument like a piano but in which the strings are not hit but pulled and let go.

harrow ('hærəʊ) *nc* a device pulled over the ground to break up the earth: see picture. ● *vt* use a harrow on. **harrowing** *adj* worrying; troubling.

harrow

harsh (hɑːʃ) *adj* **-er, -est 1** cruel. **2** rough or unpleasant to the senses: *harsh colours*. **harshly** *adv*

harvest ('hɑːvɪst) *nc* the gathering of something one has grown when it is ripe: *this year's corn harvest*. ● *vt* gather (something one has grown).

has (hæz unstressed həz, əz) *v* (used with **he, she,** or **it**) a form of **have.**

hash (hæʃ) *nc* a dish of mixed meat and vegetables cut up small. **make a hash of** *infml* do (something) badly.

hashish ('hæʃiːʃ) *nu* a drug made from the hemp plant.

hasn't ('hæzənt) *v* has not.

hasp (hɑːsp) *nc* a device for fastening a door, etc.

hast (hæst) *archaic v* (used with **thou**) a form of **have.**

haste (heɪst) *nu* speed in doing something. **hasten** ('heɪsən) *vti* (cause to) hurry. **hasty** ('heɪstɪ) *adj* **-ier, -iest** fast; hurried. **hastily** *adv*

hat (hæt) *nc* a garment for the head.

hatch¹ (hætʃ) *nc* **1** also **hatchway** a flat opening in the deck of a ship. **2** the covering for a hatchway. **3** an opening in a wall between two rooms.

hatch² *vi* **1** (of a young animal) come out of its egg. **2** (of an egg) break open and let out the young animal. *vt* **3** cause (a young animal or an egg) to hatch. **4** think up (a plan, etc.). ● *nc* **1** the act of hatching. **2** a group of animals that have just hatched.

hatchet ('hætʃɪt) *nc* a cutting tool used by hitting; small axe. **bury the hatchet** stop fighting or arguing.

hate (heɪt) *vt* dislike very strongly. ● *nu* strong dislike. **hateful** ('heɪtfʊl) *adj* causing hate. **hatred** ('heɪtrɪd) *nu* hate.

hath (hæθ) *archaic v* (used with **he, she,** or **it**) a form of **have.**

haughty ('hɔːtɪ) *adj* **-ier, -iest** unfriendly because one thinks one is better than other people. **haughtily** *adv*

haul (hɔːl) *vt* **1** pull; drag. **2** move (goods), esp. by road. ● *nc* **1** the act of hauling. **2** (the amount of) something caught. **3** a distance travelled.

haunch (hɔːntʃ) *nc* the place where a (back) leg joins the body.

haunt (hɔːnt) *vt* **1** (of a ghost) visit (a place or person). **2** be repeatedly in the thoughts of: *haunted by fear*. ● *nc* (often *pl*) a place often visited: *one of my favourite haunts*.

have (hæv unstressed həv, əv) *v* **1** (used before a past participle to express a completed action): *He has finished; I shall have gone; She would have lived.* *vt* **2** possess; own. **3** receive (a present). **4** suffer from (an illness). **5** take part in (a conversation). **6** cause to (be done): *I had my car repaired.* **7** force to (do): *I'll have him go away.* **8** eat or drink. **9** bear (children or young animals). **10** (followed by an infinitive) must: *I had to see you again.* **have back** receive (something one had before). **have in** have (someone) do a job for one: *We'll have a painter in.* **have on 1** wear (clothes). **2** have (an appointment): *What have you got on this evening?* **3** tell (someone) a lie for fun. **have out 1** settle (an argument, etc.) by fighting or discussion. **2** have (a tooth) taken out. **have round** invite (someone) to one's house. **have to do with** See under **do. have up** charge (with an offence): *John was had up for stealing.*

haven ('heɪvən) *nc* **1** a port for ships. **2** a shelter or protection.

haven't ('hævənt) *v* have not.

haversack ('hævəsæk) *nc* a strong cloth bag for carrying on the back or shoulder.

havoc ('hævək) *nu* confusion; disorder.

haw (hɔː) *nc* fruit of the hawthorn.

hawk¹ (hɔːk) *nc* **1** a bird that feeds on small animals: see picture at **birds**. **2** *infml* a person who believes in taking very strong action, esp. in military matters.

hawk² *vt* offer for sale in the street. **hawker** *nc*

hawthorn ('hɔːθɔːn) *nc* a bush with sharp points and white or pink flowers.

hay (heɪ) *nu* grass, cut and dried as food for animals. **hay fever** *nu* sneezing and watering of the eyes caused by pollen from plants. **haystack** ('heɪstæk) *nc* a large pile of hay outside.

hazard ('hæzəd) **1** *nu* danger. **2** *nc* something dangerous. **hazardous** ('hæzədəs) *adj* dangerous.

haze (heɪz) *nu* dust or tiny drops of water in the air that make it difficult to see through. **hazy** *adj* **-ier**, **-iest**.

hazel ('heɪzəl) *nc* a shrub producing round nuts that are eaten. **hazelnut** *nc* this nut.

H-bomb ('eɪtʃbɒm) also **hydrogen bomb** *nc* a very powerful atomic exploding device that uses hydrogen.

he (hiː unstressed hɪ, ɪ) *pron* (used of a male person or animal or one that might be male or female): *He is a good boy; Does everyone know what he wants?*

head (hed) *nc* **1** the part of a body containing the brain, mouth, etc. **2** a person in charge. **3** *pl* **head** one single person or animal: *£20 a head; ten head of cattle.* **4** *(usually pl)* the side of a coin showing the head of a king, etc. **5** the large end of a hammer, pin, etc. **6** the large top part of a plant such as a cabbage. **7** the upper end of a river, etc. **8** the top of something: *at the head of the list.* **9** the end of a bed on which one's head rests. **10** also **recording head** the part of a tape-recorder that actually records onto the tape. **11** an ability to apply one's mind to something: *She's got a good head for figures.* **12** *nu* a layer of bubbles on top of beer. ●*vt* **1** be at the top or front of. **2** give a title or heading to (a letter, article, etc.). **3** hit (a football) with one's head. **4** point (a ship) in a particular direction. *vi* **5** be pointed in a particular direction. **6** (followed by **for**) travel towards. **come to a head** (of a situation) come to a crisis or point when a problem must be solved, etc. **keep** or **lose one's head** remain or stop being calm. **headache** ('hedeɪk) *nc* **1** a pain in the head. **2** a problem. **headdress** ('heddres) *nc* an ornamental head covering. **headland** ('hedlənd) *nc* a point of land sticking out into the sea. **headlight** *nc* a powerful light shining forward on the front of a car, train, etc. **headline** *nc* a heading for a newspaper or magazine article. **headman** ('hedmən) *nc, pl* **-men** the chief of a

tribe. **headmaster** (hed'mɑːstə*) or **headmistress** (hed'mɪstrɪs) *nc* the man or woman in charge of a school. **headphones** ('hedfəʊnz) *n pl* a device held over the ears for listening to radio, a record, etc.: see picture. **headquarters** (hed'kwɔːtəz) *n pl* the building from which an army or other organisation is controlled.

headphones

heading ('hedɪŋ) *nc* **1** a title for a letter, article, etc. **2** the direction in which a ship is pointing.

headlong ('hedlɒŋ) *adv* head first: *He fell headlong through the window.*

headstrong ('hedstrɒŋ) *adj* not able to be persuaded to change one's mind.

headway ('hedweɪ) *nu* (esp. of a ship) progress forward.

heady ('hedɪ) *adj* **-ier**, **-iest** (esp. of alcoholic drink) likely to make one excited.

heal (hiːl) *vti* (cause to) become healthy again: *to heal the sick; That cut healed quickly.*

health (helθ) *nu* the state of not having any illnesses. **health visitor** a nurse who visits old and sick people in their homes. **healthy** *adj* **-ier**, **-iest 1** having good health. **2** helpful to good health: *a healthy meal.* **3** showing good health: *She has a healthy appearance.* **healthily** *adv*

heap (hiːp) *nc* **1** an untidy pile. **2** *infml* (often *pl*) a large number or quantity: *heaps of money.* ●*vt* (often followed by **up**) put into a heap.

hear (hɪə*) *vt* **1** notice (a sound): *He thought he heard a noise.* **2** listen to: *I heard a play on the radio.* **3** *vi* learn; receive information: *Have you heard about my accident?* **hearing 1** *nu* the ability to hear. **2** *nc* the examination of a case in law. **hearsay** ('hɪəseɪ) *nu* information that one has only heard and does not know to be true.

heard (hɜːd) past tense and past participle of **hear**.

hearse (hɜːs) *nc* a special car used to carry a dead person to be buried or burnt.

heart (hɑːt) *nc* **1** the part of the body that pumps blood. **2** the part of a person said to experience feelings, esp. love. **3** the central or most important part. **4** a shape like that of the heart. **5** a playing-card with a red shape like this on it. **break someone's heart** cause to be very sad. **by heart** so well that one can speak from memory: *Have you learnt this poem by heart?* **lose heart** stop being enthusiastic. **take something to heart** be upset about something. **heartache** (ˈhɑːteɪk) *nu* much worry or misery. **heart attack** a sudden failure of the heart to work properly. **heartbeat** (ˈhɑːtbiːt) the noise of the pumping action of the heart. **heart-breaking** (ˈhɑːtbreɪkɪŋ) *adj* (of an event) very sad. **heartburn** (ˈhɑːtbɜːn) *nu* a feeling like burning in the chest. **heartfelt** (ˈhɑːtfelt) *adj* strongly felt: *my heartfelt thanks.* **heartless** *adj* cruel; unkind.

hearth (hɑːθ) *nc* the part of a floor on which a fire is made.

hearty (ˈhɑːtɪ) *adj* **-ier, -iest 1** friendly; enthusiastic: *a hearty welcome.* **2** (of a meal) large and satisfying. **heartily** *adv*

heat (hiːt) *nu* **1** the form of energy of which the amount is measured as temperature; warmth. **2** strong feeling: *She regretted what she had said in the heat of the moment.* ●*vt* make hot or hotter. **heated** *adj* **1** made hot or hotter. **2** (of an argument, etc.) excited. **heater** *nc* a device that heats something. **heatwave** (ˈhiːtweɪv) *nc* a long period of unusually hot weather.

heath (hiːθ) *ncu* (a piece of) open, sandy land with few plants growing.

heathen (ˈhiːðən) *nc* **1** a person who is not, by religion, a Christian, Jew, or Moslem. **2** an uncivilised person. ●*adj* to do with heathens.

heather (ˈheðə*) *nc* a plant with small white, pink, or purple flowers that grows esp. on heaths.

heave (hiːv) *vt* **1** move with difficulty. **2** throw with an effort. **3** give (a sigh, etc.). **4** *vi* rise and fall strongly: *His chest heaved after his run.* **heave to 1** (of a ship) stop. **2** stop (a ship).

heaven (ˈhevən) **1** *nu* the place or state of being with God after death. *nc* **2** *(pl) literary* the sky. **3** a place or state that brings great happiness. **heavenly** *adj*

heavy (ˈhevɪ) *adj* **-ier, -iest 1** weighing a lot; not light. **2** extreme; strong, serious, or in great quantity: *heavy traffic.* **3** forceful: *a heavy blow.* **4** (of food) difficult to digest. **5** (of music or literature) serious or boring. **heavily** *adv* **heavyweight** (ˈhevɪweɪt) *nc* a heavy person or thing, esp. a boxer.

heckle (ˈhekəl) *vt* shout a question or comment at (a speaker, actor, etc.).

hectare (ˈhektɑː*) *nc* a measure of area = 10,000 sq m.

hectic (ˈhektɪk) *adj* very busy or excited.

he'd (hiːd) he had or he would.

hedge (hedʒ) *nc* **1** a row of bushes, used esp. for protection or as a border. **2** some other kind of protection. ●*vt* provide with a hedge of some kind.

hedgehog (ˈhedʒhɒg) *nc* a small animal covered with spines, usually seen only at night: see picture at **animals**.

hedgerow (ˈhedʒrəʊ) *nc* a wild hedge in the country.

heed (hiːd) *nu* attention; notice. ●*vt* pay attention to; take notice of. **heedless** *adj*

heel¹ (hiːl) *nc* **1** the back part of the foot. **2** the part of a sock, shoe, etc., round or under the heel. ●*vt* put a new heel on (a shoe). **be under the heel of** be cruelly dominated by (someone, an evil government, etc.). **take to one's heels** run away.

heel² *vi* (of a ship) lean over. ●*nu* the lean of a ship.

hefty (ˈheftɪ) *adj* **-ier, -iest** heavy, powerful, or solid.

hegemony (hɪˈgemənɪ) *nu* control of one country by another.

heifer (ˈhefə*) *nc* a young cow.

height (haɪt) *nc* **1** the distance between the top and bottom of something. **2** the distance that something is above something else, esp. the sea. **3** the highest point of something. **heighten** *vt* **1** make higher. **2** make stronger, more powerful, etc.: *a heightened sense of colour.*

heinous (ˈheɪnəs, ˈhiːnəs) *adj* evil: *a heinous crime.*

heir (eə*) *nc* a person who will receive something from someone when that person dies, esp. money, etc., or a title. **heiress** (ˈeəres) *nc* a female heir. **heirloom** (ˈeəluːm) *nc* an object that has been passed down many times within a family.

held (held) past tense and past participle of **hold¹**.

helicopter (ˈhelɪkɒptə*) *nc* a plane with large propeller blades on top with which it can travel in any direction, including straight up or down: see picture.

helicopter

helium (ˈhiːlɪəm) *nu* a chemical element that is normally a gas and is used esp. for filling balloons, because it is light and does not burn.

helix ('hiːlɪks) *nc, pl* **-lixes, -lices** ('helɪsiːz) a spiral; the shape of either a flat or a coiled spring: see picture.

helix

hell (hel) **1** *ncu* the place of punishment to which evil people are said to go when they die. *infml nu* **2** a very unpleasant experience: *That party was hell.* **3** (used to strengthen a following verb): *What the hell are you doing?* **hell of a 1** very: *a hell of a good party.* **2** very good, bad, etc.: *We had a hell of a time.*

he'll (hiːl) he will.

hellish ('helɪʃ) *adj* **1** to do with hell. **2** *infml* very bad, difficult, etc.

hello (also **hallo, hullo**) (həˈləʊ) *interj* (used when meeting someone or starting a telephone conversation.)

helm (helm) *nu* the device by which a boat is steered, esp. the wheel, etc., actually held in the hand. ● *vt* steer (a boat). **helmsman** ('helmzmən) *nc, pl* **-men** a person who steers a boat.

helmet ('helmɪt) *nc* a hat that protects the head, worn by soldiers, divers, etc.: see picture.

helmet

help (help) *vt* **1** assist (someone to do something); do something for (someone) to make his job easier or so that he can buy something, etc. **2** avoid, prevent, or prevent from being worse: *I can't help the weather.* **3** (often followed by **to**) provide (someone, or oneself) with something, esp. food: *Help yourself to bread.* ● *nu* **1** the action of helping. *nc* **2** a person employed to help. **3** something that helps. **helper** *nc* **helpful** *adj* **helping** *nc* an amount of something given, esp. food. **helpless** *adj* unable to do something alone; weak. **help out** help (someone), esp. with money.

helter-skelter (,heltəˈskeltə*) *nc* a tower with a spiral slope built round it down which one can slide on a mat for fun. ● *adj* careless; hurried.

hem (hem) *nc* an edge on a piece of cloth, made by sewing it back onto itself. ● *vt* put a hem on. **hem in** surround (something) closely. **hemline** ('hemlaɪn) *nc* the lower edge of a skirt or dress.

hemisphere ('hemɪsfɪə*) *nc* **1** half a sphere. **2** a half of the earth: *the Northern Hemisphere:* see picture.

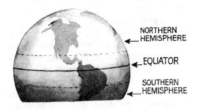

hemisphere

hemoglobin (,hiːməˈgləʊbɪn) *US n* See **haemoglobin.**

hemorrhage ('hemərɪdʒ) *US n* See **haemorrhage.**

hemp (hemp) *nu* also **cannabis, marijuana** a plant used for making rope, etc., and a drug that is smoked.

hen (hen) *nc* a female bird, esp. of the fowl, kept for its eggs and meat.

hence (hens) *adv* **1** *archaic* from here. **2** therefore. **henceforth** ('hensfɔːθ, hensˈfɔːθ) *formal adv* from now on.

henchman ('hentʃmən) *nc, pl* **-men** a follower; supporter.

hepatitis (,hepəˈtaɪtɪs) *nu* a disease; inflammation of the liver.

her (hɜː* unstressed hə*, ə*) *pron* (used for female persons and animals and sometimes ships and countries either after a preposition or when they are either the direct or indirect object of a verb): *When Mary arrived I met her; Yes, she's a fine ship—have you been on her?* ● *determiner* belonging to or to do with her: *Those are her shoes.*

herald ('herəld) *nc* a messenger or person who announces news, esp. at a royal court. **heraldry** ('herəldrɪ) *nu* the study of coats of arms.

herb (hɜːb) *nc* **1** a plant that is not woody and dies down to the ground each year. **2** any plant used to add flavour in cooking or as medicine, such as parsley or rosemary. **herbaceous** (hɜːˈbeɪʃəs) *adj* to do with plants that are not woody: *a herbaceous border.* **herbal** *adj* to do with herbs: *herbal medicine.*

herd (hɜːd) *nc* a group of animals living together, esp. cattle or sheep. ● *vt* move (animals) in a herd. **herdsman** ('hɜːdzmən) *nc, pl* **-men** a man who looks after a herd of animals.

here (hɪə*) *adv* in, at, or to this place. ●*nu* this place. **here and there** in several places. **hereabouts** (ˈhɪərəbaʊts) *adv* near here. **hereafter** (hɪərˈɑːftə*) *formal adv* in future. **hereby** (hɪəˈbaɪ) *formal adv* by means of this. **herein** (ˌhɪərˈɪn) *formal adv* in this place, thing, or document. **hereupon** (ˌhɪərəˈpɒn) *formal adv* 1 at this point or stage; as a result of this. 2 on this subject or point. **herewith** *formal adv* with this.

hereditary (hɪˈredɪtərɪ, hɪˈredɪtrɪ) *adj* (esp. of property or physical likeness) passing from parents to their children. **heredity** (hɪˈredɪtɪ) *nu* the passing of physical likeness from parents to their children.

here's (hɪəz) here is.

heresy (ˈherəsɪ) *ncu*, *pl* **-sies** (the holding of) an opinion opposite to that of a church or religion. **heretic** (ˈherətɪk) *nc* the holder of a heresy.

heritage (ˈherɪtɪdʒ) *nc* 1 something passed on, either by heredity or given when someone dies. 2 (esp. of a nation) the language, literature, art, music, etc., received from earlier times.

hermetic (hɜːˈmetik) *adj* not letting air in or out: *a hermetic seal.*

hermit (ˈhɜːmɪt) *nc* a person who lives alone and away from others. **hermitage** (ˈhɜːmɪtɪdʒ) a place where a hermit lives.

hernia (ˈhɜːnjə) *n* See **rupture** (def. 2).

hero (ˈhɪərəʊ) *nc*, *pl* **-es** 1 a boy or man who is greatly admired, esp. for his bravery. 2 the chief male character in a story. **heroic** (hɪˈrəʊɪk) *adj* to do with a hero. **heroics** *n pl* brave language or behaviour, esp. when unnecessary. **heroism** (ˈherəʊɪzəm) *nu* bravery.

heroin (ˈherəʊɪn) *nu* a drug, to which people can become highly addicted, that is used in medicine and taken for its effect on the mind.

heroine (ˈherəʊɪn) *nc* 1 a girl or woman who is greatly admired, esp. for her bravery. 2 the chief female character in a story.

heron (ˈherən) *nc* a tall bird that catches fish.

herring (ˈherɪŋ) *nc* a North Atlantic food fish: see picture at **fish**. **red herring** something irrelevant that takes away attention from the real issue.

hers (hɜːz) *pron* a person or thing belonging to her: *Hers is over there; This book is hers.*

herself (həˈself) *pron* 1 (used to refer back to a female subject): *Jane dressed herself; She did it herself.* 2 (of a female subject) in her normal state: *She hasn't been herself all day.* **by herself** (of a female) 1 without help. 2 alone.

he's (hiːz) he is or he has.

hesitate (ˈhezɪteɪt) *vi* 1 pause before or while doing something. 2 not want (to do some-

thing). **hesitant** (ˈhezɪtənt) *adj* (often) hesitating. **hesitation** (ˌhezɪˈteɪʃən) *nu* the act of hesitating.

heterogeneous (ˌhetərəʊˈdʒiːnɪəs) *adj* made up of parts that are different from each other.

heterosexual (ˌhetərəʊˈseksjʊəl) *adj*, *nc* (a person) attracted to people of the opposite sex.

hew (hjuː) *vt* 1 cut (wood, etc.), esp. with an axe. 2 make (something), esp. out of wood, etc., by hewing.

hewn (hjuːn) past participle of **hew**.

hexagon (ˈheksəgən) *nc* a shape with six sides: see picture at **shapes**.

hey (heɪ) *interj* (used to express surprise, pleasure, displeasure, etc., or to attract someone's attention.)

heyday (ˈheɪdeɪ) *nc* the period of greatest popularity, power, etc.

hi (haɪ) *chiefly US, infml interj* (used when meeting someone or to attract someone's attention.)

hibernate (ˈhaɪbəneɪt) *vi* (of an animal) spend the winter in a state like sleep.

hiccup (ˈhɪkʌp) *nc* a sudden short noise made by air being forced out of the lungs. ●*vi* make this noise.

hid (hɪd) past tense of **hide¹**.

hidden (ˈhɪdən) past participle of **hide¹**.

hide¹ (haɪd) 1 *vt* put or keep out of sight. 2 *vi* put or keep oneself out of sight. ●*nc* a place in which to hide while looking at wild animals. **hide-out** (ˈhaɪdaʊt) *nc* a hiding place, esp. used by criminals.

hide² *ncu* (a complete) animal skin, esp. made into leather. **hiding** *nc* a beating, esp. as a punishment.

hideous (ˈhɪdɪəs) *adj* very ugly.

hierarchy (ˈhaɪərɑːkɪ) *nc*, *pl* **-chies** an organisation of groups of people or things in order of importance, power, etc.

hieroglyphics (ˌhaɪərəˈglɪfɪks) *n pl* pictures representing words in a language such as ancient Egyptian: see picture.

hieroglyphics

hi-fi (ˈhaɪfaɪ) *adj*, *ncu* short for **high fidelity**. See under **high**.

high (haɪ) *adj* **-er**, **-est** 1 at a great distance above something: *high in the air.* 2 being a great distance from top to bottom; tall: *a* *high mountain.* **3** of a particular distance from top to bottom: *five metres high.* **4** great in quantity: *high prices.* **5** (of a sound) made up of fast repeated movements. **6** important: *the high table.* **7** good: *a high opinion; high spirits; high grade.* **8** (of a gear) giving the most movement for a given engine speed. ●*adv* in or to a high position. **high court** a powerful law court that can be asked to change a decision of a lower court. **high fidelity 1** the fact of sound from a record-player, etc., being very like the real sound. **2** a record-player giving such a sound. **highland** ('haɪlənd) *nc* (often *pl*) a high piece of land. **highlight** ('haɪlaɪt) *nc* the most attractive, popular, etc., part: *the highlights of a football match; the highlights of the minister's speech.* **high-powered** ('haɪpaʊəd) *adj* **1** (of a car, lens, etc.) having great power. **2** having or demanding a clever mind: *high-powered discussion.* **high-pressure** *adj* **1** to do with great pressure: *high-pressure cleaning.* **2** (of selling or a seller) trying very hard to persuade one to buy. **high-rise** *adj* (of a building): tall: *high-rise flats.* **highroad** *nc* a main road. **high spot** *infml* a highlight. **high street** the main street of a town, esp. one with many shops. **high tea** *Brit* an early evening meal. **highway** *nc* a main road. **highwayman** ('haɪweɪmən) *nc, pl* **-men** a man on a horse who used to stop travellers and rob them.

highly ('haɪlɪ) *adv* very much or well: *highly taxed; highly thought of.*

highness ('haɪnɪs) *Brit nc* (used to refer to members of the Royal Family other than the King or Queen, and to foreign princes): *His Royal Highness the Prince of Wales; Your Highnesses.*

hijack ('haɪdʒæk) *vt* seize control of (a plane, ship, lorry, etc.) in order to make it go where one wants or to steal goods. ●*nc* the act of hijacking. **hijacker** *nc*

hike (haɪk) *vi, nc* (go for) a long (country) walk. **hiker** *nc*

hilarious (hɪ'leərɪəs) *adj* very funny or amusing. **hilarity** (hɪ'lærɪtɪ) *nu*

hill (hɪl) *nc* a raised piece of land lower and usually less rocky than a mountain. **hillock** ('hɪlək) *nc* a small hill. **hillside** *nc* the sloping surface of a hill. **hilltop** *nc* the top of a hill. **hilly** *adj* **-ier, -iest.**

hilt (hɪlt) *nc* the handle of a sword.

him (hɪm unstressed ɪm) *pron* (used for male persons and animals either after a preposition or when they are either the direct or indirect object of a verb): *I saw him; This was done by him.*

himself (hɪm'self) *pron* **1** (used to refer back to a male subject): *John killed himself; He*

did it himself. **2** (of a male subject) in his normal state: *He hasn't been himself today.* **by himself** (of a male) **1** without help. **2** alone.

hind[1] (haɪnd) *nc, pl* **hinds, hind** a female deer.

hind[2] *adj* (esp. of a leg of an animal) back. **hindmost** ('haɪndməʊst) *adj* furthest back or behind.

hinder ('hɪndə*) *vt* prevent or make (something) more difficult for (someone): *to hinder progress; You shouldn't hinder the police.* **hindrance** ('hɪndrəns) *nc* a person or thing that hinders.

hindsight ('haɪndsaɪt) *nu* the ability to understand what should have been done, after something has happened.

Hindu ('hɪndu:) *nc* a follower of Hinduism. ●*adj* to do with Hindus or Hinduism. **Hinduism** ('hɪndu:ɪzəm) *nu* the main religion of India.

hinge (hɪndʒ) *nc* a device that allows one thing to swing on another, such as a door on its frame. ●*vt* **1** put a hinge on. **2** *vi* be or swing on a hinge. **hinge on** depend on.

hint (hɪnt) *nc* **1** a slight suggestion; small indication: *I can't guess—give me a hint.* **2** a helpful suggestion. **3** a small amount. ●*vi* make a **hint** (def. 1).

hinterland ('hɪntəlænd) *nu* land lying behind or near something, such as land away from the coast or near a large city.

hip[1] (hɪp) *nc* **1** the bony part on each side of the body at the top of the legs. **2** also **hip joint** the joint between each leg and the body.

hip[2] *nc* also **rosehip** the fruit of a **rose**[2] (def. 1).

hip[3] *interj* hip, hip (called out by one person to encourage others to shout 'hurrah', the whole being repeated twice more.)

hippopotamus (,hɪpə'pɒtəməs) (*infml abbrev.* **hippo**) *nc, pl* **-muses, -mi** (məsɪs, maɪ) a very large grey African animal living in or near water: see picture at **animals.**

hire (haɪə*) *vt* **1** pay for the use of (something) or the work of (someone). **2** (often followed by **out**) be paid for the use of (something) or the work of (someone). ●*nu* **1** the act of hiring: *bicycles for hire.* **2** the state of being hired: *This car's only on hire.* **hire purchase** a system of buying something by making a number of payments.

his (hɪz unstressed ɪz) *determiner* belonging to or to do with him: *Those are his shoes.* ●*pron* a person or thing belonging to him: *His is better; This one is his.*

hiss (hɪs) *nc* the sound of a long (s). ●*vi* **1** make this sound. **2** *vt* make this sound at (someone) of whom one disapproves.

histogram ('hɪstəgræm) *nc* a diagram of different quantities shown by means of bars of different heights.

history ('hɪstərɪ) *ncu, pl* **-ries** (an account or the study of) past events. **historian** (hɪ-'stɔːrɪən) *nc* a person who writes or studies history. **historic** (hɪ'stɒrɪk) *adj* (of an event) famous or important. **historical** (hɪ'stɒrɪkəl) *adj* to do with history. **historically** *adv*

hit (hɪt) *vt* **1** deliver a blow to; strike: *He hit the table with his hand.* **2** come up hard against; strike: *The ball hit the window.* **3** cause to suffer: *We've been hit by bad weather.* **4** experience; find; reach: *to hit a problem.* ● *nc* **1** the act of hitting. **2** a person or thing, esp. a song, that becomes very popular. **hit parade** the list of songs of which most records are being bought at any one time.

hitch (hɪtʃ) *vt* **1** (often followed by **up**) move (something) suddenly: *He hitched up his trousers.* **2** fasten: *The horses were hitched to the coach.* ● *nc* **1** a sudden pull or push. **2** a knot for tying a line to a post, etc. **3** a ride obtained by hitch-hiking. **hitched** *slang adj* married. **hitch-hike** ('hɪtʃhaɪk) (*infml abbrev.* **hitch**) *vi* travel by asking passing drivers for free rides.

hither ('hɪðə*) *archaic adv* to here. **hitherto** (ˌhɪðə'tuː) *formal adv* until now.

hive (haɪv) *n* short for **beehive**. **hive off** separate (something) from a larger thing or group. **hive of industry** a place where people work very hard, often with enthusiasm.

hoard (hɔːd) *nc* a collection of something stored away. ● *vt* collect into a hoard.

hoarding ('hɔːdɪŋ) *nc* **1** a fence round building works. **2** *US* **billboard** a hoarding used for sticking advertisements on.

hoarse (hɔːs) *adj* **-r, -st 1** (of a voice) sounding rough, because of shouting, a cold, etc. **2** having a hoarse voice. **hoarsely** *adv*

hoary ('hɔːrɪ) *adj* **-ier, -iest 1** (of hair) grey or white. **2** with hoary hair. **3** old and well-known: *a hoary joke.*

hoax (həʊks) *vt* deceive (someone) as a joke. ● *nc* an act of hoaxing.

hobble ('hɒbəl) **1** *vi* walk awkwardly, esp. through injury. **2** *vt* tie the legs of (a horse) together so that it cannot walk far. ● *nc* an awkward walk.

hobby ('hɒbɪ) *nc, pl* **-bies** an activity done mainly for enjoyment.

hobnail ('hɒbneɪl) *nc* a metal nail with a large head hammered into the bottoms of shoes and boots to protect them: *hobnail boots.*

hockey ('hɒkɪ) *nu* a game played on a field with a goal at each end into which the players on each side try to hit a ball with curved sticks. **ice hockey** See under **ice**.

hod (hɒd) *nc* **1** a three-sided box on a stick used for carrying bricks. **2** a container for coal.

hoe (həʊ) *nc* a tool for destroying garden weeds, etc.: see picture at **tools**. ● *vt* use a hoe on.

hog (hɒg) *nc* **1** a pig kept on a farm, esp. a male that will be killed for its meat. **2** *infml* a greedy person. ● *vt* take more than one's share of. **go the whole hog** *slang* do something completely or thoroughly.

hoist (hɔɪst) *vt* raise (something, esp. a flag). ● *nc* **1** the act of hoisting. **2** a device for hoisting. **hoist with one's own petard** ruined, defeated, etc., by something that one hoped would ruin or defeat someone else.

hold[1] (həʊld) *vt* **1** have or keep (something) with or within the hand or hands: *She stood holding the cut flowers; hold the camera steady.* **2** (be able to) contain: *This bottle holds a pint.* **3** possess; own: *He holds a degree from Leeds.* **4** carry on; arrange (a meeting, conversation, etc.). **5** believe; consider: *I hold you responsible.* **6** *vi* stay the same, esp. good. *Will the weather hold? vt* **7** keep under control; restrain: *The dam didn't hold the rising waters for long. vt* **8** support: *The branch, unable to hold his weight, suddenly broke.* ● *nc* **1** the act of holding. **2** something to hold on to. **3** control or influence: *They have a hold over us.* **holdall** ('həʊldɔːl) *nc* a bag for many different objects. **hold back 1** hesitate to do (something) or prevent (someone) from doing something. **2** keep; not give (something) up or away. **hold down 1** keep (someone or something) on something. **2** *infml* manage to keep (a job). **holder** *nc* **1** a person who holds something, such as a bank account. **2** a device that holds; container: *a toothbrush holder.* **hold in** keep (someone or something) inside something: *You're holding your stomach in!* **hold off 1** keep (someone or something) away from something. **2** not do something: *I know he owes you money, but can't you hold off a bit longer?* **hold on 1** (often followed by **to**) continue to hold. **2** *infml* wait. **hold out 1** offer or reach out. **2** (often followed by **against**) resist, esp. against an attack. **hold out for** wait for one's demands for (something) to be met. **hold out on** delay in telling (someone) something. **hold up 1** lift; raise; keep lifted or raised. **2** delay; keep waiting. **3** steal from, esp. by threatening force: *They held up a bank.* **hold-up** ('həʊldʌp) *nc* **1** a delay. **2** a robbery.

hold[2] *nc* a space for goods in a ship or aircraft.

holding ('həʊldɪŋ) *nc* a quantity of land, shares, etc. owned.

hole (həʊl) *nc* **1** an empty space or opening in something, sometimes going right through it. **2** the underground home of an animal. **3** the space into which the ball must be hit in a game such as golf. ● *vt* make a hole in.

holiday ('hɒlɪdeɪ) *nc* **1** *(often pl)* a period when one takes a rest from work or study, often spent away from home. **2** a special day on which most people in a country do not work. ● *vi* take or have a holiday. **on holiday** taking a holiday. **holiday-maker** ('hɒlɪdɪˌmeɪkə*) *nc* a person on holiday.

holiness ('həʊlɪnɪs) *nu* the quality of being holy.

hollow ('hɒləʊ) *adj* **-er, -est 1** having a space inside; empty. **2** not real: *hollow laughter; a hollow victory*. ● *vt* (often followed by **out**) make hollow. ● *nc* a hollow part.

holly ('hɒlɪ) *nc, pl* **-lies** a tree or bush with red berries and sharp-pointed leaves that are green all year.

holocaust ('hɒləkɔːst) *nc* a great destruction, esp. by fire.

holster ('həʊlstə*) *nc* a holder for a pistol, esp. worn at the waist or under an arm.

holy ('həʊlɪ) *adj* **-ier, -iest 1** to do with God. **2** pure and good in thought and behaviour. **Holy Spirit** the being or force through which Christians believe God acts on earth.

homage ('hɒmɪdʒ) *nu* a show of respect: *We paid him homage*.

home (həʊm) *nc* **1** a house or other place where someone lives. **2** a place of origin, such as one's native country. **3** a house where a number of old, poor, sick, etc., people live and are looked after: *a children's home*. **4** the place one tries to reach in a race or game. ● *adj* to do with home. ● *adv* at or to one's home. ● *vti* (often followed by **in, on,** or **in on**) travel or point at or to something: *I'll home the radio in on a strong station*. **at home 1** in one's own home. **2** at ease. **have an at home** give a party at one's home. **home help** a person who cleans, etc., in someone else's house. **homeland** ('həʊmlænd) one's native country. **home-made** ('həʊmmeɪd) *adj* (esp. of food) made at home. **Home Office** *Brit* the government department in charge of law and order, immigration, etc. **Home Secretary** *Brit* the government minister in charge of the Home Office. **homesick** ('həʊmsɪk) *adj* sad at not being at home. **homestead** ('həʊmsted) *nc* a house and land or other buildings, esp. a farm. **home truth** a fact that a person finds unpleasant when it is told to him. **homeward**

('həʊmwəd) *adj, adv* (going) towards home.

homework ('həʊmwɜːk) *nu* **1** study to be done, esp. by a child outside normal school time. **2** preparation: *He had really done his homework and knew all about the plan*.

homely ('həʊmlɪ) *adj* **-ier, -iest 1** ordinary; fitting in with an ordinary home. **2** *US* not good-looking.

homeopathy (also **homoeopathy**) (ˌhəʊmɪˈɒpəθɪ) *nu* the treatment of an illness with a very small amount of a substance that can cause it in a healthy person.

homeostasis (also **homoeostasis**) (ˌhəʊmɪəʊˈsteɪsɪs) *nu* the keeping of a balance in the workings of an animal's body by making up for changes.

homicide ('hɒmɪsaɪd) **1** *ncu* the killing of one person by another. **2** *nc* a person who kills another.

homily ('hɒmɪlɪ) *nc, pl* **-lies** a talk on a point of religion.

homing ('həʊmɪŋ) *adj* able to go home: *a homing pigeon*.

homogeneous (ˌhəʊməˈdʒiːnɪəs, ˌhɒməˈdʒiːnɪəs) *adj* the same right through; made up of parts that are the same as each other.

homonym ('hɒmənɪm) *nc* one of two or more words said or written the same but meaning something different, such as 'sail' and 'sale'.

homosexual (ˌhəʊməˈseksjʊəl, ˌhɒməˈseksjʊəl) *adj, nc* (a person) attracted to people of his or her own sex.

honest ('ɒnɪst) *adj* **1** correct and fair. **2** not lying or stealing. **honestly** *adv* **honesty** *nu*

honey ('hʌnɪ) *ncu* a (type of) sweet, dark yellow food made by bees from the nectar of flowers. **honeycomb** ('hʌnɪkəʊm) *nc* a block of wax full of six-sided holes in which bees store honey: see picture. **honeysuckle** ('hʌnɪˌsʌkəl) *nc* a climbing plant with sweet-smelling white, yellow, or pink flowers.

honeycomb

honeymoon ('hʌnɪmuːn) *nc* a holiday taken by two people who have just married. ● *vi* take a honeymoon.

honk (hɒŋk) *nc* the noise made by a goose or a car horn. ● *vi* make this noise.

honorary ('ɒnərərɪ) *adj* **1** without the work usually needed: *an honorary degree*. **2** without pay: *the honorary treasurer*.

honour US **honor** ('ɒnə*) nu 1 great respect.
2 fame. 3 a belief in always behaving correctly. 4 reputation. nc 5 a great pleasure: *It
is an honour to be here.* 6 (used after **an**)
one who brings (to someone) great respect:
He is an honour to his school. ● vt respect
highly. **Honour** (used after **Your, His,** or
Her; used to refer to someone in high position, esp. a judge): *Yes, Your Honour; His
Honour has arrived.* **in honour of** as a mark
of respect for. **honourable** US **honorable**
('ɒnərəbəl) adj 1 having **honour** (def. 3). 2
deserving **honour** (def. 1). **the Honourable**
US **the Honorable** (used as a title of
respect.)

hood (hʊd) nc 1 a covering for the head and
neck, esp. one fastened to a coat, etc. 2 *Brit*
a soft, folding roof on a car. 3 *US* See **bonnet** (def. 2).

hoodlum ('huːdləm) nc a person who behaves violently or does small crimes.

hoodwink ('hʊdwɪŋk) vt deceive.

hoof (huːf) nc, pl **hooves** (huːvz), **hoofs** the
hard growth at the end of the leg of a horse
or other animal.

hook (hʊk) nc a curved piece of metal used
for hanging something on, catching hold of
something, etc. ● vt catch or fasten to or
with a hook. **hooked on 1** unable to stop
taking (a drug). 2 very keen on or fond of.

hookworm ('hʊkwɜːm) nc a very small worm
that enters a person or animal through its
skin and causes disease.

hooligan ('huːlɪgən) nc a violent street youth.

hoop (huːp) nc a ring of wood, metal, etc.,
used as a toy, to hold a wooden barrel together, etc.

hooray (hʊˈreɪ) interj See **hurrah**.

hoot (huːt) nc 1 the noise made by an owl. 2
(the cause of) loud laughter: *He's a hoot; in
hoots of laughter.* 3 a loud noise expressing
disapproval. 4 the noise of a car horn. ● vi
1 make a hoot. 2 vti (often followed by **at**)
attract the attention of or warn off (people
or animals) by sounding a horn. **hooter**
chiefly Brit nc 1 a car horn. 2 *slang* a nose.

hooves (huːvz) plural of **hoof**.

hop¹ (hɒp) nc 1 a climbing plant. 2 (pl) the
dried flowers of the hop, used to give beer
a bitter taste.

hop² vi 1 (of a person) jump on one foot. 2
(of a bird or animal) move with short
jumps. 3 jump or move quickly: *Hop into
the car.* ● nc the action of hopping. **hop it**
Brit slang go away quickly.

hope ('həʊp) 1 ncu (often pl) a feeling of
wanting and often expecting: *I haven't
much hope that he'll come.* 2 nc a cause of
hope: *If the weather stays fine, there's a
hope that he'll come.* ● vt 1 be in hope of: *I
hope he comes.* 2 vi (followed by **for**) be in

hope: *I'm hoping for fine weather.* **raise
someone's hopes** encourage someone to
hope. **hopeful** adj 1 having hope. 2 giving
hope: *hopeful news.* **hopefully** adv 1 in a
hopeful manner. 2 it is hoped that: *Hopefully he'll come.* **hopeless** adj 1 having no
hope. 2 giving no hope; impossible to
solve, etc. 3 *infml* bad at doing something
or badly done. **hopelessly** adv

hopper ('hɒpə*) nc a container for coal,
sand, etc., with a door at the bottom for letting it out.

horde (hɔːd) nc (often pl) a very large group
of people or animals. ● vi be or move in a
horde.

horizon (həˈraɪzən) nc 1 the line that separates the earth and the sky. 2 the edge of
one's interest, understanding, etc.: *to
broaden one's horizons.*

horizontal (ˌhɒrɪˈzɒntəl) adj level; flat: *The
surface of still water is horizontal.* **horizon-
tally** adv

hormone ('hɔːməʊn) nc a chemical produced
in small amounts in one part of an animal
or plant which affects a different part or
controls growth.

horn (hɔːn) nc 1 a hard growth, often
pointed, on the head of an animal such as a
sheep or rhinoceros; (sometimes nu) the
material of which horns are made. 2 an object, container, or device made, esp. formerly, of horn: *a drinking horn.* 3 a musical
wind instrument made from a horn or from
brass tube: *a hunting horn; a French horn:*
see picture at **musical instruments**. 4 a device for giving a warning noise, as on a car.
horny adj **-ier, -iest.**

hornet ('hɔːnɪt) nc an insect with a sting;
kind of large wasp: see picture at **insects**.

horoscope ('hɒrəskəʊp) nc information that
tells someone what will happen to him in
the future, based on the positions of the
stars at the moment he was born.

horrible ('hɒrɪbəl) adj 1 causing horror. 2 unpleasant. **horribly** adv 1 in a horrible manner. 2 very: *it's horribly late.*

horrid ('hɒrɪd) adj horrible.

horrify ('hɒrɪfaɪ) vt cause to feel horror.

horror ('hɒrə*) 1 nu a feeling of disgust and
fear. 2 nc (often pl) a person or thing causing horror. **horror film** a film with a frightening story.

hors d'oeuvre (ˌɔː ˈdɜːvrə) *French* nc, pl **hors
d'oeuvres** (ˌɔː ˈdɜːvrə) a dish served before
the main dish of a meal.

horse (hɔːs) nc 1 a four-legged animal with
solid hoofs, used for riding, carrying loads,
etc.: see picture at **animals**. 2 a frame,
usually with legs, on which something is
held, put, etc.: *a clothes-horse.* **on horseback** seated on a horse. **horsehair** nu hair

from the neck or tail of a horse. **horseman** ('hɔːsmən) *nc, pl* **-men** a man riding or able to ride a horse, esp. very well. **horsepower** ('hɔːspaʊə*) *nu* the unit used to measure the power produced by an engine, etc.: *abbrev.* hp **horse-race** *nc* a race between horses with riders. **horse-racing** *nu* **horseshoe** ('hɔːsʃuː) *nc* a U-shaped strip of metal fixed to a horse's foot.

horticulture ('hɔːtɪkʌltʃə*) *nu* the art of growing flowers and vegetables; gardening. **horticultural** (,hɔːtɪ'kʌltʃərəl) *adj*

hose[1] (həʊz) *nc* a long pipe of rubber, plastic, etc., used for throwing water over a garden, putting out a fire, etc. **hosepipe** *nc* a long piece of hose: see picture. ● *vt* wash with a hose.

hosepipe

hose[2] *n pl* stockings and socks. **hosiery** ('həʊzɪərɪ) *nu* stockings and socks.

hospitable (hɒ'spɪtəbəl, 'hɒspɪtəbəl) *adj* giving comfort, a welcome, etc., to visitors.

hospital ('hɒspɪtəl) *nc* a place where ill people are treated. **hospitalise** ('hɒspɪtəlaɪz) *vt* send or take into hospital for medical care.

hospitality (,hɒspɪ'tælɪtɪ) *nu* welcoming guests, etc., in a friendly way.

host[1] (həʊst) *nc* a person who entertains or welcomes guests.

host[2] *nc* a large number of people or things: *a host of jobs to do.*

hostage ('hɒstɪdʒ) *nc* a person kept as a prisoner by someone until what is demanded has been done.

hostel ('hɒstəl) *nc* a building where students, people in training, etc., are provided with rented rooms and meals. **youth hostel** a hostel where people, usually young, can stay for one or a few nights while on walking, cycling, etc., holidays.

hostess ('həʊstɪs) *nc* a woman who entertains or welcomes guests.

hostile ('hɒstaɪl) *adj* **1** of an enemy. **2** unfriendly. **hostility** (hɒ'stɪlɪtɪ) *nc, pl* **-ties 1** *nu* hatred; strong dislike. **2** *(pl)* acts of war.

hot (hɒt) *adj* **-ter, -test 1** having great heat; very warm: *hot weather.* **2** having a sharp taste that causes a burning feeling: *a hot curry.* **3** (of feelings, etc.) intense: *a hot temper.* **4** *slang* (of stolen goods) not easy to get rid of. **hot air** *infml* words or promises that mean nothing: *He talks a lot of hot air!* **hot dog** *infml* a hot sausage in a bread roll. **hot-headed** (,hɒt'hedɪd) *adj* (of feelings)

hasty to act without much thought. **hot line** a direct link for information, news, etc., esp. between heads of governments, etc. **hot water** *infml* trouble: *He's always getting into hot water.*

hotel (həʊ'tel, əʊ'tel) *nc* a building where travellers are provided with rooms and food.

hound (haʊnd) *nc* a kind of dog used for hunting, racing, etc.: *bloodhound; greyhound.* ● *vt* **1** chase or hunt with such a dog. **2** annoy or trouble (a person) to do something, or with something.

hour ('aʊə*) *nc* one of the twenty-four periods of time into which a day is divided; sixty minutes. **hourly** ('aʊəlɪ) *adj* done or happening at every hour. ● *adv* at any hour; every hour. **hours** ('aʊəz) *n pl* a fixed time for work during the day: *school hours; office hours.*

house (haʊs) *nc* **1** a building in which people, often one family, live. **2** a building in which animals, goods, etc., are kept. **3** a building in which people meet, esp. law-makers; the law-makers themselves: *the House of Commons.* **4** the audience in a theatre. ● (haʊz) *vt* provide a house for; give room or space for. **bring the house down** cause great laughter. **houseboat** *nc* a boat built for people to live in. **housefly** *nc, pl* **-flies** a common insect with two wings that lives in houses. **household** *nc* all the people living in a house; family. **householder** *nc* a person who rents or owns, and lives in a house. **housekeeper** *nc* a woman paid to be in charge of the running of a house. **housekeeping** *nu* **1** looking after the everyday running of a house. **2** money provided for this. **housemaid** *nc* a female servant in a house. **housemaster** *nc* a teacher in a school where children live as well as being taught. **housewife** *nc, pl* **-wives** a woman, usually married, who takes care of her house, her children, etc. **housework** *nu* work done in a house, such as cleaning, cooking, etc.

housing ('haʊzɪŋ) *nu* houses for living in.

hove (həʊv) past tense and past participle of **heave**.

hovel ('hɒvəl) *nc* a house that is not fit to live in.

hover ('hɒvə*) *vi* **1** (of a bird or plane) remain in the air over a certain place. **2** (of a person) wait in an uncertain manner. **hovercraft** ('hɒvəkrɑːft) *nc* a vehicle supported by air sent out from underneath to the surface of the land or sea: see picture.

how (haʊ) *adv* **1** in what way: *How did you do it?* **2** to what extent: *How much did it cost?; How nice of you!* **how about...?** See under **about. how do you do?** See under **do.**

however (hau'evə*) (*literary abbrev.*
howe'er (hau'eə*)) *adv* whatever happens;
in whatever way: *I shall travel tomorrow,
however bad the weather is.* ●*conj* but;
nevertheless: *I must go now. However, I'll
see you tomorrow.*

hovercraft

howitzer ('hauitsə*) *nc* a short gun used for
firing shells at a high angle and at a short
distance from the enemy.

howl (haul) *nc* a long, loud cry or sound, esp.
of a dog or wolf; loud cry of pain, scornful
laughter, amusement, etc., of a person. ●*vi* 1 make such cries or sounds. 2 *vt*
make (such cries, etc.): *The crowd howled
insults at the speaker.*

how's (hauz) how is or how has?

hub (hʌb) *nc* the central part of a wheel from
which bars go to the outer edge; the central
part of interest, importance, etc., of anything.

hubbub ('hʌbʌb) *nu* a loud, confused noise.

huddle ('hʌdəl) 1 *vi* press up to someone or
something for warmth, comfort, etc. 2 *vt*
put into a confused pile. ●*nc* things or
people close together without any order.

hue (hju:) *nc* a colour, esp. how dark or how
light it is.

huff (hʌf) *nc* a fit of bad temper: *in a huff.*

hug (hʌg) *vt* hold (someone) with the arms
held tightly round, esp. in a loving
way. ●*nc* a tight hold with the arms.

huge (hju:dʒ) *adj* very large.

hulk (hʌlk) *nc* 1 the body of an old ship no
longer in use, except perhaps as a storehouse. 2 a large, awkward body of a person
or thing.

hull[1] (hʌl) *nc* the outer covering of some
seeds, esp. peas and beans. ●*vt* remove
this outer covering.

hull[2] *nc* the body or frame of a ship, plane,
etc.

hullabaloo (ˌhʌləbə'lu:) *nc* a loud, confused
noise; disturbance.

hullo (hʌ'ləu) *interj* See **hello.**

hum (hʌm) 1 *vi* make a continuous noise like
the sound made by a bee, usually with
closed lips: *She hummed as she worked.* 2 *vt*
sing (a tune, etc.) with the lips closed. *vi* 3
infml be in an active condition: *make things
start to hum.* 4 *infml* smell nasty: *This
meat's beginning to hum.* ●*nc* the sound
of humming: *the hum of voices.*

human ('hju:mən) *adj* 1 of or having to do
with man. 2 having or showing the qualities
of man, esp. the better ones. ●*nc* also
human being a person; man, woman, or
child. **human rights** those things which any
person has a right to expect, have, etc.

humane (hju:'mein) *adj* caring about the sufferings of other people; kind.

humanism ('hju:mənizəm) *nu* a system that
is interested in the study of man and morals, but not in God or spiritual matters.
humanist ('hju:mənist) *nc* a person who
believes in and supports humanism.

humanitarian (hju:ˌmæni'teəriən) *nc* a person who works to make the pain, suffering,
etc., of human beings less, or easier to
bear. ●*adj* of, or having, qualities of
kindness and mercy.

humanity (hju:'mæniti) *nu* 1 the human race.
2 the quality of caring about the sufferings
of other people; kindness. **the humanities**
the literature having to do with human development, esp. Greek and Latin literature
of times long past.

humble ('hʌmbəl) *adj* 1 having not too high
an opinion of oneself; modest. 2 not important; having a low position in society,
etc. 3 (of a thing such as a home) poor in
appearance. **humbly** *adv* ●*vt* make humble.

humbug ('hʌmbʌg) 1 *nc* a person or thing
that deceives. 2 *nu* talk or behaviour that
intends to deceive.

humdrum ('hʌmdrʌm) *adj* not very interesting; without much change.

humerus ('hju:mərəs) *anatomy nc, pl* **-ri** (rai)
the bone in the upper part of the arm.

humid ('hju:mid) *adj* (of the air) damp. **hu-
midity** (hju:'miditi) *nu* the amount of
dampness in the air.

humiliate (hju:'milieit) *vt* cause to feel ashamed. **humiliation** (hju:ˌmili'eifən) 1 *nu* the
making or being made to feel ashamed. 2
nc an example of this shame.

humility (hju:'militi) *nu* the state of not having too high an opinion of oneself; modesty.

humorist ('hju:mərist) *nc* a person who
speaks or writes in an amusing way.

humorous ('hju:mərəs) *adj* having a sense of
fun.

humour *US* **humor** ('hju:mə*) *nu* 1 a state of
mind. 2 the quality of being amusing or
funny. **sense of humour** the ability to enjoy what is funny. ●*vt* try to please (a person) by doing what he wishes, etc.

hump (hʌmp) *nc* 1 a round lump, esp. on the
back of a camel; such a lump (but not natural) on the back of a person. 2 *infml* a difficult time. ●*vt* make into the shape of a
hump.

humus ('hju:məs) *nu* the rich earth formed by dead leaves, plants, etc., rotting away.

hunch (hʌntʃ) *nc* **1** a round raised lump. **2** a feeling that something might happen: *He had a hunch that the car would crash.* ● *vt* push up to form a hump. **hunchback** ('hʌntʃbæk) *nc* a person whose back is always curved to form a hump.

hundred ('hʌndrəd) *determiner, n* the number 100. **hundredth** ('hʌndrədθ) *determiner, n, adv* **hundredweight** ('hʌndrədweɪt) *nc* a measure of weight (in Britain 50.802 kg, America 45.359 kg): *abbrev.* cwt

hung (hʌŋ) past tense and past participle of **hang** (defs. **1, 3, 4**).

hunger ('hʌŋgə*) *nu* **1** the need or wish for food. **2** any strong wish: *a hunger for affection.* ● *vi* **1** feel the need or wish for food. **2** have any strong wish. **hunger strike** refusing to eat in order to be set free from prison or to show one is not in favour of something, etc.

hungry ('hʌŋgrɪ) *adj* **-ier, -iest** feeling, showing, or causing hunger. **hungrily** *adv*

hunk (hʌŋk) *nc* a thick, solid piece of something: *a hunk of bread.*

hunt (hʌnt) **1** *vti* chase (wild animals, esp. foxes) for food or for sport. **2** *vt* search or look for (something or someone). ● *nu* **1** the act of hunting. **2** *chiefly Brit* a group of people who chase foxes, etc., for sport with horses and dogs. **hunt down** chase and find (the animal or person being hunted). **hunt for** make a search for. **hunter** *nc* a person who hunts animals. **huntsman** ('hʌntsmən) *nc, pl* **-men 1** a hunter. **2** the man in charge of the dogs when hunting.

hurdle ('hɜːdəl) *nc* **1** a frame with wooden bars for jumping over in a race. **2** *Brit* a movable frame used for a short time as a fence. **3** a difficulty that has to be overcome before progress can be made.

hurl (hɜːl) *vt* throw with force. ● *nc* a violent throw.

hurly-burly ('hɜːlɪ,bɜːlɪ) *nu* noisy activity.

hurrah (hʊ'rɑː) also **hooray** *interj* (used to show gladness, welcome, approval, etc.)

hurricane ('hʌrɪkən) *nc* a violent wind, esp. one moving in circles round a calm place: see picture. **hurricane lamp** a lamp that will not be blown out by a strong wind.

hurricane

hurry ('hʌrɪ) **1** *vi* move or do something quickly or too quickly. **2** *vt* cause to move or do (something) quickly or too quickly. ● *nu* great haste. **hurry up!** *infml* be quick!

hurt (hɜːt) **1** *vt* cause pain to (a person's body or mind). *vi* **2** feel pain of the body or mind. **3** cause pain or sorrow: *It won't hurt to wait till tomorrow before we go.* ● *nu* injury; harm.

hurtle ('hɜːtəl) *vi* rush violently and suddenly: *The rocks hurtled down the mountain.*

husband ('hʌzbənd) *nc* the man to whom a woman is married.

husbandman ('hʌzbəndmən) *archaic nc, pl* **-men** a farmer. **husbandry** ('hʌzbəndrɪ) *nu* farming.

hush (hʌʃ) **1** *vt* make quiet. **2** *vi* be quiet. ● *nc* **1** silence. **2** calm; stillness: *the hush of night.* **hush up** prevent (something) from being made known and talked about in public.

husk (hʌsk) *nc* **1** the dry outer covering of some seeds. **2** the worthless outer part of anything. ● *vt* take off the husks from.

husky ('hʌskɪ) *adj* **-ier, -iest 1** (of a voice) low and rough. **2** (of a person's body) big and tough. ● *nc, pl* **-kies** a dog used by Eskimos to pull sledges.

hustle ('hʌsəl) **1** *vt* push in a rough way; make (someone) hurry or act quickly. **2** *vi* push one's way: *He hustled through the crowd.* ● *nu* much activity.

hut (hʌt) *nc* a small, usually wooden, roughly made shelter or house.

hutch (hʌtʃ) *nc* a box for pets, such as rabbits, with the front made of crossed wire bars.

hyacinth ('haɪəsɪnθ) *nc* a sweet-smelling plant with blue, white, or pink flowers, that grows from a bulb.

hybrid ('haɪbrɪd) *nc* the young of two different kinds of animals or plants; anything with very different parts, such as a word formed from different languages. ● *adj* from parents of different kinds.

hydrant ('haɪdrənt) *nc* a large pipe, esp. in the street, with a metal end for attaching a hose, used for putting out fires, etc.

hydrate ('haɪdreɪt) *nc* a chemical formed of two parts, one of which is water.

hydraulic (haɪ'drɔːlɪk, haɪ'drɒlɪk) *adj* of water, etc., moving through pipes; worked by the power of a fluid, esp. water.

hydroelectricity (,haɪdrəʊɪlek'trɪsɪtɪ) *nu* electricity that is produced by water power. **hydroelectric** (,haɪdrəʊɪ'lektrɪk) *adj*

hydrofoil ('haɪdrəfɔɪl) *nc* a fast boat built so that it is able to lift its hull out of the water when moving.

hydrogen ('haɪdrədʒən) *nu* a gas without colour, taste, or smell, and which is the lightest substance known: symbol H

hydroxide (haɪ'drɒksaɪd) *nc* a chemical formed of an element with hydrogen and oxygen.

hyena (haɪ'iːnə) *nc* a meat-eating wild animal, like a large dog, that makes a laughing sound: see picture at **animals.**

hygiene ('haɪdʒiːn) *nu* rules for keeping healthy; cleanliness. **hygienic** (haɪ'dʒiːnɪk) *adj*

hymn (hɪm) *nc* a song praising God, esp. one used in a religious service.

hyperbola (haɪ'pɜːbələ) *mathematics nc* the curve produced when a flat surface cuts through a cone.

hyperbole (haɪ'pɜːbəlɪ) **1** *nu* an expression in words that makes something seem much bigger, better, etc., than it really is. **2** *nc* an example of this, such as 'I died laughing'.

hypermarket ('haɪpə,mɑːkɪt) *nc* a very large store, outside a town, at which customers serve themselves and pay as they leave.

hyphen ('haɪfən) *nc* the sign (-) used to join two words together, to divide a word into parts, etc. **hyphenate** ('haɪfəneɪt) *vt* join (words or parts of a word) with a hyphen.

hypnotise ('hɪpnətaɪz) *vt* make (someone) seem deeply asleep and then control his actions by the power of one's mind. **hypnotism** ('hɪpnətɪzəm) *nu* a state where someone is hypnotised; the act of causing this state. **hypnotist** *nc*

hypochondria (,haɪpə'kɒndrɪə) *nu* being very anxious about one's health, when this is not necessary.

hypocrisy (hɪ'pɒkrəsɪ) *nc, pl* **-sies 1** *nu* false behaviour; pretending to be good, nice, etc. **2** *nc* an example of this. **hypocrite** ('hɪpəkrɪt) *nc* a person who behaves in this way.

hypodermic (,haɪpə'dɜːmɪk) *adj* (of medical substances, etc.) forced under the skin. ● *n* See **syringe.**

hypotenuse (haɪ'pɒtənjuːz) *nc* the side opposite the right angle (90°) in a right-angled triangle: see picture.

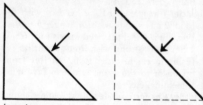

hypotenuse

hypothesis (haɪ'pɒθəsɪs) *nc, pl* **-ses** (siːz) an idea, etc., that is thought but not yet proved to be true. **hypothetical** (,haɪpə'θetɪkəl) *adj*

hyssop ('hɪsəp) *nc* a small, sweet-smelling plant, used as medicine.

hysteria (hɪ'stɪərɪə) *nu* **1** disturbance of the mind causing the feelings to become uncontrolled. **2** excitement that is uncontrolled. **hysterical** (hɪ'sterɪkəl) *adj* **hysterics** (hɪ'sterɪks) *n pl* fits of hysteria.

I

I (aɪ) *pron* (used by a speaker or writer when referring to himself or herself).

ice (aɪs) **1** *nu* water that has frozen; layer of this on top of water. **2** *nc* frozen, sweet cream, etc. ●*vi* **1** become very cold. **2** *vt* put icing on (a cake). *vi* **3** (followed by **over**) be or become covered with **ice** (def. 1). **4** (followed by **up**) freeze solid. **Ice Age** the time when much of the northern half of the earth was covered with ice. **iceberg** (ˈaɪsbɜːg) *nc* a large quantity of ice floating in the sea. **ice cream 1** frozen, sweet cream, etc. **2** a piece of this. **ice skating** the act of sliding on ice, using boots with metal blades. **ice hockey** a game played on ice by two teams of six players wearing skates and using sticks and a flat, round, piece of rubber.

icicle (ˈaɪsɪkəl) *nc* a thin, pointed, hanging piece of ice, produced by water falling off a surface in drops and freezing: see picture.

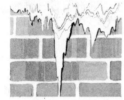

icicle

icing (ˈaɪsɪŋ) *nu* sugar mixed with the white of an egg, etc., for covering a cake.

icy (ˈaɪsɪ) *adj* **-ier, -iest 1** very cold. **2** covered with ice.

I'd (aɪd) I had or I would.

idea (aɪˈdɪə) *nc* **1** a thought. **2** an opinion; person's thoughts on a subject. **3** a plan.

ideal (aɪˈdɪəl) *adj* **1** perfect; very good. **2** (of a thought) only hopeful, not likely to become real: *an ideal world.* ●*nu* **1** something perfect, to be aimed at rather than reached. **2** *nc* an example of this. **idealise** (aɪˈdɪəlaɪz) *vt* think of (a person, thing, etc.) as being perfect. **idealism** (aɪˈdɪəlɪzəm) *nu* the act of living or trying to live in a way that is equal to what one considers perfect. **idealist** *nc* a person who believes in idealism. **ideally** *adv*

identical (aɪˈdentɪkəl) *adj* exactly the same.

identify (aɪˈdentɪfaɪ) *vt* discover or say who or what (a person or thing) is exactly. **identification** (aɪ,dentɪfɪˈkeɪʃən) *nu* the saying what somebody or something is.

identity (aɪˈdentɪtɪ) **1** *nu* the state of being exactly the same. **2** *ncu, pl* **-ties** the state of being at all times someone or something in particular: *Have you proof of your identity?*

ideology (,aɪdɪˈɒlədʒɪ) *nc, pl* **-gies** the way a person, class of people, group, etc., thinks; body or system of ideas, esp. in economics or politics. **ideological** (,aɪdɪəˈlɒdʒɪkəl) *adj* of or to do with ideology.

idiocy (ˈɪdɪəsɪ) **1** *nu* great stupidity. **2** *nc, pl* **-cies** very stupid acts, words, etc.

idiom (ˈɪdɪəm) *ncu* **1** the language of a people or country. **2** the special qualities of this language. **3** *grammar nc* a set of words, the special meaning of which can only be understood if learnt together and not separately: for example, *'bring the house down' meaning 'cause great laughter'.* **idiomatic** (,ɪdɪəˈmætɪk) *adj* (of a set of words, used) in the manner of an **idiom** (def. 3).

idiosyncrasy (,ɪdɪəˈsɪnkrəsɪ) *nc, pl* **-sies** an idea, way of behaving, etc., that belongs to a particular person's character.

idiot (ˈɪdɪət) *nc* **1** a person whose mind is so weak that he is not able to understand, have opinions, etc. **2** *infml* a stupid person; fool. **idiotic** (,ɪdɪˈɒtɪk) *adj* stupid.

idle (ˈaɪdəl) *adj* **1** lazy; not wanting to work. **2** not being used; not working. **3** of no use or worth. ●*vi* be idle. **idle away** use (time) in an idle way. **idleness** *nu* the state of being idle. **idly** (aɪdlɪ) *adv*

idol (ˈaɪdəl) *nc* **1** something of wood, stone, etc., that is worshipped because it is believed to have great power; false god. **2** someone or something greatly respected, loved, etc., sometimes unwisely. **idolatry** (aɪˈdɒlətrɪ) *ncu, pl* **-tries** the worship of idols; an example of this. **idolise** (ˈaɪdəlaɪz) *vt* love or respect (someone or something) too much.

idyllic (ɪˈdɪlɪk, aɪˈdɪlɪk) *adj* very pleasant.

if (ɪf) *conj* **1** on the condition that; supposing that: *I'll go for a walk if it stops raining.* **2** when: *If you don't understand, tell me.* **3** whether: *Ask if you may borrow his car.* **if only 1** (in a sudden, short cry showing surprise, a wish, etc.): *If only I were rich!* **2** even though there may be no other reason (than): *I shall come to the dance, if only to see who else is there.*

igloo (ˈɪgluː) *nc* a rounded shelter of hard snow in which Eskimos live: see picture.

igloo

igneous ('ɪgnɪəs) *adj* (of rocks) produced by the fire, ashes, etc., coming out of an opening in a mountain or hill.

ignite (ɪg'naɪt) 1 *vt* set fire to. 2 *vi* become on fire. **ignition** (ɪg'nɪʃən) *nc* 1 the act of setting fire to or being set on fire. 2 an electrical device in the engine of a car, etc., for igniting the gases to make it go.

ignoble (ɪg'nəʊbəl) *adj* shameful; without honour.

ignominy ('ɪgnəmɪnɪ) *ncu, pl* -**nies** shame or dishonour; a shameful act. **ignominious** (,ɪgnə'mɪnɪəs) *adj* causing or deserving shame.

ignorance ('ɪgnərəns) *nu* being without much or any knowledge. **ignorant** *adj* 1 having little knowledge. 2 behaving in a rough, awkward manner.

ignore (ɪg'nɔː*) *vt* take no notice of.

I'll (aɪl) I will or I shall.

ill (ɪl) *adj* 1 in bad health. 2 unkind. 3 bad. ●*nu* 1 evil. 2 *nc* trouble. ●*adv* badly; wrongly. **ill-advised** (,ɪləd'vaɪzd) *adj* unwise. **ill-fated** (,ɪl'feɪtɪd) *adj* bringing or fated to bring bad luck. **ill-feeling** (,ɪl'fiːlɪŋ) 1 *nu* strong dislike. 2 *nc* an example of this. **ill-treatment** (,ɪl'triːtmənt) *nu* being treated or treating in a cruel or bad way.

illegal (ɪ'liːgəl) *adj* against the law.

illegible (ɪ'ledʒəbəl) *adj* (of writing) not able to be read easily or not at all: *His writing is an illegible scrawl.*

illegitimate (,ɪlɪ'dʒɪtɪmət) *adj* 1 not lawful. 2 born of a man and woman who are not married.

illicit (ɪ'lɪsɪt) *adj* not lawful; forbidden; not proper.

illiterate (ɪ'lɪtərət) *adj* 1 not able to read or write. 2 having little education. **illiteracy** (ɪ'lɪtərəsɪ) *nu* not being able to read or write.

illness ('ɪlnɪs) 1 *nu* being in bad health. 2 *nc* a disease.

illogical (ɪ'lɒdʒɪkəl) *adj* against reason.

illuminate (ɪ'ljuːmɪneɪt) *vt* 1 give light to. 2 make clear or easier to understand. 3 decorate (streets, buildings, etc.) with bright lights. 4 decorate (a book, etc.) with gold, silver, and bright colours. **illumination** (ɪ,ljuːmɪ'neɪʃən) 1 *nu* the state of giving or being given light to. 2 *(pl)* decorations in the streets, etc.

illumine (ɪ'ljuːmɪn) *vt* 1 make bright. 2 give knowledge of God to.

illusion (ɪ'luːʒən) 1 *nc* the seeing of something that is not really there; something that does not exist. 2 *nu* the state of having a mistaken idea or belief. **be under an illusion** be deceived by illusion. **illusory** (ɪ'luːsərɪ) *adj* deceiving.

illustrate ('ɪləstreɪt) *vt* 1 explain (something) by giving an example. 2 provide (a book, etc.) with pictures. **illustration** (,ɪlə-'streɪʃən) 1 *nu* adding or being supplied with pictures. 2 *nc* a picture, drawing, etc. **illustrative** ('ɪləstrətɪv) *adj* explaining or being an example of. **illustrator** ('ɪləstreɪtə*) *nc* a person who does pictures, drawings, etc., for a book.

illustrious (ɪ'lʌstrɪəs) *adj* famous; well known.

I'm (aɪm) I am.

image ('ɪmɪdʒ) *nc* 1 something in wood or stone made to the likeness of a person or thing. 2 a great likeness. 3 a picture in the mind. 4 what a person or thing is like, as seen by the public. 5 a picture of oneself, etc., seen in a mirror, or through the lens of a camera.

imagery ('ɪmədʒərɪ) *nu* using words that bring pictures to the mind.

imagine (ɪ'mædʒɪn) *vt* 1 make a picture of (something) in the mind: *Imagine you were a millionaire!* 2 believe; guess: *I imagine he's very busy.* **imaginable** (ɪ'mædʒɪnəbəl) *adj* that can be thought of or pictured; able to be imagined. **imaginary** (ɪ'mædʒɪnərɪ) *adj* not real: only in the mind. **imagination** (ɪ,mædʒɪ'neɪʃən) *ncu* 1 the power of imagining. 2 a thing that is imagined. **imaginative** (ɪ'mædʒɪnətɪv) *adj* 1 having much power to imagine. 2 showing imagination.

imam (ɪ'mɑːm) *nc* 1 the person who leads prayers in a mosque. 2 a title of various Muslim leaders.

imbecile ('ɪmbəsiːl) *nc* a person with very little power of the mind to understand, etc. ●*adj* stupid.

imbibe (ɪm'baɪb) *formal vt* 1 drink (esp. alcohol). 2 take into the mind: *imbibe ideas.*

imbue (ɪm'bjuː) *v* **imbue with** *formal* fill with (thoughts, feelings, etc.): *imbued with confidence.*

imitate ('ɪmɪteɪt) *vt* copy the behaviour of (someone or something); take as an example. **imitation** (,ɪmɪ'teɪʃən) 1 *nu* the act of copying; taking as an example. 2 *nc* something done or made in imitation. ●*adj* not real. **imitator** *nc* a person or thing that copies.

immaculate (ɪ'mækjʊlət) *adj* pure; without fault.

immaterial (,ɪmə'tɪərɪəl) *adj* 1 (often followed by **to**) not important; not connected with. 2 not having real substance.

immature (,ɪmə'tjʊə*) *adj* not fully grown or developed.

immeasurable (ɪ'meʒərəbəl) *adj* not able to be measured; huge.

immediate (ɪ'miːdɪət) *adj* 1 most near. 2 happening at once. **immediately** *adv* at once.

immense (ɪˈmens) *adj* huge. **immensely** *adj* very; very much; to a very great degree. **immensity** (ɪˈmensɪtɪ) *ncu, pl* **-ties** 1 *nu* very large size. *nc* 2 an example of this. 3 *(pl)* things of very large size.

immerse (ɪˈmɜːs) *vt* (followed by **in**) 1 put into water, etc., until entirely covered. 2 occupy: *He's immersed in his work.* **immersion** (ɪˈmɜːʃən) *ncu* immersing or being immersed. **immersion heater** an electric device that is put into water to heat it, esp. one that is fixed in a hot-water tank.

immigrant (ˈɪmɪgrənt) *nc* a person who has left his own country to come and live permanently in another. **immigrate** (ˈɪmɪgreɪt) *vi* come to live permanently in another country. **immigration** (ɪmɪˈgreɪʃən) *ncu* the act of immigrating; an example of this.

imminent (ˈɪmɪnənt) *adj* likely to happen very soon: *imminent danger.*

immobilise (ɪˈməʊbɪlaɪz) *vt* fix or make so as to prevent movement.

immoral (ɪˈmɒrəl) *adj* of bad or evil character.

immortal (ɪˈmɔːtəl) *adj* never dying. **immortalise** (ɪˈmɔːtəlaɪz) *vt* make (someone) live or last for ever. **immortality** (ˌɪmɔːˈtælɪtɪ) *nu* the life or fame that never ends.

immovable (ɪˈmuːvəbəl) *adj* not able to be moved.

immune (ɪˈmjuːn) *adj* (followed by **from, to,** or **against**) free (from); able to resist. **immunisation** (ˌɪmjʊnaɪˈzeɪʃən) *nu* the act of making immune, esp. from a disease by injecting tiny, harmless organisms into a person or animal. **immunise** (ɪmjʊnaɪz) *vt* make able to resist infection, etc. **immunity** (ɪmjuːnɪtɪ) *nu* medicine the state of being able to resist disease. 2 the freedom, or being excused, from a duty or responsibility: *They were granted immunity from paying tax.*

imp (ɪmp) *nc* a little devil; rather naughty child.

impact (ˈɪmpækt) (followed by **on**) 1 *nc* an act of striking together; collision. *nu* 2 the force used by one thing striking against another. 3 an effect. ● (ɪmˈpækt) *vt* press or fix firmly into.

impair (ɪmˈpeə*) *vt* damage; make less strong.

impale (ɪmˈpeɪl) *vt* push into or through (something) with force, using an object with a sharp point.

impart (ɪmˈpɑːt) *formal vt* pass on (news, feelings, a message, etc.).

impartial (ɪmˈpɑːʃəl) *adj* fair, not supporting one more than another: *an impartial judge.*

impassable (ɪmˈpɑːsəbəl) *adj* (of a country, road, etc.) not able to be travelled through or on.

impasse (ˈæmpɑːs) *nc* 1 a narrow passage or street closed at one end. 2 a place or position from which there is no escape. 3 a failure to agree.

impassioned (ɪmˈpæʃənd) *adj* full of feeling: *an impassioned speech.*

impassive (ɪmˈpæsɪv) *adj* showing no sign of feeling: *an impassive face.*

impatience (ɪmˈpeɪʃəns) *nu* the state of being unable to stay calm if someone or something is slow or late; wanting things done or to happen quickly. **impatient** (ɪmˈpeɪʃənt) *adj* **impatiently** *adv*

impeach (ɪmˈpiːtʃ) *law vt* accuse (a person) of doing great wrong, esp. against the State.

impeccable (ɪmˈpekəbəl) *formal adj* without a fault; very unlikely to do wrong.

impede (ɪmˈpiːd) *vt* delay; get in the way of.

impediment (ɪmˈpedɪmənt) *nc* something that causes a delay or that causes something not to happen properly.

impel (ɪmˈpel) *vt* force; urge on.

impending (ɪmˈpendɪŋ) *adj* about to happen.

impenetrable (ɪmˈpenɪtrəbəl) *adj* 1 not able to have a way found through. 2 not able to be understood or known.

imperative (ɪmˈperətɪv) *adj* 1 urgent; greatly needed. 2 expecting to be obeyed: *an imperative manner.* ● *adj, nc* grammar (the form of the verb used when) giving a command: for example, *'do'* in *'Do it quickly'.*

imperceptible (ˌɪmpəˈseptəbəl) *adj* not to be known by just looking; almost not seen, heard, etc.

imperfect (ɪmˈpɜːfɪkt) *adj* 1 with a fault or faults. 2 not finished or complete. ● *adj, nc* grammar (the form of a verb used when) showing action still going on: *'She was dancing'* is an example of the imperfect form of the verb *'to dance'.* **imperfection** (ˌɪmpəˈfekʃən) *ncu* the state of being imperfect; a fault.

imperial (ɪmˈpɪərɪəl) *adj* of an empire or its ruler. **imperialism** (ɪmˈpɪərɪəlɪzəm) *nu* the aim of making a country or empire larger and more powerful by controlling parts of other countries. **imperious** (ɪmˈpɪərɪəs) *formal adj* too much pride in oneself; liking to use power.

imperil (ɪmˈperɪl) *literary vt* put into danger.

impersonal (ɪmˈpɜːsənəl) *adj* 1 not affected by any feelings: *impersonal behaviour.* 2 not having to do with any particular person: *an impersonal remark.*

impersonate (ɪmˈpɜːsəneɪt) *vt* pretend to be (another person) in a play, etc., or in order to deceive. **impersonation** (ɪmˌpɜːsəˈneɪʃən) 1 *nu* the act of pretending to be another person. 2 *nc* an example of this.

impertinent (ɪmˈpɜːtɪnənt) *adj* without proper respect; rude. **impertinence**

(ɪmˈpɜːtɪnəns) *ncu* the act of being impertinent; a rude act or remark.

imperturbable (ˌɪmpəˈtɜːbəbəl) *formal adj* not easily made excited; calm.

impervious (ɪmˈpɜːvɪəs) *adj* 1 (of some materials) not allowing water, etc., to pass through. 2 (of a person) not affected by.

impetuous (ɪmˈpetjʊəs) *adj* acting quickly with little thought or care.

impetus (ˈɪmpɪtəs) 1 *nc* the force that drives someone or something. 2 *nu* the force with which a body moves.

impinge (ɪmˈpɪndʒ) *vi* (often followed by **on**) have an effect (on) or strike (against).

impious (ˈɪmpɪəs) *formal adj* not showing respect, esp. for God or spiritual matters.

impish (ˈɪmpɪʃ) *adj* of or like an imp; naughty in a playful way.

implacable (ɪmˈplækəbəl) *formal adj* (of anger, an enemy, etc.) not able to be calmed or satisfied.

implant (ɪmˈplɑːnt) *vt* fix (ideas, thoughts, etc.) deeply into.

implement (ˈɪmplɪmənt) *nc* a tool: *garden implements; implements for cooking with.* ●(ˈɪmplɪment) *vt* put (a plan, promise, agreement, etc.) into action.

implicate (ˈɪmplɪkeɪt) *formal vt* show that (a person) has taken part in a crime, etc. **implication** (ˌɪmplɪˈkeɪʃən) 1 *nu* the state of being implicated in something. 2 *nc* something that is suggested but not said directly.

implicit (ɪmˈplɪsɪt) *formal adj* 1 suggested but not said directly. 2 accepted without questions; complete.

implore (ɪmˈplɔː*) *vt* ask very seriously for, esp. when in great need.

imply (ɪmˈplaɪ) *vt* 1 suggest or mean (something) without saying it directly. 2 have as a result or consequence.

impolite (ˌɪmpəˈlaɪt) *adj* not polite; rude.

import (ɪmˈpɔːt) *vt* bring (goods) into a country from a foreign country; bring (something) into use from another place. ●(ˈɪmpɔːt) *nc* 1 something brought into a country, esp. for sale. *nu* 2 importing goods. 3 meaning: *The import of his speech was very clear.* **importation** (ˌɪmpɔːˈteɪʃən) 1 *nu* importing. 2 *nc* a thing that is imported. **importer** (ɪmˈpɔːtə*) *nc* someone whose business is to import goods.

important (ɪmˈpɔːtənt) *adj* 1 (regarded as) special; particularly useful. 2 having the power to affect people or things; to be thought of in a serious way. 3 (of a person) having a high position with power. **importance** *nu* the state of being important. **importantly** *adv*

importunity (ˌɪmpɔːˈtjuːnɪtɪ) *formal nu* the act of continuing to ask for things even when this causes annoyance, anger, etc.

impose (ɪmˈpəʊz) *vt* 1 put (a tax, etc.), on something. 2 force (a task, etc.) on (a person). **imposing** (ɪmˈpəʊzɪŋ) *adj* making a deep effect on someone because of appearance, size, etc.

imposition (ˌɪmpəˈzɪʃən) 1 *nu* the putting on of a tax, etc.; the forcing of a task, etc., on. 2 *nc* a thing imposed.

impossible (ɪmˈpɒsəbəl) *adj* 1 not able to be done; not able to happen or be. 2 *infml* that cannot be put up with: *He's impossible!* **impossibility** (ɪmˌpɒsəˈbɪlɪtɪ) *nc, pl* **-ties** 1 *nu* the state of being impossible. 2 *nc* something that is impossible.

impostor (ɪmˈpɒstə*) *nc* a person pretending to be someone he is not in order to deceive someone else.

impotent (ˈɪmpətənt) *adj* 1 not able to act or have any effect. 2 (of a man) not having any sexual power. **impotence** *nu* the state of being impotent.

impoverish (ɪmˈpɒvərɪʃ) *vt* 1 make poor. 2 use up the strength and good qualities of (a person, the soil, etc.).

impracticable (ɪmˈpræktɪkəbəl) *adj* not possible or able to be done.

impractical (ɪmˈpræktɪkəl) *adj* not possible to be put into action.

impregnable (ɪmˈpregnəbəl) *adj* that can resist any attack.

impregnate (ˈɪmpregneɪt) *vt* (often followed by **with**) 1 make (a female) able to produce young, or (a tree, etc.) fruit. 2 fill with.

impress (ɪmˈpres) *vt* (followed by **on, upon,** or **with**) 1 make a mark by pressing (one thing) on another. 2 have a strong effect on (a person, the mind, etc.). **impression** (ɪmˈpreʃən) *nc* 1 a mark made by pressing. 2 the effect of someone or something on a person, the mind, feelings, etc. 3 a thought, perhaps not clear or wrong, coming into the mind. 4 a quantity of books printed at one time. 5 a picture, etc., made by printing. **impressionable** (ɪmˈpreʃənəbəl) *adj* easily affected by other people, their opinions, etc.

impressionism (ɪmˈpreʃənɪzəm) *nu* a way of painting pictures that gives an effect rather than all the details of a scene. **impressionist** (ɪmˈpreʃənɪst) *nc* a person who paints in this way.

impressive (ɪmˈpresɪv) *adj* causing feelings of admiration, etc.

imprint (ˈɪmprɪnt) *nc* a mark made by pressing or stamping. ●(ɪmˈprɪnt) *vt* (followed by **with** or **on**) press; print; stamp.

imprison (ɪmˈprɪzən) *vt* put into prison. **imprisonment** (ɪmˈprɪzənmənt) *nu* the act of putting or being put into prison.

improbable (ɪmˈprɒbəbəl) *adj* not likely to happen; not likely to be true.

impromptu (ım'prɒmptjuː) *adj, adv* done without earlier thought or preparation.

improper (ım'prɒpə*) *adj* **1** not fitting or suitable. **2** not decent. **improperly** *adv*

improve (ım'pruːv) *vti* make or become better. **improvement** **1** *nu* improving or being improved. *nc* **2** an act of improving or being improved. **3** something that improves or makes something else improve.

improvise ('ımprəvaız) **1** *vti* do or make (something) or play or write (music, etc.) without earlier thought or preparation. **2** *vt* do or make quickly, when not prepared, by using whatever one has. **improvisation** (ˌımprəvaı'zeıʃən) *nc* something done without earlier preparation.

impudent ('ımpjʊdənt) *adj* very rude; lacking any respect. **impudence** *nu* being impudent.

impulse ('ımpʌls) **1** *nc* a sudden desire to act without thinking about the results. **2** *nu* the state of mind in which this desire is a habit: *He's a man of impulse.*

impulsive (ım'pʌlsıv) *adj* acting suddenly and without a plan. **impulsively** *adv*

impunity (ım'pjuːnıtı) *nu* freedom from punishment.

impure (ım'pjʊə*) *adj* not pure; dirty. **impurity** (ım'pjʊərıtı) *ncu, pl* **-ties** being not pure; a thing that is not pure.

impute (ım'pjuːt) *vt* (often followed by **to**) consider as belonging to, being the cause of, or the act of. **imputation** (ˌımpjuː-'teıʃən) **1** *nu* imputing. **2** *nc* an accusation.

in (ın) *prep* **1** (showing a position where something is): *He's working in London.* **2** (showing when something happens): *in winter.* **3** inside; contained by: *with his hands in his pockets; twelve months in a year.* **4** during; within a space of time: *I'll return in a few days' time.* **5** at the task of: *He's done well in English.* **6** (working) for or within: *He's in the police.* ●*adv* **1** at home: *I'm staying in today.* **2** arrive: *Is the train in yet?* **3** able to be used or be present: *I will be in next week.* **4** fashionable; popular: *Hats are in this season.* **5** to, or having, a position of power: *Which party was in then?* **in all** as a total: *In all, there were ten of us.* **be in for 1** be expecting to undergo something, esp. trouble: *We're in for a hard winter.* **2** be taking part in (a competition, race, etc.) **be in with** be very friendly with. **have it in for (someone)** be waiting for the chance to punish someone. **ins and outs** all the details, both good and bad: *the ins and outs of the problem.* **day in, day out; week in, week out; year in, year out** day after day, week after week, year after year, never changing and not interesting because of this.

inability (ınə'bılıtı) *nu* the state of being unable.

inaccessible (ˌınək'sesəbəl) *adj* not able to be reached, used, etc.

inaccurate (ın'ækjʊrət) *adj* with mistakes.

inactive (ın'æktıv) *adj* not acting; lazy; slow-moving.

inadequate (ın'ædıkwət) *adj* not satisfactory; not enough; not having the power, etc., to do something.

inadmissible (ˌınəd'mısəbəl) *adj* not (to be) allowed: *inadmissible evidence.*

inadvertent (ˌınəd'vɜːtənt) *adj* done without care or attention; not intended. **inadvertently** *adv*

inalienable (ın'eılıənəbəl) *formal adj* (of a person's rights, etc.) that cannot be taken away or separated from.

inane (ın'eın) *adj* silly; worthless.

inanimate (ın'ænımət) *adj* **1** without life: *inanimate stones.* **2** without the life of a man or animal: *inanimate nature.* **3** dull; not lively: *an inanimate conversation.*

inappropriate (ˌınə'prəʊprıət) *adj* not fitting or suitable.

inarticulate (ˌınɑː'tıkjʊlət) *adj* not able to speak clearly; not able to express one's thoughts, feelings, etc., clearly and smoothly.

inasmuch (ˌınəz'mʌtʃ) *adv* **inasmuch as** since; because.

inaudible (ın'ɔːdıbəl) *adj* not able to be heard.

inaugural (ın'ɔːgjʊrəl) *adj* to do with a special occasion marking the formal beginning of a course of action or of someone's job.

inaugurate (ın'ɔːgjʊreıt) *vt* **1** introduce (a person), at a formal event, to a new job in a public position. **2** begin (a special task) or open (a new building, etc.) with a formal and public event. **3** be the beginning of. **inauguration** (ıˌnɔːgjʊ'reıʃən) *ncu* the act of being begun, or introduced, with a public and formal event.

inborn ('ınbɔːn) *adj* (of a person or animal) having a quality or ability from birth; natural.

inbred (ın'bred) *adj* **1** inborn. **2** bred within the same family for several hundred years past.

inbreeding (ˌın'briːdıŋ) *nu* (of people or farm animals) having parents who are closely related to each other.

incalculable (ın'kælkjʊləbəl) *adj* **1** too great to be measured or counted. **2** (of a person's character, feelings, etc.) often altering.

incandescent (ˌınkæn'desənt) *adj* (of light) produced by heat.

incantation (ˌınkæn'teıʃən) **1** *nu* the singing or speaking of a set of words, supposed to have magic power. **2** *nc* an example of this.

incapable (ın'keıpəbəl) *adj* not able to do something because of lack of ability, power, desire to, etc.

incapacitate (,ınkə'pæsıteıt) *vt* make unable or unfit.

incarcerate (ın'kɑːsəreıt) *formal vt* put in prison.

incarnate (ın'kɑːnıt) *adj* 1 (of a person or spirit) having a body, esp. a human one. 2 (of an idea, quality, etc.) appearing in human, or some other, form: *Beauty incarnate.* ● (ın'kɑːneıt) *vt* give bodily form to.

incarnation (,ınkɑː'neıʃən) *ncu* (esp. of a divine being) the act of taking on a bodily form.

incendiary (ın'sendjərı) *nc, pl* **-ries** a person who sets fire to buildings with an evil intention; person trying to cause serious trouble and violence. ●*adj* 1 that sets fire to buildings on purpose and with an evil intention. 2 trying to cause serious trouble and violence.

incense¹ ('ınsens) *nu* 1 a substance that smells sweet when burning. 2 smoke from this substance.

incense² (ın'sens) *vt* make angry.

incentive (ın'sentıv) *ncu* that which urges on or encourages a person to act, etc.

inception (ın'sepʃən) *formal nc* a beginning.

incessant (ın'sesənt) *adj* going on all the time without stopping.

incest ('ınsest) *nu* sexual relations between two people of the same family, such as a mother and her son.

inch (ıntʃ) *nc* a measure of length = ¹/₁₂ of a foot, or, ¹/₃₆ of a yard, or .025 m ●*vti* (often followed by **towards, nearer,** or **along**) move very gradually, almost by inches.

incidence ('ınsıdəns) *nu* the way in which something affects things or the way it falls: *The incidence of a disease shows us the number of people who catch it.*

incident ('ınsıdənt) *nc* a happening, esp. one that is less important or serious than others. **incidental** (,ınsı'dentəl) *adj* 1 done, or happening, at the same time, but not forming an essential part. 2 small and unimportant. **incidentally** *adv* 1 in an incidental way. 2 (used to introduce an unconnected remark); by the way.

incinerator (ın'sınəreıtə*) *nc* a large, enclosed fire for burning rubbish, etc.: see picture.

incipient (ın'sıpıənt) *formal adj* just at the beginning or at an early stage.

incision (ın'sıʒən) 1 *nu* the act of cutting into something. 2 *nc* a cut, esp. one made by a surgeon on a part of the body. **incisive** (ın'saısıv) *adj* 1 cutting; sharp. 2 (of a person's mind or words) sharp and quick.

incinerator

incisor (ın'saızə*) *nc* any one of the eight, sharp, cutting-teeth in the front of the mouth, four in the upper jaw and four in the lower.

incite (ın'saıt) *vt* urge on; stir up. **incitement** 1 *nu* inciting. 2 *nc* something that incites; example of inciting.

inclement (ın'klemənt) *formal adj* (of the weather or climate) bad, esp. cold or stormy.

inclination (,ınklı'neıʃən) *nc* 1 a slope; leaning or bending. 2 (often followed by **to, towards,** or **for**) a liking or desire; tendency.

incline (ın'klaın) *vt* (often followed by **to** or **towards**) 1 slope; lean; bend (one's head, body, etc.) forward or downward. 2 lean (the mind) in a particular direction; give (someone) the wish (to do something). 3 *vi* be willing or ready to; tend to. ● ('ınklaın) *nc* a slope.

include (ın'kluːd) *vt* consider as part of or belonging to. **inclusion** (ın'kluːʒən) *nu* including or being included. **inclusive** (ın'kluːsıv) *adj* including; (of the first and last, or beginning and end) being included: *I have a week's holiday from 7 June to 13 June, inclusive.*

incognito (,ınkɒg'niːtəʊ) *adj* giving oneself a different name or identity. ●*adv* with one's name, identity, etc., kept secret.

incoherent (,ınkəʊ'hıərənt) *adj* (esp. of speech) not clearly heard, or easily understood, because of some difficulty.

income ('ınkʌm) *nc* money received, esp. one's total salary for the year. **income tax** a personal tax placed on income when it gets higher than a certain level.

incomparable (ın'kɒmpərəbəl) *adj* not to be compared with anything else because so much better, greater, etc.

incompatible (,ınkəm'pætəbəl) *adj* (usually followed by **with**) (of two or more ideas, people, or things) not able to be, agree, or work together.

incompetent (ın'kɒmpıtənt) *adj* not able to do what is needed because of lack of ability, training, etc. **incompetence** (ın'kɒmpıtəns) *nu* the state of being incompetent.

incomplete (,ınkəm'pliːt) *adj* not whole or finished.

incomprehensible (ɪn,kɒmprɪˈhensəbəl) *adj* not able to be understood.

inconceivable (,ɪnkənˈsiːvəbəl) *adj* 1 that cannot be imagined. 2 *infml* impossible; difficult to believe.

inconclusive (,ɪnkənˈkluːsɪv) *adj* (of evidence, an argument, or action) not being definite or certain.

incongruous (ɪnˈkɒŋgrʊəs) *adj* not in agreement; not suitable. **incongruity** (,ɪnkɒŋˈgruːɪtɪ) *ncu, pl* **-ties** being incongruous; someone or something that is incongruous.

inconsiderate (,ɪnkənˈsɪdərət) *adj* not thinking about, or caring for, the needs, feelings, etc., of others.

inconsistent (,ɪnkənˈsɪstənt) *adj* 1 having parts that are not in agreement. 2 acting in a way that is not in agreement with one's usual way of behaviour, etc. **inconsistency** (,ɪnkənˈsɪstənsɪ) *ncu, pl* **-cies** (an example of) being inconsistent.

inconspicuous (,ɪnkənˈspɪkjʊəs) *adj* not easily seen or noticed.

incontinent (ɪnˈkɒntɪnənt) *adj* 1 lacking self-control. 2 *medicine* unable to control the passing out of waste matter from the body. **incontinence** (ɪnˈkɒntɪnəns) *nu* being **incontinent** (def. 2).

inconvenient (,ɪnkənˈviːnɪənt) *adj* causing difficulty, trouble, or discomfort. **inconvenience** (,ɪnkənˈviːnɪəns) 1 *nu* being inconvenient. 2 *nc* a cause or example of difficulty, trouble, or discomfort. ●*vt* cause trouble or annoyance to.

incorporate (ɪnˈkɔːpəreɪt) *vti* 1 make or become united in one group or body. 2 *law* form a business company.

incorrect (,ɪnkəˈrekt) *adj* 1 not true; wrong. 2 (of behaviour, the way one dresses, etc.) not suitable; not in agreement with good taste. **incorrectly** *adv*

incorrigible (ɪnˈkɒrɪdʒəbəl) *adj* (of a person, his faults, habits, etc.) that cannot be improved.

increase (ɪnˈkriːs) *vti* make or become greater in (size, number, value, etc.). ● (ˈɪnkriːs) 1 *nu* increasing. 2 *nc* an amount by which something has grown. **increasingly** (ɪnˈkriːsɪŋlɪ) *adv* more and more.

incredible (ɪnˈkredəbəl) *adj* 1 that cannot be believed. 2 *infml* that cannot be easily believed. **incredibly** (ɪnˈkredəblɪ) *adv*

incredulous (ɪnˈkredjʊləs) *adj* not willing to believe; disbelieving. **incredulity** (,ɪnkrəˈdjuːlɪtɪ) *nu* disbelief.

increment (ˈɪnkrəmənt) *nc* an example of an act of increasing; the amount of an increase. **incremental** (,ɪnkrɪˈmentəl) *adj* to do with an increment.

incriminate (ɪnˈkrɪmɪneɪt) *vt* show or cause (someone) to be accused of doing wrong.

incubate (ˈɪnkjʊbeɪt) 1 *vt* (of birds) cause (eggs) to be kept warm by sitting on them, so as to bring forth young birds, etc. 2 *vi* sit on eggs. **incubation** (,ɪnkjʊˈbeɪʃən) *ncu* the act of incubating eggs. **incubator** (ˈɪnkjʊbeɪtə*) *nc* a mechanical device for incubating eggs, or for nursing and keeping warm very small babies who are born too early: see picture.

incubator

incumbent (ɪnˈkʌmbənt) *adj* **be incumbent on** or **upon** *formal* be a duty resting on or left to (someone). ●*nc* 1 a person who holds a particular job. 2 a priest, etc., who lives on a property that produces an income and which is owned by the Church.

incur (ɪnˈkɜː*) *vt* 1 meet with (something), usually unpleasant: *incur someone's anger*. 2 cause (something) to be brought onto oneself: *incur great debts*.

incurable (ɪnˈkjʊərəbəl) *adj* that cannot be cured.

incursion (ɪnˈkɜːʃən) *nc* 1 a sudden attack. 2 entering, visiting, etc., esp. for a short time and without being invited.

indebted (ɪnˈdetɪd) *adj* (followed by **to**) owing money or gratitude.

indecent (ɪnˈdiːsənt) *adj* 1 (of behaviour, esp. sexual) likely to shock or embarrass other people. 2 *infml* not proper.

indecision (,ɪndɪˈsɪʒən) *nu* the state of not being able to decide. **indecisive** (,ɪndɪˈsaɪsɪv) *adj* not able to make decisions; hesitating.

indeed (ɪnˈdiːd) *adv* 1 really; in fact; truly: *I was indeed sorry to hear of his illness*. 2 (used to give more force to one's remarks): *Thank you very much indeed*. 3 (used to show surprise, disbelief, etc.): *He wants to become President.—Oh, does he indeed!*

indefatigable (,ɪndɪˈfætɪgəbəl) *adj* that cannot be tired out.

indefensible (,ɪndɪˈfensəbəl) *adj* that cannot be defended, or that no excuse can be given for.

indefinite (ɪnˈdefɪnɪt) *adj* not certain; not clearly stated. **indefinite article** See under **article**. **indefinitely** *adv*

indelible (ɪnˈdeləbəl) *adj* (of a mark or effect on something) that cannot be removed or rubbed out: *an indelible pencil; indelible memories*.

indelicate (ɪnˈdelɪkət) *adj* (of behaviour, talk, etc.) in bad taste; vulgar.

indemnify (ɪnˈdemnɪfaɪ) *vt* 1 *law* protect or make (a person) safe from harm or loss. 2 make good or pay back to (someone) any loss, esp. of money.

indemnity (ɪnˈdemnɪtɪ) *ncu, pl* **-ties** 1 being made safe against harm or loss; something that does this. 2 something given or received to make up for a loss, esp. money or goods paid to a country that has won in a war.

indent (ɪnˈdent) *vt* 1 make or form deep cuts in. 2 (in printing or writing) begin (a line of words) farther in than other lines from the edge, to show a new paragraph, etc. 3 order (goods) with an indent. 4 *vi* (of goods) to be ordered by an indent. ● (ˈindent) *nc* an official order made for goods. **indentation** (ˌɪndenˈteɪʃən) 1 *nu* the state of being indented. *nc* 2 a deep cut in the outline of a coast. 3 the space left at the beginning of a line of words.

indenture (ɪnˈdentʃə*) *nc* a written agreement, esp. one in which a learner of a trade agrees to work for a certain number of years, while being taught.

independent (ˌɪndɪˈpendənt) *adj* 1 not relying on or needing the support, help, etc., of other people or things. 2 free from the influence of others. 3 self-governing. **independence** (ˌɪndɪˈpendəns) *nu* being independent. **Independence Day** 4 July, when the USA remembers and celebrates the event which, on this day in 1776, made it independent of Great Britain. **independently** *adv*

in-depth (ˈindepθ) *adj* detailed; thorough.

indescribable (ˌɪndɪsˈkraɪbəbəl) *adj* too beautiful, great, etc., to be described: *indescribable joy*.

indestructible (ˌɪndɪsˈtrʌktəbəl) *adj* that cannot be destroyed.

indeterminate (ˌɪndɪˈtɜːmɪnət) *adj* not fixed.

index (ˈindeks) *nc, pl* **-dexes** or **-dices** (dɪsiːz) 1 a list of words, arranged in the order of the alphabet, at the end of a book, that tells where certain information can be found in it. 2 such a list on cards in a library. ● *vt* 1 put an index in (a book, etc.). 2 put (a word, etc.) in an index. **index finger** the first finger, next to the thumb: see picture.

index finger

indicate (ˈindɪkeɪt) *vt* 1 point to or out. 2 make known: *He indicated that he wanted me to go.* 3 be a sign of; show: *The dark skies indicate rain.* **indication** (ˌɪndɪˈkeɪʃən) 1 *nu* the act of indicating. *nc* 2 an example of this. 3 a sign that indicates. **indicative** (ɪnˈdɪkətɪv) *adj* being a sign or indication of. ● *adj, nc* grammar (to do with) the form of a verb that is used to show facts or questions, for example 'is' in 'He is here'. **indicator** *nc* (on a vehicle) a device, such as a flashing light, for showing a change of direction.

indict (ɪnˈdaɪt) *law vt* formally accuse (a person) of a crime. **indictable** (ɪnˈdaɪtəbəl) *adj* 1 (of a person) likely to be accused of a crime. 2 (of a crime) for which one may be accused. **indictment** (ɪnˈdaɪtmənt) 1 *nu* being indicted or indicting. 2 *nc* a written statement in which someone is accused of breaking the law.

indifferent (ɪnˈdɪfrənt) *adj* 1 having no interest in; neither against something nor in favour of it. 2 not very good; ordinary. **indifference** (ɪnˈdɪfrəns) *nu* being indifferent. **indifferently** *adv*

indigenisation (ˌɪndɪdʒɪnaɪˈzeɪʃən) *nu* being changed and made suitable for the needs, etc., of a certain country.

indigenous (ɪnˈdɪdʒɪnəs) *adj* belonging naturally to a certain district, country, etc.

indigestion (ˌɪndɪˈdʒestʃən) *nu* difficulty that the body has in dealing with food when it reaches the stomach; a pain caused by this difficulty. **indigestible** (ˌɪndɪˈdʒestəbəl) *adj* difficult or impossible to digest.

indignant (ɪnˈdɪgnənt) *adj* showing feelings of anger and scorn, esp. at something unjust. **indignantly** *adv* **indignation** (ˌɪndɪgˈneɪʃən) *nu* anger and scorn caused by lack of justice, etc.

indignity (ɪnˈdɪgnɪtɪ) *ncu, pl* **-ties** rude behaviour that causes shame; something said or done that causes a person to lose his self-respect.

indigo (ˈindɪgəʊ) *nu* a deep blue substance obtained from plants, used for changing the colour of cloth.

indirect (ˌɪndɪˈrekt) *adj* not going straight to a point, place, etc. **indirect object** grammar the person or thing that is affected by the verb, but is not the main object of it. **indirect speech** grammar the words of a speaker when reported to someone else, with any necessary changes of pronouns, tenses, etc. **indirectly** *adv*

indiscreet (ˌɪndɪsˈkriːt) *adj* acting without careful thought; tactless.

indiscretion (ˌɪndɪsˈkreʃən) 1 *nu* carelessness in what one says or does. 2 *nc* a careless remark or action.

indiscriminate (ˌɪndɪˈskrɪmɪnət) *adj* showing no care, thought, or taste. **indiscriminately** *adv*

indispensable (ˌɪndɪˈspensəbəl) *adj* that cannot be done without; greatly needed.

indisposed (ˌɪndɪˈspəʊzd) *adj* slightly ill; not well.

indisputable (ˌɪndɪˈspjuːtəbəl) *adj* that cannot be argued about because it is absolutely certain.

indistinct (ˌɪndɪˈstɪŋkt) *adj* not easily or clearly heard, seen, remembered, etc.

indistinguishable (ˌɪndɪˈstɪŋgwɪʃəbəl) *adj* not seen, heard, understood, etc., to be different from something else.

individual (ˌɪndɪˈvɪdʒʊəl) *adj* 1 specially of or for any one person, thing, etc. 2 having a quality that makes a person or thing different from others. ● *nc* 1 one particular person rather than a society, family, etc. 2 *infml* a person: *He's a miserable individual!*

individualism (ˌɪndɪˈvɪdʒʊəlɪzəm) *nu* the idea that every person in society should have complete freedom of thought and action. **individuality** (ˌɪndɪvɪdʒʊˈælɪtɪ) *nc, pl* -ties 1 *nu* a quality that makes a person or thing different from others. 2 *nc* a particular thing that a person likes, etc. **individually** *adv* separately.

indivisible (ˌɪndɪˈvɪzəbəl) *adj* that cannot be divided, separated, or split up.

indoctrinate (ɪnˈdɒktrɪneɪt) *vt* fill (a person's mind) with certain ideas, opinions, etc. **indoctrination** (ɪnˌdɒktrɪˈneɪʃən) *nu* being indoctrinated.

indolent (ˈɪndələnt) *adj* lazy.

indomitable (ɪnˈdɒmɪtəbəl) *adj* (of a quality of a person) that does not give in.

indoor (ˈɪndɔː*) *adj* (done, used, etc.) inside. **indoors** (ɪnˈdɔːz) *adv* inside a building.

induce (ɪnˈdjuːs) *vt* 1 persuade or cause. 2 cause to happen. **inducement** (ɪnˈdjuːsmənt) 1 *nu* inducing. 2 *nc* something that encourages or attracts a person.

induction (ɪnˈdʌkʃən) *nc* the causing of a piece of iron, etc., to be in an electric or magnetic state by being brought near something that is in an electric or magnetic state.

indulge (ɪnˈdʌldʒ) 1 *vt* please by giving what is wanted. 2 *vi* give oneself pleasure in something. **indulgence** (ɪnˈdʌldʒəns) 1 *nu* indulging. 2 *nc* something in which a person indulges. **indulgent** *adj*

industrial (ɪnˈdʌstrɪəl) *adj* to do with industry. **industrial action** action, such as a strike, taken by workers in industry or in other trades. **industrial estate** a piece of land on which factories, etc., and not houses, are built. **industrialisation** (ɪnˌdʌstrɪəlaɪˈzeɪʃən) *nu* being made or becoming industrial. **industrialise**

(ɪnˈdʌstrɪəlaɪz) 1 *vt* make industrial. 2 *vi* become industrial. **industrialist** *nc* 1 a person who owns an industry. 2 a person who strongly believes in the importance of large industries.

industrious (ɪnˈdʌstrɪəs) *adj* hard-working.

industry (ˈɪndəstrɪ) 1 *nu* being hard-working. 2 *ncu, pl* -ries trade; production of goods, materials, etc.

inebriate (ɪˈniːbrɪeɪt) *vt* make a person lose control of their actions by drinking too much alcohol.

inedible (ɪnˈedɪbəl) *adj* that is not fit to be eaten.

ineffective (ˌɪnɪˈfektɪv) *adj* having little or no effect.

ineffectual (ˌɪnɪˈfektjʊəl) *adj* without effect; not having the ability or confidence to do things well.

inefficient (ˌɪnɪˈfɪʃənt) *adj* 1 (of a machine, etc.) not working well or properly. 2 (of a person) not able to do things well because of lack of confidence, training, etc. **inefficiency** (ɪnɪˈfɪʃənsɪ) *nu* being inefficient.

ineligible (ɪnˈelɪdʒəbəl) *adj* not suitable to be chosen because of lack of training, etc.

inept (ɪˈnept) *adj* silly; said or done at the wrong time: *inept remarks.*

inequality (ɪnɪˈkwɒlɪtɪ) *ncu, pl* -ties not being equal in size, conditions, etc.; an example of this.

inert (ɪˈnɜːt) *adj* 1 not able to move or act. 2 slow-moving.

inertia (ɪˈnɜːʃə) *nu* the condition of being slow-moving; laziness; being at rest.

inescapable (ˌɪnɪˈskeɪpəbəl) *adj* that cannot be avoided or got away from.

inestimable (ɪnˈestɪməbəl) *adj* too great, valuable, etc., to be counted, judged, etc.

inevitable (ɪnˈevɪtəbəl) *adj* that is sure to happen or appear. **inevitably** (ɪnˈevɪtəblɪ) *adv*

inexcusable (ˌɪnɪkˈskjuːzəbəl) *adj* that cannot be forgiven or excused.

inexhaustible (ˌɪnɪgˈzɔːstəbəl) *adj* that cannot be used up: *inexhaustible patience.*

inexorable (ɪnˈeksərəbəl) *adj* that cannot be made to change or yield, in spite of being urgently asked, etc.

inexpensive (ˌɪnɪkˈspensɪv) *adj* not expensive; cheap.

inexperienced (ˌɪnɪkˈspɪərɪənst) *adj* lacking knowledge or skill, because of lack of practice.

inexplicable (ˌɪnɪkˈsplɪkəbəl) *adj* that cannot be explained.

infallible (ɪnˈfæləbəl) *adj* not able to make mistakes, do wrong, or be unsuccessful. **infallibility** (ɪnˌfæləˈbɪlɪtɪ) *nu* unable to be wrong.

infamous (ˈɪnfəməs) *adj* known to be wicked

or shameful. **infamy** ('ınfəmı) *nu* **1** being infamous. **2** shameful behaviour. **3** *nc, pl* **-mies** a shameful act.

infancy ('ınfənsı) *nu* **1** being a baby; time when one is a baby. **2** at the start of development or growth.

infant ('ınfənt) *nc* a child during the earliest years of its life. **infantile** ('ınfəntaıl) *adj* like or to do with infants.

infantry ('ınfəntrı) *nu* soldiers who fight on foot.

infatuated (ın'fætjʊeıtıd) *adj* liking someone or something too much or in a foolish way. **infatuation** (ın,fætjʊ'eıʃən) **1** *nu* being infatuated. **2** *nc* an example of this.

infect (ın'fekt) *vt* (often followed by **with** or **by**) **1** make diseased or dirty by touching or adding something impure. **2** pass on feelings, ideas, etc., to (a person). **infection** (ın'fekʃən) **1** *nu* being infected; spread of disease. **2** *nc* a disease that spreads. **infectious** (ın'fekʃəs) *adj* **1** (of a disease) that can be spread to others. **2** infecting with a disease. **3** (of feelings, etc.) likely to affect or spread to others.

infer (ın'fɜː*) *vt* **1** form an opinion (from something heard, seen, etc.). **2** suggest or mean. **inference** ('ınfərəns) **1** *nu* inferring. **2** *nc* the thing that is inferred.

inferior (ın'fıərıə*) *adj* lower in importance, quality, social position, etc. ●*nc* a person who is inferior in social or work position, etc. **inferiority** (ın,fıərı'ɒrıtı) *nu* being inferior.

infernal (ın'fɜːnəl) *adj* **1** of hell. **2** *infml* casuing trouble or annoyance: *What an infernal noise!*

inferno (ın'fɜːnəʊ) *nc* hell; a very hot place, esp. a great, destructive fire.

infertile (ın'fɜːtaıl) *adj* **1** (of land or plants) not producing much. **2** (of women or animals) not able to produce young ones.

infest (ın'fest) *vt* (of insects, diseases, etc.) move, or be, in large numbers in (a house, etc.).

infidel ('ınfıdəl) *nc* a person who does not believe in any particular religion, esp. in one's own religion.

infidelity (,ınfı'delıtı) *nu* **1** being disloyal or unfaithful. **2** (of a husband or wife) being sexually unfaithful. **3** *nc, pl* **-ties** an act of infidelity.

in-fighting ('ınfaıtıŋ) *infml nu* competition among people working together in the same industry, etc.

infiltrate ('ınfıltreıt) **1** *vt* make pass through, or into, by filtering. **2** *vi* pass through and into by filtering. **3** *vt* (of ideas) pass into (people's minds). **infiltration** (,ınfıl'treıʃən) *nc* an act of infiltrating or being infiltrated.

infinite ('ınfınıt) *adj* **1** without end or limits.

2 too great, large, wonderful, etc., to be measured, counted, or imagined: *infinite wisdom*. **infinitely** *adv*

infinitesimal (,ınfını'tesıməl) *adj* too small to be able to be measured; very small.

infinitive (ın'fınıtıv) *grammar adj, nc* (in the English language) (to do with) the form of a verb, sometimes used after **to**, that shows its action but says nothing about time or about the subject: *'See' in 'Let her see,' 'Allow her to see'*.

infinity (ın'fınıtı) *nu* being without end or limits.

infirm (ın'fɜːm) *adj* weak in the body or mind, esp. because of old age. **infirmity** (ın'fɜːmıtı) **1** *nu* weakness of the body or mind. **2** *nc, pl* **-ties** a weakness; disease.

infirmary (ın'fɜːmərı) *nc, pl* **-ries** a hospital; room in a building for people who are taken ill or injured, such as in a school, etc.

inflame (ın'fleım) *vti* **1** make or become angry. **2** make or become red and sore.

inflammable (ın'flæməbəl) *adj* likely to catch fire.

inflammation (,ınflə'meıʃən) **1** *nu* the condition of some part of the body in which there is redness, swelling, and pain. **2** *nc* a place on or in the body which is red, swollen, and painful.

inflammatory (ın'flæmətərı) *adj* likely to cause strong feelings, esp. of anger.

inflate (ın'fleıt) *vt* **1** fill with air, gas, etc.: *inflate a balloon*. **2** cause to become swollen: *inflated with pride*. **3** cause (prices) to become higher and the value of money to become lower.

inflation (ın'fleıʃən) *nu* inflating or being inflated; general increase in prices. **inflationary** (ın'fleıʃənərı) *adj* to do with inflation.

inflect (ın'flekt) *vt* **1** change (the quality of highness or lowness) of the voice. **2** *grammar* change the end or form of (a word) to show how it connects with other words in a sentence. **inflection 1** *nu* inflecting. **2** *ncu* the change in the quality of the highness or lowness of the voice. **3** *nc* the changed form of a word; ending added to a word, for example -*s* in *writes*.

inflexible (ın'fleksəbəl) *adj* **1** that cannot be bent. **2** (of a quality of a person) that cannot be made to change or yield.

inflict (ın'flıkt) *vt* **1** cause to suffer. **2** force (one's company) onto others. **infliction 1** *nu* inflicting or being inflicted. **2** *nc* someone or something inflicted.

inflow ('ınfləʊ) **1** *nu* flowing in. **2** *ncu* something that flows in.

influence ('ınflʊəns) *vt* have an effect on. ●*nu* **1** the power in someone or something to affect another person or thing. *nc* **2** an effect of this. **3** the person or thing that has such power. **influential** (ˌɪnflʊˈenʃəl) *adj* having influence.

influenza (ˌɪnflʊˈenzə) *(infml abbrev.* **flu***) nu* an infectious disease with fever, aching of the body, and a flow of liquid from the nose.

influx (ˈɪnflʌks) *nc* (followed by **of**) **1** *nu* the act of flowing in. **2** *nc* a flow of people or things going on all the time.

inform (ɪnˈfɔːm) **1** *vt* give information to; tell. **2** *vi* (followed by **against** or **on**) tell or show the police that someone has broken the law. **informant** *nc* a person who gives information. **informer** *nc* a person who gives the police information about someone.

informal (ɪnˈfɔːməl) *adj* not giving too much attention to the rules of behaviour; casual; without ceremony. **informally** *adv*

information (ˌɪnfəˈmeɪʃən) *nu* **1** informing; telling. **2** knowledge given; news.

informative (ɪnˈfɔːmətɪv) *adj* giving information.

infra-red (ˌɪnfrəˈred) *adj* of the line of light that is below the red band of colour in the spectrum, and that cannot be seen.

infrastructure (ˈɪnfrəˌstrʌktʃə*) *nu* a framework or the less important but necessary parts of an organisation or system, esp. fixed military equipment such as places for training, etc.

infrequent (ɪnˈfriːkwənt) *adj* not happening very often.

infringe (ɪnˈfrɪndʒ) *vt* break (a law, rule, agreement, etc.). **infringement 1** *nu* infringing. **2** *nc* an example of this.

infuriate (ɪnˈfjʊərɪeɪt) *vt* fill (someone) with great anger.

infuse (ɪnˈfjuːz) *vt* **1** pour or put a quality into: *He infused her with hope.* **2** pour hot liquid on (tea leaves, herbs, etc.), in order to obtain their juices or to add flavour. **3** *vi* (of tea, etc.) be infused. **infusion** (ɪnˈfjuːʒən) **1** *nu* infusing or being infused. **2** *nc* the liquid made by infusing.

ingenious (ɪnˈdʒiːnɪəs) *adj* **1** clever at making things, esp. in a new way. **2** (of things) cleverly made. **ingenuity** (ˌɪndʒɪˈnjuːɪtɪ) *nu* cleverness in making or doing things in a new way.

ingenuous (ɪnˈdʒenjʊəs) *adj* showing clearly one's thoughts or feelings; innocent.

ingot (ˈɪŋgət) *nc* a short, thick bar of metal, esp. of gold, silver, or steel.

ingrained (ɪnˈgreɪnd) *adj* fixed firmly in, esp. the character: *ingrained habits.*

ingratiate (ɪnˈgreɪʃɪeɪt) *vt* try to get (oneself) into the favour of someone by praising him too much.

ingratitude (ɪnˈgrætɪtjuːd) *nu* not feeling or showing thanks.

ingredient (ɪnˈgriːdɪənt) *nc* one of the parts of a mixture.

inhabit (ɪnˈhæbɪt) *vt* live in (a house, country, etc.). **inhabitant** (ɪnˈhæbɪtənt) *nc* a person living in a place.

inhale (ɪnˈheɪl) *vt* take (air, etc.) into the lungs. **inhaler** *nc* a device that produces a chemical substance, used when breathing is difficult.

inherent (ɪnˈhɪərənt) *adj* being a necessary part or quality of.

inherit (ɪnˈherɪt) *vt* **1** receive (money, a title, etc.) as a legal right when the owner dies. **2** be born with (the qualities, etc.) of the people from whom one is descended. **inheritance** (ɪnˈherɪtəns) **1** *nu* inheriting. **2** *nc* what is inherited.

inhibit (ɪnˈhɪbɪt) *vt* hold back or prevent (someone) from something or from doing something. **inhibition** (ˌɪnhɪˈbɪʃən) **1** *nu* inhibiting or being inhibited. **2** *nc* an example of this.

inhuman (ɪnˈhjuːmən) *adj* cruel; without feelings.

inimical (ɪˈnɪmɪkəl) *formal adj* not friendly; harmful.

inimitable (ɪˈnɪmɪtəbəl) *adj* that cannot be imitated because it is too good, great, etc.

iniquity (ɪˈnɪkwɪtɪ) **1** *nu* being very wicked or unjust. **2** *nc, pl* **-ties** a very wicked or unjust action.

initial (ɪˈnɪʃəl) *adj* first; at the beginning. ● *nc* the first letter of a word, esp. the first letters of the words of a person's name. ● *vt* sign (a note, etc.) with one's initials. **initially** *adv* at the beginning.

initiate (ɪˈnɪʃɪeɪt) *vt* **1** set going; begin. **2** bring (someone) into a society, group, etc., as a member. **3** give (someone) secret knowledge of or basic teaching (in something difficult). **initiation** (ˌɪnɪʃɪˈeɪʃən) *nu* the act of initiating or being initiated.

initiative (ɪˈnɪʃətɪv) *nu* the ability to see what needs to be done and to start doing it. **take the initiative** make the first move in doing something.

inject (ɪnˈdʒekt) *vt* **1** force (a liquid, medicine, etc.) into the body, using a hollow needle: see picture. **2** *infml* put some (quality, etc.) in where it is needed. **injection 1** *nu* injecting. **2** *nc* an example of this.

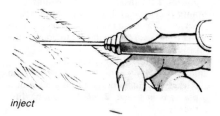

inject

injunction (ɪnˈdʒʌŋkʃən) *nc* an order given with the right to expect that it will be obeyed, esp. a written order from a law court. ·

injure (ˈɪndʒə*) *vt* cause harm to. **injurious** (ɪnˈdʒʊərɪəs) *formal adj* harmful. **injury** (ˈɪndʒərɪ) *nc, pl* **-ries 1** a wound in the body. **2** an insult; something said or done that hurts; damage to reputation. **3** *nu* harm.

injustice (ɪnˈdʒʌstɪs) **1** *nu* not being fair or just. **2** *nc* an example of this; unfair act.

ink (ɪŋk) *nu* a black, red, blue, etc., liquid for writing and printing. ● *vt* mark with ink. **inky** *adj* **-ier, -iest** marked or stained with ink.

inkling (ˈɪŋklɪŋ) *nc* a slight idea or suggestion; clue: *He gave me no inkling of his plans for the future.*

inlaid (ˌɪnˈleɪd) past tense and past participle of inlay.

inland (ˈɪnlənd) *adj* **1** placed inside a country away from the coast. **2** happening inside a country: *inland trade.* ● (ɪnˈlænd) *adv* in or towards the inside of a country. **Inland Revenue** (*US* **Internal Revenue**) *Brit* **1** money obtained from direct taxes inside a country. **2** *infml* the government department that deals with this.

in-laws (ˈɪnlɔːz) *infml n pl* relatives by marriage.

inlay (ˌɪnˈleɪ) *vt* fix (one thing) firmly into another so that the surface is smooth: *silver inlaid with gold.* ● (ˈɪnˌleɪ) *nu* **1** work of this kind. **2** *nc* the pattern of the inlay.

inlet (ˈɪnlet) *nc* **1** a narrow strip of water going into the land from the sea, a lake, etc. **2** a place of entering.

inmate (ˈɪnmeɪt) *nc* one of a number of people living together, esp. in a prison, hospital, or other building that serves a public need.

inmost (ˈɪnməʊst) *adj* **1** farthest, deepest, etc., from the outside or the surface. **2** (of a person's feelings, etc.) most secret: *my inmost thoughts.*

inn (ɪn) *nc* a place where a room and food is supplied, for payment, to travellers; public house. **inn-keeper** (ˈɪnkiːpə*) *nc* a person who owns or manages an inn.

innards (ˈɪnədz) *infml n pl* **1** the stomach and bowels. **2** the inside parts of anything.

innate (ɪˈneɪt) *adj* (of a quality) born with a person: *She has an innate kindness.*

inner (ˈɪnə*) *adj* on the inside; to do with the inside: *an inner room.*

innermost (ˈɪnəməʊst) *adj* inmost.

innings (ˈɪnɪŋz) *n pl (with singular verb)* **1** (in cricket) the time during which a team or a player is in to bat. **2** *infml* a person's lifetime.

innocent (ˈɪnəsənt) *adj* **1** not knowing of evil or sin: *as innocent as a baby.* **2** not guilty. **3** causing no harm: *innocent pleasures.* **innocence** (ˈɪnəsəns) *nu* being innocent. **innocently** *adv*

innocuous (ɪˈnɒkjʊəs) *adj* causing no harm.

innovate (ˈɪnəveɪt) *vi* make changes; start something new. **innovation** (ˌɪnəˈveɪʃən) **1** *nu* innovating. **2** *nc* a change; something new that is started. **innovator** *nc* a person who innovates.

innuendo (ˌɪnjuːˈendəʊ) *nc, pl* **-es** a remark that also suggests something else, often unpleasant.

innumerable (ɪˈnjuːmərəbəl) *adj* too many to count.

inoculate (ɪˈnɒkjʊleɪt) *vt* **1** put tiny, harmless organisms into (a person or animal) to give him or it a weak form of a disease and so become free of its danger. **2** fill (a person's mind) with ideas, etc. **inoculation** (ɪˌnɒkjʊˈleɪʃən) **1** *nu* inoculating or being inoculated. **2** *nc* an example of this: *inoculations against yellow fever.*

inorganic (ˌɪnɔːˈgænɪk) *adj* (of a substance or matter) that is of mineral origin, not containing carbon.

input (ˈɪnpʊt) *ncu* the amount of something put in, such as information supplied to a computer.

inquest (ˈɪnkwest) *nc* **1** an inquiry in a law court to find out certain facts, esp. to discover the reason for a person's death when this did not happen normally. **2** *infml* any inquiry.

inquire (also **enquire**) (ɪnˈkwaɪə*) **1** *vt* ask to be told: *I inquired what he wanted.* **2** *vi* ask for information: *inquire into the cause of the train accident.* **inquiring** *adj* wanting to find out or learn: *an inquiring mind.* **inquiry** (also **enquiry**) **1** *nu* asking. **2** *nc, pl* **-ries** a question; examination into something.

inquisition (ˌɪnkwɪˈzɪʃən) **1** *nu* a very careful examination and questioning. **2** *nc* an example of this.

inquisitive (ɪnˈkwɪzɪtɪv) *adj* too interested in other people's affairs.

inroad (ˈɪnrəʊd) *nc* **1** a sudden attack by the enemy. **2** something that intrudes, esp. so as to use up.

insane (ɪnˈseɪn) *adj* mad. **insanity** (ɪnˈsænɪtɪ) *nu* madness.

insatiable (ɪnˈseɪʃəbəl) *adj* not able to be satisfied.

inscribe (ɪnˈskraɪb) *vt* write (words) on metal, stone, paper, etc., or in a book. **inscription** (ɪnˈskrɪpʃən) *nc* something inscribed.

inscrutable (ɪnˈskruːtəbəl) *adj* of which the meaning is unknown or cannot be understood.

insects

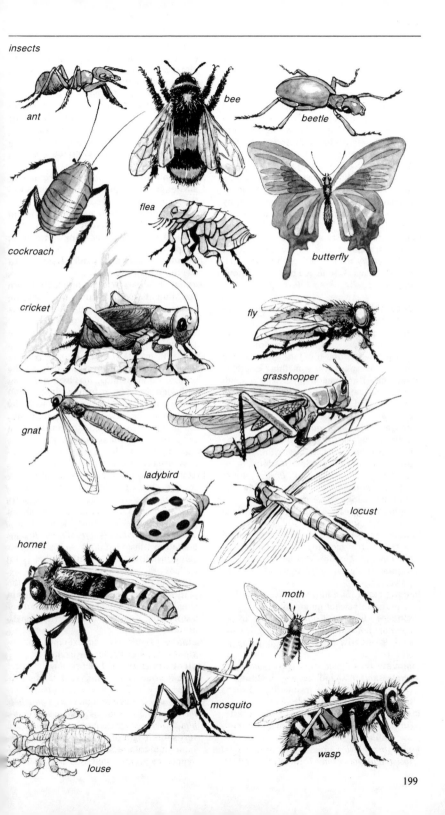

ant

bee

beetle

cockroach

flea

butterfly

cricket

fly

grasshopper

gnat

ladybird

locust

hornet

moth

mosquito

louse

wasp

insect ('ınsekt) *nc* any small animal with three pairs of legs, three separate body parts, and, usually, wings: see picture. **insecticide** (ın'sektısaıd) *nc* a substance used for killing insects.

insecure (,ınsı'kjʊə*) *adj* 1 not firmly fixed or fastened; not safe. 2 (of a person) feeling unsafe; feeling that one is wrong or is not able to do something; unprotected. **insecurity** (,ınsı'kjʊərıtı) *nu* being insecure.

insemination (ın,semı'neıʃən) *nu* putting seeds in. **artificial insemination** putting the fertilising liquid of a male person or animal into a female person or animal, by means of medical instruments, to produce young ones.

insensible (ın'sensəbəl) *adj* 1 not awake because of being struck on the head, etc. 2 (followed by **to**) not caring about the feelings of others. 3 (followed by **of**) not knowing about: *He seemed insensible of any danger.*

inseparable (ın'sepərəbəl) *adj* not able to be separated.

insert (ın'sɜːt) *vt* put or fit (something) in or into something. ●('ınsɜːt) *nc* something inserted. **insertion** (ın'sɜːʃən) 1 *nu* inserting or being inserted. 2 *nc* something inserted.

inset ('ınset) *nc* something, such as a small picture or map, that is put within the edges of a printed page or of a larger map, etc. ●(ın'set) *vt* insert.

inshore (,ın'ʃɔː*) *adj, adv* close to the shore.

inside (ın'saıd) *nc* (often followed by **of**) the inner part or surface; part within. ●*adj* placed on or in the inside. ●*adv* on, in, or to the inside: *Let's look inside.* ●*prep* within; on the inner side of. **inside out** with the inside surface on the outside.

insidious (ın'sıdıəs) *adj* doing harm without being seen.

insight ('ınsaıt) 1 *nu* the ability of the mind to see the real meaning of something; understanding. 2 *nc* an example of this.

insignia (ın'sıgnıə) *n pl* signs of honour, power, etc.

insignificant (,ınsıg'nıfıkənt) *adj* having little or no meaning; not important.

insincere (,ınsın'sıə*) *adj* (of feelings or behaviour) not truthful; not meaning what is said. **insincerity** (,ınsın'serıtı) *nu* being insincere.

insinuate (ın'sınjʊeıt) *vt* suggest (something unpleasant) in an indirect way. **insinuation** (,ınsınjʊ'eıʃən) 1 *nu* insinuating. 2 *nc* a hinting at something unpleasant.

insipid (ın'sıpıd) *adj* (of food) without taste; (of a person, behaviour, etc.) without interest; dull.

insist (ın'sıst) *vti* 1 urge in a forceful way: *I insist that you come.* 2 forcefully and re-

peatedly declare (something) to be true, etc., esp. to someone who has disbelief. **insistence** (ın'sıstəns) *nu* insisting or being insisted. **insistent** *adj*

insofar (,ınsə'fɑː*) *US adv Brit* **in so far** to the extent that: *She's very kind insofar as she's always helping others, but she doesn't give enough care to her own children.*

insolent ('ınsələnt) *adj* very rude, showing no respect; insulting. **insolence** *nu* being insolent.

insoluble (ın'sɒljʊbəl) *adj* 1 that cannot be answered or explained. 2 (of a substance) that cannot be dissolved.

insolvency (ın'sɒlvənsı) *nu* being unable to pay one's debts. **insolvent** *adj*

insomnia (ın'sɒmnıə) *nu* being not able to sleep.

insomuch (,ınsəʊ'mʌtʃ) *adv* (followed by **as**) to such an extent that.

inspect (ın'spekt) *vt* examine carefully. **inspection** (ın'spekʃən) 1 *nu* inspecting or being inspected. 2 *nc* an example of this. **inspector** *nc* a person in a public position whose work is to inspect something: *a school inspector.*

inspire (ın'spaıə*) *vt* fill (someone) with enthusiasm, high thoughts, etc., or with the urge to do something. **inspired** *adj* filled with high thoughts or feelings. **inspiration** (,ınspı'reıʃən) 1 *nu* being filled with the need to create new music, literature, art, etc. *nc* 2 a person or thing that inspires. 3 a good idea: *I've had an inspiration!*

instability (,ınstə'bılıtı) *nu* the lack of steadiness, usually of character.

install (ın'stɔːl) (also **instal**) *vt* 1 put (a person) in a new position, esp. one of authority: *He was installed (as) President.* 2 fix (machines, etc.) in place for use. 3 make (a person or oneself) comfortable in a place: *The dog installed itself in front of the fire.* **installation** (,ınstə'leıʃən) 1 *nu* installing or being installed. 2 *nc* something that is installed.

instalment (ın'stɔːlmənt) *nc* 1 any one of the parts of a payment, paid over a certain length of time. 2 any one of several parts of a story, etc., appearing over a certain length of time.

instance ('ınstəns) *nc* an example. **for instance** as an example; for example.

instant ('ınstənt) *adj* 1 happening at once: *instant defeat.* 2 (of food) that can be prepared very quickly: *instant coffee.* 3 urgent. ●*nc* 1 a certain moment: *Come here this instant!* 2 as soon as: *The instant I saw him I knew something had angered him.* 3 a very short length of time: *He came in an instant.* **instantaneous** (,ınstən'teınıəs) *adj* happening at once. **instantly** *adv*

instead (ɪnˈsted) *adv* in place of a person or of something: *Don't stay at home —come and play instead*. **instead of** in place of.

instep (ˈɪnstep) *nc* the curved, upper part of the foot between the toes and the ankle: see picture.

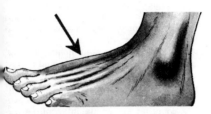

instep

instigate (ˈɪnstɪgeɪt) *vt* urge (someone) to do something; cause (something) to happen because of this.

instil (ɪnˈstɪl) *US* **instill** *vt* gradually fill (a person's mind) with (ideas, etc.).

instinct (ˈɪnstɪŋkt) **1** *nu* a natural desire to behave in a certain way without thinking about it. **2** *nc* an understanding or desire, that is in a person from birth; example of this. **instinctive** (ɪnˈstɪŋktɪv) *adj* formed on instinct, not on reason or experience. **instinctively** *adv*

institute (ˈɪnstɪtjuːt) *vt* set up (an inquiry, new rules, etc.). ●*nc* **1** an organisation set up for a public need. **2** a building used for this.

institution (ˌɪnstɪˈtjuːʃən) **1** *nu* instituting or being instituted. **2** *nc* a habit, custom, etc., that has been going on for a long time. **3** an institute.

instruct (ɪnˈstrʌkt) *vt* **1** (often followed by **in**) teach. **2** tell; inform; give (someone) orders. **instruction 1** *nu* instructing or being instructed. **2** *nc* an order; information. **instructive** *adj* teaching much. **instructor** *nc* a person who instructs.

instrument (ˈɪnstrʊmənt) *nc* **1** a tool or anything used for doing something, esp. delicate work. **2** a person used by another person for his own purpose. **3** a device on which one makes musical sounds: *a musical instrument*. **instrumental** (ˌɪnstrʊˈmentəl) *adj* **1** of use as an instrument or something to be usd. **2** (of music) played on instruments, not sung.

insubordinate (ˌɪnsəbˈɔːdɪnət) *adj* refusing to obey. **insubordination** (ˈɪnsəˌbɔːdɪˈneɪʃən) **1** *nu* being insubordinate. **2** *nc* an example of this.

insufferable (ɪnˈsʌfərəbəl) *adj* having too good an opinion of oneself; unbearable.

insufficient (ˌɪnsəˈfɪʃənt) *adj* not enough.

insular (ˈɪnsjʊlə*) *adj* **1** of an island. **2** not understanding or caring about the ideas of other people.

insulate (ˈɪnsjʊleɪt) *vt* **1** cover (a wire, etc.) with a material that will not allow the loss of heat or electricity. **2** keep (someone or something) apart from. **insulation** (ˌɪnsjʊˈleɪʃən) **1** *nu* insulating or being insulated. **2** *nc* a material that insulates: see picture. **insulator** (ˈɪnsjʊleɪtə*) *nc* a substance or device, used for insulating.

insulation

insult (ɪnˈsʌlt) *vt* speak or act in a way that will hurt the feelings or self-respect of (a person). ● (ˈɪnsʌlt) *nc* an insulting remark or action.

insuperable (ɪnˈsjuːpərəbəl) *adj* that is too difficult, etc., to be overcome: *insuperable problems*.

insupportable (ˌɪnsəˈpɔːtəbəl) *adj* that cannot be suffered; that there is no good reason for suffering.

insurance (ɪnˈʃʊərəns) *nu* **1** (the safety given by) an agreement with a company, society, etc., to pay out an agreed sum in the event of sickness, death, etc., in return for regular payments. **2** the insurance payment made to, or by, a company, etc.

insure (ɪnˈʃʊə*) *vt* obtain or give insurance on (one's life, house, etc.).

insurgent (ɪnˈsɜːdʒənt) *adj* refusing to support, and rising up against, the government in power. ●*nc* a person who rises against the government.

insurrection (ˌɪnsəˈrekʃən) **1** *nu* the violent rising of a people against the government. **2** *nc* an example of this.

insurmountable (ˌɪnsəˈmaʊntəbəl) *adj* that cannot be overcome: *insurmountable difficulties*.

intact (ɪnˈtækt) *adj* unbroken; undamaged; whole.

intake (ˈɪnteɪk) **1** *nu* the act of taking in. *nc* **2** an amount, number, etc., taken in during a certain period of time. **3** (of a pipe, etc.) the opening through which air, gas, water, etc. is taken in.

intangible (ɪnˈtændʒəbəl) *adj* that cannot be touched; that is beyond the power of the mind to understand.

integer (ˈɪntɪdʒə*) *nc* a whole number: *2 and 4 are whole numbers, 1½ is not.*

integral (ˈɪntɪɡrəl) *adj* **1** necessary in order to make something complete. **2** *mathematics* of a whole number; made up of whole numbers.

integrate (ˈɪntɪɡreɪt) *vt* **1** bring all (parts) together to form a whole. **2** bring (people) of all social classes, races, religions, etc., together as equals in society. **3** *vi* become integrated. **integration** (ˌɪntɪˈɡreɪʃən) *nu* integrating or being integrated.

integrity (ɪnˈteɡrɪtɪ) *nu* **1** complete honesty. **2** being complete.

intellect (ˈɪntəlekt) *nu* the power of the mind to know and reason. **intellectual** (ˌɪntəˈlektjʊəl) *adj* **1** of the intellect. **2** showing or using good intellect. ●*nc* a person with good powers of reasoning and interested in things of the mind.

intelligence (ɪnˈtelɪdʒəns) *nu* **1** the ability to learn, understand, and know. **2** information, esp. on important matters. **3** secret information. **intelligent** *adj* having or showing intelligence.

intelligible (ɪnˈtelɪdʒəbəl) *adj* that can be understood.

intend (ɪnˈtend) *vt* have as a purpose or a plan: *He intends to go home at five.*

intense (ɪnˈtens) *adj* **1** (of a quality or force) very great, strong, etc. **2** (of a person) having strong, deep, and serious feelings; (of feelings) very strong. **intensely** *adv*

intensify (ɪnˈtensɪfaɪ) *vti* make or become more intense.

intensity (ɪnˈtensɪtɪ) *nu* the quality or state of being intense.

intensive (ɪnˈtensɪv) *adj* thorough; deep: *intensive study.*

intent (ɪnˈtent) *nu* purpose; intention. **to all intents and purposes** so far as it appears. **intently** *adv* with great concentration.

intention (ɪnˈtenʃən) **1** *nu* intending. **2** *nc* a purpose; plan; aim. **with the intention of** with the aim or purpose of. **intentional** *adj* done on purpose.

inter (ɪnˈtɜː*) *formal vt* put (a body) in a grave; bury.

interact (ˌɪntərˈækt) *vi* act on or have an effect on each other. **interaction** (ˌɪntərˈækʃən) *nc* the act of having an effect on each other.

intercede (ˌɪntəˈsiːd) *vi* ask someone earnestly for a favour, etc., for someone else: *He interceded with him for her.*

intercept (ˌɪntəˈsept) *vt* stop and catch (someone or something) on the way from one place to another.

intercession (ˌɪntəˈseʃən) **1** *nu* interceding. **2** *nc* a request or prayer, esp. for someone else.

interchange (ˌɪntəˈtʃeɪndʒ) *vt* **1** give and receive. **2** (of two things) put (each thing) in the place of the other. ● (ˈɪntətʃeɪndʒ) *nc* an act of interchanging: *an interchange of ideas.* **interchangeable** (ˌɪntəˈtʃeɪndʒəbəl) *adj* that can be interchanged.

intercom (ˈɪntəkɒm) *infml n* short for **intercommunication.**

intercommunication (ˈɪntəkəˌmjuːnɪˈkeɪʃən) *nu* a system of passing on news, information, etc., esp. inside a plane, or in offices.

intercontinental (ˈɪntəˌkɒntɪˈnentəl) *adj* happening, etc., between the great land masses of the world.

intercourse (ˈɪntəkɔːs) *nu* the sharing of ideas, news, information, etc., between people, countries, etc. **sexual intercourse** sexual union.

interest (ˈɪntrest) **1** *nc* something that keeps one's attention. *nu* the quality that keeps one's attention. **3** the money paid by a person for the use of money he has borrowed. *nc* **4** a share in a business, etc., with a legal right to a share in the profits. ● *vt* cause (a person) to give his attention to something. **interested** *adj* **1** showing that one would like to know, learn, see, etc., more. **2** showing more favour to oneself, one person, group, etc., than to another. **interesting** *adj* keeping one's attention.

interfere (ˌɪntəˈfɪə*) *vi* **1** busy oneself with things or other people's affairs, without being asked to. **2** prevent; get in the way of. **interference** *nu* **1** the act of interfering. **2** an unwanted radio signal.

interim (ˈɪntərɪm) *n* **in the interim** in the time between two happenings. ● *adj* lasting for a short time only.

interior (ɪnˈtɪərɪə*) *adj* **1** placed inside; of the inside. **2** to do with the inside of a building **3** inland. ● *nc* **1** the inside. **2** the inland part of a country.

interject (ˌɪntəˈdʒekt) *vt* put in (a word, remark, etc.) when someone else is speaking. **interjection** *nc* a word or group of words put in to show surprise, pain, etc.

interlock (ˌɪntəˈlɒk) *vti* join firmly together see picture.

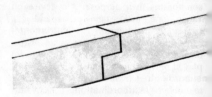

interlock

interloper (ˈɪntələʊpə*) *nc* a person who pushes in without a right to be there.

interlude ('ɪntəluːd) *nc* the time between two events, or two parts of a play, concert, etc.

intermarriage ('ɪntə'mærɪdʒ) *nu* the marriage between two people of different races, etc.

intermediary ('ɪntə'miːdɪərɪ) *nc, pl* -ries a person who carries messages, etc., between two people, or groups, who do not, or cannot, meet.

intermediate ('ɪntə'miːdɪət) *adj* coming between two things in position, level, etc.

interminable (ɪn'tɜːmɪnəbəl) *adj* seeming to last for too long a time.

intermingle ('ɪntə'mɪŋgəl) **1** *vt* mix two things together. **2** *vi* go among.

intermission ('ɪntə'mɪʃən) **1** *nu* a short stop. **2** *nc* the time between two parts of a play, film, etc.

intermittent ('ɪntə'mɪtənt) *adj* stopping, starting, stopping again, and so on. **intermittently** *adv*

intern (ɪn'tɜːn) *vt* force (a person) to live within a country, or keep him prisoner, to prevent him from doing harm. ● ('ɪntɜːn) US *nc* a young doctor living and assisting in a hospital.

internal (ɪn'tɜːnəl) *adj* **1** of or placed in the inside. **2** one's own country: *internal affairs.* **internal combustion** the way in which power is produced by the explosion of a mixture of gas and air, as in an engine: see picture.

internal combustion

international ('ɪntə'næʃənəl) *adj* to do with two or more countries: *an international agreement.*

interplanetary ('ɪntə'plænətərɪ) *adj* between bodies in the heavens: *interplanetary travel.*

interplay ('ɪntəpleɪ) *nu* the action of two things on each other.

interpolate (ɪn'tɜːpəleɪt) *vt* add (words, etc.) to a book, esp. ones that mislead.

interpose ('ɪntə'pəʊz) **1** *vi* put or come between others. **2** *vt* interfere or interrupt, by putting forward (an objection, etc.).

interpret (ɪn'tɜːprɪt) *vt* **1** explain or show the meaning of. **2** understand (something said or done) to mean: *I interpreted his silence as disapproval.* **3** *vi* explain the meaning of words of a different language. **interpretation** (ɪn'tɜːprɪ'teɪʃən) **1** *nu* the act of interpreting. **2** *nc* an explanation. **interpreter** *nc*

a person who explains the meaning of words in a different language.

interrelation ('ɪntərɪ'leɪʃən) *nc* the connection or relation between people or things.

interrogate (ɪn'terəgeɪt) *vt* question (someone) in a thorough or formal way. **interrogation** (ɪn'terə'geɪʃən) **1** *nu* the act of interrogating. **2** *nc* an example of this. **interrogative** ('ɪntə'rɒgətɪv) *adj* **1** of or to do with a question. **2** *grammar* (of a word or group of words) used in asking a question. ● *nc* an interrogative word or group of words.

interrupt ('ɪntə'rʌpt) *vt* **1** break in on (someone) while he is doing something, speaking, etc. **2** cause to stop. **3** *vi* be stopped from continuing. **interruption** ('ɪntə'rʌpʃən) **1** *nu* the act of interrupting, or being interrupted. **2** *nc* something that interrupts.

intersect ('ɪntə'sekt) **1** *vt* divide (something) by cutting or crossing. **2** *vi* (of lines) cut or cross each other. **intersection** ('ɪntə'sekʃən) **1** *nu* the act of intersecting or being intersected. **2** *nc* a place of crossing.

intersperse ('ɪntə'spɜːs) *vt* put (things) in various places among or between other things: *flowers interspersed with weeds.*

interstate ('ɪntə'steɪt) US *adj* to do with two or more States.

intertwine ('ɪntə'twaɪn) **1** *vt* twist or wind together. **2** *vi* become twisted or wound together.

interval ('ɪntəvəl) *nc* **1** the time between two happenings, esp. between two parts of a play, film, etc. **2** the space between two things.

intervene ('ɪntə'viːn) *vi* (often followed by **in** or **between**) **1** come between others or interfere to try to change things. **2** (between events or points in time) happen or come about. **intervention** ('ɪntə'venʃən) **1** *nu* the act of intervening. **2** *nc* an example of this.

interview ('ɪntəvjuː) *nc* a meeting with someone to discuss something, for example between an employer and a person applying for a job. ● *vt* (of an employer, reporter, etc.) have an interview with. **interviewer** *nc* a person, such as a reporter or employer, who interviews someone.

interweave ('ɪntə'wiːv) *vt* twist together, one with another.

intestate (ɪn'testeɪt) *adj* dying without having made a will.

intestine (ɪn'testɪn) *nc* (usually *pl)* the lower part of the food tube between the stomach and the anus: see picture. **intestinal** ('ɪn'testɪnəl) *adj* of or to do with the intestines.

intimate[1] ('ɪntɪmət) *adj* **1** very close in friendship. **2** private. **3** having a deep knowledge of. **intimacy** ('ɪntɪməsɪ) **1** *nu* being very close in friendship. **2** *nc, pl* **-cies** a familiar action, such as a kiss. **intimately** *adv*

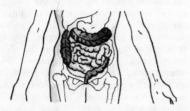

intestine

intimate² ('ıntımeıt) *vt* make known (an indirect suggestion or clear hint). **intimation** ('ıntı'meıʃən) **1** *nu* the act of intimating. **2** *nc* a suggestion; hint.

intimidate (ın'tımıdeıt) *vt* frighten (someone), esp. to make him obey. **intimidation** ('ıntımı'deıʃən) *nu* the act of intimidating or being intimidated.

into ('ıntʊ unstressed 'ıntə) *prep* **1** (showing movement or direction towards); within: *Throw it into the fire; Come into the house.* **2** (showing a change or result): *Her fear turned into relief; A tadpole changes into a frog; He swept the leaves into a large pile.*

intolerable (ın'tɒlərəbəl) *adj* that cannot be put up with: *Her rudeness is intolerable!*

intolerant (ın'tɒlərənt) *adj* not having patience with, or being willing to allow, other people's views, etc. **intolerance** (ın'tɒlərəns) *nu* the act of being intolerant.

intonation ('ıntə'neıʃən) *nu* the changes in the highness and lowness of the voice in speaking. **intone** (ın'təʊn) *vt* say (a prayer, etc.) in a singing voice.

intoxicate (ın'tɒksıkeıt) *vt* **1** cause to lose self-control because of drinking too much alcohol. **2** make too excited. **intoxicant** (ın'tɒksıkənt) *nc* beer, wine, etc., or any drink containing alcohol. ●*adj* that makes one drunk. **intoxication** ('ıntɒksı-'keıʃən) *nu* being intoxicated.

intractable (ın'træktəbəl) *adj* not easily controlled: *an intractable temper.*

intransitive (ın'trænsıtıv) *adj* (of a verb) that does not take a direct object.

intrepid (ın'trepıd) *adj* without fear.

intricate ('ıntrıkət) *adj* made up of closely connected parts and difficult to understand: *an intricate machine.* **intricacy** ('ıntrıkəsı) **1** *nc, pl* **-cies** an intricate thing. **2** *nu* being intricate.

intrigue (ın'triːg) **1** *vi* make and carry out a secret plan. **2** *vt* cause (one) to feel interested. ●('ıntriːg) *nu* secrecy; secret planning.

intrinsic (ın'trınsık) *adj* (of value, worth, etc.) to do with its real nature: *a man of intrinsic courage.*

introduce ('ıntrə'djuːs) *vt* **1** bring into use. **2** make (oneself or a person) known to another person by name. **3** make (something) known to a person for the first time. **4** bring in: *A new law was introduced.* **introduction** ('ıntrə'dʌkʃən) **1** *nu* the act of introducing or being introduced. *nc* **2** the act of making persons known to one another by name. **3** information at the beginning of a book, speech, etc., to explain what follows. **introductory** ('ıntrə'dʌktərı) *adj* with the purpose of introducing.

introspective ('ıntrə'spektıv) *adj* having the habit of examining one's own thoughts and feelings.

introvert ('ıntrəvɜːt) *nc* a person whose thoughts are always turned inward on himself. ●*vt* be always having (thoughts and feelings) about oneself.

intrude (ın'truːd) **1** *vt* force (oneself or something) upon someone or something. **2** *v* force oneself on a person, place, etc., without being invited. **intruder** *nc* a person or thing that intrudes. **intrusion** (ın'truːʒən) **1** *nu* the act of intruding. **2** *nc* an example of this.

intuition ('ıntjuː'ıʃən) **1** *nu* an understanding of something immediately without having to use reason. **2** *nc* an understanding of knowledge obtained in this way. **intuitive** (ın'tjuːıtıv) *adj* of intuition.

inundate ('ınʌndeıt) *vt* **1** cover (the land etc.) with water; flood. **2** overwhelm with a large number, amount etc.: *inundated with work.* **inundation** ('ınʌn'deıʃən) **1** *nu* inundating or being inundated. **2** *nc* a flooding **3** *nu* being overwhelmed by a large number amount, etc.

inure (ı'njʊə*) *vt* make used to: *They had become inured to hunger.*

invade (ın'veıd) *vt* **1** enter (a country) in order to attack it. **2** enter, usually in a large number or amount. **3** act towards without proper respect: *invade someone's privacy* **invader** *nc* a person or thing that invades

invalid¹ ('ınvəlıd) *nc* a person in poor health esp. one who is unable to walk through illness or injury: see picture. ●*adj* used for, or to do with, an invalid: *an invalid chair.* ●*vt* (often followed by **out of**) send home as an invalid.

invalid

of the army) send home as an invalid.

invalid² (ın'vælıd) *adj* 1 having no force; not resting on truth: *an invalid argument*. 2 of no legal force: *The marriage was invalid*.

invaluable (ın'væljʊəbəl) *adj* of too great a value or worth to be measured. **invaluably** *adv*

invariable (ın'veərıəbəl) *adj* never changing. **invariably** *adv*

invasion (ın'veıʒən) 1 *nu* the act of invading or being invaded. 2 *nc* an example of this.

invective (ın'vektıv) *nu* violent or insulting language.

inveigh (ın'veı) *vi* speak violently against someone or something.

inveigle (ın'viːgəl) *vt* use deceit, flattery, etc., to persuade (someone) (to do something).

invent (ın'vent) *vt* 1 design and make (something) that has never been made before. 2 make up (a story, excuse, etc.), esp. to deceive. **invention** (ın'venʃən) 1 *nu* the act of inventing. 2 *nc* something invented. **inventive** *adj* able to invent. **inventor** *nc* a person who invents things.

inventory ('ınvəntrı) *nc, pl* **-ries** a list of things, such as goods, furniture, etc.

inverse ('ın'vɜːs) *adj* opposite; upside-down. **inversely** *adv*

invert (ın'vɜːt) *vt* turn upside down; put in the opposite position. **inversion** (ın'vɜːʃən) 1 *nu* inverting or being inverted. 2 *nc* something inverted. **inverted commas** the signs (' ' or " ") put around spoken words.

invertebrate (ın'vɜːtıbrət) *adj* not having a backbone. ● *nc* an animal without a backbone.

invest (ın'vest) 1 *vt* use (money) to make more money by buying a part of a business and sharing the profits. 2 *infml vi* spend on something one considers to be necessary: *invest in new winter boots*. *vt* 3 clothe (a person) in robes, etc., to show high rank or office. 4 spread through, etc. (with a special quality): *a city invested with an atmosphere of learning*. **investment** 1 *nu* the act of investing money. 2 *nc* an amount of money that is invested. **investor** *nc* a person who invests money.

investigate (ın'vestıgeıt) *vt* examine carefully. **investigation** ('ınvestı'geıʃən) 1 *nu* the act of carefully examining or looking into a matter. 2 *nc* an example of this. **investigator** *nc* a person who investigates.

investiture (ın'vestıtʃə*) *nc* the ceremony of placing on someone a high rank, power, or office.

inveterate (ın'vetərət) *adj* firmly fixed as a habit or feeling: *He's an inveterate liar*.

invidious (ın'vıdıəs) *adj* likely to cause ill-feeling because of what seems to be or is unfair treatment.

invigilate (ın'vıdʒıleıt) *vi* keep a watch on (schoolchildren, students, etc.), while writing examination papers.

invigorate (ın'vıgəreıt) *vt* make lively, strong, full of energy, etc.

invincible (ın'vınsıbəl) *adj* that cannot be defeated or overcome.

inviolable (ın'vaıələbəl) *adj* that is to be treated with great reverence and great respect.

inviolate (ın'vaıələt) *adj* that is to be kept holy and treated with great respect.

invisible (ın'vızıbəl) *adj* that cannot be seen. **invisibility** (ın'vızı'bılıtı) *nu* the state of being unseen.

invite (ın'vaıt) *vt* 1 ask (a person) politely to dinner, a party, to do something, etc. 2 ask for; encourage: *He invited questions*. **invitation** ('ınvı'teıʃən) 1 *nu* inviting or being invited. 2 *nc* a polite request. **inviting** *adj* encouraging; attractive.

invocation ('ınvə'keıʃən) 1 *nu* the act of calling upon God, the law, etc., for help. 2 *nc* a prayer.

invoice ('ınvɔıs) *nc* a list of goods sent, with the price, to be paid. ● *vt* make such a list.

invoke (ın'vəʊk) *vt* 1 call upon (God, the law, etc.) for help. 2 ask very seriously for revenge, etc. 3 send for (evil spirits) by using magic powers.

involuntary (ın'vɒləntərı) *adj* done without using one's own will, choosing to, etc. **involuntarily** (ın'vɒləntərəlı) *adv*

involve (ın'vɒlv) *vt* 1 cause (someone or something) to become mixed up in difficulties, a situation, certain conditions, etc. 2 have as a necessary result: *Going to that place would involve travelling overnight*. **involved** (ın'vɒlvd) *adj* complicated. **involvement** *ncu*

invulnerable (ın'vʌlnərəbəl) *adj* that cannot be harmed or damaged.

inward ('ınwəd) *adj* placed or turned towards the inside; inner. ● *adv* also **inwards** towards the inside. **inwardly** *adv* in the mind or spirit.

iodine ('aıədiːn) *nu* a chemical substance obtained from seawater, used in medicine to destroy germs; and in photography.

ion ('aıən) *nc* an electrically charged atom or group of atoms. **ionisation** ('aıənaı'zeıʃən) *ncu* the changing or being changed into ions. **ionise** ('aıənaız) *vti* change or be changed into ions.

iota (aı'əʊtə) *nc* a very small part: *There's not an iota of truth in what he told you!*

irate (aı'reıt) *formal adj* angry.

ire ('aıə*) *poetry or formal nu* anger.

iridescent ('ırı'desənt) *adj* showing colours that change as light falls on them from different directions.

iris (ˈaɪrɪs) *nc, pl* **-ses** (sɪz) **1** the round,
coloured part of the eye, with a circular
opening in its centre that controls the
amount of light passing through: see picture. **2** a plant with brightly coloured flowers and sword-shaped leaves: see picture at
flowers.

iris

irksome (ˈɜːksəm) *adj* boring; tiresome.
iron (ˈaɪən) **1** *nu* a very common, strong
metal, grey in colour: symbol Fe **2** *nc* a flat-
based, iron tool that is heated and used for
pressing clothes, etc.: see picture. ● *adj*
made of iron. ● *vt* **1** press (clothes, material, etc.) flat with an iron. **2** *vi* (of clothes,
etc.) to be pressed flat with an iron. **Iron
Age** a certain time before recorded history
when iron tools and weapons first came
into use. **Iron Curtain** the border preventing the free passage of people, information, and trade into and out of the USSR
and countries united with it. **ironmonger**
(ˈaɪənmʌŋgə*) *nc* a person who sells metal
goods, esp. for use in the home. **iron ore** a
kind of rock from which iron may be obtained. **iron out 1** make (clothes, etc.)
smooth by pressing with an iron. **2** remove
(difficulties, etc.). **ironing board** *nc* a flat
board, with legs that can be changed in
height, on which clothes are placed for
ironing.

iron

irony (ˈaɪərənɪ) **1** *nu* the saying of something
opposite in meaning to one's thoughts, so
as to add force to one's words. **2** *nc, pl*
-nies an event, etc., that is good, or
wanted, but is wasted because it happens at
the wrong time, or in the wrong place or
circumstances. **ironic** (aɪˈrɒnɪk), **ironical**
(aɪˈrɒnɪkəl) *adj* using or showing irony.
irradiate (ɪˈreɪdɪeɪt) *vt* **1** send or cause rays of
light, sunlight, X-rays, etc., to fall upon. **2**
cause (a person's face or expression) to become bright: *A smile of joy irradiated her
face.*

irrational (ɪˈræʃənəl) *adj* **1** without reason. **2**
silly; senseless.
irregular (ɪˈregjʊlə*) *adj* **1** not behaving or
being in agreement with the usual rules,
customs, etc. **2** not even: *His teeth are very
irregular.* **3** *grammar* (of a word) not given
the usual ending: *The plural of 'leaf' is not
'leafs' but the irregular form 'leaves'.* **irregu-
larity** (ɪˈregjʊˈlærətɪ) **1** *nc, pl* **-ties** something that is irregular. **2** *nu* being irregular.
irrelevant (ɪˈreləvənt) *adj* having no connection with.
irreparable (ɪˈrepərəbəl) *adj* not able to be
put right again or repaired: *irreparable
damage.*
irreplaceable (ˈɪrɪˈpleɪsəbəl) *adj* not able to
be replaced.
irreproachable (ˈɪrɪˈprəʊtʃəbəl) *adj* that cannot be blamed or found fault with: *irreproachable behaviour.*
irresistible (ˈɪrɪˈzɪstəbəl) *adj* too tempting,
strong, etc., not to prevent or give way to.
irrespective (ˈɪrɪˈspektɪv) *adj* **irrespective
of** without considering or paying attention
to; in spite of: *He decided to buy a new car,
irrespective of the cost.*
irresponsible (ˈɪrɪˈspɒnsəbəl) *adj* not trustworthy; not caring about the results
of one's actions. **irresponsibility** (ˈɪrɪ-
ˈspɒnsəˈbɪlɪtɪ) *nu* being irresponsible.
irretrievable (ˈɪrɪˈtriːvəbəl) *adj* that can never
be as it once was.
irreverent (ɪˈrevərənt) *adj* not showing respect for sacred or holy things.
irreversible (ˈɪrɪˈvɜːsəbəl) *adj* that cannot be
changed, withdrawn, or be as it once was.
irrevocable (ɪˈrevəkəbəl) *adj* that can never
be changed. **irrevocably** *adv*
irrigate (ˈɪrɪgeɪt) *vt* take water to (land and
crops) by means of rivers, water-pipes, etc.
irrigation (ˈɪrɪˈgeɪʃən) *nu* irrigating: see picture.

irrigation

irritable (ˈɪrɪtəbəl) *adj* easily annoyed. **irrita-
bility** (ˈɪrɪtəˈbɪlɪtɪ) *nu* being irritable.
irritate (ˈɪrɪteɪt) *vt* **1** cause to become annoyed. **2** cause an unpleasant feeling or discomfort to the body; *Wool irritates her skin*
irritation (ˈɪrɪˈteɪʃən) **1** *nu* irritating or being irritated. **2** *nc* an example of this.
is (ɪz unstressed z, s) *v* (used with **he, she,** or
it) a form of **be.**

Islam ('ızlɑːm) *nu* 1 also **Mohammedanism** the religion of Muslims, followers of the Prophet Mohammed. 2 all the Muslim world. **Islamic** (ızˈlæmɪk) *adj* of Islam.

island ('aɪlənd) *nc* 1 a piece of land that has water all round it. 2 anything that is entirely separated like an island: *a traffic island*.

isle (aɪl) *nc* (used in poetry or with proper names) island: *the British Isles*.

isn't ('ızənt) *v* is not.

isobar ('aɪsəbɑː*) *nc* a line on a map joining places with the same air pressure at a certain time.

isolate ('aɪsəleɪt) *vt* put (a person or thing) apart, away from others. **isolation** ('aɪsə-ˈleɪʃən) *nu* isolating or being isolated.

isometric ('aɪsəˈmetrɪk) *adj* of equal size, quantity, etc.

isosceles (aɪˈsɒsɪliːz) *adj* (of a triangle) that has two sides equal in length: see picture.

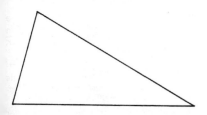

isosceles

isotherm ('aɪsəθɜːm) *nc* a line on a map that joins places with the same temperature at a certain time.

isotope ('aɪsətəʊp) *science nc* one form of an element that is chemically the same as other forms of that element, but different in nuclear qualities.

issue ('ɪsjuː) 1 *vi* come or go out from. 2 *vt* give or send out: *The soldiers were issued with new uniforms*. 3 print and sell (books, stamps, newspapers, etc.). ● *nu* 1 a flowing out. 2 *nc* that which flows out. 3 *nu* the act of giving or sending out; publishing: *the issue of a new magazine. nc* 4 that which is given out or published. 5 an important matter; subject being talked about. 6 a result. 7 *nu* law children: *He died leaving no male issue*.

isthmus ('ɪsməs) *nc* a narrow piece of land joining two larger bodies of land.

it (ɪt) *pron* 1 (used of things or animals and young children when the sex is not known): *She's just had her baby — it's beautiful*. 2 (speaking of someone or something just mentioned or just about to be): *Who is it standing at the gate?* 3 (used to supply a subject, but not meaning anything): *It's been raining all day; Is it time to go home yet?*

italics (ɪˈtælɪks) *printing n pl* letters that slope, like this: *italics*.

itch (ɪtʃ) *vi* have an unpleasant feeling on the skin that makes one want to scratch it. ● *nc* a place of discomfort on the skin, causing a need to scratch it. **itchy** *adj* of an itch.

item ('aɪtəm) *nc* 1 one of the things in a list. 2 a short piece of news in a newspaper, etc. **itemise** ('aɪtəmaɪz) *vt* give or write down every item of (a number or set of things).

itinerant (aɪˈtɪnərənt) *adj* travelling from place to place as a way of life.

itinerary (aɪˈtɪnərərɪ) *nc, pl* **-ries** a plan made for a journey.

it'll ('ɪtəl) it will.

its (ɪts) *determiner, pron* belonging to or to do with it: *She has a baby but I've forgotten its name*. **itself** (ɪtˈself) *pron* done by or concerning it. **by itself** 1 without help. 2 alone.

it's (ɪts) it is or it has.

I've (aɪv) I have.

ivory ('aɪvərɪ) *nu* a hard, white, bone-like substance obtained from the long, pointed teeth of elephants. ● *adj* the colour of ivory.

ivy ('aɪvɪ) *nu* an evergreen plant with shiny, green, five-pointed leaves, that grows and climbs on walls, etc.

J

jab (dʒæb) *vti* hit out sharply at with something pointed. ●*nc* 1 an act of jabbing. 2 *medicine, infml* an injection of a substance into the body, esp. to prevent a disease.

jabber ('dʒæbə*) *vti* speak or say fast and with little sense. ●*nu* jabbered speech.

jack (dʒæk) *nc* 1 a device for raising something heavy, esp. a car, lorry, etc. 2 also **knave** the playing-card in each suit which carries a picture of a prince. **Union Jack** the national flag of the United Kingdom. **jack up** raise with a jack.

jackal ('dʒækəl) *nc* an African and South Asian dog-like animal that hunts: see picture.

jackal

jackass ('dʒækæs) *nc* 1 a male donkey. 2 *derogatory* a stupid person.

jackdaw ('dʒækdɔː) *nc* a black bird that takes shiny objects to its nest.

jacket ('dʒækɪt) *nc* 1 a garment for the arms and upper body that fastens at the front. 2 a covering or wrapping, such as one used to keep water hot in a tank. 3 also **dust jacket** a sheet of paper wrapped round the cover of a new book. 4 the skin of a potato.

jack-knife ('dʒæknaɪf) *nc, pl* **-ves** (vz) 1 a knife of which the blade folds into the handle. 2 a dive in which the diver bends at the waist and then straightens before entering the water. ●*vi* (of an articulated lorry) accidentally fold into a V-shape while moving.

jackpot ('dʒækpɒt) *nc* a large prize, esp. of money won in a game of chance.

jade (dʒeɪd) *nu* a white or green semi-precious stone used for jewellery.

jagged ('dʒægɪd) *adj* having a rough edge or surface; rough with sharp points: *jagged rocks.*

jaguar ('dʒægjʊə*) *nc* a large American animal of the cat family.

jail (also **gaol**) (dʒeɪl) *vt* put (someone) in prison. ●*nc* a prison. **jailer** (also **jailor, gaoler**) *nc* a person in charge of prisoners.

jam[1] (dʒæm) *ncu* a (type of) sweet food made by boiling fruit with sugar until it thickens.

jam[2] *vti* 1 (cause to) be pushed in tightly: *I jammed the cork into the bottle.* 2 (cause to) be filled or blocked: *The streets were jammed with traffic.* 3 (cause to) become stuck: *The drawer's jammed because it's too full.* 4 send signals that prevent (a radio station, etc.) from being received clearly. ●*nc* 1 a blockage: *a traffic jam.* 2 the state of being jammed. 3 *infml* a difficulty; awkward situation.

jangle ('dʒæŋgəl) *vti* (of keys, a bell, etc.) (cause to) ring unmusically. ●*nu* this sound.

janitor ('dʒænɪtə*) *chiefly US nc* a person who cleans a school, the public parts of a block of flats, etc.

January ('dʒænjʊərɪ) *n* the first month of the year, before February.

jar[1] (dʒɑː*) *nc* a glass or pottery container, esp. with a wide mouth, a lid, and no handles.

jar[2] *vti* 1 (cause to) make a rough sound. 2 hit (something) and rub roughly. 3 (sometimes followed by **on**) have an unpleasant or painful effect (on) (the nerves, etc.). ●*nc* 1 a rough rubbing sound. 2 a shock.

jargon ('dʒɑːgən) *often derogatory nu* special words and expressions, used in a subject of study, profession, etc., that are hard for others to understand.

jasmine ('dʒæzmɪn) *nu* a bush with pleasant-smelling red, yellow, or white flowers used in perfume and tea.

jaundice ('dʒɔːndɪs) *nu* yellowness of the skin and the whites of the eyes, caused esp by liver diseases. ●*vt* affect (a person, his judgement, etc.) esp. so as to be unfair: *a jaundiced view.*

jaunt (dʒɔːnt) *nc* a trip made for pleasure. ●*vi* go on a jaunt.

jaunty ('dʒɔːntɪ) *adj* **-ier, -iest** quick, gay, carefree, or with such an air: *a jaunty walk.* **jauntily** *adv*

javelin ('dʒævəlɪn) *nc* a pointed stick for throwing as a weapon or, esp. made of metal, in a sports competition.

jaw (dʒɔː) *nc* 1 also **jawbone** the upper or lower bone holding the teeth. 2 the lowest part of the face, around and including the chin. ●*vi slang* talk a lot.

jay (dʒeɪ) *nc* a noisy bird with feathers of many colours including blue in the wings.

jazz (dʒæz) *nu* a type of music with characteristic rhythms and harmonies played esp by small groups and originally by United States blacks. **jazz up** *infml* 1 give to (music) some of the qualities of jazz. 2 make more lively, etc. **jazzy** *infml adj* **-ier, -iest** lively or showy.

jealous ('dʒeləs) *adj* **1** feeling that one wants something belonging to someone else: *jealous of his neighbours and their new car.* **2** determined to keep something; watchful: *jealous of her rights.* **jealously** *adv* **jealousy** *ncu, pl* **-sies** the state or an example of being jealous.

jeans (dʒiːnz) *n pl* informal or working trousers made of denim or corduroy.

jeep (dʒiːp) *nc* a small, open, army motor vehicle: see picture.

jeep

jeer (dʒɪə*) *vti* (often followed by **at**) laugh unkindly (at); make fun (of). ● *nc* a jeering laugh or shout.

Jehovah (dʒɪ'həʊvə) *n* the name given to God in the Old Testament of the Bible. **Jehovah's Witness** a member of a Christian group started in America, that believes that it is the only true Church or religion and that governments should have no control over its religion.

jelly ('dʒelɪ) *nc, pl* **-lies** *ncu* **1** a soft elastic substance, esp. a (type of) food made with gelatin obtained from the bones and skin of animals. **2** (a type or quantity of) such a food with fruit juice added. **3** (type of) sweet food made by boiling fruit juice and sugar until they set when cooled. **jellyfish** ('dʒelɪfɪʃ) *nc, pl* **-fish, -fishes** a sea-animal with a jelly-like body and long tentacles: see picture.

jellyfish

jeopardise ('dʒepədaɪz) *vt* put in jeopardy. **jeopardy** ('dʒepədɪ) *nu* danger; risk: *It was so cold that their lives were in jeopardy.*

jerk (dʒɜːk) *nc* **1** a sudden sharp pull or movement. **2** *slang, derogatory* a stupid or disliked person. ● *vti* (cause to) move with a jerk. **jerky** *adj* **-ier, -iest** moving in jerks.

jerry-built ('dʒerɪbɪlt) *adj* (of a building) badly built with cheap materials.

jersey ('dʒɜːzɪ) **1** *nc, pl* **-s** a woollen or similar garment for the arms and upper body; pullover. **2** *nu* closely knitted woollen material.

jest (dʒest) **1** *formal nc* a joke. **2** *nu* fun: *I only said it in jest.* ● *vi formal or humorous* make a jest; speak in jest.

Jesus Christ ('dʒiːzəz) *n* the Jew, believed by Christians to be the Son of God, who started Christianity. ● *slang interj* also **Jesus, Christ** (used to express surprise, disgust, etc.)

jet (dʒet) *nc* **1** a stream of liquid or gas being forced out of a hole. **2** a hole made to produce such a stream. **3** a plane with a jet engine. ● *vti* (cause to) travel in a **jet** (defs. 1, 3). **jet engine** also **jet** an engine, used esp. in planes, that works by sending a powerful jet of gas out backwards.

jetsam ('dʒetsəm) *n* See **flotsam**.

jettison ('dʒetɪsən) *vt* throw out (goods) of or let go from.

jetty ('dʒetɪ) *nc, pl* **-ties** a wall or landing-stage built out into water from the land.

Jew (dʒuː) **1** a descendant of the Hebrews of ancient Palestine. **2** a follower of Judaism. **Jewish** *adj*

jewel ('dʒuːəl) *nc* **1** a precious stone; ornament made of such stones. **2** a hard precious stone used in a watch. **3** a valued person or thing. **jeweller** *US* **jeweler** *nc* a person who makes or sells jewellery. **jewellery** *US* **jewelry** ('dʒuːəlrɪ) *nu* rings, necklaces, etc., esp. of jewels or precious metals, worn as ornaments.

jiffy ('dʒɪfɪ) *infml nc, pl* **-fies** also **jiff** a very short time: *I'll be with you in a jiffy.*

jig (dʒɪg) *nc* **1** a lively dance; tune for this. **2** a device used to hold and control a tool. ● *vi* **1** dance a jig. **2** *vti* (cause to) move rapidly up and down.

jigsaw ('dʒɪgsɔː) *nc* also **jigsaw puzzle** a picture stuck to wood or cardboard and cut into irregularly shaped pieces to be put together again for fun.

jilt (dʒɪlt) *vt* leave (a lover), esp. just before a planned marriage.

jingle ('dʒɪŋgəl) *nc* **1** a light, repeated ringing sound. **2** a short tune or song, used esp. in advertisements on radio or television. ● *vti* (cause to) make a **jingle** (def 1).

jingo ('dʒɪŋgəʊ) **by jingo** *archaic interj* (used to express surprise or determination.)

jinx (dʒɪŋks) *nc* a supposed force that brings bad luck: *So much has gone wrong with this plane that there must be a jinx on it!* ● *vt* bring bad luck to; cause to bring bad luck: *Our holiday isn't jinxed — you are!*

jive (dʒaɪv) *nu* a lively, popular dance done esp. to jazz and rock-'n'-roll in the 1940s and 1950s. ● *vi* do a jive.

job (dʒɒb) *nc* **1** a paid occupation; employment. **2** a piece of work; task. **3** *nu infml* difficulty: *I had a job getting home.* **a good job** lucky: *It was a good job I came home.*

jockey ('dʒɒkɪ) *nc, pl* **-s 1** a person who rides a horse in a race. **2** See **disc jockey** under **disc.** ● *vi* try to get a good position or obtain other advantage: *to jockey for position.*

jocund ('dʒɒkənd) *formal adj* cheerful and friendly.

jog (dʒɒg) **1** *vi* run at a gentle speed, esp. for exercise. **2** *vt* knock lightly. **jog someone's memory** make someone remember. ● *nc* the act of jogging. **jog along** move on or continue, esp. with difficulty or without enthusiasm. **jogging** *nu* the activity of jogging for exercise.

join (dʒɔɪn) **1** *vti* put or come together; unite; connect. *vt* **2** become a member of (a society, etc.). **3** come together with: *May I join you at your table?* ● *nc* a place where two things are joined: *I mended the cup — can you see the join?* **join in** take part (in) as well: *We've started, but you can still join in (the game).* **join up** become a member of (something, esp. an army, etc.).

joiner ('dʒɔɪnə*) *nc* a person who makes things in wood, esp. doors, windows, etc., for houses. **joinery** *nu* the work of or things made by a joiner.

joint (dʒɔɪnt) *nc* **1** a place where two things are joined. **2** *anatomy* a place where two or more bones meet. **3** one of the parts of an animal cut up for meat. **4** *slang* a meeting place such as a bar. ● *adj* **1** produced or owned by more than one person: *a joint effort.* **2** sharing: *the joint owner(s).* ● *vt* **1** provide with a joint. **2** cut (meat) into joints.

joist (dʒɔɪst) *nc* a long, thick piece of wood, steel, etc., used for building.

joke (dʒəʊk) *nc* **1** an amusing story or saying. **2** something done for fun; trick. **3** *infml* a situation that is thought to be funny: *A railway strike is no joke.* ● *vi* **1** tell a joke. **2** do something for fun. **joker** *nc* **1** someone who jokes. **2** *derogatory* a person one does not like or trust. **3** a playing-card that in many card games can be used as any other card. **jokingly** ('dʒəʊkɪŋlɪ) *adv* in fun; as a joke.

jolly ('dʒɒlɪ) *adj* **-ier, -iest** joyful; gay. ● *adv Brit* very: *Jolly well done!* ● *vt* (often followed by **along**) keep or make (someone) jolly.

jolt (dʒəʊlt) *vti* (cause to) shake violently and suddenly: *The train jolted to a stop.* ● *nc* a sudden shake or shock.

jostle ('dʒɒsəl) *vti* knock or push against (someone): *The crowd jostled round.*

jot (dʒɒt) *vt* (often followed by **down**) write quickly. **jotter** *nc* a book or pad for notes.

joule (dʒuːl) *physics nc* a measure of work or energy = 1 watt-second: symbol J

journal ('dʒɜːnəl) *nc* **1** a magazine or newspaper, esp. one for a profession or subject

of study. **2** a diary. **journalism** ('dʒɜːnəl-ɪzəm) *nu* the work of reporting news in a newspaper or magazine or on radio or television. **journalist** *nc* a person whose work is journalism.

journey ('dʒɜːnɪ) *nc, pl* **-s** a trip or voyage. ● *vi* travel; make a journey.

journeyman ('dʒɜːnɪmən) *nc, pl* **-men** a trained man working for another in a mechanical trade.

joust (dʒaʊst) *nc* a competition in which two men ride towards each other on horses and try to knock each other off with the points of their lances. ● *vi* take part in a joust.

jovial ('dʒəʊvɪəl) *adj* cheerful; laughing.

jowl (dʒaʊl) *nc* flesh hanging down from the neck or lower jaw of a person or animal.

joy (dʒɔɪ) *nu* **1** great happiness or gladness. **2** *infml* luck or success: *Have you had any joy in your search?* **joyful** *adj* full of, expressing, or producing joy: *joyful news.* **joyfully** *adv* **joyous** ('dʒɔɪəs) *adj* feeling, expressing, or producing joy: *in a joyous mood.*

jubilant ('dʒuːbɪlənt) *adj* feeling or expressing great joy. **jubilation** (,dʒuːbɪ'leɪʃən) *nu* (the act of feeling or expressing) great joy, esp. at a victory.

jubilee ('dʒuːbɪliː, ,dʒuːbɪ'liː) *nc* the time marking a particular number of years after an event such as the coronation of a king or queen, the starting of a society, etc.: (sixty or seventy-five years for a **diamond jubilee**, fifty years for a **golden jubilee**, and twenty-five years for a **silver jubilee**).

Judaism ('dʒuːdeɪ,ɪzəm) *n* the Jewish religion.

judge (dʒʌdʒ) *nc* **1** a person who governs in a court of law and decides punishments for people found guilty. **2** a person who decides the result of a game or competition and whether the rules are being kept. **3** a person who decides on the quality, etc., of something: *a good judge of wine.* ● *vti* act as a judge; make a decision (as): *I judged the best-behaved dog competition; They judged him guilty of murder.* **2** *vt* form an opinion of: *I can't judge his courage. I've never seen him in battle.*

judgement (also **judgment**) ('dʒʌdʒmənt) **1** *nc* a decision reached by a judge. **2** *nu* the ability to judge (well): *This eye disease affects judgement of distance; You always show good judgement.*

judicial (dʒuː'dɪʃəl) *adj* to do with judging in a court of law.

judiciary (dʒuː'dɪʃərɪ) *nc, pl* **-ries** a group of judges (**judge** def. 1).

judicious (dʒuː'dɪʃəs) *adj* sensible; showing good judgement. **judiciously** *adv*

judo ('dʒuːdəʊ) *nu* a sport, developed from the Japanese art of self-defence without weapons, in which two people try to throw each other to the ground.

jug (dʒʌg) *nc* 1 an open container with a handle, used esp. for pouring liquid. 2 *Australian* a kettle.

juggernaut ('dʒʌgənɔːt) *nc* 1 a powerful destructive force. 2 *infml, Brit* a large lorry.

juggle ('dʒʌgəl) *vti* 1 repeatedly throw up and catch (several objects) in turn as an entertainment. 2 arrange (figures, facts, or events) cleverly for one's own purposes. **juggler** *nc*

juice (dʒuːs) *ncu* 1 the liquid of a (type of) animal or plant, esp. a fruit: *tomato juice*. 2 *(usually pl)* the liquid produced by parts of the body: *stomach juices*. 3 *infml nu* electricity, petrol, etc.: *Turn on the juice and see if it goes*. **juicy** *adj* **-ier, -iest** full of juice.

jukebox ('dʒuːkbɒks) *nc* a machine that plays a chosen record when one puts a coin in.

July (dʒʊ'laɪ) *n* the seventh month of the year, after June and before August.

jumble ('dʒʌmbəl) *vt* (often followed by **up**) mix up; get out of order. ● *nc* 1 a mixed-up pile or state. 2 *Brit nu* things given for a jumble sale. **jumble sale** *Brit* a sale of given articles, esp. unwanted clothes, etc., to help a church, society, etc.

jumbo jet ('dʒʌmbəʊ) *nc* a type of large jet-powered plane with two passenger levels.

jump (dʒʌmp) 1 *vti* push oneself off the ground or other surface or over (an object) with one's legs: *jump the fence; jump two metres*. *vi* 2 rise suddenly: *Prices jumped last month*. 3 make a sudden movement, esp. from fright; start. 4 move about quickly and violently: *The children are jumping about on the chairs again*. *vt* 5 pass over; miss out: *Because he was so clever at school he jumped a year*. 6 *infml* attack suddenly, esp. in order to rob. ● *nc* 1 the act of jumping. 2 a space or object jumped.

jumper ('dʒʌmpə*) *nc* 1 a person or animal that jumps. 2 a woollen or similar garment for the arms and upper body; pullover.

jumpy ('dʒʌmpɪ) *infml adj* **-ier, -iest** likely to make sudden movements, esp. because nervous.

junction ('dʒʌŋkʃən) *nc* a place where roads, railways, etc., or electric wires meet.

juncture ('dʒʌŋktʃə*) *nu* a moment in time: *At this juncture I can't tell you his name*.

June (dʒuːn) *n* the sixth month of the year, after May and before July.

jungle ('dʒʌŋgəl) *nc* 1 a thick, mixed forest in hot, wet places near the equator. 2 a thick tangle (of plants, etc.). 3 a dangerous place.

junior ('dʒuːnɪə*) *adj* of lower age, importance, or length of time in a place: *Junior

workers should listen to those with more experience. ● *nc* a junior person: *The office junior makes the tea*.

juniper ('dʒuːnɪpə*) *nc* a bush or small tree producing cones and berries used for making the drink of gin.

junk[1] (dʒʌŋk) *nu* 1 old, unwanted, or unused belongings. 2 *infml* rubbish; nonsense.

junk[2] *nc* a Chinese flat-bottomed sailing boat: see picture.

junk

junkie ('dʒʌŋkɪ) *slang nc* a person who depends on taking drugs.

junta ('dʒʌntə, 'hʊntə) *sometimes derogatory nc* a group of military officers ruling a country, esp. after taking power by force.

jurisdiction (,dʒʊərɪs'dɪkʃən) *nu* power, esp. to judge according to laws: *Murders are outside the jurisdiction of a local court*.

juror ('dʒʊərə*) *nc* a member of a jury.

jury ('dʒʊərɪ) *nc, pl* **-ries** a group of people who decide the verdict in a court of law or who judge a competition, etc. **juryman** ('dʒʊərɪmən) *nc, pl* **-men** a male juror.

just (dʒʌst, unstressed dʒəst) *adj* 1 fair: *a just decision*. 2 rightful; proper: *his just reward*. ● *adv* 1 also **only just** (only) a short time ago: *I have (only) just arrived*. 2 also **only just** (very) nearly not; barely: *We were (only) just in time*. 3 at this moment: *I'm just finishing*. 4 only; no more than: *He's just a friend*. **just as** 1 at the moment when: *You called just as I was going out*. 2 in the same way that; while: *Just as he spends his time reading, I spend mine writing*. **just then** at that exact moment. **just the same** See under **same**.

justice ('dʒʌstɪs) *nu* 1 the quality of being just. 2 the working of the law: *He was brought to justice*. 3 *nc* a judge. **Justice of the Peace** an unpaid, part-time judge dealing with small crimes, licences, etc.

justify ('dʒʌstɪfaɪ) *vt* 1 show to be just, correct, necessary, etc.: *Her worst fears were justified; Can you justify spending so much money?* 2 *printing* make (a line of type) exactly the right width. **justifiable** ('dʒʌstɪfaɪəbəl) *adj* able to be justified. **justifiably** *adv* **justification** (,dʒʌstɪfɪ'keɪʃən) *ncu* (an example of) justifying something; a reason: *What is your justification for acting in this way?*

jut (dʒʌt) *vi* (often followed by **out**) stick out beyond something: *A shelf jutted out from the wall.*

jute (dʒuːt) *nu* material obtained from the jute plant and used to make sacks, mats, etc.

juvenile (ˈdʒuːvənaɪl) *sometimes derogatory adj* young; childish; to do with juveniles. ●*nc formal* a young person, animal, or plant. **juvenile delinquency** *nu* crimes done by juveniles.

juxtaposition (ˌdʒʌkstəpəˈzɪʃən) *nu* the placing of two things next to each other.

K

kaleidoscope (kə'laɪdəskəʊp) *nc* **1** a toy using mirrors and small coloured objects to produce ever-changing patterns. **2** a great variety. **kaleidoscopic** (kə,laɪdə'skɒpɪk) *adj*

kangaroo (,kæŋgə'ruː) *nc* a large Australian animal that travels fast by jumping and of which the young grow up in a bag on the mother's front: see picture at **animals**.

kaolin ('keɪəlɪn) *nu* a fine white earth used for making high-quality pottery and taken as a medicine for upset stomachs.

karate (kə'rɑːtɪ) *nu* a Japanese method of fighting without using weapons.

kayak ('kaɪæk) *nc* a small Eskimo boat made with animal skins: see picture.

kayak

keel (kiːl) *nc* **1** the lowest part of a boat or ship, running down its length. **2** a deep, narrow part of a boat, sticking down below it. **keel over 1** fall over or down. **2** turn over.

keen (kiːn) *adj* **-er, -est 1** enthusiastic; eager: *He's keen to go.* **2** highly developed: *a keen sense of smell.* **3** (of a wind) very cold. **4** (of pain, a desire, etc.) great. **5** (of a knife) sharp. **keen on** fond of. **keenly** *adv* **keenness** *nu*

keep (kiːp) **1** *vti* (cause to) remain, esp. in good condition: *Keep the camera still; How long does meat keep?* *vt* **2** continue to have or possess: *I sold one but kept the other.* **3** store; manage; look after: *I'll keep your watch in case you get wet.* **4** have (something, esp. animals) for one's use. **5** provide what (someone) needs to live: *Her wages keep the whole family.* **6** do something on the occasion of (a regular event, such as a holiday). **7** act according to (a promise, the law, etc.). **8** guard (a town, football goal, etc.). **9** cause to stay: *His work kept him late at the office.* **10** not tell (esp. a secret). ● *nu* **1** (the cost of) keeping someone: *earn one's keep.* **2** *nc* the strong, inner tower of a castle. **keep an eye on** *infml* look after; watch; guard. **keep oneself to oneself** avoid meeting or becoming friendly with other people. **keep at** (cause to) continue doing (something). **keep away** (often followed by **from**) not go near. **keep back 1** (cause to) stay away (from something). **2** prevent (information, water, etc.) from flowing; keep for oneself. **keep down 1** (cause to) remain low or below something. **2** control (anger, etc.). **3** cause (food) not to be forced back up out of the stomach. **keep in 1** make (a child) stay behind (at school) or indoors as a punishment. **2** cause (a fire) to stay lit all night. **keep off 1** not (allow to) go on (grass, etc.). **2** not eat (something). **3** (of rain) not start. **4** (cause to) avoid (a subject of discussion). **keep on 1** continue (doing something). **2** continue to wear or employ. **3** *infml* (often followed by **about**) continue talking or mentioning. **keep up 1** prevent from falling, sinking, or lessening. **2** cause (a house, etc.) to stay in good condition. **3** prevent (someone) from going to bed. **keep up with** travel at the same speed as; remain equal to.

keeper ('kiːpə*) *nc* a person who looks after something, esp. a shop, animals, or a museum.

keepsake ('kiːpseɪk) *nc* a present intended to remind someone of its giver or an occasion.

keg (keg) *nc* **1** a small barrel. **2** *Brit* a metal container for beer.

kelvin ('kelvɪn) *nc* a measure of temperature = 1 degree C, but with 0 at absolute zero (−273°C): symbol K

ken (ken) *n* **beyond one's ken** not within one's knowledge.

kennel ('kenəl) *nc* **1** a shelter for a dog. **2** *(pl)* a place where one can pay to have a dog kept and looked after. ● *vt* put (a dog) in kennels.

kept (kept) past tense and past participle of **keep.**

kerb (kɜːb) *US* **curb** *nc* the edge of a raised pavement.

kernel ('kɜːnəl) *nc* the softer part that is the seed in a nut or fruit-stone.

kerosene ('kerəsiːn) *US, Australian n* See **paraffin.**

kestrel ('kestrəl) *nc* a bird that hunts small animals and can stay in one place in the air to look for them.

ketchup ('ketʃʌp) *nu* also **tomato ketchup** a sauce made from tomatoes, vinegar, etc., and added to other food, esp. on one's plate.

kettle ('ketəl) *nc* a metal container with a handle and a spout, used for boiling water in.

kettledrum ('ketəldrʌm) *nc* a drum made of a metal bowl with a skin across that can be stretched more or less to alter the note it produces: see picture.

kettledrum

key (kiː) *nc, pl* **-s 1** a metal device made to fit into and undo a lock. **2** a device used to wind a clock, work a switch, etc. **3** any of the parts of a typewriter, musical instrument, etc., pressed with the fingers. **4** a system of musical notes, based on one particular note, on which a piece of music is built up: *a piece in the key of C.* **5** the most important thing for obtaining, reaching, or understanding something: *Ambition is the key to success.* **6** a list of explanations of the signs on a map, etc. **keyboard** ('kiːbɔːd) *nc* a set of keys (**key** def. 3) esp. on a musical instrument such as a piano. **keyhole** ('kiːhəʊl) *nc* the hole in a door, etc., through which a key is put into its lock. **keynote** ('kiːnəʊt) *nc* **1** the note on which a **key** (def. 4) is based. **2** the central idea or subject of a meeting, etc. **keystone** ('kiːstəʊn) *nc* **1** a central idea on which everything else depends. **2** the stone at the top of an arch.

khaki ('kɑːkɪ) *nu* a yellowish-brown colour used esp. for soldiers' clothes.

kick (kɪk) *vt* **1** hit and esp. move with the foot. **2** get (a goal) by kicking a football. **3** *infml* stop or give up (a habit). **4** *vi* (of a gun, etc.) move sharply back when fired, etc. ●*nc* **1** the act of kicking. **2** the sharp movement of a gun, etc., when fired. **3** *infml* a feeling of enjoyment: *I did it for kicks.* **kick the bucket** *slang* die. **kick off 1** remove (a shoe, etc.) by kicking. **2** start (a game of football). **3** *infml* start: *Who'll kick off with the first question?* **kick-off** ('kɪkɒf) **1** *nc* the start of a game of football. **2** *infml nu* a start: *You weren't there, for a kick-off.*

kid¹ (kɪd) *nc* **1** a young goat. **2** *infml* a child. **3** *nu* leather made from the skin of a kid: *kid gloves.*

kid² *infml vti* deceive; pretend.

kidnap ('kɪdnæp) *vt* carry off and hold (someone), esp. threatening to kill unless one is paid. ●*nc* an instance of kidnapping. **kidnapper** *nc*

kidney ('kɪdnɪ) *anatomy nc, pl* **-s** either of the two parts of the body that clean the blood and make urine.

kill (kɪl) *vt* **1** cause to die. **2** cause to end; destroy. **3** *infml* cause great pain to: *My new shoes are killing me.* **4** *infml* make very tired: *That walk killed me.* ●*nc* **1** an act of killing, esp. at the end of a hunt. **2** the animal or animals killed in a hunt or shoot. **3** the destruction in war of a plane, ship, etc. **killer** *nc*

kiln (kɪln) *nc* a large heated container for burning or drying something or for firing pots, etc.

kilogram ('kɪləgræm) (often shortened to **kilo**) *nc* a measure of weight = 1000 g

kilometre *US* **kilometer** ('kɪlə,miːtə*, kɪ'lɒmɪtə*) *nc* a measure of length = 1000 m

kilowatt ('kɪləwɒt) *nc* a measure of power = 1000 W

kilt (kɪlt) *nc* a knee-length skirt worn by men from the Scottish Highlands.

kimono (kɪ'məʊnəʊ) *nc, pl* **-s** a long Japanese garment with short, wide sleeves: see picture.

kimono

kin (kɪn) *nu* one's family or relations. **kith and kin** See **kith**. **next of kin** See under **next**.

kind¹ (kaɪnd) **1** *nc* a sort; type: *I like this kind of food.* **2** *nu* goods: *payment in kind.* **a kind of** a sort (esp. not good) of: *We were given a kind of a breakfast.*

kind² *adj* **-er, -est** friendly; generous; helpful. **kindly** *adv* in a kind way. ●*adj* **-ier, -iest** also **kind-hearted** (of a person) kind. **kindness** *nu*

kindergarten ('kɪndə,gɑːtən) *nc* a school for young children under the normal school age.

kindle ('kɪndəl) *vti* **1** (cause to) start to burn. **2** (cause to) start: *His anger was easily kindled.* **kindling** *nu* material such as small pieces of dry wood used for starting a fire.

kindred ('kɪndrɪd) *adj* **1** (of people) related. **2** similar; alike: *My neighbour proved to be a kindred spirit.* ●*nu* one's family.

kinetic (kaɪ'netɪk, kɪ'netɪk) *formal adj* to do with movement.

king (kɪŋ) *nc* **1** a male ruler of a country who is normally the son of the king or queen before him. **2** the best or most important person, animal, or thing: *the king of oranges.* **3** the playing-card in each suit carrying a picture of a king. **4** the chess piece whose inability to escape from an attacked square loses the game. **kingfisher** ('kɪŋfɪʃə*) *nc* a bird with mainly shiny blue feathers that catches fish: see picture. **kingpin** ('kɪŋpɪn) *nc* the most important person in an organisation, point in an argument, etc. **king-size** ('kɪŋsaɪz) *adj* extra large.

kingfisher

kingdom ('kɪŋdəm) *nc* **1** a country ruled by a king or queen. **2** all of something: *the animal kingdom.*

kink (kɪŋk) *nc* a small bend or twist in a pipe, wire, etc. ● *vti* get or put a kink in.

kinship ('kɪnʃɪp) *formal nu* a family relationship.

kinsman ('kɪnzmən) *archaic nc, pl* **-men** a family relation.

kiosk ('kiːɒsk) *nc* **1** a small building used for selling cigarettes, newspapers, etc. **2** *chiefly Brit* a public telephone box.

kipper ('kɪpə*) *nc* a salted and smoked herring.

kiss (kɪs) **1** *vt* touch with the lips. **2** *vti* touch or hit gently against. **3** *vi* (of two people) kiss each other's lips or cheeks. ● *nc* an instance of kissing. **kiss of life** a way of keeping someone alive who has stopped breathing by blowing into his mouth.

kit (kɪt) **1** *nc* a set of tools, parts, etc., for doing a job, building something, etc.: *a tool kit; I made my boat from a kit.* **2** *nu* clothes and other necessary things: *sports kit; a bag for a soldier's kit.* ● *vt* provide with kit. **kit out** or **up** obtain or provide (someone) with kit.

kitchen ('kɪtʃɪn) *nc* a room used for preparing and cooking food. **kitchenette** (ˌkɪtʃɪ'net) *nc* a small room or part of a room used as a kitchen.

kite (kaɪt) *nc* **1** a toy made of a light frame covered with thin paper or cloth, tied to a long piece of string and allowed to rise in the wind. **2** a type of bird that feeds on small animals.

kith (kɪθ) *n* **kith and kin** one's friends and relations.

kitten ('kɪtən) *nc* a young cat.

kitty ('kɪtɪ) *nc, pl* **-ties** a pool of money provided by two or more people, esp. in a gambling game.

kiwi ('kiːwiː) *nc* a New Zealand bird that cannot fly: see picture.

kiwi

kleptomaniac (ˌkleptəʊ'meɪnɪæk) *nc* a person who cannot stop stealing things.

knack (næk) *nc* **1** a method that enables one to do something more easily: *The knack is to hold your needle like this.* **2** an ability to do something: *He'll never do very well—he just hasn't the knack.*

knapsack ('næpsæk) *nc* a bag carried on the back by soldiers, etc.

knave (neɪv) *nc* **1** *archaic* a dishonest man. **2** See **jack** (def. 2).

knead (niːd) *vt* repeatedly press and fold (dough).

knee (niː) *nc* **1** the joint halfway up each leg. **2** the part of a garment covering a knee. ● *vt* push or knock with a knee. **kneecap** ('niːkæp) *n* See **patella. knee-deep** (ˌniː'diːp) *adj* **1** (of water, etc.) reaching up to the knees. **2** standing in or filled with something that reaches up to the knees: *The room was knee-deep in papers.*

kneel (niːl) *vi* fall or rest on one's knees or one knee only.

knell (nel) *nu* the sound of a bell, esp. rung to tell of someone's death. ● *vi* (of a bell) ring a knell.

knelt (nelt) past tense and past participle of **kneel.**

Knesset ('knesɪt) *n* the parliament of Israel.

knew (njuː) past tense of **know.**

knickerbockers ('nɪkəˌbɒkəz) *n pl* trousers reaching to and gathered tight just below the knees.

knickers ('nɪkəz) *infml, Brit n pl* a woman's garment worn next to the body from the waist to the tops of the legs.

knick-knack ('nɪknæk) *nc* a useless ornament.

knife (naɪf) *nc, pl* **-ves** (vz) a metal blade with a sharp edge and a handle, used chiefly for cutting or as a weapon. ● *vt* stick a knife into (someone).

knight (naɪt) *nc* **1** (in the Middle Ages) an important man serving as a horse-soldier in heavy armour. **2** (in Britain and the Commonwealth) a man given a high position and the title 'Sir' before his name by a king or queen as a reward. **3** a chess piece that can move two squares in one direction and then one square at right angles. ●*vt* make (someone) a **knight** (defs. **1, 2**). **knighthood** (ˈnaɪthʊd) *ncu* the state or title of being a **knight** (defs. **1, 2**).

knit (nɪt) *vt* **1** make (a garment, etc.) by repeatedly looping a yarn, esp. of wool, over itself, esp. using knitting-needles. **2** connect; join closely. ●*nc* any type or pattern of knitting. **knitting** *nu* **1** partly knitted garments. **2** the activity of knitting. **knitting-needle** (ˈnɪtɪŋ,niːdəl) *nc* a long, thick needle with no hole in it, used for knitting.

knob (nɒb) *nc* **1** a rounded part on the end or side of something, esp. as a handle. **2** a rounded piece of something, such as butter. **knobby** *adj* **-ier, -iest 1** covered in knobs (**knob** def. **1**). **2** sticking out.

knock (nɒk) *vt* **1** hit sharply. **2** hit several times: *knock a nail into a wall.* **3** *infml* criticise (esp. a play, etc.) as bad. **4** *vi* (often followed by **at** or **on**) knock (esp. a door) with the hand to ask to go in. ●*nc* **1** a sound of knocking. **2** a blow. **knock down 1** hit (someone) to the ground. **2** take down (a building). **3** sell at an auction. **knock out 1** make (someone) unconscious, esp. with a blow. **2** destroy or damage. **3** defeat (someone) in a competition. **knockout** (ˈnɒkaʊt) *nc* **1** a blow that knocks someone out. **2** a competition in which the winner of each game plays another winner. **knock together** make quickly and esp. not very well: *knock together a table.*

knoll (nɒl) *nc* a small hill.

knot (nɒt) *nc* **1** a fastening or ornament made by tying string, rope, etc. **2** a hard lump in part of a plant or animal, esp. in wood where a branch grew out. **3** a measure of the speed of a ship or plane = 1 nautical mile per hour. **4** a group, esp. of people. ●*vt* make a **knot** (def. **1**) in. **knotty** *adj* **-ier, -iest 1** (of rope, etc.) full of knots. **2** (of a problem) difficult.

know (nəʊ) *vt* **1** have (a fact, etc.) in one's mind: *I knew that he would come; I know nothing about cars.* **2** have met or had experience of; be familiar with: *I know most of her friends as well.* **3** recognise: *They all knew me in spite of my disguise.* **4** be able to use (a language). **know-how** (ˈnəʊhaʊ) *nu* knowledge, esp. practical or technical. **know how to** know the way in which to (do something).

knowing (ˈnəʊɪŋ) *adj* **1** knowing what one is doing or what is happening: *a knowing member of an unlawful group.* **2** suggesting that one knows more than one has said, etc.: *a knowing look.* **knowingly** *adv*

knowledge (ˈnɒlɪdʒ) *nu* **1** the state of knowing or understanding. **2** all the things that are known (by one person, on a subject, etc.). **knowledgeable** (ˈnɒlɪdʒəbəl) *adj* having or showing much knowledge.

known (nəʊn) past participle of **know.**

knuckle (ˈnʌkəl) *nc* **1** *anatomy* a finger joint, esp. joining the finger to the hand. **2** a joint of meat from the leg below the knee of an ox, pig, etc. **knuckle down to** *infml* set about (work) seriously.

kobo (ˈkəʊbəʊ) *nc, pl* **-s** See appendix.

kopeck (ˈkəʊpek) *nc* See appendix.

Koran (kɔːˈrɑːn) *n* the holy book of Islam, believed by Muslims to be the words of God to Mohammed.

Kremlin (ˈkremlɪn) *n* (the old buildings in the centre of Moscow housing) the government of the Soviet Union.

Krishna (ˈkrɪʃnə) *n* a popular Hindu god.

L

label ('leɪbəl) *nc* 1 a piece of paper, metal, etc., fixed to and giving information about an object. 2 a word or name applied to something or someone. ● *vt* fix a label to.

laboratory (lə'bɒrətrɪ) (*infml abbrev.* **lab**) (læb) *nc, pl* **-ries** a room used for scientific experiments.

laborious (lə'bɔːrɪəs) *adj* needing much or hard work.

labour *US* **labor** ('leɪbə*) *nu* 1 work. 2 workers as a class. 3 the pain and process of giving birth. 4 *nc* a task. ● *vi* 1 work, esp. hard or with difficulty. 2 *vt* talk or write about (something) a great deal: *Don't labour the point—I've understood.* **labourer** *US* **laborer** *nc* a person doing physical work as a job. **hard labour** the punishment of being forced to work while in prison.

labyrinth ('læbərɪnθ) *nc* 1 a number of connecting tunnels, paths, etc.; maze. 2 a confusing place, state of affairs, etc.

lace (leɪs) 1 *nc* a type of string used to tie a shoe, boot, etc. 2 *nu* a fine material made with a pattern of holes in it. ● *vt* 1 (often followed by **up**) tie (a shoe, boot, etc.) with a lace. 2 add some alcohol to (a drink).

lacerate ('læsəreɪt) *vt* tear (esp. flesh) roughly.

lack (læk) *nu* an absence or shortage: *a lack of interest.* ● *vt* be without: *This picture lacks colour.* **for lack of** because of not having.

lackey ('lækɪ) *nc, pl* **-s** 1 a male servant, esp. in characteristic clothes. 2 an unthinking political follower.

laconic (lə'kɒnɪk) *adj* using few words.

lacquer ('lækə*) *nu* 1 a liquid that dries to a hard shiny coat on objects it is used to protect. 2 also **hair lacquer** a substance sprayed onto hair to hold it in place. ● *vt* coat with lacquer.

lacrosse (lə'krɒs) *nu* a game played by two teams using a ball and small nets on sticks.

lacy ('leɪsɪ) *adj* **-ier, -iest** to do with or having the appearance of **lace** (def. 2).

lad (læd) *nc* 1 a boy or young man. 2 *infml* a boy or man, esp. a mischievous one.

ladder ('lædə*) *nc* 1 a set of steps held between two wooden or metal posts or two ropes and used for climbing up and down. 2 a row of stitches that have come undone in knitted material, esp. stockings. ● *vti* (cause to) develop a **ladder** (def. 2).

laden ('leɪdən) *adj* loaded: *a heavily laden lorry.*

ladle ('leɪdəl) *nc* a deep spoon with a long handle for serving soup, etc.

lady ('leɪdɪ) *nc, pl* **-dies** 1 *polite* a woman. 2 a woman with a high position in society. **ladies** *infml, Brit nc, pl* **ladies** *(often with singular verb)* a public toilet for women. **Lady** (a title for a woman of the aristocracy or the wife of a knight): *Lady Churchill.* **Ladyship** ('leɪdɪʃɪp) *nc* (used to refer to Ladies): *Her Ladyship; Your Ladyships.*

ladybird ('leɪdɪbɜːd) *nc* a flying insect with wing-cases that are red with black spots: see picture at **insects**.

lag[1] (læg) *vi* (sometimes followed by **behind**) go more slowly than someone or something else; fall (behind). ● *nc* a delay.

lag[2] *vt* wrap (a pipe, boiler, etc.) to prevent it losing heat.

lager ('lɑːgə*) *ncu* (a type or drink of) pale beer.

lagoon (lə'guːn) *nc* an area of seawater (partly) cut off from the sea by sand or coral.

laid (leɪd) past tense and past participle of **lay**[2].

lain (leɪn) past participle of **lie**[2].

lair (leə*) *nc* the place where a wild animal rests.

laissez faire (ˌleɪseɪ 'feə*) *nu* the fact or attitude of not interfering, esp. by a government.

laity ('leɪɪtɪ) *nu* laymen (see **layman** under **lay**[3]).

lake (leɪk) *nc* a body of water surrounded by land and usually fed and emptied by a river.

lamb (læm) 1 *nc* a young sheep. 2 *nu* meat from a sheep or lamb. ● *vi* (of a female sheep) give birth.

lame (leɪm) *adj* **-r, -st** 1 unable to walk normally because of disease, injury, etc. 2 not satisfactory or effective: *a lame argument.* ● *vt* make lame. **lame duck** 1 a weak person or thing. 2 *Brit* a firm not making enough money to stay in business. **lamely** *adv*

lament (lə'ment) *vt* feel or express grief about. ● *nc* an expression, esp. in song, of grief. **lamentable** ('læməntəbəl) *adj* regrettable; very bad: *Your work in the examination was lamentable.* **lamentation** (ˌlæmən'teɪʃən) *ncu* (an example of) lamenting.

laminated ('læmɪneɪtɪd) *adj* (of glass, metal, etc.) made of two or more sheets stuck together.

lamp (læmp) *nc* a device for producing light from electricity, oil, etc. **lamppost** ('læmppəʊst) a post supporting a lamp lighting a street. **lampshade** ('læmpʃeɪd) a frame covered with cloth, paper, etc., surrounding a lamp to spread the light and prevent it being too bright to look at.

lance (lɑːns) *nc* a weapon made of a metal point on a long stick. ●*vt medicine* cut into (a boil, etc.) to remove poisonous matter.

land (lænd) *nu* **1** those parts of the earth's surface not covered with water. **2** land used for farming, etc., not building towns: *working on the land. nc* **3** a country; nation. **4** a piece of land belonging to someone. ●*vti* **1** go or put onto land: *The soldiers were landed from small boats; We're landing in Riyadh soon. vt* **2** *infml* obtain or win: *You've landed a good job.* **3** *infml* put (someone) in (a difficult position): *His temper landed us all in trouble.* **landlady** (ˈlænd,leɪdɪ) *nc, pl* **-ladies** or **landlord** (ˈlænd,lɔːd) *nc* **1** a woman or man who runs a pub, boarding-house, etc. **2** a woman or man who rents out property for others to use. **landlocked** (ˈlændlɒkt) *adj* surrounded by land: *Zimbabwe is a landlocked country.* **landmark** (ˈlændmɑːk) *nc* **1** a building, hill, etc., that is well known and easy to recognise. **2** an important event: *a landmark in the history of medicine.* **landscape** (ˈlændskeɪp) *nc* **1** (a picture of) a view of the countryside. **2** a wide view of anything: *the literary landscape.* **landslide** (ˈlændslaɪd) *nc* **1** the sliding of a lot of earth or rock down the side of a mountain or cliff. **2** a win by a large majority in an election: *a landslide victory.*

landing (ˈlændɪŋ) *nc* **1** the action of or a place for landing. **2** a platform at the top of or between sets of stairs. **landing-stage** (ˈlændɪŋsteɪdʒ) *nc* a platform used for landing passengers and goods from a ship.

lane (leɪn) *nc* **1** a narrow road between rows of buildings, trees, etc. **2** a strip of road, sea, air, etc., to which traffic, ships, or planes must keep.

language (ˈlæŋgwɪdʒ) **1** *ncu* (a particular system of) spoken sounds and usually also written signs used to pass information, express feelings, etc. **2** *nu* words and expressions used by a particular person or group or in particular situations: *polite language; religious language.* **3** *nc* also **computer language** a system of letters and numbers used to make a computer work. **4** *nu* impolite words: *Such terrible language!* **language laboratory** a room containing tape-recorders, etc., used for learning foreign languages.

languid (ˈlæŋgwɪd) *adj* slow-moving, weak, or unenthusiastic.

languish (ˈlæŋgwɪʃ) *vi* **1** be or become languid. **2** exist (in bad conditions).

lank (læŋk) *adj* **-er, -est** **1** (of a person) tall and thin. **2** (esp. of hair or grass) long and straight.

lanky (ˈlæŋkɪ) *adj* **-ier, -iest** (of a person or legs) tall or long and thin.

lantern (ˈlæntən) *nc* **1** a lamp containing a candle. **2** the top part of a lighthouse or other building, with windows all round.

lap¹ (læp) *nc* the flat surface of the upper parts of the legs of a person who is seated: *The baby lay on her lap.*

lap² *nc* the act of going once round a continuous track: *a race of twenty laps.* ●*vt* overtake (another slower racer), getting one whole lap ahead.

lap³ **1** *vt* (often followed by **up**) (of an animal) drink (water, etc.) by picking it up with the tongue. **2** *vti* (of waves) strike softly: *We heard the waves lapping on the shore.*

lapel (ləˈpel) *nc* the part folded back on either side of the front of a coat or jacket.

lapse (læps) *vi* **1** (often followed by **into**) fail to keep up a standard set: *He was too slow at French so lapsed into his own language.* **2** come to an end, because of failure to do something: *If you don't pay, your membership will lapse.* ●*nc* **1** an instance of lapsing. **2** a delay; break: *After a lapse of two years he wrote to me again.*

larceny (ˈlɑːsənɪ) *law ncu, pl* **-nies** (a) theft; robbery.

larch (lɑːtʃ) *nc* a tree that produces cones and loses its leaves each year.

lard (lɑːd) *nu* grease obtained from pig fat. ●*vt* **1** add lard to (food). **2** add extra words or phrases to (one's normal speech, etc.): *His talk was larded with difficult expressions.*

larder (ˈlɑːdə*) *nc* a room or cupboard in which food is kept.

large (lɑːdʒ) *adj* **-r, -st** big, esp. broad; great. **at large** **1** (of a criminal or wild animal) free; escaped or not captured. **2** in general; as a whole: *The public at large know nothing about politics.* **largely** *adv* chiefly; on the whole. **large-scale** (ˈlɑːdʒskeɪl) **1** (of a map or model) larger than most maps or models of the same place or thing. **2** in large amounts: *The plant was built for large-scale car production.*

lark¹ (lɑːk) *nc* a small brown bird that is noted for its song and can stay in one place in the air.

lark² *nc* **1** a piece of fun or little adventure. **2** *infml, Brit* an activity of a particular kind: *This is a stupid lark—I'm stopping.* ●*vi* (often followed by **about** or **around**) have a **lark²** (def. 1).

larva (ˈlɑːvə) *nc, pl* **-vae** (viː) an insect in its first form after hatching from an egg.

larynx ('lærɪŋks) *anatomy nc, pl* **-nges** (ndʒiːz) also **voice-box** a part of the throat containing the mechanism used for speaking.

lascivious (lə'sɪvɪəs) *adj* feeling or showing great, esp. unwelcome, sexual desire.

laser ('leɪzə*) *nc* a device producing a powerful beam of invisible light used for measuring, healing eyes, etc.

lash (læʃ) *vt* **1** move (an arm, tail, etc.) forcefully. **2** hit hard, esp. with a whip as a punishment. **3** fasten by tying with rope, etc.: *The prisoner was lashed to a chair.* ●*nc* **1** a blow with a whip, etc. **2** the end of a whip.

lashing *nc* **1** a whipping. **2** *(pl) infml, Brit.* a lot: *toast with lashings of butter.* **3** *nu* rope, etc., used for lashing (**lash** def. **3**).

lass (læs) *poetry or chiefly Northern Brit nc* a girl.

lasso (læ'suː) *nc, pl* **-s, -es** a rope with a loop in the end, used for catching horses and cattle, esp. in America. ●*vt* catch with a lasso.

last (laːst) *adj, adv* **1** at the end; after all others: *He came last in the race.* **2** most recent(ly): *last week.* ●*vti* remain; be enough (for someone or something); continue to exist, work etc. (for a period): *This food will last us a month; How long can you last under the water?* **at last** in the end; finally. **lastly** *adv* at the end; finally. **last-minute** ('laːst,mɪnɪt) *adj* done at the last possible moment: *a last-minute change of clothes.*

latch (lætʃ) *nc* **1** a small bar worked by a handle on a door, serving to keep it shut: see picture. **2** a door lock on a spring, worked by a key. ●*vt* fasten with a latch.

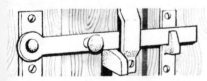

latch

late (leɪt) *adj* **-r, -st,** *adv* **1** (happening, arriving, etc.) after the proper or usual time: *The train is ten minutes late already.* **2** (happening, etc.) far on in a period of time: *She worked late into the night.* ●*adj* (used before a noun) **1** having died recently: *the late Mr Smith.* **2** being no longer as described: *The late president is living abroad.* **lately** *adv* also **of late** recently.

latent ('leɪtənt) *adj* hidden; capable of developing: *a latent musical ability.*

lateral ('lætərəl) *adj* to do with the side.

latex ('leɪteks) *nu* a milky liquid obtained from a plant, esp. the rubber plant.

lath (laːθ) *nc* a thin strip of wood, esp. used to make a wall on which plaster is spread.

lathe (leɪð) *nc* a machine for shaping wood, metal, etc., by turning it round and round against a movable cutter.

lather ('laːðə*) *nu* bubbles produced by rubbing soap in water. ●*vti* make a lather (on).

latitude ('lætɪtjuːd) **1** *nc* the distance from a point on the earth to the equator, expressed as an angle: *Peking lies at about latitude forty degrees North.* **2** *nu* variety of expected behaviour, results, etc.: *I ought to be at work by half-past nine, but luckily there's some latitude.*

latter ('lætə*) *pron, adj* the second of two already mentioned: *Of Mary and Alison, I prefer the latter.* ●*adj* later; nearer the end: *the latter part of last year.*

lattice ('lætɪs) *nc* an arrangement of crossing or joined strips of metal or wood serving as an ornamental fence, etc.

laud (lɔːd) *literary vt, nu* praise. **laudable** *adj* deserving praise.

laugh (laːf) *vi* make a sound expressing amusement, usually while smiling. ●*nc* **1** an instance of laughing. **2** a manner of laughing. **laughable** *adj* (of an offer, demand, etc.) deserving laughter, not serious consideration. **laugh at 1** laugh because of (a joke, etc.). **2** make fun of. **laughter** ('laːftə*) *nu* (the sound of) laughing.

launch (lɔːntʃ) *vt* **1** put (a boat or ship) into the water, esp. for the first time. **2** start (oneself, a spacecraft, etc.) moving through the air. **3** start (a company, collection, etc.). ●*nc* **1** an instance of launching. **2** a motorboat usually used for taking people short distances. **launching-pad** ('lɔːntʃɪŋ,pæd) *nc* a place from which rockets are launched.

launder ('lɔːndə*) *vt* wash and often iron (clothes, etc.). **laundry** ('lɔːndrɪ) **1** *nc, pl* **-dries** a place where clothes, etc., are laundered. **2** *nu* clothes, etc., that are to be, are being, or have just been laundered. **launderette** (lɔːn'dret) *nc* a place where one can wash and dry clothes in machines worked by coins.

laurel ('lɒrəl) *nc* also **bay** a tree with shiny dark green leaves. **rest on one's laurels** be satisfied with one's past efforts or successes.

lava ('laːvə) *nu* rock in a hot liquid form that flows from a volcano and then cools.

lavatory ('lævətrɪ) *nc, pl* **-tories** also **toilet** (a room containing) a bowl, connected to a drain, where one gets rid of solid and liquid waste from the body.

lavender ('lævɪndə*) *nu* a plant of which the mauve flowers are used for their pleasant smell, being either dried or used for making an oil.

lavish (ˈlævɪʃ) *adj* in great quantity; generous: *a lavish meal.*

law (lɔ:) **1** *ncu* (one of) a set of rules governing behaviour in a country or other society, with punishments laid down for breaking them. *nc* **2** a rule of an activity, such as a game. **3** a statement of the way something behaves in nature: *the laws of science.* *nu* **4** laws as a social system: *He studied law at university.* **5** knowledge of law. **6** the social state produced by people not breaking laws: *law and order.* **law-abiding** (ˈlɔ:*ə-ˌbaɪdɪŋ) *adj* not breaking the law. **lawful** *adj* not forbidden by law. **lawfully** *adv* **lawgiver** (ˈlɔ:ˌgɪvə*) *nc* a person who makes laws. **lawless** *adj* **1** without laws. **2** breaking the law: *lawless behaviour.* **lawsuit** (ˈlɔ:sju:t, ˈlɔ:su:t) *nc* a claim or complaint by one person, company, etc., against another in a court of law.

lawn¹ (lɔ:n) *ncu* (a piece of land covered with) grass that is kept cut short. **lawnmower** (ˈlɔ:n,məʊə*) *nc* a device, esp. powered by a motor, for cutting a lawn.

lawn² *nu* a fine cotton or linen cloth.

lawyer (ˈlɔ:jə*) *nc* a person in a job to do with the law, esp. a solicitor or barrister.

lax (læks) *adj* **1** loose; not decisive: *a rather lax arrangement.* **2** not firm or strict: *He's very lax about getting to work on time.*

laxative (ˈlæksətɪv) *nc, adj* (a medicine) causing one to get rid of solid waste from the body more easily.

lay¹ (leɪ) past tense of **lie².**

lay² *vt* **1** put, esp. carefully and in a flat or level position: *Lay the dress on the bed.* **2** put things for a meal on (a table). **3** (of a bird, etc.) produce (an egg). **4** make (a bet). **5** *not standard vi* **lie².** ●*nc* the way or position in which something lies. **lay aside 1** stop doing, using, etc.; give up. **2** keep; store up. **lay by** store up. **lay off 1** *infml* stop annoying (someone). **2** *infml* stop using, doing, etc.: *to lay off cigarettes.* **3** stop employing (someone) for a time. **lay up 1** store up or keep (esp. a ship) for the future. **2** *infml* (of an illness) prevent (someone) from leading a normal life: *He was laid up with a cold.*

lay³ *adj* **1** to do with people who are not priests. **2** to do with people without special knowledge of a subject. **layman** (ˈleɪmən) *nc, pl* **-men** a lay person.

lay-by (ˈleɪbaɪ) *nc, pl* **-s** a piece of ground, at the side of a road, on which traffic can stop.

layer (ˈleɪə*) *nc* a thickness or coat of a substance, such as paint spread over a surface. ●*vt* arrange in layers.

layout (ˈleɪaʊt) *nc* an arrangement of things, such as the type and photographs in a newspaper.

lazy (ˈleɪzɪ) *adj* **-ier, -iest 1** not wanting to work or take exercise. **2** causing or to do with laziness: *a lazy day on holiday.* **lazily** *adv* **laziness** *nu*

lea (li:) *poetry nc* a field of grass.

lead¹ (li:d) *vt* **1** show the way to (someone) by going in front; guide. **2** direct or control (a meeting, etc.). **3** pass; spend: *He led a life of evil.* **4** (followed by an infinitive) cause (to do something): *I was led to believe the story was true.* **5** *vti* be at the top or front (of): *He's leading the race.* **6** *vi* (of a road, etc.) be a way: *The path led up the hill to the castle.* ●*nu* **1** the first or leading place in a race, etc. **2** guidance or example: *Follow my lead.* **3** a distance by which one is leading a race, etc.: *He has a lead of ten metres.* *nc* **4** also **leash** a chain, strip of leather, etc. with one end fastened round the neck of a dog or other animal to control it. **5** the main part in a play or film. **6** the set of wires leading to an electrical device. **7** a piece of information that could help solve a crime, etc. **lead to** be the cause of: *Doing two things at once could lead to confusion.* **lead up to 1** be an introduction to; come before. **2** be about to mention or discuss.

lead² (led) **1** *nu* a chemical element; a soft, heavy, grey metal used for roofs, batteries, paints, etc. **2** *ncu* (a piece of) graphite used for writing within pencils. **leaden** (ˈledən) *adj* **1** made of **lead** (def. 1). **2** grey: *a leaden sky.* **3** slow or lifeless.

leader (ˈli:də*) *nc* **1** a person or animal who leads, rules, or guides. **2** *US* **concertmaster** the chief violinist of an orchestra. **3** *US* **leading article** an article in a newspaper giving the opinion of the editor. **leadership** (ˈli:dəʃɪp) *nu* the condition of being or ability to be a leader.

leading (ˈli:dɪŋ) *adj* **1** most important or best known. **2** in front. **leading question** a question that suggests an expected answer, such as 'Don't you think it's expensive?'

leaf (li:f) *nc, pl* **-ves 1** a usually broad, thin, green part of a plant. **2** a sheet of paper in a book. **3** part of a table that can be put in the top to make it bigger. **leaf through** look quickly (at a book), etc., by turning the pages rapidly. **turn over a new leaf** improve one's behaviour, give up a habit, etc. **leafless** *adj* having no leaves. **leafy** *adj* **-ier, -iest** having many leaves; full of plants: *a leafy garden.*

leaflet (ˈli:flɪt) *nc* a folded sheet of paper printed with advertising or information, usually given free.

league (li:g) *nc* **1** an organisation of countries, towns, etc., that join to help or protect each other. **2** a group of sports teams that play each other.

leak (li:k) *nc* **1** an unwanted hole in a container, boat, etc., through which a gas or liquid passes. **2** a piece of secret information published esp. by a newspaper. ● *vti* (allow to) pass through a leak: *Water is leaking from the pipe; He leaked the news of the battle to the press.* **leakage** *nc* **1** an instance of leaking. **2** something leaked. **leaky** *adj* **-ier, -iest** having a leak or leaks.

lean¹ (li:n) *vti* **1** (cause to) rest on or against something. **2** (cause to) slope or be not upright. ● *nu* the state or amount of leaning. **leaning** *nc* the quality of being likely to do or be something: *strong political leanings.* **lean on** or **upon** depend on (someone), esp. for advice or help.

lean² *adj* **-er, -est 1** not fat. **2** not producing profits; marked by shortages: *a lean year in business.* ● *nu* meat containing little fat.

leant (lent) past tense and past participle of **lean¹**.

leap (li:p) *vti* jump (over). ● *nc* a jump. **leap year** a year with 366 days in, 29 February being added; every fourth year.

leapt (lept) past tense and past participle of **leap**.

learn (lɜ:n) *vt* **1** obtain knowledge of or become able (to do): *I learn French; He learned to drive.* **2** store in one's memory: *to learn a poem.* **3** *vi* (often followed by **about** or **of**) come to know (about or of). **learned** ('lɜ:nɪd) *adj* having or showing great knowledge. **learning** *nu* knowledge obtained by study.

learnt (lɜ:nt) past tense and past participle of **learn**.

lease (li:s) *nc* an arrangement by which property belonging to someone is held by someone else for a limited period: *a ninety-nine-year lease.* ● *vt* give or receive (property) under a lease. **leasehold** ('li:shəʊld) *nu* the way in which leased property is held.

leash (li:ʃ) *n* See **lead¹** (def. 4). ● *vt* control or fasten with a leash.

least (li:st) *adj* smallest, slightest, smallest amount of, or fewest: *He's got the least money of us all.* ● *nu* the least amount: *The least you could do is be polite.* ● *adv* also **the least** the least amount; in the least quantity: *I talk Russian least.* **at least 1** also **at the least** as the smallest quantity or amount: *It will cost at least £1000.* **2** if nothing else: *At least the weather was fine.*

leather ('leðə*) *nu* skin from an animal, prepared for use in jackets, bags, shoes, etc.; (sometimes *nc*) a type or piece of leather. ● *vt* cover or wipe with leather. **leathery** *adj* like, esp. as tough as, leather.

leave¹ (li:v) **1** *vti* go away (from): *I left London yesterday.* *vt* **2** cause to remain: *I left the book on the table.* **3** give (to someone) to deal with: *Leave that job to me.* **4** stop belonging to (a club), attending (a school), etc. **5** have (belongings) given (to someone) after one's death: *He left all his money to his wife.* **6** cause to be or remain: *He was left very poor.* **leave alone 1** allow to be alone. **2** not annoy or disturb. **leave off 1** stop: *Leave off asking questions!* **2** fail to put on or wear: *You left off the last word.* **leave out 1** fail to include. **2** allow to remain outside.

leave² *nu* **1** permission to be away or on holiday, esp. from army service, etc.: *He's on leave.* **2** *formal* permission (to do something): *by your leave.* **take one's leave** *formal* say goodbye.

leaves (li:vz) plural of **leaf**.

lecture ('lektʃə*) *nc* **1** a formal talk to university students, etc. **2** a long talk, esp. giving a warning or telling someone off. ● *vti* give a lecture (to). **lecturer** ('lektʃərə*) *nc* **1** a person who gives a lecture. **2** a university teacher: *Senior Lecturer in English.*

led (led) past tense and past participle of **lead¹**.

ledge (ledʒ) *nc* a narrow flat surface like a shelf sticking out from a wall, rock face, etc.

ledger ('ledʒə*) *nc* a book in which the accounts of a business are kept.

lee (li:) *nu, adj* (on) the side of a boat, island, etc., away from the wind.

leech (li:tʃ) *nc* **1** a worm that feeds on the blood of animals. **2** *archaic* a doctor.

leek (li:k) *nc* a kind of vegetable like a large onion but with a long white stem: see picture at **vegetables**.

leer (lɪə*) *vi* look or smile unpleasantly (at). ● *nc* an unpleasant look.

left¹ (left) past tense and past participle of **leave¹**. **leftover** ('left,əʊvə*) *nc, adj* (something left) unused, uneaten, etc.

left² *adj, nu* (to do with) the side of something facing west when its front faces north. ● *nu* the left side: *on your left.* **the left** also **the Left** supporters of changes intended to put power in the hands of the state to help its people. **left-hand** ('left-hænd) *adj* (used before a noun) to do with the left side: *left-hand drive.* **left-handed** (,left'hændɪd) *adj* **1** able to use one's left hand for writing, etc., more easily than one's right. **2** to do with the left hand. ● *adj, adv* (done) with the left hand. **left-wing** ('leftwɪŋ) *adj* to do with **the left**: *left-wing politics.*

leg (leg) *nc* **1** *anatomy, zoology* a long lower body part used for standing and walking. **2** the part of a garment covering a leg. **3** an upright supporting part of a chair, table, etc. **4** a stage of a journey. **pull someone's leg** tell someone a lie for fun.

legacy ('legəsɪ) *nc, pl* **-cies** something, esp. money, given to others after one's death, according to one's will.

legal ('liːgəl) *adj* to do with, esp. allowed by, the law. **legalise** (liːˈgəlaɪz) *vt* make legal. **legality** (liːˈgælɪtɪ) *nu* **legally** *adv*

legation (lɪˈgeɪʃən) *nc* (the building used by) a group of people representing one country in another.

legend ('ledʒənd) *nc* **1** a popular old story supposed to be true. **2** an explanation or other note on a map, coin, etc. **legendary** ('ledʒəndərɪ) *adj* **1** described in a legend. **2** remarkable; famous.

leggings ('legɪŋz) *n pl* an extra covering, esp. to protect, for the legs from the knees to the ankles.

legible ('ledʒɪbəl) *adj* (of writing, printing, etc.) able to be read.

legion ('liːdʒən) *nc* **1** a group of 3000 to 6000 men in the ancient Roman army. **2** another military or former military group: *the French Foreign Legion.* ● *adj formal* great in number.

legislate ('ledʒɪsleɪt) *vi* make laws. **legislation** (ˌledʒɪsˈleɪʃən) *nu* (the making of) laws. **legislative** ('ledʒɪslətɪv) *adj* to do with legislation. **legislator** *nc* a person who has a part in legislating. **legislature** ('ledʒɪsleɪtʃə*) *nc* a body of people with the power to legislate.

legitimate (lɪˈdʒɪtɪmət) *adj* **1** born of married parents. **2** reasonable; having the right to be considered; correct: *a legitimate claim to the money.* **legitimacy** (lɪˈdʒɪtɪməsɪ) *nu* **legitimately** *adv*

legume ('legjuːm) *nc* (a plant that produces) a fruit in a pod, eaten as a vegetable, esp. a pea or bean.

leisure ('leʒə*) *nu* free time used for hobbies, games, etc. **leisurely** *adj, adv* (done or acting) without hurry.

lemon ('lemən) *nc* the yellow, oval, citrus fruit of the lemon tree: see picture at **fruits**. **lemonade** (ˌleməˈneɪd) *nu* a drink made either from lemon juice, sugar, and water, or from fizzy water and a bitter liquid.

lend (lend) *vt* **1** allow someone to use (something): *The bank lent me the money; Will you lend me your car tonight?* **2** provide; add: *The good news lent joy to the occasion.* **lend oneself to** be useful or suitable for: *His poetry lends itself to being read aloud.*

length (leŋθ) *nc* **1** the distance between the two ends of something, esp. the longest side of an object; this distance used as a measurement: *The horse won by two lengths.* **2** the time taken for something: *The length of each lesson is the same.* **3** the distance a garment reaches down the body. **4** a piece of something long and thin, such as cloth. **at length 1** in great detail: *He talked at length about his holiday.* **2** finally; after a long time. **lengthen** *vt* make longer. **lengthways** ('leŋθweɪz) *US* **lengthwise** ('leŋθwaɪz) *adv* along or to do with the longest side: *Turn the bed lengthways so that it will go through the door.* **lengthy** *adj* **-ier, -iest** (too) long.

lenient ('liːnɪənt) *adj* showing mercy, esp. in being or giving a light punishment.

lens (lenz) *nc* **1** a piece of glass with one or more curved surfaces, used to focus rays of light in cameras, glasses, etc. **2** the jelly-like substance at the front of the eye that acts like this. **3** a number of lenses set in a tube and used on a camera.

Lent (lent) *n* the period of the Christian year in the weeks before Easter, when many Christians give up some luxuries.

lent (lent) past tense and past participle of **lend**.

lentil ('lentɪl) *nc* a small, flat, round seed cooked and eaten as a vegetable, in soup, etc.: see picture at **vegetables**.

leopard ('lepəd) *nc* also **panther** a large African and South Asian animal of the cat family, with a dark yellow coat with black spots: see picture at **animals**.

leprosy ('leprəsɪ) *nu* a disease of the skin and nerve tissue, in which affected parts of the body waste away. **leper** ('lepə*) *nc* **1** a person with leprosy. **2** a person who others keep away from.

less (les) *determiner, pron* a smaller amount (of): *I have less (money) than you.* ● *adv* **1** in a smaller amount: *You should talk less.* **2** minus: *4 less 3 equals 1.*

lessen ('lesən) *vti* make or become less. **lessening** *nu* the act of becoming less.

lesser ('lesə*) *adj* **1** not as famous, important, good, etc.: *A lesser man would have run away.* **2** not as large as (one other thing): *the lesser of the two evils.*

lesson ('lesən) *nc* **1** a teaching period, esp. at school. **2** an example, event, etc., that serves to teach: *Let that be a lesson to you not to talk in class.* **3** (*pl*) school work.

lest (lest) *old-fashioned conj* so that. . . not; for fear that: *I've written it down lest I forget it.*

let (let) *vt* **1** allow (someone) to (do something): *I let him go.* **2** (used in front of a verb to indicate a suggestion, order, etc.): *Let's go now.* **3** charge rent for the use of (a shop, house, etc.). **4** allow to move: *Shut* *the door or you'll let the heat out.* **5** (as a command) allow (something to happen): *Let them attack—they'll soon wish they hadn't!* **let alone 1** See under **alone. 2** stop annoying: *Let me alone or I'll call the police!* **let down 1** lower. **2** disappoint; fail to keep a promise to (someone). **let go** stop holding (onto). **let in** allow to enter. **let off 1** fail to punish. **2** allow (someone) not to do: *I was let off having to go.* **3** fire or explode (a gun, firework, etc.). **let on** allow to be known: *Don't let on that I'm here!* **let out 1** allow to go out (of prison, etc.). **2** allow (a secret) to be known. **3** give (a cry, etc.). **let (someone) know** give information to (someone): *I'll let you know if you win.* **let through** allow to go through. **let up** become less or stop: *Has the rain let up at all?*

lethal ('li:θəl) *adj* (of a weapon, etc.) able to kill.

lethargy ('leθədʒɪ) *nu* lack of interest or energy. **lethargic** (lɪ'θɑ:dʒɪk) *adj*

let's (lets) let us.

letter ('letə*) *nc* **1** a single written or printed character, such as *d* or *W*. **2** a written message from one person, business, etc., to another, usually sent by post. **the letter of the law** what the actual words of a law, agreement, etc., say, rather than the meaning it was intended to have. **letterbox** ('letəbɒks) a box or a hole in a door, wall, etc., for letters being posted or delivered. **lettering** *nu* the letters written on something such as a sign.

lettuce ('letɪs) *nc* a plant with broad, light green leaves: see picture at **vegetables;** *(also nu)* these leaves, usually eaten raw as a salad.

leukaemia (luː'kiːmɪə) *nu* a disease in which the body makes too many white blood cells.

level ('levəl) *adj* **-ler, -lest 1** flat; not sloping. **2** (of a surface) smooth. **3** as high, far forward, etc., as something else: *Put the shelf level with the window.* ●*vt* **1** make level. **2** (often followed by **at**) aim (a gun, criticism, a remark, etc.). ●*nc* **1** a height. **2** a value or amount: *a high level of government support.* **3** an instrument used to test whether something is level. **4** a flat piece of land. **level crossing** a place where a road and a railway cross at the same level, usually with gates with which to close the road when a train comes. **level-headed** (ˌlevəl'hedɪd) *adj* sensible; reliable: *a level-headed judgement.*

lever ('liːvə*) *nc* a bar held or resting somewhere along its length so that when one end is moved, the other moves in the opposite direction and can be made to lift an object, etc. ●*vt* move with a lever.

leviathan (lɪ'vaɪəθən) *nc* something huge, esp. in the sea.

levy ('levɪ) *vt* demand and collect (a tax, etc.). ●*nc, pl* **-vies 1** something levied. **2** *ncu* (an example of) levying.

lewd (luːd) *adj* **-er, -est** indecent; rude; obscene.

lexicon ('leksɪkən) *nc* a dictionary, esp. of Latin or ancient Greek.

liability (ˌlaɪə'bɪlɪtɪ) **1** *nu* the state of being liable. *nc, pl* **-ties 2** an amount of money owed, esp. by a business. **3** a person or thing for which one is responsible and that gets in one's way.

liable ('laɪəbəl) *adj* **1** likely: *He's liable to change his mind.* **2** *law* responsible; answerable: *If someone is hurt at work, his employer is liable.* **3** (often followed by **for**) to be considered with respect to: *What you earn is liable for tax.*

liaison (lɪ'eɪzən) *nu* the passing of messages and information between groups, parts of an army, etc.

liar ('laɪə*) *nc* a person who lies (**lie**[1]).

libel ('laɪbəl) *ncu* (the printing of) untrue statements that harm a person's reputation. ●*vt* make such statements about (someone).

liberal ('lɪbərəl) *adj* **1** to do with the political opinion that people should have more freedom. **2** generous. **3** not minding much what other people do. ●*nc* a person with **liberal** (def. 1) opinions. **liberalism** *nu* **liberal** (def. 1) opinions. **liberally** *adv*

liberate ('lɪbəreɪt) *vt* make free, esp. from occupation by a foreign army. **liberation** (ˌlɪbə'reɪʃən) *nu*

liberty ('lɪbətɪ) **1** *nu* freedom. **2** *nc, pl* **-ties** an action that is not proper or allowed: *Asking to be invited is taking a liberty.*

library ('laɪbrərɪ) *nc, pl* **-ries 1** a building, esp. public, containing books, newspapers, etc., to be read there or borrowed. **2** a room for books in a house. **librarian** (laɪ'breərɪən) *nc* a person who organises or runs a library.

lice (laɪs) plural of **louse.**

licence *US* **license** ('laɪsəns) **1** *nc* a piece of paper acting as proof that one may do something, has paid a tax, etc.: *a driving licence.* **2** *nu* freedom of thought or action, esp. when used to do something other people dislike.

license ('laɪsəns) *vt* give a licence to or for: *a licensed car.*

lick (lɪk) *vt* **1** rub with the tongue, esp. in eating or to make wet. **2** (of waves or flames) move lightly over or round. **3** *infml* beat, esp. in competition. ●*nc* an instance of licking.

licorice ('lɪkərɪs) *US n* See **liquorice.**

lid (lɪd) *nc* **1** a movable cover, either loose or fixed at one side, for something such as a tin or suitcase. **2** short for **eyelid**.

lie¹ (laɪ) *vi* knowingly say something that is untrue. ●*nc* something untrue, said knowingly.

lie² *vi* **1** be or put oneself in a flat position, as on a bed. **2** be placed or situated; be found: *London lies on the Thames.* **3** (of a dead person) be buried: *Here lies John Smith.* ●*nc* the manner or place in which something lies. **lie down** put oneself in a lying position, esp. to sleep. **lie in** stay late in bed in the morning.

liege (liːʒ) *archaic nc* a person whom one has to serve: *my liege.*

lien (lɪən) *nc* the right to hold someone's property until he pays one a debt.

lieu (ljuː, luː) *n* **in lieu of** instead of: *I get extra pay in lieu of some of my holiday.*

lieutenant (lefˈtenənt *US* luːˈtenənt) *nc* an officer in a navy or an army.

life (laɪf) *nu* **1** the quality that plants and animals have but objects do not. **2** liveliness; energy. **3** living things. **4** a style or way of living: *Village life is slow. nc, pl* **-ves 5** the period between birth and death or that part of it up to or after a certain time. **6** the period for which something lasts: *the life of this government.* **7** a human being: *loss of lives in battle.* **8** a book describing someone's life (def. **5**). **true to life** (of a story, etc.) correct; like the real thing. **take someone's life** kill someone. **lifebelt** (ˈlaɪfbelt) *nc* a ring that floats in water, used to save someone from drowning. **lifeboat** (ˈlaɪfbəʊt) *nc* **1** a boat sent from land to rescue people from wrecked ships, etc. **2** a boat carried by a ship in case it sinks. **lifeguard** (ˈlaɪfgɑːd) *nc* a person ready to rescue people from drowning in the sea or a swimming pool. **lifeless** *adj* **1** without life; dead. **2** lacking energy or interest. **lifelike** (ˈlaɪflaɪk) *adj* very like life or something living. **lifelong** (ˈlaɪflɒŋ) *adj* lasting for one's life. **life-saving** (ˈlaɪfˌseɪvɪŋ) *nu* methods of rescuing someone in danger of drowning. **lifetime** (ˈlaɪftaɪm) *nc* the period for which someone or something is alive or lasts.

lift (lɪft) **1** *vti* (cause to) move upwards. **2** *slang vt* steal. ●*nu* **1** upward force. *nc* **2** a free ride in a car or other vehicle, esp. someone else's. **3** a box that moves up and down inside a building to carry people and things from floor to floor. **lift off 1** take (something) off (something else). **2** (of a rocket) leave the ground. **lift-off** (ˈlɪftɒf) *nc* the act of lifting off by a rocket.

ligament (ˈlɪgəmənt) *anatomy nc* a piece of tough tissue holding bones together at a joint.

light¹ (laɪt) **1** *nu* brightness. *nc* **2** a device that gives off light; lamp. **3** something that can be used to set fire to something, esp. a cigarette. ●*adj* **-er, -est 1** (of a room, etc.) full of light. **2** (of a colour) reflecting a lot of light; pale. ●*vt* **1** set fire to. **2** shine light on. **come to light** be discovered; become known. **in the light of** in view of; considering. **shed** or **throw light on** make clearer; help to explain. **lighthouse** (ˈlaɪthaʊs) *nc* a tower with a flashing light on top to help people in ships know where they are. **lightship** (ˈlaɪtʃɪp) *nc* a ship that stays in one place and has a light like that of a lighthouse. **light-year** (ˈlaɪtjɪə*) *nc* a measure of distance = 9.46 million million km (the distance that light travels in a year).

light² *adj* **-er, -est 1** weighing little; not heavy. **2** for small loads: *a light railway.* **3** (of work) easily done. **4** (of a punishment) easy to put up with. **5** small in force, quantity, number, etc.: *light rain.* **6** not containing much alcohol: *a light beer.* **7** intended only for entertainment; not serious: *light music.* ●*adv* with not much luggage: *to travel light.* **make light of** not treat as important or take seriously. **light-hearted** (ˌlaɪtˈhɑːtɪd) *adj* cheerful; not serious. **lightly** *adv* **lightweight** (ˈlaɪtweɪt) *adj* **1** (of a person or animal) weighing little. **2** not important or serious. ●*nc* a light person or animal.

lighten¹ (ˈlaɪtən) *vti* make or become **light¹** or lighter.

lighten² *vti* make or become **light²** or lighter.

lighter (ˈlaɪtə*) *nc* a device that produces a flame for lighting a cigarette, etc.

lightning (ˈlaɪtnɪŋ) *nu* a flash of light in the sky, caused by a discharge of electricity held in the clouds.

likable (ˈlaɪkəbəl) *adj* liked; pleasant.

like¹ (laɪk) *adj* (used before a noun) similar; alike. ●*prep* **1** similar to; in a like manner to: *Your writing is like mine; The child was like its mother; The animal roared like a bull.* **2** such as; for example: *I sell lots of things, like furniture.* ●*adv* in the same way as: *You walk like he does.* ●*n* **the like** such a thing or such things: *I never heard the like!* **feel like 1** feel as though one were. **2** want: *I feel like a cup of tea; Do you feel like going out?* **look like 1** have a similar appearance to. **2** appear likely that. . . will come or happen: *It looks like rain; He looks like giving up.* **what is. . . like?** what sort of (a person or thing) is. . .? **likeness 1** *ncu* (a) similarity. **2** *nc* a copy or picture.

like² *vt* be attracted by or fond of. ●*nc* (usually *pl*) what one likes; a fondness. **would like** want; wish.

likelihood ('laɪklɪhʊd) *nu* 1 the quality of being likely. 2 something likely.

likely ('laɪklɪ) *adj* **-ier, -iest** 1 probable: *the likely result.* 2 to be expected: *He is likely to win.* 3 likely to succeed: *a likely candidate.* ● *adv* probably.

liken ('laɪkən) *vt* compare: *He likened me to a thief!*

likewise ('laɪkwaɪz) *adv* in a similar way.

liking ('laɪkɪŋ) *nc* a fondness.

lilac ('laɪlək) *nc* a tree with large numbers of white or pale purple flowers. ● *adj* pale purple.

lilt (lɪlt) *nc* an attractive, flowing rhythm, esp. in music. ● *vi* (of music) have or move with a lilt.

lily ('lɪlɪ) *nc, pl* **-lies** (a flower of) a plant that grows from a bulb and has large flowers on long stems.

limb (lɪm) *nc* 1 an arm, leg, or wing. 2 a branch of a tree.

limber ('lɪmbə*) *v* **limber up** loosen one's body with gentle exercise before a race, etc.

limbo ('lɪmbəʊ) *n* **in limbo** left alone; not being dealt with.

lime¹ (laɪm) *nu* a chemical; a calcium compound, esp. calcium hydroxide, used as fertiliser, in cement, etc. ● *vt* put lime on.

limelight ('laɪmlaɪt) *n* **the limelight** the position to which most attention is given: *The news of his discovery has really put him in the limelight.* **limestone** ('laɪmstəʊn) *nu* a rock of mainly calcium carbonate, much used for building with.

lime² *nc* the small, oval, green citrus fruit of the lime tree.

limerick ('lɪmərɪk) *nc* a type of humorous poem with five lines, esp. with a joke in the last line.

limit ('lɪmɪt) *nc* the furthest point, greatest value, etc. of something: *Unfortunately the price is over my limit.* ● *vt* fix a limit for. **limitation** (ˌlɪmɪ'teɪʃən) 1 *nc* something, esp. a weakness, that limits an attempt, opinion, result, etc. 2 *nu* the act of limiting. **limitless** *adj*

limousine (ˌlɪmə'ziːn) *nc* a large, powerful car used by a king, president, etc.

limp¹ (lɪmp) *adj* **-er, -est** not stiff or strong: *a book in limp covers.*

limp² *vi* walk, stepping more heavily with one foot than with the other because of injury. ● *nc* such a walk.

limpet ('lɪmpɪt) *nc* a shellfish that sticks to rocks: see picture.

limpid ('lɪmpɪd) *adj* (of water, air, or writing) clear.

line¹ (laɪn) *nc* 1 a long narrow mark, either occurring naturally or made with a pen, etc. 2 the edge of a shape, esp. in a picture. 3 a rope, wire, etc.: *fishing line; a power*

line. 4 a row of people or objects, esp. in war: *soldiers in the front line.* 5 a row of written or printed words. 6 a telephone connection: *Is there an outside line free?* 7 one of the narrow parts of a television picture running across it. 8 a travel or transport company; part of this: *a bus line.* 9 a railway track. 10 a course of action: *This line of questioning won't tell us anything.* 11 an occupation or field of knowledge: *Is this job in your line?* ● *vt* 1 mark with lines. 2 cause to be positioned along the sides of: *The streets were lined with happy people.* **draw the line** set a limit: *I draw the line at your spending so much money.* **in** or **out of line** doing or not doing what is expected of one. **line up** 1 put or come into a line. 2 prepare; plan: *I'm lining up a holiday for us all.* **line-up** ('laɪnʌp) *nc* a row or choice of people for a football team, etc.

line² *vt* put a coating or layer inside (something): *a jacket lined with fur.*

limpet

lineage ('lɪnɪɪdʒ) *nu* one's descent from other people; one's ancestors.

linear ('lɪnɪə*) *adj* to do with lines: *linear measurement.*

linen ('lɪnɪn) *nu* 1 a cloth made from flax. 2 sheets, shirts, and other things that are or could be made of linen.

liner ('laɪnə*) *nc* 1 a large passenger ship. 2 something that forms a layer inside something else, esp. to protect it.

linesman ('laɪnzmən) *nc, pl* **-men** a person who decides whether the ball has gone out of the playing area, etc., in a game such as football.

linger ('lɪŋɡə*) *vi* stay; not go away.

lingerie ('lænʒərɪ) *formal nu* women's underclothes.

lingo ('lɪŋɡəʊ) *often derogatory or humorous ncu, pl* **-es** (a) foreign or unfamiliar language.

lingua franca ('lɪŋɡwə 'fræŋkə) *nc* a language used between people with different native languages.

linguist ('lɪŋɡwɪst) *nc* 1 a person good at learning or using foreign languages. 2 a person who studies linguistics. **linguistic** (lɪŋ'ɡwɪstɪk) *adj* to do with language or linguistics. **linguistics** *nu (with singular verb)* the study of the development, nature, learning, etc., of language.

liniment ('lɪnɪmənt) *nu* a liquid made of alcohol, oil, etc., rubbed into the skin to relieve pain in a joint or muscle.

lining ('laɪnɪŋ) *ncu* (a piece of) material used to line something, such as a coat.

link (lɪŋk) *nc* 1 a single part of a chain. 2 a connection between roads, facts, etc. ● *vti* (often followed by **up**) connect.

linoleum (lɪ'nəʊlɪəm) (often shortened to **lino**) ('laɪnəʊ) *nu* a floor covering made of tough cloth covered with a hardened mixture of tiny pieces of cork, oil, etc.

linseed ('lɪnsiːd) *nu* seeds of the flax plant, used to make linseed oil, which is used in paint, ink, etc.

lint (lɪnt) *nu* a soft cotton material, smoother on one side, used for dressing wounds.

lion ('laɪən) *nc* 1 a large, dark yellow, African and Asian animal of the cat family, the male of which has long hair on its neck: see picture at **animals**. 2 someone who is admired by others. **lioness** ('laɪənes) a female lion. **lion's share** the greatest part.

lip (lɪp) *nc* 1 *anatomy* either of the two fleshy parts forming the entrance to the mouth. 2 something like a lip, such as the turned-over top edge of a glass. **lip service** insincere respect or pretended obedience. **lipstick** ('lɪpstɪk) *ncu* a (stick of) coloured substance used for ornamenting the lips.

liquefy ('lɪkwɪfaɪ) *vti* make or become liquid.

liqueur (lɪ'kjʊə*) *nc* a strong, sweet, alcoholic drink, esp. made from fruit.

liquid ('lɪkwɪd) *nc* a substance that flows and cannot be made to take up more or less space, such as water. ● *adj* 1 able to flow. 2 flowing smoothly.

liquidate ('lɪkwɪdeɪt) *vt* 1 end the existence of (a company or business) by selling things owned, paying people owed money to, etc. 2 sell to get money. **liquidation** (ˌlɪkwɪ'deɪʃən) *nu*

liquidity (lɪ'kwɪdɪtɪ) *nu* the state of having money to be able to pay all one's debts.

liquor ('lɪkə*) *chiefly US nu* alcoholic drink. **liquor store** *US* a shop selling liquor.

liquorice *US* **licorice** ('lɪkərɪs) *nu* a black, sweet food made from the root of the liquorice plant.

lisp (lɪsp) *ncu* (a manner of speaking marked by) the saying of (θ) instead of (s), and (ð) instead of (z). ● *vi* speak with a lisp.

list[1] (lɪst) *nc* a number of written names of people or things. ● *vt* make a list of.

list[2] *vi* (of a ship) lean to one side. ● *nc* a state or amount of listing.

listen ('lɪsən) *vi* (often followed by **to**) pay attention to hearing (something): *to listen to the radio*. **listener** *nc*

listless ('lɪstlɪs) *adj* lacking interest or energy. **listlessly** *adv*

lit (lɪt) past tense and past participle of **light**[1].

litany ('lɪtənɪ) *nc, pl* **-nies** a number of short, similar, Christian prayers said one after the other.

liter ('liːtə*) *US n* See **litre**.

literacy ('lɪtərəsɪ) *nu* the ability to read and write.

literal ('lɪtərəl) *adj* to do with the exact or simplest meaning of a word or expression: *a literal translation*. **literally** *adv* in a literal sense: *We literally laughed at his jokes till it hurt*.

literary ('lɪtərərɪ) *adj* to do with literature.

literate ('lɪtərət) *adj* 1 able to read and write. 2 educated.

literature ('lɪtrətʃə*) 1 *ncu* (a type or period of) writing, esp. plays, poetry, and novels: *English literature. nu* 2 the study of this. 3 writing on a particular subject, esp. giving information.

lithe (laɪð) *adj* **-r, -st** (esp. of a person or animal) able to bend easily.

litigation (ˌlɪtɪ'geɪʃən) *nu* the act of bringing or contesting a claim in a court of law.

litmus ('lɪtməs) *nu* a substance that is turned red by acid and blue by an alkali.

litre *US* **liter** ('liːtə*) *nc* a measure for liquids: *abbrev.* l

litter ('lɪtə*) *nu* 1 rubbish dropped by people in the street, etc. 2 an untidy collection of objects. 3 a material, such as straw, given to animals to lie on. *nc* 4 the young animals produced at one birth. 5 a bed or seat with handles for carrying a person. ● *vt* 1 put (objects) all over (a place): *The room was littered with papers*. 2 (of objects) be all over (a place).

little ('lɪtəl) *adj* **-r, -st** small; short. ● *adv* 1 not very: *little used*. 2 scarcely. ● *determiner* not much: *We have little money; I drive very little*. **a little** a small amount; some. **little by little** a bit at a time. **make little of** act as though (something is) unimportant. **little-known** ('lɪtəlnəʊn) *adj* not well-known.

live[1] (lɪv) 1 *vi* be alive; spend one's life (in a particular manner or place): *They lived happily ever after. vt* 2 spend (one's life, etc.). 3 be alive for (a certain length of time). **live down** be able not to mind the reputation brought to one by a mistake, etc. **live off** have the food, etc., of (someone else). **live on** 1 continue to live or exist: *His name lived on after his death*. 2 manage to live by eating or spending (something): *I live on very little*. **live through** experience: *My father lived through two wars*. **live up to** be as good as or do as well as (someone, an expectation, etc.): *You have your reputation to live up to*.

live² (laɪv) *adj* **1** alive: *Live chickens for sale.* **2** (of a wire, etc.) connected to an electricity supply. **3** (of a bomb) able to explode. **4** able to be seen or heard on television or radio at the time of the event: *a live discussion on recent events.*

livelihood ('laɪvlɪhʊd) *nc* an occupation by which one lives.

lively ('laɪvlɪ) *adj* **-ier, -iest 1** fast-moving; energetic; busy. **2** interesting. **3** (of a colour) bright. **liveliness** *nu*

liver ('lɪvə*) *nc* a part inside the body that alters chemical substances in the blood.

livery ('lɪvərɪ) *nc, pl* **-ries** a characteristic suit of clothes worn by male servants of a noble family, etc.

lives (laɪvz) plural of **life.**

livestock ('laɪvstɒk) *nu* animals kept or raised on a farm.

livid ('lɪvɪd) *adj* **1** (esp. of skin over a bruise) bluish-grey. **2** *infml* very angry.

living ('lɪvɪŋ) *adj* alive. ●*nu* **1** the state of being alive. **2** *nc* an occupation by which one earns what one needs: *This work is my living; How do you make a living?* **living-room** ('lɪvɪŋrʊm) *nc* a room in a house for general use during the day.

lizard ('lɪzəd) *nc* an animal with four short legs and a long tail; a reptile: see picture at **reptiles.**

llama ('lɑːmə) *nc* a South American animal kept for its wool: see picture.

llama

lo (ləʊ) *archaic interj* look! **lo and behold** (expression of surprise): *I was just beginning to think I'd lost him when lo and behold—he suddenly appeared!*

load (ləʊd) *nc* **1** something carried or supported by a person, vehicle, etc. **2** a force borne by part of a building, bridge, etc., or resisted by a machine, etc. **3** an electric current being delivered. ●*vt* **1** put (goods) on a lorry, ship, train, etc. **2** put a charge into (a gun). **3** put (a film) into (a camera). **4** apply force to. **a loaded question** a question suggesting a particular answer. **loads** *infml n pl, adv* a lot: *loads of money; loads better.*

loadstone ('ləʊdstəʊn) *n* See **lodestone.**

loaf¹ (ləʊf) *nc, pl* **-ves** (vz) **1** a quantity of bread, other than a small one, baked in one piece. **2** a shaped quantity of sugar or cooked meat. **3** *nu slang* brain; ability to think: *If you used your loaf, you'd know it was wrong.*

loaf² *vi* spend time doing nothing useful or interesting. **loafer** *nc*

loam (ləʊm) *nu* good earth for growing plants in, because it contains clay, sand, and rotting plant matter.

loan (ləʊn) *vt* lend (esp. money). ●*nc* **1** something loaned. **2** *ncu* (an instance of) loaning.

loath (ləʊθ) *adj* See **loth.**

loathe (ləʊð) *vt* hate strongly. **loathsome** ('ləʊðsəm) *adj* causing hatred or disgust.

lob (lɒb) *vt* throw in a high curve. ●*nc* a high, curving throw.

lobby ('lɒbɪ) *nc, pl* **-bies 1** a small room leading to a larger one. **2** *chiefly Brit* a room in a parliament where the public can speak to members. **3** a group of people who lobby on a particular subject: *the fishing lobby.* ●*vti* try to influence (people making laws).

lobe (ləʊb) *anatomy nc* a rounded part of something larger, esp. of a part of the body such as the ear or brain.

lobster ('lɒbstə*) *nc, pl* **lobsters, lobster** a large shellfish that has two double claws and is caught for food: see picture.

lobster

local ('ləʊkəl) *adj* **1** to do with a particular place: *a local newspaper.* **2** affecting only one part: *local pain.* ●*nc* **1** a person living locally. **2** *infml, Brit* a nearby pub. **local authority** *Brit* the group of people dealing with the affairs of a part of the country. **local government** the governing of a part of a country by locally elected people. **locally** *adv*

localise ('ləʊkəlaɪz) *vt* make local, esp. by keeping within a particular place.

locality (ləʊ'kælɪtɪ) *nc, pl* **-ties 1** a neighbourhood; the area around a place. **2** the scene of an event.

locate (ləʊ'keɪt) *vt* **1** find. **2** place; position: *Where is the house located?* **location** (ləʊ'keɪʃən) *ncu* **1** (an example of) locating. **2** the place where something is. **3** a place used for making a film, other than a studio built for the purpose: *filmed on location in Spain.*

loch (lɒk) *Scottish nc* a lake or a part of the sea nearly surrounded by land.

loci ('ləʊsaɪ) plural of **locus.**

lock¹ (lɒk) *nc* **1** a device fixed to a door, drawer, etc., that prevents it being opened except with a correct key. **2** a part of a canal or river, shut in by gates, by means of which boats can be moved between parts at different levels: see picture. **3** a device which prevents something moving: *a steering lock.* ● *vt* **1** fasten (a lock); fasten with a lock. **2** *vti* (cause to) become fixed or stuck: *My jaws have locked.* **lock in** shut (a person or thing) in (a place) by means of a lock: *We'll lock ourselves in the room so we're not disturbed.* **lock out 1** shut (a person or thing) out of a place by means of a lock. **2** prevent (employees) from going to work by locking up a factory, etc. **lock-out** ('lɒkaʊt) *nc* an instance of locking employees out. **lock up 1** shut (a person or thing) in a place, esp. a prison, by means of a lock. **2** lock the doors of (a building). **3** put out of reach; make unable to be used, spent, etc.: *Money locked up in property.*

lock 2

lock² *nc* a curl or small bunch of hair.
locker ('lɒkə*) *nc* a cupboard, usually one of many, for luggage left at a railway station, one's belongings at work, etc.
locket ('lɒkɪt) *nc* a small container for a picture, etc., worn on a chain round the neck.
locomotion (,ləʊkə'məʊʃən) *nu* (the power of) movement from one place to another.
locomotive (,ləʊkə'məʊtɪv) *nc* a powered railway vehicle for pulling a train: see picture. ● *adj* to do with locomotion.

locomotive

locus ('ləʊkəs) *science nc, pl* **loci** an exact place or point.
locust ('ləʊkəst) *nc* an African and Asian flying insect that travels in large numbers and eats great quantities of plants: see picture at **insects.**
lodestone (also **loadstone**) ('ləʊdstəʊn) *nc* a piece of stone containing iron that, being magnetic, can be used to find direction.

lodge (lɒdʒ) *nc* **1** a house in the country used for some activity: *a hunting lodge.* **2** *chiefly Brit* a house at the entrance to the grounds of a larger one. **3** the home built by beavers in a river or lake. ● *vti* **1** (cause to) be provided with somewhere to live, esp. in an already partly occupied private house. **2** *vt* bring (a complaint, etc.) against someone. **3** *vi* become stuck. **lodger** *nc* a person who lodges in someone else's house. **lodging** *nc* **1** somewhere to live. **2** (*pl*) a room or rooms to live in in someone else's house.
loft (lɒft) *nc* the space inside a roof. ● *vt* hit or throw (something) high in the air.
lofty ('lɒftɪ) *adj* **-ier, -iest 1** high; towering. **2** grand; noble.
log (lɒg) *nc* **1** a piece of a cut-up branch or trunk of a tree. **2** also **logbook** a book used to enter movements and events, esp. on a ship. **3** a device used to measure the speed of a ship. ● *vt* **1** enter (a journey or event) in a logbook. **2** *vi* cut down trees for their wood.
logarithm ('lɒgərɪðəm) (often shortened to **log**) *nc* the number of times a number (the base) must be multiplied by itself to give another number: *The logarithm of 100 to the base 10 is 2; $log_{10}\ 100 = 2.$*
loggerheads ('lɒgəhedz) *n* **at loggerheads** in strong disagreement.
logic ('lɒdʒɪk) *nu* **1** the study of how one uses reason to arrive at a proof, conclusion, etc. **2** the reasoning used to support an argument, etc.: *I don't see the logic of what you are saying.* **3** correct reasoning. **4** the arrangement of the parts of a computer that lets it do its job. **logical** *adj* **1** correctly reasoned. **2** to do with logic. **logically** *adv*
loin (lɔɪn) *n* **1** *ncu* (meat from) the back, below or behind the ribs. **2** (*pl*) the part of the body from the waist to just below the hips. **loincloth** ('lɔɪnklɒθ) *nc* a simple garment wrapped round the loins.
loiter ('lɔɪtə*) *vi* stand around doing nothing useful.
loll (lɒl) *vi* lie or lean lazily.
lollipop ('lɒlɪpɒp) *nc* a boiled sweet on a small stick.
lone (ləʊn) *adj* (used before a noun) alone; single: *There were no buildings except a lone house.*
lonely ('ləʊnlɪ) *adj* **-ier, -iest 1** (unhappy because) alone. **2** causing a feeling of loneliness. **loneliness** *nu*
lonesome ('ləʊnsəm) *chiefly US adj* lonely.
long¹ (lɒŋ) *adj* **-er** ('lɒŋgə*), **-est** ('lɒŋgɪst) **1** measuring much in distance or time: *a long road; a long life.* **2** (used after a noun) reaching or lasting. . . : *a lesson two hours long.* **3** unlikely: *a long chance.* **4** (of a drink) containing a spirit and a large

amount of a non-alcoholic drink. ●*adv* (for) a long time: *long ago; Have you been here long?* **as** or **so long as 1** for the time that. **2** provided that. **before long** soon. **in the long run** in the end; after some time. **long-distance** (lɒŋˈdɪstəns) *adj* travelling or reaching a long way: *a long-distance telephone call.* **long-playing record** a gramophone record 30 or 25 cm across and played at 33⅓ revolutions per minute: *abbrev.* LP. **long-range** (lɒŋˈreɪndʒ) *adj* **1** able to travel far: *a long-range plane.* **2** (of a weather forecast, etc.) dealing with the future. **long-sighted** (ˌlɒŋˈsaɪtɪd) *adj* unable to see close things clearly. **long-standing** (lɒŋˈstændɪŋ) *adj* existing for a long time. **long-suffering** (lɒŋˈsʌfərɪŋ) *adj* not complaining at unhappiness, annoyance, etc. **long-term** (ˌlɒŋˈtɜːm) *adj* lasting until or to do with the distant future: *a long-term plan.* **long²** *v* **long for** want very much. **longing** *adj* ●*nu* **1** the state of wanting something. **2** *nc* an urge. **longingly** *adv*

longitude (ˈlɒndʒɪtjuːd, ˈlɒŋɡɪtjuːd) *nc* the distance from a point on the earth to the line between the North and South Poles that passes through Greenwich, England, expressed as an angle: *Peking lies at about longitude 116 degrees East.* **longitudinal** (ˌlɒndʒɪˈtjuːdɪnəl, ˌlɒŋɡɪˈtjuːdɪnəl) *adj* **1** to do with longitude. **2** to do with length.

look (lʊk) *vi* **1** (often followed by **at**) position one's eyes so as to see: *Look at this view!* **2** (often followed by **for**) search. **3** (of a thing) face; allow one to look: *My room looks onto the garden.* **4** (sometimes followed by an infinitive) seem or appear (to be): *You look tired.* **5** *infml* (followed by an infinitive) hope; expect: *He's looking to finish today.* **6** *vt* look at in a particular way: *He looked me in the eye.* ●*nc* **1** an instance of looking: *I'll have a look.* **2** (often *pl*) an appearance: *The painting has a strange look to it; The beard spoils his looks.* **look after** take care of. **look at** watch; see or examine (in order to give an opinion, judgement, etc.). **look down on** act towards or consider as worse than oneself. **look forward to** be glad or hope that one is going to be, experience (doing something): *I'm looking forward to going on holiday.* **look in** (often followed by **on**) visit for a short time. **looking-glass** (ˈlʊkɪŋɡlɑːs) *archaic nc* a mirror. **look into** find out about. **look on 1** watch an event. **2** consider: *I look on this as a waste of time.* **look out 1** be careful. **2** (usually followed by **for**) watch: *Look out for our turning.* **3** find by looking: *He looked out a book I wanted.* **look-out** (ˈlʊkaʊt) *nu* **1** the act of looking out (**look out** def. 2). **2** *infml* worry; busi-

ness: *You must buy your own food—that's your look-out.* **3** chance of success or a happy result: *In this bad weather there's a poor look-out for the missing men. nc* **4** a person who keeps watch. **5** a place where a **look-out** (def. 4) is positioned. **look over** examine (a house, patient, etc.). **look through 1** examine (a book, etc.) quickly. **2** search among. **look up 1** look for (information about something) in a book such as a dictionary or encyclopedia. **2** visit (someone one has not seen before or for some time): *Look me up if you come to Australia.* **3** (appear to) improve: *The market for cars is looking up.* **look up to** respect.

loom¹ (luːm) *nc* a machine for weaving cloth. **loom²** *vi* **1** appear unclearly, esp. also large or threatening: *dark clouds looming in the sky.* **2** (of an unwelcome event) be about to happen.

loop (luːp) *nc* **1** (the shape of) the part of a line, rope, etc., between two points where it crosses or (nearly) touches itself. **2** also **loop line** a railway line that leaves a main line and rejoins it further along. **3** a strip of cloth tape, etc., sewn at each end to a garment, towel, etc., to hang it by. **4** a circle of tape or film that can be played or shown continuously. ●*vt* **1** make a loop in (rope, etc.). **2** contain or fasten with a loop. **3** *vi* move in loops.

loophole (ˈluːphəʊl) *nc* something not thought of in the making of a law, etc., that allows one to avoid obeying it: *a tax loophole.*

loose (luːs) *adj* **-r, -st 1** not tight: *loose clothes.* **2** not fixed or contained: *a loose cover; The cattle have got loose.* **3** not pressed together: *loose earth.* **4** not exact: *a loose expression.* **5** considered bad by society: *a loose woman.* ●*vt* also **let loose** cause to be **loose** (def. 2). **at a loose end** with nothing useful or interesting to do. **loosely** *adv* **loosen** *vti* make or become **loose** (defs. 1, 3) or looser.

loot (luːt) *nu* **1** goods that are stolen, esp. during fighting. **2** *slang or humorous* money. ●*vti* take (goods) from (a place) as loot.

lop (lɒp) *vt* (usually followed by **off**) cut (esp. a branch of a tree).

lop-sided (ˌlɒpˈsaɪdɪd) *adj* with one side higher or bigger than the other.

loquacious (ləˈkweɪʃəs) *formal adj* able or keen to talk a lot.

lord (lɔːd) *nc* **1** *Brit* a man given the title 'Lord': *Lord Wilmington.* **2** a master, ruler. **the Lord** God. **lordship** (ˈlɔːdʃɪp) *nu* the state of being a lord. **Lordship** *Brit nc* (used to refer to a judge, bishop, or lord): *Your Lordship; Their Lordships.*

Lords (lɔːdz) *n* **the (House of) Lords** the upper house in the British parliament, in which lords sit.

lore (lɔː*) *nu* knowledge (of a subject) collected over a long time: *weather lore.*

lorry (ˈlɒrɪ) *chiefly Brit nc, pl* **-ries** a large road vehicle for goods.

lose (luːz) *vt* **1** fail to continue to possess or have: *to lose one's advantage.* **2** become unable to find: *I've lost my umbrella—will you help me find it?* **3** fail to win (a game, etc.). **4** (of a clock) run slow (by): *My watch loses a minute a day.* **be lost 1** die or be killed. **2** (often followed by **in**) be totally interested: *He's lost in the newspaper.* **loser** *nc*

loss (lɒs) **1** *ncu* (an example of) losing. **2** *nc* something or someone lost. **at a loss** unable to decide what to do, through surprise, anger, etc.

lost (lɒst) past tense and past participle of **lose**.

lot (lɒt) *nu* **1** *infml* a group or collection: *His family are a pleasant lot.* **2** what will happen to one in one's life: *His is a humble lot.* *nc* **3** one of a number of objects, the choice of which decides who does something: *Let's draw lots to see who goes first.* **4** a thing or group of things together, offered for sale at an auction. **5** *chiefly US* a piece of land with a particular use: *a parking lot.* **a lot** also **lots 1** a large quantity: *lots of food; A lot of the cars are new.* **2** very much or often: *I eat a lot.* **the lot** everything.

loth (also **loath**) (ləʊθ) *adj* unwilling: *loth to talk much.*

lotion (ˈləʊʃən) *nc* a liquid put on the skin or hair to heal, clean, etc.

lottery (ˈlɒtərɪ) *nc, pl* **-ries** a game of chance in which some of those who pay to enter are chosen to win prizes.

lotus (ˈləʊtəs) *nc* a lily with large pink flowers: see picture at **flowers**.

loud (laʊd) *adj* **-er, -est 1** (of sound) strong; easy to hear. **2** making a lot of noise. **3** (of a colour) too bright; ugly. **4** (of clothes, a person, etc.) unpleasantly noticeable. **loudly** *adv* **loudness** *nu* **loudspeaker** (ˌlaʊdˈspiːkə*) *nc* a device that turns electrical signals from a record-player, etc., into sound. **out loud** See under **out**.

lounge (laʊndʒ) *nc* **1** a living-room in a house. **2** a room for reading, conversation, etc., in a hotel. ●*vi* (often followed by **about** or **around**) spend time lazily, esp. sitting or lying.

louse (laʊs) *nc, pl* **lice** a small wingless insect that lives on other animals and sucks their blood: see picture at **insects**. **louse up** *slang* fail; do (something) badly. **lousy** (ˈlaʊzɪ) *adj* **-ier, -iest 1** having lice. **2** *slang* bad or ill.

lout (laʊt) *nc* an unpleasant, bad-mannered person.

lovable (ˈlʌvəbəl) *adj* deserving love.

love (lʌv) *nu* **1** a strong feeling of attraction and fondness, esp. between a man and a woman. **2** affection or respect. **3** no points (in a game such as tennis): *love-thirty.* **4** *nc* a loved person or thing. **5** *infml, Brit* (expression used to address someone): *Cup of tea, love?* ●*vt* feel love for. **be** or **fall in love** (often followed by **with**) (of a man, or woman, or both) (start to) feel love (for each other). **make love to 1** have sex with. **2** *archaic* make loving approaches to. **love affair** a relationship, esp. short, between two people who fall in love.

lovely (ˈlʌvlɪ) *adj* **-ier, -iest 1** beautiful; attractive. **2** very pleasant. **loveliness** *nu*

lover (ˈlʌvə*) *nc* **1** (usually *pl*) a person in love. **2** a person, esp. a man, having a sexual relationship outside marriage. **3** a person who likes something particular: *doglovers.*

loving (ˈlʌvɪŋ) *adj* showing or feeling love. **lovingly** *adv*

low¹ (ləʊ) *adj* **1** set deep in; at a not very high level: *low in the valley.* **2** being a small distance from top to bottom: *a low building.* **3** small in quantity: *low prices.* **4** (of a sound) made up of slow repeated movements; deep. **5** bad: *a low opinion; low grade.* **6** not generally considered nice or acceptable: *low entertainment.* **7** (of a gear) producing little movement but much power. ●*adv* in or to a low position. ●*nc* a time, place, etc., when someone or something is low. **lowland** (ˈləʊlənd) *nc* (often *pl*) a low piece of land. **low-lying** (ˈləʊˌlaɪɪŋ) *adj* (of land) low, esp. near sea level.

low² *nc* the sound made by cattle. ●*vi* make this sound.

lower (ˈləʊə*) *adj* in or to the bottom part. ●*vti* **1** make or become smaller in amount, price, etc.; decrease. **2** make or become lower in height. **lower oneself** bring oneself down in the opinion of others: *I wouldn't lower myself to do such a thing.*

lowly (ˈləʊlɪ) *adj* **-ier, -iest** humble; modest.

loyal (ˈlɔɪəl) *adj* faithful or true (to an employer, friend, country, etc.). **loyalist** (ˈlɔɪəlɪst) *nc* a person loyal to his king, queen, or government. **loyalty 1** *nu* the ability to be or quality of being loyal. **2** *nc* (usually *pl*) something or someone to which one is loyal: *Where do her loyalties lie?*

lozenge (ˈlɒzɪndʒ) *nc* a piece of solid medicine sucked to turn it liquid.

lubricate (ˈluːbrɪkeɪt) *vt* cover or spread (part of a machine, etc.) with oil or grease to make run smoothly. **lubrication** (ˌluːbrɪ-

'keɪʃən) *nu* **1** the act of lubricating. **2** a substance used for lubricating.

lucid ('luːsɪd) *adj* (of writing, a mind, etc.) clear.

luck (lʌk) *nu* **1** chance; fortune: *How this will turn out is just a matter of luck.* **2** good luck; success. **bad luck!** (used to express sorrow that someone has not had good luck.) **good luck!** (used to wish someone success.) **luckily** *adv* **lucky** *adj* **-ier, -iest** to do with or having good luck.

lucrative ('luːkrətɪv) *adj* bringing a good profit or good earnings.

ludicrous ('luːdɪkrəs) *adj* so odd or silly as to cause laughter: *What a ludicrous suggestion!*

lug (lʌg) *nc* a part of something that sticks out and by which it can be lifted. ● *vt* pull or carry with an effort.

luggage ('lʌgɪdʒ) *nu* **1** bags, suitcases, etc., in which to put clothes, etc., for travel. **2** one's own belongings packed in this way: *lost luggage.*

lukewarm ('luːk,wɔːm) *adj* **1** slightly warm. **2** not enthusiastic.

lull (lʌl) *vt* calm (a person, suspicions, a storm, etc.): *The noise of the water lulled him to sleep.* ● *nc* a short period of calm, esp. during fighting or in bad weather.

lullaby ('lʌləbaɪ) *nc, pl* **-bies** a gentle song intended to send a child to sleep.

lumbago (lʌm'beɪgəʊ) *nu* pain in the lower back.

lumber¹ ('lʌmbə*) *nu* **1** *chiefly US* trees cut down for their wood. **2** *Brit* unused or unwanted belongings. ● *vt infml, Brit* give something that is unpleasant or a nuisance to (someone): *I've been lumbered with showing people round all day.* **lumberjack** ('lʌmbədʒæk) *nc* a person who cuts down trees.

lumber² *vi* move slowly, heavily, and awkwardly.

luminous ('luːmɪnəs) *adj* **1** giving off light in the dark: *luminous hands on a watch.* **2** bright; shining.

lump (lʌmp) *nc* **1** an amount or piece of something solid with no particular shape: *a lump of coal; a lump of butter.* **2** a rounded raised part of a surface: *I've got a lump on my head where I hit it.* ● *vt infml* **1** (often followed by **together**) consider or act towards as a group: *I'll lump the English together with the French, Germans, etc., as Europeans.* **2** put up with, without complaining about: *Like it or lump it.* **lumpy** *adj* **-ier, -iest** having or full of lumps.

lunar ('luːnə*) *adj* to do with the moon.

lunatic ('luːnətɪk) *infml or archaic nc, adj* (a person) with a sick mind. **lunatic asylum** *archaic* See **asylum** (def. 2).

lunch (lʌntʃ) (also *formal* **luncheon**) ('lʌntʃən) *nc* a midday meal, esp. when the main meal of the day is in the evening. ● *vi* eat lunch.

lung (lʌŋ) *nc* either of two spongy organs inside the body into which air is taken, so that oxygen can be put into the blood and carbon dioxide removed.

lunge (lʌndʒ) *vti* move or push (something) forward suddenly. ● *nc* an act of lunging.

lurch¹ (lɜːtʃ) *vi* move (forward and) suddenly or hard to one side. ● *nc* an act of lurching.

lurch² *n* **leave someone in the lurch** leave someone to deal with problems without help.

lure (ljʊə*) *vt* tempt (someone) by leading to expect some pleasure, profit, or advantage. ● *nc* a thing that lures.

lurid ('ljʊərɪd, 'lʊərɪd) *adj* **1** (of a colour) unpleasantly bright. **2** shocking.

lurk (lɜːk) *vi* be hidden, esp. for an evil purpose.

luscious ('lʌʃəs) *adj* (of food) sweet or juicy.

lush (lʌʃ) *adj* **-er, -est** (of plants) growing in great quantity.

lust (lʌst) *nu* a strong feeling of wanting something, esp. sexual pleasure. ● *vi* (often followed by **after** or **for**) feel lust (for).

lustre *US* **luster** ('lʌstə*) *nu* **1** shine. **2** splendour; glory. ● *vt* give lustre to. **lustrous** ('lʌstrəs) *adj*

lute (luːt) *nc* a stringed musical instrument played by pulling at the strings.

luxury ('lʌkʃərɪ) **1** *nu* great comfort (in one's home, food, clothes, etc.). **2** *nc, pl* **-ries** something enjoyable but not necessary. ● *adj* luxurious. **luxuriant** (lʌg'ʒʊərɪənt) *adj* (esp. of plants) rich; growing in great quantity. **luxurious** (lʌg'ʒʊərɪəs) *adj* providing luxury: *a luxurious home.*

lymph (lɪmf) *anatomy nu* a clear liquid leaked out of and returning to the blood, that passes round the body, supplying and cleaning the body cells. **lymphatic** (lɪm'fætɪk) *adj*

lynch (lɪntʃ) *vt* (of a crowd) kill, esp. hang (someone) by the neck because he is thought to have performed a crime.

lynx (lɪŋks) *nc, pl* **lynxes, lynx** an animal of the cat family with a short tail and grey-brown spotted fur: see picture at **animals.**

lyre (laɪə*) *nc* an ancient stringed musical instrument played by pulling at the strings.

lyric ('lɪrɪk) *adj* also **lyrical** (of poetry) **1** expressing the writer's feelings. **2** written to be sung. ● *nc* **1** a poem or song. **2** (usually *pl*) the words of a (popular) song. **lyrical** *adj* **1** lyric. **2** enthusiastic; full of praise.

M

ma (mɑ:) *infml n* short for **mother**.

ma'am (mæm, mɑ:m) *n* short for **madam**.

macadam (məˈkædəm) *nu* small stones laid and pressed down in layers, often with tar, to form a road surface. **macadamise** (məˈkædəmaɪz) *vt* surface (a road) with macadam.

macaroni (ˌmækəˈrəʊnɪ) *nu* a food made from wheat flour, in the form of tubes.

mace¹ (meɪs) *nc* **1** a stick with a round metal head with sharp points, once used as a weapon. **2** an ornamental stick used as a sign of someone's position or office.

mace² *nu* the dried outer covering of nutmeg seeds, used in food for its taste.

machine (məˈʃiːn) *nc* **1** a mechanical device, such as a pump or a food mixer, making use of power to do a task. **2** a powerful group of people or organisation that does not seem to care about individual people. ● *vt* shape (an object) by cutting it with a machine tool. **machine-gun** (məˈʃiːngʌn) *nc* a gun that fires bullets and reloads itself automatically: see picture.

machine-gun

machinist (məˈʃiːnɪst) *nc* a person who works a machine, esp. a sewing-machine.

machinery (məˈʃiːnərɪ) **1** *nu* machines, considered together. **2** *nc, pl* **-ries** a system for doing something: *the machinery for dealing with complaints.*

mackerel (ˈmækrəl) *nc, pl* **mackerel, mackerels** a North Atlantic oily food fish: see picture at **fish**.

mackintosh (ˈmækɪntɒʃ) *nc* a raincoat, esp. made of cloth covered with rubber.

macroeconomics (ˌmækrəʊˌiːkəˈnɒmɪks) *nu (with singular verb)* the study of the economy of a whole country or society.

mad (mæd) *adj* **-der, -dest 1** sick in the mind; insane. **2** *infml* (usually followed by **about** or **on**) very enthusiastic or keen: *He's mad about cars.* **3** *infml* very angry. **4** odd; strange in behaviour: *I know I may seem a bit mad.* **madly** *adv* **madness** *nu*

madman (ˈmædmən) *nc, pl* **-men** a **mad** (def. 1) person.

madam (ˈmædəm) *polite nu* (used to speak to a woman, esp. a customer in a shop, etc.).

madden (ˈmædən) *vt* make **mad** (defs. 1, 3).

made (meɪd) past tense and past participle of **make**.

Madonna (məˈdɒnə) **1** *n* the Virgin Mary; the mother of Jesus Christ. **2** *nc* a picture or statue of the Virgin Mary.

madrigal (ˈmædrɪgəl) *nc* a song for several different voices, without instruments.

magazine (ˌmægəˈziːn) *nc* **1** a thin, paper-covered, regularly produced book, usually having large pages containing articles, photographs, news, etc.: *a music magazine.* **2** a store for ammunition and explosives. **3** a container for holding bullets for a gun, slides for a projector, etc.

maggot (ˈmægət) *nc* the soft, young form of a fly, found esp. in rotten food.

magic (ˈmædʒɪk) *nu* **1** the art of influencing people or events by mysterious means. **2** the art of entertaining people with tricks that deceive their eyes. **3** anything that has a powerful, strange effect: *The doctor cured me so quickly—it was magic.* ● *adj* also **magical** to do with magic. **magician** (məˈdʒɪʃən) *nc* a person who practises magic.

magistrate (ˈmædʒɪstreɪt) *nc* a person who decides simple law cases and makes court orders but is not a judge.

magnanimous (mægˈnænɪməs) *adj* generous, willing to forgive, etc. **magnanimity** (ˌmægnəˈnɪmɪtɪ) *nu*

magnate (ˈmægneɪt) *nc* a wealthy or powerful person: *an oil magnate.*

magnesium (mægˈniːzɪəm) *nu* a chemical element; a metal that burns with a bright white flame.

magnet (ˈmægnɪt) *nc* **1** a piece of iron, steel, etc., that attracts iron. **2** a person or thing that attracts and is difficult to resist. **magnetic** (mægˈnetɪk) *adj* to do with, esp. having, magnetism. **magnetise** (ˈmægnɪtaɪz) *vt* make magnetic. **magnetism** (ˈmægnɪtɪzəm) *nu* the property of a magnet; power to attract.

magnificent (mægˈnɪfɪsənt) *adj* splendid; excellent. **magnificence** *nu* **magnificently** *adv*

magnify (ˈmægnɪfaɪ) *vt* make (something) appear larger. **magnification** (ˌmægnɪfɪˈkeɪʃən) **1** *nu* the act of magnifying. *nc* **2** the amount by which something is magnified or can magnify. **3** something magnified, such as a picture. **magnifying glass** a piece of glass, thick in the middle and thin at the edges, usually with a handle, used to magnify objects.

magnitude ('mægnɪtjuːd) **1** *nu* size. **2** *nc* the brightness of a star.

magnolia (mæg'nəʊlɪə) *nc* a tree with large, mainly white or pink flowers.

magpie ('mægpaɪ) *nc* **1** a black and white European and North American bird that is believed to steal things: see picture at **birds. 2** a person who collects and keeps things for no clear reason.

mahogany (mə'hɒgənɪ) *nc, pl* **-nies** an American tree; *(also nu)* the reddish-brown wood of this tree, much used for making furniture.

maid (meɪd) *nc* **1** a female servant. **2** short for **maiden**.

maiden ('meɪdən) *nc archaic or poetry* also **maid** a girl or unmarried woman. ● *adj* first: *a maiden voyage; a maiden speech.* **maiden name** a woman's last or family name before she married.

mail[1] (meɪl) *nu, vt* See **post**[3]. **mail bag** a sack in which mail is carried. **mailbox** ('meɪlbɒks) *US n* See **postbox** under **post**[3]. **mailman** *US n* See **postman** under **post**[3]. **mail-order** *nu, adj* (the method of) selling goods by post: *a mail-order firm.*

mail[2] *nu* a material made of connected metal rings, once worn as protection in battle.

maim (meɪm) *vt* injure (a person or animal) permanently.

main (meɪn) *adj* chief; largest or most important. ● *nc* **1** a main water pipe, electric wire, etc. **2** *(pl)* a water, gas, or electricity supply or a system of waste pipes. **mainland** ('meɪnlənd) *nu* a large piece of land as compared with islands near it. **mainly** ('meɪnlɪ) *adv* generally; for the most part. **mainmast** ('meɪnmɑːst) *nc* the tallest mast supporting sails on a boat. **mainsail** ('meɪnseɪl) *nc* the sail at the bottom or back of a mainmast. **mainstay** ('meɪnsteɪ) *nc* **1** a wire or rope supporting a mainmast, fixed further forward on the boat. **2** the chief support of something. **mainstream** ('meɪnstriːm) *nu* the most popular opinions, music, fashions, etc.: *the mainstream of science.*

maintain (meɪn'teɪn) *vt* **1** cause to continue (to exist). **2** keep in good condition: *A car must be maintained to be reliable.* **3** provide with the means to live. **4** claim (to be true): *I maintain that I am right.* **maintenance** ('meɪntənəns) *nu* **1** the act of maintaining. **2** (money paid to provide) the means to live.

maize (meɪz) *Brit n* See **corn**[1] (def. 2).

majestic (mə'dʒestɪk) *adj* grand; splendid. **majestically** *adv*

majesty ('mædʒəstɪ) *nu* the quality of being majestic. **Majesty** *nc, pl* **-ties** (used to refer to the King or Queen): *Your Majesties; Her Majesty.*

major ('meɪdʒə*) *adj* **1** large, larger, or largest: *the major part of the day.* **2** (more or most) important: *a major road; My major subject at university was English.* **3** (of a musical key) with the higher of the two possible third notes. ● *nc* **1** an officer in an army or an air force. **2** *US, Australian* a university student's major subject. **3** *US, Australian* a student having a particular major subject: *an English major.* ● *vi US, Australian* (usually followed by **in**) study as one's major subject: *I major in English.*

majority (mə'dʒɒrɪtɪ) *nc, pl* **-ties 1** a greater or the greatest number: *The majority of people have cars.* **2** the number by which a political party has more members in a parliament than the next strongest party or all other parties together. **3** the number of votes which separates the winner of an election from the best loser. **4** *nu* the age at which one is allowed to vote, etc.

make (meɪk) *vt* **1** cause (to exist); create: *I'll make the tea.* **2** cause to become: *Who made the floor dirty?* **3** force or cause to (do something): *Make him go away.* **4** be; be turned into: *He makes a good soldier.* **5** arrive in time for; arrange to have: *I didn't make my train.* **6** prepare (a bed) for sleeping in. **7** win; earn: *I made £100 on that sale.* **8** add up to: *3 and 4 make 7.* **9** reckon to be: *What time do you make it?* ● *nc* a type of something according to who made it: *I know several makes of car.* **make-believe** ('meɪkbɪˌliːv) *adj, nu* (something) pretended. **make for 1** travel towards. **2** help to bring about. **make of 1** consider to be the purpose or importance of: *I don't know what to make of him.* **2** make (something) using (a material): *a table made of wood.* **make off** leave or go away in a hurry. **make off with** steal. **make out 1** see and recognise: *I can't make it out so far away.* **2** write (a cheque, etc.). **3** (try to) show to be: *The film made him out to be a coward.* **4** pretend: *Don't make out that you're rich.* **make out of** get, esp. sense or a reason) out of (an answer, statement, etc.): *Make some sense out of this report.* **maker** *nc* **1** a person who makes. **2 the Maker** God. **makeshift** ('meɪkʃɪft) *adj* intended to serve for only a short time: *sheets pinned over the windows as makeshift curtains.* **make up 1** put together; prepare (esp. something pretended or false): *That story is completely made up.* **2** be the parts of; be what (something) is made of: *Eleven people make up a football team.* **3** complete: *One more will make up the number we need.* **4** end (a disagreement, argument, etc.). **5** put **make-up** (def. 1) on. **make-up** ('meɪkʌp) **1** *nu* substances put on the skin of the face to change its appearance. **2** *nc* the combined parts of a person's character. **make up for** do or give something as a replacement for something lost or an unkind act: *I brought you a present to make up for coming home late.*

maladjusted (ˌmælə'dʒʌstɪd) *adj* unable to deal with normal life and problems.

malady ('mælədɪ) *formal nc, pl* **-dies** an illness; disease.

malaria (mə'leərɪə) *nu* a disease carried by mosquitoes that produces fever.

male (meɪl) *adj, nc* **1** (to do with) a man, boy, or other animal of the sex that produces the seeds used in creating its young. **2** (to do with a plant producing) a flower with stamens, producing pollen.

malformation (ˌmælfɔː'meɪʃən) *ncu* (an example of) not being normally formed.

malfunction (mæl'fʌŋkʃən) *vi* (of a machine, etc.) fail to work normally. ●*nc* an instance of malfunctioning.

malice ('mælɪs) *nu* unkind thoughts towards someone. **malicious** (mə'lɪʃəs) *adj*

malignant (mə'lɪgnənt) *adj* **1** (of a growth in the body) spreading; doing harm. **2** feeling hate.

malleable ('mælɪəbəl) *adj* (esp. of metal) able to be shaped by hammering or pressing.

mallet ('mælɪt) *nc* a hammer-like tool with a wooden head: see picture at **tools.**

malnutrition (ˌmælnjuː'trɪʃən) *nu* the condition resulting from not eating enough (of the right) food.

malt (mɔːlt) *nu* seeds, esp. of barley, dried after being wetted and allowed to start growing, used esp. in beer. ●*vt* make into malt.

mama (also **mamma**) (mə'mɑː) *old-fashioned, formal nc* mother.

mammal ('mæməl) *nc* any animal of which the female produces milk to feed its young.

mammoth ('mæməθ) *nc* a type of hairy elephant that has died out. ●*adj* huge.

man (mæn) *nc, pl* **men** (men) **1** a grown-up male human. **2** any person. **3** *(pl)* members of armed forces who are not officers. **4** a male servant or employee. **5** *nu* the human race: *Man rules the world.* ●*vt* (prepare to) work; look after: *Man the guns!* **the man in the street** an average or ordinary person. **man-made** (ˌmæn'meɪd) *adj* made by man; not natural: *a man-made lake.*

manage ('mænɪdʒ) *vt* **1** succeed in being able (to do something): *I managed to come home early.* **2** have room, time, etc., for: *Can you manage another drink?* **3** control or be in charge of (a business, etc.). **manageable** *adj* able to be managed or easily handled. **management 1** *nu* the act or skill of managing. **2** *nc* managers as a group. **manager** *nc* **manageress** *nc* **managerial** (ˌmænɪ'dʒɪərɪəl) *adj* to do with a manager or management.

mandate ('mændeɪt) *nc* **1** an order made by a legal power. **2** power given by voters to a person or party winning an election. **3** power to govern the land of a defeated enemy. **4** land for which such power is given. ●*vt* **1** give a **mandate** (defs. 1, 2, 3) to. **2** make (land) a mandate. **mandatory** ('mændətrɪ) *adj* ordered by a mandate; that must be done, given, etc.

mane (meɪn) *nc* the long hair growing on the neck of an animal, esp. a horse or lion.

maneuver (mə'nuːvə*) *US n, v* See **manoeuvre.**

manganese ('mæŋgəniːz) *nu* a chemical element; a grey metal used in making steel.

manger ('meɪndʒə*) *nc* a long, open box for food given to cattle or horses.

mangle¹ ('mæŋgəl) *vt* damage or destroy by cutting, pressing, or tearing.

mangle² *nc* a device with two rollers, between which wet clothes are squeezed to remove water from them.

mango ('mæŋgəʊ) *nc, pl* **-es, -s** the soft yellowish fruit of the Asian mango tree: see picture at **fruits.**

mangrove ('mæŋgrəʊv) *nc* a tree that grows in shallow coastal water in hot parts of the world and has roots that divide above the water: see picture.

mangrove

mangy ('meɪndʒɪ) *adj* **-ier, -iest** (esp. of an animal) having a skin disease that makes hair fall out.

manhole ('mænhəʊl) *nc* a covered hole in the ground leading down to a tunnel, passage, etc.

manhood ('mænhʊd) *nu* the condition of being a man.

mania ('meɪnɪə) **1** *nu* an illness of the mind, causing excitement and sometimes violence. **2** *nc* great fondness or enthusiasm: *He has a mania for collecting furniture.*

maniac ('meɪnɪæk) *nc* **1** person with a mania. **2** *infml* a wild, violent person.

manicure ('mænɪkjʊə*) *ncu* (a short time given to) care of the hands, esp. to make them look nicer. ●*vt* carry out manicure on.

manifest ('mænɪfest) *adj, vt* (make) plain to see or recognise. ● *nc* a list of the goods or passengers on a ship, plane, or train. **manifestation** (,mænɪfe'steɪʃən) *ncu* (an example of) manifesting.

manifesto (,mænɪ'fəstəʊ) *nc, pl* **-es, -s** a list of the things a political party says it intends to do if elected.

manifold ('mænɪfəʊld) *adj* many and various. ● *nc* a part of an engine that divides a flow of fuel entering it or collects a flow of gas leaving it.

manioc ('mænɪɒk) *n* See **cassava**.

manipulate (mə'nɪpjʊleɪt) *vt* 1 handle or use (an instrument, machine, etc.). 2 influence the behaviour of (someone). **manipulation** (mə,nɪpjʊ'leɪʃən) *nu*

mankind (mæn'kaɪnd) *nu* 1 all humans. 2 all men.

manly ('mænlɪ) *adj* **-ier, -iest** 1 (of a man) brave, attractive, or tough. 2 (of a woman) like a man. **manliness** *nu*

manna ('mænə) *nu* 1 food mysteriously supplied to the Israelites in the desert, as told in the Bible. 2 anything good or helpful, esp. unexpected.

mannequin ('mænɪkɪn) *nc* 1 a woman employed to show off clothes for sale by wearing them. 2 a model of a person used for making or showing clothes.

manner ('mænə*) 1 *nc* a way of doing something. 2 *nu* a person's general behaviour: *He has an unpleasant manner.* **all manner of** all kinds of: *There were all manner of people.* **mannered** *adj* 1 having manners as described: *well-mannered.* 2 having or marked by mannerisms. **manners** *n pl* (good) behaviour when one is with other people: *Don't forget your manners; bad manners.*

mannerism ('mænərɪzəm) *nc* a characteristic quality or habit.

manoeuvre *US* **maneuver** (mə'nuːvə*) *nc* 1 a planned movement, esp. of armed forces. 2 an action or plan intended to influence someone to one's own advantage. ● *vti* carry out a manoeuvre (on): *He's manoeuvring to get elected leader.*

manor ('mænə*) *nc* also **manor house** the house of a lord or landowner.

manpower ('mæn,paʊə*) *nu* the people able or needed to do a task: *Have we got the manpower to build the house in a month?*

mansion ('mænʃən) *nc* a large, grand house.

manslaughter ('mæn,slɔːtə*) *nu* the crime of killing someone without having planned to do.

mantelpiece ('mæntəlpiːs) *nc* a shelf above a fireplace.

mantle ('mæntəl) *nc* 1 *archaic* a long, loose garment covering the whole body from the neck down. 2 the part of a lamp round the flame that becomes hot and makes more light.

manual ('mænjʊəl) *adj* to do with, used with, or done by the hands: *manual work.* ● *nc* a book describing how to use or repair a machine, etc.

manufacture (,mænjʊ'fæktʃə*) *vt* 1 make with machines. 2 make up (something that is not true). ● *nu* the act of manufacturing. **manufacturer** *nc*

manure (mə'njʊə*) *nu* a substance, esp. animal waste, used to help plants grow. ● *vt* put manure on.

manuscript ('mænjʊskrɪpt) *nc* 1 something written by hand or sometimes typed. 2 the first writing down of a book, etc.

many ('menɪ) *determiner, pron* a large number (of): several. **how many** what number of: *How many chairs are there?—Five.*

map (mæp) *nc* a drawn representation of (part of) the surface of the earth or the moon, the arrangement of stars, etc. ● *vt* make a map of.

maple ('meɪpəl) *nc* a tree with winged seeds, of which the wood is used for furniture, etc.: see picture at **trees**; (also *nu*) this wood.

mar (mɑː*) *vt* spoil.

marathon ('mærəθən) *nc* 1 a running race over 42.195 km. 2 a lengthy task.

maraud (mə'rɔːd) *vti* attack and steal (from a place).

marble ('mɑːbəl) 1 *nu* a kind of limestone that can be highly polished and is much used for building. 2 *nc* a small stone or glass ball used in various children's games. ● *vt* give an irregularly mixed coloured appearance to (paper).

March (mɑːtʃ) *n* the third month of the year, after February and before April.

march (mɑːtʃ) *vti* 1 (esp. of a group of soldiers), (cause to) walk with a firm, regular step. 2 walk in a determined way. ● *ncu* 1 (an example of) marching. 2 *nc* a piece of music for marching to.

mare (meə*) *nc* a female horse.

margarine (,mɑːdʒə'riːn) *nu* a soft, greasy, yellowish food made from vegetable and sometimes also animal fats, used for cooking and eaten on bread.

margin ('mɑːdʒɪn) *nc* 1 an edge or border of a surface. 2 a strip free of writing or printing at the side of a page. 3 an extra amount: *a profit margin.* **marginal** *adj* 1 to do with a margin. 2 (of a seat in a parliament) held by a member who got only a few votes more than another candidate.

marijuana (also **marihuana**) (,mærɪjʊ'wɑːnə) *n* See **hemp**.

marine (mə'riːn) *adj* to do with the sea. ● *nc* a soldier who fights on land or at sea. **mariner** ('mærɪnə*) *formal, poetry* *nc* a sailor.

marital ('mærɪtəl) *adj* to do with marriage or a marriage partner: *marital duty*.

maritime ('mærɪtaɪm) *adj* to do with the sea, esp. sailing and ships.

mark (mɑːk) *nc* 1 a line, scratch, spot, etc., on a surface. 2 a sign adding information (esp. to written language): *a postmark; a question mark*. 3 a characteristic quality or influence: *He left his mark everywhere he worked*. 4 a point given for a correct answer in school work, etc. 5 a number, esp. a total of marks (**mark** def. 4), or letter used to indicate the standard of school work, etc. ● *vt* 1 put a **mark** (def. 1) on (a surface). 2 give (something) a particular or special character: *Let's have a party to mark the occasion*. 3 give a **mark** (def. 5) to. 4 put a label or other object by (an object or place) so as to be able to find the place again: *I've marked my place in the book*. 5 notice. **marked** (mɑːkt) *adj* (easily) noticeable: *a marked improvement*. **markedly** ('mɑːkɪdlɪ) *adv* **marker** *nc* 1 a thing (esp. a pen) that marks a thing or place. 2 a person who marks work or a game. **mark out** make (something, such as a games field) by marking the ground. **mark time 1** move the feet up and down as in marching but without moving forward. 2 do nothing (to something) for a particular reason: *We're marking time on this until we are told we can have more money*. **mark up** add to the price of (something) to produce a profit.

market ('mɑːkɪt) *nc* 1 a gathering of people to buy and sell goods. 2 a place where goods are bought and sold. 3 possible buyers for a product. 4 a trade: *The cotton market has been better lately*. ● *vt* put (a product) on sale. **on the market** for sale. **marketing** *nu* the science and practice of selling goods. **market-place 1** *nc* an open space in a town where a market is held. 2 *nu* the world of buying and selling. **market research** working out the probable number of possible buyers of a product.

marksman ('mɑːksmən) *nc, pl* **-men** a person trained to shoot well.

marmalade ('mɑːməleɪd) *nc* a kind of jam made from bitter oranges or sometimes lemons, limes, or grapefruit and eaten esp. at breakfast.

maroon¹ (mə'ruːn) *vt* (usually passive) leave or abandon (someone) in a lonely position: *They were marooned on their farm until the snow melted*.

maroon² *adj* dark brownish-red. ● *ncu* a maroon colour.

marquee (mɑː'kiː) *nc* a large tent used for holding meals, exhibitions, etc.

marquess (also **marquis**) ('mɑːkwɪs) *nc* a nobleman next below a duke.

marriage ('mærɪdʒ) *nc* 1 the joining together of a man and a woman as husband and wife; the state of being married. 2 a ceremony of marriage; wedding.

marrow ('mærəʊ) 1 *nu* the substance inside hollow bones. 2 *nc* a large green vegetable with soft yellow flesh: see picture at **vegetables**.

marry ('mærɪ) *vt* 1 take (a person) as one's husband or wife. 2 (of a priest, etc.) join in marriage.

marsh (mɑːʃ) *ncu* (a stretch of) watery land; swamp. **marshy** *adj* **-ier, -iest**

marshal ('mɑːʃəl) *nc* 1 an army or air force officer of the highest rank. 2 a person who organises processions, controls crowds, etc. 3 (in the USA) an officer of the law whose duty is to put into action the decisions of the courts. 4 (in the USA) the head of a police or fire department. ● *vt* organise, put in order, or gather (thoughts, people, etc.).

marsupial (mɑː'suːpɪəl) *nc* an animal, such as the kangaroo, that carries its young in a pouch.

mart (mɑːt) *formal nc* a market(-place); centre of trade.

martial ('mɑːʃəl) *adj* to do with war, soldiers, etc.: *martial music*. **martial law** government by an army.

martyr ('mɑːtə*) *nc* 1 a person who is killed because of his beliefs. 2 a person who suffers greatly: *She is a martyr to poor health*. 3 *humorous* a person who complains a lot about small troubles. ● *vt* (usually passive) kill (someone) because of his beliefs. **martyrdom** ('mɑːtədəm) 1 *nc* being martyred. 2 *nu* great suffering.

marvel ('mɑːvəl) *nc* something to wonder at: *the marvels of space travel*. ● *vi* (often followed by **at**) wonder; be amazed. **marvellous** *US* **marvelous** *adj* wonderful. **marvellously** *US* **marvelously** *adv*

Marxism ('mɑːksɪzəm) *nu* the system of ideas started by Karl Marx. **Marxist** *adj* to do with Marxism. ● *nc* a follower of Marxism.

masculine ('mæskjʊlɪn) *adj* 1 to do with or like a man. 2 (in some languages) of a class of nouns usually including male people and animals.

mash (mæʃ) *vt* press and mix (potatoes, etc.) until they are soft. ● *nu* 1 mashed vegetables, meat, etc. 2 a mixture of water and corn, etc., fed to animals. 3 *infml* mashed potatoes.

mask (mɑːsk) *nc* 1 a covering for the face, used as disguise, for protection, to breathe a gas with, etc. 2 anything used to hide the real nature of something: *Behind his gentle* *mask, he was a violent man.* ● *vt* **1** cover (the face). **2** hide the real nature of.

mason ('meɪsən) *nc* a person who builds with stone. **masonry** ('meɪsənrɪ) *nu* **1** stonework. **2** the art of building with stone.

masque (maːsk) *nc* a play with songs and dances, popular in the sixteenth and seventeenth centuries.

masquerade (ˌmæskəˈreɪd) *nc* **1** a gathering of people in fancy dress and masks. **2** a pretence; action intended to deceive. ● *vi* (usually followed by **as**) pretend to be (something one is not).

Mass (mæs) *nc* **1** the Christian service of Holy Communion, esp. in the Roman Catholic Church. **2** a musical setting of parts of the Mass.

mass (mæs) *nc* **1** the size or volume of something; amount of matter. **2** a large solid block. **3** a great crowd or quantity. **4** *(pl) infml* a great quantity: *There's masses of food left over.* **5** *nu* the greatest number; majority. ● *vti* bring or come together in large quantities. **mass media** See **media**. **mass production** production of goods in large quantities, with each worker doing only part of the work on each piece. **the masses** people in general; less educated people.

massacre ('mæsəkə*) *nc* the killing of many people, often without a plan. ● *vt* kill in large numbers; slaughter.

massage ('mæsaːʒ) **1** *nu* the science of rubbing parts of the body to improve health. **2** *nc* a treatment of massage. ● *vt* give massage to (a person or a part of the body). **masseur** (mæˈsɜː*) *nc* a man who gives massage. **masseuse** (mæˈsɜːz) *nc* a woman who gives massage.

massive ('mæsɪv) *adj* **1** huge; bulky; heavy. **2** large; impressive; powerful.

mast (maːst) *nc* **1** an upright pole or post on a ship, to which sails or flags are attached: see picture. **2** a tall metal post which supports a radio or television aerial.

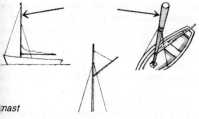

mast

master ('maːstə*) *nc* **1** a man in charge: *I am master in my own house.* **2** the man in charge of a merchant ship. **3** a male schoolteacher. **4** a man who is fully qualified in a trade and employs others: *a master builder.*

5 a person who is very clever at something: *a master of disguise.* **6** a great painter. ● *vt* **1** gain a thorough knowledge of (a subject). **2** get the better of or learn to control (a person or situation). **Master of Arts** or **Science** a man or woman who has passed the examinations for usually a second degree in arts or science. **masterful** *adj* able to master someone or something. **masterly** *adj* with thorough knowledge and skill: *His handling of that complicated subject was masterly.* **masterpiece** ('maːstəpiːs) *nc* **1** an outstanding object or piece of work. **2** the best object in a collection or in the work of a writer or artist. **3** a work or product of genius. **mastery** ('maːstərɪ) *nu* **1** charge; control. **2** thorough knowledge.

mat¹ (mæt) *nc* **1** a small floor covering. **2** a small piece of cloth, cork, etc., placed under objects to prevent damage to the furniture on which they are standing.

mat² *adj* See **matt.**

match¹ (mætʃ) *nc* **1** a competition between persons or teams playing a game or sport. **2** a marriage. **3** an equal; someone of the same ability: *She's a match for any of them.* **4** something that is the same as or goes well with something else: *This carpet is a very good match for the one you already have.* ● *vti* **1** be the same (as) or go well (with): *I want a hat to match this coat; Their ideas match. vt* **2** (be) equal (to): *His courage matches hers.* **3** offer competition to. **matchless** *adj* without equal.

match² *nc* a small wooden stick with one end covered in a substance that catches fire when rubbed sharply against the special strip on a matchbox: see picture. **matchbox** ('mætʃbɒks) *nc* a box for matches with this special strip along its side.

match

mate (meɪt) *nc* **1** a companion, esp. friend or fellow worker. **2** a marriage partner; an animal's sexual partner. **3** a ship's officer who is next highest to the captain. ● *vti* (cause to) become a sexual mate (of).

material (məˈtɪərɪəl) *nc* **1** a substance from which things can be made or with which things can be done. **2** a cloth; fabric. **3** *nu* the ideas and information used in writing a book, etc. ● *adj* **1** made of matter. **2** important: *You've given me very material help.*

materialise (mə'tıərıəlaız) vi 1 come about; really happen. *I wonder whether his offer of money will materialise.* 2 (of the spirit of a dead person) become visible.

materialism (mə'tıərıəlızəm) nu 1 the overvaluing of money or material goods. 2 the belief that only material things exist. **materialistic** (mə,tıərıə'lıstık) adj

maternal (mə'tɜːnəl) adj 1 like or to do with a mother; motherly. 2 on one's mother's side of the family: *my maternal grandfather.*

mathematics (,mæθə'mætıks) *(infml abbrevs.* **maths** US **math)** nu 1 *(with singular verb)* the science of numbers. 2 *(with plural verb)* a person's ability to do mathematics: *His mathematics are not to be trusted.* **mathematical** adj 1 to do with mathematics. 2 that can be worked out by mathematics: *a mathematical certainty.* **mathematically** adv **mathematician** (,mæθəmə'tıʃən) nc a person who studies or is an expert in mathematics.

matinée ('mætıneı) nc a theatre or cinema performance in the afternoon.

matriculate (mə'trıkjʊleıt) vi (pass an examination that qualifies one to) enter a university. **matriculation** nu 1 this examination. 2 the act of matriculating.

matrimonial (,mætrı'məʊnıəl) adj to do with marriage. **matrimony** ('mætrımənı) nu the state of marriage.

matrix ('mætrıks, 'meıtrıks) nc, pl **-trixes, -trices** (trısiːz) a mould; a hollow inside which a thing can take shape.

matron ('meıtrən) nc 1 (in the UK) the person in charge of nursing in a hospital. 2 the woman in charge of nursing, clothes, etc., in a boarding school, etc. 3 a married woman who is no longer young.

matt (also **mat**) (mæt) adj (of a surface) dull; not shining or polished.

matted ('mætıd) adj (of hair) tangled; not having been combed for some time.

matter ('mætə*) nu 1 all the substances of which objects, animals, and plants are made. 2 liquid that collects in a wound that goes bad, etc. 3 nc a subject; question: *I must see you about a very important matter.* ● vi be important: *Does it matter?* **as a matter of course** according to the usual practice; automatically. **as a matter of fact** actually; to be correct. **matter-of-fact** (,mætərəv'fækt) adj factual; without expressing feelings. **no matter** without taking any notice of. **what's the matter?** what's the trouble?; what's wrong? **what's the matter with him? 1** what has upset him? **2** what illness has he got?

matting ('mætıŋ) nu a rough material used for mats, packing goods, etc.

mattress ('mætrəs) nc a thick, firm pad covered with cloth made to fit on a bed, for lying on: see picture.

mattress

mature (mə'tjʊə*) adj **-r, -st 1** (of a person, animal, or plant) fully grown. **2** (of fruit, wine, etc.) ripe to eat or drink. **3** wise with experience. ● vti **1** (cause to) become mature. **2** vi (of a bill) become due to be paid. **maturity** (mə'tjʊərıtı) nu **1** the state of being mature. **2** the date on which a bill matures.

maul (mɔːl) vt (esp. of a wild animal) handle roughly or violently.

mausoleum (,mɔːsə'lıəm) nc a grand building in which a royal or other famous person is buried.

mauve (məʊv) adj light purple, like lavender. ● ncu a mauve colour.

maxim ('mæksım) nc a short, wise remark about life; proverb.

maximum ('mæksıməm) nc, pl **-ima** (ımə), adj the greatest (amount) reached, possible, etc.: *today's maximum temperature.* **maximise** ('mæksımaız) vt make (profits, production, etc.) as great as possible.

May (meı) n the fifth month of the year, after April and before June.

may (meı) v **1** shall or will perhaps: *I may come; It might rain.* **2** be permitted (to): *May I leave early?* **3** would do well to: *You might shut the door.* **4** *formal* I hope that... shall or will: *May we have luck!* **5** (used in expressing a purpose) can: *Stand up so that you may see better.* **6** be no reason against: *We may as well go now.* **maybe** ('meıbiː) adv perhaps.

mayn't (meıənt) v may not.

mayonnaise (,meıə'neız) nu a sauce for salads, made from eggs, oil, vinegar, etc.

mayor (meə*) nc the elected head of usually a large town.

maze (meız) nc **1** a puzzle in the form of many paths, esp. between high hedges, along which one has to find one's way to the middle, etc. **2** something complicated or confusing: *The law is a maze.*

me (miː) pron (used for the speaker or writer either after a preposition or when the object of a verb): *Give it to me; It won't do me any good.*

meadow ('medəʊ) nc a field of grass, esp cut for hay.

meagre *US* **meager** ('miːgə*) *adj* **1** (of food) small in amount. **2** (of ideas, etc.) poor; weak. **3** (of a person) thin.

meal¹ (miːl) *nc* **1** a taking of food (usually of several kinds) and drink: *three meals a day.* **2** the food and drink eaten at a meal. **mealtime** ('miːltaɪm) *nc* the time when a meal is usually eaten.

meal² *nu* grain that has been broken up small, esp. to feed animals.

mean¹ (miːn) *vt* **1** have the sense of: *'Quick' means 'fast'.* **2** give (an expression) its exact sense: *When I say 'at once', I mean 'now'.* **3** be as important as: *Music means everything to him.* **4** indicate or be a sign of (something coming): *A north wind can mean snow.* **5** intend: *I didn't mean it; She doesn't mean to be rude.* **mean business** be serious about a matter.

mean² *adj* **-er, -est 1** not generous, esp. with money. **2** (of an action) low; unkind. **3** (of a house, etc.) poor; dirty.

mean³ *adj, nc* (an) average; middle: *yesterday's mean temperature.*

meander (mɪ'ændə*) *vi* **1** (of a river) wind; have many turns. **2** wander; walk around with no clear aim. ●*nc* **1** a curve in a river. **2** a meandering path or course.

meaning ('miːnɪŋ) *nc* **1** the sense of or idea behind an expression. **2** the sense or idea a person wants to make clear: *Do you get my meaning?* **3** an indication: *The election has a clear meaning: the President is losing popularity.* **meaningful** *adj* having some use or meaning. **meaningless** *adj*

means (miːnz) *nc, pl* **means 1** anything that makes one able to do something: *A bicycle is a means of transport.* **2** (*pl*) money: *She has private means; a man of means.* **by all means** certainly; with my full approval: *May I have a biscuit?—By all means.* **by means of** by using: *I got in by means of a ladder.* **by no means** not at all; far from: *They are by no means rich.*

meant (ment) past tense and past participle of **mean.**

meantime ('miːntaɪm) also **meanwhile** ('miːnwaɪl) *adv, nu* (in) the period between two events.

measles ('miːzəlz) *nu (with singular verb)* a disease caught mainly by children, causing fever and a rash.

measure ('meʒə*) *nc* **1** an exact amount of a substance. **2** a necessary amount of a quality: *You need a measure of patience to deal with children.* **3** an instrument or container for measuring. **4** *(often pl)* an action; step; move: *Strong measures will be taken against law-breakers.* **5** a law: *a measure passed by Parliament.* **6** *nu* the proof, indication: *It is a measure of his success that everyone is*

happier. **7** *nc* the metre or rhythm of a poem. ●*vt* find the exact size or quantity of. **measure up (to)** prove oneself equal (to): *He measured up well to the other players.* **made-to-measure** *adj* (of clothes) specially made to fit a particular customer. **measurable** *adj* large enough to be measured. **measurement 1** *nu* the act of measuring. **2** *nc* a size or quantity found by measuring.

meat (miːt) **1** *nc* the flesh of animals other than birds and fish, eaten as food. *nu* **2** solid food: *meat and drink.* **3** the important part of a speech, etc.

mechanic (mɪ'kænɪk) *nc* a worker who makes or repairs machines: *a car mechanic.* **mechanical** (mɪ'kænɪkəl) *adj* **1** to do with machines. **2** to do with mechanics. **3** (of behaviour) done as if by a machine. **mechanically** *adv*

mechanics (mɪ'kænɪks) *nu* **1** *(with singular verb)* the science of movement and force; the science of machines. **2** *(with plural verb)* how something works: *The mechanics of this election are beyond my understanding.*

mechanise ('mekənaɪz) *vt* use machines to do: *The sorting of letters in the post office is mechanised now.* **mechanisation** (ˌmekənaɪ'zeɪʃən) *nu*

mechanism ('mekənɪzəm) *nc* **1** all the parts of a mechanical process working as a whole. **2** a system of parts that work together like the parts of a machine: *the mechanism of government.* **3** a way in which something can be done: *A secret vote is a good mechanism for the free expression of opinion.*

medal ('medəl) *nc* a piece of metal, usually like a coin and often on a ribbon, given to a person as a reward or to remember a special occasion by: see picture.

medal

meddle ('medəl) *vi* interfere in someone's affairs.

media ('miːdɪə) *n pl* also **mass media** the chief means of informing and entertaining large numbers of people; newspapers, radio and television.

median ('miːdɪən) *nc, adj* (the) middle; halfway (point).

mediate ('miːdɪeɪt) *vi* act as a mediator.

mediator ('miːdɪeɪtə*) *nc* person who tries to settle an argument between others.

medical ('medɪkəl) *adj* to do with medicine. ● *nc infml* an examination by a doctor.

medicinal (mɪ'dɪsɪnəl) *adj* to do with or acting as medicine: *for medicinal use.*

medicine ('medsɪn, 'medɪsɪn) **1** *nu* the art and science of the prevention and cure of disease. **2** *nc* something to be eaten or drunk to help cure an illness. **medicineman** ('medsɪn,mæn) *nc, pl* **-men** a man who practises an unscientific kind of medicine.

medieval (also **mediaeval**) (,medɪ'iːvəl) *adj* to do with the **Middle Ages**.

mediocre (,miːdɪ'əʊkə*) *chiefly derogatory adj* ordinary; not particularly good or bad; second-rate.

meditate ('medɪteɪt) **1** *vi* (often followed by **on**) think deeply; reflect (on something). **2** *vt* consider doing (something). **meditation** (,medɪ'teɪʃən) *ncu* (a) deep thought; reflection.

Mediterranean (,medɪtə'reɪnɪən) *adj* being or having a warm climate like that of the countries round the Mediterranean Sea.

medium ('miːdɪəm) *adj* average; middle: *a man of medium height.* ● *nu* **1** the middle point between two opposites. *nc* **2** *pl* **-s** a person who claims to have contact with the spirits of dead people. **3** *pl* **-dia** (dɪə) a means (of giving information, entertainment, etc.): *Films are a good teaching medium.* **medium-sized** ('miːdɪəm-saɪzd) *adj* neither large nor small.

medley ('medlɪ) *nc, pl* **-s** a mixture of different things.

meek (miːk) *adj* humble; patient. **meekly** *adv* **meekness** *nu*

meet¹ (miːt) **1** *vi* come together; gather together. *vti* **2** come into contact (with); get to know (each other). **3** come across (each other) by chance or on purpose. *vt* **4** go to welcome (someone who is arriving). **5** satisfy (demands). **6** deal or cope with (a challenge). **meeting** *nc* a gathering of people at which decisions are made or business is done.

meet² *literary adj* suitable or fit for a purpose.

megaphone ('megəfəʊn) *nc* a funnel-shaped device for making a person's voice sound louder, used for speaking to crowds.

melancholy ('melənkɒlɪ) *adj* sad; depressed. ● *nu* sadness; depression.

mellow ('meləʊ) *adj* **1** (of a person) kind; gentle. **2** (of a colour) warm; rich. **3** (of fruit) ripe. ● *vti* make or become (more) mellow.

melodious (mɪ'ləʊdɪəs) *adj* tuneful; pleasant to listen to. **melodic** (mɪ'lɒdɪk) *adj* to do with melody.

melodrama ('melədrɑːmə) *nc* a kind of play with over-simplified characters, violent actions, and a happy ending. **melodramatic** (,melədrə'mætɪk) *adj*

melody ('melədɪ) *nc, pl* **-dies** a tune; air.

melon ('melən) *nc* a large, sweet, usually round fruit: see picture at **fruits**.

melt (melt) *vi* **1** (of a solid) become liquid. **2** (of a person) become kinder; change one's hard intentions. *vt* **3** cause (a solid substance) to become liquid. **4** soften (someone's heart). **melt away 1** become liquid and disappear. **2** (of anger, etc.) disappear.

member ('membə*) *nc* **1** a person or group that belongs to an organisation, church, team, etc. **2** one of a class of people or things: *a member of the human race.* **Member of Parliament** a person who has been elected to represent the voters of a district in a country's parliament. **membership** ('membəʃɪp) *nc* **1** the state of being a member. **2** members as a whole. **3** the number of members: *Membership in the local chess club fell last year.*

membrane ('membreɪn) *nc* **1** the skin-like material that lines, covers, or connects parts of animals or plants. **2** any skin-like substance.

memoir ('memwɑː*) *nc* **1** a short account of one's personal memories of a dead person. **2** a learned article on a specialist subject. **memoirs** a person's own memories of his or her life; autobiography.

memorable ('memərəbəl) *adj* worth remembering.

memorandum (,memə'rændəm) (often shortened to **memo**) *nc, pl* **-s, -anda** (ændə) a written note bringing a subject to someone's attention.

memorial (mɪ'mɔːrɪəl) *nc, adj* (something) done, built, or started in memory of a person or event.

memorise ('meməraɪz) *vti* learn and remember (words, music, etc.).

memory ('memərɪ) *nu* **1** the ability to remember things that are past: *Memory sometimes plays tricks with us.* **2** the place where information is stored in a computer. **3** *nc, pl* **-ries** something remembered from the past: *I have happy memories of India.* **in memory of** (done, built, etc.) so that people will remember (someone or something). **within living memory** recent enough for people still living to remember.

men (men) plural of **man**.

menace ('menɪs) *nc* a threat; danger. ● *vt* threaten (a person, jobs, peace, etc.). **menacingly** *adv* making menaces; in a threatening way.

menagerie (mɪ'nædʒərɪ) *nc* a collection of wild animals kept in cages.

mend (mend) 1 *vt* repair (something worn or broken). 2 *vti* improve (a relationship, etc.). 3 *vi* (of a broken bone, etc.) heal. **on the mend** *infml* getting better; recovering (from illness).

menial ('miːnɪəl) *sometimes derogatory adj* 1 (of a task) simple; humble. 2 to do with or suitable for a servant. ● *nc* a servant.

meningitis (ˌmenɪn'dʒaɪtɪs) *nu* a dangerous disease of the brain and spinal cord.

menopause ('menəpɔːz) *nu* the ending of menstruation in women.

menstruation (ˌmenstrʊ'eɪʃən) *nu* the monthly bleeding from a woman's womb.

mental ('mentəl) *adj* 1 to do with the mind. 2 *slang* mentally ill; mad. **mental hospital** a hospital for the mentally ill. **mental illness** any disease of the mind; madness. **mentally** *adv* **the mentally ill** those who have diseases of the mind; mad people.

mentality (men'tælɪtɪ) *nc, pl* **-ties** 1 a type of mind. 2 a view of or outlook on life.

mention ('menʃən) *vt* 1 refer to; speak or write briefly about (a subject). 2 name (a person) in a good or bad connection. ● *nc* the act of mentioning: *He received honourable mention.* **don't mention it** 1 it's a pleasure; there's no need to thank me. 2 there's no need to apologise.

menu ('menjuː) *nc* a list of the food that can be ordered in a restaurant.

mercantile ('mɜːkəntaɪl) *adj* to do with trade.

mercenary ('mɜːsənərɪ) *adj* 1 hired for money. 2 eager to make money. ● *nc, pl* **-ries** a soldier who fights only for money.

merchandise ('mɜːtʃəndaɪz) *nu* goods for sale.

merchant ('mɜːtʃənt) *nc* 1 a person who trades. 2 a shopkeeper. ● *adj* commercial. **merchantman** ('mɜːtʃəntmən) *old-fashioned nc, pl* **-men** a merchant ship.

merciful ('mɜːsɪfʊl) *adj* showing mercy; forgiving.

merciless ('mɜːsɪlɪs) *adj* without mercy; cruel.

mercury ('mɜːkjərɪ) *nu* a poisonous, silver-coloured metal that is liquid at normal temperatures: symbol Hg

mercy ('mɜːsɪ) 1 *nu* pity; compassion; unwillingness to punish. 2 *nc, pl* **-cies** a welcome event or situation. **at the mercy of** in the power of.

mere (mɪə*) *adj* **-st** plain; simple; no more than: *It's a mere ten minutes' walk; He made not the merest mention of the trouble.* **merely** ('mɪəlɪ) *adv* just; only.

merge (mɜːdʒ) *vti* 1 (cause to) become one (with) or join together. 2 cause to change slowly (into). **merger** *nc* the merging of two commercial companies.

meridian (mɪ'rɪdɪən) *nc* 1 a line that goes round the earth through the North and South Poles. 2 the height of a person's success. ● *adj* to do with a meridian.

meringue (mɪ'ræŋ) *ncu* a very light, breakable food made of white of egg and sugar.

merit ('merɪt) 1 *nu* high quality; (great) worth. 2 *nc* a quality; good point. ● *vt* deserve.

mermaid ('mɜːmeɪd) *nc* an imaginary being, a young woman above the waist and a fish below it.

merry ('merɪ) *adj* **-ier, -iest** 1 jolly; cheerful; happy. 2 *infml* slightly drunk. **merry-go-round** ('merɪɡəʊˌraʊnd) *nc* also **roundabout** a revolving machine with toy horses on which children ride: see picture. **merrily** *adv* **merriment** ('merɪmənt) *nu* fun; cheerfulness.

merry-go-round

mesh (meʃ) *nc* 1 a net. 2 the space between the threads or wires of a net. 3 a trap: *the mesh of crime.* ● *vt* 1 catch in a net. 2 *vi* (of cog-wheels) fit into each other.

mess (mes) *nc* 1 a dirty, untidy state; muddle. 2 (in the armed forces) (the people who use) a room or building for eating or spending free time in. ● *vt* make dirty or untidy. **mess about** *infml* 1 do small tasks in a leisurely way. 2 waste time. 3 treat (someone) casually: *They've messed me about for months over this work.* **mess up** *infml* make (something) into a muddle or a difficult situation.

message ('mesɪdʒ) *nc* 1 a piece of news or information sent from one place to another. 2 the point made by (a book, etc.): *I've got the message.*

messenger ('mesɪndʒə*) *nc* a person who takes messages.

Messiah (mɪ'saɪə) *n* 1 the deliverer expected by the Jews. 2 a title given by Christians to Jesus Christ.

Messrs. ('mesəz) *determiner* a title for the name of a business company or the names of two or more men: *Messrs. Macmillan Limited; Messrs. Harry and Charles Brown.*

met (met) past tense and past participle of **meet¹**.

metabolism (mɪ'tæbəlɪzəm) *nu* the processes by which substances are changed in the bodies of animals and plants. **metabolic** (ˌmetə'bɒlɪk) *adj*

metal ('metəl) 1 *ncu* any of several substances obtained from under the ground, such as iron and gold, that are mostly hard at normal temperatures. 2 *nu* broken stones used in making roads. ● *adj* made of **metal** (def. 1). ● *vt* cover with **metal** (def. 2): *a metalled road*. **metallic** (mɪ'tælɪk) *adj* (sounding) like **metal** (def. 1).

metallurgy (mɪ'tælədʒɪ) *nu* the science of obtaining pure metals and the art of working in metal. **metallurgist** *nc* a person who studies metallurgy.

metamorphosis (ˌmetə'mɔːfəsɪs) *nc, pl* **-ses** (siːz) a change of shape or form, esp. in an animal.

metaphor ('metəfɔː*) *nc* a manner of speaking in which a thing is said actually to be something which it is like, such as 'She's a cat'.

metaphysical (ˌmetə'fɪzɪkəl) *adj* 1 to do with the philosophy of existence and thought. 2 *infml* (of ideas) abstract and complicated.

mete (miːt) *formal vt* (often followed by **out**) measure out (punishment, etc.).

meteor ('miːtɪə) *nc* a small piece of material that enters the earth's atmosphere from space and is quickly burnt up. **meteoric** (ˌmiːtɪ'ɒrɪk) *adj* 1 to do with a meteor. 2 (of a rise to fame, etc.) sudden.

meteorology (ˌmiːtɪə'rɒlədʒɪ) *nu* the science of weather and of saying what it will be. **meteorological** (ˌmiːtɪərə'lɒdʒɪkəl) *adj* **meteorologist** *nc* a person who studies meteorology.

meter¹ ('miːtə*) *nc* 1 an instrument for measuring something passing through it, such as electricity: see picture. 2 an instrument for measuring the passage of time, such as a parking meter: see picture. ● *vt* measure by means of a meter.

meter

meter² *US n* See **metre¹,²**.

methane ('miːθeɪn) *nu* a natural gas burnt for cooking and heating.

methinks (mɪ'θɪŋks) *archaic* I think.

method ('meθəd) 1 *nc* a (regular or orderly) manner of doing something. *nu* 2 order; organisation; tidiness. 3 *theatre* a way of acting as living a part rather than taking it on. **methodical** (mɪ'θɒdɪkəl) *adj* orderly; (done) using a method.

Methodist ('meθədɪst) *adj* of a Christian Church started by John Wesley in Britain in the eighteenth century. ● *nc* a member of this Church. **Methodism** *nu* the teachings and practices of the Methodist Church.

methylated ('meθɪleɪtɪd) *adj* **methylated spirits** (*infml abbrev.* **meths**) alcohol with methyl alcohol added, used for heating and lighting.

meticulous (mɪ'tɪkjələs) *adj* very careful, attentive to detail. **meticulously** *adv*

metre¹ *US* **meter** ('miːtə*) *nc* a measure of length: *abbrev.* m **metric** ('metrɪk) *adj* to do with the metre or the metric system. **metric system** the system of measures based on the metre, the gram, and the litre. **metric ton** See **tonne**.

metre² *US* **meter** *ncu* a pattern and rhythm of the syllables in poetry. **metrical** ('metrɪkəl) *adj* (of words) arranged in a metre.

metropolis (mɪ'trɒpəlɪs) *nc* the chief city of a country or district. **metropolitan** (ˌmetrə'pɒlɪtən) *adj* to do with a metropolis. ● *nc* the chief bishop of a province of an Eastern Church.

mettle ('metəl) *nu* courage; spirit.

mew (mjuː) *vi* (of a cat) give its high-pitched cry. ● *nc* the cry of a cat.

mews (mjuːz) *nu (with singular verb)* 1 buildings used for the horses of a private house. 2 a street of houses made from a mews.

miaow (mɪ'aʊ) *nc, interj* the high-pitched cry of a cat. ● *vi* (of a cat) give a miaow.

mica ('maɪkə) *nu* a substance obtained from under the ground and made into thin sheets that are like glass but will stand higher temperatures.

mice (maɪs) plural of **mouse**.

microbe ('maɪkrəʊb) *nc* a germ; tiny animal or plant that can cause disease.

microcosm ('maɪkrəkɒzəm) *ncu* a situation, group of people, etc., taken to represent a larger one.

microeconomics (ˌmaɪkrəʊˌiːkə'nɒmɪks) *nu (with singular verb)* the study of the economics of particular areas or problems and the relationships between them.

microfilm ('maɪkrəʊfɪlm) *nc* a film on which newspapers, books, etc., are photographed very small. ● *vt* photograph on microfilm.

micrometer (maɪ'krɒmɪtə*) *nc* an instrument for measuring very small thicknesses.

microorganism ('maɪkrəʊˌɔːgənɪzəm) *nc* a very tiny animal or plant.

microphone ('maɪkrəfəʊn) (*infml abbrev.* **mike**) *nc* a device which changes sound waves into electrical signals for a telephone, radio, etc.

microprocessor ('maɪkrəʊˌprəʊsesə*) *nc* the central part of a small computer.

microscope ('maikrəskəup) *nc* an instrument that makes objects put under it look a lot larger: see picture. **microscopic** (,maikrə'skɒpik) *adj* **1** too tiny to see without a microscope. **2** to do with a microscope.

microscope

microwave ('maikrəuweiv) *nc* a very short wave, used for radio, cooking, etc.

mid (mid) *literary adj* in the middle of. **midpoint** ('mid,pɔint) *nc* the point halfway between two others.

midday (,mid'dei) *nu* noon or the middle of the day. ● ('middei) *adj* at noon or in the middle of the day: *It is too hot to go out in the midday sun.*

middle ('midəl) *adj* **1** at the centre. **2** between others; neither first nor last. **3** (of opinions, etc.) away from the extremes; moderate: *the middle ground.* ●*nc* **1** a centre or place away from the edges. **2** *infml* the waist. **middle-aged** between youth and old age; aged between about forty and sixty. **Middle Ages** the years between 1100 and 1500. **middle class** the class of people between the upper class and the working class. **Middle East** See under **east. middleman** ('midəlmæn) *nc, pl* -**men** a trader who buys goods from their makers and sells them to people or shops.

midget ('midʒit) *nc* an unusually small person. ●*adj* very small.

midnight ('midnait) *nu* **1** twelve o'clock at night. **2** the middle of the night. ●*adj* at midnight or in the middle of the night: *a midnight feast.*

midst (midst) *literary nu* the middle: *He appeared in our midst.*

midsummer (,mid'sʌmə*) *nu* the middle of the summer. ● ('midsʌmə*) *adj* happening at midsummer. **Midsummer Day** the longest day of the year.

midway (,mid'wei) *adv* halfway (between two places).

midwife ('midwaif) *nc, pl* -**wives** (waivz) a person who helps women to give birth.

midwinter (,mid'wintə*) *nu* the middle of the winter. ● ('midwintə*) *adj* happening at midwinter.

mien (mi:n) *literary nu* an appearance; expression on a person's face.

might¹ (mait) past tense of **may**.

might² *nu* power; strength; force. **mighty** -**ier**, -**iest** *adj* powerful; strong. ●*adv infml, chiefly US* very: *That's mighty good of him.* **mightily** *adv* **1** powerfully; strongly. **2** very: *She was mightily pleased.*

mightn't ('maitənt) *v* might not.

migraine ('mi:grein) *nc* a very bad headache, usually on only one side of the head or face.

migrate (mai'greit) *vi* **1** go to live in another country. **2** (of birds, etc.) go to a warmer or cooler part of the world according to the season. **migrant** ('maigrənt) *adj* migrating. ●*nc* **1** a migrating person or animal. **2** *Australian* a person who has (just) arrived from another country to live. **migration** (mai'greiʃən) *nc* **migratory** ('maigrətəri) *adj* (of birds, etc.) that migrate.

mike (maik) *infml n* short for **microphone**.

mild (maild) *adj* -**er**, -**est** **1** (of a person, manners, etc.) gentle. **2** (of weather) fairly warm. **3** (of food, drink, or tobacco) not strong or bitter. **4** (of interest, surprise, etc.) not great or excited. **mildly** *adv*

mildew ('mildju:) *nu* a layer of fungus growing on things that are damp. ●*vt* cover with mildew.

mile (mail) *nc* a measure of length = 1.609 km **mileage** ('mailidʒ) *nu* **1** the total number of miles a car has been driven. **2** *infml* unused capacity or wear: *There's plenty of mileage in that coat yet.* **milestone** ('mailstəun) *nc* **1** a stone at the roadside that gives the distance in miles from the nearest town. **2** an important event in a person's life or in history.

militant ('militənt) *adj, nc* (a) fighting or aggressive (person). **militancy** *nu* **militantly** *adv*

military ('militəri) *adj* **1** to do with war or armies. **2** to do with soldiers. **the military** *(with plural verb)* soldiers.

militia (mi'liʃə) *nu* an army, sometimes of volunteer soldiers, that serves only in its own country.

milk (milk) *nu* **1** the whitish liquid with which mammals feed their young. **2** cow's milk. ●*vt* **1** draw the milk from (cows, etc.) to feed people. **2** take the resources of (a person, organisation, etc.). **milkman** ('milkmən) *nc, pl* -**men** (in the UK) a man who delivers milk to his customers' houses.

milky ('milki) *adj* -**ier**, -**iest** **1** like milk, esp. in colour. **2** containing milk: *milky coffee.* **Milky Way** a strip of very faint stars across the sky.

mill (mil) *nc* **1** a machine for breaking grain, pepper, etc., up small: *a flour mill.* **2** a factory using or making a particular material: *a cotton mill; a paper mill.* ●*vt* **1** break up small. **2** *vi* (usually followed by **about** or

around) (of a crowd) move about within a space. **miller** (ˈmɪlə*) a person who works a flour mill.

millennium (mɪˈleniəm) **1** nc, pl **-nia** (nɪə) (the end of) a thousand years. **2** nu a future time of peace and happiness.

millet (ˈmɪlɪt) nu **1** a grass producing small seeds that can be eaten. **2** these seeds.

millimetre (ˈmɪlɪˌmiːtə*) nc a measure of length = 0.001 m: abbrev. mm

milliner (ˈmɪlɪnə*) nc a maker or seller of hats. **millinery** nu **1** hats. **2** the art of making hats.

million (ˈmɪljən) determiner, n the number 1,000,000; a thousand thousand. **millionaire** (ˌmɪljəˈneə*) a person who has a million pounds, dollars, etc. **millionth** (ˈmɪljənθ) determiner, adv (placed) after 999,999 others. ●nc the whole of a quantity divided by a million.

millipede (also **millepede**) (ˈmɪlɪpiːd) nc a long, small animal with very many legs.

mime (maɪm) vt act without speaking. ●nu **1** acting without speaking. **2** nc an actor who mimes.

Mimeograph (ˈmɪmɪəɡrɑːf) Trademark nc a machine that produces copies of written or typed material from a stencil. ●vt copy with a Mimeograph.

mimic (ˈmɪmɪk) vti imitate the behaviour of. ●nc a person or animal that mimics (well). **mimicry** (ˈmɪmɪkrɪ) nu the act of mimicking.

mimosa (mɪˈməʊzə) nu any of several kinds of tree or bush, esp. one with small, yellow, ball-like flowers.

minaret (ˌmɪnəˈret) nc the tower of a mosque, from which people are called to prayer.

mince (mɪns) **1** vt cut up (meat, etc.) very small, esp. with a machine. **2** vi walk with short, affected steps. ●nu **1** minced meat. **2** short for **mincemeat**. **mince one's words** use weaker words than one would like to.

mincemeat (ˈmɪnsmiːt) (often shortened to **mince**) nu a mixture of apples, dried fruit, fat, etc., made esp. into pies: mince pies.

mind (maɪnd) nc **1** the ability to think; intelligence; thoughts: the power of mind over matter. **2** opinion: We are not of the same mind. nu **3** wish; intention: I've (half) a mind to send him away. **4** memory: I can't call it to mind. ●vti **1** be upset (by), feel offended (by). **2** object (to): I don't mind your going. vt **3** look after or care for (a child, etc.). **4** take care not to damage or be damaged by: Mind my best hat!; Mind the traffic! **bear** or **keep in mind 1** remember. **2** take into account. **change one's mind** alter one's decision or opinion. **make up**

one's mind make a decision. **mind out!** be careful!; stand clear! **mind you** but then; though: I don't eat much... mind you, I do like my food. **mind your own business!** keep out of my affairs! **never mind!** it doesn't matter!; forget it! **never you mind!** it's nothing to do with you! **mindful** literary adj (usually followed by **of**) remembering; having in mind. **mindless** adj not according to reason; senseless: mindless cruelty.

mine¹ (maɪn) pron a person or thing belonging to me: Mine is on the table; It is mine.

mine² nc **1** a place underground where something such as coal, gold, or salt is dug out. **2** a rich source: a mine of information. **3** a metal case containing explosive, left in water or in the ground to explode when a vehicle, ship, etc., comes near it. **4** a passage dug under an enemy's camp, etc., in which explosive can be placed. ●vt **1** dig out (coal, gold, salt, etc.) from mines. **2** make underground passages or tunnels in (a place). **3** place mines in (water or land). **minefield** (ˈmaɪnfiːld) nc **1** a piece of land that has been mined (**mine²** def. 3). **2** a subject or situation that has many hidden dangers. **miner** nc a person who works in an underground mine, esp. a coalmine.

mineral (ˈmɪnərəl) nc, adj (being or to do with) one of many substances without life that come out of the ground, such as rocks and metals. **mineral water** water that contains health-giving minerals and comes out of the ground.

mingle (ˈmɪŋɡəl) vti (cause to) mix.

miniature (ˈmɪnɪtʃə*) adj very small, esp. much smaller than the normal article: A miniature camera is easy to hide. ●nc **1** a very small painting of someone's head. **2** any miniature thing.

minibus (ˈmɪnɪbʌs) nc a small bus with room for about twelve people.

minim (ˈmɪnɪm) US **half note** nc a musical note that is twice as long as a crotchet.

minimal (ˈmɪnɪməl) adj very small; the least possible.

minimise (ˈmɪnɪmaɪz) vt **1** keep (bad effects, etc.) as small as possible. **2** make (disadvantages, etc.) seem as unimportant as possible.

minimum (ˈmɪnɪməm) nc, pl **-ima** (ɪmə), adj the smallest (amount) reached, possible, etc.: We need a minimum of ten people; the minimum wage.

mining (ˈmaɪnɪŋ) nu the digging of mines to obtain coal, gold, salt, etc.

minion (ˈmɪnjən) nc an unimportant servant or assistant.

minister (ˈmɪnɪstə*) nc **1** a Christian priest, esp. in some churches such as the Methodist. **2** the head of a government department. ● *vi* (usually followed by **to**) take care of or give help to (someone). **ministerial** (ˌmɪnɪsˈtɪərɪəl) *adj* of or to do with a minister.

ministry (ˈmɪnɪstrɪ) **1** *nu* the job of a minister of religion. **2** *nc, pl* **-ries** a government department with a minister as its head.

mink (mɪŋk) *nc* **1** a small animal with fur. **2** a coat of mink fur.

minnow (ˈmɪnəʊ) *nc* a small European fish found in freshwater.

minor (ˈmaɪnə*) *adj* **1** unimportant; lesser. **2** (of a musical key) with the lower of the two possible third notes. ● *nc* a person who is too young to have full legal rights and responsibilities.

minority (maɪˈnɒrɪtɪ) *nc, pl* **-ties 1** a smaller or the smallest number: *A small minority voted against the new law; We are in the minority.* **2** the period for which one is a minor.

minstrel (ˈmɪnstrəl) *nc* a travelling musician of the Middle Ages.

mint[1] (mɪnt) *nu* a plant with strongly flavoured leaves used in food.

mint[2] **1** *nc* a place where coins are made. **2** *infml nu* a huge quantity of money. ● *vt* make (coins).

minuet (ˌmɪnjʊˈet) *nc* **1** a dance popular in the seventeenth and eighteenth centuries. **2** a piece of music for this dance.

minus (ˈmaɪnəs) *prep* **1** with (a number) taken away: *Seven minus four equals three.* **2** *infml* without: *She arrived minus her luggage.* ● *adj* below zero: *We had minus temperatures yesterday.* ● *nc* **1** a sign indicating minus(−). **2** *infml* a disadvantage; point against someone or something.

minute[1] (ˈmɪnɪt) *nc* **1** a measurement of time = a sixtieth of an hour. **2** *infml* a very short time. **3** a sixtieth of a degree in an angle. **4** a short note. **5** (*pl*) a written record of the business of a meeting. ● *vt* make a written record of the business of (a meeting).

minute[2] (maɪˈnjuːt) *adj* **1** tiny. **2** exact; in great detail: *a minute study of these plants.*

miracle (ˈmɪrəkəl) *nc* **1** a wonderful event that one would not have thought possible. **2** anything particularly good or wonderful.

miraculous (mɪˈrækjʊləs) *adj* like a miracle: *miraculous happenings.* **miraculously** *adv*

mirage (mɪˈrɑːʒ) *nc* **1** a false vision, esp. of water in a desert, caused by the state of the air. **2** anything that is not as good as it appears.

mire (maɪə*) *nc* a wet, muddy place. **in the mire** in trouble or difficulty.

mirror (ˈmɪrə*) *nc* **1** a surface, esp. glass with one side covered in silver, that reflects light and can be used to look at oneself with. **2** a

reflection of the life around: *Dickens' books are a mirror of his time.* ● *vt* reflect; give a true impression of.

mirth (mɜːθ) *nu* amusement; laughter.

misadventure (ˌmɪsədˈventʃə*) *nc* an unlucky event; accident: *death by misadventure.*

misbehave (ˌmɪsbɪˈheɪv) *vi* behave badly; have bad manners.

miscarriage *nc* **1** (ˈmɪsˌkærɪdʒ, ˌmɪsˈkærɪdʒ) the death of a baby through being born too early. **2** (ˌmɪsˈkærɪdʒ) a situation where the right result is not produced: *a miscarriage of justice.*

miscellaneous (ˌmɪsɪˈleɪnɪəs) *adj* mixed, various: *miscellaneous notes; a miscellaneous collection.*

mischance (ˌmɪsˈtʃɑːns) *ncu* (an) unlucky chance; (piece of) bad luck.

mischief (ˈmɪstʃɪf) *nu* **1** children's tricks or naughtiness. **2** harm. **3** trouble; bad relations: *He made mischief between his sisters.* **mischievous** (ˈmɪstʃɪvəs) *adj* causing mischief.

misconception (ˌmɪskənˈsepʃən) *nc* a misunderstanding; mistaken idea of something: *You're under a misconception.*

misconduct (mɪsˈkɒndʌkt) *nu* improper behaviour, esp. in one's work: *The doctor was found guilty of misconduct.*

misdemeanour *US* **misdemeanor** (ˌmɪsdɪˈmiːnə*) *nc* **1** a minor offence against the law. **2** a small act of wrongdoing.

miser (ˈmaɪzə*) *nc* a person who likes to have money but not to spend it. **miserly** *adj*

miserable (ˈmɪzərəbəl) *adj* **1** unhappy; depressed; wretched; pitiable. **2** depressing: *miserable weather.* **3** poor, mean, inferior: *miserable food.* **miserably** *adv* **misery** (ˈmɪzərɪ) *nu* the state of being miserable; suffering. ● *nc, pl* **-ries 1** a cause of misery. **2** *infml* a person who often complains.

misfire (mɪsˈfaɪə*) *vi* **1** (of a gun) fail to fire (correctly). **2** (of an engine) fail to fire at exactly the right time. **3** (of a plan) go wrong or out of control and produce unexpected results.

misfortune (mɪsˈfɔːtʃən) *ncu* (a piece of) bad luck.

misgiving (mɪsˈgɪvɪŋ) *nc* a doubt about the good sense of something; reservation.

misguided (mɪsˈgaɪdɪd) *adj* acting or done under the influence of unwise ideas.

mishap (ˈmɪshæp) *nc* an accident; unlucky event.

misinterpret (ˌmɪsɪnˈtɜːprɪt) *vt* misunderstand the sense or intention of (orders, etc.).

mislaid (mɪsˈleɪd) past tense and past participle of **mislay**.

mislay (mıs'leı) *vt* lose (something) for a short time, esp. by forgetting where it is.

mislead (mıs'liːd) *vt* give incorrect information or advice to (someone).

misled (mıs'led) past tense and past participle of **mislead.**

mismanagement (mıs'mænıdʒmənt) *nu* failure to handle the affairs of a business, etc., well.

misplace (mıs'pleıs) *vt* **1** direct (one's confidence, enthusiasm, etc.) towards an unworthy object. **2** put (something) in the wrong place.

misprint ('mısprınt) *nc* a mistake in printing. ● (mıs'prınt) *vt* print (a word, etc.) wrongly.

mispronounce (,mısprə'naʊns) *vt* pronounce (a word) wrongly.

Miss (mıs) *determiner* **1** a title to put before the name of an unmarried woman. **2** the title of the winner of a beauty competition: *Miss World.* ● *nc* **miss** sometimes derogatory a girl; young woman.

miss (mıs) *vt* **1** feel sad at the absence of. **2** become aware of the absence of. **3** fail to be in time for (a train, etc.). **4** fail to take advantage of (an opportunity). **5** fail to hit (a ball). **6** fail to see (a person or thing): *We missed each other at the station.* **7** be absent from; not attend (an occasion). ● *nc* a failure to hit, reach, etc. **miss out 1** leave out; omit. **2** *infml* (usually followed by **on**) lose; fail to get. **missing** ('mısıŋ) *adj* **1** absent or lost. **2** (of soldiers, etc.) absent after fighting but not yet known to be dead.

missile ('mısaıl) *nc* **1** something that is thrown or shot through the air. **2** a container of explosive, driven by a rocket.

mission ('mıʃən) *nc* **1** a party of people sent to carry out a particular task. **2** a task that a person or group is ordered to do, or sees as a duty to carry out. **3** a group of people who represent their national government in a foreign country. **4** an organisation that employs missionaries. **5** a centre of missionary or welfare work. **missionary** ('mıʃənrı) *nc, pl* **-ries** a religious worker who tries to spread his faith among non-believers, usually abroad. ● *adj* to do with missionaries.

misspell (mıs'spel) *vt* spell wrongly.

misspelt (mıs'spelt) past tense and past participle of **misspell.**

mist (mıst) *nu* **1** a kind of thin cloud just above the ground. **2** tiny drops of water on glass, preventing one from seeing through. ● *vti* cover or be covered with mist. **misty** *adj* **-ier, -iest** covered with mist.

mistake (mıs'teık) *nc* something that is done wrongly; an error: *We've made a mistake.* ● *vt* **1** be wrong about (something): *We have mistaken our way.* **2** (followed by **for**) suppose (someone or something) to be (someone or something else): *I mistook you for your sister.* **mistaken** (mıs'teıkən) past participle of **mistake.** ● *adj* **1** wrong; in error: *He was mistaken about her age.* **2** wrongly supposed: *mistaken identity.* **3** unwise: *In a mood of mistaken jealousy she sent him away.*

mistletoe ('mısəltəʊ) *nu* a plant with small white berries that grows on various trees in the winter in Europe.

mistook (mıs'tʊk) past tense of **mistake.**

mistress ('mıstrəs) *nc* **1** a woman who employs servants. **2** a woman teacher. **3** a woman who has a lover to whom she is not married. **4** *nu* a woman in charge: *She was mistress of the situation.*

mistrust (mıs'trʌst) *vt* have no confidence in; suspect. ● *nu* lack of confidence; suspicion.

misunderstand (,mısʌndə'stænd) *vt* fail to understand properly. **misunderstanding** *ncu* (a) failure to understand properly.

misunderstood (,mısʌndə'stʊd) past tense and past participle of **misunderstand.**

misuse (,mıs'juːz) *vt* **1** treat badly. **2** use for an unsuitable purpose. ● (,mıs'juːs) **1** *nu* bad treatment. **2** *nc* an unsuitable use.

mite (maıt) *nc* **1** *archaic* a coin of very low value. **2** a small child. **3** any of many kinds of tiny animals similar to spiders. **4** *nu* a tiny bit.

mitigate ('mıtıgeıt) *vt* lessen; make (a punishment, etc.) less severe.

mitre *US* **miter** ('maıtə*) *nc* **1** a tall hat worn by Christian bishops, etc. **2** a joint made between two pieces of wood, etc., in the middle of the angle between them: see picture. ● *vt* make a mitre joint between (two pieces).

mitre

mitten ('mıtən) *nc* **1** a glove that reaches only to the bottom of each finger. **2** a glove with one cover for all four fingers together and a separate one for the thumb.

mix (mıks) *vt* **1** put (substances, liquids, etc.) together, esp. by stirring. **2** make (a substance) by mixing others together: *I'll mix you a drink.* *vi* **3** be able to be mixed: *Oil* *and water don't mix.* **4** meet people: *One should try to mix at a party.* ● *nc infml* See **mixture.** **mixed** *adj* **1** made by mixing. **2** for people of both sexes, different races, etc.: *a mixed school; mixed sport.* **mixer** *nc* a machine for mixing food, cement, etc. **a good** or **bad mixer** a person who gets on well or badly with all kinds of people. **mixture** ('mɪkstʃə*) *nc* also **mix** a combination of different elements; blend; variety. **mix up 1** confuse: *I mix him up with his brother.* **2** involve: *mixed up in crime.*

mnemonic (nɪ'mɒnɪk) *nc, adj* (a word, phrase, rhyme, etc.) that helps one to remember something.

moan (məʊn) *nc* **1** a cry of pain; groan. **2** *infml* a complaint or grumble: *We're having a moan about working hours.* ● *vi* **1** cry or groan with pain. **2** *infml* complain or grumble.

moat (məʊt) *nc* a broad ditch full of water surrounding a castle.

mob (mɒb) *nc* a crowd excited by friendliness or hostility. ● *vt* crowd excitedly round (a famous person, building, etc.) in friendliness or hostility.

mobile ('məʊbaɪl) *adj* **1** able to move or be moved. **2** provided with a means of transport. **3** that can change expression quickly: *He has mobile features.* ● *nc* a hanging ornament made of parts that spin round in a current of air. **mobilise** ('məʊbɪlaɪz) *vti* gather (armed forces, etc.) together for action. **mobility** (mə'bɪlɪtɪ) *nu* ability to move. **social mobility** movement from one social class to another.

moccasin ('mɒkəsɪn) *nc* a soft leather shoe originally worn by North American Indians.

mock (mɒk) *vti* (when *vi,* often followed by **at**) make fun (of): *Don't mock him—he's doing his best.* ● *adj* imitation; pretended: *A mock exam is a practice for the real thing.* **mockery** ('mɒkərɪ) **1** *nu* the act of mocking. **2** *nc, pl* -**ries** a meaningless performance of something serious.

mode (məʊd) *nc* **1** a means; method; way: *Many modes of transport are used in the mountains.* **2** a fashion; fashionable style.

model ('mɒdəl) *nc* **1** a pattern; example to be copied; person whose picture is painted by an artist. **2** a tiny copy of something. **3** a perfect example: *He was a model of good behaviour.* **4** an article of dress designed to set a style. **5** a person who wears new fashions at shows or for advertisement: *a fashion model.* ● *adj* deserving to be copied. ● *vt* **1** form (clay, etc.) into the shape of (someone's head, etc.). **2** make a tiny copy of. **3** wear (clothes) as a fashion model. **4** *vi* act as an artist's model.

moderate ('mɒdərɪt) *adj* **1** medium; neither strong nor weak, etc. **2** (of opinions, etc.) reasonable; not extreme. ● *nc* a person with moderate political views. ● ('mɒdəreɪt) *vti* (cause to) become moderate: *You ought to moderate your drinking.* **moderately** *adv* **moderation** (,mɒdə'reɪʃən) *nu* the state of being moderate; reasonableness.

modern ('mɒdən) *adj* **1** to do with the present or the recent past. **2** of the time since the end of the Middle Ages (about 1500). **modernise** ('mɒdənaɪz) *vt* make modern; bring up to date; add a bathroom, etc., to (a house). **modernisation** (,mɒdənaɪ'zeɪʃən) *nu*

modest ('mɒdɪst) *adj* **1** (of a person) who does not boast of his qualities; humble. **2** fairly small; moderate: *modest beginnings; a modest house.* **3** decent; pure. **modestly** *adv* **modesty** *nu*

modify ('mɒdɪfaɪ) *vt* change the sense, character, etc., of. **modification** (,mɒdɪfɪ'keɪʃən) *ncu* **modifier** *nc* a word that modifies another.

modulate ('mɒdjʊleɪt) **1** *vt* alter the pitch or frequency of (a sound, electrical signal, etc.). **2** *music vi* move into another key.

module ('mɒdjuːl) *nc* **1** a separate part of a spacecraft: *a landing module.* **2** an original unit of size from which larger parts of things are designed.

mohair ('məʊheə*) *nu* a hairy cloth made from the long hair of the Angora goat.

Mohammedan (mə'hæmɪdən) *n, adj* See **Muslim. Mohammedanism** *n* See **Islam** (def. 1).

moist (mɔɪst) *adj* damp; slightly wet. **moisten** ('mɔɪsən) *vt* make moist. **moisture** ('mɔɪstʃə*) *nu* dampness, slight wetness.

molar ('məʊlə*) *nc, adj* (to do with) one of the large teeth near the back of the mouth.

molasses (mə'læsɪz) *nu* a thick brown liquid obtained from raw sugar, esp. fed to cattle.

mold (məʊld) *US n, v* See **mould**[1,2].

molder ('məʊldə*) *US v* See **moulder**.

molding ('məʊldɪŋ) *US n* See **moulding**.

mole[1] (məʊl) *nc* **1** a small furry animal that lives underground. **2** *infml* an employee of a government organisation who gives its secrets to an enemy of his nation. **molehill** ('məʊlhɪl) *nc* a small pile of earth pushed above the surface by a mole as it digs. **make a mountain out of a molehill** make a great fuss over a small matter.

mole[2] *nc* a black or brown spot on the skin.

molecule ('mɒlɪkjuːl) *nc* the smallest possible quantity of a chemical compound. **molecular** (mə'lekjʊlə*) *adj*

molest (mə'lest) *vt* **1** annoy or trouble (someone). **2** interfere with (someone) sexually.

mollusc ('mɒləsk) *nc* one of a class of animals with shells and soft bodies, including snails and oysters.

molt (məʊlt) *US v, n* See **moult**.

molten ('məʊltən) *adj* **1** (of metals, etc.) melted; liquid. **2** made from melted metal.

moment ('məʊmənt) **1** *nc* a very short time. **2** *nu* importance. **at the moment** just now; at present. **for the moment** for now; for the present. **the moment** as soon as: *The moment he comes, you can go.* **momentary** ('məʊməntərɪ) *adj* lasting only a moment. **momentarily** ('məʊməntərəlɪ) *adv*

momentous (mə'mentəs) *adj* fateful; very important: *a momentous decision.*

momentum (mə'mentəm) *nu* the force that causes a moving object to continue moving.

monarch ('mɒnək) *nc* **1** a king, queen, emperor, etc. **2** a ruler: *He is monarch of all around him.* **monarchy** ('mɒnəkɪ) **1** *nu* the existence of a monarch. *nc, pl* **-chies 2** a system of monarchy. **3** a country with a monarch.

monastery ('mɒnəstrɪ) *nc, pl* **-ries** a place where monks live together.

Monday ('mʌndɪ) *nc* the second day of the week, after Sunday and before Tuesday.

monetary ('mʌnɪtərɪ) *adj* to do with money. **monetarist** *nc, adj* (a person) believing that the best way to control the economy of a country is by controlling the supply of money.

money ('mʌnɪ) *nu* **1** banknotes and coins, for which things are sold and with which things are bought. **2** wealth. **money-box** *nc* a locked box in which to save or collect coins, which can be put in through a narrow hole. **money order** an order to a post office for money to be paid to a named person at another post office.

mongoose ('mɒnguːs) *nc, pl* **-s** a small animal, found esp. in India, that kills poisonous snakes: see picture at **animals.**

mongrel ('mʌngrəl) *nc, adj* (an animal, esp. a dog) of mixed breeds.

monitor ('mɒnɪtə*) *nc* **1** a person or machine that checks or makes a record of an activity. **2** a child at school who helps a teacher, esp. by organising other children. **3** a television used to observe and check the programmes being sent out. ●*vt* check or make a record of (an activity).

monk (mʌŋk) *nc* a man who joins others in leading a simple, religious life.

monkey ('mʌŋkɪ) *nc, pl* **-s 1** any of many kinds of animal that are closely related to man: see picture at **animals. 2** *infml* a playful or naughty person, esp. a child. ●*vi* *infml* (often followed by **about, with,** etc.) play naughtily; interfere (with machines, etc.).

monochrome ('mɒnəkrəʊm) *nu, adj* **1** (of paintings, printing, etc.) (in) one colour. **2** (of films, television, etc.) black and white.

monogamy (mə'nɒgəmɪ) *nu* marriage to one wife or husband at a time.

monogram ('mɒnəgræm) *nc* a pattern made from two or more letters, usually the first letters of a person's names, and used to ornament handkerchiefs, etc.

monologue ('mɒnəlɒg) *theatre nc* **1** a long speech by one actor in a play. **2** a piece written for only one actor to speak.

monopoly (mə'nɒpəlɪ) *nc, pl* **-lies 1** control of all sales of a particular product. **2** a company that has a monopoly. **3** the largest claim (on); the greatest part: *Her children have the monopoly of her attention.* **Monopoly** *Trademark nu* a board game for two or more players, concerned with buying property in any of several large cities of the world.

monotony (mə'nɒtənɪ) *nu* **1** lack of variety; dullness. **2** (of music or a voice) sameness of tone. **monotonous** *adj*

monoxide (mə'nɒksaɪd) *nc* a chemical compound containing one atom of oxygen in each molecule: *carbon monoxide (symbol CO).*

monsoon (mɒn'suːn) *nc* a strong, seasonal wind in south-east Asia, esp. one bringing heavy rain in the summer.

monster ('mɒnstə*) *nc* **1** a huge, esp. imaginary animal: *the Loch Ness Monster.* **2** a very cruel or evil person. ●*adj* huge; larger than life.

monstrous ('mɒnstrəs) *adj* **1** huge; enormous. **2** shocking; disgraceful: *a monstrous crime.*

montage (mɒn'tɑːʒ) **1** *nu* choosing and putting together material for a film. **2** *ncu* (the preparing of) several photographs which are made into one.

month (mʌnθ) *nc* **1** one of the twelve divisions of the year, of between twenty-eight and thirty-one days. **2** the time between a date in one month and the same date in the next month, such as from 6 May to 6 June. **monthly** ('mʌnθlɪ) *adj, adv* (that happens) every month; once a month. ●*nc, pl* **-lies** a monthly magazine, etc.

monument ('mɒnjʊmənt) *nc* **1** a statue or other memorial built in honour of a dead person. **2** a permanent reminder of people or events of the past: *The laws he brought in are a monument to his efforts.* **monumental** (ˌmɒnjʊ'mentəl) *adj* **1** serving as a monument. **2** great; lasting: *a monumental piece of work.* **3** remarkable: *a monumental failure.*

moo (muː) *nc, interj* a sound made by a cow. ●*vi* (of a cow) give a moo.

mood¹ (muːd) *nc* a state of mind or feeling. **moody** *adj* **-ier, -iest** (of a person) **1** whose state of mind or feeling varies a lot. **2** bad-tempered.

mood² *grammar nc* any of the classes into which verbs are divided according to whether they express statements, wishes, orders, etc.

moon (muːn) **1** *nc* a planet that moves around a larger planet. *nu* **2** the moon that goes around Earth. **3** the moon as seen from Earth: *There will be a full moon tonight.* **moon about** wander about without an aim. **moonlight** (ˈmuːnlaɪt) *nu* the light of the moon. ● *vi infml* do an extra job in the evenings to earn more money.

moor¹ (mʊə*) *ncu* (a stretch of) open, bare land.

moor² **1** *vt* tie up (a ship). **2** *vi* (of a ship) be tied up.

moose (muːs) *nc, pl* **moose** a large kind of deer found in the north of America and Europe: see picture.

moose

mop (mɒp) *nc* **1** a number of pieces of thick string, etc., on the end of a long handle, used to soak up liquid, clean floors, etc.: see picture. **2** *infml* hair that is untidy like the head of a mop. ● *vt* clean (a floor) with a mop. **mop up 1** soak up (water on the floor, etc.) with a mop. **2** deal with: *The army mopped up the last pockets of resistance.*

mop

mope (məʊp) *vi* be miserable or depressed.

moped (ˈməʊped) *nc* a bicycle powered by a small petrol engine.

moral (ˈmɒrəl) *adj* **1** to do with (a sense of) right and wrong. **2** (of actions, etc.) right; good. ● *nc* a lesson that can be learned from an experience, story, etc. **morals** principles; ideas of how to behave. **morally** *adv*

morale (məˈrɑːl) *nu* confidence; belief in one's cause: *Soldiers' morale is good after a victory.*

morality (məˈrælɪtɪ) **1** *nc, pl* **-ties** a system of morals. **2** *nu* rightness.

morass (məˈræs) *nc* a bog; stretch of muddy land.

morbid (ˈmɔːbɪd) *adj* **1** diseased; to do with disease: *a morbid growth.* **2** unusually concerned with death: *morbid thoughts.*

more (mɔː*) *determiner, pron* **1** a larger quantity (of): *I have more books than you.* **2** a further quantity (of): *Would you like some more?* ● *adv* **1** (used to form comparatives) to a greater degree: *The town is more crowded than I had expected.* **2** further; else; besides: *There's nothing more to be said.* **3** again: *We've been there once more.* **more and more** even more; increasingly. **more or less 1** roughly; approximately: *There are twenty, more or less.* **2** near enough; as good as: *The battle is more or less over.*

moreover (mɔːˈrəʊvə*) *adv* besides; also.

morgue (mɔːg) *n* See **mortuary.**

Mormon (ˈmɔːmən) *nc, adj* (a member) of the Church of Jesus Christ of Latter-day Saints, started in the USA in 1830.

morn (mɔːn) *poetry nc* a morning.

morning (ˈmɔːnɪŋ) *nc* **1** the part of a day between dawn and noon. **2** *poetry* the early part: *the morning of life.* ● *adj* of the morning; that happens in the morning.

moron (ˈmɔːrɒn) *nc* a person with the mental age of a child.

morose (məˈrəʊs) *adj* bad-tempered; moody.

morphine (ˈmɔːfiːn) also **morphia** (ˈmɔːfɪə) *nu* a pain-killing drug.

morrow (ˈmɒrəʊ) *literary nu* **1** tomorrow. **2** the next day.

Morse (mɔːs) *nu* also **Morse code** a system of dots and dashes that represent the letters of the alphabet for signalling.

morsel (ˈmɔːsəl) *nc* a mouthful; small piece of food.

mortal (ˈmɔːtəl) *adj* **1** whose life will end in death; subject to death: *We are all mortal.* **2** that causes death: *a mortal wound.* **3** until death: *They are mortal enemies.* ● *nc* a human being. **mortally** *adv* **1** in such a way, or to such an extent, as to cause death: *He is mortally ill.* **2** very; greatly: *She was mortally offended.* **mortality** (mɔːˈtælɪtɪ) *nu* **1** the quality of being **mortal** (def. 1). **2** the number of deaths in a period: *The child mortality figures are improving.*

mortar (ˈmɔːtə*) **1** *nu* a mixture of lime, sand, and water that sets hard when it dries and is used to keep the bricks or stones of a building together. *nc* **2** a short heavy gun that can fire shells at high angles. **3** a strong bowl in which substances are broken up into powder.

mortgage (ˈmɔːgɪdʒ) *nc* a loan made to a person so that he can buy a house, the house being the security for the loan. ● *vt* offer (a house) as security for a loan of money.

mortify (ˈmɔːtɪfaɪ) *vt* make (someone) feel shame: *He was mortified by her dislike of him.*

mortuary (ˈmɔːtjʊərɪ) *nc, pl* **-ries** also **morgue** a place where dead bodies are kept before being buried.

mosaic (məˈzeɪɪk) *nc* a picture or pattern made from small pieces of coloured stone.

Moslem (ˈmɒzləm) *n, adj* See **Muslim.**

mosque (mɒsk) *nc* a building where Muslims have religious services.

mosquito (mɒsˈkiːtəʊ) *nc, pl* **-s, -es** one of several kinds of insect that can give people malaria when they suck blood from them: see picture at **insects.**

moss (mɒs) *nc, pl* **-es** any of various soft, thick plants that grow on wet surfaces. **mossy** *adj* **-ier, -iest** covered with moss.

most (məʊst) *determiner, pron* **1** the greatest quantity (of): *The big towns have the most television sets.* **2** the greater number (of); majority (of): *Most people eat cake sometimes.* ● *adv* **1** very: *That's most kind of you.* **2** (used to form superlatives) to the greatest degree: *the most beautiful flower I have seen.* ● *nu* the best thing: *The most one can say of him is that he is kind.* **at the most** at the highest guess or estimate: *There were fifty people there at the most.*

mostly *adv* **1** also **for the most part** chiefly; mainly: *The people here are mostly farmers.* **2** usually; most often: *We mostly go away for the weekend.*

motel (məʊˈtel) *chiefly US nc* a hotel for motorists where one can park a car just outside each room.

moth (mɒθ) *nc* any of many kinds of dull-coloured insects that fly by night: see picture at **insects.**

mother (ˈmʌðə*) (*infml abbrevs.* **ma, mum, mummy**) *nc* **1** a female parent. **2** the source; origin: *Greece, the mother of the arts.* ● *vt* look after (someone) like a mother. **mother country 1** one's native country. **2** the home country from which people have gone to develop new countries. **mother-in-law** (ˈmʌðərɪnˌlɔː) *nc, pl* **mothers-in-law** the mother of one's husband or wife. **mother tongue** the language one learns as a small child. **motherhood** (ˈmʌðəhʊd) *nu* the state of being a mother. **motherly** (ˈmʌðəlɪ) *adj* to do with or like a mother.

motion (ˈməʊʃən) **1** *ncu* (a) movement. **2** *nc* a proposal for discussion at a meeting. **3** an emptying of the bowels. **set in motion** start

(a machine or chain of events). **motionless** (ˈməʊʃənlɪs) *adj* completely still; not moving. **motion-picture** *nc* a film for the cinema.

motivate (ˈməʊtɪveɪt) *vt* provide (someone) with a motive; encourage. **motivation** (ˌməʊtɪˈveɪʃən) *nu*

motive (ˈməʊtɪv) *nc* a reason (for an action). ● *adj* causing motion; that makes someone act: *motive force.*

motley (ˈmɒtlɪ) *adj* **1** mixed; varied: *a motley crowd of people.* **2** of many colours.

motor (ˈməʊtə*) *nc* **1** a kind of engine that makes vehicles move. **2** also **electric motor** a device in which electricity produces a turning movement. **3** *infml* a car, motor car. ● *adj* to do with movement; that causes movement in the body: *motor nerves.* ● *vi* go by car. **motorbike** *infml n* See **motorcycle. motorboat** (ˈməʊtəbəʊt) *nc* a small boat powered by a motor. **motorcade** (ˈməʊtəkeɪd) *nc* a procession of cars containing important people. **motor car** See **car. motorcycle** (ˈməʊtəˌsaɪkəl) *nc* also **motorbike** a vehicle with two wheels and an engine: see picture. ● *vi* ride a motorcycle. **motorise** (ˈməʊtəraɪz) *vt* provide (someone) with motor vehicles. **motorist** (ˈməʊtərɪst) *nc* a person who drives a car. **motor-racing** *nu* racing among drivers of very fast cars. **motorway** (ˈməʊtəweɪ) *nc* a specially built road for fast motor traffic only.

motorcycle

motto (ˈmɒtəʊ) *nc, pl* **-es** a phrase chosen by a family or an organisation to express its aims.

mould¹ *US* **mold** (məʊld) *nc* **1** a container into which a hot liquid is poured and from which it takes its shape when it cools and becomes solid. **2** a particular way in which a person has been trained or influenced: *a politician in the Marxist mould.* ● *vt* **1** shape in a mould: *moulded plastic.* **2** influence or train (someone).

mould² *US* **mold** *nu* a growth of fungus on things that have been warm and damp.

moulder *US* **molder** (ˈməʊldə*) *vi* be destroyed by mould; decay.

moulding *US* **molding** (ˈməʊldɪŋ) **1** *nu* shaping, influencing. **2** *nc* a piece of shaped wood or stone on or around a door, etc.

moult *US* **molt** (məʊlt) *vi* (of some birds and animals) lose its feathers, skin, etc. ● *nc* the process of losing feathers or skin.

mound (maʊnd) *nc* **1** a very small hill. **2** a bank of earth or stones built as a protection. **3** *infml* a huge heap: *a mound of papers to be read.*

mount¹ (maʊnt) *vt* **1** get up onto (a horse, etc.). **2** climb or go up (stairs, a hill, etc.). **3** arrange and fix (pictures, jewels, heavy guns, etc.) in position. **4** prepare (a play, exhibition, etc.) for public showing. **5** put (an operation) into action. **6** *vi* increase; grow; rise: *mounting excitement.* ● *nc* **1** an animal to ride on. **2** a support or frame for guns, pictures, etc.

mount² *nc* **1** *sometimes poetry* a mountain. **2** *(with capital letter)* the title of a mountain: *Mount Tabor.*

mountain (ˈmaʊntɪn) *nc* **1** a high hill. **2** *infml* a huge heap: *She gets through a mountain of work every day.* **mountain range** a group or row of mountains. **mountaineer** (ˌmaʊntɪˈnɪə*) *nc* a person who climbs mountains. **mountaineering** (ˌmaʊntɪˈnɪərɪŋ) *nu* the sport of climbing mountains. **mountainous** (ˈmaʊntɪnəs) *adj* **1** (of country) with many mountains. **2** like a mountain. **mountainside** (ˈmaʊntɪnˌsaɪd) *nu* the sloping side of a mountain.

mourn (mɔːn) *vti* grieve (for), lament (anything sad, esp. a death). **mourner** *nc* **1** a relative or friend of a dead person who attends the funeral. **2** a person who mourns. **mournful** *adj* sad; full of grief. **mournfully** *adv* **mourning** *nu* **1** grieving; lamenting. **2** black clothes worn as a sign of grief.

mouse (maʊs) *nc, pl* **mice 1** an animal with a long tail, like a rat but smaller: see picture. **2** a timid quiet person. ● (maʊz) *vi* (of a cat) hunt mice.

mouse

moustache *US* **mustache** (məsˈtɑːʃ) *nc* hair that grows on a man's upper lip.

mouth (maʊθ) *nc, pl* **-ths** (ðz) *nc* **1** the opening in an animal's head through which it makes sounds and takes in food. **2** a person considered as an eater of food: *There are six mouths to feed in this house.* **3** the place where a river reaches the sea. **4** the opening of a bay, etc. ● (maʊð) *vt* move one's mouth to make (words) but without speaking. **mouthful** *nc* **1** the amount of food a person can chew and swallow comfortably at a time. **2** *infml* a long and complicated word. **mouthpiece** (ˈmaʊθpiːs) *nc* **1** the part of a musical instrument, etc., which the player or user puts to or into his mouth. **2** a person who speaks for an organisation.

movable (ˈmuːvəbəl) *adj* able to be moved. **movable feast** one of the important dates in the Christian calendar that occur on a different date each year.

move (muːv) *vti* **1** go or take from one place to another. **2** go to live in another (house). *vi* **3** go to another job. **4** take action. *vt* **5** cause (someone) (to do something). **6** affect the feelings of: *The audience was deeply moved by her singing.* **7** recommend or propose (an action) formally at a meeting. ● *nc* **1** an action: *He made a move to obtain control of the company.* **2** a change of house or job. **3** a moving of a counter, etc., in a game: *It's your move.* **get a move on** *infml* hurry. **move along 1** walk on; keep walking. **2** go further along (a bus, etc.). **move in 1** come or go to live in a house. **2** move closer (to deal with something): *The soldiers moved in to capture the town.* **move off** start off; (of a procession, etc.) leave the place where it has gathered. **move out 1** leave (a house where one has been living). **2** (of an army, etc.) leave (a town).

movement (ˈmuːvmənt) *nc* **1** a change of one's position. **2** some or all of the moving parts of a machine: *the movement of a clock.* **3** an organised activity: *a youth movement.* **4** a section of a long piece of instrumental music. **5** an emptying of the bowels.

movie (ˈmuːvɪ) *chiefly US, infml nc* a film for the cinema. **the movies** a cinema: *Let's go to the movies.*

mow (məʊ) *vt* cut the (grass) in (a field, etc.). **mow down** knock or shoot (people) down.

mown (məʊn) past participle of **mow.**

much (mʌtʃ) *adv* a lot; greatly. ● *determiner, pron* a lot (of); a large quantity (of). **how much 1** how great a quantity (of money): *How much does that fruit cost?* **2** to what extent. **make much of 1** make a fuss of or pay a lot of attention to (someone). **2** treat (something) as important. **3** succeed in understanding: *I couldn't make much of what he said.* **much the same** nearly the same; similar. **not think much of** have a low opinion of. **think too much of** have a higher opinion of (a person or thing) than he or it deserves.

muck (mʌk) *nu* dirt, esp. manure. ● *v* **muck in** *infml* share work (with others). **muck out** clean out (buildings where horses are kept). **muck up** *infml* **1** make (something) dirty. **2** spoil; handle (a situation) badly.

mucous ('mjuːkəs) *adj* **1** like mucus. **2** that produces mucus.

mucus ('mjuːkəs) *nu* a sticky substance produced by the lining of the throat, nose, etc.

mud (mʌd) *nu* very wet earth. **muddy** *adj* **-ier, -iest 1** full of or covered with mud. **2** not clear: *a muddy colour.* ● *vt* get mud on (something). **mudguard** ('mʌdgɑːd) *US* **fender** *nc* a metal cover for each wheel of a vehicle to stop mud from flying up.

muddle ('mʌdəl) *nc* a state of untidiness or confusion. ● *vt* confuse; get (someone or something) into a muddle. **muddle through** overcome a problem in a disorganised way.

muffin ('mʌfin) *nc* a kind of small bread roll, eaten hot, with butter.

muffle ('mʌfəl) *vt* **1** wrap (oneself) up to be warm. **2** quieten the sound of. **muffler** *nc* a long, narrow scarf.

mug¹ (mʌg) *nc* **1** a large kind of cup with straight sides: see picture. **2** *infml, derogatory* face; mouth.

mug

mug² *infml nc* a person who is easily deceived.

mug³ *vti* attack (a person) in order to steal from him. **mugger** *nc* **mugging** *ncu*

muggy ('mʌgɪ) *adj* **-ier, -iest** (of the air) unpleasantly warm and damp.

mulatto (mjʊ'lætəʊ) *old-fashioned nc, pl* **-s** *US* **-es** a person of mixed black and white race.

mulberry ('mʌlbərɪ) *nc, pl* **-ries 1** a small dark purple fruit that can be eaten. **2** the tree on which this fruit grows.

mule (mjuːl) *nc* **1** an animal that has a horse and a donkey for parents. **2** a shoe that covers only the front part of the foot.

mull¹ (mʌl) *v* **mull over** consider (an idea) carefully, think (a thing) over thoroughly.

mull² *vt* heat and add spices, etc. to (wine, etc.).

mullet ('mʌlɪt) *nc* any of various kinds of sea-fish that can be eaten.

multicoloured ('mʌltɪˌkʌləd) *adj* of many colours.

multifarious (ˌmʌltɪ'feərɪəs) *adj* (of activities, etc.) many and varied.

multilateral (ˌmʌltɪ'lætərəl) *adj* **1** having many sides. **2** (of discussions, etc.) in which many people or sides take part.

multinational (ˌmʌltɪ'næʃənəl) *nc, adj* (a business company) which operates in more than one country.

multiple ('mʌltɪpəl) *adj* more than one: *multiple births.* ● *nc* a quantity which contains another quantity an exact number of times: *Fourteen is a multiple of seven.*

multiply ('mʌltɪplaɪ) **1** *vt* increase (a number) by a given number of times: *Two multiplied by three is six.* **2** *vti* (cause to) increase (greatly): *They have multiplied their profits since they opened their new factory.* **multiplication** (ˌmʌltɪplɪ'keɪʃən) *nu* **multiplicand** (ˌmʌltɪplɪ'kænd) *nc* a number being multiplied. **multiplier** *nc* a number by which another is multiplied.

multitude ('mʌltɪtjuːd) *nc* **1** a large crowd. **2** a large number (of things). **the multitude** the common people.

mum¹ (mʌm) *infml n* short for **mother.**

mum² *infml adj* silent or quiet about a subject: *Keep mum; Mum's the word.*

mumble ('mʌmbəl) *vti* say (words) quietly and unclearly. ● *nc* something mumbled.

mummy¹ ('mʌmɪ) *infml n, pl* **-mies** short for **mother.**

mummy² *nc, pl* **-mies** a preserved dead body, esp. from Egypt long ago.

mumps (mʌmps) *nu (with singular verb)* disease which is caught from other people and causes the neck to swell.

munch (mʌntʃ) *vti* chew (food) thoroughly.

municipal (mjuː'nɪsɪpəl) *adj* to do with a town or city (council). **municipality** (mjuːˌnɪsɪ'pælɪtɪ) *nc, pl* **-ties** a town that has its own local council.

munitions (mjuː'nɪʃənz) *n pl* weapons of war.

mural ('mjʊərəl) *nc* a large picture painted on a wall. ● *adj* to do with walls.

murder ('mɜːdə*) **1** *nc* the unlawful killing of a person. **2** *infml nu* a painful, dangerous, etc., experience. ● *vt* **1** kill (a person) unlawfully. **2** *infml* play (music), read (a poem, etc.) very badly. **murderer** *nc* **murderous** ('mɜːdərəs) *adj* **1** to do with murder. **2** violent or dangerous enough to kill: *a murderous blow.*

murky ('mɜːkɪ) *adj* **-ier, -iest 1** dark. **2** mysterious: *his murky past.*

murmur ('mɜːmə*) *nc* **1** a slight continuing sound not clearly heard: *a murmur of conversation.* **2** something said very quietly. **3** a complaint: *murmurs of discontent.* ● *vt* **1** say (something) in a murmur. **2** *vi* (of a stream) make a gentle sound as it flows.

muscle ('mʌsəl) **1** *ncu* a particular piece of tissue in a body which can be made to shorten itself to move a part of the body. **2** *nu* strength; power. **muscle in** (often followed by **on**) push or force one's way (into). **muscular** ('mʌskjʊlə*) *adj* 1 to do with muscles. 2 (of a man) with powerful muscles.

muse (mju:z) *vi* reflect; think; meditate. ● *nc* also **Muse** one of the nine spirits believed by the ancient Greeks to inspire art and learning.

museum (mju:'zɪəm) *nc* a building where works of art or interesting objects of any kind are collected and displayed to the public.

mush (mʌʃ) *nu* partly liquid food that is easy to swallow. **mushy** *adj* **-ier, -iest** 1 (of food) partly liquid. 2 (of music, etc.) over-sentimental.

mushroom ('mʌʃrʊm) *nc* fungi with thick stems and flat or pointed tops, some of which can be eaten: see picture. ● *vi* (of businesses, etc.) start or appear very quickly.

mushroom

music ('mju:zɪk) *nu* 1 a connected series of sounds that are pleasant to listen to. 2 a beautiful sound: *The news of the victory was music to their ears.* 3 the art of playing or writing music. 4 the written or printed notes of music. **musical** ('mju:zɪkəl) *adj* 1 to do with music. 2 (of sounds) pleasant to listen to. 3 (of persons) able to play music or sing pleasantly. ● *nc* a film with many songs and dances. **musician** (mju:'zɪʃən) *nc* 1 a person who plays an instrument or sings, esp. in public to make a living. 2 a person who understands and interprets music well. 3 a person who writes music.

musk (mʌsk) *nu* a substance used in perfumes, obtained from the glands of male deer.

musket ('mʌskɪt) *nc* a long shoulder-gun formerly used by soldiers.

Muslim ('mʊzlɪm) also **Mohammedan, Moslem** *nc* a follower of Islam. ● *adj* to do with Muslims; Islamic.

muslin ('mʌzlɪn) *nu* a thin, open, cotton cloth used for garments and to strain butter and cheese.

mussel ('mʌsəl) *nc* a shellfish that can be eaten, with a black shell in two halves.

must (mʌst unstressed məst, məs) *v* 1 be obliged to, have it as one's duty to: *We must pay the price.* 2 be certain to: *You must win some time.* **must not** not be allowed to: *We must not smoke here.* ● *nc* something that must be done, bought, etc.

mustache (məs'tɑ:ʃ) *US n* See **moustache.**

mustang ('mʌstæŋ) *nc* a wild North American horse.

mustard ('mʌstəd) 1 *ncu* (a type of) sharp-tasting yellow or brown paste used in food. 2 *nu* the plant of which the seeds are made into mustard.

muster ('mʌstə*) 1 *vt* gather (soldiers, supporters, etc.) together. 2 *vi* (of soldiers, supporters, etc.) gather together. ● *nc* such a gathering.

mustn't ('mʌsənt) *v* must not.

musty ('mʌstɪ) *adj* **-ier, -iest** smelling or tasting mouldy or stale.

mutation (mju:'teɪʃən) *ncu* 1 (a) change in a new plant or animal. 2 (in language) a sound change under certain conditions.

mute (mju:t) *adj*, **-r, -st** 1 dumb; unable to speak. 2 silent. 3 not said: *a mute e.* ● *nc* a person who cannot speak.

mutilate ('mju:tɪleɪt) *vt* seriously injure or damage. **mutilation** (,mju:tɪ'leɪʃən) *ncu*

mutiny ('mju:tɪnɪ) *ncu, pl* **-nies** (a) revolt or rebellion in the armed forces. ● *vi* take part in a mutiny. **mutineer** (,mju:tɪ'nɪə*) *nc* a person who mutinies.

mutter ('mʌtə*) 1 *vti* speak (words) quietly and unclearly. 2 *vi* complain quietly. ● *nc* 1 something spoken quietly and unclearly. 2 a quiet complaint.

mutton ('mʌtən) *nu* meat from a sheep.

mutual ('mju:tjʊəl) *adj* 1 (of an emotion, etc.) felt by each of two people for each other: *mutual respect.* 2 to do with or belonging to both or all; shared: *This is in our mutual interest.* **mutually** *adv*

muzzle ('mʌzəl) *nc* 1 the projecting mouth and nose of some animals. 2 a cage or strap that is put over a dog's muzzle to prevent it from biting people. 3 a limit on freedom, esp. of expression. 4 the mouth of a gun. ● *vt* 1 put a muzzle on (a dog). 2 limit the freedom of: *muzzled press.*

my (maɪ) *determiner* belonging or to do with me: *This is my house.* ● *interj* what a surprise!

myopia (maɪ'əʊpɪə) *nu* short-sightedness; inability to see distant things clearly.

myriad ('mɪrɪəd) *literary nc* a large number. ● *adj* in large numbers: *There were myriad flowers in the field.*

myrrh (mɜ:) *nu* a kind of gum used in some perfumes.

myrtle ('mɜ:təl) *nu* a large evergreen plant with shiny leaves and sweet-smelling white flowers.

myself (maɪ'self) *pron* 1 (used to refer back to the speaker or writer): *I made myself work; I did it myself.* 2 in my normal state: *I don't feel myself today.* **by myself** 1 without help. 2 alone.

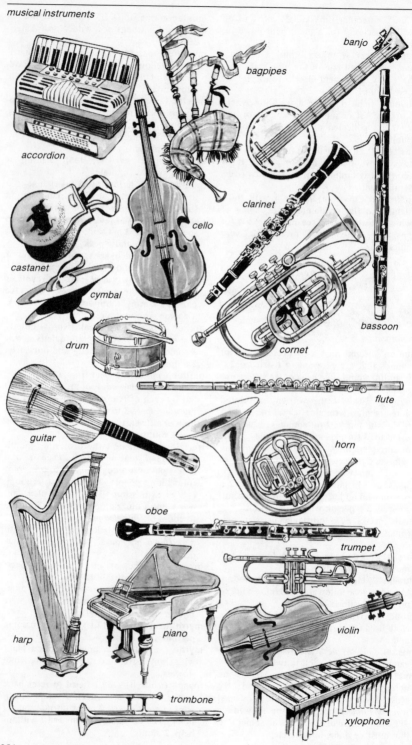

mystery ('mɪstərɪ) **1** *nu* the state of being un-known or secret. *nc, pl* **-ries 2** an unsolved puzzle. **3** a story describing the solving of a crime of murder. **mysterious** (mɪ'stɪərɪəs) *adj* **1** that cannot be explained. **2** puzzling. **mysteriously** *adv*

mystic ('mɪstɪk) *nc* a person who feels, or seeks to be, united to God. ● *adj* also **mystical 1** of a mystic. **2** to do with mysti-cism. **mysticism** ('mɪstɪsɪzəm) *nu* **1** a feel-ing of union with God. **2** beliefs about, and experiences of, this feeling.

mystify ('mɪstɪfaɪ) *vt* puzzle or confuse (a person).

mystique (mɪ'stiːk) *nu* fear of or wonder at the power or ability of someone or some-thing: *People are attracted by the mystique of the theatre.*

myth (mɪθ) *nc* **1** an ancient story that ex-presses important truths. **2** *infml* an in-vented person or thing. **mythical** ('mɪθɪkəl) *adj*

mythology (mɪ'θɒlədʒɪ) **1** *nc, pl* **-gies** a body of myths. **2** *nu* the study of myths. **mytho-logical** (ˌmɪθə'lɒdʒɪkəl) *adj*

255

N

'n' (ən) *infml conj* short for **and:** *fish 'n' chips.*

nab (næb) *infml vt* get (hold of); seize quickly: *You nab a seat while I get in the queue.*

nag¹ (næg) *nc* **1** a small horse. **2** *derogatory* a horse.

nag² *vti* keep complaining (at) (someone).

nail (neɪl) *nc* **1** a layer of horn on the end of each finger and toe. **2** a long thin piece of metal, pointed at one end and with a head at the other, which can be hammered into a wall, etc.: see picture. ● *vt* fix (something) to a wall, etc., with a nail. **hit the nail on the head** say or do something that is exactly right.

nail

naive (naɪˈiːv) *adj* new to the ways of the world; innocent.

naked (ˈneɪkɪd) *adj* **1** without any clothes on. **2** with no defence or protection. **3** (of evil intentions, etc.) undisguised: *naked aggression.* **nakedness** *nu*

name (neɪm) **1** *nc* the word by which a person, animal, plant, or thing is called and known. **2** *nu* reputation: *It's a shop with a very good name.* ● *vt* **1** give a name to: *I name this child Elizabeth.* **2** put the correct name to. **3** appoint (someone): *He has been named the new president.* **call (someone) names** insult (someone). **make a name for oneself** become well known; make a reputation. **nameless** *adj* **1** without a name; unnamed. **2** too horrible to describe: *nameless crimes.* **namesake** (ˈneɪmseɪk) *nc* a person who has the same name as someone else.

namely (ˈneɪmlɪ) *adv* that is to say: *He was somewhere else, namely at home.*

nap¹ (næp) *nc, vi* (take) a short sleep during the day.

nap² *nu* a hairy finish on cloth.

nape (neɪp) *nc* the back of the neck.

napkin (ˈnæpkɪn) *nc* a piece of cloth used to protect one's clothes while eating.

nappy (ˈnæpɪ) *nc, pl* **-pies** a thick towel or paper pad wrapped around a baby to collect its waste.

narcotic (nɑːˈkɒtɪk) *nc, adj* (a substance) that makes a person sleepy or relieves pain.

narrate (nəˈreɪt) *vt* tell (a story). **narration** (nəˈreɪʃən) *ncu* the telling of a story. **narrative** (ˈnærətɪv) *nc* a story. ● *adj* that tells a story: *a narrative poem.* **narrator** *nc* **1** a storyteller. **2** a person who reads aloud the background story of a radio play, etc.

narrow (ˈnærəʊ) *adj* **-er, -est 1** not wide; thin. **2** (of opinions, etc.) ungenerous; not broad. **3** close: *a narrow escape.* ● *vti* make or become narrow(er). **narrowly** *adv* only just; barely: *We narrowly avoided an accident.* **narrow-minded** *adj* (of a person) with narrow opinions; intolerant.

nasal (ˈneɪzəl) *adj* **1** to do with the nose. **2** spoken or sung through the nose: *a nasal voice.* ● *nc* a nasal sound.

nasty (ˈnɑːstɪ) *adj* **-ier, -iest 1** unpleasant: *a nasty cold.* **2** disagreeable: *He was quite nasty about it.* **3** ugly: *The wrecked plane was a nasty sight.* **4** dangerous: *This is a nasty stretch of road on a wet day.* **nastily** *adv*

nation (ˈneɪʃən) *nc* a group of people, usually with their own language and government. **national** (ˈnæʃənəl) *adj* of or to do with a nation or its country. ● *nc* a citizen of a particular country. **nationality** (ˌnæʃəˈnælɪtɪ) *ncu* the fact of belonging to a particular country. **nationally** *adv* **nationwide** (ˈneɪʃənˌwaɪd) *adj, adv* (applying) over a whole country.

nationalise (ˈnæʃənəlaɪz) *vt* bring (a business or industry) under the ownership of a national government. **nationalisation** (ˌnæʃənəlaɪˈzeɪʃən) *nu*

nationalism (ˈnæʃənəlɪzəm) *nu* **1** the feeling of belonging to a nation. **2** a nation's wish for independence. **nationalist** *adj* to do with nationalism. ● *nc* a supporter of nationalism. **nationalistic** (ˌnæʃənəˈlɪstɪk) *adj*

native (ˈneɪtɪv) *adj* **1** of the place where a person was born: *my native country; their native language.* **2** (of animals and plants) living naturally (in): *a native bird; a bird native to America.* ● *nc* **1** a person born or living in a particular place: *a native of Calcutta.* **2** *old-fashioned, now chiefly derogatory* a local person.

natural (ˈnætʃrəl) *adj* **1** according to nature. **2** to do with nature. **3** given by nature. **4** without artificial additions or procedures: *in its natural state; natural childbirth.* **5** simple and unforced: *natural manners.* **6** (of a musical note) neither sharp nor flat. ● *nc* **1** *music* a note that is neither sharp nor flat.

2 the sign that indicates this in written music. **3** *infml* a person naturally suited (for something). **naturally** *adv* **1** in a natural way. **2** of course: *Naturally, she expected him to come and meet her.* **natural gas** a gas that is found in underground deposits ready to use for heating and cooking. **natural history** the study of animals and plants.

naturalise ('nætʃrəlaɪz) *vt* give nationality to (a foreigner).

naturalist ('nætʃrəlɪst) *nc* a person who studies animals and plants.

nature ('neɪtʃə*) *nu* **1** life and all its processes. **2** the forces that control the working of the physical world. **3** a simple way of life. *nc* **4** a person's character. **5** the character or particular features of a plan, idea, etc. **6** a kind; sort: *We don't want any trouble of that nature.*

naught (nɔːt) *literary or archaic n* See **nought** (def. 2).

naughty ('nɔːtɪ) *adj* **-ier, -iest 1** (of children) behaving badly; not obeying a parent, teacher, etc. **2** indecent; intended to shock: *She sang some rather naughty songs.*

nausea ('nɔːsɪə) *nu* the feeling that one is going to vomit.

nautical ('nɔːtɪkəl) *adj* to do with ships, sailors, or sailing. **nautical mile** a measure of length used for shipping and flying = 1.852 km

naval ('neɪvəl) *adj* **1** to do with a navy. **2** to do with ships.

navel ('neɪvəl) *nc* the place on the abdomen where a cord connected a baby or young animal to its mother before and during birth.

navigable ('nævɪgəbəl) *adj* **1** (of a waterway) able to be sailed along. **2** (of a boat, etc.) able to be steered.

navigate ('nævɪgeɪt) *vti* plan and direct the course of (a ship or plane). **navigation** (ˌnævɪˈgeɪʃən) *nu* **navigator** *nc*

navy ('neɪvɪ) *nc, pl* **-ies** a national force of warships. **navy blue** (a) very dark blue (colour).

nay (neɪ) *adv* **1** *archaic* no. **2** no, rather: *difficult, nay, impossible.* ● *nc* a no.

near (nɪə*) *adj* **-er, -est 1** close: *Go away—you're too near!* **2** just avoided: *a near failure.* ● *prep, adv* close (to). ● *vti* approach; come close (to). **nearby** (nɪəˈbaɪ) *adv,* ('nɪəbaɪ) *adj* not far away. **nearly** *adv* **1** almost. **2** closely. **3** anywhere near: *I'm not nearly tall enough to see over.* **nearness** *nu* closeness. **near-sighted** (ˌnɪəˈsaɪtɪd) *adj* unable to see distant things clearly.

neat (niːt) *adj* **-er, -est 1** tidy; in order. **2** (of an action) smoothly done; efficient. **3** (of alcoholic drinks) with nothing added. **neatly** *adv* **neatness** *nu*

nebula ('nebjʊlə) *nc, pl* **-lae** (liː) a faint, hazy light that comes from very distant stars or gas in space.

nebulous ('nebjʊləs) *adj* (of ideas, etc.) not clearly thought out or expressed; vague.

necessary ('nesəsərɪ) *adj* **1** needed. **2** that must be; inescapable. **necessarily** ('nesəsərɪlɪ, ˌnesəˈserɪlɪ) *adv* unavoidably.

necessitate (nɪˈsesɪteɪt) *vt* cause a need for; make necessary.

necessity (nɪˈsesɪtɪ) **1** *nc, pl* **-ties** a thing that is needed: *the necessities of life. nu* **2** need. **3** poverty.

neck (nek) *nc* **1** the part of the body between the head and the rest of the body. **2** a narrow connecting part of anything. ● *vi infml* kiss or cuddle lovingly. **neck and neck** (of competitors in a race) level with each other. **necklace** ('neklɪs) *nc* an ornamental chain, string of pearls, etc., that a woman wears around her neck. **necktie** ('nektaɪ) *US* See **tie** (def. 2).

nectar ('nektə*) *nu* **1** a substance in flowers that bees collect to make honey. **2** a delicious drink.

née (neɪ) *adj* (of a married woman) born with the name: *Sarah Jones, née Evans.*

need (niːd) *nc* **1** the fact of having to have something: *We must satisfy their needs.* **2** a necessary thing. **3** *nu* poverty. ● *vt* **1** have to have: *Everyone needs food.* **2** be without; lack. **3** *(chiefly interrogative or negative)* have to: *Need we take all this luggage?* **in need of 1** without; lacking. **2** needing: *in need of repair.* **needless** *adj* unnecessary; pointless. **needy** *adj* **-ier, -iest** poor.

needle ('niːdəl) *nc* **1** a metal pin with a point at one end and a hole at the other for a thread, used in sewing: see picture. **2** any of various other kinds of pointed pin used for knitting, playing records, etc. **3** a moving pin that indicates the reading on a measuring instrument, etc. **4** a hollow pin that is stuck into the skin in order to pass a liquid into the body, take blood out, etc. ● *vt* remind (someone) sharply of a duty. **needlework** ('niːdəlwɜːk) *nu* **1** sewing by hand. **2** something sewn by hand.

needle

needn't ('niːdənt) *v* need not.

ne'er (neə*) *poetry adv* short for **never**.

negation (nɪˈgeɪʃən) **1** *nc* a refusal; denial. *nu* **2** the act of undoing; neutralisation. **3** the opposite.

negative ('negətɪv) *adj* **1** (of a number such as −2) less than nothing. **2** (of a verb, statement, etc.) expressing a denial, refusal, failure, etc., through the addition of a word such as 'not', as in 'We shall not be going'. **3** (of an attitude, etc.) not active or helpful; lacking enthusiasm. **4** the opposite of: *A negative tax is really a payment to people.* **5** (of an electric charge) like that of an electron. ●*nc* **1** a photographic film or plate on which light and dark are in the opposite places. **2** a negative verb, statement, etc. ●*vt* **1** reduce to nothing; cancel out. **2** refuse to accept. **negatively** *adv*

neglect (nɪ'glekt) *vt* **1** fail to care for. **2** fail (to do) (something). ●*nu* (followed by **of**) failure to care (for); lack of attention (to). **negligence** ('neglɪdʒəns) *nu* carelessness, failure to take touble. **negligible** ('neglɪdʒəbəl) *adj* so small that it need not be considered.

negotiate (nɪ'gəʊʃɪeɪt) *vt* **1** reach (an agreement) by discussion. **2** make one's way through, round, etc. (a difficulty, etc.). **negotiation** (nɪ,gəʊʃɪ'eɪʃən) *ncu*

Negro ('niːgrəʊ) *nc, pl* **-es**, *adj* (of or to do with) a black person, of African origin. **Negroid** ('niːgrɔɪd) *adj* to do with the black races of African origin with thick lips and very curly hair.

neigh (neɪ) *vi* (of a horse) give a cry. ●*nc* the cry of a horse.

neighbour *US* **neighbor** ('neɪbə*) *nc* **1** a person who lives in the next house to, or not far from, oneself. **2** a person or thing next to or near another: *The Moon is Earth's nearest neighbour.* ●*vti* (when *vi*, often followed by **on**) be close or next to (something or someone else). **neighbourhood** *US* **neighborhood** ('neɪbəhʊd) *nc* a district. ●*adj* local. **neighbouring** *US* **neighboring** *adj* close; nearby: *the neighbouring villages.*

neither ('naɪðə*, 'niːðə*) *determiner, pron* not the one nor the other of two: *Neither story is correct; Neither came to see us again.* ●*conj* **1** (used to introduce the first of a choice) not: *Neither he nor she knows anything about it.* **2** See **nor** (def. 2).

neon ('niːɒn) *nu* a chemical element; gas used to produce coloured electric lighting in tubes for advertisements: symbol Ne

nephew ('nevjuː, 'nefjuː) *nc* the son of a person's brother or sister.

nerve (nɜːv) *nc* **1** a collection of fibres that carry signals between the brain and different parts of the body. **2** (*pl*) *infml* excitability; the control of one's state of mind: *My nerves won't take another shock like that.* **3** self-confidence; boldness: *He's lost his nerve.* **4** *infml* cheek; insolence. ●*vt* give

(someone) courage to do something. **get on one's nerves** annoy one greatly.

nervous ('nɜːvəs) *adj* **1** to do with nerves. **2** restless; excitable. **3** afraid. **nervous breakdown** a collapse of the body's central nervous system through exhaustion. **nerviousness** *nu*

nest (nest) *nc* **1** a structure built by a bird, mouse, etc., from feathers, leaves, etc., in which to lay its eggs or give birth and then bring up its young: see picture. **2** a comfortable place. **3** a set of objects that fit together: *a nest of tables.* ●*vi* (of a bird or animal) build and live in a nest.

nest

nestle ('nesəl) *vi* shelter oneself comfortably: *The town nestled in the valley.*

net¹ (net) *nc* **1** a set of crossing, regularly knotted strings used for catching fish, etc. **2** a trap: *The net was closing round the thief.* ●*vt* catch (fish, a husband, etc.). **netball** ('netbɔːl) *nu* a game in which each of two teams of seven players aims to throw a large ball into a small net on the other side's half of the ground. **network** ('netwɜːk) *nc* a complicated system of communications: *the railway network.*

net² (also **nett**) *adj* **1** after all taxes, etc., have been taken away: *net profit.* **2** (of weight) without the container or wrappings. **3** final; actual: *The net result was that everyone became healthier.*

nettle ('netəl) *nc* a plant of which one type has hairy leaves that sting the skin. ●*vt* annoy.

neurosis (njʊə'rəʊsɪs) *nc, pl* **-ses** (siːz) a disturbance of the mind causing fear and worry. **neurotic** (njʊə'rɒtɪk) *nc, adj* (a person) with a neurosis or subject to neurosis.

neuter ('njuːtə*) *adj* **1** (in some languages) belonging to a class of nouns including generally no animals of which the sex is described. **2** (of an animal or plant) sexually undeveloped. ●*vt* castrate (an animal, esp. a cat).

neutral ('njuːtrəl) *nc, adj* **1** (a person, country, etc.) that does not join either side in a dispute. **2** (of a colour, such as grey or cream) quiet; weak. ●*nu* (of a car gearbox) in a position in which no power is transmitted. **neutralise** ('njuːtrəlaɪz) *vt* **1** destroy the power or strength of; put out of action. **2** declare (a place) neutral.

neutron ('nju:trɒn) *nc* a particle of an atom that has no electric charge.

never ('nevə*) *adv* at no time. **never mind!** See under **mind. nevermore** (,nevə'mɔ:*) *adv* never again.

nevertheless (,nevəðə'les) *adv* however; just the same.

new (nju:) *adj* **-er, -est** 1 fresh; appearing for the first time. 2 just bought or obtained. 3 unknown before. 4 another: *We are starting a new term at school.* **newborn** ('nju:bɔ:n) *adj* (of a baby) just born. **newcomer** ('nju:,kʌmə*) *nc* a person who has just come to a place. **newfangled** (,nju:'fæŋgəld) *derogatory adj* (of an idea, etc.) new and disapproved of by the person speaking. **newly** ('nju:lɪ) *adv* (only) just, very recently: *newly married.* **newness** *nu* **New Year** the beginning of next year: *See you in the New Year!* **New Year's Day** 1 January.

news (nju:z) *nu* (*with singular verb*) information about recent events: *We have had news of an attack; Have you heard the news?* **newsagent** ('nju:z,eɪdʒənt) *nc* a person who sells newspapers in a shop. **news bulletin** *US* **newscast** ('nju:zkɑ:st) *nc* a news report on television or radio. **newspaper** ('nju:s,peɪpə*) (often shortened to **paper**) *nc* a daily or weekly set of large folded printed sheets of paper containing news, photographs, articles, advertisements, etc.

newt (nju:t) *nc* a small animal with a long tail and short legs that lives mostly in water: see picture.

newt

next (nekst) *adj* 1 nearest (in space): *the next house.* 2 (of a period) immediately following: *next year; The next hours were unforgettable.* ●*adv* in the next place; on the next occasion: *I'll see you next; when next I see him.* **next door** (in) the next house or room. **next of kin** a person's closest relative. **next to** beside; nearest to: *the building next to the church.*

nibble ('nɪbəl) *vti* (when *vi*, often followed by **at**) 1 take small bites (at something). 2 show slight interest (in an offer, etc.). ●*nc* 1 *infml* a little food; snack. 2 *nu* the act of nibbling.

nice (naɪs) *adj* **-r, -st** 1 (of persons) pleasant, likable. 2 (of things) of good quality. 3 (of occasions) enjoyable. 4 fine, delicate: *a nice point for discussion.* **nice and** pleasantly: *The weather's nice and dry.* **nice-looking** (naɪs'lʊkɪŋ) *adj* attractive; beautiful. **nicely** *adv*

niche (nɪtʃ, ni:ʃ) *nc* 1 a situation where a person fits in and feels at home: *She's found a niche for herself.* 2 a hollow in a wall.

nick (nɪk) *vt* 1 make a slight cut in the edge of (something). 2 *chiefly Brit, infml* steal. ●*nc* 1 a slight cut. 2 *Brit, slang* prison. 3 *Brit, slang* a police station.

nickel ('nɪkəl) 1 *nu* a chemical element; silver-coloured metal often mixed with other metals to make coins, etc.: symbol Ni 2 *US nc* a five-cent coin.

nickname ('nɪkneɪm) *nc* a person's familiar name or one invented to make fun of him. ●*vt* give a person a nickname: *He was nicknamed Fatty.*

niece (ni:s) *nc* the daughter of a person's brother or sister.

nigger ('nɪgə*) *derogatory nc* a black person; Negro.

nigh (naɪ) *archaic or literary prep, adv, adj* near.

night (naɪt) 1 *ncu* the period of darkness between two days. 2 *nc* an evening: *tomorrow night.* **nightcap** ('naɪtkæp) *nc* 1 a woollen cap worn in bed. 2 a drink taken before going to bed. **nightclub** ('naɪtklʌb) *nc* a place open till late at night offering food, drink, and entertainment. **nightdress** ('naɪtdres) *nc* a loose dress worn in bed by women. **nightfall** ('naɪtfɔ:l) *literary nu* the coming of darkness. **nightgown** ('naɪtgaʊn) *nc* a long loose garment worn in bed by men or women. **nightly** *adj, adv* 1 (happening, etc.) at night. 2 (happening, etc.) every night. **nighttime** *nu* the time during which it is night.

nightingale ('naɪtɪŋgeɪl) *nc* a small bird that sings at night.

nightmare ('naɪtmeə*) *nc* 1 a horrible dream. 2 a horrible experience.

nil (nɪl) *nu* (used esp. in scores for sport) nothing; zero. *The score is three goals to nil.*

nimble ('nɪmbəl) *adj* **-r, -st** quick-moving; with easy movements.

nine (naɪn) *determiner, n* the number 9. **ninth** (naɪnθ) *determiner, n, adv* **nineteen** (,naɪn'ti:n) *determiner, n* 19. **nineteenth** *determiner, n, adv* **ninety** ('naɪntɪ) *determiner, n* 90. **ninetieth** ('naɪntɪəθ) *determiner, n, adv*

nip (nɪp) *nc* 1 a bite; pinch. 2 a little alcoholic drink: *a nip of whisky.* 3 *nu* coldness: *There's a nip in the air.* ●*vt* 1 bite; pinch. 2 cut off the end of. 3 *Brit, infml vi* go quickly: *I nipped down to the shops.* **nip in the bud** put an end to (something troublesome) before it develops very far.

nitrate (ˈnaɪtreɪt) *nc* a salt of nitric acid; chemical substance in which nitrogen and oxygen are combined with a metal, essential for plants to grow.

nitric (ˈnaɪtrɪk) *adj* containing nitrogen. **nitric acid** a strong acid; nitrate of hydrogen: symbol HNO₃

nitrogen (ˈnaɪtrədʒən) *nu* a chemical element; gas that makes up most of the earth's air: symbol N

no (nəʊ) *adv* (used to express refusal, disagreement, disapproval, etc., in answer to a question, or to indicate that a negative statement is correct): *Can I go out?—No; He didn't win—No, I saw.* ● *determiner* not any; not a: *We have no oranges; It was no surprise to see them.* ● *nc* (a person who gives) an answer or vote of 'no'.

nobility (nəʊˈbɪlɪtɪ) *nu* 1 the quality of being noble. 2 titled people.

noble (ˈnəʊbəl) *adj*, **-r, -st** 1 with high moral qualities; unselfish. 2 with a title; belonging to a titled family. 3 (of buildings, etc.) splendid; majestic. ● *nc* also **nobleman** (ˈnəʊbəlmən) *nc, pl* **-men** a man with a title such as Lord. **nobly** *adv*

nobody (ˈnəʊbədɪ) *pron* no person; no-one. ● *nc, pl* **-dies** an unimportant person.

nocturnal (nɒkˈtɜːnəl) *adj* 1 that happens at night. 2 (of animals) active at night.

nod (nɒd) *nc* a bending forward and raising again of the head in greeting, agreement, etc. ● *vti* 1 bend (one's head) forward and raise it again. 2 *infml vi* (often followed by **off**) go to sleep.

nodule (ˈnɒdjuːl) *nc* a small, hard lump or swelling.

noise (nɔɪz) 1 *nc* a sound, esp. an unpleasant or unmusical one. 2 *nu* shouting. **noise abroad** *literary* make (news, etc.) public. **noiseless** *adj* making no noise. **noisy** *adj* **-ier, -iest** full of or making a lot of noise.

nomad (ˈnəʊmæd) *nc* a member of a tribe that lives a wandering life. **nomadic** (nəʊˈmædɪk) *adj* wandering.

nomenclature (nəʊˈmenklətʃə*) *nu* the system of names used in a science or other subjects.

nominal (ˈnɒmɪnəl) *adj* 1 in name only; so-called: *a nominal believer.* 2 much smaller than is owed or expected: *a nominal payment.* **nominally** *adv*

nominate (ˈnɒmɪneɪt) *vt* 1 suggest that (a person) be elected to a position. 2 appoint (a person) to a position. **nomination** (ˌnɒmɪˈneɪʃən) *ncu* **nominee** (ˌnɒmɪˈniː) *nc* a person suggested for, or appointed to, a position.

nonchalant (ˈnɒnʃələnt) *adj* not worried; carefree.

none (nʌn) *pron* 1 not one; not any; *None of our planes is missing.* 2 *literary* no-one: *None can describe its beauty.* ● *adv* not at all; not a bit: *They came none too soon.*

nonetheless (ˌnʌnðəˈles) *adv* in spite of that.

non-fiction (ˌnɒnˈfɪkʃən) *nu* any writing to do with facts, as compared with stories, poetry, etc.

non-iron (ˌnɒnˈaɪən) *adj* (of cloth) that does not need to be ironed after being washed.

nonplussed *US* **nonplused** (ˌnɒnˈplʌst) *adj* confused and unable to answer a question, do something, etc.

non-resident (ˌnɒnˈrezɪdənt) *nc, adj* (a person) not living in a particular place, such as a house that he owns or his place of work.

nonsense (ˈnɒnsəns) *nu* 1 something without sense or meaning. 2 stupidity.

non-smoker (ˌnɒnˈsməʊkə*) *nc* 1 a person who does not smoke tobacco. 2 (part of) a public vehicle where smoking is forbidden.

non-stop (ˈnɒnˈstɒp) *adj, adv* without stopping: *a non-stop train to London.*

noodle (ˈnuːdəl) *nc* (usually *pl*) a paste made from flour and eggs, in long strips for use in soups, etc.

nook (nʊk) *nc* a sheltered or hidden corner.

noon (nuːn) *nu* twelve o'clock in the day; midday. **noonday** (ˈnuːndeɪ), **noontide** (ˈnuːntaɪd) *US* **noontime** (ˈnuːntaɪm) *nu, adj* (of or to do with) noon.

no-one (ˈnəʊwʌn) *pron* nobody.

noose (nuːs) *nc* a loop of rope which can be pulled tight, esp. used for hanging a person by the neck. ● *vt* catch in a noose.

nor (nɔː*) *conj* 1 (used after **neither**) and not: *Neither he nor I knew; He is neither rich nor poor.* 2 also **neither** (used after any negative expression) (and) not... either; (and) no more: *I don't know what is going on and nor does anyone else.*

norm (nɔːm) 1 *nc* a normal amount or quality of work. 2 *nu* normal behaviour.

normal (ˈnɔːməl) *adj* usual; average; common. **normally** *adv* **normality** (nɔːˈmælɪtɪ) *nu* the normal state of affairs.

north (nɔːθ) *n* **the north** 1 the direction that is on the left of a person facing the east. 2 the direction in which a compass needle points. **the North** 1 the northern part of a country, etc. 2 the richer countries of the world. ● *adj* 1 in or towards the north. 2 (of the wind) coming from the north. ● *adv* towards the north. **north-east** (ˌnɔːθˈiːst) *n* the direction halfway between north and east. ● *adj* 1 in or towards the north-east. 2 (of the wind) coming from the north-east. ● *adv* towards the north-east. **northerly** (ˈnɔːðəlɪ) *adj* in or from the north. **northern** (ˈnɔːðən) *adj* in or to the north. **northernmost** (ˈnɔːðənməʊst) *adj* (of a place) the furthest (towards the) north. **northward(s)** (ˈnɔːθwəd(z)) *adj, adv* towards the north. **north-west** *n* the direction halfway between north and west. ● *adj* 1 in or towards the north-west. 2 (of the wind) coming from the north-west. ● *adv* towards the north-west.

nose (nəʊz) *nc* 1 the part of the head through which humans and animals breathe and smell. 2 the front part of something such as a plane, that sticks out. **follow one's nose** 1 do what seems right. 2 go where seems right. **have a nose for** have a natural ability to find or recognise. **look down one's nose at** regard as inferior. **turn up one's nose at** scorn or refuse (something one considers beneath one's dignity). **under someone's nose** very close to but unnoticed by someone.

nostalgia (nɒsˈtældʒə) *nu* 1 regret and longing for the past. 2 longing to be at home or with one's family: *While living abroad, she felt a nostalgia for England.*

nostril (ˈnɒstrɪl) *nc* either of the two openings in the nose.

not (nɒt) *adv* (used to make words mean the opposite): *The book is not on the table but on the chair.* **not at all** 1 not in the least; not even slightly. 2 there is no need to thank me. 3 there is no need to apologise.

notable (ˈnəʊtəbəl) *adj* worth taking note of; remarkable. ● *nc* an important person. **notably** (ˈnəʊtəblɪ) *adv* particularly; especially.

notary (ˈnəʊtərɪ) *nc, pl* **-ries** also **notary public** a law official who witnesses the signing of papers.

notation (nəʊˈteɪʃən) *nu* a system of expressing numbers, musical notes, etc., in writing by means of signs or symbols.

notch (nɒtʃ) *nc* a slight cut or nick in wood, etc. ● *vt* make a notch in. **notch up** *infml* reach a total of: *I've notched up twenty years' service.*

note (nəʊt) *nc* 1 a short letter; memorandum. 2 a written reminder to oneself: *I've made a note of it.* 3 *(pl)* the main points of a speech, etc., written down. 4 a banknote. 5 a written remark or comment on a point in a book. 6 a musical sound at a particular pitch. 7 a written sign that represents such a sound. 8 a sign. **of note** worth mentioning; important. ● *vt* 1 take notice of; give attention to. 2 (sometimes followed by **down**) make a **note** (def. 2) of. **notebook** (ˈnəʊtbʊk) *nc* a small book for writing notes in. **noted** *adj* known; famous. **note-paper** (ˈnəʊtˌpeɪpə*) *nu* paper for writing letters on. **noteworthy** (ˈnəʊtˌwɜːðɪ) *adj* worth mentioning.

nothing (ˈnʌθɪŋ) *nu* 1 not anything: *Nothing can be done; It's nothing serious.* 2 completely unimportant: *It's nothing.* 3 no points, goals, etc., in a game: *They won six-nothing.* **come to nothing** (of a plan, etc.) fail to develop or succeed. **nothing like** or **near** not in the least: *nothing like as good as the old one.* **nothing to do with** 1 without any connection with. 2 not the business of: *This is private—it's nothing to do with you.*

notice (ˈnəʊtɪs) *nc* 1 a written or printed announcement. 2 a criticism of a play, etc. *nu* 3 a warning that one's job is going to end, that one must leave a rented house, etc.: *They will have to give us a month's notice.* 4 attention: *This has been brought to my notice.* ● *vt* see; observe:. **take no notice (of)** pay (no) attention (to). **noticeable** *adj* easily seen. **notice-board** (ˈnəʊtɪsbɔːd) *nc* a board on which notices (**notice** def. 1) are put up, usually for the members of an organisation.

notify (ˈnəʊtɪfaɪ) *vt* tell or inform (someone) in a formal way. **notification** (ˌnəʊtɪfɪˈkeɪʃən) *ncu*

notion (ˈnəʊʃən) *nc* an idea or opinion.

notorious (nəʊˈtɔːrɪəs) *adj* well known for something shocking or evil.

notwithstanding (ˌnɒtwɪðˈstændɪŋ) *prep, adv* in spite of (that).

nought (nɔːt) 1 *nc* the figure 0. 2 *literary or archaic nu* also **naught** nothing; an end: *It's all come to nought.*

noun (naʊn) *nc* a word that is a name for something, such as 'book', 'ambition', or 'Nairobi'.

nourish (ˈnʌrɪʃ) *vt* 1 feed; build up the strength of. 2 encourage or maintain (feelings, etc.). **nourishment** *nu* 1 the act of nourishing. 2 something that nourishes; food.

novel¹ (ˈnɒvəl) *nc* a long, invented, written story. **novelist** (ˈnɒvəlɪst) *nc* a person who writes novels.

novel² *adj* new and interesting. **novelty** (ˈnɒvəltɪ) 1 *nu* the excitement of newness. 2 *nc, pl* **-ties** a new and interesting thing.

November (nəʊˈvembə*) *n* the eleventh month of the year, after October and before December.

novice (ˈnɒvɪs) *nc* 1 a beginner in some activity. 2 a person who has just joined a religious order and is still on trial.

now (naʊ) *adv* 1 at this moment. 2 at this time; at present. 3 after all that has happened: *He won't stand for election now.* ● *conj* (followed by **that**) since at this time; because. **(every) now and again** or **then** occasionally; from time to time. **for now** for the present; for the time being.

just now 1 a moment ago. **2** *US* at this moment. **now, now! 1** calm down! **2** (used as a warning): *Now, now, children—don't start fighting!*

nowadays ('naʊədeɪz) *adv* in these times.

nowhere ('nəʊweə*) *adv* in no place; not anywhere. **get nowhere** fail to make any progress; have no success.

noxious ('nɒkʃəs) *adj* (esp. of chemicals, etc.) harmful.

nozzle ('nɒzəl) *nc* a fitting on the end of a pipe, used to direct the gas or liquid coming through it.

n't (nt) short for **not**: *Don't do it!*

nuclear ('njuːklɪə*) *adj* **1** to do with energy produced by splitting an atom. **2** to do with a nucleus; that consists of a nucleus only: *the nuclear family.* **nuclear disarmament** getting rid of nuclear weapons. **nuclear-powered** (,njuːklɪə'paʊəd) *adj* driven by nuclear energy. **nuclear reactor** See under **reactor.**

nucleus ('njuːklɪəs) *nc, pl* **-lei** (lɪaɪ) **1** the centre of an atom. **2** the most important people in an organisation. **3** a small centre from which a larger thing can develop. **4** a cell body which contains chromosomes.

nude (njuːd) *adj* naked; without clothes on. **in the nude** naked. *nc* (a painting, etc. of) a nude person.

nudge (nʌdʒ) *vt* push (someone) gently with an elbow. ●*nc* a gentle push with an elbow.

nugget ('nʌgɪt) *nc* **1** a small lump of a precious metal found in rock. **2** a small valuable thing.

nuisance ('njuːsəns) *nc* a person or thing that causes annoyance or trouble.

null (nʌl) *adj* also **null and void** (of a law, etc.) not in force; not binding. **nullify** ('nʌlɪfaɪ) *vt* make null.

numb (nʌm) *adj* **-er, -est** without feeling because of cold, shock, etc. ●*vt* make numb. **numbness** *nu*

number ('nʌmbə*) *nc* **1** a quantity of things: *a large number of people.* **2** a figure representing a number, such as any from 0 to 9. **3** a figure or figures representing a position in an order: *This house is number four; What's your telephone number?* **4** an issue of a magazine. **5** a piece of music, esp. a song within an opera or musical. ●*vt* **1** give a number or numbers to. **2** be... in number: *The crowd numbered three thousand.* **3** consider; put in a group: *I was numbered among his followers.* **a number of** several.

number plate a metal or plastic plate on the front and back of a vehicle showing its official number: see picture.

numeral ('njuːmərəl) *nc* any of the figures 0 to 9.

number plate

numerator ('njuːməreɪtə*) *nc* the number above the line in a fraction, such as 1 in ½.

numerical (njuː'merɪkəl) *adj* to do with numbers.

numerous ('njuːmərəs) *adj* **1** many: *Numerous lives were saved.* **2** made of many parts: *a numerous collection.*

nun (nʌn) *nc* a woman who joins others in leading a simple, religious life. **nunnery** ('nʌnərɪ) *nc, pl* **-ries** a place where nuns live.

nuptial ('nʌpʃəl) *adj* to do with a wedding. ●*nc (pl)* a wedding.

nurse (nɜːs) *nc* **1** a person who looks after people who are ill, esp. in a hospital. **2** a person who looks after children in their family home. ●*vt* **1** look after (someone ill). **2** try to cure (an illness): *I'm nursing a cold.* **3** help (a plant, an organisation, jealousy, etc.) to grow or develop.

nursery ('nɜːsərɪ) *nc, pl* **-ries 1** a room kept for use by children. **2** a piece of ground where plants are grown, esp. for sale. **nursery rhyme** a short simple poem or song for children.

nursing ('nɜːsɪŋ) *nu* the art and practice of looking after ill people. **nursing home** a kind of hospital, usually a private organisation, where ill people are looked after.

nurture ('nɜːtʃə*) *nu* care, attention, and training given to children. ●*vt* bring up or care for (children).

nut (nʌt) *nc* **1** the hard fruit of many kinds of tree and shrub: see picture. **2** a small piece of metal for screwing onto the end of a bolt: see picture. **3** *infml* a crazy person. **4** *slang* a human head. **nutcracker** ('nʌtkrækə*) *nc* a device for cracking the shells of nuts. **nutshell** ('nʌtʃel) *nc* the hard outer covering of a nut. **(put) in a nutshell** (explain or describe) very briefly.

nut 1

nutmeg ('nʌtmeg) *ncu* the scented seed of an East Indian tree, which is made into a powder and used in food.

nut 2

nutrient ('nju:triənt) *nc* a nourishing (substance in) food.

nutrition (nju:'trɪʃən) *nu* **1** food. **2** the study of food and its effects on health. **3** the system by which an animal or plant takes in and uses food. **nutritious** (nju:'trɪʃəs) *adj* (of food) nourishing; useful to the body.

nuzzle ('nʌzəl) *vti* (of a child or animal) put its nose or head close up to (a person or thing).

nylon ('naɪlɒn) **1** *nu* a man-made plastic material used for cloth, combs, etc. **2** *nc (pl)* nylon stockings.

nymph (nɪmf) *nc* **1** (in Greek and Roman stories) a beautiful girl who lived in trees, rivers, hills, etc. **2** an undeveloped insect.

O

o (əʊ) *interj* See **oh.**

oak (əʊk) *nc* a large tree with acorns as its fruit and leaves with a wavy outline: see picture at **trees;** (also *nu*) the wood of this tree. ● *adj* made of oak.

oar (ɔː*) *nc* a shaped board on a long handle used to move a boat through the water: see picture.

oar

oasis (əʊˈeɪsɪs) *nc, pl* **-ses** (siːz) a place in a desert where plants grow because water is there.

oat (əʊt) *nc* **1** *(often pl)* a grass grown for its seeds, which are eaten. **2** *(pl)* these seeds. **oatmeal** (ˈəʊtmiːl) *nu* oats broken up small for eating in porridge, etc.

oath (əʊθ) *nc, pl* **-ths** (ðz) **1** the act of calling on God, a dead person, or some object to show that one is making a sincere promise: *He made an oath that he would never give up his search.* **2** a disrespectful use of the name of God, etc., to add force to a statement.

obdurate (ˈɒbdjʊrət) *adj* very unlikely to change one's mind: *You can ask him again, but I think he's obdurate.*

obedient (əˈbiːdɪənt) *adj* obeying; doing as one is told. **obedience** *nu* **in obedience to** according to; as ordered by. **obediently** *adv*

obelisk (ˈɒbəlɪsk) *nc* a tall, thin stone monument with four sides that come to a point at the top.

obesity (əʊˈbiːsɪtɪ) *nu* the state of being very fat.

obey (əʊˈbeɪ, əˈbeɪ) *vti* do as one is told (by someone or in an order, etc.): *Children should obey their parents.*

obituary (əˈbɪtjʊərɪ) *nc, pl* **-ries** a report in a newspaper of someone's death, often also describing his life.

object (ˈɒbdʒɪkt) *nc* **1** a thing that can be seen or touched. **2** an aim; purpose: *the object of my visit.* **3** the person or thing towards which something is directed: *an object of hate.* **4** the part of a sentence that receives the action of a verb, such as 'the apple' in 'I ate the apple'. **no object** no problem: *Time is no object—take as long as you like.* ● (əbˈdʒekt) *vti* (when *vi,* often followed by **to**) say or write that one dislikes something: *I object to bad laws; She objected that she had not had enough time to get ready.*

objection (əbˈdʒekʃən) **1** *ncu* (an instance of) objecting. **2** *nc* a reason for objecting. **objectionable** *adj* unpleasant.

objective (əbˈdʒektɪv) *adj* (of a person, description, etc.) to do only with what is known, plain to see, etc., and not with personal feelings. ● *nc* an aim, purpose, or place one wishes to reach. **objectively** *adv*

obligation (ˌɒblɪˈɡeɪʃən) **1** *nc* something one has to do; a duty. **2** *nu* the state of having an obligation: *I'm under no obligation to him.*

obligatory (əˈblɪɡətrɪ) *adj* that must be done, etc.; binding.

oblige (əˈblaɪdʒ) *vt* **1** (usually passive) force or bind (someone to do something): *I was obliged by law to give my name.* **2** (passive) be grateful (to one, or in someone's debt: *I'm obliged to you for helping.* **3** *vti* help (someone); do as one is asked: *They obliged (us) by carrying our bags.* **obliging** *adj* helpful.

oblique (əˈbliːk) *adj* **1** sloping; not upright or in line with something. **2** (of an answer, etc.) unclear. **3** *geometry* at or being an angle other than a right angle. ● *n* See **stroke** (def. 4). **obliquely** *adv*

obliterate (əˈblɪtəreɪt) *vt* destroy; rub out.

oblivion (əˈblɪvɪən) *nu* **1** the state of forgetting; unconsciousness. **2** the state of having been forgotten or disregarded. **oblivious** *adj* (usually followed by **of** or **to**) forgetful; unconscious.

oblong (ˈɒblɒŋ) *adj, nc* (a figure) with square corners and longer in one direction than the other.

obnoxious (əbˈnɒkʃəs) *adj* very unpleasant: *an obnoxious smell.*

oboe (ˈəʊbəʊ) *nc* a musical wind instrument with keys and a double reed: see picture at **musical instruments.**

obscene (əbˈsiːn) *adj* (of a photograph, book, etc.) not decent; unpleasant. **obscenity** (əbˈsenɪtɪ) **1** *nu* the quality of being obscene. **2** *nc, pl* **-ties** something obscene.

obscure (əbˈskjʊə*) *adj* **1** unclear; hard to understand. **2** hidden or far away. **3** unimportant or little known. **4** dark or difficult to see. ● *vt* make **obscure** (defs. 1, 2, 4) **obscurity 1** *nu* the state of being obscure. **2** *nc, pl* **-ties** someone or something that obscures or is obscure.

observable (əb'zɜːvəbəl) *adj* able to be observed.

observance (əb'zɜːvəns) *ncu* (an instance of) observing (**observe** def. 3). **observant** *adj* 1 good at observing (**observe** def. 1). 2 dutiful over one's observance.

observation (,ɒbzə'veɪʃən) 1 *nu* the act of observing (**observe** def. 1). 2 *nc* a remark or opinion (esp. made after one has studied something carefully).

observatory (əb'zɜːvətərɪ) *nc, pl* -**ries** a building for observing something, esp. the stars.

observe (əb'zɜːv) *vt* 1 watch or notice. 2 remark. 3 keep, follow, etc., (a law, custom, holiday, etc.). **observer** *nc* someone who observes, esp. by watching without taking part.

obsess (əb'ses) *vt* occupy or take over (the mind of) completely: *He is obsessed with becoming rich.* **obsession** (əb'seʃən) 1 *nu* the act of obsessing or state of being obsessed. 2 *nc* something that obsesses one.

obsolete ('ɒbsəliːt) *adj* out-of-date; no longer in use. **obsolescence** (,ɒbsə'lesəns) *nu* the process of becoming obsolete.

obstacle ('ɒbstəkəl) *nc* something that gets in the way.

obstetrics (əb'stetrɪks) *nu* (*with singular verb*) the part of medicine to do with childbirth. **obstetrician** (,ɒbste'trɪʃən) *nc* a doctor who practises obstetrics.

obstinate ('ɒbstɪnɪt) *adj* 1 difficult to persuade to act differently. 2 (of dirt, an illness, etc.) difficult to get rid of. **obstinacy** ('ɒbstɪnəsɪ) *nu* **obstinately** *adv*

obstruct (əb'strʌkt) *vt* block; make movement, etc., difficult for. **obstruction** 1 *nc* a person or thing that obstructs. 2 *ncu* (an instance of) obstructing.

obtain (əb'teɪn) 1 *vt* get (possession of). 2 *formal vi* (of a law, etc.) apply; be used. **obtainable** *adj*

obtrusive (əb'truːsɪv) *adj* annoyingly noticeable.

obtuse (əb'tjuːs) *adj* 1 stupid; slow to understand. 2 (of an angle) of between 90 and 180 degrees.

obviate ('ɒbvɪeɪt) *vt* get rid of (danger, a necessity, etc.).

obvious ('ɒbvɪəs) *adj* easy to see or understand. **obviously** *adv*

occasion (ə'keɪʒən) 1 *nc* a time at which something is or may be done: *She came here many times—on the last occasion I told her not to come again.* 2 *nu* reason; cause: *There is no occasion to laugh!* 3 *nc* a special or splendid event: *The Queen's visit was quite an occasion.*

occasional (ə'keɪʒənəl) *adj* 1 infrequent or irregular: *occasional visits.* 2 *formal* to do with special occasions: *occasional clothes.* **occasionally** *adv*

occult ('ɒkʌlt, ə'kʌlt) *adj* magical; mysterious. **the occult** occult events, beliefs, etc.

occupant ('ɒkjʊpənt) *nc* a person occupying a place or holding a position.

occupation (,ɒkjʊ'peɪʃən) 1 *nc* an activity, esp. a job or regular work. 2 *ncu* (an instance of) occupying or being occupied. **occupational** *adj* to do with an **occupation** (def. 1).

occupy ('ɒkjʊpaɪ) *vt* 1 live or be in (a house, position, space, etc.). 2 enter and stay in (someone else's country or property, during a war or to express a complaint, dislike, etc.). 3 keep busy; give (someone or oneself) something to do.

occur (ə'kɜː*) *vi* 1 happen; take place. 2 exist; be found. 3 (followed by **to**) be thought of (by): *It occurs to me that we may be going the wrong way.* **occurrence** (ə'kʌrəns) *nc* an event. **of... occurrence** happening as stated: *of frequent occurrence.*

ocean ('əʊʃən) *ncu* (one of the large areas of) sea: *the Atlantic Ocean.* **ocean-going** (of a ship) able to sail in the open sea. **oceanic** (,əʊʃɪ'ænɪk) *adj*

o'clock (ə'klɒk) *adv* (used after a number to give the time of day, but only whole hours): *six o'clock.*

octagon ('ɒktəgən) *nc* a figure, building, etc., with eight sides.

octane ('ɒkteɪn) *nu* a measure of the grade of petrol: *98-octane petrol gives more power than 94-octane.*

octave ('ɒktɪv) *nc* (the gap or the notes between) two musical notes known by the same letter of which one is twice as high as the other.

October (ɒk'təʊbə*) *n* the tenth month of the year, after September and before November.

octopus ('ɒktəpəs) *nc* a sea-animal with eight tentacles coming directly from its head: see picture.

octopus

odd (ɒd) *adj* -**er**, -**est** 1 strange or unusual. 2 (of a number) not able to be divided by two. 3 not (part of) a pair or set: *wearing odd socks.* 4 occasional; extra: *doing odd* *jobs.* **5** left over: *If you've taken all you want, I'll give the odd ones away.* **6** and a little or few more: *two kilos odd of butter.* ●*nc* an odd number. **oddity 1** *nc, pl* **-ties** something **odd** (def. 1). **2** *nu* the quality of being **odd** (def. 1). **oddly** *adv* **oddment** ('ɒdmənt) *nc* something **odd** (def. 5).

odds (ɒdz) *n pl* **1** the amount paid to a person who wins a bet, compared to the amount betted: *odds of five to one.* **2** a chance; probability: *What are the odds that he won't come?* **odds and ends** oddments or a mixture of objects.

ode (əʊd) *nc* a poem written as if spoken to someone or something: *Ode to Music.*

odious ('əʊdɪəs) *adj* hateful; disgusting: *odious comparisons.*

odour *US* **odor** ('əʊdə*) *nc* a smell. **odourless** *adj* **odorous** *adj* having a smell.

o'er (əʊə*, 'ʊə*) *poetry prep, adv* short for **over.**

oesophagus *US* **esophagus** (ɪ'sɒfəgəs) *nc, pl* **-gi** (gaɪ) also **gullet** the tube down which food travels from the throat to the stomach.

of (ɒv unstressed əv) *prep* **1** belonging to or to do with: *the danger of flying.* **2** with; having: *a man of wealth.* **3** from: *within a mile of my house.* **4** about: *Tell me of your life.* **5** made with or containing: *a window of glass; a book of rules.* **6** (used in expressing a quantity): *a litre of milk.* **7** done to: *the arranging of flowers.* **8** done by: *the shouting of a hundred voices.* **9** who or that is or are: *the Republic of China.* **10** *US* See **to¹** (def. 6). **11** because of: *plants dying of cold.* **12** from among: *two of you.* **13** on the part of: *That was nice of him.*

off (ɒf) *prep* **1** away from: *Get off the floor.* **2** not wanting or liking: *I've gone off drink.* **3** near; connected to: *the farm off the main road.* ●*adv* **1** away; so as to be no longer in the same place: *He just walked off.* **2** so as to stop, get rid of, separate, etc.: *Turn the light off; Will you cut me off a piece of meat?* **3** away from work: *I've got the day off.* ●*adj* **1** away from work: *I'm afraid Mr Jones is off sick.* **2** not happening (yet): *The concert is off.* **3** provided with money or (followed by **for**) something else: *He's very well off, but badly off for friends.* **4** poor; disappointing: *I'm having rather an off day.* **5** not able to be had, served etc.: *Soup's off.* **6** (of food) gone rotten or sour. **the off** the start of a race, etc. **be off** go away. **off and on** or **on and off** occasionally, from time to time. **off chance** a faint possibility. **off colour** not feeling well. **off-licence** ('ɒf,laɪsəns) a shop where alcoholic drink may be bought but not drunk.

offence *US* **offense** (ə'fens) **1** *nc* a wrong or crime. **2** *nu* the hurting of one's feelings.

offend (ə'fend) *vt* **1** hurt the feelings of. **2** be very unpleasant to. **3** *vi* do wrong. **offender** *nc*

offensive (ə'fensɪv) *adj* **1** hurting someone's feelings. **2** very unpleasant. **3** to do with attack. ●*nc* an attack. **the offensive** an attacking position or state: *to take the offensive.*

offer ('ɒfə*) *vt* **1** allow (someone) to choose to accept or take (something): *I was offered a free ticket.* **2** say or write that one would be glad (to do something): *She offered to take me there.* ●*nc* **1** an act of offering. **2** something offered, such as a service or the chance to buy something cheap. **offering** *nc* something offered, such as money for the work of a church. **offer up** give, esp. to God.

offhand (,ɒf'hænd) *adj, adv* **1** without warning or time to think. **2** without thought or respect.

office ('ɒfɪs) *nc* **1** (a building containing) a room for working at a desk in: *He's gone to the office; a large office.* **2** a part of a government: *the Foreign Office.* **3** an important position: *an office in the Government.* **4** a duty; job; service: *the most important office of a president.* **5** a place where a particular kind of business is done: *a railway ticket office.* **6** a religious service. **7** *(pl)* formal help. **office-bearer** a person who holds an **office** (def. 3). **office block** a large building containing offices.

officer ('ɒfɪsə*) *nc* **1** a member of one of the armed forces or person working on a ship who is responsible for others of whom he is in charge. **2** a person with a job as described: *a police officer; an information officer.* **3** a person in a responsible position in a society, such as its treasurer.

official (ə'fɪʃəl) *adj* to do with or coming from someone in charge of something: *official approval to spend public money.* ●*nc* a person holding an **office** (def. 3), esp. in a government. **officially** *adv*

officiate (ə'fɪʃɪeɪt) *vi* do an official job or action.

officious (ə'fɪʃəs) *derogatory adj* so eager to help one do the right thing as to be annoying.

offing ('ɒfɪŋ) *n* **in the offing** expected soon.

offset ('ɒfset) *vt* act as a balance against: *The extra business will offset our earlier losses.* ●*nu, adj, adv* (to do with or by) printing by putting ink onto a metal plate that transfers it to a rubber roller that then presses the ink onto the paper.

offshore (,ɒf'ʃɔː*) *adj, adv* away from the coast; out at or out to sea.

offspring ('ɒfsprɪŋ) *nu* children or animal young.

oft (ɒft) *chiefly archaic or poetry adv* short for **often**.

often ('ɒfən) *adv* frequently; many times. **oftentimes** *archaic adv* frequently.

ogre ('əʊgə*) *nc* 1 (in stories) a huge man who eats people. 2 a fierce frightening person.

oh (also **o**) (əʊ) *interj* (used to express surprise, doubt, pleasure, etc.)

oil (ɔɪl) 1 *nc* any of several mostly thick, smooth liquids obtained from plants, animals, or from under the ground and used in foods, for greasing machines, for burning for heat and light, etc. 2 *nu* also **petroleum** an oil found under the ground and made esp. into petrol. 3 *(pl)* paint containing oil. ● *vt* apply oil to (a machine, etc.) to make it run smoothly. **oilcloth** ('ɔɪlklɒθ) *nu* cloth coated with oil to stop it letting water through. **oilfield** ('ɔɪlfiːld) *nc* a piece of land under which oil is found. **oil painting** a picture made with oils. **oil-producing** *adj* (of a country) exporting oil. **oil rig** the machinery used for making an oil well: see picture. **oilskin** ('ɔɪlskɪn) *ncu* (a garment made of) cloth coated with oil to stop it letting water through. **oil slick** a large quantity of oil floating on the sea. **oil tanker** a ship or road vehicle for carrying oil. **oil well** a deep hole in the ground or bottom of the sea for obtaining oil. **oily** *adj* **-ier, -iest** like, covered with, or containing oil.

oil rig

ointment ('ɔɪntmənt) *nc* a creamy or oily substance put onto the skin to heal it.

OK (also **okay**) (,əʊ'keɪ) *infml interj* (used to express or ask for agreement or approval.) ● *adj, adv* all right; good or well enough. ● *vt* agree to or approve of. ● *ncu* (an expression of) agreement or approval.

old (əʊld) *adj* **-er, -est** 1 having lived or existed for some, esp. a long, time; no longer young. 2 of age: *fifty years old.* 3 damaged or worn through age or use: *Wear old clothes in case you get dirty.* 4 former: *Your old copy of the book.* 5 familiar; dear: *We're old friends.* 6 not new or modern. **the old** (def. 1) old people. **old-fashioned** (,əʊld-'fæʃənd) *adj* belonging to former times; not

thought of value now. **old hand** an experienced person. **old-time** ('əʊld-taɪm) *adj* as done or seen in former times: *old-time dancing.*

olden ('əʊldən) *archaic or literary adj* old: *in olden times.*

olfactory (ɒl'fæktərɪ) *formal or medicine adj* to do with the sense of smell.

oligopoly (,ɒlɪ'gɒpəlɪ) *nc, pl* **-lies** a situation in which there are few producers and sellers of goods and there can be little competition between them.

olive ('ɒlɪv) *nc* 1 a tree with green or black fruit that is eaten or made into oil. 2 one of these fruits. ● *adj* 1 (of skin) brown. 2 also **olive green** pale green.

omelette ('ɒmlət) *nc* a food made of eggs, beaten and cooked flat with oil or butter in a pan.

omen ('əʊmən) *nc* an event believed to indicate another, esp. bad, in the future. **ominous** ('ɒmɪnəs) *adj* indicating something bad to come.

omit (əʊ'mɪt) *vt* 1 miss or leave out. 2 fail (to do something). **omission** (əʊ'mɪʃən) 1 *ncu* (an instance of) omitting. 2 *nc* something omitted.

omnibus ('ɒmnɪbəs) *old-fashioned nc* See **bus**. ● *nc, adj* (a book) containing several stories, plays, etc.

on (ɒn) *prep* 1 touching the top of or supported by; upon: *sitting on a chair.* 2 against (something upright): *on the wall.* 3 during: *on Monday.* 4 by means of: *I came on foot; We spoke on the telephone.* 5 close to: *a house on the river.* 6 in (a street, etc.): *on Oxford Street.* 7 against: *the war on crime.* 8 at the time of; after: *On arrival, please collect your luggage.* 9 in a state, action, or place described: *on the move.* 10 about; to do with: *a book on gardening.* 11 occupied in: *on a long journey.* 12 held by: *a dog on a lead.* 13 according to: *on your recommendation.* 14 *infml* carried by: *Have you a pen on you?* ● *adv* 1 working; running: *You left the water on.* 2 touching or surrounding something: *I've no shoes on.* 3 without stopping: *He just talks on (and on).* 4 further: *We drove on towards the town.* 5 happening: *Is there a meeting on inside?* **and so on** See under **so**. **off and on** or **on and off** See under **off**.

once (wʌns) *adv* 1 one time; in one case. 2 formerly: *There was once a castle here.* 3 ever: *If once it goes, it'll never come back.* ● *conj* when; as soon as: *Once you start, it's easy.* ● *nu* one time: *I saw him just the once.* **at once** 1 at the same time. 2 immediately; straightaway. **once and for all** for the only or last time. **once in a while** occasionally; not often. **once more**

(yet) another time; again. **once or twice** only a few times. **once upon a time** (used to start children's stories) in former times.

oncoming (ˈɒn,kʌmɪŋ) adj approaching: oncoming traffic.

one (wʌn) determiner, n the number 1. ●determiner 1 a single; each. 2 (used after **the**) only: the one way to make more friends. 3 some: One day you'll know what I mean. ●pron 1 a single person or thing. 2 (used after **the**) only person or thing. 3 formal any person, representing people generally: One puts petrol in a car. 4 (used to avoid repeating something): Do you like that plant?— Yes, I have one in my garden. **one another** each other: They talked to one another. **one or two** a few. **one-legged** (ˌwʌnˈlegd, ˌwʌnˈlegɪd) adj with only one leg. **oneness** nu 1 the state of being one. 2 agreement. **oneself** (wʌnˈself) pron 1 (the reflexive form of **one** (pron def. 3)): One should not blame oneself. 2 (the emphatic form of **one** (pron def. 3)): Can one do it oneself? **by oneself** 1 without help. 2 alone. **one-sided** (ˌwʌnˈsaɪdɪd) adj 1 larger, better, etc., on one side than the other. 2 (of a fight, etc.) with one side at an advantage. 3 considering only one side; unfair: a one-sided view of the argument. **one-way** (ˌwʌnˈweɪ) adj travelling or allowing travel in only one direction: a one-way street.

onerous (ˈɒnərəs, ˈəʊnərəs) adj causing a lot of work or trouble.

ongoing (ˈɒn,gəʊɪŋ) adj continuing; in progress.

onion (ˈʌnjən) nc a plant bulb with many layers, widely used as food: see picture at **vegetables**.

onlooker (ˈɒn,lʊkə*) nc a person just watching.

only (ˈəʊnlɪ) adv 1 no more than: He is young—only twelve. 2 merely; simply: I only want to see. 3 alone; no other than: Only you could do that. 4 no longer ago than: I only did it yesterday. ●adj 1 being the whole number or quantity of or the one: The only bread I have is very dry; the only soldier I know. 2 (of a child) with no brothers or sisters. ●conj but: I would do it, only I don't know how to. **if only** See under **if**. **not only... but also...** not just... but... as well: not only naughty but also proud of it. **only just** See under **just**.

onset (ˈɒnset) nc 1 an attack. 2 a start, esp. of something bad.

onshore (ˌɒnˈʃɔː*) adv, adj (blowing) from the sea towards land.

onslaught (ˈɒnslɔːt) nc a fierce attack.

onto (ˈɒntu: unstressed ˈɒntə) prep 1 to a position on: I walked onto the stage. 2 infml knowing about; making use of: I'm onto

your little tricks, so behave yourself! 3 infml into contact with: I'll get onto the police.

onus (ˈəʊnəs) nu responsibility: The onus is on you to prove what you are saying.

onward (ˈɒnwəd) adv, adj (moving or pointing) further forward. **onwards** adv further forward.

ooze (uːz) vti 1 (allow to) flow out gently. 2 (cause to) be squeezed out. ●nc 1 a gentle flow. 2 old-fashioned or poetic mud.

opal (ˈəʊpəl) ncu a precious stone appearing to be any of several colours.

opaque (əʊˈpeɪk) adj 1 not letting light through. 2 hard to understand.

open (ˈəʊpən) adj 1 not closed; free to be passed through, etc.: an open gate. 2 closed but not locked: Come in—the door's open. 3 spread out; unfolded: an open book. 4 not covered in: an open boat. 5 (of a shop, etc.) ready to do business, let in visitors, etc. 6 (of a meeting, competition, etc.) allowing anyone to enter. 7 without natural shelter: open country; open sea. 8 not yet decided: an open question; an open mind. 9 not hidden or disguised: open dishonesty. ●vti 1 make or become (wider) open. 2 start: The music opens with a horn call. ●nc an **open** (def. 6) competition. **the open** open land; outside: The soldiers came out of the house into the open. **open-air** (ˌəʊpənˈeə*) adj not in a building: an open-air concert. **opening** nc 1 a space or hole, esp. for going or looking through. 2 a start or first part. 3 an opportunity, esp. for employment. **opening hours** the period(s) for which a shop, office, etc., is open. **openly** adv in an **open** (def. 9) manner. **open out** spread out; unfold. **open up** 1 allow someone or something to come through or into (something): We are police—open this door up! 2 infml start shooting or throwing.

opera (ˈɒpərə) nc a musical work for singers and instruments that is acted like a play.

operate (ˈɒpəreɪt) 1 vti (cause to) work or do a job: Can you operate this machine? 2 v (often followed by **on**) do an **operation** (def. 2).

operation (ˌɒpəˈreɪʃən) 1 ncu the act or a manner of operating. nc 2 an act of using instruments on a person's body, esp. by cutting into it to repair damage, remove a diseased part, etc. 3 an action of the armed forces. 4 nu the state of operating or being in force. **operational** adj 1 to do with operation (defs. 1 and 3). 2 to do with, esp. able to carry out, an **operation** (def. 3).

operative (ˈɒpərətɪv) adj 1 in force; in operation. 2 important; that matters: 'Must' is the operative word. 3 to do with operations (operation def. 2). ●nc polite a person who does unskilled work.

operator (ˈɒpəreɪtə*) *nc* **1** a person who operates a machine, etc. **2** a person who connects telephone calls. **3** *infml* a person who is successful but usually dishonest: *a smooth operator.*

operetta (ˌɒpəˈretə) *nc* a light or funny opera.

opinion (əˈpɪnjən) *nc* what a person thinks about a subject; a view. **opinion poll** the act of asking a number of people their opinions on something.

opium (ˈəʊpɪəm) *nu* a drug made from poppy seeds, used in medicine or smoked.

opponent (əˈpəʊnənt) *nc* a person fighting or playing against one.

opportune (ˈɒpətjuːn) *adj* **1** (of a time) good for a particular purpose. **2** (of an event) done or happening at a good time.

opportunity (ˌɒpəˈtjuːnɪtɪ) *nc, pl* **-ties** a situation in which something can be done; chance: *Do it while there is the opportunity.*

oppose (əˈpəʊz) *vt* **1** fight against; resist. **2** take the opposite view to.

opposite (ˈɒpəzɪt) *adj* **1** facing (each other): *in opposite directions.* **2** exactly what something else is not; totally different: *We hold opposite opinions—he agrees with it and I do not.* ●*adv* on opposite sides. ●*prep* also **opposite to** facing. ●*nc* an opposite person or thing: *Black is the opposite of white.*

opposition (ˌɒpəˈzɪʃən) *nu* **1** the act of opposing; resistance: *We wrote a letter in opposition to the plan.* **2** the main party not in power in a parliament, whose job is to oppose the government. **3** a person or group of people who oppose.

●**oppress** (əˈpres) *vt* **1** control (a people) by force and cruelty. **2** trouble, worry: *oppressed by feelings of doubt.* **oppression** *nu* **oppressive** *adj* **oppressor** *nc*

●**opt** (ɒpt) *vt* (followed by an infinitive) also **opt for** choose. **opt out (of)** choose to avoid (something).

●**optic** (ˈɒptɪk) *adj* to do with the eye. **optical** *adj* to do with light or the eye. **optician** (ɒpˈtɪʃən) *nc* a person who makes or sells optical instruments, esp. glasses.

●**optimism** (ˈɒptɪmɪzəm) *nu* the practice of looking for the good in everything and hoping for the best. **optimist** *nc* a person who has optimism. **optimistic** (ˌɒptɪˈmɪstɪk) *adj*

●**optimum** (ˈɒptɪməm) *adj, nu* (the) best (thing) for something: *optimum conditions for plant growth.*

●**ption** (ˈɒpʃən) *ncu* (a) choice. **optional** *adj* that one is free to choose or not: *Leather seats are optional on this car.*

●**r** (ɔː* unstressed ə*) *conj* (used to join things of which any may be chosen, true, etc.): *Robert, or Bob, as he is usually called;*

Do you want these or those? **or else** See under **else. or so** about: *There are thirty or so people.*

oracle (ˈɒrəkəl) *nc* a person or thing mysteriously able to answer questions and give information about the future.

oral (ˈɔːrəl) *adj* **1** spoken. **2** to do with the mouth. ●*nc* a spoken examination. **orally** *adv*

orange (ˈɒrɪndʒ) **1** *nc* a large, round, juicy, reddish-yellow fruit grown in fairly hot parts of the world: see picture at **fruits. 2** *ncu* an orange colour. ●*adj* of a colour between red and yellow.

oration (əˈreɪʃən) *nc* a formal public speech.

orator (ˈɒrətə*) *nc* a (good) public speaker.

oratorio (ˌɒrəˈtɔːrɪəʊ) *nc, pl* **-s** a religious musical work for singers and instruments that is theatrical but not acted.

orb (ɔːb) *nc* **1** a ball with a cross fixed to it, held by a king or queen as a sign of power. **2** *poetry* a star or planet.

orbit (ˈɔːbɪt) *nc* a path taken by a planet, spacecraft, etc., travelling around the sun, earth, etc. ●*vt* (of a moon, spacecraft, etc.) travel in an orbit around. **orbital** *adj*

orchard (ˈɔːtʃəd) *nc* a piece of land used for growing fruit trees.

orchestra (ˈɔːkɪstrə) **1** *nc* a large group of musicians, usually playing several different types of instrument. **2** *nu* the place in front of the stage in a theatre where the orchestra sits. **orchestral** (ɔːˈkestrəl) *adj*

orchid (ˈɔːkɪd) *nc* **1** any of several plants with unusual, brightly-coloured flowers. **2** one of these flowers.

ordain (ɔːˈdeɪn) *vt* **1** make (someone) a priest. **2** appoint; decide on: *the ordained time when each of us will die.*

ordeal (ɔːˈdiːl) *nc* a testing or unpleasant experience.

order (ˈɔːdə*) *nc* **1** a direction to do something, given to a soldier, made by a judge, etc. **2** the act of asking a shop, restaurant, etc., to supply goods, serve food, etc. **3** a way, esp. the correct way, of arranging things one after or behind the other: *in order.* **4** a group of people who have a common purpose, esp. religious, or have been given the same rank by a king or queen. **5** *nu* a state in which things are as they should be; control: *in order.* ●*vt* **1** give an order for (something) to be done, supplied, etc., for (someone) to go (away, out, etc.), or that (someone) is (to do something): *We ordered two cups of tea; The king ordered his army to advance.* **2** put in order. **in order that** so that: *We agreed in order that war should be avoided.* **in order to** so as to; so that one can or could: *He works in order to earn money.* **of the order of** about: *of the* *order of 1000 people.* **on order** (of goods) ordered but not yet supplied. **out of order 1** not in **order** (defs. 3, 5). **2** (of a machine) not working. **order about** give orders unnecessarily or unpleasantly to (someone).

orderly (ˈɔːdəlɪ) *adj* **1** arranged in order. **2** behaving properly. ●*nc, pl* **-lies 1** a helper or cleaner in a hospital. **2** a soldier who attends upon an officer.

ordinal (ˈɔːdɪnəl) *nc* also **ordinal number** a number such as 1st, 2nd, or 3rd, as compared with 1, 2, and 3.

ordinance (ˈɔːdɪnəns) *nc* an order, rule, etc., made by someone in charge.

ordinary (ˈɔːdənrɪ) *adj* **1** normal; usual. **2** unexciting; boring. **ordinarily** (ˈɔːdənərəlɪ, ˌɔːdənˈerəlɪ) *adv*

ore (ɔː*) *ncu* (a type of) rock from which a metal or other useful substance can be obtained: *iron ore.*

organ (ˈɔːgən) *nc* **1** a musical instrument with keys to be pressed by the fingers and usually also some for the feet, the notes being produced by air being blown through pipes of different lengths or sometimes electrically. **2** a part of an animal or plant, such as a heart. **3** a part of a large oganisation. **organist** *nc* a person who plays the organ.

organic (ɔːˈgænɪk) *adj* **1** to do with animals or plants. **2** to do with chemical substances containing carbon. **3** (of food) grown using only natural substances to help growth and prevent plant diseases.

organise (ˈɔːgənaɪz) **1** *vt* put in order; arrange (a meeting, etc.). **2** *vti* (of members of a group), (cause to) form into an association. **organisation** (ˌɔːgənaɪˈzeɪʃən) **1** *nu* the act of organising or state of being organised. **2** *nc* a business, society, etc., with a particular purpose. **organiser** *nc*

organism (ˈɔːgənɪzəm) *nc* any animal or plant; anything which may be considered to be alive.

orgy (ˈɔːdʒɪ) *nc, pl* **-gies** a period of having too much of something pleasurable, esp. drinking or sexual activity.

orient (ˈɔːrɪənt) *n* **the Orient** *literary* the East. **oriental** (ˌɔːrɪˈentəl) *adj* from or to do with the East. ●*nc* usually **Oriental** an oriental person.

orientate (ˈɔːrɪənteɪt) *vt* **1** cause to get used to new surroundings or conditions. **2** turn to face the right way. **orientation** (ˌɔːrɪənˈteɪʃən) *ncu* (a position achieved by) orientating.

orifice (ˈɒrɪfɪs) *formal nc* a hole or opening in the body, a wall, a machine, etc.

origin (ˈɒrɪdʒɪn) *nc* a starting-point; place from which something comes or is developed: *a word of Latin origin.*

original (əˈrɪdʒɪnəl) *adj* **1** to do with an origin or beginning; earliest. **2** (of an idea, fashion, etc.) new; unusual. **3** having original ideas. ●*nc* something that copies may be made from. **originality** (əˌrɪdʒɪˈnælɪtɪ) *nu* **originally** *adv*

originate (əˈrɪdʒɪneɪt) *vti* start; come or bring into being.

Orlon (ˈɔːlɒn) *Trademark nu* a man-made cloth.

ornament (ˈɔːnəmənt) *nc* anything used to decorate or make something beautiful. ● (ˈɔːnəment) *vt* decorate or make beautiful. **ornamental** (ˌɔːnəˈmentəl) *adj*

ornate (ɔːˈneɪt) *adj* greatly ornamented.

ornithology (ˌɔːnɪˈθɒlədʒɪ) *nu* the study of birds.

orphan (ˈɔːfən) *nc* a child, both of whose parents are dead. **be orphaned** have both one's parents die while one is a child. **orphanage** (ˈɔːfənɪdʒ) *nc* a home for orphans.

orthodox (ˈɔːθədɒks) *adj* doing, believing, etc., what is approved, esp. in religion.

orthography (ɔːˈθɒgrəfɪ) *ncu* (a system of) spelling.

orthopaedic *US* **orthopedic** (ˌɔːθəˈpiːdɪk) *adj* to do with healing bones, joints, and muscles.

oscillate (ˈɒsɪleɪt) *science vti* move from side to side regularly. **oscillation** (ˌɒsɪˈleɪʃən) *ncu*

oscilloscope (əˈsɪləskəʊp) *science nc* an instrument that gives a representation of electrical signals on a screen.

osmosis (ɒzˈməʊsɪs) *science nu* the process by which water passes through a membrane from a weak solution to a stronger one.

ostensible (ɒˈstensɪbəl) *adj* made to look real but actually pretended: *The ostensible purpose of this advertisement is to give advice, but it is really meant to make you buy their goods.*

ostentatious (ˌɒstenˈteɪʃəs) *derogatory adj* showing off; attracting attention on purpose.

ostrich (ˈɒstrɪtʃ) *nc, pl* **ostriches, ostrich** a large African bird that cannot fly but runs fast.

other (ˈʌðə*) *determiner, pron* (one(s)) different from the one(s) already mentioned or under consideration. See also **another every other** every second: *I have a bath every other day.* **one after the other** one at a time; separately. **on the one** or **other hand** See under **hand. or other** no known: *someone or other; He went somewhere or other—I don't know exactly.* **the other day, week, afternoon, etc.** only a few days, weeks, afternoons, etc., ago.

otherwise (ˈʌðəwaɪz) *adv* **1** differently: *I could not have spoken otherwise.* **2** in other respects: *It is too sweet, but otherwise quite nice.* **3** if not: *Put it back, otherwise there will be trouble.*

otter (ˈɒtə*) *nc* a furry animal that eats fish: see picture.

otter

ouch (aʊtʃ) *interj* (used to express sudden pain.)

ought (ɔːt) *v* (followed by an infinitive) **1** (used to express what it is advisable, one's duty, etc., to do): *You ought to go to the theatre more often.* **2** (used to express what is probable and often also wanted): *It ought to be sunny today.*

oughtn't (ˈɔːtənt) *v* ought not.

ounce (aʊns) *nc* **1** a measure of weight = a sixteenth of a pound or 28.349 g **2** a small amount: *every last ounce of freedom.*

our (aʊə* unstressed ɑː*) *determiner* belonging to or to do with us: *Our army is winning.* **ours** (ˈaʊəz) *pron* a person or thing belonging to or to do with us. **ourselves** (aʊəˈselvz) *pron* **1** (the reflexive form of **us**): *We dressed ourselves.* **2** (the emphatic form of **us**): *We read it ourselves.* **by ourselves** (of the speaker or writer and one or more others) **1** without help. **2** alone.

oust (aʊst) *vt* put or drive out: *The government will be ousted at the next election.*

out (aʊt) *adv* **1** at or to a place not in something: *He just walked out.* **2** (used to show removal): *I rubbed out my name on the list.* **3** (used to show an increase in length, size, etc.): *The days are drawing out.* **4** (used to show a conclusion or exhaustion): *That family died out long ago.* ●*adv, adj* **1** (so as to be) no longer burning: *The light went out.* **2** (so as to be) unconscious: *He was knocked out cold.* **3** (so as to be) away from home: *a day out with the family.* **4** (so as to be) (far) away: *a ship out at sea.* **5** (so as to be) able to be seen, bought, etc., by the public: *His new book has just come out.* **6** (so as to be) not in place or accurate: *Your guess was a long way out.* **7** (so as to be) no longer fashionable: *Shoes like those went out last year.* **8** (so as to be) on strike: *The whole factory is out.* ●*adj* **1** not allowed: *Speaking when you're not asked to is out!* **2** no longer possible: *A holiday is out, as we've no money.* **3** finished: *before the day is out.* **4** (followed by **for** or

an infinitive) hoping or trying: *out to get rich.* ●*prep* out of; out through: *He went out the door.* **out loud** aloud; using the voice. **out of 1** at or to a point not in: *He walked out of the room.* **2** because of: *I shouted at him out of anger.* **3** no longer having a supply of: *Sorry, we're out of petrol.* **4** from; using: *I've made curtains out of sheets.* **out-of-date** (ˌaʊtəvˈdeɪt) *adj* See under **date**[1]. **out-of-doors** (ˌaʊtəvˈdɔːz) *adv, adj* outside; not in a building. **out-of-the-way** (ˌaʊtəvðəˈweɪ) *adj* in a place that is difficult to reach or not visited much.

outboard (ˈaʊtbɔːd) *nc* also **outboard motor** an engine that is fixed to the back of a boat and is easily removable: see picture.

outboard motor

outbreak (ˈaʊtbreɪk) *nc* a sudden happening or start of something, such as a disease or a war.

outbuilding (ˈaʊtˌbɪldɪŋ) *nc* a building separate from but belonging to another one.

outburst (ˈaʊtbɜːst) *nc* a sudden show of feeling, esp. anger.

outcast (ˈaʊtkɑːst) *nc, adj* (a person) avoided by the rest of society.

outcome (ˈaʊtkʌm) *nc* a result.

outcrop (ˈaʊtkrɒp) *nc* a part of a layer of rock that pushes up or out from the surface.

outcry (ˈaʊtkraɪ) *nc, pl* **-cries** a strong general protest or complaint.

outdated (aʊtˈdeɪtɪd) *adj* no longer in use or in fashion.

outdo (aʊtˈduː) *vt* do better than (someone).

outdoor (ˈaʊtdɔː*) *adj* (done, used, etc.) outside. **outdoors** (aʊtˈdɔːz) *adv, nu* (the world) outside or not in a building.

outer (ˈaʊtə*) *adj* **1** on the outside. **2** further from the middle. **outermost** (ˈaʊtəməʊst) *adj* farthest from the middle.

outfit (ˈaʊtfɪt) *nc* **1** a set of things intended to be used together. **2** a set of clothes worn together. **3** *infml* a group of people working together, such as a business or part of an army ●*vt* provide with an outfit.

outgoing (ˈaʊtˌgəʊɪŋ, ˌaʊtˈgəʊɪŋ) *adj* **1** friendly. **2** leaving a job or position: *the outgoing president.*

outgrow (aʊtˈgrəʊ) *vt* **1** grow faster than. **2** grow too big for (clothes, etc.). **3** develop beyond (childish ideas, etc.).

271

outhouse ('aʊthaʊs) *nc* a small building separate from but belonging to another one.

outing ('aʊtɪŋ) *nc* a short journey to somewhere and back, made for pleasure.

outlandish (aʊt'lændɪʃ) *adj* shockingly unusual.

outlaw ('aʊtlɔ:) *nc* a person who has had the protection of the law taken away from him, esp. a hunted criminal. ● *vt* 1 make into an outlaw. 2 forbid.

outlet ('aʊtlet) *nc* 1 a place or means for escape, esp. of strong feelings. 2 a place or means for selling something.

outline ('aʊtlaɪn) *nc, vt* 1 (give) a short description (of). 2 (draw) a line in the shape of the outside of (something).

outlive (aʊt'lɪv) *vt* live longer than.

outlook ('aʊtlʊk) 1 *nc* a feeling towards something: *We have different outlooks on life.* 2 *nu* the probable future of something: *There's not much outlook for peace.*

outlying ('aʊt,laɪɪŋ) *adj* far from a centre such as a town.

outnumber (aʊt'nʌmbə*) *vt* exist in a greater number than.

outpost ('aʊtpəʊst) *nc* a far-off settlement or army camp.

output ('aʊtpʊt) 1 *ncu* (an example of) the amount of something produced, such as electricity: *These two power stations have different outputs—one generates more than the other.* 2 *nu* information got out of a computer.

outrage ('aʊtreɪdʒ) 1 *nc* a serious insult, injury, or act of cruelty done on purpose. 2 *nu* great anger or hurt caused by an outrage. ● *vt* cause outrage in (someone). **outrageous** (aʊt'reɪdʒəs) *adj* causing outrage.

outright ('aʊtraɪt) *adj* complete; done all at once: *an outright sale.* ● (aʊt'raɪt) *adv* completely; all at once.

outrun (aʊt'rʌn) *vt* run faster or farther than.

outset ('aʊtset) *nc* a beginning.

outshine (aʊt'ʃaɪn) *vt* 1 do better or get a better result than. 2 shine more brightly than.

outside (aʊt'saɪd, 'aʊtsaɪd) *prep, adv* at or to a place not inside. ● *prep* apart from. ● ('aʊtsaɪd) *adj* outside something: *outside help.* ● (aʊt'saɪd, 'aʊtsaɪd) *nc* the side of something that faces outwards or the part of something near its edge; the farthest limit: *the outside of a bend in the road; It will cost twenty pounds at the outside.* **outsider** (aʊt'saɪdə*) *nc* 1 a person or thing not a member of some group. 2 a person or animal thought unlikely to win a race or other competition.

outskirts ('aʊtskɜ:ts) *n pl* the district near the edge of a town, etc.

outspoken (aʊt'spəʊkən) *adj* speaking or spoken boldly and plainly.

outspread (aʊt'spred) *vt, adj* spread out.

outstanding (aʊt'stændɪŋ) *adj* 1 remarkable, esp. very good. 2 not yet paid or decided.

outstretched (aʊt'stretʃt) *adj* stretched or reaching out.

outstrip (aʊt'strɪp) *vt* do better, esp. go faster, than.

outward ('aʊtwəd) *adv* also **outwards** towards the outside. ● *adj* 1 on the outside. 2 able to be seen; not deep or hidden: *He showed no outward signs of fear.* 3 (esp. of the first half of a journey to somewhere and back) (travelling) away from somewhere: *Your outward flight leaves at six tonight.* **outwardly** *adv*

outweigh (aʊt'weɪ) *vt* be more important than: *Our joy outweighed the sorrow.*

outwit (aʊt'wɪt) *vt* be cleverer than; deceive.

oval ('əʊvəl) *adj, nc* (having) a flat shape similar to that of an egg: see picture at **shapes.**

ovary ('əʊvərɪ) *nc, pl* **-ries** 1 the part of a female body that produces eggs. 2 the part of a plant from which fruit develops.

ovation (əʊ'veɪʃən) *nc* an enthusiastic reception, esp. with clapping.

oven ('ʌvən) *nc* a heated container like a box or cupboard for cooking food, heating or drying substances, etc.

over ('əʊvə*) *prep* 1 above, but not touching; above, esp. to cover: *Put a cloth over the bird's cage.* 2 about: *He argued over the price.* 3 more than: *over 100 people.* 4 during: *Come and stay with us over next week.* 5 (showing higher rank): *She's over us at work.* 6 recovered from (an illness, etc.). ● *prep, adv* across: *I jumped over the gate; The plane flew over (the city); Come over and see us.* ● *adv* 1 so as to (cause to) fall: *The bottle was knocked over.* 2 so as to leave one side showing: *Turn the page over.* 3 from beginning to end: *I'll read the letter over to you.* ● *adj* finished: *Let's get this job over.* **over and above** besides: *He gets this money over and above his normal pay.* **over and over** (**again**) a great many times.

overall ('əʊvər,ɔ:l) *adj* complete; taking everything into account: *overall length.* ● (,əʊvər'ɔ:l) *adv* taking everything into account. ● ('əʊvərɔ:l) *nc* 1 *Brit* a work garment worn over other clothes to protect them. 2 (*pl*) trousers with shoulder straps, or a complete one-piece garment, worn over other clothes to protect them.

overboard (,əʊvə'bɔ:d) *adv* from a ship into the sea.

overcast (,əʊvə'kɑ:st) *adj* (of the sky) covered with (dark) clouds.

overcharge (,əʊvə'tʃɑːdʒ) *vti* charge (someone) too much money.

overcoat ('əʊvəkəʊt) *nc* a warm coat worn over other clothes.

overcome (,əʊvə'kʌm) *vt* 1 beat (an enemy), get over (a difficulty), etc. 2 (usually passive) (of smoke, laughter, etc.) make one helpless or powerless.

overdo (,əʊvə'duː) *vt* 1 work too hard at: *Don't overdo your welcome.* 2 cook for too long.

overdose ('əʊvədəʊs) *nc* too much of a drug taken at once.

overdraft ('əʊvədrɑːft) *nc* an arrangement or situation in which one draws more money from a bank account than one has in it.

overdue (,əʊvə'djuː) *adj* late; expected, owed, etc., but not yet arrived or paid.

overeat (,əʊvər'iːt) *vi* eat too much.

overflow (,əʊvə'fləʊ) 1 *vti* (of a liquid, crowd, etc.) flow over the top of; more than fill. 2 *vi* (of a container, room, etc.) be filled so that the contents overflow: *The house is overflowing with visitors.* ● ('əʊvəfləʊ) *nc* a pipe, etc., that carries away overflowing liquid.

overgrown (,əʊvə'grəʊn) *adj* covered with wild plants.

overhang (,əʊvə'hæŋ) *vti* stick out (over): *an overhanging rock.* ● ('əʊvəhæŋ) *nc* something that overhangs.

overhaul (,əʊvə'hɔːl) *vt* 1 examine (and repair) (a machine, etc.). 2 overtake (another car, etc.). ● ('əʊvəhɔːl) *nc* an examination (and repair).

overhead (,əʊvə'hed) *adj, adv* above one's head, esp. in the sky. **overheads** ('əʊvəhedz) *n pl* general business costs, such as rent, that are not caused by any one job or sale.

overhear (,əʊvə'hɪə*) *vt* hear (a person, conversation, etc.) by chance or without the speaker knowing.

overjoyed (,əʊvə'dʒɔɪd) *adj* very happy.

overland (,əʊvə'lænd) *adj, adv* (travelling) across land.

overlap (,əʊvə'læp) 1 *vt* partly cover. 2 *vi* (of two things) lie so that one partly covers the other. ● ('əʊvəlæp) *nc* an overlapping part of something.

overload (,əʊvə'ləʊd) *vt* put too much load on. ● ('əʊvələʊd) *nc* a load that is too great.

overlook (,əʊvə'lʊk) *vt* 1 fail to see. 2 choose not to take (a mistake, etc.) into account; forgive. 3 allow one to look out over: *My room overlooks the garden.*

overly ('əʊvəlɪ) *adv* too (much).

overnight (,əʊvə'naɪt) *adv, adj* 1 at night or for a night. 2 immediate(ly); sudden(ly): *an overnight success.*

overpower (,əʊvə'paʊə*) *vt* overcome (an enemy, etc.) by force, or with smoke, laughter, etc.

overrate (,əʊvə'reɪt) *vt* have too high an opinion of.

overriding (,əʊvə'raɪdɪŋ) *adj* (of a consideration, claim, etc.) more important than any other.

overrule (,əʊvə'ruːl) *vt* not allow (a decision, argument, etc.) of (someone).

overrun (,əʊvə'rʌn) *vt* 1 attack and beat (an army, town, etc.). 2 (of animals or plants) spread quickly over (ground). 3 use or occupy more than (the time or space allowed).

overseas (,əʊvə'siːz) *adv, adj* abroad, esp. across the sea.

overseer ('əʊvəsɪə*) *nc* a person who makes sure that others work properly.

overshadow (,əʊvə'ʃædəʊ) *vt* seem more important than.

overshoot (,əʊvə'ʃuːt) *vti* shoot or go too far or past (something) by mistake.

oversight ('əʊvəsaɪt) *nc* a mistake, esp. something overlooked or forgotten.

overstep (,əʊvə'step) *vt* go beyond (a mark, etc.).

overt ('əʊvɜːt, əʊ'vɜːt) *adj* openly done; observable.

overtake (,əʊvə'teɪk) *vt* 1 *chiefly Brit* pass (someone or something moving in the same direction) by travelling faster. 2 pass in some other way, such as in value. 3 come upon; surprise.

overthrow (,əʊvə'θrəʊ) *vt* destroy; get rid of (a government, society, etc.). ● ('əʊvəθrəʊ) *nu* the act of overthrowing.

overtime ('əʊvətaɪm) *adv* outside normal working hours. ●*nu* time spent working overtime; pay for this.

overtones ('əʊvətəʊnz) *n pl* extra, unexpressed meaning.

overture ('əʊvətjʊə*) *nc* 1 a piece of music for orchestra, usually written to be played before an opera or play. 2 (*pl*) an offer to start talks or business.

overturn (,əʊvə'tɜːn) *vti* (cause to) fall or turn over.

overweight (,əʊvə'weɪt) *adj* weighing more than is healthy or allowed. ● ('əʊvəweɪt) *nu* weight that is more than is healthy or allowed.

overwhelm (,əʊvə'welm) *vt* 1 astonish, esp. with something pleasant: *I was overwhelmed by their generosity.* 2 overcome (an enemy, etc.) by great force, quantity, or numbers: *An overwhelming number of people said 'no'.*

overwork (,əʊvə'wɜːk) *vti* (cause to) work too hard. ●*nu* the act of overworking (oneself).

273

overwrought (ˌəʊvəˈrɔːt) *adj* very excited or nervous.

ovule (ˈəʊvjuːl) *nc* the part of a plant that develops into its seed.

ovum (ˈəʊvəm) *nc, pl* **ova** (ˈəʊvə) an animal's egg that has not (yet) started growing into a new animal.

owe (əʊ) *vt* **1** be or feel bound to give (money, thanks, etc.) (to someone). **2** have to be grateful (to someone or something) for: *We owe our victory to luck.* **owing to** because of; as a result of: *We stayed at home, owing to the bad weather.*

owl (aʊl) *nc* a large bird that hunts small animals at night: see picture.

owl

own (əʊn) *determiner, pron* **1** (used as an intensifier after **my,** etc.) and not another's: *The house has its own garden; David bought one of his own.* **2** for or to do with oneself: *I'll make my own way there.* ● *vt* have the right to possess; have as one's property: *I own this land.* **get one's own back (on)** do harm, etc., to (someone who has done harm to one). **on one's own 1** alone. **2** without help. **own up (to)** confess (to a crime, doing something wrong, etc.).

owner (ˈəʊnə*) *nc* a person who owns something. **ownership** (ˈəʊnəʃɪp) *nu* the fact of owning something.

ox (ɒks) *nc, pl* **-en** (ən) **1** any animal of the cattle family. **2** a castrated male of the type of cattle kept on farms: see picture at **animals.**

oxide (ˈɒksaɪd) *nc* any chemical compound containing oxygen with another substance: *iron oxide.* **oxidise** (ˈɒksɪdaɪz) *vti* (cause to) combine with oxygen, esp. to form an oxide.

oxygen (ˈɒksɪdʒən) *nu* a chemical element; colourless gas that is necessary for respiration and makes up part of the air: symbol O

oyster (ˈɔɪstə*) *nc* a shellfish that is eaten and from which pearls are obtained.

ozone (ˈəʊzəʊn) *nu* a colourless gas formed from oxygen.

P

pa (pɑː) *infml n* See **father**.

pace (peɪs) *nc* **1** a step in walking or running. **2** a speed, esp. of walking or running. **3** a manner of walking or running. ● *vti* **1** walk (about on (something)), esp. slowly, as if in thought: *He nervously paced the corridor.* **2** *vt* set a speed for (a runner in a race, etc.).

pacific (pə'sɪfɪk) *adj* peaceful; peace-loving.

pacifism ('pæsɪfɪzəm) *nu* the belief that violence, esp. war, is wrong. **pacifist** *nc, adj*

pack (pæk) *nc* **1** a load carried on the back. **2** a set of playing-cards. **3** a group of animals, esp. ones that hunt. **4** a wrapped or boxed quantity of something such as food for selling. ● *vti* **1** put (objects) into (a container), esp. clothes, etc., into a suitcase for a journey. **2** crowd or press tightly together (into): *The hall was packed for the meeting.*

package ('pækɪdʒ) *nc* **1** anything wrapped or boxed; parcel. **2** a number of offers, conditions, etc., made as a whole: *a package holiday.* ● *vt* wrap as or make into a package.

packet ('pækɪt) *nc* **1** (a quantity of something in) a small box or wrapping: *a packet of cigarettes.* **2** *slang* a lot of money: *That cost a packet!* **3** *archaic* a boat carrying mail and passengers. ● *vt* wrap as or put into a **packet** (def. 1).

packing ('pækɪŋ) *nu* **1** material used to pack goods in. **2** the act of packing clothes, etc., for a journey.

pact (pækt) *nc* an agreement, esp. between countries, to help one another.

pad (pæd) *nc* **1** a thick piece of soft material used as a cushion or to hold a cleaning liquid, ink, etc. **2** a pile of sheets of paper joined at one edge, to be torn off as each is written on. **3** See **launching-pad** under **launch**. **4** a soft part of the foot of an animal. ● *vt* **1** use soft material to shape or protect. **2** *vi* walk quietly and steadily. **padding** *nu* material used to pad with.

paddle

paddle¹ ('pædəl) *nc* **1** a shaped board with a handle, used to move a boat through water: see picture. **2** a period of paddling. ● *vt* move (a boat) with a paddle.

paddle² *vi* walk about in shallow water. ● *nc* a period of paddling.

paddock ('pædək) *nc* a small field used esp. for horses.

paddy ('pædɪ) **1** *nu* rice that is growing or has just been harvested. **2** *nc, pl* **-dies** also **paddy field** a field used for growing rice.

padlock ('pædlɒk) *nc* a lock used by passing its closable ring through the ends of a chain, etc.: see picture.

padlock

paediatrics *US* **pediatrics** (ˌpiːdɪ'ætrɪks) *nu* (*with singular verb*) the branch of medicine to do with children's diseases. **paediatrician** (ˌpiːdɪə'trɪʃən) *nc* a doctor who practises paediatrics.

pagan ('peɪgən) *nc, adj* (a person) with no apparent religion.

page¹ (peɪdʒ) *nc* (one side of) a leaf of a book.

page² *nc* (esp. in older times) a boy employed to carry messages, etc. ● *vt* call out the name of (someone) so that he can be given a message when he answers.

pageant ('pædʒənt) *nc* a colourful show or procession, esp. illustrating events from history. **pageantry** *nu* the show and splendour of pageants.

pagoda (pə'gəʊdə) *nc* a religious building, tall and narrowing towards the top, seen in India, China, etc.: see picture.

pagoda

paid (peɪd) past tense and past participle of **pay**.

pail (peɪl) *nc* a bucket.

pain (peɪn) *ncu* (an instance of) suffering or hurt in body or mind: *a pain in my foot.* **painful** *adj* causing pain. **painfully** *adv* **painless** *adj*

pains (peɪnz) *n pl* care: *He took great pains to get everything right.* **painstaking** (ˈpeɪnz-ˌteɪkɪŋ) *adj* (of work, etc.) very careful; in great detail.

paint (peɪnt) *nc* a liquid that is spread and dries on surfaces to colour or protect them. ● *vt* 1 spread paint onto (a surface), esp. with a brush. 2 make (a picture) of (something) by brushing paint onto paper, cloth, etc. **painter** *nc* 1 a person who paints houses, etc. 2 an artist who makes paintings. **painting** *nc* a painted picture.

pair (peə*) *nc* 1 a set of two things: *a pair of shoes.* 2 an object (as if) made of two similar parts: *a pair of trousers; a pair of scissors.* 3 a man and a woman who are in love or married; couple. 4 one member of a pair: *Have you got the pair to this shoe?* ● *vti* (sometimes followed by **off**) form (into) pairs.

pajamas (pəˈdʒɑːməz) *n* See **pyjamas**.

pal (pæl) *infml nc* a friend. **pal up (with)** become friends (with).

palace (ˈpælɪs) *nc* the official home of a king, queen, bishop, etc.

palate (ˈpælɪt) *nc* 1 the roof of the mouth. 2 a person's taste or liking.

palatial (pəˈleɪʃəl) *adj* like a palace; splendid.

pale (peɪl) *adj* -**r**, -**st** not strong in colour; whitish: *pale blue; He was pale from lack of sleep.* ● *vti* make or become pale or paler.

palette (ˈpælɪt) *nc* a board on which an artist mixes paints: see picture.

palette

palindrome (ˈpælɪndrəʊm) *nc* a word or group of words that is spelt the same forwards and backwards, such as 'radar'.

pall¹ (pɔːl) *nc* 1 a thick cloth spread over anything containing a dead body. 2 a thick, heavy covering: *a pall of smoke.*

pall² *vi* (often followed by **on**) become uninteresting (to someone).

pallid (ˈpælɪd) *adj* (of a person's appearance, etc.) pale.

pally (ˈpælɪ) *infml adj* friendly.

palm¹ (pɑːm) *nc* 1 the inner surface of the hand between the wrist and fingers. 2 the part of a glove covering the palm. ● *vt* cleverly hide (something) in or with one's hand. **palm off** (often followed by **on**) *infml* get rid of: *I palmed the job off on my assistant.*

palm² *nc* a tree that grows in hot parts of the world and of which all the branches and leaves grow out of the top: see picture.

palm

palpitate (ˈpælpɪteɪt) *vi* (esp. of the heart) tremble; flutter.

palsy (ˈpɔːlzɪ) *nc, pl* -**sies** a disease that prevents movement, control, or use of a part of the body.

paltry (ˈpɔːltrɪ) *derogatory adj* -**ier**, -**iest** worthless; too little to be of (much) use: *I got paid a paltry amount.*

pampas (ˈpæmpəs) *n pl (sometimes singular)* the grassy plains of southern South America.

pamper (ˈpæmpə*) *vt* be too kind to; give (someone) anything that is asked for.

pamphlet (ˈpæmflɪt) *nc* a small book with a paper cover, esp. on a subject of current interest.

pan¹ (pæn) *nc* a container, esp. shallow and of metal, for cooking, etc. ● *vi* wash soil in a pan to try to find precious stones or metals.

pan² *vt* swing (a film or television camera) sideways, esp. to follow something moving. ● *nc* an instance of panning.

pancake (ˈpænkeɪk) *nc* a thin, flat cake of egg, milk, and flour, cooked in a pan.

pancreas (ˈpæŋkrɪəs) *nc* a part of the body, near the stomach, that produces juices to break down the food one eats.

panda (ˈpændə) *nc* 1 also **giant panda** a large black and white bear-like animal from China: see picture at **animals**. 2 a reddish-brown furry Indian animal.

pandemonium (ˌpændɪˈməʊnɪəm) *nu* great confusion and noise.

pander (ˈpændə*) *vi* (followed by **to**) completely satisfy (someone's wishes, esp. bad).

pane (peɪn) *nc* a sheet of glass in a window or door.

panel (ˈpænəl) *nc* 1 a sheet of metal, wood, etc., that is part of something else: *a door panel; car-body panel.* 2 a group of people who choose someone for a job, answer questions from an audience, etc. ● *vt* make or fit (a wall, etc.) with panels.

pang (pæŋ) *nc* a sudden painful or unpleasant feeling: *pangs of hunger.*

panic (ˈpænɪk) *nu* sudden great fear causing foolish behaviour, esp. among a group of people. ● *vti* (cause to) feel panic.

panorama (ˌpænəˈrɑːmə) *nc* a long, wide, unbroken view of surrounding land.

pansy (ˈpænzɪ) *nc, pl* **-sies** a garden plant with yellow, purple, or white flowers.

pant (pænt) **1** *vi* breathe fast after exercise, etc. **2** *vt* say while panting. ●*nc* an instance of panting.

panther (ˈpænθə*) *n* See **leopard.**

panties (ˈpæntɪz) *n pl* a light garment worn next to the skin by women, reaching from (below) the waist to the tops of the legs.

pantomime (ˈpæntəmaɪm) *nc* **1** *Brit* a children's entertainment produced around Christmas. **2** a play without words.

pantry (ˈpæntrɪ) *nc, pl* **-ries** a small room either for food or for plates, glasses, etc.

pants (pænts) *n pl* also **pair of pants 1** short for **underpants. 2** *chiefly US* See **trousers.**

papa (pəˈpɑː) *archaic nc* a father.

papal (ˈpeɪpəl) *adj* to do with the pope.

paper (ˈpeɪpə*) **1** *ncu* a (type of) substance made from wood, cotton, etc., and used in thin sheets for writing, printing, wrapping, etc. *nc* **2** short for **newspaper. 3** a piece of writing on some subject. **4** also **examination paper** a set of questions, or someone's answers to them, in a written examination. **5** *(pl)* a person's letters, diaries, etc. **6** *(pl)* pieces of paper giving one's name, one's permission to visit somewhere, etc. **7** short for **wallpaper.** ●*vt* cover (a wall or the walls of a room) with wallpaper. **paperback** (ˈpeɪpəbæk) *nc* a cheap book with paper covers. **paper bag** a bag made from paper, esp. used for wrapping goods bought in a shop.

paprika (ˈpæprɪkə, pəˈpriːkə) **1** *nu* a powder, made from a hollow red fruit, used to add taste to food. **2** *nc* one of these fruits: see picture.

paprika

par (pɑː*) *nu* a set value or standard.

parable (ˈpærəbəl) *nc* a story that explains a religious point.

parabola (pəˈræbələ) *nc* a curve made by, for example, something thrown up through the air and falling to the ground again.

parachute (ˈpærəʃuːt) *(infml abbrev.* **chute)** *nc* a large, shaped cloth attached by lines to a person, box of supplies, etc., to slow its fall through the air: see picture. ●*vti* drop by parachute. **parachutist** *nc*

parachute

parade (pəˈreɪd) *nc* **1** a gathering or procession of soldiers, etc. **2** a public street or row of shops. **3** *nu* show: *on parade.* ●*vti* **1** (cause to) gather or march in a procession. **2** show (oneself) off.

paradise (ˈpærədaɪs) *nu* **1** heaven. **2** a place, state, or time of great happiness.

paradox (ˈpærədɒks) *nc* something that at first does not appear true or possible but when thought about is found to be so. **paradoxical** (ˌpærəˈdɒksɪkəl) *adj* **paradoxically** *adv*

paraffin (ˈpærəfɪn) *US, Australian* **kerosene** *nu* a light oil burnt in lamps, heaters, plane engines, and, as paraffin wax, in candles.

paragraph (ˈpærəɡrɑːf) *nc* a part of a piece of writing or printing that starts a new line, usually a little way in from the edge.

parakeet (ˈpærəkiːt) *nc* a bird; a small, esp. long-tailed, parrot.

parallel (ˈpærəlel) *adj* **1** (of lines, etc.) always the same distance away (from each other): *parallel railway lines.* **2** similar; matching: *There has been a parallel improvement in our other factories.* ●*nc* **1** one of two or more parallel lines. **2** a parallel fact, development, etc. ●*vt* be a parallel to; match. **parallelogram** (ˌpærəˈleləɡræm) *nc* a four-sided figure whose opposite sides are parallel: see picture at **shapes.**

paralyse *US* **paralyze** (ˈpærəlaɪz) *vt* cause (someone or a part of the body) to be unable to move. **paralysis** (pəˈrælɪsɪs) *nc, pl* **-lyses** (lɪsiːz) a state of being paralysed; a condition causing this.

paramount (ˈpærəmaʊnt) *adj* chief; most important: *The wishes of the local people are paramount.*

parapet (ˈpærəpɪt) *nc* a low wall along the edge of a roof, bridge, etc.

paraphernalia (ˌpærəfəˈneɪlɪə) *n pl* **1** belongings; equipment. **2** useless objects.

paraphrase (ˈpærəfreɪz) *vt* express (something written or spoken) in a different way. ●*nc* a piece of language produced by paraphrasing.

parasite (ˈpærəsaɪt) *nc* **1** a plant or animal that lives and feeds in or on another one. **2** *derogatory* a person who lives on the money or work of others. **parasitic** (ˌpærəˈsɪtɪk) *adj*

parasol (ˈpærəsɒl) *nc* a light umbrella used to give protection from the sun.

paratroops (ˈpærətruːps) *n pl* soldiers who can parachute in to where they are needed.

parcel (ˈpaːsəl) *nc* 1 something wrapped up, esp. to be sent by post. 2 *law* a piece of land. ●*vt* 1 (often followed by **up**) wrap as a parcel. 2 (often followed by **out**) divide or share something out. **parcel post** a postal service delivering parcels.

parch (paːtʃ) *vt* (of the sun, etc.) dry (something or someone) up.

parchment (ˈpaːtʃmənt) *ncu* (a sheet of) thin leather from a sheep or goat, or thick, good-quality paper, used for writing on.

pardon (ˈpaːdən) *vt* forgive (someone) for (a mistake, crime, etc.). ●*nu* 1 forgiveness. 2 *nc* the stopping of someone's punishment for a crime. ●*interj* also **I beg your pardon** 1 excuse me; sorry. 2 what did you say?

pare (peə*) *vt* cut away (the outside or edges) of (fruit, one's nails, etc.).

parent (ˈpeərənt) *nc* a father or mother. **parental** (pəˈrentəl) *adj*

parenthesis (pəˈrenθɪsɪs) *nc, pl* **-theses** (θɪsiːz) 1 a group of words that are separate from the main flow of a sentence, usually within brackets. 2 *(pl)* See **bracket** (def. 5). **parenthetical** (ˌpærənˈθetɪkəl) *adj*

parish (ˈpærɪʃ) *nc* 1 a district having its own church and priest. 2 (in England) the smallest district for local government.

park (paːk) *nc* 1 a piece of open or wooded land kept for people's enjoyment. 2 a place where vehicles, etc., are kept. ●*vt* 1 position (a motor vehicle), esp. so that it can be left for a time. 2 *infml* put; leave: *Can I park the kids with you?*

parliament (ˈpaːləmənt) *nc* a gathering of people who represent the population in deciding how a country should be run. **parliamentary** (ˌpaːləˈmentrɪ) *adj*

parlour *US* **parlor** (ˈpaːlə*) *nc* 1 *old-fashioned* a room for receiving visitors in. 2 *chiefly US* a room or shop for a particular business: *a beauty parlor.*

parody (ˈpærədɪ) *nc, pl* **-dies** a piece of writing or music imitating and making fun of another writer's or composer's works. ●*vt* write or be a parody of.

parole (pəˈrəʊl) *nu* the early freeing of a prisoner if he behaves well in prison. ●*vt* free (a prisoner) early.

parrot (ˈpærət) *nc* 1 any of various brightly coloured birds that live in hot parts of the world and can learn to repeat words: see picture at **birds**. 2 a person who repeats or imitates words or actions without thinking or understanding. ●*vt* repeat or imitate without thinking or understanding.

parsley (ˈpaːslɪ) *nu* a plant whose leaves are added to food for their taste.

parsnip (ˈpaːsnɪp) *nc* a long pointed plant root, eaten cooked.

parson (ˈpaːsən) *nc* a priest, esp. of the Church of England.

part (paːt) *nc* 1 a piece or not the whole of something: *He only told a part of the story.* 2 a character played by an actor: *a good part in a play.* 3 a share in an activity: *I shall do my part.* 4 one of several equal quantities: *Use one part of butter to two parts of flour.* 5 a set of musical notes for one of two or more voices or instruments: *This song has a piano part.* 6 *(pl)* a district: *I'm a stranger in these parts.* ●*vti* 1 separate; divide. 2 *vi* leave each other: *They parted as enemies.* **part with** give (something) up or away. **for the most part** See under **most. in part** partly. **on the part of** done by; coming from: *There were no complaints on the part of the local people.* **part of speech** a class of words in a language that may be used in similar places in sentences, such as verb and noun. **take part (in)** help (in an activity).

partake (paːˈteɪk) *vi* 1 (often followed by **in**) join in or take part (in). 2 (often followed by **of**) take a share, esp. of food or drink.

partial (ˈpaːʃəl) *adj* 1 to do with only a part; not complete: *the partial agreement of the group.* 2 (often followed by **to**) liking: *I'm quite partial to ice cream.* 3 unfair: *a partial judgement.* **partially** *adv*

participate (paːˈtɪsɪpeɪt) *vi* take part. **participant** *nc* **participation** (paˌtɪsɪˈpeɪʃən) *nu*

participle (ˈpaːtɪsɪpəl) *nc* a form of a verb, used in some tenses and as an adjective: *The present participle of 'go' is 'going', and the past participle is 'gone'.*

particle (ˈpaːtɪkəl) *nc* 1 a very small piece (of something): *dust particles.* 2 *grammar* a word like 'to', 'and', or 'but' that joins the other important words in a sentence.

particular (pəˈtɪkjʊlə*) *adj* 1 being or to do with one and no other; special: *a report on a particular case.* 2 unusual: *of particular importance.* 3 difficult to please: *He is particular about what he eats.* ●*nc* (often *pl*) a detail: *correct in every particular.* **in particular** specially. **particularly** *adv*

parting (ˈpaːtɪŋ) 1 *ncu* (an instance of) separating or going away. 2 *Brit nc* a line of skin showing on the head, on either side of which the hair is combed in a different direction.

partisan (ˌpaːtɪˈzæn, ˈpaːtɪzæn) *nc* 1 an armed person fighting an army that has occupied his country. 2 a member of a party, follower of a cause, etc. ●*adj* unthinkingly following one cause, etc.

partition (paː'tɪʃən) **1** *nc* a thin wall dividing one room from another. **2** *nu* the act of dividing a country, etc., into parts. ● *vt* divide into parts.

partly ('paːtlɪ) *adv* in part; not completely.

partner ('paːtnə*) *nc* **1** a companion; someone who shares in something with another or others. **2** a husband, boyfriend, wife, or girlfriend. **3** a person one dances with. ● *vt* be a partner to (someone). **partnership 1** *nu* the state of being partners. **2** *nc* a business carried on by two or more people together.

partridge ('paːtrɪdʒ) *nc, pl* **partridges, partridge** a brown bird shot for food: see picture.

partridge

part-time (ˌpaːt'taɪm) *adj, adv* for less time than most people spend working: *a part-time job.*

party ('paːtɪ) *nc, pl* **-ties 1** a social gathering, esp. of friends invited to someone's home: *a dinner party; a birthday party.* **2** also **political party** a group of people with common aims regarding the running of their country. **3** a person having a part in an agreement such as insurance or marriage. **4** a group of people doing something together: *a shooting party.*

pass (paːs) *vt* **1** move past or to beyond (something). **2** cause to move, esp. with the hand: *Pass me the sugar.* **3** do well enough in (an examination). **4** say that (someone) has done well enough in an examination. **5** allow or approve (a law, measure, etc.). **6** spend (time, a season, etc.): *They passed two happy weeks by the sea.* **7** give a (judgement). *vi* **8** move; lead: *He passed along the line of soldiers.* **9** (of a law, measure, etc.) be allowed or approved. **10** happen: *What passed between you?* **11** come to an end; finish: *The illness soon passed.* ● *nc* **1** the act of passing **2** a piece of paper giving someone permission to visit somewhere, etc. **3** a route between high mountains. **pass away 1** come slowly to an end. **2** euphemistic die. **pass by 1** walk or go past (something). **2** take no notice of. **pass for** be taken for or thought to be: *This will have to pass for an answer.* **pass off 1** take place; be carried on: *The discussion passed off smoothly.* **2** cause to be thought to be

(something else) in order to deceive: *He passed the painting off as his own.* **pass on 1** give (news, an object, etc.) to (yet) another person. **2** euphemistic die. **pass out** infml become unconscious.

passable ('paːsəbəl) *adj* fair; just good enough.

passage ('pæsɪdʒ) *nc* **1** a way for someone or something to pass down or along. **2** also **passageway** a long, narrow room off which other rooms lead; corridor. **3** the act of travelling; a journey. **4** a piece of writing in a book: *Find the passage about the second battle.*

passenger ('pæsɪndʒə*) *nc* **1** a traveller in a vehicle that he is not driving, flying, etc. **2** infml a member of a team who is not doing his share of its work, etc.

passer-by (ˌpaːsə'baɪ) *nc, pl* **passers-by** a person passing something, esp. on foot.

passion ('pæʃən) **1** *nc* a strong liking. *nu* **2** strong sexual love. **3** strong feeling. **passionate** ('pæʃənɪt) *adj* feeling or showing passion. **passionately** *adv*

passive ('pæsɪv) *adj* **1** not taking part; inactive: *passive behaviour.* **2** to do with a verb of which the action is done to, not by, its subject: *In 'The book was written by me', 'was written' is a passive verb.*

Passover ('paːsˌəʊvə*) *n* the time of the year at which Jews remember God's sparing of the Israelites in Egypt.

passport ('paːspɔːt) *nc* a small book given to someone by a country's government to say that he is from that country and may travel abroad.

past (paːst) *adj* **1** having passed; over; finished. **2** to do with former times: *past history.* **3** former: *a past leader.* **4** to do with a verb describing a past event. ● *nu* **1** **the past** time that has passed. *nc* **2** someone's past life. **3** a verb describing a past event. ● *prep* **1** (by the side of and) beyond. **2** *US* **after** (used in giving the time of day) beyond: *twenty past two.* ● *adv* so as to go past something or someone.

paste (peɪst) *nu* **1** a substance made from flour and water and used for sticking paper. **2** any soft, stiff substance made for eating, cleaning one's teeth with, etc. **3** a hard glass-like material used for making imitation jewels and pearls. ● *vt* stick with **paste** (def. 1). **pasteboard** *nu* cardboard.

pastel ('pæstəl) *nc* **1** an artist's coloured drawing stick. **2** a picture drawn with these. ● *adj* (of a colour) soft or pale.

pasteurise ('pæstʃəraɪz, 'pæstəraɪz) *vt* heat (milk) in a particular way to kill anything in it that might cause disease.

pastime ('paːstaɪm) *nc* a hobby, sport, or other activity done for enjoyment.

pastor ('pɑːstə*) *nc* a priest in charge of the church or people of a district.

pastoral ('pɑːstərəl) *adj* 1 to do with life in the country. 2 to do with the work of a pastor.

pastry ('peɪstrɪ) *ncu, pl* **-ries** (a piece of food made with) a baked mixture of flour, fat, salt, and water.

pasture ('pɑːstʃə*) *ncu* (a piece of) land covered with grass. ● *vt* keep (animals) on pasture.

pasty[1] ('peɪstɪ) *adj* **-ier, -iest** (of a face) pale; unhealthy-looking.

pasty[2] ('pæstɪ) *nc* a pie containing meat and vegetables with a covering of pastry.

pat (pæt) *vt* hit lightly, esp. with the inside of an open hand. ● *nc* 1 an instance of patting. 2 a small quantity of butter. **off pat** exactly remembered or done: *He said the long speech from the play off pat.*

patch (pætʃ) *nc* 1 a piece of cloth, leather, metal, etc., fixed onto a larger piece to repair it or make a pocket. 2 a part of a surface such as land or skin. ● *vt* fix a patch to. **patch up** 1 mend (something) quickly or roughly. 2 settle (a quarrel, etc.). **patchwork** ('pætʃwɜːk) *nu* material made of many small pieces of cloth sewn together.

patella (pə'telə) *nc, pl* **-lae** (liː) also **kneecap** the small, nearly flat bone in front of the knee-joint.

patent ('peɪtənt, 'pætənt) *nc* a right to be the only maker of an invention. ● *vt* obtain a patent for. ● *adj* 1 patented: *a patent invention.* 2 (of a medicine) sold under a name chosen by its maker. 3 ('peɪtənt) clear for all to see.

paternal (pə'tɜːnəl) *adj* 1 like or to do with a father. 2 on one's father's side of the family: *My paternal grandfather emigrated to Australia in 1925.*

path (pɑːθ) *nc, pl* **-ths** (ðz) 1 a track for walking along. 2 the route or direction followed by something moving. 3 a course of action.

pathetic (pə'θetɪk) *adj* 1 causing sadness or pity: *The homeless children were a pathetic sight.* 2 *Brit, derogatory, slang* useless, uninteresting, etc.: *a pathetic attempt to be funny.*

pathology (pə'θɒlədʒɪ) *nu* the study of the causes and nature of diseases.

pathos ('peɪθɒs) *nu* a **pathetic** (def. 1) quality in language.

pathway ('pɑːθweɪ) *nc* a **path** (def. 1).

patience ('peɪʃəns) *nu* 1 the ability to stay calm when annoyed, in pain, repeatedly failing to do something, etc. 2 *Brit* a card game for only one person.

patient ('peɪʃənt) *adj* having or showing patience. ● *nc* a person receiving medical treatment or care. **patiently** *adv*

patio ('pætɪəʊ) *nc, pl* **-s** a piece of ground with a hard surface put on it, next to a house, and esp. used for sitting in the sunshine.

patriarch ('peɪtrɪɑːk) *nc* 1 the male leader of a family or people. 2 an important person in some churches.

patriot ('pætrɪət, 'peɪtrɪət) *nc* a person loyal to his country. **patriotic** (ˌpætrɪ'ɒtɪk, ˌpeɪtrɪ'ɒtɪk) *adj* **patriotism** *nu*

patrol (pə'trəʊl) *nc* (a person or group that carries out) a regular tour of a town, army camp, etc., to guard or observe. ● *vt* go on a patrol of (a place).

patron ('peɪtrən) *nc* 1 a customer of a shop, restaurant, etc., esp. a frequent one. 2 a person who protects or supports (an artist, organisation that helps others, etc.). **patronage** ('pætrənɪdʒ) *nu* the support or custom of a patron.

patronise ('pætrənaɪz) *vt* 1 be a patron of. 2 behave towards (someone) as if he is inferior or less clever than oneself. **patronising** *adj* tending to **patronise** (def. 2).

patter[1] ('pætə*) *vi, nu* (make) the quick tapping noise of rain falling on a window, etc.

patter[2] *nu* the fast speech of an entertainer, salesman, etc. ● *vi* speak quickly, esp. without much meaning.

pattern ('pætən) *nc* 1 a (regular) arrangement of objects, marks, places, events, etc.: *a pattern of behaviour.* 2 an ornamental arrangement of lines, shapes, and colours on cloth, etc. 3 a model or plan of something to be made: *a dress pattern.* ● *vt* put a **pattern** (def. 2) on. **pattern oneself on** copy (someone).

pause (pɔːz) *nc* a wait; a break for a short time. ● *vi* make a pause.

pave (peɪv) *vt* cover (a road, floor, etc.) with flat stones or a material that sets hard. **pavement** *US* **sidewalk** *nc* a paved path for people walking next to a road.

pavilion (pə'vɪljən) *nc* 1 a building used for entertainment, putting something on show, etc. 2 *Brit* a building beside a cricket or football ground used by players to change their clothes, etc.

paw (pɔː) *nc* a foot of an animal such as a dog or lion. ● *vt* 1 (of a horse, bull, or other animal) scrape (the ground) with the feet. 2 *infml* feel with the hands.

pawn (pɔːn) *vt* borrow money by leaving (a possession) with the lender. **pawnbroker** ('pɔːnˌbrəʊkə*) *nc* a person who lends money to the owners of possessions left with him.

pay (peɪ) *vt* 1 give (money) to (someone) for work or goods. 2 make (a visit). 3 give (attention, one's respects, etc.). 4 *vti* be profitable or worth the trouble (to someone):

will pay you to take your time; Does the business pay? ●*nu* money paid for work. **payable** *adj* to be paid: *Your rent is payable monthly.* **pay back 1** give (someone) back (money one has borrowed). **2** do something, esp. harm, to (someone who has done something similar to one). **payee** (peɪˈiː) *nc* the person to whom a cheque, etc., is payable. **payer** *nc* **pay in** put (money) into a bank account. **payload** (ˈpeɪləʊd) *nc* (the weight of) the goods, passengers, etc., carried by a plane, etc. **payment 1** *ncu* (an instance of) paying. **2** *nc* something paid. **pay off 1** (of an action) succeed; turn out to be profitable: *It was a risk, but it paid off.* **2** pay (someone) all the money owed at the end of a job. **3** pay (a debt) completely. **pay out 1** pay (money), esp. to several people. **2** let (a rope, etc.) fall or be pulled away from one. **payroll** (ˈpeɪrəʊl) *nc* a list of employees receiving regular pay. **pay up** pay (a debt) at once or when asked to do so.

pea (piː) *nc* a round green seed eaten as a vegetable: see picture at **vegetables**.

peace (piːs) *nu* **1** absence of war. **2** order within a country. **3** agreement between people. **4** quietness; calmness. **at peace 1** not at war. **2** in agreement. **3** calm. **peaceable** *adj* **1** wanting peace. **2** peaceful. **peaceful** *adj* **1** not at war. **2** calm. **3** to do with peace. **peacefully** *adv* **peacetime** *nu* a period of peace.

peach (piːtʃ) *nc* a soft, juicy fruit with a large stone and furry, red and yellow skin: see picture at **fruits**.

peacock (ˈpiːkɒk) *nc* a bird of which the male has long tail feathers that it can raise and spread out: see picture.

peacock

peak (piːk) *nc* **1** the flat part sticking out at the front of a cap. **2** (the top of) a pointed mountain. **3** the point or time of greatest power, activity, etc.: *Travelling at peak times takes longer.*

peal (piːl) *nc* **1** a loud noise, esp. of thunder, laughter, etc. **2** a series of notes made by bells ringing. ●*vi* **1** sound in a peal. **2** *vti* ring (bells) in a peal (as a welcome, etc.).

peanut (ˈpiːnʌt) *nc* also **ground-nut** the nut-like seed, which is eaten or made into oil, of a plant grown in hot parts of the world.

pear (peə*) *nc* a juicy fruit, with a brown or greenish-yellow skin, that gets narrower towards the top: see picture at **fruits**.

pearl (pɜːl) *nc* **1** a small, white, valuable, stone-like ball found in some oysters and used in jewellery. **2** a person one admires and respects. **pearly** *adj* **-ier, -iest.**

peasant (ˈpezənt) *nc* **1** a person living and working in the country, esp. on a farm. **2** *infml, derogatory* a person who does not understand or like civilised things.

peat (piːt) *nu* a brown substance formed from dead plants that is dug out of the ground and either used to help plants grow or dried and burnt for heat.

pebble (ˈpebəl) *nc* a small stone rounded by being in moving water.

peck (pek) **1** *vti* (esp. of a bird) strike with its beak (at). **2** *vt* make (a hole) by pecking. ●*nc* an instance of pecking.

peculiar (pɪˈkjuːlɪə*) *adj* **1** strange; odd. **2** special; particular: *Everyone has his own peculiar likes; Lions are not peculiar to Africa.* **peculiarity** (pɪˌkjuːlɪˈærɪtɪ) **1** *ncu, pl* **-ties** (an instance of) being peculiar. **2** *nc* something that is peculiar. **peculiarly** *adv*

pedal (ˈpedəl) *nc* a part of a machine or musical instrument pressed or sometimes lifted with the foot. ●*vt* **1** move (a bicycle, boat, etc.) by working the pedals. **2** *vi* work the pedals of a machine or instrument.

peddle (ˈpedəl) *vt* **1** travel around selling (something). **2** sell (illegal drugs). **peddler** *US n* See **pedlar.**

pedestal (ˈpedɪstəl) *nc* a block of stone, wood, etc., on which a statue, pillar, etc., is supported.

pedestrian (pɪˈdestrɪən) *nc* a person travelling on foot. ●*adj* **1** for, or to do with, walking. **2** ordinary or boring.

pediatrics (ˌpiːdɪˈætrɪks) *US n* See **paediatrics.**

pedigree (ˈpedɪgriː) *nc* a line of descent, esp. of an animal. ●*adj* having a good pedigree.

pedlar *US* **peddler** (ˈpedlə*) *nc* a person who peddles something.

peek (piːk) *vi* look quickly or secretly. ●*nc* a quick or secret look.

peel (piːl) *vt* **1** cut or pull the skin or covering off (fruit, etc.). *vi* **2** (of a tree, the body, etc.) lose its skin or covering. **3** (of paint, tree bark, etc.) come away. ●*nu* the skin of an apple, orange, etc.

peep (piːp) *vi* look secretly, esp. through a narrow hole, etc. ●*nc* such a look.

peer¹ (pɪə*) *vi* look hard or with difficulty.

peer² *nc* **1** (chiefly in the UK) a noble person. **2** someone of the same age or class as oneself. **peerage** (ˈpɪərɪdʒ) *nu* peers (**peer²** def. 1) as a group.

peg (peg) *nc* **1** a thick pin of wood, metal, etc., fixed to something to hold it together, hang a coat on, fix a tent to the ground, etc. **2** *Brit* also **clothes peg** a split wooden pin or device with a spring for holding washing on a line to dry. ● *vt* **1** fix with a peg. **2** fix (prices, etc.) at a constant level.

pelican ('pelɪkən) *nc* a large water bird that traps fish in a bag under its mouth: see picture at **birds**.

pellet ('pelɪt) *nc* a small hard ball of something.

pelt¹ (pelt) *nc* the skin and fur of an animal.

pelt² **1** *vt* throw a large number of things at (someone): *He was pelted with stones.* *vi* **2** rain heavily. **3** travel or run fast.

pelvis ('pelvɪs) *nc, pl* **-vises, -ves** (viːz) the circle of bones to which, in man, the legs are joined.

pen¹ (pen) *nc* a writing instrument using ink. **the pen** writing; literature: *The pen is mightier than the sword.* ● *vt formal* write (a letter). **pen-friend** *nc* a friend, esp. abroad, with whom one exchanges letters but whom in most cases one does not meet.

pen² *nc* a small piece of land with a fence round it to keep farm animals such as sheep in. ● *vt* shut or keep in a pen.

pen³ *nc* a female swan.

penalty ('penəltɪ) *nc, pl* **-ties 1** a punishment. **2** a disadvantage brought on one or one's team by one's own action.

penance ('penəns) *nc* the act of punishing oneself for a sin or other wrong.

pence (pens) plural of **penny**.

pencil ('pensəl) *nc* **1** a writing instrument made of 'lead' (actually graphite) in a tube of wood that is cut away as the lead is used up. **2** a long, narrow shape. ● *vt* write with a pencil.

pendant ('pendənt) *nc* a piece of jewellery made up of an ornament hanging from a chain.

pending ('pendɪŋ) *adj* not yet settled or decided: *That decision is still pending.* ● *prep* until: *I shall allow this pending a final decision by the board.*

pendulum ('pendjʊləm) *nc* a hanging weight that is free to swing, esp. one controlling a clock.

penetrate ('penɪtreɪt) *vt* **1** make one's way into or through: *We soon penetrated the enemy's defences.* **2** see through (darkness, mist, etc.). **3** understand (an idea, someone's mind, etc.). **penetrating** *adj* **1** (of a noise) unpleasantly loud. **2** (of someone's mind) able to understand quickly or easily. **penetration** *nu*

penguin ('peŋgwɪn) *nc* a sea-bird in the cold southern part of the world that cannot fly but swims underwater: see picture.

penguin

penicillin (ˌpenɪ'sɪlɪn) *nu* a drug made from a fungus and used to kill tiny organisms that cause disease.

peninsula (pɪ'nɪnsjʊlə) *nc* a piece of land sticking out into the sea or a lake.

penis ('piːnɪs) *nc, pl* **-nises, -nes** (niːz) the part of a male body used for putting seed into a female and for getting rid of liquid body waste.

penitent ('penɪtənt) *adj* sorry; feeling regret.

penknife ('pennaɪf) *nc, pl* **-ves** (vz) a small knife of which the blade(s) fold(s) into the handle.

pennant ('penənt) *nc* a small flag narrowing towards one side, esp. used on ships for signalling, etc.

penniless ('penɪlɪs) *adj* having no money or very poor.

penny ('penɪ) *nc, pl* **pennies, pence** See appendix. **spend a penny** *infml* go to the lavatory. **the penny dropped** the meaning of what was said was understood at last.

pension ('penʃən) *nc* **1** a regular payment made by a government or former employer to someone when he stops work or reaches a certain age. **2** a boarding-house. ● *vt* (start to) pay a pension to. **pensioner** *nc* a person receiving a pension, esp. on account of old age.

pensive ('pensɪv) *adj* deep in thought, esp. sad.

pentagon ('pentəgən) *nc* a five-sided figure. **the Pentagon** the building in the USA from which orders are given to its armed forces.

Pentecostal (ˌpentɪ'kɒstəl) *adj* to do with Christian churches that consider the influence of the Holy Spirit as very important.

pent-up ('pent.ʌp) *adj* shut in; not allowed out: *pent-up anger.*

penultimate (pɪ'nʌltɪmət) *adj* last but one.

penumbra (pɪ'nʌmbrə) *nc, pl* **-brae** (briː). **-bras** the part of a shadow where some light falls: see picture.

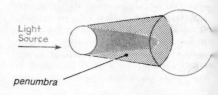

Light Source

penumbra

people ('pi:pəl) plural of **person**. *nc* **1** a race or nation. **2** a large number, group, or class of persons: *the common people*. **3** one's family. ● *vt* provide or occupy (land, etc.) with people.

pepper ('pepə*) *ncu* **1** (a type of) seed that is dried, powdered, and added to food for its sharp taste. **2** a hollow red, green, or yellow fruit eaten cooked or in salad. ● *vt* **1** add **pepper** (def. 1) to. **2** provide (something) plentifully (with something else): *His talk is peppered with jokes*. **3** hit (someone or something) repeatedly (with small objects).

peppermint ('pepəmint) *ncu* ((a sweet made from) the oil of) a particular mint plant.

pep (pep) *nu* energy; spirit. ● *vt* (usually followed by **up**) add pep to: *He looks so sad—he needs pepping up*.

per (pɜ:* unstressed pə*) *prep* **1** in or for each: *ten kilometres per hour*. **2** *formal* by: *as per your wishes*. **per annum** ('ænəm) each year. **per cent** See under **cent**.

peradventure (,pɜ:rəd'ventʃə*) *archaic adv* perhaps. ● *nu* a chance; doubt: *If, by some peradventure, this happens,...*

perambulator (pə'ræmbjʊ,leitə*) *formal n* See **pram**.

perceive (pə'si:v) *vt* **1** learn of or discover, esp. by seeing. **2** understand.

percentage (pə'sentidʒ) *nc* **1** a number's relationship to another number expressed as a number per hundred: *A half, expressed as a percentage, is fifty per cent*. **2** *infml* a share: *What's my percentage of the profits?*

perceptible (pə'septəbəl) *adj* able to be perceived.

perception (pə'sepʃən) *nu* **1** the act of perceiving. **2** the ability to perceive. **perceptive** (pə'septiv) *adj* good or quick at perceiving.

perch¹ (pɜ:tʃ) *nc* **1** a branch, etc., on which a bird rests, off the ground. **2** any similar high place. ● *vti* (cause to) land or rest on a perch.

perch² *nc* a freshwater fish with sharp points on its fins.

perchance (pə'tʃɑ:ns) *archaic adv* **1** by chance. **2** perhaps.

percolate ('pɜ:kəleit) *vti* **1** (of a liquid), (cause to) flow slowly through something solid. **2** (of coffee), (cause to) be made by percolating.

percussion (pə'kʌʃən) **1** *nc* (the noise of) a blow or hit. **2** *nu* musical instruments played by hitting, such as a drum or piano.

perennial (pə'reniəl) *adj* **1** lasting for a long time or for ever. **2** lasting all year. ● *nc* a plant that lives for several years.

perfect ('pɜ:fikt) *adj* **1** good or correct in every way. **2** complete; total: *a perfect stranger*. **3** to do with a verb describing a completed past event, such as 'I have sung'. ● *nu* **1** the class of perfect verbs. **2** *nc* a verb in the perfect. ● (pə'fekt) *vt* make **perfect** (def. 1). **perfection** (pə'fekʃən) *nu* **1** the act of perfecting. **2** the state of being **perfect** (def. 1). **perfectly** *adv* in a **perfect** (defs. 1, 2) way.

perforate ('pɜ:fəreit) *vt* make holes in (something, esp. paper to make it easy to tear). **perforation** (,pɜ:fə'reiʃən) *ncu* (a hole or holes made by) perforating.

perforce (pə'fɔ:s) *formal adv* of necessity; unavoidably.

perform (pə'fɔ:m) *vti* **1** carry out (a task). **2** act in (a play, etc.). **3** behave, esp. well. **performance** (pə'fɔ:məns) **1** *nu* the act of performing. *nc* **2** an occasion on which a play, etc., is performed: *We give two performances a night*. **3** a quality of performance: *a car with good performance*. **4** *infml* a troublesome task. **performer** *nc*

perfume ('pɜ:fju:m) **1** *ncu* (a type of) liquid made from flowers, etc., and used to give a pleasant smell to the body. **2** *nc* a pleasant smell. ● (pə'fju:m) *vt* give a pleasant smell to.

perhaps (pə'hæps) *adv* possibly; it may be.

peril ('peril) *ncu* (a) danger or risk. **perilous** ('periləs) *adj* dangerous; risky.

perimeter (pə'rimitə*) *nc* (a line round) the edge of something.

period ('piəriəd) *nc* **1** an amount of time. **2** a school lesson. **3** *chiefly US* a full stop. **4** an instance of menstruation. ● *adj* to do with a (particular) period of history: *The actors were in period dress*. **periodic** (,piəri'ɒdik) *adj* **1** happening occasionally. **2** happening regularly. **periodical** (,piəri'ɒdikəl) *adj* periodic. ● *nc* a magazine that appears regularly, esp. every week or month. **periodically** (,piəri'ɒdikli) *adv*

periphery (pə'rifəri) *nc, pl* **-ries** the outside edge of something.

periscope ('periskəʊp) *nc* a device made, for example, of mirrors in a tube, that allows one to see over something, esp. over the water from inside a submarine while it is beneath the surface.

perish ('periʃ) *vi* **1** (of rubber, leather, etc.) rot. **2** die; be destroyed. **perishable** *adj* that rots easily or quickly. ● *nc (often pl)* a perishable substance, esp. food such as fruit.

perjury ('pɜ:dʒəri) *nc, pl* **-ries** the act of telling a lie in a law court when one has sworn to tell the truth.

perk¹ (pɜ:k) *v* **perk up** make or become lively or confident.

perk² *infml nc (often pl)* money, an advantage, etc., obtained from one's job other than one's normal pay: *His company car is a good perk.*

permanent ('pɜːmənənt) *adj* lasting or intended to last for an unknown, esp. long, time. **permanence** *nu* **permanently** *adv* **Permanent Under-Secretary** See under **Secretary.**

permeable ('pɜːmɪəbəl) *adj* able to be permeated by a liquid, gas, etc.

permeate ('pɜːmɪeɪt) **1** *vt* (of a liquid) flow slowly through (a solid). **2** *vti* spread (through); fill: *The party was gradually permeated with her joy.*

permissible (pə'mɪsəbəl) *adj* allowable or allowed.

permission (pə'mɪʃən) *nu* the state of being allowed to do something: *Have you permission to leave?*

permit (pə'mɪt) *vt* allow (something), (someone to do something), etc. ● ('pɜːmɪt) *nc* a paper giving permission for something.

pernicious (pə'nɪʃəs) *adj* causing great harm or ruin.

perpendicular (ˌpɜːpən'dɪkjʊlə*) *adj* **1** at right angles. **2** upright. ●*nc* a line at right angles to another.

perpetrate ('pɜːpɪtreɪt) *formal vt* carry out or cause (a crime, etc.).

perpetual (pə'petjʊəl) *adj* **1** permanent. **2** frequent. **perpetually** *adv* **perpetuate** (pə'petjʊeɪt) *vt* cause to last.

perplex (pə'pleks) *vt* puzzle or confuse (someone). **perplexity 1** *nu* the state of being perplexed. **2** *nc, pl* **-ties** something that perplexes.

persecute ('pɜːsɪkjuːt) *vt* harm or trouble (someone) unfairly. **persecution** (ˌpɜːsɪ'kjuːʃən) *nu* **persecutor** *nc*

persevere (ˌpɜːsɪ'vɪə*) *vi* continue in spite of difficulties. **perseverance** *nu* the act of persevering or ability to persevere.

persist (pə'sɪst) *vi* continue, esp. in spite of difficulties or not being allowed to do something: *Why do you persist in telling lies?* **persistence** *nu* the act of persisting or ability to persist. **persistent** *adj* having or showing persistence.

person ('pɜːsən) *nc* **1** *pl* **-s, people** a single, particular human: *that person; person or persons unknown.* **2** *pl* **-s** any of the three classes of pronouns and verbs, divided according to whether they refer to the speaker or writer (first person), someone spoken or written to (second person), or someone or something else (third person). **3** a human body; self: *He will be here in person to explain his views.*

personage ('pɜːsənɪdʒ) *nc* an important person.

personal ('pɜːsənəl) *adj* **1** with the person actually appearing, taking part, etc.: *a per-*sonal appearance. **2** for or to do with one particular person: *my personal opinion.* **3** rude: *Don't make personal remarks.* **4** private: *a personal letter from a friend.* **5** to do with the body. **personalise** *vt* make personal, esp. by marking with someone's name. **personally** *adv*

personality (ˌpɜːsə'nælɪtɪ) **1** *ncu, pl* **-ties** a person's character or nature. **2** *nc* a famous person.

personnel (ˌpɜːsə'nel) *nu* the people employed by a company, army, etc.

perspective (pə'spektɪv) *nu* **1** the way of painting or drawing objects so that they appear to be positioned and as large, far away, etc., as they really are. **2** a view of the world in which everything is given its correct importance: *Let's get this issue in perspective.* **3** *nc* a way of looking (at something); view: *We have very different perspectives on this matter.*

perspex ('pɜːspeks) *Trademark nu* a plastic material similar to but less easily breakable than glass.

perspire (pə'spaɪə*) *polite vti* sweat. **perspiration** (ˌpɜːspə'reɪʃən) *nu* **1** sweat. **2** the act of sweating.

persuade (pə'sweɪd) *vt* **1** cause (someone to do something): *I persuaded him to let us go.* **2** cause (someone) to believe: *He persuaded me that he was right.* **persuasion** (pə'sweɪʒən) *nu* **1** the ability to persuade. **2** the act of persuading. **3** *ncu* (a) belief: *Are you of the same persuasion as us?* **persuasive** (pə'sweɪsɪv) *adj* able to persuade people.

pert (pɜːt) *adj* **-er, -est 1** naughty and not having proper respect. **2** cheerful and confident.

pertain (pə'teɪn) *formal vi* (often followed by **to**) belong (to) or have to do with.

pertinent ('pɜːtɪnənt) *adj* to do with the matter being considered.

perturb (pə'tɜːb) *vt* disturb; trouble; throw into confusion.

peruse (pə'ruːz) *vt* read; examine.

pervade (pə'veɪd) *vt* spread slowly through: *Smoke pervaded the room.*

perverse (pə'vɜːs) *adj* differing on purpose from what is normal or expected.

pervert (pə'vɜːt) *vt* **1** use for a wrong purpose. **2** turn from right actions.

pessimism ('pesɪmɪzəm) *nu* the practice of looking for the bad in everything and expecting the worst. **pessimist** *nc* a person who has pessimism. **pessimistic** (ˌpesɪ'mɪstɪk) *adj*

pest (pest) *nc* **1** an animal that damages plants being grown by man or harms his animals. **2** an annoying person or thing: *My little brother is a pest.*

pester ('pestə*) *vt* annoy (someone) by asking a lot of questions, etc.

pestilence ('pestɪləns) *nc* **1** *chiefly archaic* a disease caught by large numbers of people at the same time. **2** *infml, humorous* a nuisance.

pet (pet) *nc* **1** a tame animal kept in or around one's house for pleasure. **2** *derogatory* a favourite person: *the teacher's pet.* ●*adj* favourite; particular personal: *a pet hate.* ●*vt* **1** treat as a pet. **2** stroke lovingly.

petal ('petəl) *nc* any of the leaf-like parts of a flower, usually coloured and forming a ring.

peter ('piːtə*) *v* **peter out** (of a road, or a flow or supply of something) get narrower or smaller and come to an end.

petition (pə'tɪʃən) *nc* a paper signed usually by many people asking a king, government, etc., to do or not do something. ●*vti* ask (someone) formally (for something).

petrify ('petrɪfaɪ) **1** *vt* frighten greatly. **2** *vti* turn into stone.

petrol ('petrəl) *US* **gasoline** *ncu* a (type of) light, explosive oil made from petroleum and used to power car engines, etc. **petrol station** a place where petrol is sold.

petroleum (pɪ'trəʊlɪəm) *n* See **oil** (def. 2).

petticoat ('petɪkəʊt) *nc* a women's garment like a dress or skirt but worn under one of these.

petty ('petɪ) *adj* **-ier, -iest 1** unimportant. **2** having or showing meanness or spite. **petty cash** money in coins and notes used for or received as small payments. **petty officer** a member of a navy, just below a full officer.

petulant ('petjʊlənt) *adj* annoyingly impatient or not doing as one is told.

petunia (pɪ'tjuːnɪə) *nc* a plant grown for its white or purple flowers.

pew (pjuː) *nc* **1** a wide seat for several people in a church. **2** *infml* a seat.

pewter ('pjuːtə*) *nu* a metal made of tin mixed with lead.

phantom ('fæntəm) *nc* something, esp. the figure of a person, that can be seen but has no material form.

pharmacy ('faːməsɪ) **1** *nc, pl* **-cies** a place where medicines are prepared and given out. **2** *nu* the practice of preparing and giving out medicines. **pharmacist** *nc* a person who practises pharmacy.

pharynx ('færɪŋks) *medicine nc, pl* **-rynxes, -rynges** (rɪn'dʒiːz) the top part of the tube leading from the mouth to the stomach; throat.

phase (feɪz) *nc* **1** a stage or period of a change or development. **2** a fixed period describing the appearance of a moon or planet from the earth. ●*vt* spread (a change) over a period. **phase in** or **out** bring in or get rid of (something) slowly or bit by bit.

pheasant ('fezənt) *nc* a long-tailed, mainly brown bird that is shot for food: see picture.

pheasant

phenomenon (fɪ'nɒmɪnən) *nc, pl* **-mena** (mɪnə) **1** any thing or event that can be seen, smelt, touched, etc. **2** a remarkable person, thing, or event. **phenomenal** *adj* huge; very surprising.

philanthropic (ˌfɪlən'θrɒpɪk) *adj* showing care or love for other people.

philosophy (fɪ'lɒsəfɪ) **1** *nu* the study of the nature of truth, existence, etc. *nc, pl* **-phies 2** a system of thought. **3** one's ideas about life. **philosopher** *nc* a person who studies philosophy. **philosophical** (ˌfɪlə'sɒfɪkəl) *adj* **1** to do with philosophy. **2** calm; unworried by difficulties. **philosophically** *adv*

phlegm (flem) *nu* a thick liquid coat to the inside of the throat, mouth, etc. **phlegmatic** (fleg'mætɪk) *adj* calm; not easily excited.

phone (fəʊn) *infml n, v* short for **telephone**. **phone back** See **ring back** under **ring**.

phonetics (fə'netɪks) *nu (with singular verb)* the study of the sounds of language.

phosphate ('fɒsfeɪt) *nc* any of several chemicals containing phosphorus, used esp. to make plants grow better.

phosphorus ('fɒsfərəs) *nu* a chemical element used, for example, in matches: symbol P

photocopy ('fəʊtəʊˌkɒpɪ) *nc, pl* **-pies** a photographically-made copy of something written or drawn. ●*vt* make a photocopy of.

photograph ('fəʊtəgrɑːf) *nc (infml abbrev.* **photo.** ('fəʊtəʊ) *pl* **-s**) a picture produced chemically by light falling on the film in a camera. ●*vt* take a photograph of. **photographer** (fə'tɒgrəfə*) *nc* **photographic** (ˌfəʊtə'græfɪk) *adj* **photography** (fə'tɒgrəfɪ) *nu* the art or practice of taking photogaphs.

photosynthesis (ˌfəʊtəʊ'sɪnθəsɪs) *nu* the formation by plants of new material using the energy of light.

phrase (freɪz) *nc* **1** a group of words that makes sense but is usually not a whole sentence. **2** a group of notes in music. ●*vt* express in words.

phylum ('faɪləm) *nc, pl* **-la** (lə) any of the broad divisions of the animal or plant world.

physical ('fɪzɪkəl) *adj* 1 to do with what can be seen, touched, etc.: *the physical world*. 2 to do with the body: *physical exercise*. 3 to do with nature: *a physical impossibility*. 4 to do with physics: *physical chemistry*. **physically** *adv*

physician (fɪ'zɪʃən) *nc* a doctor, esp. one healing diseases with medicine.

physics ('fɪzɪks) *nu (with singular verb)* the science of matter and energy; study of light, heat, electricity, sound, etc. **physicist** ('fɪzɪsɪst) *nc* a person who studies physics.

physiology (,fɪzɪ'ɒlədʒɪ) *nu* the study of the workings of plants and animals. **physiological** (,fɪzɪə'lɒdʒɪkəl) *adj*

physiotherapy (,fɪzɪəʊ'θerəpɪ) *nu* the healing of diseases and injuries by exercise, etc., not medicines.

physique (fɪ'ziːk) *nc* the size, shape, strength, etc., of the body.

piano (pɪ'ænəʊ) *nc, pl* **-s** a musical instrument with strings hit by pressing the keys: see picture at **musical instruments. pianist** ('pɪənɪst) *nc*

pick¹ (pɪk) *vt* 1 choose. 2 take (fruit or flowers) from their trees or plants. 3 open (a lock) with an instrument other than the proper key. 4 get into (a fight, etc.) on purpose. 5 make (one's way) carefully. 6 remove loose bits from (bones, one's teeth, nose, etc.). 7 *vi* (often followed by **at**) eat little of. ● *nu* 1 something picked, esp. the best of a quantity. 2 the act of picking. **pick out** 1 choose. 2 recognise from among others. 3 cause to be noticeable: *The doors are picked out in a different colour.* **pick up** 1 take hold of and lift up. 2 buy (something). 3 collect (people or goods) to deliver somewhere. 4 improve: *Business will soon pick up.* 5 learn, esp. while doing something else. 6 receive (a signal). **pick-up** ('pɪkʌp) *nc* 1 a small, open goods vehicle. 2 a device on a record-player, etc., that turns movements into electrical signals.

pick² *nc* a tool with a long handle and a long, curved metal head for digging up the ground, etc.

picket ('pɪkɪt) *nc* a person or group of people trying to prevent employees, customers, or suppliers from entering a factory or business. ● *vt* act as picket outside (a factory or business).

pickle ('pɪkəl) *nc* 1 (often *pl*) a food, esp. a vegetable, kept good in vinegar, salty water, etc. 2 *infml* a difficult situation; trouble. ● *vt* put (food) in vinegar, salty water, etc., to keep it good.

pickpocket ('pɪk,pɒkɪt) *nc* a person who steals from people's pockets.

picnic ('pɪknɪk) *nc* 1 a meal eaten in the open air. 2 an easy or pleasant thing: *Fighting in deep mud is no picnic.* ● *vi* have a picnic (def. 1).

pictogram ('pɪktəgræm) *nc* a picture or sign representing one or more words, as in Chinese or on signs at airports, etc.

pictorial (pɪk'tɔːrɪəl) *adj* to do with pictures.

picture ('pɪktʃə*) *nc* 1 a drawing, painting, photograph, or other flat representation of something. 2 an idea in one's mind of what something is or looks like. 3 a beautiful person or thing. 4 a cinema film. 5 an example; copy: *a picture of happiness.* ● *vt* 1 imagine. 2 describe. 3 make a picture of. **the pictures** *chiefly Brit* a cinema.

picturesque (,pɪktʃə'resk) *adj* 1 strikingly attractive. 2 (of language) very descriptive; vivid.

pidgin ('pɪdʒɪn) *nc, adj* (being or to do with) a language made from parts of two different languages: *pidgin English.*

pie (paɪ) *nc* a food, esp. with fruit or meat, baked in a dish lined, covered, or both, with pastry. **pie chart** *mathematics* a picture representing percentages as if they were slices of a round pie.

piebald ('paɪbɔːld) *adj, nc* (an animal, esp. a horse) with markings in black and white.

piece (piːs) *nc* 1 a separate part of something: *The pieces of the model train have to be stuck together; a piece of cheese.* 2 a work of art, music, writing, etc. 3 a coin: *a ten-pence piece.* 4 an object used to mark a player's position in a board game. **in pieces** cut or broken up or not yet put together. **to pieces** into separate parts. **piecemeal** ('piːsmiːl) *adv, adj* (done, etc.) bit by bit or in stages. **piece together** put (something) together piece by piece. **piecework** ('piːswɜːk) *nu* work paid for according to results, not the time spent.

pier (pɪə*) *nc* 1 a long platform built out into but never the sea for landing goods or walking on. 2 an upright of brick, stone, etc., supporting a bridge.

pierce (pɪəs) *vt* 1 make a hole with a pointed object. 2 of (a pointed object) make a hole in. **piercing** *adj* (of a sound) high and painfully loud.

piety ('paɪətɪ) *nu* the quality of being pious.

pig (pɪg) *nc* 1 a four-legged animal, esp. pink, widely raised for its meat. 2 *infml, derogatory* a greedy, dirty, or annoying person. ● *vt* *infml* eat greedily. **pig iron** iron in large blocks, ready to be shaped, used in steel, etc. **pigsty** ('pɪgstaɪ) *nc, pl* **-sties** 1 a covered or open space for pigs. 2 *derogatory* a dirty or untidy place. **pigtail**

('pɪgteɪl) *nc* hair held twisted together, hanging from any point on the head.

pigeon ('pɪdʒɪn) **1** *nc* a very common, usually grey bird: see picture at **birds**. **2** *infml nu* (someone's) responsibility: *You'll be taken there, but getting home again is your pigeon.*

piggy (pɪgɪ) *nc, pl* **-gies** *infml, children* **1** a (small) pig. **2** a toe. ● *adj infml* **1** like a pig: *piggy little eyes.* **2** greedy.

pigment ('pɪgmənt) *nc* a substance giving colour to plant or animal material or to paints, inks, etc.

pigmy ('pɪgmɪ) *n* See **pygmy**.

pike¹ (paɪk) *nc* a long wooden pole with a sharp metal point at one end, formerly used as a weapon.

pike² *nc, pl* **pike**, **pikes** a fierce freshwater fish that eats other fish and animals: see picture at **fish**.

pile¹ (paɪl) *nc* a collection of things put one on top of another; heap. ● *vti* **1** arrange or be arranged in a pile. **2** *vi* (followed by **in(to)**, **off**, **out (of)**, etc.) (of a large number of people) move quickly: *We all piled into the cars.* **pile-up** *infml nc* an accident involving several cars, etc.

pile² *nc* a long post driven into the ground to support a building, etc.

pile³ *nu* hairs or threads sticking out from the surface of cloth, etc.

pilfer ('pɪlfə*) *vt* steal small quantities of.

pilgrim ('pɪlgrɪm) *nc* a person who makes a pilgrimage. **pilgrimage** *nc* a journey to a holy or special place.

pill (pɪl) *nc* a small hard piece of medicine, swallowed whole. **the pill** a pill taken by women to prevent them having children.

pillage ('pɪlɪdʒ) *vt* steal from (a place) during war. ● *nu* the act of pillaging.

pillar ('pɪlə*) *nc* **1** a thick post supporting part of a building, etc. **2** someone or something that gives important support: *a pillar of society.*

pillow ('pɪləʊ) *nc* a cloth case filled esp. with feathers to rest one's head on in bed. **pillowcase** ('pɪləʊkeɪs) *nc* a washable cloth bag used to cover a pillow with.

pilot ('paɪlət) *nc* **1** a person who flies a plane, helicopter, etc. **2** a person who steers a ship, esp. only into or out of ports. **3** something used as a guide or experiment. ● *vt* act as pilot in (a plane), for (someone), etc.

pimple ('pɪmpəl) *nc* a small, red, painful, raised spot on the skin.

pin (pɪn) *nc* **1** a small piece of thin, stiff wire, flattened at one end and sharpened at the other for holding cloth, paper, etc., together. **2** any of various long, narrow pieces of wood, metal, etc., for fastening with. **3** any of nine or ten bottle-shaped objects

knocked over with a ball in a game. ● *vt* fasten with a pin or pins. **pin down 1** stop (an enemy army, etc.) from moving away. **2** make (someone) tell the truth, give more information, etc.: *Can you pin him down to a definite time?* **pinhole** ('pɪnhəʊl) *nc* a very small hole. **pin-up** ('pɪnʌp) *nc* a picture of a popular person or pretty girl.

pinafore ('pɪnəfɔː*) *nc* a garment worn by women to protect the front of their other clothes: see picture.

pinafore

pincers ('pɪnsəz) *n pl* **1** a tool with jaws used for pulling nails out of wood, etc.: see picture at **tools**. **2** the part of the body of a crab, lobster, etc., used for holding.

pinch (pɪntʃ) *vt* **1** hold a small quantity of, esp. the flesh of (someone), tightly between two surfaces, esp. the finger and thumb: *That boy pinched me.* **2** *infml* take or steal. ● *nc* **1** an act of pinching. **2** an amount of something, esp. salt, that one can hold between one finger and thumb.

pine¹ (paɪn) *nc* any of several types of tree with dark green needle-shaped leaves, which do not fall in the autumn, and cones containing seeds: see picture at **trees**; *(also nu)* the wood of this tree.

pine² *vi* **1** (often followed by **for** or an infinitive) long; want sadly: *an old woman pining for her lost sons.* **2** (often followed by **away**) become slowly weaker through worry, sadness, etc.; waste away.

pineapple ('paɪn,æpəl) *nc* a large fruit, yellow inside, with leaves coming out of the top: see picture at **fruits**.

pinion¹ ('pɪnjən) *nc* **1** *poetry* a bird's wing. **2** a large feather. ● *vt* hold (someone's arms) to stop him moving.

pinion² *nc* a small wheel with teeth that fit into those of a larger one, so that the two wheels move at the same time.

pink (pɪŋk) *adj* **-er**, **-est** pale red. ● *ncu* a pink colour.

pinnacle ('pɪnəkəl) *nc* the highest point of something.

pinpoint ('pɪnpɔɪnt) *nc* **1** the point of a pin. **2** something very tiny. ● *vt* find the exact position of.

pint (paɪnt) *nc* a measure for liquids (in Britain 0.568 litres, America 0.473 litres).

pioneer (,paɪə'nɪə*) *nc* 1 one of the first people to do something, esp. go to live in unknown country. 2 a soldier who makes roads, etc. ●*vt* be a **pioneer** (def. 1) of: *This hospital pioneered many modern practices.*

pious ('paɪəs) *adj* (pretending to be) religious.

pip (pɪp) *nc* a seed of a fruit such as an apple or an orange.

pipe (paɪp) *nc* 1 a tube or hollow rod through which a liquid or gas is moved. 2 (a part of) a musical wind instrument made from a pipe. 3 a small bowl attached to a pipe with which tobacco is smoked. ●*vt* 1 move (a liquid or gas) through a pipe. 2 *vi* play (music) on a pipe. **piper** *nc*

pipeline ('paɪplaɪn) *nc* a long, large pipe laid to carry water, oil, or gas across land or under the sea. **in the pipeline** about to be produced, brought out, etc.

pipette (pɪ'pet) *nc* a narrow glass tube for moving or measuring liquid chemicals, etc.: see picture.

pipette

pique (piːk) *vt* annoy (someone); wound (someone's) pride. ●*nu* bad feeling towards someone.

pirate ('paɪərət) *nc* 1 a person who robs ships at sea. 2 a person who copies (something, esp. a book or film) and sells copies without the permission needed. ●*vt* produce (goods, esp. copies of someone else's) without permission.

pistol ('pɪstəl) *nc* a small gun held in one hand.

piston ('pɪstən) *nc* a machine part that fills and can slide up and down a tube so as to turn movement into pressure or pressure into movement.

pit (pɪt) *nc* 1 a hole in the ground, esp. made for digging out coal, etc. 2 a sunken part of a surface, esp. on the body. 3 a lower part of the floor of a theatre, esp. occupied by an orchestra. 4 *(usually pl)* the place where a racing car is prepared or repaired during a race. ●*vti* 1 mark or be marked with pits (**pit** def. 2). 2 *vt* (usually followed by **against**) use (one's strength, wits, etc.) (against another's).

pitch¹ (pɪtʃ) *vt* 1 throw. 2 set up (a tent or camp). 3 sing or play a note: *He pitched that note too low.* 4 aim at a particular level: *Pitch the book at intelligent people.* *vi* 5 slope downwards. 6 move or fall heavily. 7 (of a ship) move up and down at the front and back. ●*nc* 1 an angle of slope. 2 the height of a musical note. 3 *chiefly Brit* a field of play for cricket, football, etc. **pitchfork** ('pɪtʃfɔːk) *nc* a long-handled fork used for moving hay, etc.

pitch² *nu* a black or dark brown substance made from tar that melts when heated and is used esp. to stop water getting between the boards of wooden boats.

pitcher ('pɪtʃə*) *nc* a large container for water, with either one or two handles.

piteous ('pɪtɪəs) *adj* causing pity: *piteous cries for help.*

pitfall ('pɪtfɔːl) *nc* a danger or problem that one does not know about before meeting it.

pith (pɪθ) *nu* 1 the soft white material just inside the outer covering of a fruit such as an orange or lemon. 2 the important part of (a talk, article, etc.). 3 the centre of a stem in a plant.

pitiable ('pɪtɪəbəl) *adj* deserving pity.

pitiful ('pɪtɪfʊl) *adj* 1 deserving pity. 2 *derogatory* useless; not worthy of respect.

pitiless ('pɪtɪlɪs) *adj* showing no pity.

pity ('pɪtɪ) 1 *nu* sorrow caused by someone else's bad luck or suffering. 2 *nc* a fact about which one feels sorry: *What a pity it broke!* ●*vt* feel pity for (someone). **have** or **take pity on** show mercy to or help (someone for whom one feels pity).

pivot ('pɪvət) *nc* 1 a pin or rod on which something turns. 2 an important person or thing on which something depends. ●*vt* 1 fit with a pivot. 2 *vti* move on a pivot.

pixie ('pɪksɪ) *nc* an imaginary little person.

pizza ('piːtsə) *nc* a baked dish of cheese, tomatoes, etc., spread on a round sheet of a kind of bread.

placard ('plækɑːd) *nc* a large notice put up in public or carried by someone.

place (pleɪs) *nc* 1 a point in or a part of space. 2 a position in an order or arrangement: *second place.* 3 the proper position for someone or something: *Put the salt in its place.* 4 a town, village, house, etc.: *a place in the country.* 5 a square in a town: *a market place.* 6 a chance to enter a school, university, career, etc. 7 a page in a book that one had been reading: *I've lost my place.* ●*vt* 1 put. 2 find or show the place of. 3 remember a connection with: *I've seen that man before but I can't place him.* 4 make (an order for goods, a bet, etc.). 5 find a home, job, etc., for. **in** or **out of place** 1 in or not in the correct place. 2 in or not in keeping; suitable or unsuitable. **in place of** instead of. **in the first, second,**

etc., **place** as the first, second, etc., point in an argument, etc. **take place** happen. **take the place of** act or serve instead of. **placement 1** *nu* the act of placing or being placed. **2** *nc* the act or state of being found a job, home, etc.

placid ('plæsɪd) *adj* calm; untroubled.

plague (pleɪg) *nc* a dangerous disease caught by many people at once. ● *vt* annoy or trouble.

plaice (pleɪs) *ncu* a kind of flat fish used for food; see picture at **fish.**

plaid (plæd) *nc* a long, woollen cloth with a square pattern worn over one shoulder by Scotsmen. ● *adj* having a pattern consisting of squares and lines in various sizes and colours.

plain (pleɪn) *adj* **-er, -est 1** clear; easy to see or understand. **2** flat; smooth. **3** ordinary. **4** with no pattern; all one colour. **5** not pretty or beautiful. **6** not mixed. **7** honest. ● *nc* a large piece of flat, open land. **plainly** *adv*

plaintiff ('pleɪntɪf) *nc* a person who brings a lawsuit against someone else.

plaintive ('pleɪntɪv) *adj* sad-sounding.

plait (plæt) *vt* cross three bunches or lines of (hair, etc.) repeatedly over each other to make one bunch. ● *nc* a plaited bunch of hair, etc.

plan (plæn) *nc* **1** an intended method for doing something. **2** a map, esp. of a town or the rooms in a building. ● *vt* **1** make a plan of or for. **2** intend (to do something).

plane[1] (pleɪn) *nc* **1** short for **aeroplane. 2** a flat surface. **3** a level of thought, knowledge, ability, etc. ● *adj* (of a surface) flat. ● *vi* **1** fly without power. **2** (of a boat) travel higher in the water when going faster.

plane[2] *nc* a tool with a blade sticking slightly out underneath for smoothing or levelling wood: see picture at **tools.** ● *vt* use a plane on.

plane[3] *nc* also **plane tree** a tree with broad leaves, often planted in towns.

planet ('plænɪt) *nc* one of the large objects in space which move round the sun, including the earth. **planetarium** (,plænɪ'teərɪəm) *nc, pl* **-riums, -ria** (rɪə) (a building containing) a device that produces a picture of the night sky by shining lights onto the curved ceiling. **planetary** ('plænɪtərɪ) *adj*

plank (plæŋk) *nc* a long, thick wooden board.

planner ('plænə*) *nc* a person who plans something, esp. where buildings may be put up, roads built, etc.

plant (plɑːnt) *nc* **1** any living thing that is not an animal; tree, flower, or vegetable. **2** any plant that has leaves and roots and is smaller than a tree. **3** a factory. **4** *nu* heavy machines for a particular purpose. **5** *infml nc* someone or something placed so as to provide information or cause trouble. ● *vt* **1** put (seeds or plants) into the ground. **2** put (an idea, etc.) in someone's mind. **3** *infml* place as a plant (def. **5**).

plantain ('plæntɪn) *nc* the green banana-like fruit of a tree grown in many hot parts of the world.

plantation (plæn'teɪʃən, plɑːn'teɪʃən) *nc* a large piece of land where coffee, rubber, tea, etc., is produced.

planter ('plɑːntə*) *nc* the owner or manager of a plantation.

plaque (plæk, plɑːk) **1** *nc* a sheet of stone, wood, etc., with writing on, marking the place where something famous happened, etc. **2** *nu* a substance that forms on teeth if they are not cleaned.

plasma ('plæzmə) *nu* the clear liquid in blood.

plaster ('plɑːstə*) *nu* **1** a mixture of lime and sand that is wetted and spread smoothly over walls and ceilings and then sets hard. **2** also **plaster of Paris** a white powder that is wetted and shaped and then sets hard, used esp. round parts of the body to make broken bones heal properly. **3** *Brit ncu* (a piece of) cloth that is stuck to the skin to cover a wound. ● *vt* **1** cover (a wall or ceiling) with plaster. **2** spread (something) thickly with (something).

plastic ('plæstɪk) *nc* a man-made material that is shaped when hot and firm when cold. ● *adj* **1** made of plastic. **2** able to be shaped. **3** to do with shaping: *plastic surgery.*

plate (pleɪt) *nc* **1** a round, shallow dish for eating from. **2** a sheet of metal or other substance, used as a cover or protection. **3** a sheet of metal with one's name on, on a door, etc. **4** a sheet, usually of metal, used for printing from. **5** a picture printed from a plate. **6** *nu* also **plating** a thin layer of metal, esp. silver or gold, put chemically all over an object of another metal. ● *vt* **1** cover with metal plates (**plate** def. **2**). **2** coat with metal plate.

plateau ('plætəʊ) *nc, pl* **-s, -x** (z) a large piece of high, level ground.

platform ('plætfɔːm) *nc* **1** a level raised (part of a) surface, such as a stage. **2** *Brit* a strip of raised ground at a railway station, from which passengers get onto trains. **3** a set of aims, ideas, etc., expressed esp. by a political party.

platinum ('plætɪnəm) *nu* a chemical element; silvery metal used in jewellery, etc.: symbol Pt

platter ('plætə*) *nc* a large plate for serving food.

plausible ('plɔːzəbəl) *adj* **1** (of an argument, etc.) seeming to be true or reasonable. **2** (of a person) seeming to be telling the truth.

play (pleɪ) *vt* **1** take part in (a game) against (someone). **2** act (a part) in (a play). **3** produce (music) on (an instrument). **4** carry out (a joke or trick) on someone. **5** use (a playing-card) in a game. **6** cause (a radio, · record, etc.) to give out sound. **7** pretend to be: *play dead*. *vi* **8** (of a radio, record, etc.) give out sound. **9** (often followed by **with**) amuse oneself. **10** *vti* direct or be directed: *I played water on the flames*. ●*nc* **1** a written work acted and spoken by actors in a theatre or on television or only spoken on the radio. *nu* **2** games and other amusement, carried on esp. by children. **3** the playing of a game: *Rain stopped play*. **4** freedom of movement, esp. between two connected parts of a machine. **5** a pun: *play on words*. **play at 1** play (a game). **2** pretend to be: *What are you playing at?* **play back** play (the sound) on (a recorded tape). **play-back** ('pleɪbæk) *nu* the act of playing sound or tape back. **play down** cause other people to think (something) less important than it is. **player** *nc* **1** a person taking part in a game. **2** someone who acts, performs on a musical instrument, etc. **playful** *adj* **1** wanting to play or have fun. **2** (of a remark, etc.) funny; not serious. **playground** ('pleɪgraʊnd) *nc* a piece of land where children play. **playing-card** ('pleɪɪŋkɑːd) *nc* any of a set of fifty-two small cards used in several games. **playmate** ('pleɪmeɪt) *nc* a companion in children's play. **play on 1** continue to play. **2** use (someone's feelings) for one's own advantage. **playroom** ('pleɪrʊm) *nc* a room used by children during the day. **plaything** ('pleɪθɪŋ) *nc* a toy. **playtime** ('pleɪtaɪm) *nc* a break between school lessons for small children. **play up** *chiefly Brit* **1** be naughty (with (someone)). **2** (of a machine) not work properly.

plea (pliː) *nc* **1** the act of asking urgently for something. **2** the answer to a charge, made by someone at his trial: *a plea of guilty*.

plead (pliːd) **1** *vi* ask urgently (for something). **2** *vt* say that one is (guilty or not guilty) in answering a charge at one's trial.

pleasant ('plezənt) *adj* giving pleasure; agreeable. **pleasantly** *adv* **pleasantry** ('plezəntrɪ) *nc, pl* **-ries** *(often pl)* an unimportant but polite remark.

please (pliːz) *vt* **1** give pleasure to. **2** like: *Take what you please*. ●*adv* **1** (used for politeness in asking someone for or to do something): *Please go away; Would you close the door, please?* **2** also **yes please** (used to accept an offer or invitation politely.) **pleased** *adj* happy (about, at, or with something). **pleasing** *adj* giving pleasure.

pleasure ('pleʒə*) *ncu* (something or someone that gives) enjoyment or happiness. ●*vi* (often followed by **in**) take pleasure. **pleasurable** ('pleʒərəbəl) *adj* giving pleasure.

pleat (pliːt) *nc* a fold, esp. shaped like a 'Z', in cloth to shorten it. ●*vt* make a pleat in.

pledge (pledʒ) *vt, nc* (make) a formal or serious promise (of): *He pledged his support to the movement.*

plentiful ('plentɪfʊl) *adj* existing in large quantities.

plenty ('plentɪ) *nu, pron* a lot; enough; large number.

pliable ('plaɪəbəl) *adj* easy to bend or influence.

pliers ('plaɪəz) *n pl* a tool with two jaws used for holding something tight: see picture at **tools.**

plight (plaɪt) *nc* a dangerous or hopeless situation.

plod (plɒd) *vi* **1** walk heavily. **2** work slowly and steadily. ●*nc* the act or sound of plodding.

plop (plɒp) *vi, nc* (make) the sound of a small object falling into a liquid.

plot¹ (plɒt) *nc* **1** a secret plan to do something, esp. dishonest or unlawful. **2** the story of a play, etc. ●*vti* **1** (of several people) plan (something dishonest or unlawful) secretly. **2** *vt* mark (a point, course, etc.) on a map.

plot² *nc* a small piece of land.

plough *US* **plow** (plaʊ) *nc* a farm machine with a curved blade that turns the earth over when pulled through it: see picture. **the Plough** *US* **the Big Dipper** a group of stars thought to resemble a plough. ●*vt* **1** turn (earth) over with a plough. **2** *vi* move like a plough: *The car left the road and ploughed into the bushes.* **plough back** use (profits) to build up the business from which they came.

plough

pluck (plʌk) **1** *vti* (when *vi*, often followed by **at**) pull at or off lightly. *vt* **2** pull or pick (feathers) from (a bird). **3** pull (the strings of a musical instrument) and let them go. ●*nc* **1** the act of plucking. **2** *nu* courage. **pluck up one's courage** become confident enough to do something. **plucky** *adj* **-ier, -iest** brave.

plug (plʌg) *nc* **1** an object used to block off a pipe, esp. to stop water flowing out of a bath, etc. **2** a small box with one or more metal pins coming from it, attached to the end of the cable leading to an electrical device and used to connect the device to an electricity supply. ●*vt* put a **plug** (def. 1) in (a pipe, etc.).

plum (plʌm) *nc* a soft, roundish, yellow or dark red fruit with a stone: see picture at **fruits**.

plumage (ˈpluːmɪdʒ) *nu* a bird's feathers.

plumb (plʌm) *nc* a small metal weight lowered on a line to measure the depth of water or to indicate what is exactly upright. ●*adj* exactly upright. ●*adv* straight down. ●*vt* **1** find the bottom of; solve (a mystery). **2** put esp. water pipes in (a building). **plumber** *nc* a person who plumbs buildings and repairs pipes. **plumbing** *nu* **1** the practice or business of a plumber. **2** water, gas, etc., pipes in a building.

plume (pluːm) *nc* **1** a large brightly-coloured feather. **2** something shaped like a plume: *a plume of smoke*.

plump (plʌmp) *adj* **-er, -est** fat or well filled. ●*vt* make plump. **plump for** *infml* choose.

plunder (ˈplʌndə*) *vti* steal (goods) from (a place), esp. in war. ●*nu* **1** something taken in plundering. **2** the act of plundering.

plunge (plʌndʒ) *vti* push or dive deep into something, esp. quickly and without thinking. ●*nc* the act of plunging. **plunger** *nc* a device that pushes or plunges.

plural (ˈplʊərəl) *adj* **1** (of a number) more than one. **2** (of a word) indicating a plural number: *a plural verb*. ●*nc* a plural word.

plus (plʌs) *prep* **1** added to: *Two plus two equals four.* **2** with: *I got another car out of them, plus some money back.* ●*adj* above zero: *a plus figure*. ●*nc* **1** a sign indicating plus (+). **2** *infml* an advantage.

plush (plʌʃ) *infml adj* **-er, -est** smart and expensive-looking. ●*nu* silk or cotton cloth with short, soft hairs on one side.

ply¹ (plaɪ) **1** *vi* (of a ship, bus, etc.) go regularly between one place and another. *vt* **2** work at (a job or trade). **3** offer or supply repeatedly.

ply² *nc, pl* **plies 1** a layer of wood, cloth, etc. **2** one of the threads twisted together with other threads into wool, rope, etc. **plywood** (ˈplaɪwʊd) *nu* thin, strong board made of thin sheets of wood stuck together.

pneumatic (njuːˈmætɪk) *adj* to do with, esp. worked by or containing, air: *a pneumatic tyre*.

pneumonia (njuːˈməʊnɪə) *nu* a serious lung illness.

poach¹ (pəʊtʃ) *vt* **1** cook (an egg) without its shell in boiling water. **2** cook (fish, etc.) in liquid that is almost boiling.

poach² *vt* kill and steal (animals and birds) without permission on someone else's land.

pocket (ˈpɒkɪt) *nc* **1** a small bag in a garment in which to keep money, a handkerchief, etc. **2** a small quantity of something surrounded by something else: *an air pocket*. ●*adj* of the right size for putting in a pocket: *a pocket-knife*. ●*vt* **1** put into one's pocket. **2** take for oneself, esp. steal. **pocket-book** *nc* **1** a small notebook. **2** *US* a small case for money, papers, etc. **pocket money** a small amount of money given regularly, esp. to children.

pod (pɒd) *nc* the long seed-case of a plant, esp. a pea or bean: see picture. ●*vt* take (peas, etc.) out of their pods.

pod

poem (ˈpəʊɪm) *nc* a piece of writing, often arranged in lines of regular length and sound, showing deep feelings, etc., in beautiful language.

poet (ˈpəʊɪt) *nc* a person who writes poetry. **poetic** (pəʊˈetɪk) *adj* to do with poetry.

poetry (ˈpəʊɪtrɪ) *nu* poems collectively.

poignant (ˈpɔɪnjənt) *adj* disturbing the feelings.

point (pɔɪnt) *nc* **1** a sharp end: *the point of a pencil*. **2** an idea; matter: *We have three points to discuss*. **3** an exact place. **4** a special quality: *Her eyes are her best point*. **5** a unit won in a game, the side that wins the most being the winner. **6** *nu* a purpose; aim: *What was the point of doing that?* ●*vt* **1** (often followed by **at**) hold or position (a finger, gun, etc.) along the direction towards someone or something: *Don't point the gun at me!* **2** *vi* (often followed by **at** or **to**) indicate where someone or something is by pointing something at him or it: *He pointed to the guilty man*. **be on the point of doing something** do something soon. **make a point of doing something** do (something one believes to be necessary). **point of view** See under **view**. **to the point** directly connected with the matter being talked about. **point out** show. **pointed** *adj* **1** having a point. **2** aimed directly at a person: *a pointed remark*. **pointless** *adj* without any meaning or purpose. **pointer** *nc* **1** a stick, etc., used for pointing at something. **2** a kind of needle indicating the reading on a measuring instrument. **3** a large dog, used in hunting, that stands with its nose pointing to where a bird or small animal is.

poise (pɔɪz) *nu* **1** calmness of mind and behaviour; quiet self-control. **2** being balanced or steady. **3** a way of walking and holding the head. ● *vti* (cause to) balance or keep steady.

poison (ˈpɔɪzən) *nc* a substance that can harm, destroy, or kill when taken in by an animal or plant. ● *vt* give poison to. **poisonous** *adj* that acts as a poison.

poke (pəʊk) **1** *vt* push (a finger, stick, etc.) into, out of, or through (something): *He poked me in the back with his gun; Don't poke your head out of the window.* **2** *vi* (of a finger, stick, etc.) be pushed into, out of, or through something. ● *nc* a push with a finger, stick, etc.

poker¹ (ˈpəʊkə*) *nu* a card game for two or more players.

poker² *nc* a strong metal tool used for stirring up a fire to keep it burning.

polar (ˈpəʊlə*) *adj* to do with the North or South Pole. **polar bear** a large bear with white fur that lives near the sea round the North Pole. **polarity** (pəˈlærɪtɪ) *nu* the state of having poles (**pole**² defs. 2, 3, 4).

polarise (ˈpəʊləraɪz) **1** *vt* divide (a group) into two, each with opposite or very different opinions, etc. **2** *vi* (of a group) be divided in this way. **polarisation** (ˌpəʊləraɪˈzeɪʃən) *nu* polarising or being polarised.

pole¹ (pəʊl) *nc* a long, strong stick, esp. used as a support: *a flagpole.*

pole² *nc* **1** the most northerly or southerly point of the earth: *the North Pole.* **2** either of two places carrying an opposite electric charge. **3** either end of a magnet. **4** either of two opposite or very different opinions, etc. **Pole Star** a star that is always to the north.

police (pəˈliːs) *nu* a group of people trained and paid to keep public order and peace. ● *vt* control or keep in order with, or as if with, the help of the police. **police station** a building in which the police of a district have their offices. **policeman** (pəˈliːsmən) *nc, pl* **-men** a male member of the police. **policewoman** (pəˈliːsˌwʊmən) *nc, pl* **-women** a female member of the police.

policy (ˈpɒlɪsɪ) *nc, pl* **-cies 1** an action decided upon, esp. by a government or big organisation. **2** also **insurance policy** an insurance agreement, esp. between a person and an insurance company. **3** *nu* wise or sensible behaviour.

poliomyelitis (ˌpəʊlɪəʊˌmaɪəˈlaɪtɪs) (*infml abbrev.* **polio** (ˈpəʊlɪəʊ)) *nu* a disease, esp. affecting children and young adults, that is caught from other people and can damage nerves and so destroy the ability to move parts of the body.

polish (ˈpɒlɪʃ) *vt* **1** rub (a surface) until it shines. **2** make (something) even better or perfect: *a polished result.* **3** *vi* (of a surface) be rubbed until it shines. ● *nu* **1** a shine on a surface. **2** *nc* a wax or other substance used for polishing: *shoe polish.* **3** *nu* the act of polishing. **polish off** finish or use (something) up completely or quickly.

polite (pəˈlaɪt) *adj* giving thought to the feelings and wishes of other people in one's manners, behaviour, etc. **politely** *adv* **politeness** *nu*

political (pəˈlɪtɪkəl) *adj* to do with politics. **politically** *adv*

politician (ˌpɒlɪˈtɪʃən) *nc* **1** a person who is or who wants to be occupied in the government of a country. **2** *derogatory, chiefly US* a person who takes part in the government of a country for his own advantage.

politics (ˈpɒlɪtɪks) **1** *nu* (*with singular verb*) the practice or study of government and authority. **2** *n pl* political opinions, affairs, etc.

poll (pəʊl) *nc* **1** the voting at an election; result of this voting; place where this voting takes place. **2** See **opinion poll** under **opinion.** ● *vt* **1** receive (a number of votes). **2** *vti* give (one's vote) at an election.

pollen (ˈpɒlən) *nu* a powder in a flower that causes other flowers to produce seeds when it is taken to them by the wind, etc.

pollinate (ˈpɒlɪneɪt) *vt* take pollen to (a flower). **pollination** (ˌpɒlɪˈneɪʃən) *nu*

pollute (pəˈluːt) *vt* make dirty or impure: *The sea was polluted with oil.* **pollution** (pəˈluːʃən) **1** *nu* polluting or being polluted. **2** *nc* something that pollutes.

polo (ˈpəʊləʊ) *nu* a game played on horseback using long-handled wooden hammers and a wooden ball.

polygamy (pəˈlɪgəmɪ) *nu* the practice of having more than one wife at the same time.

polygon (ˈpɒlɪgən) *nc* a figure having many straight sides, usually more than five: see picture at **shapes.**

polytechnic (ˌpɒlɪˈteknɪk) *nc* a college that teaches many subjects, esp. those connected with science and industry.

polythene (ˈpɒlɪθiːn) *nu* a strong, plastic material used for wrapping, keeping heat in, making pipes, etc.

pomegranate (ˈpɒmɪˌgrænɪt) *nc* **1** a round fruit with a tough, orange skin containing juicy red flesh and many seeds. **2** a tree bearing this fruit.

pomp (pɒmp) *nu* **1** stately, splendid show, esp. in public. **2** something that seems splendid and worthy of pride but is not really so.

pompous ('pɒmpəs) *adj* thinking oneself to be very important and worthy.

pond (pɒnd) *nc* a hollow place in the ground filled with water used by cattle for drinking, by ducks, etc.

ponder ('pɒndə*) *vti* (when *vi*, often followed by **over**) think (something) over carefully.

ponderous ('pɒndərəs) *adj* **1** heavy. **2** awkward in movement. **3** dull: *a ponderous speech*.

pontoon (pɒn'tuːn) **1** *nc* a boat used as a floating support for a bridge, etc. **2** *nu* a card game.

pony ('pəʊnɪ) *nc, pl* **-nies** a small kind of horse.

poodle ('puːdəl) *nc* a kind of dog with curly hair that is usually cut.

pool¹ (puːl) *nc* **1** a small hollow in the ground filled with water. **2** a small amount of liquid lying on a surface. **3** See **swimming-pool** under **swim.**

pool² *nc* **1** an amount of money that people have joined together to provide in a game or for a business. **2** a game played with balls and long, thin sticks on a table with cushions and holes along its edges. **the (football) pools** a gambling game in which many people risk money on the results of football matches.

poor (pʊə*) *adj* **1** not rich; having little money. **2** of little value. **3** not enough: *a poor night's sleep.* **4** not lucky; unhappy: *Both of the poor child's parents are dead.* **the poor** poor people. **poorly** *adj* not in good health. ●*adv* in a poor manner; badly: *The family has little money so the children are very poorly dressed.*

pop¹ (pɒp) *nc* the sound of a light explosion: *The cork came out of the bottle with a pop.* ●*adv* with such a sound. ●*vti* **1** (cause to) make this sound. **2** *infml* move quickly or for a short time: *I'm just popping upstairs.*

pop² *infml adj* short for **popular.** ●*nu* popular music.

pope (pəʊp) *nc* the head of the Roman Catholic Church.

poplar ('pɒplə*) *nc* a tall, narrow tree; (also *nu*) wood from this tree.

poppy ('pɒpɪ) *nc, pl* **-pies** a plant with red, orange, or white flowers and a milky liquid.

populace ('pɒpjʊləs) *formal nc* all the members of the public, esp. except for those in important positions.

popular ('pɒpjʊlə*) *adj* **1** admired or well-liked by many people. **2** made suitable for most ordinary people's tastes, needs, etc.: *the popular press.* **3** to do with the people: *popular opinion.* **popularise** ('pɒpjʊləraɪz) *vt* make popular. **popularity** (,pɒpjʊ'lærɪtɪ) *nu* **popularly** *adv*

populate ('pɒpjʊleɪt) *vt* **1** live in (a place). **2** supply (a place) with people. **population** (,pɒpjʊ'leɪʃən) *nc* the (number of) people living in a place.

populous ('pɒpjʊləs) *adj* filled with people.

porcelain ('pɔːsəlɪn) *nu* (cups, plates, etc., made from) a delicate kind of baked clay with a glass-like surface.

porch (pɔːtʃ) *nc* an entrance with a roof built outside the door of a house, church, etc.

porcupine ('pɔːkjʊpaɪn) *nc* an animal covered with needle-like parts: see picture.

porcupine

pore¹ (pɔː*) *v* **pore over** read or study (something) very carefully.

pore² *nc* one of the many tiny openings in the skin through which liquids that are given off by the body may pass.

pork (pɔːk) *nu* the flesh of a pig used for food.

pornography (pɔː'nɒgrəfɪ) *nu* books, films, etc., describing sexual activity in an indecent way so as to stir up sexual feelings.

porous ('pɔːrəs) *adj* that allows liquid to pass through.

porpoise ('pɔːpəs) *nc* a sea-animal that is not a fish but related to whales, though much smaller.

porridge ('pɒrɪdʒ) *nu* oats boiled in water or milk and eaten as a soft, hot food.

port¹ (pɔːt) *nc* **1** a place in a river or sea in which ships shelter; harbour. **2** a town with a harbour.

port² *nc* an opening in the side of a ship through which goods are taken in or brought out. **porthole** ('pɔːthəʊl) *nc* a round window in the side of a ship or plane.

port³ *nu, adj* (on) the left-hand side of a ship or plane as one faces the front.

port⁴ *nu* a strong, sweet wine.

portable ('pɔːtəbəl) *adj* that can easily be carried about: *a portable radio.*

portal ('pɔːtəl) *nc* a grand or splendid door or entrance to a building.

portend (pɔː'tend) *formal vt* be a sign or warning of something to happen in the future.

porter ('pɔːtə*) *nc* a person at a railway station, hotel, etc., whose job is to carry luggage.

portfolio (pɔːt'fəʊlɪəʊ) *nc* **1** a flat case in which to keep sheets of paper, drawings, etc. **2** the job of a person in a chief position in a government.

portion ('pɔːʃən) *nc* **1** a part or share. **2** a quantity of food served to one person; helping. ● *vt* divide into shares or parts.

portly ('pɔːtlɪ) *adj* rather fat and heavy.

portrait ('pɔːtrɪt) *nc* a painting, drawing, photograph, etc., of a person, esp. of the face.

portray (pɔː'treɪ) *vt* **1** make a picture of. **2** describe in great detail. **portrayal** (pɔː'treɪəl) **1** *nu* the act of portraying. **2** *nc* a picture or description.

pose (pəʊz) **1** *vt* put forward or bring up (a question, problem, etc.). **2** *vti* (cause to) stand, sit, etc., in a certain position to be painted, photographed, etc. **pose as** pretend to be.

position (pə'zɪʃən) *nc* **1** the place where someone or something is. **2** the way in which someone or something is standing, etc., or is placed. **3** a person's place and reputation in society, at work, etc. **4** a job; employment. **5** an opinion; point of view. **6** a state of affairs: *What's the position at home?* ● *vt* place in position.

positive ('pɒzɪtɪv) *adj* **1** sure; with no doubts: *a positive view of things; a positive statement.* **2** helpful; good: *positive criticism.* **3** complete: *positive stupidity.* **4** (of a number) greater than nothing. **5** (of an electric charge) like that of a proton. ● *nc* a photograph in which light and dark are the right way round, as in real life. **positively** *adv*

possess (pə'zes) *vt* have as belonging to one; own. **in possession of** having or owning. **possession** (pə'zeʃən) **1** *nu* the state of having or owning. **2** *nc* a thing that is owned. **possessive** *adj* **1** to do with possession. **2** wanting possession, control or influence, esp. over another person. **3** *grammar* showing who something belongs to: in 'a child's toy', 'child's' is possessive.

possible ('pɒsəbəl) *adj* that can be done or may be or may happen. **possibility** (,pɒsə'bɪlɪtɪ) **1** *nu* the state of being possible. **2** *nc*, *pl* **-ties** a thing that is possible.

possibly *adv* **1** perhaps; maybe. **2** at all: *I cannot possibly do what you ask.*

post¹ (pəʊst) *nc* a strong, upright piece of wood or metal used as a support or for marking something: *a lamppost.* ● *vt* put up (a notice, etc.) in a public place.

post² *nc* a position in employment; job.

post³ also **mail** *nu* **1** letters, parcels, etc., delivered by a postal service to the houses to which they are addressed. **2** a service that delivers post: *The post is very slow.* ● *vt* take or hand in (a letter, etc.) to be delivered as post. **postbox** ('pəʊstbɒks) *nc* a box in a public place into which letters are posted. **postcard** ('pəʊstkɑːd) *nc* a piece of card with a short message, and sometimes a picture on one side, sent by post without an envelope. **postcode** ('pəʊstkəʊd) *US* **zip code** *nc* a group of letters and numbers added to an address to help a post office in sorting the mail. **postman** ('pəʊstmən) *nc*, *pl* **-men** a person whose job is to deliver mail. **postmark** ('pəʊstmɑːk) *nc* a mark printed over the stamps on letters by a post office giving the date and place where they were collected and preventing the stamps from being used again. **postmaster** ('pəʊst,mɑːstə*) or **postmistress** ('pəʊst,mɪstrɪs) *nc* a man or woman who is paid to be in charge of a post office. **post office** ('pəʊst,ɒfɪs) *nc* **1** a room or building where stamps are sold, etc., and other business connected with the post is dealt with. **2** a service that delivers post. **postpaid** (,pəʊst'peɪd) *adj*, *adv* with the postage paid before posting.

postage ('pəʊstɪdʒ) *nu* the money charged for delivering a letter, etc. **postage stamp** a paper stamp stuck on a letter, parcel, etc. to show that postage has been paid.

postal ('pəʊstəl) *adj* to do with (the) **post³**; post. **postal order** a written order to a post office to pay a certain amount of money to a particular person.

poster ('pəʊstə*) *nc* **1** a printed notice shown in a public place. **2** a large printed picture used as decoration.

posterior (pɒ'stɪərɪə*) *adj* **1** placed at the back of or behind something. **2** coming later in time or order. ● *nc humorous* the part of the body on which one sits.

posterity (pɒ'sterɪtɪ) *nu* **1** all the people in the future. **2** one's descendants.

postgraduate (,pəʊst'grædjʊət) *adj*, *nc* (to do with) a student who continues studying after successfully finishing a university course.

posthumous ('pɒstjʊməs) *adj* happening after one's death. **posthumously** *adv*

post-mortem (,pəʊst'mɔːtəm) *nc*, *adj* (to do with) the examination of a dead body to find out the cause of death.

postpone (pəs'pəʊn) *vt* put off until a later time.

postscript ('pəʊstskrɪpt) (*infml abbrev.* **PS**) *nc* a piece of writing added to a letter after the signature.

postulate ('pɒstjʊleɪt) *vt* put forward (a idea, statement, etc., one considers to be true) in order to reason from it.

posture ('pɒstʃə*) *nc* a way of holding one's head and body. ● *vi* behave in an unnatural or vain way to impress people.

post-war (,pəʊst'wɔː*) *adj* happening, built, etc., after a war.

posy ('pəʊzı) *nc, pl* **-sies** a small bunch of flowers.

pot (pɒt) *nc* a round container made of glass, metal, baked clay, etc.: *a cooking pot; a teapot; Plants can be kept in flowerpots.* ● *vt* **1** put (a plant) with soil in a pot. **2** put meat, butter, etc., in a pot to keep it from decay. **go to pot** *infml* be ruined. **pothole** ('pɒthəʊl) *nc* **1** a hole in a road caused by traffic, rain, etc. **2** a deep hole or cave under the ground caused by running water. ● *vi* explore potholes under the ground.

potash ('pɒtæʃ) *nu* any of several substances containing potassium, esp. used to help plants grow.

potassium (pə'tæsıəm) *nu* a chemical element; soft, silver-white metal: symbol K

potato (pə'teɪtəʊ) *nc, pl* **-es** a root that is nearly white inside, has brown or red skin, and is cooked and eaten as a vegetable: see picture at **vegetables. potato crisp** *US* **potato chip** See **crisp.**

potent ('pəʊtənt) *adj* powerful.

potentate ('pəʊtənteɪt) *nc* a ruler; powerful person.

potential (pə'tenʃəl) *adj* that may happen or be; possible: *a potential danger.* ● *nc* **1** a possibility. **2** *nu* an ability that has not yet been developed or is not yet active. **potentiality** (pə,tenʃı'ælıtı) *nc, pl* **-ties** an ability or power that is present but needs developing. **potentially** *adv*

potter[1] ('pɒtə*) *nc* a person who makes pots out of baked clay. **pottery** ('pɒtərı) **1** *nu* articles made of baked clay. **2** *nc, pl* **-ries** a place where such articles are made.

potter[2] *vi* (often followed by **about**) move about doing various things in one's house, etc., with little purpose but in a pleasant manner.

pouch (paʊtʃ) *nc* **1** a small bag: see picture. **2** the bag in which an animal such as a kangaroo keeps its young.

pouch

poultry ('pəʊltrı) *nu* birds, such as hens, kept by man to provide him with eggs and meat.

pounce (paʊns) *vi* (often followed by **on**) jump or come down on suddenly.

pound[1] (paʊnd) *nc* See appendix.

pound[2] *nc* a measure of weight = 0.454 kg

pound[3] *nc* **1** a place where animals found loose are kept until their owners fetch them. **2** a place where vehicles are taken if left where they should not have been.

pound[4] *vti* **1** beat heavily with the fists again and again (on). **2** *vt* break into very small pieces. *vi* **3** walk, run, or make one's way in a heavy manner. **4** (of one's heart) beat heavily because of fear, after running, etc.

pour (pɔː*) **1** *vt* cause (liquid, etc.) to flow, esp. from one container to another. **2** *vi* (of a liquid, etc.) flow. **3** *vti* (cause to) flow down, out, etc.: *Rain was pouring down.*

pout (paʊt) **1** *vti* push (the lips) out to show displeasure. **2** *vi* (of the lips) be pushed out to show displeasure.

poverty ('pɒvətı) *nu* being poor. **poverty-stricken** ('pɒvətı,strıkən) *adj* made very poor.

powder ('paʊdə*) *ncu* a substance, such as soap or medicine, in tiny, dry pieces. ● *vt* **1** make into powder. **2** cover with powder; put powder on. **powder-room** ('paʊdərʊm) *euphemistic nc* a ladies' lavatory in a hotel, cinema, etc.

power ('paʊə*) *nu* **1** ability to do something: *He did all in his power to help us.* **2** strength; force. **3** control or authority: *He has us in his power.* **4** the ability of glasses, etc., to make things look larger than they really are. **5** energy used to make machines work. *nc* **6** a person, country, etc., with control, influence, or authority. **7** *mathematics* the number of times another number is to be multiplied by itself: *Two to the power of three (written 2^3) is eight.* **powerful** *adj* having great power; strong. **powerless** *adj*

practicable ('præktıkəbəl) *adj* that can be done or used.

practical ('præktıkəl) *adj* **1** of or to do with action rather than just ideas. **2** meant for use; useful: *a practical device.* **3** (of a person) experienced in the practice of something. **practically** *adv* **1** in a practical way. **2** almost.

practice ('præktıs) *nu* **1** the doing of something rather than just thinking about it. **2** a custom; regular habit. **3** the doing of something often and regularly in order to improve: *music practice.* **4** *nc* a job as a dentist, lawyer, family doctor, etc.: *A new doctor has taken over the practice.* **in** or **out of practice** having or not having worked hard at one's skill, etc., often and lately.

practise *US* **practice** ('præktıs) *vt* **1** do (something) often to improve at it and become skilful. **2** do (something) as a regular habit. **3** work at (a profession, etc.): *to practise medicine.*

practitioner (præk'tɪʃənə*) *nc* a person who works at a profession or art, esp. in medicine.

pragmatic (præg'mætɪk) *adj* **1** interested in being practical and keeping to facts rather than ideas. **2** accepting beliefs, etc., as true without reasoning them out.

prairie ('preərɪ) *nc* a large area of grassland without trees.

praise (preɪz) *vt* **1** say that one admires. **2** give honour to (God, a hero, etc.). ● *nu* praising. **praiseworthy** ('preɪz,wɜːðɪ) *adj* worthy of praise.

pram (præm) *nc* a four-wheeled hand-vehicle for carrying a baby lying down.

prance (prɑːns) *vi* **1** walk about in a self-important way. **2** jump around. **3** (of a horse) take lively steps.

prank (præŋk) *nc* a playful, not serious or harmful trick.

prate (preɪt) *vi* talk foolishly or too much.

prattle ('prætəl) *vi* talk in a childish or foolish way.

prawn (prɔːn) *nc* a small sea-animal with a shell, used for food: see picture.

prawn

pray (preɪ) *vti* (when *vt*, often followed by **that**; when *vi*, often followed by **to** or **for**) speak or think prayers: *I pray that I may go to heaven; We prayed to God for the war to end.*

prayer (preə*) *ncu* (set of words spoken or thought in) praying to God.

preach (priːtʃ) *vi* **1** give a serious talk or speech, esp. in church about God and religious teachings. **2** give advice about what is right or wrong. **preacher** ('priːtʃə*) *nc* a person who preaches, esp. in church.

preamble (priː'æmbəl) *nc* the first part of a speech, law, etc., introducing the main part.

precarious (prɪ'keərɪəs) *adj* not certain or safe, likely to lead to danger or failure.

precaution (prɪ'kɔːʃən) *ncu* care or an action taken to avoid an accident, danger, etc.

precede (,prɪ'siːd) *vt* come before in time, order, or importance. **precedent** ('presɪdənt) *nc* something that has happened or been done earlier, taken as an example or rule for what comes later. **preceding** *adj* coming before.

precept ('priːsept) *nc* a rule of behaviour, esp. concerning what is right or wrong.

precinct ('priːsɪŋkt) *nc* a piece of land, part of a building, etc., that is enclosed or marked off. **precincts** the surrounding district.

precious ('preʃəs) *adj* **1** of great value. **2** very dear to a person, whether valuable or not. **3** (of behaviour, language, or a person) not natural or real; trying to make an effect. ● *adv* very.

precipice ('presɪpɪs) *nc* the steep side of a cliff or rock.

precipitate (prɪ'sɪpɪteɪt) *vt* **1** cause (something) to happen sooner than it would have done. **2** throw down with force. **3** *chemistry* cause (a substance dissolved in a liquid) to be separated and left in its solid form at the bottom of a liquid. ● (prɪ'sɪpɪtɪt) *nc* a solid form after precipitation. ● (prɪ'sɪpɪtɪt) *adj* done or said too quickly. **precipitation** (prɪ,sɪpɪ'teɪʃən) *nu* **1** precipitating or being precipitated. **2** (an amount of fallen) rain, snow, etc.

precipitous (prɪ'sɪpɪtəs) *adj* **1** like a precipice; covered with precipices. **2** very steep. **3** hasty.

précis ('preɪsiː) *nc, pl* **précis** ('preɪsiːz) a piece of writing, speech, etc., made shorter by giving only the main points. ● *vt* make a précis of.

precise (prɪ'saɪs) *adj* **1** exact. **2** (of language, etc.) careful and clear. **precisely** *adv* **precision** (prɪ'sɪʒən) *nu*

preclude (prɪ'kluːd) *vt* make (something) impossible, esp. before it would happen.

precocious (prɪ'kəʊʃəs) *adj* (of a child, mind, etc.) having developed earlier than is normal.

predator ('predətə*) *nc* a predatory animal. **predatory** ('predətərɪ) *adj* **1** (of an animal) living by hunting, killing, and eating other animals. **2** to do with stealing, often by force, or living off others.

predecessor ('priːdɪ,sesə*) *nc* someone or something that has come before: *The new headmaster is not as good as his predecessor.*

predetermine (,priːdɪ'tɜːmɪn) *vt* decide that (something) will happen.

predicament (prɪ'dɪkəmənt) *nc* an upsetting, difficult, or dangerous situation from which there seems to be no escape.

predicate ('predɪkət) *nc* the part of a sentence saying something about its subject, such as 'ran away' in 'The boy ran away'.

predict (prɪ'dɪkt) *vt* say that (something) will happen. **predictable** *adj* that can be predicted. **prediction** (prɪ'dɪkʃən) **1** *ncu* (an example of) predicting. **2** *nc* something that is predicted.

predominant (prɪ'dɒmɪnənt) *adj* **1** most easily seen or noticed. **2** having the most control over other people; most important. **predominance** *nu* **predominantly** *adv*

predominate (prɪ'dɒmɪneɪt) *vi* **1** (often followed by **over**) have or use power or influence over another person, etc. **2** be greater in number or stronger, have more influence, etc.

pre-eminent (pri:'emɪnənt) *adj* doing or being better than others.

prefabricate (pri:'fæbrɪkeɪt) *vt* make the parts of (a building, etc.) in a factory before they are fitted together where the building, etc., is to be.

preface ('prefəs) *nc* a statement at the front of a book explaining its subject, etc. ● *vt* supply with a preface; begin.

prefect ('pri:fekt) *nc* **1** (in Rome, long ago) a governor or army officer. **2** (in France) the head of a police force. **3** *Brit* an older boy or girl given some control over the other children in a school.

prefer (prɪ'fɜ:*) *vt* (often followed by **to**) like better; choose (one thing) rather than another: *I prefer fish to meat.*

preferable ('prefərəbəl) *adj* to be preferred; better. **preferably** ('prefərəblɪ) *adv*

preference ('prefərəns) *nu* **1** preferring. **2** special consideration. **3** *nc* something that is preferred.

prefix ('pri:fɪks) *nc* a group of letters, such as 're-' or 'dis-', joined to the front of a word in order to change its meaning. ● *vt* put a prefix in front.

pregnant ('pregnənt) *adj* **1** (of a woman or female animal) carrying a child, children, or other young yet to be born. **2** full of meaning.

prehistoric (,pri:hɪ'stɒrɪk) *adj* before the events of history were put down in writing.

prejudice ('predʒʊdɪs) **1** *nc* an opinion made before knowing or examining all the facts. **2** *nu* the practice of having such opinions. **prejudiced** *adj* having a prejudice.

preliminary (prɪ'lɪmɪnərɪ) *adj* happening before; getting ready for something that is to come; *He made a few preliminary remarks before introducing the speaker.* ● *nc, pl* **-ries** a preliminary action.

prelude ('prelju:d) *nc* **1** a piece of music played before the main or a longer one. **2** anything that comes before or introduces something else.

premature ('premətʃə*) *adj* happening, done, or born before the usual or proper time; too early.

premier ('premɪə*) *adj* first in importance, order, etc. ● *nc* the head of a government.

première ('premɪeə*) *nc* the first public performance of a new play, film, etc.

premise ('premɪs) *nc* a set of facts, views, etc., believed to be true and from which an opinion or conclusion can be reached. **premises** *n pl* a house or other building and the land on which it is built.

premium ('pri:mɪəm) *nc* **1** an extra payment, in addition to what is usual or expected; reward. **2** the money paid for an insurance policy.

preoccupation (pri:,ɒkjʊ'peɪʃən) **1** *nu* a state of having all one's attention or thoughts occupied with something. **2** *nc* something that occupies all one's attention or thoughts. **preoccupied** (pri:'ɒkjʊpaɪd) *adj* being in a state of preoccupation.

prepare (prɪ'peə*) **1** *vti* make or get ready: *Prepare yourself for a shock.* **2** *vt* make (a meal). **preparation** (,prepə'reɪʃən) **1** *nu* preparing or being prepared. *nc* **2** something done to prepare. **3** a prepared substance or material, such as a medicine. **preparatory** (prɪ'pærətərɪ) *adj* making prepared; leading to something else.

preposition (,prepə'zɪʃən) *nc* a word, such as 'in' or 'to', used in front of a noun or pronoun to indicate its relationship to another part of its sentence.

preposterous (prɪ'pɒstərəs) *adj* completely foolish; *What a preposterous idea!*

prerogative (prɪ'rɒgətɪv) *nc* a special right enjoyed only by a certain person, class, etc.

presbyopia (,prezbɪ'əʊpɪə) *nu* a condition in old age of being unable to see things near one clearly.

Presbyterian (,prezbɪ'tɪərɪən) *adj* of or to do with a church governed by the elder members of the people who worship there. ● *nc* a member of the Presbyterian Church.

prescribe (prɪ'skraɪb) *vt* **1** recommend (a medicine or other treatment). **2** direct or order that (an action) be taken. **prescription** (prɪ'skrɪpʃən) **1** *nu* prescribing. **2** *nc* something that is prescribed.

presence ('prezəns) *nu* **1** being present. **2** a person's appearance, way of walking, etc., esp. of a kind that deserves or gets respect.

present¹ ('prezənt) *adj* **1** being in a certain place: *He was present when the accident happened.* **2** now passing, in existence, being dealt with, etc.: *the present year.* ● *adj, nc* grammar (to do with) a form of a verb used to describe the present time: *present tense.* **at present** now. **the present** the present time; now.

present² *nc* a gift; something given: *birthday presents.* ● (prɪ'zent) *vt* **1** introduce; *May I present my parents to you?* **2** give (something) to someone formally on a special occasion: *He was presented with a large cheque when he retired from his job.* **3** show or give (a theatre play, etc.).

presentable (prɪ'zentəbəl) *adj* fit or suitable to be seen.

presentation (ˌprezən'teɪʃən) **1** *nu* presenting or being presented. **2** *nc* something that is presented.

presently ('prezəntlɪ) *adv* **1** soon. **2** *chiefly US* now.

preserve (prɪ'zɜːv) *vt* **1** keep from going bad: *preserved fruit.* **2** protect from danger or harm: *Heaven preserve us!* **3** keep safe from change, loss, or destruction: *We like to preserve old buildings.* ● *nc* **1** a jam. **2** a piece of land in which the animals, birds, and fish are protected. **preservation** (ˌprezə-'veɪʃən) *nu* **1** preserving or being preserved. **2** the state of being well or badly cared for: *The old house was in a poor state of preservation.* **preservative** (prɪ'zɜːvətɪv) *nc, adj* (a substance) that helps to preserve something, esp. food.

preside (prɪ'zaɪd) *vi* have control: *to preside over a meeting.*

president ('prezɪdənt) *nc* **1** the head of a government such as that of the USA. **2** the head of some colleges, societies, etc. **3** *US* the head of a bank or business company. **presidency** ('prezɪdənsɪ) *nc, pl* **-cies 1** the post of a president. **2** the length of time for which one person is president. **presidential** (ˌprezɪ'denʃəl) *adj*

press (pres) **1** *vti* push steadily (against). *vt* **2** use force and heat to make (clothes) smooth and flat; iron. **3** urge. ● *nu* **1** pressing or being pressed. *nc* **2** a device or machine used for pressing: see picture. **3** short for **printing press. 4** a cupboard used for storing clothes, bed-sheets, etc. **be pressed for** not have enough of (esp. time, money, or space). **press for** keep on asking for: *The workers are pressing for higher wages.* **press on 1** hurry. **2** continue firmly to do something. **the press** newspapers, magazines, etc., as a whole. **pressing** *adj* **1** urgent. **2** always asking for something.

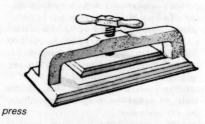

press

pressure ('preʃə*) **1** *nu* pressing or being pressed. *nc* **2** an amount of force applied to a given area. **3** something that causes trouble or difficulty. **pressurise** ('preʃəraɪz) *vt* **1** put under pressure. **2** try to force (someone) into doing something.

prestige (pre'stiːʒ) *nu* a good reputation due to being successful, wealthy, etc.

presume (prɪ'zjuːm) **1** *vt* take to be true before there is proof. **2** *vi* be too self-confident or bold in one's behaviour. **presumably** *adv* **presumptuous** (prɪ'zʌmptʃuəs) *adj* bold and badly behaved.

presuppose (ˌpriːsə'pəuz) *vt* **1** accept as true before proof or reason is given. **2** have as a necessary condition.

pretence *US* **pretense** (prɪ'tens) *nu* **1** pretending. *nc* **2** false behaviour intended to impress, etc. **3** a false reason.

pretend (prɪ'tend) **1** *vt* claim (something untrue): *He pretends that he is rich.* **2** *vti* play at (being or doing something): *The children pretended to be soldiers.*

pretentious (prɪ'tenʃəs) *adj* pretending or claiming, without good reason, to be important or very worthy.

pretext ('priːtekst) *nc* a pretended reason.

pretty ('prɪtɪ) *adj* **-ier, -iest** of pleasing or nice appearance. ● *adv infml* quite; rather: *The weather was pretty bad last week.* **prettily** *adv*

prevail (prɪ'veɪl) *vi* **1** have the most influence, power, etc.: *Truth will prevail.* **2** be generally current or in use: *the prevailing opinion.* **prevail upon** persuade (someone) to do something.

prevalent ('prevələnt) *adj* seen, found, or accepted generally.

prevent (prɪ'vent) *vt* **1** stop (something) happening. **2** stop (someone) from doing something. **prevention** (prɪ'venʃən) *nu* **preventive** (prɪ'ventɪv), **preventative** (prɪ'ventətɪv) *adj, nc* (something, esp. a medicine) used to prevent something, esp. disease.

preview ('priːvjuː) *nc* the act of seeing a film, new car, etc., before the public do.

previous ('priːvɪəs) *adj* **1** coming earlier in time or order. **2** acting, done, etc., too soon. **previously** *adv*

prey (preɪ) *nu* **1** an animal or bird that is hunted by another one for food. **2** a person or thing that suffers under an enemy, disease, etc.: *She's a prey to ill health.* **prey (up)on 1** hunt for as food. **2** worry greatly.

price (praɪs) *nc* **1** the amount of money for which something is bought or sold. **2** that which must be done to obtain anything: *Death can be the price of victory.* **3** *nu* value. ● *vt* **1** give (goods) a price. **2** find out the price of (goods) by asking. **3** mark the price on (goods). **priceless** ('praɪslɪs) *adj* **1** of too great a value to be priced. **2** *infml* very funny.

prick (prɪk) *vt* **1** make a tiny hole or holes in with something sharp-pointed: *I've pricked my finger on a needle.* **2** cause a sharp pain to (the body or mind). **3** *vi* (of the body or mind) feel a sharp pain. ● *nc* **1** a tiny hole made by pricking. **2** a pain made by pricking. **prickle** ('prɪkəl) *nc* one of many sharp-pointed growths on a plant or the skin of an animal. ● *vti* (cause to) have feelings of being pricked. **prickly** *adj* **-ier, -iest 1** covered with prickles. **2** *infml* easily made angry.

pride (praɪd) *nu* **1** the state of having too high an opinion of oneself. **2** being satisfied or pleased with what one, or another person, has done. **3** self-respect. **4** a person or thing with which one is very satisfied or pleased. **5** *nc* a group of lions. **pride oneself on** be proud of.

priest (priːst) *nc* a person, esp. a man, trained to lead prayers and talk on religious matters in a Christian Church. **priesthood** ('priːsthʊd) *nu* **1** the state of being a priest. **2** all priests.

prim (prɪm) *adj* **-mer, -mest** too concerned with what is correct, right, or suitable.

primary ('praɪmərɪ) *adj* first in importance, order, or time. **primarily** *adv*

primate ('praɪmeɪt) *nc* one of the highest class of animals, which includes man and the monkeys.

prime (praɪm) *adj* **1** chief in importance. **2** of the best kind; very good. **3** (of a number such as 2, 3, or 41) that cannot be divided except by itself and the number 1. ● *nu* the time when a person or thing is at his or its best: *He's in the prime of life.* ● *vt* **1** prepare for use. **2** prepare (a person) before an event by supplying him with information, etc., about it. **3** put a first coat of special paint, etc., onto (a surface) to prevent following coats from being taken in through the surface. **prime minister** the head of a government.

primer ('praɪmə*) *nc* **1** a child's first school book. **2** a paint used for priming. **3** a device for setting off an explosion.

primitive ('prɪmɪtɪv) *adj* **1** to do with the earliest period of man's existence. **2** not civilised. **3** not highly developed; simple: *primitive weapons.*

primrose ('prɪmrəʊz) *nc* a wild yellow flower.

prince (prɪns) *nc* **1** the son of a king or queen. **2** the ruler of a small country. **princely** *adj* **1** to do with a prince. **2** generous.

princess (prɪn'ses) *nc* **1** the daughter of a king or queen. **2** the wife of a prince.

principal ('prɪnsɪpəl) *adj* first in importance. ● *nc* **1** a person who is first in importance, esp. the head of a college. **2** an amount of money lent on which interest is paid. **principally** *adv*

principle ('prɪnsɪpəl) *nc* **1** a rule of behaviour. **2** a general truth, rule, or law. **3** a natural law that controls how a machine, etc., works. **in principle** in the main facts, but not necessarily in the details. **on principle** because of one's principles.

print (prɪnt) *vt* **1** make (books, pictures, patterns, etc.), esp. in large numbers, by pressing ink onto (paper, cloth, etc.,) in a machine. **2** fix (ideas, feelings, etc.) firmly and deeply in the mind. **3** write (the letters) of (a word) separately instead of joining them as in usual handwriting. **4** make a photographic print from (a negative or film). ● *nu* **1** printed matter. *nc* **2** a printed picture. **3** a cloth printed with a pattern. **4** a photograph on paper. **in print** (of a book) printed and ready to be sold. **out of print** (of a book) no longer being printed. **printer** *nc* **printing press** a machine for printing.

prior ('praɪə*) *adj* earlier; coming before; **prior to** before. ● *nc* the head of a house in which men live and serve God.

priority (praɪ'ɒrɪtɪ) **1** *nu* the right to have or do something before other people. **2** *nc, pl* **-ties** something that must be dealt with first or early.

prise (also **prize**) (praɪz) *vt* force (something) open or away from something, esp. by using a strong tool.

prism ('prɪzəm) *nc* a solid block with five or more flat sides and with ends that are regular and equal, esp. one made of glass that refracts light or breaks it up into its colours: see picture at **shapes.**

prison ('prɪzən) **1** *nc* a building in which people who have broken the law are kept locked up for a certain time. **2** *nu* being kept in such a building. **prisoner** *nc* **1** a person who is kept in prison for breaking the law. **2** anyone who is put under control, shut in, etc., for some reason.

prithee ('prɪðiː) *archaic interj* please: *Prithee, will you marry me?*

private ('praɪvɪt) *adj* **1** to do with one person or a few people and not the public: *a private letter.* **2** secret: *private business.* ● *nc* a common soldier. **privacy** ('prɪvəsɪ) *nu* **1** being alone and undisturbed by other people. **2** being secret. **privately** *adv* **private secretary** See under **secretary.**

privilege ('prɪvɪlɪdʒ) *nc* **1** a special right that only a certain person or a few particular people can have. **2** a special favour. **privileged** *adj* having special rights.

prize[1] (praɪz) *nc* a reward for winning a race, competition, etc. ● *vt* have a very high opinion of; value greatly.

prize[2] *v* See **prise.**

pro[1] (prəʊ) *infml adj, n* short for **professional.**

pro² *n* **pros and cons** arguments for and against something.

probable (ˈprɒbəbəl) *adj* that is likely to happen or be true. **probability** (ˌprɒbə-ˈbɪlɪtɪ) **1** *nu* being probable. **2** *nc, pl* **-ties** something that is probable. **probably** *adv*

probation (prəˈbeɪʃən) *nu* **1** a time of a person's behaviour, abilities, etc., being tested to find out if he is suitable for a job, etc. **2** the system of allowing people, esp. young people, who have broken the law to stay out of prison as long as they keep out of trouble. **probationary** *adj* to do with probation.

probe (prəʊb) *nc* **1** *medicine* a narrow metal tool for examining wounds, etc. **2** a very careful inquiry. ●*vt* examine very carefully.

problem (ˈprɒbləm) *nc* a difficult question; anything that is difficult to understand, deal with, or work out.

procedure (prəˈsiːdʒə*) *nc* a way of doing something, esp. the usual way.

proceed (prəˈsiːd) *vi* **1** go on, esp. after stopping; continue: *He proceeded to tell me the rest of the story.* **2** formal or old-fashioned come or start from: *Serious trouble could proceed from evil talk.* **proceeds** (ˈprəʊ-siːdz) *n pl* money taken at some event, etc.: *The proceeds from the concert are to be given away.*

proceeding (prəˈsiːdɪŋ) *nc* an action taken.

process (ˈprəʊses) *nc* **1** a set of actions aimed at the same result or state. **2** a way of doing something. ●*vt* treat (a substance) in a special way or with special devices: *processed cheese; You process a camera film so that the picture can be seen.* **in the process of** occupied in: *He's in the process of buying a house.* **processing** *nu* See **data processing** under **data**.

procession (prəˈseʃən) *nc* a number of people, vehicles, etc., following each other in order: see picture.

procession

proclaim (prəˈkleɪm) *vt* **1** make known to the public; declare. **2** clearly show. **proclamation** (ˌprɒkləˈmeɪʃən) **1** *nu* proclaiming. **2** *nc* something that is proclaimed.

procure (prəˈkjʊə*) *vt* obtain, esp. after trying hard.

prod (prɒd) *vt* **1** push into with one's finger or something pointed. **2** urge (someone) into doing something. ●*nc* a sharp push.

prodigious (prəˈdɪdʒəs) *adj* **1** huge. **2** most unusual; wonderful.

produce (prəˈdjuːs) *vt* **1** bring forward to be shown: *Can you produce proof of who you are?* **2** bring into being: *This tree produces good fruit.* **3** cause. **4** give birth to. **5** make (goods). **6** show a film, play, etc., to the public. ● (ˈprɒdjuːs) *nu* anything that is produced, esp. grown on a farm, etc. **producer** (prəˈdjuːsə*) *nc* **1** a person or thing that produces. **2** a person in charge of producing a play, film, etc.

product (ˈprɒdʌkt) *nc* **1** something produced by man or by natural means. **2** *mathematics* the amount obtained by multiplying two or more numbers together.

production (prəˈdʌkʃən) *nu* **1** producing or being produced. **2** the amount produced. **3** the speed at which something is produced. **4** *nc* something that is produced.

productive (prəˈdʌktɪv) *adj* having the power to produce; producing much. **productivity** (ˌprɒdʌkˈtɪvɪtɪ) *nu* being productive.

profane (prəˈfeɪn) *adj* **1** feeling or showing lack of respect for God or sacred things. **2** to do with the world, not religious or spiritual matters. ●*vt* treat God's name or sacred place with disrespect.

profess (prəˈfes) *vt* **1** claim (to be or be able to do something). **2** pretend. **3** declare openly.

profession (prəˈfeʃən) *nc* **1** a declaration or claim. **2** a kind of work for which a person has to have higher education.

professional (prəˈfeʃənəl) *adj* **1** to do with a profession (def. 2). **2** to do with professionals. ●*nc* a person who is an expert at a sport and plays or teaches it for money.

professor (prəˈfesə*) *nc* **1** a teacher of the highest grade in a university or college. **2** chiefly US any teacher in a university or college.

proffer (ˈprɒfə*) *vt* offer (a gift, thanks, etc.).

proficient (prəˈfɪʃənt) *adj* able to do something very well: *He's a proficient teacher.* **proficiency** *nu*

profile

profile ('prəʊfaɪl) *nc* **1** something seen from the side, esp. someone's head; the outside edge of anything: see picture. **2** a short account of a person's life, interests, or work, in a magazine, etc. **keep a low profile** stay quiet or hidden for a certain length of time.

profit ('prɒfit) **1** *nc (often pl)* money gained from a business, etc. **2** *nu* advantage. **profitable** *adj* providing profit. **profitably** *adv*

profound (prə'faʊnd) *adj* (of thought, feeling, knowledge, etc.) deep. **profoundly** *adv*

profuse (prə'fjuːs) *adj* generous or in great plenty: *profuse thanks*. **profusion** (prə'fjuː-ʒən) *nu* a very large number or amount.

program ('prəʊgræm) *nc* **1** a set of orders in code fed into a computer to make it do something to information it is given. **2** *US* See **programme**. ● *vt* feed a program into (a computer).

programme *US* **program** ('prəʊgræm) *nc* **1** a notice describing an event such as a play, concert, sports meeting, etc. **2** a show or service on radio or television. **3** a plan for an event or set of events.

progress ('prəʊgres) *nu* forward movement; development. **in progress** being done or happening. ● (prə'gres) *vi* move forward; develop. **progression** (prə'greʃən) *nu* **progressive** (prə'gresɪv) *adj* **1** making continual progress. **2** improving. **3** continually increasing. **progressively** *adv*

prohibit (prə'hɪbɪt) *vt* forbid by rules or laws; stop. **prohibition** (ˌprəʊɪ'bɪʃən) **1** *nu* prohibiting. **2** *nc* a rule, law, or order that prohibits. **prohibitive** *adj* **1** likely to prohibit. **2** (of prices) so high as to prevent sale.

project ('prɒdʒekt) *nc* a plan, esp. for a group of people to take part in a scheme or activity together. ● (prə'dʒekt) *vt* **1** throw forwards. **2** cause (a picture, light, etc.) to fall onto a surface: *project a film*. **3** *vi* stick or stand out.

projectile (prə'dʒektaɪl) *nc* something that is sent forward with force, esp. from a gun.

projection (prə'dʒekʃən) **1** *nu* projecting or being projected. **2** *nc* something that sticks or stands out.

projector (prə'dʒektə*) *nc* a device for throwing out pictures onto a screen by means of rays of light.

proletariat (ˌprəʊlə'teərɪət) *nc* all the people in society who are wage-earners; all workers.

proliferate (prə'lɪfəreɪt) **1** *vi* increase very quickly. **2** *vt* produce (cells) quickly and in great numbers. **proliferation** (prəˌlɪfə'reɪ-ʃən) *nu* **1** proliferating or being proliferated. **2** something that proliferates.

prolific (prə'lɪfɪk) *adj* producing much.

prologue ('prəʊlɒg) *nc* **1** the opening lines of a poem or speech. **2** anything said or done to prepare for what is to follow.

prolong (prə'lɒŋ) *vt* make longer; cause to last longer: *He prolonged his holiday by another week*. **prolongation** (ˌprəʊlɒn'geɪʃən) **1** *nu* making or being made longer. **2** *nc* something that is added to prolong something else.

promenade (ˌprɒmə'nɑːd) *nc* **1** a place where people can walk for pleasure, esp. by the side of the sea. **2** a pleasant walk. ● *vi* **1** take a promenade. **2** *vt* show (oneself or someone else) off.

prominent ('prɒmɪnənt) *adj* **1** that clearly stands out; easily seen: *a prominent nose*. **2** important: *He's in a prominent position in the government*. **prominence 1** *nu* being prominent. **2** *nc* (a part of) something that is prominent. **prominently** *adv*

promiscuous (prə'mɪskjʊəs) *adj* **1** behaving without care, or taste, esp. in having many sexual relationships. **2** disordered; mixed up in confusion.

promise ('prɒmɪs) *vt* **1** say or write to (someone) that one certainly will or will not do something: *I promise that I will come tomorrow; I promise to come*. **2** cause a person to hope for or expect (something) in the future. ● *nc* **1** a written or spoken agreement to do or not to do something. **2** *nu* a sign of something good, hopeful, etc., in the future: *His work shows great promise*. **promising** *adj* having signs of success, etc., for the future. **promisingly** *adv*

promontory ('prɒməntərɪ) *nc, pl* **-ries** a high point of land sticking out into the sea: see picture.

promontory

promote (prə'məʊt) *vt* **1** give (someone) a higher position in his job or in life. **2** support or urge the start of (a business, cause, etc.). **promoter** *nc* **promotion** (prə'məʊ-ʃən) *ncu* (an example of) promoting or being promoted.

prompt (prɒmpt) *adj* done immediately: *prompt action*. ● *vt* **1** urge or cause (someone) to do something. **2** help (an actor, speaker, etc.) by telling him his words if he forgets them. **promptly** *adv*

promulgate ('promǝlgeɪt) *vt* 1 make (laws, etc.) known to the public. 2 spread (ideas, teachings, etc.).

prone (prǝʊn) *adj* lying with the face or front downwards; lying stretched out on the ground. **prone to** likely to (do something).

prong (prɒŋ) *nc* a sharp-pointed end on a tool, esp. a fork.

pronoun ('prǝʊnaʊn) *nc* a word such as 'she' or 'them' used instead of a noun to point out a person or thing just spoken or written about.

pronounce (prǝ'naʊns) *vt* 1 make known, esp. officially or in a solemn way. 2 make the sound of (words): *Some foreign words are difficult to pronounce.* **pronounced** *adj* easily noticeable. **pronouncement** *nc* something solemn or official that is made known.

pronunciation (prǝˌnʌnsɪ'eɪʃǝn) *nc* 1 a person's way of speaking. 2 the way a word is spoken. 3 *nu* the way a language is spoken.

proof (pru:f) 1 *nu* showing that something is or is not true. *nc* 2 a thing or reason that shows this. 3 the first printing of a book, etc., that will be corrected before being finally printed and published. 4 *nu* a fixed measure of the strength of alcoholic drinks or other liquids. **proof against** able to resist: *a paint that is proof against oil.*

prop (prɒp) *nc* 1 a support, esp. a stick used to keep something up. 2 a person who greatly helps someone or something. ● *vt* support.

propaganda (ˌprɒpǝ'gændǝ) *nu* information, claims, etc., spread about to advertise a political movement, etc.

propagate ('prɒpǝgeɪt) 1 *vt* cause (plants, etc.) to increase in numbers in a natural way. 2 *vi* (of plants, etc.) increase in a natural way. 3 *vt* spread (ideas, beliefs, etc.). **propagation** (ˌprɒpǝ'geɪʃǝn) *nu*

propane ('prǝʊpeɪn) *nu* a colourless gas made from oil and burnt for light or heat.

propel (prǝ'pel) *vt* drive or push forward. **propeller** (prǝ'pelǝ*) *nc* a device with two or more curved blades that is made to turn in air or water to drive a plane or ship: see picture.

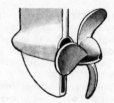

propeller

propensity (prǝ'pensɪtɪ) *nc, pl* -**ties** a natural leaning to behave in a particular way.

proper ('prɒpǝ*) *adj* 1 correct; suitable: *Is he the proper man for the job?* 2 fitting; polite; decent: *proper behaviour.* **proper noun** *grammar* the name of a particular person, animal, place, etc. **properly** *adv*

property ('prɒpǝtɪ) 1 *nu* goods belonging to a person. *nc, pl* -**ties** 2 a building or piece of land owned by someone. 3 a quality of a person or thing.

prophecy ('prɒfɪsɪ) *ncu, pl* -**cies** (an example of) prophesying.

prophesy ('prɒfɪsaɪ) *vt* tell of (future events), esp. claiming that one has learned of these from God.

prophet ('prɒfɪt) *nc* 1 a person who teaches on religious matters, esp. one who has been inspired by God directly. 2 a person who prophesies. **prophetic** (prǝ'fetɪk) *adj* to do with a prophet or a prophecy.

prophylaxis (ˌprɒfɪ'læksɪs) *nu* medical treatment that controls or prevents disease.

propitious (prǝ'pɪʃǝs) *adj* helpful; favourable; suitable.

proportion (prǝ'pɔ:ʃǝn) 1 *nu* the relationship between a part of something and the whole thing. *nc* 2 *(pl)* the size of something: *a house of huge proportions.* 3 a share or part. ● *vt* put into proportion; put into a correct and satisfactory arrangement. **in proportion to** in relation to. **proportional** (prǝ'pɔ:ʃǝnɪl) *adj* of or to do with being in proportion; equal. **proportionately** (prǝ'pɔ:ʃǝnɪtlɪ) *adv* in proper proportion.

propose (prǝ'pǝʊz) *vt* 1 put forward an idea, plan, etc. 2 propose that (someone) be appointed to a position. 3 *vti* suggest (marriage) to someone: *He proposed to her and she said yes.* **proposal** (prǝ'pǝʊzǝl) 1 *nu* proposing. 2 *nc* something proposed; a suggestion: *a proposal of marriage.*

proposition (ˌprɒpǝ'zɪʃǝn) *nc* 1 a matter for discussion. 2 *infml* a problem; plan that may be impossible to carry out. 3 an offer, esp. an indecent one made to a woman by a man.

proprietary (prǝ'praɪǝtǝrɪ) *adj* 1 being privately owned or controlled. 2 of or to do with an owner.

proprietor (prǝ'praɪǝtǝ*) *nc* 1 an owner, esp. of a shop, hotel, or other business that is not a company. 2 the only person or company that by law has the right to own something.

propriety (prǝ'praɪǝtɪ) *nu* suitable, fitting, and correct behaviour. **the proprieties** the rules of such behaviour.

propulsion (prǝ'pʌlʃǝn) *nu* driving or being driven forward by force.

pro rata (ˌprǝʊ'rɑ:tǝ) *Latin* in proportion: *Twenty sheets cost a pound, and any extra are charged pro rata.*

prose (prəʊz) *nu* writing that is not in the form of poetry. **prosaic** (prəˈzeɪɪk) *adj* uninteresting; ordinary; dull.

prosecute (ˈprɒsɪkjuːt) *vt* take action against (someone) in a court of law. **prosecution** (ˌprɒsɪˈkjuːʃən) *ncu* (an example of) prosecuting or being prosecuted. **prosecutor** *nc*

prospect (ˈprɒspekt) *nc* 1 a hope or chance of something, esp. success, in the future: *a job with good prospects.* 2 a view: *a window with a wide prospect.* **in prospect** expected. ● (prəˈspekt) *vi* search for gold or other precious metals, etc. **prospector** *nc*

prospective (prəˈspektɪv) *adj* expected; looked forward to, esp. with pleasure.

prosper (ˈprɒspə*) *vi* be successful. **prosperity** (prəˈsperɪtɪ) *nu* being successful; wealth. **prosperous** *adj* successful.

prostitute (ˈprɒstɪtjuːt) *nc* also **whore** a woman who has sexual intercourse for money. ●*vt* 1 offer (oneself or someone) as a prostitute. 2 offer (something) to be used for an unworthy purpose.

prostrate (ˈprɒstreɪt) *adj* 1 stretched out face down on the ground, esp. to show obedience or respect. 2 very tired and weak in body or mind. ● (prɒˈstreɪt) *vt* 1 put or stretch out on the ground to show obedience or respect. 2 overcome with tiredness or weakness of the body or mind.

protagonist (prəʊˈtægənɪst) *nc* 1 the chief person in a play or story. 2 *infml* the chief supporter of a cause, political party, etc.

protect (prəˈtekt) *vt* keep safe from danger or harm. **protection** 1 *nu* protecting or being protected. 2 *nc* person or thing that protects. **protective** *adj* that protects. **protector** *nc*

protectorate (prəˈtektərɪt) *nc* a country that is under the protection of a stronger one.

protein (ˈprəʊtiːn) *nc* a food essential to living things, found in milk, meat, eggs, fish, etc.

protest (prəˈtest) 1 *vti* argue against; refuse to agree or accept: *I protest at the government's actions.* 2 *vt* say that (something) is definitely real or true. ● (ˈprəʊtest) *nc* an act of protesting.

Protestant (ˈprɒtɪstənt) *nc* a member of one of the Christian churches that separated from the Church of Rome in the sixteenth century. ●*adj* to do with Protestants.

protocol (ˈprəʊtəkɒl) 1 *nu* the rules of usual, generally accepted behaviour. 2 *nc* a written account of an agreement about to be made, esp. between nations.

proton (ˈprəʊtɒn) *nc* one of several tiny amounts of matter with a positive charge that form part of the nucleus of an atom.

prototype (ˈprəʊtətaɪp) *nc* the first example of something that can be improved or copied.

protozoan (ˌprəʊtəʊˈzəʊən) *nc, pl* **-zoa** (zəʊə) a tiny animal formed of a single cell, such as an amoeba.

protract (prəˈtrækt) *vt* make longer; cause to last longer: *a protracted holiday.* **protractor** *nc* a device, usually semi-circular in shape, for measuring angles: see picture.

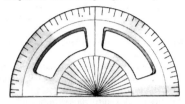

protractor

protrude (prəˈtruːd) *vti* (cause to) stick out from a surface: *protruding eyes.*

proud (praʊd) *adj* 1 being pleased and satisfied with what one has or has done: *proud of one's work.* 2 having too good an opinion of oneself. 3 making people **proud** (def. 1): *a proud day for the family.* **proudly** *adv*

prove (pruːv) *vt* 1 show that (something) is true by giving reasons, arguments, etc. 2 *mathematics* test whether or not (an answer) is correct. 3 *vi* be found (to be): *He proved to be the right man for the job; This could prove useful.*

proven (ˈpruːvən) past participle of **prove**.

proverb (ˈprɒvɜːb) *nc* a well-known, short, wise saying generally accepted as true.

provide (prəˈvaɪd) *vt* supply (someone or something) with (something): *We'll provide you with clothes; Can you provide a car for us to go in?* **provided** or **providing** (**that**) only if. **provide for** supply (someone) with enough money to live on.

providence (ˈprɒvɪdəns) 1 *ncu* (a sign or example of) God's protection. 2 *nu* care taken, esp. in planning for the future.

provident (ˈprɒvɪdənt) *adj* taking care to provide for future needs, esp. for when one is old. **providential** (ˌprɒvɪˈdenʃəl) *adj* to do with God's protection.

province (ˈprɒvɪns) *nc* 1 a large district of a country. 2 a person's interests, activities, particular knowledge, etc. **the provinces** the part of a country outside the city that governs it. **provincial** (prəˈvɪnʃəl) *adj* 1 to do with a **province** (def. 1) or the provinces. 2 thinking or behaving in a way that is not open to greater ideas, etc.

provision (prəˈvɪʒən) 1 *nu* providing for something, esp. future needs. *nc* 2 amount of something supplied. 3 a condition of an agreement. 4 *(pl)* food for a household, journey, etc. **provisional** *adj* for the present time only; until some other arrangement has been made.

proviso (prə'vaizəʊ) *nc, pl* **-s, -es** a condition, esp. in a legal agreement.

provoke (prə'vəʊk) *vt* 1 make angry. 2 cause (certain behaviour): *He provokes laughter.* **provocation** (ˌprɒvə'keɪʃən) *nu* provoking or being provoked. **provocative** (prə'vɒkətɪv) *adj* provoking or likely to provoke something, esp. anger or sexual feelings.

prow (praʊ) *nc* the pointed front end of a boat or ship.

prowess ('praʊɪs) *nu* 1 great courage. 2 great ability or skill.

prowl (praʊl) *vi* move about carefully and quietly in search of animals to kill, goods to steal, etc. **on the prowl** hunting.

proximity (prɒk'sɪmɪtɪ) *nu* nearness.

proxy ('prɒksɪ) 1 *nu* the power given to a person to act for someone else. *nc, pl* **-xies** 2 a printed document that gives this power. 3 a person given this power.

prudent ('pruːdənt) *adj* careful and wise, esp. with money or in planning for the future. **prudence** *nu*

prune[1] (pruːn) *nc* a dried plum.

prune[2] *vt* 1 cut (branches, etc.) off (a tree, bush, etc.). 2 get rid of (unwanted parts): *to prune a book of unnecessary facts.*

pry (praɪ) *vi* take too much interest in other people's affairs.

PS ('piː'es) *infml n* short for **postscript**.

psalm (sɑːm) *nc* a religious poem sung in praise of God.

pseudonym ('sjuːdənɪm) *nc* a name used instead of one's real name, esp. when writing a book.

psychiatry (saɪ'kaɪətrɪ) *nu* the treatment of illnesses of the mind. **psychiatrist** *nc* a person who practises psychiatry.

psychic ('saɪkɪk) *adj* to do with the soul or the mind.

psychology (saɪ'kɒlədʒɪ) *nu* the study of behaviour. **psychological** (ˌsaɪkə'lɒdʒɪkəl) *adj* to do with psychology or the mind. **psychologist** (saɪ'kɒlədʒɪst) *nc* a person who studies psychology.

pub (pʌb) *nc* short for **public house**.

public ('pʌblɪk) *adj* to do with people in general: *a public library.* **in public** not in private or in secret. **the public** people in general. **public house** (often shortened to **pub**) *Brit* a place in which alcoholic drinks are sold and drunk. **public relations** the practice of building up friendly feelings between the public and business companies, etc. **public school** *Brit* a school for children over thirteen whose parents have to pay to send them there. **publicly** *adv*

publican ('pʌblɪkən) *Brit nc* a person who owns or is in charge of a public house.

publication (ˌpʌblɪ'keɪʃən) 1 *nc* a book, etc., that is published. *nu* 2 the act of publishing

a book, etc. 3 the act of making information, etc., known to the public.

publicity (pʌb'lɪsɪtɪ) *nu* information given to the public about someone or something to stir up interest.

publish ('pʌblɪʃ) *vt* 1 print, advertise, and sell (a book, etc.). 2 make (a fact, etc.) known to the public. **publisher** *nc* a business company or a person who publishes books, etc.

puck (pʌk) *nc* a flat, round piece of rubber used instead of a ball in the game of ice-hockey.

pucker ('pʌkə*) 1 *vt* gather (something soft, such as lips, eyebrows, cloth, etc.) into small folds or wrinkles. 2 *vi* (of lips, etc.) be gathered into small folds or wrinkles.

pudding ('pʊdɪŋ) *nc* 1 any sweet food served after the main course of a meal. 2 any of several foods made with flour, eggs, etc.

puddle ('pʌdəl) *nc* 1 a small amount of water left on the ground after rain. 2 a small amount of any liquid lying on a surface: *a puddle of milk on the kitchen floor.*

puff (pʌf) *nc* a short, quick giving out of breath, wind, air, smoke, etc. ● *vti* give out a puff of (breath, wind, air, smoke, etc.): *He was puffing at a cigarette; The train puffed smoke.*

pull (pʊl) *vt* 1 use force on (something) to draw it towards or along behind one. 2 damage (a muscle) by straining it. ● *nc* 1 the act of pulling. 2 a deep gulp of liquid. *nu* 3 force applied by pulling. 4 *infml* influence: *He has a lot of pull with the government.* 5 something used to pull with, such as a handle on a door. **pull down** destroy: *Those old houses are to be pulled down.* **pull in** 1 (of a train) arrive at a station and stop. 2 (of a car, etc.) move to the edge of the road, etc. **pull off** 1 take off clothing with some effort. 2 *infml* succeed in (a task). **pull on** put on (clothes). **pull out** 1 take out, esp. with some effort. 2 move out: leave. **pull through** win or succeed after some difficulty or trouble. **pull up** 1 drag up (a plant) by the roots. 2 (of a car, etc.) come to a stop. 3 speak sharp words to.

pulley ('pʊlɪ) *nc, pl* **-s** a wheel with a curved hollow round the outside for a rope, etc. used for lifting heavy weights: see picture.

pulley

pullover ('pʊl,əʊvə*) *nc* a garment, usually knitted, that is put on the arms and upper body by pulling it over the head.

pulmonary ('pʌlmənərɪ) *adj* to do with the lungs.

pulp (pʌlp) *nu* 1 the soft part of fruit. 2 a soft mixture with no regular shape, esp. one made from wood and turned into paper. ● *vti* make or be made into pulp.

pulpit ('pʊlpɪt) *nc* a raised box, with sides about a metre high, from which a priest speaks to the people in a church.

pulsate (pʌl'seɪt) *vi* beat, esp. regularly, like the heart.

pulse (pʌls) *nc* the beat of the heart.

pulverise ('pʌlvəraɪz) *vti* crush or be crushed to powder.

pumice ('pʌmɪs) *nu* also **pumice stone** a light stone full of tiny holes, used for polishing or cleaning with.

pump (pʌmp) *nc* a device for moving a liquid or gas, such as a bicycle pump, which is used for forcing air into tyres: see picture. ● *vt* use a pump to move a liquid or gas.

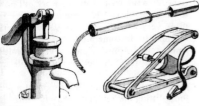

pump

pumpkin ('pʌmpkɪn) *nc* a large, soft, round, orange-coloured fruit used as food.

pun (pʌn) *nc* a humorous use of words which have the same sounds, or of a word which has two meanings; a play on words. ● *vi* make a play on words.

punch¹ (pʌntʃ) *vt* strike with the hand tightly closed. ● *nc* the act of punching.

punch² *nc* 1 a tool for cutting out holes or printing designs. 2 a tool for knocking out nails, etc., from holes. ● *vt* 1 make (a hole) in (something) with a punch. 2 knock (a nail, etc.) out with a punch.

punch³ *nu* a drink made of wine or strong alcohol with hot water, sugar, spices, etc.

punctual ('pʌŋktjʊəl) *adj* arriving or happening at the exact time arranged. **punctually** *adv*

punctuate ('pʌŋktjʊeɪt) *vt* 1 put punctuation marks into a piece of writing. 2 interrupt frequently: *His speech was punctuated by shouts from the audience.* **punctuation** (,pʌŋktjʊ'eɪʃən) *nu* 1 also **punctuation marks** signs such as commas and full stops added to words in writing sentences. 2 the act of punctuating.

puncture ('pʌŋktʃə*) *nc* a small hole caused by something sharp, esp. one that lets the air out of a tyre. ● *vt* 1 make a puncture in. 2 *vi* be punctured.

pungent ('pʌndʒənt) *adj* 1 (of a smell or taste) sharp; bitter. 2 (of something said to or about someone) hurtful; bitter.

punish ('pʌnɪʃ) *vt* 1 make (someone) suffer for doing wrong. 2 treat in a rough manner. **punishment** 1 *nu* punishing or being punished. 2 *nc* a way of punishing.

puny ('pjuːnɪ) *adj* **-ier, -iest** small and weak; useless: *a puny effort.*

pup (pʌp) *infml n* short for **puppy**.

pupil¹ ('pjuːpəl) *nc* a schoolchild or other person who is being taught.

pupil² *nc* the black, circular opening in the centre of the eye that controls the amount of light entering: see picture.

pupil

puppet ('pʌpɪt) *nc* 1 a doll that is made to move by working the strings attached to its body or by a hand pushed inside it. 2 a person controlled by someone else.

puppy ('pʌpɪ) *nc, pl* **-pies** a young dog.

purchase ('pɜːtʃɪs) *vt* buy. ● *nu* 1 buying. 2 *nc* something that is bought. **purchase tax** *Brit* a tax on goods sold, added to prices by shopkeepers. **purchaser** *nc*

pure (pjʊə*) *adj* **-r, -st** 1 with no other substance added: *pure water.* 2 without any bad quality: *She has a pure heart.* 3 complete: *pure nonsense.* **purely** *adv*

purge (pɜːdʒ) *vt* 1 make pure; make clean in body or mind. 2 show (oneself or someone else) to be innocent of wrongdoing. ● *nc* 1 purging. 2 a medicine used to get rid of waste matter from the body.

purify ('pjʊərɪfaɪ) *vt* make pure. **purification** (,pjʊərɪfɪ'keɪʃən) *nu*

purist ('pjʊərɪst) *nc* a person who urges purity, esp. in music, art, the use of language, etc.

puritan ('pjʊərɪtən) *nc* a person who is very strict in his views on religion and morals and believes most pleasures to be sinful.

purity ('pjʊərɪtɪ) *nu* being pure.

purl (pɜːl) *nu* a knitting stitch made with the needle moving in the opposite direction to the usual one. ● *vt* knit with purl stitches.

purple ('pɜːpəl) *adj* red and blue mixed together. ● *ncu* a purple colour.

purpose (ˈpɜːpəs) *nc* **1** an intention; plan. **2** a reason for the existence of something. **3** *nu* the ability to keep to a firmly fixed plan or intention. **on purpose** with intention.

purr (pɜː*) *vi* (of a cat) make a low, continuous throbbing sound showing pleasure.

purse (pɜːs) *nc* **1** a small bag for money, esp. carried by a woman. **2** *US* a woman's handbag. ● *vt* move (the lips) into a small, round shape.

pursue (pəˈsjuː) *vt* **1** follow in order to catch. **2** be always with: *He is pursued by bad luck wherever he goes.* **3** give one's attention, interest, etc., to. **pursuit** (pəˈsjuːt) **1** *nu* pursuing. **2** *nc* something to which one gives one's attention, interest, time, etc. **in pursuit of** pursuing.

pus (pʌs) *nu* thick, yellowish matter that comes out of a poisonous wound, etc.

push (pʊʃ) *vt* **1** use force to move (something) away from oneself; press against. **2** urge (someone) to buy (goods), do (something), etc. ● *nc* **1** pushing. **2** *nu* the ability to get things done, to get what one wants in life, etc. **push button** an electrical switch worked by pressing. **pushing** *adj* being inclined to be ambitious or get oneself noticed.

pussy (ˈpʊsɪ) *infml, children nc, pl* **-sies** a cat.

put (pʊt) *vt* move or place (something) into a certain place or position. **put across** teach or do (something) etc., in a way that can be fully understood. **put aside** put (something) down to be dealt with later. **put away** put (something) back into its usual place. **put back 1** return something to its usual place. **2** delay; move to a later time: *My holiday had to be put back because I was ill.* **put by** save (money) to be used in the future. **put down 1** place (something) on something else. **2** put an animal to death because of a serious illness. **3** write down. **4** consider: *They put her down as a fool.* **5** suppress; crush: *The rebellion was put down by the army.* **6** humiliate: *He enjoys putting his wife down in public.* **put forward** suggest (an idea, etc.). **put in for** apply for. **put off 1** delay; move to a later time. **2** upset; confuse:

She was put off by all the shouting. **3** cause (someone) to lose an appetite for: *The smell put me off my dinner.* **put on 1** clothe oneself in. **2** pretend. **3** increase or add: *She's put on a lot of weight.* **4** arrange for (something) to happen. **put out 1** confuse; upset. **2** make angry. **3** switch off (a light); stop a fire burning. **put through 1** cause (someone) to go through a test, trial, etc. **2** connect by telephone. **put up 1** build. **2** obtain or provide food and shelter for (someone). **3** increase (prices, fares, etc.). **put up with** behave in a patient way during (difficulties, etc.).

putrid (ˈpjuːtrɪd) *adj* **1** rotten; having a bad smell. **2** *infml* of very poor quality.

putt (pʌt) *vt* hit (a ball) gently in the game of golf so that it will roll into a hole. ● *nc* a gentle hit of the ball in golf.

putty (ˈpʌtɪ) *nu* a soft substance of white powder and oil, used for fixing glass into windows, filling up cracks, etc.

puzzle (ˈpʌzəl) *nc* **1** a question or problem that is not easy to understand or answer. **2** a toy specially made to test skill and patience. ● *vi* **1** try to solve or work out how to do something. **2** *vt* cause one to have to think very hard in order to solve or work out how to do something.

pygmy (also **pigmy**) (ˈpɪgmɪ) *nc, pl* **-mies** one of a race of very small people in Africa.

pyjamas (also **pajamas**) (pəˈdʒɑːməz) *n pl* a loose-fitting jacket and trousers worn in bed.

pylon (ˈpaɪlən) *nc* a tall, steel frame for supporting electric wires high above the ground.

pyramid (ˈpɪrəmɪd) *nc* **1** one of the huge stone buildings in ancient Egypt with four sloping sides that meet at the top, used for the dead bodies of rulers. **2** any object with such a shape: see picture at **shapes**.

pyre (ˈpaɪə*) *nc* a large heap of wood for burning, esp. one on which to burn a dead body.

python (ˈpaɪθən) *nc* a large snake that kills by twisting itself round its victim and crushing it.

Q

quack¹ (kwæk) *nc* the sound a duck makes. ● *vi* make this sound.

quack² *nc* a person who pretends to have knowledge, esp. medical knowledge, that he really does not have. ● *adj* to do with such a person: *a quack doctor*.

quadrangle ('kwɒˌdræŋgəl) *nc* **1** a flat figure with four sides, esp. a square, or a rectangle. **2** (*infml abbrev.* **quad**) a large, four-sided, open space inside a castle, college, etc. **quadrangular** (kwɒ'dræŋgjʊlə*) *adj* having the shape of a quadrangle.

quadrant ('kwɒdrənt) *nc* **1** a quarter of a circle. **2** a piece of metal shaped like a quarter of a circle, used for measuring the heights of stars: see picture.

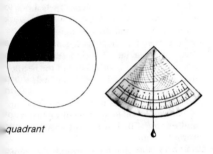

quadrant

quadratic (kwɒ'drætɪk) *mathematics adj* (of an equation) containing no unknown number to the power of more than two.

quadrilateral (ˌkwɒdrɪ'lætərəl) *nc, adj* (a flat figure) with four sides.

quadruped ('kwɒdrʊped) *nc* an animal with four legs.

quadruple ('kwɒdrʊpəl, kwɒ'druːpəl) *adj* **1** having four parts. **2** four times as much or as many. ● *nc* a number that is four times greater than another. ● (kwɒ'druːpəl) *vti* increase or be increased by four times.

quagmire ('kwægmaɪə*, 'kwɒgmaɪə*) *nc* a piece of soft, wet land.

quail¹ (kweɪl) *nc, pl* **quail, quails** a small bird that is shot for food.

quail² *vi* draw back in fear.

quaint (kweɪnt) *adj* **-er, -est** attractive in an unusual or old-fashioned way.

quake (kweɪk) *vi* shake; tremble: *The earth quaked; She was quaking with fear.*

Quaker ('kweɪkə*) *nc* a member of the Society of Friends, a Christian group that has informal meetings instead of fixed religious services and is against war.

qualification (ˌkwɒlɪfɪ'keɪʃən) *nc* **1** a training, quality, or ability that makes a person suitable for a job, etc. **2** something that qualifies. **3** *nu* qualifying.

qualify ('kwɒlɪfaɪ) *vti* **1** make (oneself) suitable to be chosen for a job, etc., by getting or giving the qualities needed. **2** *vt* make (something said or done) more moderate or less general.

quality ('kwɒlɪtɪ) *nc, pl* **-ties 1** the worth, value, or goodness of something: *She wears clothes of poor quality; different qualities of cloth.* **2** something essential or special in a person or a thing: *the qualities of chemicals; He has many good qualities.*

qualm (kwɑːm) *nc* **1** a feeling of doubt; uncomfortable feeling in the mind, esp. as to whether one is doing right or wrong. **2** a sudden feeling of sickness lasting only for a short time.

quantitative ('kwɒntɪtətɪv) *adj* to do with quantity.

quantity ('kwɒntɪtɪ) *nc, pl* **-ties** *nc* **1** a particular amount or number. **2** a large amount or number. **3** *nu* the quality of things that can be weighed, counted, measured, etc.

quantum ('kwɒntəm) *nc, pl* **-ta** (tə) an amount, esp. an exact or fixed one.

quarantine ('kwɒrəntiːn) *nu* (a period of) being kept separate from other people or animals to prevent the spread of disease.

quarrel ('kwɒrəl) *nc* **1** an angry disagreement. **2** a cause for disagreement or complaint: *I have a quarrel with his way of teaching.* ● *vi* have a quarrel (with). **quarrelsome** ('kwɒrəlsəm) *adj* likely to quarrel.

quarry¹ ('kwɒrɪ) *nc, pl* **-ries** a place where stone, etc., is dug up for building: see picture.

quarry

quarry² *nc, pl* **-ries 1** an animal, bird, or fish that is hunted. **2** anything that is hunted.

quart (kwɔːt) *nc* a measure for liquids (in Britain 1.136 litres, America 0.946 litres).

quarter ('kwɔːtə*) nc **1** a fourth equal part of anything: *She cut the apple into quarters.* **2** a period of three months: *The gas bill is paid at the end of every quarter.* **3** a district of a town, esp. one lived in by particular people: *the Indian quarter; the industrial quarter.* **4** *US* one fourth of a dollar; twenty-five cents. ● *vt* **1** divide into quarters. **2** provide (soldiers) with **quarters**. **quarter note** *music, US* See **crotchet**. **quarter past** or **to** fifteen minutes after or before (an hour in the day). **quarterly** ('kwɔːtəlɪ) *adj, adv* (happening, etc.) once every three months: *quarterly payments.* ● *nc, pl* **-lies** a paper, magazine, etc., that is printed and sold once every three months.

quarters ('kwɔːtəz) *n pl* a place for someone, esp. a soldier, to live in. **at close quarters** very near or close up: *It's not very pleasant, seen at close quarters.*

quartet (kwɔːˈtet) *nc* **1** a group of four singers or musicians. **2** a piece of music for such a group.

quartz (kwɔːts) *nu* a hard, shiny mineral found in many rocks.

quash (kwɒʃ) *vt* put an end to, esp. by the power of law.

quaver ('kweɪvə*) *vi* **1** speak or sing with a shaking voice. **2** (of music) tremble; shake. ● *nc* a musical note lasting half as long as a crotchet.

quay (kiː) *nc* a place to which ships are tied up for goods to be loaded or unloaded.

queen (kwiːn) *nc* **1** the wife of a king. **2** the woman ruler of a country. **3** a woman thought to be the best of a certain group: *a beauty queen.* **4** the playing-card in each suit carrying the picture of a queen.

queer (kwɪə*) *adj* **1** not usual or normal; strange. **2** suspicious; probably not proper or honest: *There's some queer business going on.* **3** (feeling) ill or faint. **4** *slang* homosexual. ● *nc slang* a homosexual. ● *vt slang* spoil or cause to go wrong.

quell (kwel) *vt* overcome; put an end to; bring under control: *The police quelled the trouble.*

quench (kwentʃ) *vt* **1** satisfy (one's thirst, desires, etc.). **2** put out (fire or flames).

query ('kwɪərɪ) *nc, pl* **-ries** a question, esp. one showing doubt. ● *vt* show doubt or uncertainty about the truth, etc., of (something).

quest (kwest) *nc* a search: *the quest for truth.*

question ('kwestʃən) *nc* **1** a sentence asking for an answer. **2** an affair; matter to be discussed. ● *vt* **1** ask a question of (someone). **2** express doubt about. **in question** being discussed or talked about. **out of the question** impossible; not even to be thought about. **question mark** the sign (?)

used in writing at the end of a question.

questionable ('kwestʃənəbəl) *adj* of doubtful truth or honesty.

questionnaire (ˌkwestʃəˈneə*) *nc* a list of printed questions put to a number of people in order to collect information.

queue (kjuː) *US* **line** *nc* a line of people, vehicles, etc., waiting to be served in a shop, continue their journey, etc. ● *vi* (often followed by **up**) form or wait in a queue.

quibble ('kwɪbəl) *vi* argue about or object to a small, unimportant thing, esp. to avoid a matter. ● *nc* such an argument or objection.

quick (kwɪk) *adj* **-er**, **-est** **1** (moving) fast; taking a short time. **2** thinking fast; eager: *a quick mind.* ● *adv infml* quickly. **quicken** ('kwɪkən) *vti* make or become quick or quicker. **quicklime** ('kwɪklaɪm) *nu* a white solid used in making steel, paper, etc. **quicksand** ('kwɪksænd) *nc* deep, wet sand that draws things down inside it. **quicksilver** ('kwɪkˌsɪlvə*) *nu* another name for mercury.

quiet ('kwaɪət) *adj* **-er**, **-est** **1** with little or no noise. **2** with little or no movement or disturbance; calm. **3** secret; private: *I'll have a quiet word with him.* ● *nu* the state of being quiet. **quietly** *adv* **quietness** *nu*

quill (kwɪl) *nc* **1** a whole, large feather from a bird's wing or tail. **2** such a feather made into a pen to write with. **3** one of the needle-like parts on the back of some animals, such as a hedgehog.

quilt (kwɪlt) *nc* a thick bed-covering made up of two layers filled with wool or feathers. **quilted** *adj* filled with soft material for warmth, comfort, etc.

quinine (kwɪˈniːn) *nu* a sharp-tasting medicine for fevers, made from the bark of a tree.

quire ('kwaɪə*) *nc* twenty-four sheets of paper.

quit (kwɪt) *vt* **1** stop ((doing) something). **2** give up: *He quit his job.* **3** go away from.

quite (kwaɪt) *adv* **1** completely; entirely: *You're quite wrong.* **2** almost; to some extent; rather: *He's quite nice.* **3** *chiefly Brit* (used to show complete agreement with a suggestion, etc.): *'I always think that a cup of tea is very refreshing on a hot day.' 'Yes, quite!'*

quiver[1] ('kwɪvə*) *vi* tremble; shake: *Her voice quivered with anger; The wind made the leaves quiver.* ● *nc* the sound or movement of quivering.

quiver[2] *nc* a container for arrows.

quiz (kwɪz) *vt* question (someone) in a thorough way. ● *nc* a game, esp. on television or radio, in which players are asked questions to test their knowledge. **quizzical**

quota ('kwəʊtə) *nc* **1** a share that is given out to or received from a person or group. **2** an amount or number fixed by a rule or law: *The college has its full quota of students for this year.*

quotation (kwəʊ'teɪʃən) **1** *nu* quoting. *nc* **2** a sentence or group of words that is quoted. **3** an opinion, reached after some thought, on the cost of work to be done: *We shall get several quotations and choose the lowest.*

quotation marks the signs (" ") or (' ') used in writing to separate a quotation from a piece of writing.

quote (kwəʊt) **1** *vt* say or write (words) from (a book, poem, etc.) or repeat (words) said by (someone else): *He quoted several writers to support the point he was making.* **2** *vti* (often followed by **for**) give (a price) as a **quotation** (def. **3**): *Will you quote for this job, please?*

quoth (kwəʊθ) *archaic vt* (used only with **I, we, he, she,** or **they**) said: *'It was well done,' quoth I.*

quotient ('kwəʊʃənt) *mathematics nc* the result of dividing one number into another.

R

rabbi ('ræbaɪ) *nc* a Jewish teacher or religious leader.

rabbit ('ræbɪt) *nc* a four-legged animal with long ears and a round white tail that lives in a hole in the ground.

rabble ('ræbəl) *nc* a crowd of people in disorder.

rabies ('reɪbiːz) *nu* a disease that can cause death and is carried esp. by dogs.

race¹ (reɪs) *nc* 1 a competition of speed between people, vehicles, horses, etc. 2 any competition: *the arms race.* ● *vi* 1 move very quickly. 2 *vt* have a race with. **race-course** ('reɪskɔːs) *nc* a place, usually of grass, where horse-races are run. **race-horse** ('reɪshɔːs) *nc* a horse used for racing on. **racetrack** ('reɪstræk) *nc* a path or road made for racing, esp. one used for cars. **racing** *nu* the practice or hobby of running horses, dogs, or cars in races. **racing-car** ('reɪsɪŋkɑː*) *nc* a car specially built for racing.

race² *nc* 1 a group of people of common descent, generally having the same colour eyes, skin, and hair as each other: *the white race.* 2 a group of people having the same language and history. **the human race** all people. **racial** ('reɪʃəl) *adj* to do with the division of human beings into races or with the differences between them. **racialism** ('reɪʃəlɪzəm) or **racism** ('reɪsɪzəm) *nu* 1 believing that one's own race is better than all others. 2 unjust behaviour because of this. **racialist** ('reɪʃəlɪst) or **racist** ('reɪsɪst) *nc* a person who believes in or supports racialism. ● *adj* to do with racialism.

rack (ræk) *nc* a frame for holding things, hanging things on, etc.: *a luggage rack in a train.* ● *vt* cause great suffering of the mind or body to: *His whole body was racked with pain.*

racket¹ ('rækɪt) 1 *nu* a loud, confused noise. 2 *infml nc* a dishonest means of getting money.

racket² (also **racquet**) ('rækɪt) *nc* a bat used for hitting the ball in games such as tennis.

racy ('reɪsɪ) *adj* **-ier, -iest** lively; full of energy: *a writer with a racy style.*

radar ('reɪdɑː*) *nu* a device used for finding out the position, speed, etc., of ships, planes, etc.

radial ('reɪdɪəl) *adj* to do with the radius of a circle or with a ray.

radiant ('reɪdɪənt) *adj* 1 sending out rays of light or heat without flames. 2 (of a person) happy, healthy, excited, etc. **radiance** ('reɪdɪəns) *nu*

radiate ('reɪdɪeɪt) 1 *vi* (of light or heat) be sent out in rays. *vt* 2 send out (light or heat) in rays. 3 show (happiness, health, excitement, etc.): *Her smile radiated pleasure.*

radiation (,reɪdɪ'eɪʃən) 1 *nu* radiating or being radiated. 2 *nc* something that is radiated.

radiator ('reɪdɪeɪtə*) *nc* a device that gives off heat without flames, used for heating a room, cooling an engine, etc: see picture.

radiator

radical ('rædɪkəl) *adj* 1 forming a very important part of something: *There is a radical difference between them.* 2 affecting the basis or deepest part of something: *radical change.* 3 wanting to see great changes made, esp. in laws and government. ● *nc* a **radical** (def. 3) person. **radically** *adv*

radio ('reɪdɪəʊ) 1 *nu* the passing on of messages, information, news, etc., by means of electrical waves. 2 *nc* a device for sending or receiving messages, etc., by such means ● *vti* send (a message) to (a person or place) by radio.

radioactive (,reɪdɪəʊ'æktɪv) *adj* (of a substance) having some of the central parts of its atoms that can change and break up sending out harmful rays. **radioactivity** (,reɪdɪəʊæk'tɪvɪtɪ) *nu*

radish ('rædɪʃ) *nc* a red or white root with a sharp taste that is eaten uncooked in salad.

radium ('reɪdɪəm) *nu* a radioactive metal symbol Ra

radius ('reɪdɪəs) *nc, pl* **-dii** (dɪaɪ) 1 the straight line from the centre of a circle to its edge: see picture. 2 the length of this line.

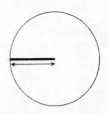

radius

raffia ('ræfɪə) *nu* a straw-like substance from the leaves of the palm-tree, used for making baskets, mats, etc.

raffle ('ræfəl) *nc* a game of luck in which tickets with numbers on are sold and the winners are those whose ticket numbers are drawn by chance.

raft (rɑːft) *nc* several logs of wood tied firmly together to make a flat surface, used as a boat.

rafter ('rɑːftə*) *nc* any of the sloping beams of wood that form the frame of a roof.

rag[1] (ræg) *nc* **1** a piece of cloth, esp. one torn from a garment no longer used. **2** *infml* a newspaper thought to be of little worth.

rag[2] *vt* annoy (someone) playfully by reminding him of a fault or failure.

rage (reɪdʒ) **1** *ncu* (a period of) great anger. **2** *nu* violent movements: *the storm's rage.* ● *vi* **1** be greatly angry. **2** be violent in action.

ragged ('rægɪd) *adj* **1** (of clothes) with badly worn edges. **2** wearing ragged clothes. **3** with rough, uneven edges: *a ragged haircut; ragged rocks.*

raid (reɪd) *nc* **1** a sudden attack made by soldiers, police, etc., in order to attack or catch someone by surprise. **2** a sudden attack made in order to steal: *a bank raid.* ● *vt* make a raid on (a person or place).

rail (reɪl) *nc* **1** a metal or wooden bar fixed to upright posts as a barrier, support for people walking, etc. **2** a bar, fixed to a wall, on which to hang things: *a picture rail; a towel rail.* **3** one of two metal bars that form a track for a train to run on. **4** *nu* short for **railway**: *Travel by rail.* **railing** ('reɪlɪŋ) *nc* a fence, support, etc., made up of rails. **railway** ('reɪlweɪ) *US* **railroad** ('reɪlrəʊd) *nc* **1** a track made up of rails on which trains run. **2** a whole system of tracks, trains, stations, etc., and the people who organise it.

raiment ('reɪmənt) *archaic or poetry nu* clothing.

rain (reɪn) *nu* **1** water falling from the clouds in drops. **2** anything that falls in a large amount: *a rain of arrows.* ● *vi* **1** send down rain: *It is raining; It has rained a lot.* **2** fall like rain: *Her tears rained down her face.* **3** *vt* send down like rain: *He rained presents on her.* **rainbow** ('reɪnbəʊ) *nc* a curved band of all the colours that appears in the sky when the sun shines on rain or mist. **raincoat** ('reɪnkəʊt) *nc* a coat made of material that does not let water through. **raindrop** ('reɪndrɒp) *nc* a drop of water falling as rain. **rainfall** ('reɪnfɔːl) *nu* the amount of rain falling in a particular place (in a particular period). **rainstorm** ('reɪnstɔːm) *nc* a storm with much rain. **rainwater** ('reɪn,wɔːtə*) *nu* soft, pure water

that has fallen as rain. **rainy** *adj* **-ier, -iest** with much rain: *rainy days.*

raise (reɪz) *vt* **1** move to a higher position. **2** increase in amount, value, etc.: *Prices were raised.* **3** educate; bring up: *They raised seven children.* **4** lift or cause to be in an upright position. **5** cause: *to raise a smile.* **6** bring to attention; cause to be heard: *Serious subjects were raised at the meeting.* **7** cause (animals or plants) to grow. ● *nc US* a pay increase; rise.

raisin ('reɪzən) *nc* a dried grape.

rake (reɪk) *nc* a tool with a long handle and teeth like those on a fork, used for gathering leaves into piles, smoothing soil, etc.: see picture at **tools**. ● *vt* use a rake to collect, smooth, etc. **rake in** *infml* receive money in large quantities. **rake up** bring up (memories, information, etc., that had been forgotten).

rally ('rælɪ) **1** *vi* (of a group) come together, esp. after being split up, for a common purpose. **2** *vt* cause (a group) to do this. **3** *vi* (of health, strength, courage, etc.) be regained or called up. **4** *vt* regain or call up (health, strength, courage, etc.). ● *nc, pl* **-lies 1** a large meeting of people for a special purpose. **2** *tennis, etc.* the hitting of a ball backwards and forwards by two players before a point is won by one of them. **3** a car race on public roads.

ram (ræm) *nc* **1** a male sheep. **2** any of several devices for pushing forcefully. ● *vt* push suddenly or violently.

Ramadan (,ræmə'dæn) *nu* the ninth month of the Muslim year when Muslims go without food during daylight.

ramble ('ræmbəl) *vi* **1** go for a quiet, unhurried walk in no particular direction: *rambling in the countryside.* **2** keep changing the subject while speaking. **3** (of a plant) grow in all or changing directions. ● *nc* a quiet, unhurried walk taken for pleasure.

ramification (,ræmɪfɪ'keɪʃən) *nc* any of the many parts of a complicated system.

ramp (ræmp) *nc* a slope that leads from one level surface to another.

rampage (ræm'peɪdʒ) *vi* rush about in an excited, wild, or angry way. ● ('ræmpeɪdʒ, ræm'peɪdʒ) *n* **on the rampage** active in rampaging. **rampant** ('ræmpənt) *adj* existing, or growing in an uncontrolled way.

rampart ('ræmpɑːt) *nc* a wall made of earth as a defence round a castle, etc.

ramshackle ('ræm,ʃækəl) *adj* (esp. of a building) badly built or shaky.

ran (ræn) past tense of **run.**

ranch (rɑːntʃ) *nc* a large farm in North America, esp. for cattle.

rancour *US* **rancor** ('ræŋkə*) *nu* a deep feeling of unforgiving hatred; spite.

random (ˈrændəm) adj without any definite plan or order. **at random** in an aimless way; not in any particular order.

rang (ræŋ) past tense of **ring²**.

range (reɪndʒ) nc 1 a line or row of mountains. 2 the distance between the points, places, values, etc., between which something exists, moves, works, etc.: a good range of vision; a wide range of prices. 3 the distance something, esp. a gun or rocket, can shoot or be shot forward. 4 a large iron cooker with one or more ovens and a surface for boiling pans, etc. ● vti 1 (be) put in a row or in a certain order. vi 2 extend over a certain area. 3 vary within a **range** (def. 2): The price ranges between ten and twenty pounds. 4 vt wander here and there in. **ranger** nc a person who guards or is in charge of a park, forest, etc.

rank¹ (ræŋk) ncu 1 (a) social position. 2 (a) position in a group or class, esp. in an army, etc.: the rank of Captain. 3 nc a line of people or things: a taxi rank. ● vt 1 put (people or things) in rows or lines. 2 vti give or be given a particular position in a group, class, or society: He ranks among the best tennis players in the world.

rank² adj 1 evil-smelling. 2 complete: a rank coward. 3 (of plants) growing plentifully.

ransack (ˈrænsæk) vt 1 make a thorough search of. 2 steal from (a town, etc.), esp. in war.

ransom (ˈrænsəm) nc an amount of money paid in return for a prisoner's being set free. ● vt pay a ransom for (a prisoner).

rap (ræp) vti give a quick, sharp blow (on or to): Someone rapped at the door. ● nc 1 a quick, sharp blow. 2 infml blame or punishment: He took the rap for what his friend did.

rape¹ (reɪp) vt 1 (of a man) have sexual intercourse with (a woman) against her will. 2 rob or spoil (a country, etc.), esp. in war. ● nc the act of raping.

rape² nu a plant fed to animals or grown for its seeds, which are used to make oil.

rapid (ˈræpɪd) adj fast-moving. **rapidity** (rəˈpɪdɪtɪ) nu **rapidly** adv **rapids** n pl part of a river where the water is very fast and violent.

rapier (ˈreɪpɪə*) nc a sword with a point but no cutting edge.

rapture (ˈræptʃə*) nc great joy or delight. **rapturous** (ˈræptʃərəs) adj feeling or showing rapture: They gave him a rapturous welcome.

rare¹ (reə*) adj -r, -st 1 unusual; not happening often. 2 of high value because of being uncommon. 3 (of a substance, esp. air) thin: Air is rare in mountain districts. **rarely** adv not often.

rare² adj (of meat) cooked for only a short time so as to keep it red inside.

rarefy (ˈreərɪfaɪ) 1 vt cause (a substance, esp. air) to become thinner. 2 vi (of a substance, esp. air) become thinner.

rarity (ˈreərɪtɪ) 1 nu being unusual or rare. 2 nc a rare person or thing.

rascal (ˈrɑːskəl) nc 1 a wicked man. 2 (used playfully) a naughty person, esp. a child.

rash¹ (ræʃ) adj acting without thought; too hasty: a rash promise. **rashly** adv

rash² nc 1 a red patch or collection of red spots on the skin. 2 a set of unpleasant events: a rash of strikes.

rasp (rɑːsp) 1 nc a metal tool with a rough surface, used for shaping wood, etc. 2 nu an unpleasant rough noise. ● vt 1 scrape or rub with a rasp. 2 vi make a rasp: a rasping voice.

raspberry (ˈrɑːzbərɪ) nc, pl -ries a small, juicy, red fruit containing many seeds: see picture at **fruits**.

rat (ræt) nc 1 an animal like a large mouse. 2 slang a worthless person. 3 infml a person who does not help a friend in trouble or who helps a friend's enemy. ● vi 1 hunt and kill rats. 2 (usually followed by **on**) give away secrets about (someone): He ratted on us to the police.

rate (reɪt) 1 nc an amount or number measured in relation to another: a rate of two dollars to one pound. 2 nu the quality of something when compared with another thing; class: His work is first-rate. ● vti 1 (be) put in a particular place in an order: We rate as the biggest producer of cars. 2 consider or be considered to be: I rate him among my very best friends. 3 Brit vt fix the **rates** to be paid on (property). **at any rate** anyway. **at this** or **that rate** infml if this or that continues to happen or is true. **ratepayer** (ˈreɪtˌpeɪə*) Brit nc a person who pays **rates** on property that he owns. **rates** Brit n pl a tax on buildings and land paid to the local government.

rather (ˈrɑːðə*) adv 1 quite: He's rather nice. 2 more; better: This is called a mat rather than a carpet. **would rather** would prefer.

ratify (ˈrætɪfaɪ) vt agree or settle formally. **ratification** (ˌrætɪfɪˈkeɪʃən) nu

rating (ˈreɪtɪŋ) nc 1 (in some navies) an ordinary sailor without authority. 2 the class into which something is put.

ratio (ˈreɪʃɪəʊ) nc the relation of one thing to another as decided by the number of times one contains the other: The ratio of men to women in my office is three to one.

ration (ˈræʃən) nc (often pl) a fixed amount of food, etc., given to a person. ● vt allow (a person) no more than a ration of (food, etc.).

rational ('ræʃənəl) *adj* **1** to do with reason. **2** having or showing good sense. **rationalise** ('ræʃənəlaɪz) *vt* **1** show something to be, or treat it as if it were, reasonable. **2** make (production, a factory, etc.) more efficient.

rattle ('rætəl) *vti* (cause to) make short, sharp sounds, esp. by shaking or being shaken. ● *nc* **1** a sound made by rattling. **2** a musical instrument, baby's toy, or other device that rattles when shaken. **rattlesnake** ('rætəlsneɪk) *nc* a poisonous American snake that shakes its tail to produce a rattling noise.

raucous ('rɔːkəs) *adj* (of a voice, laugh, etc.) loud, harsh, and unpleasant.

ravage ('rævɪdʒ) *vt* destroy or damage: *a country ravaged by war.* ● *nu* destruction; damage. **ravages** *n pl* destroying action: *the ravages of time.*

rave (reɪv) *vi* **1** talk wildly when or as if mad or with a high fever. **2** *infml* talk or write very enthusiastically about something, such as a play.

raven ('reɪvən) *nc* a large bird with shiny black feathers and a harsh cry.

ravenous ('rævənəs) *adj* **1** very hungry. **2** greedy for power, money, etc.

ravine (rə'viːn) *nc* a deep, narrow valley: see picture.

ravine

ravish ('rævɪʃ) *vt* **1** fill with delight: *ravishing beauty.* **2** rape.

raw (rɔː) *adj* **1** (of food) not cooked. **2** without experience or training. **3** in a natural state; before being treated: *Iron is the main raw material for making steel.* **4** (of the weather) cold and damp. **5** (of the skin, an injury, etc.) painful, esp. where the skin has been scraped off.

ray[1] (reɪ) *nc* **1** a thin beam of light. **2** a small amount: *a ray of hope.*

ray[2] *nc* a large sea-fish with a flat body.

rayon ('reɪɒn) *nu* a silk-like material made from cellulose.

raze (reɪz) *vt* destroy (buildings), esp. until level with the ground.

razor ('reɪzə*) *nc* a tool with one or more sharp blades used for shaving off hair, esp. from the face.

re (riː) *prep* with reference to; to do with.

reach (riːtʃ) *vt* **1** arrive at (a place, person, etc.). **2** stretch out the hand for: *Can you reach that book on the top shelf?* **3** *vti* (often followed by **out**) stretch or be stretched out. **4** *vi* apply; have an effect; spread: *Rain will reach across the whole country.* ● *nc* **1** act of stretching out the hand. **2** the distance to which a thing can reach or be stretched. **3** *(often pl)* a part of a river between bends: *the upper reaches of the Nile.* **out of reach 1** too far away to reach. **2** not obtainable.

react (rɪ'ækt) *vi* **1** (often followed by **to**) behave or act in a certain way because of the behaviour or action of another person or thing. **2** (often followed by **with**) *chemistry* change when put together: *Acid reacts with metal.* **reaction** (rɪ'ækʃən) *nc* **1** an action or effect that results from something that has happened earlier: *Her tiredness is a reaction to the weeks she spent studying for her examination.* **2** *chemistry* the effect one substance has on another. **reactor** (rɪ'æktə*) *n* **nuclear reactor** a device producing nuclear power.

read (riːd) *vt* **1** look at, understand, (and speak) something written or printed: *I can read German; Will you read the letter to me?* **2** (of a measuring instrument) indicate: *The thermometer is reading 110.* **3** *vti* study (a subject), esp. at university: *He's reading history at Oxford; Are you reading for a degree?* ● *nc* **1** reading. **2** written or printed material for reading: *This book is a very good read.* **readable** ('riːdəbəl) *adj* **1** (of a book, story, etc.) interesting and easy to read. **2** (of writing or printing) possible to read. **reader** *nc* **1** a person who reads, esp. one who is fond of reading. **2** *Brit* a person who is in a senior position at a university. **3** a book used in teaching. **reading** *nu* **1** the act of a person who reads. **2** being able to read. *nc* **3** the way in which something said or written is explained or understood. **4** the figure indicated on a measuring instrument.

ready ('redɪ) *adj* **-ier, -iest 1** prepared; suitable for use or for doing something: *Are you ready for your journey?* **2** willing to do what is needed, etc. **3** quick: *a ready mind; a ready reply.* **4** near; easily obtained: *ready to hand.* **ready-made** (,redɪ'meɪd) *adj* ready for immediate use or wear: *If he complains, I've got a ready-made answer; a ready-made suit.* **ready reckoner** a list of numbers in a book that provide answers, used in business, etc. **readily** *adv* **1** willingly. **2** easily. **readiness** *nu*

real (rɪəl) *adj* **1** being a fact; existing. **2** not false. **reality** (rɪ'ælɪtɪ) **1** *nu* being real. **2** *nc, pl* **-ties** something that is real.

realise (ˈrɪəlaɪz) vt 1 understand; have knowledge of: *Do you realise how much a new car will cost?* 2 change (hopes, dreams, plans, etc.) into facts: *His aim to become a doctor was realised.* 3 sell (belongings) for money. 4 (of belongings) be sold for (money). **realisation** (ˌrɪəlaɪˈzeɪʃən) *nu*

realism (ˈrɪəlɪzəm) *nu* 1 looking at things as they really are; rejecting things that are impractical. 2 (in art, literature, etc.) showing things as they are in real, familiar, daily life. **realist** *nc* a person who believes in realism. **realistic** (rɪəˈlɪstɪk) *adj* 1 looking like the real thing. 2 to do with realism. **realistically** *adv*

really (ˈrɪəlɪ) *adv* 1 truly: *I'm really sorry.* 2 in fact: *It's really nothing to do with us.*

realm (relm) *nc* 1 a country ruled by a king or queen: *the laws of the realm.* 2 an area of interest, activity, study, etc.: *the realms of science.*

ream (riːm) *nc* 1 500 sheets of paper. 2 *(usually pl) infml* a large quantity, esp. of writing.

reap (riːp) *vt* 1 cut and gather (corn, etc.) from (a field, etc.). 2 get (a profit or advantage) as a result of one's own or other people's actions.

rear[1] (rɪə*) *nc* the back part of anything. ● *adj* of or at the rear: *the rear lights of a car.*

rear[2] *vt* 1 care for and bring up (children). 2 grow or produce (plants or animals). 3 cause to be lifted or built up. 4 *vi* (esp. of a horse) lift the front legs.

reason (ˈriːzən) *nc* 1 a cause for an action. 2 an argument that something is right or reasonable: *I have reason to doubt what you say.* *nu* 3 the power of understanding, thinking, etc. 4 good sense: *He won't listen to reason.* **within reason** sensible: *He'll do anything within reason.* ● *vt* 1 think over something and form (an opinion): *He reasoned that it would be better to go now rather than later.* *vti* 2 (often followed by **with**) try to work (something) out or decide (something) by using one's powers of understanding and thinking. 3 try to persuade (someone) of something. **by reason of** because of. **reasonable** (ˈriːzənəbəl) *adj* 1 having good sense; willing to listen to reason. 2 done, said, etc., according to reason. 3 fair; quite good: *reasonable prices; reasonable weather.*

reassure (ˌriːəˈʃʊə*) *vt* lessen or remove the worries of. **reassurance** *ncu*

rebate (ˈriːbeɪt) *nc* a small amount of money that is taken off a price or given back after some has been paid.

rebel (ˈrebəl) *nc* 1 a person who fights against the government. 2 a person who re- fuses to accept rules, etc., that are generally accepted. ● (rɪˈbel) *vi* 1 fight against the government. 2 fight against any power, control, or authority. **rebellion** (rɪˈbeljən) *ncu* (an example of) rebelling. **rebellious** (rɪˈbeljəs) *adj* behaving like a rebel.

rebirth (ˌriːˈbɜːθ) *nc* 1 a total change of a person's religious beliefs. 2 the bringing back of something into use.

rebound (riːˈbaʊnd) *vi* 1 spring back after striking something. 2 (of an action) go wrong, so as to harm the person who did it. ● (ˈriːbaʊnd) *ncu* (an example of) rebounding.

rebuff (rɪˈbʌf) *nc* a cold, painful refusal to accept someone's offer of friendship, help, etc. ● *vt* give a rebuff to.

rebuke (rɪˈbjuːk) *vt* speak sharply to (someone) for doing something wrong; scold. ● *nc* a scolding.

recall (rɪˈkɔːl) *vt* 1 bring back (a memory): *I recall going there once.* 2 order (someone) to return. ● (rɪˈkɔːl, ˈriːkɔːl) 1 *nu* the ability to remember. 2 *nc* an order to return.

recapitulate (ˌriːkəˈpɪtʃʊleɪt) *vt* repeat the main ideas of (something that has been said). **recapitulation** (ˌriːkəˌpɪtʃʊˈleɪʃən) *ncu* (an example of) recapitulating.

recede (rɪˈsiːd) *vi* 1 go farther back. 2 slope back from the front: *a receding chin.* 3 lessen: *Hopes of peace receded.*

receipt (rɪˈsiːt) 1 *nu* receiving or being received. *nc* 2 a written or printed paper showing that something, esp. money, has been received. 3 *(usually pl)* money taken at an event such as a concert.

receive (rɪˈsiːv) *vt* 1 get or accept (something) that is sent, offered, or given to one: *Did you receive my letter?; The matter is receiving attention.* 2 suffer; experience: *He received serious head injuries.* 3 allow (someone) to enter or join something: *She was received into the society.* 4 welcome formally: *The king received his guests at the palace gate.* **receiver** *nc* a person appointed by a court of law to manage esp. a failing company.

recent (ˈriːsənt) *adj* that happened or began not long ago. **recently** *adv* lately.

receptacle (rɪˈseptəkəl) *nc* a container.

reception (rɪˈsepʃən) 1 *nu* receiving or being received. 2 *nc* a formal party for guests: *a wedding reception.* 3 *nu* the receiving of sounds on a radio or television.

receptive (rɪˈseptɪv) *adj* 1 ready to accept new ideas, etc. 2 (of the mind) quick.

receptor (rɪˈseptə*) *nc* any of a number of devices that receive information, etc.

recess (rɪˈses, ˈriːses) *nc* 1 a short time during which work is stopped. 2 a part of a room that is set farther back: *a recess with a* *bed in it:* see picture. **3** a secret place. ● *vt* put (something) in a recess.

recess

recession (rɪ'seʃən) *nc* a time when business, trade, etc., is less active.

recipe ('resɪpɪ) *nc* a list of instructions on how to make a particular food dish.

recipient (rɪ'sɪpɪənt) *nc* a person who receives something.

reciprocal (rɪ'sɪprəkəl) *adj* given by each of two people, etc., to the other: *reciprocal friendship.* ● *nc mathematics* the number which, when multiplied by a given number, makes 1: *The reciprocal of 3 is ⅓.*

reciprocate (rɪ'sɪprəkeɪt) *vti* feel or give in return (for something): *I hope to reciprocate your help some day.*

recital (rɪ'saɪtəl) *nc* **1** a concert given by one or a small number of musicians. **2** an account of something with all the details.

recite (rɪ'saɪt) *vti* **1** speak (a poem, etc.), esp. from memory. **2** tell of (something), including all the details. **recitation** (ˌresɪ'teɪʃən) **1** *ncu* (an example of) reciting. **2** *nc* a poem, etc., that is recited.

reckless ('reklɪs) *adj* having or showing no thought for the results of one's actions: *reckless driving.* **recklessly** *adv* **recklessness** *nu*

reckon ('rekən) *vt* **1** work with numbers to find out (something). **2** think; be of the opinion: *Do you reckon he'll come?* **reckoning 1** *nu* counting. **2** *nc* a punishment or suffering for one's actions. **reckon on** depend on: *I'm reckoning on everyone's support.* **reckon with** or **without** take or fail to take into account: *I reckoned without rain at this time of year.*

reclaim (rɪ'kleɪm) *vt* **1** make (waste land) useful again. **2** make (someone) change from bad to good ways. **reclamation** (ˌreklə'meɪʃən) *nu*

recline (rɪ'klaɪn) *vti* (cause to) lie or lean back in a comfortable position.

recognise ('rekəgnaɪz) *vt* **1** see and remember seeing (someone or something) before. **2** be willing to accept that something is real or that someone has a right: *The college recognises that qualification.* **recognisable** ('rekəgnaɪzəbəl) *adj* able to be recognised. **recognition** (ˌrekəg'nɪʃən) *nu*

recoil (rɪ'kɔɪl) *vi* **1** draw back in fear, disgust, etc. **2** (of a gun) jump back on being fired. ● *nc* the backward jump of a gun on being fired.

recollect (ˌrekə'lekt) *vt* remember, esp. after some effort. **recollection** (ˌrekə'lekʃən) **1** *nu* remembering. **2** *nc* something remembered: *recollections of his schooldays.*

recommend (ˌrekə'mend) *vt* **1** speak well of; say to be suitable, etc.: *I can recommend the hotel at which I stayed.* **2** advise: *The doctor recommended this medicine.* **recommendation** (ˌrekəmen'deɪʃən) **1** *nu* recommending. *nc* **2** something that recommends. **3** something that is recommended.

recompense ('rekəmpens) *vt* **1** reward (someone) for work, etc. **2** pay (someone) for a loss, etc. ● *nu* a reward.

reconcile ('rekənsaɪl) *vt* **1** cause (people) to become friendly again after a quarrel. **2** make (oneself) accept something unpleasant: *She reconciled herself to her son's death.* **3** make (differing things) match or agree. **reconciliation** (ˌrekən,sɪlɪ'eɪʃən) *ncu* (an example of) reconciling or being reconciled.

reconnoitre *US* **reconnoiter** (ˌrekə'nɔɪtə*) *vt* search (a district) to find out an enemy's position, etc. **reconnaissance** (rɪ'kɒnɪsəns) *ncu* (an example of) reconnoitring.

record (rɪ'kɔːd) *vt* **1** set down in writing or some other permanent form. **2** (of a measuring instrument) show (information). ● ('rekɔːd) *nc* **1** an account of something kept in a permanent form. **2** the best score, mark, etc., reached or known of, esp. in sport: *the world land speed record; The number of tourists here reached a record last year.* **3** a flat plastic disc on which sound is recorded. **record-player** ('rekɔːdpleɪə*) *nc* a machine for playing records (**record** def. 3) on. **recorder** *nc* **1** a pipe-like musical instrument blown at one end. **2** a device that records: *a tape-recorder.* **3** *Brit* a government officer who acts as a judge in the lower courts. **recording** (rɪ'kɔːdɪŋ) *nc* recorded sound or television pictures.

recount (rɪ'kaʊnt) *vt* tell (a story, one's adventures, etc.).

re-count (ˌriː'kaʊnt) *vt* count again. ● ('riːkaʊnt) *nc* another count.

recourse (rɪ'kɔːs) *nu* a person, action, etc., that is turned to for help. **have recourse to** turn to or use when in need of action or help.

recover (rɪ'kʌvə*) **1** *vt* get back (what was lost, out of use, etc.). **2** *vi* become healthy or calm after an illness, surprise, shock, etc. **recovery** (rɪ'kʌvərɪ) *ncu, pl* **-ries** (an example of) recovering.

re-cover (ˌriː'kʌvə*) *vt* cover again.

315

recreation (ˌrekrɪ'eɪʃən) **1** *nu* play or amusement that brings new strength to mind and body when one's work is done. **2** *nc* anything done to pass the time pleasantly. **recreational** (ˌrekrɪ'eɪʃənəl) *adj*

recrimination (rɪˌkrɪmɪ'neɪʃən) *ncu* (an example of) blaming someone for a fault, crime, etc., after being blamed for this oneself.

recruit (rɪ'kruːt) *nc* **1** a person who has just joined an army. **2** any new member of a group, society, etc. ● *vt* take in or obtain (new members), esp. for an army. **recruitment** *nu* recruiting.

rectangle ('rektæŋgəl) *nc* a flat, four-sided figure with four right angles and opposite sides equal: see picture at **shapes. rectangular** (rek'tæŋgjʊlə*) *adj* having the shape of a rectangle.

rectify ('rektɪfaɪ) *vt* correct; put right.

rectilinear (ˌrektɪ'lɪnɪə*) *adj* to do with a straight line or straight lines.

rector ('rektə*) *nc* **1** a Church of England priest in charge of a parish. **2** the head of some schools, colleges, or universities. **rectory** ('rəktərɪ) *nc, pl* **-ries** the house provided for a rector to live in.

recuperate (rɪ'kjuːpəreɪt) **1** *vi* become well again after an illness or loss of strength. **2** *vt* get back (something that was lost).

recur (rɪ'kɜː*) *vi* **1** happen again. **2** (of an idea, thought, etc.) come back into one's mind. **recurrence** (rɪ'kʌrəns) *ncu* (an example of) recurring. **recurrent** (rɪ'kʌrənt) *adj* happening often.

recycle (ˌriː'saɪkəl) *vt* use (a substance, such as glass or paper) again.

red (red) *adj* **-der, -dest** of the colour of blood or the rising or setting sun. ● *ncu* a red colour. **be in the red** owe money to a bank. **Red Cross** an international organisation formed to care for people sick and wounded in war and in terrible accidents such as earthquakes, etc. **catch (someone) red-handed** catch (someone) in the act of doing wrong. **red-hot** (ˌred'hɒt) *adj* **1** very hot. **2** very excited. **red tape** *nu* (esp. in business or an army) unimportant rules that get in the way. **redden** ('redən) *vti* make or become red. **reddish** ('redɪʃ) *adj* quite red.

redeem (rɪ'diːm) *vt* **1** get (something) back that once belonged to one, esp. by payment. **2** (in Christianity) save from the punishment of sin by Jesus' death. **3** save from being completely bad, ugly, etc.: *She's ugly, her one redeeming feature being beautiful eyes.* **4** carry out (a promise, duty, etc.). **redemption** (rɪ'dempʃən) *nu*

redouble (rɪ'dʌbəl) *vti* make or become even greater, stronger, etc.

redress (rɪ'dres) *vt* make (something) right that was wrong. ● *nu* **1** the setting right of a wrong. **2** something that does this.

reduce (rɪ'djuːs) **1** *vt* make less in size, number, weight, etc. **2** *infml vi* become less in weight: *She's always trying to reduce.* **3** *vt* bring by force or need to a certain action, way of living, etc.: *He became so poor he was reduced to begging.* **reduction** (rɪ'dʌkʃən) *ncu* (an example of) reducing or being reduced.

redundant (rɪ'dʌndənt) *adj* not needed or wanted, esp. in a job; more than is needed. **redundancy** *ncu, pl* **-cies** (an example of) being (made to be) redundant.

reed (riːd) *nc* **1** a tall, thin grass that grows by or in water. **2** a thin piece of cane or metal in some musical instruments that produces sound when air is blown over it.

reef (riːf) *nc* a line of rocks near to the surface of the sea.

reek (riːk) *vi* smell strongly and unpleasantly: *The room reeks of cigarette smoke.* ● *nu* a strong, unpleasant smell.

reel[1] (riːl) *nc* **1** a wooden, metal, etc., device on which cotton, string, wire, etc., is wound: *a reel of film:* see picture. **2** a Scot-

reel

tish dance. ● *vt* wind (cotton, etc.) onto a reel.

reel[2] *vi* move in an unsteady way.

refectory (rɪ'fektərɪ) *nc, pl* **-ries** a large room in which meals are eaten in a college or religious institution.

refer (rɪ'fɜː*) **1** *vt* hand over (a matter) to someone else to deal with. *vi* (often followed by **to**) **2** make mention of; apply to; concern: *Did that rude remark refer to me?* **3** go to (a person, book, etc.) for information. **referee** (ˌrefə'riː) *nc* **1** a person from whom an opinion or decision is sought. **2** a person who acts as a judge in various sports. **reference** ('refərəns) *ncu* (an example of) referring: *The book contains many references to the Middle East.* **with reference to** about; to do with. **reference book** a book from which one may obtain information, such as a dictionary.

referendum (ˌrefə'rendəm) *nc, pl* **-dums, -da** (də) a public vote on an important political matter.

refill (ˌriː'fɪl) *vt* fill again. ● ('riːfɪl) *nc* another filling; substance put in the place of one that has been used up.

refine (rɪ'faɪn) *vt* 1 make (oil, etc.) pure. 2 cause to improve in tastes, manners, etc. *vi* 3 (of oil, etc.) become pure. 4 improve in tastes, manners, etc. **refinement** 1 *nu* refining or being refined. 2 *nc* an example of purity, improvement in tastes, etc. **refinery** (rɪ'faɪnərɪ) *nc, pl* **-ries** a place where something is refined: *a sugar refinery*.

reflect (rɪ'flekt) 1 *vt* throw back (light, heat, or sound) from a surface. *vi* 2 (usually followed by **on**) throw honour or dishonour on: *His bad manners reflect on his background.* 3 think about something. 4 *vt* show: *Her smile reflected her joy; Television reflects what society is like.* **reflection** 1 *nu* reflecting or being reflected. 2 *nc* something reflected. **reflector** *nc* a device that reflects light, heat, or sound, such as a piece of glass or metal on the back of a vehicle that reflects the lights of a vehicle behind it.

reflex ('ri:fleks) *adj* done without intention: *Coughing and sneezing are reflex actions.*

reflexive (rɪ'fleksɪv) *adj* of a word that shows the object of a sentence is the same as the subject: *In 'He drove himself to the station', the word 'himself' is reflexive.*

reform (rɪ'fɔ:m) *vti* change or be changed for the better. ● *nu* 1 reforming. 2 *nc* an improvement made. **reformation** (ˌrefə'meɪʃən) *nu* reforming or being reformed. **the Reformation** a movement in Europe in the sixteenth century to make changes in the Roman Catholic Church. **reformer** *nc* a person who favours or works for reform.

refract (rɪ'frækt) *vt* make a beam of light bend by passing it through a substance: see picture. **refraction** (rɪ'frækʃən) *nu*

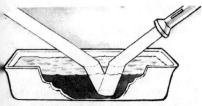

refract

refrain[1] (rɪ'freɪn) *vi* stop oneself from (doing) something: *to refrain from anger; I refrained from singing too loud.*

refrain[2] *nc* a part of a song that is repeated, usually after each verse.

refresh (rɪ'freʃ) *vt* make fresh; make stronger, less weary, less thirsty, etc. **refresh one's memory** go back to something learnt once before in order to remember it better. **refreshing** *adj* 1 giving new strength, rest, or relief. 2 different in a pleasing way. **refreshment** 1 *nu* refreshing

or being refreshed. 2 *(pl)* food and drink.

refrigerate (rɪ'frɪdʒəreɪt) *vt* make or keep (food) cold to prevent it from going bad. **refrigerator** (rɪ'frɪdʒəreɪtə*) (often shortened to **fridge**) *nc* a machine or room in which food and drink are kept cold.

refuge ('refju:dʒ) 1 *nu* shelter or protection from trouble, danger, etc. 2 *nc* a place that gives shelter, etc.

refugee (ˌrefjʊ'dʒi:) *nc* a person who has run away from danger, trouble, his own country, etc., to find protection elsewhere.

refund (rɪ'fʌnd) *vt* give back (money) to someone. ● ('ri:fʌnd) *ncu* (an amount of) money returned.

refuse[1] ('refju:s) *formal nu* waste matter; rubbish.

refuse[2] (rɪ'fju:z) 1 *vt* say or show that one will not agree, accept, or do something. 2 *vi* say no; not agree to, accept, or allow something. **refusal** (rɪ'fju:zəl) *ncu* (an example of) refusing. **first refusal** the chance to accept or refuse an offer before it is made to anyone else.

regain (rɪ'geɪn) *vt* get back (something lost, etc.).

regal ('ri:gəl) *adj* of, to do with, or suitable for a king or queen; royal.

regard (rɪ'gɑ:d) *vt* 1 look at closely. 2 consider. ● *nu* 1 a long, close look. 2 opinion; respect. 3 attention. **in** or **with regard to** concerning. **as regards** See **as for** under **as**. **regards** *n pl* good wishes. **regarding** *prep* concerning. **regardless** *adj* without caring about or taking any notice of.

regatta (rɪ'gætə) *nc* a set of races for boats that are rowed, sailing-boats, etc.

regent ('ri:dʒənt) *nc* a person chosen to take on the duties of a ruler if the real king is too young, too ill, or absent. **regency** ('ri:dʒənsɪ) *nc, pl* **-cies** 1 *nu* the job of a regent. 2 *nc* the length of time a regent rules.

regime (reɪ'ʒi:m) *nc* a way of government or the control of public affairs; social system.

regiment ('redʒɪmənt) *nc* 1 a unit of the army consisting of six or more companies of soldiers. 2 a large number of anything.

region ('ri:dʒən) *nc* a part of the country or any surface or space, the limits of which are uncertain. **regional** *adj* of a region.

register ('redʒɪstə*) *nc* 1 a written list; book containing this. 2 the range of the voice or a musical instrument. 3 a machine that stores information, adds numbers, etc.: *a cash register.* ● *vt* 1 put down (a person's name, etc.) in a register. 2 (of an instrument) show (an amount, etc.). 3 show (a certain emotion) on one's face: *He registered anger.* 4 send (an important letter, etc.) by special post. 5 *infml vi* have an effect; be noticed. **registrar** (ˌredʒɪ'strɑ:*) *nc* a person who keeps written registers. **registration** (ˌredʒɪˈstreɪʃən) **1** *nu* registering or being registered. **2** *nc* an entry in a register. **registry** (ˈredʒɪstrɪ) *nc, pl* **-tries** a place where registers are kept. **registry office** *Brit* a place where registers are kept and where marriages take place without a religious service.

regret (rɪˈgret) *vt* **1** feel sorrow for (something one did or did not do). **2** feel sorry or upset about. ●*nu* **1** feeling of sorrow or guilt over something done or not done; grief. **2** *(pl)* sadness, apology, or sorrow about something. **regretfully** (rɪˈgretfʊlɪ) *adv* **regrettable** (rɪˈgretəbəl) *adj* to be regretted.

regular (ˈregjʊlə*) *adj* **1** happening or done at fixed or steady intervals. **2** even: *regular teeth.* **3** according to usual behaviour or ways of doing things. **4** *grammar* (of a word or its ending) having the usual form. ●*nc infml* a person who is a regular customer at a pub, etc. **regularity** (ˌregjʊˈlærɪtɪ) *nu* being regular. **regularly** *adv*

regulate (ˈregjʊleɪt) *vt* **1** slightly alter (a machine, etc.) to set it right. **2** control, esp. by means of rules. **regulation** (ˌregjʊˈleɪʃən) **1** *nu* regulating or being regulated. **2** *nc* a rule. ●*adj* as ordered by a rule.

rehabilitate (ˌriːhəˈbɪlɪteɪt) *vt* **1** make almost as new again: *rehabilitate old buildings.* **2** put back to former rank or importance. **3** help (someone who is disabled) to live a normal life. **rehabilitation** (ˌriːhəbɪlɪˈteɪʃən) *nu* rehabilitating.

rehearse (rɪˈhɜːs) *vt* **1** practise (a play) before acting to an audience. **2** repeat aloud from memory. **rehearsal** *ncu* (an instance of) rehearsing.

reign (reɪn) *nc* **1** the time when a king, etc., rules a country. **2** the time when a person or thing is powerful. ●*vi* rule as or like a king, etc.

reimburse (ˌriːɪmˈbɜːs) *vt* pay back (an amount already spent) to (someone). **reimbursement** *ncu* repayment.

rein (reɪn) *nc* **1** one of the long, leather straps used to control the movements of a horse: see picture. **2** something used to control (esp. a person or animal): *Keep your husband on a tight rein—don't let him do as he likes.*

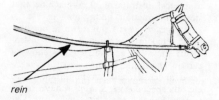

rein

reindeer (ˈreɪndɪə*) *nc, pl* **reindeer** a kind of large deer with branched horns living in northern parts of Europe: see picture at **animals.**

reinforce (ˌriːɪnˈfɔːs) *vt* give extra strength or support to. **reinforcement 1** *nu* reinforcing or being reinforced. **2** *nc (usually pl)* something, esp. soldiers, that reinforces.

reiterate (riːˈɪtəreɪt) *vt* repeat.

reject (rɪˈdʒekt) *vt* **1** refuse to accept or consider. **2** throw out as not being good enough. **3** show no interest in or care for (someone). **rejection 1** *nu* rejecting or being rejected. **2** *nc* a refusal.

rejoice (rɪˈdʒɔɪs) *vi* feel great joy and gladness. **rejoicing 1** *nu* joy. **2** *nc (pl)* joyful happenings.

rejoin (ˌriːˈdʒɔɪn) *vt* **1** join (the company of someone or something) again. **2** put or join together again. **3** (rɪˈdʒɔɪn) *formal* answer quickly, sharply, or humorously.

relapse (rɪˈlæps) *vi* fall back (into bad habits, evil ways, illness, etc.). ●*nc* such a falling back.

relate (rɪˈleɪt) *vt* **1** tell (a story); give the facts, details, etc., of. **2** show the connection in thought or meaning between (two or more things). **3** understand; sympathise: *I can't relate to him at all.* **be related to** be connected to by family.

relation (rɪˈleɪʃən) *nu* **1** the connection between two or more people or things. **2** the connection between people by family or marriage. **3** *nc* a person connected in this way. **4** *(pl)* connections: *good business relations.* **in** or **with relation to** concerning.

relationship (rɪˈleɪʃənʃɪp) **1** *nu* the connection between one person or thing and another or others. **2** *nc* an example of this: *The relationship between husband and wife is a happy one.*

relative (ˈrelətɪv) *adj* **1** showing a comparison. **2** being connected in some way. **3** *grammar* of a word or group of words that connect: *'Who' in 'The girl who played with me was kind' is a relative pronoun.* ●*nc* a person who belongs to one's family. **relatively** *adv* to a certain extent. **relativity** (ˌreləˈtɪvɪtɪ) *nu* **1** the quality of being **relative** (def. 2). **2** *science* the theory dealing with space, time, and movement.

relax (rɪˈlæks) **1** *vti* (of muscles, etc.), (cause to) become looser, less stiff, or tense. **2** *vi* not do work; enjoy oneself in a lazy way. **3** *vt* make less strict. **relaxation** (ˌriːlækˈseɪʃən) *ncu* (an instance of) relaxing; rest.

relay (ˈriːleɪ) *nc* **1** a fresh set of horses or group of men to replace tired ones. **2** *radio* a device that receives messages, programmes, etc., and sends them out again in order to lengthen the distance they travel. **3** a race in which members of a team take turns to run, swim, etc. ●(rɪˈleɪ) *vt* receive and send out (messages, etc.).

release (rɪˈliːs) *vt* **1** set free; let go one's hold of: *release a prisoner; release one's grip on a rope.* **2** make (news, information, etc.) known to the public. ●*ncu* (an example of) releasing or being released.

relegate (ˈrelɪgeɪt) *vt* move to a position of less importance.

relent (rɪˈlent) *vi* change one's mind and become less harsh or cruel. **relentless** *adj* **1** without mercy. **2** *infml* not stopping: *relentless noise.*

relevant (ˈrelɪvənt) *adj* to do with the subject being discussed. **relevance** *nu* being relevant.

reliable (rɪˈlaɪəbəl) *adj* that can be depended on; trustworthy. **reliance** (rɪˈlaɪəns) *nu* trust.

relic (ˈrelɪk) *nc* something that has continued to exist from times long past.

relief¹ (rɪˈliːf) *nu* **1** a lessening or removal of worry, fear, etc.; something that brings this about. **2** help given to the poor or those in trouble. **3** something that adds variety to make more interesting: *light relief from a boring task.* **4** a person or thing that takes over another's work for a few hours.

relief² *nu* a way of carving or drawing in which designs appear to stand out from the surface; *nc* such a carving or drawing. ● *adj* using relief.

relieve (rɪˈliːv) *vt* **1** lessen or remove (worry, fear, pain, etc.). **2** take over (someone's work) for a few hours.

religion (rɪˈlɪdʒən) **1** *nu* the belief in a spiritual power that has created and is in control of the world. *nc* **2** one of a number of groups that believe this and have formed a system of worship. **3** something to which one gives time and care (esp. more than is proper). **religious** (rɪˈlɪdʒəs) *adj* of or to do with religion.

relinquish (rɪˈlɪŋkwɪʃ) *vt* give up; let go.

relish (ˈrelɪʃ) *vt* fully enjoy (an experience, taste, etc.). ●*nu* **1** eager enjoyment. **2** *nc* something that adds taste or enjoyment, esp. a sauce or pickle.

reluctant (rɪˈlʌktənt) *adj* not eager or willing. **reluctance** *nu* being reluctant. **reluctantly** *adv*

rely (rɪˈlaɪ) *v* **rely on** or **upon** depend on; have confidence in: *Don't rely too much on what your friends say.*

remain (rɪˈmeɪn) **1** *vi* stay behind or be left after part has gone, been used, etc. **2** *vt* stay; continue to be. **remainder** *nu* a part that is left. **remains** *n pl* **1** the pieces or parts left. **2** the body of a dead person.

remark (rɪˈmɑːk) **1** *formal vt* notice. **2** *vi* speak or write an opinion or thought. ● *nu* **1** *formal* notice. **2** *nc* an expression of opinion or thought, esp. not a forceful one. **remark (up)on** express an opinion on. **remarkable** (rɪˈmɑːkəbəl) *adj* attracting notice; unusual. **remarkably** *adv*

remedial (rɪˈmiːdɪəl) *adj* of or to do with a cure for an illness, or the setting right of something that is wrong: *remedial treatment.*

remedy (ˈremɪdɪ) *nc, pl* **-dies** anything that cures an illness or puts right what is wrong. ● *vt* put right.

remember (rɪˈmembə*) *vt* **1** not forget; keep in the memory. **2** do something on the occasion of (a regular event, such as a birthday). **3** not forget to give a tip or present to: *Remember your friends this Christmas!* **remember to** say hello to (someone) from (a friend who is not there): *Remember me to her when you see her again.*

remembrance (rɪˈmembrəns) **1** *nu* remembering or being remembered. **2** *nc* something that reminds one of someone or something.

remind (rɪˈmaɪnd) *vt* cause someone to remember: *Remind me to take my bag; His face reminds me of his mother.* **reminder** *nc* something that helps one to remember something, esp. a letter sent by someone waiting for something: *I got a reminder about the gas bill today.*

reminisce (ˌremɪˈnɪs) *vi* think or talk about something that happened in the past. **reminiscence** **1** *nu* reminiscing. **2** *(pl)* some past events or experiences thought or talked about. **reminiscent** *adj* that causes one to remember.

remit (rɪˈmɪt) *vt* **1** *archaic* (of God) forgive. **2** send (money, etc.) by post. **3** free (someone) from a debt or punishment. **4** *formal vti* make or become less in amount, degree, etc. **remittance 1** *nu* the remitting of money. **2** *nc* payment sent by post.

remnant (ˈremnənt) *nc* a small part that is left after the rest has been used, lost, etc.

remonstrate (ˈremənstreɪt) *vi* make a protest; complain. **remonstrance** (rɪˈmonstrəns) *ncu* (a) protest.

remorse (rɪˈmɔːs) *nu* **1** a feeling of sorrow and guilt for one's wrongdoing. **2** pity. **remorseless** *adj* without remorse.

remote (rɪˈməʊt) *adj* **-r, -st** far away: *a remote village; in the remote past.*

remove (rɪˈmuːv) *vt* **1** take or move (one's belongings, etc.) to another place. **2** take off. **3** get rid of. **removable** *adj* that can be removed. **removal** *ncu* (an instance of) removing. ●*adj* of or for a removal: *a removal van.*

remunerate (rɪˈmjuːnəreɪt) *formal or humorous vt* pay (someone) for work, etc., done; reward. **remuneration** (rɪˌmjuːnəˈreɪʃən) *nu* a payment; reward. **remunerative** (rɪˈmjuːnərətɪv) *adj* that pays well.

renaissance (rəˈneɪsəns) *nc* a new direction or interest in something, esp. learning or the arts. **the Renaissance** the time in Europe, about 1300 to 1500, when there was a new birth in art and learning.

rend (rend) *literary vt* 1 tear. 2 divide in two or in pieces.

render (ˈrendə*) *formal vt* 1 give what is due: *render payment.* 2 cause to become: *render it useless.* 3 perform: *render service.*

rendezvous (ˈrɒndɪvuː, ˈrɒndeɪvuː) *nc, pl* **rendezvous** 1 a meeting or arrangement to meet at an agreed place. 2 a place where people meet.

rendition (renˈdɪʃən) *nc* a performance (of a play, piece of music, etc.).

renegade (ˈrenɪgeɪd) *derogatory nc* a person who deserts his religious faith, the political party he supports, etc.; traitor.

renew (rɪˈnjuː) *vt* 1 make as if new again; bring to a new and fresh condition. 2 replace something used up, worn out, etc. **renewal** *ncu* (an instance of) renewing or being renewed.

renounce (rɪˈnaʊns) *vt* say that one will have nothing more to do with (someone or something): *renounce one's faith.*

renovate (ˈrenəveɪt) *vt* bring back to a good condition: *renovate old paintings.* **renovation** (ˌrenəˈveɪʃən) *ncu* (an instance of) renovating or being renovated.

renown (rɪˈnaʊn) *nu* fame. **renowned** *adj* famous.

rent¹ (rent) *ncu* (an amount of) money paid regularly for the use of a house, flat, land, etc. ● *vt* 1 pay rent to live in or use (a house, land, etc.). 2 (of a house, land, etc.) allow to be rented. **rental** (ˈrentəl) *nc* an amount paid as rent.

rent² past tense and participle of **rend**. ● *nc* a tear in cloth, etc.

renunciation (rɪˌnʌnsɪˈeɪʃən) 1 *nu* the giving up of a belief, right, habit, etc. 2 *nc* an act or example of this.

repair (rɪˈpeə*) *vt* 1 put in a good condition again after damage, much use, etc.: *repair shoes.* 2 *formal* put right (a wrong, etc.). ● *nu* 1 a state: *in good repair.* 2 *nc* an act or example of repairing.

reparation (ˌrepəˈreɪʃən) *formal ncu* something given or done to make up for a loss, injury, etc.

repast (rɪˈpɑːst) *formal nc* a meal.

repatriate (riːˈpætrɪeɪt) *vt* send back (a person) to his own country. **repatriation** (ˌriːpætrɪˈeɪʃən) *nu*

repay (rɪˈpeɪ) *vt* 1 pay back (money that has been borrowed) to (the lender). 2 give or do something in return for: *repay kindness.* **repayment** *ncu* (an amount of money for) repaying.

repeal (rɪˈpiːl) *vt* stop the effectiveness of (a law, etc.).

repeat (rɪˈpiːt) *vt* say or do (something) again: *repeat one's words; repeat a poem; repeat an action.* ● *nc* anything that is repeated: *a repeat of a radio programme.* **repeatedly** (rɪˈpiːtɪdlɪ) *adv* again and again.

repel (rɪˈpel) *vt* 1 drive back (someone or something): *repel an attacker.* 2 cause a feeling of disgust in. **repellent** *adj* causing disgust.

repent (rɪˈpent) *vti* feel sorrow and regret for (a wrong one has done). **repentance** *nu* regret for doing wrong.

repercussion (ˌriːpəˈkʌʃən) *nc (often pl)* an important, esp. unexpected effect that continues long after the event that caused it.

repertoire (ˈrepətwɑː*) *nc* a set of plays, pieces of music, etc., that an actor, musician, etc., has practised and is ready to perform.

repertory (ˈrepətrɪ) *nu* the system by which a group of actors give performances of plays for several days at a time in the same theatre.

repetition (ˌrepɪˈtɪʃən) *ncu* (an instance of) repeating or being repeated. **repetitive** (rɪˈpetɪtɪv) *adj* marked by repetition.

replace (rɪˈpleɪs) *vt* 1 put (something) back in its former place. 2 take the place of.

replenish (rɪˈplenɪʃ) *vt* fill up again.

replica (ˈreplɪkə) *nc* an exact copy, esp. of a work of art.

reply (rɪˈplaɪ) *vti* answer in words or by an action. ● *ncu, pl* **-plies** (an) answer.

report (rɪˈpɔːt) 1 *vt* give an account of (something seen or heard). 2 *vi* go to an agreed place for a purpose: *report for duty.* 3 *vt* complain about (someone) to someone in power. ● *nc* 1 an account of something seen or heard. 2 a sharp, loud sound: *the report of a gun.* **reported speech** a report of something said or written, giving the meaning but not the exact words. **reporter** *nc* a person who gets news for a newspaper, etc.: *the crime reporter.*

represent (ˌreprɪˈzent) *vt* 1 be a sign or example of. 2 show by a picture (what something is like). 3 act for; speak for. **representation** (ˌreprɪzenˈteɪʃən) *ncu* (an instance of) representing or being represented. **representative** (ˌreprɪˈzentətɪv) *adj* being a sign, example, or picture of; typical. ● *nc* a person chosen to act for another or others.

repress (rɪ'pres) *vt* keep under control; put down: *repress one's anger; repress a rebellion.* **repression 1** *nu* repressing or being repressed. **2** *nc* a feeling which is being repressed.

reprieve (rɪ'priːv) *vt* **1** put off or delay a punishment: *He was reprieved from hanging.* **2** give a time of relief from something unpleasant. ●*nc* **1** an order that puts off or delays a punishment. **2** a delay.

reprint ('riːprɪnt) *nc* a book, etc., published again with no changes made. ●(riː'prɪnt) *vt* print again, esp. a new, unchanged copy of (a book or magazine).

reprisal (rɪ'praɪzəl) *ncu* (an instance of) ill-treatment given as repayment for injury done to oneself: *We killed their leader in reprisal for the death of our soldiers.*

reproach (rɪ'prəʊtʃ) *vt* blame or find fault with (a person) because they have caused one shame or sorrow. ●*ncu* **1** (words of) blame. **2** a cause of disgrace. **beyond** or **above reproach** with no faults.

reproduce (ˌriːprə'djuːs) *vt* **1** cause (something) to be seen or heard again: *music reproduced on a record-player.* **2** make an exact copy of. **3** *vti* produce (children, young, or new plants). **reproduction** (ˌriːprə'dʌkʃən) **1** *nu* the act or process of reproducing. **2** *nc* something that is reproduced or copied. **reproductive** (ˌriːprə'dʌktɪv) *adj* of or to do with reproduction.

reproof (rɪ'pruːf) *formal ncu* (an act or expression of) blame.

reprove (rɪ'pruːv) *formal vt* find fault with (someone).

reptile ('reptaɪl) *nc* a cold-blooded animal that lays eggs and crawls: *Snakes and lizards are reptiles:* see picture. **reptilian** (rep'tɪlɪən) *adj* of or to do with a reptile.

republic (rɪ'pʌblɪk) *nc* a political system in which the power is held by a government chosen by the people; country with this system. **republican** *adj* of or to do with a republic. ●*nc* a person who supports or wishes for such a government.

repudiate (rɪ'pjuːdɪeɪt) *vt* **1** say that one will have nothing to do with (someone or something). **2** refuse to admit that one owes (a debt) or that one has done (something). **repudiation** *nu*

repulse (rɪ'pʌls) *vt* **1** drive back: *repulse the enemy.* **2** turn away in a cold manner (someone's offer of help, friendship, etc.). **repulsion** *nu* a feeling of disgust. **repulsive** *adj* disgusting.

repute (rɪ'pjuːt) *nu* reputation: *a person of bad repute.* **reputable** ('repjʊtəbəl) *adj* having a good reputation; trustworthy. **reputation** (ˌrepjʊ'teɪʃən) *nu* the general opinion about the qualities of someone or something: *the reputation of being a bad loser.*

request (rɪ'kwest) *vt* ask for. ●*ncu* **1** (an instance of) asking or being asked. **2** *nc* a thing that is asked for.

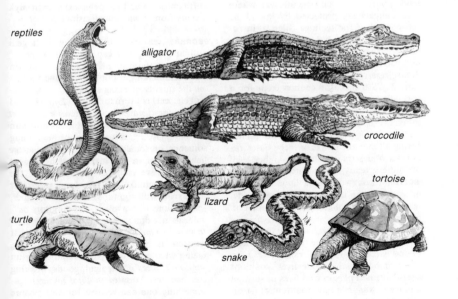

reptiles

alligator

cobra

crocodile

tortoise

lizard

turtle

snake

require (rɪˈkwaɪə*) vt 1 need; depend upon. 2 formal order. **requirement** nc something ordered or needed.

requisite (ˈrekwɪzɪt) adj very necessary. ● nc something that is very necessary. **requisition** (ˌrekwɪˈzɪʃən) nc a written demand, esp. a formal one.

requite (rɪˈkwaɪt) formal vt pay back (something) (with something): requite love with hate.

rescind (rɪˈsɪnd) law vt put an end to (a law, agreement, etc.).

rescue (ˈreskjuː) vt save from danger; set free. ● ncu (an example of) rescuing or being rescued.

research (rɪˈsɜːtʃ) ncu (a) scientific or other investigation to get new information. ● vti do research (into). **researcher** nc a person who is doing research work.

resemble (rɪˈzembəl) vt be or look like. **resemblance** 1 nu likeness. 2 nc a degree of likeness: The sisters show a strong resemblance.

resent (rɪˈzent) vt feel bitter or angry about (something bad done to one by someone). **resentful** adj feeling or showing resentment. **resentment** nu bitterness; anger.

reserve (rɪˈzɜːv) vt 1 put aside or keep back for future use or for another occasion: reserve one's opinion. 2 obtain a promise of having (something) by special arrangement or by paying in advance: reserve two seats for the theatre. ● nc 1 a supply of something being kept for later use. 2 a piece of land kept for a special purpose, esp. where wild animals are protected by law. 3 nu self-control of the feelings; silence. **in reserve** kept back, but ready for use if needed. **reservation** (ˌrezəˈveɪʃən) 1 ncu (an instance of) keeping back. nc 2 a doubt: I have reservations about your friend's honesty. 3 US a piece of country kept for a special purpose: a Red Indian reservation. 4 a special arrangement to obtain something, esp. by paying beforehand: a reservation for the flight to Paris. **reserved** adj not saying all that one thinks or feels; quiet. **reserves** n pl extra amount or number, esp. of soldiers, ready for later use.

reservoir (ˈrezəvwaː*) nc a large container or a lake that is natural or man-made, where water is collected and stored, esp. for the use of a city.

reside (rɪˈzaɪd) formal vi live, stay for a long time, or have one's home (in a place). **residence** (ˈrezɪdəns) 1 nu residing. 2 nc a place or house where one lives. **resident** (ˈrezɪdənt) nc a person who lives or stays in a place. ● adj residing. **residential** (ˌrezɪˈdenʃəl) adj suitable for living in: a residential part of the town.

residue (ˈrezɪdjuː) nc a part that is left. **residual** (rɪˈzɪdjʊəl) adj of or to do with a residue.

resign (rɪˈzaɪn) vt give up (a job, office, right, etc.). **resign oneself to** accept something unpleasant without complaining. **resignation** (ˌrezɪgˈneɪʃən) nu 1 the giving up of a job, right, etc.; nc an example of this. 2 the acceptance of something unpleasant without complaining.

resilient (rɪˈzɪlɪənt) adj 1 able to spring back to its proper shape after being bent, pulled, etc. 2 (of a person) recovering quickly from illness, trouble, etc.

resin (ˈrezɪn) ncu (a) sticky substance obtained from almost all trees and plants and used in making varnishes, plastics, etc., and in medicine.

resist (rɪˈzɪst) vt 1 use force in order not to give in to: resist the enemy. 2 try not to give in to: resist temptation; resist disease. **resistance** ncu (an example of) resisting; ability to resist. **resistant** adj showing resistance. **resistor** nc a device that puts a known amount of resistance in the path of an electrical current.

resolute (ˈrezəluːt) adj firmly decided in purpose. **resolutely** adv

resolution (ˌrezəˈluːʃən) 1 nu being resolute. 2 nc something, esp. a planned change of habit, that is firmly decided on.

resolve (rɪˈzɒlv) 1 vti firmly decide on (an action, etc.). 2 vt find an answer to (a problem, etc.) or a way of dealing with (a difficulty). ● nc 1 something that is firmly decided on. 2 nu firm decision: full of resolve.

resonant (ˈrezənənt) adj 1 (of a sound) large, full, and filling a place: a resonant voice. 2 (of a large room or place) sending sound back and making it last longer. **resonance** nu the quality of being resonant.

resort (rɪˈzɔːt) vi 1 turn for help. 2 go, esp. to somewhere pleasant; go often. ● nc 1 a place, esp. near the sea, to which people go for a holiday. 2 nu a turning to for help. 3 nc someone or something that provides such help. **as a** or **in the last resort** as a last effort when everything else has failed.

resound (rɪˈzaʊnd) vi 1 (of a large room or place) ring with sound; send back echoes. 2 (of a sound) fill a place. **resounding** adj without any doubt; great: a resounding victory; a resounding success.

resource (rɪˈzɔːs, rɪˈsɔːs) 1 nu cleverness in seeing what needs to be done and doing it well. nc 2 (often pl) the land, goods, wealth, etc., esp. of a country: natural resources. 3 something one can turn to for help when needed. **resourceful** adj clever at finding ways of doing things.

respect (rɪ'spekt) *nu* 1 honour. 2 proper attention to: *respect for people's feelings. nc* 3 a detail; quality: *In many respects the two brothers are very alike.* 4 *(pl)* greetings: *give one's respects.* ●*vt* have respect for; treat with due attention. **in respect of** or **with respect to** concerning.

respectable (rɪ'spektəbəl) *adj* 1 deserving honour. 2 (of a person or his behaviour) decent. 3 fairly good: *He earns a respectable wage.*

respectful (rɪ'spektfʊl) *adj* showing respect.

respective (rɪ'spektɪv) *adj* belonging to each of several: *We each went our respective ways home.* **respectively** *adv* separately and in the stated order: *He and I got our examination results today, seventy-five per cent and fifty-two per cent respectively.*

respiration (ˌrespə'reɪʃən) *ncu* 1 (an act of) breathing in and out. 2 *science* the series of chemical changes that occur in all the cells of the body, by which energy is released from food material. **respiratory** (rɪ'spɪrətərɪ) *adj* of breathing.

respite ('respaɪt) *nc* a short time of being free from work, pain, trouble, etc.

resplendent (rɪ'splendənt) *adj* bright or splendid in appearance.

respond (rɪ'spɒnd) *vi* 1 answer. 2 be affected by, esp. in a successful way: *The sick man responded to treatment.*

response (rɪ'spɒns) 1 *nc* a reply. 2 *ncu* an effect produced by something: *Did you get much response to your advertisement?*

responsibility (rɪˌspɒnsə'bɪlɪtɪ) *ncu, pl* -ties 1 the state of being responsible: *The job carries much responsibility.* 2 a duty: *His new job has many responsibilities.*

responsible (rɪ'spɒnsəbəl) *adj* 1 having a duty that must be done for moral or legal reasons. 2 expected to take the blame for mistakes. 3 trustworthy. 4 (followed by **for**) being the cause or reason (of): *Who is responsible for making this mess?*

responsive (rɪ'spɒnsɪv) *adj* replying quickly and readily to (a suggestion, etc.).

rest¹ (rest) 1 *vi* be quiet and still, stopping work, movement, etc., for a short time. *vt* 2 give rest to. 3 put (something) in a position where it is supported or made steady. ● *nu* 1 being quiet and still; relief. 2 *nc* a place to support or steady something. **at rest** 1 calm and still. 2 *polite* dead. **restroom** *US* a public lavatory.

rest² *n* **the rest** something that remains; remainder.

restaurant ('restərɒŋ, 'restərɒnt) *nc* a place where people are served meals for which they pay.

restful ('restfʊl) *adj* giving rest; calm and peaceful.

restitution (ˌrestɪ'tjuːʃən) *nu* the giving back of something that was lost or stolen.

restive ('restɪv) *adj* restless; not willing or able to stay still.

restless ('restlɪs) *adj* not willing or able to stay still; anxious.

restore (rɪ'stɔː*) *vt* 1 give back. 2 bring back to a good condition: *restore an old painting; restored to health.* **restoration** (ˌrestə'reɪʃən) *nu* restoring or being restored.

restrain (rɪ'streɪn) *vt* hold back; control. **restrained** *adj* kept under control: *restrained laughter.* **restraint** *nu* restraining or being restrained.

restrict (rɪ'strɪkt) *vt* keep within certain limits. **restriction** *ncu* (an example of) restricting or being restricted. **restrictive** *adj* that restricts.

result (rɪ'zʌlt) *ncu* (the amount or an instance of) something that happens because of an earlier cause or action. ● *vi* 1 happen because of an earlier cause: *sadness resulting from disappointment.* 2 end in a certain way: *The game resulted in a victory for us.* **resultant** *adj* happening as a result.

resume (rɪ'zjuːm) 1 *vti* begin (a meeting) again after a short stop. 2 *vt* occupy again; take back (a title, office, etc.): *resume one's seat; resume the office of President.* **resumption** (rɪ'zʌmpʃən) *nu* beginning again after a short stop.

résumé ('rezjuːmeɪ) *nc* a short account giving the main points of a speech, event, etc.

resurrect (ˌrezə'rekt) *vt* 1 bring back into use or action. 2 bring (someone) back to life again. **resurrection** *nu* being brought back to life, use, or activity.

resuscitate (rɪ'sʌsɪteɪt) *vt* bring back to a normal condition (a person or thing that was almost dead). **resuscitation** (rɪˌsʌsɪ'teɪʃən) *nu* the act or method of resuscitating.

retail ('riːteɪl) 1 *vt* sell (goods) in small quantities to customers. 2 *vi* (of goods) be sold: *This jacket retails at ten pounds.* ● *nc* the sale of goods in small quantities. ● *adj* of or to do with such selling. **retailer** *nc* a shopkeeper who sells by retail.

retain (rɪ'teɪn) *vt* keep; keep within. **retainer** *nc* 1 a servant, esp. one who has been with the same family for a long time. 2 a sum of money paid to make firm an arrangement, etc.

retaliate (rɪ'tælɪeɪt) *vi* do wrong in return for having been done wrong to. **retaliation** (rɪˌtælɪ'eɪʃən) *nu* retaliating.

retard (rɪ'tɑːd) *vt* delay the progress or development of. **retardation** (ˌriːtɑː'deɪʃən) *ncu* (an example of) retarding or being retarded: *The youth suffered from mental retardation.*

retention (rɪˈtenʃən) *nu* retaining or being retained. **retentive** (rɪˈtentɪv) *adj* able to retain or keep, esp. in the mind: *a retentive memory*.

reticence (ˈretɪsəns) *nu* the keeping of one's feelings or thoughts to oneself.

retina (ˈretɪnə) *nc, pl* **-nas** or **-nae** (niː) the covering at the back of the eye that is sensitive to light: see picture.

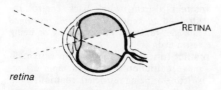

retina

retinue (ˈretɪnjuː) *nc* the servants, assistants, etc., travelling with an important person.

retire (rɪˈtaɪə*) *vi* 1 go away; draw back. 2 *formal* go to bed. 3 (of someone) give up work, esp. on reaching a certain age. 4 *vt* cause (someone) to give up work. **retirement** 1 *nu* retiring or being retired. 2 *nc* an example of this.

retort (rɪˈtɔːt) *vti* answer quickly and sharply. ●*nc* 1 a quick, sharp answer. 2 a glass container with a long, narrow neck that is bent down, used in scientific experiments: see picture.

retort

retrace (rɪˈtreɪs) *vt* go back over (past events or actions) either in one's mind or in reality: *retrace one's steps*.

retract (rɪˈtrækt) *vt* 1 take back (something said) saying it was not true or right. 2 draw back, esp. a part of one's body.

retreat (rɪˈtriːt) *vi* move back or away: *an army retreating from an enemy*. ●*nu* 1 the act of moving back, esp. of an army from an enemy. *nc* 2 an example of this. 3 a place to which one goes for peace or to rest after an illness.

retribution (ˌretrɪˈbjuːʃən) *nu* punishment for doing wrong.

retrieve (rɪˈtriːv) *vt* 1 get back (esp. something that was lost). 2 bring back to a better or more successful condition.

retrograde (ˈretrəgreɪd) *adj* 1 moving backwards. 2 likely to make conditions worse.

retrogression (ˌretrəˈgreʃən) *nu* a move backward to an earlier, worse condition.

retrospect (ˈretrəspekt) *nu* the act of considering things that have passed. **in retrospect** looking back at the past. **retrospective** (ˌretrəˈspektɪv) *adj* remembering past events, esp. in one's own experience.

return (rɪˈtɜːn) 1 *vi* come or go back to a former place or condition: *She returned home yesterday; He has returned to his evil ways*. 2 *vt* give or send back. ●*ncu* 1 (an example of) returning or being returned. 2 (an example of) giving or sending back. ●*adj* of or to do with a return. **in return for** in payment for; as thanks for. **return ticket** a ticket for a journey able to be used to go and to come back.

reunion (ˌriːˈjuːnɪən) 1 *nu* coming or being brought together again. 2 *nc* a meeting of people, esp. friends, who have not met for a long time.

reveal (rɪˈviːl) *vt* 1 show (something which is usually or has been hidden). 2 make known (a secret, etc.).

revel (ˈrevəl) *vi* 1 have a lively, merry time. 2 (followed by **in**) enjoy very much: *She revels in making me unhappy*. **revelry** *ncu, pl* **-ries** (the spirit of) a revelling, sometimes not kept under control.

revelation (ˌrevəˈleɪʃən) 1 *nu* the making known of something that was secret or hidden. 2 *nc* something made known, esp. that causes surprise.

revenge (rɪˈvendʒ) *vt* punish someone to pay back (a wrong done to oneself, one's family, etc.) esp. with the same wrong. ●*nu* the punishment given.

revenue (ˈrevenjuː) *nu* money paid by the people for public needs; part of the government that collects this money.

reverberate (rɪˈvɜːbəreɪt) 1 *vi* (of sound) be thrown backwards and forwards: *The music reverberated in the huge hall*. 2 *vt* throw back (sound). **reverberation** (rɪ,vɜːbəˈreɪʃən) *ncu* (an example of) reverberating or being reverberated.

revere (rɪˈvɪə*) *formal vt* respect deeply; honour.

reverence (ˈrevərəns) *nu* deep respect.

reverend (ˈrevərənd) *n* the title of a priest. ●*adj* 1 worthy of being treated with deep respect. 2 being a priest.

reverent (ˈrevərənt) *adj* feeling or showing great respect. **reverently** *adv*

reverse (rɪˈvɜːs) 1 *vt* turn something upside-down or inside-out. 2 *vi* (of something) be turned in this way. 3 *vti* move or be moved backwards or in the opposite direction: *reverse one's car*. ●*nu* 1 the back or opposite of something. 2 *nc* a disappointment. **reversal** 1 *nu* reversing or being reversed. 2 *nc* an example of this. **reversible** *adj* that can be reversed.

revert (rɪ'vɜːt) *vi* go back (to a former condition, subject, etc.).

review (rɪ'vjuː) *vt* **1** examine (something) again: *review the situation.* **2** write an account of (a new book, film, etc.) giving opinions on it for a newspaper, etc. ●*ncu* **1** reviewing or being reviewed; an example of this. *nc* **2** a written account, with opinions on a new book, film, etc. **3** a magazine that is published weekly, monthly, etc., with such pieces of writing. **reviewer** *nc* a person who writes reviews.

revile (rɪ'vaɪl) *formal vt* use cruel and unjust language against.

revise (rɪvaɪz) **1** *vt* change or alter. **2** *vti* read carefully (through a subject), esp. before an examination. **3** *vt* correct (a book already printed) for a new edition. **revision** (rɪ'vɪʒən) **1** *nu* revising or being revised. **2** *nc* something revised.

revive (rɪ'vaɪv) **1** *vt* bring (a person or thing) back to life or strength. **2** *vi* (of a person) come back to life or strength. **3** *vti* make or become active or useful again. **revival** (rɪ'vaɪvəl) *ncu* (an example of) reviving or being revived.

revoke (rɪ'vəʊk) **1** *vt* take back or cancel (a law, one's permission, etc.). **2** *vi* (in card games) break a rule by not playing the right card when able to do so.

revolt (rɪ'vəʊlt) *vi* **1** get ready to fight against the government, etc. **2** be filled with disgust. **3** *vt* fill with disgust. ●*nu* **1** disgust. **2** *nc* a **revolution** (def. 2). **revolting** *adj* disgusting.

revolution (ˌrevə'luːʃən) *nc* **1** a turning-round movement in, or as if in, a circle: *the revolutions of a wheel.* **2** a complete change in conditions, esp. on the defeat of a government. **revolutionary** (ˌrevə'luːʃənərɪ) *adj* of or to do with a complete change in conditions. ●*nc* a person who wants a revolution, esp. a political one. **revolutionise** (ˌrevə'luːʃənaɪz) *vt* make great changes in: *Computers have revolutionised modern business*

revolve (rɪ'vɒlv) *vti* (cause to) move round a centre or in a circle: *The earth revolves round the sun.*

revolver (rɪ'vɒlvə*) *nc* a pistol that holds several bullets in a ring that turns round after each one is fired: see picture.

revolver

evue (rɪ'vjuː) *nc* an entertainment in the theatre that consists of short, amusing plays, songs, and dancing, esp. one that makes fun of present-day events.

revulsion (rɪ'vʌlʃən) *nu* sudden and violent change in feeling, esp. to one of disgust.

reward (rɪ'wɔːd) *nc* something that is given or received for work or services, or to show gratitude. ●*vt* give a reward to.

rhetoric ('retərɪk) *nu* **1** the art of using words well in writing or in speech. **2** *derogatory* showy use of words, suggesting the speaker is not sincere.

rheumatism ('ruːmətɪzəm) *nu* a kind of disease causing pain and stiffness of the joints. **rheumatic** (ruː'mætɪk) *adj* of or to do with rheumatism.

rhinoceros (raɪ'nɒsərəs) *nc, pl* **-es** or **rhinoceros** an animal of Africa or Asia with a large, heavy body, thick skin, and one or two horns.

rhombus ('rɒmbəs) *nc, pl* **-es** or **-bi** (biː) a figure with four angles, none of which are right angles, and four equal sides: see picture at **shapes.**

rhubarb ('ruːbɑːb) *nu* a garden plant with sharp-tasting thick stalks that are usually cooked before being eaten as a fruit.

rhyme (raɪm) **1** *nu* the state produced by two or more words having the same sound or ending sound, esp. at the end of each line of poetry. *nc* **2** a short poem. **3** a word with the same sound as another: *'Cry' and 'sigh' are rhymes.* ●*vt* **1** put into the form of rhyme: *You can rhyme 'cry' with 'sigh'.* *vi* **2** write verses with rhymes. **3** be in rhyme.

rhythm ('rɪðəm) **1** *nu* the coming of one thing, esp. sound, movement, etc., after another in a regular way: *a dance rhythm.* **2** *nc* a particular kind of rhythm. **rhythmic** ('rɪðmɪk) *adj* **rhythmical** *adj* of or to do with rhythm.

rib (rɪb) *nc* **1** one of the several curved bones forming and supporting the chest part of the body. **2** anything like a rib in appearance or action: *the ribs of an umbrella.* ●*vt infml* make fun of.

ribbon ('rɪbən) **1** *nu* cloth, esp. silk, in a long strip, used for decoration, tying things, etc.; *nc* a piece of this. **2** *nc* a long strip of anything.

rice (raɪs) *nu* a plant grown in E Asia with a white grain; this grain cooked and eaten.

rich (rɪtʃ) *adj* **-er, -est 1** having much wealth or property. **2** (of food) having a large amount of fat, oil, etc. **3** producing much: *a rich soil.* **4** costly: splendid: *rich silks and furs.* **5** (of colours or sounds) deep and full. **6** large; plentiful: *a rich blood supply.* **the rich** people with much wealth or property. **riches** ('rɪtʃɪz) *n pl* wealth. **richly** *adv* in a rich way. **richness** *nu* being rich.

rickets ('rɪkɪts) *nu (with singular or plural verb)* a disease caused by lack of vitamin D and found mainly in children in whom the bones soften.

rickety ('rɪkətɪ) *adj* **1** likely to break: *a rickety chair.* **2** (of the body) weak because of illness or old age.

rid (rɪd) *vt* also **get rid of** get free of. ●*adj* free: *I'm finally rid of you.*

ridden ('rɪdən) past participle of **ride.**

riddle¹ ('rɪdəl) *nc* **1** an amusing puzzle or difficult question that needs cleverness to solve. **2** a mystery.

riddle² *vt* make full of holes: *the woodwork of a ship riddled by worms; a body riddled with bullets.*

ride (raɪd) *vi* **1** sit on a horse and cause it to move along: *Let's ride today.* **2** sit in a car, public vehicle, etc., and be carried along. *vt* **3** sit on (a horse, bicycle, etc.) and cause to move along. **4** travel over or across, esp. on horseback: *He rode many miles; ride a race.* **5** float: *A boat was riding the waves.* **let it ride** leave it as it is; let it pass. ●*nc* a journey on a horse, bicycle, etc., or in a car or public vehicle. **rider** ('raɪdə*) *nc* **1** a person who rides, esp. on a horse, bicycle, or motorbike. **2** *law* a statement added to a decision, law, etc., to give an opinion, recommend change, etc.

ridge (rɪdʒ) *nc* **1** a long, narrow piece of high land with sloping sides. **2** any long, raised line: *the ridge along the top of a roof.*

ridicule ('rɪdɪkju:l) *vt* laugh rudely at (someone or something). ●*nu* being made or making fun of. **ridiculous** (rɪ'dɪkjʊləs) *derogatory adj* deserving to be made fun of; stupid.

rifle¹ ('raɪfəl) *nc* a long gun that is put to the shoulder when being fired.

rifle² *vt* search through (something) in order to steal from it: *All the drawers had been rifled by the thief.*

rift (rɪft) *nc* **1** a large crack: *a rift in the ice.* **2** a break or separation caused by disagreement between friends, friendly countries, etc.

rig (rɪg) *vt* **1** fit (a ship) with sails, ropes, etc. **2** supply with anything that is needed. **3** arrange (something, esp. an election) to get an unfair result. ●*nc* a set or system of sails. **rigging** ('rɪgɪŋ) *nu* all the ropes and sails on a ship.

right (raɪt) *adj* **1** true; correct; not wrong: *the right answer.* **2** to do with the side of something facing east when its front faces north. **3** (of behaviour) just; fair: *Try to do what is right.* ●*adv* **1** straight: *Go right on until you reach the main road.* **2** all the way: *right to the top of the hill.* **3** completely: *She turned right round to look at it.* **4** correctly:

Do it right this time. ●*nc* **1** a claim that is due to a person by law or because it is just. **2** *nu* the right side or part of anything: *Turn to the right at the end of the road.* **the right** also **the Right** supporters of political parties that are against change or development. ●*vt* **1** make correct. **2** put into the correct position: *The boat righted itself.* **right away** immediately. **by rights** if right were done; justly. **go right** **1** turn to the right. **2** go properly. **put right** bring back to a good, correct, etc., condition. **right angle** an angle of 90°. **right-hand** ('raɪthænd) *adj* (used before a noun) to do with the right side: *right-hand drive.* **right-handed** (,raɪt-'hændɪd) *adj* **1** able to use one's right hand for writing, etc., more than one's left. **2** to do with the right hand. ●*adj, adv* (done) with the right hand. **rightly** *adv* justly; correctly; with good reason. **rights** (raɪts) *n pl* **1** the true facts. **2** something that a person has a just claim to. **right-wing** ('raɪtwɪŋ) *adj* to do with **the right:** *right-wing party.*

righteous ('raɪtʃəs) *adj* being or shown to be morally right; just. **righteousness** *nu* being righteous.

rightful ('raɪtfʊl) *adj* **1** having a legal and just claim: *the rightful owner.* **2** just; proper. **rightfully** *adv*

rigid ('rɪdʒɪd) *adj* **1** that does not bend; stiff. **2** strict: *rigid rules.* **rigidity** (rɪ'dʒɪdɪtɪ) *nu* **1** being stiff. **2** strictness. **rigidly** *adv*

rigour *US* **rigor** ('rɪgə*) *n* **1** *nu* harshness; severity. **2** *(usually pl)* conditions that cause suffering. **rigorous** *adj* harsh.

rill (rɪl) *literary nc* a small stream.

rim (rɪm) *nc* the edge of something circular, such as a cup. ●*vt* form or put a rim on.

rind (raɪnd) *nu* the hard outer covering on some foods and fruit: see picture.

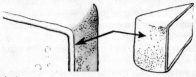

rind

ring¹ (rɪŋ) *nc* **1** a circular band usually of some precious metal and sometimes with jewels fixed in, worn on the finger: *a wedding ring.* **2** anything that is circular: *rings of smoke from a cigarette.* **3** a circular closed-in space: *a circus ring.* ●*vt* form or make a circle round. **ringleader** (rɪŋ,li:də*) *nc* a person who is responsible for leading others into mischief, trouble, etc. **ringmaster** ('rɪŋ,mɑ:stə*) *nc* the man in charge of activities in a circus ring. **ring road** a road that goes round a town instead of through it.

ring² 1 *vt* cause (a bell) to send out a sound. *vi* 2 (of a bell) send out a sound. 3 make a clear, echoing sound like that of a bell: *ringing laughter.* 4 (of a place, building, etc.) echo with sound; be filled with continuing sound. 5 *infml, chiefly Brit* vti telephone. **ring** (or **phone**) **back** make a telephone call to (someone) who has telephoned one earlier. **ring off** end a telephone conversation. **ring** (or **phone**) **up** make a telephone call to (someone). ●*nc* 1 an act of ringing; a sound made in this way: *Give the doorbell a ring.* 2 *infml, chiefly Brit* a telephone call. 3 *nu* a sound like that of a bell: *the ring of voices singing.*

rink (rɪŋk) *nc* a place in or outside a building, that has been covered with a layer of ice for skating.

rinse (rɪns) *vt* get rid of soap, etc., from (clothes, hair, etc., just washed) with clear, clean water. ●*nc* 1 an act of rinsing. 2 a substance used to colour hair while it is wet. **rinse out** get rid of unwanted substances by rinsing.

riot (ˈraɪət) 1 *nc* a loud and violent disturbance against the law made by a crowd of people. 2 *nu* loud, noisy behaviour. ●*adj* of or to do with a riot: *riot police.* ●*vi* take part in a riot. **riotous** (ˈraɪətəs) *adj* likely to stir up a riot; (of behaviour) without control: *riotous laughter.*

rip (rɪp) 1 *vt* tear (something), esp. in a rough, uneven way. 2 *vi* (of something) be torn in this way. ●*nc* a torn place.

ripe (raɪp) *adj* -r, -st 1 (of fruit, grain, etc.) ready to be eaten or used. 2 arising from full development of body or mind: *ripe judgement.* 3 ready; suitable.

ripen (ˈraɪpən) *vti* make or become ripe: *The apples ripen in the sun.*

ripple (ˈrɪpəl) *nc* 1 a small wave. 2 a gentle, faintly-heard or felt movement: *a ripple of sound; a ripple of laughter.* ●*vti* (cause to) move in ripples.

rise (raɪz) *vi* 1 get up (from a chair, bed, etc.). 2 move up into a higher position or level: *The sun rose; smoke rising from chimneys.* 3 reach a higher rank or position: *He's risen in the world!* 4 increase: *rising prices.* 5 (of land) slope upward. 6 **revolt** (def. 1). ●*nc* 1 an increase in something: *a rise in temperature.* 2 a move up in pay, rank, or position. 3 a small hill or sloping ground. **give rise to** cause; suggest. **rise to the occasion** show one is well able to deal with a difficult or unexpected situation, etc.

risen (ˈrɪzən) past participle of **rise**.

risk (rɪsk) *vt* dare to do something even if it puts (one's life, money, etc.) in danger: *He risked everything he had to help us.* ●*ncu* (a source of) danger, trouble, etc. **at (a per-**

son's) own risk taking responsibility for oneself, one's property, etc., having been warned of certain risks. **take risks** act, even though there are risks in doing so. **risky** *adj* -ier, -iest full of risks.

rite (raɪt) *nc* a solemn act, esp. a religious one: *the marriage rite.*

ritual (ˈrɪtʃʊəl) 1 *nu* a set of rites. 2 *nc* a special form of ritual. ●*adj* of or to do with rites.

rival (ˈraɪvəl) *nc* a person who wants the same thing as another or who is taking part in the same race, competition, etc.: *They were rivals for her love.* ●*adj* being a rival: *rival teams.* ●*vt* be equal to or as good as. **rivalry** (ˈraɪvəlrɪ) 1 *nu* being rivals. 2 *nc, pl* **-ries** an example of this.

river (ˈrɪvə*) *nc* 1 a long, wide, natural stream of water, usually flowing into the sea. 2 any large, steady flow: *rivers of blood.* **riverbank** (ˈrɪvəbæŋk) *nc* the land along each side of a river.

rivet (ˈrɪvɪt) *nc* a small metal pin used to fasten pieces of metal together and flattened with a hammer when this is done. ●*vt* 1 fasten with rivets. 2 fix firmly: *His eyes were riveted to the film on television.*

rivulet (ˈrɪvjʊlɪt) *nc* a small river.

road (rəʊd) *nc* 1 a wide way or large street with a hard man-made surface for the use of traffic. 2 one's way or direction: *You're in my road; a road to ruin.* **road-block** (ˈrəʊdblɒk) *nc* something put across a road to stop traffic. **roadside** (ˈrəʊdsaɪd) *nc, adj* (at) the edge of a road: *a roadside café.* **roadworks** (ˈrəʊdwɜːks) *n pl* a place where the road is being repaired, etc., by workmen. **roadworthy** (ˈrəʊd,wɜːðɪ) *adj* (of a vehicle) fit to be used on the roads.

roam (rəʊm) 1 *vi* wander. 2 *literary vt* walk about in an aimless way with no fixed purpose: *roam the green hills.*

roar (rɔː*) 1 *vi* make a loud, deep, rough sound: *The traffic roared along the motorway; He roared in pain.* 2 *vt* say (something) loudly: *He roared an order to the soldiers.* ●*nc* a deep, loud, rough sound. **roaring** *adj* quick and active: *roaring trade.* ●*adv infml* noisily and greatly: *roaring drunk.*

roast (rəʊst) *vt* 1 cook (meat, etc.) inside an oven or over a hot fire. 2 warm oneself (perhaps too much) in the sun or in front of a hot fire. ●*nc* a piece of roasted meat.

rob (rɒb) *vt* 1 steal something from (a person or place), esp. by force: *rob a bank.* 2 take away from (a person) or prevent him from having something that is due to him: *robbed of all pleasure in life by his illness.* **robber** (ˈrɒbə*) *nc* a person who robs. **robbery** (ˈrɒbərɪ) *ncu, pl* **-ries** (an instance of) robbing.

327

robe (rəʊb) *nc* **1** a long, loose garment: *a bath robe*. **2** a long, loose garment worn by an important person on a great occasion.

robin ('rɒbɪn) *nc* also **robin redbreast** a small, brown bird marked with red on its breast: see picture at **birds**.

robot ('rəʊbɒt) *nc* **1** a machine built to carry out some human activities: see picture. **2** a person who works or behaves as if without normal feelings.

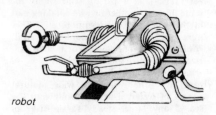

robot

robust (rəʊ'bʌst) *adj* **1** strong and healthy. **2** strongly made or built.

rock¹ (rɒk) **1** *ncu* (a type of) a hard mass of stone: *rocks formed by dead sea creatures*. **2** *nc* a large piece of stone separated from a mass: *Rocks fell onto the road*.

rock² *vti* (cause to) move from side to side. ● *nc* a rocking movement.

rock³ also **rock-'n'-roll** *nu* popular music with a strong, regular rhythm played esp. on guitars, for dancing to. ● *vi* dance to this music.

rocket ('rɒkɪt) *nc* **1** a tube-like device filled with gunpowder, etc., used as a firework, signal, etc. **2** a space vehicle. ● *vi* go up high and quickly, like a rocket: *Prices are rocketing again*.

rocky ('rɒkɪ) *adj* **-ier, -iest** **1** covered in rocks; as hard as rock. **2** *infml* not steady; likely to fall.

rod (rɒd) **1** *nc* a thin, straight stick of wood, metal, etc.: *a fishing rod*. **2** *nu* beating, esp. of children: *Don't threaten to use the rod—treat your children as friends*.

rode (rəʊd) past tense of **ride**.

rodent ('rəʊdənt) *nc* a small animal with very sharp teeth, such as a mouse or rat.

rodeo ('rəʊdɪəʊ, rəʊ'deɪəʊ) *chiefly US nc* **1** a cowboy show in which wild horses are ridden, cattle caught with long ropes, etc. **2** a bringing together of cattle to be counted, etc.

roe¹ (rəʊ) **1** *nu* the eggs in a female fish. **2** *nc* a mass of these.

roe² *nc, pl* **roes** or **roe** a small red-brown deer of Europe and Asia.

rogue (rəʊg) *nc* **1** a dishonest person, esp. a man. **2** (playful use) a mischievous person or child. ● *adj* very different from others of its kind; behaving strangely.

role (rəʊl) *nc* **1** the part taken by an actor in a play. **2** a person's usual duty or activity.

roll (rəʊl) **1** *vti* (cause to) move along by turning over and over, round and round, or travelling on wheels. *vt* **2** make, esp. into a ball or cylinder, by turning over and over: *roll a cigarette*. **3** make flat by rolling something heavy over. *vi* **4** move from side to side: *rolling about with laughter*. **5** go smoothly: *rolling along in the car*. ● *nc* **1** anything rolled up into the shape of a cylinder: *a roll of camera film; bread roll; sausage roll*. **2** a deep, echoing sound: *a roll of thunder*. **3** an official list of names. **4** a rolling or unsteady movement. **roll in** *infml* come in large quantities or numbers. **roll up** *infml* arrive.

roller ('rəʊlə*) *nc* a device of metal, wood, etc., in the shape of a cylinder, usually as part of a machine: *a paint roller; a garden roller to flatten grass*.

rollicking ('rɒlɪkɪŋ) *adj* noisy, merry, and carefree: *in rollicking mood*.

rolling ('rəʊlɪŋ) *adj* rising and falling in gentle slopes: *rolling hills*. **rolling-pin** ('rəʊlɪŋpɪn) *nc* a kitchen tool, often of wood, used for rolling pastry, etc., flat.

Roman ('rəʊmən) *adj* of or to do with Rome. ● *nc* **1** *history* a citizen of the Roman Empire. **2** *infml* a Roman Catholic. **Roman Catholic** (often shortened to **Catholic**) *nc* a member of the Christian Church of which the pope is the head. ● *adj* of or to do with the Roman Catholic Church. **Roman numeral** a sign used by the Romans, and still sometimes in use today, to stand for a number: *I, II, III are the Roman numerals for 1, 2, 3*.

romance (rəʊ'mæns) *nc* **1** a love affair between a man and a woman. **2** a story, film, etc., that deals with love and adventure, esp. in a way that is not like real life; *nu* the kind of literature made up of such stories. **3** *ncu* a fanciful idea of something based on imagination, not on truth. ● *vi* add untrue details to an account or story to make it more interesting. **romantic** (rəʊ'mæntɪk) *adj* of or to do with romance.

romp (rɒmp) *vi* **1** (esp. of children) play and jump about, esp. in a rather rough way. **2** win or succeed easily: *Our team romped home at five goals to one*. ● *nc* a time of romping.

roof (ruːf) *nc* **1** the top outside covering of a building, car, etc. **2** a house: *live under the same roof*. ● *vt* provide or cover with a roof. **roofing** ('ruːfɪŋ) *nu* the material used for building a roof. **rooftop** ('ruːftɒp) *nc* a roof.

rook (rʊk) *nc* a large black bird: see picture at **birds**.

room (ruːm) *n* **1** *nc* one of the parts with walls, a floor, and a ceiling into which a building is divided. *nu* **2** space not already filled: *Is there room for three in your car?* **3** opportunity for action: *We still have room to change our minds.* **4** (*usually pl*) rented lodgings. ●*vi* live in a room, esp. one that is rented. **roommate** (ˈruːmmeɪt) *nc* a person with whom one shares a room or flat.

roomy *adj* **-ier, -iest** with much space: *a roomy house; a roomy cupboard.*

roost (ruːst) *nc* a place, branch, etc., where birds, esp. hens, sit and rest or sleep. ●*vi* rest or sleep in this way.

rooster (ˈruːstə*) *chiefly US nc* a male hen; cock.

root[1] (ruːt) *nc* **1** the underground part of a plant or tree that provides it with minerals and water. **2** the most necessary part, cause, or beginning of anything. **3** *grammar* a word from which other words can be made by adding beginnings and endings: *'Change' is the root of 'unchangeable'.* **4** *mathematics* a number which gives another number when multiplied by itself a certain number of times: *4 is the square root of 16.* ●*vti* **1** (of plants, etc.), (cause to) send out roots and grow. **2** (of ideas, feelings, etc.), (cause to) be made firm: *It was rooted in his mind that you were evil.* ●*adj* having or grown for roots: *a root crop.*

root[2] *vi* **1** search for, moving things about and turning them over. **2** (followed by **out**) find.

rope (rəʊp) *ncu* (a piece of) thick, strong string made esp. of plant fibres or pieces of wire twisted together. ●*vt* fasten with a rope. **know the ropes** understand the rules, the way things are done, etc., in a particular activity.

rosary (ˈrəʊzərɪ) *nc, pl* **-ries** (in the Roman Catholic Church) a set of prayers counted on a string of beads.

rose[1] (rəʊz) past tense of **rise**.

rose[2] **1** *nc* a plant, usually with sharp points on its stem, bearing beautiful sweet-smelling flowers: see picture at **flowers**. **2** *ncu* (a shade of) pinkish-red colour. ●*adj* pinkish-red. **rosehip** See **hip**[2].

rosette (rəʊˈzet) *nc* a rose-shaped ornament made of ribbons given as a prize or worn as a badge: see picture.

rosette

rostrum (ˈrɒstrəm) *nc* a raised part of the floor on which a person stands to give a public speech.

rosy (ˈrəʊzɪ) *adj* **-ier, iest** of a pinkish-red colour.

rot (rɒt) **1** *vti* (cause to) decay from natural causes, becoming rotten or useless: *rotting leaves.* **2** *vi* become weak or come to an end through lack of action, use, etc. ●*nu* **1** decay. **2** *Brit, slang* nonsense: *Don't talk such rot!*

rota (ˈrəʊtə) *chiefly Brit nc* a list of the names of people who take it in turn to do a certain duty.

rotary (ˈrəʊtərɪ) *adj* **1** turning round in a circle. **2** (of a machine) working with such a movement.

rotate (rəʊˈteɪt) *vti* **1** (cause to) turn round in a circle. **2** (cause to) follow one thing after another in order. **rotation** (rəʊˈteɪʃən) **1** *nu* rotating or being rotated. **2** *nc* an example of this movement.

rotor (ˈrəʊtə*) *nc* the part of a machine that turns round and round, esp. a group of such parts fitted together to drive a helicopter.

rotten (ˈrɒtən) *adj* **1** decayed. **2** *infml* very unpleasant; bad.

rouge (ruːʒ) *nu* a red substance used to add colour to the face. ●*vt* put rouge on.

rough (rʌf) *adj* **-er, -est** **1** (of a surface) not smooth; not even. **2** not calm; uncontrolled: *a rough sea; rough, noisy children.* **3** done quickly and without much detail, esp. as a preparation to being done properly: *a rough drawing.* **4** harsh; sharp: *a rough voice; rough manners.* **5** not exact; about right: *Have you a rough idea of the cost?* ●*adv* in a rough way. ●*vt* make a rough plan or drawing of. **in rough** not exactly. **rough it** *infml* put up with or live under harsh conditions. **roughage** (ˈrʌfɪdʒ) *nu* plant fibre in coarse food that helps the bowels to get rid of waste matter. **roughen** (ˈrʌfən) *vti* make or become rough. **roughly** *adv* **1** in a rough way. **2** about: *roughly a thousand sheep.* **roughness** *ncu* being rough.

round (raʊnd) *adj* **1** having a shape like a circle. **2** with a circular movement. **3** complete. **4** not exactly, but nearly: *a round hundred.* ●*prep, adv* a less formal word for **around**. ●*nc* **1** a complete, thin, flat piece of bread cut off a loaf of bread. **2** a set of drinks, visits, or activities: *a doctor's round; a round of parties.* **3** one of the parts into which a game, match, etc., is divided: *a boxing round.* **4** a song for several people to sing, each beginning to sing the tune at different times until all are singing. ●*vti* **1** make or become round. **2** *vt* go around:

You see it as you round the bend in the road.
roundabout (ˈraʊndəbaʊt) *adj* not the quickest or most direct way. ●*nc* 1 *Brit* a road junction at which cars go round in a circular direction before turning. 2 See **merry-go-round. round about** 1 on all sides of. 2 very near to: *I'll see you round about six tonight.* **roundly** *adv* thoroughly. **roundness** *nu* being round. **round off** finish off in a satisfactory way. **rounds** *n pl* **go** or **make the rounds** 1 go from place to place making visits. 2 (of news, gossip, etc.) be passed around. **roundtrip** *nc* a journey that finishes at the place from which it started. ●*adj US* return: *a round-trip ticket.* **round up** bring or collect together. **round-up** *nc* a bringing or collecting together: *a round-up of today's news on the radio.* **roundworm** (ˈraʊndwɜːm) *nc* a worm that can live in the bowels of humans and animals.

rounders (ˈraʊndəz) *Brit n pl* a ball game in which a player hits a ball and tries to run round a marked-out square before the ball is thrown back.

rouse (raʊz) *vt* 1 wake up. 2 stir or excite (someone) into some action.

rout (raʊt) *nc* 1 a complete and disorderly defeat. 2 *archaic or law* a crowd of disorderly people. ●*vt* defeat and cause the disorderly flight of: *rout an enemy.*

route (ruːt) *nc* a direction or way taken to get to a place. ●*vt* plan the route of; make go: *They routed us around the place where the accident was.*

routine (ruːˈtiːn) *ncu* (an example of) the usual, fixed order of work or doing things: *daily routine.* ●*adj* to do with routine.

row¹ (rəʊ) *nc* a number of people or things arranged in a line.

row² 1 *vti* move (a boat) forward by using oars. 2 *vt* take (a person or thing) in a boat with oars. ●*nc* a journey in such a boat. **rowing** *nu* the sport or activity of rowing a boat with oars.

row³ (raʊ) *infml* 1 *nc* a noisy quarrel. 2 *nu* a lot of noise. ●*vi* make or have a row.

rowdy (ˈraʊdɪ) *adj* **-ier, -iest** rough and noisy.

royal (ˈrɔɪəl) *adj* of or to do with a king or queen. **royalist** (ˈrɔɪəlɪst) *nc* a person who supports a king or queen, or the royal family. **royalty** (ˈrɔɪəltɪ) *nu* 1 a member of the royal family. 2 the position, power, etc., of a king or queen. 3 *nc, pl* **-ties** (a sum of) a part of the money made on every copy of a book, record, etc., sold which is paid to the author; such a payment to writers of plays, inventors, etc.: *a ten per cent royalty.*

rub (rʌb) 1 *vt* press on (a surface) and move something over, esp. to clean, polish, etc.:

rub one's wet face with a towel. 2 *vti* (of a surface), (cause to) press and move against another surface. ●*nc* an act of rubbing.
rub down 1 make a surface smooth or ready for painting by rubbing. 2 dry with a towel by rubbing. **rub in** 1 spread something with force so that it will be taken in through the surface. 2 *infml* keep reminding someone of (something unpleasant). **rub out** get rid of (marks, esp. pencil marks) by rubbing.

rubber (ˈrʌbə*) 1 *nu* an elastic substance obtained from a milky liquid produced by some trees and used for car tyres, elastic bands, etc. 2 *nc* a piece of rubber, plastic, etc., for rubbing out pencil marks, etc.

rubbish (ˈrʌbɪʃ) *nu* 1 waste material; useless, worthless, or unwanted things. 2 *infml* nonsense: *Don't talk such rubbish!*

rubble (ˈrʌbəl) *nu* pieces of broken stone, rock, etc.: *The house had been knocked down and was now just a pile of rubble.*

rubella (ruˈbelə) *nu* also **German measles** a disease producing fever, a sore throat, and tiny red spots on the skin.

ruby (ˈruːbɪ) *nc, pl* **-bies** 1 a precious stone, bright-red in colour. 2 *nu* a bright-red colour. ●*adj* bright-red.

rucksack (ˈrʌksæk) *nc* a large bag carried on the back by means of straps, used for carrying things for a holiday on foot: see picture.

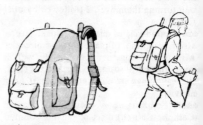

rucksack

rudder (ˈrʌdə*) *nc* 1 a flat, wooden, or metal device on the back of a boat or ship that is used to control the direction it takes: see picture. 2 a device to control direction on a plane: see picture.

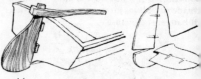

rudder

rude (ruːd) *adj* **-r, -st** 1 (of behaviour) showing lack of respect; not polite. 2 roughly made: *a rude hut.* 3 in bad taste: *rude joke.*

4 sudden and shocking: *a rude awakening.* **5** *old-fashioned* not (yet) civilised. **rudely** *adv* **rudeness** *nu* being rude.

rudimentary (ˌruːdɪˈmentərɪ) *adj* simple; not formed or developed; basic: *a rudimentary language system.*

ruefully (ˈruːfəlɪ) *adv* regretfully; sorrowfully.

ruff (rʌf) *nc* **1** a collar of stiff folds of material, worn in the sixteenth century. **2** long, coloured feathers or hair around the necks of some birds and animals.

ruffian (ˈrʌfɪən) *nc* a wicked, lawless man.

ruffle (ˈrʌfəl) **1** *vt* disturb (feathers, hair, a person's feelings or temper, etc.). **2** *vi* become disturbed or annoyed. ●*nc* material in folds, forming part of a garment at the neck or ends of the sleeves.

rug (rʌg) *nc* **1** a floor covering, usually of wool, and smaller than a carpet. **2** a form of blanket for the legs, etc., when travelling.

rugby (ˈrʌgbɪ) *Brit nu* football between teams of fifteen or thirteen players using an oval ball that may be kicked or picked up and carried by the players.

rugged (ˈrʌgɪd) *adj* **1** having sharp points and uneven surfaces: *rugged rocks.* **2** rough; not smooth or even: *a rugged face.*

ruin (ˈrʊɪn) **1** *nu* the state of being completely destroyed or greatly damaged. **2** *ncu* (the cause of) something having been destroyed, damaged, or decayed. ●*vt* **1** destroy. **2** take all one's money: *He was ruined by the fire.* **ruins** *nu* what is left of a building, town, etc., that has been ruined. **in ruins** in a state of ruin: *The building was in ruins; Her life is in ruins.*

rule (ruːl) *nc* **1** a law or custom that controls the behaviour or activity of someone or something: *school rules; rules of mathematics.* **2** a way of doing something that is usual; habit: *He makes it a rule to take the dog for a walk every day.* **3** See **ruler** (def. 2). **4** *nu* control, esp. by the government. **as a rule** usually. **work to rule** give too much attention to rules on purpose to slow down the amount of work done. ●*vti* **1** govern or control (a country, oneself, etc.): *We rule here; He rules his country badly.* **2** (of someone with the power to do so) make a decision, order, or judgement (on something). **3** *vt* make (straight lines) with a ruler (def. 2). **rule out** say that something is not possible, cannot be considered etc. **ruler** *nc* **1** a person who rules (**rule** defs. 1, 2). **2** also **rule** a piece of wood, metal, etc., with a straight edge, used for drawing straight lines or for measuring if marked for this. **ruling** *adj* that rules. ●*nc* a decision, judgement, etc., made by someone with the power to do so.

rum (rʌm) *nu* an alcoholic drink made from sugar.

rumble (ˈrʌmbəl) **1** *vi* make a deep, low sound like thunder. **2** *infml, Brit vt* understand (something that someone tried to keep hidden). ●*nc* a sound like thunder: *the rumble of heavy traffic.*

rummage (ˈrʌmɪdʒ) *vi* search, turning things over and causing disorder among them: *rummage through papers.* ●*nu* such a search.

rumour (ˈruːmə*) **1** *nu* talk, usually unpleasant and untrue, about the future, other people's affairs, etc. **2** *nc* a story, account, etc., that may or may not be true. ●*vt* tell or spread rumour.

rump (rʌmp) *nc* **1** the back part of an animal, nearest the tail. **2** *infml* a person's buttocks.

rumple (ˈrʌmpəl) *vti* (cause to) wrinkle or become untidy: *This thin material rumples easily; rumpled hair.*

rumpus (ˈrʌmpəs) *infml nu* noisy disturbance.

run (rʌn) *vi* **1** move quickly, faster than walking. **2** go from one place to another: *The trains are running late; Rumours ran through the town.* **3** be spread in all directions: *The colours ran when I washed the dress.* **4** escape: *run away; Teacher's coming, we'd better run!* **5** (of an engine, etc.) go smoothly. *vt* **6** control; be in charge of: *His daughter runs the home since his wife died; to run a business.* **7** move over (a distance) by running: *run a race.* **8** *infml* take (someone) in a car: *I'll run you to the shops later.* ●*nu* **1** the act of moving quicker than walking. **2** distance moved or travelled: *The town is an hour's run by car; go for a five-mile run.* *nc* **3** a continuous set of actions: *The play had a long run; a run of luck.* **4** a short journey or visit. **5** a space, usually with a fence, for hens, etc., to move about in: *a chicken run.* **6** *sport* a unit of scoring: *He made twenty runs.* **run across** meet by chance. **run away with 1** take as true before there is proof: *Don't run away with that idea!* **2** steal; carry off. **3** win. **runaway** (ˈrʌnəwəɪ) *nc* a person that runs away from justice, etc. ●*adj* moving fast, esp. out of control: *a runaway train.* **run down 1** knock down with a vehicle. **2** (of a clock, engine, etc.) come to a stop. **3** say unpleasant things about (someone or something). **run-down** (ˈrʌndaʊn) *infml nu* information on what has happened. ● (rʌnˈdaʊn) *adj* weak; tired. **run into 1** meet unexpectedly. **2** come together with force. **3** get into: *run into debt.* **run off 1** leave hastily. **2** produce, esp. print, quickly. **3** (cause to) flow away. **run out** come to an end. **run out of** use up a supply of something: *run out of food; run* *out of patience.* **run over 1** (of a vehicle) knock (a person) down. **2** spill. **3** read through quickly.

rung[1] (rʌŋ) past participle of **ring**[2].

rung[2] *nc* one of the bars that form the steps of a ladder.

runner ('rʌnə*) *nc* **1** a person or animal that runs, esp. in a race. **2** a person who carries messages: *a bank runner.* **3** one of the two strips of metal that a sledge runs on. **4** a plant with a long stem that runs along something, esp. the surface of the soil. **runner-up** (ˌrʌnə'rʌp) *nc, pl* **runners-up** a person who finishes second in a race.

running ('rʌnɪŋ) *nu* the control or working of: *the running of a business.* ● *adj* **1** moving continuously. **2** (of water) flowing. **3** done while moving fast: *a running jump.*

runway ('rʌnweɪ) *nc* a hard level surface for planes to take off from and land on.

rupture ('rʌptʃə*) **1** *ncu* (an example of) bursting or breaking apart. **2** *nc* also **hernia** a breaking of a part in the front of the body, causing a swelling where the bowel pushes through. ● *vt* **1** cause to break or burst. **2** *vi* be broken or burst.

rural ('rʊərəl) *adj* to do with the countryside.

rush[1] (rʌʃ) **1** *vi* move rapidly. *vt* **2** cause to move rapidly. **3** make a sudden attack on. **4** force (someone) to act quickly: *Don't rush me!* ● *ncu* (an example of) rapid movement; sudden movement forward. **rush-**

hour ('rʌʃaʊə*) *nc* a time of day when crowds of people are rushing to and from work.

rush[2] *nc* a tall, grass-like plant without leaves that grows in wet places.

rusk (rʌsk) *nc* a kind of hard biscuit; a piece of bread baked until it is brown and hard.

rust (rʌst) *nu* **1** a red-brown coating that forms on iron or steel if allowed to become wet. **2** a plant disease causing red-brown spots. ● *vti* (cause to) become coated with rust. **rusty** *adj* **-ier, -iest 1** covered with rust. **2** *infml* out of practice; largely forgotten: *My French is rusty.*

rustic ('rʌstɪk) *adj* **1** of or to do with the country or country people. **2** rough; lacking in good taste. ● *nc* **1** a person who lives in or comes from the country. **2** a person who does not appreciate fine things.

rustle ('rʌsəl) *vti* (cause to) make a low gentle sound like dry leaves. ● *nc* a sound like this: *the rustle of a heavy silk dress.*

rut (rʌt) *nc* a deep track made by a wheel esp. in mud. **be in a rut** be in a fixed way of life, boring because it does not vary ● *vt* make ruts in.

ruthless ('ruːθlɪs) *adj* without pity; cruel **ruthlessly** *adv*

rye (raɪ) *nu* **1** a grass-like plant that produces grain used for making flour and whisky and as cattle-food. **2** whisky made from rye.

S

Sabbath ('sæbəθ) *nc* a day of worship and rest from work.

sable ('seɪbəl) **1** *nc* a small, meat-eating animal with beautiful, dark brown fur. **2** *nu* its fur.

sabotage ('sæbətɑːʒ) *nu* the damage done purposely to machines, buildings, etc., by enemies in wartime or by workers not satisfied with conditions, etc. ● *vt* damage or destroy. **saboteur** (ˌsæbə'tɜː*) *nc* a person who does wrong in this way.

sabre *US* **saber** ('seɪbə*) *nc* a strong sword with a curved blade, used by soldiers on horses.

sac (sæk) *nc* a bag-like membrane in an animal or plant.

sachet ('sæʃeɪ) *nc* a small bag, usually of plastic or waxed paper, for containing some sweet-smelling substance: *a sachet of shampoo.*

sack¹ (sæk) *nc* **1** a large bag of strong, rough cloth for containing goods. **2** the amount a sack contains: *two sacks of coal.* ● *vt infml* send (someone) away permanently from his employment: *The manager sacked him.* **the sack** *infml* being sent away permanently from one's employment: *He's been given the sack; He's got the sack.*

sack² *vt* steal goods, etc., from (a town, etc.) by force and violence, esp. in times of war. ●*nc* (of a place) the sacking.

sacrament ('sækrəmənt) *nc* one of the religious ceremonies of a Church in which it is believed that God gives to those taking part a special favour to do with the spirit.

sacred ('seɪkrɪd) *adj* **1** of or to do with God or religion. **2** solemn; causing great respect.

sacrifice ('sækrɪfaɪs) **1** *nu* the offering of something to God or to a god as a sign of worship. **2** *nc* an example of this; person, animal, or thing that is offered. **3** *ncu* the giving up of something one values for a special purpose or worthy reason. **4** *nc* a thing that is given up. ● *vti* **1** make an offering (to God or to a god). **2** give up (something) one values.

sacrilege ('sækrɪlɪdʒ) *nu* the wrong or wicked treatment of something that is sacred or worthy of great respect.

sacrosanct ('sækrəʊsæŋkt) *adj* **1** very sacred. **2** *infml* to be treated with respect.

sad (sæd) *adj* **-der**, **-dest** feeling unhappy; causing such a feeling. **sadden** ('sædən) **1**

vt make sad. **2** *vi* become sad. **sadly** *adv* **sadness** *nu*

saddle ('sædəl) *nc* **1** a strong leather seat for riding on a horse: see picture. **2** a seat, usually of leather, on a bicycle, motorbike, etc. **3** a long stretch of high land that slopes at each end to a higher point. ● *vt* **1** put a saddle on (a horse, etc.). **2** put a heavy responsibility on (someone): *After the flood, he was saddled with the job of providing shelter for everyone.* **saddlebag** ('sædəlbæg) *nc* a small bag fixed to the saddle of a bicycle, horse, etc.

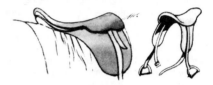

saddle

sadistic (sə'dɪstɪk) *adj* taking pleasure in being cruel.

safari (sə'fɑːrɪ) *ncu* a long journey over one or more countries, esp. to hunt wild animals in Africa.

safe (seɪf) *adj* **-r**, **-st 1** protected from danger or harm. **2** not dangerous: *a safe place to swim.* **3** that can be trusted. **4** not hurt. ● *nc* a special box in which money or things of value are locked away for safety. **safeguard** ('seɪfgɑːd) *nc* something that gives protection. ● *vt* protect. **safely** *adv*

safety ('seɪftɪ) *nu* being safe; freedom from danger or injury. **safety belt** See **seat belt** under **seat.**

saffron ('sæfrən) *nu* **1** an orange-red substance obtained from the flowers of the autumn crocus in order to colour food, sweets, etc. **2** an orange-red colour.

sag (sæg) *vi* **1** sink in, esp. in the middle: *a sagging bed.* **2** hang unevenly. **3** become tired; lose courage: *Her spirits sagged.*

saga ('sɑːgə) *nc* **1** an old, long story of brave actions, esp. of great men in Norway or Iceland. **2** a long story, esp. one told in several books, about a family, etc. **3** *infml* a long account of some experience.

sagacious (sə'geɪʃəs) *adj* wise; (of animals) intelligent. **sagacity** (sə'gæsɪtɪ) *nu* good judgement; ability to see clearly with the mind.

sage¹ (seɪdʒ) *nc* a wise man.

sage² *nu* a plant, the grey-green leaves of which are used in cooking to give more taste to food.

said (sed) past tense and past participle of **say.**

sail (seɪl) *nc* **1** a large piece of strong cloth spread out in a certain position to catch the wind and move a boat, etc., forward. **2** a journey on water, esp. for pleasure. ● *vi* **1** travel in a boat, etc. **2** (of a ship) move over water. **3** *vt* control a boat or ship. (**set**) **sail for** start a journey by water. **sailor** ('seɪlə*) *nc* a seaman; any person who sails.

saint (seɪnt *Brit* unstressed as a title sənt) *nc* **1** a holy person, esp. one now dead. **2** *infml* a person deserving praise. **saintly** *adj*

saith (seθ) *archaic v* (used with **he, she,** or **it**) a form of **say.**

sake (seɪk) *nc* **1** the good, benefit, advantage, or interest. **2** a purpose; aim. **for the sake of** for the advantage or help of; in order to obtain (something): *He would do anything for his sister's sake.*

salad ('sæləd) **1** *nu* uncooked vegetables flavoured with oil, salt, etc., and eaten with cold meat, eggs, etc. **2** *nc* a dish of this.

salary ('sæləri) *nc, pl* **-ries** a fixed payment made, usually each month, to a person in regular, esp. professional, employment.

sale (seɪl) **1** *nu* the act of selling. *nc* **2** an example of this; amount sold. **3** an event when goods are sold at lower prices than usual. **4** a public event when goods are sold to those offering the most money for them. **for** or **on sale** that can be bought. **salesclerk** ('seɪlzklɑːk) (often shortened to **clerk**) *US nc* a shop assistant. **salesman** ('seɪlzmən), **saleswoman** ('seɪlzwʊmən) *nc, pl* **-men** a person who sells goods in a shop.

saliva (sə'laɪvə) *nu* the liquid that is naturally produced in the mouth.

sallow ('sæləʊ) *adj* (of the skin) of an unhealthy, yellow-white colour.

sally ('sæli) *vi* (often followed by **forth**) go out on a journey, etc.; go or set out, esp. in a lively way. ● *nc, pl* **-lies 1** a sudden attack, esp. by soldiers. **2** a clever remark.

salmon ('sæmən) **1** *nc, pl* **salmon** a large fish hunted for sport and for food: see picture at **fish.** *nu* **2** its dark pink flesh used for food. **3** a dark pink colour.

saloon (sə'luːn) *nc* **1** a public room in a ship, hotel, etc. **2** *US* a place where alcoholic drink is sold and drunk.

salt (sɔːlt) *nu* a white, powder-like substance found in seawater and added to food to give it flavour or prevent it from going bad. ● *vt* add salt to (food) to give it flavour or to prevent it from going bad. **saltwater** ('sɔːlt,wɔːtə*) *adj* of the sea. **salty** *adj* **-ier, -iest** containing or tasting of salt.

salutary ('sæljʊtəri) *adj* having a good effect: *salutary advice.*

salutation (,sæljʊ'teɪʃən) **1** *nu* a greeting or welcome. **2** *nc* an action or words used to express a greeting.

salute (sə'luːt) **1** *vt* give (someone) a greeting or welcome. **2** *vi* make a salute. ● *nc* **1** action used in welcome. **2** (of a soldier) the raising of the right arm to show respect.

salvage ('sælvɪdʒ) *nu* **1** the saving of goods from being destroyed or lost. **2** the goods saved. **3** the payment made for saving goods. ● *vt* save from damage or loss.

salvation (sæl'veɪʃən) *nu* **1** saving or being saved. **2** the person or thing that saves. **3** the saving of one's soul from everlasting punishment. **Salvation Army** a body of people that spreads the Christian religion and helps the poor.

same (seɪm) *adj* **1** not different: *We went back home the same way we had come.* **2** exactly alike. **3** being the one that is mentioned: *He travels on the same train every day.* ● *nu* being not different; not changed. ● *adv* in the same way. **all** or **just the same** in spite of that; however. **at the same time 1** together; at once. **2** however; yet. **be all the same to** make no difference to; be of no real importance to. **sameness** ('seɪmnɪs) *nu* **1** being the same. **2** being boring because of always being the same.

sample ('sɑːmpəl) *nc* an example; small part of something meant to show what the rest of it is like. ● *vt* take a sample of; try (something) to test it.

sanctify ('sæŋktɪfaɪ) *vt* make sacred or holy.

sanctimonious (,sæŋktɪ'məʊnɪəs) *adj* pretending that one is very holy or very religious.

sanction ('sæŋkʃən) **1** *nu* the right or permission to do something. **2** *nc* the punishment given to a country by others for breaking an international agreement. **3** *nu* the support of certain behaviour, etc., by custom. ● *vt* allow; agree to.

sanctity ('sæŋktɪtɪ) **1** *nu* holiness. **2** *nc, pl* **-ties** something that is considered sacred or to be treated with great respect.

sanctuary ('sæŋktjʊərɪ) *nc, pl* **-ries 1** a holy place. **2** a place that gives protection to people in trouble or danger. **3** *nu* the protection or freedom given. **4** *nc* a place where, by law, animals can live and breed in safety.

sand (sænd) *n* **1** *nu* a loose substance made up of many tiny pieces of broken rock, found on the seashore, in deserts, etc. **2** *(often pl)* the wide and open area of the seashore or desert. **sandbank** ('sændbæŋk) *nc* a long, raised mass of sand that is usually beneath the surface of the water. **sandpaper** ('sænd,peɪpə*) *nu* strong paper with sand fixed to it, used for rubbing surfaces to make them smooth. **sandstone** ('sænd stəʊn) *nu* stone or rock made up of sand grains tightly pressed together. **sandstorm** ('sændstɔːm) *nc* a strong wind that stirs up sand and blows it around. **sandy** *adj* **-ier, -iest 1** covered with, containing, or consisting of sand. **2** (esp. of hair) yellow-red.

sandal ('sændəl) *nc* a kind of shoe held onto the foot with leather straps: see picture.

sandal

sandwich ('sænwɪdʒ) *nc* two pieces of bread, usually buttered, with meat, cheese, etc., between them. ● *vt* put or press (someone or something) between two others, leaving hardly any space.

sane (seɪn) *adj* **1** not mad. **2** having or showing good sense.

sang (sæŋ) past tense of **sing**.

sanguine ('sæŋgwɪn) *adj* **1** hopeful; expecting the best. **2** having a red face.

sanitary ('sænɪtərɪ) *adj* **1** clean; free from germs. **2** of or to do with the protection of health. **sanitary towel** a pad of cloth that takes in liquid, worn by a woman during her monthly loss of blood.

sanitation (ˌsænɪ'teɪʃən) *nu* the planning and putting into practice of ways to protect the health of the public.

sanity ('sænɪtɪ) *nu* **1** being sane. **2** good sense.

sank (sæŋk) past tense of **sink**.

sap¹ (sæp) *nu* the liquid that moves around in a plant keeping it alive and healthy. **sapling** ('sæplɪŋ) *nc* a young tree.

sap² *vt* **1** weaken the walls of (a fort, etc.) by digging tunnels underneath them. **2** weaken (a person's strength, beliefs, etc.).

sapphire ('sæfaɪə*) **1** *nc* a bright-blue precious stone. **2** *nu* the bright-blue colour of sapphire.

sarcasm ('saːkæzəm) **1** *nu* words used in order to hurt the feelings. **2** *nc* a remark of this kind. **sarcastic** (saː'kæstɪk) *adj* of or using sarcasm.

sardine (saː'diːn) *nc* a small sea-fish, often packed in tins to be preserved until eaten.

sari ('saːrɪ) *nc* the dress of an Indian woman that consists of a long piece of silk or cotton cloth wrapped round the body.

sash¹ (sæʃ) *nc* the frame into which a window is fitted.

sash² *nc* a long, broad, strip of silk, etc., worn round the waist or over one shoulder.

sat (sæt) past tense and past participle of **sit**.

Satan ('seɪtən) *nu* the Devil.

satchel ('sætʃəl) *nc* a leather or cloth bag with a long strap, esp. for carrying schoolbooks.

satellite ('sætəlaɪt) *nc* **1** a heavenly body moving in a certain line or path round a planet. **2** a man-made object put into space to move round the earth, etc., for a purpose: *a communications satellite:* see picture.

satellite

satiate ('seɪʃɪeɪt) *vt* **1** fill; satisfy. **2** have too much of (something): *satiate oneself with food.*

satin ('sætɪn) *nu* silk material, one side of which is smooth and shiny.

satire ('sætaɪə*) *ncu* a play, novel, etc., that ridicules the foolishness or evil of certain ideas, subjects, etc. **satirical** (sə'tɪrɪkəl) *adj* of or containing satire.

satisfaction (ˌsætɪs'fækʃən) *nu* **1** satisfying or being satisfied; something that satisfies. **2** something done or given to put right a wrong done: *He demanded satisfaction.* **satisfactorily** (ˌsætɪs'fæktərɪlɪ) *adv* **satisfactory** (ˌsætɪs'fæktərɪ) *adj* **1** adequate or suitable. **2** that gives pleasure or satisfaction.

satisfy ('sætɪsfaɪ) **1** *vt* give (someone) what he wants or needs. **2** *vi* (followed by **with** or **by**) give pleasure or satisfaction. *vt* **3** be accepted as enough or suitable for what one wants or needs. **4** make free from doubt: *This information satisfies me that the man is guilty.*

saturate ('sætʃəreɪt) *vt* **1** make completely wet. **2** cause to be filled with or to take in as much as possible: *saturated with knowledge.* **saturation** (ˌsætʃə'reɪʃən) *nu* the state of being saturated.

Saturday ('sætədɪ) *nc* the seventh day of the week, after Friday and before Sunday.

sauce (sɔːs) *nu* **1** a liquid with a sharp or sweet taste, cooked with or added to food. **2** *nc* an example of this. **3** *infml nu* disrespectful talk or behaviour, but not done with the intention to hurt. **saucy** *adj* **-ier, -iest** disrespectful in a playful way; rude.

saucepan ('sɔːspən) *nc* a deep pan with a long handle, and sometimes a lid, in which food is cooked.

saucer ('sɔːsə*) *nc* a small, round dish on which a cup is placed.

saunter ('sɔːntə*) *vi* walk without hurrying. ● *nc* a slow, unhurried walk.

335

sausage ('sɒsɪdʒ) *nc* a piece of meat, mixed with other substances to add taste and put into a tube of skin.

savage ('sævɪdʒ) *adj* **1** in an uncivilised state: *a savage tribe.* **2** cruel: *a savage temper.* **3** wild: *savage animals.* ● *nc* a person who belongs to a savage tribe. ● *vt* attack and cause injury: *The child was savaged by the mad dog.* **savagely** *adv* **savagery** ('sævɪdʒərɪ) *nu* the state of being savage; savage action.

savanna (also **savannah**) (sə'vænə) *nc* a piece of flat, grassy country with few trees found in hot parts of the world.

save¹ (seɪv) *vt* **1** rescue or protect from danger, trouble, or harm. **2** keep (money, etc.) for future use. **3** prevent from being lost or wasted: *He caught the bus instead of walking in order to save time.* **4** (in Christianity) make safe from everlasting punishment for sin. ● *nc* the act of preventing a point being made by stopping a kicked ball in football, etc. **savings** ('seɪvɪŋz) *n pl* money that has been kept aside for future use.

save² *prep* except.

saviour *US* **savior** ('seɪvɪə*) *nc* a person who saves or sets free a person or thing.

savour ('seɪvə*) **1** *vt* enjoy the taste of, esp. in an unhurried way. **2** *vi* have a sign that something is present: *His unusual behaviour savours of guilt.* ● *nc* **1** the taste and smell of something. **2** a sign that something is present.

savoury ('seɪvərɪ) *adj* **1** pleasing to the taste or smell. **2** sharp or spicy; not sweet. ● *nc, pl* **-ries** *chiefly Brit* a savoury dish eaten at the beginning or end of a meal.

saw¹ (sɔː) past tense of **see¹**.

saw² *nc* a tool with a blade that has a tooth-like edge, used for cutting wood, etc.: see picture at **tools.** ● *vt* **1** cut (wood, etc.) with a saw. **2** *vti* (of wood, etc.) cut or be cut with a saw. **saw off** saw (a piece of wood) from a larger piece. **saw up** saw (wood) into pieces. **sawdust** ('sɔːdʌst) *nu* very small bits of wood that fall when it is being sawn. **sawmill** ('sɔːmɪl) *nc* a building in which saws are worked by machinery.

sawn (sɔːn) past participle of **saw²**.

saxophone ('sæksəfəʊn) (often shortened to **sax**) *nc* a musical instrument of metal that produces sound when blown.

say (seɪ) *vt* **1** speak (a word, etc.). **2** express (an idea, thought, etc.) in words. **3** *vi* give an opinion about something: *I don't want to say.* *vt* **4** suppose: *It is said to be very old.* **5** show: *The clock says one.* **that is to say** in other words. **be hard to say** be difficult to give an opinion. **saying** ('seɪɪŋ) *nc* a well-known expression; group of words commonly used together.

scab (skæb) *nc* a mass of dried blood formed over an injury or sore.

scabbard ('skæbəd) *nc* a container for the blade of a sword.

scabies ('skeɪbiːz) *nu* a kind of skin disease that causes much itching.

scaffold ('skæfəʊld) *nc* **1** a frame put up round a building that is being built or repaired. **2** a raised wooden platform on which criminals used to be put to death. **scaffolding** ('skæfəldɪŋ) *nu* the materials used for a frame put round a building being built or repaired: see picture.

scaffolding

scald (skɔːld) *vti* boil or burn with hot liquid or steam. ● *nc* a burn on the skin caused by scalding.

scale¹ (skeɪl) *nc* one of the thin, hard plates, each partly over the other, that cover the skin of a fish, snake, etc.: see picture. **scaly** *adj* covered with scales.

scale

scale² *nc* **1** a set of marks at regular spaces for measuring. **2** a tool, ruler, etc., marked in this way. **3** the relation between the real size of something and a map, plan, etc., or it. **4** a system of things arranged in order, in classes, steps, etc.: *the social scale; scale of wages.* **5** a group of musical notes, esp. a set of eight, arranged in order of highness or lowness. **6** a relative amount, step, etc.: *Our house is built on a rather small scale in comparison with theirs.* ● *vt* **1** make or draw a copy of (something) in relation to something else. **2** increase or decrease in size, etc., in proportion.

scale³ *vt* climb up, esp. to the top: *scale a mountain.*

scales (skeɪlz) *n pl* a machine or device for weighing.

scallop ('skɒləp) *nc* a kind of shellfish with a hard, fan-shaped shell.

scalpel ('skælpəl) *nc* a short, sharp knife used by a surgeon.

scamper ('skæmpə*) *vi* (esp. of children and small animals) run quickly.

scan (skæn) *vt* **1** look at very carefully, examining every part: *scan someone's face.* **2** look at quickly and not very carefully: *scan the contents of a book.* **3** examine the beat of (a line of poetry) by dividing it up into units. **4** *vi* (of a line of poetry) be examined in this way.

scandal ('skændəl) **1** *nu* foolish or wrong behaviour that shocks the public. **2** *nc* a shameful action. **scandalise** ('skændəlaız) *vt* shock. **scandalous** *adj* that causes shock.

scant (skænt) *adj* almost not enough. **scanty** *adj* **-ier**, **-iest** small; not large enough.

scapegoat ('skeıpgəʊt) *nc* a person who takes the blame for another person's wrong behaviour.

scar (skɑː*) *nc* a mark left on the body where there has been an injury in the past; mark left on anything through past damage. ●*vt* **1** mark with a scar. *vi* **2** be marked with a scar. **3** form a scar on.

scarce (skeəs) *adj* **-r**, **-st** difficult to get or find, because not enough for everyone: *Fresh vegetables are scarce in the winter.* **scarcely** *adv* only just enough; not quite. **scarcity** ('skeəsıtı) **1** *nu* the state of being scarce. *nc*, *pl* **-ties** **2** an example of this. **3** a time when something is scarce.

scare (skeə*) **1** *vt* frighten. **2** *vi* become frightened. ●*nc* a sudden feeling of fear. **scarecrow** *nc* a figure made out of sticks and old clothes put in a field to frighten birds away from eating the crop.

scarf (skɑːf) *nc* a long, narrow piece of cloth worn round the neck or shoulders for warmth or decoration.

scarlet ('skɑːlət) *adj* bright-red. ●*ncu* a bright-red colour. **scarlet fever** a disease that causes a fever and scarlet marks on the body.

scary ('skeərı) *infml adj* **-ier**, **-iest** causing fear.

scathing ('skeıðıŋ) *adj* that makes someone or something seem to be of no value or not worthy of respect: *a scathing remark; a scathing attack.*

scatter ('skætə*) *vt* **1** throw about in various places. **2** send in different directions. **3** *vi* be sent in different directions.

scavenger ('skævındʒə*) *nc* an animal that feeds on flesh that is going bad or on waste food.

scene (siːn) *nc* **1** the place of a real or imaginary action or event. **2** a view; anything spread out to be seen. **3** an outburst of feelings: *The child made a scene when her mother told her to go to bed.* **4** the painted view, picture, etc., at the back of the stage in a theatre. **5** one of the parts into which a play, film, etc., is divided. **behind the scenes 1** not in front of the audience. **2**

not generally known about. **scenery** ('siːnərı) *nu* **1** the general, natural appearance of a district. **2** the painted view, furniture, etc., used on the stage in a play.

scent (sent) **1** *nu* a smell, esp. a pleasant one: *The scent of roses. nc* **2** a particular smell. **3** a pleasant-smelling liquid made from flowers, etc.; perfume: *a bottle of scent.* **4** the smell left by an animal that other animals can follow. ●*vt* **1** find out, or begin to find out, that something is present or exists. **2** put perfume on. **scented** ('sentıd) *adj* having a perfumed smell.

sceptic *US* **skeptic** ('skeptık) *nc* a person whose habit is to distrust people and things. **sceptical** *US* **skeptical** ('skeptıkəl) *adj* doubtful; in the habit of doubting beliefs, etc.

sceptre *US* **scepter** ('septə*) *nc* a staff carried by a king or ruler as a sign of power and used on grand occasions.

schedule ('ʃedjuːl *US* 'skedʒʊəl) *nc* a list, esp. one showing at what times events will take place. ●*vt* put in a schedule; make a schedule of. **ahead of schedule** in front of the planned time. **behind schedule** later than the planned time. **on schedule** at the right, planned time.

scheme (skiːm) *nc* **1** a careful plan for work or an activity. **2** a careful arrangement of parts that go well together. **3** a secret and dishonest plan. ●*vi* make a plan, esp. a dishonest one.

scholar ('skɒlə*) *nc* **1** a person with great learning, esp. in old languages and literature. **2** *old-fashioned* a schoolchild. **3** a student who is chosen, after examination, etc., to attend a college, university, etc. **scholarly** *adj* showing much learning. **scholarship** ('skɒləʃıp) **1** *nu* the learning obtained by much studying. **2** *nc* the money given to a student likely to succeed to help him to continue learning. **scholastic** (skə'læstık) *adj* of or to do with schools, scholars, or education.

school[1] (skuːl) *nc* **1** a building in which children are educated. **2** one of the several colleges that form part of a university. **3** all the children and teachers of a school: *The whole school is on holiday.* **4** the time during which the children are taught: *School finishes at 4.30pm.* **5** a group of people who admire or copy a certain painter, etc.; group who have the same ideas, style, etc. ●*vt* teach; control. **schoolboy** ('skuːlbɔı), **schoolchild** ('skuːltʃaıld) *pl* **schoolchildren**, or **schoolgirl** ('skuːlgɜːl) *nc* a boy or girl at school. **schoolhouse** ('skuːlhaʊs) *nc* **1** a small school building, esp. one in a village. **2** a house joined onto a school building. **schoolmaster** ('skuːlˌmɑːstə*) or

schoolmistress ('skuːlˌmɪstrɪs) *nc* a man or woman who teaches in a school. **schoolteacher** ('skuːlˌtiːtʃə*) *nc* a person who teaches in a school. **schooling** ('skuːlɪŋ) *nu* education.

school² *nc* a large group of fish swimming together.

schooner ('skuːnə*) *nc* a kind of sailing-ship.

science ('saɪəns) **1** *nu* the knowledge obtained from the discovery, examination, and testing of facts. **2** *ncu* a branch of such knowledge. **science fiction** books, films, etc., dealing with imaginary scientific happenings, esp. in space. **scientific** (ˌsaɪən-'tɪfɪk) *adj* **1** of or to do with science. **2** making careful use of a knowledge of science. **scientifically** *adv* **scientist** ('saɪəntɪst) *nc* a person who studies or is an expert in science.

scissors

scoff (skɒf) **1** *vi* talk to or laugh at someone, with scorn. **2** *infml vt* eat greedily.

scold (skəʊld) **1** *vt* speak angrily and sharply to. **2** *vi* find fault with a person.

scone (skɒn, skəʊn) *nc* a small flat cake made from flour.

scoop (skuːp) *nc* **1** a deep, spade-like tool with a short handle used for taking up sugar, flour, etc.; deep spoon-like tool with a long handle for taking up liquids, etc. **2** the action of or an action like that of a scoop. **3** *infml* an important piece of news first given in one newspaper, or on one radio or television station, before all the others. ●*vt* **1** lift up with or as if with a scoop. **2** make (a hole) with or as if with a scoop.

scooter ('skuːtə*) *nc* **1** a child's toy with two wheels, moved along by pushing one foot against the ground. **2** a kind of motorbike with small wheels.

scope (skəʊp) *nu* **1** the opportunity to make full use of something. **2** the range of thought, action, or observation (on a subject, etc.): *the scope of an inquiry.*

scorch (skɔːtʃ) **1** *vt* burn (the surface) slightly so as to change the colour or taste or cause pain. **2** *vi* (of the surface) be slightly burnt.

score (skɔː*) **1** *vt* win (a point, etc.) in a sport or game. **2** *vi* make a point in a sport or game. *vt* **3** make cuts or marks in or on (a surface). **4** make a piece of music suitable for particular instruments or voices. ●*nc* **1** a point, goal, etc., won in a game or sport. **2** *pl* **score** twenty; group of twenty. **3** a cut or mark made on a surface. **4** written or printed music in which the instruments or voices are shown what to play or sing. **on that score** on that particular subject or point. **scoreboard** ('skɔːbɔːd) *nc* a board on which the points, etc., won in a sport are recorded. **scorer** *nc* a person who keeps a record of the points, etc., made in a game or contest.

scorn ('skɔːn) *vt* **1** treat without respect. **2** refuse to do (something), considering it worthless. ●*nu* **1** a feeling of disrespect. **2** an object considered worthless. **scornful** ('skɔːnfʊl) *adj* feeling or showing scorn. **scornfully** *adv*

scorpion ('skɔːpɪən) *nc* a small creature of the spider group with poison in its tail.

Scotch (skɒtʃ) *adj* of or to do with Scotland, its people, or their language. ●*nu* whisky.

scoundrel ('skaʊndrəl) *nc* **1** a wicked man; wrongdoer. **2** (playful use) a mischievous little boy.

scour¹ ('skaʊə*) **1** *vt* clean (a surface) by rubbing. **2** *vi* (of a surface) be cleaned by rubbing.

scour² **1** *vi* go along quickly, esp. looking for something. **2** *vt* search quickly all over (a place).

scourge (skɜːdʒ) *nc* **1** a whip for beating (someone) with as a punishment. **2** a person or thing that punishes or causes great harm.

scout (skaʊt) *nc* a person, ship, or plane sent ahead to get information about the enemy. **Scout** *nc* a member of the Scouts, an international organisation that helps boys to develop skills and responsibility. **scout around** search around or look for.

scowl (skaʊl) *nc* an angry frown. ●*vi* look frowning and bad-tempered.

scramble ('skræmbəl) *vi* **1** climb, crawl, or move, esp. with haste. **2** struggle with others or take part in a competition to get something. **3** *vt* beat up (eggs) and cook them in butter and milk. ●*nc* **1** a climb, etc., over difficult ground. **2** a struggle with others to get something.

scrap¹ (skræp) **1** *nc* a small piece. **2** *nu* waste material. ●*vt* throw away as unwanted or useless. **scrapbook** ('skræpbʊk) *nc* a book of blank pages in which to fix pictures, pieces cut from newspapers, etc.

scrap² *infml nc* a fight or argument. ●*v* fight; argue.

scrape (skreɪp) *vt* **1** make (a surface) smooth or level by moving a rough or sharp edge over it: *The hungry child scraped his plate clean.* **2** cause a scratch or injury to (a surface): *scrape one's knee by falling.* **3** *vi* move near and along something so as to touch it or almost touch it. ●*nc* **1** the act or sound of scraping. **2** *infml* a difficult situation. **3** a scraped place. **scraper** *nc* a tool for scraping paint, etc., from a surface.

scratch (skrætʃ) *vt* **1** make long, thin marks on (a surface) with something pointed or with nails or claws. **2** scrape (the skin) with the nails to relieve an itch. **3** get (a part of one's body) marked with a pointed thing or things. ●*nc* **1** a mark, sound, or injury made by scratching. **2** *nu* the act of scratching. **scratch out** draw a line through (a word or words) to cancel them. **scratch the surface** not get deeply into a subject. **start from scratch** start from the very beginning. **up to scratch** of the quality wanted; good enough. **scratchy** *adj* **-ier, -iest** that scratches.

scrawl (skrɔːl) *vti* write or draw in a careless or hurried way. ●*nu* **1** careless handwriting. **2** *nc* a piece of careless handwriting.

scream (skriːm) **1** *vi* give a loud, sharp cry to show fear or pain. **2** *vt* speak or shout in a loud, sharp voice. ●*nc* a loud, sharp cry or sound.

screech (skriːtʃ) **1** *vi* make a loud, sharp noise: *screech with laughter.* **2** *vt* scream in a sharp or frightening way. ●*nc* such a cry or noise.

screen (skriːn) *nc* **1** a frame, sometimes able to be moved or folded, and covered with cloth, paper, etc., used to hide or protect someone or something; anything used to protect or shelter. **2** the surface onto which a cinema film falls or a television picture is seen. **3** a frame with a net put over an opening to keep out insects: *a window screen.* ●*vt* **1** hide; protect; shelter. **2** examine (a person's character) to see if he is suitable for a job, etc.

screw (skruː) *nc* **1** a nail-like device with a slotted head and a spiral thread that is fixed into wood, etc., by twisting it round and round: see picture. **2** a twisting movement; turn. ●*vt* **1** fasten with a screw. **2** twist round, like a screw: *screw the lid on*

tightly. **screwdriver** (ˈskruːˌdraɪvə*) *nc* a tool with a flat end that fits into the head of a screw to turn it: see picture at **tools.**

scribble (ˈskrɪbəl) *vti* write in a careless, hurried, or meaningless way. ●*nu* **1** careless or hurried handwriting. **2** *nc* a piece of such writing.

scribe (skraɪb) *nc* **1** a person who writes; writer. **2** a person who wrote out copies of important papers, etc., esp. before printing was invented.

script (skrɪpt) **1** *nu* handwriting, not printing; letters used in writing by hand. **2** *nc* the written text of a play, film, etc.

scripture (ˈskrɪptʃə*) *nc* a holy book or piece of writing.

scroll (skrəʊl) *nc* a roll of paper, skin, etc., for writing on; ancient book in such a form: see picture.

scroll

scrub¹ (skrʌb) **1** *vt* rub (a surface) hard, esp. with soap, water, and a brush, to clean it: *scrub the floor.* **2** *vi* (of a surface) be cleaned by rubbing hard with a brush, etc. ●*nc* **1** an act of scrubbing. **2** a thorough wash: *Give your face a scrub!* **scrubbing brush** a brush for scrubbing floors, etc.

scrub² *nu* dry land with trees and bushes not fully or properly grown because of little rain.

scruple (ˈskruːpəl) **1** *nu* doubt as to whether something is morally right. **2** *nc* such a feeling. ●*vi* be uncertain because of scruples. **scrupulous** (ˈskruːpjʊləs) *adj* **1** very careful to do what is morally right. **2** giving much care and attention to details.

scrutinise (ˈskruːtɪnaɪz) *vt* examine very carefully. **scrutiny** (ˈskruːtɪnɪ) *ncu, pl* **-nies** a very careful examination.

scud (skʌd) *vi* move smoothly and quickly: *clouds scudding across the sky.*

scuffle (ˈskʌfəl) *vi* take part in a confused fight. ●*nc* such a fight.

scullery (ˈskʌlərɪ) *chiefly Brit nc, pl* **-ries** a room in which kitchen tools are kept and dishes, etc., are washed.

sculptor (ˈskʌlptə*) *nc* a person who makes models of people, animals, and things out of stone, metal, etc.

sculpture (ˈskʌlptʃə*) **1** *nu* the art of making figures or designs from stone, metal, etc. **2** *nc* an example of such work. ●*vt* also **sculpt** (skʌlpt) **1** carve out of stone, etc. **2** *vi* be a sculptor.

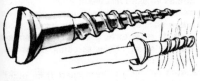

screw

scum (skʌm) *nu* dirt that comes to the surface of a liquid, esp. after it has been boiled; dirt on the surface of still water.

scurry ('skʌrɪ) *vi* hurry. ●*nu* **1** the act or sound of scurrying. **2** *nc, pl* **-ries** a whirl: *a scurry of snow.*

scurvy ('skɜːvɪ) *nu* a skin condition caused by lack of vitamin C which occurs in fresh fruit and vegetables.

scuttle¹ ('skʌtəl) *nc* also **coal scuttle** a container for coal kept by the fireside.

scuttle² *vi* (often followed by **about** or **from**) hurry, esp. from trouble or danger.

scuttle³ *vt* sink (a ship) on purpose by letting in water through openings or cutting holes in the bottom.

scythe (saɪð) *nc* a tool with a curved blade and a long handle used for cutting grass, etc.: see picture at **tools.** ●*vt* cut with a scythe.

sea (siː) **1** *nu* (*with singular verb*) the mass of saltwater on most of the surface of the earth: not land or freshwater. **2** *nc* a particular piece of sea. **at sea 1** in a ship, etc., on the sea. **2** in a confused state of mind. **by sea** in a ship, etc. **go to sea** become a sailor. **put to sea** set off on a journey by sea. **seaboard** ('siːbɔːd) *chiefly US nc* the land that borders the sea; coast. **seacoast** ('siːkəʊst) *nc* seaboard. **seafaring** ('siːfeərɪŋ) *adj* of work or travelling on the sea. **seafood** ('siːfuːd) *nc* shellfish or seafish suitable for eating. **sea-going** ('siːˌgəʊɪŋ) *adj* (of ships) built for travelling long distances at sea. **seagull** ('siːgʌl) *nc* a common sea-bird, usually white, with long wings. **sea level** the level of the sea's surface between high tide and low tide. **seaman** ('siːmən) *nc, pl* **-men 1** an ordinary sailor, not an officer. **2** a person who has much knowledge of ships, etc. **seaport** ('siːpɔːt) *nc* the place from which ships leave and to which they return; town situated at such a place. **seashell** ('siːʃel) *nc* the empty shell of a small sea-animal. **seashore** ('siːʃɔː*) *nc* the land on the edge of the sea. **seasick** ('siːsɪk) *adj* made sick by the movement of a ship, etc., at sea. **seaside** ('siːsaɪd) *nc* a place by the sea, esp. one to visit for a holiday. ●*adj* of or to do with the seaside. **sea urchin** a small sea-animal with many sharp points on its shell. **seaward** ('siːwəd) *adj* towards the sea. **seawater** ('siːwɔːtə*) *nu* water in or from the sea. **seaweed** ('siːwiːd) *ncu* kinds of plants that grow in or near the sea.

seal¹ (siːl) *nc* **1** a piece of wax with a special mark on it used to fasten a letter, packet, etc. **2** any device used to close tightly. **3** an act or event that gives a solemn promise or agreement. ●*vt* **1** close (a letter, etc.) with a seal of hot wax. **2** put a special mark on hot wax. **3** close tightly. **4** make a decision that cannot be changed: *His fate was sealed.* **seal off** close (a piece of land, etc.) so that it cannot be entered.

seal² *nc* a large sea-animal that eats fish and is hunted for its skin: see picture at **animals.** **sealskin** ('siːlskɪn) *ncu* the skin of a fur seal.

seam (siːm) *nc* **1** the line where two pieces of cloth, etc., are joined together by stitches. **2** a line of coal, metal, etc., lying between level layers of rock. ●*vt* **1** join together (two pieces of cloth) with a seam. **2** cover with lines: *His face was seamed with old age.* **seamstress** ('siːmstrɪs) *nc* a woman who sews, esp. for a living.

sear (sɪə*) *vt* **1** burn or scorch (the surface) of, esp. with a hot iron. **2** make hardhearted. **searing** ('sɪərɪŋ) *adj* burning: *a searing pain.*

search (sɜːtʃ) **1** *vt* look carefully through, in, or at (something) to find someone or something. **2** *vi* examine or look closely in order to find. ●*ncu* the act of searching. **searchlight** ('sɜːtʃlaɪt) *nc* a device that throws out a powerful light in a particular direction. **searching** *adj* thorough.

season ('siːzən) *nc* **1** one of the parts into which the year is divided, according to the weather, such as spring or summer. **2** the time of year when something particular happens: *the football season; rainy season.* ●*vt* **1** make (wood, etc.) fit for use. **2** *vi* (of wood, etc.) become fit for use. **3** *vt* add salt, etc., to (food) to make it tastier. **in** or **out of season** (esp. of fruit, vegetables, etc.) able or not able to be obtained. **season ticket** a ticket that the owner can use as often as he likes on a particular journey for a certain period of time. **seasonal** ('siːzənəl) *adj* happening at a certain season of the year. **seasoning** ('siːzənɪŋ) *ncu* salt, pepper, etc., used to add taste to food.

seat (siːt) *nc* **1** a piece of furniture made for sitting on; any place on which to sit. **2** the part of the body or a chair, etc., on which one sits. **3** a place for which one has paid to sit: *two theatre seats.* **4** the place where something is or where something happens: *the seat of government.* ●*vt* **1** sit down: *be seated.* **2** have enough seats for: *How many does the bus seat?* **seat belt** also **safety belt** a belt worn in a car or plane to protect from harm if an accident should occur.

secede (sɪ'siːd) *vi* (of a person, group, etc.) formally cease to be a member of. **secession** (sɪ'seʃən) **1** *nu* seceding. **2** *nc* an example of this.

seclude (sɪ'kluːd) *vt* keep apart from other people. **secluded** *adj* kept away from other

people or other places: *a secluded garden.*
seclusion (sɪˈkluːʒən) *nu* secluding or being secluded.

second[1] (ˈsekənd) *adj* **1** the next after the first in order, time, etc. **2** extra; another: *a second chance.* ●*nc* **1** a person or thing that comes next after the first. **2** (in a boxing-match, etc.) a person who attends to one of the fighters. **second-best** (ˌsekəndˈbest) *adj* of second, not best, quality. **second-class** (ˌsekəndˈklɑːs) *adj* **1** (of a class) second in quality, etc., to the best or first: *a second-class seat in a train.* **2** of poor quality, value, etc. **secondhand** (ˌsekəndˈhænd) *adj* owned or known about by someone else first. **secondly** *adv* also. **second-rate** (ˌsekəndˈreɪt) not of the best quality. **Second World War** see **World War II** under **world**.

second[2] *nc* **1** one of the sixty parts into which a minute is divided. **2** *infml* a very short time; moment.

second[3] (sɪˈkɒnd) *Brit vt* move (a person), such as an army officer, from his usual duty to another one. **secondment** *ncu*

secondary (ˈsekəndərɪ) *adj* not of the first importance; coming after. **secondary school** a school that children attend after the age of eleven.

secrecy (ˈsiːkrəsɪ) *nu* being secret; not telling about something secret; habit of keeping things secret.

secret (ˈsiːkrɪt) *adj* **1** that is not to be told about to others; known only to a few. **2** (of a place) hidden; not known about by many. ●*nc* **1** something secret. **2** a reason or explanation that is not easily seen: *the secret of her success.* **secret agent** a person whose business is to try and get secret information about another country. **Secret Service** a department of the government that gathers and deals with information about enemies, etc. **in secret** without others knowing. **keep a secret** not tell others. **secretly** *adv*

secretary (ˈsekrətərɪ) *nc, pl* **-ries 1** a person who assists his or her employer in business affairs by doing office work, shorthand and typing, etc. **2** someone who is in charge of the writing and answering of letters, etc., for an organisation. **General Secretary** (in some organisations, esp. the trade unions) the person in charge. **Permanent Under-Secretary** *Brit* the chief civil servant in a government department. **private secretary** a special secretary who works only for one person in an organisation. **Secretary-General** (in some organisations) the person in charge: *the Secretary-General of the United Nations.* **Secretary of State** *Brit* a person who is head of one of the

government departments: *the Secretary of State for Defence.* **secretarial** (ˌsekrəˈteərɪəl) *adj* of or to do with the work of a secretary.

secrete (sɪˈkriːt) *vt* **1** produce (a substance) for use in the body. **2** hide or keep in a secret place. **secretion** (sɪˈkriːʃən) **1** *nu* actions in the body that cause certain substances to be given out. **2** *nc* such a substance.

sect (sekt) *nc* a group of people who have the same religious beliefs that are in some ways different from the usual ones.

section (ˈsekʃən) *nc* **1** a part of a whole that is cut off or separated from it. **2** one of the parts of a country; a group of people living in a district, etc. **sectional** *adj* of or to do with a section; made up of several parts.

sector (ˈsektə*) *nc* **1** the part of a circle between two lines drawn from the centre to the edge. **2** a part, esp. of the business affairs of a society: *the public sector of industry.*

secular (ˈsekjʊlə*) *adj* **1** to do with the affairs of this life and not with spiritual matters. **2** (of priests, etc.) not living in a monastery.

secure (sɪˈkjʊə*) *adj* **1** safe from danger, anxiety, fear, etc. **2** firmly fixed; not likely to fail: *Make sure the ladder is secure.* ●*vt* make firm, safe, or well-fastened. **securely** *adv* **security** (sɪˈkjʊərɪtɪ) **1** *nu* safety. **2** *nc, pl* **-ties** something that makes safe or free from anxiety, fear, etc. **3** *ncu* something of value given to someone as a promise that money he has lent, or a duty done, will be repayed. **4** *nc* a printed paper to show that one owns shares, etc.

sedan (sɪˈdæn) also **sedan chair** *nc* a closed chair for one person, carried on two poles by two men.

sedate (sɪˈdeɪt) *adj* calm and serious in behaviour.

sedative (ˈsedətɪv) *nc* a medicine given to someone who is very nervous in order to make him calm. ●*adj* having a calming effect.

sedentary (ˈsedəntərɪ) *adj* **1** done sitting down: *sedentary work.* **2** in the habit of not taking much exercise. **3** not moving.

sediment (ˈsedɪmənt) *nu* matter that settles to the bottom of a liquid. **sedimentary** (ˌsedɪˈmentərɪ) *adj* of, like, or containing sediment. **sedimentation** (ˌsedɪmenˈteɪʃən) *nu* the production of sediment.

seduce (sɪˈdjuːs) *vt* **1** persuade (someone) into doing something wrong. **2** persuade (someone) into having sexual relations with one.

see[1] (siː) **1** *vi* use one's eyes: *A blind man cannot see.* *vt* **2** notice (someone) by using one's eyes: *Can you see him in the crowd?* **3**

understand: *I see what you mean.* **4** visit: *He came to see us yesterday.* **5** meet in order to talk: *Have you seen your lawyer about it yet?* **6** *vi* find out from printed papers: *He saw from the papers that the bad weather was expected to continue.* **7** *vti* (often followed by **to it**) make sure: *He saw (to it) that the door was properly locked.* **8** *vt* know or experience. **see about 1** deal with. **2** inquire into. **see off** say goodbye to (someone) about to leave on a journey. **see through** not be deceived by. **see to** deal with. **seeing that** as; because: *Seeing that it's raining, we'll stay at home.*

see² *nc* the district under the control of a bishop in the Christian Church.

seed (si:d) **1** *nc, pl* **seeds, seed** the part of a plant that produces new plants. **2** *nu* a part of the fluid from a male animal that helps to produce young. ●*vt* **1** put or plant in the ground. **2** remove seeds from (fruit, etc.). **3** *vi* (of a plant) produce seeds. **seedling** ('si:dlɪŋ) *nc* a very young plant.

seek (si:k) *vt* **1** look for; try to find. **2** ask for; ask to be told: *seek help; seek information.* **seeker** *nc* a person who seeks.

seem (si:m) *vi* appear to be; look as if: *He seems to be a very nice man.* **seeming** *adj* appearing to be real or true but perhaps not so. **seemingly** *adv* **seemly** *adj* **-ier, -iest** (of behaviour) not suitable or proper.

seen (si:n) past participle of **see¹**.

seep (si:p) *vi* (of a liquid) pass slowly into, through, or out of.

seer ('si:ə*) *nc* a person who is supposed to be able to see what will happen in the future; prophet.

seesaw ('si:so:) **1** *nc* a board supported in the middle and a seat at each end, for riding up and down. **2** *nu* an up-and-down movement. ●*vi* move like this.

seethe (si:ð) *vi* **1** boil. **2** (of a person's feelings) be very excited or disturbed: *seethe with anger.*

segment ('segmənt) *nc* a part that is cut off or separated from the whole; portion. ●*vti* (seg'ment) divide into segments.

segregate ('segrɪgeɪt). *vt* separate one (group) from another. **segregation** (,segrɪ'geɪʃən) *nc* segregating or being segregated.

seismic ('saɪzmɪk) *adj* of or to do with earthquakes. **seismograph** ('saɪzməgrɑ:f) *nc* an instrument that shows the qualities and the distance away of an earthquake.

seize (si:z) *vt* **1** get hold of suddenly and quickly. **2** take possession of by law. *vi* **3** understand clearly and quickly: *She seized on his idea.* **4** suddenly and eagerly make use of: *He seized on the unexpected event as an opportunity to escape.* **seizure** ('si:ʒə*) **1**

nu seizing or being seized. *nc* **2** an example of this. **3** a sudden attack of illness causing the loss of the power to feel or think.

seldom ('seldəm) *adv* not often.

select (sɪ'lekt) *vt* choose (one) as being more suitable than another. ●*adj* **1** carefully chosen. **2** for specially chosen people; not for anyone. **selection 1** *nu* the act of selecting or being selected. **2** *nc* a group of things that have been selected. **selective** (sɪ'lektɪv) *adj* careful in choosing. **selector** *nc* a person or thing that selects.

self (self) *ncu, pl* **selves** (selvz) **1** a person's nature or character; one's own character. **2** one's own interests, happiness, or wishes: *Always considering the needs of others, he has no thought of self.* **self-confident** (,self'kɒnfɪdənt) *adj* believing in oneself and in one's abilities. **self-conscious** (,self'kɒnʃəs) *adj* being uncomfortable in the company of others. **self-contained** (,selfkən'teɪnd) *adj* **1** keeping one's feelings to oneself. **2** (of a flat) complete in itself, not having to share a bathroom, etc., with people living in other flats. **self-control** (,selfkən'trəʊl) *nu* the control over one's feelings or behaviour. **self-defence** (,selfdɪ'fens) *nu* the defence of one's own body or property against attack. **self-determination** ('selfdɪ,tɜ:mɪ'neɪʃən) *nu* being able to make one's own decisions. **self-employed** (,selfɪm'plɔɪd) *adj* offering one's own services for money; having one's own business. **self-evident** (,self'evɪdənt) *adj* clear and plain, without need of proof. **self-governing** (,self'gʌvənɪŋ) *adj* **1** (of the government of a country) being controlled by the people. **2** having control of one's feelings or behaviour. **self-help** (,self'help) *nu* the use of one's own powers to get something done. **self-interest** (,self'ɪntrest) *nu* one's own advantage or profit. **self-pity** (,self'pɪtɪ) *nu* caring too much for one's own troubles. **self-respect** (,selfrɪ'spekt) *nu* the proper feeling that one's own behaviour will cause no shame to oneself. **self-righteous** (,self'raɪtʃəs) *adj* thinking that oneself is better or more right than others. **self-same** ('selfseɪm) *adj* very same: *We both had the self-same idea!* **self-service** (,self'sɜ:vɪs) *adj* (of a shop, restaurant, etc.) one in which a person serves himself. **self-sufficient** (,selfsə'fɪʃənt) *adj* not depending on help from others. **self-supporting** (,selfsə'pɔ:tɪŋ) *adj* able to earn enough to take care of oneself. **selfish** ('selfɪʃ) *adj* thinking mainly of one's own needs, and not caring much for the needs of others. **selfishness** *nu* being selfish. **selfless** ('selflɪs) *adj* having little care for one's own needs. **selfmade** (,self'meɪd) *adj* having made a success in life by one's own efforts.

sell (sel) *vt* **1** give (goods) in return for money. **2** offer (goods, etc.) in return for money: *We sell all kinds of clothes.* *vt* **3** gain a sale; gain satisfactory sales: *Her books sell very well.* **4** (followed by **at** or **for**) have a certain price: *The car sells at £10,000.* **sell off** sell (goods) cheaply. **sold out of** sold all one's supply of goods. **seller** (ˈselə*) *nc* **1** a person who sells. **2** something that is sold: *So many copies of that book have been sold that it is now a best-seller.*

semantics (sıˈmæntıks) *nu (with singular verb)* the study of the meaning of words and sentences.

semaphore (ˈseməfɔː*) *nu* a system of sending messages by moving the arms (sometimes holding flags) to various positions, each one representing a letter: see picture.

semaphore

semblance (ˈsembləns) *nu* a likeness; appearance.

semester (sıˈmestə*) *chiefly US nc* either of the two divisions of a university, college, etc., year.

semi-circle (ˈsemı,sɜːkəl) *nc* one half of a circle. **semi-circular** (,semıˈsɜːkjʊlə*) *adj* of a semi-circle.

semi-colon (,semıˈkəʊlən) *nc* the mark (;) used in writing and printing to separate those parts of a sentence where a longer pause is needed than that marked by a comma.

semi-detached (,semıdıˈtætʃt) *adj* (of a house) joined on one side to another house.

semi-final (,semıˈfaınəl) *nc* the match or round that comes just before the final one.

seminar (ˈsemınɑː*) *nc* a small group of students meeting to discuss a subject with a teacher.

seminary (ˈsemınərı) *nc, pl* **-ries** a college where priests are trained.

senate (ˈsenət) *nc* **1** (in ancient Rome) a body of people with the highest power chosen to manage affairs of government. **2** the governing body in some universities. **Senate** a body of people chosen as lawmakers in some countries, such as Canada, USA.

send (send) *vt* **1** cause (someone or something) to go to some place. **2** post (a letter, etc.). **3** cause to move quickly: *The crash sent me through the car window.* **4** cause to become: *His words sent me wild with anger.*

5 pass (good wishes) to someone: *Send her my regards.* **send for** ask for or order (someone or something) to come. **send in 1** cause (someone or something) to go in or enter. **2** enter (someone or something) for a competition, etc. **send off 1** get (a letter, etc.) posted. **2** cause (someone or something) to leave. **3** be present at the departure of (someone) to wish him a good journey, etc. **send-off** (ˈsendɒf) *nc* **1** a good beginning to an event. **2** the act of being present at someone's departure to wish him well: *They gave her a good send-off.* **send on 1** send (something) so that it will reach a place before oneself. **2** (of a letter) change the address and post it again: *His mother sent on all his letters to his university.* **send out 1** cause (someone) to leave, esp. a room. **2** give out; produce.

sender (ˈsendə*) *nc* a person or thing that sends.

senile (ˈsiːnaıl) *adj* weak in mind or body because of old age.

senior (ˈsiːnıə*) *adj* older; higher in rank. ● *nc* a senior person.

sensation (senˈseıʃən) **1** *ncu* feeling. **2** *nu* sudden excitement: *Some newspapers deal more in sensation than serious news.* **3** *nc* something that causes this excitement. **sensational** *adj* causing strong feelings.

sense (sens) **1** *nc* one of the body's special powers—sight, hearing, smell, taste, and touch. *nu* **2** a feeling: *a sense of warmth.* **3** a feeling in the mind or heart: *a sense of joy.* **4** use or purpose: *He saw no sense in going on.* **5** *nc* meaning: *Can you make sense of this?* **6** *nu* good judgement. ● *vt* feel with one of the senses. **make sense** able to be understood. **senseless** *adj* **1** foolish. **2** without feeling of the mind or body, as if asleep.

sensibility (,sensıˈbılıtı) *nu* the power of feeling. **sensibilities** *n pl* delicate feelings.

sensible (ˈsensıbəl) *adj* **1** having good judgement; useful at doing things. **2** great enough to be noticed: *a sensible difference.* **sensibly** *adv*

sensitive (ˈsensıtıv) *adj* **1** easily affected or irritated: *a sensitive skin that burns in the sun.* **2** (of the feelings) easily hurt. **3** easily noting very small changes: *a sensitive measuring instrument.* **sensitivity** (,sensıˈtıvıtı) *nu* being sensitive.

sensory (ˈsensərı) *adj* of the senses of sight, hearing, taste, smell, and touch; of the feelings.

sensual (ˈsensjʊəl) *adj* of the pleasures of the bodily feelings; too much enjoyment in regard to these feelings, esp. sexual ones.

sensuous (ˈsensjʊəs) *adj* pleasing to, noticed by, or affecting the senses.

sent (sent) past tense and past participle of **send.**

sentence ('sentəns) *nc* 1 a group of words, including a verb, that together make a statement, ask a question, give an order, etc. 2 a punishment decided by a judge in a law court. ● *vt* give such a punishment: *The judge sentenced the man to three years' imprisonment.*

sentiment ('sentɪmənt) 1 *nc* a feeling of the mind, opinion, or thought on a matter. 2 *nu* a (perhaps too) tender feeling. 3 *nc* an expression of feeling. **sentimental** (ˌsentɪ-ˈmentəl) *adj* 1 of or to do with the feelings. 2 causing, having, or showing too much feeling: *a sentimental tune.*

sentinel ('sentɪnəl) *nc* a sentry.

sentry ('sentrɪ) *nc, pl* **-tries** a soldier who guards a place: see picture.

sentry

separate ('sepərət) *adj* not joined; not shared with another; apart: *separate interests; sleep in separate beds; problem with three separate parts.* ● ('sepəreɪt) *vti* 1 (often followed by **into**) divide: *We were separated into groups.* 2 (often followed by **from** or **by**) be or make apart: *The two countries are separated from each other by a wide river.* **separately** *adv* **separation** (ˌsepəˈreɪʃən) 1 *nu* the act of separating or being separated. 2 *nc* an example of this.

separatist ('sepərətɪst) *nc* a member of a group in favour of separation from an organisation or country.

September (sepˈtembə*) *n* the ninth month of the year, after August and before October.

septic ('septɪk) *adj* of or to do with poison in the body: *a septic injury.*

sequel ('siːkwəl) *nc* 1 that which results from something happening earlier: *a sequel of events.* 2 a story, film, etc., that follows on with the same story from an earlier one.

sequence ('siːkwəns) 1 *nu* the coming of one thing after another. 2 *nc* an action or event that follows another or others.

seraph ('serəf) *nc, pl* **seraphs, seraphim** (fɪm) 1 a being in heaven, represented as a child with wings. 2 a pretty or small child.

serenade (ˌserəˈneɪd) *nc* a piece of music to be played or sung outside in the evening, esp. by a lover to his lady. ● *vt* play or sing a serenade to (someone).

serene (sɪˈriːn) *adj* peaceful and calm: *a serene smile.* **serenely** *adv* **serenity** (sɪˈrenɪtɪ) *nu* the state of being serene.

serf (sɜːf) *nc* (in older times) a land-worker who was not allowed to leave the land on which he worked.

sergeant ('saːdʒənt) *nc* 1 an army officer. 2 a police officer.

serial ('sɪərɪəl) *nc* a story, play, etc., appearing in parts in a magazine, on television, etc., weekly, monthly, etc. ● *adj* of or to do with a series.

series ('sɪəriːz) *nc, pl* **series** a group of things, events, etc., each connected in some way to the other and usually arranged in order: *a television series on politics.*

serious ('sɪərɪəs) *adj* 1 thoughtful; solemn: *a serious person.* 2 needing careful thought: *a serious problem.* 3 important because dangerous: *a serious illness; in serious trouble.* 4 sincere. 5 lacking a sense of humour or fun. **seriously** *adv* **seriousness** *nu* the state or quality of being serious.

sermon ('sɜːmən) *nc* a speech that teaches on religious matters, esp. one given by a Christian priest in church.

serpent ('sɜːpənt) *literary nc* snake.

serrated (səˈreɪtɪd) *adj* having tooth-like cuts on the edge, like a saw.

serum ('sɪərəm) *nu* 1 the clear, yellowish, liquid part of the blood. 2 this liquid, taken from the blood of an animal that has been made free from a disease, put into a person to prevent him getting the disease seriously by giving him a weak form of it.

servant ('sɜːvənt) *nc* 1 a person who is paid to do housework in the home of his employer. 2 someone who works for a government or other public organisation: *a public servant.* 3 a person who uses his work as an opportunity to serve others.

serve (sɜːv) *vt* 1 deal helpfully and politely with customers in a shop, restaurant, etc.: *Can I serve you, sir?* 2 be suitable or useful for: *This car no longer serves my needs.* *vt* 3 work as a servant to. *vi* 4 be a servant. 5 work for, esp. give one's loyalty to: *serve one's country.* 6 prepare (a meal) and give it out: *Breakfast in this hotel is served between 7 and 9 am.* **serve out** put (food) on a table ready for a meal. **serve up** offer (food) that has been prepared in a particular way: *The apple-pie was served up with ice cream.*

service ('sɜːvɪs) *nc* 1 an act done to help others. 2 a system that supplies a public need: *a bus service.* 3 a government department; people who work for this department: *the Civil Serivce.* 4 a fixed form of religious worship: *a burial service.* **5** a complete set of dishes: *a dinner service.* **6** (esp. of a car, aircraft, etc.) a general repair or making fit for further use. *nu* **7** the way of dealing with customers: *poor service.* **8** being a servant; position and work of a servant: *She was in service for many years.* **the Services** the army, navy, and air force. ● *vt* repair or make fit for use: *service a car.* **at your service** ready to help you. **service charge** the money paid for help given, added to the bill at a restaurant, etc. **service station** a place that provides petrol and often repair work, etc., for road vehicles. **serviceable** (ˈsɜːvɪsəbəl) *adj* **1** strong and solid: *a pair of serviceable boots.* **2** useful.

servitude (ˈsɜːvɪtjuːd) *nu* the condition of being a slave; being forced to work for others.

session (ˈseʃən) *nc* **1** a meeting of a court of law, parliament, etc.; set of such meetings. **2** any single meeting of a group of people for some purpose. **3** *chiefly US* a university term.

set (set) **1** *vt* put into a place or condition: *set food on the table.* **2** *vi* (of the sun, etc.) to go down in the evening. **3** *vti* turn from a liquid state to a solid state: *A jelly sets quickly in the cold.* *vt* **4** cause (someone or something) to be in a certain condition: *The house was set on fire.* **5** put (the hands of a clock, etc.) to the right time. **6** put back or fix in the right position: *set a broken leg; have one's hair set.* **7** show; offer: *The quality of his work set an example to everyone.* **8** *vi* be put back or fixed into the right position. ● *nc* **1** a number of people or things that belong together or are grouped together: *He is in the top set for science; set of tools; tea set.* **2** a device that sends or receives radio waves: *a television set.* **3** the furniture, painted background, etc., at the back of the stage in a theatre-play; scenery. **4** fixing of the hair by a hairdresser. ● *adj* fixed: *set ideas.* **all set (to)** be quite ready (to). **set about 1** start. **2** attack. **set back 1** be placed away from. **2** move back. **3** delay. **setback** (ˈsetbæk) *nc* something that gets in the way of progress. **set down 1** put down. **2** write down. **set in** likely to continue: *The rain seems to have set in for the night.* **set off** (often followed by **for** or the infinitive) **1** begin a journey. **2** (esp. of events, explosions, etc.) cause. **set out 1** (often followed by **for** or the infinitive) start on a journey. **2** arrange (things) in order to show to others: *The food was beautifully set out on the table.* **3** have as a main or first aim. **set to 1** begin working. **2** start to quarrel or fight. **set up 1** start (a business, etc.). **2** build or place (something) in

position. **set-up** (ˈsetʌp) *infml nc* the way in which something, esp. an organisation, is arranged.

set-square (ˈsetskweə*) *nc* a thin, flat piece of plastic or wood in the shape of a triangle, used in drawing plans for technical work: see picture.

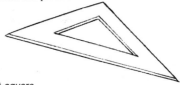

set-square

settee (seˈtiː) *nc* a long, comfortable seat with a back and arms, for two or more persons.

setting (ˈsetɪŋ) *nc* **1** a scene; the surroundings in which something is placed: *a house in a beautiful woodland setting.* **2** the furniture, etc., used on the stage in a play.

settle (ˈsetəl) *vti* **1** decide to live in a place, usually permanently: *He settled in London.* **2** agree; decide: *That's settled; After much discussion, they settled on a plan to end the war quickly.* **3** make or become calm and not likely to change: *settled weather.* **4** *vi* sink to the bottom or come down onto a surface: *Dust had settled on the furniture.* **5** *vt* pay (a bill, etc.). *vi* **6** (of a bill, etc.) be paid. **7** (followed by **for**) agree to have or accept something when that which is better cannot be obtained: *He had to settle for the less well-paid of the two jobs.* **settle down 1** make one's home, usually permanently, in a place. **2** become calm and peaceful after some activity. **settle in** or **into** start to get used to (a new home, job, etc.). **settled** *adj* decided; fixed; not likely to change. **settlement** (ˈsetəlmənt) **1** *nu* the ending of a quarrel, etc. **2** *nc* an example of this. **3** *nu* the making of a new life in a new country. *nc* **4** a place, esp. in a new country, where people settle. **5** the land, goods, etc., given to someone for use in his lifetime. **6** a legal, printed paper giving such rights. **settler** *nc* a person who moves to a new country in order to live there permanently.

seven (ˈsevən) *determiner, n* the number 7. **seventh** (ˈsevənθ) *determiner, n, adv* **seventeen** (ˌsevənˈtiːn) *determiner, n* 17. **seventeenth** (ˌsevənˈtiːnθ) *determiner, n, adv* **seventy** (ˈsevəntɪ) *determiner, n* 70. **seventieth** (ˈsevəntɪəθ) *determiner, n, adv* **Seventh Day Adventist** a member of a Christian group that believes Jesus Christ's Second Coming will be soon.

sever (ˈsevə*) *vt* **1** cut off: *The rope had been severed.* **2** break off: *sever a friendship.* **3** *vi* be parted or broken.

several ('sevrəl) *determiner* more than two but less than many. ●*adj* separate. ●*pron* a few: *Several of them began to laugh.*

severe (sɪ'vɪə*) *adj* **1** without much pity for others; stern. **2** dangerous: *a severe illness.* **3** hard to do; needing much effort. **4** very plain in dress, etc. **severely** *adv* **severity** (sɪ'verɪtɪ) **1** *nu* being severe. **2** *nc, pl* **-ties** an example of this.

sew (səʊ) *vti* fasten or decorate (pieces of cloth, etc.) with a needle and thread. **sewing-machine** ('səʊɪŋmə,ʃiːn) *nc* a machine, esp. one used in the home, for sewing.

sewage ('sjuːɪdʒ) *nu* waste matter from houses or other buildings that is carried away in pipes.

sewer ('sjuːə*) *nc* a pipe, esp. one under the ground, or tunnel that takes waste matter away from a city, etc. **sewerage** ('sjuːərɪdʒ) *nc* a system of sewers.

sewn (səʊn) past participle of **sew.**

sex (seks) **1** *nu* being male or female. **2** *nc* either of the two groups, males or females. *nu* **3** matters to do with satisfying the urge for bodily union with someone (usually) of the opposite sex. **4** *infml* the satisfying or the attempt to satisfy this urge. ●*adj* to do with sex. **sexual** ('seksjʊəl) *adj* of the sexes or sexual activity. **sexy** *adj* **-ier, -iest** *infml* causing or trying to cause sexual desire.

sextant ('sekstənt) *nc* an instrument used in order to set the course of a ship.

shabby ('ʃæbɪ) *adj* **-ier, -iest 1** (esp. of clothes) much worn and faded. **2** wearing such clothes. **3** (of behaviour) mean.

shack (ʃæk) *nc* a small, poor, roughly-made hut.

shackle ('ʃækəl) *nc* **1** one of two metal rings on a chain for fastening a prisoner round the wrists or ankles. **2** anything of the mind or body that prevents the freedom to act. ●*vt* prevent an escape or action.

shade (ʃeɪd) *nu* **1** slight darkness caused by the shutting out of some light. **2** a place made darker in this way: *He sat in the shade of a tree. nc* **3** something that shuts out some light: *a lamp-shade.* **4** strength or weakness of colour; a colour that is lighter or darker than usual. ●*vt* **1** protect from direct or too much light. **2** make darker by the use of some device. **3** *vi* (of colour, etc.) be gradually made darker. **4** *vt* make (colour, etc.) gradually darker.

shadow ('ʃædəʊ) *nc* **1** a slightly dark place. **2** the dark shape of something thrown onto a surface when something cuts off direct light: see picture. **3** *nu* the condition of being protected from direct light. ●*vt* **1** darken. **2** follow (someone) secretly. **shad-**

owy *adj* **1** having a shadow or shadows. **2** not clearly seen; like a shadow.

shadow

shady ('ʃeɪdɪ) *adj* **-ier, -iest 1** in the shade; giving shade from the sun. **2** *infml* dishonest or seeming so.

shaft (ʃɑːft) *nc* **1** the long, main part of an arrow, etc. **2** the long handle of a hammer or other tool. **3** one of two wooden poles by which a horse is fastened to a cart, etc. **4** a long, narrow passage for going down into a mine or for a lift in a building. **5** a long, narrow line of light.

shaggy ('ʃægɪ) *adj* **-ier, -iest 1** (of hair) rough; untidy. **2** having rough hair.

shah (ʃɑː) *nc* a ruler of Iran.

shake (ʃeɪk) **1** *vt* move (someone or something) quickly up and down or from side to side: *She shook the tablecloth to get rid of the crumbs.* **2** *vi* (of someone or something) be moved in this way. **3** *vti* tremble or cause to tremble. **4** *vt* make weaker or less firm: *shake one's courage.* ●*nc* shaking or being shaken. **shake hands** greet someone by holding his hand and shaking it. **shake off** get rid of him. **shake up 1** move (something) quickly in order to mix it well. **2** cause (someone) to be stirred up or have a shock. **3** cause (someone) to be more active. **shake-up** ('ʃeɪkʌp) *nc* **1** an example of having a shock or being made more active or stirred up. **2** a big reorganisation. **shaky** ('ʃeɪkɪ) *adj* **-ier, -iest 1** not steady in movements. **2** unsure.

shaken ('ʃeɪkən) past participle of **shake.**

shale (ʃeɪl) *nu* a dark, soft rock formed of thin sheets of earth.

shall (ʃæl unstressed ʃəl) *v* **1** (used esp. with **I** or **we** to express the future tense): *I shall see you soon.* **2** (used with **you, he, she, it,** or **they** to express the speaker's determination): *You shall do as I say!*

shallow ('ʃæləʊ) *adj* **1** not deep: *a shallow dish; shallow water.* **2** not going deeply into ideas, subjects, etc.: *a shallow conversation; a shallow mind.*

shalt (ʃælt) *archaic, poetry v* (used with **thou**) a form of **shall.**

sham (ʃæm) *vti* pretend to be, have, or feel. ●*nc* **1** a person who shams. **2** *nu* pretended behaviour. ●*adj* pretended.

shame (ʃeɪm) *nu* **1** a feeling of sorrow, disgust, loss of self-respect, etc., caused by wrong, dishonour, failure, etc. **2** dishonour.

3 a person or thing that causes shame. **4** the power of feeling shame: *He has no sense of shame.* ●*vt* cause such a feeling to (someone). **what a shame!** how disappointing! **shamefaced** (,ʃeɪm'feɪst) *adj* looking ashamed. **shameful** *adj* deserving or causing shame. **shamefully** *adv* **shameless** *adj* without shame; not pure in behaviour, etc.

shampoo (ʃæm'puː) **1** *ncu* the washing of the hair with special soap, liquid, etc. **2** *nc* this special soap or liquid, etc. ●*vt* wash (the hair).

shank (ʃæŋk) *nc* **1** the part of the leg between the knee and the ankle. **2** the part of a tool between the working end and the handle.

shan't (ʃɑːnt) *v* shall not.

shanty ('ʃæntɪ) *nc, pl* **-ties 1** a roughly-made hut. **2** a song sung by sailors while working.

shape (ʃeɪp) *ncu* **1** form; outward appearance: see picture. **2** *infml* condition. ●*vt* give form to. **out of shape 1** in an unhealthy condition. **2** not in the right shape. **take shape** become clear and certain in form: *Our plans are taking shape.* **shapeless** ('ʃeɪplɪs) *adj* without shape. **shapely** *adj* **-ier, -iest** pleasing in shape.

share (ʃeə*) *nc* **1** a part of something given or received: *I have done my share of the work.* **2** an equal part in the owning of a business company with the right to an equal share in the profits: *He owns 500 shares in the company.* ●*vt* **1** give out or divide among other people; give away part of: *He shared his lunch with me.* **2** *vi* (often followed by **in**) give or receive a part: *We all shared in his happiness.* **shareholder** ('ʃeə,həʊldə*) *nc* an owner of one or more shares in a company. **share-out** ('ʃeəraʊt) *nc* giving each person, etc., a share of profits, something stolen, etc.

shark (ʃɑːk) *nc* **1** a large, fierce sea-fish. **2** a person who cheats others out of money.

sharp (ʃɑːp) *adj* **-er, -est 1** with an edge that cuts: *a sharp knife.* **2** coming to a fine point: *a sharp needle.* **3** stern; harsh: *sharp words.* **4** quick to see, hear, or notice: *sharp ears.* **5** changing direction suddenly: *a sharp bend in the road.* **6** giving a feeling as if one is being cut: *a sharp pain.* **7** almost sour: *a sharp apple.* **8** with clear edges; clearly marked: *This photograph isn't sharp because you moved the camera.* **9** *music* raised above the true or natural note. **10** (of a sound) on a high note: *a sharp cry of pain.* **11** not honest or fair: *sharp business practice.* ●*nc music* a sharp note. ●*adv* **1** exactly: *Come at six o'clock sharp.* **2** sharply: *Turn sharp left.* **sharpen** *vti* make or become sharp. **sharply** *adv*

shatter (ʃætə*) **1** *vti* break or be broken suddenly and violently into pieces. **2** *vt* destroy: *Our hopes were shattered.*

shave (ʃeɪv) **1** *vti* cut (hair) from (the face, etc.) with a razor: *He shaved off his beard.* *vt* **2** cut (thin pieces) off (something, esp. wood) to make it smooth. **3** go very close to without touching. ●*nc* shaving the face. **a close** or **narrow shave** a lucky escape from harm, danger, etc. **shaver** *nc* an electric razor. **shavings** *n pl* very thin pieces of wood, cut off when making it smooth.

shaven ('ʃeɪvən) *adj* having had hair removed from the face, etc.: *clean-shaven.*

shawl (ʃɔːl) *nc* a piece of cloth or material worn round the shoulders or head by women.

she (ʃiː unstressed ʃɪ) *pron* **1** (used of a female person or animal): *My mother said she felt ill.* **2** (sometimes used of a ship, country, machine, etc.)

sheaf (ʃiːf) *nc, pl* **-ves** (vz) a bundle of things tied or held together, esp. corn after being gathered from the field.

shear (ʃɪə*) *vt* cut (the wool) off (a sheep). **shears** *n pl* also **pair of shears** any of several tools like large scissors, used for shearing sheep, cutting cloth, etc.: see picture at **tools.**

sheath (ʃiːθ) *nc* a cover that fits closely, esp. one for the blade of a weapon or tool.

sheathe (ʃiːð) *vt* put into a sheath.

shed¹ (ʃed) *nc* a building made esp. of wood, used for storing things or doing work in: *a coal-shed.*

shed² *vt* **1** let drop off or fall: *Trees shed their leaves; He shed tears of sorrow.* **2** send out (love, warmth, etc.).

she'd (ʃiːd) she had or she would.

sheen (ʃiːn) *nu* being shiny; brightness: *the sheen of silk.*

sheep (ʃiːp) *nc, pl* **sheep** an animal kept for its wool and its meat. **sheepish** ('ʃiːpɪʃ) *adj* **1** feeling foolish because of doing something wrong, stupid, etc. **2** not wanting to do something for fear of drawing attention to oneself. **sheepskin** ('ʃiːpskɪn) *nc* a sheep's skin with the wool on it, esp. made into a coat, rug, etc.

sheer (ʃɪə*) *adj* **1** very steep. **2** (of cloth) fine enough to be almost seen through. **3** complete: *You are talking sheer nonsense!*

sheet (ʃiːt) *nc* **1** a large piece of cloth, esp. cotton, used on a bed. **2** a thin, flat piece of some material: *a sheet of paper.* **3** a rope tied to a bottom corner of a sail and used to control its position.

sheik (also **sheikh**) (ʃeɪk) *nc* an Arab chief or ruler.

shelf (ʃelf) *nc, pl* **-ves** (vz) **1** a narrow, flat board, sheet of glass, etc., fixed to a wall,

shapes

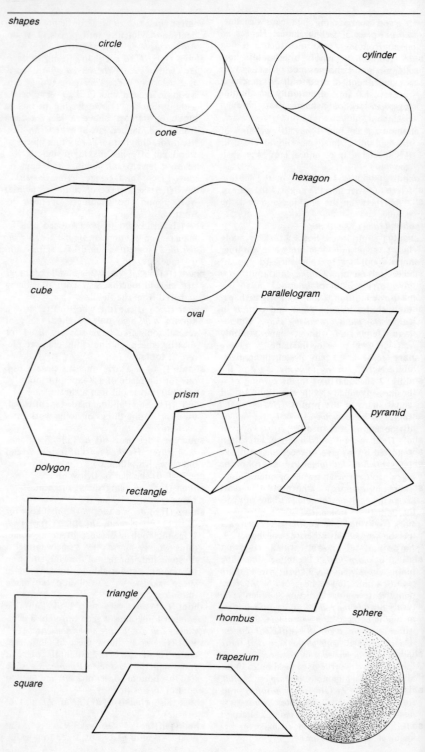

circle

cone

cylinder

cube

oval

hexagon

parallelogram

polygon

prism

pyramid

rectangle

triangle

rhombus

sphere

square

trapezium

etc., and used for putting things on. **2** a step-like piece of rock under water or sticking out from the side of a cliff, etc.

shell (ʃel) *nc* **1** the hard outside covering of an egg, a nut, or some small animals, such as a snail or crab. **2** the frame of a building, ship, etc., that is being built or has been destroyed inside. **3** a metal container of material that explodes after being fired from a big gun. ● *vt* **1** take out of a shell or other seed-container: *to shell peas.* **2** fire shells at.
shellfish (ˈʃelfiʃ) *nc, pl* **-fish, -fishes** any of several kinds of small animal covered with a hard shell, mostly living in water.
she'll (ʃiːl) she will.
shelter (ˈʃeltə*) **1** *nu* being protected, covered, etc.: *We found shelter under a tree when it rained.* **2** *nc* something, esp. a building, that gives shelter. ● *vt* **1** protect; be a shelter to: *The tree sheltered us from the storm.* **2** *vi* take cover, shelter, etc.
shelve (ʃelv) *vt* **1** put off dealing with (a problem, plan, etc.) until another time. **2** put (a book, etc.) on a shelf.
shepherd (ˈʃepəd) *nc* a man who guards and looks after sheep. ● *vt* take care of; guide or show the way: *The children were shepherded across the road.* **shepherdess** (ˈʃepədis) *nc* a woman who guards and looks after sheep.
sheriff (ˈʃerif) *nc* **1** (in England and Wales) the chief officer in a county. **2** (in the USA) the elected chief law officer in a county.
sherry (ˈʃeri) *nc, pl* **-ries** (a type or a drink of) a strong yellow or brown wine.
she's (ʃiːz) she is or she has.
shew (ʃəʊ) *archaic* See **show.**
shied (ʃaid) past tense and past participle of **shy**[2].
shield (ʃiːld) *nc* **1** a mainly flat piece of metal, plastic, leather, etc., held in front of one for protection when fighting. **2** anything, such as a piece of machinery, that protects. ● *vt* protect: *to shield one's eyes from the sun.*
shift (ʃift) **1** *vti* move or be moved from one place to another. **2** *vt* change (gear) in a car, etc. ● *nc* **1** a movement. **2** a change. **3** a period of time for which someone works in turn with others. **4** a group of such workmen who start work as another group finish: *I'm on the night shift.* **shifty** *adj* **-ier, -iest** not to be trusted.
shilling (ˈʃiliŋ) *nc* **1** See appendix. **2** (in the UK) (a former coin worth) one twentieth of a pound or five new pence.
shimmer (ˈʃimə*) *vi, nc* (shine with) an unsteady or weak light: *the shimmer of moonlight on the water.*
shin (ʃin) *nc* the front of the leg between the knee and the ankle.

shine (ʃain) *vi* **1** give out or reflect light. **2** be bright: *The sun was shining; His face shone with joy.* **3** (past tense and past participle **shined**) *vt* make bright, esp. by polishing. ● *nu* brightness; polish. **shiny** *adj* **-ier, -iest** having a shine; polished.
shingle (ˈʃiŋgəl) *nu* small round pebbles on a beach.
Shinto (ˈʃintəʊ) *n* Japanese religion that honours nature and the earlier members of one's family.
ship (ʃip) *nc* a very large boat that can cross any sea. ● *vt* take or send (passengers or goods), esp. by ship. **shipbuilding** (ˈʃip-ˌbildiŋ) *nu* the business of building ships. **shipment** (ˈʃipmənt) *nc* an amount of goods sent on a ship. **shipper** *nc* a person or company that ships goods. **shipping** *nu* ships: *Here is a warning to all shipping.* **shipwreck** (ˈʃiprek) *nc* the destroying or sinking of a ship. ● *vt* **1** cause (a ship) to be wrecked. **2** *vi* be in a ship that is wrecked. **shipyard** (ˈʃipjɑːd) *nc* a place where ships are built.
shirk (ʃɜːk) *vt* avoid doing (something) because of laziness, fear, etc.: *Do not shirk your duty.*
shirt (ʃɜːt) *nc* a garment for the top part of the body and the arms, worn with trousers or a skirt.
Shiva (ˈʃiːvə) *n* a Hindu god.
shiver (ˈʃivə*) *vi* tremble with cold or fear. ● *nc* the act of shivering.
shoal (ʃəʊl) *nc* a large group of fish swimming together.
shock (ʃɒk) *nc* **1** a sudden blow; violent shaking, esp. by an explosion. **2** (the reason for) a sudden upset of the mind or feelings: *The news of his death came as a shock.* **3** the effect of electricity passing through the body: *an electric shock.* **4** *nu* a state in which the body does not work normally because of cold, pain, etc. ● *vt* fill with horror, fear, disgust, etc.: *I was shocked by his behaviour.* **shocking** *adj* **1** very bad: *shocking manners.* **2** causing feelings of horror, fear, disgust, etc.
shod (ʃɒd) past tense and past participle of **shoe.**
shoddy (ˈʃɒdi) *adj* **-ier, -iest** badly made or done: *a shoddy piece of work; shoddy material.*
shoe (ʃuː) *nc* a tough covering for the foot, esp. made chiefly of leather. ● *vt* provide with shoes, esp. (a horse) with horseshoes. **shoelace** (ˈʃuːleis) *nc* a piece of string, cord, etc., used to tie a shoe over the front of the foot. **shoemaker** (ˈʃuːˌmeikə*) *nc* a person who makes boots and shoes. **shoeshine** (ˈʃuːʃain) *chiefly US nu* polishing of shoes. **shoestring** (ˈʃuːstriŋ) *nc* shoelace.

on a shoestring *infml* with very little money: *living on a shoestring.*

shone (ʃɒn) past tense and past participle of **shine** (defs. 1, 2).

shoo (ʃuː) *interj* (used to make people or animals go away.) ● *vt* make (someone or something) go away by calling 'shoo'.

shook (ʃʊk) past tense of **shake.**

shoot (ʃuːt) *vt* **1** fire (something) from (a gun, etc.). **2** hit, and esp. kill, with something fired from a gun, etc. **3** photograph; film. **4** *vti* (cause to) move quickly: *The dog shot across the road.* **5** *vi* (of a gun, etc.) be fired. **6** *vti* (in a game such as football) hit or kick (the ball, etc.) towards the right place to win a point. **7** *vi* (of a plant) put out a shoot or shoots. ● *nc* a new young part growing on a plant. **shooting star** a small star rushing towards the earth and becoming bright as it burns up.

shop (ʃɒp) *nc* **1** a room or building in which goods are shown and sold to customers. **2** a place where goods are made or repaired: *I work in the paint shop of a car factory.* ● *vi* buy goods in shops: *Let's go shopping.* **talk shop** talk about one's work, business, etc. **shop assistant** a person who works in a shop. **shopkeeper** (ˈʃɒpˌkiːpə*) *nc* a person who owns a shop. **shoplifter** (ˈʃɒpˌlɪftə*) *nc* a person who steals things from a shop. **shoplifting** (ˈʃɒpˌlɪftɪŋ) *nu* **shopping** *nu* goods bought at a shop or shops: *My shopping is heavy.* **shopping centre** a group of shops, often where cars are not allowed. **shop steward** a workman chosen by other workmen to represent them when dealing with their employer.

shore¹ (ʃɔː*) *nc* the land at the edge of a sea or lake.

shore² *nc* a support for a wall, a ship that is being built or repaired, etc. **shore up** support (something).

shorn (ʃɔːn) past participle of **shear.**

short (ʃɔːt) *adj* **-er, -est 1** not tall or long. **2** not enough: *Time is short.* **3** (of a person) using few words; not really polite: *He was short with me.* **4** (of pastry) containing a lot of fat for the amount of flour, and therefore easily broken. ● *adv* suddenly: *stop short.* **in short** in a few words, esp. expressing the main points. **in the short run** over a short period of time. **short of 1** except for; apart from: *Nothing short of complete success is good enough.* **2** lacking; missing: *We can't play if we are short of enough men.* **shortage** (ˈʃɔːtɪdʒ) *nc* a lack; not having enough: *food shortages.* **shortcoming** (ˈʃɔːtˌkʌmɪŋ) *nc* a failure to do or be what is expected. **short cut 1** a way of going somewhere that is shorter than the usual way. **2** a way of doing something that is quicker

than the usual way. **shorten** (ˈʃɔːtən) *vti* make or become shorter. **shortening** *nu* fat used in making pastry, cake, etc. **shorthand** (ˈʃɔːthænd) *nu* a system of writing at great speed using special signs instead of letters. **shortly** *adv* **1** soon. **2** in a few words. **3** rudely. **shorts** *n pl* trousers with legs that reach down to the knees or anywhere above. **short-sighted** (ˌʃɔːtˈsaɪtɪd) *adj* **1** unable to see distant things clearly. **2** unable to think and prepare for the future. **short story** a story that is shorter than a normal book. **short-term** (ˌʃɔːtˈtɜːm) *adj* for or happening in a short period of time: *the short-term borrowing of money.* **short wave** a radio wave with a wavelength of between 10 and 100 metres, used for sending radio over long distances.

shot¹ (ʃɒt) *nc* **1** the firing of a gun. **2** *infml* an attempt to do something: *Have a shot at solving this problem.* **3** a single photograph or an uninterrupted part of a moving film. **4** *nu* a number of small metal balls, fired from a gun at a bird or small animal. **shotgun** (ˈʃɒtgʌn) *nc* a gun used for firing shot over short distances.

shot² past tense and past participle of **shoot.**

should (ʃʊd unstressed ʃəd) *v* **1** ought to; have it as a duty to: *You ought to say you are sorry.* **2** shall or will probably: *He should be there by now.* **3** (used to form a conditional verb with **I** or **we**): *I should go if I were you.* **4** (used to show what is possible, esp. with **if**): *If that should be so, I shall know what to do.*

shoulder (ˈʃəʊldə*) *nc* the part of the body where either arm is joined on. ● *vt* **1** put or carry on the shoulder or shoulders: *He shouldered the heavy sack.* **2** take (blame, responsibility, etc.) on oneself. **3** push with the shoulder or shoulders: *He shouldered me to one side.*

shouldn't (ˈʃʊdənt) *v* should not.

shout (ʃaʊt) *nc* a loud cry. ● *vti* call or say loudly: *He shouted with joy; She shouted a warning.*

shove (ʃʌv) **1** *vti* push violently. **2** *infml vt* put: *Shove your books in the cupboard.* ● *nc* a violent push.

shovel (ˈʃʌvəl) *nc* a broad, flat tool with a long handle, used for picking up and moving coal, snow, etc. ● *vt* move with a shovel.

show (ʃəʊ) **1** *vti* (allow or cause to) be seen. *vt* **2** use actions to explain (something) to (someone): *I'll show you what to do.* **3** guide: *The visitors were shown round the city.* **4** prove: *This shows that I am right.* ● *nu* **1** showing or being shown. *nc* **2** a collection of things put out for the public to see: *a motor show; a flower show.* **3** an entertainment such as a play or a musical. **4** *nu* an appearance: *When he was being watched he made a great show of working hard.* **on show** put somewhere to be seen. **show business** the business of entertaining people in the theatre, on television, etc. **showcase** (ˈʃəʊkeɪs) *nc* a fixed container with glass sides for showing things in a shop, exhibition, etc. **showdown** (ˈʃəʊdaʊn) *infml nc* a final decision or argument at which everything is made known. **show-jumping** (ˈʃəʊˌdʒʌmpɪŋ) *nu* riding a horse over fences, hedges, etc., in a competition. **showman** (ˈʃəʊmən) *nc, pl* **-men** the manager of a circus of other show. **show off 1** allow (something) to be seen so as to invite admiration: *He's glad to show off his stamp collection to other people.* **2** try to attract attention by one's behaviour. **show-off** (ˈʃəʊɒf) *nc* a person who shows off (**show off** def. 2). **showroom** (ˈʃəʊrʊm) *nc* a room in which goods can be looked at. **show up 1** (cause to) be easily seen. **2** *infml* arrive; appear. **showy** *adj* **-ier, -iest** likely to attract attention, but often tasteless.

shower (ˈʃaʊə*) *nc* **1** a light, short fall of rain, snow, etc. **2** (a room containing) a device with small holes through which water comes down over a person for washing. **3** the act of washing in a shower: *to have or take a shower.* **4** a number of things coming or falling together: *a shower of letters; a shower of blows.* ● *vti* **1** send or travel in a **shower** (def. 4): *He showered presents on me.* **2** *vi* take a **shower** (def. 3).

shown (ʃəʊn) past participle of **show.**

shrank (ʃræŋk) past tense of **shrink.**

shred (ʃred) *nc* **1** a small piece of something that has been torn or cut off: *His shirt was torn to shreds.* **2** a small amount: *without a shred of comfort.* ● *vt* tear or cut into shreds.

shrewd (ʃruːd) *adj* **-er, -est** having good powers of judgement, esp. in business matters.

shriek (ʃriːk) *nc* a high, loud cry. ● *vi* **1** give a shriek. **2** *vt* say in a shriek: *She shrieked her answer.*

shrill (ʃrɪl) *adj* **-er, -est** (of a sound) high and sharp: *a shrill whistle.*

shrimp (ʃrɪmp) *nc* a small sea-animal with a hard shell, used for food: see picture.

shrimp

shrine (ʃraɪn) *nc* a place or building honoured for its connection with a holy person, etc.

shrink (ʃrɪŋk) *vti* (cause to) become smaller: *My dress shrank in the wash.* **shrink from** draw back from (something) or from (doing something) because of fear, disgust, etc. **shrinkage** (ˈʃrɪŋkɪdʒ) *nu* **1** shrinking. **2** the amount by which something shrinks.

shrivel (ˈʃrɪvəl) *vti* (cause to) become smaller and wrinkled because of heat, dryness, old age, or frost: *shrivelled skin.*

shroud (ʃraʊd) *nc* **1** a cloth put round a dead person. **2** something that covers and hides: *A shroud of mist hid the mountain from view.* ● *vt* **1** cover (a dead body) with a shroud. **2** cover and hide.

shrub (ʃrʌb) *nc* a plant like a small tree that branches near the ground; bush. **shrubbery** (ˈʃrʌbərɪ) *nc, pl* **-ries** a group of shrubs.

shrug (ʃrʌg) *vt* raise (one's shoulders) for a moment to show one does not know, is not interested, etc. ● *nc* such a movement of the shoulders: *He answered with a shrug.* **shrug off** put (something) out of one's mind as not being important.

shrunk (ʃrʌŋk) past tense and past participle of **shrink. shrunken** (ˈʃrʌŋkən) *adj* having been shrunk: *a shrunken head from South America.*

shudder (ˈʃʌdə*) *vi* shake suddenly and quickly from fear, disgust, etc. ● *nc* such a sudden, quick shake.

shuffle (ˈʃʌfəl) **1** *vi* walk slowly, dragging the feet. *vt* **2** slide (one's feet) around while standing or sitting. **3** mix (things) up so that their positions are changed, esp. (playing-cards) on purpose. ● *nc* the act of shuffling.

shun (ʃʌn) *vt* avoid; keep away from: *You shun responsibility; After his crime he was shunned by society.*

shunt (ʃʌnt) *vt* move (a train, etc.) onto another track.

shush (ʃʊʃ) *interj* be quiet! ● *vt* make (someone) be quiet by saying 'shush'.

shut (ʃʌt) **1** *vt* move (a door, lid, etc.) to cover an opening. **2** *vi* (of a door, lid, etc.) move so as to cover an opening. *vti* **3** bring or be brought into a closed state: *Shut your book and listen.* **4** stop business (at): *The shop shuts at five every day.* **5** *vt* keep (someone or something) in a place by shutting a door, etc.: *We shut the dog outside.* **shut down** (cause to) stop working: *The factory where I work is being shut down.* **shut-down** (ˈʃʌtdaʊn) *nc* the closing of a factory, etc. **shut up** *infml* stop talking.

shutter (ˈʃʌtə*) *nc* **1** a door-like cover put up outside a window to keep thieves or light out. **2** a device in a camera that opens to let light onto the film. ● *vt* put up shutters over (a window).

shuttle (ˈʃʌtəl) *nc* **1** a tool with pointed ends, used for carrying thread across and back again in making cloth. **2** a bus, plane, etc., that takes people between two places, esp. as often as needed: *There's a shuttle service between the city and the airport.* ● *vi* travel as a **shuttle** (def. 2).

shy¹ (ʃaɪ) *adj* **-er, -est; shier, shiest 1** uncomfortable in the company of other people; not wanting to attract attention. **2** (of an animal) easily frightened. **shyly** *adv* **shyness** *nu*

shy² *vi* (of a horse) turn away in sudden fear.

sick (sɪk) *adj* **-er, -est** not well; ill. **be sick** bring food back up from the stomach and through the mouth. **feel sick** feel that one is about to be sick. **the sick** (all) sick people. **sicken** (ˈsɪkən) **1** *vi* begin to be ill. **2** *vti* (cause to) feel sick or be disgusted. **sickening** (ˈsɪkənɪŋ) *adj* disgusting. **sickly** *adj* **-ier, -iest** often ill; not healthy: *a sickly child.* **2** causing a feeling of sickness: *a sickly smell.* **sickness 1** *ncu* (an) illness; disease. **2** *nu* being or feeling sick.

sickle (ˈsɪkəl) *nc* a tool with a curved blade and a short handle for cutting corn, grass, etc.: see picture at **tools.**

side (saɪd) *nc* **1** a surface of an object: *Most boxes have six sides: an egg has only one.* **2** the place near an edge: *Cross to the other side of the road.* **3** a line forming an edge: *A square has four sides.* **4** one of two groups of people who are playing, fighting, arguing, etc., against each other; team. **5** a surface that is (roughly) upright: *the side of a mountain.* **6** the left or right half of a body. **7** a way of looking at something: *Try to see my side of the problem.* **8** a family line: *She looks more like her mother's side of the family.* **on all sides** all round. **side by side** close together. **take sides** (start to) support one team, political party, etc. **sideboard** (ˈsaɪdbɔːd) *nc* a piece of furniture with drawers and cupboards, kept in a dining-room. **side-effect** an effect, esp. an unpleasant one, other than the main one of a medicine, etc. **sidelines** (ˈsaɪdlaɪnz) *n pl* a space next to that used for games of football, tennis, etc. **sidetrack** (ˈsaɪdtræk) *vt* turn (someone) away from what he intended to do, say, etc. **sidewalk** (ˈsaɪdwɔːk) *US n* See **pavement** under **pave. sideways** (ˈsaɪdweɪz) *adv, adj* moving or facing towards one side: *A train won't go sideways; a sideways look.* **side with** support (one side of an argument, etc.) **siding** *nc* a short railway track leading off a main one, used for storage, etc.

sidle (ˈsaɪdəl) *vi* walk in a nervous way or as if one did not want to be noticed: *He sidled up to me.*

siege (siːdʒ) *nc* a method used by an army to capture a town by surrounding (and attacking) it. **lay siege to** try to capture (a town) by means of a siege.

sieve (sɪv) *nc* a tool with a wire net through which liquids, etc., are passed, leaving solid matter behind. ● *vt* put through a sieve.

sift (sɪft) *vt* **1** put through a sieve. **2** examine carefully: *We must sift all the arguments.*

sigh (saɪ) *vi* take in and let out a loud breath showing that one is sad, tired, bored, relieved, etc. ● *nc* the act of sighing.

sight (saɪt) *nu* **1** the power of seeing: *He lost his sight.* **2** seeing or being seen. **3** the distance one can see: *Wait till they come within sight.* **4** *infml* a person or thing that is untidy, ugly, etc.: *She looked a sight!* *nc* **5** something seen, esp. something worth seeing. **6** a device for guiding the eye when one fires a gun, looks through a telescope, etc. ● *vt* **1** see or notice. **2** observe the position of (a star, etc.). **catch** or **lose sight of** begin or no longer be able to see. **in** or **out of sight** able or not able to be seen. **sights** *n pl* the most attractive or interesting parts of a town, etc., to be visited. **sightseeing** (ˈsaɪtˌsiːɪŋ) *nu* visiting sights. **sightseer** (ˈsaɪtˌsiːə*) *nc*

sign (saɪn) *nc* **1** a mark or object used to represent something. **2** an action or movement giving information, an order, etc. **3** something that points out or makes something known; indication: *Her face showed signs of grief.* **4** a board giving directions, information, etc.: *Can you see a sign to the car park?* ● *vt* **1** write one's name on (a letter, cheque, etc.) to show that one formally approves it. **2** make (something) known by a movement of the hand, head, etc.

signal (ˈsɪɡnəl) *nc* **1** any sign giving information, an order, etc., esp. to someone far away. **2** an event that causes an action: *The shooting was a signal for general disturbances.* **3** a movement of electricity or set of radio waves carrying information. ● *vt* make a signal sending (information, an order, etc.) to (someone). **signal box** *chiefly Brit nc* a building from which signals to railway trains are controlled.

signatory (ˈsɪɡnətərɪ) *nc, pl* **-ries** a person, state, country, etc., that signs an agreement.

signature (ˈsɪɡnɪtʃə*) *nc* a person's name written by himself when signing a letter, etc.

signet (ˈsɪɡnɪt) *nc* a small metal stamp, esp. part of a ring for a finger, used for pressing into hot wax, etc., to indicate one's approval of a letter, etc.

significance (sɪgˈnɪfɪkəns) *nu* **1** importance. **2** having (a) meaning. **significant** *adj* **significantly** *adv*

signify (ˈsɪgnɪfaɪ) **1** *vt* indicate; mean; be a sign of. **2** *infml vi* be of importance.

signpost (ˈsaɪnpəʊst) *nc* a sign, esp. where roads meet, with arms showing the names of places and pointing in the direction of each one.

silage (ˈsaɪlɪdʒ) *nu* a food, such as grass, for cattle, kept good without drying.

silence (ˈsaɪləns) *nu* **1** being quiet; being without sound. **2** not speaking. ● *vt* make silent. **in silence** without a sound; without speaking. **silencer** *nc* device that makes a car engine, gun, etc., quieter. **silent** *adj* **1** quiet; with no sound. **2** saying nothing or very little. **silently** *adv*

silhouette (ˌsɪluːˈet) *nc* **1** the outline of someone or something seen against the light. **2** a picture like this, esp. in black on white: see picture. ● *vt* show or cause to be seen as a silhouette.

silhouette

silicon (ˈsɪlɪkən) *nu* a chemical element that is not a metal, found, for example, in sand: symbol Si

silk (sɪlk) *nu* (cloth made from) the fine, soft thread made by silkworms. **silken** (ˈsɪlkən) *adj* **1** made of silk. **2** like silk; soft or shining: *silken hair*. **silkworm** (ˈsɪlkwɜːm) *nc* an insect that makes a covering of silk to protect itself. **silky** *adj* **-ier, -iest**.

sill (sɪl) *nc* a narrow shelf of wood or stone at the bottom of a window.

silly (ˈsɪlɪ) *adj* **-ier, -iest 1** foolish. **2** pointless; useless.

silo (ˈsaɪləʊ) *nc* a tower or a hole in the ground in which silage is stored.

silt (sɪlt) *nu* sand, mud, etc., left at the mouth of a river, on the bottom of a lake, etc.

silver (ˈsɪlvə*) *nu* **1** a chemical element; bright, light grey, valuable metal used for coins, ornaments, etc.: symbol Ag **2** coins made of silver or a metal or mixture of metals with the colour of silver **3** knives, plates, etc., made of silver. **4** the colour of silver. ● *adj* **1** made of silver. **2** having the colour of silver. ● *vt* **1** cover with silver. **2** *vti* (cause to) become silver in colour. **silver paper** *infml* very thin metal, esp. aluminium, used for wrapping chocolate, cigarettes, etc. **silversmith** (ˈsɪlvəsmɪθ) *nc* a

person who makes things out of silver. **silverware** (ˈsɪlvəweə*) *nu* plates or knives made out of silver. **silvery** *adj*

similar (ˈsɪmɪlə*) *adj* alike; of the same kind: *That pen is similar to mine*. **similarity** (ˌsɪmɪˈlærɪtɪ) **1** *nu* being similar. **2** *nc, pl* **-ties** a way in which things are similar. **similarly** *adv*

simile (ˈsɪmɪlɪ) *nc* an expression comparing one thing to another, such as 'like a horse' in 'He eats like a horse'.

simmer (ˈsɪmə*) *vi* **1** (of food, water, etc.) be almost boiling; boil gently. **2** control one's anger, laughter, etc., so that it is not seen: *He simmered with excitement*. **3** *vt* cause (food, water, etc.) to simmer.

simple (ˈsɪmpəl) *adj* **-r, -st 1** easy to do or understand. **2** plain; with not much decoration: *simple cooking*. **3** foolish. **4** not connected to others; with only a few parts: *a simple machine*. **5** without difficulties or complicated things: *the simple life*. **simple interest** money paid for borrowing money, worked out only on the actual amount borrowed. **simpleton** (ˈsɪmpəltən) *nc* a foolish, easily deceived person. **simplicity** (sɪmˈplɪsɪtɪ) *nu* **simply** *adv*

simplify (ˈsɪmplɪfaɪ) *vt* make simple or simpler. **simplification** (ˌsɪmplɪfɪˈkeɪʃən) **1** *nu* simplifying. **2** *nc* a way in which something is simplified.

simulate (ˈsɪmjʊleɪt) *vt* pretend to be: *a film of a simulated attack*. **simulation** (ˌsɪmjʊˈleɪʃən) *ncu* (an instance of) simulating.

simultaneous (ˌsɪməlˈteɪnɪəs) *adj* happening or done at the same time. **simultaneously** *adv*

sin (sɪn) **1** *ncu* (an instance or way of) breaking the laws of God. **2** *infml nc* an act against good taste or good sense. ● *vi* **1** break God's laws. **2** do wrong.

since (sɪns) *prep* for or during the time after: *I haven't been home since yesterday*. ● *conj* **1** since the time when. **2** because; as. ● *adv* since then.

sincere (sɪnˈsɪə*) *adj* **1** (of feelings) true; not pretended. **2** (of a person) honest; truthful; not pretending. **sincerely** *adv* **yours sincerely** (used before one's name at the end of a letter, usually to someone one has met.) **sincerity** (sɪnˈserɪtɪ) *nu*

sinew (ˈsɪnjuː) *nc* **1** a tough, string-like part of the body that joins a muscle to a bone; tendon: see picture. **2** *(pl) literary* muscles; strength of the body.

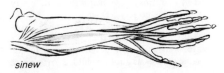

sinew

sinful ('sınfʊl) *adj* wrong; evil.

sing (sıŋ) **1** *vti* produce (words, a song, etc.) as a tune. *vi* **2** (of a bird, etc.) make a tuneful sound. **3** make a humming, whistling, ringing, etc., sound: *The noise has set my ears singing.* **singer** *nc* **singing** *nu*

singe (sındʒ) **1** *vti* burn or be burnt slightly. **2** *vt* burn off the ends of (hair, etc.).

single ('sıŋgəl) *adj* **1** one only. **2** for the use of one person only: *a single bed.* **3** not married. ● *nc* **1** also **single ticket** a ticket for a journey to a place but not back again. **2** *(pl)* a game, such as tennis, with only one person on each side. **single-handed** (,sıŋgəl'hændıd) *adj, adv* (done) alone or without help: *He captured the town single-handed.* **single-minded** (,sıŋgəl'maındıd) *adj* with one's mind on one purpose only.

singly ('sıŋglı) *adv* one by one; separately.

singular ('sıŋgjʊlə*) *adj* **1** (of a noun, verb, etc.) used in writing or speaking of only one person or one thing. **2** odd; unusual. ● *nc* a singular word: *'Foot' is the singular of 'feet'.* **singularly** *adv* oddly; unusually.

sinister ('sınıstə*) *adj* looking evil or as if evil is intended.

sink (sıŋk) *vti* (cause to) go slowly down, esp. below a surface: *The sun is sinking; The ship was sunk by the enemy.* ● *nc* a fixed container of stone, steel, etc., with a pipe for carrying away dirty water, used for washing dishes in a kitchen.

sinner ('sınə*) *nc* a person who sins.

sinuous ('sınjʊəs) *adj* with many twists and bends.

sip (sıp) *vt* drink in small mouthfuls. ● *nc* a small mouthful of a drink.

siphon (also **syphon**) ('saıfən) *nc* **1** a curved tube used to draw liquid up and out of a container. **2** See **soda siphon** under **soda**.

sir (sɜ:* unstressed sə*) *n* a polite and respectful way of speaking to a man. **Sir** *nc* **1** (used to begin a formal letter to a man or a company): *Dear Sir(s).* **2** a title put before the name of a knight: *Sir Seretse Khama.*

sire (saıə*) *nc* **1** (used when speaking to a king or other male ruler.) **2** the father of an animal, esp. a horse. ● *vt* (of an animal, esp. a horse) become the father of.

siren ('saıərən) *nc* a device that makes a loud, sharp sound to give a warning, etc., as on a police car.

sirloin ('sɜ:lɔın) *nc* beef from the back of the animal above the back legs.

sirrah ('sırə) *old-fashioned n* (used in a way that shows no respect) sir.

sissy ('sısı) *nc, pl* **-sies**, *adj* (a) weak, cowardly, or woman-like (boy or man).

sister ('sıstə*) *nc* **1** a female child of the same parents as another child. **2** *Brit* a nurse

in charge of others in a hospital. **3** one of a group of women living a religious life together; nun. **sisterhood** ('sıstəhʊd) **1** *nu* the state of being a sister or sisters. **2** *nc* a society of religious sisters. **sister-in-law** ('sıstərınlɔ:) *nc, pl* **sisters-in-law 1** one's brother's wife. **2** one's wife's or husband's sister. **sisterly** ('sıstəlı) *adj* like or to do with a sister.

sit (sıt) *vi* **1** (often followed by **down**) (lower the body so as to) rest one's bottom on a chair, the ground, etc. **2** (of a bird) settle or rest on a branch or nest. **3** (of clothes) fit: *The jacket sits badly on your shoulders.* *vt* **4** put in a sitting position: *She sat the baby on her knee.* **5** do (an examination). **sit down** have a seat. **sit for 1** hold the body in a particular position while (an artist) paints (a picture) of one. **2** be a member of a parliament for (a town or district). **sit-in** ('sıtın) *nc* an action by workers, students, etc., who occupy a building to protest against something. **sitter** *nc* a person having his picture painted. **sitting-room** ('sıtıŋrʊm) *nc* a room for entertaining and general use. **sit up 1** get up from lying down. **2** delay going to bed at night. **3** sit with a straight back.

site (saıt) *nc* **1** a piece of land on which a building, town, etc., stood, is standing, or is about to be built. **2** a place where something happened, is happening, or will happen: *the site of a battle.*

situated ('sıtjʊeıtıd) *adj* **1** placed: *Our house is situated on top of a hill.* **2** (of a person) in a particular situation: *He's been badly situated since he lost his job.* **situation** (,sıtjʊ'eıʃən) *nc* **1** the position or place where a town, building, etc., is. **2** the state a person or thing is in: *a difficult situation.* **3** a position or job.

six (sıks) *determiner, n* the number 6. **sixth** (sıksθ) *determiner, n, adv* **sixteen** (,sıks-'ti:n) *determiner, n* 16. **sixteenth** (sıks'ti:nθ) *determiner, n, adv* **sixty** ('sıkstı) *determiner, n* 60. **sixtieth** ('sıkstııθ) *determiner, n, adv*

size (saız) **1** *nu* the bigness or amount of something. **2** *nc* one of the fixed measures of the size of something: *These shoes come in several sizes.* **size up** form an opinion of, esp. quickly. **sizable** ('saızəbəl) *adj* quite large.

sizzle ('sızəl) *infml vi* make a sound like that of water falling on a hot surface or of something cooking in hot fat. ● *nu* this sound.

skate (skeıt) *nc* one of two steel blades fastened to boots and used for sliding over ice. ● *vi* slide over on skates. **skating** *nu* also **ice skating** See under **ice**.

skeleton ('skelıtən) *nc* **1** the complete bones of a human or animal. **2** the framework or most important part of a building, idea, plan, etc.

skeptic ('skeptɪk) *US n, adj* See **sceptic.**

sketch (sketʃ) *nc* **1** a rough drawing with few details. **2** a short account or description ●*vt* give or draw a sketch of.

skew (skju:) *adj* not straight or in the usual position.

ski (ski:) *nc* one of two long, flat pieces of wood, plastic, metal, etc., fastened to boots and worn for sliding over snow. ● *vi* slide over the snow wearing skis. **skier** *nc*

skid (skɪd) *vi* **1** (of a wheel of a car, etc.) slide without turning. **2** (of a car, etc.) slide out of control. ●*nc* an instance of skidding.

skies (skaɪz) plural of **sky.**

skiff (skɪf) *nc* a small rowing boat.

skill (skɪl) *nc* **1** an ability to do something well. **2** an activity needing skill. **skilful** *US* **skillful** ('skɪlfʊl) or **skilled** *adj* having or needing skill. **skilfully** *adv*

skim (skɪm) *vt* **1** take floating matter from the top of (a liquid), esp. cream from (milk). **2** move smoothly over (a surface) without touching it. **3** *vti* (when *vi*, usually followed by **through**) read quickly and not completely: *He skimmed the pages of the newspaper.*

skin (skɪn) **1** *nu* the outer covering of a human or animal body. *nc* **2** an animal skin made into leather, esp. with the fur or wool on. **3** the outer covering of a fruit. **4** a layer that forms on top of boiled milk. ● *vt* **1** take the skin off. **2** *vi* lose skin. **3** *vt infml* cheat (someone), esp. of his money. **by the skin of one's teeth** *infml* only just: *I caught the train by the skin of my teeth.* **skinny** *adj* **-ier, -iest** **1** (of a person) very thin. **2** not wanting to give or spend.

skip (skɪp) *vi* **1** jump about lightly. **2** jump over a piece of rope which is swung under the feet and over the head. **3** *vt* miss out (a meal, part of a book, etc.). ●*nc* a skipping movement.

skipper ('skɪpə*) *infml nc* **1** the person in charge of a ship; captain. **2** the leader of a sports team; captain. ● *vt infml* be captain of.

skirmish ('skɜ:mɪʃ) *nc* **1** a small, short, esp. unexpected, fight. **2** an argument that is soon over. ● *vi* take part in a skirmish.

skirt (skɜ:t) *nc* **1** a one-piece women's garment hanging from the waist. **2** the part of a dress or long coat below the waist. ● *vt* be on or go round the edge of: *The woods skirt the town.* **skirting-board** ('skɜ:tɪŋbɔːd) *US* **baseboard** *nc* a wooden board fixed to the bottom of a wall inside a building.

skit (skɪt) *nc* an amusing piece of writing that shows the faults or foolishness of a person, society, etc.

skulk (skʌlk) *vi* move secretly or hide, esp. because of cowardice or in order to do wrong, avoid work, etc.

skull (skʌl) *nc* the bony case around the brain.

skunk (skʌŋk) *nc* a small, black and white, furry, bushy-tailed American animal that gives off a nasty smell when in danger.

sky (skaɪ) *nc, pl* **-ies** the space above the earth that contains clouds and the sun, moon, and stars. **skylark** ('skaɪlɑ:k) *nc* a small bird that sings as it flies high. **skyline** ('skaɪlaɪn) *nc* the shape of buildings, hills, etc., seen against the sky. **skyscraper** ('skaɪˌskreɪpə*) *nc* a very tall building.

slab (slæb) *nc* a flat, broad, esp. square-cornered, piece of stone, cake, wood, etc.

slack (slæk) *adj* **-er, -est** **1** loose; not tight. **2** lazy or careless. **3** (of trade or business) not active. ●*vi* work without care or effort: *Stop slacking!*

slacken ('slækən) *vti* (often followed by **off**) make or become slower, looser, less active, etc.: *Slacken your belt; Business is slackening off.*

slacks (slæks) *n pl infml* trousers.

slag (slæg) *nu* **1** waste matter left when metal has been obtained from rock. **2** waste matter left when coal has been dug out of the ground.

slain (sleɪn) past participle of **slay.**

slake (sleɪk) *vt* satisfy or lessen (one's thirst, revenge, etc.).

slam (slæm) *vti* **1** (cause to) shut hard and loudly: *He slammed the door angrily.* **2** force, be forced, throw, or be thrown hard against something: *The car slammed into the wall.* ●*nc* the noise of something slamming or being slammed.

slander ('slɑːndə*) *ncu* something untrue said in order to harm someone's reputation. ● *vt* speak slander about (someone).

slang (slæŋ) *nu* words, meanings, etc., in common use but not thought suitable for formal or good writing. ● *vt* use rude or bad language to (someone).

slant (slɑːnt) *vti, nc* ((cause to) have) a lean or slope: *Your writing slants.*

slap (slæp) *vt* **1** hit with the open hand or something flat. **2** bring (the open hand or something flat) down hard onto something: *He slapped the money down on the table.* ●*nc* the noise or act of slapping.

slash (slæʃ) *vt* **1** make long cuts in. **2** greatly lower (a price). ●*nc* a long cut.

slat (slæt) *nc* one of a number of long, thin strips of wood or plastic set in a door or window to allow the movement of air in between them.

slate (sleɪt) **1** *nu* a blue-grey stone that breaks easily into thin sheets. *nc* **2** a sheet of slate used in a roof. **3** a sheet of slate framed in wood, once used for writing on. ●*vt* **1** cover (a roof) with slates. **2** *infml* find much fault with.

slaughter ('slɔːtə*) *nu* **1** the killing of animals for food. **2** the killing of people in large numbers. ●*vt* **1** kill (an animal) for food. **2** kill (people) in large numbers. **slaughter-house** ('slɔːtəhaʊs) *nc* also **abattoir** a place where animals are killed for food.

slave (sleɪv) *nc* **1** a person who is owned by another and has no freedom. **2** a person under the control of another or some other influence: *a slave to fashion.* ●*vi* work very hard. **slavery** ('sleɪvərɪ) *nu* **1** being a slave. **2** *infml* very hard, unpleasant work.

slay (sleɪ) *often literary or humorous vt* kill; murder.

sledge (sledʒ) *nc* also **sled** a vehicle with two long strips of wood or metal underneath, used for travelling over snow. ●*vti* go or take in a sledge.

sledgehammer ('sledʒ,hæmə*) *nc* a large, heavy hammer with a long handle: see picture.

sledgehammer

sleek (sliːk) *adj* **-er, -est 1** (of hair, fur, etc.) smooth and shiny; well-brushed. **2** too eager to please: *sleek manners.*

sleep (sliːp) **1** *nu* a state of complete rest of the body and mind, as in bed every night. **2** *nc* a period of sleep: *Get a good night's sleep.* ●*vi* **1** be in a state of sleep. **2** *vt* have beds, etc., for: *Our room sleeps three.* **go to sleep** go into a state of sleep. **sleeper** *nc* **1** a person who sleeps. **2** *chiefly Brit* a heavy piece of wood that supports the rails on a railway track. **3** (a part of) a train with beds in. **4** a bed on a train. **sleepily** *adv* **sleepiness** *nu* **sleeping-car** ('sliːpɪŋkɑː*) *nc* a part of a train with beds in it. **sleepy** *adj* **-ier, -iest 1** feeling tired. **2** with little activity: *a sleepy town.*

sleet (sliːt) *nu* partly frozen rain.

sleeve (sliːv) *nc* **1** a part of a garment that covers the arm or part of it. **2** a cover for a record.

sleigh (sleɪ) *nc* a sledge, esp. one pulled by a horse.

sleight (slaɪt) *n* **sleight of hand** cleverness in using the hands, esp. doing magic tricks.

slender ('slendə*) *adj* **-est 1** small in width; slim: *a girl with a slender waist.* **2** not enough; small in amount: *slender hopes.*

slept (slept) past tense and past participle of **sleep.**

slew (sluː) past tense of **slay.**

slice (slaɪs) *nc* **1** a thin, flat piece cut off bread, meat, etc. **2** a piece or share: *a slice of the profits.* ●*vt* cut into slices.

slick (slɪk) *adj* **-er, -est** acting or done in a quick, smooth, but perhaps insincere, way. ●*nc* a layer of oil on the ground or the sea.

slid (slɪd) past tense and past participle of **slide.**

slide (slaɪd) **1** *vti* (cause to) move smoothly along: *Don't slide on the ice.* **2** *vi* go from one state, thing, etc., to another without really noticing: *to slide into bad habits.* ●*nc* **1** an instance of sliding. **2** a slope built for esp. children to slide down. **3** See **transparency** (def. 1). **slide-rule** ('slaɪdruːl) *nc* a long, straight device with a central part that slides, used for working out problems with numbers: see picture.

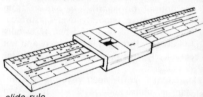

slide-rule

slight (slaɪt) *adj* **-er, -est 1** looking as if not strongly made; slender: *a slight figure.* **2** not serious; small: *She had a slight cold.* ●*vt* be rude to, esp. by avoiding. **slightly** *adv*

slim (slɪm) *adj* **-mer, -mest 1** narrow; quite thin. **2** small: *a slim hope.* ●*vti* make or become slim, esp. by eating less.

slime (slaɪm) *nu* soft mud or other slippery, wet matter. **slimy** *adj* **-ier, -iest** like or covered with slime.

sling (slɪŋ) *vt* **1** throw with force. **2** support with a **sling** (def. 1). ●*nc* **1** a belt, strip of material, etc., put under and round something to support it: *She had her broken arm in a sling.* **2** a strip of leather held in a loop for throwing stones with.

slink (slɪŋk) *vi* move in a quiet, secret way from guilt or shame.

slip (slɪp) *vi* **1** (nearly) fall over. **2** go quietly without being noticed: *Let's slip away.* **3** escape, fall, etc., because not easy to hold: *The soap slipped out of my hand.* **4** make a mistake through being careless. *vt* **5** put quickly: *He slipped the money into his pocket.* **6** escape from: *I forgot to go—it slipped my mind.* ●*nc* **1** an instance of slipping. **2** a mistake caused by being careless. **3** a small piece of paper. **4** a woman's garment like a sleeveless dress, worn under a dress. **let slip 1** miss (a chance). **2** make known (a secret, etc.) by mistake. **slip on** pull on (a garment, etc.) with a quick, sliding movement. **slip up** *infml* make a mistake.

slipper ('slɪpə*) *nc* a soft, loose shoe worn in the house.

slippery ('slɪpərɪ) *adj* **1** smooth, wet, etc.; easy to slip on: *slippery roads*. **2** (of a person) not to be trusted.

slipshod ('slɪpʃɒd) *adj* **1** (of a person) untidy. **2** (of work) careless.

slit (slɪt) *nc* a long, narrow opening or cut. ● *vt* make a slit in: *to slit open an envelope*.

slither ('slɪðə*) *vi* slide in a slippery way.

sliver ('slɪvə*) *nc* a long, thin piece, esp. of wood. ● *vti* break or be broken into slivers.

slog (slɒg) **1** *vt* hit (a ball, etc.) hard, esp. without control. **2** *infml vi* work hard and long: *He's always slogging away*. ● *nc* a period of hard work: *It was a real slog*.

slogan ('sləʊgən) *nc* an easily remembered expression advertising something or used by a group, party, etc., to state its purpose.

sloop (slu:p) *nc* a sailing boat with one mast.

slop (slɒp) **1** *vi* (of a liquid) fall over the side of a container. **2** *vt* cause (a liquid) to slop. ● *nc* a quantity of slopped liquid. **slops** kitchen waste, esp. fed to pigs.

slope (sləʊp) *nc* **1** a position that is between being flat and being upright. **2** a place on a slope: *mountain slopes*. ● *vti* (cause to) have a slope.

sloppy ('slɒpɪ) *adj* **-ier, -iest 1** wet with dirty pools of rain or water. **2** *infml* acting or done without care or thought: *a sloppy piece of work*. **3** *infml* foolish; without deep feeling: *sloppy talk*.

slosh (slɒʃ) **1** *vi* (of a liquid) be poured or thrown. *vt* **2** pour or throw (a liquid). **3** *Brit, slang* hit. **sloshed** *chiefly Brit, slang adj* drunk.

slot (slɒt) *nc* a narrow opening into which something is dropped, fitted, or put. ● *vt* **1** make a slot in. **2** put into a slot. **slot-machine** ('slɒtmə,ʃi:n) *nc* a machine that provides something, such as cigarettes, tickets, etc., when a coin is put into it: see picture.

slot-machine

sloth (sləʊθ) **1** *nu* laziness. **2** *nc* a furry South American animal that moves very slowly and hangs from the branches of trees. **slothful** ('sləʊθfʊl) *adj* lazy.

slouch (slaʊtʃ) *vi* move, stand, or sit in a lazy, awkward way. ● *nc* a slouching way of moving.

slovenly ('slʌvənlɪ) *adj* (of a person, his work, etc.) very untidy, dirty, or careless.

slow (sləʊ) *adj* **-er, -est 1** not quick in movement. **2** not quick to understand. **3** rather boring: *What a slow game!* **4** (of a watch or clock) behind the right time: *My watch is ten minutes slow*. ● *adv* slowly. ● *vti* (often followed by **down** or **up**) make or become slower. **slowly** *adv* **slowness** *nu* **slow motion** action that is slower than normal, as in a slowed-down film.

slug (slʌg) *nc* a small, soft animal that moves slowly and is like a snail without a shell.

sluggish ('slʌgɪʃ) *adj* slow in movement; lazy: *a sluggish stream; a sluggish person*.

sluice (slu:s) *nc* a way for a flood of water to flow, controlled by a gate: see picture. ● *vt* **1** send or pour water over. **2** wash out or wash away with water. **3** *vi* (of water) rush.

sluice

slum (slʌm) *nc* (usually *pl*) an area of a city in which the houses are in a very bad condition and, usually, in which too many people live.

slumber ('slʌmbə*) *esp. poetry vi, nc* sleep.

slump (slʌmp) *vi* **1** fall or drop down heavily: *He slumped into a chair*. **2** (of prices, business activity, etc.) drop suddenly. ● *nc* a drop in prices, business, trade activity, etc.

slung (slʌŋ) past tense and past participle of **sling**.

slunk (slʌŋk) past tense and past participle of **slink**.

slur (slɜ:*) *vt* run (words) into one another in a careless way so that one's speech is unclear. ● *nc* something said or done that harms someone's reputation.

slush (slʌʃ) *nu* any watery substance, such as melting snow.

slut (slʌt) *nc* a dirty, untidy woman.

sly (slaɪ) *adj* **-er, -est; slier, sliest** deceiving in a clever way. **slyly** *adv* **slyness** *nu*

smack[1] (smæk) *nc* **1** a blow given by the front of the hand. **2** the sound made in doing this. ●*vt* hit with the front of the hand.

smack[2] *nu* something that can only just be tasted, felt, etc.: *The food had a smack of spice in it.* ●*vi* (followed by **of**) taste or show the presence or influence: *This whole business smacks of dishonesty.*

small (smɔːl) *adj* **-er, -est 1** not large; little. **2** not important: *a small problem.* **small arms** weapons that are small and light enough to be carried by one man. **smallholding** ('smɔːl,həʊldɪŋ) *Brit nc* a small piece of land used as a farm. **small-scale** ('smɔːlskeɪl) *adj* (of a model or map) made in a size that is small when compared to the real size. **small talk** talk about unimportant things.

smallpox ('smɔːlpɒks) *nu* a disease that spreads to other people, causing fever and nasty spots that damage the skin.

smart (smɑːt) *adj* **-er, -est 1** neat; tidy; well-kept. **2** clever; sharp: *a smart answer.* **3** quick; lively: *a smart walk.* ●*vti* feel or cause a sharp, lasting pain in the body or the mind: *She smarted with anger; My finger is smarting where I burnt it.* ●*nu* a smarting pain. **smartly** *adv* **smartness** *nu*

smash (smæʃ) *vti* **1** break or be broken violently into pieces. **2** (cause to) crash: *The car smashed into the back of a lorry.* ●*nc* an instance of smashing.

smear (smɪə*) *vt* **1** spread (something dirty, sticky, etc.) over (something): *His face was smeared with oil.* **2** spoil the reputation of. ●*nc* **1** something smeared on something else. **2** words that **smear** (def. 2) a person.

smell (smel) **1** *nu* noticing by means of the nose. **2** *nc* something noticed by the nose, pleasant or unpleasant: *the smell of cooking.* ●*vt* **1** notice a smell of (something). **2** *vi* give out a smell: *The flowers smell lovely.* **smelly** *adj* **-ier, -iest** with an unpleasant smell.

smelt[1] (smelt) *vt* get (metal) out of (rock) by melting the metal.

smelt[2] past tense and past participle of **smell**.

smile (smaɪl) **1** *vi* turn up the ends of the mouth to show one is pleased, happy, amused, etc. **2** *vt* show (one's feelings) by smiling: *She smiled a welcome.* ●*nc* the act of smiling.

smirk (smɜːk) *vi* smile because one is satisfied with oneself. ●*nc* a smile of this kind.

smite (smaɪt) *chiefly archaic vt* **1** strike; hit. **2** have an effect on: *He was smitten with a pretty girl.* **3** *vi* come with force: *The sun smote down without mercy.*

smith (smɪθ) *nc* a person who makes things from metal, esp. iron. **smithy** ('smɪðɪ) *nc, pl* **-thies** the place of work of a smith who uses iron.

smitten ('smɪtən) past participle of **smite**.

smock (smɒk) *nc* a loose-fitting outer garment.

smog (smɒg) *nu* very thick mist mixed with smoke.

smoke (sməʊk) **1** *nu* cloud-like matter produced by something burning. **2** *nc* the act of smoking a cigarette, pipe, etc. ●*vi* **1** give out smoke or something like it. *vt* **2** breathe in and breathe out the smoke from (a cigarette, etc.). **3** dry and keep (meat, fish, etc.) good with smoke. **smokeless** *adj* (of coal, etc.) that produces no smoke. **smoker** *nc* **1** a person who smokes cigarettes, etc. **2** a part of a train where smoking is allowed. **smokestack** ('sməʊkstæk) *nc* a tall chimney. **smoky** ('sməʊkɪ) *adj* **-ier, -iest.**

smooth (smuːð) *adj* **-er, -est 1** with a surface that is even and not rough: *a smooth skin.* **2** (of movement) without being shaken about: *a smooth journey by sea.* **3** (of a person, his manner, etc.) calm and polite but not always sincere. ●*vti* make or become smooth. **smoothly** *adv* **smoothness** *nu*

smote (sməʊt) past tense of **smite**.

smother ('smʌðə*) *vt* **1** kill by keeping the air from or by covering the nose and mouth to prevent breathing. **2** put out (a fire) by covering it. **3** cover: *She smothered him with kindness.*

smoulder ('sməʊldə*) *vi* **1** burn with smoke but without flames. **2** (of feelings) exist without being known or seen: *smouldering hatred.*

smudge (smʌdʒ) *nc* a dirty mark, esp. one made by rubbing: *an ink smudge.* ●*vt* make a smudge on or with.

smug (smʌg) *adj* **-ger, -gest** over-satisfied with oneself.

smuggle ('smʌgəl) *vt* take secretly and unlawfully in or out of a country. **smuggler** *nc*

snack (snæk) *nc* a small meal, esp. one eaten in a hurry. **snack bar** a place where such a meal is bought and eaten.

snag (snæg) *nc* **1** an unexpected difficulty. **2** something rough or sharp, like a broken tooth or a piece of rock, on which something may become caught or torn. ●*vt* cause to become caught or torn on a snag.

snail (sneɪl) *nc* a small, soft shell-fish.

snake (sneɪk) *nc* any of several kinds of long, thin animal without legs, some of which have a poisonous bite: see picture at **reptiles**.

snap (snæp) *vti* **1** break or be broken sharply, esp. with a noise. **2** (cause to) shut

with a sharp noise: *I snapped the box shut.*
3 *vi* try to seize something with the teeth:
The dog snapped at his leg. **4** *infml vt* take a
photograph of. ● *nc* **1** the act or sound of
snapping. **2** *infml* a photograph. **snappy**
infml adj **-ier, -iest** quick; lively. **snapshot**
('snæpʃɒt) *nc* a photograph taken quickly.
snap up buy or take quickly and eagerly.

snare (sneə*) *nc* **1** a trap for catching birds
or small animals. **2** something that tempts
and often leads to failure, loss, etc. ● *vt*
catch in a snare.

snarl (snɑːl) **1** *vi* (of an animal such as a dog)
show the teeth and make an angry noise. **2**
vti (of a person) say (something) angrily. ● *nc* the act or sound of snarling.

snatch (snætʃ) *vt* take eagerly and suddenly. ● *nc* **1** the act of snatching. **2** a short
period of something: *I heard snatches of
their conversation.*

sneak (sniːk) *vi* **1** move in a quiet and secret
manner. **2** *schoolchildren slang, Brit* tell the
teacher what someone else has done
wrong. ● *nc schoolchildren slang, Brit* a
child who sneaks. **sneaking** *adj* **1** secret: *I
have a sneaking hate of this music.* **2** slight
but lasting: *a sneaking suspicion.*

sneakers ('sniːkəz) *chiefly US n pl* also **pair
of sneakers** cloth shoes with soft rubber
underneath.

sneer (snɪə*) *vi* show one's disrespect by
words or an unpleasant smile. ● *nc* sneering words or a sneering smile.

sneeze (sniːz) *nc* a sudden pushing out of air
through the nose and mouth making a
short noise. ● *vi* give a sneeze.

sniff (snɪf) **1** *vi* draw air in loudly through the
nose, esp. to stop it running, or to show disrespect. **2** *vt* smell: *The dog sniffed the ball.*
● *nc* the act of sniffing.

sniffle ('snɪfəl) *vi* make sniffing sounds. ●
nc a sniffing sound.

snigger ('snɪgə*) *vi* laugh in a quiet and secret way, esp. at something that is not
proper, or to show disrespect. ● *nc* such a
laugh.

snip (snɪp) *vt* cut with short, quick cuts.
● *nc* a short, quick cut.

snipe (snaɪp) *vti* shoot (at) from a place
where one is hidden. **sniper** *nc*

snob (snɒb) *nc* **1** a person with too much respect for wealth, fashionable people and
behaviour, etc. **2** a person who thinks he is
better than other people. **snobbish**
('snɒbɪʃ) *adj*

snooker ('snuːkə*) *nu* a game played with
long sticks, fifteen red balls, six balls of
other colours, and one white ball on a table
with cushions and holes round the edge.

snoop (snuːp) *vi* look secretly into other people's affairs.

snooze (snuːz) *vi, nc* (have) a short sleep,
esp. in the daytime.

snore (snɔː*) *vi* breathe in a noisy way while
asleep. ● *nc* the act of snoring.

snorkel ('snɔːkəl) *nc* a device for supplying a
submarine or diver with air from above the
water.

snort (snɔːt) *vi* force air out through the nose
with a small noise, showing anger, refusal
to believe something, etc. ● *nc* an instance
of snorting.

snout (snaʊt) *nc* the pointed nose of an animal such as a pig.

snow (snəʊ) **1** *nu* frozen water falling from
the sky in small, white, delicate pieces. **2** *nc*
a fall of snow. ● *vi* (of snow) fall from the
sky: *It's snowing heavily.* **snowball**
('snəʊbɔːl) *nc* an amount of snow pressed
into a hard ball for throwing in a game.
snowdrift ('snəʊdrɪft) *nc* a large amount of
snow piled up by the wind. **snowflake**
('snəʊfleɪk) *nc* a single piece of snow.
snowman ('snəʊmæn) *nc, pl* **-men** a figure
of a man made of snow by children. **snow-
plough** ('snəʊplaʊ) *nc* a device for clearing
roads or railways of snow. **snowshoe**
('snəʊʃuː) *nc* one of a pair of devices
strapped to the foot for walking on snow
without sinking in. **snowstorm**
('snəʊstɔːm) *nc* a heavy fall of snow,
usually with wind. **snowy** *adj* **-ier, -iest** **1**
covered with snow. **2** pure white.

snub (snʌb) *vt* insult (someone) on purpose.
● *nc* an instance of snubbing. ● *adj* (of a
nose) turned up at the end.

snuff[1] (snʌf) *nu* powdered tobacco breathed
up the nose: *Do you take snuff?*

snuff[2] *vt* (often followed by **out**) **1** put out (a
flame, candle, etc.). **2** put an end to: *His
hopes were snuffed out.*

snug (snʌg) *adj* **-ger, -gest** **1** warm and
comfortable: *snug in bed.* **2** (of clothes) fitting closely and neatly. **snugly** *adv*

snuggle ('snʌgəl) *vi* lie or move close to
someone or something for warmth and
comfort: *The boy snuggled up to his mother.*

so (səʊ) *adv* **1** to such an amount, point, extent, etc.: *He felt so ill that he stayed in bed.*
2 in this or that way: *Do it so.* **3** also: *I
passed and so did you.* **4** very: *You're so
kind!* ● *conj* **1** therefore: *He wanted a
newspaper, so he went to the shop.* **2** (used to
express surprise, horror, pain, etc.): *So
you're not coming after all!* **and so on** and
other things of the same kind. **or so** See
under **or**. **so as to** See under **as**. **so far as**
See under **far**. **so long as** See under **long**[1].
so-called ('səʊkɔːld) *adj* so named but perhaps wrongly: *I don't like this so-called improvement.* **so that 1** in order that. **2** with
the result that.

soak (səʊk) *vt* **1** make very wet. **2** (usually followed by **up**) draw in (a liquid). **3** *vi* (usually followed by **in** or **into**) (of a liquid) be drawn in by a solid: *The wine soaked into the carpet.* ● *nc* an instance of being soaked: *Give the dirty clothes a good long soak.*

soap (səʊp) *nu* a substance made from fat or oil, used with water for washing. ● *vt* put soap on. **soapy** *adj* **-ier, -iest.**

soar (sɔː*) *vi* **1** fly high in the air. **2** rise: *Prices have soared.*

sob (sɒb) *vi* take quick, sharp breaths, esp. when crying. ● *nc* an instance of sobbing.

sober ('səʊbə*) *adj* **1** not drunk. **2** reasonable; serious. **3** (of a colour) plain; dull. ● *vti* (usually followed by **up**) make or become sober. **sobriety** (sə'braɪɪtɪ) *nu*

soccer ('sɒkə*) *n* See **association football** under **associate.**

sociable ('səʊʃəbəl) *adj* liking the company of other people; friendly.

social ('səʊʃəl) *adj* **1** living in groups, not apart. **2** to do with human society. ● *nc* an informal gathering of people in a club, etc. **social security** money given by the government to poor people. **social services** services provided by the government, such as education, health, and housing. **social worker** a person employed by a government to help the poor, the old, people with social problems, etc. **socially** *adv*

socialism ('səʊʃəlɪzəm) *nu* the belief that a government should produce, own, and control the wealth that comes from its industries, land, transport, etc., and that this wealth should be fairly divided. **socialist** *adj* to do with socialism. ● *nc* a person who believes in and supports the doctrine of socialism.

society (sə'saɪətɪ) **1** *nu* the way of life, customs, etc., of a group of people living in one place, district, or country. *nc, pl* **-ties 2** such a group of people. **3** a group of people coming together with the same purpose or interest; club. *nu* **4** being together with other people, esp. one's friends: *I always enjoy her society.* **5** fashionable and wealthy people.

sociology (,səʊsɪ'ɒlədʒɪ) *nu* the study of human societies. **sociological** (,səʊsɪə-'lɒdʒɪkəl) *adj*

sock (sɒk) *nc* a covering, esp. of wool or cotton, for the foot and part of the leg.

socket ('sɒkɪt) *nc* a hollow place for something to turn round in or fit into: *an eye socket; an electric light bulb socket.*

sod (sɒd) *nc* a piece of earth with grass and its roots growing in it.

soda ('səʊdə) *nu* a white substance used in making soap, glass, etc. **soda siphon** a glass or metal container for making and keeping soda water in, and from which soda water is forced out by the gas inside when the handle is pressed: see picture. **soda water** water filled with gas to make it bubble, drunk esp. mixed with an alcoholic drink, etc.

soda siphon

sodden ('sɒdən) *adj* made completely wet.

sodium ('səʊdɪəm) *nu* a chemical element; silver-white metal found in soda, salt, etc.: symbol Na

sofa ('səʊfə) *nc* a comfortable seat, with a back and arms, for two or more people.

soft (sɒft) *adj* **-er, -est 1** not hard; easily pressed into a different shape: *a soft bed.* **2** not rough to touch; smooth: *soft hair; soft fur.* **3** gentle; having sympathy for others: *soft words; a soft heart.* **4** *infml* foolish: *He's gone soft over his new girlfriend.* **5** not loud: *soft music.* **6** (of water) good for washing and cooking because it does not contain substances out of the ground: *nice, soft rainwater.* **7** (of light and colours) not too bright. **soft drink** a sweet drink without alcohol. **soften** ('sɒfən) *vti* make or become soft. **softly** *adv* **softness** *nu* **software** ('sɒftweə*) *nu* computer programs.

soggy ('sɒgɪ) *adj* **-ier, -iest** soft because very wet.

soil (sɔɪl) *ncu* (a type of) the top part of earth in which plants grow. ● *vti* make or become dirty.

sojourn ('sɒdʒɜːn) *literary vi, nc* (a) stay in a place.

solace ('sɒlɪs) **1** *nu* comfort when one is in trouble. **2** *nc* something that gives solace. ● *vt* give solace to.

solar ('səʊlə*) *adj* to do with the sun. **solar system** the sun and the planets, such as earth, that move round it.

sold (səʊld) past tense and past participle of **sell.**

solder ('səʊldə*) *nu* a mixture of metals that is easily melted, used to join other metals together. ● *vt* join with solder. **soldering iron** *nc* a heated tool used to join such metals.

soldier ('səʊldʒə*) *nc* a person in an army.

sole¹ (səʊl) *nc* the underneath part of a foot, shoe, sock, etc. ● *vt* put a sole on a shoe, boot, etc.

sole² *adj* one and only. **solely** ('səʊllɪ) *ad* alone; only.

sole³ *nc* a flat sea-fish used for food.

solemn ('sɒləm) *adj* **1** done with seriousness and respect. **2** very serious; (pretending to be) very important. **solemnity** (sə'lemnɪtɪ) **1** *nu* being solemn. **2** *nc, pl* **-ties** a solemn event or practice. **solemnly** *adv*

solicit (sə'lɪsɪt) **1** *vt* invite; ask (someone) for (something): *I shall solicit his help.* **2** *vi* (followed by **for**) ask.

solicitor (sə'lɪsɪtə*) *nc* **1** *Brit* a lawyer who gives advice on the law and prepares cases for barristers. **2** *US* a person who goes about asking for votes, orders for goods, etc.

solid ('sɒlɪd) *adj* **1** not a liquid or gas. **2** firm; strong: *solid rock.* **3** not hollow. **4** that can be depended on: *a man of solid character.* **5** going on without a break: *He slept for eight solid hours.* ●*nc* a solid substance or object. **solidity** *nu*

solidarity (,sɒlɪ'dærɪtɪ) *nu* being united by the same interests or purpose.

solidify (sə'lɪdɪfaɪ) *vti* make or become solid.

solitary ('sɒlɪtrɪ) *adj* **1** living or being on one's own. **2** lonely. **3** only one.

solitude ('sɒlɪtjuːd) *nu* being on one's own.

solo ('səʊləʊ) *nc* **1** *pl* **solos, soli** ('səʊlɪ) a piece of music played, sung, or danced to by one person. **2** *pl* **-s** anything special done by one person. **soloist** ('səʊləʊɪst) *nc* a person who plays, sings, or dances a solo.

soluble ('sɒljʊbəl) *adj* able to be dissolved in a liquid. **solubility** (,sɒljʊ'bɪlɪtɪ) *nu*

solution (sə'luːʃən) *nc* **1** the explanation of a problem, puzzle, etc.; answer. *nu* **2** the finding of an answer, explanation, etc. **3** the change of a solid or gas into a liquid by adding it to a liquid. **4** *nc* a substance that results from this.

solve (sɒlv) *vt* find the answer to (a problem, puzzle, etc.).

solvent ('sɒlvənt) *adj* **1** having enough money to pay one's debts. **2** being a liquid in which something will dissolve. ●*nc* a **solvent** (def. 2).

sombre ('sɒmbə*) *adj* sad; miserable; dark in colour: *sombre clothes; a sombre winter's day.*

some (sʌm unstressed səm) *determiner, pron* **1** (an) unknown or unnamed: *Some kind person mended it for me; Some of you know what I mean.* **2** an unknown or unnamed number or amount (of): *I have bought some apples.* **3** a little: *Do make some effort!* ● *determiner* **1** a large number or amount: *some days ago; some distance away.* **2** about: *some ten people.*

somebody ('sʌmbədɪ) also **someone** *pron* some person. ●*nc, pl* **-dies** a person of importance: *You might have been somebody if you had worked harder.*

somehow ('sʌmhaʊ) *adv* by some means or another.

someplace ('sʌmpleɪs) *infml, US adv* somewhere.

somersault ('sʌməsɔːlt) *nc, vi* (make) a jump or fall, turning the body completely over before landing on one's feet again.

something ('sʌmθɪŋ) *pron* some thing: *Have you lost something?* **have something to do with** be connected with: *I don't know what his job is exactly, but it has something to do with teaching.* **something like 1** about: *It's something like five miles to the nearest town.* **2** rather like.

sometime ('sʌmtaɪm) *adv* at some time in the past or future: *I saw him sometime last year.*

sometimes ('sʌmtaɪmz) *adv* at some times; occasionally.

somewhat ('sʌmwɒt) *adv* rather: *His clothes are somewhat old.*

somewhere ('sʌmweə*) *adv* in, at, or to some place.

son (sʌn) *nc* someone's male child. **son-in-law** ('sʌnɪnlɔː) *nc, pl* **sons-in-law** the husband of someone's daughter.

sonata (sə'nɑːtə) *nc* a piece of music for one or two instruments, such as a piano and violin, divided into three or four parts.

song (sɒŋ) **1** *nc* a piece of music with words to be sung to it. **2** *nu* singing: *the song of a bird.*

sonic ('sɒnɪk) *adj* to do with sound: *a sonic boom.*

sonnet ('sɒnɪt) *nc* a poem with fourteen lines arranged in a certain pattern: *The poet wrote a sonnet.*

soon (suːn) *adv* **1** in a short time: *We'll be home soon.* **2** early: *Why did you come so soon?* **as soon as** at the moment that; not later than: *I'll come as soon as I can.* **no sooner... than** at the very moment that: *He had no sooner arrived at his destination than he left again.* **sooner or later** at some future time.

soot (sʊt) *nu* a black powder left by smoke. **sooty** *adj* **-ier, -iest 1** covered with soot. **2** as black as soot.

sooth (suːθ) *archaic n* **in sooth** truly.

soothe (suːð) *vt* **1** calm (a person who is troubled). **2** lessen (pain).

sophisticated (sə'fɪstɪkeɪtɪd) *adj* **1** with highly developed tastes and habits. **2** (of a machine, etc.) complicated; highly developed.

soprano (sə'prɑːnəʊ) **1** *nu* the highest female or boy's singing voice. **2** *nc, pl* **-s** a person with such a voice.

sorcerer ('sɔːsərə*) *nc* a man who can do magic tricks, helped by evil spirits. **sorcery** *nu* the practices of a sorcerer.

sordid ('sɔːdɪd) *adj* **1** dirty; without comfort: *a sordid district of the town.* **2** (of a person, behaviour, etc.) shameful; mean.

sore (sɔː*) *adj* **-r, -st 1** painful when touched; hurting: *a sore throat.* **2** feeling annoyance: *He's very sore about failing to get the job.* ●*nc* a tender, painful place on the body. **sorely** *adv* greatly.

sorghum ('sɔːgəm) *nu* a grass grown for its seeds, which are eaten, and for hay.

sorrow ('sɒrəʊ) **1** *nu* sadness; grief. **2** *nc* a cause of grief or sadness. **sorrowful** *adj* **sorrowfully** *adv*

sorry ('sɒrɪ) *adj* **-ier, -iest 1** feeling sad because of loss, for doing wrong, etc. **2** pitiful: *What a sorry mess he's in!* ●*interj* **1** (used to say no or to show disagreement or apology.) **2** *Brit* (used to ask someone to say something again.)

sort (sɔːt) *nc* a kind, type, or group of people or things that are alike in some way. ●*vt* arrange (people or things) into groups of the same type. **sort out 1** solve (a problem, etc.). **2** make (a mess, etc.) tidy. **3** separate (something) from a group.

soufflé ('suːfleɪ) *French nc* a baked dish made mainly of eggs, with the whites beaten stiff.

sought (sɔːt) past tense and past participle of **seek**.

soul (səʊl) *nc* **1** the spiritual part of a person that is believed to live for ever. **2** the true nature of a person: *He hated war with all his soul!* **3** a person: *I didn't see a soul.* **soulful** ('səʊlfʊl) *adj* having or seeming to have deep feelings: *soulful eyes.* **soulless** *adj* with no noble or deep feelings.

sound[1] (saʊnd) **1** *nc* something that can be heard; (a) noise: *the sound of voices.* **2** *nu* the effect made on the mind by something said or read: *I don't like the sound of it.* ●*vti* **1** (cause to) give out a noise: *It sounds as if it's raining.* **2** *vt* feel or examine by tapping and listening. **sound effects** sounds, other than those of speech and music, made for a film, play, etc. **sound-track** ('saʊndtræk) *nc* the track at the side of a cinema film on which sound is recorded. **sound-wave** ('saʊndweɪv) *nc* a wave-like movement in the air, etc., by which sound is carried.

sound[2] *adj* **-er, -est 1** healthy; not injured or rotten: *a sound body; sound fruit.* **2** showing or having good sense: *sound ideas.* **sound asleep** in a complete, deep sleep. **soundly** *adv* **soundness** *nu*

sound[3] *vt* measure the depth of (the sea, etc.). **sound out** try, in a careful way, to find out the ideas, feelings, etc., of (a person) about something. **sounding** *nc* a measurement of depth.

sound[4] *nc* a long, narrow strip of water that joins two larger bodies of water.

soup (suːp) *nu* a liquid food made by cooking meat, vegetables, etc., in water.

sour (saʊə*) *adj* **1** having a sharp taste: *a sour apple.* **2** (of milk, etc.) gone bad. **3** having a bad temper. ●*vti* make or become sour.

source (sɔːs) *nc* **1** the point from which a river starts. **2** the place from which something comes or is obtained.

south (saʊθ) *n* **the south** the direction that is on the right of a person facing the east. **the South 1** the southern part of a country, etc. **2** the poorer countries of the world. ●*adj* **1** in or towards the south. **2** (of the wind) coming from the south. ●*adv* towards the south. **south-east** (ˌsaʊθˈiːst) *n* the direction halfway between south and east. ●*adj* **1** in or towards the south-east. **2** (of the wind) coming from the south-east. ●*adv* towards the south-east. **southerly** ('sʌðəlɪ) *adj* in or from the south. **southern** ('sʌðən) *adj* in or to the south. **southernmost** ('sʌðənməʊst) *adj* (of a place) the furthest (towards the) south. **southward(s)** ('saʊθwəd(z)) *adj, adv* towards the south. **south-west** (ˌsaʊθˈwest) *n* the direction halfway between south and west. ●*adj* **1** in or towards the south-west. **2** (of the wind) coming from the south-west. ●*adv* towards the south-west.

souvenir (ˌsuːvəˈnɪə*) *nc* something kept, given, or bought to remind one of a person, place, or event.

sovereign ('sɒvrɪn) *nc* **1** a chief ruler, esp. a king, queen, or emperor. **2** (in the UK) a former gold coin worth £1. ●*adj* having the highest power: *a sovereign state.* **sovereignty** ('sɒvrəntɪ) *nu* complete or the highest power.

sow[1] (saʊ) *nc* a grown-up female pig.

sow[2] (səʊ) *vt* put (seeds) in the earth in order to grow plants, etc. **sower** *nc*

sown (səʊn) past participle of **sow**[2].

soya ('sɔɪə) *nu* a plant grown for its seeds. **soya bean** one of the these seeds, which are eaten or made into oil or flour.

space (speɪs) **1** *nu* that in which everything exists and through which everything moves, esp. the region beyond the earth. **2** *nc* the distance between objects. *nu* **3** a length of time: *in the space of two weeks.* **4** a place that has or might have nothing in it; room: *Is there enough space in your car for five people?* ●*vt* set out with regular spaces between. **spacecraft** ('speɪskrɑːft) or **spaceship** ('speɪsʃɪp) *nc* a vehicle for travelling in space. **space shuttle** a spacecraft that can be used more than once, as for journeys between earth and another planet.

spacious ('speɪʃəs) *adj* having plenty of room: *a spacious house.*

spade (speɪd) *nc* **1** a tool with a long handle and a broad metal blade, used for digging: see picture at **tools. 2** a playing-card with a black shape like a painted leaf on it.

spaghetti (spə'getɪ) *Italian nu* long, thin, strings made from flour, eggs, and water that are boiled and eaten.

spake (speɪk) *archaic* past tense of **speak.**

span[1] (spæn) *nc* **1** the distance between the end of the little finger and the end of the thumb when stretched out. **2** the distance between two supports, esp. of a bridge. **3** a distance in time, from the beginning to the end: *man's span of life.* ● *vt* **1** stretch from one side to another of: *Many bridges span the river.* **2** (of a life, memory, etc.) extend across. **3** measure with the hand stretched out.

span[2] past tense of **spin.**

spangle ('spæŋgəl) *nc* one of many tiny, round, shiny decorations sewn onto a dress, etc.

spaniel ('spænjəl) *nc* a kind of dog with short legs, long hair, and long ears.

spank (spæŋk) *vt* punish (esp. a child) by hitting on the bottom with the front of the hand. ● *nc* a slap on the bottom. **spanking** *adj* **1** good; splendid: *We had a spanking time!* **2** quick.

spanner ('spænə*) *Brit nc* a tool used for turning nuts on screws, etc.: see picture at **tools.**

spar[1] (spɑ:*) *nc* a strong pole used on a ship for supporting a sail or for keeping it stretched out.

spar[2] *vi* make movements with the hands as if boxing.

spare (speə*) *adj* **1** extra; not in use but there if needed: *a spare wheel for a car.* **2** not used for work: *spare time.* ● *vt* **1** hold oneself back from hurting, killing, etc.: *Spare my life; Spare his feelings.* **2** do without: *I can't spare him.* **3** protect from; not cause to suffer: *I'll spare you the trouble.* **spare part** a part of a machine used to replace one that is damaged or worn out. **sparing** *adj* careful in the spending of money, time, etc. **sparingly** *adv*

spark (spɑ:k) *nc* **1** a tiny piece thrown off from something burning or produced when metal is struck on stone. **2** a flash of bright light produced when electricity jumps through air. **3** a small sign that something exists: *a spark of life; He hasn't a spark of wit in him.* ● *vi* give off sparks of fire or electricity. **sparking-plug** ('spɑ:kɪŋplʌg) *nc* a device in a petrol engine that makes a **spark** (def. 2), which causes the petrol to explode.

sparkle ('spɑ:kəl) *vi* give out flashes of light; shine: *Her eyes sparkled with happiness.* ● *nc* a flash of light. **sparkling** *adj* **1** (of wine) giving off bubbles of gas. **2** brilliant; very good: *a sparkling performance.*

sparrow ('spærəʊ) *nc* a small brown or grey bird found in many parts of the world: see picture at **birds.**

sparse (spɑ:s) *adj* **-r, -st** not many or much: *a sparse population; a sparse meal.* **sparsely** *adv*

spasm ('spæzəm) *nc* **1** a sudden tightening of the muscles. **2** a sudden burst of pain, excitement, etc. **spasmodic** (spæz'mɒdɪk) *adj* done or happening occasionally.

spat (spæt) past tense and past participle of **spit.**

spate (speɪt) *nc* **1** a flood in a river. **2** a sudden large amount: *a spate of words.*

spatial ('speɪʃəl) *adj* to do with space.

spatter ('spætə*) **1** *vt* throw drops of (water, mud, etc.) onto (something): *His coat was spattered with blood.* **2** *vti* (of water, mud, etc.) be thrown in drops (onto): *Rain spattered the window.* ● *nc* something spattered: *a spatter of rain.*

spatula ('spætjʊlə) *nc* a flat tool with a broad blade, used for mixing or spreading substances: see picture.

spatula

spawn (spɔ:n) *nu* the eggs of a fish or some other water animals. ● *vt* **1** produce (eggs). **2** produce; cause.

speak (spi:k) *vi* **1** use one's voice to talk, not sing: *Don't speak so fast!* **2** talk to a person: *I'll speak to him about the matter.* **3** make a speech. *vt* **4** be able to use a language that is not one's own: *He speaks several languages.* **5** make known; say: *He always speaks the truth.* **speak for** speak as a representative of. **speak up 1** speak louder. **2** give one's opinion. **speaker** *nc* **1** a person who makes a speech. **2** short for **loudspeaker.**

spear (spɪə*) *nc* a weapon made from a long stick with a metal point at the end.

special ('speʃəl) *adj* **1** of a particular sort: *There is a special tool for this job.* **2** particularly good: *Special qualities are needed for this important job.* **specially** *adv*

specialise ('speʃəlaɪz) **1** *vi* (often followed by **in**) give all one's attention, time, study, etc., to a particular subject. **2** *vt* make suitable for a special use. **specialisation** (,speʃəlaɪ'zeɪʃən) *ncu*

specialist ('speʃəlɪst) *nc* a person who specialises in a certain type of study, work, etc., esp. medicine: *a heart specialist.*

speciality (,speʃɪ'ælɪtɪ) *US* **specialty** ('speʃəltɪ) *nc, pl* **-ties** an interest, activity, etc., in which someone or something specialises.

species ('spiːʃiːz) *nc, pl* **species** a similar type of animal or plant: *The lion and tiger are different species of cat.*

specific (spɪ'sɪfɪk) *adj* **1** having to do with one particular thing, subject, etc.: *a disease specific to humans.* **2** exact; particular: *one specific thing.* **specifically** *adv*

specify ('spesɪfaɪ) *vt* give exact details of. **specification** (,spesɪfɪ'keɪʃən) **1** *nu* specifying. **2** *nc* details of something to be done.

specimen ('spesɪmɪn) *nc* a part of something, member of a group, etc., taken to represent the whole thing: *a blood specimen.*

specious ('spiːʃəs) *adj* seeming to be right or true but actually wrong or false: *a specious argument.*

speck (spek) *nc* a tiny spot, mark, piece of dirt, etc. **speckled** ('spekəld) *adj* covered with tiny marks or spots.

spectacle ('spektəkəl) *nc* **1** a special public event, procession, etc. **2** something seen, esp. something splendid. **spectacles** *n pl* also **pair of spectacles** a device containing two pieces of glass worn in front of the eyes to correct one's sight or protect the eyes; glasses.

spectacular (spek'tækjʊlə*) *adj* splendid; striking: *a spectacular view.*

spectator (spek'teɪtə*) *nc* a person who watches a game, public show, etc.

spectrum ('spektrəm) *nc, pl* **-tra** (trə) a set of bands of different-coloured light formed when white light is divided up.

speculate ('spekjʊleɪt) *vi* **1** form an opinion before knowing all the facts; guess. **2** take risks in business in the hope of making profits later. **speculation** (,spekjʊ'leɪʃən) *ncu* **speculator** *nc*

sped (sped) past tense and past participle of **speed.**

speech (spiːtʃ) **1** *nu* the power of speaking. **2** *nc* a talk given in public. **speechless** *adj* unable to speak because of some deep feeling such as anger, disappointment, etc.

speed (spiːd) **1** *nu* fast movement. **2** *nc* a distance travelled measured against the time taken: *The car was travelling at a speed of forty kilometres an hour.* ● *vti* (cause to)

go quickly. **speed up** (cause to) go or work faster: *The engine speeded up.* **speed-boat** ('spiːdbəʊt) *nc* a boat with an engine, built to go fast. **speedometer** (spiː'dɒmɪtə*) *nc* a device that shows how fast a vehicle is travelling. **speedy** *adj* **-ier, -iest** quick.

spell[1] (spel) *vt* **1** say or write letters to form (a word): *How do you spell 'politician'?* **2** (of letters) form (a word): *C-A-T spells cat.* **spell out 1** manage to read (words) letter by letter. **2** explain clearly. **spelling** *nc* the way a word is spelt.

spell[2] *nc* a set of words believed to have magic power. **spellbound** ('spelbaʊnd) *adj* with all the interest or attention held, as if by magic words.

spell[3] *nc* a period of time, esp. short.

spelt (spelt) past tense and past participle of **spell.**

spend (spend) *vt* **1** pay out (money). **2** pass (time): *Where did you spend your holiday?* **spendthrift** ('spendθrɪft) *nc* a person who is in the habit of wasting money.

spent (spent) past tense and past participle of **spend.**

sperm (spɜːm) *nu* the liquid of a male human or animal that causes a female to produce young.

spew (spjuː) *vt* **1** bring back (food, etc.) from the stomach and out through the mouth. **2** *vti* send or be sent out in a violent stream.

sphere (sfɪə*) *nc* **1** an object shaped like a ball: see picture at **shapes. 2** a star; planet. **3** the interests, activities, etc., of a person. **spherical** ('sferɪkəl) *adj* shaped like a ball.

sphinx (sfɪŋks) *nu* a stone figure with a woman's head, a lion's body, and wings: see picture.

sphinx

spice (spaɪs) **1** *nc* a sweet-smelling or sharp-tasting plant substance used in food to give it more taste. **2** *nu* something that adds excitement, interest, etc. ● *vt* add spice to. **spicy** *adj* **-ier, -iest 1** (of food) with spice added. **2** exciting.

spider ('spaɪdə*) *nc* a small animal with eight legs that makes a net in which to catch flying insects for food. **spidery** *adj* (esp. of handwriting) thin and with sharp corners.

spied (spaɪd) past tense and past participle of **spy.**

spike (spaɪk) *nc* a sharp point, esp. of metal. ● *vt* **1** put on a spike. **2** provide with spikes: *spiked shoes.*

spill (spɪl) *vt* **1** allow (liquid, etc.) to run out of its container accidentally. **2** (of a horse or vehicle) cause (its rider or passenger) to be thrown off. **3** *vi* (of a liquid) be upset. ● *nc* a fall from a horse, etc.

spilt (spɪlt) past tense and past participle of **spill.**

spin (spɪn) *vt* **1** make (threads) by twisting (wool, cotton, silk, etc.). **2** (of a spider) make (a web) to catch insects in. **3** *vti* (cause to) move round like a wheel. ● *nc* **1** a turning movement. **2** *infml* a short ride in a car, on a bicycle, etc. **spin out** make (something) last longer: *Try to spin out your money until you get your wages.* **spin-dryer** (ˌspɪnˈdraɪə*) *nc* a machine for drying washed clothes, etc., by spinning them round and forcing the water out. **spinner** *nc* **spinning-wheel** (ˈspɪnɪŋwiːl) *nc* a simple machine used for spinning.

spinach (ˈspɪnɪdʒ) *nu* a green vegetable with leaves that are cooked and eaten.

spinal (ˈspaɪnəl) *adj* to do with the spine.

spindle (ˈspɪndəl) *nc* a bar that turns round or on which something, such as a wheel, turns.

spine (spaɪn) *nc* **1** the line of bones that go down the middle of the back. **2** one of the needle-like parts of some plants and animals. **3** the part of a book's cover that is seen when in a row on a shelf. **spineless** *adj* **1** having no spine. **2** not having enough power of the mind to decide things. **spiny** *adj* **-ier, -iest** having needle-like parts.

spinster (ˈspɪnstə*) *nc* a woman who has not married.

spiral (ˈspaɪərəl) *nc* a shape or line that curves round and round while moving away from a point: see picture. ● *adj* in the shape of a spiral. ● *vi* have the shape of or move in a spiral.

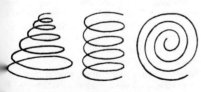

spiral

spire (ˈspaɪə*) *nc* tall, pointed part of a building, esp. on a church tower.

spirit (ˈspɪrɪt) **1** *nu* the soul. *nc* **2** the soul of a person without the body: *the spirits of the dead.* **3** a liquid obtained from another by boiling it off and collecting it, such as a strong alcoholic drink. **4** a person's real nature or qualities. *nu* **5** the quality of courage, energy, liveliness, etc.: *men of fine spirit.* **6** the real meaning of the words, esp. of a law: *obey the spirit of the law.* **spirited** *adj* lively. **spirits** a state of mind: *She's in high spirits.* **spiritual** (ˈspɪrɪtjʊəl) *adj* of the soul, religion, or the church: caring for things of the soul. **spiritually** *adv*

spirits (ˈspɪrɪts) *n pl* strong alcoholic drinks, such as whisky and brandy.

spit¹ (spɪt) **1** *vi* throw out liquid from the mouth. *vt* **2** throw out (something unpleasant) from the mouth. **3** say violently or angrily: *She spat out her hatred of him.* *vi* **4** (of a fire) throw out tiny pieces. **5** rain very lightly. ● *nu* liquid spat from the mouth. **spit out** *infml* say quickly (what one wants to say).

spit² *nc* a long, thin, metal bar on which meat is fixed to be cooked over a fire.

spite (spaɪt) *nu* a strong wish to harm someone's feelings or reputation; hatred. **in spite of** not paying any attention to: *He went out in spite of being ill.* **spiteful** *adj* having feelings of spite.

splash (splæʃ) **1** *vt* cause (water, mud, etc.) to fly about or onto (someone or something). *vi* **2** (of water, mud, etc.) fly about over someone, the floor, etc. **3** fall or move in water causing it to fly about: *The child was splashing about in the pool.* ● *nc* **1** a noise or mark made by splashing: *splashes of mud on my coat.* **2** a small patch of colour.

splendid (ˈsplendɪd) *adj* **1** fine, esp. to look at. **2** greatly to be admired: *What a splendid idea!* **splendidly** *adv*

splendour *US* **splendor** (ˈsplendə*) **1** *nu* the quality of being splendid. **2** *nc* a splendid quality: *the splendours of the royal palace.*

splint (splɪnt) *nc* a piece of wood, etc., tied to a broken arm, leg, etc., to keep it in the right position.

splinter (ˈsplɪntə*) *nc* a small, sharp piece of wood, glass, etc., broken off a larger piece: *get a splinter in one's finger.* ● *vti* break or be broken into splinters.

split (splɪt) **1** *vti* break or be broken apart: *The wood split down the middle.* **2** *vt* divide into parts: *Let's split the money between us.* ● *nc* **1** splitting. **2** a tear caused by bursting open or splitting. **split hairs** make too much of unimportant or small points in an argument, etc.

splutter (ˈsplʌtə*) *vt* speak quickly and unclearly because of excitement, etc.

spoil (spɔɪl) *vt* **1** make (a person's enjoyment) less; make useless: *Our holiday was spoilt by heavy rain.* **2** harm (someone's) character by letting him have his own way too often: *a spoilt child.* **3** *vi* (of food, etc.) go bad. **spoils** *n pl* stolen goods; goods taken by force in war.

spoilt (spɔɪlt) past tense and past participle of **spoil.**

spoke¹ (spəʊk) past tense of **speak.**

spoke² *nc* one of the bars coming from the centre of a wheel to its outer edge.

spoken ('spəʊkən) past participle of **speak.**

spokesman ('spəʊksmən) *nc, pl* **-men** a person chosen to speak for or represent others.

sponge (spʌndʒ) *nc* **1** a kind of simple sea-animal that is soft and yellow, with a structure full of holes able to take in water easily. **2** a piece of this, or something made like it, used for washing, cleaning, etc. ● *vt* clean with a sponge. **spongy** *adj* **-ier, -iest** soft, like a sponge.

sponsor ('spɒnsə*) *nc* **1** a person who promises to be responsible for another person. **2** a person who puts forward a plan, idea, etc., and promises to support it. **3** a person, business, etc., that offers to pay for a radio or television programme if his goods are advertised on it. ● *vt* be a sponsor for.

spontaneous (spɒn'teɪnɪəs) *adj* done or happening without being planned or suggested by anyone or anything. **spontaneity** (ˌspɒntə'neɪɪtɪ) *nu* **spontaneously** *adv*

spool (spuːl) *nc* a small device on which cotton thread, wire, photographic film, etc., is wound: see picture.

spool

spoon (spuːn) *nc* a tool with a cup-shaped part on the end of a handle, used for eating, stirring, etc. **spoon out** serve (food) with a spoon. **spoonfeed** ('spuːnfiːd) *vt* **1** feed (a baby, an ill person, etc.) with a spoon. **2** do things for (someone) without his asking for help. **spoonful** ('spuːnfʊl) *nc* as much food, etc., as will fill a spoon.

sporadic (spə'rædɪk) *adj* happening only occasionally.

spore (spɔː*) *nc* a seed by which a plant without flowers increases itself.

sport (spɔːt) **1** *ncu* a (type of) outside activity or game done for amusement and exercise, such as running or football. **2** *nu* amusement: *We did it for sport.* **sporting** *adj* **1** to do with or interested in sports. **2** with a risk of losing: *a sporting chance.* **sports** *n pl* a meeting of people taking part in outdoor games. **sports car** a small car built to go very fast. **sportsman** ('spɔːtsmən) *nc, pl* **-men** a person who is fond of sports. **sportsmanship** ('spɔːtsmənʃɪp) *nu*

spot (spɒt) *nc* **1** a small mark: *a blue skirt with white spots.* **2** a stain; dirty mark: *Mud caused spots on her coat.* **3** a place: *Here's a*

good spot to park the car. **4** a small, red mark on the skin: *Her face is covered in spots.* ● *vt* **1** mark or stain with spots. **2** see or recognise (someone or something).

spotless ('spɒtlɪs) *adj* very clean. **spotlight** ('spɒtlaɪt) **1** *nc* a lamp that gives a strong light pointed at a particular person or place, esp. in a theatre. **2** *nu* a place or person to whom everyone's attention is given: *He loves to be in the spotlight.* **spotted** ('spɒtɪd) *adj* marked with spots: *Her dress is of a spotted material.* **spotty** *adj* **-ier, -iest** covered with spots, esp. on the skin.

spouse (spaʊz, spaʊs) *formal nc* a husband or wife.

spout (spaʊt) **1** *vt* throw out (liquid). **2** *vi* (of liquid) be thrown out: *Blood spouted from his wound.* **3** *infml vt* speak as if making a speech, instead of talking in a usual manner. ● *nc* **1** a pipe, etc., through which liquid is poured: *the spout of a kettle.* **2** a stream of water thrown out with force.

sprain (spreɪn) *vt* twist (one of the joints of the body) so that damage and pain is caused. ● *nc* such an injury.

sprang (spræŋ) past tense of **spring.**

sprawl (sprɔːl) *vi* **1** sit with the arms and legs loosely and ungracefully spread out. **2** spread out in an untidy manner: *a sprawling town.* ● *nc* **1** a sprawling manner of sitting, etc. **2** a sprawling movement.

spray¹ (spreɪ) **1** *nu* water, etc., flying about in small drops: *sea spray.* *nc* **2** liquid forced out of a small device, in the form of a fine mist: *a spray of scent.* **3** a device used for producing this fine mist. ● *vt* throw or sprinkle (water, etc.) in the form of a spray.

spray² *nc* a small branch of a tree or plant, used as an ornament.

spread (spred) **1** *vt* cover the surface of (something) with (something): *Spread the table with a cloth; Spread butter on the bread.* **2** *vi* (cause to) cover a large surface. **3** *vti* (cause to) pass from person to person. ● *nc* **1** a measurement from one side to the other side: *the spread of a bird's wings.* **2** *nu* spreading to a larger area, greater number of people, etc.: *the spread of knowledge.* *nc* **3** a food made for spreading on bread. **4** a table laid out with food: *What a lovely spread!*

spree (spriː) *nc* a lively, happy time: *a shopping spree.*

sprig (sprɪg) *nc* a very small branch of a tree or plant with leaves, flowers, etc.

sprightly ('spraɪtlɪ) *adj* **-ier, -iest** lively and active.

spring (sprɪŋ) *vi* **1** jump up suddenly from the ground: *The cat sprang onto the wall.* **2** move suddenly: *He sprang out of bed.* **3** v.

cause or produce suddenly when not expected: *to spring a surprise on someone.* ●*nc* **1** the season between winter and summer in which flowers, leaves, etc., appear. **2** a piece of coiled metal wire that goes back to its normal shape after being pulled, pressed down, etc.: *the springs of a bed.* **3** a flow of water coming up from the earth; place where this happens. **4** a jump up.

springboard ('sprɪŋbɔːd) *nc* **1** a board, easily bent without breaking, from which someone jumps. **2** a point from where to start off: *This job will be a springboard to your future.* **spring from** come from suddenly: *Where did you spring from?* **springtime** ('sprɪŋtaɪm) *nu* the season of spring. **spring up** grow or appear suddenly; arise: *Another problem has sprung up.*

sprinkle ('sprɪŋkəl) *vt* throw (something) all around in small drops or pieces: *I sprinkle water over the garden to make it grow.* **sprinkler** ('sprɪŋklə*) *nc* a device for sprinkling water onto a lawn, etc., or fixed in a building for putting out a fire.

sprint (sprɪnt) *vi* run a short distance as fast as possible. ●*nc* a short fast run. **sprinter** *nc*

sprite (spraɪt) *nc* a fairy.

sprout (spraʊt) *vti* (cause to) begin to grow. ●*nc* a new growth on a plant.

spruce[1] (spruːs) *adj* **-r**, **-st** smart and neat in appearance. **spruce oneself up** make oneself look neat and smart.

spruce[2] *nc* a kind of fir-tree; *(also nu)* the wood of this tree.

sprung (sprʌŋ) past participle of **spring.**

spry (spraɪ) *adj* **-ier**, **-iest** quick-moving; lively: *a spry old man.*

spun (spʌn) past tense and past participle of **spin.**

spur (spɜː*) *nc* **1** one of a pair of sharp devices worn on a rider's boots to make the horse go faster: see picture. **2** something

spur 1

that urges a person on to do things with greater effort. **3** a sharp, hard point on a male bird's leg. **4** a hill on the top of a line of hills or mountains: see picture. ●*vt* (often followed by **on**) urge on (a person or a horse) to try harder, do better, etc. **on the spur of the moment** on a sudden desire to act.

spur 4

spurn (spɜːn) *vt* refuse with contempt: *She spurned his offer of marriage.*

spurt (spɜːt) *vi* **1** (of water, blood, etc.) flow out suddenly with force. **2** make a sudden, extra effort, esp. in running a race. ●*nc* **1** a sudden flow. **2** a sudden, harder effort.

spy (spaɪ) *nc, pl* **-ies 1** a person who goes into other countries to get secret information, esp. in times of war. **2** a person who secretly watches the activities of other people. ●*vt* **1** see, by looking carefully: *He spied someone in the garden.* **2** *vi* work as a spy.

squabble ('skwɒbəl) *vi, nc* (have) an unimportant, noisy quarrel.

squad (skwɒd) *nc* a small group of men being trained together or employed for the same purpose.

squadron ('skwɒdrən) *nc* a group of warships or warplanes.

squalid ('skwɒlɪd) *adj* dirty and uncared for. **squalor** ('skwɒlə*) *nu*

squall (skwɔːl) *nc* **1** a noisy cry of fear or pain, esp. from a baby. **2** a sudden burst of wind and rain. ●*vi* cry out noisily.

squander ('skwɒndə*) *vt* waste (esp. money or time).

square (skweə*) *nc* **1** a figure with four equal sides and four equal angles: see picture at **shapes. 2** anything with this shape. **3** an open space with four sides in a town, in which trees and grass are planted, or round which are buildings. **4** the result of a number when it is multiplied by itself: *The square of three is nine.* **5** *slang* an old-fashioned person. ●*adj* **-r**, **-st 1** having the shape of a square. **2** (of one's accounts, debts, etc.) attended to and settled. **3** honest; fair: *I'll be square with you.* ●*vt* **1** make square. **2** multiply a number by itself: *Three squared is nine.* **square deal** *infml* a fair piece of business. **squarely** *adj* **1** honestly. **2** straight. **square root** a number whose square (def. 4) is a number that is mentioned: *Three is the square root of nine.* **square up** pay what is owing; settle an account, etc. **square up to** face (something) bravely.

squash (skwɒʃ) **1** *vt* make flat by pressing; press into too small a space. **2** *vi* become pressed flat. **3** *vt* crowd in very small space

•*nu* 1 a crowd of people squashed together: *It was a bit of a squash in our small car.* 2 also **squash rackets** a game played with rackets and a rubber ball in a place with walls on all sides. *nc* 3 a sweet fruit drink. 4 *pl* **squash** a fruit, eaten as a vegetable.

squat (skwɒt) *vi* 1 sit on the ground on one's heels or with one's legs drawn up near to the body. 2 occupy public land, an empty building, etc., without permission. •*adj* **-ter, -test** short and thick. **squatter** *nc* 1 a person who squats (**squat** def. 2). 2 *Australian* a sheep-farmer.

squaw (skwɔː) *nc* a North American Indian woman or wife.

squawk (skwɔːk) *vi, nc* (esp. of a bird), (give) a loud, sharp cry of pain or fear.

squeak (skwiːk) *vi, nc* (give) a short, high cry as of a mouse, or a noise like this as of a door that needs oiling. **squeaky** *adj* **-ier, -iest** giving squeaks.

squeal (skwiːl) *nc* a long, high cry, louder than a squeak, showing great fear or pain. •*vi* 1 give a squeal. 2 *vt* say (something) with a squeal. 3 *slang vi* give information to the police, esp. about someone who has broken the law.

squeamish ('skwiːmɪʃ) *adj* 1 easily made to feel sick; feeling sick: *The movement of the ship made her feel very squeamish.* 2 too easily feeling disgust.

squeeze (skwiːz) *vt* 1 press tightly: *He squeezed my hand.* 2 press tightly in order to get (water, etc.) out of: *Squeeze the juice out of an orange.* 3 *vti* push (someone or oneself) into a small space: *We squeezed into the lift.* •*ncu* (an instance of) squeezing or being squeezed.

squid (skwɪd) *nc* a sea-animal with ten long, thin arms on the head.

squint (skwɪnt) *vi* 1 look with each eye pointing in a different direction. 2 look sideways or with the eyes half-shut. •*nc* 1 a position of the eyes that is not normal. 2 *infml* look: *Let's have a quick squint at it.*

squire ('skwaɪə*) *nc* 1 *Brit* a country gentleman, esp. one owning the most land in a district. 2 *archaic* a young man who served a knight. 3 *US* a local judge.

squirm ('skwɜːm) *vi* twist the body with small movements because of feeling uncomfortable, ashamed, shy, etc.

squirrel ('skwɪrəl) *nc* a small tree-climbing animal like a rat with grey or red fur and a thick tail.

squirt (skwɜːt) 1 *vt* force out a thin stream of (water, powder, etc.). 2 *vi* (of water, powder, etc.) be forced out in a thin stream. •*nc* 1 a thin stream of water, powder, etc. 2 a device that forces out liquid, etc.

stab (stæb) *vt* wound with a sharp-pointed weapon. •*nc* 1 a blow from a sharp-pointed weapon. 2 *infml* a try.

stable[1] ('steɪbəl) *nc* a building in which horses are kept.

stable[2] *adj* 1 firm in position; not changing. 2 (of a person) faithful; not likely to change. **stabilise** ('steɪbɪlaɪz) *vt* make firm or steady. **stability** (stə'bɪlɪtɪ) *nu*

stack (stæk) *nc* 1 a pile or heap of anything, esp. neatly arranged. 2 *infml* a large amount: *a stack of work.* 3 a pile of stored hay, etc., with a pointed top. 4 a number of chimneys together. •*vt* pile up; put one on top of another.

stadium ('steɪdɪəm) *nc, pl* **-diums, -dia** (dɪə) a sports ground with rows of seats, one behind and higher than another, for people to watch games, competitions, etc.

staff (stɑːf) *nc* 1 a strong stick used as a support when walking or climbing. 2 a group of people working together under a manager, head, etc.: *school staff.* 3 a group of army officers who organise the army. •*vt* provide with staff.

stag (stæg) *nc* a male deer with branch-like horns.

stage (steɪdʒ) *nc* 1 the raised part in a theatre where the acting takes place. 2 a certain point in progress or development: *Our baby is just at the walking stage.* 3 a distance between two stopping places on a journey. •*vt* 1 put (a play) on the theatre stage. 2 arrange (an event, esp. a sudden or exciting one). **the stage** the activity of acting in plays. **stagecoach** ('steɪdʒkəʊtʃ) *nc* a vehicle with horses that used to take passengers at fixed times from one stopping place on a journey to another.

stagger ('stægə*) 1 *vi* walk very unsteadily moving from one side to another, because of being drunk, carrying something heavy etc. *vt* 2 greatly shock, surprise, etc. 3 arrange (holidays, times of work, etc.) so that not everyone's are the same: *We staggered our work so that the office was never empty.* •*ncu* (an instance of) staggering.

stagnant ('stægnənt) *adj* 1 (of water) not flowing. 2 (of business, etc.) not busy; not changing. **stagnate** (stæg'neɪt) *vi* 1 (of water, etc.) be or become without movement. 2 (of a person, business, etc.) be or become slow-moving or dull because of lack of change, activity, etc. **stagnation** *nu*

staid (steɪd) *adj* (of a person) serious; not liking change.

stain (steɪn) *vt* 1 change the colour of; make a dirty mark on: *clothes stained with blood. Smoking can stain the fingers.* 2 colour (wood, etc.) with a special substance that goes into it. 3 *vi* (of material) become dirt-

or have its colour spoiled. ●*nc* **1** a liquid used for colouring wood. **2** a dirty mark. **stained glass** coloured glass, esp. used in church windows. **stainless** *adj* without a stain, esp. on one's reputation. **stainless steel** steel that will not rust.

stairs (steəz) *n pl* a set of fixed steps in a building. **staircase** ('steəkeɪs) or **stairway** ('steəweɪ) *nc* a set of stairs.

stake¹ (steɪk) *nc* **1** a strong stick with a sharp point driven into the ground as part of a fence, as a support for a young tree, etc. **2** a piece of wood to which a person was tied and burnt to death as a punishment. ●*vt* **1** mark out (a place) with stakes. **2** support with a stake.

stake² *nc* an amount of money risked on the result of some future race, event, etc. ●*vt* risk (money) on some future event, etc. **at stake** at risk: *There is a lot at stake here.*

stalactite ('stæləktaɪt) *nc* a natural, long, pointed, white object hanging from the roof of a cave, formed by water falling in drops: see picture.

stalactite

stalagmite ('stæləgmaɪt) *nc* a natural, long, pointed, white object on the floor of a cave, formed by water falling in drops: see picture.

stalagmite

stale (steɪl) *adj* **-r**, **-st** **1** (of food) not fresh; dry: *stale bread.* **2** not interesting because already heard, known, etc.: *stale news.* ● *vi* become stale.

stalk¹ (stɔːk) *nc* the part of a plant that supports the leaves, flowers, fruits, etc.

stalk² **1** *vi* walk in a stiff, proud, etc., manner. **2** *vt* follow slowly and carefully in order to take as a prisoner or kill.

stall¹ (stɔːl) *nc* **1** one of the divisions of a stable, etc., in which a horse, cow, etc., is kept. **2** a small shelter-like shop, esp. in a market. **3** *Brit (usually pl)* one of the seats nearest to the stage in a theatre. **4** a wooden seat with a back and sides in a church.

● *vi* **1** (of a vehicle or its engine) stop moving because of lack of power. **2** *vt* cause (a vehicle or engine) to stall.

stall² *vi* delay answering a question in order to have more time to think of an answer.

stallion ('stæljən) *nc* a male horse, esp. used for the producing of young.

stalwart ('stɔːlwət) *adj* showing no fear; firm; *stalwart supporters.* ●*nc* a stalwart person.

stamen ('steɪmən) *nc* the male part of a flower containing the yellow powder called pollen: see picture.

stamen

stamina ('stæmɪnə) *nu* strength of body and mind that enables a person to work for a long time, etc.

stammer ('stæmə*) *vi* speak in a hesitating way often repeating a word or sound, as in 'M-m-may I g-go h-h-home?' ●*nc* a habit of doing this.

stamp (stæmp) **1** *vti* bring (the foot) down with force. **2** *vi* stamp while walking: *He stamped out of the room.* *vt* **3** press or print (something) on (a surface). **4** prepare (a letter, parcel, etc.) for posting by putting a postage stamp on it. ●*nc* **1** the act of stamping with the foot. **2** a device for printing a mark, etc., on a surface: *a date stamp.* **3** short for **postage stamp.** See under **postage.**

stampede (stæm'piːd) *nc* a sudden rush made by people or animals because of fear. ●*vti* (cause to) take part in a stampede.

stand (stænd) **1** *vti* (often followed by **up**) (cause to) be or become upright: *I stood up when they came in; I'll stand the brush up against the wall.* *vi* **2** be in a certain condition: *This is how the situation stands.* **3** be in a certain place: *The house stands in a large garden.* **4** *vt* bear: *She can't stand pain.* ●*nc* **1** a piece of furniture on which something can be held or supported: *a hat stand; a music stand.* **2** a shelter-like place where something is sold: *a newspaper stand.* **3** a structure on which people sit or stand to watch sports, etc. **stand back** move away from something. **stand by 1** watch something without interfering: *I won't stand by and see them go hungry.* **2** be ready for when help, action, etc., is needed.

standby ('stændbaɪ) *nc, pl* **-s** a person or thing that can be used if another does not arrive, work, etc. **stand for 1** put up with; support: *I won't stand for cruelty to animals.* **2** *Brit* try to be chosen for a particular office: *He is standing for Parliament.* **3** be a sign of; mean: *In this dictionary, 'n' stands for 'noun'.* **stand-in** ('stændɪn) *nc* a person who stands in for another, esp. an actor. **stand in (for)** take the place of; represent. **standing** *nu* **1** the length of time that something lasts or is. **2** a person's reputation or place in society. ●*adj* fixed, remaining unchanged: *a standing rule.* **stand out** be easily noticed or seen. **stand-up** ('stænd-ʌp) *adj* **1** (of a meal) eaten while one is standing. **2** (of a fight) violent. **3** (of a shirt collar) stiff and upright. **stand up for** support. **stand up to 1** face bravely. **2** (of a thing) stay in good condition in spite of (much use, etc.).

standard ('stændəd) *nc* **1** an accepted or approved size, quality, etc., with which others are compared. **2** a special flag: *the royal standard.* ●*adj* of the accepted or approved size, quality, etc.: *the standard weight.* **standardise** ('stændədaɪz) *vt* make standard.

standpoint ('stændpɔɪnt) *nc* a way of looking at a question, situation, etc.: *He takes the standpoint that an election is necessary.*

standstill ('stændstɪl) *nu* an end; short stop: *The project has come to a standstill.*

stank (stæŋk) past tense of **stink**.

stanza ('stænzə) *nc* a division of a poem consisting of a fixed number of lines.

staple[1] ('steɪpəl) *nc* a piece of metal wire in a U-shape with pointed ends, used for fastening wood, paper, etc., by hammering or pressing it in. ●*vt* fasten with a staple.

staple[2] *adj, nc* (the) most important or chief (goods, food, etc., produced): *Rice is the staple food of India.*

star (stɑː*) *nc* **1** one of the many bodies seen shining in the sky at night. **2** a figure with five or more points coming out from it, such as (*). **3** a famous actor, actress, singer, etc. ●*vt* **1** decorate or mark with a **star** (def. 2). *vi* **2** take one of the main parts in a film, play, etc. **Stars and Stripes** the national flag of the USA. **stardom** ('stɑːdəm) *nu* fame as an actor, actress, singer, etc. **starfish** ('stɑːfɪʃ) *nc, pl* **-fish, -fishes** a sea-animal shaped like a star, with five or more arms. **starlight** ('stɑːlaɪt) *nu* light from the stars.

starboard ('stɑːbəd) *nu, adj* (on) the right-hand side of a ship or plane when a person faces the front.

starch (stɑːtʃ) *nu* **1** a white food substance without smell or taste, found in potatoes,

corn, etc. **2** this substance as a powder used for making clothes, etc., stiff. ● *vt* make stiff with starch. **starchy** *adj* **-ier, -iest 1** (of a food) containing starch. **2** (of a person) rather formal in manner.

stare (steə*) *vi* look steadily with the eyes wide open: *She stared at him in surprise; It's rude to stare!* ●*nc* a steady, wide-eyed look.

stark (stɑːk) *adj* **-er, -est 1** deserted-looking; bare: *That wall is very stark without a picture on it.* **2** complete: *stark madness.* ●*adv* completely: *stark naked.*

starling ('stɑːlɪŋ) *nc* a small European bird with bright, black feathers that often lives near buildings.

starry ('stɑːrɪ) *adj* **-ier, -iest** covered with or shining like stars: *a starry night; starry eyes.*

start (stɑːt) **1** *vti* (cause to) begin, come into being, or begin to move: *I've started the clocks; When does school start?* **2** *vi* make a sudden movement from surprise: *He started at the loud noise.* ●*nc* **1** a beginning. **2** a sudden movement from surprise, fear, etc. **start off** begin to move. **start out 1** *infml* begin something with a particular intention: *He started out wanting to become rich.* **2** *chiefly US* begin a journey. **start up 1** get up suddenly, esp. from one's seat. **2** (cause to) begin suddenly to do something: *Get the engine started up.* **starter** *nc* **1** a person who gives the signal for a race to begin. **2** a horse or person taking part in a race. **3** a device for starting up an engine.

startle ('stɑːtəl) *vt* surprise (a person), esp. so that he starts (**start** def. 2). **startling** *adj*

starve (stɑːv) *vti* **1** (cause to) die from hunger. **2** (cause to) eat too little food. **3** *infml vi* be very hungry. **4** *vt* cause to lack something important: *The engine is being starved of air.* **starvation** (stɑː'veɪʃən) *nu*

state (steɪt) **1** *nu* the condition in which something is; what something is like: *a happy state of mind; Your room is in a very untidy state!* **2** *nc* also **State** (a part of) a country with its own political government: *the United States of America.* **3** *nu* ceremony: *the Queen travels in state.* ●*vt* say, esp. clearly and firmly: *He stated his opinion on the matter.* **stately** *adj* **-ier, -iest** serious; grand.

statement ('steɪtmənt) *nc* something stated.

statesman ('steɪtsmən) *nc, pl* **-men 1** a person who takes an important part in managing state business. **2** a respected politician. **statesmanship** ('steɪtsmənʃɪp) *nu* cleverness in dealing with state business or public affairs.

static ('stætɪk) *adj* not moving: *static electricity.* ●*nu* **1** static electricity. **2** unwanted radio noise.

station ('steɪʃən) *nc* **1** a place where a public service is provided: *a fire station; a police station.* **2** a building where trains or buses stop. **3** a person's place in society. **4** *Australian* a large sheep or cattle farm. ●*vt* put in position.

stationary ('steɪʃənrɪ) *adj* **1** not intended to be moved about. **2** not moving: *a stationary vehicle.*

stationery ('steɪʃənrɪ) *nu* writing materials, such as notepaper, envelopes, pens, etc.

statistics (stə'tɪstɪks) *nu* (*with singular verb*) the study of facts in the form of numbers. **statistic** *nc* such a fact. **statistical** *adj* **statistically** *adv* **statistician** (,stætɪs'tɪʃən) *nc* a person who deals with statistics.

statue ('stætʃuː) *nc* a figure of a person or animal made out of stone, wood, etc.

stature ('stætʃə*) *nu* **1** a person's height. **2** a person's quality or greatness.

status ('steɪtəs) *nu* a person's place in society or in relation to others. **status quo** (kwəʊ) *Latin* an unchanged state or position. **status symbol** something thought to be a sign of high position, wealth, success, etc., such as owning a car.

statute ('stætjuːt) *nc* a written law examined and accepted by a law-making body, esp. a parliament.

statutory ('stætjʊtərɪ) *adj* fixed, done, or demanded by law: *one's statutory duty.*

staunch (stɔːntʃ) *adj* **-er, -est** loyal; firm: *a staunch supporter.* ●*vt* hold back or stop (a flow, esp. of blood).

stave (steɪv) *nc* **1** one of the curved pieces of wood forming the sides of a barrel: see picture. **2** *music* a set of five lines on and between which notes are written. **stave in** break a hole in (a boat, barrel, etc.). **stave off** keep off; prevent: *We staved off an attack.*

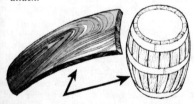

stave

stay[1] (steɪ) *vi* **1** remain: *stay at home.* **2** pass a short time in or at a place, esp. as a guest: *We stayed with friends; He's staying in London for the weekend.* *vt* **3** continue to be: *He stays happy whatever happens.* **4** stop; hold back; keep off: *to stay one's hunger.* ●*nc* a period spent at a place, esp. as a guest: *a short stay in London.* **stay in** remain at home; not go outside: *I'll stay in to watch television.* **stay out** remain outdoors or

away from home: *Don't stay out late.* **stay put** remain where put: *My hat won't stay put.*

stay[2] *nc* **1** a support: *His daughter has been the stay of his old age.* **2** a rope supporting a ship's mast.

stead (sted) *n* **in someone's stead** in someone's place: *I'll go in your stead.* **stand someone in good stead** be useful to someone when needed.

steadfast ('stedfɑːst) *adj* firm; never changing; loyal.

steady ('stedɪ) *adj* **-ier, -iest 1** not shaking; still: *a steady hand.* **2** regular, not changing, etc.: *a steady flow of traffic.* ●*vti* make or become steady. **steadily** *adv*

steak (steɪk) *nc* a thick piece of meat or fish.

steal (stiːl) *vt* **1** take away secretly and unlawfully (something that belongs to someone else). **2** get by surprise; do in secret: *to steal a kiss; She stole a glance at herself in the mirror.* **3** *vi* move quietly or secretly: *He stole away.*

stealth (stelθ) *nu* secret action. **stealthily** *adv* **stealthy** *adj* **-ier, -iest.**

steam (stiːm) *nu* **1** the gas into which water is changed when boiled. **2** *infml* energy; force. ●*vi* **1** give out steam: *The kettle was steaming away.* **2** move (as if) by the power of steam: *The ship steamed down the river; Our plans steamed ahead.* **3** *vt* cook (food) by steam: *steamed fish.* **steamboat** ('stiːmbəʊt) *nc* a boat driven by a steam-engine. **steam-engine** ('stiːm,endʒɪn) *nc* a railway engine or a fixed engine driven or worked by steam. **steamer** *nc* **1** a ship driven by a steam-engine. **2** a cooking pot for steaming food. **steamship** ('stimʃɪp) *nc* a ship driven by a steam-engine. **steamy** *adj* **-ier, -iest.**

steed (stiːd) *archaic or literary nc* a horse.

steel (stiːl) *nc* a hard metal made of iron, carbon, and sometimes another metal, used for making knives, tools, machinery, etc. ●*vt* make (oneself) determined or fixed in purpose. *He steeled himself for action.*

steep[1] (stiːp) *adj* **-er, -est 1** having a very sharp slope: *a steep hill.* **2** *infml* too much; too great: *steep prices.* **steeply** *adv*

steep[2] **1** *vti* (cause to) become and stay full of liquid for a time. **2** *vt* take in or fill with as much as possible: *a town steeped in history.*

steeple ('stiːpəl) *nc* the tall, pointed part on the roof of a church tower.

steer[1] ('stɪə*) **1** *vt* guide (a ship, vehicle etc.) in the right direction **2** *vi* (of a ship, vehicle, etc.) allow to be guided in the right direction.

steer[2] a young castrated male of the cattle family. **steering-wheel** ('stɪərɪŋwiːl) *nc* wheel, turned by the driver, for guiding the course of a ship, car, etc.

stem[1] (stem) *nc* **1** the main, central part of a plant that carries the flowers, leaves, etc. **2** anything that is shaped like a stem. **3** *grammar* the main part of a word on which other forms of that word are built: *'Time' is the stem of 'timetable'.*

stem[2] *vt* control or stop (the flow of a liquid).

stench (stentʃ) *nc* a strong, unpleasant smell.

stencil ('stensəl) *nc* a piece of paper, metal, etc., in which patterns or letters are cut, through which ink is put onto a surface as a form of printing. ● *vt* make a pattern, words, etc., with a stencil.

stenographer (stɪ'nɒgrəfə*) *chiefly US nc* a person who writes very quickly by using signs to represent words.

step (step) *vi* move one foot and then the other forward, as in walking. ● *nc* **1** such a movement of the foot; a distance moved in stepping. **2** one of a set of actions, stages, etc., coming one after the other. **3** a short distance up or down; place for the foot when going up or down. **4** a sound made by stepping. **step aside** move to one side. **step by step** gradually. **step down** to give up one's job or position, esp. to someone else. **step in** come forward to help sort out an argument, etc.; busy oneself with. **step up** increase. **in** or **out of step 1** putting or not putting the correct foot down when dancing, marching, etc., with others. **2** behaving or not behaving like other people in a group. **stepladder** ('step,lædə*) *nc* a ladder, with wide, flat steps, that folds up when not in use. **stepping-stone** ('stepɪŋstəʊn) *nc* **1** one of several flat stones put in a small stream, etc., and used as a path across it. **2** something that helps towards one's purpose, ambition, etc. **steps** *n pl* a stepladder.

steppe (step) *nc (usually pl)* a flat land without trees, esp. in Russia.

stereo ('steriəʊ) *infml adj* short for **stereophonic**. ● *nc* a stereophonic record-player, tape-recorder, etc. **stereophonic** (,steriə'fɒnɪk) *adj* (of broadcast and recorded sound) making sound seem to come from all directions by using two or more loudspeakers. **stereotype** ('steriətaɪp) *nc* an idea of what a sort of person or thing is that has become fixed and often uninteresting because of this: *the stereotype of a naughty little boy.* ● *vt* use or have fixed ideas about.

sterile ('steraɪl) *adj* **1** unable to produce crops, seeds, or young. **2** without new ideas or progress: *a sterile business meeting.* **3** free from germs that cause disease. **sterilisation** (,steraɪlaɪ'zeɪʃən) *nu* sterilising. **sterilise** ('steraɪlaɪz) *vt* make sterile.

sterling ('stɜːlɪŋ) *adj* **1** (to do with gold and silver) of fixed value; pure. **2** honest and good: *a man of sterling qualities.* ● *nu* the sort of money used in Britain.

stern[1] (stɜːn) *adj* **-er, -est 1** expecting obedience. **2** firm and harsh in manner. **sternly** *adv*

stern[2] *nc* the back end of a boat or ship.

stethoscope ('steθəskəʊp) *medicine nc* an instrument for listening to sounds inside the body, esp. those of the heart: see picture.

stethoscope

stew (stjuː) *vti* (of meat and vegetables) (cause to) cook slowly in liquid in a closed pan. ● *ncu* (a type of) stewed meat and vegetables.

steward ('stjuəd) *nc* **1** a man whose job is to wait on passengers in a ship, plane, or train. **2** a man in charge of another person's large house, etc. **3** a man in charge of a public event, such as a dance, etc. **stewardess** (,stjuːə'des) *nc* a woman **steward** (def. 1).

stick[1] (stɪk) *nc* **1** a thin branch cut or broken off a tree. **2** anything shaped like a stick. **3** a branch cut into a special shape or used for a special purpose: *a walking-stick for an old man.*

stick[2] *vt* **1** push something pointed into something. **2** fix or fasten, esp. with glue, etc.: *stick a poster on a wall.* **3** *infml* put: *Stick your book in my bag.* **4** *infml* put up with: *I can't stick the way he looks at her.* *vi* **5** be fastened or fixed, esp. with glue. **6** be fixed in by its point: *He had a feather sticking in his hat.* **stick at** continue doing something, esp. with an effort. **stick out** be easily seen among others. **stick out for** demand (something) and refuse to give way until one gets it. **stick to** keep to (one's promise, etc.). **stick together** *infml* stay loyal or friendly with each other. **stick up** be in an upright position. **stick up for** *infml* speak in support of. **sticky** *adj* **-ier, -iest 1** that sticks or may stick. **2** *infml* difficult or awkward: *a sticky situation.*

stiff (stɪf) *adj* **-er, -est 1** not easily bent: *a stiff neck.* **2** difficult: *a stiff examination.* **3** great or strong: *a stiff wind.* **4** (of a person or behaviour) formal. **stiffly** ('stɪflɪ) *adv* **stiffen** *vti* (cause to) become stiff.

stifle ('staɪfəl) 1 *vti* (cause someone to) find it difficult to breathe. 2 *vt* hold back; prevent from being seen or heard: *stifle a cough*.

stigma ('stɪgmə) *nc* 1 a mark of disgrace. 2 the top of the seed-producing part of a flower.

stile (staɪl) *nc* a step or set of steps for climbing over a fence or wall: see picture.

stile

still[1] (stɪl) *adv, adj* **-er -est** not moving: *still water* ●*adj* 1 peaceful: *a still night*. 2 (of wine) without bubbles. ●*nu* 1 the state of being peaceful. *nc* 2 a set of devices and containers for making strong alcohol. 3 a photograph made from one frame of a motion-picture. ●*vt* make still. **stillness** *nu*

still[2] *adv* 1 even up till now or then: *I'm still hoping to work abroad; Do you still work at the same place?* 2 even; yet: *Still more strikes are expected*. 3 in spite of that: *I don't want to go... still, I promised, so I must*.

stilt (stɪlt) *nc* one of two long poles with foot supports to make the user appear taller: *Stilts are used by circus clowns*.

stimulant ('stɪmjʊlənt) *nc* 1 a drink, medicine, etc., that increases activity of the body or mind. 2 something that encourages a person.

stimulate ('stɪmjʊleɪt) *vt* excite; stir into activity. **stimulating** *adj*

stimulus ('stɪmjʊləs) *nc, pl* **-li** (liː) something that stimulates.

sting (stɪŋ) *vt* 1 cause a wound by forcing poison through the skin of. 2 cause pain to the body or mind of. 3 *infml* ask for money, esp. too much, from. 4 *vi* be able to sting. ●*nc* 1 a wound, often poisonous, caused by being stung. 2 the part of a bee, etc., that causes this. 3 *ncu* (a) pain in the body or mind.

stingy ('stɪndʒɪ) *infml adj* **-ier, -iest** mean; not giving freely, esp. money.

stink (stɪŋk) *vi* give out a strong, unpleasant smell. ●*nc* a strong, unpleasant smell.

stint (stɪnt) *vt* keep (oneself) within a certain small amount: *There's plenty of food, so don't stint yourself!*

stipulate ('stɪpjʊleɪt) *vt* say that (certain conditions, etc.) must be met before something can be done.

stir (stɜː*) 1 *vti* (cause to) move slightly: *The baby stirred in its sleep. vt* 2 move (liquid) round with a tool to mix it: *stir one's tea with a spoon; stir a pot of paint*. 3 excite or move (feelings, etc.). ●*nc* 1 an act of stirring. 2 a fuss. **stirring** *adj* exciting.

stirrup ('stɪrəp) *nc* one of two supports hanging from the leather seat on a horse for the feet of the rider.

stitch (stɪtʃ) 1 *nc* (in sewing) an amount of thread seen on cloth after the passing in and out of a needle through it. 2 *ncu* (a type of) stitching. *nc* 3 (in knitting) a loop of wool over the needle. 4 a loop of thread, etc., used to hold the sides of a wound together. 5 *nu* a pain in the side caused by too much activity. ●*vt* sew with stitches.

stock (stɒk) *nu* 1 the goods kept by a shop or business. 2 the starting-point in times past from which a family has begun: *She's of Welsh stock*. 3 juice from the meat, bones, etc., of an animal, used for cooking. *ncu* 4 (an amount of) money lent to a government. 5 (a number of) shares in the money owned by a company. *nc* 6 an amount of something kept in good supply for future use. 7 the handle of a tool, etc.: *the stock of a whip*. ●*vt* keep or provide with (goods). ●*adj* usual and rather boring: *a stock response*. **in** or **out of stock** (of goods) available or not available for purchase from a shop or business.

stockade (stɒˈkeɪd) *nc* a tall fence round something as a defence. ●*vt* put a stockade around.

stockbroker ('stɒkbrəʊkə*) *nc* a person whose job is to buy and sell shares.

stock exchange also **stock market** a place where shares are bought and sold.

stockholder ('stɒkhəʊldə*) *chiefly US nc* a person who owns shares.

stocking ('stɒkɪŋ) *nc* one of a pair of nylon, wool, etc., garments fitting closely over the foot and leg.

stockist ('stɒkɪst) *nc* a person who owns a supply of certain goods for sale.

stockpile ('stɒkpaɪl) *nc* a large supply of important goods kept in store for future use. ●*vt* build up and keep a stockpile of.

stockroom ('stɒkrʊm) *nc* a room in a shop, school, factory, etc., where a supply of goods is kept.

stockstill (ˌstɒkˈstɪl) *adv* without any movement: *stand stockstill*.

stock-taking ('stɒkteɪkɪŋ) *nu* the examining and making of a list of goods that are available in a shop, etc.

stocky ('stɒkɪ) *adj* **-ier, -iest** (esp. of a person) short and broad.

stoical ('stəʊɪkəl) *adj* able to bear pain, trouble, etc., without complaining.

stoke (stəʊk) **1** *vt* put coal, etc., onto (a fire) in a building, engine, etc. **2** *vi* look after such a fire.

stole[1] (stəʊl) past tense of **steal**.

stole[2] *nc* a woman's loose scarf-like garment worn round the shoulders with each end hanging down at the front.

stolen (ˈstəʊlən) past participle of **steal**.

stomach (ˈstʌmək) *nc* a bag-like part of the body where food goes after being swallowed, to be broken down by acid juices. ● *vt* put up with without feeling ill, angry, etc.: *She can't stomach all that rubbish he talks.*

stone (stəʊn) **1** *nu* a hard substance in the ground; rock. *nc* **2** a small piece of rock, broken off the main rock. **3** a jewel: *precious stones.* **4** something hard and round, esp. the large seed in the centre of a fruit. **5** a measure of weight = 14 lbs, 6.350 kg ● *vt* **1** throw small rocks at. **2** take out stones from (fruit). **Stone Age** a time before history was written down when weapons, etc., were made of stone. **stony** *adj* **-ier, -iest 1** having many stones: *a stony road.* **2** cold and hard: *a stony stare.*

stood (stʊd) past tense and past participle of **stand**.

stool (stuːl) *nc* a small, backless seat, with three or four legs.

stoop (stuːp) *vi* **1** bend the body forward and downward, esp. from the waist. **2** (followed by **to**) behave in a way so as to be less deserving of respect. ● *nc* a bending of the body.

stop (stɒp) *vt* **1** put an end to the movement of (a person or thing). **2** fill up (a hole, etc.): *stop a tooth.* **3** cause to cease for a time: *His wages have been stopped.* **4** prevent: *You can't stop me from running away.* *vi* **5** come to an end; cease moving: *My watch has stopped.* **6** remain; stay: *stop at home.* ● *nc* **1** an example of stopping or being stopped. **2** a place where a public vehicle waits for people to climb on and off: *a bus stop.* **3** the sign (.) used in writing, esp. at the end of a sentence; full stop. **stop behind** remain in a place after others have left. **stop in** stay at home. **stop off** break a journey for a short time. **stop over** break a journey for one or two days. **stopover** (ˈstɒpəʊvə) *nc* a break in a journey. **stop press** the latest news added to a newspaper after the printing of it has begun. **stop up** not go to bed until late. **stopcock** (ˈstɒpkɒk) *nc* a device in a pipe that controls the flow of liquid or gas going through it. **stopgap** (ˈstɒpgæp) *nc* a person or thing filling the place of another person or thing for a short time only. **stopwatch** (ˈstɒpwɒtʃ) *nc* a watch that can be stopped and started, used for measuring the time taken in races, etc.

stoppage (ˈstɒpɪdʒ) **1** *ncu* (an example of) stopping or being stopped. **2** *nc* something that makes movement or action difficult or impossible.

stopper (ˈstɒpə*) *nc* a cork, etc., fitted in the top of a bottle, etc., to keep the contents in.

store (stɔː*) *vt* **1** put away for future use. **2** provide; supply: *a mind stored with information.* ● *nc* **1** a supply of something kept for future use. **2** *(pl)* such goods. **3** a large shop which sells a great variety of goods: *a department store.* **4** *chiefly US* a shop. **set (great) store by** think of as important or of great value. **storehouse** (ˈstɔːhaʊs) *nc* a place where goods are kept. **storekeeper** (ˈstɔːkiːpə*) *nc* **1** a person who owns or is in charge of a storehouse. **2** *chiefly US* a person in charge of a shop. **storeroom** (ˈstɔːrʊm) *nc* a room where supplies are kept.

storey *US* **story** (ˈstɔːrɪ) *nc* (all the rooms on) a floor or level of a building: *The hotel in the old part of the city was eight storeys high.*

stork (stɔːk) *nc* a large bird that has very long legs and walks about in water.

storm (stɔːm) *nc* **1** a period of heavy rain, strong winds, etc. **2** a show of very strong feeling: *a storm of protest.* ● *vi* **1** show very strong feelings: *He stormed out of the room in anger.* **2** *vt* attack and capture (a place). **stormy** *adj* **-ier, -iest 1** (of weather) showing violence. **2** full of strong feelings: *a stormy meeting.*

story (ˈstɔːrɪ) *nc, pl* **-ries 1** an account of a set of events told in a book, etc.: *Some stories are true, some are imaginary.* **2** *infml* an untrue account. **storybook** (ˈstɔːrɪbʊk) *nc* a book of imaginary happenings, esp. for children. ● *adj* convenient and pleasing, but unlikely: *a storybook ending to their troubles.* **storyteller** (ˈstɔːrɪˌtelə*) *nc* **1** a person who tells stories. **2** a person who tells lies. **storytelling** (ˈstɔːrɪˌtelɪŋ) *nu* telling stories.

stout (staʊt) *adj* **-er, -est 1** strongly made: *a pair of stout shoes.* **2** rather fat: *a stout woman.* **3** brave. ● *nu* beer of the strongest kind. **stoutly** *adv*

stove[1] (stəʊv) *nc* a device heated by gas, electricity, etc., for warming a room or cooking food.

stove[2] past tense and past participle of **stave**.

stow (stəʊ) *vt* put (things) away, usually closely packed together. **stowaway** (ˈstəʊəweɪ) *nc* a person who hides on a ship or a plane in order to make a journey without paying.

straddle ('strædəl) *vt* sit on or stand over something with one's legs wide apart: *He straddled his horse.*

straggler ('stræglə*) *nc* a person who goes so slowly as to be left behind the others in a group.

straight (streɪt) *adj* **-er, -est 1** without a bend or bends: *a straight line.* **2** honest. **3** placed in an upright or level position. **4** in good order; tidy. ●*adv* directly; in a straight line: *The children were told to come straight home.* ●*nc* a straight part of a racetrack.

straighten ('streɪtən) *vti* make or become straight.

straightforward (ˌstreɪt'fɔːwəd) *adj* **1** honest. **2** easily understood: *a straightforward question.*

strain (streɪn) *vt* **1** stretch by pulling tightly. **2** stretch (one's powers) too much, esp. damaging part of the body: *to strain one's eyes by reading in a weak light.* **3** *vi* make a great effort (to do something). **4** *vti* (of a liquid), (cause to) be passed through a wire framework or cloth to remove any solid matter. ●*ncu* **1** (an example of) being strained. *nc* **2** anything that strain one's powers. **3** *(pl)* music: *the strains of a guitar heard through an open window.* **4** a natural tendency in a person's character: *a strain of weakness in the family.* **5** *nu* great tiredness of body or mind. **strainer** *nc* a device through which liquid is passed to remove solid matter.

strait (streɪt) *nc* **1** a narrow piece of sea between two larger seas. **2** *(pl)* great difficulty or need: *in desperate straits.*

strand¹ (strænd) *chiefly poetry nc* a seashore. ●*vti* (of a ship), (cause to) become stuck in shallow water. **stranded** *adj* helpless because of being left without money, transport, etc., esp. in a foreign place.

strand² *nc* one of several threads of string, wire, etc., that are twised together to form a rope, cable, etc.

strange (streɪndʒ) *adj* **-r, -st 1** unknown; foreign: *a strange noise; in a strange land.* **2** unusual: *What a strange man!* **strangeness** *nu* being strange. **stranger** *nc* **1** a person one does not know. **2** a person in a place that is unknown to him. **strangely** *adv*

strangle ('stræŋgəl) *vt* kill by tightly pressing the throat of.

strap (stræp) *nc* a thin strip of leather or of a material easily bent, used for fastening, holding, etc.: *a watch strap; handbag with a shoulder strap.* ●*vt* **1** fasten or hold with a strap. **2** use a strap to beat (someone).

strapping ('stræpɪŋ) *adj* tall, strong, and showing good health: *a strapping lad.*

stratagem ('strætədʒəm) *nc* a plan or trick to deceive, esp. an enemy.

strategy ('strætɪdʒɪ) *nc, pl* **-gies 1** *ncu* (a plan made by) the art of planning the positions of armies and their likely behaviour, etc., in war. **2** *nu* the art of using plans or stratagems in business, etc. **strategic** (strə'tiːdʒɪk) *adj* of or to do with strategy, esp. to gain an advantage. **strategically** *adv*

stratify ('strætɪfaɪ) *vti* form into layers: *stratified rock.* **stratification** (ˌstrætɪfɪ'keɪʃən) *nu* arrangement in layers.

stratosphere ('strætəsfɪə*) *nc* a layer of mixed gases lying above the surface of the earth.

stratum ('strɑːtəm) *nc, pl* **-ta** (tə) **1** a layer of rock in the earth's surface: see picture. **2** a group in society that is of the same class.

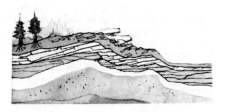

stratum

straw (strɔː) **1** *nu* dried stalks of wheat, etc., used for making hats, baskets, etc., and as food for cattle. *nc* **2** one of these stalks. **3** a thin, hollow tube for sucking up liquid into the mouth.

strawberry ('strɔːbərɪ) *nc, pl* **-ries** (a plant producing) a juicy, red fruit with small, yellow seeds on its surface: *strawberry jam:* see picture at **fruits.**

stray (streɪ) *vi* **1** wander away from the rest of a group or from the right path. **2** wander away from the main subject when speaking. ●*nc* a person or animal who has wandered away, esp. a child. ●*adj* seen, heard, etc., occasionally.

streak (striːk) *nc* **1** a long, thin line of something: *a streak of light.* **2** a quality in someone's character. ●*vi* **1** move very quickly. **2** *vt* mark with streaks.

stream (striːm) *nc* **1** a very small river. **2** a continual movement in one direction of people or things: *a stream of traffic.* **3** *chiefly Brit* a group of children separated by level of ability from others of the same age in a school: *There are three streams in the first year—stream A is for the cleverest.* ●*vi* **1** flow or move continually in one direction; flow steadily: *Blood streamed from his nose.* **2** flow or move freely. **3** *vt* divide into streams (**stream** def. **3**).

streamer *nc* a long, coloured ribbon of paper. **streamline** (ˈstriːmlaɪn) *vt* 1 give a shape to (a vehicle, plane, etc.) that makes it move more efficiently. 2 *business* make (a system) smoother by removing unnecessary activities, etc. **streamlined** *adj* 1 having a shape that allows air, etc., to flow over surfaces more easily. 2 smooth in operation.

street (striːt) *nc* a road in a town or village with houses on both sides.

strength (strenθ) *nu* 1 the quality of being strong in mind or body. 2 someone or something that gives help or power. 3 the full or total power of a group of people: *The army was below strength.* **strengthen** (ˈstrenθən) *vti* make or become stronger.

strenuous (ˈstrenjʊəs) *adj* needing or using much effort or strength: *a strenuous game.*

stress (stres) 1 *ncu* (an example of) force put on a word or part of a word to make the meaning stronger or more important; force placed on anything for this purpose: *He laid yet more stress on the importance of justice.* 2 *nu* pressure or great influence; time or conditions of difficulty: *Stress because of too much work caused his illness.* ● *vt* put stress on.

stretch (stretʃ) *vt* 1 make tight, straight, and longer or larger by pulling. 2 *infml* make something include more than is really right or true: *stretch the rules.* *vi* 3 become longer, etc., by being pulled. 4 spread out between two points or from one point: *The road stretches a long way.* ● *ncu* 1 (an example of) stretching or being stretched. 2 *nc* a length of time or piece of country, etc., that is uninterrupted. **stretch out** lie flat and spread out one's body. **stretcher** *nc* a frame of two poles with strong cloth between for carrying a sick or injured person.

strew (struː) *vt* spread (esp. small things) in various directions over a surface.

strewn (struːn) past participle of **strew**.

stricken (ˈstrɪkən) *adj* (of a person's feelings) much affected (by): *stricken with grief.*

strict (strɪkt) *adj* -er, -est 1 expecting to be obeyed; firm. 2 exact; total: *the strict truth.* **strictly** *adv*

stridden (ˈstrɪdən) past participle of **stride**.

stride (straɪd) *vi* walk with long steps, esp. as when in a hurry. ● *nc* a long step; distance covered in such a step. **take (something) in one's stride** do (something) without any difficulty; accept without complaint.

strife (straɪf) *nu* quarrelling; violent argument.

strike (straɪk) *vt* 1 hit: *The ball struck him on the arm.* 2 enter suddenly into (one's mind): *It struck me that I'd seen him before somewhere.* 3 find (something, esp. oil). 4

make (a coin, etc.). *vti* 5 (of a match), (cause to) light by scraping against something hard. 6 (cause to) sound: *The clock struck three.* 7 *vi* (of employees) stop working for an employer as a protest against something, in order to get better wages, etc. ● *nc* 1 a stoppage of work. 2 an example of striking oil, etc. 3 an attack, esp. by planes. **be (out) on strike** be taking part in a **strike** (def. 1). **strike down** cause to be very ill or die: *He was struck down by a serious illness.* **strike off** remove (esp. a name) from (a list). **strike out** 1 cross out, as with a pen. 2 begin something new. **strike up** 1 begin to play (music). 2 start (a new friendship). **striking** *adj* getting much attention or interest; impressive. **strikingly** *adv*

string (strɪŋ) 1 *ncu* (a piece of) strong thread used for tying, hanging, etc.; *nc* a piece of this. *nc* 2 a tightly stretched piece of wire, etc., on a musical instrument. 3 a set of things arranged on a thread: *a string of beads.* 4 any set of people or things in a line or connected in some: *a string of insults; string of cars; string of racehorses.* 5 (usually *pl*) a musical instrument with strings, which is played in an orchestra. ● *vt* 1 put (beads, etc.) on a string. 2 hang (something) on a string. **string along** accompany someone. **with no strings attached** without conditions. **stringy** (ˈstrɪŋɪ) *adj* -ier, -iest (of a person's body) thin but tough, like string.

stringent (ˈstrɪndʒənt) *adj* 1 that demands obedience: *stringent rules.* 2 lacking in money, esp. public money.

strip (strɪp) 1 *vt* remove the covering of (something): *strip a bed and put on clean sheets.* 2 *vti* take off (someone's) clothes. ● *nc* a long, narrow piece of something: *a strip of land.* **strip (someone) of** take away a person's (possessions, rights, etc.).

stripe (straɪp) *nc* 1 a long, narrow band of colour that is different from the colour of the cloth or surface that surrounds it. 2 a thin band, worn esp. on the sleeve, to show rank. **striped** (straɪpt) *adj* marked with stripes.

stripling (ˈstrɪplɪŋ) *nc* a boy, not yet a man.

strive (straɪv) *vi* work hard for some purpose or aim; make much effort.

striven (ˈstrɪvən) past participle of **strive**.

strode (strəʊd) past tense of **stride**.

stroke (strəʊk) *nc* 1 a blow: *a stroke of the whip; a hammer stroke.* 2 one of a set of movements in writing, drawing, etc.: *a stroke of the pen.* 3 something that happens suddenly, by an effort or by chance: *a good stroke of business; stroke of luck.* 4 the sign (/) used in writing, esp. as in a fraction or instead of the word 'or'. 5 a sudden attack that damages the brain. 6 one of a set of movements in sport: *a good tennis stroke.* **7** a sound made by a clock striking, esp. on the hour. ●*vt* move the hand gently, slowly, and frequently over a surface: *stroke one's beard.*

stroll (strəʊl) *vi* walk without haste. ●*nc* a walk: *go for a stroll in the park.*

strong (strɒŋ) *adj* **stronger** (ˈstrɒŋgə*), **strongest** (ˈstrɒŋgɪst) **1** having strength of body or mind. **2** difficult to break. **3** with a powerful taste or smell: *strong coffee; Onions have a strong smell.* **stronghold** (ˈstrɒŋhəʊld) *nc* a place, such as a fort, that is made to be defended. **strongly** *adv*

strove (strəʊv) past tense of **strive.**

struck (strʌk) past tense and past participle of **strike.**

structure (ˈstrʌktʃə*) **1** *nu* the way in which something is built or made up. **2** *nc* a building. ●*vt* give order or form to. **structural** (ˈstrʌktʃərəl) *adj* of a structure or its most important parts.

struggle (ˈstrʌgəl) *vi* **1** make great efforts, esp. under difficulties. **2** fight. **3** try to get free from: *the fish struggling in the net.* ●*nc* an instance of struggling.

strum (strʌm) *vt* play (a musical instrument) in a careless, esp. unskilled, way.

strung (strʌŋ) past tense and past participle of **string.**

strut (strʌt) *often derogatory vi* walk about with one's head held in a proud way, as if one were very important.

stub (stʌb) *nc* **1** the end of something that is almost used up: *the stub of a pencil.* **2** anything short and not pointed: *a stub of a tail.* **3** the part of a ticket, cheque, etc., remaining after the rest has been used. ●*vt* **1** knock (one's toe) against something. **2** put out (a cigarette) by pressing its end down on a surface.

stubble (ˈstʌbəl) *nu* the short ends of wheat, etc., remaining after a field has been cut; anything that looks like this: *a stubble of beard.*

stubborn (ˈstʌbən) *adj* **1** not easily changing one's opinion or giving in. **2** difficult to treat or deal with. **stubbornly** *adv*

stubby (ˈstʌbɪ) *adj* **-ier, -iest** short and thick.

stuck (stʌk) past tense and past participle of **stick².**

stud¹ (stʌd) *nc* **1** a button-like device that passes through two holes to fasten a shirt collar, etc.: see picture. **2** a nail, pin, etc., with a large head, esp. used as an ornament on something. ●*vt* decorate or cover with studs or as if with studs: *a sky studded with stars.*

stud² *nc* a group of horses kept for mating and producing young; place where such horses are kept.

stud

student (ˈstjuːdənt) *nc* a person who studies, esp. at a college, university, etc.

studio (ˈstjuːdɪəʊ) *nc, pl* **-s 1** a large room used for work that needs light and space: *an artist's studio.* **2** a room or set of rooms, esp. very large, where television programmes and films are made.

studious (ˈstjuːdɪəs) *adj* **1** in the habit of studying. **2** done carefully and on purpose.

study (ˈstʌdɪ) *nc, pl* **-dies 1** *ncu* (an example of) learning about a subject, esp. by reading about: *the study of English literature; How are your studies going at school? nc* **2** a room in which one studies, reads, etc. **3** something drawn or played on an instrument as a form of practice. ●*vt* **1** learn about (a subject), esp. by reading about it. **2** look at carefully. **3** *vi* give one's attention to study.

stuff (stʌf) *nu* **1** the cloth or substance of which something is made. **2** any substance that is worthless or the name of which is unknown: *What's this sticky stuff in your pocket?* ●*vt* **1** pack things very tightly into (something) until very full. **2** fill (a dead animal's empty skin) with material to make it look as it did alive. **3** prepare (a chicken, piece of meat, etc.) for cooking by putting herbs, etc., into it. **4** *infml vti* (cause to) eat too much. **stuffy** *adj* **-ier, -iest 1** lacking fresh or free-flowing air. **2** uninteresting; old-fashioned.

stumble (ˈstʌmbəl) *vi* **1** almost fall when walking or running by making a wrong step or tripping. **2** walk in an unsure and unsteady way. **3** get one's words mixed up, make mistakes, etc., when speaking. **stumbling block** *nc* something that causes difficulty or gets in the way of progress.

stump (stʌmp) *nc* **1** the part of a tree left in the ground after it has fallen or been cut down; anything similarly left after the main part has been removed by some means. **2** *cricket* one of the three upright sticks that form part of the wicket. ●*vt* **1** *infml* puzzle: *This question stumps me!* **2** *vi* walk in a heavy way.

stun (stʌn) *vt* **1** make unconscious, esp. by a blow on the head or a fall. **2** cause great surprise to; shock.

stung (stʌŋ) past tense and past participle of **sting.**

stunk (stʌŋk) past participle of **stink.**

stunt (stʌnt) *vt* cause (the growth or development) (of) to go slowly or stop. ● *nc* something done to get public attention, esp. something dangerous, exciting, or skilful.

stupefy ('stju:pɪfaɪ) *vt* make unable to think clearly.

stupendous (stju:'pendəs) *adj* very great in size or in importance.

stupid ('stju:pɪd) *adj* **-er, -est** slow to understand; foolish. **stupidity** (stju:'pɪdɪtɪ) *ncu* being stupid; something done that is stupid. **stupidly** *adv*

stupor ('stju:pə*) *ncu* a state almost like sleep, caused by shock, drugs, too much alcohol, etc.

sturdy ('stɜ:dɪ) *adj* **-ier, -iest** strong and healthy: *a sturdy little boy.*

stutter ('stʌtə*) *vi* have difficulty in making the sound of a word when speaking. ● *nc* (an instance or habit of) stuttering.

sty[1] (staɪ) *n* See **pigsty** under **pig.**

sty[2] *nc, pl* **sties** a septic place on the edge of the eyelid.

style (staɪl) *ncu* **1** (a) way of doing things, writing, speaking, etc.: *furniture in the modern style; I like the style of the book he has written.* **2** (a) fashion in clothes and hairdressing. **3** *nu* the quality of being different or behaving in a superior or fashionable way: *You may not like him, but you've got to agree he has style!* **4** *nc* the part joined to the seed container in a plant. ● *vt* arrange or design. **stylish** ('staɪlɪʃ) *adj* fashionable; different in a superior or fashionable way. **stylistic** (staɪ'lɪstɪk) *adj* of style in writing or art.

stylus ('staɪləs) *nc* a needle-like device used for playing sound on a record: see picture.

stylus

suave (swɑ:v) *adj* **-r, -st** (of a person's speech or manners) very polite, sometimes in a false way.

sub (sʌb) *infml n* short for **submarine** or **subscription.**

subconscious (ˌsʌb'kɒnʃəs) *adj* (of a thought, etc.) so deep in the mind that one is unaware of its presence. ● *nu* the part of the mind containing such thoughts, etc. **subconsciously** *adv* without active thought.

subcontinent (ˌsʌb'kɒntɪnənt) *nc* a large mass of land that is not big enough to be called a continent.

subdivide (ˌsʌbdɪ'vaɪd) *vti* divide (something already divided) into still smaller parts. **subdivision 1** (ˌsʌbdɪ'vɪʒən) *nu* subdividing. **2** (ˌsʌbdɪvɪʒən) *nc* one of the parts, etc., obtained by subdividing.

subdue (səb'dju:) *vt* **1** bring under control. **2** make lower in spirits; make (a colour or sound) quieter or softer.

subject ('sʌbdʒɪkt) *adj* under the control of a foreign government, person, or thing. ● *nc* **1** any person, except the king or ruler, belonging to a country: *a British subject.* **2** a person or matter being talked or written about, etc.: *Keep to the subject!* **3** *grammar* the part of a sentence that does the action: *'He' is the subject of 'He told us what to do'.* ● (səb'dʒekt) *vt* **1** cause (someone) to undergo something. **2** bring (a country, person, etc.) under one's control. **subject to 1** likely to do or to suffer something. **2** on the condition that. **subjection** (səb'dʒekʃən) *nu* bringing under control or being brought under control.

subjective (səb'dʒektɪv) *adj* based on feelings.

subjunctive (səb'dʒʌŋktɪv) *grammar adj, nc* (to do with) the form of a verb that is used to show wishes or situations that might happen, for example 'were' in 'I wish he were here'.

sublime (sə'blaɪm) *adj* **-r, -st** of the most noble kind; causing feelings of honour, admiration, etc.

submarine (ˌsʌbmə'ri:n, 'sʌbməri:n) (*infml abbrev.* **sub**) *nc* a boat that is able to travel under water, used esp. in war: see picture.

submarine

submerge (səb'mɜ:dʒ) **1** *vt* put under water; cover with water. **2** *vi* (of something lying on the surface) go under water.

submit (səb'mɪt) **1** *vti* give (oneself, someone, or something) over to the control or power of someone or something. **2** *vt* put forward for people to think about, discuss, etc.: *submit one's opinion; submit an examination paper.* **3** *vi* give in: *submit to temptation.* **submission** (səb'mɪʃən) *ncu* (an instance of) submitting. **submissive** (səb'mɪsɪv) *adj* easily giving in to the power or control of someone or something.

subordinate (sə'bɔːdɪnət) *adj* less important in value, position, etc. ● *nc* a person in a less important position, and esp. under one's command. ● (sə'bɔːdɪneɪt) *vt* make or treat as less important.

subscribe (səb'skraɪb) *vti* 1 (followed by **to**) agree with (a general opinion, etc.). 2 join in with others by paying (money) (for something or for a cause). **subscriber** *nc* a person who joins with others to pay money for something. **subscription** (səb'skrɪpʃən) 1 *nu* subscribing or being subscribed. 2 *(infml abbrev.* **sub***) nc* an amount of money paid to join a club, for a cause, etc.

subsequent ('sʌbsɪkwənt) *adj* coming later in time or order and esp. as a result: *Subsequent events showed the foolishness of his earlier actions.* **subsequently** *adv*

subset ('sʌbset) *mathematics nc* a set of things of the same kind within a larger set.

subside (səb'saɪd) *vi* 1 (of water or land) sink to a lower or normal level. 2 (of strong feelings, storms, etc.) become calmer and quieter.

subsidiary (səb'sɪdjərɪ) *adj* not of first importance but a useful support to one that is. ● *nc* a subsidiary thing, esp. a business.

subsidise ('sʌbsɪdaɪz) *vt* (esp. of the government, a society, etc.) agree to give money as a help towards (a person or a cause).

subsidy ('sʌbsɪdɪ) *nc, pl* **-dies** money that the government, a society, etc., agrees to pay to help a cause or to keep down the prices of goods sold to the public.

subsistence (səb'sɪstəns) *nu* existence; way of keeping oneself alive or earning one's living, esp. at the lowest possible level.

subsoil ('sʌbsɔɪl) *nu* the soil that lies just below the soil on the surface

substance ('sʌbstəns) 1 *ncu* (an example of) the matter of which something is made; *nc* an example of this. *nu* 2 the real or main points of a subject, etc. 3 weight; firmness: *an idea without substance.* 4 property; wealth: *a man of substance.*

substandard (,sʌb'stændəd) *adj* of a lower quality than is usual or wanted.

substantial (səb'stænʃəl) *adj* 1 well and solidly made: *a substantial house.* 2 (of a person) rather rich. 3 large: *substantial prices; a substantial meal.* **substantially** *adv* largely; a lot.

substantiate (səb'stænʃɪeɪt) *vt* support (something said, claimed, etc.) by giving further facts.

substitute ('sʌbstɪtjuːt) *nc* a person or thing put in the place of another. ● *vt* 1 put or use (someone or something) in the place of another. 2 *infml vi* be a substitute for. **substitution** (,sʌbstɪ'tjuːʃən) *nu* substituting or being substituted.

subterfuge ('sʌbtəfjuːdʒ) 1 *nc* an excuse, lie, or trick used to avoid blame, discovery, or trouble. 2 *nu* the use of such deception.

subterranean (,sʌbtə'reɪnɪən) *adj* under the surface of the ground: *subterranean caves.*

sub-title ('sʌbtaɪtəl) *nc* 1 a second title coming after the main title of a book. 2 *(usually pl)* words printed on a film made in a foreign language, giving the meaning of the words spoken in it.

subtle ('sʌtəl) *adj* **-r, -st** 1 not easily noticed because delicate or slight: *a subtle smell; subtle changes.* 2 clever. **subtly** ('sʌtlɪ) *adv*

subtract (səb'trækt) *vt* take away (a number or a quantity) from a larger one. **subtraction** (səb'trækʃən) *ncu* (an example of) subtracting.

suburb ('sʌbɜːb) *nc* an outer district of a town or city, esp. where people live. **suburban** (sə'bɜːbən) *adj* 1 of or to do with a suburb. 2 having fixed interests; unchanging and dull.

subvert (sʌb'vɜːt) *vt* overthrow (a government, religion, etc.) by causing people to lose trust or faith in it. **subversive** (sʌb'vɜːsɪv) *adj* likely or planned to overthrow a government, etc.

subway ('sʌbweɪ) *nc* 1 a tunnel built underground for people to get from one side of a road to the other. 2 *US* See **underground**.

succeed (sək'siːd) 1 *vi* do what one has wanted to do; do very well. 2 *vti* come next in order to and take the place of (someone or something). 3 *vi* (followed by **to**) have (a title, money, etc.) when the owner dies.

success (sək'ses) 1 *nu* a result that one hoped or planned for: *success in life.* 2 *nc* someone or something that succeeds. **successful** *adj* having success. **successfully** *adv*

succession (sək'seʃən) *nu* 1 the coming of one thing or person after another in time or in order; *nc* an example of this. 2 having a title, money, etc., when the owner dies. **in succession** one after the other. **successive** *adj* coming one after the other. **successor** (sək'sesə*) nc* a person or thing that comes after another and takes his, her, or its place.

succinct (sək'sɪŋkt) *adj* (capable of) saying much in a very few words. **succinctly** *adv*

succour *US* **succor** ('sʌkə*) literary nu* help, esp. in a time of difficulty. ● *vt* give help to.

succulent ('sʌkjʊlənt) *adj* 1 (esp. of fruit) full of juice; having a pleasant taste. 2 (of plants) having thick, fleshy leaves and stems. ● *nc* a succulent plant.

succumb (sə'kʌm) *vi* 1 give way (to temptation, etc.). 2 die.

such (sʌtʃ) *determiner* **1** of the same kind or degree: *Such languages as French and German are taught in schools; Such beauty as hers is not often seen.* **2** of a kind already mentioned or known about: *He wanted to see it but had no such luck.* **3** (adding force to); very: *We had such nice times!* **such a** so great; so much of, etc.: *I had such a shock!; in such a hurry.* **such as 1** of a kind that or like that. **2** for example. **as such 1** in itself or in themselves: *A beautiful face as such isn't certain to bring happiness.* **2** in a particular position already mentioned or known of: *A teacher as such doesn't know everything.* **such... that** so great; to so high a degree: *It was such a hot day that we had to sit down and rest.*

suck (sʌk) *vti* **1** draw (liquid) through the mouth by making a small hole with the lips. **2** take in (ideas, knowledge, etc.). **3** draw (liquid) (from): *a baby sucking its mother's breast; suck a sweet; Plants suck moisture from the soil.* ● *nc* an act of sucking. **sucker** *nc* **1** a device, usually of rubber, with a surface that clings to another surface by suction. **2** *chiefly US, infml* a person silly enough to trust someone or something not worthy of trust. **3** a new shoot of a plant growing out from a root.

suckle (ˈsʌkəl) *vti* feed (a baby or young animal) on milk from the breast.

suction (ˈsʌkʃən) *nu* **1** the action of sucking. **2** the holding together of two surfaces because of removal of the air between them.

sudden (ˈsʌdən) *adj* happening quickly and with no warning: *sudden death.* **all of a sudden** without warning. **suddenly** *adv* **suddenness** *nu*

suds (sʌdz) *n pl* (bubbles on top of) soapy water.

sue (suː) **1** *vt* make a claim against (someone) in a law court. **2** *vi old-fashioned or law* ask (for): *sue for mercy.*

suede (sweɪd) *nu* a soft leather with one rough or brushed surface. ● *adj* of suede: *a suede jacket.*

suet (ˈsuːɪt) *nu* hard fat from the insides of sheep and cattle, used in cooking.

suffer (ˈsʌfə*) *vi* **1** feel pain, grief, etc. **2** get worse or less in quality: *When you hurry, the work suffers.* *vt* **3** undergo (something causing) (pain, sadness, etc.). **4** *formal or old-fashioned* allow to happen; put up with: *Why do you suffer such a rude man?* **sufferer** (ˈsʌfərə*) *nc* a person who suffers, esp. from an illness.

sufferance (ˈsʌfərəns) *n* **on sufferance** being allowed or put up with, but without being wanted or liked.

suffice (səˈfaɪs) *vti* be enough to satisfy.

sufficient (səˈfɪʃənt) *adj* enough. **sufficiency** (səˈfɪʃənsɪ) *nu* a sufficient amount or quantity. **sufficiently** *adv*

suffix (ˈsʌfɪks) *grammar nc* a group of letters joined to the end of a word in order to change its meaning: *'-ery' is the suffix in 'bakery'.*

suffocate (ˈsʌfəkeɪt) *vti* **1** (cause to) die by stopping breathing. **2** (cause to) have difficulty in breathing. **suffocation** (ˌsʌfəˈkeɪʃən) *nu* suffocating or being suffocated.

suffrage (ˈsʌfrɪdʒ) *nu* the right to vote in political elections.

sugar (ˈʃʊgə*) *nu* a sweet substance found in many plants and used to give a sweet taste to food. ● *vt* make sweet by adding or mixing with sugar. **sugar beet** or **cane** *nu* plants from which sugar is obtained.

suggest (səˈdʒest) *vt* **1** mention (an idea, plan, etc.) to be thought about or discussed. **2** show; cause to come into the mind: *Her red face suggested that she was guilty.* **suggestion** (səˈdʒestʃən) *nc* **1** an idea, plan, etc., that is suggested. **2** a small sign: *a suggestion of a smile.* **suggestive** (səˈdʒestɪv) *adj* **1** that brings ideas, memories, etc., into the mind. **2** that suggests something likely to shock or embarrass.

suicide (ˈsjuːɪsaɪd) *nu* **1** the killing of oneself; *nc* an example of this or a person who does this. **2** any act in which one ruins or puts an end to one's own interests or chances for future success. **suicidal** (ˌsjuːɪˈsaɪdəl) *adj* **1** of or likely to lead to suicide. **2** wanting to commit suicide.

suit (sjuːt, suːt) *nc* **1** a set of clothes of the same material made to be worn together: see picture; any set of clothes or piece of clothing, for a special purpose: *a swimsuit.* **2** See **lawsuit** under **law**. **3** one of the four sets of playing-cards in a pack. **4** *formal* a request. ● *vt* **1** satisfy; be all right for: *Your plan suits me.* **2** *vti* look well on: *I like your dress, blue suits you.* **3** *vt* make right for the purpose. **suited** *adj* suitable; having the right qualities: *Is he suited for the job?*

suit

suitable (ˈsjuːtəbəl) *adj* right or fitting for the purpose. **suitably** *adv*

suitcase (ˈsjuːtkeɪs) (often shortened to **case**) *nc* a flat-sided case with a handle, for carrying clothes when travelling.

suite (swiːt) *nc* **1** a set of rooms in a hotel. **2** a set of pieces of furniture designed to go well together. **3** a piece of music consisting of several parts.

suitor ('sjuːtə*) *nc* **1** *old-fashioned* a man who tries to win the love of a woman so that she will marry him. **2** *formal* a person making a claim in a court of law.

sulfur ('sʌlfə*) *US n* See **sulphur**.

sulk (sʌlk) *vi* be bad-tempered in a silent way. **sulky** *adj* **-ier, -iest** silent and unfriendly because bad-tempered.

sullen ('sʌlən) *adj* **1** bad-tempered and not willing to talk. **2** dark and unpromising: *a sullen sky*.

sulphur *US* **sulfur** ('sʌlfə*) *nu* an element that is not metal and that burns with a blue flame and a strong smell: symbol S

sultan ('sʌltən) *nc* a ruler of a Muslim country.

sultana (səl'tɑːnə) *nc* **1** a small, dried, seedless fruit used in cooking. **2** a wife or woman connected with a sultan.

sultry ('sʌltrɪ) *adj* **-ier, -iest** (of the weather) hot and uncomfortable.

sum (sʌm) *nc* **1** the total obtained when numbers, etc., have been added together. **2** *arithmetic* a problem. **3** an amount of money. **sum up 1** make a total of by adding together. **2** give, in a few words at the end of a speech, trial, etc., the main points again. **3** form an opinion of.

summary ('sʌmərɪ) *nc, pl* **-ries** the main points of a speech, book, etc., given in a few words. ● *adj* **1** giving the main points. **2** done quickly without thinking about it properly; done without delay. **summarise** ('sʌməraɪz) *vt* make or be a summary of.

summer ('sʌmə*) *nc* the season between spring and autumn, in which the temperature is at its highest. **summer time** the time when clocks are made to show one hour ahead of normal time so that darkness falls later. **summertime** ('sʌmətaɪm) *nu* the season of summer.

summit ('sʌmɪt) *nc* **1** a pointed top: *the summit of a mountain:* see picture. **2** the highest point or aim: *the summit of her hopes and ambition*. **summit conference** a very important meeting of those people with the highest power.

summon ('sʌmən) *vt* order (a person) to come to or attend. **summons** ('sʌmənz) *nc* **1** a written order to come to or attend a court of law. **2** an order to do or attend something. ● *vt* order (a person) to attend at a court of law.

sumptuous ('sʌmptjʊəs) *adj* splendid; expensive and beautiful.

sun (sʌn) *nu* **1** the nearest star, that gives out heat and light to the earth. **2** heat and light from the sun: *sit outside in the sun*. **3** *nc* any fixed star with smaller bodies moving round it. ● *vt* put (oneself) into the sunshine. **sunbathe** ('sʌnbeɪð) *vi* uncover part or all of one's body and enjoy the sun's warmth. **sunbeam** ('sʌnbiːm) *nc* a line or ray of light from the sun. **sunburn** ('sʌnbɜːn) *nu* the state of having let too much sun on the skin, making it very red and sore; place on the skin where this has happened. **sundial** ('sʌndaɪəl) *nc* a device on which the time can be read when a bar on its surface casts a shadow during times of sunlight. **sunflower** ('sʌnflaʊə*) *nc* a very tall plant with a large, yellow flower: see picture at **flowers**. **sunlight** ('sʌnlaɪt) *nu* the light coming from the sun. **sunrise** ('sʌnraɪz) **1** *nc* the daily rising of the sun. **2** *nu* the time when this happens. **sunset** ('sʌnset) or **sundown** ('sʌndaʊn) **1** *nc* the daily going down of the sun below the horizon. **2** *nu* the time when this happens. **sunshine** ('sʌnʃaɪn) *nu* the light or warmth from the sun. **sunspot** ('sʌnspɒt) *nc* **1** *infml* a place where the weather is warm and sunny. **2** one of the dark spots that sometimes appear on the sun's surface. **suntan** ('sʌntæn) (*abbrev.* **tan**) *nc* a brown colour on the skin due to its being uncovered in sunlight. **sunny** ('sʌnɪ) *adj* **-ier, -iest 1** having bright sunlight. **2** cheerful.

sundae ('sʌndeɪ) *nc* an ice cream with fruit, nuts, etc., and a sweet sauce and whipped cream on top.

Sunday ('sʌndɪ) *nc* the first day of the week, before Monday.

sunder ('sʌndə*) *archaic or literary vt* break apart; separate.

sundry ('sʌndrɪ) *adj* various.

sung (sʌŋ) past participle of **sing**.

sunk (sʌŋk) past tense and past participle of **sink. sunken** ('sʌŋkən) *adj* below the usual level or surface: *sunken eyes*.

super ('suːpə*) *infml adj* **1** very good: *What a super idea!* **2** of the best quality.

superb (sʊ'pɜːb) *adj* **1** extremely good: *He's a superb singer*. **2** very grand in appearance; splendid.

superficial (,suːpə'fɪʃəl) *adj* **1** on or of the surface only. **2** without deep thought, feeling, learning, etc. **superficially** *adv*

summit

superfluous (su'pɜːfluəs) *adj* more than is needed or wanted; not needed.

superimpose (ˌsuːpərɪmˈpəʊz) *vt* put (something) directly over and onto (something else).

superintendent (ˌsuːpərɪnˈtendənt) *nc* 1 a person who is in charge of a place or controls people at work, etc. 2 a police officer in a middle rank.

superior (su'pɪərɪə*) *adj* 1 better than usual in quality or level. 2 greater in number. 3 higher; higher in social or official position. 4 *often derogatory* considering that one is better in some way than everyone else. ● *nc* a person who is higher in position or better than another or others. **superior to** 1 better than. 2 higher in official or social position. **superiority** (su,pɪərɪˈɒrɪtɪ) *nu* being superior.

superlative (su'pɜːlətɪv) *adj* of the highest degree, amount, or quality. ● *nc, adj* (to do with) the form of an adjective or adverb meaning 'most': *'best' and 'slowest' are the superlatives of 'good' and 'slow'.*

supermarket ('suːpəˌmɑːkɪt) *nc* a large store selling a variety of goods, usually food, which customers collect as they walk round and pay for as they leave: see picture.

supermarket

supernatural (ˌsuːpəˈnætʃərəl) *adj* of events, etc., that are outside the natural or normal way of things and cannot be explained by the laws of nature.

supersede (ˌsuːpəˈsiːd) *vt* take the place of; put or be used in the place of.

supersonic (ˌsuːpəˈsɒnɪk) *adj* faster than the speed that sound travels: *a supersonic plane.*

superstition (ˌsuːpəˈstɪʃən) 1 *nu* belief in magic, the unknown, etc., based on fear or ignorance and not on reason. 2 *nc* an instance of this. **superstitious** (ˌsuːpəˈstɪʃəs) *adj* 1 of or to do with superstition. 2 believing in superstition.

supervise ('suːpəvaɪz) *vt* be in charge of or watch and control (people at work). **supervision** (ˌsuːpəˈvɪʒən) *nu* supervising or being supervised. **supervisor** ('suːpəvaɪzə*) *nc* a person who supervises. **supervisory** ('suːpəvaɪzərɪ) *adj* supervising.

supper ('sʌpə*) *nc* the last meal of the day.

supplant (səˈplɑːnt) *vt* take the place of; supersede.

supple ('sʌpəl) *adj* **-r, -st** bending or moving easily: *a supple body.*

supplement ('sʌplɪmənt) *nc* 1 something added to give extra information or to improve. 2 extra pages or a magazine added to a newspaper. ● ('sʌplɪment) *vt* add to.

supplication (ˌsʌplɪˈkeɪʃən) *ncu* a humble but urgent request.

supply (səˈplaɪ) *vt* give, sell, etc. (what is wanted or needed). ● *nc, pl* **-plies** 1 something supplied. 2 *(pl)* a store of food, etc., for an activity, need, or journey. 3 an amount of something for use or for sale; stock. 4 *nu* the availability of supplies: *in short supply, so hard to obtain.* **supplier** (səˈplaɪə*) *nc* a person or business that supplies goods.

support (səˈpɔːt) *vt* 1 carry the weight of; hold up. 2 give help for someone or something to continue: *support a political party.* 3 provide the necessary things of life for. ● *nu* 1 supporting or being supported. 2 *nc* someone or something that supports. **supporter** (səˈpɔːtə*) *nc* a person that supports.

suppose (səˈpəʊz) *vt* 1 take to be true before knowing for sure; imagine: *Let us suppose that you have passed your examination, what are your future plans?* 2 believe; think: *I don't suppose he'll be late.* 3 *formal* require that (something) exists: *Guilt supposes an awareness of crime.* ● *conj* (used to suggest something): *Suppose I told you I was lying— would you believe me?* **be supposed to** 1 be expected to: *You're supposed to be in bed by nine.* 2 be allowed to: *You're not supposed to stay out after nine.* **supposing** (səˈpəʊzɪŋ) *conj* if. **supposition** (ˌsʌpəˈzɪʃən) 1 *nu* supposing. 2 *nc* something expected or put forward as likely.

suppress (səˈpres) *vt* 1 put an end to with force or power: *suppress a riot.* 2 prevent from happening or being seen: *suppress a laugh.* **suppression** (səˈpreʃən) *nu* suppressing or being suppressed.

supreme (su'priːm) *adj* highest in importance, power, or quality. **supremacy** (su'preməsɪ) *nu* being supreme; highest power. **supremely** *adv*

surcharge ('sɜːtʃɑːdʒ) *nc* an amount of money added to the basic price.

sure (ʃʊə*) *adj* 1 without doubt; feeling certain. 2 that can be depended on or trusted. 3 steady; not shaking: *sure steps.* **as sure as** as certain as. **be sure to** 1 be certain to. 2 don't forget to. **make sure** make certain. **surely** *adv* 1 certainly; steadily. 2 (used to express hope that something is or is not true): *Surely you didn't believe him!*

surety (ˈʃʊərətɪ) *ncu, pl* **-ties** 1 (a person) promising to pay the debt or bear any blame for the behaviour of another person. 2 (a written) formal agreement that something will be done.

surf (sɜːf) *nu* waves with many white bubbles breaking on the seashore: see picture. **surfboard** (ˈsɜːfbɔːd) *nc* a long, narrow board used for standing on while allowing waves, esp. large, to carry one toward the shore. **surfing** (ˈsɜːfɪŋ) *nu* the sport of riding on a surfboard.

surf

surface (ˈsɜːfɪs) *nc* 1 the top of a liquid; outside of anything: *The sea's surface was calm; A cube has six surfaces.* 2 what is seen on the outside only: *He appears to be happy on the surface, but deep down he is not.* ● *adj* of the surface only. ● *vt* 1 put a surface on: *a path surfaced with cement.* 2 *vi* rise to the surface.

surfeit (ˈsɜːfɪt) *nc* too much of anything, esp. eating and drinking. ● *vt* have too much of (anything).

surge (sɜːdʒ) *vi* move or rush forward like a wave in the sea. ● *nc* a movement or rush forward: *a surge of anger; surge of waves onto the shore.*

surgeon (ˈsɜːdʒən) *nc* a doctor who cuts into the body to cure a disease.

surgery (ˈsɜːdʒərɪ) 1 *nu* the treatment of injuries and disease by cutting into the body. 2 *Brit nc, pl* **-ries** the room in which one asks for advice or gets treatment from a doctor or dentist.

surgical (ˈsɜːdʒɪkəl) *adj* of or to do with surgery.

surly (sɜːlɪ) *adj* **-ier, -iest** bad-tempered and rude.

surmise (səˈmaɪz) *formal vti* make a guess (about). ● *nc* a guess.

surmount (səˈmaʊnt) *vt* 1 overcome (difficulties, problems, etc.). 2 climb up and over the other side of. 3 lie on top of.

surname (ˈsɜːneɪm) *nc* a family name.

surpass (səˈpɑːs) *vt* 1 be better, greater, etc., than. 2 go further than.

surplus (ˈsɜːpləs) *nc* an amount of something left over that is more than is needed. ● *adj* more than is needed or used: *surplus to requirements.*

surprise (səˈpraɪz) 1 *nu* the feeling caused by something sudden or unexpected. 2 *nc* a sudden or unexpected event, gift, etc. ● *adj* unexpected; sudden. ● *vt* 1 cause a feeling of surprise to. 2 make a sudden attack on; come upon suddenly. **surprising** *adj* causing surprise. **surprisingly** *adv*

surrender (səˈrendə*) *vti* 1 give up (oneself or something) to someone else's control: *surrender the city to the enemy.* 2 give in to (one's feelings, a habit, influence, etc.): *She surrendered to grief and killed herself.* 3 *formal vt* give (something) up through force, influence, or necessity: *Please surrender your ticket as you leave.*

surround (səˈraʊnd) *vt* be or come all round or on all sides of something: *The pretty girl was surrounded by admirers; a town surrounded by the enemy.* ● *nc* something that surrounds, esp. a carpet in a room. **surrounding** *adj* that is all around. **surroundings** *n pl* everything that is round and about a person or place: *He woke and began to notice his surroundings.*

surveillance (sɜːˈveɪləns) *nu* a very careful watch kept on someone, esp. believed to have done or be doing wrong.

survey (səˈveɪ) *vt* 1 take a general look at: *He surveyed the beautiful scene before him.* 2 measure and make a map of (a piece of land). 3 examine (a building) to find out its condition and value. ● (ˈsɜːveɪ) *nc* 1 a general view. 2 a map or report resulting from surveying. **surveyor** (səˈveɪə*) *nc* a person whose job is to survey land or buildings.

survive (səˈvaɪv) 1 *vi* continue to live in spite of death being near. 2 *vt* continue to live after (someone else's death, an accident, war, etc.). **survival** (səˈvaɪvəl) 1 *nu* (the skill of) surviving. 2 *nc* a person or thing that seems to belong to the past but has continued to survive. **survivor** (səˈvaɪvə*) *nc* a person who has survived: *There were no survivors of the plane crash.*

susceptible (səˈseptəbəl) *adj* easily influenced, esp. by one's feelings. **susceptible to** likely to be troubled or affected by: *susceptible to bad colds.*

suspect (səˈspekt) *vt* 1 feel (something unpleasant) to be possible or probable. 2 have doubt about the truth or honesty of. 3 believe (someone) to be guilty of something. ● (ˈsʌspekt) *nc* a person suspected of wrongdoing. ● *adj* causing doubt, because possibly untrue, dishonest, etc.

suspend (səˈspend) *vt* 1 hang up from 2 cause to stay still or float in air, a liquid, etc. 3 delay; stop for a certain length of time. 4 stop (someone) from enjoying special favours or prevent him from doing his duties for a time, as a punishment. **suspenders** *n pl Brit* 1 devices that hang from a belt to fasten on and hold up women's stockings; a similar device hanging from a band round the leg to hold up men's socks. **2** *US* See **brace** (def. 2).

suspense (sə'spens) *nu* an anxious or impatient feeling caused by uncertainty.

suspension (sə'spenʃən) *nu* **1** suspending or being suspended. **2** the parts in a car that stop passengers being shaken about when driving over rough ground. **3** *nc* a liquid with very small pieces floating evenly in it. **suspension bridge** a bridge that is hung between two towers by steel ropes: see picture.

suspension bridge

suspicion (sə'spɪʃən) **1** *nu* a feeling of doubt about someone or something; feeling that something is wrong. *nc* **2** an example of this. **3** a small amount: *A suspicion of doubt showed on his face.* **suspicious** (sə'spɪʃəs) *adj* having or causing suspicion. **suspiciously** *adv*

sustain (sə'steɪn) *vt* **1** *formal* hold up; keep from falling. **2** help to continue in some way: *Her courage sustained her when her husband died.* **3** keep up; keep going: *sustain an argument.* **4** suffer (a loss, etc.). **5** *law* agree with; hold to be right. **sustenance** ('sʌstɪnəns) *often humorous nu* **1** food and drink. **2** the ability of food and drink to sustain a person.

swab (swɒb) *nc* **1** a small piece of cloth used for cleaning a wound or other medical purpose. **2** a cloth, etc., tied to a long handle for cleaning floors. ● *vt* clean or wipe with a swab.

swagger ('swægə*) *vi* walk or behave in a proud, important way. ● *nc* a proud kind of walk or behaviour.

swain (sweɪn) *archaic or poetry nc* a young man living in the country who loves a girl and is often with her.

swallow¹ ('swɒləʊ) *vt* **1** put (food) into one's mouth and allow it to go down the throat. **2** hold back (esp. one's feelings): *swallow one's pride.* **3** *infml* believe (something): *How could you swallow such a story!* **4** use up: *wages swallowed up by debts to be paid.* **5** *vi* make a movement in the throat as if swallowing food, esp. because anxious. ● *nc* an act of swallowing.

swallow² *nc* a small, fast-flying bird with long wings and a V-shaped tail, that flies to a warmer country for the winter: see picture at **birds.**

swam (swæm) past tense of **swim.**

swamp (swɒmp) **1** *nu* very wet, soft ground. **2** *nc* a piece of land like this. ● *vt* (of water) flood into (a boat, house, etc.). **be swamped with** be given too much to do or deal with: *be swamped with work.* **swampy** *adj* **-ier, -iest** like a swamp.

swan (swɒn) *nc* a large bird with a long neck and (usually) white feathers, living on or near water.

swap (also **swop**) (swɒp) *infml vti* give (something) and receive (something else in its place). ● *nc* **1** such an exchange. **2** something exchanged.

swarm (swɔːm) *nc* **1** a large group (of insects, esp. bees, etc.) moving about together. **2** large crowd of people when moving. ● *vi* move in large numbers; crowd around.

swarthy ('swɔːðɪ) *adj* **-ier, -iest** (of a person or his face) having a dark skin.

swash (swɒʃ) *vi* (of water) move up and down, making splashing noises.

swathe (sweɪð) *literary vt* wrap round with cloth.

sway (sweɪ) *vti* **1** (cause to) move in different directions, esp. from one side to the other. **2** (cause to) be influenced. ● *nu* **1** swaying movement. **2** power; influence: *under the sway of.*

swear (sweə*) *vti* **1** say or promise (something) very seriously. **2** (cause to) make a promise using a sacred name or object to strengthen it. **3** *vi* use sacred or sexual words in a wrong way to show strong, esp. angry feelings.

sweat (swet) *nu* **1** the liquid given off by the body through the skin, esp. after great activity or when one is hot. **2** similar drops of liquid on the surface of anything. ● *vi* **1** give out sweat. **2** *vti* (cause to) work hard. **sweaty** *adj* **-ier, -iest** causing, wet with, or smelling of sweat.

sweater ('swetə*) *nc* a garment, esp. of wool, pulled over the head and covering the top part of the body: see picture.

sweater

sweep (swiːp) *vt* **1** clean up (dust, dirt, etc.) from (a place) with a brush: *sweep the floor;*

sweep dead leaves from the garden. **2** take off or away with a strong movement: *The wind swept her hat off.* **3** move quickly over and esp. touch gently. *vi* **4** stretch in a curve that is unbroken: *a huge garden sweeping down to a river.* **5** move in a smooth and continuous way: *She swept out of the room.* ●*nc* **1** an act of sweeping. **2** an example of removal with or as if with a brush. **3** a sweeping movement: *with a sweep of his arm.* **4** a stretch of unbroken country, river, etc., esp. in a curve. **5** *infml* a person who sweeps chimneys. **sweeper** *nc* a person or device that sweeps. **sweeping** *adj* **1** far-reaching: *sweeping changes.* **2** including much, but with not enough attention to details: *He makes sweeping statements about bad laws, but never suggests how they should be changed.*

sweet (swi:t) *adj* **-er, -est 1** having or being like the taste of sugar. **2** pleasant; nice: *a sweet smile; sweet music.* **3** fresh: *the sweet smell of clean sheets.* ●*nc Brit* **1** a small piece of boiled sugar, a piece of chocolate, etc. **2** *Brit* a sweet dish served as a part of a meal. **sweetheart** ('swi:tha:t) *nc* a person who is loved by another of the opposite sex. **sweeten** ('swi:tən) *vti* make or become sweet or sweeter. **sweetly** *adv* **sweetness** *nu* being sweet.

swell (swel) *vti* **1** (cause to) become larger in size, amount, force, etc. **2** (cause to) become fuller or blown out with air, etc.: *boat sails swelled by the wind.* ●*nu* **1** the increasing loudness of a musical instrument. **2** the rising up and falling of waves: *The heavy swell made everyone in the boat feel sick.* ●*adj infml, US* good. **swelling** ('sweliŋ) **1** *nc* a swollen place on the body. **2** *nu* swelling or being swollen.

swelter ('sweltə*) *vi* be hot and uncomfortable: *a sweltering day.*

swept (swept) past tense and past participle of **sweep.**

swerve (swɜ:v) *vti* (cause to) turn to one side suddenly from the direct or usual direction: *The car swerved to avoid hitting the child.* ●*nc* such a movement.

swift¹ (swift) *adj* **-er, -est** fast; done without delay. **swiftly** *adv*

swift² *nc* a kind of small bird with long wings, that eats insects.

swill (swil) **1** *vti* drink greedily. **2** *chiefly Brit vt* wash out with clean water. ●*nc* **1** a washing out. **2** *nu* waste food, esp. in liquid form, for pigs.

swim (swim) **1** *vi* move through water by movements of the body: *They swam in the sea; fish swim.* **2** *vt* cross (a distance of water) in this way. *vi* **3** feel as if everything is turning round and round: *His head swam*

with the noise. **4** be too full or be flowing over with liquid: *eyes swimming with tears.* ●*nc* an act of swimming. **swimmer** *nc* a person who swims. **swimming** *adj* flowing over with or too full of liquid. ●*nu* the sport of swimmers. **swimming-bath** or **pool** *nc* an indoor or outdoor pool for swimming in: *In Britain, swimming-baths are public places for swimming, but a swimming-pool is often in someone's private garden.* **swimming costume** a garment worn, esp. by women and girls, for swimming. **swimming trunks** a short garment worn by men and boys for swimming. **swimsuit** (swimsju:t) *nc* a swimming costume.

swindle ('swindəl) **1** *vt* cheat (a person) out of his money. **2** *vi* get money by deceiving. ●*nc* **1** a dishonest plan. **2** something that is of much less value than it is claimed to be. **swindler** *nc*

swine (swain) *nc, pl* **swine 1** *formal* a pig. **2** *slang* a nasty person.

swing (swiŋ) *vti* **1** (cause to) move backwards and forwards, or with a curving movement; sway. **2** (cause to) turn quickly, in a curving movement: *He swung round to see who was behind him.* **3** *vi* move in an easy, loose way: *swinging along the road.* ●*nc* **1** a swinging movement. **2** a seat hanging by ropes or chains for a child to swing on.

swipe (swaip) *infml vt* **1** hit very hard. **2** steal.

swirl (swɜ:l) *vti* (cause to) move in a circular twisting way. ●*nc* such a movement: *a swirl of smoke.*

swish (swiʃ) **1** *vt* move (a stick, etc.) quickly through the air making a hissing sound. **2** *vi* move with or make such a sound. ●*nc* a sound of something being swished: *the swish of a whip.*

switch (switʃ) *nc* **1** a device for sending a train from one railway line onto another. **2** a device for turning an electric current on or off. **3** a thin stick that is easily bent without breaking, esp. used for punishment. **4** a change: *a sudden switch in our plans.* ●*vt* **1** turn (an electric current) on or off. **2** change or turn suddenly. **3** exchange. **4** *vti* (of a train), (cause to) move onto another line. **switchboard** *nc* a board with several electrical switches, esp. one where telephone calls are received and connected.

swivel ('swivəl) *nc* a device that connects two things, allowing each to move freely and on its own: *a swivel chair.* ●*vti* (cause to) move by means of a swivel.

swollen ('swəulən) past participle of **swell.** ●*adj* having become greater in size.

swoon (swu:n) *literary vi* faint. ●*nc* a sudden attack of fainting.

swoop (swuːp) *vi* come down with a sudden rush. ●*nc* such a movement.

swop (swɒp) *v* See **swap**.

sword (sɔːd) *nc* a weapon with a long, steel blade fixed in a short handle: see picture.

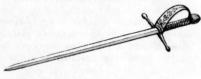

sword

swore (swɔː*) past tense of **swear**.

sworn (swɔːn) past participle of **swear**.

swum (swʌm) past participle of **swim**.

swung (swʌŋ) past tense and past participle of **swing**. .

sycamore (ˈsɪkəmɔː*) *nc* a large tree grown for its wood and its beauty: see picture at **trees**; (sometimes *nu*) valuable wood of this tree.

sycophant (ˈsɪkəfənt) *nc* a person who flatters and shows too much respect for powerful people, hoping for favours.

syllable (ˈsɪləbəl) *nc* a set of sounds that form a part of a word, each part containing a vowel: *'Marvellous' has three syllables.*

syllabus (ˈsɪləbəs) *nc, pl* **-es** or **-bi** (baɪ) a list of things arranged, esp. of work to be done or a course of subjects to be taught.

syllogism (ˈsɪlədʒɪzəm) *nc* a way of reasoning in which a result is reached from two strong ideas that have something in common.

sylph (sɪlf) *nc* **1** a kind of female fairy believed to live in the air. **2** a slender girl or young woman.

sylvan (ˈsɪlvən) *adj* of or to do with woods and forests.

symbol (ˈsɪmbəl) *nc* something that is a sign, mark, example, or picture of something else, esp. an idea: *A lion is sometimes used as a symbol for strength or bravery.* **symbolic** (sɪmˈbɒlɪk) *adj* **1** of or to do with a symbol. **2** acting as a symbol. **symbolise** (ˈsɪmbəlaɪz) *vt* be a symbol of. **symbolism** (ˈsɪmbəlɪzəm) *nu* the showing of ideas, etc., by the use of symbols.

symmetry (ˈsɪmɪtrɪ) *nu* the pleasing arrangement or similarity of two halves of something; beauty that is a result of this; exact agreement in design, size, etc., of all parts with each other. **symmetrical** (sɪˈmetrɪkəl) *adj* having symmetry. **symmetrically** *adv*

sympathetic (ˌsɪmpəˈθetɪk) *adj* having or showing sympathy. **sympathetically** *adv*

sympathise (ˈsɪmpəθaɪz) *vi* share the feelings of other people; feel pity. **sympathiser** (ˈsɪmpəθaɪzə*) *nc* a person who sym-

pathises: *He found there were many sympathisers for his cause.*

sympathy (ˈsɪmpəθɪ) *ncu, pl* **-thies 1** ability to share the feelings of other people. **2** a feeling of pity, agreement, etc., with another's similar feeling. **3** *(pl)* feelings of sympathy or support.

symphony (ˈsɪmfənɪ) *nc, pl* **-nies** a long piece of music to be played by a large group of musicians with a variety of musical instruments.

symptom (ˈsɪmptəm) *nc* a sign showing that something is present, esp. a change in the body showing illness: *A high temperature is a symptom of fever; There were symptoms of trouble before the strike.*

synagogue (ˈsɪnəgɒg) *nc* a building in which Jews meet to pray and in which religion is taught.

synchronise (ˈsɪŋkrənaɪz) *vti* (cause to) happen at the same time, agree as to time, etc.: *We synchronised our watches.*

syndicate (ˈsɪndɪkət) *nc* a group of people or businesses joined together for a common purpose, esp. one needing a large amount of money. ● (ˈsɪndɪkeɪt) *vt* **1** form into a syndicate. **2** publish (stories, pictures, etc.) in several newspapers at the same time.

synonym (ˈsɪnənɪm) *nc* a word that has the same or almost the same meaning as another, such as 'light' and 'lamp'.

synopsis (sɪˈnɒpsɪs) *nc, pl* **-ses** (siːz) a short account of the main points of a book, etc.

syntax (ˈsɪntæks) *nu* rules for the proper arrangement of words in a sentence.

synthesis (ˈsɪnθəsɪs) *nc, pl* **-ses** (siːz) **1** *nu* a way of joining up parts, substances, etc., into a whole. **2** *nc* a whole produced by doing this.

synthetic (sɪnˈθetɪk) *adj* made by synthesis; man-made: *synthetic drugs.* ●*nc* a substance or material made by man, not occurring naturally.

syphon (ˈsaɪfən) *n* See **siphon**.

syringe (sɪˈrɪndʒ) *nc* also **hypodermic** a device for taking in liquid and pushing it out through a needle into something, such as medicine into the body.

syrup (ˈsɪrəp) *nu* a thick, sweet liquid made from sugar, used in cooking, sweetening fruit, etc.

system (ˈsɪstəm) *nc* **1** a group of parts, facts, ideas, etc., that together form a whole: *a system of government.* **2** a number of things arranged to work well together: *the post-office system; system of the human body.* **3** *nu* being carefully arranged and in good order: *You can't work well without some system.* **systematic** (ˌsɪstəˈmætɪk) *adj* done with order. **systematically** *adv*

T

ta (tɑ:) *infml, Brit interj* thank you.

tab (tæb) *nc* a small piece of cloth fixed to a coat, etc., for hanging it up or to show which it belongs to; any small flap. **keep tabs on** keep a careful watch on (someone or something).

tabernacle ('tæbənækəl) *nc* **1** any place, that is not called a church, in which to praise God. **2** (in the Bible) a tent containing sacred objects carried by the Israelites on their journey to Palestine.

table ('teibəl) *nc* **1** a piece of furniture with a flat surface standing on (usually) four legs. **2** a list of numbers, words, facts, etc., usually arranged in columns. ● *vt formal* put forward or offer for discussion. **table-cloth** ('teibəlklɒθ) *nc* a cloth spread over the surface of a table, esp. for meals. **table-spoon** ('teibəlspu:n) *nc* a large spoon used for serving food. **table tennis** a game like tennis but played on a table with small bats and a light ball. **tabletop** ('teibəltɒp) *nc* **1** the surface of a table. **2** the flat top of a hill, etc.

tablet ('tæblɪt) *nc* **1** a small ball of medicine. **2** a small piece of substance: *a tablet of soap*. **3** a piece of stone, wood, etc., on which words are carved.

taboo (tə'bu:) *ncu* something that is forbidden to speak of, touch, do, etc., because of religious reasons or because it is not the custom. ● *adj* forbidden. ● *vt* forbid.

tabulate ('tæbjʊleit) *vt* arrange (numbers, facts, etc.) into lists. **tabulation** (,tæbjʊ-'leiʃən) *nc* tabulating or being tabulated.

tacit ('tæsit) *adj* meant or understood without any words being spoken: *a tacit agreement*.

tack (tæk) *nc* **1** a short nail with a flat head. **2** a long loose stitch made in making clothes, etc., to hold cloth together for a short time. ● *vt* **1** fasten pieces of cloth together. **2** *vi* sail a boat into the wind (and turn, esp. several times) so that the wind is on the opposite side.

tackle ('tækəl) **1** *ncu* ropes, chains, etc., for use on a ship. **2** *nu* the things needed for a particular purpose: *fishing tackle*. ● *vt* **1** deal with (something) and try to overcome it: *tackle a problem*. **2** seize and stop (someone): *tackle a thief*.

tact (tækt) *nu* the understanding of other people's feelings, and being careful not to upset them. **tactful** *adj* having tact. **tactless** *adj* without tact.

tactics ('tæktiks) *nu (with singular verb)* the ability to organise the movements of armies for or during a battle; any plans that need skill. **tactical** ('tæktikəl) *adj* to do with tactics.

tadpole ('tædpəʊl) *nc* the form a frog takes between coming out of the egg and becoming fully grown: see picture.

tadpole

tag (tæg) *nc* a small piece of paper, card, etc., fastened at one end to something as a label: *a price tag*.

tail (teil) *nc* **1** the part of an animal, bird, fish, etc., at and beyond the lower end of its body, that moves. **2** anything like a tail in shape or position: *the tail of an aircraft*. **3** the side of a coin opposite to the side with the head of a king or ruler. ● *vt* secretly follow (someone). **tail-light** ('teillait) *chiefly US nc* a light at the back of a vehicle. **tail off** become less in sound, numbers, size, etc.

tailor ('teilə*) *nc* a person who makes or repairs clothes. ● *vt* make (clothes). **tailoring** ('teiləriŋ) *nu* the act or business of making or repairing clothes. **tailor-made** *adj* (of clothes) made to fit exactly.

take (teik) *vt* **1** grasp; seize: *Take the knife in your hand*. **2** make use of; use: *If you're in a hurry, do take my car*. **3** carry: *The bus will take you to town*. **4** go with: *Take the children for a walk*. **5** be affected by; cause to be made: *He's been taken ill with a fever*. **6** (followed by **it**) understand; suppose: *I take it that you've heard the news?* **7** accept: *Can't you take a joke?* **8** photograph (someone or something): *take a picture*. **9** write down or copy (something): *take notes*. **10** allow oneself to have: *take a walk; take a holiday*. **11** steal: *Someone has taken my pen!* **12** need or require: *It will take about a week to finish the work*. **13** obtain by force; make a prisoner of: *We took many prisoners during the battle*. **14** regularly buy and read: *I take three newspapers every day*. **take after** be like someone else in appearance or in behaviour. **take apart** separate into parts. **take away** remove. **take back** say that something one said was not meant or was not true. **take down 1** pull or tear down. **2** write down. **take for** consider to be. **take in 1** understand. **2** deceive. **3** include. **4** alter a dress, etc., by making it smaller. **5** have lodgers. **take off 1** remove a garment. **2** (of a plane) leave the ground. **3** imitate, esp. to make others laugh. **take-off** ('teɪkɒf) *nc* an imitation of someone's behaviour to make others laugh. **take on 1** agree to do. **2** employ. **take out 1** remove. **2** obtain. **take out of** make one feel weak and tired: *Too much hard work has taken it out of him.* **take over** (begin to) take control in the place of someone else. **take place** happen. **take to** like or begin to like (someone or something). **take to pieces 1** divide (something) into its parts. **2** find much fault with. **take up 1** start to interest oneself in: *take up a new hobby.* **2** (of time or space) fill. **3** continue with. **4** lift up. **takings** ('teɪkɪŋz) *n pl* money earned by a shop, business, etc.

taken ('teɪkən) past participle of **take.**

talcum ('tælkəm) *n* **talcum powder** pleasant-smelling powder made from a natural substance, talc, used for dusting on the skin.

tale (teɪl) *nc* **1** story. **2** an account of something seen, done, heard, etc. **3** a piece of talk, often unpleasant, about someone else.

talent ('tælənt) **1** *nu* the ability to do something very well, esp. an ability one is born with. **2** *nc* an example of this.

talk (tɔːk) *vi* **1** speak; say something: *talk with a friend.* **2** have the power of speech: *The baby has started to talk.* **3** *vt* discuss: *talk politics.* ●*nu* **1** a conversation; discussion. **2** *nc* an example of this. **3** *nu* a conversation about other people that is often worthless or unpleasant. **4** *nc* a speech or lecture. **talk back** reply in a rather rude or disobedient way. **talk down to** speak to (someone) as if he is not so clever as oneself. **talk into** or **out of** persuade (someone) into or out of doing something. **talk over** discuss. **talking-point** *nc* a subject likely to be discussed and cause argument.

talkative ('tɔːkətɪv) *adj* fond of talking a lot.

tall (tɔːl) *adj* **1** high: *a tall building.* **2** (of a person) more than the average height. **a tall order** something difficult to do. **a tall story** a story that is difficult to believe or is untrue.

tallow ('tæləʊ) *nu* the hard fat, chiefly obtained from animals, used for making soap, candles, etc.

tally ('tælɪ) *nc, pl* **-lies 1** *in former times* a stick with cuts in one side to show the amount of a debt or a payment. **2** anything that records a debt or payment. ●*vi* be in agreement.

Talmud ('tælmʊd) *nc* a full account of Jewish law.

talon ('tælən) *nc* one of the sharp, hooked points on the foot of a bird that kills and eats animals or other birds.

tambourine (ˌtæmbə'riːn) *nc* a small drum with metal rings round the edge that make a ringing sound when it is hit and shaken.

tame (teɪm) *adj* **-r, -st 1** (of animals) used to living with humans; not wild or fierce. **2** dull; not exciting or interesting: *a tame football match; a tame sort of man.* ●*vt* make (animals) used to living with humans.

tamper ('tæmpə*) *v* **tamper with** interfere with (something) without the right or lawful power to do so.

tan (tæn) *adj* yellow-brown. ●*ncu* a yellow-brown colour. ●*vt* **1** make (an animal's skin) into leather. **2** cause (the skin) to go brown in the sun. **3** *vi* (of the skin) go brown in the sun. **tanner** *nc* a person who makes animal skins into leather.

tandem ('tændəm) *nc* a bicycle with two sets of pedals and two seats, one behind the other, for two people to ride on.

tang (tæŋ) *nc* a strong taste or smell: *a tang of the sea.*

tangent ('tændʒənt) *nc* a straight line touching a curve at one point but not going through it.

tangible ('tændʒəbəl) *adj* **1** that can be touched or felt; of real substance. **2** that is able to be clearly understood.

tangle ('tæŋgəl) *nc* a mass of wool, string, etc., in disorder: *The wind blew her hair into tangles.* ●*vt* **1** cause (someone or something) to become disordered or confused. **2** *vi* become disordered or confused.

tango ('tæŋgəʊ) *nc* a dance with long, slow steps and sudden stops, for two people.

tank (tæŋk) *nc* **1** a large container for liquid or gas. **2** a large vehicle covered in metal for protection and which has guns: see picture.

tank

tantalise ('tæntəlaɪz) *vt* make (someone) hope for something that is unlikely to become a fact.

tantrum ('tæntrəm) *nc* an outburst of bad temper, esp. from a child.

Taoism ('taʊɪzəm) *nu* a Chinese system of religion based on the teachings of Lao-tse. **Taoist** *nc* a person who believes in the teachings of Lao-tse.

tap¹ (tæp) **1** *vt* strike lightly. **2** *vi* strike a light blow or blows: *The old man's stick tapped along the road.* ● *nc* a light blow.

tap² *US* **faucet** *nc* a device fitted to a pipe, used to control the flow of liquid or gas.

tape (teɪp) **1** *nu* a strip of material for stitching to clothes, carpets, etc., to prevent the edges being pulled into loose threads. *nc* **2** a piece of this or any such strip for fastening, tying, etc. **3** a long, plastic strip that is made magnetic and used to record sound or vision. ● *vt* **1** tie, fasten, strengthen, measure, etc., with tape. **2** record sounds on magnetic tape. **tape-measure** *nc* a strip of metal or cloth marked out in inches, etc., for measuring with. **tape-recorder** *nc* an electrical device for recording sounds on and playing them back on special tape. **tapeworm** (ˈteɪpwɜːm) *nc* a kind of long, flat worm that lives in the stomach and bowels of man and other animals.

taper (ˈteɪpə*) **1** *vt* make slowly narrower or smaller towards one end. **2** *vi* become narrower or smaller towards one end.

tapestry (ˈtæpəstrɪ) *pl* **-ries 1** *nu* the art of making a picture or design by weaving cloth with different coloured wools. **2** *nc* a picture or design made in this way: *The walls were hung with beautiful tapestries.*

tar (tɑː*) *nu* a black, sticky substance obtained from coal, wood, etc., used in road-making or to protect wooden fences, etc.

tarantula (təˈræntjʊlə) *nc* a kind of large, hairy poisonous spider of southern Europe.

tardy (ˈtɑːdɪ) *adj* **-ier, -iest 1** coming later than expected or hoped for: *tardy payments.* **2** slow in moving or developing.

target (ˈtɑːgɪt) *nc* **1** something to be aimed at with a gun or an arrow; anything one is aiming for. **2** a person or thing that is being found fault with.

tariff (ˈtærɪf) *nc* **1** a list of prices, esp. for food and rooms, at a hotel. **2** a list of taxes on goods brought into the country, and sometimes on goods going out.

Tarmac (ˈtɑːmæk) *Trademark nu* a mixture of tar and crushed stone, used for making road surfaces, etc.

tarnish (ˈtɑːnɪʃ) *vti* (cause to) lose the shine of: *tarnished silver; tarnished reputation.* ● *nc* a dull surface; loss of shine.

tarpaulin (tɑːˈpɔːlɪn) **1** *nu* a strong, heavy cloth treated with tar to keep out water, used for tents, boat sails, etc. **2** *nc* a sheet of this.

tarry (ˈtærɪ) *literary vi* stay for a short time; delay.

tart¹ (tɑːt) *nc* baked pastry with fruit, jam, etc., on top or inside.

tart² *adj* **1** sharp to the taste. **2** sharp: *a tart remark.*

tartar (ˈtɑːtə*) *nu* a hard substance formed by food, dirt, etc., left on teeth.

task (tɑːsk) *nc* a piece of work that is to be done, esp. one that is hard or unpleasant.

tassel (ˈtæsəl) *nc* a bunch of threads tied together at one end and hanging loosely as an ornament: see picture.

tassel

taste (teɪst) **1** *nc* the sense by which we notice the quality of what we eat. **2** *ncu* this quality: *This milk has a sour taste.* **3** *nc* a small amount of something to eat or drink. **4** *ncu* a liking for one thing more than or rather than another. **5** *nu* good judgement in what is beautiful or not, in how to behave etc. **6** *nc* a sensation; experience: *He's having his first taste of responsibility.* ● *vt* **1** learn or recognise the taste of a substance. **2** *vi* have a taste: *This tea tastes good.* **3** *vt* test the taste of: *The cook tasted the food.*

tasteless *adj* **1** (of food) having no taste. **2** without good judgement or good quality.

tasty *adj* **-ier, -iest** (of food) having a pleasant taste.

tatters (ˈtætəz) *n pl* torn pieces, esp. of cloth.

tattoo¹ (təˈtuː) **1** *nc* a public show of music and marching given by soldiers, usually at night. **2** *nu* a beating on a drum calling soldiers back to camp.

tattoo² *nc* a picture made on the skin by making tiny holes in it and putting in colours that cannot be removed. ● *vt* mark (someone) in this way.

taught (tɔːt) past tense and past participle of **teach**.

taunt (tɔːnt) *vt* find fault with (someone) in a disrespectful, sneering way. ● *nc* a sneering remark.

taut (tɔːt) *adj* **1** tightly stretched: *a taut rope.* **2** not relaxed: *taut nerves.*

tavern (ˈtævən) *nc* a public house.

tawny (ˈtɔːnɪ) *adj* (of a colour) yellow-brown.

tax (tæks) **1** *nu* money to be paid to the government for public needs. *nc* **2** a certain amount of this money. **3** something that weakens one's nerves, strength, etc., or that is difficult to bear. ● *vt* **1** put a tax on; make (a person) pay a tax. **2** be a strain on. **taxable** (ˈtæksəbəl) *adj* that can be taxed. **taxation** (tækˈseɪʃən) *nu* the obtaining of money for public needs by taxes; money to be paid as taxes. **taxpayer** *nc* a person who pays taxes.

taxi ('tæksɪ) *nc* a car for hire with a driver and a device for measuring the distance travelled and the money to be paid. ●*vi* (of aircraft) slowly move along the ground. **taxi cab** a taxi.

tea (tiː) **1** *nu* an evergreen plant of Asia, Africa, etc.; drink made by pouring boiling water onto these leaves: *a cup of tea. ncu* **2** *Brit* a time in the afternoon when tea is drunk. **3** *Brit* a light meal at this time of tea, cakes, biscuits, etc. **teacup** ('tiːkʌp) *nc* a cup from which tea is drunk. **teapot** ('tiːpɒt) *nc* a container with a handle and a short pipe in which tea is made and from which it is poured. **teaspoon** ('tiːspuːn) *nc* a small spoon for stirring tea in the cup.

teach (tiːtʃ) **1** *vt* try to make (a person) learn or show how to do something. **2** *vi* give lessons in a subject, esp. at school. **teacher** *nc* a person whose job is to teach, esp. by giving lessons at school. **teaching 1** *nu* the skill or work of teaching. **2** *nc* something that is taught.

teak (tiːk) **1** *nc* a tall evergreen Indian tree. **2** *nu* the hard wood of this tree, used for making furniture, building ships, etc.

team (tiːm) *nc* **1** a group of people on the same side in a game: *a football team.* **2** any group of people working together. **3** two or more horses, etc., pulling a cart, etc.: *a team of dogs pulling a sledge over snow.* **team up with** work together with. **teammate** ('tiːmmeɪt) *nc* a person in the same team as oneself. **teamwork** ('tiːmwɜːk) *nu* the work done together by a team.

tear[1] (tɪə*) *nc* a drop of saltwater coming from the eye, esp. as a sign of sorrow. **teardrop** ('tɪədrɒp) *nc* a tear. **tearful** *adj* about to cry; crying; wet with tears: *a tearful face.*

tear[2] (teə*) *vt* **1** pull apart quickly with some force. **2** damage by pulling sharply. *vi* **3** be pulled apart or damaged in this way. **4** rush: *He tore down the road to catch the bus.* ●*nc* a torn place or hole caused by tearing. **tear up** tear into pieces.

tease (tiːz) *vt* make fun of (someone) in a playful or unkindly way. ●*nc* a person who likes to tease. **teaser** *nc* **1** a person who likes to tease. **2** *infml* a difficult question or problem.

teat (tiːt) *nc* **1** the part of the female breast from which a baby gets its mother's milk. **2** the rubber device on the end of a baby's feeding-bottle.

technical ('teknɪkəl) *adj* of or to do with machines or industry; of or to do with a special method, art, or skill. **technically** ('teknɪkəlɪ) *adv*

technician (tek'nɪʃən) *nc* a person who is an expert in a particular art or skill.

Technicolor ('teknɪkʌlə*) *Trademark nu* the way of producing photographs in colour, used for cinema films.

technique (tek'niːk) **1** *nu* the special skill given to a particular task. **2** *nc* a way of doing something expertly.

technology (tek'nɒlədʒɪ) *nu* the study of ways of using scientific knowledge to produce goods by machines, etc. **technological** (‚teknə'lɒdʒɪkəl) *adj* of or to do with technology. **technologist** (tek'nɒlədʒɪst) *nc* a person who is an expert in technology.

tectonic (tek'tɒnɪk) *adj* of or to do with buildings or the way things are built.

tedious ('tiːdɪəs) *adj* seeming to be slow-moving, long, etc., because uninteresting: *a tedious journey; a tedious book.*

tee (tiː) *golf nc* **1** a space from which the ball is struck at the beginning of the game. **2** the support on which the ball is placed to be struck.

teem[1] (tiːm) *vi* have or be found in great numbers: *rivers teeming with fish.*

teem[2] *vi* (of rain) fall fast and heavily: *It's teeming down; It's teeming with rain.*

teenage ('tiːneɪdʒ) *adj* of or to do with young people between and including the ages of thirteen and nineteen. **teenager** ('tiːneɪdʒə*) *nc* a teenage boy or girl. **teens** (tiːnz) *n pl* the numbers or ages between and including thirteen and nineteen: *two sisters, both in their teens.*

tee-shirt ('tiːʃɜːt) *n* See **T-shirt.**

teeth (tiːθ) plural of **tooth.**

teethe (tiːð) *vi* (of a baby) produce its first teeth.

teetotal (tiː'təʊtəl) *adj* not drinking or not allowing oneself to drink alcohol.

telecommunications (‚telɪkə‚mjuːnɪ'keɪʃənz) *n pl* the passing on of news, information, or messages by means of the telephone, radio, etc.

telegram ('telɪɡræm) *nc* a message sent by the use of electricity along wires or by radio.

telegraph ('telɪɡrɑːf) *nc* a device or system by which messages can be sent over a distance by the use of electricity along wires or by radio. ●*vt* send (messages, etc.) by telegraph. **telegraphic** (‚telɪ'ɡræfɪk) *adj* of or to do with the telegraph. **telegraphy** (tə'legrəfɪ) *nu* the science or use of the telegraph.

telepathy (tə'lepəθɪ) *nu* the passing on of feelings, thoughts, etc., from one person's mind to another's, without the use of speech or signs.

telephone ('telɪfəʊn) (*infml abbrev.* **phone**) *nu* the system of sending and receiving messages, etc., with the human voice, by means of electricity. **2** *nc* an electrical device for this purpose. ●*vt* **1** speak to (someone) on the telephone. **2** *vi* send a message by speaking on the telephone. **on the telephone** speaking to someone by means of a telephone. **telephone booth** or **box**) a small enclosure containing a telephone which the public can pay to use. **telephone directory** (*infml abbrev.* **phone book***)* a book with a list of names, addresses, and telephone numbers of people in a particular district. **telephone exchange** a place where all the telephone wires are connected, giving the means for people to speak to each other. **telephone number** the special set of figures which connects to a particular telephone or group of telephones.

telephonic (ˌtelɪˈfɒnɪk) *adj* of or to do with the telephone.

telephonist (təˈlefənɪst) *nc* a person who works in a telephone exchange.

telephony (təˈlefənɪ) *nu* the system for sending and receiving messages by telephone.

teleprinter (ˈtelɪprɪntə*) *nc* a telegraph apparatus that changes a typed message into code as it passes along a wire and then prints it out again at the other end.

telescope (ˈtelɪskəʊp) *nc* an instrument that can make distant objects seem closer by looking into it with one eye through a lens: see picture. ●*vti* make shorter by sliding

telescope

one section of (something) into another. **telescopic** (ˌtelɪˈskɒpɪk) *adj* **1** of or to do with a telescope. **2** having parts that, when pushed, fit into each other to make the whole object shorter and compact: *a telescopic umbrella*.

television (ˈtelɪˌvɪʒən) (*infml abbrev.* **TV**) **1** *nu* the system of sending pictures by radio waves to a distant apparatus that receives them and causes sound at the same time. **2** *nc* such an apparatus. **televise** (ˈtelɪvaɪz) *vt* send (pictures, programmes, etc.) by television.

telex (ˈteleks) *nu* the passing on of information by means of teleprinters.

tell (tel) *vt* **1** make (something) known: *Tell me your name.* **2** express in words; say: *Tell*

the truth. **3** order (someone) to do something: *I told him to go away.* **4** *vi* have an effect that is clearly noticed: *Too much work began to tell on his health.* **5** *vt* know or discover: *I can never tell which twin is which!* **tell apart** see the difference between. **tell off** speak angrily to (someone) about his faults, etc.

teller (ˈtelə*) *nc* **1** a person who receives, pays out, and counts money in a bank. **2** a person who counts votes.

telltale (ˈtelteɪl) *nc* a person who talks of other people's secrets, affairs, etc.; something that makes known a person's thoughts, feelings, etc. ●*adj* making known: *A telltale blush showed her guilt.*

temper (ˈtempə*) **1** *nc* the condition of one's feelings: *in a good temper.* **2** *nu* the condition of a metal, esp. its hardness: *the temper of steel.* ●*vt* **1** bring (metal) to the right hardness by treating it with heat. **2** *vi* (of metal) be brought to the right hardness. **3** *vt* make less severe, cruel, etc.: *He tempered his anger with some sympathy.* **lose one's temper** become angry.

temperament (ˈtemprəmənt) *nc* a person's usual and natural state of mind, qualities, and feelings. **temperamental** (ˌtemprəˈmentəl) *adj* likely to suddenly become excited.

temperate (ˈtempərət) *adj* **1** in control of oneself. **2** (of the weather, etc.) warm and gentle.

temperature (ˈtemprətʃə*) **1** *nu* the degree of heat or cold. **2** *nc* a measure of this. **have a temperature** have a fever.

tempest (ˈtempɪst) *nc* a violent storm. **tempestuous** (temˈpestʃʊəs) *adj* (of the weather or the feelings) violent; stormy.

temple[1] (ˈtempəl) *nc* **1** a building or place for the worship of God or a god. **2** *rare* any Christian church.

temple[2] *nc* a flat part on each side of the head just above and in front of the ear.

tempo (ˈtempəʊ) *nc, pl* **-s**, *music* **-pi** (piː) **1** the speed at which a piece of music is played. **2** the rate of any activity.

temporal (ˈtempərəl) *adj* **1** of or to do with time. **2** of the affairs of this life; not spiritual.

temporary (ˈtempərərɪ) *adj* lasting for a short time only; not permanent. **temporarily** (ˈtempərəlɪ *US* ˌtempəˈrearəlɪ) *adv*

tempt (tempt) *vt* **1** try to persuade (someone) into doing something, esp. something wrong. **2** be the cause of the desire in (someone) to have or do something; attract (someone). **temptation** (tempˈteɪʃən) **1** *nu* tempting or being tempted. **2** *nc* something that tempts. **tempting** *adj* that attracts.

ten (ten) *determiner, n* the number 10. **tenth** (tenθ) *determiner, n, adv*

tenacious (tɪˈneɪʃəs) *adj* holding firmly; not letting go: *The sick man had a tenacious hold on life; a tenacious memory.* **tenacity** (tɪˈnæsɪtɪ) *nu* being tenacious.

tenant (ˈtenənt) *nc* a person who pays rent for the use of a house, land, etc. ● *vt* live in or use as a tenant.

tend[1] (tend) *vi* be likely to do something: *He tends to visit us in the summer instead of in the winter.*

tend[2] *vt* look after; give care to: *tend the sick; tend sheep.*

tendency (ˈtendənsɪ) *nc, pl* **-cies** a turning or leaning towards a particular action, state, etc.: *She has a tendency to be fat.*

tender[1] (ˈtendə*) *adj* 1 kind and loving: *a tender heart.* 2 painful when touched; sore. 3 not tough: *a tender piece of meat.* **tenderly** *adv* **tenderness** *nu* being tender.

tender[2] *vt* 1 *formal* give or offer: *tender one's apologies.* 2 offer (money or goods) for what one owes. 3 *vi* make an offer of work or goods for a certain price.

tendon (ˈtendən) *nc* a string-like mass of skin the fixes a muscle to a bone.

tendril (ˈtendrɪl) *nc* the long, stem-like part of a climbing plant that clings to any support that is near.

tenement (ˈtenəmənt) *nc* a large building divided into rooms or flats for rent, esp. for poor people.

tennis (ˈtenɪs) *nu* a game for two or four people hitting a ball backwards and forwards over a net.

tenor (ˈtenə*) 1 *ncu* the male singing voice that is higher than the baritone and lower than the alto. *nc* 2 a man who has such a voice. 3 music for such a voice. 4 a musical instrument with the same extent between the highest and lowest notes as the tenor voice. 5 the general meaning or direction.

tense[1] (tens) *adj* (of the nerves, a rope, etc.) not relaxed; tightly stretched; tight. ● *vti* (cause to) make (the body, etc.) tense.

tense[2] *grammar nc* the form of a verb that shows time: *the present tense.*

tension (ˈtenʃən) *nu* 1 the state or degree of being tense. 2 stretching or being stretched. 3 *nc* a state when feelings, etc., are being stretched: *racial tensions.*

tent (tent) *nc* a shelter made of strong cloth supported by poles and fixed to the ground with ropes.

tentacle (ˈtentəkəl) *nc* an arm-like part growing from some animals, used for feeding, holding, etc.

tentative (ˈtentətɪv) *adj* said or done in a careful way as a test to see the effect: *a tentative suggestion.* **tentatively** *adv*

tenuous (ˈtenjʊəs) *adj* 1 delicate and slender. 2 not good enough: *a tenuous chance.*

tenure (ˈtenjʊə*) 1 *nu* the holding of or the right to hold an office, house, or land. 2 *nc* the length of time that an office or the holding of a house or land lasts.

tepid (ˈtepɪd) *adj* 1 (esp. of water) slightly warm. 2 not showing much enthusiasm.

term (tɜːm) *nc* 1 a certain or fixed length of time: *a school term; term of office.* 2 a word or expression used for some particular thing, esp. in a certain occupation, study, etc.: *a medical term.* 3 any word or expression. ● *vt* describe as; name: *This may be termed a synonym.* **come to terms with** be willing to accept (a situation, etc.). **in terms of** as expressed by. **terms** *n pl* 1 the conditions of an agreement. 2 words: *He spoke of your work in terms of praise!*

terminal (ˈtɜːmɪnəl) *adj* of, being, or placed at the end: *She has a terminal disease so has not long to live.* ● *nc* 1 the last station of a railway or bus line. 2 a building in a town used by people going to or coming from an airport.

terminate (ˈtɜːmɪneɪt) 1 *vt* put an end to. 2 *vi* come to an end. **termination** (ˌtɜːmɪˈneɪʃən) 1 *nu* terminating or being terminated. 2 *nc* something that causes or comes to an end.

terminology (ˌtɜːmɪˈnɒlədʒɪ) *nc, pl* **-gies** 1 *nu* the study of words or expressions used for a particular subject. 2 *nc* a group of such words or expressions.

terminus (ˈtɜːmɪnəs) *nc, pl* **-ni** (niː) or **-es** the place where buses, trains, planes, etc., reach the end of their route.

termite (ˈtɜːmaɪt) *nc* a white, ant-like insect that chiefly lives in hot countries and feeds on wood.

terrace (ˈterəs) *nc* 1 a flat piece of ground cut in the form of large steps in the side of a hill: see picture. 2 a row of houses that

terrace

look alike and are joined together. 3 a piece of ground given a hard surface next to a house. 4 *usually pl* rows of standing places each row rising one above the other, for people to watch football, etc. ● *vt* make or form terraces in. **terraced** *adj* formed into terraces.

terrain (təˈreɪn) *nc* a piece of land, esp. concerning its special qualities or its suitability as a battlefield.

terrestrial (təˈrestrɪəl) *adj* 1 of or to do with the earth. 2 living on or belonging to the earth or land: *terrestrial creatures*.

terrible (ˈterəbəl) *adj* 1 causing great fear. 2 very serious: *a terrible illness*. 3 *infml* very poor in quality; very bad: *a terrible meal*. **terribly** *adv* very: *He's terribly nice!*

terrier (ˈterɪə*) *nc* a kind of small hunting dog full of life and action.

terrific (təˈrɪfɪk) *adj* 1 causing great fear. 2 *infml* very good: *a terrific pop group*. 3 very great: *driving at a terrific speed*.

terrify (ˈterɪfaɪ) *vt* greatly frighten.

territory (ˈterɪtərɪ) *ncu, pl* **-ries** 1 (a piece of) land ruled by one person or government. 2 any piece of such land. 3 *nu* an area of land lived in or defended by a certain animal or animals. **territorial** (ˌterɪˈtɔːrɪəl) *adj* of or to do with a territory. **Territorial** *Brit nc* a member of the Territorial Army. **Territorial Army** *Brit* the body of mainly part-time soldiers organised and trained to help the full-time defence forces. **territorial waters** the sea near a country's coast over which it has control and special rights.

terror (ˈterə*) 1 *nu* great fear. *nc* 2 someone or something that causes great fear. 3 *infml, sometimes humorous* a person who causes worry or trouble, esp. a child. **terrorise** (ˈterəraɪz) *vt* cause terror by using force or making known that one will cause harm, etc. **terrorism** (ˈterərɪzəm) *nu* the use of violent force, esp. to bring about political changes. **terrorist** (ˈterərɪst) *nc* a person who supports or takes part in acts of terrorism.

terse (tɜːs) *adj* 1 saying much in a few words. 2 rather rude and brief: *a terse reply*.

tertiary (ˈtɜːʃərɪ) *adj* third in degree or order of importance, etc.

Terylene (ˈterəliːn) *Trademark, Brit nu* a fibre made by man and used for clothes, sheets, etc.

test (test) *nc* an examination or trial to get knowledge of a person's powers, find out the quality of something, etc. ● *vt* examine; put to the test. **test-tube** (ˈtesttjuːb) *nc* a glass tube open at one end used in scientific experiments.

testament (ˈtestəmənt) *law nc* a written paper saying who is to receive property after the owner's death: *This was his last will and testament*. **New Testament, Old Testament** the two main parts of the Bible.

testicle (ˈtestɪkəl) *nc* one of the two parts of a man's, and of a male animal's, sex organ that forms a liquid for producing young.

testify (ˈtestɪfaɪ) *vti* 1 give proof of (something), esp. in a law court. 2 speak in support of (someone). 3 *vt* be proof of.

testimonial (ˌtestɪˈməʊnɪəl) *nc* 1 a letter in support of a person's abilities, qualities, etc.: *For the job he wanted he needed three testimonials*. 2 something given to someone by a group of people to show their respect and thanks for his hard work, etc.

testimony (ˈtestɪmənɪ) *nu* 1 *law* proof given by a person, esp. in a law court, that something is true. 2 the making known that something is true.

tetanus (ˈtetənəs) *nu* a disease causing tightening of some muscles.

tether (ˈteðə*) *nc* a rope or chain to which an animal is tied while feeding on grass, etc. ● *vt* tie up (an animal) with a tether. **at the end of one's tether** with nothing left to turn to for help, support, etc.

text (tekst) *nc* 1 the main part of a book, not the notes, pictures, etc. 2 the words actually used by a writer before being improved on, etc., by someone else. 3 a short piece chosen from a book to discuss, etc. **textbook** (ˈtekstbʊk) *nc* a book that teaches or gives information on a particular subject.

textile (ˈtekstaɪl) *nc* any cloth, esp. made from threads by a machine. ● *adj* of or to do with the making of cloth.

texture (ˈtekstʃə*) *ncu* 1 the way the threads are arranged in a textile. 2 the surface of a material, esp. how it feels. 3 the way the parts of something are put together.

than (ðæn unstressed ðən) *conj* when compared with: *She is much shorter than her sister*.

thank (θæŋk) *vt* show (someone) that one is grateful by saying so. **no thank you** (used to refuse something.) **thanks** *n pl* the showing of one's gratitude. ● *interj* (an expression of being thankful): *Thanks! It is a very nice gift*. **give thanks** make known by speech or action that one is thankful for what has been received or done. **thanks to** because of. **thank you** (used to show one is grateful.)

thankful (ˈθæŋkfʊl) *adj* grateful. **thankfully** *adv* **thankfulness** *nu* being thankful.

thankless (ˈθæŋklɪs) *adj* 1 ungrateful. 2 (of an action) not receiving thanks or praise: *a thankless job*.

thanksgiving (ˌθæŋksˈgɪvɪŋ) *nu* an expression of thanks, esp. to God. **Thanksgiving** *US nc* also **Thanksgiving Day** a day in November of every year when there is a public holiday to give thanks to God.

that¹ (ðæt) *determiner, pron, pl* **those** a person or thing pointed at; person or thing just mentioned or noticed: *That's the house, over there; Where's that noise coming from?*

that² (ðæt unstressed ðət) *pron* (often used in place of *which, whom,* or *who*): *Please return the book that I lent you.*

that³ *conj* **1** (used to introduce a group of words that make up the second part of a sentence): *He said that he won't be able to come to the party.* **2** (used to introduce a result): *I felt so tired that I went to bed early.* **so that** See under **so. that is 1** in other words. **2** for example.

thatch (θætʃ) *nu* **1** also **thatching** the material for making a roof made up of dried straw, reeds, etc. **2** a roof of this material: see picture. ● *vt* cover (a roof, house, etc.) with thatch.

thatch

that'll ('ðætəl) that will.

that's (ðæts) that is.

thaw (θɔː) **1** *vi* (of snow, ice, or anything frozen) melt. **2** *vt* cause (snow, ice, or anything frozen) to melt. **3** *vi* (of a person's behaviour) become more friendly.

the (ði: unstressed ðə before consonants, ðɪ before vowels) *determiner* **1** (used before a noun that has just been mentioned or already known about): *Here is the book I suggested you read; Is the pain any better?* **2** *(used with a singular noun)* a class or group with common qualities, of people or things: *Lions belong to the cat family; Do you play the guitar?* **3** (with superlative): *the best way to learn.* **4** the only one existing: *the African continent.* **the** (**more**)... **the** (**more**) by so much; by that much: *The more you study the more you will know.*

theatre *US* **theater** ('θɪətə*) *nc* **1** a building where plays, operas, etc., can be seen by the public. **2** a large room with each row of seats placed behind and higher than the one before, used for lectures, etc. **3** a place where important events happen. **theatrical** (θɪ'ætrɪkəl) *adj* **1** of or to do with the theatre. **2** (of behaviour, etc.) false and wanting to impress.

thee (ði:) *archaic or literary pron* object form of **thou.**

theft (θeft) **1** *nu* the act of stealing. **2** *nc* an example of this.

their (ðeə*) *determiner* of or to do with them.

theirs (ðeəz) *pron* someone or something belonging to or to do with them.

them (ðem unstressed ðəm) *pron* (used for people, animals, and things either after a preposition or when they are either the direct or indirect object of a verb.) **themselves** (ðəm'selvz) *pron* **1** (where the object of the verb is the same as the subject): *People who swim in a rough sea put themselves in danger.* **2** in their normal state: *They are not themselves today.* **by themselves 1** without help. **2** alone.

theme (θi:m) *nc* **1** an idea or subject for discussion or for writing or thinking about. **2** a tune that is often repeated, developed, etc., in a piece of music.

then (ðen) *adv* **1** at that time (in the past or future). **2** if that happens; if that is so: *If he's offered the job then he'll accept it.* **3** next; afterwards: *They travelled first by plane and then by car on their journey.* **now and then** See under **now.**

thence (ðens) *formal adv* from there. **thenceforth** (,ðens'fɔ:θ), **thenceforward** (,ðens'fɔ:wəd) *adv* from that time on.

theology (θi:'ɒlədʒɪ) *nu* the study of the truths known about God and of religious teachings. **theologian** (,θɪə'ləʊdʒɪən) *nc* a person who is an expert in the study of theology. **theological** (,θɪə'lɒdʒɪkəl) *adj* of or to do with theology.

theorem ('θɪərəm) *nc* **1** a written statement to be proved true by skilled reasoning. **2** *mathematics* a statement in signs or numbers for which proof by skilled reasoning is required.

theoretical (θɪə'retɪkəl) *adj* of or based on ideas, not on facts. **theoretically** *adv*

theory ('θɪərɪ) *ncu, pl* **-ries 1** a set of general ideas or truths to explain an art or science. *nc* **2** an idea based on reason to explain certain facts, etc. **3** an opinion, etc., reached without proper experience or reasoning or without knowing all the facts.

therapeutic (,θerə'pju:tɪk) *adj* of or to do with the treatment of disease; able to or helping to cure disease.

therapy ('θerəpɪ) *nc, pl* **-pies** the treatment of disease or ill health. **therapist** ('θerəpɪst) *nc* a person who is an expert in some form of therapy.

there (ðeə*) *adv* **1** in, at, or to that place: *Hang your coat up there; He goes there every week; They've lived there for years.* **2** (used as a sudden exclamation): *There he is!* **3** (used with, and to give, extra force): *There goes the last train tonight.* **4** on or at that point or matter: *You are quite right there.* ● *pron* (used as an indefinite pronoun subject at the beginning of a sentence): *There is someone in the room; There seems to be someone in the room.* **here and there** See under **here. thereabouts**

('ðeərəbaʊts) *adv* near that place; a little more or less than that number, amount, etc. **thereafter** (ðeər'ɑːftə*) *formal adv* afterwards. **thereby** (ðeə'baɪ) *formal adv* by that means; because of that. **therefore** ('ðeəfɔː*) *adv* because of that reason. **therein** (ðeər'ɪn) *formal adv* in or into that place or thing: *Therein is the answer.* **thereof** (ðeər'ɒv) *formal adv* of that or it. **thereupon** (,ðeərə'pɒn) *formal adv* because of that; immediately after that.

there'd (ðeəd) there had or there would.

there'll (ðeəl) there will.

there's (ðeəz) there is.

thermal ('θɜːməl) *adj* 1 of or to do with heat. 2 warm or hot.

tnermodynamics (,θɜːməʊdaɪ'næmɪks) *nu (with singular verb)* the science of the way heat is affected by or united with other forms of power.

thermometer (θə'mɒmɪtə*) *nc* an instrument with a set of marks on it for measuring temperature: see picture.

thermometer

Thermos ('θɜːməs) *n* also **Thermos flask** *Trademark* See under **vacuum.**

thermostat ('θɜːməstæt) *nc* a device that is able to control the temperature in a heating system.

these (ðiːz) plural of **this.**

thesis ('θiːsɪs) *nc, pl* **-ses** (siːz) an idea based on reason, esp. in the form of a long piece of writing put forward for the purpose of getting a university higher degree.

they (ðeɪ) *pron* 1 (used of people or things, not of the speaker or the people being spoken to): *We expected them to visit us but they didn't.* 2 (used of people in general): *In New Zealand they have Christmas in the summer.* 3 *not standard* (used with a word such as **anyone**): *If anyone wants to come, they can.*

they'd (ðeɪd) they had or they would.

they'll (ðeɪl) they will.

they're ('ðeɪə*) they are.

they've (ðeɪv) they have.

thick (θɪk) *adj* **-er, -est** 1 not thin; broad, fat, or deep when compared with something of the same sort. 2 not flowing quickly: *thick cream.* 3 not easily seen through: *a thick mist.* 4 arranged closely together: *thick hair.* 5 *infml* stupid. ● *nu* a thick part of any-

thing. **thick-headed** *adj* stupid. **thick-skinned** *adj* not easily hurt in the feelings or the spirit; lacking in feeling. **thickly** *adv* **thickness** *ncu*

thicken ('θɪkən) 1 *vt* make thick or thicker. 2 *vi* become thick or thicker.

thicket ('θɪkɪt) *nc* a place where trees and bushes are growing closely together.

thief (θiːf) *nc, pl* **-ves** (vz) a person who steals.

thigh (θaɪ) *nc* the part of the human leg above the knee.

thimble ('θɪmbəl) *nc* a cap of metal, plastic, etc., that fits on the end of the finger to protect it when sewing.

thin (θɪn) *adj* **-ner, -nest** 1 not thick; not broad, fat, or deep when compared with something of the same sort: *a thin slice of bread.* 2 (of liquids) like water: *thin soup.* 3 not fat; with not much flesh. 4 not arranged close together: *thin hair.* 5 not dense: *a thin mist.* ● *vti* make or become thin. **thinly** *adv* **thin-skinned** *adj* easily hurt in the feelings or the spirit.

thine (ðaɪn) *archaic adj* (coming before a vowel) your. ● *pron* yours.

thing (θɪŋ) *nc* 1 any material object: *What's that thing on the floor?* 2 event; act; happening: *That was a silly thing to do!; The next exciting thing will be my birthday party.* 3 a person or animal regarded with feeling of some kind: *You poor thing; The new baby's a lovely little thing.* 4 an idea; thought: *He has things on his mind.* 5 a subject: *That's the very thing we mustn't talk about.* **first thing** *infml* before anything else. **for one thing** for one of several reasons. **things** *n pl* belongings.

think (θɪŋk) 1 *vi* use the mind: *Give me time to think before I decide.* 2 *vt* believe; have an opinion; consider: *I think you're wrong; Do you think he will come?* ● *nc infml* act of thinking. **think about** use the mind to form an opinion, etc. **think of** 1 consider. 2 have as a possible intention: *She's thinking of leaving her job.* 3 remember. 4 suggest. 5 invent. **think better of** change one's mind. **think out** consider something carefully; make a plan. **think over** consider carefully before deciding, etc. **thinker** *nc* a person who uses his mind. **thinking** *adj* using the mind in an intelligent way. ● *nc* a thought.

third (θɜːd) *determiner, n, adv* the next after the second. ● *nc* one of three equal parts. **thirdparty** another person as well as the two, more important, people. **third-rate** *adj* of rather poor quality. **Third World** those parts of the world that have not yet been developed in agriculture, building, etc., or been brought into shared power with other countries. **thirdly** *adv*

thirst (θɜːst) *nu* **1** the feeling that one wants or needs a drink. **2** the suffering caused by lack of a drink. **3** a strong desire: *a thirst for knowledge.* ●*vt* feel a thirst. **thirsty** *adj* **-ier, -iest** causing or having thirst: *thirsty work; feel thirsty*

thirteen (θɜːˈtiːn) *determiner, n* 13. **thirteenth** (θɜːˈtiːnθ) *determiner, n, adv*

thirty (ˈθɜːtɪ) *determiner, n* 30. **thirtieth** (ˈθɜːtɪɪθ) *determiner, n, adv*

this (ðɪs) *determiner, pron, pl* **these 1** a person or thing that is near, closer, or here: *Do you prefer this house or that one over there?; He's lived in this country for ten years.* **2** *infml* (used instead of *a* or *the* to add force) a certain: *We drove until we came to this pretty village.* ●*adv infml* to this degree: *I've never seen such a plant grow this high before.*

thistle (ˈθɪsəl) *nc* a kind of wild plant with sharp-pointed leaves and pink, purple, white, or yellow flowers.

thither (ˈðɪðə*) *archaic adv* to that place; in that direction.

tho' (ðəʊ) *adj, conj* short for **though.**

thong (θɒŋ) *nc* a thin strip of leather, esp. for fastening: *a thong on a sandal.*

thorax (ˈθɔːræks) *nc, pl* **-xes** (sɪz) the part of the body between the neck and the stomach.

thorn (θɔːn) *nc* the sharp, pointed part of a plant growing from the stem. **thorny** *adj* **-ier, -iest 1** having thorns. **2** difficult; causing trouble: *a thorny problem.*

thorough (ˈθʌrə) *adj* complete; taking great care not to forget or miss anything. **thoroughbred** (ˈθʌrəbred) *nc* an animal, esp. a horse, of pure breed. ●*adj* of pure breed.

thoroughfare (ˈθʌrəfeə*) *nc* a main road or street, much used by traffic. **thoroughgoing** (ˈθʌrəgəʊɪŋ) *adj* complete. **thoroughly** *adv* **thoroughness** *nu* the condition or act of being thorough.

those (ðəʊz) plural of **that**¹.

thou (ðaʊ) *archaic pron* you.

though (ðəʊ) *conj* **1** in spite of the fact that: *Though she studied hard she failed her examinations.* **2** even if; although. ●*adv* however; nevertheless: *She said she would write to him: she didn't, though.* **as though** as if.

thought¹ (θɔːt) past tense and past participle of **think.**

thought² **1** *nu* the act, way, or power of thinking. **2** *nc* an idea, opinion, etc., formed in the mind: *Have you any thoughts on the subject? nu* **3** attention of the mind given to something. **4** care for others; kindness. **5** *nc* intention: *They had no thought of harming him.* **on second thoughts** having formed a different opinion after considering something for a second time. **thoughtful** (ˈθɔːtfʊl) *adj* **1** deep in thought; showing thought. **2** caring about the feelings of others. **thoughtfully** *adv* **thoughtfulness** *nu* the state of being thoughtful. **thoughtless** (ˈθɔːtlɪs) *adj* **1** without thought. **2** not caring for the feelings of others.

thousand (ˈθaʊzənd) *n* the number 1000. **thousandth** (ˈθaʊzəndθ) *determiner, n, adv*

thrall (θrɔːl) **1** *nu* being in the power of someone or something. **2** *nc* a slave.

thrash (θræʃ) *vt* **1** beat with a stick, whip, etc. **2** *infml* win a victory over a team, etc., in a game. **3** *vi* move violently about: *His fever caused the sick man to thrash about on his bed.* **thrash out** deal with (a problem, etc.) by discussing it until it is settled. **thrashing** *nc* a beating.

thread (θred) **1** *nu* cotton, wool, silk, etc. *nc* **2** a piece of this. **3** any fine, thin line: *a thread of smoke; threads of silver in the old lady's hair.* **4** something that unites or connects parts of a whole: *the threads of a story.* **5** the long, hollow cut round the length of a screw. ●*vt* put a piece of thread through the tiny hole of (a needle). **threadbare** (ˈθredbeə*) *adj* (of material) with thin or broken threads; worn out.

threat (θret) *nc* **1** the expression of the intention to cause harm or pain, esp. if one is not obeyed. **2** a sign that danger or trouble is likely.

threaten (ˈθretən) *vt* **1** use threats against. **2** give a warning sign of danger, trouble, etc. **threatening** *adj* showing trouble, danger, etc., to come.

three (θriː) *determiner, n* the number 3. **three-dimensional** *adj* having or seeming to have length, width, and height.

thresh (θreʃ) **1** *vi* beat out or separate the seeds from the husks of wheat, etc. **2** *vt* beat (wheat, etc.) to separate the seeds.

threshold (ˈθreʃhəʊld) *nc* **1** a flat block of wood or stone under a doorway; any entrance. **2** the start of an experience, happening, etc.

threw (θruː) past tense of **throw.**

thrice (θraɪs) *archaic adv* three times.

thrift (θrɪft) *nu* carefulness in dealing with money matters. **thrifty** *adj* **-ier, -iest** careful in the use of money; not wasteful.

thrill (θrɪl) *nc* **1** a sudden feeling of excitement and pleasure. **2** a thing that causes such a feeling. **thriller** *nc* an exciting book, film, or play, esp. one about crime.

thrive (θraɪv) *vi* **1** do well; be successful. grow in a strong and healthy way.

thriven (ˈθrɪvən) archaic past participle of **thrive.**

thro' (θruː) *prep* short for **through.**

throat (θrəʊt) *nc* **1** the front part of the neck. **2** the opening at the back of the mouth leading down to the stomach and lungs. **throaty** *adj* **-ier, -iest** rough; deep: *a throaty voice.*

throb (θrɒb) *vi* **1** beat, like the heart, again and again, esp. in a regular way. **2** (of the heart) beat faster and with greater force than usual.

throes (θrəʊz) *n pl* a condition of feeling sudden, sharp pains.

throne (θrəʊn) **1** *nc* the seat on which a king, ruler, etc., sits during great, stately occasions or events: see picture. **2** *nu* the power and duties of a royal person.

throne

throng (θrɒŋ) *nc* a crowd. ● *vti* crowd.

throttle ('θrɒtəl) *vt* **1** cause (someone) to stop breathing by pressing on his throat; strangle. **2** control the flow of steam, petrol, etc., in an engine. ● *nc* a device for controlling the flow of steam, etc., in an engine.

through (θruː) *prep* **1** going in at one side or end and coming out at the other; from one end or side to the other: *a road through the village; look through a window.* **2** during: *all through the night.* **3** because of: *It was through his help that she got the job.* ● *adv* **1** from side to side, end to end, beginning to end: *He read the newspaper all through; Let's go through.* **2** to the end. **3** (of making a telephone call) connected: *At last, I'm through to London.* **4** completely: *He was wet through.* **5** all the way: *Book a ticket from London through to Rome.* ● *adj* that goes all the way; continuous: *a through train.* **be through (with)** be finished (with). **through and through** completely.

throughout (θruː'aʊt) *adv* all the way through; in every part of; through the whole time.

throve (θrəʊv) archaic past tense of **thrive.**

throw (θrəʊ) *vt* **1** send (something) through the air with some force, using the hand and arm or some device. **2** move in a quick, careless, or violent way: *He threw his legs over the chair; throw on a coat.* **3** cause to fall: *He was thrown off his horse.* **4** cause to be suddenly in some condition: *The news threw her into anger.* **5** send (light or sound) in a particular direction. ● *nc* the act of throwing; distance something is thrown: *That was a good throw!* **throw away** get rid

of as useless or unwanted. **throw off** become free from. **throw on** put on clothes carelessly or quickly. **throw out 1** get rid of. **2** say (something), esp. in a casual way. **throw up 1** *infml* be sick. **2** give up (one's job, position, etc.).

thrown (θrəʊn) past participle of **throw.**

thrush (θrʌʃ) *nc* a kind of bird noted for its song: see picture at **birds.**

thrust (θrʌst) **1** *vt* push suddenly or with force. **2** *vi* make a sudden, forward movement with the body, a weapon, etc.

thud (θʌd) *nc* a dull, heavy sound as of something being dropped or falling onto something soft. ● *vi* strike, fall, etc., with a thud.

thug (θʌg) *nc* a dangerous and violent man, esp. a criminal.

thumb (θʌm) *nc* the short, and usually thickest, finger of the hand, separate from the other four. **thumbtack** ('θʌmtæk) *US nc* See **drawing-pin** under **drawing.**

thump (θʌmp) **1** *vt* beat with the hand tightly closed, using some force. **2** *vi* strike heavily and often: *His heart thumped with excitement.*

thunder ('θʌndə*) *nu* **1** a deep, heavy sound or a sharp, loud sound in the sky. **2** any deep, loud noise. ● *vi* **1** send out thunder. **2** make a noise like thunder. **3** *vt* speak in a loud, angry voice. **thunderbolt** ('θʌndəbəʊlt) *nc* a flash of light in the sky together with thunder. **thunderstorm** ('θʌndəstɔːm) *nc* a storm with thunder and lightning, and often heavy rain. **thunder-struck** ('θʌndəstrʌk) *adj* completely surprised. **thunderous** ('θʌndərəs), **thundery** ('θʌndərɪ) *adj* making a noise like thunder.

Thursday ('θɜːzdɪ) *nc* the fifth day of the week, after Wednesday and before Friday.

thus (ðʌs) *adv* in this way; so.

thwart (θwɔːt) *vt* prevent someone's (hopes, plans, aims, etc.) from coming true.

thy (ðaɪ) *archaic determiner* your. **thyself** (ðaɪ'self) *archaic pron* yourself.

thyme (taɪm) *nu* a plant of which the leaves are added to food for their taste.

thyroid ('θaɪrɔɪd) *anatomy, zoology nc* also **thyroid gland** a part of the body, in the neck, producing chemicals that control esp. growth.

tick[1] (tɪk) *nc* **1** the sharp, light, repeated noise made by a clock, etc. **2** a bent line written to mark something on a list or to indicate that something is correct. ● *vi* **1** make a **tick**[1] (def. 1). **2** *vt* put a **tick**[1] (def. 2) by (something). **tick off 1** mark with a **tick**[1] (def. 2) (something that has been done, finished with, etc.). **2** *infml* scold (someone).

tick[2] *nc* a very small animal that lives and feeds on a larger one, such as a dog.

ticket ('tɪkɪt) *nc* 1 a piece of paper or card showing that the holder may (and usually has paid to) use transport, attend an entertainment, etc. 2 a piece of paper or cloth giving the price or other information of the thing it is fixed to. 3 a notice given to a driver who has broken the law: *a parking ticket*. **ticket collector** a person employed on a railway to take back used tickets and check that they were correct. **ticket office** a place where tickets are sold.

tickle ('tɪkəl) *vt* 1 touch (someone) in a place and way that makes him move suddenly and laugh. 2 amuse or please: *He was quite tickled by the idea*. 3 *vi* experience a tickling feeling: *My nose tickles*. **ticklish** ('tɪklɪʃ) *adj* 1 easily made to laugh when tickled. 2 delicate; difficult: *a ticklish problem*.

tide (taɪd) *nc* 1 the rise and fall of the sea about every twelve hours. 2 a flow of water caused by this rise and fall: *a strong tide*. 3 a general movement: *the tide of opinion*. **tidal** ('taɪdəl) *adj* to do with tides. **tidal wave** an unusually large and dangerous wave in the sea: see picture. **tide over** provide or be just enough for (someone) to live on (for a while).

tidal wave

tidings ('taɪdɪŋz) *literary n pl* news; information.

tidy ('taɪdɪ) *adj* -ier, -iest 1 neat; in order: *a tidy girl; a tidy room*. 2 *infml* (of an amount of money) large. ●*vti* (often followed by **up**) make tidy. **tidiness** *nu*

tie (taɪ) *vti* 1 (often followed by **up**) fasten or be held tight (as if) with string, rope, etc.: *Tie the horse to the gate; He's tied up in a meeting*. 2 make (a knot, etc.) in (string or rope). 3 *vi* (of someone in a competition) get the same result (as someone else): *We tied with a team from another school in third place*. ●*nc* 1 a string, etc., used for tying something. 2 *US* **necktie** a strip of cloth worn mainly by men, tied round the neck under the collar of a shirt. 3 a link; connection. 4 an equal result. 5 something that prevents free movement.

tier (tɪə*) *nc* 1 one of several rows, esp. of seats, placed behind and above one another. 2 a stage or level: *a two-tier system*.

tiger ('taɪgə*) *nc* a large Asian member of the cat family that is yellow with black stripes: see picture at **animals**.

tight (taɪt) *adj* -er, -est 1 closely or firmly put together: *a tight knot; The lid of this jar is tight*. 2 (of a rope, wire, etc.) pulled or stretched until firm. 3 closely fitting: *tight clothes*. 4 *infml* not generous: *tight with his money*. 5 *infml* drunk. ●*adv* tightly. **tighten** *vti* make or become tight or tighter. **tightly** *adv* **tightness** *nu* **tightrope** ('taɪtrəʊp) *nc* a rope or wire pulled tight on which balancing acts are done, esp. for entertainment at a circus. **tights** *n pl* a tight garment covering the body from the waist down, worn by women and also by dancers, etc.

tile (taɪl) *nc* a thin flat piece of baked mud, rubber, cork, etc., used esp. to cover a roof, floor, or wall. ●*vt* cover with tiles.

till[1] (tɪl) *conj, prep* short for **until**.

till[2] *nc* a container, esp. a drawer, for money in a bank or shop.

till[3] *old-fashioned vt* work (land) to grow food.

tiller ('tɪlə*) *nc* the handle used to steer a small boat.

tilt (tɪlt) *vti* (cause to) lean not flat or upright. ●*nc* a slope or lean.

timber ('tɪmbə*) *nu* wood, esp. used for building; (also *nc*) a type or piece of such wood.

timbre ('tæmbə*) *nc* the quality of the sound of a voice or musical instrument.

time (taɪm) *nu* 1 the fact that events will happen, then are happening, and then have happened; continued existence: *Time cannot be stopped*. 2 rhythm: *beat time*. *nc* 3 a particular point in time: *The time is two o'clock; He comes at the same time every day*. 4 a period of time: *Five days is a long time*. 5 an occasion: *This is the fourth time I've come*. 6 a proper occasion: *Is it time for us to go?* ●*vt* 1 measure how long (something) lasts or takes. 2 choose a moment for (something) to happen. **all the time** without stopping. **at times** (of a state) occasionally; sometimes. **at the same time** 1 at the same moment; together. 2 however; in spite of that. **behind the times** old-fashioned. **by the time** before or when: *It was dark by the time I finished work*. **for the time being** temporarily; until something better can be found, etc. **from time to time** (of an event) occasionally; sometimes. **have a good time** enjoy oneself. **in time** 1 early (enough): *We were just in time to see the Queen*. 2 eventually; sometime in the future. 3 following the beat or speed of music, etc.: *We walked in time to the music*. **on time** (happening, etc.) at the appointed moment: *Is the train on time?* **take one's time** not hurry. **time and (time) again** many times; very often. **time-consuming** ('taɪm-

kən‚sjuːmɪŋ) *adj* needing a lot of time.
timekeeper ('taɪm‚kiːpə*) *nc* a person who writes down or tells someone the time he spends working, playing a game, etc. **timeless** ('taɪmlɪs) *adj* not changing: *her timeless beauty.* **timely** *adv, adj* **-ier, -iest** at the right or a good moment. **timer** *nc* a person or device that measures or indicates time. **times** *n pl* (used to indicate a multiplication): *Two times three is six.* **timetable** ('taɪm‚teɪbəl) *nc* a list showing the times when events, esp. departures of buses, trains, etc., are supposed to happen. **timing** *nu* the act of doing things at the best time in sport, entertainment, etc.

timid ('tɪmɪd) *adj* easily frightened. **timidity** (tɪ'mɪdɪtɪ) *nu* **timidly** *adv*

timorous ('tɪmərəs) *adj* frightened or timid.

tin (tɪn) **1** *nu* a chemical element; a metal used in bronze and for making containers for food. *nc* **2** a sealed metal container for keeping food good, esp. made of tin plate. **3** a metal box. ●*vt* **1** put (beans, peas, etc.) into a **tin** (def. 2). **2** give (another metal) a coat of tin. **tinfoil** ('tɪnfɔɪl) *nu* very thin tin or aluminium. **tinny** *adj* **-ier, -iest 1** to do with tin. **2** cheaply or badly made. **3** (of a sound) unpleasantly light. **tin-opener** ('tɪn‚əʊpənə*) *nc* a tool for opening tins (**tin** def. 2). **tin plate** thin steel with a coat of tin.

tincture ('tɪŋktʃə*) *nc* a medicine dissolved in alcohol.

tinder ('tɪndə*) *nu* dry wood used for lighting a fire. **tinderbox** ('tɪndəbɒks) *nc* a box for tinder and a flint and steel for making a spark to light the tinder with.

tinge (tɪndʒ) *nc* **1** a small amount of a colour. **2** a small amount of something else: *a tinge of sadness.* ●*vt* give a tinge to.

tingle ('tɪŋgəl) *vi* experience a light stinging feeling. ●*ncu* (an example of) this feeling.

tinker ('tɪŋkə*) *vi* (often followed by **with**) play or experiment (with a machine such as a car), esp. while repairing it. ●*nc* **1** an example of tinkering. **2** a person who used to mend pots and pans.

tinkle ('tɪŋkəl) *vti* (cause to) ring lightly. ●*nc* **1** a light ringing sound. **2** *Brit infml* a telephone call: *I'll give you a tinkle.*

tinsel ('tɪnsəl) *nu* string with strips of very thin metal fixed to it, used as an ornament.

tint (tɪnt) *nc* **1** a light variety of a colour. **2** a hair colouring. ●*vt* give a tint to.

tiny ('taɪnɪ) *adj* **-ier, -iest** very small.

tip¹ (tɪp) *nc* the end of something, esp. pointed or the top: *the tip of the tongue.* ●*vt* give a **tip¹** to. **tiptoe** ('tɪptəʊ) *n* **on tiptoe** without one's heels touching the ground. ●*vi* walk on tiptoe. ●*adv* on tiptoe. **tiptop** ('tɪptɒp) *adj* very good.

tip² **1** *vti* (cause to) slope or lean. **2** *vt* pour or empty: *Tip the coal over there.* ●*nc* **1** an act of tipping. **2** a place for tipping, esp. rubbish. **tip over** tip (something) so that it falls over. **tip up** tip (something) so as to empty it, etc.

tip³ *nc* **1** money given to a waiter, etc., as a reward for service on top of any normal charge. **2** a piece of advice. ●*vt* give a **tip³** (def. 1) to.

tip⁴ *vt* hit lightly, esp. with the edge of something. ●*nc* an act of tipping.

tipple ('tɪpəl) *vti* take (alcoholic drink) frequently. ●*ncu* (an) alcoholic drink.

tipsy ('tɪpsɪ) *adj* **-ier, -iest** slightly drunk.

tirade (taɪ'reɪd) *nc* a long, angry, or criticising speech.

tire¹ ('taɪə*) *vti* make or become less active or energetic through any sort of activity. **tired** *adj* no longer able or wanting to be active; ready for sleep. **tired of** bored with or annoyed by: *I'm tired of London.* **tireless** *adj* unable to be tired. **tire out** tire (someone) completely. **tiresome** ('taɪəsəm) *adj* boring or annoying.

tire² *US n* See **tyre.**

'tis (tɪz) *archaic or literary* it is.

tissue ('tɪsjuː, 'tɪʃuː) *nu* **1** material of a particular type in a plant or animal: *skin tissue.* **2** soft paper used as a handkerchief, towel, etc.; (sometimes *nc*) a paper handkerchief. **tissue paper** thin paper used esp. for wrapping delicate objects.

tit (tɪt) *nc* one of several small birds, such as a bluetit (see picture at **birds**) or coal tit.

titbit ('tɪt‚bɪt) *nc* a small, tasty piece of food.

tithe (taɪð) *nc* a tenth of what one is paid, what a farm produces, etc., given esp. to support a church.

title ('taɪtəl) *nc* **1** the name given to a book, film, etc. **2** a description of a person indicating his job, position in society, etc. **3** *law* a claim of ownership. **4** a position of being the best in a particular class of sport: *He holds the World Heavyweight title.* **titled** *adj* having a title, esp. a noble one. **title role** the character in a play, film, etc., after whom it is named.

to¹ (tuː unstressed tʊ, tə) *prep* **1** (used to indicate direction): *I went to Africa.* **2** (used to indicate an indirect object): *Why are you telling this to me?* **3** (used to indicate a comparison or relationship): *We have six to your two; doing exercises to music.* **4** until: *from January to April.* **5** against; onto; as far as: *stuck on the floor.* **6** *US* of before the hour of: *twenty to seven.* ●*adv* **1** (of a door) shut or neary shut: *Please pull the door to.* **2** conscious: *I was knocked out and came to half an hour later.* **to and fro** See under **fro.**

to² 1 (used to show the infinitive of a verb, or to indicate this when the verb is not spoken or written): *We don't want to go; He asked us to go, but we don't want to.* 2 (used with the infinitive to show purpose or the flow of events): *She did it to please him; I looked up to find him gone.*

toad (təʊd) *nc* an animal that lives in water and on land and has long powerful back legs. **toadstool** ('təʊdstuːl) *nc* a plant with a flat top like an umbrella.

toast¹ (təʊst) *nu* cut bread turned brown by heat. ● *vt* turn (bread, etc.) brown in this way.

toast² *vt* (of a group of people) indicate, by raising a glass and drinking, one's wishes for the health, success, etc., of (someone or something). ● *nc* an act of toasting.

tobacco (tə'bækəʊ) *ncu, pl* -**s**, -**es** a (type of) plant of which the leaves are dried and smoked, esp. in cigarettes. **tobacconist** (tə'bækənɪst) *nc* a person who sells tobacco and things made from tobacco.

toboggan (tə'bɒgən) *nc* a wooden frame used for sliding down snow-covered slopes. ● *vi* slide on a toboggan.

today (tə'deɪ) *adv, n* 1 (during) this day. 2 (during) the present.

toddle ('tɒdəl) *vi* (esp. of a small child) walk unsteadily with short steps. ● *nc infml* a short walk. **toddler** *nc* a child of two or three.

to-do (tə'duː) *infml nc, pl* -**s** a state of confused activity; a disturbance.

toe (təʊ) *nc* 1 one of the five separate parts of the front of the foot. 2 a part like this on an animal's foot. 3 the part of a shoe, sock, etc., covering the toes. ● *vt* touch with the toes. **toe the line** do as one is told or expected to do. **toenail** ('təʊneɪl) *nc* the hard, nearly flat growth on top of the end of each toe.

toffee ('tɒfɪ) *ncu* a (piece of) hard or soft sweet food chiefly made from sugar and butter.

together (tə'geðə*) *adv* 1 in or into company or union: *They live together; The pages are bound together.* 2 at the same time: *They said it together.* **together with** as well as.

toggle ('tɒgəl) *nc* a wooden or metal bar tied by its middle and used for fastening by being pushed through a hole or loop.

toil (tɔɪl) *formal nu* hard work. ● *vi* 1 work hard. 2 travel slowly and with difficulty.

toilet ('tɔɪlɪt) *nc* 1 See **lavatory**. 2 *old-fashioned ncu* (an example of) getting dressed, brushing one's hair, etc.

token ('təʊkən) *nc* 1 an indication or sign: *This present is just a token of my thanks.* 2 an object like a coin, used to work a public telephone, for gambling, etc. 3 a card that is given as a present and can be used to pay for something in a shop: *a book token.*

told (təʊld) past tense and past participle of **tell.**

tolerate ('tɒləreɪt) *vt* allow or not mind. **tolerable** ('tɒlərəbəl) *adj* that can be tolerated. **tolerant** ('tɒlərənt) *adj* able to tolerate something. **tolerance** ('tɒlərəns) *nu* 1 the quality of being tolerant. 2 *science ncu* (an example of) the ability of a substance, plant, etc., to put up with a measured amount of stress.

toll¹ (təʊl) 1 *vi* (of a bell) ring repeatedly. 2 *vt* ring (a bell) repeatedly. ● *nu* the sound or act of tolling.

toll² *nc* an amount of money charged, esp. for using a road or bridge.

tomahawk ('tɒməhɔːk) *nc* a North American Indian axe used for fighting with.

tomato (tə'mɑːtəʊ) *nc, pl* -**es** the round red fruit of the tomato plant, used as food.

tomb (tuːm) *nc* a place where a dead person is buried, esp. a room under the ground. **tombstone** ('tuːmstəʊn) *nc* a piece of stone over a tomb or grave giving the name of the person buried in it.

tomboy ('tɒmbɔɪ) *nc, pl* -**s** a girl who dresses or behaves like a boy.

tomcat ('tɒmkæt) *nc* also **tom** a male cat.

tomorrow (tə'mɒrəʊ) *adv, n* (on) the day after today.

ton (tʌn) *nc* 1 a measure of weight (in Britain 1016.047 kg, America 907.2 kg). 2 *infml* a very heavy weight. 3 (of a ship) a measurement of size or of cargo capacity. 4 *infml* 100 miles per hour: *doing a ton down the motorway.* 5 *infml (pl)* a very large amount: *tons of interesting things.*

tone (təʊn) *nc* 1 the quality of a sound. 2 a variety of a colour. 3 the general character of something: *the tone of the meeting.* ● *v* 1 (often followed by **with**) match in colour: *Your coat tones well with your dress.* 2 *vt* give a **tone** (def. 2) to. **tonal** ('təʊnəl) *adj* to do with tone. **tone down** make (something esp. likely to cause anger or offence) more ordinary or (a colour) less bright: *His article was toned down before it was printed.*

tongs (tɒŋz) *n pl* also **pair of tongs** a device made of two arms squeezed together to hold an object.

tongue (tʌŋ) *nc* 1 *anatomy, zoology* the part of the body inside the mouth used for tasting and licking food, and, in humans, for talking. 2 a language: *What is your mother tongue?* 3 the piece of leather under the lace on a shoe. 4 anything shaped like tongue. 5 *nu* the tongue(s) of an animal esp. an ox, cooked and eaten as food. **tongue-tied** ('tʌŋtaɪd) *adj* unable to speak esp. because of shyness.

tonic ('tɒnɪk) *nc* **1** a medicine that improves the general working of the body. **2** also **tonic water** fizzy water containing quinine, often drunk mixed with gin.

tonight (tə'naɪt) *adv, n* (during) the evening of or night following today.

tonnage ('tʌnɪdʒ) *nc* a weight expressed in tons.

tonne (tʌn, tɒn) *nc* also **metric ton** a measure of weight = 1000 kg

tonsil ('tɒnsəl) *anatomy nc* either of two small parts at each side of the back of the mouth.

too (tu:) *adv* **1** also: *I wrote this too.* **2** more than is good or than one would like: *It's too cold to go outside.*

took (tʊk) past tense of **take.**

tool (tu:l) *nc* **1** an instrument, usually held in the hand, such as a hammer or saw: see picture: *The engineer carried all his tools in a case.* **2** a person who is used by another, often to do unpopular or unpleasant things. **3** a means of or help in doing something: *Books are a tool of learning.* ● *vt* work or ornament (something, esp. the leather cover of a book) with tools.

toot (tu:t) *vti* (of a horn, whistle, etc.), (cause to) sound briefly. ● *nc* such a sound.

tooth (tu:θ) *nc, pl* **teeth 1** one of the set of bone-like parts of the mouth used chiefly for biting and chewing. **2** a tooth-like object on a comb, gear, etc. **toothache** ('tu:θeɪk) *nc* a pain in or near a tooth. **toothbrush** ('tu:θbrʌʃ) *nc* a small brush with a long handle used for cleaning the teeth. **toothpaste** ('tu:θpeɪst) *ncu* a (type of) soft preparation used when brushing the teeth. **toothpick** ('tu:θpɪk) *nc* a thin pointed piece of wood for cleaning food from between the teeth.

top¹ (tɒp) *nc* **1** the highest part of something: *the top of the tree.* **2** a lid or cap: *a bottle top.* *nu* **3** the best, most important, etc., part or member: *at the top of his class at school.* **4** the greatest possible extent: *at the top of one's voice.* ● *adj* to do with or at the top: *a top lawyer.* ● *vt* **1** put a top on. **2** reach the top of. **3** remove the top of. **4** be greater, higher than: *He topped me by only one point.* **from top to bottom** thoroughly; completely: *We cleaned the house from top to bottom.* **on top of 1** on; over. **2** as well as: *There's a tax on top of the selling price.* **3** *infml* in control: *He got on top of the situation by hard work.* **topcoat** ('tɒpkəʊt) *nc* **1** a coat worn over a dress, jacket, etc. **2** a last coat of paint. **topheavy** (tɒp'hevɪ) *adj* heavier at the top than at the bottom and so likely to tip over. **topmost** ('tɒpməʊst) *adj* highest, most important, etc. **top secret** very secret. **topsoil** ('tɒpsɔɪl) *nu* the surface

earth in the ground. **top up** fill (a container that is not empty).

top² *nc* a toy that stays upright when it is spun: see picture.

top

topaz ('təʊpæz) *ncu* (a piece of) coloured (mostly common yellow) or clear precious stone.

topic ('tɒpɪk) *nc* a subject of a discussion, book, etc. **topical** *adj* to do with a topic, esp. a local or current one: *a topical report.*

topography (tə'pɒgrəfɪ) *ncu, pl* **-phies** the study (or a description) of the shape of the surface of an area of land.

topple ('tɒpəl) *vti* (often followed by **over**) (cause to) fall.

topsy-turvy (,tɒpsɪ'tɜ:vɪ) *adj, adv* upside-down; in confusion.

Torah ('tɔ:rə) *n* the first five books of the Bible, as read in synagogues.

torch (tɔ:tʃ) *nc* **1** *US* **flashlight** a small electric lamp containing its own battery. **2** a wooden stick or mass of other material soaked with a substance that burns, which is carried, burning, for its light.

tore (tɔ:*) past tense of **tear².**

torment (tɔ:'ment) *vt* cause to suffer great pain or worry. ● ('tɔ:ment) *ncu* (a cause of) great pain or worry.

torn (tɔ:n) past participle of **tear².**

tornado (tɔ:'neɪdəʊ) *nc, pl* **-s, -es** a very strong wind blowing round and round a moving point.

torpedo (tɔ:'pi:dəʊ) *nc, pl* **-es** a bomb used against ships that travels by its own power under water: see picture.

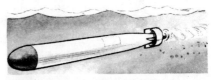

torpedo

torque (tɔ:k) *nu* a twisting force.

torrent ('tɒrənt) *nc* a large, fast rush or stream, esp. of water. **torrential** (tə'renʃəl) *adj* to do with or in a torrent: *torrential rain.*

torrid ('tɒrɪd) *adj* (of land, weather, etc.) very hot and dry.

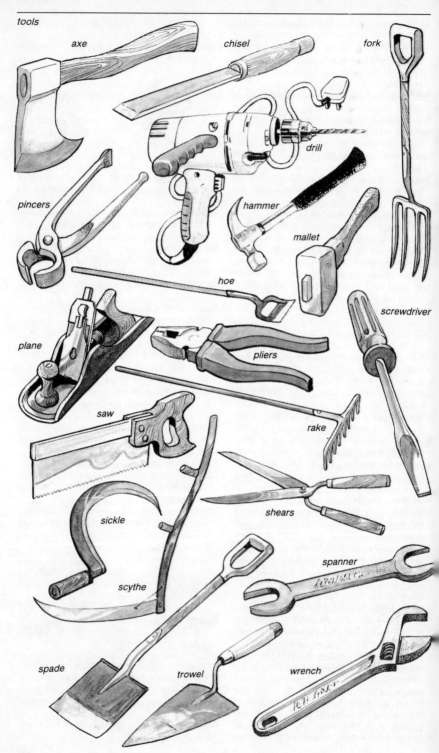

tools
axe
chisel
fork
drill
pincers
hammer
mallet
hoe
plane
screwdriver
pliers
saw
rake
sickle
shears
scythe
spanner
spade
trowel
wrench

torsion ('tɔːʃən) *nu* the twisting of something.

tortoise ('tɔːtəs) *nc* an animal that moves very slowly and has a shell into which it can draw its head and legs: see picture at **reptiles.**

tortuous ('tɔːtjʊəs) *adj* 1 twisting and turning: *a tortuous route.* 2 difficult to follow or understand: *a tortuous argument.*

torture ('tɔːtʃə*) *vt* hurt (someone) very badly in order to persuade or punish. ● *nu* 1 the act of causing pain in this way. 2 *nc* a way of torturing.

toss (tɒs) 1 *vt* throw, esp. up. *vti* 2 (often followed by **up**) throw (a coin) up in order to let the way it lands decide something. 3 (cause to) move wildly about: *He tossed in his sleep; The ship was tossed by the storm.* ● *nc* the act of tossing. **toss-up** ('tɒsʌp) *nc* 1 an instance of tossing a coin. 2 *infml* an affair which might develop in either of two ways.

tot¹ (tɒt) *nc* 1 a small child: *tiny tots.* 2 a small measure of an alcoholic drink.

tot² *vti* (often followed by **up**) add up.

total ('təʊtəl) *adj* complete. ● *nc* a number or amount reached by adding up several numbers or amounts. ● *vt* 1 add up the total of: *to total one's costs.* 2 *vi* amount to: *The houses in this street total ten.* **totally** *adv*

totalitarian (təʊ,tælɪ'teərɪən) *adj* to do with a political system in which one leader or party alone decides the affairs of the country, and no opposition is allowed.

totter ('tɒtə*) *vi* 1 walk unsteadily. 2 be about to fall or fail.

touch (tʌtʃ) 1 *vti* come or be up against or in contact with (something): *His foot touched the ball; Are the cars touching? vt* 2 have to do with: *I won't touch drink.* 3 affect: *a life touched by sadness.* 4 affect with feeling: *Her letter touched me; a touching remark.* 5 come close to; reach: *Our speed touched 90 kph.* ● *nu* 1 the ability to feel by touching. *nc* 2 an act or state of touching. 3 a small amount: *a touch of heat.* 4 the quality of something as felt by touch. 5 a way of handling or touching. **in** or **out of touch** 1 aware or not aware of; in or out of contact with: *He's out of touch with events abroad; I'll put you in touch with a friend of mine.* 2 *sport* (of a ball or player) inside or outside the playing area. **touch down** (of a plane or spacecraft) land. **touchdown** ('tʌtʃdaʊn) *nc* the act or moment of touching down. **touch on** deal with or refer to (a subject) briefly. **touch up** do small repairs on the final work on (a painting, photograph, etc.). **touchy** ('tʌtʃɪ) *adj* **-ier, -iest** easily annoyed.

tough (tʌf) *adj* **-er, -est** 1 strong; hard to break, bite, etc. 2 able to survive rough treatment or bad conditions. 3 difficult; awkward: *a tough question; Don't get tough with me!* ● *nc* a rough, violent person. **toughen** *vti* (often followed by **up**) make or become tough or tougher. **toughness** *nu*

toupee ('tuːpeɪ) *nc* a small mat of false hair to cover a part of the head that has lost its hair.

tour (tʊə*) *nc* 1 a journey visiting many places, esp. either for pleasure or to give a concert, play, etc., in each. 2 a short journey around a city, house, etc. 3 (esp. of businessmen or the armed forces) a period of working abroad: *a business tour of America.* ● *vt* visit (a number of places) or travel around in (a place) on a tour.

tourist ('tʊərɪst) *nc* a person making a tour, esp. on holiday away from home. **tourism** ('tʊərɪzəm) *nu* the business connected with tourist travel.

tournament ('tʊənəmənt) *nc* a competition between a number of players or teams.

tourniquet ('tʊənɪkeɪ) *nc* a device, such as a rolled-up cloth, for tightening round a part of the body to stop bleeding.

tousle ('taʊzəl) *vt* make (something, esp. hair) untidy.

tow (təʊ) *vt* (esp. of a boat or vehicle) pull (something, esp. another boat or vehicle) with a rope, etc. ● *nc* an act of towing. **towpath** ('təʊpɑːθ) *nc* a path beside a river or canal from which a boat can be towed.

towards (tə'wɔːdz) *prep* also **toward** 1 in the direction of: *He walked towards the house.* 2 with respect to: *his love towards her.* 3 to help with: *Here's some money towards your new house.* 4 near: *towards the end of the month.*

towel ('taʊəl) *nc* a piece of cloth or paper that soaks up water and is used for drying oneself after washing, swimming, etc. ● *vt* dry with a towel. **throw in the towel** give up; admit defeat.

tower ('taʊə*) *nc* a tall building or other structure, such as one that is part of a church or castle: *a church tower; a water tower; the control tower of an airport.* ● *vi* (often followed by **above** or **over**) be very high: *He was so tall he towered over his friends.* **tower block** a very tall building of flats or offices.

town (taʊn) *nc* a fairly large group of houses, shops, factories, etc. **town hall** the chief building where the affairs of a town are dealt with, often also used for public meetings, etc. **town planning** the activity of deciding where buildings may be built, what land may be used for, etc.

township ('taʊnʃɪp) *nc* a small town.

toxic ('tɒksɪk) *adj* poisonous or to do with poison.

toy (tɔɪ) *nc* **1** an object made to be played with, esp. by a child. **2** a small animal, esp. a kind of dog, kept as a pet. **toyshop** ('tɔɪʃɒp) *nc* a shop selling toys. **toy with 1** play with. **2** consider: *I'm toying with the idea of going abroad.*

trace (treɪs) *nc* **1** a track or mark left by someone or something: *disappear without a trace.* **2** a small amount. **3** a line drawn by a measuring instrument, etc. ● *vt* **1** follow or discover the track or position of: *Have you traced where the gun was bought?* **2** copy (a drawing, etc.) by drawing on a piece of paper through which the original can be seen underneath. **tracing** *nc* a drawing made by tracing another.

trachea (trə'kiːə) *anatomy, zoology nc, pl* **-cheae** ('kiːiː) also **windpipe** the tube through which breath travels between the mouth and the lungs.

track (træk) *nc* **1** a set of marks or a line left by a moving vehicle, animal, etc. **2** a path or way, either rough or one used for racing. **3** a railway line. **4** a separate part of the recording on a gramophone record. **5** also **caterpillar track** an endless set of connected metal plates running round the wheels of a vehicle such as a tank. ● *vt* follow the track of (something moving). **keep** or **lose track of** follow or fail to follow the progress of. **off the beaten track** See under **beaten**. **track down** find by hunting or following. **tracker** *nc* **tracksuit** *nc* a suit made of soft material and worn by sportsmen, esp. while training.

tract¹ (trækt) *nc* **1** a piece of land; region. **2** *anatomy* a set of parts of the body forming a particular system: *the digestive tract.*

tract² *nc* a piece of writing, esp. religious.

traction ('trækʃən) *nu* **1** the act or power of pulling, esp. by a vehicle. **2** *medicine* the pulling of a part of the body to help something, esp. a broken bone, to heal.

tractor ('træktə*) *nc* a vehicle used to pull a load, farm machine, etc.

trade (treɪd) **1** *nu* the act of buying and selling as a business. *nc* **2** an occupation or business, esp. a mechanical one, such as making furniture or repairing bicycles. **3** the people working in a trade: *This information is for the trade only.* ● *vt* buy and sell (goods); exchange. **trademark** ('treɪd-mɑːk) *nc* **1** a name, picture, etc., that is shown on goods made by one firm and may not be used by another. **2** something characteristic of someone or something. **trader** *nc* **tradesman** ('treɪdzmən) *nc, pl* **-men** a person in (a) trade, esp. a shopkeeper. **trade union** also **trades union** an organi-

sation of workers in a particular trade, having the aim of improving their pay, etc. **trade wind** a wind blowing towards the equator from either the north-east or the south-east.

tradition (trə'dɪʃən) *ncu* (an example of) the passing down of opinions or customs to descendants or successors. **traditional** *adj*

traffic ('træfɪk) *nu* **1** the vehicles using a road. **2** the transport of people or goods: *a lot of air traffic.* **3** trade, esp. unlawful. ● *vi* (often followed by **in**) trade, esp. unlawfully: *trafficking in illegal drugs.* **traffic light(s)** a set of red, green, and usually also yellow lights used to indicate whether road traffic must stop or may go on.

tragedy ('trædʒədɪ) *nc, pl* **-dies 1** a sad or unlucky event, such as an accident. **2** a play with a sad ending. **tragic** ('trædʒɪk) *adj* to do with a tragedy. **tragically** *adv*

trail (treɪl) *nc* **1** the track left by a person, animal, or anything considered to be moving: *This affair is leaving a trail of confusion.* **2** a road or path through wild country. ● *vti* **1** drag along behind, esp. on the ground. **2** *vt* hunt or chase by following a **trail** (def. 1). **3** *vi* (esp. of plants) reach out, esp. across the ground.

trailer ('treɪlə*) *nc* **1** a road vehicle used for carrying and towed by one with an engine. **2** a short film containing parts of another which it is advertising. **trailer truck** *US* See **articulated lorry** under **articulate**.

train (treɪn) **1** *vti* teach, guide, or prepare for or to do something: *I'm training my dog to obey me; a trained soldier.* **2** *vt* (often followed by **on**) aim (a gun, etc.). ● *nc* **1** a number of railway vehicles pulled by a locomotive. **2** the long back of a skirt or other garment that trails on the ground. **3** a row or number: *a train of events.* **trainer** *nc* **training** *nu*

trait (treɪt, treɪ) *nc* a characteristic of appearance or behaviour.

traitor ('treɪtə*) *nc* a person who helps an enemy of his country or of a friend, breaks a promise, or lets out a secret.

trajectory (trə'dʒektərɪ) *nc, pl* **-ries** the path taken by an object, esp. a bomb, spacecraft, etc., moving through the air or in space.

tram (træm) *nc* a passenger vehicle running like a railway engine on lines in the road.

tramp (træmp) *vi* **1** walk a long way. **2** walk or step heavily. **3** live as a **tramp** (def. 1). ● *nc* **1** a person who walks around the country asking for money or doing occasional work. **2** a long walk. **3** the sound of heavy walking.

trample ('træmpəl) *vti* knock or press down with the feet: *He trampled all over the flowers.*

trampoline ('træmpə,liːn) *nc* a flat sheet of cloth connected by springs to a frame and used for jumping on as exercise: see picture.

trampoline

trance (trɑːns) *nc* a state when one is conscious but behaving as if unaware of one's surroundings: *Ever since she met him she's been going around in a trance.*

tranquil ('træŋkwɪl) *adj* calm; restful: *a tranquil mind; a tranquil sea.* **tranquillity** (træŋ'kwɪlɪtɪ) *nu*

tranquilliser ('træŋkwɪlaɪzə*) *medicine nc* a drug used to make someone calmer or less worried.

transact (træn'zækt) *vt* do or carry out (business). **transaction** (træn'zækʃən) *nc* 1 an act of transacting. 2 something transacted.

transatlantic (,trænzət'læntɪk) *adj* from, on, or to the other side of the Atlantic Ocean.

transcend (træn'send) *vt* be above or beyond (experience, understanding, etc.): *She transcends beauty.* **transcendent** (træn-'sendənt) *adj* also **transcendental** (,trænsen'dentəl) transcending human experience.

transcontinental (,trænzkɒntɪ'nentəl) *adj* from, at, or to the other side of a continent.

transcribe (træn'skraɪb) *vt* write again or differently; copy: *transcribe notes into a book; a song transcribed for instruments.* **transcript** ('trænskrɪpt) *nc* a transcribed copy.

transfer (træns'fɜː*) *vti* move or change from one person or thing, esp. place, to another: *I'll transfer some money from my bank account to yours; I transferred from the bus to the train.* ● ('trænsfɜː*) *nc* an act of transferring or being transferred.

transfigure (træns'fɪgə*) *vt* change the shape or appearance of, esp. to make appear ideal.

transfix (træns'fɪks) *vt* 1 stick a sword, pin, etc., through. 2 cause (someone) to stand still through fear, shock, etc.

transform (træns'fɔːm) *vt* 1 change the form, appearance, etc., of. 2 change the voltage of (electricity). **transformation** (,trænsfə'meɪʃən) *nc* a great change. **transformer** *nc* 1 a person or thing that transforms. 2 a device that changes electric voltage.

transfusion (træns'fjuːʒən) *nc* 1 an instance of causing something, esp. liquid, to flow from one thing into another. 2 *medicine* an instance of replacing blood lost by a patient with some from someone else.

transgress (træns'gres) *formal or humorous vt* break (a law, custom, understanding, etc.). **transgression** (træns'greʃən) *ncu*

transient ('trænzɪənt) *adj* not permanent; lasting only a short time.

transistor (træn'zɪstə*) *nc* 1 an electrical device used in radios, etc., to control current. 2 a radio containing transistors.

transit ('trænzɪt) *nu* the movement of people or goods: *They're still in transit.*

transition (træn'zɪʃən) *ncu* (an example of) change from one place or state to another. **transitional** *adj*

transitive ('trænzɪtɪv) *grammar adj* (of a verb) (usually) able to have a direct object: *'Ring' is transitive in the sense of 'make (a bell) sound'.*

transitory ('trænzɪtərɪ) *adj* not permanent; lasting only a short time.

translate (træns'leɪt) *vt* 1 say or write in a different language: *a Hindi novel translated into English.* 2 explain, esp. in simpler language. 3 turn or change into something else. 4 *formal* move from one place to another. **translation** (træns'leɪʃən) 1 *nu* the act of translating. 2 *nc* something translated. **translator** *nc*

translucent (træns'luːsənt) *adj* (of a substance such as thin cloth) allowing light through but not clear enough to see through.

transmit (trænz'mɪt) *vt* 1 pass on (a message, disease, radio programme, etc.). 2 allow (light, etc.) to pass through. **transmission** (trænz'mɪʃən) 1 *nu* the act of transmitting or being transmitted. *nc* 2 something transmitted, esp. a radio signal. 3 a set of parts in a motor vehicle that transmits power to the wheels. **transmitter** *nc* a person or thing that transmits radio or television signals.

transparent (træns'pærənt) *adj* 1 (of a substance such as glass) clear enough to see through. 2 easily understood, discovered, etc.: *a transparent disguise.* **transparency** (træns'pærənsɪ) 1 *nc, pl* -cies also **slide** a transparent picture for looking at with the light behind it and esp. projected onto a screen. 2 *nu* the quality of being transparent.

transpire (træn'spaɪə*) *vi* 1 *infml* happen: *What transpired then?* 2 become known: *It transpired that he had not told the truth.* 3 *vt* (of a plant) give off (water) from the leaves.

transplant (træns'plɑːnt) *vt* put (a plant) in another place or (a part of the body) into a different body. ● ('trænsplɑːnt) *nc* an instance of transplanting.

transport (træn'spɔːt) *vt* **1** move or carry from one place to another. **2** send (someone) somewhere abroad to serve a punishment. ● ('trænspɔːt) *nu* **1** the act or business of transporting. **2** a means of transport; *(sometimes nc)* a vehicle, plane, or ship used to carry soldiers. **transportation** (ˌtrænspɔːˈteɪʃən) *nu* **1** *US* transport. **2** the act of transporting (**transport** *v* def. 2). **transporter** *nc* a person or thing that transports, esp. a very long vehicle for carrying cars on two levels.

transpose (trænsˈpəʊz) *vt* **1** put (things) in each other's places. **2** write or play (music) in a different key.

transversal (trænzˈvɜːsəl) *adj* (of a line) crossing two or more other lines. ● *nc* a transversal line.

transverse (trænzˈvɜːs) *adj* arranged, pointing, etc., across something: *a transverse car engine.*

trap (træp) *nc* **1** a cage, pit, mechanical device, etc., used to catch animals or people. **2** a way of tricking someone into making a mistake. **3** a light two-wheeled vehicle pulled by a horse. **4** *slang* a mouth: *Shut your trap!* ● *vt* catch in a **trap** (defs. 1, 2). **trap-door** (ˌtræpˈdɔː*) *nc* also **trap** a door in a floor or ceiling. **trapper** *nc* a person who traps wild animals, esp. for their fur.

trapeze (trəˈpiːz) *nc* a bar hanging by two ropes used for swinging on, esp. as a circus act.

trapezium (trəˈpiːzɪəm) *geometry nc, pl* **-ziums, -zia** (zɪə) a four-sided figure with one opposite pair of sides both pointing in the same two directions: see picture at **shapes.**

trash (træʃ) *nu* **1** something of poor quality. **2** nonsense. **3** *chiefly US* waste; rubbish.

trauma (ˈtrɔːmə) *nc, pl* **-mas, mata** (mətə) **1** a serious shock to the mind. **2** an injury to the body. **traumatic** (trɔːˈmætɪk) *adj*

travail (ˈtræveɪl) *literary or archaic nu* **1** the pain of giving birth to a child. **2** very hard or painful work. ● *vi* work very hard or in pain.

travel (ˈtrævəl) *vt* **1** make a journey or journeys: *He travels around Europe a lot.* **2** (sometimes followed by **for**) move, esp. for a period: *We travelled for two days; Sound travels in water.* **3** (often followed by **in**) be employed to go from place to place selling: *He travels in toys.* **4** move or be sent, remaining in a good condition. **5** *infml* move fast. *vt* **6** move (a distance): *The ball only travelled ten metres!* **7** pass over or through: *I travelled the country looking for work.* ● *nu* **1** the act of travelling. **2** *nc* (usually *pl*) a journey or journeys. **travel agency** a business that gives advice on tra-

vel (esp. holidays), obtains tickets, etc. **travelled** *US* **traveled** *adj* having done (much) travelling: *well-travelled.* **traveller** *US* **traveler** *nc* **traveller's cheque** *US* **traveler's check** a cheque bought from a bank in one country and changed for money in another.

traverse (trəˈvɜːs) *vt* move across (something, such as the side of a mountain). ● *nc* an act of traversing.

travesty (ˈtrævəstɪ) *nc, pl* **-ties** something that tries to copy or pretends to be something else, but fails completely: *This food is a travesty of French cooking.* ● *vt* make a travesty of.

trawler (ˈtrɔːlə*) *nc* a fishing boat that pulls a net through the water: see picture.

trawler

tray (treɪ) *nc* **1** a board or sheet of metal with a raised edge, used for carrying. **2** a shallow, open container for papers on a desk.

treacherous (ˈtretʃərəs) *adj* **1** tricking, cheating, letting out a secret, etc., or likely to do so. **2** dangerous; untrustworthy: *a treacherous road.* **treachery** (ˈtretʃərɪ) *ncu, pl* **-ies** (an instance of) treacherous behaviour.

treacle (ˈtriːkəl) *nu* a dark brown, sticky, sweet liquid made from sugar.

tread (tred) **1** *vti* step (on): *Don't tread on the grass; to tread a road.* **2** *vt* press or squash by treading: *treading grapes.* ● *nc* **1** an act or manner of treading. **2** the flat part of a step or stair. **3** the raised parts of the surface of a tyre.

treason (ˈtriːzən) *nu* the act of being disloyal to one's king, queen, or country, esp. by helping an enemy.

treasure (ˈtreʒə*) **1** *nu* a collection of precious metals or stones. **2** *infml nc* a highly valued person or thing. ● *vt* **1** value highly. **2** *vi* (often followed by **up**) save or store (something valuable).

treasurer (ˈtreʒərə*) *nc* a person in charge of the money of a club, town, etc.

treasury (ˈtreʒərɪ) *nc, pl* **-ries** a place where money or treasure is kept. **Treasury** a government department controlling how public money is spent.

treat (triːt) *vt* **1** behave towards: *He treats her badly.* **2** deal with (a sick person or an illness) by using medicine, etc.: *He treated me for a broken leg.* **3** use a chemical substance on: *Fruit is often treated with chemicals.* **4** pay for (someone) to have: *I'll treat you to* *a meal.* **5** deal with: *treat problems as they arise.* ● *nc* **1** something enjoyable, esp. to which one is treated. **2** an act of treating (**treat** def. **4**).

treatise ('tri:tɪs) *nc* a formal piece of writing on a particular subject.

treatment ('tri:tmənt) *ncu* the act or a way of treating someone or something.

treaty ('tri:tɪ) *nc, pl* **-ties** an agreement, esp. between countries.

treble ('trebəl) *adj* to do with high sound, esp. a high instrument or a boy's singing voice. ● *vti* make or become three times as many: *If you treble three you get nine.* ● *nc* **1** a trebled quantity or thing. **2** a boy singer. **3** *nu* the high part of music or sound.

tree (tri:) *nc* a large woody plant, such as an oak, with a trunk from which branches and leaves grow at a distance from the ground: see picture. **treetop** ('tri:tɒp) *nc* the top (part) of a tree.

trek (trek) *nc* a long journey, esp. in wild country. ● *vi* make a trek.

trellis ('trelɪs) *nc* a fence made of crossed sloping bars, used esp. to support plants: see picture.

trellis

tremble ('trembəl) *vi* **1** shake, esp. from fear, anger, cold, etc. **2** be very afraid: *He trembled at the thought of what might happen.* ● *nc* an act of trembling.

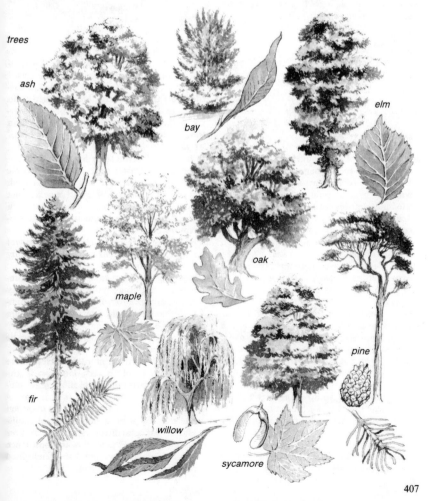

trees

ash

bay

elm

oak

maple

pine

fir

willow

sycamore

tremendous (trɪ'mendəs) *adj* **1** huge; very big. **2** *infml* very good or unusual. **tremendously** *adv*

tremor ('tremə*) *nc* a shake or tremble: *an earth tremor.*

tremulous ('tremjʊləs) *adj* trembling; shaking.

trench (trentʃ) *nc* a long narrow hole in the ground, esp. dug for soldiers to shelter in. ● *vti* dig a trench (in or for).

trend (trend) *nc* the general direction of a change in behaviour, dress, etc.: *a trend towards longer skirts.* ● *vi* follow a trend.

trepidation (ˌtrepɪ'deɪʃən) *nu* fear or worry.

trespass ('trespəs) *vi* **1** (often followed by **on**) enter (someone else's property) without permission. **2** (followed by **on** or **upon**) disturb (someone's privacy, rights, etc.). ● *nc* an act of trespassing. **trespasser** *nc*

tress (tres) *chiefly literary nc (usually pl)* a part of a woman's hair when it is arranged.

trestle ('tresəl) *nc* a folding wooden stand used in pairs to support a table: see picture.

trestle

trial ('traɪəl) *nc* **1** an examination of a case in law to discover whether someone is guilty. **2** a test or experiment. **3** an annoying or worrying person or thing. **on trial 1** being tried in a court of law. **2** being tested before being bought, employed, etc. **trial and error** discovering how to do something by seeing which methods work and which do not: *If there's no-one to teach you, you'll have to learn by trial and error.* **trial run** an experiment, esp. the first time a vehicle or other machine is worked.

triangle ('traɪæŋgəl) *nc* **1** *geometry* a three-sided figure: see picture at **shapes**. **2** three objects or points not in a straight line. **3** a musical instrument consisting of a metal bar in the shape of a triangle which is hit with another metal bar. **triangular** (traɪ-'æŋgjʊlə*) *adj* to do with a **triangle** (defs. **1, 2**).

tribe (traɪb) *nc* a group of related people, esp. living together in a place little affected by industrial society. **tribal** *adj* **tribesman** ('traɪbzmən) *nc, pl* **-men** a member of a tribe.

tribulation (ˌtrɪbjʊ'leɪʃən) *ncu* (a cause of) suffering or worry.

tribunal (traɪ'bjuːnəl) *nc* **1** a law court. **2** a group of people appointed to decide an argument over employment, rent, etc.

tributary ('trɪbjʊtərɪ) *nc, pl* **-ries 1** a river, stream, etc. that flows into a larger one. **2** a person, country, etc., that pays **tribute** (def. 1). ● *adj* to do with a tributary.

tribute ('trɪbjuːt) *ncu* **1** (an amount of) money paid by one country to another that controls or attacks it. **2** (an expression of) admiration, thanks, etc.

trice (traɪs) *n* **in a trice** very quickly.

trick (trɪk) *nc* **1** an action intended to deceive or cheat. **2** an action learned by a person or animal: *to teach a dog a new trick.* **3** a playful action; joke: *He plays tricks like putting things in people's shoes.* **4** the cards played by all the players in one round of a card game. **5** a habit, esp. a useful one: *She has a trick of smiling and making you forget you were angry.* ● *vt* deceive; cheat: *I was tricked into buying something I didn't want.* ● *adj* made as a trick, to confuse, etc.: *a trick question.* **tricky** *adj* **-ier, -iest 1** difficult; needing great care: *a tricky business.* **2** to do with tricks; deceitful.

trickle ('trɪkəl) *vi* (of a liquid) flow slowly or in small quantities. ● *nc* a slow or small flow.

tricycle ('traɪsɪkəl) *nc* a three-wheeled vehicle, esp. for carrying one person and driven with the legs.

tried (traɪd) past tense and part participle of **try.**

trifle ('traɪfəl) **1** *nc* something small, unimportant, or worthless. **2** *nu* a little: *It's a trifle hot in here.* **3** *ncu* a (dish of) cold, sweet food made with sponge cake, jam, fruit, sherry, and custard. ● *vi* **1** (often followed by **with**) treat something as if unimportant etc.: *Don't trifle with me—I mean what I say!* **2** *vt* waste: *He trifled his money away on useless things.* **trifling** *adj* unimportant or worthless.

trigger ('trɪgə*) *nc* **1** a small part of a gun, pulled with a finger to fire the gun. **2** a mechanical device that lets a spring go, starts a machine, etc. **3** an action that causes another. ● *vt* **1** fire (a gun), start (a machine), etc. **2** also **trigger off** be the cause or the start of; bring about.

trigonometry (ˌtrɪgə'nɒmɪtrɪ) *mathematics nu* the study of the relationships of the sides and angles of triangles.

trill (trɪl) *nc* **1** *music* the quick, repeated playing or singing of two notes close together, one after the other. **2** the high song of some birds. ● *vi* make a trill; sing with trills.

trillion ('trɪljən) *nc, pl* **trillion, trillions 1** *Bri* a million million million(s). **2** *US* a million million(s).

trilogy ('trɪlədʒɪ) *nc, pl* **-gies** a group of three connected plays, books, etc.

trim (trɪm) *adj* **-mer, -mest** in good order; neat. ●*vt* 1 make trim, esp. by cutting away: *I'll have my hair trimmed.* 2 cut away: *He trimmed the edge to make it fit.* 3 alter the position in which (a boat or plane) travels by moving its load, etc. 4 alter the position of (a boat's sail) to make best use of the wind. 5 ornament: *a hat trimmed with ribbons.* ●*nu* 1 order; neatness: *put everything in trim. nc* 2 an act of trimming. 3 the position in which a boat or plane travels. 4 an ornament, esp. on a garment. **trimming** *nc* 1 a trim (def 4). 2 *(pl)* pleasant additions, esp. vegetables, sauces, etc., to go with meat: *roast beef with all the trimmings.*

trinity ('trɪnɪtɪ) *formal* 1 *nc, pl* **-ties** a group of three. 2 *nu* the state of being three. **Trinity** *n* the three persons (Father, Son, and Holy Spirit) that make up the Christian God.

trinket ('trɪŋkɪt) *nc* an ornament or piece of jewellery that is worth little.

trio ('triːəʊ) *nc, pl* **-s** 1 a group of three, esp. musicians. 2 a piece of music written for a trio.

trip (trɪp) 1 *vt* (often followed by **up**) cause to fall or nearly fall: *He tripped me up with a stick. vi* 2 (often followed by **on, over,** or **up**) fall or nearly fall: *I tripped over that shoe on the stairs.* 3 *formal or literary* step or dance lightly. 4 *vti* (often followed by **up**) (cause to) make a mistake. ●*nc* 1 a journey. 2 an act of tripping. 3 *infml* a state of altered consciousness produced by taking a certain kind of drug.

tripe (traɪp) *nu* 1 part of a stomach of a cow, etc., used as food. 2 *infml* nonsense.

triple ('trɪpəl) *adj* 1 being three in number or in three parts. 2 three times as much. ●*nc* a triple quantity or thing. ●*vti* make or become three times as much or many.

tripod ('traɪpɒd) *nc* a three-legged stand, esp. for a camera: see picture.

tripod

trite (traɪt) *adj* **-r, -st** (of an idea, expression, etc.) having lost its force through being used too much.

triumph ('traɪəmf) 1 *ncu* (a) victory or success. 2 *nu* happiness at a victory or success. ●*vi* 1 win or be successful. 2 enjoy a

triumph. **triumphal** (traɪ'ʌmfəl) *adj* to do with (a) triumph. **triumphant** (traɪ'ʌmfənt) *adj* 1 victorious or successful. 2 experiencing the joy of victory. **triumphantly** *adv*

trivial ('trɪvɪəl) *adj* of little value or importance.

trod (trɒd) past tense and past participle of **tread.**

trodden ('trɒdən) past participle of **tread.**

trolley ('trɒlɪ) *nc, pl* **-s** a small stand or container on wheels for moving things such as luggage at an airport or food about to be served. **trolley bus** an electric bus that gets its power from cables over the streets.

trombone (trɒm'bəʊn) *nc* a brass musical wind instrument with a sliding tube: see picture at **musical instruments.**

troop (truːp) *nc* 1 a large group of people or animals. 2 *(pl)* soldiers. ●*vi* collect or move in a crowd: *We all trooped off to school.* **trooper** *nc* a soldier in a cavalry or armoured unit.

trophy ('trəʊfɪ) *nc, pl* **-phies** an object given or taken to remind one of a victory or success.

tropic ('trɒpɪk) *nc* either of two lines of latitude around the earth, at twenty-three and a half degrees North (tropic of Cancer) and twenty-three and a half degrees South (tropic of Capricorn). **the tropics** the part of the earth's surface between the two tropics. **tropical** *adj* 1 to do with or coming from the tropics. 2 (esp. of weather) hot.

trot (trɒt) *nu* 1 the third fastest step of a horse, between a walk and a canter. 2 a slow run. ●*vi* 1 (of a horse or person) move at a trot. 2 *infml* go: *I'll trot down to the shops.* 3 *vt* cause (a horse or person) to move at a trot. **trot out** produce, esp. repeatedly, for approval, examination, etc.

troth (trəʊθ) *archaic nu* a promise to be faithful, esp. in marriage.

trouble ('trʌbəl) *nu* 1 worry: *trouble with my car.* 2 effort or thought: *He took a lot of trouble over his work.* 3 the condition of being likely to be punished: *He got into trouble with the law. nc* 4 a cause of worry: *The trouble with your car is its age.* 5 *(often pl)* disturbance; disorder: *the troubles amongst the workers.* 6 a disease or pain: *back trouble.* ●*vti* cause trouble for or be caused trouble: *My back troubles me; These are troubled times; Don't trouble to get up; Can I trouble you to help me?* **troublemaker** ('trʌbəl,meɪkə*) *nc* a person who causes trouble, esp. disagreement. **troublesome** ('trʌbəlsəm) *adj* causing trouble.

trough (trɒf) *nc* 1 a long, narrow, open container, esp. for animals' food or water. 2 a long, narrow hollow in the ground, between waves, etc.

troupe (truːp) *nc* a company of actors, dancers, etc.

trousers ('traʊzəz) *n pl* also **pair of trousers** *chiefly US* **pants** a garment reaching from the waist down to any point on the legs, which it covers separately: see picture. **trouser** *nu* trousers: *trouser material.*

trousers

trout (traʊt) *nc, pl* **trout** a food fish found usually in freshwater and often caught for sport: see picture at **fish.**

trowel ('traʊəl) *nc* **1** a small hand tool with a flat metal blade used in laying bricks: see picture at **tools.** **2** a small hand tool with a pointed curved metal blade used in gardening.

truant ('truːənt) *adj* away from school without permission. ● *nc* a truant child.

truce (truːs) *nc* an agreement to stop fighting, esp. just for a short time.

truck (trʌk) *nc* **1** *Brit* a railway vehicle for goods. **2** a lorry. ● *vt* move (goods) in a truck.

trudge (trʌdʒ) *vi* walk heavily, esp. when tired. ● *nc* a long tiring walk.

true (truː) *adj* **-r, -st 1** according to fact: *a true story.* **2** real; being as the name suggests: *a true oak desk.* **3** loyal; faithful: *true to his friends.* **4** exactly in position: *a true note.* ● *adv* **1** *archaic* truly: *Tell me true.* **2** exactly (in position): *The wheel is running true.* **truly** *adv* **1** in a true manner. **2** really: *truly a great day.* **yours truly** (used before one's name at the end of a letter, usually to someone one has not met).

trump (trʌmp) *nc* a playing-card of the suit that is trumps. ● *vt* beat (another card) by playing a trump. **trumps** *nu* (*with singular verb*) the suit, in a card game, of which a card can beat any card of any other suit.

trumpet ('trʌmpit) *nc* a brass musical wind instrument, esp. with three valves: see picture at **musical instruments.** ● *vi* (of an elephant) make a noise like a trumpet.

truncheon ('trʌnʃən) *nc* a stick used as a weapon, esp. by policemen.

trundle ('trʌndəl) *vti* (of something heavy and esp. large) move slowly on wheels.

trunk (trʌŋk) *nc* **1** the main solid part of a tree, between the roots and the branches. **2** a large case for carrying belongings. **3** *anatomy* most of a body, not including the head, neck, arms, and legs. **4** the long nose of an elephant. **5** *US* See **boot** (def. 2).

trunk call *chiefly Brit* a long-distance telephone call. **trunk road** *Brit* a main road.

trunks *n pl* short for **swimming trunks.**

truss (trʌs) *vt* **1** (sometimes followed by **up**) tie up. **2** tie the wings and legs of (a chicken, etc.) for cooking. **3** support (a roof, etc.) with a **truss** (def. 1). ● *nc* **1** a supporting part of a roof, etc. **2** *medicine* a device, esp. a type of belt, worn to keep a part inside the body in place.

trust (trʌst) *nu* **1** belief in the truth, reliability, value, etc., of someone or something. **2** responsibility brought by people's trust: *in a position of trust.* *nc* **3** an arrangement by which money, etc., is held by one person, etc., to be used for another's good. **4** a group of people, company, etc., in charge of such an arrangement. ● *vt* **1** believe in: *I don't trust his story.* **2** expect or hope: *I trust that all is well.* **3** rely on to look after: *I wouldn't trust him with my life.* **4** *vi* (often followed by **in**) have trust: *Trust in your friends.* **trustworthy** ('trʌst‚wɜːði) *adj* able to be trusted; reliable. **trusty** *adj* **-ier, -iest** faithful or reliable.

trustee (trʌsˈtiː) *nc* a person who holds property in trust for another.

truth (truːθ) *nu* **1** the quality of being true: *the truth of your story.* **2** what is true: *Are you telling the truth?* **3** *nc* something true. **truthful** *adj* honest; telling the truth. **truthfully** *adv*

try (traɪ) **1** *vi* (often followed by **to** or, but not often in a past tense, **and**) make an attempt: *I tried to hit it; Do try and come.* *vt* **2** (often followed by **out**) test: *Would you like to try my pen?* **3** examine and decide (a case in law); decide whether (someone) is guilty. ● *nc, pl* **tries 1** an attempt. **2** a test. **trying** *adj* difficult or annoying: *Children can be trying.* **try on 1** put on (a garment) to see whether it fits. **2** do (something) to see whether it will be allowed, go unnoticed, etc.: *Don't try anything on with your new teacher.*

tsar (also **czar**) (zɑː*) *nc* the ruler of Russia until 1917.

T-shirt ('tiːʃɜːt) *nc* a light, simple, short-sleeved garment for the upper body: see picture.

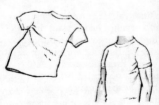

T-shirt

tub (tʌb) *nc* **1** a large, open container for washing, etc. **2** a small plastic or cardboard container for ice cream, etc. **3** short for **bathtub** (see **bath** def. 1). **4** *derogatory* a ship or boat, esp. an old one.

tube (tjuːb) *nc* **1** a long, round, hollow object, used esp. to run a liquid through. **2** a tube of soft metal or plastic, flattened at one end and with a cap at the other, for holding a stiff liquid or substance such as toothpaste. **3** a part shaped like a tube in the body. **4** also **inner tube** a hollow rubber ring filled with air inside a tyre. **5** short for **cathode-ray tube**. **the tube** *Brit, infml* the London underground railway. **tubing** *nu* a number, system, or kind of tubes. **tubeless** *adj* (of a tyre) having no inner tube.

tuber ('tjuːbə*) *nc* the solid, rounded part, usually under the ground, of a plant such as a potato.

tuberculosis (tjʊ,bɜːkjʊ'ləʊsɪs) *nu* a disease that can be passed from one person to another and usually affects the lungs.

tubular ('tjuːbjʊlə*) *adj* to do with a tube.

tuck (tʌk) *vt* **1** fold or force into a small or tight place: *Tuck the money in your pocket.* **2** draw together; put a tuck in. ● *nc* **1** a fold made in a garment to shorten it. **2** *nu* schoolchildren slang, Brit food, esp. sweet foods: *the tuck shop.* **tuck in** or **into** 1 fold or force (something) into a small or tight place. **2** tuck bedclothes in around (someone), esp. so that he goes to sleep. **3** *infml* (start to) eat heartily.

Tuesday ('tjuːzdɪ) *nc* the third day of the week, after Monday and before Wednesday.

tuft (tʌft) *nc* a bunch of hair, grass, etc., growing or held together at one end.

tug (tʌg) *vti* pull sharply: *The dog tugged at the rope.* ● *nc* **1** a sharp pull: *Give it a tug.* **2** also **tugboat** a boat with a powerful engine used for moving either large ships or boats without engines: see picture.

tug

tuition (tjuːˈɪʃən) *nu* teaching.

tulip ('tjuːlɪp) *nc* **1** a plant that grows from a bulb and produces brightly coloured, bell-shaped flowers: see picture at **flowers. 2** one of these flowers.

tumble ('tʌmbəl) **1** *vti* (cause to) fall, esp. hard or then rolling over and over. **2** *vi* do jumps, balancing acts, etc., as an entertainment. ● *nc* an act of tumbling. **tumbledown** ('tʌmbəldaʊn) *adj* (of a building) in a very bad state of repair.

tumbler ('tʌmblə*) *nc* **1** a flat-bottomed drinking glass with no handle. **2** a person who tumbles (**tumble** def. 2).

tummy ('tʌmɪ) *children or infml nc, pl* **-mies** stomach.

tumour *US* **tumor** ('tjuːmə*) *medicine nc* a growth that is not normal in the body.

tumult ('tjuːmʌlt) *ncu* (a) loud noise, esp. from a crowd shouting. **tumultuous** (tjuːˈmʌltjʊəs) *adj* noisy; enthusiastic.

tuna ('tjuːnə) *nc, pl* **tuna, tunas** also **tunny** ('tʌnɪ) *pl* **tunny, tunnies** a large sea fish.

tundra ('tʌndrə) *nu* treeless land in northern North America, Europe, and Asia, where the earth freezes in winter.

tune (tjuːn) *nc* **1** a piece of music in which only one note is played or sung at a time. **2** the chief part in a piece of music in which more than one note is played or sung at a time. ● *vt* **1** put (a musical instrument) in tune. **2** alter (an engine, etc.) so that it works as efficiently as possible. **in** or **out of tune** with the notes set exactly at the right pitch or not quite right: *Stringed instruments go out of tune very quickly.* **in tune with** with the notes set exactly the same as those of: *All the instruments are in tune with each other.* **tuneful** *adj* having a pleasant tune. **tune in** (often followed by **to**) 1 alter (a radio or television) so as to receive a particular station or programme. **2** listen to: watch. **tuner** *nc* 1 a person who tunes musical instruments. **2** the part of a radio or television set that receives or can be altered to receive different stations.

tungsten ('tʌŋstən) *nu* a chemical element; a metal used in steel and for the wire that gives off light in electric light bulbs.

tunic ('tjuːnɪk) *nc* any of several garments reaching from the shoulders down to about the top part of the legs, and usually without sleeves.

tunnel ('tʌnəl) *nc* a long hole dug under the ground, esp. for a road, railway, etc. ● *vi* dig a tunnel.

turban ('tɜːbən) *nc* a garment for the head worn esp. by Muslim and Sikh men and made of a long piece of cloth wound round the head itself or a cap.

turbine ('tɜːbaɪn) *nc* a machine driven by a flow of gas or liquid, esp. water.

turbulent ('tɜːbjʊlənt) *adj* (esp. of air or water) moving in a confused or disordered way. **turbulence** *nu*

tureen (tjʊˈriːn) *nc* a large dish with a cover for serving soup, etc.

turf (tɜːf) *ncu, pl* **-s, -ves** (vz) (a cut piece of) grass with its roots and the earth in which they are growing. ● *vt* plant (ground) with turf. **the turf 1** a grass racetrack for horses. **2** horseracing.

turkey (ˈtɜːkɪ) *ncu, pl* **-s** (meat from) a bird that is widely kept and eaten: see picture.

turmoil (ˈtɜːmɔɪl) *nu* confusion: *His mind was in turmoil.*

turn (tɜːn) *vti* **1** (cause to) move around; spin; twist: *Wheels turn.* **2** (cause to) change direction: *Turn right onto the road.* *vt* **3** become: *She turned pale with fear; He's turned ninety.* **4** give a shape to (a material) or make (an object) by cutting into it as it is turned round and round by a machine. ● *nc* **1** an act of turning (**turn** defs. **1, 2**): *a quick turn of the page.* **2** a bend in a road. **3** also **turning** a place where roads meet: *Take the next turn on the right.* **4** a change: *a turn for the better.* **5** an opportunity or right to do something in a particular order: *We'll take turns; You missed your turn; The boys took it in turns to ride the bike.* **6** *old-fashioned* a short walk or ride: *Take a turn round the garden.* **7** something turned: *Put a turn of rope round that post.* **8** an action that helps or causes difficulty for someone: *It's nice to do someone a good turn.* **9** *infml* a strange, esp. frightened feeling: *I had a funny turn when they said that ship had sunk.* **in** or **out of turn** in or out of order when taking turns (**turn** def. **5**): *Wait—don't go out of turn.* **turn back 1** fold (the end of a sheet on a bed, etc.) back onto itself. **2** start to return: *The weather was so bad we had to turn back.* **turn down 1** refuse to accept, appoint, etc.: *I've been turned down for the job.* **2** lower (the strength, volume, brightness, etc.) of (a radio, light, etc.). **3** fold (the end of a sheet on a bed, etc.) back onto itself. **turn in 1** hand in or give up: *Turn in your gun if you haven't permission to own it.* **2** *infml* go to bed at night. **turn into** (cause to) change into: *I've turned my garage into a bedroom.* **turn off 1** cause (a machine, etc.) to stop working, esp. by switching off the power supply. **2** leave (a road, path, etc.). **3** *infml* be disliked by: *Cold rice turns me off.* **turn on 1** cause (a machine, etc.) to start working, esp. by switching it on. **2** suddenly attack or become angry with: *As soon as we were alone he stopped being kind and turned on me.* **3** *infml* make (someone) pleased or interested, esp. sexually: *Her dancing at the party turned him on.* **turn out 1** switch (an electric light, etc.) off. **2** produce: *This factory turns out ten cars a day.* **3** empty (things) out of (something): *Turn out your pockets.* **4** prove to be: *It's turned out sunny.* **5** dress; present (someone or oneself): *She's always nicely turned out.* **6** go out (to

do something): *We all turned out to meet him.* **turn-out** (ˈtɜːnaʊt) *nc* **1** the way in which one is dressed. **2** the number of people who turn out to do something. **turn over 1** (cause to) change position, bringing the bottom to the top: *He turned the paper over to read the other side.* **2** pass on; give up: *He'll turn his house over to me when he leaves.* **3** receive (money) in business: *I turn over about £400 a week.* **4** (of an engine) work without producing movement. **5** cause (an engine) to work esp. in order to get it running smoothly. **6** consider carefully: *He turned the problem over in his mind.* **turnover** (ˈtɜːn,əʊvə*) *nc* **1** the amount of money turned over by a business. **2** a sheet of pastry folded over to hold fruit, jam, etc. and cooked. **turn to** go to for advice or help. **turn up 1** arrive; appear: *He turned up late again.* **2** find or be found by chance. **3** increase (the volume, brightness, etc.) of (a radio, lamp, etc.). **turn-up** (ˈtɜːnʌp) *nc* the material folded up at the bottom of a trouser leg.

turner (ˈtɜːnə*) *nc* a person who turns (**turn** def. **4**).

turning-point (ˈtɜːnɪŋpɔɪnt) *nc* a point or moment at which a change, esp. of direction, takes place.

turnip (ˈtɜːnɪp) *nc* a plant of which the large white root is eaten.

turnpike (ˈtɜːnpaɪk) *archaic or US nc* a road that one has to pay to use.

turntable (ˈtɜːn,teɪbəl) *nc* a stand that can be turned round, esp. to point a locomotive in a different direction or for playing a record.

turpentine (ˈtɜːpəntaɪn) (*infml abbrev.* **turps**) *nu* a light oil made from pine trees and used in paint and medicine.

turquoise (ˈtɜːkwɔɪz) *ncu* (a) greenish-blue precious stone. ● *adj* having the colour of turquoise.

turret (ˈtʌrɪt) *nc* **1** a small tower, esp. set in the wall of a castle. **2** also **gun turret** See under **gun**.

turtle (ˈtɜːtəl) *nc* an animal that can swim and has a strong shell on its back: see picture at **reptiles**.

turves (tɜːvz) plural of **turf**.

tusk (tʌsk) *nc* a long, curved, pointed tooth growing out of the mouth of an elephant, etc.

tussle (ˈtʌsəl) *vi, nc* (a) struggle; fight.

tut (tʌt) *vi* make the noise 'tut-tut'. **tut-tut** *interj* (said as two clicks made with the tip of the tongue behind the top front teeth and used to scold someone.)

tutor (ˈtjuːtə*) *nc* **1** a teacher, esp. of one person or a small group. **2** a university teacher responsible for the general progress of a few students. ● *vt* teach, esp. as a tutor.

twain (twein) *archaic determiner, n* two.

twang (twæŋ) *nc* **1** a sharp ringing sound, made esp. by pulling a stretched string and letting it go. **2** a way of speaking that makes it sound as if the speaker is talking through his nose. ● *vti* (cause to) make a twang.

'twas (twɒz) *archaic or literary* it was.

tweak (twi:k) *nc* a sudden sharp pull or twist (esp. to a part of the body). ● *vt* give a tweak to.

tweed (twi:d) *nu* a thick woollen cloth.

tweezers (ˈtwi:zəz) *n pl* also **pair of tweezers** a tool for picking up small objects.

twelve (twelv) *determiner, n*, the number 12. **twelfth** (twelfθ) *determiner, n, adv*

twenty (ˈtwentɪ) *determiner, n* the number 20. **twentieth** (ˈtwentɪθ) *determiner, n, adv*

'twere (twɜ:*) *archaic or literary* it were.

twice (twais) *adv* two times: *He called twice; This one is twice as good.*

twiddle (ˈtwɪdəl) *vt* twist or spin, esp. to no useful purpose. **twiddle one's thumbs** have nothing to do.

twig¹ (twig) *nc* a small branch of a tree.

twig² *infml, Brit vti* understand.

twilight (ˈtwailait) *nu* light from the sun when it is just below the horizon, esp. in the evening.

'twill (twɪl) *archaic or literary* it will.

twin (twin) *nc* **1** one of two people or animals formed and born together. **2** one of a pair. **3** also **twin town** one of two towns, in different countries, that arrange visits and other contacts between themselves. ● *adj* being (one of) a pair: *twin engines.* ● *vt* make into a pair: *Our town is twinned with one in Germany.*

twine (twain) *nu* string made by twisting cotton, etc. together. ● *vt* twist or wind: *Twine the ribbon round your hat.*

twinge (twindʒ) *nc* a short, sharp pain.

twinkle (ˈtwiŋkəl) *vi* **1** (esp. of a star) shine, seeming brighter and less bright quickly and irregularly. **2** (of the eyes) shine from happiness, amusement, etc. ● *nc* **1** an irregular brightness. **2** a look of amusement, etc., in the eyes.

twirl (twɜ:l) *vti* spin or twist fast. ● *nc* an act of twirling.

twist (twist) *vt* **1** cause one end of (something) to turn (in the opposite direction to the other end): *Your belt is twisted.* **2** bend awkwardly and painfully: *I twisted my knee jumping off the wall.* **3** *vi* become twisted (**twist** def. 1). *vti* **4** wind or be wound: *Twist the rope round your arm; The path twists through the wood.* **5** (cause to) go round; spin; turn: *To open the jar, twist the lid off.* ● *nc* **1** an act of twisting. **2** something made by twisting, such as cotton for sew-

ing. **3** a bend in a path, etc. **4** an unexpected event in a story. **twister** *old-fashioned, Brit nc* a person who cheats others.

twitch (twitʃ) *vti* (cause to) move sharply: *She twitched her scarf from her face.* ● *nc* a sudden, sharp movement, esp. a movement of part of the body, esp. the face, that one cannot prevent.

twitter (ˈtwitə*) *vi* **1** (esp. of a bird) make a high, irregular sound. **2** *derogatory* talk a great deal, esp. in a nervous way. ● *nc* **1** a sound of twittering. **2** *nu* an anxious or excited state: *The women were all in a twitter.*

'twixt (twikst) *archaic or literary prep* short for **betwixt.**

two (tu:) *determiner, n* the number 2. **twofold** (ˈtu:fəʊld) *adj* double; in two parts or of two kinds. ● *adv* doubly. **two-way** (ˈtu:wei) *adj* moving or allowing movement, etc., in both directions: *two-way traffic; two-way radio.*

tycoon (taiˈku:n) *nc* a powerful businessman.

type (taip) **1** *nc* a sort; kind; class: *What type of wine do you like? nu* **2** printed letters: *not in handwriting, but in type.* **3** metal or wooden letters used for printing. ● *vti* write with a typewriter. **typewriter** (ˈtaip-ˌraitə*) *nc* a machine for writing with, in which levers with **type** (def. 3) press a ribbon containing ink onto the paper. **typing** *nu* writing done with a typewriter. **typist** (ˈtaipist) *nc* a person who uses a typewriter. **typography** (taiˈpɒɡrəfɪ) *nu* the art of choosing and arranging type for printing.

typhoid (ˈtaifɔid) *nu* also **typhoid fever** a serious disease carried in food and water and causing high temperature, red spots, and pain around the stomach.

typhoon (taiˈfu:n) *nc* a very violent storm with strong winds, esp. at sea in the East.

typhus (ˈtaifəs) *nu* also **typhus fever** a serious disease causing high temperature, purple spots, and headache.

typical (ˈtipikəl) *adj* representative; serving as an example: *A mistake like that is typical of a beginner.* **typically** *adv*

typify (ˈtipifai) *vt* be representative or typical of: *Arriving late typifies your approach to work.*

tyranny (ˈtirəni) **1** *nu* cruel, unjust government or rule. *nc, pl* **-nies 2** a tyrannical act. **3** a country under tyrannical rule. **tyrannical** (tiˈrænikəl) *adj*

tyrant (ˈtaiərənt) *nc* a tyrannical ruler.

tyre *US* **tire** (ˈtaiə*) *nc* a rubber ring, esp. hollow and filled with air under pressure, round the outside of a wheel.

U

ubiquitous (ju:'bɪkwɪtəs) *adj* 1 being or appearing to be everywhere. 2 *infml* frequent or common.

udder ('ʌdə*) *nc* the bag hanging near to the back legs of a cow, female goat, etc., that produces milk for its young.

ugh (u:, ɜ:) *interj* (a noise made to express disgust.)

ugly ('ʌglɪ) *adj* **-ier, -iest** 1 unpleasant to look at; not beautiful. 2 harmful, dangerous, or threatening: *ugly clouds*. **ugliness** *nu*

ukelele (,ju:kə'leɪlɪ) *nc* a four-stringed musical instrument like a small guitar.

ulcer ('ʌlsə*) *nc* a sore in the stomach, etc.

ultimate ('ʌltɪmət) *adj* 1 last; final: *War is our ultimate defence*. 2 most, largest, best, etc.: *the ultimate furniture for luxury*. **ultimately** *adv* in the end.

ultimatum (,ʌltɪ'meɪtəm) *nc, pl* **-matums, -mata** ('meɪtə) a final offer or demand made by a person, group, or country, that is threatening to strike, go to war, etc., if it is not accepted or allowed.

ultraviolet (,ʌltrə'vaɪələt) *nu, adj* (to do with) radiation of a slightly higher frequency than light that can be seen.

umbilical (ʌm'bɪlɪkəl) *nc, adj* (to do with) an umbilical cord. **umbilical cord** the tube connecting a human or other mammal to its mother until birth.

umbra ('ʌmbrə) *nc, pl* **-s, -rae** (ri:) *astronomy* the part of a shadow, esp. of the moon on the earth, that is completely dark.

umbrella (ʌm'brelə) *nc* a device made of cloth fixed to metal arms that can be raised and lowered on a stick, used as a protection from rain or sun: see picture.

umbrella

umpire ('ʌmpaɪə*) *nc* a person appointed to see that rules are kept, esp. in a game such as cricket or tennis. ● *vt* act as umpire in (a game, etc.).

unable (ʌn'eɪbəl) *adj* not able (see **be able**

414

(to do something) under **able**): *He was unable to speak.*

unaccountable (,ʌnə'kaʊntəbəl) *adj* not accountable.

unaccustomed (,ʌnə'kʌstəmd) *adj* not accustomed.

unaffected (,ʌnə'fektɪd) *adj* not affected.

unanimous (ju:'nænɪməs) *adj* with everyone agreeing: *a unanimous decision*. **unanimously** *adv*

unarmed (,ʌn'ɑ:md) *adj* not armed (**arm²** def. 1).

unattended (,ʌnə'tendɪd) *adj* 1 with no-one present or in charge: *an unattended car*. 2 not being looked after, served, etc.

unavoidable (,ʌnə'vɔɪdəbəl) *adj* not avoidable.

unaware (,ʌnə'weə*) *adj* not aware. **unawares** *adv* 1 unexpectedly. 2 accidentally.

unbearable (,ʌn'beərəbəl) *adj* not bearable.

unbecoming (,ʌnbɪ'kʌmɪŋ) *adj* not becoming.

unbend (,ʌn'bend) *vti* 1 (cause to) become straight again. 2 *infml* (cause to) become less formal or more friendly.

unbent (,ʌn'bent) past tense and past participle of **unbend**.

unborn (,ʌn'bɔ:n) *adj* not yet born: *an unborn child*.

unbroken (,ʌn'brəʊkən) *adj* 1 not broken; whole. 2 continuous; uninterrupted. 3 (of a record, esp. in sport) not beaten.

unbutton (,ʌn'bʌtən) *vt* undo (a garment, etc.) that is fastened with buttons.

uncalled-for (,ʌn'kɔ:ldfɔ:*) *adj* unnecessary, undeserved, or unwelcome.

uncanny (ʌn'kænɪ) *adj* **-ier, -iest** mysterious: *It's uncanny how you're always right.*

uncertain (ʌn'sɜ:tən) *adj* 1 not sure or confident. 2 not known for sure. 3 unreliable; changeable: *uncertain weather*. **uncertainly** *adv* **uncertainty** 1 *nc, pl* **-ties** something uncertain. 2 *nu* the quality of being uncertain.

unchanged (,ʌn'tʃeɪndʒd) *adj* not changed.

uncivilised (,ʌn'sɪvɪlaɪzd) *adj* 1 not (yet) civilised. 2 rude.

uncle ('ʌŋkəl) *nc* 1 a brother of one's father or mother. 2 the husband of an aunt. 3 (used by and to children in naming a male friend of their parents.)

unclean (,ʌn'kli:n) *adj* 1 not pure spiritually. 2 not fit to be eaten, for religious reasons.

uncomfortable (ʌn'kʌmftəbəl) *adj* 1 not comfortable. 2 embarrassed; guilty: *He looked uncomfortable when the farmer asked who had left the gate open.*

uncommon (ʌn'kɒmən) *adj* unusual.

uncompromising (ʌn'kɒmprəmaɪzɪŋ) *adj* not trying or wanting to **compromise** (def. 1).

unconcerned (ˌʌnkənˈsɜːnd) *adj* not **concerned** (def. 2).

unconscious (ʌnˈkɒnʃəs) *adj* not conscious; senseless. ● *nu* the group of mental activities not under conscious control. **unconsciously** *adv*

unconventional (ˌʌnkənˈvenʃənəl) *adj* not conventional.

uncouth (ʌnˈkuːθ) *adj* (of behaviour or a person) rough, awkward, or not polite.

uncover (ʌnˈkʌvə*) *vt* 1 take the cover, lid, etc., off. 2 discover: *They uncovered a plan to kill the president.*

uncut (ˌʌnˈkʌt) *adj* 1 not (yet) cut. 2 (of a film, book, etc.) not shortened; complete. 3 (of a precious stone) having not (yet) been given a regular shape. 4 (of a book) not (yet) having had the edges of its pages cut since they were folded.

undaunted (ˌʌnˈdɔːntɪd) *adj* not daunted.

undecided (ˌʌndɪˈsaɪdɪd) *adj* 1 not having made a decision. 2 not (yet) settled or agreed on: *His future here is undecided.*

undeniable (ˌʌndɪˈnaɪəbəl) *adj* unable to be denied: *a woman of undeniable beauty.* **undeniably** *adv*

under (ˈʌndə*) *prep, adv* below or beneath. ● *prep* 1 governed by; under the control of: *I work under the owner of the factory.* 2 less than: *Can you do it in under four minutes?* 3 having: *I travel under a false name.* 4 in the process of: *under consideration by the council.*

underclothes (ˈʌndəˌkləʊðz) *n pl* also **underwear** clothes worn inside others, esp. next to the skin.

undercurrent (ˈʌndəˌkʌrənt) *nc* 1 a current below the surface, esp. in the sea. 2 an opinion or influence disguised by or different to a more common one.

underdeveloped (ˌʌndədɪˈveləpt) *adj* 1 (esp. of a photograph) not developed enough. 2 (of a country) not as advanced as it could be.

underestimate (ˌʌndərˈestɪmeɪt) *vt* make too low an estimate of. ● (ˌʌndərˈestɪmət) *nc* an estimate that is too low.

underfoot (ˌʌndəˈfʊt) *adv* on the ground; under one's feet.

undergo (ˌʌndəˈɡəʊ) *vt* experience; suffer: *The town underwent a great change.*

undergone (ˌʌndəˈɡɒn) past participle of **undergo**.

undergraduate (ˌʌndəˈɡrædjʊət) *nc* a university student who has not yet obtained a **degree** (def. 4).

underground (ˈʌndəɡraʊnd) *adj* (ˌʌndəˈɡraʊnd) *adv* 1 below the surface of the ground. 2 (in) secret or in(to) hiding. ● (ˈʌndəɡraʊnd) *nc US* **subway** an underground railway.

undergrowth (ˈʌndəɡrəʊθ) *nu* bushes or small trees growing beneath larger ones: see picture.

undergrowth

underline (ˌʌndəˈlaɪn) *vt* 1 draw a line under. 2 draw special attention to; give force to.

underlying (ˌʌndəˈlaɪɪŋ) *adj* 1 hidden but suggested or suspected: *the underlying reason for his action.* 2 central; original: *The underlying cause of crime is the shape of modern society.*

undermine (ˌʌndəˈmaɪn) *vt* 1 dig or wear away the supporting ground underneath. 2 weaken: *They undermined his position by telling lies about him.*

underneath (ˌʌndəˈniːθ) *prep, adv* below; under. ● *adj, nc* (a) lower (side or part).

undernourished (ˌʌndəˈnʌrɪʃt) *adj* not eating enough of the right foods for health and normal growth.

underpants (ˈʌndəpænts) also **pair of underpants** (often shortened to **pants**) *n pl* a man's garment reaching from the waist to the tops of the legs and worn inside other clothes.

undershirt (ˈʌndəʃɜːt) *US n* See **vest** (def. 1).

underside (ˈʌndəsaɪd) *nc* a lower side; bottom.

understand (ˌʌndəˈstænd) *vt* 1 (come to) know the meaning of: *Do you understand what I'm saying?* 2 believe; learn: *I understand that the meeting is tomorrow.* 3 consider without expressing: *It is understood that everyone attends without being told to.* 4 see the point of (another person's feelings): *I can understand why it matters to you.* **understandable** *adj* able to be understood.

understanding 1 *nu* the ability to understand things; sympathy. 2 *nc* an opinion; way of understanding: *What is your understanding of the law on this point?* 3 *ncu* (an) agreement. ● *adj* able to **understand** (def. 4); sympathetic.

understatement (ˈʌndəˌsteɪtmənt) *ncu* (an example of) representing or describing something as less, smaller, less important, etc., than it is.

understood (ˌʌndəˈstʊd) past tense and past participle of **understand**.

undertake (ˌʌndəˈteɪk) *vt* 1 promise: *He undertook to finish in a week.* 2 agree to take, do, etc.: *I'll undertake that job.* **undertaking** *nc* 1 a job, esp. large, undertaken. 2 a promise (to do something).

undertaken (ˌʌndəˈteɪkən) past participle of **undertake.**

undertaker (ˈʌndəˌteɪkə*) *nc* a person who arranges funerals.

undertone (ˈʌndətəʊn) *nc* 1 a quiet voice: *He spoke in an undertone.* 2 an underlying quality: *His praise had undertones of jealousy.*

undertook (ˌʌndəˈtʊk) past tense of **undertake.**

underwater (ˌʌndəˈwɔːtə*) *adj, adv* below the surface of water, esp. the sea.

underwear (ˈʌndəweə*) *nu* See **underclothes.**

underweight (ˌʌndəˈweɪt) *adj* weighing too little.

underwent (ˌʌndəˈwent) past tense of **undergo.**

underworld (ˈʌndəwɜːld) *nu* 1 the world of criminals. 2 the place where dead people's souls are thought to go.

underwrite (ˌʌndəˈraɪt) *economics vt* 1 provide insurance for (property or a risk). 2 promise to buy the part of (an issue of a company's shares) not bought by the public. **underwriter** (ˈʌndəˌraɪtə*) *nc*

underwritten (ˌʌndəˈrɪtən) past participle of **underwrite.**

underwrote (ˌʌndəˈrəʊt) past tense of **underwrite.**

undesirable (ˌʌndɪˈzaɪərəbəl) *adj* not desirable.

undid (ˌʌnˈdɪd) past tense of **undo.**

undisturbed (ˌʌndɪˈstɜːbd) *adj* not disturbed.

undo (ˌʌnˈduː) *vt* 1 open (a coat, button, knot, etc.). 2 change (the effect of an earlier action): *You'll have to undo your own mistake.* **undoing** *nu* the cause of someone's ruin or failure: *Carelessness was his undoing.*

undone (ˌʌnˈdʌn) past participle of **undo.** ● *adj* not done: *The washing of last week's laundry is still undone.*

undoubtedly (ʌnˈdaʊtɪdlɪ) *adv* without doubt or question: *He was undoubtedly the winner.*

undress (ˌʌnˈdres) 1 *vi* take one's clothes off. 2 *vt* take off the clothes of. ● *nu* being (partly) undressed: *in a state of undress.*

undue (ˌʌnˈdjuː) *adj* 1 not fitting or necessary. 2 more than is fitting or necessary: *with undue haste.* **unduly** *adv* more than is fitting or necessary: *unduly fast.*

undulate (ˈʌndjʊleɪt) *vti* (cause to) move in or look like waves: *undulating country.*

unearth (ˌʌnˈɜːθ) *vt* 1 dig up out of the ground. 2 find after a long or difficult search.

uneasy (ʌnˈiːzɪ) *adj* **-ier, -iest** 1 (of a person) not at ease; disturbed. 2 disturbing; worrying: *an uneasy silence.* **uneasily** *adv* **uneasiness** *nu*

unemployed (ˌʌnɪmˈplɔɪd) *adj* 1 with no paid job. 2 not in use. **the unemployed** unemployed people. **unemployment** *nu* 1 the state of not having a paid job. 2 the state of there being too few jobs: *There is high unemployment around this town.*

unequal (ˌʌnˈiːkwəl) *adj* not equal.

unexpected (ˌʌnɪkˈspektɪd, before a noun ˈʌnɪkˌspektɪd) *adj* not expected. **unexpectedly** *adv*

unfair (ˌʌnˈfeə*) *adj* not **fair**[1] (def. 1).

unfaithful (ˌʌnˈfeɪθfʊl) *adj* not **faithful** (def. 1).

unfamiliar (ˌʌnfəˈmɪljə*) *adj* not **familiar** (defs. 1, 2); not knowing about.

unfavourable *US* **unfavorable** (ˌʌnˈfeɪvərəbəl) *adj* not favourable.

unfeeling (ˌʌnˈfiːlɪŋ) *adj* not feeling.

unfinished (ˌʌnˈfɪnɪʃt) *adj* not finished.

unfit (ˌʌnˈfɪt) *adj* not **fit**[1]. **unfit for** not **fit for** (see under **fit**[1]).

unfold (ʌnˈfəʊld) *vti* 1 open up or come out of a folded state: *Unfold the map so that I can see it all at once.* 2 (cause to) develop; reveal or be revealed: *The story slowly unfolded.*

unforgettable (ˌʌnfəˈgetəbəl) *adj* unable to be forgotten.

unfortunate (ʌnˈfɔːtʃənɪt) *adj* not fortunate. **unfortunately** *adv* unluckily.

unfounded (ˌʌnˈfaʊndɪd) *adj* not based on fact; groundless: *an unfounded accusation of dishonesty.*

unfriendly (ˌʌnˈfrendlɪ) *adj* **-ier, -iest** not friendly.

unfurl (ˌʌnˈfɜːl) *vt* bring (esp. a flag, umbrella, or sail) out of a rolled-up state; open out.

ungrateful (ʌnˈgreɪtfʊl) *adj* 1 not grateful. 2 *formal* not likely to be appreciated or rewarded: *an ungrateful task.*

unguarded (ˌʌnˈgɑːdɪd) *adj* not guarded.

unhappy (ʌnˈhæpɪ) *adj* **-ier, -iest** 1 not happy. 2 not suitable: *an unhappy choice of dress for a funeral.*

unhealthy (ʌnˈhelθɪ) *adj* **-ier, -iest** not healthy.

unheard (ˌʌnˈhɜːd) *adj* not heard. **unheard-of** (ˌʌnˈhɜːdɒv) *adj* not known or experienced before: *It's unheard-of for him to admit he's wrong.*

unicorn (ˈjuːnɪkɔːn) *nc* an imaginary animal; a horse with a long, straight horn.

unification (ˌjuːnɪfɪˈkeɪʃən) *nu* the act of unifying.

uniform (ˈjuːnɪfɔːm) *nc* a characteristic set of clothes worn by a member of a group or organisation, such as a soldier or nurse: see picture. ● *adj* the same; not changing or differing: *men of uniform height.* **uniformity** (ˌjuːnɪˈfɔːmɪtɪ) *nu* **uniformly** *adv*

uniform

unify (ˈjuːnɪfaɪ) *vt* make (things) one or uniform.

unilateral .(ˌjuːnɪˈlætərəl) *adj* done by or affecting only one side, person, country, etc.: *a unilateral decision to become independent.*

union (ˈjuːnɪən) *nu* 1 the act of uniting or the act or state of being united. 2 agreement. *nc* 3 a group of people, countries, etc., that join together for a purpose, esp. political: *the Soviet Union.* 4 a club, esp. a university students' organisation for social activities. 5 short for **trade union.** 6 a device for joining things, esp. pipes. **Union Jack** See under **jack.**

unique (juːˈniːk) *adj* 1 being the only one of its kind: *Since everyone is different, you are unique!* 2 *infml* unusual: *a unique opportunity to buy a historic house.* **uniqueness** *nu*

unisex (ˈjuːnɪseks) *adj* for men or women: *unisex clothes.*

unison (ˈjuːnɪsən) *nu* 1 the singing or playing of the same note(s) at the same time by more than one voice or musical instrument: *to sing in unison.* 2 agreement.

unit (ˈjuːnɪt) *nc* 1 one of something: *One ten and three units make thirteen.* 2 a quantity used for measuring, such as an hour or a kilogram. 3 a device, group, piece of furniture, etc., that is part of a larger one: *an army unit, a kitchen unit.* **unitary** (ˈjuːnɪtərɪ) *adj* 1 to do with a unit or units. 2 to do with unity.

unite (juːˈnaɪt) *vti* (cause to) join or become one. **united** *adj* 1 joined. 2 in agreement. **the United Nations** an organisation of independent countries that tries to bring about international peace.

unity (ˈjuːnɪtɪ) 1 *nu* the quality or state of being united. 2 *nc, pl* **-ties** something that is united or considered as a unit.

universal (ˌjuːnɪˈvɜːsəl) *adj* 1 to do with the whole world. 2 to do with everyone or everything in a particular class: *a universal oil for all engines.* 3 general: *universal suffering.* **universally** *adv*

universe (ˈjuːnɪvɜːs) 1 *nu* everything material that exists. 2 *nc* a system like the universe:

Scientists think that a universe of negative matter may exist.

university (ˌjuːnɪˈvɜːsɪtɪ) *nc, pl* **-ties** a place of higher education, chiefly for students studying for degrees.

unjust (ˌʌnˈdʒʌst) *adj* not just.

unkempt (ˌʌnˈkempt) *adj* 1 (of the hair) uncombed. 2 untidy: *an unkempt garden.*

unkind (ʌnˈkaɪnd) *adj* **-er, -est** not **kind²**.

unknown (ʌnˈnəʊn) *adj* not known. ● *nc* an unknown person, thing, or quantity.

unlawful (ʌnˈlɔːfʊl) *adj* not lawful.

unless (ənˈles) *conj* ... not; except if: *I shall go unless I'm told not to.*

unlike (ˌʌnˈlaɪk) *adj, prep* not **like¹**; different from.

unlikely (ʌnˈlaɪklɪ) *adj* not likely.

unload (ˌʌnˈləʊd) *vt* 1 remove (a load) from (a ship, lorry, etc.). 2 remove the bullet, charge, etc., from (a gun). 3 get rid of; *Can I unload that job onto you?*

unlock (ˌʌnˈlɒk) *vt* undo the lock of (a door, room, etc.).

unlucky (ʌnˈlʌkɪ) *adj* **-ier, -iest** not lucky.

unmanned (ˌʌnˈmænd) *adj* (of a ship, etc.) not manned.

unmistakable (ˌʌnmɪˈsteɪkəbəl) *adj* not mistakable; clear. **unmistakably** *adv*

unnatural (ʌnˈnætʃrəl) *adj* 1 not according to nature; not normal. 2 very cruel. 3 false; affected: *an unnatural smile.*

unnecessary (ʌnˈnesəsərɪ) *adj* 1 not necessary. 2 more than is necessary: *unnecessary cost.* 3 unwelcome: *an unnecessary remark.*

unpaid (ˌʌnˈpeɪd) *adj* not (being) paid.

unpleasant (ʌnˈplezənt) *adj* not pleasant. **unpleasantness** 1 *nu* the quality of being unpleasant. 2 *nc* an unpleasant event.

unpopular (ˌʌnˈpɒpjʊlə*) *adj* not **popular** (def. 1).

unprecedented (ʌnˈpresɪdentɪd) *adj* having no precedent.

unpredictable (ˌʌnprɪˈdɪktəbəl) *adj* not predictable.

unprepared (ˌʌnprɪˈpeəd) *adj* 1 not having made (enough) preparations. 2 done without preparation.

unproductive (ˌʌnprəˈdʌktɪv) *adj* not productive.

unprofitable (ˌʌnˈprɒfɪtəbəl) *adj* not profitable.

unqualified (ˌʌnˈkwɒlɪfaɪd) *adj* 1 without qualifications. 2 complete; not limited in any way: *an unqualified success.*

unquestionable (ʌnˈkwestʃənəbəl) *adj* not questionable; definite. **unquestionably** *adv*

unravel (ʌnˈrævəl) *vt* 1 sort out (something knotted or mixed up). 2 undo (cloth, knitting, etc.) into single threads. 3 solve (a mystery, etc.).

417

unreal (ˌʌnˈrɪəl) *adj* imaginary; not in existence.

unreasonable (ʌnˈriːzənəbəl) *adj* 1 unfair: *It's unreasonable to make him go.* 2 not wanting or prepared to be sensible.

unremitting (ˌʌnrɪˈmɪtɪŋ) *adj* not slowing or pausing.

unrest (ˌʌnˈrest) *nu* a lack of peace or calm: *The unrest in the country could bring about civil strife.*

unruly (ʌnˈruːlɪ) *adj* -ier, -iest disorderly; troublesome.

unsatisfactory (ˌʌnsætɪsˈfæktərɪ) *adj* not satisfactory.

unscathed (ˌʌnˈskeɪðd) *adj* without injury.

unscrew (ˌʌnˈskruː) *vt* 1 loosen (something) by removing a screw. 2 remove (a lid, etc.) by turning it like a screw.

unscrupulous (ʌnˈskruːpjʊləs) *adj* (of a person or behaviour) not keeping to what is right or honest.

unseemly (ʌnˈsiːmlɪ) *adj* -ier, -iest not proper or in good taste.

unseen (ˌʌnˈsiːn) *adj* 1 not seen. 2 (of something written) not seen or prepared before one has to read or translate it. ●*nc Brit* a piece of writing that one has not seen before, to be translated into one's own language.

unsettle (ˌʌnˈsetəl) *vt* disturb; make worried or unsteady.

unsightly (ʌnˈsaɪtlɪ) *adj* unattractive or ugly.

unskilled (ˌʌnˈskɪld) *adj* not skilled.

unsound (ˌʌnˈsaʊnd) *adj* 1 not firm or solid: *an unsound wall.* 2 unwise; unreliable: *unsound advice.* 3 sick; confused: *of unsound mind.*

unspeakable (ʌnˈspiːkəbəl) *adj* bad or awful, esp. too much so to be described.

unstable (ˌʌnˈsteɪbəl) *adj* not **stable**².

unsuspected (ˌʌnsəˈspektɪd) *adj* not suspected.

untidy (ʌnˈtaɪdɪ) *adj* -ier, -iest not tidy. ●*vt* make untidy.

untie (ˌʌnˈtaɪ) *vt* undo (something tied or tied up).

until (ənˈtɪl) (often shortened to **till**) *conj, prep* 1 up to (the time that): *I'll work until five o'clock or until I'm tired.* 2 (used with a negative) before: *You mustn't stop until tomorrow or until I do.*

untimely (ʌnˈtaɪmlɪ) *adj* not timely.

unto (ˈʌntʊ) *archaic prep* **to**¹.

untold (ˌʌnˈtəʊld) *adj* 1 very great or many: *untold damage.* 2 not told.

untrue (ˌʌnˈtruː) *adj* not **true** (defs. 1, 3).

unused¹ (ˌʌnˈjuːzd) *adj* not used.

unused² (ˌʌnˈjuːst) *adj* not used. See **used to** under **use**.

unusual (ʌnˈjuːʒʊəl) *adj* not usual; uncommon. **unusually** *adv*

unveil (ˌʌnˈveɪl) *vt* 1 uncover (a statue, etc.) for a first official showing. 2 make known: *The government unveiled its plans for the railways.* 3 *vti* take a veil off one's (or someone else's) face.

unwelcome (ʌnˈwelkəm) *adj* not welcome.

unwieldy (ʌnˈwiːldɪ) *adj* too big or heavy to use or hold easily.

unwilling (ˌʌnˈwɪlɪŋ) *adj* not willing. **unwillingly** *adv* **unwillingness** *nu*

unwind (ˌʌnˈwaɪnd) 1 *vti* stretch out after having been wound. 2 *infml vi* relax; become rested.

unwise (ˌʌnˈwaɪz) *adj* not **wise**¹.

unwitting (ʌnˈwɪtɪŋ) *adj* 1 not knowing or conscious: *He was an unwitting part of their plan.* 2 unintended: *unwitting criticism.* **unwittingly** *adv*

unworthy (ʌnˈwɜːðɪ) *adj* not worthy.

unwound (ˌʌnˈwaʊnd) past tense and past participle of **unwind**.

up (ʌp) *prep* at or to a higher point in or on: *There's a bird up the chimney; Go up the stairs.* ●*adv* 1 moving from a lower position to a higher one: *Look up.* 2 (used to indicate that an action is complete or final): *Eat up your dinner; Your time is up.* 3 to a particular place or to the speaker: *He drove up (to the house) in his new car.* 4 in a higher or more important place: *We're going up to London.* 5 (used to show a greater intensity): *Speak up—we can't hear you!* ●*vt* raise (esp. a price). ●*adj* 1 (still or already) out of bed. 2 higher (in price): *Butter is up this week.* **ups and downs** periods of good and bad luck. **up to** 1 doing or intending to do: *He's up to his tricks.* 2 until: *It's been cold up to now.* 3 to a limit of: *up to ten miles.* 4 capable of: *Are you up to a walk?* 5 to be decided by: *It's up to you where we go.* 6 the duty of: *It's up to us to do our best.* 7 as good as: *This isn't up to his best work.* **what's up?** *infml* what's the matter?

upbraid (ʌpˈbreɪd) *formal vt* scold angrily.

upbringing (ˈʌpbrɪŋɪŋ) *ncu* (an example of) the educating of a person in general behaviour.

upgrade (ˌʌpˈgreɪd) *vt* raise in importance, pay, etc.

upheaval (ʌpˈhiːvəl) *nc* a violent disturbance.

upheld (ʌpˈheld) past tense and past participle of **uphold**.

uphill (ˌʌpˈhɪl) *adv* 1 (moving) up a slope. 2 against great difficulties. ●*adj* 1 sloping upwards. 2 difficult; needing great effort: *uphill work.*

uphold (ʌpˈhəʊld) *vt* 1 agree with; approve: *The judgement was upheld by a higher court.* 2 support (a person, cause, etc.).

upholstery (ʌpˈhəʊlstərɪ) *nu* 1 the cloth, soft filling material, etc., used in furniture. 2 the work of upholstering. **upholster** *vt* fit (furniture) with upholstery.

upkeep (ˈʌpkiːp) *nu* (the cost of) keeping something in good condition.

upland (ˈʌplənd) *nc, adj* (to do with) a high piece of land.

uplift (ʌpˈlɪft) *vt literary* raise. ● (ˈʌplɪft) *nu* 1 the condition of being raised; power to do this. 2 *nc* something that makes one feel better, happier, etc.

upon (əˈpɒn) *formal prep* on; onto.

upper (ˈʌpə*) *adj* higher (part of): *the upper air.* ● *nc* the part of a shoe or boot above the sole and heel: see picture. **uppermost** (ˈʌpəməʊst) *adj, adv* highest.

upper

upright (ˈʌpraɪt) *adj* 1 standing up; not lying down, bent, or folded. 2 honest; honourable. ● *nc* 1 an upright, esp. supporting part of something such as a chair or roof. 2 also **upright piano** a piano in which the strings are upright, not flat.

uprising (ˈʌpˌraɪzɪŋ) *nc* an act of fighting, causing disturbances, etc., by a large number of people in order to overthrow a government; rebellion.

uproar (ˈʌprɔː*) *nu* confused, noisy disturbance: *There was uproar at his speech.* **uproarious** (ʌpˈrɔːrɪəs) *adj* 1 (of laughter) loud. 2 very funny. 3 to do with uproar.

uproot (ʌpˈruːt) *vt* 1 pull (a plant) from the ground, with its roots. 2 move (someone) from his home or country. 3 find and destroy: *uproot corruption.*

upset (ʌpˈset) 1 *vti* tip over; overturn. 2 *vt* disturb (the mind or body of): *Shouting upsets me; an upset stomach.* ● *nc* 1 the act of upsetting or the act or state of being upset. 2 an unexpected defeat.

upshot (ˈʌpʃɒt) *nc* a result or effect.

upside-down (ˌʌpsaɪdˈdaʊn) *adj, adv* 1 completely turned over. 2 *infml* in confusion or disorder: *an upside-down world.*

upstairs (ˌʌpˈsteəz) *adv, adj* up (the) stairs; to or on an upper floor. ● *nu* an upstairs floor.

upstream (ˌʌpˈstriːm) *adv, adj* in the opposite direction to the current of a river.

up-to-date (ˌʌptəˈdeɪt) *adj* modern; current.

upturned (ˌʌpˈtɜːnd) *adj* 1 (of a nose) with the end pointing upwards. 2 turned over.

upward (ˈʌpwəd) *adv* also **upwards**, *adj* (moving or pointing) towards a higher place, value, etc.

uranium (juˈreɪnɪəm) *nu* a chemical element; a radioactive metal used for nuclear power.

urban (ˈɜːbən) *adj* to do with a town or city. **urbanise** (ˈɜːbənaɪz) *vt* 1 make (esp. a piece of country) more urban. 2 make (a person or group of people) used to town or city life. **urbanisation** (ˌɜːbənaɪˈzeɪʃən) *nu*

urchin (ˈɜːtʃɪn) *nc* 1 a naughtily playful child, esp. poorly dressed. 2 short for **sea urchin.**

urge (ɜːdʒ) *vt* 1 recommend strongly: *We were urged to leave quickly; I urge silence.* 2 drive; hurry: *Urge the horses on.* ● *nc* a strong wish to do something.

urgent (ˈɜːdʒənt) *adj* 1 needing quick action or attention: *an urgent parcel.* 2 showing that something is urgent. **urgency** *nu* **urgently** *adv*

urine (ˈjʊərɪn) *nu* liquid waste from the body.

urn (ɜːn) *nc* 1 a type of pot used to hold the ashes of the burnt body of a dead person. 2 a large metal container with a tap at the bottom, used for tea, coffee, etc.: see picture.

urn

us (ʌs unstressed əs) *pron* (used to indicate the speaker or writer together with one or more other people either after a preposition or when they are the object of a verb): *He paid us quickly; She is waving to us.*

usable (ˈjuːzəbəl) *adj* able to be used.

usage (ˈjuːzɪdʒ, ˈjuːsɪdʒ) *ncu* (a) way of using something; use.

use (juːz) *vt* 1 cause to serve a purpose; employ: *I use a pen for writing.* 2 treat or behave towards, esp. for one's own good: *He uses his friends shamefully.* ● *nu* 1 the act of using or the state of being used: *The new guns are in use against the enemy.* 2 custom or practice: *This new idea has come into use recently; It is an old word now going out of use.* 3 value. 4 *nc* a purpose for using something: *A knife has many uses.* **it's no use** it is useless: *It's no use complaining.* **used** (juːst) or **usedn't** (ˈjuːsənt) **to** at an earlier time make or not make it one's practice to: *I used to walk more before I had a car.* **used** (juːst) **to** familiar with: *You quickly get used to foreign food.* **use up** employ (something that is destroyed by use); finish: *We used up nearly all the ink.*

useful ('juːsfʊl) *adj* **1** able to be used for a purpose. **2** *infml* good; praiseworthy: *He played a useful game.* **usefulness** *nu*

useless ('juːslɪs) *adj* **1** serving no purpose. **2** *infml* having no ability: *You're useless at swimming.*

usher ('ʌʃə*) *nc* **1** a person who shows people to their seats in a theatre or cinema: see picture. **2** (in England) a person who keeps

usher

order in a court of law. ● *vt* show the way to or lead (someone). **usher in** be just before in time or be present at the arrival of: *The Boer War ushered in the twentieth century.*

usual ('juːʒʊəl) *adj* normal; most common: *My usual drink is tea.* **as usual** as (nearly)

always; again: *He's late, as usual.* **usually** *adv*

usurp (juːˈzɜːp) *vt* take over or seize (someone's power, property, etc.) wrongfully.

utensil (juːˈtensəl) *nc* a tool, instrument, or container used esp. for cooking, eating, or writing.

uterus ('juːtərəs) *anatomy nc, pl* **-ri** (raɪ) also **womb** the part of the body of a female human or other mammal in which its young grow.

utilise ('juːtɪlaɪz) *vt* put to use. **utilisation** (ˌjuːtɪlaɪˈzeɪʃən) *nu*

utility (juːˈtɪlɪtɪ) **1** *nu* usefulness. **2** *nc, pl* **utilities** also **public utility** a public service, such as a water supply or bus service. ● *adj* made chiefly with utility in mind: *utility furniture.*

utmost ('ʌtməʊst) *adj* greatest or furthest possible: *with the utmost care.* ● *nu* the most possible: *I did my utmost to find it.*

utter¹ ('ʌtə*) *vt* express in sound: *He uttered a long cry and then these words.* **utterance 1** *formal nu* the act of uttering. **2** *nc* something uttered.

utter² *adj* complete; total: *in utter admiration.* **utterly** *adv*

V

vacancy ('veɪkənsɪ) **1** *nc, pl* **-cies** a job not being done by anyone. **2** *nu* the state of being vacant.

vacant ('veɪkənt) *adj* **1** empty; unoccupied. **2** (appearing to be) not occupied in thought: *a vacant expression on his face.*

vacate (və'keɪt) *vt* leave (a place) vacant by going away from it.

vacation (və'keɪʃən, veɪ'keɪʃən) *ncu* **1** *Brit* (a) holiday for universities or law courts. **2** *US* (a) holiday from work, esp. spent away from home. **3** *nu* the act of vacating. ● *vi* *US* take a **vacation** (def. 2).

vaccinate ('væksɪneɪt) *vt* give a vaccine to. **vaccination** (ˌvæksɪ'neɪʃən) *ncu* **vaccine** ('væksiːn) *ncu* a (particular) substance taken or injected into the body to prevent a disease: *measles vaccine.*

vacillate ('væsɪleɪt) *vi* keep changing one's mind.

vacuum ('vækjuːm) *nc, pl* **-s, -ua** (jʊə) a space containing nothing or less air than normal. ● *vti* clean (a room, etc.) with a vacuum cleaner. **vacuum cleaner** a machine that cleans by sucking dirt into a bag. **vacuum flask** also **Thermos flask** *Trademark* a bottle with a double wall containing a vacuum, used to keep drinks, etc., hot or cold.

vagabond ('vægəbɒnd) *often derogatory nc* a person with no fixed home.

vagrant ('veɪgrənt) *nc* a person with no fixed home or work. **vagrancy** *nu* the state of being a vagrant.

vague (veɪg) *adj* **-r, -st** not clear or exact: *I can see the vague outline of a building.* **vaguely** *adv*

vain (veɪn) *adj* **-er, -est** **1** too proud or pleased with one's appearance or success. **2** pointless: *a vain attempt.* **in vain** without result or success. **take someone's name in vain** talk about someone without showing proper respect and esp. without them knowing. **vainly** *adv*

vale (veɪl) *archaic or literary nc* a valley.

valency ('veɪlənsɪ) *chemistry nc, pl* **-cies** the number of hydrogen atoms that an atom or group can combine with or replace: *Oxygen has a valency of two.*

valentine ('væləntaɪn) *nc* **1** a loved one. **2** a card sent to a loved one on St Valentine's Day (14 February), esp. without the sender's signature.

valet ('væleɪ) *nc* a man's personal male servant, employed to look after clothes, etc.

valiant ('væliənt) *formal adj* brave.

valid ('vælɪd) *adj* **1** (of a ticket, licence, etc.) (still) usable; able to be accepted. **2** (of an argument, reason, etc.) forceful or sensible. **3** *law* properly done; able to be accepted by a law court. **validate** *vt* make valid. **validity** (və'lɪdɪtɪ) *nu*

valley ('vælɪ) *nc, pl* **-s** a long hollow between hills, usually with a river flowing down it: see picture.

valley

valour *US* **valor** ('vælə*) *formal nu* bravery, esp. in battle.

valuable ('væljʊəbəl) *adj* of great worth or value.

valuation (ˌvæljʊ'eɪʃən) **1** *nc* a price or value arrived at by valuing. **2** *nu* the act of valuing.

value ('væljuː) **1** *nu* the quality of something, esp. in terms of worth, usefulness, or desirability. *nc* **2** the worth of something expressed as money. **3** an amount or quantity: *The temperature reaches very high values in the desert.* **4** *(pl)* the importance a person places on standards of behaviour: *They have strange values—they don't think that stealing is really a crime.* ● *vt* **1** guess the value of, with knowledge of other values. **2** consider to be valuable. **Value-Added Tax** a tax on the difference between the cost of making or buying something and the price it is sold for: *abbrev.* VAT **valueless** ('væljʊlɪs) *adj* of no value; not worth anything.

valve (vælv) *nc* **1** a device for stopping or controlling the flow of a gas or liquid in a pipe, esp. for allowing flow in only one direction. **2** a device in a radio or television set, used to control the flow of electricity.

vampire ('væmpaɪə*) *nc* a dead person supposed to come alive again at night and drink the blood of living people.

van (væn) *nc* **1** a closed-in motor vehicle used to carry goods. **2** a railway carriage, esp. used for goods.

vandal ('vændəl) *nc* a person who damages public or other people's property on purpose. **vandalism** *nu* the acts of vandals.

vane (veɪn) *nc* **1** a flat or curved blade in a stream of gas or liquid, either fixed to direct the flow, or free to move to indicate direction or produce power. **2** a weathercock.

vanguard ('vængɑːd) *nc* the leading part or members of an army, artistic movement, etc.

vanilla (və'nɪlə) *nu* a plant of which the seed pods are cooked with food, esp. sweet, for their taste.

vanish ('vænɪʃ) *vi* disappear or stop existing.

vanity ('vænɪtɪ) *ncu, pl* **-ties** (an example of) being vain.

vanquish ('væŋkwɪʃ) *chiefly archaic or literary vt* defeat; overcome.

vaporise ('veɪpəraɪz) *vti* (cause to) turn into vapour.

vapour *US* **vapor** ('veɪpə*) *nc* a gas or cloud of tiny drops of a substance, such as steam.

variable ('veərɪəbəl) *adj* **1** likely to change. **2** able to be varied. ●*nc* a variable quantity: *There are so many variables that I don't know what will happen.*

variant ('veərɪənt) *adj, nc* (something) different from a particular or the normal form or type: *a variant spelling.*

variation (ˌveərɪ'eɪʃən) **1** *ncu* (an example of) varying or being different. *nc* **2** something different. **3** a part of a piece of music made up of ornamentations on one simple tune.

varied ('veərɪd) *adj* showing variety; mixed.

variegated ('veərɪgeɪtɪd) *adj* (esp. of a plant) having two or more different colours: *variegated leaves.*

variety (və'raɪɪtɪ) *nu* **1** the quality of varying or being mixed: *the variety of all human life.* **2** a mixed or varied group: *There's a variety to choose from.* **3** an entertainment made up of many short pieces, such as songs, dances, and the telling of jokes. **4** *nc, pl* **-ties** *often science* a type within a mixed group: *Which variety of apple does this belong to?*

various ('veərɪəs) *determiner* several: *There are various ways of doing this.* ●*adj* several; different; varying: *His experiences are many and various.* **variously** *adv*

varnish ('vɑːnɪʃ) *ncu* a (type of) liquid usually made of oil, resin, and spirit that dries to give a hard, shiny, clear finish to wood, etc. ●*vt* coat with varnish.

vary ('veərɪ) *vti* (cause to) change or be different.

vase (vɑːz) *nc* a glass or china container, esp. for cut flowers: see picture.

vassal ('væsəl) *nc* (esp. in the Middle Ages) a person given protection and the use of land in return for service.

vast (vɑːst) *adj* **-er, -est** very large; huge. **vastly** *adv* **vastness** *nu*

vase

vat (væt) *nc* a large, esp. open, container for liquid.

vault[1] (vɔːlt) *nc* **1** an arched roof or ceiling. **2** a room under the ground for burying dead people in: *a family vault.* **3** a room for something valuable, such as silver or money: *a bank vault.*

vault[2] *vti* jump over (something), using a pole or the arms for support. ●*nc* such a jump.

veal (viːl) *nu* meat from a young bull or cow.

vector ('vektə*) *nc* **1** *mathematics* a quantity having both size and direction, such as force. **2** something, esp. an insect, that spreads disease between humans or animals.

Vedas ('veɪdəz) *n pl* the four oldest sacred Hindu writings.

veer (vɪə*) *vi* **1** change direction. **2** change a subject, opinion, etc.: *The discussion veered away from politics.* **3** (of the wind) change direction clockwise: *veering from south-east to south.*

vegetable ('vedʒtəbəl) *nc* a non-woody plant used as food, such as the pea, cabbage, or potato: see picture. ●*adj* from or to do with any plant: *vegetable oil.*

vegetarian (ˌvedʒɪ'teərɪən) *nc, adj* (to do with) a person who eats no meat or fish, and sometimes no animal products, such as cheese or eggs.

vegetate ('vedʒɪteɪt) *vi* **1** *infml* lead a life without interest or variety. **2** grow as a vegetable does.

vegetation (ˌvedʒɪ'teɪʃən) *nu* plants. **vegetative** ('vedʒɪtətɪv) *adj*

vehement ('vɪəmənt) *adj* with very strong feeling; forceful: *a vehement defence of freedom.* **vehemence** *nu* **vehemently** *adv*

vehicle ('vɪəkəl) *nc* **1** a device for carrying people or goods, esp. one using roads. **2** a means of expressing or communicating, such as music or a newspaper. **3** a substance mixed with and used to carry and distribute another: *Oil is the main vehicle in printing ink.*

veil (veɪl) *nc* **1** a piece of cloth, through which it is possible for the wearer to see, worn in front of the face. **2** something that covers or hides. ●*vt* **1** put a veil over the face of. **2** cover or hide: *The plot was veiled in secrecy.*

vegetables

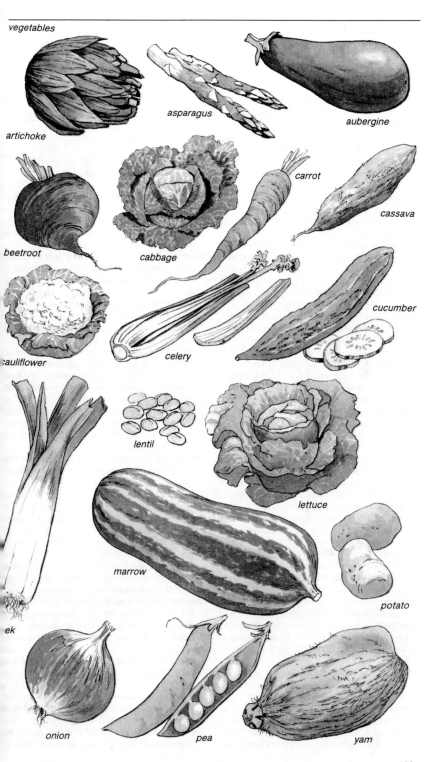

artichoke

asparagus

aubergine

beetroot

cabbage

carrot

cassava

cauliflower

celery

cucumber

lentil

lettuce

marrow

potato

ek

onion

pea

yam

vein (vein) *nc* **1** a tube that carries blood to the heart. **2** mood; general feeling: *Our talk was in a serious vein.* **3** a layer of coal, metal ore, etc., in the ground.

velocity (vɪˈlɒsɪtɪ) *nc, pl* **-ties** speed of movement.

velvet (ˈvelvɪt) *nu* a thick, soft cloth with threads sticking up on one side. **velvety** *adj*

vendetta (venˈdetə) *nc* **1** a long quarrel or fight, esp. between two families. **2** a state when one person tries to make another's work, life, etc., difficult.

vendor (ˈvendə*, ˈvendɔː*) *nc* a person who sells something: *the vendor of a house.*

veneer (vəˈnɪə*) **1** *ncu* a thin layer of (a type of) fine wood stuck onto furniture, etc., made of a cheaper wood. **2** *nc* something that seems good but is actually put on to hide something less pleasant: *a place with a thin veneer of civilisation.* ● *vt* cover with (a) veneer.

venerate (ˈvenəreɪt) *vt* hold in great respect on account of character, great age, religious connections, etc. **venerable** *adj* worthy of veneration. **veneration** (ˌvenəˈreɪʃən) *nu*

venereal (vəˈnɪərɪəl) *adj* (of a disease) caught from another person during sexual intercourse.

vengeance (ˈvendʒəns) *nu* punishment brought on someone by a person he has wronged. **with a vengeance** a lot; more than usual: *It's raining with a vengeance.*

venison (ˈvenɪsən) *nu* meat from a deer.

venom (ˈvenəm) *nu* poison from a snake, scorpion, etc.

vent (vent) *nc* a hole allowing the passage, esp. escape, of air, a liquid, etc. ● *vt* **1** also **give vent to** express or let out (a feeling): *He gave vent to his anger by hitting me.* **2** allow (air, a liquid, etc.) through a vent. **3** provide with a vent.

ventilate (ˈventɪleɪt) *vt* **1** allow fresh air into (a room, etc.). **2** allow public consideration or discussion of (a subject). **ventilation** (ˌventɪˈleɪʃən) *nu* **1** a system for bringing fresh air into a building. **2** the act of ventilating. **ventilator** *nc* a device for ventilating a room.

ventral (ˈventrəl) *anatomy, zoology adj* to do with the front or underside of the body.

ventricle (ˈventrɪkəl) *anatomy nc* **1** one of the two lower spaces in the heart. **2** any of several spaces, esp. filled with liquid, in the body.

ventriloquist (venˈtrɪləkwɪst) *nc* a person who can make his speech appear to come from someone else or an object.

venture (ˈventʃə*) *vt* **1** *formal* risk: *to venture one's life.* **2** dare to put forward (an opinion, etc.): *I venture to suggest that you're lying.* **3** *vi* dare to go: *I wouldn't venture out in this weather.* ● *nc* an action with an element of risk, such as the starting of a business.

veranda (also **verandah**) (vəˈrændə) *nc* a covered and sometimes partly walled space along the side of a house: see picture.

veranda

verb (vɜːb) *nc* a word describing a state or an action, such as 'be', 'make', or 'fly'.

verbal (ˈvɜːbəl) *adj* **1** in speech not writing: *only a verbal agreement.* **2** to do with verbs. **3** to do with words or language. **verbally** *adv*

verdant (ˈvɜːdənt) *literary adj* (of a field, etc.) green (with many healthy plants).

verdict (ˈvɜːdɪkt) *nc* a judgement or decision, esp. on someone's guilt in a law court.

verdure (ˈvɜːdʒə*) *literary nu* green plants.

verge (vɜːdʒ) *nc* an edge, esp. one of grass along the side of a road. ● *vt* be next or on edge to: *Our garden verges the road.* **on the verge of** on the point of; close to: *I'm on the verge of finishing; on the verge of an important discovery.* **verge on** approach; be almost: *Such behaviour verges on stupidity.*

verify (ˈverɪfaɪ) *vt* **1** find out whether (something) is true. **2** show to be true. **verification** (ˌverɪfɪˈkeɪʃən) *nu*

veritable (ˈverɪtəbəl) *adj* real; absolute: *That meal was a veritable feast.*

vermilion (vəˈmɪljən) *adj* bright red. ● *ncu* a vermilion colour.

vermin (ˈvɜːmɪn) *n pl* **1** small animals, such as rats and many insects, that can harm man, animals that he keeps, or plants that he grows. **2** *derogatory* people who are useless or harmful to the rest of society.

vernacular (vəˈnækjʊlə*) *nc, adj* (to do with) the language spoken in a particular place: *The vernacular of England is English.*

vernal (ˈvɜːnəl) *adj* to do with the season of spring.

versatile (ˈvɜːsətaɪl) *adj* able to do many different things: *a versatile writer; a versatile tool.*

verse (vɜːs) **1** *nu* poetry. *nc* **2** a separate part of a poem or song. **3** a short, numbered paragraph of the Bible.

versed (vɜːst) *adj* (usually followed by **in**) experienced (in) or knowledgeable (about).

version ('vɜːʃən) *nc* a (different) form or type of something, esp. an account or story: *The other witness gave quite a different version of the accident.*

versus ('vɜːsəs) *chiefly law or sport prep* against: *abbrev.* **v.** or **vs**: *England v. Brazil.*

vertebra ('vɜːtɪbrə) *nc, pl* **-brae** (briː) any of the bones making up the spine. **vertebrate** ('vɜːtɪbrət) *nc, adj* (an animal) with a spine.

vertex ('vɜːteks) *nc, pl* **-tices** (tɪsiːz), **-texes** the highest point of something, esp. a figure such as a triangle.

vertical ('vɜːtɪkəl) *adj* upright; at an angle of 90° to something level or to another line. ● *nc* a vertical line, surface, etc. **vertically** *adv*

very ('verɪ) *adv* a lot; much: *very angry; very badly; very much better.* ● *adj* (used to add force to a following adjective or noun: *the very first time; at the very end of the book; the very thing I want.*

vessel ('vesəl) *nc* **1** *formal* a container, esp. for liquids. **2** *formal* a ship or boat, esp. a large one. **3** a tube in the body carrying a liquid, esp. blood.

vest (vest) *nc* **1** *US* **undershirt** a garment worn under other clothes on the upper body. **2** *US, Australian* See **waistcoat**. ● *vt formal* (followed by **in**) allow someone to use: *The greatest power is vested in the governor of the district.*

vestibule ('vestɪbjuːl) *nc* a small room at or near an entrance.

vestige ('vestɪdʒ) *nc* **1** something that remains, showing that a person or thing was once there. **2** a very small amount: *There's not a vestige of freedom left in the country since he took power.*

vestment ('vestmənt) *nc* a garment worn to indicate position, authority, etc., esp. by Christian priests.

vet (vet) *infml n* short for **veterinary surgeon**. ● *vt* examine before acceptance: *Before we get married, you'll have to be vetted by my family!*

veteran ('vetərən) *nc* **1** a person, esp. a soldier, or a thing, esp. a car, that has done long service. **2** *US* a former soldier. ● *adj* to do with or being a veteran.

veterinary ('vetərɪnərɪ) *adj* to do with medicine for animals. **veterinary surgeon** (*infml abbrev.* **vet**) a person who treats sick or injured animals.

veto ('viːtəʊ) *nc, pl* **-es** the right to forbid a measure, law, etc., wanted by others. ● *vt* use one's veto to forbid.

vex (veks) *vt* anger or annoy. **vexation** (vek'seɪʃən) **1** *nc* something that vexes. **2** *nu* the act of vexing; the state of being vexed.

via ('vaɪə) *prep* through; by way of: *We flew to Australia via America.*

viable ('vaɪəbəl) *adj* **1** (of a plan, suggestion, etc.) workable; of use. **2** (of an unborn child or animal) able to live if born.

viaduct ('vaɪədʌkt) *nc* a bridge, built on a row of arches, carrying a road or railway across a valley.

vibrate (vaɪ'breɪt) *vti* (cause to) move quickly to and fro. **vibration** *nu* the act of vibrating. **vibrations** *infml n pl* a feeling one gets about a place or another person.

vicar ('vɪkə*) *nc* an Anglican priest usually in charge of a parish.

vice¹ (vaɪs) *nc* **1** an evil habit or quality. **2** *humorous* a bad habit: *What are his favourite vices?* **3** *nu* immoral behaviour, esp. sexual.

vice² *US* **vise** *nc* a device for holding an object being worked on: see picture.

vice

vice versa (ˌvaɪs 'vɜːsə, ˌvaɪsɪ 'vɜːsə) the other way round.

vicinity (vɪ'sɪnɪtɪ) *nu* the region close to or around a place: *in the vicinity of London.*

vicious ('vɪʃəs) *adj* cruel, esp. also violent. **vicious circle** a situation in which solving one problem causes a second and solving that causes the first again. **viciously** *adv*

vicissitude (vɪ'sɪsɪtjuːd) *nc* a change in one's situation: *One learns to deal with the vicissitudes of life.*

victim ('vɪktɪm) *nc* a person who suffers on account of a natural event or someone's actions: *the victims of war.*

victor ('vɪktə*) *nc* the winner of a war etc. **victorious** (vɪk'tɔːrɪəs) *adj*

victory ('vɪktərɪ) *ncu, pl* **-ries** (an example of) defeating someone.

video ('vɪdɪəʊ) *nu, adj* (to do with) the recording and showing of pictures, esp. moving: *a video link for the football match.* **videotape** ('vɪdɪəʊˌteɪp) *ncu* (a piece of) tape for recording pictures. ● *vt* record on videotape.

view (vjuː) *nc* **1** an act or opportunity of seeing or looking at something. **2** a scene, esp. of pretty countryside: *There's a lovely view from the top of the hill.* **3** an opinion: *give one's views on a subject.* **4** *nu* vision; sight: *to come into view.* ● *vt* **1** look at. **2** consider: *He views the matter differently.* **3** watch (television). **in view of** on account of; considering. **point of view** also **viewpoint** a way of considering a matter. **with a**

view to 1 with the intention of. **2** in the hope of. **viewer** *nc* **1** a person who views. **2** a device used for viewing something. **viewpoint** ('vju:pɔint) *nc* **1** See **point of view. 2** a place from which there is a good **view** (def. 2).

vigil ('vidʒil) *nc* the act of staying awake at night, either on guard or as a religious custom.

vigilant ('vidʒilənt) *adj* watchful; keeping guard. **vigilance** *nu*

vigorous ('vigərəs) *adj* possessing or showing great energy: *a vigorous sport.* **vigorously** *adv*

vigour *US* **vigor** ('vigə*) *nu* the quality of being vigorous.

vile (vail) *adj* **-r, -st 1** disgusting. **2** evil.

villa ('vilə) *nc* a comfortable country house, esp. used for holidays.

village ('vilidʒ) *nc* a group of houses smaller than a town. **villager** *nc* a person who lives in a village.

villain ('vilən) *nc* **1** an evil person. **2** *Brit* a criminal. **villainy** *nu* evil behaviour.

vindicate ('vindikeit) *vt* show to be just, right, or not guilty: *History will vindicate our actions.* **vindication** (,vindi'keiʃən) **1** *nu* the act of vindicating. **2** *nc* something that vindicates.

vindictive (vin'diktiv) *adj* wanting (too much) to harm someone who has wronged one.

vine (vain) *nc* a plant on which grapes grow. **vineyard** ('vinjəd) *nc* a place where vines are grown.

vinegar ('vinigə*) *nu* a sour liquid made from wine, beer, etc., and used in food.

vintage ('vintidʒ) *nc* (the wine, esp. a good quality one, made from) a particular year's harvest of grapes. ● *adj* of lasting quality: *a vintage car.*

vinyl ('vainil) *nu* a type of plastic material.

viola (vi'əulə) *nc* a stringed musical instrument slightly larger than a violin.

violate ('vaiəleit) *vt* **1** break (a law, agreement, etc.). **2** not respect (a holy place). **3** disturb or interrupt: *to violate someone's privacy.* **4** rape. **violation** (,vaiə'leiʃən) *ncu* (an example of) violating.

violent ('vaiələnt) *adj* **1** using force to cause injury, etc.: *He got violent and hit me.* **2** forceful: *in violent disagreement.* **3** caused by force: *a violent death.* **violence** *nu* **violently** *adv*

violet ('vaiələt) *adj* reddish-blue. ● *ncu* **1** a violet colour. **2** *nc* a plant with small, often sweet-smelling, white or violet flowers.

violin (,vaiə'lin) *nc* a stringed musical instrument played with a bow: see picture at **musical instruments. violinist** *nc* a person who plays a violin.

viper ('vaipə*) *n* See **adder.**

virgin ('vɜːdʒin) *nc* a person, esp. a woman, who has not had sexual intercourse. ● *adj* natural; untouched: *virgin forest.* **virginity** (və'dʒiniti) *nu* the quality or state of being (a) virgin.

virile ('virail) *adj* (of a man) young and healthy; attractive. **virility** (və'riliti) *nu*

virtual ('vɜːtjuəl) *adj* with the effect or nature but not the name or form of; amounting to: *We had to work in virtual darkness.* **virtually** *adv*

virtue ('vɜːtju:) **1** *ncu* (a particular type of) goodness or uprightness of behaviour: *the virtue of generosity.* **2** *nc* a good quality; advantage: *This plan has the virtue of simplicity.* **3** effectiveness. **by virtue of** on account of; on the strength of: *He is allowed such freedom by virtue of his important position.* **virtuous** *adj* having or showing **virtue** (def. 1).

virus ('vaiərəs) *nc* a tiny creature that multiplies in living cells.

visa ('vi:zə) *nc* a note made in a passport allowing the holder to enter a particular country: *an American visa.*

visage ('vizidʒ) *literary or humorous nc* a face.

vis-à-vis (,vi:zɑː'vi:) *prep* in respect of; regarding. ● *prep, adv* opposite; facing.

viscount ('vaikaunt) *nc* (in the UK) a nobleman above a baron and below an earl.

viscous ('viskəs) *adj* (of a liquid) sticky; not flowing easily. **viscosity** (vis'kɒsiti) *ncu, pl* **-ties** (a measure of) the quality of being viscous.

vise (vais) *US n* See **vice².**

Vishnu ('viʃnu:) *n* a Hindu god.

visible ('vizibəl) *adj* **1** able to be seen. **2** noticeable: *visible danger.* **visibility** (,vizi'biliti) **1** *nu* the quality of being visible. **2** *ncu, pl* **-ties** ease of seeing or a distance that one can see.

vision ('viʒən) *nu* **1** the ability to see; sight. **2** the ability to imagine, esp. the future and plan for it. *nc* **3** something seen in a dream or a religious experience. **4** *(often pl)* an act of imagining something: *I used to have visions of being rich.*

visionary ('viʒənəri) *adj* given to having visions; fanciful. ● *nc, pl* **-ries** a visionary person.

visit ('vizit) *vt* **1** come or go to see (a person or place). **2** go to (a place) in order to examine something. **3** (of a disease, disaster, etc.) come upon (someone). **4** *formal or literary* bring (a punishment, etc.) on (someone): *Their sins were visited on us.* ● *nc* an act of visiting (**visit** defs. **1, 2**). **pay a visit to** come or go to see. **visit with** *US* come or go to talk with (someone).

visitation (ˌvɪzɪˈteɪʃən) *nc* 1 a visit to inspect or examine. 2 a disease or disaster seen as a punishment.

visitor (ˈvɪzɪtə*) *nc* a person who visits.

visor (ˈvaɪzə*) *nc* 1 a guard fixed at the top of the front window of a car, etc., that can be swung down to protect the passengers' eyes from bright light. 2 a part on a helmet that can be swung down to protect the wearer's face: see picture.

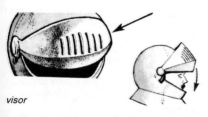

visor

visual (ˈvɪzjʊəl) *adj* to do with seeing. **visualise** (ˈvɪzjʊəlaɪz) *vt* imagine; see in one's mind. **visually** *adv*

vital (ˈvaɪtəl) *adj* 1 necessary, esp. for life: *A water supply is vital.* 2 of great importance: *a vital decision.* 3 full of life or energy; lively. **vitally** *adv*

vitality (vaɪˈtælɪtɪ) *nu* 1 the power to live. 2 liveliness; energy.

vitamin (ˈvɪtəmɪn, ˈvaɪtəmɪn) *nc* any of several substances present in food that are necessary in small quantities for health: *Fruit contains vitamin C.*

vivacious (vɪˈveɪʃəs) *adj* full of life; lively.

vivid (ˈvɪvɪd) *adj* 1 (of a colour) bright. 2 (of a description, the imagination, etc.) powerful; clear: *a vivid account of events.* **vividly** *adv*

vivisection (ˌvɪvɪˈsekʃən) *nu* cutting into live animals in order to do experiments with them.

vixen (ˈvɪksən) *nc* 1 a female fox. 2 a nasty woman.

vocabulary (vəˈkæbjʊlərɪ) *nc, pl* **-ries** 1 a set of words used by one person. 2 a set of words used by a particular group: *scientific vocabulary.* 3 a list of words used in a book, printed in the book with an explanation of their meanings.

vocal (ˈvəʊkəl) *adj* 1 to do with the voice: *vocal music.* 2 expressing oneself forcefully: *Several very vocal people complained.* **vocalist** *nc* a singer. **vocally** *adv*

vocation (vəʊˈkeɪʃən) 1 *nc* a job; occupation. 2 *nu* a calling or urge to take up a particular occupation, esp. a religious one. **vocational** *adj*

vodka (ˈvɒdkə) *nu* a strong, clear alcoholic drink made esp. from corn, originally in Russia.

vogue (vəʊg) *nc* a fashion; popularity: *The vogue for this kind of hat went out last summer—nobody wears one now.*

voice (vɔɪs) *nc* 1 the sound, made in the throat, that humans use for speaking and singing. 2 the quality or power of this: *a good singing voice; a quiet voice.* 3 *grammar* a set of forms of verbs that shows the relationship between subject and verb: *English has active and passive voices.* ● *vt* express (an opinion or feeling). **give voice to** voice (an opinion or feeling). **lose one's voice** not be able to speak normally, through illness, shouting, etc. **with one voice** with everyone agreeing. **voice-box** (ˈvɔɪsbɒks) *n* See **larynx.**

void (vɔɪd) *adj* 1 empty. 2 (followed by **of**) lacking; without: *an expression void of meaning.* 3 without force or not binding in law: *Their marriage has been proved void.* ● *vt* 1 *law* make void. 2 get rid of. ● *nc* 1 an empty space. 2 *nu* the space between the stars and planets.

volatile (ˈvɒlətaɪl) *adj* 1 (of a liquid) easily turning to vapour. 2 likely to change one's mind or ideas.

volcano (vɒlˈkeɪnəʊ) *nc, pl* **-es** a mountain through which liquid rock, gases, and sometimes ashes come out of the inside of the earth: see picture. **volcanic** (vɒlˈkænɪk) *adj*

volcano

volley (ˈvɒlɪ) *nc, pl* **-s** 1 the firing of several guns together. 2 (in cricket, tennis, football, etc.) the hitting or kicking of a ball in play before it hits the ground. ● *vi* 1 (of guns) fire together. 2 *vti* hit or kick (a ball) with a volley. **volleyball** (ˈvɒlɪbɔːl) *nu* a game for two teams of six players who knock a large ball back and forth over a high net with their hands.

volt (vəʊlt) *nc* a measure of electric force = the force needed to produce 1 watt at 1 amp: symbol V **voltage** (ˈvəʊltɪdʒ) *nc* electric force expressed in volts. **voltmeter** (ˈvəʊltˌmiːtə*) *nc* an instrument for measuring voltage.

voluble (ˈvɒljʊbəl) *adj* talking easily: *A voluble speaker.*

volume (ˈvɒljuːm) 1 *nu* the amount of space taken up by something: *the volume of a* room; *Milk is sold by volume.* 2 *nc* a book, esp. one of a set: *Where is volume three of this series?* *nu* 3 loudness: *shouting at full volume.* 4 an amount; quantity: *a great volume of business.*

voluminous (vəˈluːmɪnəs, vəˈljuːmɪnəs) *adj* great or lengthy: *his voluminous writings.*

voluntary (ˈvɒləntrɪ) *adj* 1 acting by choice, esp. also not for payment: *a voluntary worker.* 2 able to continue because of voluntary work: *a voluntary organisation.* 3 carried out consciously: *a voluntary movement of the hand.* ● *nc, pl* **-ries** a piece of music played before or after a church service. **voluntarily** *adv*

volunteer (ˌvɒlənˈtɪə*) *nc* a person who does or offers to do something voluntarily. ● *vti* (when *vi, often followed by* **for**) offer (to do something) voluntarily: *He volunteered for the job; May I volunteer my help?*

voluptuous (vəˈlʌptʃʊəs) *adj* 1 to do with pleasures of the body. 2 (of a woman) sexually attractive.

vomit (ˈvɒmɪt) *vti* bring (the contents of the stomach) up through the mouth. ● *nu* vomited matter.

vortex (ˈvɔːteks) *nc, pl* **-tices** (tɪsiːz), **-texes** 1 a mass of spinning gas or liquid. 2 a situation or activity regarded as sucking in people who take part in it.

vote (vəʊt) *nc* 1 a formal expression of a preference or choice, such as for or against a plan of action or between people standing in an election. 2 a number of votes made: *a high vote.* ● *vti* 1 express (a preference or choice) by vote: *We voted to accept the plan; Vote for Smith!* *vt* 2 place in or remove from a position by voting: *He was voted off the council.* 3 approve by vote: *We voted them more money.* 4 *infml* decide that (something) is: *The play was voted a failure.* **voter** *nc*

vouch (vaʊtʃ) *v* **vouch for** answer for; guarantee: *I'll vouch for his honesty.*

voucher (ˈvaʊtʃə*) *nc* a receipt for goods or services not yet obtained: *a meal voucher.*

vouchsafe (ˌvaʊtʃˈseɪf) *formal or literary vt* promise or agree (to give): *He vouchsafed me no answer.*

vow (vaʊ) *nc* a serious promise: *They took a vow of silence.* ● *vt* make a vow: *I vow never to go there again.*

vowel (ˈvaʊəl) *nc* 1 a speech sound produced without even partly stopping the flow of air through the mouth. 2 any of the letters *a, e, i, o, u,* and sometimes *y.*

voyage (ˈvɔɪdʒ) *nc* a journey, esp. a long one, by sea or air or in space. ● *vti literary* make a voyage (across). **voyager** *nc*

vulcanise (ˈvʌlkənaɪz) *vt* heat (rubber) with sulphur to make it strong and elastic.

vulgar (ˈvʌlɡə*) *adj* 1 showing lack of taste or manners: *vulgar clothes; a vulgar word.* 2 *chiefly archaic* to do with ordinary people.

vulnerable (ˈvʌlnərəbəl) *adj* open to being wounded, captured, criticised, etc.

vulture (ˈvʌltʃə*) *nc* a large African and Asian bird that feeds on dead animals: see picture at **birds.**

W

wad (wɒd) *nc* a lump of soft material, such as cotton, used to pack something, fill a hole, etc. ● *vt* pack, fill, etc., with a wad.

waddle ('wɒdəl) *vi* walk, rolling from side to side, like a duck.

wade (weɪd) **1** *vti* walk through (water, snow, etc., which comes above the knees): *We waded across the river.* *vi* **2** *infml* (followed by **through**) read (something long or boring). **3** (followed by **in** or **into**) attack with force.

wafer ('weɪfə*) *nc* a thin slice of something, esp. of biscuit eaten with ice cream.

waffle¹ ('wɒfəl) *infml, chiefly Brit vi* talk or write at great length and vaguely. ● *nu* lengthy, vague talk or writing.

waffle² *chiefly US nc* a kind of small flat cake usually eaten with syrup.

waft (wɒft) *vti* carry or travel (as easily and smoothly as) on water or in the air: *Smoke wafted in through the window.* ● *nc* a smell, quantity of smoke, etc., carried in the air.

wag (wæg) *vti* shake back and forth: *The dog wagged its tail.* ● *nc* **1** an instance of wagging. **2** *old-fashioned* a person who makes jokes, funny remarks, etc.

wage (weɪdʒ) *nc (usually pl)* payment for work, esp. worked out by the hour and paid every week. ● *vt* start and carry on (esp. a war).

wager ('weɪdʒə*) *n, v* See **bet**.

wagon (also **waggon**) ('wægən) *nc* **1** a goods vehicle of various kinds, esp. with four wheels and pulled by a tractor. **2** *Brit* an open railway goods vehicle.

wail (weɪl) *vi, nc* (make) a long, high noise, esp. indicating grief or pain.

waist (weɪst) *nc* **1** (the part of a garment covering) the part of the body between the ribs and the hip-bones. **2** the (narrower) middle part of an object. **waistcoat** ('weɪstkəʊt) *US, Australian* **vest** *nc* a buttoned, sleeveless, man's upper garment worn esp. under a jacket. **waistline** ('weɪstlaɪn) *nc* **1** the shape or measurement of a person's waist. **2** the waist of a garment.

wait (weɪt) **1** *vti* (when *vi*, often followed by **for**) delay action or stay somewhere in expectation (of); be ready (for): *Wait here till I come back; They waited for the next attack; You must wait your turn.* **2** *vi* work as a waiter or waitress: *wait at table.* ● *nc* an

instance of waiting (**wait** def. 1). **lie in wait (for)** wait (for) in order to attack. **waiting-list** ('weɪtɪŋlɪst) *nc* a list of people waiting to obtain something. **waiting-room** ('weɪtɪŋrʊm) *nc* a room in which to wait for a train, one's turn to see a doctor, etc. **wait on 1** serve, esp. as a waiter. **2** *chiefly US* wait for.

waiter ('weɪtə*) *nc* a man who serves food in a restaurant, etc. **waitress** ('weɪtrɪs) *nc* a woman who does this work.

waive (weɪv) *formal or law vt* **1** disregard or not apply (a rule, etc.). **2** give up (a right).

wake¹ (weɪk) **1** *vti* (often followed by **up**) stop sleeping: *You woke me up; I woke early.* **2** *vi* (followed by **to** or **up to**) start to take notice (of): *We must wake up to new ideas.* **wakeful** ('weɪkfʊl) *adj* awake; not able to sleep. **waking** *adj* awake.

wake² *nc* a track, esp. that left in water by a moving boat.

walk (wɔːk) *vi* **1** move on foot, always with at least one foot on the ground. **2** (of a horse) move with its slowest step. *vt* **3** walk on, along, across, etc.: *to walk the streets.* **4** cause (a horse, dog, etc.) to walk. **5** walk with: *Let me walk you home.* ● *nc* **1** an instance or manner of walking. **2** a place intended for walking. **walk of life** a job; occupation: *people from all walks of life.* **walkabout** ('wɔːkəbaʊt) *nc* **1** an informal walk made by a royal person, etc., to talk to people. **2** *Australian* a period spent walking in the bush by a native Australian. **walker** *nc* **walking-stick** ('wɔːkɪŋstɪk) *nc* a stick carried in the hand to lean on while walking. **walk off with** *infml* **1** win (a prize, etc.) easily. **2** steal. **walk out 1** go away suddenly or angrily. **2** go on strike. **walk-out** ('wɔːkaʊt) *nc* an act of going on strike. **walkover** ('wɔːk,əʊvə*) *infml nc* an easy win.

walkie-talkie (,wɔːkɪ'tɔːkɪ) *infml nc* a small radio, for talking and listening to others, that can be used while one moves about.

wall (wɔːl) *nc* **1** a usually tall, long, narrow structure made of bricks, stones, concrete, wood, etc., to separate fields or rooms, support a roof, etc. **2** anything that divides, separates, or encloses in this way. ● *vt* put a wall around: *a walled garden.* **go to the wall** fail or be ruined, esp. in business. **up the wall** crazy or angry: *He drives me up the wall.* **wallflower** ('wɔːl,flaʊə*) *nc* **1** a plant often found on old walls and grown for its flowers. **2** a shy person who does not become involved at social occasions. **wallpaper** ('wɔːl,peɪpə*) *ncu* (a kind of) paper, usually printed with a coloured pattern, that is stuck onto walls and ceilings. ● *vti* put wallpaper on (the walls of a room).

wallet ('wɒlɪt) *nc* a small, flat, folding case, esp. of leather, for paper money, etc.: see picture.

wallet

wallow ('wɒləʊ) *vi* 1 roll about in water, mud, etc. 2 *infml* take a kind of pleasure (in): *He wallowed in grief.* ●*nc* an instance of or place for wallowing.

walnut ('wɔːlnʌt) *nc* 1 a tree grown for its nuts, which are eaten, and its wood. 2 a nut from this tree. 3 *nu* the wood of this tree.

walrus ('wɔːlrəs) *nc, pl* **walruses, walrus** a large grey animal that lives in the sea and on land in cold parts of the world: see picture.

walrus

waltz (wɔːls) *nc* (a piece of music written for) a simple, popular dance for couples. ●*vi* dance a waltz.

wan (wɒn) *adj* **-ner, -nest** (of a person or their face) pale.

wand (wɒnd) *nc* a narrow stick used in magic, carried as a sign of one's position.

wander ('wɒndə*) *vi* 1 travel or move from place to place without purpose. 2 leave a set path or course. 3 (of a person or of speech or writing) leave the main subject; appear confused and hard to understand. **wanderer** *nc*

wane (weɪn) *vi* (esp. of the moon, as it appears from earth) lessen or become smaller. ●*nu* the act of waning.

want (wɒnt) *vt* 1 feel a need (for); wish (to have): *I want a dog; Do you want to go home?* 2 need: *This job wants doing properly.* 3 be without; lack: *The film wants only a good ending.* ●*nc* 1 something wanted. *nu* 2 the act of wanting. 3 lack: *We walked for want of a car.* 4 need: *Poor people are in great want of help.* **wanted** *adj* 1 needed. 2 being looked for on suspicion of being a criminal. **want for** be without: *We want for nothing.* **wanting** *adj* 1 absent. 2 not good enough: *They were examined and found wanting.*

wanton ('wɒntən) *adj* 1 to no purpose: *wanton destruction.* 2 not proper in the opinion of society: *a wanton woman.*

war (wɔː*) 1 *ncu* (a period of) armed fighting between countries or between forces within a country: *a civil war; the Second World War.* 2 *nc* any fight: *the war on crime.* ●*vi* fight a war. **at war** fighting a war. **warfare** ('wɔːfeə*) *nu* the act of fighting a war. **warhead** ('wɔːhed) *nc* the explosive front end of a shell, missile, etc. **warlike** ('wɔːlaɪk) *adj* 1 threatening war. 2 often going to war. **warpath** ('wɔːpɑːθ) *n* **on the warpath** looking or preparing for a fight. **warship** ('wɔːʃɪp) *nc* a ship armed, etc., for use in war. **wartime** ('wɔːtaɪm) *nu* a period of war: *wartime cooking.*

warble ('wɔːbəl) *vti* (esp. of a bird) sing with a note that varies in pitch. ●*ncu* (an instance of) warbling. **warbler** *nc* 1 a small insect-eating bird, not all kinds of which are noted for their song. 2 a person or thing that warbles.

ward (wɔːd) *nc* 1 a separate room in a hospital. 2 a division of an area: *a parliamentary ward.* 3 a person who has a **guardian** (def. 1).

warden ('wɔːdən) *nc* a person in charge of people or a building: *the Warden of an Oxford College.*

warder ('wɔːdə*) *nc* a person in charge of prisoners.

wardrobe ('wɔːdrəʊb) *nc* 1 a tall cupboard for clothes to be hung up in. 2 a person's clothes.

warehouse ('weəhaʊs) *nc* a building in which goods are stored.

wares (weəz) *n pl* goods for sale.

warm (wɔːm) *adj* **-er, -est** 1 fairly hot. 2 (of clothes, etc.) keeping one warm. 3 (of a colour) containing red or yellow. 4 close to finding or guessing something: *You're getting warm.* 5 friendly; enthusiastic: *a warm welcome.* ●*vti* 1 (often followed by **up**) make or become warm or warmer. 2 (usually followed by **to**) become sympathetic or friendly: *He soon warmed to our new neighbours.* ●*nu* an instance of warming. **the warm** a warm place: *Come into the warm.* **warm-blooded** *adj* (of an animal) having a blood temperature that stays almost the same, whatever the outside temperature. **warm-hearted** (,wɔːm'hɑːtɪd) *adj* kind or sympathetic. **warmly** *adv* **warmth** (wɔːmθ) *nu* **warm up** 1 make or become warm or warmer. 2 prepare for something esp. a race.

warn (wɔːn) *vt* 1 make (someone) be careful (of or about): *We were warned of the danger.* 2 give (someone) notice: *I warn you that I may not come.* 3 advise: *I warned* *them not to break the law again.* **warning** *nc* 1 an instance of warning. 2 something that warns.

warp (wɔːp) *vti* make or become bent out of shape: *The wood got wet and warped.* ●*nc* 1 an instance of being warped. 2 *nu* the threads, laid lengthwise, across and in between which others are fed in weaving cloth.

warrant ('wɒrənt) *nc* permission, esp. written, or directions to pay someone money, search a house, etc.: *a warrant for an arrest.* ●*vt* 1 promise that (something) is of good quality: *warranted used cars.* 2 *infml* say for certain: *I'll warrant he's lying.* 3 be sufficient reason for: *His foolish remark didn't warrant her anger.* **warranty** *nc, pl* **-ties** a promise to repair or replace something bought if it proves not to be of good quality.

warrior ('wɒrɪə*) *nc* a fighter in war.

wart (wɔːt) *nc* a small, firm lump sticking out on the skin.

wary ('weərɪ) *adj* **-ier, -iest** careful; looking out for trouble.

was (wɒz unstressed wəz) *v* (used with **I, he, she,** or **it**) past tense of **be.**

wash (wɒʃ) 1 *vti* clean (clothes, oneself, etc.) with a liquid, esp. water and usually soap or some other substance. *vt* 2 remove (dirt, etc.) by washing. 3 (of a liquid) carry (something) along or away: *The flood washed the bridge away.* *vi* 4 (of a liquid) flow onto or splash: *Waves washed right over the ship.* 5 (of clothes, etc.) be able to be washed without losing colour or being damaged. 6 *infml, chiefly Brit* stand up to examination: *This story of yours just won't wash.* ●*nc* 1 an instance of washing. 2 a collection of clothes washed together. 3 the waves produced by a moving boat. **washbasin** ('wɒʃ,beɪsən) *nc* a bowl with taps and a pipe for letting out dirty water, for washing the hands, etc., in. **washed-out** (wɒʃt'aut) *adj* pale, esp. also tired. **washer** *nc* 1 a person or thing that washes. 2 a flat ring of metal, rubber, etc., used to help a screw, bolt, or tap to be tightened. **washing** *nu* clothes that are to be, are being, or have just been washed. **washing-machine** ('wɒʃɪŋmə,ʃiːn) *nc* a machine for washing clothes. **washing-powder** ('wɒʃɪŋ,paudə*) *ncu* a (type of) powder used in washing clothes, etc. **washing-up** (,wɒʃɪŋ'ʌp) *Brit nu* 1 dirty plates, etc., that are to be washed up. 2 the act of washing up. **wash out** 1 wash the inside of. 2 remove (dirt, etc.) by washing. 3 (of dirt, etc.) be removed by washing. **washout** ('wɒʃaut) *infml nc* 1 a failure. 2 a useless person. **wash up** 1 *chiefly Brit* wash (plates, knives, forks, etc.)

after a meal. 2 *US* wash one's hands and face.

wasn't ('wɒzənt) *v* was not.

wasp (wɒsp) *nc* a winged insect with yellow and black stripes and a sting: see picture at **insects.**

wast (wɒst) *archaic v* (used with **thou**) past tense of **be.**

wastage ('weɪstɪdʒ) *nu* 1 something lost or wasted. 2 the act of wasting.

waste (weɪst) 1 *vt* use to no purpose or unnecessarily: *Don't waste your money on useless things.* 2 *vti* (often followed by **away**) wear away or (cause to) get smaller or weaker. ●*nu* 1 the act of wasting. 2 something wasted or thrown away. 3 *nc* also **wasteland** wild or unused land: *the icy wastes of Russia.* **go** or **run to waste** be wasted. **lay waste** ruin or destroy: *The town was laid waste by the war.* **wasteful** ('weɪstful) *adj* causing waste. **waste paper** paper thrown away after use. **waste-paper basket** a basket, tin, etc., for waste paper, etc.

watch (wɒtʃ) *vt* look at or observe carefully: *to watch television.* ●*nc* 1 a small clock worn on the wrist or carried in a pocket. 2 a period of being on duty, guarding, etc.: *There are soldiers on watch.* 3 a person or group keeping watch. **watchdog** ('wɒtʃdɒg) *nc* 1 a dog kept to guard property. 2 a person or group that makes sure that a government department, etc., acts properly. **watcher** *nc* **watchful** ('wɒtʃful) *adj* watching carefully; keeping a good watch. **watchman** ('wɒtʃmən) *nc, pl* **-men** a man who guards a factory, etc., esp. at night. **watch (out) (for)** be on one's guard (against): *Watch out for the holes in the road!* **watchword** ('wɒtʃwɜːd) *nc* a word or phrase, esp. secret, that shows someone that one is a friend, member of the same group, etc.

water ('wɔːtə*) *nu* 1 the clear liquid that forms sea, rain, rivers, etc.; *(also pl)* water forming a river, part of the sea, etc.: *the waters of the Nile; international waters.* 2 *polite* yellow liquid body waste; urine. 3 the height of a sea or river at a place at certain times: *low water.* ●*vt* 1 supply (land, plants, animals, etc.) with water. *vi* 2 (of the eyes) fill with tears. 3 (of the mouth) produce saliva. 4 (of a ship, etc.) take on water. **water closet** *archaic* (a room containing) a lavatory: *abbrev. (not archaic)* **WC water-colour** ('wɔːtə,kʌlə*) *nc* 1 paint made ready for use for painting pictures by mixing with water. 2 a painting done with watercolours. **watercress** ('wɔːtəkres) *nu* a plant that grows in water and which is eaten, esp. as salad. **water down** 1 mix with water. 2

431

make less unpleasant, shocking, etc. **waterfall** ('wɔːtəfɔːl) *nc* a river falling down a steep, rocky drop: see picture. **waterfront**

waterfall

('wɔːtəfrʌnt) *nc* the land or part of a town near the sea, a lake, or a river. **water level** the level of the surface of a body of water. **watermark** ('wɔːtəmɑːk) *nc* a word, picture, etc., formed in paper by making some parts thinner than the rest. ●*vt* put a watermark in (paper). **watermelon** ('wɔːtə,melən) *nc* a very large fruit with a hard green outside and very juicy red flesh. **waterproof** ('wɔːtəpruːf) *adj* (of cloth, a joint,etc.) that does not let water through. ●*nc (often pl)* a waterproof garment. ●*vt* make waterproof. **watershed** ('wɔːtəʃed) *nc* 1 high land on either side of which the rivers flow to different seas or lakes. 2 a time or point of change, esp. in someone's life. **water-ski** ('wɔːtəskiː) *nc* a board on which one can stand and be towed across water by a boat. ●*vi* travel on one or two water-skis: see picture. **watertight** ('wɔːtətaɪt) *adj* (of a

water-ski

door, boat, etc.) closed, built, etc., so as not to let water through. **waterway** ('wɔːtəweɪ) *nc* a river or canal used by boats. **waterworks** ('wɔːtəwɜːks) *nu (with singular verb)* a place supplying water to a town, etc. **watery** *adj* 1 covered with water; under water. 2 (esp. of food or drink) thin or weak. 3 (esp. of colours) pale.

watt (wɒt) *nc* a measure of electric power = the power produced by 1 amp at 1 volt: symbol W

wattle ('wɒtəl) 1 *nu* branches and twigs pushed and twisted together to make a fence, wall, or roof. 2 *nc* a loose fold of skin hanging from the throat of some birds.

wave (weɪv) *vti* 1 (cause to) move to and fro with a continuous movement. 2 (be) put in

curves: *waved hair.* 3 wave (one's hand) as a greeting, etc. 4 *vt* direct by waving: *The policeman waved us on.* ●*nc* 1 an instance of waving. 2 a long, raised body of water moving across the surface of the sea, etc. 3 a movement like a wave: *The attack came in three waves.* 4 a sudden extra quantity: *a heat wave.* 5 *physics* a movement within a substance by means of which light, heat, sound, etc., travels: *radio waves.* 6 a curve made in hair. etc. **wavelength** ('weɪvleŋθ) *nc* the distance between matching points on neighbouring waves (**wave** def. 5), as used to describe where to find a particular station on a radio, etc. **wavy** *adj* **-ier, -iest** shaped or moving in or like waves.

waver ('weɪvə*) *vi* 1 be undecided: *I'm wavering between going now and staying another week.* 2 become unsteady: *The tower wavered and fell.*

wax¹ (wæks) *ncu* a (type of) smooth substance, made from a plant or animal, got from petroleum, or made by bees, that melts when heated and is used for burning, polishing, sealing, etc. ●*vt* coat, polish, etc. with wax.

wax² *vi* (esp. of the moon, as it appears from earth) increase or become larger.

way (weɪ) *nc* 1 a method or means of doing something: *Which way do you do this?* 2 a means of going somewhere; road, path, etc. 3 a degree; respect: *We're similar in many ways, though we argue.* 4 a direction: *It points that way.* 5 a manner of behaving: *He has a way with awkward customers.* nu 6 a distance: *a long way away.* 7 the state of going somewhere: *Let's be on our way.* 8 **in** or **out of the way** preventing or not preventing someone or something from moving forward. ●*adv* far: *That remark was way off the subject.* **by the way** in passing; as an unconnected remark. **by way of 1** passing through: *to Japan by way of Hong Kong.* 2 (to serve) as: *The letter was by way of an apology.* **get** or **have one's (own) way** get what one wants. **give way 1** break down: *The gate gave way when he kicked it.* 2 change one's mind and allow someone to have what they want. **in a bad way** in a bad state (of health, etc.). **in a way** in one respect. **lose one's way** no longer know in which direction to travel or what to do. **make way (for)** allow (someone) space to move through. **no way** *infml* certainly not. **under way** in progress; moving. **way of life** a method of organising or set of ideas behind one's whole life. **way out** the door, road, etc., by which one leaves somewhere.

wayfarer ('weɪ,feərə*) *literary nc* a traveller. **waylay** (,weɪ'leɪ) *vt* stop (someone) to attack or talk to.

wayside ('weɪsaɪd) *nc* the side of a road.

wayward ('weɪwʊd) *adj* wanting to have one's own way.

we (wi: unstressed wɪ) *pron* 1 (used of two or more people, one of whom is the speaker or writer, as the subject of a verb): *We all went together.* 2 (used by editors and by kings and queens) I. 3 *infml* you: *We're being naughty, aren't we?*

weak (wi:k) *adj* **-er, -est** 1 not strong. 2 watery: *weak orange juice.* 3 not up to a good or usual standard. 4 (of a verb) forming different parts by adding sounds and not changing a vowel. **weaken** *vti* make or become weak or weaker. **weakling** ('wi:klɪŋ) *nc* a weak person. **weakly** *adv* **weakness** 1 *nu* the quality of being weak. *nc* 2 a bad quality of a person, plan, machine, etc. 3 a liking or habit about which one feels slightly guilty: *I have a weakness for buying old books.*

weal (wi:l) *nc* a raised mark produced on the body by a blow with a stick, whip, etc.

wealth (welθ) *nu* 1 (much) money; riches. 2 the state of being rich. 3 a large quantity. **wealthy** *adj* **-ier, -iest** rich.

wean (wi:n) *vt* cause (a child or young animal) to start taking food and drink other than its mother's milk.

weapon ('wepən) *nc* 1 a device or instrument, such as a knife, a gun, or an animal's horn, used to cause harm to people or things. 2 an idea, plan, etc., used to bring victory in a quarrel, argument, etc.

wear (weə*) *vt* 1 be dressed in (clothes, etc.). 2 have on or as part of one's person: *She wears her hair long; wearing a smile.* 3 *vti* (often followed by **away**) rub or be rubbed (away): *The rocks have been worn away by the weather.* 4 *vi* last; resist being worn away or out: *Good clothes wear well.* ●*nu* 1 the state of wearing or being worn away. 2 clothes: *formal wear.* 3 ability to resist being worn out: *There's still a lot of wear in my old coat.* **wear away** remove or be removed by rubbing. **wear down** 1 remove or be removed by rubbing. 2 overcome by continued effort. **wear off** 1 rub or be rubbed away. 2 (of a feeling) gradually cease to exist: *The pain will soon wear off.* **wear out** 1 make or become useless through wear. 2 make very tired: *I'm worn out!*

weary ('wɪərɪ) *adj* **-ier, -iest** *vti* (make or become) tired. **wearily** *adv* **weariness** *nu* **wearisome** ('wɪərɪsəm) *adj* tiring or annoying.

weasel ('wi:zəl) *nc* a small, fast, fierce, furry animal: see picture.

weather ('weðə*) *nu* natural conditions; the state or presence or absence of sun, rain, temperature, cloud, dampness of the air, etc. ●*vti* 1 (cause to) change colour, etc., or wear away through the action of the weather. 2 *vt* come safely through (a storm or other difficulty). **weather-beaten** ('weðə,bi:tən) *adj* (esp. of a person, face, etc.) much affected by the action of the weather. **weathercock** ('weðəkɒk) *nc* a moving pointer, esp. in the shape of a cock, that indicates wind direction. **weatherman** ('weðəmæn) *nc, pl* **-men** a man who finds out or announces what weather to expect.

weasel

weave (wi:v) *vt* 1 make (cloth, a basket, etc.) by repeatedly crossing (threads, sticks, etc.) over and under each other. 2 make (something) by combining (things): *He wove all his experiences into a book.* 3 *vti* make (one's way, etc.) by moving forward and from side to side: *The procession weaved its way through the town.* ●*nc* a style of weaving. **weaver** *nc* **weaving** 1 *nu* the occupation of weaving. 2 *ncu* (an example of) something being or having been woven. **get weaving** *infml* act quickly.

web (web) 1 *nu* cloth which is being woven. *nc* 2 also **spider's web** a net made by a spider to catch flies, etc., to eat. 3 skin between toes, as on a duck. 4 a complicated arrangement, esp. of something bad: *a web of corruption.* ●*vt* cover with a web.

wed (wed) 1 *vti* marry. 2 *vt* join closely.

we'd (wi:d) we had or we would.

wedding ('wedɪŋ) *nc* the occasion of a marriage: *I'm going to their wedding next week.*

wedge (wedʒ) *nc* a piece of wood, metal, etc., shaped like a triangle that gets narrower towards one sharp edge, used for splitting wood, for putting under a door to keep it open, etc. ●*vt* 1 fasten with a wedge. 2 push into a small or tight space.

wedlock ('wedlɒk) *chiefly formal nu* the state of being married.

Wednesday ('wenzdɪ) *nc* the fourth day of the week, after Tuesday and before Thursday.

wee (wi:) *adj* very small: *a wee bit.* ●*vi* *infml, children* pass urine.

weed (wi:d) *nc* 1 a wild plant, esp. an unwanted one in a garden, etc. 2 *infml* a weak person. ●*vti* remove weeds from (ground). **weedy** *adj* **-ier, -iest.**

week (wi:k) *nc* a period of seven days, esp. beginning with Sunday. **weekday** ('wi:kdeı) *nc* any day of the week other than Sunday and sometimes Saturday. **weekend** (ˌwiːkˈend) *nc* a period from about Friday evening to Sunday evening. **weekly** *adj, adv* (happening, produced, etc.) once a week. ● *nc, pl* **-lies** a weekly newspaper, magazine, etc.

weep (wiːp) *vti* **1** produce (tears); cry. **2** (of cheese, a wound, etc.) produce (drops of liquid). ● *nc* a period of weeping. **weeping** *adj* (of a tree) having branches curving downwards.

weevil (ˈwiːvɪl) *nc* a small insect that eats plants including many of man's foods.

weft (weft) *nu* the threads fed across and in between others in weaving cloth.

weigh (weı) *vt* **1** measure the weight of. **2** (often followed by **up**) consider carefully: *to weigh up the advantages and disadvantages.* **3** *vti* have a certain weight: *He weighs seventy kilos; You weigh more than me.* **weigh down** press down with a heavy weight. **weighing-machine** (ˈweıŋməˈʃiːn) *nc* a device for weighing with. **weigh on** trouble; worry: *a problem that is weighing on my mind.* **weigh out** take (one or more weighed quantities) from a larger one of (something): *I'll weigh out a kilo for everyone.*

weight (weıt) *nc* **1** the amount that something weighs. **2** an object, esp. of metal, made to weigh a certain amount, such as a kilogram. **3** an object used to hold something down. *nu* **4** the force produced by the action of gravity on an object. **5** importance; influence: *That argument carries a lot of weight.* ● *vt* **1** add weight to. **2** take account of something when considering: *Your pay is weighted to allow for your living in London.* **put on weight** become heavier or fatter. **weightless** *adj* weighing nothing, as in space. **weightlessness** *nu* **weightlifting** (ˈweıtˌlıftıŋ) *nu* the sport of lifting weighted metal bars. **weighty** *adj* **-ier, -iest 1** heavy. **2** important; considerable.

weir (wıə*) *nc* a wall built across a river to raise the water level, control the flow, etc.: see picture.

weir

weird (wıəd) *adj* **-er, -est** strange or odd, esp. in a frightening way.

welcome (ˈwelkəm) *vt* show one's pleasure at receiving (someone). ● *adj* **1** received

with pleasure. **2** free; invited: *Anyone is welcome to call.* ● *interj* (used to welcome someone.) ● *nc* the act of welcoming. **you're welcome!** (used to accept someone's thanks) not at all!; don't mention it!

weld (weld) *vti* (of metal or plastic) (cause to) join by pressing pieces together while they are softened by heat. **welder** *nc*

welfare (ˈwelfeə*) *nu* **1** the state of having good health, education, etc., and the means to live comfortably. **2** *US* government money paid to people in need. **welfare state** a system in which the government is responsible for the welfare of the people.

well¹ (wel) *adv* **better, best 1** in a good way: *a job well done.* **2** thoroughly; considerably: *well over a hundred.* **3** certainly; indeed: *He could well be right.* ● *interj* (used esp. at the start of a sentence, to show surprise, agreement, expectation, etc.) ● *adj* **better, best 1** healthy. **2** in good order: *All's well.* **as well (as)** in addition (to); besides. **do well 1** get a good result. **2** be right (to do something). **well done!** (used to congratulate someone on a good result.) **well-being** (ˌwelˈbiːıŋ) *nu* a general state of health and happiness. **well-known** (ˌwelˈnəʊn) *adj* famous; known by most people. **well-nigh** (ˈwelnaı) *adv* almost. **well off** rich or having some other advantage. **well to do** rich.

well² *nc* a hole in the ground for obtaining water, oil, etc. ● *vi* (often followed by **up**) flow up and out.

we'll (wiːl) we shall or we will.

wench (wentʃ) *archaic or humorous nc* a girl or young woman.

wend (wend) *vti* make (one's way).

went (went) past tense of **go**.

wept (wept) past tense and past participle of **weep**.

were (wɜː* unstressed wə*) *v* past tense of **be**.

we're (wıə*) we are.

weren't (wɜːnt) *v* were not.

wert (wɜːt unstressed wət) *archaic v* (used with **thou**) past tense of **be**.

west (west) *n* **the west** the direction in which the sun sets. **the West 1** the western part of the world, esp. Europe and North America. **2** the western part of the United States, esp. at the time when it was being colonised. ● *adj* **1** in or towards the west. **2** (of the wind) coming from the west. ● *adv* towards the west. **westerly** (ˈwestəlı) *adj* in or from the west. **western** (ˈwestən) *adj* in or to the west. ● *nc* a book or film about **the West** (def. 2). **westerner** (ˈwestənə*) *nc* a person from the west of somewhere, esp. from **the West** (def. 1). **westward(s)** (ˈwestwəd(z)) *adj, adv* towards the west.

wet (wet) *adj* **-ter, -test 1** full of or covered with water or some other liquid. **2** (of weather, etc.) rainy. **3** (of paint, ink, etc.) not yet dry. **4** *infml. Brit* weak or stupid. ●*vt* make wet. ●*nu* **1** wetness; dampness. **2** *infml. Brit nc* a weak or stupid person. **3** *nu* rainy weather.

we've (wiːv) we have.

whack (wæk) *infml vt* **1** hit sharply. **2** *Brit* tire out. ●*nc* **1** a sharp blow. **2** *infml* a try: *Have a whack!* **3** *infml* a share of a task: *Do your whack.*

whale (weɪl) *nc, pl* **whales, whale** any of several very large sea animals, such as the blue whale (see picture), that are not fish

wheat

blue whale

but mammals. **whaler** *nc* a ship used for whaling. **whaling** *nu* the hunting and killing of whales.

wharf (wɔːf) *nc, pl* **-ves** (vz) **-s** a platform at which ships load and unload goods.

what (wɒt) *determiner, pron* **1** (used to ask for something, esp. something selected from all others of its kind): *What (book) are you reading?* **2** the (people, thing(s), etc.) that: *What audience we had was interested; Let's see what you have done.* ●*determiner* (showing surprise at the quality of something): *What a good boy!* **so what?** *infml* what importance, use, or meaning does that have? **what about?** See under **about**. **what... for?** (used to ask the reason for or purpose of something): *What is that device used for?*

whatever (wɒt'evə*) (*literary abbrev.* **whate'er** (wɒt'eə*)) *determiner, pron* **1** the or any (people, things, etc.) at all that: *You can keep whatever you find.* **2** no matter what: *He'll go, whatever the weather.* **3** also **what ever** (used to add force to one's words) just what exactly?: *Whatever have you done?* ●*adj* also **whatsoever** at all: *This has nothing whatever to do with us.* ●*pron infml* something else: *Fetch your money or cheque book or whatever.*

what'll ('wɒtəl) what will or what shall?

what's (wɒts) what is or what has?

wheat (wiːt) *nu* **1** a grass grown for its seeds, which are made into flour: see picture. **2** these seeds.

wheedle ('wiːdəl) *vt* **1** (try to) persuade (someone) by being very polite or friendly: *I was wheedled into paying.* **2** obtain by wheedling: *They wheedled the secret out of him.*

wheel (wiːl) *nc* **1** a flat, round object or frame able to spin around its fixed centre and used as part of a machine, for a vehicle to run on, etc. **2** short for **steering-wheel**. **3** an act of wheeling (**wheel** def. 2). ●*vti* **1** (cause to) move on wheels. *vi* **2** (of a line of marching soldiers, etc.) turn as if fixed to a point. **3** move in circles or curves: *The birds wheeled in the air.* **wheelbarrow** ('wiːl-ˌbærəʊ) *nc* a one-wheeled hand vehicle used in building, gardening, etc. **wheelchair** ('wiːltʃeə*) *nc* a chair on wheels used by a person who cannot walk.

wheeze (wiːz) *vti* breathe or speak with a whistling sound. ●*nu* **1** whistling breathing. **2** *slang, Brit nc* a plan, esp. for a trick or joke. **wheezy** *adj* **-ier, -iest.**

when (wen) *adv* **1** at what time?: *When did this happen?* **2** at or on which (time): *There was a time when I enjoyed this.* ●*conj* **1** at the or any time at which: *I'll write when I can.* **2** if; since: *Why did you say it, when you knew it was wrong?* **3** although: *He said it, when he knew it was wrong.* ●*pron* which time: *By when will he come?*

whence (wens) *archaic or formal adv, conj* from where (?): *Whence did it come?*

whenever (wen'evə*) (*literary abbrev.* **whene'er** (wen'eə*)) *conj* every time; no matter when: *Whenever she writes, she has bad news.* ●*adv* **1** also **when ever** (used to add force) just when exactly?: *Whenever did that fall over?* **2** *infml* at some other time: *Come on Sunday or whenever.*

when's (wenz) when is or when has?

where (weə*) *adv* in or to what place?: *Where are you going?* ●*conj* in or to the place in which: *I like living where I do.* ●*pron* **1** in or to which (place): *the place where we live.* **2** which place?: *Where do you come from?* **whereabouts** ('weər-əbaʊts) *adv* (roughly) where. ●*nu* position: *Do you know Brian's whereabouts?*

whereas (weər'æz) *conj* **1** but (on the other hand): *I drive, whereas he goes by train.* **2** *formal or law* since; because.

whereat (weər'æt) *archaic adv* where? ● *pron* at which (time or place).

whereby (weə'baɪ) *pron* by which (means). ● *adv archaic* how?

where'er (weər'eə*) *literary conj, pron, adv* short for **wherever**.

wherefore ('weəfɔ:*) *archaic or formal conj* for which reason. ● *adv archaic* why? ● *n* **whys and wherefores** reasons.

wherein (weər'ɪn) *archaic or formal pron* in which (place or respect). ● *adv* in what place or respect?

whereof (weər'ɒv) *archaic or formal pron* of which (thing) or of whom. ● *adv* of what or of whom?

whereon (weər'ɒn) *archaic pron* on which (thing). ● *adv* on what?

where's (weəz) where is or where has?

whereupon (,weərə'pɒn) *conj* at which; as a result of which: *I refused to go, whereupon he went alone.*

wherever (weər'evə*) (*literary abbrev.* **where'er**) *conj* in or to every place; no matter where: *Wherever you look there are people.* ● *pron* every place in or to which: *Wherever we go is crowded.* ● *adv* **1** also **where ever** (used to add force) just where exactly?: *Wherever did you get that hat?* **2** *infml* in or to some other place.

wherewith (weə'wɪð) *archaic or formal pron* with which. ● *conj* after or as a result of which. ● *adv* with what?

wherewithal ('weəwɪðɔ:l) *n* **the wherewithal** the necessary things: *the wherewithal for a long journey.* ● *pron archaic* with which.

whet (wet) *vt* **1** sharpen (a knife, etc.). **2** increase (an appetite or other feeling).

whether ('weðə*) *conj* if... (or not): *I don't know whether he did it; Have you decided whether to go or not?* **whether... or** (**whether**) if... or (if): *It will happen, whether the weather is wet or dry.*

which (wɪtʃ) *determiner, pron* **1** (used to ask for something, esp. selected from only some of its kind or from a group of which all are known): *Which (countries) have you visited?* **2** the one that: *Take which you want.* ● *pron* (used to stand for a noun other than a person in a relative clause): *She enjoyed herself, which made me glad; His books, about which I know nothing, sell very well.*

whichever (wɪtʃ'evə*) *determiner, pron* **1** any at all that: *I'll have whichever (one) I'm given.* **2** no matter which: *Whichever it is, I don't want it.* **3** also **which ever** (used to add force) just which exactly?: *Whichever did you choose?*

whiff (wɪf) *nc* a brief current of air, a smell, etc. ● *vti* **1** blow gently. **2** *vi slang, Brit* smell unpleasant.

while (waɪl) *conj* also **whilst** (waɪlst) **1** during (all) the time that: *While I'm away, take care of the plants and water them once.* **2** although: *While that's the normal method, I wouldn't use it.* **3** but (on the other hand): *I went home, while Jane stayed at work.* ● *prep* also **whilst** when; during: *I think a lot while walking.* ● *nu* a period of time: *a long while ago; all the while.* ● *v* **while away** pass (time), esp. pleasantly.

whim (wɪm) *nc* a sudden, esp. odd, idea.

whimsical ('wɪmzɪkəl) *adj* with or full of odd ideas.

whimper ('wɪmpə*) *vi* cry nervously, sadly, or in fear. ● *nu* the sound of whimpering.

whine (waɪn) *vti, nc* **1** (make) a long, high sound. **2** (make) an annoying complaint.

whinny ('wɪnɪ) *nc, pl* **-nies** the soft noise made by a horse. ● *vi* (of a horse) make this noise.

whip (wɪp) *nc* **1** a rope, thin strip of leather, etc., on a handle, used for driving animals, hitting someone as a punishment, etc. **2** a blow with a whip. **3** a stiff, sweet food made from egg whites, cream, fruit, etc. **4** a member of a parliament who makes sure that members of his party vote when necessary. **5** a direction to a member of a parliament from his party whip to attend. ● *vt* **1** hit with a whip. **2** (followed by **on**, etc.) drive with a whip. **3** (followed by **off**, **out**, etc.) take or move quickly: *I whipped the gun off the table before he could pick it up.* **4** wind thin string round (the end of a rope, etc.) to hold it together. **5** beat (cream, egg white, etc.) to make stiff. **6** *infml vi* come or go quickly or for a short time: *I'll whip over and fetch it.* **whip up 1** excite (a feeling, crowd, etc.). **2** *infml* make or prepare (food, etc.) quickly.

whirl (wɜ:l) *vti* (cause to) spin or turn quickly. ● *nc* a whirling movement. **whirlpool** ('wɜ:lpu:l) *nc* a current of water going round and round. **whirlwind** ('wɜ:lwɪnd) *nc* a tall body of air blowing round quickly.

whisk (wɪsk) **1** *vti* move or carry with a fast, sweeping movement: *We whisked the visitors round the factory.* **2** *vt* beat (eggs, milk, etc.) to get air bubbles in. ● *nc* **1** an act of whisking. **2** a tool for whisking food. **3** a short brush or soft whip: *a fly whisk.*

whisker ('wɪskə*) *nc* **1** a stiff, straight hair, used for feeling, that grows on the face of an animal such as a cat. **2** a hair growing on a man's face.

whisky ('wɪskɪ) *ncu, pl* **-kies** (a type of) strong, alcoholic drink made, esp. in Scotland, from corn.

whisper ('wɪspə*) *vti* **1** speak very quietly; speak without using the full voice. **2** spread (a rumour or secret) to a stated degree: *The* *fight they had has been whispered every-where.* **3** *vi* (esp. of leaves) make a soft rustling sound. ● *nc* **1** whispered speech. **2** something whispered.

whist (wɪst) *nu* a card game played by two pairs of players.

whistle ('wɪsəl) **1** *vi* make a sharp clear sound, as by blowing through a small hole between the lips. **2** *vt* make (a tune, etc.) by whistling. ● *nc* **1** a device or musical instrument that whistles. **2** a sound or a period of whistling.

white (waɪt) *adj* **-r, -st 1** having the colour of snow, milk, etc. **2** (of a person) of a race with pale (pinkish) skin. **3** (of coffee) with milk. **4** (of glass, plastic, etc.) colourless; clear. ● *ncu* **1** a white colour. *nc* **2** a white person. **3** the white part of an egg. **4** the white part of the eyeball. **white-collar** (ˌwaɪt'kɒlə*) *adj* doing an office or desk job. **white elephant** See under **elephant**. **White House** the home, in Washington, of the President of the USA. **whiteness** *nu* **whitewash** ('waɪtwɒʃ) **1** *nu* a mixture of water and a substance such as lime, used for making walls white. **2** *nc* an attempt to disguise wrongs, mistakes, etc. ● *vt* **1** cover with whitewash. **2** disguise wrongs, etc. **whitish** *adj*

whither ('wɪðə*) *archaic or literary adv* to what place? ● *conj* **1** to which (place). **2** to whatever place: *Go whither I show you.*

whittle ('wɪtəl) *vt* shape or cut down (a stick, etc.) by shaving off small pieces. **whittle down** lessen or get rid of bit by bit.

whiz also **whizz** (wɪz) *infml vti, nc* ((cause to) move with) great speed together with the sound of something moving fast through the air.

who (huː unstressed hʊ) *pron* **1** what or which person(s)? **2** (used to stand for a person in a relative clause): *The man who was here is my brother.* **3** the person(s) who: *Talk to who you like.*

who'd (huːd) who had or who would.

whoever (huː'evə*) *pron* **1** the or any person(s) who: *Whoever did this must be caught.* **2** no matter who: *It is wrong, whoever did it.* **3** also **who ever** (used to add force) just who exactly?: *Whoever can that be?* **4** *infml* someone else.

whole (həʊl) *adj* **1** complete; with nothing missing or removed: *I was there a whole week; whole flour is good for you.* **2** (of a number) containing no fraction: *You can buy only a whole number of eggs.* ● *ncu* (an example of) something whole. **on the whole** all things considered. **wholehearted** (ˌhəʊl'hɑːtɪd) *adj* enthusiastic or sincere. **whole-heartedly** *adv* **wholly** ('həʊlɪ) *adv*

wholesale ('həʊlseɪl) *nu* the business of buying goods from their makers and selling them to shopkeepers. ● *adj, adv* in large quantities. ● *vt* sell wholesale. **wholesaler** *nc*

wholesome ('həʊlsəm) *adj* good for the development of health or a good character: *wholesome food; wholesome entertainment.*

who'll (huːl) who will or who shall.

whom (huːm) *pron* (used instead of **who** when it is an object in its own clause): *Whom did you see?; Did he say whom he gave it to?*

whoop (huːp) *vi, nc* (give) a shout of excitement, etc. **whooping cough** a disease that is caught from someone else and makes one cough and then breathe in noisily.

whore (hɔː*) *esp. derogatory n* See **prostitute**. ● *vi* **1** be a prostitute. **2** have sexual intercourse with a prostitute.

who're (huːə*) who are.

whorl (wɜːl) *nc* a ring of leaves, petals, etc., on a plant.

who's (huːz) who is or who has.

whose (huːz) *determiner, pron* **1** of or belonging to whom?: *Whose is this?* **2** of or belonging to whom or which: *the cupboard whose doors are missing.*

why (waɪ) *adv* for what reason?: *Why have you come here?* ● *pron* for which: *the reason why you did that.* ● *interj* (used to express surprise, etc.): *Why, that's a good idea!* ● *n* **whys and wherefores** See under **wherefore**.

wick (wɪk) *nc* a kind of loose string used in a candle or cigarette lighter, etc., to bring wax or oil to the flame.

wicked ('wɪkɪd) *adj* **1** evil or harmful. **2** *often humorous* (of a person) naughty. **wickedly** *adv* **wickedness** *nu*

wicker ('wɪkə*) *nu* bendy twigs from a tree, esp. the willow, repeatedly crossed over each other to make baskets, chair seats, etc.

wicket ('wɪkɪt) *nc* **1** (in the game of cricket) a set of three upright sticks in the ground, with two small ones across the top which it is the aim of the bowler to knock over. **2** a small gate or door, esp. next to or within a larger one.

wide (waɪd) *adj* **-r, -st 1** measuring a larger amount than usual from side to side: *a wide road.* **2** (used after a noun) measuring... from side to side: *a road five metres wide.* **3** reaching far; including much: *a wide public.* **4** (of eyes, mouth, etc.) fully open. **5** far from the target: *Your shot was very wide.* ● *adv* **1** fully: *wide awake.* **2** over a great distance: *I searched far and wide.* **3** far from the target: *Your shot went wide.* **wide-eyed** (ˌwaɪd'aɪd) *adj* very surprised. **widely** *adv* **1** far apart. **2** to a great extent.

widen *vti* make or become wide or wider.

widespread ('waɪdspred) *adj* widely occurring, held, etc.

widow ('wɪdəʊ) *nc* a woman whose husband has died and who has not remarried. ●*vt* make (someone) a widow or widower. **widower** *nc* a man whose wife has died and who has not remarried.

width (wɪdθ) *nc* **1** the distance from one side of something to the other. **2** *nu* the state of being wide.

wield (wiːld) *vt* hold or use (power, a weapon, etc.).

wife (waɪf) *nc, pl* **-ves** (vz) a woman to whom a man is married.

wig (wɪg) *nc* a mat of false hair to cover the head.

wiggle ('wɪgəl) *vti* (cause to) move repeatedly from side to side. ●*nc* an act of wiggling, a place where something wiggles, etc.

wigwam ('wɪgwæm) *nc* a North American Indian's house made of animal skins stretched round sticks: see picture.

wigwam

wild (waɪld) *adj* **-er, -est 1** (of plants or animals) living in a natural state; not grown or kept on a farm, etc. **2** uncontrolled; disorderly: *wild behaviour.* **3** violent: *a wild storm.* **4** very excited or disturbed: *wild enthusiasm.* **5** (of country) deserted-looking; uninviting. ●*nc* wild country. ●*adv* wildly: *He was shooting wild.* **wildcat** ('waɪldkæt) *nc, pl* **wildcat, wildcats** a middle-sized European animal of the cat family. **wildfire** ('waɪldfaɪə*) *n* **like wildfire** very quickly. **wildlife** ('waɪldlaɪf) *nu* wild animals. **wildly** *adv*

wilderness ('wɪldənɪs) *nc* a deserted, unused piece of land.

wile (waɪl) *nc (usually pl)* a trick; deceit.

wilful ('wɪlfʊl) *adj* **1** intentional: *wilful damage.* **2** determined to do as one likes.

will¹ (wɪl unstressed əl) *v* **1** (used to form the future tense, expressing determination when used with **I** or **we**): *He will be there; I will go, whatever happens.* **2** (used to ask someone to do something): *Will you do this for me?* **3** (used to express ability): *Will the engine start?* **4** (used to give an order): *You will do as you're told.* **5** (used to express expectation): *The letter will be for me.* **6** (used

to express what is usual): *The weather will stay like this for weeks at a time.* **7** (used to express what is bound to happen): *Things will go wrong at the last minute.*

will² *nc* **1** a written list of who one wants one's possessions to be given to when one dies. **2** something decided on; an intention. **3** *nu* the mental ability to want, choose, or do something. ●*vt* **1** want or intend: *I willed it to happen and it did!* **2** leave (someone something) in one's will: *He willed everything to his wife.* **at will** when one chooses. **willpower** ('wɪl‚paʊə*) *nu* strength of the mind, esp. to make one's body do something difficult.

willing ('wɪlɪŋ) *adj* glad or ready (to do something). **willingly** *adv* **willingness** *nu*

willow ('wɪləʊ) *nc* a tree with long, thin, bendy branches that grows esp. near water: see picture at **trees**; *(*also *nu)* the elastic wood of this tree.

wilt¹ (wɪlt) *vti* (of a plant, leaf, etc.), (cause to) become soft and hang down.

wilt² *archaic v* (used with **thou**) a form of **will¹**.

wily ('waɪlɪ) *adj* **-ier, -iest** clever; full of trickery or deceit.

win (wɪn) **1** *vti* come first, defeat one's enemy, etc., in (a race, war, etc.). *vt* **2** obtain (a prize, etc.) as a result of winning (a race, war, etc.). **3** *formal* get or reach, esp. with an effort. **4** (often followed by **over**) persuade (someone) to agree with one. ●*nc* an instance of winning. **win the day** win a battle, argument, etc.

wince (wɪns) *vi* make a sudden quick movement from pain, horror, etc. ●*nc* an act of wincing.

winch (wɪntʃ) *nc* a device for winding in a rope or cable. ●*vt* pull with a winch.

wind¹ (wɪnd) **1** *ncu* a current of air. **2** *nc* a force: *the wind of change.* *nu* **3** a report, indication: *He got wind of our plans.* **4** breath needed in exercise, singing, etc.: *short of wind.* **5** the state of having too much air in the stomach or bowels. **6** *infml* empty talk: *Don't believe his promises, they're just wind.* **7** the part of an orchestra, band, etc., playing instruments that are blown into to produce music. ●*vt* cause (someone) to have difficulty breathing, esp. by hitting just below the ribs. **windbreak** ('wɪndbreɪk) *nc* fence, row of trees, etc., that protects from the wind. **windfall** ('wɪndfɔːl) *nc* **1** an apple etc., blown early from the tree. **2** money received unexpectedly. **windmill** ('wɪndmɪl) *nc* a machine for making corn into flour pumping water, etc., worked by sails or blades blown round by the wind: see picture. **windpipe** ('wɪndpaɪp) *n* See **trachea**. **windscreen** ('wɪndskriːn) *US* **windshield**

windmill

('wɪndʃiːld) *nc* the front window of a motor vehicle. **windscreen wiper** (often shortened to **wiper**) a mechanical arm with a rubber strip to wipe water off a windscreen. **windswept** ('wɪndswept) *adj* (of a place, person's hair, etc.) blown by strong winds. **windy** *adj* **-ier, -iest.**

wind² (waɪnd) **1** *vti* turn or lead (a string, wire, etc.) round (something): *a cloth wound round the head; Wind him in a blanket.* *vi* **2** (of a string, wire, etc.) be turned or led round something. **3** (of a path, river, etc.) curve from side to side. *vt* **4** (often followed by **up**) tighten (the spring) or raise (the weights) of (a clock, watch, etc.). **5** move (a window, etc.) by turning or twisting (a handle). **wind up 1** wind (a clock, watch, etc.). **2** finish; bring or come to an end: *The company was making no profit and was wound up; We wound up going after all.* **3** *infml* make angry or anxious.

windlass ('wɪndləs) *nc* a device for winding in a rope or cable.

window ('wɪndəʊ) *nc* a frame containing glass, set in the wall of a building. **windowpane** ('wɪndəʊpeɪn) *nc* a single piece of glass in a window. **window-sill** ('wɪndəʊsɪl) *nc* a shelf at the bottom of a window.

wine (waɪn) *ncu* (a type of) alcoholic drink made from grape juice or another fruit, flower, or vegetable. **wineglass** ('waɪnglɑːs) *nc* a glass for drinking wine from, esp. with a rounded bowl on top of a thin stem.

wing (wɪŋ) *nc* **1** a thin, flat part on the side of a bird or aircraft, used for flying. **2** *US* **fender** a part of a car covering a wheel. **3** a side part of a building: *the north wing of the palace.* **4** *(often pl)* the space on either side of the stage in a theatre. **5** (in a game such as football) (a player who uses) the side of the field. **6** a part of a political party, esp. with more extreme views than the rest of that party. ● *vti* **1** (cause to) fly or move fast. **2** *vt* wound slightly.

wink (wɪŋk) *vi* **1** close and open one eye quickly, esp. as a sign of amusement or to be friendly. **2** (of a light) flash quickly. ● *nc* an act of winking.

winner ('wɪnə*) *nc* **1** a person or thing that wins. **2** *infml* a successful person or thing.

winnings ('wɪnɪŋz) *n pl* something won, esp. money.

winsome ('wɪnsəm) *adj* (of a person, smile, etc.) attractive.

winter ('wɪntə*) *nc* the season between autumn and spring; the coldest season, in which plants that have lost their leaves stay bare and snow may fall. ● *vi* spend the winter (in a particular place). **winter sports** sports done on snow or ice, such as skiing and skating. **wintertime** ('wɪntətaɪm) *nu* the winter season. **wintry** ('wɪntrɪ) *adj* **-ier, -iest.**

wipe (waɪp) *vt* **1** rub (a cloth, hand, etc.) across (a surface). **2** clean (dirt, water, etc.) off (something) by wiping. ● *nc* an act of wiping. **wipe off** remove or cancel (a debt, etc.). **wipe out 1** destroy or kill. **2** clean by wiping. **wiper** *nc* **1** something or someone that wipes. **2** short for **windscreen wiper. wipe up** dry (plates, etc., that have been washed up) by wiping with a cloth.

wire (waɪə*) **1** *ncu* (a length of) thread-like bendy metal, used esp. to carry electricity or electric signals. **2** *infml, chiefly US nc* a telegram. ● *vt* **1** fasten, provide, etc., with wire. **2** put in wires to make an electric circuit. **3** *infml, chiefly US* send a telegram, message, etc. to (someone). **wiring** *nu* wires used in or for electric devices.

wireless ('waɪəlɪs) *chiefly Brit, old-fashioned n* See **radio.**

wisdom ('wɪzdəm) *nu* great knowledge, experience, and good sense. **wisdom tooth** any of the four teeth, at the back of each side of each jaw, that are the last to grow.

wise¹ (waɪz) *adj* **-r, -st 1** showing wisdom and good judgement. **2** (followed by **to**) *infml* understanding the ways, esp. tricks, of: *I'm wise to you, son.* **wisely** *adv*

wise² *archaic nc* a way; manner: *I am in no wise unhappy.*

wish (wɪʃ) **1** *vti* (when *vi*, often followed by **for**) want and hope (for): *I wish he would go away; I couldn't wish for better weather; Wish us luck!* **2** *vt* want (something that one can expect to bring about): *I wish to see the manager.* ● *nc* **1** an act of wishing. **2** something wished for. **wishful** ('wɪʃfʊl) *adj* having a wish or wishes. **wishful thinking** believing something unlikely because one wants it to be true.

wisp (wɪsp) *nc* a thin, delicate piece of something such as cloud or hair.

wistful ('wɪstfʊl) *adj* sadly thoughtful or wanting something. **wistfully** *adv*

wit (wɪt) **1** *nu* (the ability to make) amusing, unexpected connections between ideas and expressions. *nc* **2** a person with **wit** (def. 1). **3** *(also pl)* intelligence, understanding, and ability to act quickly.

witch (wɪtʃ) *nc* **1** a person, esp. a woman, practising magic or serving the devil. **2** an attractive, esp. dangerous, woman. **witchcraft** (ˈwɪtʃkrɑːft) *nu* the practices of a **witch** (def. **1**).

with (wɪð) *prep* **1** in the company of: *I went abroad with friends.* **2** using: *Hit it with the hammer.* **3** because of: *eyes wet with tears.* **4** having: *a house with two chimneys.* **5** (used after a verb to indicate that the action is also being done by the following noun): *I agree with you; They discussed it with the others.* **6** following or understanding what someone says or writes: *I'm not with you.* **7** supporting or agreeing with: *If you're not with us, you're against us.*

withdraw (wɪðˈdrɔː) **1** *vti* take or move back or away. **2** *vt* take (a sum of money) from a bank account. **withdrawal** *nc* **1** an act of withdrawing, esp. by an army, etc. **2** the period of pain, etc. after one stops taking a habit-forming drug. **3** an amount of money withdrawn.

withdrawn (wɪðˈdrɔːn) past participle of **withdraw.** ● *adj* unwilling to meet or talk to others; thoughtful.

withdrew (wɪðˈdruː) past tense of **withdraw.**

wither (ˈwɪðə*) *vti* (of a flower, etc.), (cause to) dry up.

withheld (wɪðˈheld) past tense and past participle of **withhold.**

withhold (wɪðˈhəʊld) **1** *vt* keep back; prevent someone from having. **2** *vi* (followed by **from**) keep from (doing something).

within (wɪˈðɪn) *prep* **1** inside: *within the castle walls.* **2** before the end of: *Come back within a year.* **3** no more than: *within fifty kilometres.* ● *adv archaic* inside.

without (wɪˈðaʊt) *prep* not having, with, or using: *completely without money; I can't see it without moving.* ● *prep, adv archaic* outside.

withstand (wɪðˈstænd) *vt* resist; fight off; put up with.

withstood (wɪðˈstʊd) past tense and past participle of **withstand.**

witness (ˈwɪtnɪs) *nc* **1** a person who sees or hears an event, etc. **2** a person who says what he knows in a court of law. **3** an account of an event. **4** proof. **5** a person present at the signing of a legal document. ● *vt* **1** see or hear (an event, etc.). **2** be present when a legal document is signed. **3** show: *The blood on his clothes witnesses his guilt.*

witty (ˈwɪtɪ) *adj* **-ier, -iest** showing **wit** (def. **1**).

wives (waɪvz) plural of **wife.**

wizard (ˈwɪzəd) *nc* **1** a male witch. **2** a person very clever at something. ● *adj old-fashioned, infml* wonderful: *a wizard idea.*

wizened (ˈwɪzənd) *adj* (esp. of a person or face) looking dried up through age.

wobble (ˈwɒbəl) *vti* (cause to) move or shake unsteadily. ● *nc* an act of wobbling.

woe (wəʊ) **1** *nc (often pl)* a piece of bad luck; trouble: *Tell me all your woes.* **2** *chiefly archaic or literary nu* great grief. **woeful** *adj* causing or showing grief. **woefully** *adv*

woke (wəʊk) past tense of **wake.**

woken (ˈwəʊkən) past participle of **wake.**

wolf (wʊlf) *nc, pl* **-ves** (vz) a wild hunting animal of the dog family: see picture at **animals.** ● *vt* eat greedily. **cry wolf** raise a false alarm.

woman (ˈwʊmən) *nc, pl* **women** (ˈwɪmɪn) a grown-up female human. **womanhood** *nu* the condition of being a woman. **womanly** *adj*

womb (wuːm) *n* See **uterus.**

won (wʌn) past tense and past participle of **win.**

wonder (ˈwʌndə*) *ncu* (something that causes) a mixture of surprise, curiosity, and sometimes admiration. ● *vti* **1** (when *vi* often followed by **about**) be curious about; wish that one knew (about). **2** *vi* (usually followed by **at**) feel wonder. **wonderful** *adj* very good; splendid. **wonderfully** *adv* **wondrous** (ˈwʌndrəs) *archaic or literary adj* causing wonder.

wont (wəʊnt) *chiefly archaic adj* used; likely *He is wont to complain.* ● *nu* habit.

won't (wəʊnt) *v* will not.

woo (wuː) *vt* **1** *formal or old-fashioned* try to win the love of (a woman). **2** try to obtain (fame, etc.).

wood (wʊd) **1** *nu* the hard material in the trunks and branches of trees. **2** *nc* a large group of trees. **the wood** a barrel: *beer from the wood, not a bottle.* **woodcraft** (ˈwʊdkrɑːft) *nu* knowledge of woods and the ability to live in them. **woodcutter** (ˈwʊd,kʌtə*) *nc* a man who cuts down trees or cuts wood. **wooded** *adj* (of land) covered with trees. **wooden** (ˈwʊdən) *adj* made of wood. **2** (of a person or his behaviour) stiff or expressionless. **woodland** (ˈwʊdlənd) *ncu* (an area of) wooded country. **woodpecker** (ˈwʊd,pekə*) *nc* a bird that digs with its beak into tree trunks for insects: see picture at **birds. woodsman** (ˈwʊdzmən) *nc, pl* **-men** a person who lives in woods or is good at woodcraft. **woodwind** (ˈwʊdwɪnd) *adj* (of a musical instrument, such as the flute) blown, but not brass. ● *nu (with plural verb)* woodwind instruments. **woodwork** (ˈwʊdwɜːk) *nu* making things from wood. **2** things made from wood. **woody** *adj* **-ier, -iest.**

woof (wʊf) *nc* the short sharp noise made by a dog. ● *vi* (of a dog) make this noise.

wool (wʊl) *ncu* (a type of) animal hair, usually from sheep, used to make warm clothes, etc. **woollen** *US* **woolen** ('wʊlən) *adj* made of wool. ●*nc (usually pl)* a woollen garment. **woolly** *adj* **-ier, -iest** 1 like wool. 2 unclear; mixed up: *a woolly argument.* ●*nc, pl* **-lies** a woollen garment, esp. a pullover or cardigan.

word (wɜːd) *nc* 1 a short piece of language written with a space either side: *'Word' and 'language' are words.* 2 *(often pl)* something spoken, esp. in anger, to tell someone off, etc.: *I had a word with him; words of warning. nu* 3 a promise: *I shall keep my word.* 4 news: *They sent word of the victory.* ●*vt* say or write in words: *a carefully worded answer.* **in a word** in short; using few words. **in other words** expressed differently. **take (someone) at his word** believe that (someone) means what he says. **word for word** 1 exactly as spoken or written: *The speech is printed word for word in the newspaper.* 2 with each word translated separately into another language: *a word-for-word translation.* **wording** *nu* 1 the way in which something is worded. 2 the writing on a sign, etc.

wore (wɔː*) past tense of **wear.**

work (wɜːk) *nu* 1 an effort of the body or mind put to a purpose. 2 employment; a job: *What work do you do?* 3 a task: *There's work to be done.* 4 *physics* movement brought about by a force. 5 *nc* something made by work, esp. a book, painting, piece of music, etc. ●*vti* 1 produce (something) by doing work: *I can't work wonders.* 2 make (one's way): *He worked through the crowd. vt* 3 cause (a machine) to do its job: *Can you work this kind of radio?* 4 make something (esp. from metal) by shaping. *vi* 5 (of a machine) do what it should: *The clock isn't working.* 6 do work: *Where do you work?* **at work** 1 in action; working. 2 at the place where one does one's job. **out of work** unemployed. **workable** *adj* able to be put into practice. **worked up** angry; annoyed. **worker** *nc* **workman** ('wɜːkmən) *nc, pl* **-men** a man who does his job with his hands. **workmanship** ('wɜːkmənʃɪp) *nu* the quality of the work done on something. **work of art** anything well or beautifully made. **work out** 1 find (an answer, figure, etc.) using numbers or by thought. 2 think up or invent (a plan, etc.). 3 happen (as planned or hoped): *Did everything work out (all right)?* **works** 1 *n pl* the moving parts of a machine. 2 *nu (with singular verb)* a factory or other place where something is made or processed: *a gas works.* **workshop** ('wɜːkʃɒp) *nc* a room or building used for building and repairing machines, etc. **work**

surface also **worktop** ('wɜːktɒp) a flat space for working on, esp. about one metre high against the wall of a kitchen. **work up** 1 (cause to) develop: *I've worked up quite a thirst.* 2 (cause to) become angry or excited. **work up to** move towards (an action): *You're working up to asking me to do you a favour.*

working ('wɜːkɪŋ) *nc (often pl)* 1 the way something works. 2 (a part of) a place where coal, etc., is dug out of the ground. ●*adj* 1 to do with work or workers. 2 useful: *a working knowledge.* **in working order** able to work (def. 5). **working class** people who work mainly with their hands for a living, together with their families. **working hours** periods during which most people work. **working party** a group of people who find out about and report on something.

world (wɜːld) *nu* 1 the earth and all the people on it. 2 all human society and its affairs, esp. seen as outside a small group, such as the family: *Children grow up and go out into the world. nc* 3 any planet, esp. one with life on it. 4 a part of the world or its people: *the Third World.* 5 a division of activity, culture, life, etc.: *the animal world; the world of music.* **on top of the world** very happy or excited. **world-famous** (,wɜːld'feɪməs) *adj* known in all parts of the world. **worldly** *adj* **-ier, -iest** of the world, esp. to do with pleasure in this life. **World War I** also **First World War, Great War** the war from 1914 to 1918 fought by Britain, France, Italy, Russia, and the United States against Germany, Austro-Hungary, and Turkey. **World War II** also **Second World War** the war from 1939 to 1945 fought by Britain, France, the Soviet Union, and the United States against Germany, Italy, and Japan. **worldwide** (,wɜːld'waɪd) *adj* to do with the whole world.

worm (wɜːm) *nc* a usually small, long, thin animal without legs that lives in the ground or in a larger animal. ●*vt* 1 make (one's way) by creeping, sliding, etc. 2 (followed by **out of**) get (information) from someone. 3 get worms out of (a dog, etc.).

worn (wɔːn) past participle of **wear.** ●*adj* damaged by wear.

worry ('wʌrɪ) 1 *vt* disturb or annoy: *I shan't worry you with the news now.* 2 *vti* (cause to) become anxious: *I'm worried about the future; a worrying time.* ●*ncu, pl* **-ries** (something that causes) anxiety.

worse (wɜːs) *adj, adv* more bad(ly). ●*nu* something worse. **the worse for wear** 1 worn. 2 *polite* drunk. **worse off** in a worse state, esp. with less money. **worsen** ('wɜːsən) *vti* make or become worse.

worship (ˈwɜːʃɪp) *vt* **1** have or show great respect for (a god, etc.). **2** admire or love greatly. ●*ncu* (an act of) worshipping. **worshipper** *nc*

worst (wɜːst) *adj, adv* the most bad(ly). **the worst** the worst person or thing. ●*vt* old-fashioned defeat (someone).

worsted (ˈwʊstɪd) *ncu* (a type of) woollen cloth.

worth (wɜːθ) *adj* **1** deserving: *It's not worth the trouble.* **2** having the value of: *a hat worth £10.* **3** (of a person, company, etc.) owning money or property of a certain value: *They're worth millions.* ●*nu* **1** value. **2** an amount of a particular value: *twenty dollars' worth of food.* **worthless** (ˈwɜːθlɪs) *adj* **1** having no value. **2** (of a person) not having a good character. **worthwhile** (ˌwɜːθ-ˈwaɪl) *adj* worth the effort, time, money, etc., needed.

worthy (ˈwɜːðɪ) *adj* **-ier, -iest 1** deserving: *worthy of praise.* **2** of greath worth: *a worthy way to spend one's time.* ●*nc* an important person, esp. in one time or place.

would (wʊd *unstressed* wəd, əd) *v* **1** (used in reported speech in place of **shall** (def. 2) or **will**[1] (def. 1)): *He said he would go.* **2** past tense of **will**[1] (defs. 3, 5, 6, 7). **3** (used to form a conditional verb): *Would you go if you had time?* **4** (used to ask someone politely to do something): *Would you help me, please?* **5** *formal or literary* used to: *I would visit her often.* **6** *formal* if only: *Would that you had been there!* **would-be** (ˈwʊdbiː) *adj* wanting, claiming, or intended to be: *a would-be leader of his people.*

wouldn't (ˈwʊdənt) *v* would not.

wound[1] (wuːnd) *nc* **1** an injury to the body caused by a knife, bullet, etc. **2** an injury to the feelings. ●*vt* cause a wound to.

wound[2] (waʊnd) past tense and past participle of **wind**[2].

wove (wəʊv) past tense of **weave**.

woven (ˈwəʊvən) past participle of **weave**.

wrangle (ˈræŋgəl) *vi, nc* (have) a loud or angry argument.

wrap (ræp) *vt* **1** (often followed by **up**) cover (something) by winding paper, cloth, etc., round it: *a parcel wrapped in brown paper.* **2** wind (paper, cloth, etc.) round something: *with a blanket wrapped round him.* ●*nc* chiefly US a garment wrapped around the shoulders and upper body. **wrapped up in 1** occupied with; thinking only of. **2** connected with; in a close relationship with. **wrapper** chiefly US *nc* a sheet of something, esp. paper, wrapped round a book, sweet, etc. **wrapping** *nc* material used for wrapping.

wrath (rɒθ) chiefly archaic or literary *nu* anger. **wrathful** (ˈrɒθfʊl) *adj* angry.

wreath (riːθ) *nc, pl* **-ths** (ðz, θs) a ring of flowers or leaves used to show honour or respect, esp. for a dead person.

wreathe (riːð) often literary **1** *vti* (cause to) form a ring or wreath. **2** *vt* form a ring round: *Cloud wreathed the mountains.* **3** *vi* (of smoke, cloud, etc.) move in twists and curves.

wreck (rek) *vt* ruin or destroy (hopes, a ship, etc.). ●*nc* **1** something, esp. a ship, that has been wrecked. **2** someone who looks ill. **3** *nu* ruin; destruction. **wreckage** (ˈrekɪdʒ) *nu* **1** the remains of something wrecked. **2** wrecking or being wrecked.

wren (ren) *nc* a very small brown bird with a tail pointing upwards.

wrench (rentʃ) *vt, nc* (give (something) or remove (something) with) a violent twist or pull: *The gun was wrenched from his hand.* ●*nc* a tool for turning nuts and bolts, esp. of many different sizes: see picture at **tools**.

wrest (rest) *vt* take by force or with an effort.

wrestle (ˈresəl) **1** *vti* (when *vi*, often followed by **with**) fight (someone) by holding, twisting, and throwing. **2** *vi* (followed by **with**) deal or struggle (with a problem, one's feelings, etc.). **wrestler** *nc* **wrestling** *nu* the sport of wrestling.

wretch (retʃ) *nc* **1** an annoying person. **2** a miserable or unlucky person.

wretched (ˈretʃɪd) *adj* **1** annoying. **2** of poor quality. **3** miserable; unlucky. **wretchedness** *nu*

wriggle (ˈrɪgəl) *vti* (cause to) make or move with short twisting movements. ●*nc* a wriggling movement. **wriggle out of** *infml* manage to avoid (doing something, etc.).

wring (rɪŋ) *vt* **1** twist or press (a chicken's neck, wet clothes, etc.) forcefully. **2** (often followed by **out** or **out of**) remove or obtain (water out of clothes, information from someone, etc.) by force. ●*nc* an act of wringing.

wrinkle (ˈrɪŋkəl) *nc* an unevenness in old skin, wet paper, etc. ●*vti* form wrinkles (in).

wrist (rɪst) *nc* **1** the joint between the hand and the arm. **2** the part of a garment covering this. **wristwatch** (ˈrɪstwɒtʃ) *nc* a watch worn on a strap or band around the wrist.

writ (rɪt) *nc* a formal order made by a law court telling someone to do something or to stop doing something.

write (raɪt) *vt* **1** mark (letters, a language one's name, etc.), esp. on paper with a pen etc. **2** produce (a letter, a book, music, etc.) by writing. **write away** send a letter, order etc.: *I've written away for information.* **write down** make a written note of. **write in** send an order, suggestion, etc., to a busi ness, radio station, etc. **2** add in writing: *Please write in your name on the form.* **write off 1** send an order, etc. to a business, etc. **2** (esp. of money or something that has a value) consider as completely lost, destroyed, or non-existent. **write-off** (ˈraɪtɒf) *nc* something written off, esp. a car too badly damaged to be worth repairing. **write out** write (an abbreviation, etc.) in full. **writer** *nc* **write up 1** describe (events) in (a diary, etc.). **2** turn (notes, etc.) into a full report.

writhe (raɪð) *vi* twist or roll about in pain, etc.

writing (ˈraɪtɪŋ) **1** *nu* the practice of representing language by means of marks on paper, stone, etc. **2** *nc* (often *pl*) something written: *the writings of Shakespeare.* **writing paper** sheets of good quality paper used for letters to people.

written (ˈrɪtən) past participle of **write**.

wrong (rɒŋ) *adj* **1** not correct or true. **2** (of behaviour, etc.) bad. **3** not intended or not the best: *You went the wrong way.* ● *adv* not working properly: *My car has gone wrong again.* ● *ncu* (an example of) bad or unfair action. ● *vt* be unfair or cause trouble to (someone). **in the wrong 1** having made a mistake. **2** having done wrong. **wrong-doer** (ˈrɒŋˌduːə*) *nc* a person who breaks the law or does something else bad. **wrongly** *adv*

wrote (rəʊt) past tense of **write**.

wrought (rɔːt) *adj* (of metal) shaped by hammering or rolling: *wrought iron.*

wrung (rʌŋ) past tense and past participle of **wring**.

wry (raɪ) *adj* **-er, -est; wrier, wriest** twisted, esp. (of a smile, etc.) expressing dislike or disgust. **wryly** *adv*

X

Xmas ('eksməs, 'krısməs) *infml n* short for **Christmas**.

X-ray also **x-ray** ('eks,reı) *nc* **1** *(pl)* radiation that can go through substances which light cannot. **2** a photograph taken with X-rays, esp. of bones inside the body: see picture. ● *vt* take an X-ray of.

X-ray

xylophone ('zaıləfəʊn) *nc* a musical instrument with blocks of wood of different lengths which are hit with hammers: see picture at **musical instruments**.

Y

yacht (jɒt) *nc* **1** a sailing boat used for pleasure or racing. **2** a motor boat or small ship used for pleasure. **yachting** *nu* sailing in a **yacht** (def. 1). **yachtsman** ('jɒtsmən) *nc, pl* **-men** a person who sails a **yacht** (def. 1).

yak (jæk) *nc* a long-haired, Tibetan type of cattle: see picture.

yak

yam (jæm) *nc* **1** a plant in hot parts of the world, of which the thick root parts are eaten: see picture at **vegetables**. **2** one of these root parts.

yank (jæŋk) *infml vt, nc* (give) a sharp pull (to).

yap (jæp) *vi* **1** (of a dog, esp. small) make short, high, sharp noises. **2** *infml* talk a lot. ● *nc* an instance of yapping.

yard[1] (jɑːd) *nc* **1** a measure of length = 0.914 m **2** a long pole fixed across the mast of a ship to support a sail.

yard[2] *nc* a piece of closed-in land with a hard surface, esp. behind a house, shop, etc., or used for a particular purpose: *our back yard; a railway goods yard.*

yarn (jɑːn) **1** *ncu* (a length or type of) thread made from wool, cotton, etc., for making into material. **2** *nc infml* a story, esp. untrue.

yawn (jɔːn) *vi* **1** open the mouth wide and breathe in deeply on account of being tired or bored: see picture. **2** be wide open: *The*

yawn

mouth of the cave yawned in front of us. ● *nc* an act of yawning (**yawn** def. 1).

yaws (jɔːz) *nu* a disease caught from other people in hot parts of the world and producing red skin growths and painful joints.

ye (jiː) *archaic pron (pl)* you.

yea (jeı) *archaic adv, nc* (a) yes.

year (jıə*) *nc* **1** a period of 365 or 366 days, esp. from 1 January to 31 December. **2** a group of students entering a university etc., in the same year: *He was in the year above me at school.* **all the year round** during the whole year. **yearly** *adv, adj* (happening, done, paid, etc.) once a year. **year-round** ('jıəraʊnd) *adj* open, existing, etc. all the year round. **years** *n pl* **1** age: *He doesn't show his years.* **2** time: *in years to come.* **3** *infml* a long time.

yearn (jɜːn) *vi* (usually followed by **after, for** or infinitive) want very much: *to yearn for home.*

yeast (jiːst) *nu* a kind of tiny plant used in making beer, wine, raised bread, etc.

yell (jel) *vti, nc* (say with or give) a loud, high shout.

yellow ('jeləʊ) *adj* **-er, -est 1** of the colour of, for example, a ripe banana or an egg yolk. **2** *infml* cowardly; afraid. ● *ncu* a yellow colour. ● *vti* make or become yellow. **yellow fever** a disease caught from other people in hot parts of the world and causing fever and coughing of blood. **yellowish** ('jeləʊıʃ) *adj*

yelp (jelp) *vi* (esp. of a dog) give a short, sharp, high noise, esp. indicating pain. ● *nc* an act of making this noise.

yen (jen) *nc, pl* **yen** See appendix.

yeoman ('jəʊmən) *nc, pl* **-men** (in former times) a man who owned the land he farmed.

yes (jes) *adv* **1** (used to express approval or agreement or to indicate correctness or that a negative statement is incorrect): *Will you do it?—Yes; He wasn't there—Yes, he was.* **2** (used as a question to ask someone what he wants or to continue speaking): *Yes? Can I help you?* ●*nc* (a person who gives) an answer or vote of 'yes'.

yesterday ('jestədeɪ) *adv, nu* (during) the day before today. ●*nc* (often *pl*) the recent past: *yesterday's leaders.*

yet (jet) *adv* **1** now or then: *I haven't finished yet; It wasn't yet ready.* **2** even; still: *yet another surprise; yet bigger than the last.* **3** still; in the time remaining: *I'll finish yet.* ●*conj* also **and yet** but: *I saw him yet didn't recognise him.* **as yet** so far: *This method has worked as yet.*

yield (ji:ld) **1** *vti* (often followed by **to**) give up; surrender: *The defenders yielded (the town) to the enemy.* **2** *vt* produce; return: *a trade that yields a good profit.* **3** *vi* bend; come open; burst: *The door yielded as he pushed it.* ●*nc* an amount produced or returned as a profit, harvest, etc.

yogurt also **joghurt** ('jɒgət, 'jəʊgət) *ncu* (a type or helping of) a thick liquid or soft food made from milk, often with fruit added.

yoke (jəʊk) *nc* **1** a wooden bar, fixed across the backs of their necks, by which two oxen or other animals pull a vehicle, plough, etc.: see picture. **2** the part of a garment

yoke

around the neck and shoulders if made from a separate piece of material. ●*vt* join with a **yoke** (def. 1).

yolk (jəʊk) *nc* the yellow part inside an egg, which feeds the young animal.

yon (jɒn) *literary or northern Brit adj, adv* (that. . .) over there.

yonder ('jɒndə*) *archaic or literary adj, adv* (that. . .) over there.

yore (jɔː*) *chiefly literary n* **of yore** in the past: *in days of yore.*

you (ju: unstressed jʊ, jə) *pron* **1** the person(s) or thing(s) to whom one is talking or writing: *I'll tell you a story; You coward!* **2** any person: *You hold a hammer like this.*

you'd (ju:d) you had or you would.

you'll (ju:l) you will.

young (jʌŋ) *adj* **younger** ('jʌŋgə*), **youngest** ('jʌŋgɪst) having lived or existed for a short time; not yet old. ●*nu* (with plural verb) young people or animals: *a cat with her young.* **youngster** ('jʌŋstə*) *nc* a young person or animal.

your (jɔː*, jʊə* unstressed jə*) *determiner* **1** belonging to or to do with you: *Is this your car, sir?* **2** belonging to or to do with one: *You wear a hat on your head.* **3** *infml, often derogatory* the. . . in general: *Your oak is a difficult wood to use.*

you're (jɔː*, jʊə* unstressed jə*) you are.

yours (jɔːz, jʊəz) *pron* the one(s) belonging to or to do with you.

yourself (jɔː'self, unstressed jə'self) *pron, pl* **-ves** (vz) **1** (the reflexive form of 'you'): *Have you cut yourself?* **2** (the emphatic form of 'you'): *Do it yourself!* **3** in your normal state: *You're not looking yourself today— had a late night?* **by yourself** (of the person(s) spoken or written to) **1** without help. **2** alone.

youth (ju:θ) *nu* **1** the quality of being young. **2** the period when a person or thing is young. **3** (with plural verb) young people. **4** *nc, pl* **-ths** (ðz) a young man. **youthful** ('ju:θfʊl) *adj* **1** to do with the young. **2** feeling, looking, etc., young. **youth hostel** See under **hostel**.

you've (ju:v) you have.

Z

zeal (zi:l) *nu* great enthusiasm, esp. in religious or political matters. **zealous** ('zeləs) *adj* enthusiastic; ambitious; eager.

zebra ('zebrə) *nc, pl* **zebra, zebras** a wild African horse with black and white stripes: see picture at **animals**. **zebra crossing** (in the UK) a road crossing, marked by black and white stripes and flashing yellow lights, where people on foot have right of way over vehicles.

Zen (zen) *nu* also **Zen Buddhism** a mainly Chinese and Japanese form of Buddhism in which meditation is important.

zenith ('zenɪθ) *nc* **1** the point in the sky directly above one. **2** the highest point or time of greatest power, happiness, etc.

zephyr ('zefə*) *chiefly poetry nc* a very light wind.

zero ('zɪərəʊ) *nc, pl* **-s, -es** **1** the figure 0, indicating nothing. **2** a point on a scale between plus and minus values. ●*adj* no; none; at zero. ●*vt* alter (a measuring instrument) to read zero.

zest (zest) *nu* 1 enthusiasm; keen interest: *a zest for living*. 2 added taste, interest, etc.: *A good dressing gives salad some zest*. 3 the thin layer of outer skin of an orange or lemon.

zigzag ('zɪgzæg) *nc, adj, adv, vi* ((move in) a course) turning sharply from side to side.

zinc (zɪŋk) *nu* a chemical element; white metal used in brass, in batteries, and for coating iron: symbol Zn

zip (zɪp) *nc* 1 also **zip fastener, zipper** a device for closing a garment, bag, etc., by means of two rows of plastic or metal teeth which are joined and separated by a slide pulled along them: see picture. 2 a noise made by very fast movement through

zip

air. ●*vt* 1 (often followed by **up**) close with a **zip** (def. 1). 2 *vi* move with a **zip** (def. 2) or very fast. **zip code** (in the USA) See **postcode** under **post³**.

zither ('zɪðə*) *nc* a flat musical instrument with strings that are pulled slightly and let go.

zodiac ('zəʊdɪæk) *n* **signs of the zodiac** 1 twelve signs representing groups of stars along the path which the sun appears to take across the sky each year. 2 the importance of these signs, believed by some people to affect character and events.

zone (zəʊn) *nc* a district or division, esp. of land. ●*vt* divide into zones.

zoo (zuː) *nc* also **zoological garden** a place where living animals are kept for study and showing to visitors.

zoology (zəʊ'ɒlədʒɪ, zuː'ɒlədʒɪ) *nu* the science of studying animals. **zoological** (ˌzəʊə'lɒdʒɪkəl, ˌzuːə'lɒdʒɪkəl) *adj* **zoologist** *nc*

zoom (zuːm) *vi* move fast, esp. with a buzzing noise. ●*nc* an act or noise of zooming. **zoom lens** a lens system on a camera, etc., that can be altered so as to get less or more into the picture. **zoom in** or **out** alter a zoom lens so as to get less or more into the picture.

APPENDIX
Currency Units

Country	Unit of currency		
Algeria	dinar		= 100 centimes
Argentina	peso		= 100 centavos
Australia	dollar		= 100 cents
Austria	schilling		= 100 groschen
(The) Bahamas	dollar		= 100 cents
Bahrain	dinar		= 1000 fils
Bangladesh	taka		= 100 paisa
Barbados	dollar		= 100 cents
Belgium	franc		= 100 centimes
Bermuda	dollar		= 100 cents
Bolivia	peso		= 100 centavos
Botswana	pula		= 100 thebe
Brazil	cruzeiro		= 100 centavos
Brunei	dollar		= 100 cents
Burma	kyat		= 100 pyas
Canada	dollar		= 100 cents
Chile	peso		= 100 centavos
China	yuan	= 10 chiao	= 100 fen
Colombia	peso		= 100 centavos
Cuba	peso		= 100 centavos
Cyprus	pound		= 1000 mils
Czechoslovakia	koruna		= 100 halérů
Denmark	krone		= 100 øre
Ecuador	sucre		= 100 centavos
Egypt	pound	= 100 piastres	= 1000 millemes
El Salvador	colón		= 100 centavos
Ethiopia	birr		= 100 cents
Finland	markka		= 100 pennia
France	franc		= 100 centimes
(The) Gambia	dalasi		= 100 butut
Germany (Federal Republic and German Democratic Republic)	mark		= 100 pfennig
Ghana	cedi		= 100 pesewas
Gibraltar	pound		= 100 pence
Greece	drachma		= 100 lepta
Guatemala	quetzal		= 100 centavos
Guinea	syli		= 100 cauris
Guyana	dollar		= 100 cents
Honduras	lempira		= 100 centavos
Hong Kong	dollar		= 100 cents
Hungary	forint		= 100 fillér
Iceland	króna		= 100 aurar
India	rupee		= 100 paise
Indonesia	rupiah		= 100 sen
Iran	rial		= 100 dinars
Iraq	dinar		= 1000 fils
(Republic of) Ireland	pound		= 100 pence
Israel	shekel		= 100 new agorot
Italy	lira		= 100 centesimi
Jamaica	dollar		= 100 cents
Japan	yen	= 100 sen	= 1000 rin
Jordan	dinar		= 1000 fils
Kampuchea	riel		= 100 sen
Kenya	shilling		= 100 cents

CURRENCY UNITS

Country	Unit of currency		
Korea (People's Democratic Republic)	won		= 100 jun
Korea (Republic)	won		= 100 chon
Kuwait	dinar		= 1000 fils
Laos	kip		= 100 at
(The) Lebanon	pound		= 100 piastres
Liberia	dollar		= 100 cents
Libya	dinar		= 1000 millemes
Luxembourg	franc		= 100 centimes
Madagascar	franc		= 100 centimes
Malawi	kwacha		= 100 tambala
Malaysia	dollar (ringgit)		= 100 cents
Malta	pound	= 100 cents	= 1000 mils
Mauritius	rupee		= 100 cents
Mexico	peso		= 100 centavos
Monaco	franc		= 100 centimes
Morocco	dirham		= 100 centimes
Mozambique	metical		= 100 centavos
Nepal	rupee		= 100 paisa
The Netherlands	guilder		= 100 cents
New Zealand	dollar		= 100 cents
Nicaragua	córdoba		= 100 centavos
Nigeria	naira		= 100 kobo
Norway	krone		= 100 øre
Oman	rial		= 1000 baiza
Pakistan	rupee		= 100 paise
Panama	balboa		= 100 centésimos
Papua New Guinea	kina		= 100 toca
Paraguay	guaraní		= 100 céntimos
Peru	sol		= 100 centavos
Philippines	peso		= 100 centavos
Poland	zloty		= 100 groszy
Portugal	escudo		= 100 centavos
Qatar	riyal		= 100 dirhams
Romania	leu		= 100 bani
Saudi Arabia	rial	= 20 qursh	= 100 halalas
Sierra Leone	leone		= 100 cents
Singapore	dollar		= 100 cents
South Africa	rand		= 100 cents
Spain	peseta		= 100 céntimos
Sri Lanka	rupee		= 100 cents
(The) Sudan	pound	= 100 piastres	= 1000 millièmes
Sweden	krona		= 100 öre
Switzerland	franc		= 100 centimes
Syria	pound		= 100 piastres
Tanzania	shilling		= 100 cents
Thailand	baht		= 100 satang
Trinidad and Tobago	dollar		= 100 cents
Tunisia	dinar		= 1000 millimes
Turkey	lira		= 100 kurus
Uganda	shilling		= 100 cents
Union of Soviet Socialist Republics	rouble		= 100 kopecks
United Arab Emirates	dirham		= 100 fils
United Kingdom	pound		= 100 pence
United States of America	dollar		= 100 cents
Uruguay	peso		= 100 centésimos
Venezuela	bolívar		= 100 céntimos
Vietnam	dong		= 100 hao
Yemen (Arab Republic)	riyal		= 100 rial
Yemen (People's Democratic Republic)	dinar		= 1000 fils

Country	Unit of currency	
Yugoslavia	dinar	= 100 para
Zaïre	zaïre	= 100 makuta
Zambia	kwacha	= 100 ngwee
Zimbabwe	dollar	= 100 cents

Continents and countries of the world

Continent or country	Adjective, person
Afghanistan (æf,gænɪ'staːn)	Afghan ('æfgæn)
Africa ('æfrɪkə)	African (-kən)
Albania (æl'beɪnɪə)	Albanian (-nɪən)
Algeria (æl'dʒɪərɪə)	Algerian (-rɪən)
Andorra (æn'dɔːrə)	Andorran (-rən)
Angola (æŋ'gəʊlə)	Angolan (-lən)
Antarctica (ænt'aːktɪkə)	Antarctic (ænt'aːktɪk)
Antigua (æn'tiːgə)	Antiguan (-gən)
Argentina (,aːdʒən'tiːnə),	Argentinian (-'tɪnɪən),
The Argentine ('aːdʒəntaɪn)	Argentine ('aːdʒəntaɪn)
Asia ('eɪʃə, 'eɪʒə)	Asian (-ʃən, -ʒən)
Australia (ɒ'streɪlɪə)	Australian (-lɪən)
Austria ('ɒstrɪə)	Austrian (-strɪən)
(The) Bahamas (bə'haːməz)	Bahamian (bə'heɪmɪən)
Bahrain (baː'reɪn)	Bahraini (-reɪnɪ)
Bangladesh (,bæŋgləˈdeʃ)	Bangladeshi (-'deʃɪ)
Barbados (baː'beɪdəs)	Barbadian (-dɪən)
Belgium ('beldʒəm)	Belgian (-dʒən)
Belize (be'liːz)	Belizian (-zɪən)
Benin (be'niːn)	Beninese (benɪ'niːz)
Bermuda (bə'mjuːdə)	Bermudan (-dən), Bermudian (-dɪən)
Bhutan (buː'taːn)	Bhutanese (-niːz)
Bolivia (bə'lɪvɪə)	Bolivian (-vɪən)
Botswana (bɒ'tswaːnə)	Tswana ('tswaːnə)
Brazil (brə'zɪl)	Brazilian (-lɪən)
Brunei ('bruːnaɪ)	Bruneian (bruː'naɪən)
Bulgaria (bʌl'geərɪə)	Bulgarian (-rɪən)
Burma ('bɜːmə)	Burmese (,bɜː'miːz)
Burundi (bʊ'rʊndɪ)	Burundian (-dɪən)
Cameroon (,kæmə'ruːn)	Cameroonian (-nɪən)
Canada ('kænədə)	Canadian (kə'neɪdɪən)
Chad (tʃæd)	Chadian (-dɪən)
Chile ('tʃɪlɪ)	Chilean (-lɪən)
China ('tʃaɪnə)	Chinese (,tʃaɪniːz)
Colombia (kə'lɒmbɪə)	Colombian (-bɪən)
Congo ('kɒŋgəʊ)	Congolese (,kɒŋgə'liːz)
Costa Rica (,kɒstə 'riːkə)	Costa Rican (-kən)
Cuba ('kjuːbə)	Cuban (-bən)
Cyprus ('saɪprəs)	Cyprian ('sɪprɪən), Cypriot ('sɪprɪət)
Czechoslovakia (,tʃekəʊslə'vækɪə)	Czech (tʃek), Czechoslovak (,tʃekəʊ'sləʊvæk), Czechoslovakian (,tʃekəʊslə'vækɪən)
Denmark ('denmaːk)	Danish ('deɪnɪʃ), Dane (deɪn)
Dominican Republic (də'mɪnɪkən rɪ'pʌblɪk)	Dominican (-kən)
Ecuador ('ekwədɔː*)	Ecuadorian (,ekwə'dɔːrɪən)
Egypt ('iːdʒɪpt)	Egyptian (ɪ'dʒɪpʃən)
El Salvador (el 'sælvədɔː*)	Salvadorean (,sælvə'dɔːrɪən)

CONTINENTS AND COUNTRIES OF THE WORLD

Continent or country	Adjective, person
England ('ɪŋglənd)	English ('ɪŋglɪʃ)
Eritrea (ˌerɪ'treɪə)	Eritrean (-eɪən)
Ethiopia (ˌiːθɪ'əʊpɪə)	Ethiopian (-pɪən)
Europe ('jʊərəp)	European (ˌjʊərə'pɪən)
Fiji (ˌfiː'dʒiː)	Fijian (ˌfiː'dʒiːən)
Finland ('fɪnlənd)	Finnish ('fɪnɪʃ), Finn (fɪn)
France (frɑːns)	French (frentʃ), Frenchman ('frentʃmən)
Gabon (gæ'bɒn)	Gabonese (ˌgæbə'niːz)
(The) Gambia ('gæmbɪə)	Gambian (-bɪən)
German Democratic Republic (ˌdʒɜːmən deməˌkrætɪk rɪ'pʌblɪk)	(East) German ('dʒɜːmən)
Federal Republic of Germany (ˌfedərəl rɪˌpʌblɪk əv 'dʒɜːmənɪ)	(West) German ('dʒɜːmən)
Ghana ('gɑːnə)	Ghanaian (gɑː'neɪən)
Gibraltar (dʒɪ'brɔːltə*)	Gibraltarian (ˌdʒɪbrɔːl'teərɪən)
Great Britain (ˌgreɪt 'brɪtən)	British ('brɪtɪʃ), Briton ('brɪtən)
Greece (griːs)	Greek (griːk)
Grenada (grɪ'neɪdə)	Grenadian (-dɪən)
Guatemala (ˌgwɑːtə'mɑːlə)	Guatemalan (-lən)
Guinea ('gɪnɪ)	Guinean (-nɪən)
Guyana (gaɪ'ænə)	Guyanese (ˌgaɪə'niːz)
Haiti ('heɪtɪ)	Haitian ('heɪʃən)
Honduras (hɒn'djʊərəs)	Honduran (-rən)
Hong Kong (ˌhɒŋ 'kɒŋ)	
Hungary ('hʌŋgərɪ)	Hungarian (hʌŋ'geərɪən)
Iceland ('aɪslənd)	Icelandic (aɪs'lændɪk), Icelander ('aɪsləndə*)
India ('ɪndɪə)	Indian (-dɪən)
Indonesia (ˌɪndə'niːzɪə)	Indonesian (-zɪən)
Iran (ɪ'rɑːn)	Iranian (ɪ'reɪnɪən)
Iraq (ɪ'rɑːk)	Iraqi (ɪ'rɑːkɪ)
(Republic of) Ireland ('aɪələnd)	Irish ('aɪərɪʃ), Irishman ('aɪərɪʃmən), Irishwoman ('aɪərɪʃˌwʊmən)
(Republic of) Israel ('ɪzreɪəl)	Israeli (ɪz'reɪlɪ)
Italy ('ɪtəlɪ)	Italian (ɪ'tælɪən)
Jamaica (dʒə'meɪkə)	Jamaican (-kən)
Japan (dʒə'pæn)	Japanese (ˌdʒæpə'niːz)
Java ('dʒɑːvə)	Javanese (ˌdʒɑːvə'niːz)
Jordan ('dʒɔːdən)	Jordanian (dʒɔː'deɪnɪən)
Kampuchea (kæmpʊ'tʃɪə)	Kampuchean (-'tʃɪən)
Kashmir (kæʃ'mɪə*)	Kashmiri (kæʃ'mɪərɪ)
Kenya ('kenjə)	Kenyan (-jən)
Korea (kə'rɪə)	Korean (-'rɪən)
Kuwait (kʊ'weɪt)	Kuwaiti (-tɪ)
Laos ('lɑːɒs)	Laotian ('lɑːɒʃən)
(The) Lebanon ('lebənən)	Lebanese (ˌlebə'niːz)
Lesotho (lə'suːtuː)	Sotho ('suːtuː), Basotho (bə'suːtuː)
Liberia (laɪ'bɪərɪə)	Liberian (-rɪən)
Libya ('lɪbɪə)	Libyan (-bɪən)
Liechtenstein ('lɪktənstaɪn)	Liechtenstein, Liechtensteiner (-nə*)
Luxembourg ('lʌksəmbɜːg)	Luxembourg, Luxembourger (-gə*)
Madagascar (ˌmædə'gæskə*)	Madagascan (-kən)
Malawi (mə'lɑːwɪ)	Malawian (-wɪən)
Malaya (mə'leɪə)	Malay (mə'leɪ)
Malaysia (mə'leɪzɪə)	Malaysian (-zɪən)
Mali ('mɑːlɪ)	Malian (-lɪən)
Malta ('mɔːltə)	Maltese (mɔːl'tiːz)
Mauritania (ˌmɒrɪ'teɪnɪə)	Mauritanian (-nɪən)
Mauritius (mə'rɪʃəs)	Mauritian (-'rɪʃən)
Mexico ('meksɪkəʊ)	Mexican (-kən)

450

Continent or country	Adjective, person
Monaco ('mɒnəkəʊ)	Monegasque (ˌmɒnə'gæsk)
Mongolia (mɒŋ'gəʊlɪə)	Mongolian (-lɪən), Mongol ('mɒŋgɒl)
Montserrat (ˌmɒntsə'ræt)	Montserratian (-'ræʃən)
Morocco (mə'rɒkəʊ)	Moroccan (-kən)
Mozambique (ˌməʊzæm'biːk)	Mozambican (-'biːkən)
Namibia (nə'mɪbɪə)	Namibian (-bɪən)
Nauru (naːˈuːruː)	Nauruan (-ruːən)
Nepal (nɪ'pɔːl)	Nepalese (ˌnepə'liːz)
The Netherlands ('neðələndz),	Dutch (dʌtʃ), Hollander
Holland ('hɒlənd)	('hɒləndə*), Dutchman ('dʌtʃmən)
New Zealand (ˌnjuː 'ziːlənd)	New Zealand, New Zealander (-də*)
Nicaragua (ˌnɪkə'rægjʊə)	Nicaraguan (-ən)
Niger ('naɪdʒə)	
Nigeria (naɪ'dʒɪərɪə)	Nigerian (naɪ'dʒɪərɪən)
North America (ˌnɔːθ ə'merɪkə)	North American (-kən)
Northern Ireland (ˌnɔːðən'aɪələnd)	Northern Irish ('aɪərɪʃ), Ulsterman ('ʌlstəmən),
	Ulsterwoman ('ʌlstəˌwʊmən)
Norway ('nɔːweɪ)	Norwegian (nɔː'wiːdʒən)
Oman (əʊ'maːn)	Omani (əʊ'maːnɪ)
Pakistan (ˌpɑːkɪ'staːn)	Pakistani (-nɪ)
Panama (ˌpænə'maː)	Panamanian (ˌpænə'meɪnɪən)
Papua New Guinea ('pæpjʊə njuː 'gɪnɪ)	Papuan ('pæpjʊən)
Paraguay ('pærəgwaɪ)	Paraguayan (ˌpærə'gwaɪən)
Peru (pə'ruː)	Peruvian (-'ruːvɪən)
(The) Philippines ('fɪlɪpiːnz)	Philippine ('fɪlɪpiːn), Filipino (ˌfɪlɪ'piːnəʊ)
Poland ('pəʊlənd)	Polish ('pəʊlɪʃ), Pole (pəʊl)
Portugal ('pɔːtʃʊgəl)	Portuguese (ˌpɔːtʃʊ'giːz)
Qatar ('kʌtaː*)	Qatari (-aːrɪ)
Romania (rə'meɪnɪə)	Romanian (-nɪən)
Russia ('rʌʃə)	Russian (-ʃən)
Rwanda (rʊ'ændə)	Rwandan (-dən)
Samoa (sə'məʊə)	Samoan (-ən)
San Marino (ˌsæn mə'riːnəʊ)	San Marinese (ˌsæn ˌmærɪ'niːz)
Sarawak (sə'raːwæk)	Sarawakian (ˌsærə'wækɪən)
Saudi Arabia (ˌsaʊdɪ ə'reɪbɪə)	Saudi Arabian (-bɪən)
Scotland ('skɒtlənd)	Scottish ('skɒtɪʃ), Scot (skɒt), Scotsman
	('skɒtsmən)
Senegal (ˌsenɪ'gɔːl)	Senegalese (ˌsenɪgə'liːz)
(The) Seychelles ('seɪʃelz)	Seychellois (seɪ'ʃelwaː)
Sierra Leone (sɪˌerə lɪ'əʊn)	Sierra Leonean (-nɪən)
Singapore (ˌsɪŋgə'pɔː*)	Singaporean (ˌsɪŋgə'pɔːrɪən)
Somalia (sə'maːlɪə)	Somalian (-lɪən), Somali (-li)
South Africa (ˌsaʊθ 'æfrɪkə)	South African (-kən)
South America (ˌsaʊθ ə'merɪkə)	South American (-kən)
Spain (speɪn)	Spanish ('spænɪʃ), Spaniard ('spænɪəd)
Sri Lanka (ˌsrɪ 'læŋkə)	Sri Lankan (ˌsrɪ 'læŋkən)
(The) Sudan (suː'daːn)	Sudanese (ˌsuːdə'niːz)
Sumatra (suː'maːtrə)	Sumatran (-trən)
Swaziland ('swaːzɪlænd)	Swazi ('swaːzɪ)
Sweden ('swiːdən)	Swedish ('swiːdɪʃ), Swede (swiːd)
Switzerland ('swɪtsələnd)	Swiss (swɪs)
Syria ('sɪrɪə)	Syrian (-rɪən)
Tahiti (taː'hiːtɪ)	Tahitian (-'hiːʃən)
Taiwan (taɪ'waːn)	Taiwanese (ˌtaɪwə'niːz)
Tanzania (ˌtænzə'nɪə)	Tanzanian (-'nɪən)
Thailand ('taɪlænd)	Thai (taɪ)
Tibet (tɪ'bet)	Tibetan (-tən)
Tobago (tə'beɪgəʊ)	Tobagonian (ˌtəʊbə'gəʊnɪən)
Togo ('təʊgəʊ)	Togolese (ˌtəʊgə'liːz)

Continent or country	Adjective, person
Tonga (ˈtɒŋə)	Tongan (-ən)
Trinidad (ˈtrɪnɪdæd)	Trinidadian (ˌtrɪnɪˈdeɪdɪən)
Tunisia (tjuːˈnɪzɪə)	Tunisian (-ən)
Turkey (ˈtɜːkɪ)	Turkish (ˈtɜːkɪʃ), Turk (tɜːk)
Uganda (juːˈgændə)	Ugandan (-dən)
Union of Soviet Socialist Republics (ˌjuːnɪən əv ˌsəʊvɪət ˌsəʊʃəlɪst rɪˈpʌblɪks)	Soviet (ˈsəʊvɪət)
United Arab Emirates (juːˌnaɪtɪd ˈærəb eˈmɪərəts)	
United Kingdom (juːˌnaɪtɪd ˈkɪŋdəm)	
United States of America (juːˌnaɪtɪd ˌsteɪts əv əˈmerɪkə)	American (-kən)
Uruguay (ˈjʊərəgwaɪ)	Uruguayan (ˌjʊərəˈgwaɪən)
Venezuela (ˌvenɪˈzweɪlə)	Venezuelan (-lən)
Vietnam (ˌvɪetˈnæm)	Vietnamese (ˌvɪetnəˈmiːz)
Wales (weɪlz)	Welsh (welʃ), Welshman (ˈwelʃmən)
(The) West Indies (ˌwest ˈɪndɪz)	West Indian (-dɪən)
Yemen (ˈjemən)	Yemeni (-nɪ)
Yugoslavia (ˌjuːgəʊˈslɑːvɪə)	Yugoslavian (-vɪən), Yugoslav (ˈjuːgəʊslɑːv)
Zaïre (zɑːˈɪə)	Zaïrean (-rɪən)
Zambia (ˈzæmbɪə)	Zambian (-bɪən)
Zimbabwe (zɪmˈbɑːbwɪ)	Zimbabwean (-wɪən)

Abbreviations

A ampere
AA anti-aircraft; Automobile Association
AB able-bodied (seaman)
ABM anti-ballistic missile
A/C; a/c account
a.c. alternating current
ACAS Advisory, Conciliation, and Arbitration Service
AD *anno Domini* (Latin), in the year of our Lord
ADC aide-de-camp
AFL-CIO American Federation of Labor and Congress of Industrial Organisations
AGM Annual General Meeting
AH *anno Hegirae* (Latin), in the year of Hegira
A level Advanced level (of GCE)
AM amplitude modulation
a.m. *ante meridiem* (Latin), before noon
anon. anonymous
AP Associated Press
approx. approximately
Apr. April
arr. arrives
a.s.a.p. as soon as possible
ASEAN Association of South-East Asian Nations
Assoc. Association
asst. assistant
Aug. August
AV Audio-Visual
Ave. Avenue
AWOL absent without leave

B. Bachelor; Blessed; British
b. born; bowled
BA Bachelor of Arts; British Airways
BAOR British Army of the Rhine
BBC British Broadcasting Corporation
BC before Christ
B.Ed. Bachelor of Education
b/f brought forward
BFPO British Forces' Post Office
bk. book
BL British Leyland; British Library
BM Bachelor of Medicine; British Museum
BMA British Medical Association
B.Mus. Bachelor of Music
bn billion
BP British Petroleum
b.p. blood-pressure; boiling point
BR British Rail
Bros Brothers
BS British Standard
B.Sc. Bachelor of Science
BSI British Standards Institution
BST British Summer Time
BTA British Tourist Authority
BTU British Thermal Unit

C carbon; Celsius; centigrade; (Roman numeral) 100
C. Conservative
c. caught; cent; century; cubic
c. *circa* (Latin), about
ca. *circa* (Latin), about
CAB Citizens' Advice Bureau

Cantab. *Cantabrigiensis* (Latin), of Cambridge (University)
Capt. Captain
CAT College of Advanced Technology
CB citizens' band (radio); Companion (of the Order) of the Bath
CBE Commander (of the Order) of the British Empire
CBI Confederation of British Industry
cc copies; cubic centimetre(s)
CCF Combined Cadet Force
cent. century
Cento Central Treaty Organisation
cert. certificate; certified
cf. *confer* (Latin), compare
c/f carried forward
CGS Chief of General Staff
c.g.s. centimetre-gram-second system
ch. chapter
CIA Central Intelligence Agency
CID Criminal Investigation Department
cif cost, insurance, freight
C.-in-C. Commander-in-Chief
cl. class
cm centimetre(s)
CND Campaign for Nuclear Disarmament
CO Commanding Officer; conscientious objector
Co. Company; County
c/o care of
COD cash on delivery
Cons. Conservative (Party)
cont'd continued
Co-op Co-operative (Society)
cp. compare
Cr. credit; creditor; Crown
CSE Certificate of Secondary Education
cu. cubic
c.v. curriculum vitae
cwt. hundredweight

D (Roman numeral) 500
d. daughter; died; *denarius,* (Latin), (old) penny
dB decibel(s)
d.c. direct current
DD Doctor of Divinity
DDR *Deutsche Demokratische Republik* (German), German Democratic Republic
DDT dichloro-diphenyl-trichloro-ethane insecticide)
Dec. December
dep. departs
Dept Department
DES Department of Education and Science
DHSS Department of Health and Social Security
Dip Ed Diploma in Education
Dir. Director
DIY do-it-yourself
DJ dinner-jacket; disc-jockey

D.Litt. Doctor of Letters
DM Deutsche Mark (German currency)
D.Mus. Doctor of Music
DNA deoxyribonucleic acid
D.o.E. Department of the Environment
D.Phil. Doctor of Philosophy
Dr Doctor
Dr. debtor
D.Sc. Doctor of Science
DV *Deo volente* (Latin), God willing

E. east; eastern
Ed. edited (by); editor
EDP electronic data processing
EEC European Economic Community (the Common Market)
EFTA European Free Trade Association
e.g. *exempli gratia* (Latin), for example
e.m.f. electromotive force
encl. enclosed
Eng. Engineering; England; English
ENT ear, nose, and throat
ER *Elizabetha Regina* (Latin), Queen Elizabeth
ESN educationally subnormal
ESP extra-sensory perception
esp. especially
Esq. Esquire
ETA estimated time of arrival
etc. *et cetera* (Latin), and the rest
et seq. *et sequentia* (Latin), and what follows
excl. excluding

F Fahrenheit
f. female; feminine; following; franc
f *forte* (Italian), loud(ly)
FA Football Association
FAO Food and Agriculture Organisation
FBI Federal Bureau of Investigation
FC Football Club
FD *fidei defensor* (Latin), Defender of the Faith
Feb. February
Fed. Federal; Federation
fem. female; feminine
ff *fortissimo* (Italian), very loud(ly)
FIFA *Fédération Internationale de Footbal Association* (French)
fig. figurative; figure
fl. fluid
fl. *floruit* (Latin), flourished
FM frequency modulation
f.p. freezing-point
Fr Father; franc; France; French
Fri. Friday
FRS Fellow of the Royal Society
ft. feet; foot
fwd forward

g gram(s); (acceleration due to) gravity

GATT General Agreement on Tariffs and Trade
GB Great Britain
GBH grievous bodily harm
GC George Cross
GCE General Certificate of Education
Gdn(s) Garden(s)
GDR German Democratic Republic
Gen. General
GHQ General Headquarters
Gk Greek
GLC Greater London Council
GM George Medal
gm gram(s)
GMT Greenwich Mean Time
GNP gross national product
govt government
GP general practitioner
GPO General Post Office
gr. gross
gt great

ha hectare(s)
h. & c. hot and cold (water)
HB hard and black (pencil lead)
HCF highest common factor
HE Her or His Excellency; high explosive; His Eminence
h.f. high frequency
HM Her or His Majesty('s)
HMI Her or His Majesty's Inspector
HMS Her or His Majesty's Ship
HMSO Her or His Majesty's Stationery Office
HNC Higher National Certificate
HND Higher National Diploma
Hon. Honorary; Honourable
HP hire-purchase
hp horsepower
HQ Headquarters
hr hour(s)
HRH Her or His Royal Highness
h.t. high tension
Hz hertz

I Island; (Roman numeral) 1
IATA International Air Transport Association
ib.; ibid. *ibidem* (Latin), in the same place
IBA Independent Broadcasting Authority
ICBM inter-continental ballistic missile
id. *idem* (Latin), the same
i.e. *id est* (Latin), that is; in other words
ILO International Labour Organisation
IMF International Monetary Fund
in. inch(es)
Inc Incorporated
incl. included; inclusive
inst. institute; institution
IOU I owe you
IPA International Phonetic Alphabet

IQ intelligence quotient
IRA Irish Republican Army
Ital. Italian; Italy
ITV Independent Television
Jan. January
JP Justice of the Peace
jr. junior
Jul. July
Jun. June
jun. junior

kg kilogram(s)
km kilometre(s)
KO; k.o. knock-out
kW kilowatt

L learner
L. Lady; Lake; Latin; left; (Roman numeral) 50
l line; litre(s)
LA Los Angeles
Lab. Labour (party)
lang. language
Lat. Latin
lat. latitude
lb. *libra(e)* (Latin), pound(s) (weight)
lbw leg before wicket
LCM least (or lowest) common multiple
LEA Local Education Authority
l.h. left-hand
Lib. Liberal (Party)
lit. literally; literature
ll lines
LL B Bachelor of Laws
LL D Doctor of Laws
long. longitude
LP long-playing (record)
LSD or **£.s.d.** *librae, solidi, denarii* (Latin), pounds, shillings, and pence
Lt Lieutenant
l.t. low tension
Ltd. Limited
LV luncheon voucher

M motorway; (Roman numeral) 1000
M. member; *Monsieur* (French), Mr
m. male; married; masculine; metre(s); mile(s); million(s)
MA Master of Arts
Mar. March
masc. masculine
max. maximum
MBE Member of (the Order of) the British Empire
MC Master of Ceremonies; Military Cross
MCC Marylebone Cricket Club
MD *Medicinae Doctor* (Latin), Doctor of Medicine
Med Mediterranean
MEP Member of the European Parliament
mg milligram(s)

min. minimum; minute(s)
MIRV multiple independently targeted re-entry vehicle
mkt market
ml millilitre(s)
Mlle *Mademoiselle* (French), Miss
MM *Messieurs* (French), Messrs
mm millimetre(s)
Mme *Madame* (French), Mrs
MO Medical Officer; money order
MOH Medical Officer of Health
Mon. Monday
MOT Ministry of Transport
MP Member of Parliament
m.p.g. miles per gallon
m.p.h. miles per hour
M.Phil. Master of Philosophy
Mr title before a man's name
Mrs title before a married woman's name
MS manuscript
Ms title before a woman's name
M.Sc. Master of Science
MSS manuscripts
Mt Mount

N newton (unit of force)
N. north; northern
n. noun
NAAFI Navy, Army, and Air Force Institutes
NASA (US) National Aeronautics and Space Administration
NATO North Atlantic Treaty Organisation
NB *nota bene* (Latin), note well
NCB National Coal Board
NCO non-commissioned officer
NE north-east
NEB National Enterprise Board
NHS National Health Service
NI National Insurance; Northern Ireland
No.; no. number
Nov. November
nr. near
NSB National Savings Bank
NSPCC National Society for the Prevention of Cruelty to Children
NT New Testament; National Trust
NUS National Union of Students
NW north-west
NY New York
NZ New Zealand

OAP old-age pensioner
OAS Organisation of American States
OAU Organisation of African Unity
OBE Officer of the Order of the British Empire
Oct. October
OECD Organisation for Economic Co-operation and Development
OHMS On Her Majesty's Service

O level Ordinary level (of GCE)
OM (Member of the) Order of Merit
ONC Ordinary National Certificate
OND Ordinary National Diploma
o.n.o. or nearest offer
op cit *opere citato* (Latin), in the work cited
OPEC Organisation of Petroleum Exporting Countries
opp opposite
OT occupational therapy; Old Testament
OU Open University
Oxfam Oxford Committee for Famine Relief
Oxon. *Oxoniensis* (Latin), of Oxford (University)
oz. ounce(s)

P parking(-place)
p pence; pennies; penny
p. page; participle; past
p *piano* (Italian), soft(ly)
PA personal assistant; Press Association; public address
pa *per annum* (Latin), per year
p. & p. postage and packing
para paragraph
PAYE pay-as-you-earn (tax-collection)
PC Police Constable; Privy Councillor
p.c. postcard
PE physical education
per pro. *per procurationem* (Latin), on behalf of
Ph.D. *Philosophiae Doctor* (Latin), Doctor of Philosophy
PLC Public Limited Company
PM post-mortem; Prime Minister
p.m. *post meridiem* (Latin), after noon
PO postal order; post office
POW prisoner of war
pp. pages
p.p. past participle; *per procurationem* (Latin), on behalf of
pp *pianissimo* (Italian), very soft(ly)
PR Public Relations
PRO Public Relations Office or Officer
PS postscript
PT physical training
PTA Parent-Teacher Association
PTO please turn over
Publ.; publ. published (by); publisher

QC Queen's Counsel
QED *quod erat demonstrandum* (Latin), which was to be proved
Qu question
q.v. *quod vide* (Latin), which see

R. Railway; *Regina* (Latin), Queen; *Rex* (Latin), King; right; River
RA Royal Academician; Royal Academy
RAC Royal Automobile Club

ABBREVIATIONS

RADA Royal Academy of Dramatic Art
RAF Royal Air Force
RC Red Cross; Roman Catholic
Rd. Road
rec(d) received
ref. reference
ret(d). retired
RFC Rugby Football Club
r.h. right-hand
RIP *requiescat* (or *requiescant*) *in pace*
(Latin), may he or she (or they) rest in peace
rly railway
RM Royal Mail; Royal Marines
rm room
RN Royal Navy
RNLI Royal National Lifeboat Institution
r.p.m. revolutions per minute
RSA Royal Society of Arts
RSPCA Royal Society for the Prevention
of Cruelty to Animals
RSVP *répondez, s'il vous plaît* (French),
please reply
rt right
Rt. Hon. Right Honourable

S. Saint; Society; south; southern
s. second(s); shilling(s); singular; son
SA South Africa; South America
s.a.e stamped addressed envelope
SALT Strategic Arms Limitation Talks
Sat. Saturday
SAYE save as you earn
sch school
SCM State Certified Midwife
SDP Social-Democratic Party
SE south-east
SEATO South-East Asia Treaty
Organisation
sec. second(s); secretary
SEN State Enrolled Nurse
Sept. September
SF science fiction
Sgt Sergeant
SI *Système International* (French),
International System (of Units)
Sn(r) Senior
Soc. Society
SOS save our souls (distress signal)
sp spelling
sq. square
SRN State Registered Nurse
SS Saints; steamship
St. Saint; Street
st. stone(s)
STD Subscriber Trunk Dialling
Sun. Sunday
Suppl. Supplement
Supt Superintendent
s.v. *sub verbo* or *sub voce* (Latin), under
the word or heading
SW south-west

t. ton(s)
TA Territorial Army
TB tuberculosis
tel. telephone
temp. temperature
Thurs. Thursday
TNT trinitrotoluene
trans. translated
TT teetotal(ler); tuberculin tested
TUC Trades Union Congress
Tues. Tuesday
TV television

UAE United Arab Emirates
UDI unilateral declaration of independence
UFO unidentified flying object
UHF ultra high frequency
UK United Kingdom
UN United Nations
Unesco United Nations Educational,
Scientific, and Cultural Organisation
Unicef United Nations (International)
Children's (Emergency) Fund
Univ. University
UNO United Nations Organisation
UPI United Press International
UPU Universal Postal Union
US United States
USA United States of America
USSR Union of Soviet Socialist Republics

V volt(s); (Roman numeral) 5
v. verb; verse; versus; very
v. *vide* (Latin), see
VAT value-added tax
VC vice-chancellor; vice-consul;
Victoria Cross
VCR video-cassette recorder
VDU visual display unit
VHF very high frequency
VIP very important person
viz *videlicet* (Latin), namely
vol. volume
vs versus
VSO Voluntary Service Overseas
VTOL vertical take-off and landing
VTR videotape recorder
vv. verses

W watt(s)
W. west; western
WEA Workers' Educational Association
Weds. Wednesday
wef with effect from
WHO World Health Organisation
WI West Indies; Women's Institute
wk week; work
WP word-processing
w.p.b. waste-paper basket
wpm words per minute
WRAF Women's Royal Air Force

WRNS Women's Royal Naval Service	**YHA** Youth Hostels Association
WRVS Women's Royal Voluntary Service	**YMCA** Young Men's Christian Association
wt weight	**yr.** year; your
X (Roman numeral) 10	**YWCA** Young Women's Christian Association
yd. yard	

Punctuation

This section has been adapted from *Current English Usage* by Frederick T. Wood, R.H. Flavell, and L.M. Flavell (Macmillan 1981).

Full stop (*US* period) (.)

It indicates the end of a sentence. Any sentence which follows begins with a capital letter:

☐ He left the hotel. It was raining outside.

If a sentence ends with a question mark or exclamation mark, no full stop is added:

☐ Do you want to come with us tomorrow?

Question mark (?)

It is used at the end of direct questions:

☐ 'May I come with you tomorrow?'

It is not used after indirect questions:

☐ She asked if she could have a glass of water.

Exclamation mark (*US* exclamation point) (!)

1 After interjections It is used after interjections and words which are meant to imitate a sudden, sharp sound:

☐ Ah! Oh! Bang! Crash! You stupid boy!

After *how* or *what* It is used after sentences which use *how* or *what* as exclamations to show surprise or indignation:

☐ *How* rude he is! ☐ *What* an awful mess!

Comma (,)

1 Where adjectives qualify the same noun Compare these two sentences:

☐ She was a tall, slim girl. ☐ She was a pretty little girl.

Commas are used in the first sentence because the adjectives have equal weight in qualifying the same noun. There are no commas in the second sentence because *little girl* has the force of a compound.

2 To separate repeated words It is used to separate words which are repeated for the sake of emphasis:

☐ He speaks very, very quickly.

3 To indicate a parenthesis It indicates a parenthesis or an interruption and separates it from the rest of the sentence. The parenthesis may consist of a single word or a group of words:

☐ This, however, is certain.

☐ The story, such as it is, may be summarised as follows.

Since a parenthesis is an insertion into a sentence, *two commas* are needed to separate it from the sentence.

4 To distinguish defining and non-defining expressions It is used to distinguish a non-defining expression from one which defines. This is a very important use and must be carefully observed. Compare these two sentences:

☐ My brother who is an engineer has gone to Australia.

☐ My brother, who is an engineer, has gone to Australia.

The first sentence implies I have several brothers. The clause *who is an engineer* defines: it describes the brother I am talking about. Here there are no commas. The implication of the second sentence is that I have only one brother. The clause *who is an engineer* merely adds extra information about that brother. The information is like a parenthesis and is separated off by two commas.

5 To mark off a noun in direct address It is used to mark off a noun or pronoun in direct address:
☐ Is that you, Mary?
Where the phrase occurs internally, two commas are needed:
☐ And now, ladies and gentlemen, we come to the most interesting exhibit of all.
6 To separate participial phrases It is used to separate participial phrases from the rest of the sentence:
☐ The horse, seeing how high the fence was, refused to jump.
7 To separate verbs like *say* from direct speech: It separates the verbs *say, shout, reply,* etc., from direct speech:
☐ 'Your dinner is on the table,' she shouted.   ☐ 'All right,' he replied, 'I'm coming now.'
8 To separate co-ordinate clauses It may be used to separate two co-ordinate clauses joined by a conjunction, though there is a tendency in modern usage to leave the comma out:
☐ I am going out now, but I hope to find everything ready when I get back.
If the subjects of the clauses are different, the comma is more likely to be kept:
☐ I have to go now, but Mr Haverall will arrive shortly.
9 To separate a main and subordinate clause Where the main clause follows the subordinate clause, a comma may be used to separate the two:
☐ Although it was raining heavily, the match continued.
A comma is never used when the main clause comes first.

Colon (:)

1 It separates two co-ordinate clauses where the second clause explains the first:
☐ Martin had never felt so happy: Sheila loved him.
2 It separates two clauses where one is in contrast to the other:
☐ Speech is silver: silence is golden.
3 It introduces a list or an example:
☐ The box contained a collection of articles: a few books, various papers, foreign coins, stamps and paperclips.
Where the list introduced starts on the following line, the colon may be followed by a dash:
☐ The following candidates passed with distinction:—
J C Andrews, W A Barsley, J Charlesworth, P G Dutton.
4 It introduces a fairly long passage of direct speech, as a comma would introduce a shorter passage:
☐ Introducing the speaker, the Chairman said: (Here follows an actual report of his speech, or the relevant parts of it, in inverted commas.)
5 It introduces a literary or documentary quotation within the body of the paragraph. In this case the quotation should not be more than one sentence long:
☐ If I may quote from the Managing Director's last report: 'Property revaluation shows a surplus of £21.7 million over book value.'

Semi-colon (;)

1 Usage It separates two clauses not joined by a conjunction, which are closely connected in thought:
☐ You couldn't expect it to last very long; it was too cheap.
2 Comma or semi-colon? Sometimes it is hard to decide whether to use a comma or a semi-colon. The sense we wish to express is the best guide. Generally the semi-colon, being a heavier punctuation mark than the comma, throws more emphasis on the words that follow it. Compare these sentences:
☐ I knew he would fail, and he did.   ☐ I knew he would fail; and he did.
3 Other use It separates items in a list where commas are ineffective because they have been used within the items themselves:
☐ To avoid sunburn you need: a big, shady sun-hat; a good, protective, cream; a cool, cotton shirt as a cover-up; and self-discipline not to stay out in the sun too long.

Inverted commas (or quotation marks) ('...' or "...")

They are used in direct speech. Note the following:
1 Inverted commas are only used around words actually spoken:
☐ 'I really can't think why Martin's so late,' said Sheila. 'He must have been held up in the traffic.'

2 Where the words inside the inverted commas form a complete sentence, the full stop comes inside the inverted commas:

☐ 'He must have been held up in the traffic.'

The exception to this is where the sentence is followed by words such as *she said*, in which case the full stop follows them:

☐ 'I really can't think why Martin's so late,' said Sheila with a sigh.

When a sentence is interrupted by words such as *she said, he replied*, etc., then these words are marked off by commas:

☐ 'Yes,' said the secretary, 'Mr Hopkins will see you at ten tomorrow.'

3 Any punctuation of direct speech belongs inside the inverted commas:

☐ 'You clumsy boy!' the fat lady exclaimed. 'Who told you to ride your bicycle on the pavement?'

4 Where there is a quotation within a quotation, it is marked off by double inverted commas. You must be careful that any further punctuation, such as a question mark, is correctly placed:

☐ 'Did he say "I refuse to do it"?' asked the magistrate.

Hyphen (-)

1 With prefixes It links prefixes to nouns to form new words: *ex-soldier, non-intervention, sub-let, pro-British, anti-aircraft*. In long-established compounds the two elements are now written as one word, but the hyphen continues to be used if its absence would lead to a duplication of letters: *co-operating, re-employ, mis-shapen*. A hyphen is always necessary when a prefix is attached to a noun or adjective beginning with a capital letter: *pro-German, anti-Nazi, un-English*.

2 To prevent ambiguity The hyphen is used to prevent ambiguity where words are similar. Compare:

☐ I am going to *re-cover* that old cushion.   ☐ I *recovered* the cushion from the dustbin.

3 To group words The hyphen is used to group words so as to avoid ambiguity: *an Irish-linen manufacturer* (the linen is Irish, not the manufacturer). *An old factory-cleaner* (the cleaner is old, not the factory).

4 With adjectives before a noun In phrases consisting of an adjective + noun or an adjectival phrase, a hyphen is used before a noun: *nineteenth-century poetry, our next-door neighbours*. But they are not hyphenated after a noun or verb: *poetry of the nineteenth century, our neighbours next door*.

5 With adjectives modified by adverbs Usually, no hyphen is necessary when an adverb modifies an adjective: *a badly behaved child, an incredibly foolish act*. But with combinations such as *well-known, ill-behaved, wide-open, half-hearted* where the first element might not at once be recognised as an adverb, the hyphen is necessary before a following noun: *a well-known fact, a well-acted play, a wide-open window, a half-hearted attempt*. No hyphen is required when the combination follows the noun and verb: *The fact is well known; the play was well acted*.

6 With adjective-participle combinations Adjective-participle combinations like *hard-boiled, new-born*, are hyphenated whether used before the noun or after the noun and verb:

☐ Pack some *hard-boiled* eggs for the picnic.   ☐ These eggs are *hard-boiled*.

7 With compounds ending in *-ed* Compound adjectives made from an adjective followed by a noun with *-ed* added take the hyphen: *a good-sized house, a four-wheeled vehicle*.

8 With compound cardinal numbers Compound cardinal numbers like *twenty-one, fifty-three*, etc., are hyphenated; so are the corresponding ordinals: *one's twenty-first birthday*. With multiples there is no hyphenation of the cardinals *(two hundred, five thousand, three score and ten)*, but the ordinals have a hyphen: *the two-hundredth anniversary*. Fractions are hyphenated when they denote a single amount: *two-thirds of a mile, three-quarters of a pound*.

9 At the end of a line As far as possible, avoid splitting words at the end of a line, but if splitting is necessary, then (a) place the hyphen at the end of the first line, not at the beginning of the second, and (b) see that the word is so split that the part of it on the first line is recognisable as a sense unit. Thus *wonder-ing*, not *won-dering* or *wond-ering*.

10 Unnatural hyphens Avoid the unsightly and unnatural hyphens in *schoolboys and -girls, Englishmen and -women, grandfathers and -mothers*. Write *schoolboys and schoolgirls*, etc.

Dash (—)

It is longer than a hyphen and separates parts of sentences, whereas a hyphen joins parts of words.

1 It separates a parenthesis from the main body of the sentence. For this use two dashes are needed, one at each end:

☐ Those who knew Pop—and there were few who did not know him—learnt to love him.

2 It attaches an afterthought or comment to the end of a sentence. The dash is used here only when the comment which follows is not a complete clause:

☐ Of the young men going into industry, many can scarcely write their name or read a simple sentence of English—a sad commentary on our educational system.

3 To attach a final summing-up to a sentence. Here the words that follow the dash may, and usually do, constitute a complete clause, or even several clauses:

☐ Friends, money, power, position — all these he had before he reached middle age.

4 To show that a sentence is unfinished or has been interrupted:

☐ A: I was about to say—

☐ B: I'm not interested in what you were about to say.

Apostrophe (')

There are three uses:

1 In omissions To indicate the omission of one or more letters from the spelling of a word, as in *can't, isn't.* Remember *it's* is short for *it is.* The possessive adjective *its* has no apostrophe.

2 In plurals For the plural of words which, not being nouns or pronouns, do not normally have a plural form: *if's, and's* and *but's; he gets mixed up with his will's and shall's.* It is also used for the plural of letters of the alphabet; *Mind your p's and q's; how many l's are there in travelling?* An apostrophe may also be used for the plurals of numbers when they are written as figures: *He makes his 8's like 3's; the 1980's,* but the modern tendency is to omit the apostrophe here: *8s like 3s; the 1980s.*

3 In possessives To indicate the possessive (or genitive case) of a noun.

a The apostrophe is placed before the *s* for the genitive singular: *my father's car* and after the *s* for the genitive plural: *a girls' school, a dogs' home.*

b Those nouns which do not make their plural in *s (child/children, woman/women, man/ men)* add an *'s* to the singular and the plural forms: *a child's toys, children's toys, a woman's hat, a women's college.*

c For personal names ending in *s,* add an *'s* if an additional syllable is pronounced for the possessive: *Jones's, James's, Charles's,* but if no extra syllable is pronounced, then place the apostrophe after the existing *s: Mr Humphreys' house.*

d When two names are to be taken together as a 'joint' possessive, the possessive ending is added only to the last: *Gilbert and Sullivan's operas* (joint authorship) but *Trollope's and Thackeray's novels* (the novels of Trollope and Thackeray considered separately).

e Note the 'free' or independent genitive in *St Paul's; she was staying at her aunt's; I am going to the butcher's/baker's/barber's.*

f Use the *'s* or *s'* in phrases such as *an hour's time, a day's journey, two weeks' wages, three weeks' holiday,* etc.

g Note the use of the apostrophe in such expressions as *a friend of my father's, a poem of Shelley's, a relative of her husband's.*